French
Cinema

FRENCH CINEMA

The
First
Wave,
1915-
1929

Richard
Abel

PRINCETON
UNIVERSITY
PRESS

Copyright © 1984 by Princeton University Press,
Published by Princeton University Press, 41 William Street, Princeton, New Jersey 08540
In the United Kingdom: Princeton University Press, Guildford, Surrey

All Rights Reserved

Library of Congress Cataloging in Publication Data will be found on the last
printed page of this book

ISBN 0-691-05408-8

Publication of this book has been aided by a grant from the Paul Mellon Fund
of Princeton University Press

This book has been composed in Linotron Garamond

Clothbound editions of Princeton University Press books are printed on acid-free paper, and
binding materials are chosen for strength and durability.

Printed in the United States of America by Princeton University Press, Princeton, New Jersey

"When you wake up in the morning, Pooh," said Piglet at last, *"what's the first thing you say to yourself?"*

"What's for breakfast?" said Pooh. "What do you *say, Piglet?"*

"I say, I wonder what's going to happen exciting today?*" said Piglet.*

Pooh nodded thoughtfully.

"It's the same thing," he said.

—A. A. Milne, *Winnie the Pooh* (1926)

For Barbara,
with love and gratitude

Contents

The discovery of the cinema is as important as the discovery of printing.
—Adolphe Brisson (1914)

Ça, c'est du cinéma!—Louis Delluc (1921)

It is from the cinema that our era borrows its color, its picturesqueness, and the moral atmosphere in which it breathes; one lives as a function of the other. . . .
—Albert Valentin (1927)

To paraphrase Jean Epstein, the book that one writes is never the book that one initially conceives. A book that presumes to be a history is especially both less and more. Less than one had hoped for in all sorts of ways: in the consistency and comprehensiveness of its design; in the thoroughness of its investigation of sources; in the articulation of its findings; in the balance of its mediation between past, present, and future. But also more: for the misconceptions corrected (one's own as well as others), the new questions posed, the conceptual models considered, the discoveries made in progress, and the ways found to speak them. The process of writing a history, in fact, can be so engrossing, stimulating, and open-ended that to close it off seems little more than arbitrary and expedient.

Any project that aims to reconstruct the past, of course, is fraught with difficulties. If we tend to iron out ambiguities in the light of more recent developments and the questions raised by them, as John Berger has noted,[1] it is imperative that we recognize the interests and patterns of thinking that guide our work. Here, Shoshana Felman's pedagogical questions may be helpful: "What is the 'navel' of my own theoretical dream of understanding? What is the specificity of my own incomprehension? What is the riddle which I in effect here pose under the guise of knowledge?"[2] Such questions may keep us from repeating the fable of a history already agreed upon or from accepting the illusory idealism of an absolute knowledge (and the mastery it bestows) as well as allow us to counter the conclusion that all things deeply searched merely become confusing.

The project for this book had its origin in the summer of 1976. A sabbatical leave from Drake University permitted me to travel to Paris where I could continue a study, begun three years earlier, of French films and critical writings from the 1920s. At the Cinémathèque française, Marie Epstein (with the approval of the late Henri Langlois and Mary Meerson) generously agreed to let me examine closely and repeatedly a large number of French films, especially those of her brother, Jean Epstein, on an old, hand-cranked editing machine in one of the dark, cluttered offices on rue Courcelles. Within a month, I discovered that my stay chanced to coincide with an extensive retrospective of early French films—"Eighty years of French cinema (part 2)"—mounted, with the then usual lack of publicity, by the Cinémathèque française.[3] From late July to the middle of September, for three to five hours, five afternoons a week (with the legendary delays and substitutions of film prints), I perched uncomfortably on what passed for cushions in the black-walled Petite Salle at Chaillot and madly took notes as film after film unreeled in the darkness and silence. The idea of writing a history of the French cinema of the 1920s already tempted me, but I preferred first to do a number of studies of individual filmmakers and film texts before tackling such an immense project. Gradually, after more and more editing-machine sessions and screenings, conversations with Stuart Liebman (then a graduate student at New York University), Dugald Williamson (then a graduate student at Griffith University in Australia), and Peter Cowie (Tantivy Press) made me realize the unique opportunity at hand. By the time I returned to the United States in December, 1976, I was committed to an historical project that would occupy over five years of research and writing.

During the course of that writing, I came to see that the project actually covered more than a decade and was marked off by two major disruptions—the halt in French film production (from 1914 to 1915) that resulted from the outbreak of World War I and the slowdown that came from the industry's belated acceptance of the "sound film revolution" in 1929. I also realized that, to more clearly differentiate between the commercial and avant-garde cinema during this fifteen-year period, I needed to distribute the work into two major sections. The first would focus on the dominant film industry and the commercial feature films that were the staple of its production. The second would focus on the alternate cinema network which developed in parallel to the industry and on the narrative and non-narrative avant-garde films that were determined, in part, by that network.

In effect, this project gradually has grown into a major reassessment and, if I may presume, a much-needed "revisionist" history of the French cinema during the period, 1915 to 1929. The absence of prior studies—with the exception of Georges Sadoul's mammoth yet uneven *Histoire générale du cinéma* (six volumes) as well as Jean Mitry's slightly less imposing *Histoire du cinéma* (now five volumes)—demanded that I give more space than originally planned to the changing material conditions and policies of the French film industry and to the (previously unexamined) generic nature of its output of commercial feature films. Futhermore, the general lack of sustained close analysis of the narrative avant-garde films (both in French and English) led me to sacrifice not only the short non-narrative avant-garde works (many of which have received a good deal of attention in the United States) but also the usual auteur-based study of those films. Instead, I decided to position the theory and practice of the narrative avant-garde within the context of the conventions of narrative film discourse then operating in the French as well as the American cinema. This somewhat original working definition then provided the framework for a series of individual textual studies of the narrative avant-garde's exploration of the cinema's systems of signification, the means to what they saw as a new aesthetic practice.

Some years ago, Jean Mitry defined a proper history of the cinema as, simultaneously, a history of its industry, its technologies, its systems of expression (or, more precisely, signification), and its aesthetic structures, all bound together by the forces of the economic, psychosocial, and cultural order.[4] Writing such an inclusive history is perhaps an impossible task. As one French film historian confessed recently, "It is already too late to write the history of the silent cinema."[5] In my case, the received level of knowledge about the early French cinema (in English) as well as the constraints of time, access to sources, intellectual acumen, and personal interest have led me to emphasize certain subjects and lines of inquiry at the expense of others. Still, the purpose of this history is multiple. First of all, for English-speaking viewers, it provides a good deal of "new information" about this neglected period of French film history. That information includes not only data on specific films and filmmakers, on industry policies and practices, on institutional as well as individual relations, on ideological and aesthetic constructs, but also resource references—as a means of stimulating further inquiry. It also singles out particular areas of historical development for special attention, either because of a lack in prior histories and critical studies or because of serious misconceptions and misrepresentations. That is why so much space is given over to the industry and its more commercial products and why even more is given to the narrative avant-garde practice. Finally, it continually raises questions of historical accuracy, conceptual formulation, and textual reading and interpretation in an attempt to offer directions for further research on the French cinema of the silent period.

May at least some of this work meet the challenge thrown down, in another context, by Walter Benjamin:

A writer who does not teach other writers teaches nobody. The crucial point, therefore, is that a writer's production must have the character of a model: it must be able to instruct other writers in their production and, secondly, it must be able to place an improved apparatus at their disposal. This apparatus will be the better, the more consumers it brings in contact with the production process—in short, the more readers or spectators it turns into collaborators.[6]

The American researcher interested in the French cinema of the 1910s and 1920s faces a number of obstacles. Access to existing films and written sources is severely limited because the best archives are in Europe. The largest repository of French silent films is the product of Henri Langlois's extraordinary, lifelong passion for film collecting, the Cinémathèque française in Paris. Until recently, however, the Cinémathèque had shown little interest in (nor could it probably afford) providing viewing facilities for historians and critics, except on an irregular, rather personal basis. Specific films had to be "caught" in their infrequent public screenings at Chaillot or Beaubourg (and previously at rue d'Ulm). Now that the Cinémathèque's relationships with the French government and with the state Archives du Film at Bois d'Arcy have stabilized and become more clear, that attitude has begun to change. Smaller collections of French silent films are housed at Bois d'Arcy, at the Royal Film Archive of Belgium in Brussels, at the National Film Archive in London, and at the Cinémathèque de Toulouse. Except for the latter, all provide (at some cost) excellent viewing facilities for visiting researchers. The most important libraries for written sources pertaining to the period are also located in Paris: the Bibliothèque de l'Arsenal, the Bibliothèque d'IDHEC, the Bibliothèque nationale, and the Bibliothèque de la Cinémathèque française (just recently opened for the first time to the public). Another valuable collection is housed at the Cinémathèque de Toulouse. For a list of sources consulted for this history, see the appended bibliography, especially the section on film journals.

In the United States, the most important collection of French silent films is at the Museum of Modern Art in New York. During the past few years, the museum has been adding excellent prints of 1920s French films to its archives; and, beginning in January, 1983, it included these as well as prints from other archives in an extensive retrospective of the French cinema.[7] Smaller collections of French silent films are housed at the George Eastman House in Rochester, at Anthology Film Archives in New York, at the Library of Congress in Washington, at the UCLA Film Archives in Los Angeles, and at the State Historical Society of Wisconsin in Madison. Along with the Museum of Modern Art, all provide superb viewing facilities for researchers. Written sources pertaining to the period are less easy to come by. The best collection of material related to the narrative and non-narrative avant-garde films is housed at the Museum of Modern Art, while those related to the commercial film industry can be found at the New York Public Library, the Library of Congress, and the University of Southern California. For researchers seriously interested in the French cinema of the 1910s and 1920s, consequently, it is almost imperative to arrange to study in Europe.

If access to sources presents a problem, the number and condition of existing film prints presents one even more severe. No one seems to know exactly how many of the several thousand films (excluding newsreels, educational films, and other short works) produced in France from 1915 to 1929 still exist and in what condition.[8] Raymond Borde recently reported that his queries to some thirty film archives around the world had turned up only 222 titles of the approximately 1,400 French films produced just between 1919 and 1929.[9] Although most of the films of the narrative avant-garde were diverted from the industry's economic cycle of production, exhibition, and destruction—through the action of ciné-clubs, specialized cinemas, and private collectors—the more commercial products usually had less chance of survival. A good number of important films seem irretrievably lost—for example, Baroncelli's *Ramuntcho* (1919), Hervil's *Paris* (1924), Grémillon's *Tour au large* (1927), Renoir's *Marquitta* (1927), Feyder's *Thérèse Raquin* (1928), Bernard's *Tarakanova* (1930). Others, though listed as surviving, actually exist in incomplete or condensed versions—e.g., several of Antoine's films for Pathé-Consortium; several of Poirier's films for Gaumont; Dulac's *La Mort du soleil* (1922); Roussel's *Les Opprimés* (1923), *Violettes impériales* (1924), and *La Terre promise* (1925); Luitz-Morat's *La Cité foudroyée* (1924); Perret's *Madame Sans-Gêne* (1925); Volkoff's *Michel Strogoff* (1926); Bernard's *Joueur d'échecs* (1927). And this list does not even consider the popular serials, comic shorts, and other lesser films.[10] Despite the special attention paid to them, several of the narrative avant-garde films are also lost or survive in less than complete versions—e.g., Dulac's *La Fête espagnole* (1920), Delluc's *Le Silence* (1920), Feyder's *L'Image* (1926) and Epstein's *Sa Tête* (1930).

Added to this destruction and dismemberment is the loss of two features considered essential to the films' exhibition. The first to be lost were the musical arrangements and special scores (for large orchestras, organs, or small chamber groups) which accompanied the film screenings. These were particularly important to the films of Marcel L'Herbier, to Bernard's *Le Miracle des loups* (1924), to Marodon's *Salammbô* (1925), to Epstein's *La Chute de la maison Usher* (1928), and to others as well. Only recently has any attention been given to this specialized music, and very few scores have yet been found.[11] Perhaps the most important "reconstruction" to come out of this effort has been Clair's *Entr'acte* (1924), meticulously timed to synchronize with Erik Satie's music. The second feature to disappear was color. Most French films of the period were tinted in a half-dozen different colors according to a conventional set of codes—blue for night scenes and seascapes, mauve for early evening scenes, light green for daylight exteriors, amber for interiors, red for passionate scenes or those lit by firelight.[12] Some were even toned (in the dark areas of the frame) as well as tinted (in the light areas), producing a relatively refined two-color process. In scenes of horror, for instance, the light areas were tinted red while the dark areas were toned green; in Gance's *Napoléon* (1927), the general's reaction to the burning of the French fleet off Toulon was described in a close shot of his face (tinted orange-red) against a background (toned deep blue).[13] Certain Pathé films—e.g., from *La Sultane de l'amour* (1919) to *Casanova* (1927)—were even printed in a complicated stencil process that could accommodate three or four different colors within a single frame.[14] Tragically, very few film prints survive with their original color intact, and it is quite expensive to reproduce it. I myself have seen only a half-dozen or so original prints—Gance's *J'Accuse* (1919), Pouctal's *Travail* (1919-1920), L'Herbier's *El Dorado* (1921), Poirier's *Jocelyn* (1922), Le Somptier's *La Dame de Monsoreau* (1923), Epstein's *Pasteur* (1922) and *Mauprat* (1926), and a brief fragment of Volkoff's *Casanova* (1927). The loss of these features changes the works drastically—the parallel to Greek and Roman statues is both presumptuous and apt. Futhermore, it lessens the impact of those few films that were exhibited in sepia—e.g., Clair's *Un Chapeau de paille d'Italie* (1928)—and in stark black-and-white—e.g., Feyder's *Thérèse Raquin* (1928), Dreyer's *La Passion de Jeanne d'Arc* (1928), and Epstein's *La Chute de la maison Usher* (1928) and *Finis terrae* (1929)—as well as those that may have included scored moments of silence.

Consequently, writing a history of the French cinema of the 1910s and 1920s is a treacherous operation, somewhat like constructing a work of landscape art over partially visible terrain. Not only is one sometimes cut off from the "primary evidence"—the individual film texts—and forced to rely on written documents for description and analysis, but one can rarely view even those films that survive under conditions of their original projection and as frequently as one would wish. Nearly all of the films I have selected for extended analysis are those I have been able to study closely on a viewing machine or view several times projected on a screen. The section on the narrative avant-garde is predicated exclusively on the shot-by-shot descriptions that this kind of study allows. As scrupulous as it may seem, such a method inevitably produces gaps and misrepresentations. I have tried to keep these to a minimum; and, whenever discrepancies between archive prints have cropped up, I have taken note of them.

January, 1983

Any work of history is collective in its dependence on the generosity, resource material, ideas, and constructive criticism of others. This book is no exception.

Of all those who made this work possible, the most important was Marie Epstein, the former director of technical services at the Cinémathèque française. Without her trust and her devotion to her brother's films and to the work of the narrative avant-garde generally (characteristically, she downplays her own considerable work as a filmmaker), I would not have been able to make the shot-by-shot descriptions of so many rare films that were essential to my analysis. She was like a fairy godmother to me during the months I sat hunched over that ancient "visionneuse" and during our countless conversations and more formal interviews. I will forever be indebted to her. At the Cinémathèque française, I must also thank the late Henri Langlois, Mary Meerson, and especially Lucie and Renée Lichtig (who have taken over Marie Epstein's position now that she has finally retired) for their generous assistance in arranging special screenings of particular films.

Other archivists and archives were no less helpful—especially Charles Silver of the Film Study Center at the Museum of Modern Art; Jeremy Boulton and Elaine Burrows of the National Film Archive in London; James Card, George Pratt, and Marshall Deutelbaum, all formerly of the George Eastman House in Rochester; Jacques Ledoux of the Royal Film Archive of Belgium in Brussels; Maxine Fleckner of the Film Archive at the State Historical Society of Wisconsin in Madison; Patrick Sheehan of the Motion Picture Section of the Library of Congress in Washington, D.C.; and Edouard Chamard of the Centre national du cinéma in Paris.

For written sources, I am indebted to the staffs of the Bibliothèque de l'Arsenal, the Bibliothèque d'IDHEC, and the Bibliothèque nationale in Paris; the library of the Museum of Modern Art in New York; the library of the University of Iowa in Iowa City; the library of the University of Southern California in Los Angeles; and the Inter-Library Loan Services of Cowles Library at Drake University.

For frame stills and production photographs, I would like to thank Sylvie de Luze of the Cinémathèque française, Mary Corliss of the Museum of Modern Art, Donald Crafton of Yale University, the National Film Archive, the State Historical Society of Wisconsin, and David Phipps (who prepared many of the actual stills) of the Educational Media Services Center at Drake University. Whenever possible, I have tried to use frame stills rather than publicity photographs, especially for the narrative avant-garde films, even if that meant sacrificing image quality. Any gaps and omissions are due either to space limitations or to the absence or inaccessibility of sources.

I am indebted also to several people who graciously opened their personal collections of films, photographs, and written materials to my use—Jean Dréville, Gérard Troussier, Kevin Brownlow, Stuart Liebman, Armand Panigel, Bernard Eisenschitz, and Mme. Ruta Sadoul (who arranged for me to examine part of the late Georges Sadoul's private library). Particularly helpful were the transcripts of interviews that Armand Panigel conducted in 1973 with some dozen French film celebrities from the silent period.[1]

Those who read all or part of the manuscript at various stages and made numerous emendations and provocative suggestions include Kevin Brown-

ACKNOWLEDGMENTS low, Barry Salt, Kristin Thompson, Rick Altman, Alan Williams, Douglas Gomery, Donald Crafton, Stuart Liebman, David Bordwell, Dudley Andrew, and Janet Altman. Others who contributed information and ideas were Bernard Eisenschitz, Dugald Williamson, Sandy Flitterman, Ernest Callenbach, Glenn Myrent, Wendy Dozoretz, Phil E. Brown, William Lafferty, Jon Gartenberg, Robert Hammond, Charles Ford, Claude Autant-Lara, and Lotte Eisner. Whether accepted in toto or not, their responses were valuable in shaping this book.

At Princeton University Press, I am grateful for Joanna Hitchcock's enthusiastic and unstinting support for the manuscript as well as her helpful suggestions and patience during its final revision. I was also delighted to have Marilyn Campbell's highly efficient and consistently well-judged assistance in preparing the manuscript for production.

Support for my research and writing came from several quarters at Drake University—from Carol J. Guardo (the former Dean of Liberal Arts) and the English Department, for a partial leave of absence one semester, and from the Graduate Research Council for several summer grants as well as typing services. In Paris, my efforts to contact various people, conduct interviews, and do some writing was facilitated by the Bureau d'Accueil des Professeurs d'Universités Etrangères (formerly the Centre Universitaire International).

Finally, my deepest appreciation goes to the person who has encouraged me most throughout this period of writing, who has read and reread, corrected and commented upon, every version of the manuscript—my best reader and collaborator, Barbara Hodgdon.

Permission has been granted to reprint portions of this book, which originally appeared in different formats, in *Quarterly Review of Film Studies* 1 (1976) and 2 (1977); *Wide Angle* 3 (1979); *Film Quarterly* 25 (1982); and *Cinema Journal* 22 (1983).

Personal collection of Richard Abel: 1, 2, 3, 4, 6, 7, 8, 9, 10, 13, 14, 15, 17, 18, 19, 23, 29, 32, 35, 45, 47, 48, 55, 56, 62, 63, 64, 68, 69, 70, 72, 78, 86a, 89, 90, 96, 97, 98, 99, 100, 102, 103, 104, 105, 107, 109, 111, 113, 117, 118, 119, 120, 121, 127, 128, 129, 130, 131, 132, 134, 135, 136, 138, 140, 147, 150, 151, 155, 156, 157, 158, 159, 160, 162, 173, 175, 177, 184, 194, 196, 198, 199a-k, 200, 201, 202a-c, 209, 210, 211, 214, 216, 217, 222, 225a, 225c, 233, 234, 239a-f, 240, 241, 242, 243, 244, 245a-d, 246, 247, 248, 249, 250a-c, 251, 252a-b, 253a-b, 254, 255a-b, 256a-b, 257a-b, 258a-b, 259a-b, 260, 261a-i, 262a-b, 263a-b, 264a-g, 265a-h, 266, 267a-c, 272, 275

Cinémathèque française: 20, 21, 22, 25, 26, 28, 30, 33, 37, 39, 42, 43, 44, 46, 51, 52, 61, 65, 66, 67, 71, 73, 74, 75, 77, 81, 83, 86b, 87, 88, 92, 108, 110, 112, 116, 123, 139, 142, 143, 144, 161, 174, 178, 179, 180, 186, 204, 205, 228, 229, 277, 278, 279, 280, 281

State Historical Society of Wisconsin: 53, 54, 93, 124, 125, 126, 163, 164, 165a-c, 166, 167a-d, 168a-h, 169, 170, 185a-e, 235, 236, 237a-c, 238

National Film Archive: 24, 27, 38, 41, 79, 80, 82, 84, 106, 114, 115, 145, 153, 171, 172, 176, 187, 188, 189, 190, 191, 206, 207, 208, 212, 219, 268, 269, 271

Museum of Modern Art: 11, 12, 16, 31, 36, 40, 76, 91, 94, 95, 122, 141, 148, 181, 182, 183, 192, 203, 220, 253, 270, 273, 274

Personal collection of Jean Dréville: 5, 137, 146, 213, 215, 221, 223, 225, 226, 230, 231, 232, 282

Personal collection of Stuart Liebman: 34, 133, 154, 193, 195, 197, 276

Yale University Film Stills Collection: 49, 50, 57, 85, 149

Images Film Archives: 101, 218, 224, 227a-c

Personal collection of Barry Salt: 58, 59, 60, 152

Personal collection of Donald Crafton: 10

In the interests of reading ease, I have translated nearly all of the French quotations into English; the translations are my own unless otherwise indicated. In the interests of accuracy, however, I have kept the French titles of books and essays as well as the original titles of the French films under discussion, adding the English translations only when I thought it required or when reference is made to the American release print of the film. Otherwise, I have used the original titles of American films and the English titles of German, Italian, Swedish, and Soviet films, along with their French release titles when it seemed appropriate.

The date given for each French film is the date of its public release in Paris. At the end of the war, serials and feature films were presented to the cinema owners and critics about five weeks prior to their planned release.[1] By the middle twenties, the period between private presentation or preview and public release had been extended to three to six months. And actual production generally began anywhere from six months to a year before the presentation. Whenever there was an exception to this pattern, usually a delay of a year or more, the dates of both production and exhibition are noted.

Occasionally, I call attention to the length of a film—in reels, meters, minutes, or hours. The standard reel of a French film was approximately 300-400 meters in length and ran close to fifteen minutes (that is, at 18 frames per second or fps).[2] However, the cranking speeds of silent films increased gradually during the 1920s so that the screening time of a reel of film became shorter and shorter. According to Barry Salt, American films were being shot and projected at the speed of 22 fps by as early as 1924, whereas French films did not reach that speed until 1929.[3] Most French films made at the end of the decade, consequently, were projected at close to sound film speed and should be projected at that speed today.

Finally, in the sections of the book devoted to close textual analysis, my descriptions of specific shots resort to notational acronyms designating camera distance and angle that have become familiar and necessary in film criticism. They include the following:

ECU   extreme close-up (the shot of an eye, a pair of eyes, or part of a body or small object)
CU   close-up (the shot of a face or object)
MCU   middle close-up (the shot of a person from the chest up)
MS   middle shot (the shot of a person from the waist up)
FS   full shot (the shot of a person from the knees up [American shot] or from the feet up, or the shot of a large object)
LS   long shot (the shot of a full interior space or of a large exterior space)
ELS   extreme long shot (the shot of a mammoth interior space or of an extensive landscape)
HA   high angle (a shot taken from above chest level, looking down)
LA   low angle (a shot taken from below chest level, looking up)

When a film's mise-en-scène combines two or more planes of interest within the frame, I resort to a double acronym—e.g., MS/LS. Only one other acronym appears frequently—POV—for point-of-view shot.

French
Cinema

FRENCH
FRENCH
CINEMA

The
French
Film
Industry

The cinema: two drawers—one marked expenses, the other receipts—and between them this mysterious little box in which films are filed as index cards. . . .
—Louis Aubert (1923)

The facts do not speak for themselves. . . . {The} historian speaks for them, speaks on their behalf, and fashions the fragments of the past into a whole whose integrity is— in its representation—a purely discursive one.
—Hayden White (1976)

At the outset a question: How was the French film industry structured during the period from 1915 to 1929, and how did it function? Like the cinemas of other advanced industrial societies, by then the French cinema had become a mass art constituted from a new technological apparatus of perception and representation and thus had acquired some degree of cultural importance. That importance derived, in part, from its emergence within a number of already existing social structures, each of which helped shape its organization and operation as an industry. But the shaping of the French film industry was unique. A good way of grasping that shaping process, Gérard Talon suggests, "is to put in play once more the series of economic and ideological mutations that made the French film industry produce the films that it produced."[1] To begin reconstructing this period of the French cinema's history, therefore, let me sketch a framework of those mutations.[2]

The years between the beginning of the Great War and the end of the twenties can be divided politically into four more or less distinct periods. The war years were dominated nominally by the Radicals, who had controlled the French legislature and its cabinet ministries since 1899. The real government leaders, however, were the Moderate Raymond Poincaré (in the hitherto ceremonial post of president), who had become the symbol of the "nationalist revival" just prior to the war, and the aging Tiger, Prime Minister Georges Clemenceau, who for the last two years of the war turned France into a virtual civilian dictatorship. In 1919-1920, partly as a result of internal divisions that wracked the Radicals and the Socialists, a coalition of rightist parties and Moderates, for the first time since the 1870s, achieved a brief, clear-cut majority in the National Assembly. This *Bloc national* or *horizon bleu* coalition soon gravitated into a Moderate-Radical alliance, led most prominently by Poincaré, from 1922 to 1924. It adopted a rather harsh foreign policy, especially toward German war reparations, and held strictly conservative domestic positions. The elections of 1924, however, gave power to a *Cartel des gauches* organized by left-leaning Radicals and Socialists. This government reversed its predecessor's policies by adopting Aristide Briand's strategy of rapprochement with Germany and by half-heartedly advancing Prime Minister Edouard Herriot's program of economic reforms. In 1926, in the face of escalating inflation and a "capital strike," partly occasioned by overextended government loans for reconstruction, a Radical-Moderate coalition, the *Union nationale*, assumed political control of the cabinet ministries. Leading this "restoration of confidence" once again was Prime Minister Poincaré, who quickly reestablished more conservative positions on internal matters but who also allowed Briand to continue his foreign policy of rapprochement. This return to an "era of stability" was formalized in the elections of 1928. Despite these political changes, which, as we will see, did have a considerable effect on the French cinema throughout the period, the government's attitude toward the film industry was consistently one of benign neglect. As a new industry, like the more important synthetic textiles industry, for example, it was expected to make its own way. That attitude was particularly telling in the areas of film production financing and the regulation, or lack of regulation, of film imports.

France's economic development during this period coincided, in part, with these political changes. Inflation and unemployment, for instance, were highest in the years immediately following the war, from 1919 to 1921, and in the middle of the decade, from 1924 to 1926. At no time, however, did either reach the disastrous levels experienced in Germany. Furthermore, the revolutionary dreams of the working-class movement were shattered by the failure of the 1920 general strike and by the bitter ideological debates that split the Confédération Générale du Travail and the Socialists and gave rise to a fledgling Communist Party (and its trade-union arm, the Confédération Générale du Travail Unitaire). But the seeming stability of the period could not mask a persistent sense of stagnancy and a fear that the country was on the verge of bankruptcy. In 1919, for instance, industrial production was no more than 60 percent of what it had been in 1914, and much of the country's extensive foreign investments had been lost, particularly in Russia. The following decade was marked, especially compared to Germany, by the slow development of key industries—for example, that of hydroelectric power and the concomitant commercial and domestic uses of electricity. The cautious reinvestment strategies and the resistance to new production and marketing strategies that too often characterized this development also showed up in the French film industry. Although the French tended to be chauvinistic in resisting the intervention of foreign enterprises—despite the lack of economic regeneration from within—the French film industry actually encouraged foreign capital and business organizations, almost out of necessity. In the overall economy, however, the industry was small, capital-deficient, and played a distinctly minor role (in contrast to its American counterpart, which was, for some time, among the top forty industries in the United States).[3] Also, in comparison to the Americans, the French film industry's structure exhibited much less concentration and vertical integration, and the industry invested much less of its capital in film production and more in distribution and exhibition.

Finally, the Great War severely strained the ideological bases of French society. Instead of celebrating its victory after the Armistice, France evidenced, paradoxically, a national mood of suffering and defeat. "The war played the role of catalyst," writes Jacques Petat. "It burst the nationalist gut strings. The uniforms and flamboyant rhetoric could no longer hide the shit of the trenches. We were disappointed, disgusted. We had been swindled."[4] Its economic effects, adds José Baldizzone, completely undermined "bourgeois morality."[5] Stripped of the ideological trappings that decked out the prewar Belle Epoque revival, the French nation seemed in search of its own collective identity. As a popular spectacle, the French cinema gave representation to this search or reexamination in an operation that was doubly motivated by the industry's own sense of defeat or loss. Before the war, according to then accepted, though unreliable statistics, "90 percent of the films exhibited throughout the world were French films." By 1919, only 10 to 15 percent of the films projected in Paris alone were French.[6] "If the French cinema is stripped of its glories, it will perish," wrote *Mon-Ciné*, "and we will have to resign ourselves to being a country that no longer makes good films."[7] Thus, the industry had its own related question of identity to confront: What was or should be French about the French cinema?

Can there be any wonder, then, that, from the beginnings of the Great War to the end of the 1920s, the French cinema found itself in a state of crisis. Year after year, the epithet echoed through the French press devoted to the cinema.

The crisis preceded the war, which precipitated it rather than being its principal cause. It was inevitable. . . .—Henri Diamant-Berger, 1919[8]

Cognizant of the pitiful state of our cinema, in both men and material, today we must demolish these badly lit, enclosed buildings, scrap this obsolete equipment, banish from the screen all that which admits of the theater or promenade, expel the cads and the unfit.—Pierre Henry, 1919[9]

The first question posed . . . : what remedies do you recommend for the real crisis of the cinema?—René Jeanne, 1921[10]

The present situation is clear; we are faced with ruin. . . .—Jean Sapène, 1925[11]

It has become banal and even a bit ridiculous to speak of the crisis of the cinema.—Hubert Revol, 1927[12]

1. Charles Pathé

Despite rather steadily growing box office receipts and intermittent reports of a renaissance of the French cinema, the crisis was perceived as chronic and persistent, infecting all levels of the film industry from production to exhibition.

What exactly had happened? And was the film industry really as moribund, disorganized, and second- or even third-rate as was imagined? Or could the crisis be read as a sign of healthy ferment? To discover more precise answers, to better understand the French cinema of the period, one can begin by looking more closely at the double-edged effect of the war.

The War: Collapse and Reconstruction

On the eve of World War I, the French film industry seemed almost as consolidated and powerful as was its counterpart in the United States. The early artisan-based production-distribution companies of the Lumière brothers and of Georges Méliès had been superseded by a different kind of company, modeled on the corporations that were beginning to monopolize other more important industries. At first, these new companies employed a strategy of horizontal integration to ensure their success. They sought to control the material conditions of the young industry by manufacturing camera and projector equipment, producing and developing film stock, and constructing studios. Soon, however, as the commodity nature of the cinema, with its dependence on rapid change in consumer interest, was recognized, this strategy gave way to one of vertical integration. Control was now sought over each stage of film production, distribution, and exhibition. The company that led this transformation and thus came to dominate the industry, both in France and abroad, was Pathé-Frères.

Under the direction of Charles Pathé, Pathé-Frères had grown out of selling and exhibiting films (Edison Kinetoscope films, in fact) at traveling fairs in the French provinces. Backed by loans from the Neyret-Grivolas group of the Crédit Lyonnais, Pathé soon expanded the company's operations to sell cinematographic equipment (in alliance with Continsouza, developers of the Maltese cross device to advance the film in the camera), to produce its own film stock and films (at Vincennes and Montreuil), to open foreign exchanges for distribution (in Germany and Russia, it dominated the market until the war), and to exhibit its product through its own network of cinemas (which were organized into six regional circuits whose principal manager was Edmond Benoît-Lévy). In 1907, as part of its vertical integration strategy, Pathé made the crucial decision to begin renting film prints rather than selling them outright, as had been the practice—a decision that quickly forced the industry to adopt international standards of distribution and exhibition. Within a year, through its exchange in New York and its studio in Jersey City (which became the center of a French emigré film colony), the company was allegedly distributing more films in the United States than any of the American film companies. Even Louis B. Mayer, when he was managing a nickelodeon in Boston around 1912, confessed that he could double his receipts simply by showing Pathé films. By 1914, in France alone, Pathé-Frères employed 5,000 people. The company trademark (a crowing red cock) was seen by more audiences throughout the world than any other.[1]

Etablissements Gaumont, founded by Léon Gaumont, quickly followed Pathé's example by shifting its business from photography to all the different stages of cinematography. From 1905 to 1907, the company transformed itself from a family firm into a limited liability corporation, dictated in part by Pierre Azaria and the Banque Suisse et Française (later the Crédit Commercial de France). Previously, Gaumont's films had been written and directed almost exclusively by Alice Guy (perhaps the first woman filmmaker); now film production was turned over to Louis Feuillade—in the world's largest studio at Buttes-Chaumont (La Cité-Elgé, after Gaumont's initials). Besides producing films and cinematographic equipment as well as experimenting with color processing and sound synchronization, the company expanded into distribution and exhibition. It, too, put together a chain of cinemas that included the grand Gaumont-Palace (the former Hippodrome Theater, remodeled in 1911 to seat close to 6,000 people). By 1914, under the sign of the marguerite (the tiny white French daisy), Gaumont had 52 agencies and 2,100 employees around the world.[2]

Despite their success, Pathé and Gaumont were model French companies in that they refused to monopolize the film industry by destroying their smaller competitors.[3] Consequently, although other film companies had to limit themselves to one or two areas of operation within the industry, they could compete almost equally with Pathé and Gaumont within those limitations. Eclipse (headed by Louis Mercanton), a former British company, and Eclair (headed by Marcel Vandal) concentrated chiefly on film production, including newsreels. Eclair had even set up a second studio in Fort Lee, New Jersey, as well as a distribution exchange in Germany.[4] Another important production company was the prestigious Film d'Art, originally founded by the Lafitte brothers (one of whom was a successful magazine publisher) and then taken over by Charles Delac [Ben-Kaled]. Film d'Art had an explicit "cultural mission"—to elicit original scenarios from Comédie Française dramatists for Comédie Française actors and directors.[5] Soon after its debut, the Société cinématographique des auteurs et gens des lettres (S.C.A.G.L.) was established by Pierre Decourcelle and Eugene Guggenheim, from an idea developed by Edmond Benoît-Lévy.[6] As a subsidiary company to Pathé-Frères, S.C.A.G.L. produced adaptations of literary classics, most of them nineteenth-century novels and short stories, directed by André Capellani. One of the two major film distribution rivals to Gaumont and Pathé-Frères was the Agence générale cinématographique (A.G.C.), which generally handled the films of Eclipse, Eclair, and Film d'Art.[7] The other was Etablissements Aubert, headed by Louis Aubert, whose operation depended chiefly on film imports. In 1913, Aubert was fortunate enough to distribute the record-breaking Italian film, *Quo Vadis?*, which incited him to embark on a major program of cinema construction.[8]

2. Léon Gaumont

The French film industry seemed to be in a very lucrative position. It could produce and market films and equipment almost anywhere in the world through its own foreign exchange offices, and it could saturate its own markets in France, thus inhibiting foreign companies from directly distributing their products. While Pathé and Eclair made and, along with Gaumont, distributed films profitably in the American market, most American films sold to France (except those of Vitagraph) initially came through Aubert or Pathé, whose American exchange, in 1908, had helped set up the Motion Pictures Patents Company (or simply the Trust).[9] Even before 1914, however, this position had begun to suffer erosion. Pathé left the Trust and soon lost some of its influence in a bitter rivalry with the Eastman Company over the production and marketing of film stock in the United States.[10] Then, as the financial risks increased, French banks began to curtail their support for any film production company.[11] The film industries of the United States, Denmark, Sweden, and Italy began to flourish, and French film production dropped to 30 to 35 percent of the world's total production.[12] American film companies such as Vitagraph (especially) and Biograph (briefly) established distribution offices in Paris, and many cinemas (e.g., the Tivoli, Colisée, and Cosmograph) began to exhibit American, Italian, and other foreign films on a regular basis. The crucial fact was that, although more French films were being made, relatively fewer were being shown, even in France. In early June, 1914, for instance, of the 20,000 meters of film being exhibited in Paris, 17,000 meters were foreign films.[13] The French position collapsed completely in August, 1914, when the declaration of war paralyzed the film industry almost overnight.

All branches of the industry immediately closed down. The general mobilization emptied the studios of directors, actors, and technicians. Even the French film star, Max Linder, although rejected by the army, left for the front in his own limousine to deliver military dispatches before eventually going off to make films in the United States. The deserted spaces of the studios were requisitioned for military stores and horse barns, and Pathé's film-stock factory at Vincennes was transformed into a war plant. The cinemas, along with all other shows, closed their doors in the national interest. But everyone expected that the war would be brief and that life would soon resume as before. Soldiers going off to the front shouted, "To Berlin!" and "Home for Christmas!" It was not to be.

As the war settled down to a grim, protracted struggle late in the year, the film industry sought to reestablish itself. In November and December, after the "race to the sea" had ended in a stalemate and trench warfare began in earnest, the cinemas (along with some theaters) began to reopen, for the official purpose of maintaining the morale of the people.[14] Early in 1915, in order to supply the cinema owners' demands for film programs, each of the major

9

companies resumed production, but well below prewar levels. For nearly two years, most of their work was geared to the war effort. Pathé and Film d'Art especially felt compelled to propagandize their audiences by producing historical and fictional films on patriotic themes connected with the war.[15] Two of the most publicized were Film d'Art's *Alsace* (by Henri Pouctal) and *Mères françaises* (by René Hervil and Louis Mercanton), the latter of which posed Sarah Bernhardt at the foot of Jeanne d'Arc's statue before the ruined cathedral at Rheims. When the Service photographique et cinématographique de l'armée was created in February, 1915, each of the four major companies assigned a cameraman to it—Pathé: Alfred Machin; Gaumont: Edgar Costil; Eclair: Georges Maurice; Eclipse: Emile Pierre—and together they turned out a weekly newsreel on the war, *Annales de la Guerre* (though they were confined to activity behind the lines until the summer of 1916).[16] The French public soon tired of all this attention to the fighting and demanded what they had begun to enjoy just prior to the war. Given the obvious opportunities for cinema exhibition—compared to some of the other spectacles (particularly the opera and theater) that remained shut down—the way was prepared for the American invasion.

Philippe Soupault has written one of the best descriptions of the French reaction to the new American films and their publicity posters.

We walked the cold and deserted streets seeking an accidental, a sudden, meeting with life. To distract ourselves we found it necessary to yoke the imagination to sensational dreams. For a time we found distraction in lurid periodicals—those papers which are more highly-colored than picture postcards. We scoured the world for them, and by means of them we participated in marvelous and bloody dramas which illuminated for an instant various parts of the earth.

Then one day we saw hanging on the walls great posters as long as serpents. At every street-corner a man, his face covered with a red handkerchief, leveled a revolver at the peaceful passersby. We imagined that we heard galloping hoofs, the roar of motors, explosions, and cries of death. We rushed into the cinemas, and realized immediately that everything had changed. On the screen appeared the smile of Pearl White—that almost ferocious smile which announced the revolution, the beginning of a new world.[17]

It all began during the spring of 1915 when Aubert released the first Mack Sennett Keystone comedies starring Mabel Normand, Fatty Arbuckle, and Charlie Chaplin. By the summer and fall, Chaplin or Charlot (his French nickname) was the rage throughout France. In December, Pathé began distributing the first episodes of *Les Mystères de New York*, starring Pearl White, in conjunction with Pierre Decourcelle's daily serialization of the film's story in the Paris newspaper, *Le Matin*. The posters advertising the film publicized the image of Pearl White to such an extent that they created a fashion out of the heroine's costume—a simple skirt, black vest, narrow-brimmed hat, and white gloves.[18] The following year, in addition to the continuing series of Sennett/Chaplin comedies and Pearl White serials, came the Triangle films produced by Thomas Ince (especially the westerns of William S. Hart) and Famous Players' adaptations directed by Cecil B. De Mille (e.g., *The Cheat*, starring Sessue Hayakawa).

Most of the genres specifically developed by the French prior to the war—the burlesque (André Deed, Prince Rigadin, Max Linder), the serial (from

Eclair's *Nick Carter* series to Gaumont's *Fantômas*), the adventure film (Jean Durand and Joë Hamman's westerns), and the dramatic film or literary adaptation (Film d'Art and S.C.A.G.L. productions)—had been taken over by the Americans.[19] Moreover, technically (in set design, lighting, and editing), the imported films were consistently superior to the French films, and their acting style was strikingly more natural and spontaneous.[20] "*Forfaiture {The Cheat}, Pour sauver sa race {The Aryan}, Molly*, then a hundred other films," wrote Jean-Louis Bouquet, "provided the evidence for French technicians. We could no longer explain away such success as isolated incidents. We were surely in the presence of superior methods."[21] Given the limited quantity and variety of French film production, the exhibitors turned increasingly to the highly popular American films. By 1917, American films comprised over 50 percent of the cinema programs in Paris.[22]

The rapid influx of American films and the resumption of French film production wrought immediate changes within the French film industry. Although established distributors such as Aubert and A.G.C. handled many of the Triangle and Mutual films, they simply could not accommodate the demand.[23] Several American companies, Jesse Lasky and Adolph Zukor's Famous Players, for instance, opened offices in Paris to join Vitagraph in marketing their films more directly. More importantly, a multitude of European import companies (Monat-Film, Mundus-Film, Harry, Georges Petit, and especially Western Imports or Jacques Haik), sprang up to profit from the tide. At the production end of the industry, the personnel who had been conscripted into the armed forces or who had gone to the United States—e.g., Maurice Tourneur and André Capellani transformed the Eclair studio at Fort Lee; Léonce Perret became a director at Paramount—were replaced by a new generation of directors, actors, and technicians.[24] From the theater came André Antoine (to direct for Pathé), Léon Poirier, Jacques Feyder, and Raymond Bernard (all to write and direct for Gaumont), Marcel L'Herbier (to write scenarios for Eclipse), and Abel Gance (to direct for the new production head of Film d'Art, Louis Nalpas). Several stars and young directors formed their own independent production companies, perhaps in imitation of Camille de Morlhon, whose Valetta Films had been a prewar subsidiary of Pathé. René Navarre (the star of *Fantômas*), Musidora (the star of *Les Vampires*), and Renée Carl all broke away from Gaumont to head short-lived production units. Several journalists turned from writing to directing. Jacques de Baroncelli set up Lumina Films, in alliance with Film d'Art and A.G.C., and Germaine Albert-Duluc (an interviewer and critic for the first French feminist magazines, *La Fronde* and *La Française*) founded Film D.-H., in conjunction with her husband and the poet-scenarist, Irene Hillel-Erlanger. The practice of independent or semi-independent production would become standard during the next decade.

The full impact of the American films did not come until the crucial years of 1918-1919. By the end of the long, costly, but victorious war, the industry was faced with a situation aptly summed up by the posters advertising Mundus-Film (the distributors in France for Selig, Goldwyn, First National, etc.): a cannon manned by American infantrymen fired film title after film title into the center of a French target.[25] According to the *Cinématographie française*, for every 5,000 meters of French films presented weekly in France there were 25,000 meters of imported films, mostly American.[26] One of the reasons was

11

3. An early Pathé camera

4. A Debrie camera (circa 1920)

obviously economic. Whereas one meter of film exported to the United States or England cost the French the equivalent of .18 to .35 centimes in customs duties, one meter of film imported into France cost only .02 centimes.[27] It was simply better business to risk a little money on American imports than to risk a lot more on producing French films. Consequently, by 1918, French film production had fallen so low that it made up only 20 percent of the Paris cinema programs. In the words of Henri Diamant-Berger, the publisher of *Le Film*, France was in danger of becoming "an American cinematographic colony."[28] How the industry would respond to that threat was determined in large part by Charles Pathé.

Early in 1918, perhaps spurred by the recent foundation of UFA in Germany, Pathé proposed "the organization of a cartel of manufacturers, which while allowing competition to continue, would enjoin all the French cinematographic companies to assure the normal existence of some film producers in our country."[29] In order to do this, he recommended "the institution of a percentage on cinema receipts as well as a quota system for the importation of foreign film negative into France." Although producers such as Louis Nalpas and Henri Diamant-Berger supported Pathé, most of his colleagues in the film industry, especially the distributors and exhibitors, opposed the idea, out of short-sighted self-interest and probably also out of fear that Pathé would turn such a cartel to his own advantage. After all, ten years earlier he had opposed a cartel of European production in the United States, only to sign up Pathé-Exchange as part of the Trust.[30] Moreover, early in the war Pathé had realized that the world banking center had shifted from Paris to New York and that the New York branch office was now the real source of financial power and stability for his company.[31] It was Pathé-Frères, after all, which, unable to get much film stock for its own productions, had begun importing Pathé-Exchange films (particularly serials such as *Les Mystères de New York*) and had thus opened the way for the flood of American films into France.[32] Louis Delluc wondered sarcastically if Charles Pathé ever really went to the cinema.[33]

Pathé's proposals marked the initial step of a retreat and a reversion to more conservative business methods.[34] Soon after their possibly inevitable rejection, he embarked on a reorganization of Pathé-Frères to ensure its financial security (the accumulation of capital) and his own semi-retirement, once the war ended. In November, 1918, Pathé-Cinéma was established according to the traditional French principles of limited production, high profit margins, and market-sharing arrangements. Because the French money and material available for film production seemed paltry compared to the American resources—and the German as well, since its film industry had expanded greatly due to the war—and because production had become a financial adventure with unusually high risks, Pathé-Cinéma would concentrate on distribution and exhibition.[35] Also, because the French exhibition market was relatively small (2,400 cinemas to 18,000 in the United States, 3,730 in Germany, and 3,000 in England), any French film project the company might finance would have to have "a sure commercial appeal beyond France itself"—which meant that it should cater to the interests and tastes of the American or English-speaking public.[36] For Pathé, disingenuously, the only crisis facing the French film industry was a "scenario crisis." Consequently, Pathé-Cinéma cut back production (by 1920, S.C.A.G.L. had dwindled to financing André Antoine's last films), sold off

its foreign exchanges, and expanded its network of cinemas in France and nearby lands.[37] To Georges Sadoul, Pathé's new company was a twentieth-century version of Count Ugolin, prospering by devouring its own children.[38]

Most of the other major film companies accepted Pathé's analysis and conclusions. "Everything is beginning again, thanks to the Americans," Gaumont told Léon Poirier. "While our factories produced material for the war, theirs made films; and they have conquered the market."[39] Recognizing the superiority of American film technique ("technique . . . is the key to success") and the French public taste for American films ("the Gaumont-Palace never made more money than when it played a Chaplin comedy or a William Hart western"), Gaumont also turned increasingly to distributing American film imports and closed most of the company's foreign exchange offices.[40] Louis Feuillade's highly profitable serials would be continued, but Gaumont's prescription for the rest of his company's product was simply, "American technique and French subtitles, that is what must be done now."[41]

For its part, Eclair ceased commercial film production and became the Société française du cinéma and then the Société industrielle cinématographique. Although it continued to produce the newsreel, *Eclair-Journal*, and to distribute a few films through Union-Eclair, the company sold its moribund foreign exchange in Germany (which became Erich Pommer's Decla-Bioskop, soon part of the UFA system), made its two studios at Epinay-sur-Seine available on a rental basis, and concentrated on camera equipment and film processing.[42] Eclair's four-lens-turret camera, developed in 1921, together with Debrie's "Parvo" camera (with its automatic dissolve facility) competed on a par with

7. Pathé studio at Vincennes (circa 1920): notice the two-camera setup, with Pathé cameras

8. (facing page) Pathé studio at Monteuil-sous-bois (circa 1920): notice the one-camera setup

Bell and Howell's cameras on the world market.[43] Eclipse halted production entirely and gambled on distributing the films of several stars—René Navarre (briefly), René Cresté (the star of *Judex*), and Suzanne Grandais (perhaps the most popular French film actress of her day).[44] When Suzanne Grandais was killed in an auto accident in September, 1920, the French cinema lost its third top film star in less than a year—the music hall star of Mercanton's *Bouclette* (1918) and Pouctal's *Dieu du hasard* (1919), Gaby Deslys, had died the year before; and Max Linder had returned a second time to the United States.[45] In 1919, Eclipse built a new studio at Boulogne-sur-Seine (short-sightedly following the prewar glass window design that primarily used sunlight for illumination) and rented it out to the other production companies.

Thus, a wave of pessimism, coinciding with the defeatist mood of the country, swept through the French film industry at the crucial moment of its reconstruction. The lack of capital for film production, the lag in advanced technological resources (*Ciné-pour-tous*'s review of French studio facilities, early in 1920, was dismal),[46] the loss of exhibition markets and of control over even those in France—all these contributed to the perceived crisis in 1919. And they would remain more or less unchanged throughout the next decade. Perhaps the best way to consider the various ways the industry responded to these economic and political conditions is to examine separately—since they now functioned separately—the different phases of the industry's operation: production, distribution, and exhibition. For one of the chief characteristics of the French film industry during this period was the fragmentation, decentralization, and lack of coordination in policy and practice among its constituent parts. Yet these presumed disadvantages, in part, proved advantageous.

14

In the production sector, the French film industry underwent a paradoxical series of metamorphoses during the 1920s. It found itself reacting to encroachments by foreign companies and financing and, in the process, saw at least one faction—the Russian emigré film colony—turn into a crucial source of production. It became dependent, in equal measure, on a cottage industry of small companies and individual producer-directors, on several big studios, and on an increasing number of co-production deals with other European countries. And it created fertile conditions for a range of experimental production strategies as well as gambling and profit-taking by opportunistic speculators.

When the French fully realized the power and influence of the American cinema in France at the end of the Great War, one of the first things they did was attempt to imitate or associate themselves with it. Much like Louis Renault's engineers who before the war had studied F. W. Taylor's management methods in the American automobile industry,[1] a stream of producers and filmmakers crossed the Atlantic to study the American film industry, particularly the methods and techniques of its factory system of production. They included Charles Pathé, of course, Henri Diamant-Berger, Germaine Dulac, Abel Gance, Jacques de Baroncelli, Marcel Vandal, and Charles Delac (the last two having now taken joint control of Film d'Art).

In 1918, with Charles Pathé's approval, Diamant-Berger launched the first effort to link up with the Americans. Familiar with Pathé-Exchange's failure to sign a contract with Chaplin after he had left Mutual, Diamant-Berger took as his model instead Louis Mercanton's production of *Queen Elizabeth* (1912), which Adolph Zukor had made such a success in the United States. Zukor was now president of Paramount Pictures, the new leader (in quantity, at least)

Production: From Independent Artisan to International Consortium

15

of American film production. After extensive talks with Zukor, Otto Kahn (Paramount's chief financier), and Adolphe Osso (affiliated with Pathé-Exchange), Diamant-Berger proposed an alliance—"an exchange of stars, directors, technicians, and a limited common market of exhibition."[2] Zukor agreed, and they drew up a plan:

a French-American association based on absolute equality: each will invest one million dollars and hold 49 percent of the shares of the new company; the remaining 2 percent will be put at the disposal of the French partners for the first two years, as long as there are profits; otherwise, the 2 percent will pass to the American partners. . . .[3]

Although personally uninterested in the plan, Pathé arranged for Diamant-Berger to secure financial backing from the bankers supporting Edmond Benoît-Lévy's chain of cinemas. Initially enthusiastic, the bankers cooled to the idea as the postwar inflation began to drive down the value of the French franc. At his end, Zukor agreed to wait, but the French bankers remained adamant—the risk was too great.[4] The collapse of this project was a sign of things to come.

Several subsequent French initiatives got much further along, but they, too, came to naught. In 1919, after returning from the United States, Vandal and Delac embarked on a series of film projects supposedly made according to American production methods and calculated to be marketable in the United States. They hired the American actress, Fanny Ward (who had starred in *The Cheat*), and assigned their new "artistic director," Jacques de Baroncelli, to direct her in two bourgeois melodrama adaptations, *La Rafale* (1920) and *Le Secret du Lone Star* (1920).[5] Unfortunately, it turned out, Fanny Ward was no longer a star in the United States, and not one American distributor agreed to buy the films. Trying another tack, the two producers attempted to reestablish a vertically integrated corporation in France. Their plan was to merge Film d'Art with Eclair, A.G.C., and the circuit of cinemas controlled by Benoît-Lévy, particularly the newly opened Salle Marivaux. This merger, la Compagnie Générale Française de Cinématographie, lasted but a couple of months and produced only one film, Jacques de Baroncelli's *Le Rêve* (1921).[6]

Another ill-fated venture was the Franco-American Cinematographic Corporation, launched in the summer of 1920. Initially, this was announced as a trust, with 300 million francs in capital, that would operate much like the newly formed UFA in Germany and UCI (Union Cinematografica Italiana) in Italy.[7] Its supporters, financial and otherwise, gave the corporation an aura of unusual prestige: the banker Henri de Rothschild, the new auto magnate André Citroën, the Minister of Education, and the director of the Comédie Française. And its scenario department, including the likes of Tristan Bernard, Albert Carré, and André Antoine, showed a good deal of promise. Interestingly, just three months after an elaborate banquet inauguration, the corporation's young secretary-general, André Himmel, was arrested for embezzlement; and the whole project collapsed, without a single film to its credit.[8]

Finally, Diamant-Berger made a second effort to exploit his American connections. On his second trip to the United States, late in 1919, he convinced Adolphe Osso (who had spent seven years with the Pathé-Exchange) to return to France and become an independent producer. The two men quickly agreed on a joint film project, *Le Secret de Rosette Lambert* (1920). Diamant-Berger would provide the scenario (by Tristan Bernard), the director (Raymond Bernard), and half the financing; Osso would provide the other half as well as the distribution and the American star. Unfortunately, the star turned out to be an unknown actress, Lois Meredith, otherwise qualified as Osso's mistress, and Osso's money ran out before the film could be distributed. When Diamant-Berger had to take over the film's distribution at the last minute, he resorted to an American-style publicity campaign, including special poster ads in the film magazines and widely distributed postcards. Although *Le Secret de Rosette Lambert* played at several major Paris cinemas—e.g., the Lutetia, Marivaux, Tivoli, Colisée, Select—it apparently did not regain the filmmaker's investment.[9]

With the failure of these joint French-American ventures and the cutbacks at Pathé-Cinéma, Gaumont, Eclair, and Eclipse, the burden of French film production fell on a diverse group of smaller production companies and independent producers.

9. Louis Nalpas

The most important opposition to what was seen as a full-scale retreat by the French film industry came from a loose band of newly independent producers and filmmakers. At least two of these men dreamed of becoming "American-style producers" within the French film industry structure.[10] They and their colleagues were convinced that, since the American "superproductions" now determined the course of world film production, distribution, and exhibition, the French would have to engage in large-scale productions beyond the budgets of their serials and conventional feature films in order to survive even in their home markets.[11] Since the median budget for a French film in 1920 was about 100,000 to 200,000 francs (or 20,000 to 40,000 dollars, a mere 10 to 20 percent of a comparable American film), the French superproductions would demand budgets of a half million to one million francs.[12] Paradoxically, both of these dreamers received encouragement and financial support from Charles Pathé.

Perhaps the most important of the two was Louis Nalpas, the former production head of Film d'Art, who, with the financial backing of Pathé and Serge Sandberg, an important cinema manager for Aubert, set up his own production company in January, 1919. Films Louis Nalpas was launched with a superproduction of an exotic Arabian Nights story, *La Sultane de l'amour*, which was filmed at the villa Liserb in Nice. Directed by René Le Somptier and Charles Burguet, *La Sultane de l'amour* had a rousing preview in May, 1919, and was a tremendous commercial success when it opened in November, playing for over two months in several major Paris cinemas. Encouraged, Nalpas quickly initiated a series of high- and low-budgeted projects, including Maurice Mariaud's *Tristan et Yseut* (1921) ["six songs" of 650 meters each] and Germaine Dulac's *La Fête espagnole* (1920), from a brief Louis Delluc scenario. He and Sandberg also purchased an area west of Nice called Victorine and constructed an immense studio there for Henri Fescourt's serial superproduction of *Mathias Sandorf* (1921). Nalpas's dream was to create a French version of Hollywood around Victorine. Although Gaumont, Pathé, and the Société des Cinéromans (René Navarre and Jean Durand's company) had small studios around Nice, most of the French film production was still done in and around Paris. But a combination of technological short-sightedness and political resistance (Victorine was only minimally electrified, and the local authorities reneged on several promised commercial concessions) dashed Nalpas's hopes. In the summer of 1920, while Serge Sandberg assumed control of Victorine (for René Navarre's Société des Cinéromans), Nalpas took his films off to the United States in order to sell them there in person. [13]

The other American-style producer was Henri Diamant-Berger, the former editor of *Le Film* and a protégé of Charles Pathé. After his first plan for joint French-American film production fell through, Diamant-Berger set himself up as an independent "executive producer" in Films Diamant. With a budget of 165,000 francs, personally underwritten by Pathé, he engaged the famous French comic, Max Linder (just back from the United States), to make a film of Tristan Bernard's popular boulevard comedy, *Le Petit Café*, at one of Eclair's studios in Epinay. From Gaumont, he hired Raymond Bernard (the play-wright's son) to direct the production. Against great odds (only four Paris cinemas contracted to exhibit it in December, 1919), the film ended up nearly as successful as *La Sultane de l'amour*—eventually bringing in grosses of over a million francs. Undermined by Adolphe Osso, Diamant-Berger's second French-American project, *Le Secret de Rosette Lambert*, immediately depleted most of those profits. [14] But his credit was still good, as we shall see, particularly with Pathé.

Of the established filmmakers who also formed their own production units at this time (e.g., Luitz-Morat from Gaumont, Louis Mercanton from Eclipse, Henry Roussel from Film d'Art), perhaps the most promising were Abel Gance and Jacques Feyder. Gance, it turns out, was also a protégé of Pathé. After making several very successful films during the war for Film d'Art—*Mater Dolorosa* (cost: 48,000 francs/receipts: 181,000), *La Dixième Symphonie* (cost: 63,000 francs/receipts: 343,000)—Gance began the first of a trilogy of films, *Ecce Homo*. [15] Film d'Art became alarmed at the film's costs and closed the production down, leaving the stranded director with a 50,000-franc debt. Pathé personally settled that debt and then arranged for Pathé-Cinéma to finance Gance's war epic superproduction, *J'Accuse* (1919). [16] When that film proved extraordinarily profitable (3,510,000 francs by 1923), [17] the young filmmaker founded Films Abel Gance (again with Pathé's backing) in the summer of 1919. He, too, acted as executive producer for someone else's film, Robert Boudrioz's *L'Atre* (1920-1923). But his energy went primarily into writing and directing (with the poet Blaise Cendrars's assistance) a scenario originally entitled *La Rose du rail*. Late in 1919, Gance constructed an on-location studio in the Gare Saint-Roch railyard outside Nice and began the unexpected year-long shooting schedule on his film, which would finally end in the snowy wastes below Mont Blanc. Three years and 3 million francs later—after the deaths of his leading actor, Séverin-Mars, and of his young wife, Ida Danis—the film opened as *La Roue* (1922-1923) and soon surpassed even *J'Accuse* in popularity.

About the same time in 1919, Jacques Feyder found himself fired at Gaumont, either because of the company's cutback in production or because of a dispute over his direction of *La Faute d'orthographie* (1919) as a comedy. Aware that Gaumont had turned down an option to produce a film from Pierre Benoit's best-seller, *L'Atlantide*, Feyder bought the rights to the novel and was fortunate enough to borrow 600,000 francs from a rich cousin, Alphonse Frédérix, director of the Banque Thalman. Deciding to shoot the film entirely

18

on location, he and his cast and crew filmed all of the interiors and exteriors in various parts of Algeria from March, 1920, to January, 1921. By the time *L'Atlantide*, premiered at the Gaumont-Palace on 4 June 1921, its cost had soared to nearly 2 million francs. Everywhere in Paris, the film's posters proclaimed Feyder as "One man [who] dared." The risk proved worth it, for *L'Atlantide* was a smashing success.[18]

Another group of independent producers and filmmakers opted for a strategy of production quite different from that of the superproductions. This strategy found its most radical advocate in Pierre Henry, the editor of *Ciné-pour-tous*.[19] Since the French could not produce enough quality films to compete with the large-scale American films, Henry argued, they should instead produce top quality short films of two to three reels each (600 to 900 meters). Given the cinema program format of the time, these short films, even made in quantity, would be guaranteed exhibition as a complement to the serials and the American or French superproductions. Henry pointed to several short films then ready for release as worthy examples—Dulac's *La Fête espagnole* (for Louis Nalpas), Baroncelli's *La Rose* and Delluc's *Le Silence* (for Film d'Art), and E. E. Violet's *Le Main* (for Aubert). Although none of the smaller film companies adopted Henry's idea exclusively, several integrated it into their strategy of producing a varied series of low- and medium-budget films.

10. Abel Gance (circa 1917)

As the only major established company to buck the trend toward fewer films, Film d'Art had the potential in the spring of 1920 to act as the leader of this group. The failure of the Fanny Ward films, together with the collapse of the ambitious Compagnie Générale Française de Cinématograhie project, however, seems to have curtailed whatever influence Vandal and Delac may have exerted. Still, their work, along with that of Louis Nalpas, encouraged several others to try their hand at film production. In May, 1920, for instance, Franz Toussaint split away from Films Louis Nalpas to form a company called Jupiter (Société Française des Films Artistiques). Besides distributing Italian film imports and collaborating on several projects with Stoll Films in England, Jupiter set up a schedule of French film production that resulted in about ten completed films in little more than a year. Included in its production were Toussaint's own *Le Destin rouge* (1921), Roussel's *Visages voilés . . . âmes closes* (1921), and Delluc's short feature, *Fièvre* (1921).[20] About the same time, Legrand and Tarieux, a pair of producers who took Vandal and Delac as their model, formed Films André Legrand. For several years, they financed and sometimes wrote scenarios for a number of medium-budget films—René Hervil's *Blanchette* (1921) and *Le Crime de Lord Arthur Saville* (1922), Séverin-Mars's *Le Coeur magnifique* (1921), Dulac's *La Mort du soleil* (1922), and Feyder's *Crainquebille* (1923).[21]

Almost unnoticed at the time (unlike Diaghilev's Ballets russes a decade earlier) a small band of Russian exiles led by Joseph Ermolieff took over an abandoned studio, once built by Méliès and later used by Pathé, at Montreuil-sous-bois. Ermolieff had controlled one of the three major Russian film production companies prior to the 1917 Revolution, and his films had been distributed in Russia by Pathé's exchange office. Initially based in Moscow, Ermolieff had moved to Yalta and then fled to France when the Civil War broke out in 1918. Now reorganized as Films Ermolieff, his company began turning out a series of French films for distribution through Pathé-Consortium. The company's prestige grew quickly as its output increased—Protozanoff's *L'Angoissante Aventure* (1920) and *L'Ombre du péché* (1922), Mosjoukine's *L'Enfant du carnaval* (1921), Tourjansky's *L'Ordonnance* (1921) and *Les Milles et Une Nuits* (1922), Boudrioz's *Tempêtes* (1922), and Volkoff's *La Maison du mystère* (1922).[22]

While Film d'Art was encountering difficulties in its reorganization, Louis Aubert was expanding his company's operations to include film production. His strategy was to draw a number of independent film producers into his orbit of influence by offering them partial financial backing as well as a guaranteed outlet for distribution. By June, 1920, Aubert was acting as a consortium for at least five independent producers: René Hervil, Le Somptier's Cinégraphie d'Art, Delluc's Parisia-Film, Violet's Films Lucifer, and Pierre Marodon's Monte-Carlo Films. Although Hervil soon left the fold to work for Films André Legrand, the rest each had at least one film ready for the fall season. These included Delluc's *Fumée noire* (1920), Violet's *Li-Hang le cruel* (1920), Dulac's *Malencontre* (1920), Charles Maudru's *Le Lys rouge* (1920), and Le Somptier's *La Montée vers l'Acropole* (1920). What Aubert called his "Artistic Effort" nearly suffered the same fate as Jupiter's. But just as his production money was beginning to dry up, in the summer of 1921, he had the foresight to take over the distribution rights to Feyder's *L'Atlantide* (1921).[23]

11. Louis Aubert

This upsurge of independent film production, especially in the face of the continuing flood of American films, even had an effect, momentarily, on Gaumont and Pathé-Cinéma. Despite cutting back on film production (especially its series of short comedies), Gaumont was receptive to several strategies. For instance, he put up 40,000 francs for Marcel L'Herbier's first film, *Rose-France* (1919), a "cantilène" on the war which played briefly at just two Paris cinemas and bombed ignominiously.[24] More important, he used some of the profits from Louis Feuillade's popular series—*Judex* (1917), *La Nouvelle Mission de Judex* (1918), *Tih-Minh* (1919), *Barrabas* (1920), and *Les Deux Gamines* (1921)— to initiate a series of medium-budget quality films called "Séries Pax."[25] Edgar Costil was named the series' executive producer, and Léon Poirier was elevated to the position of "artistic director."[26] Besides himself, Poirier was able to engage L'Herbier and H. Desfontaines as directors for the series, but Gaumont refused his request to add Louis Delluc as well. Over the next three years, Séries Pax produced some of the most imaginative and critically successful French films of the period: Poirier's *Le Penseur* (1920) and *Jocelyn* (1922), L'Herbier's *L'Homme du large* (1920) and *El Dorado* (1921).

The effect of the independent producers on Pathé-Cinéma is more complex. In September, 1920, Charles Pathé announced a further reorganization of his enterprises by dividing Pathé-Cinéma into two separate companies. Under the direction of Ferdinand Zecca, Pathé-Cinéma would henceforth concern itself with amateur camera equipment (the 9.5mm Pathé-Baby), film stock, and film processing. A new company, Pathé-Consortium, was cut loose to manage the commercial film-stock factory at Vincennes, to rent out the old studios at Vincennes and Nice, and to concern itself only with the distribution and exhibition of films. The reason for this division was (and still is) less than clear. There is some evidence to indicate that, earlier in 1920, S.C.A.G.L. was replaced by a production unit called the Société d'Editions Cinématographiques. This unit seems to have adopted a systematic strategy of producing long films divided into several episodes or "chapters." That summer, it initiated a series of expensive superproductions, including Henri Pouctal's *Gigolette* (1921), Bernard-Deschamps's *L'Agonie des aigles* (1921), and René Leprince's *L'Empereur des pauvres* (1922). Perhaps Pathé wanted to nip this speculative venture in the bud. Or rather, to protect his investors with the assurance of growing assets and steady dividends (he was fond of quoting these), he would limit any high-risk speculation in film production to his own personal resources (through S.E.C.). Yet, apparently, it was Pathé who immediately involved Pathé-Consortium in financing an even larger superproduction.[27]

That superproduction was *Les Trois Mousquetaires* (1921-1922), to be directed by Pathé's young friend, Henri Diamant-Berger. Diamant-Berger adapted Dumas's novel as a twelve-hour film divided into hour-long chapters, designed to be released in consecutive weeks over a three-month period. For this gigantic serial, Diamant-Berger was allotted an enormous budget of 2½ million francs.[28] From December, 1920, to September, 1921, the film's shooting ranged widely across France and ended in the studios at Vincennes. There Diamant-Berger installed a battery of mobile ceiling arc lights mounted on rails and transformed it into one of the earliest electrified studios in France.[29] Given an unprecedented gala premiere that lasted three evenings at the Trocadéro, *Les Trois Mousquetaires* went on to become one of the most profitable films of the decade—quickly accumulating an astounding 17 million francs.[30] Its success was aided, to be sure, by an arrangement with United Artists that kept Douglas Fairbanks's *The Three Musketeers* (1921) from being distributed in France and much of Europe.[31] Still, the strategy of balancing the high risk of superproductions with the low risk of serials (consistently the most profitable films in France) looked like a sure bonanza. Before the film was even finished, Pathé-Consortium underwent an important internal transformation that seemed to put it in a position to exploit Diamant-Berger's success.

According to Georges Sadoul, Pathé-Consortium was controlled initially by three major interests: Pathé, the Lyon Banque Bauer et Marchal, and the Gounouilhou-Bourrageas families of Marseille and Bordeaux. In a surprise move, shortly after the company's inauguration, the Gounouilhou-Bourrageas faction seized power. Besides increasing the cinema circuits under its control, the new administration, headed by Denis Richaud, decided to invest heavily in superproductions similar to Diamant-Berger's film. In anger over what he took to be foolhardiness and insubordination (although, ironically, he himself in part was its cause), Pathé resigned from the board of the company he had created. Unflinchingly, Richaud and his "artistic director," M. Fourel, drew up plans to continue the expensive superproductions announced the previous summer. Bernard-Deschamps's *L'Agonie des aigles* (1921) was budgeted at two million francs; Leprince's *L'Empereur des pauvres* (1922) at one million; and Diamant-Berger's second adaptation of Dumas, *Vingt Ans après* (1922-1923), at another two million. Furthermore, they reaffirmed the company's support of Abel Gance's *La Roue*, which had then reached the editing stage. The sum of this capital investment was staggering. Pathé-Consortium's strategy had all the appearances of a strong challenge to the American cinema, but it was dependent on relatively unmodernized technical facilities, dubious scenarios, and directors (excepting Gance) whose styles were distinctly old-fashioned. The stage was set for another fall.[32]

By 1922, French film production had risen to 130 feature-length films per year (up from 80 and 100 films during the two years before). Although this figure was still quite small compared to the production levels of the United States (706 films) and Germany (474 films), it seemed, given the industry's severe limitations, a clear sign of health. Below the surface, however, several of the major production companies were experiencing serious problems and undergoing drastic reorganizations. By 1924, partly because of these changes, the annual production figure had fallen to only 68 films. This drop may have represented a setback for the industry, but it was also a bit deceptive, for the French films were now "larger" (longer and more highly budgeted) and there were more production companies making major films.[33]

All three of the production companies that had survived the war suffered relapses in 1922. When Jacques de Baroncelli left his position as "artistic director" at Film d'Art, Vandal and Delac did not replace him. Instead, they themselves assumed the role of independent producers (to make three or four films per year) and opened negotiations to link Film d'Art with Louis Aubert for distribution purposes.[34] At La Cité Elgé, Léon Gaumont quietly folded his tent in capitulation to the American films. Decision-making power seems to have passed to Edgar Costil and the company's financiers, the Compagnie Générale d'Electricité and the Crédit Commercial de France; Gaumont himself became little more than a board member.[35] Production was reduced to Feuillade's serials and a few low-budget films as the company turned increasingly to the distribution of American films. With Séries Pax halted, Poirier and L'Herbier were let go as directors. In fact, L'Herbier's last film for the series, *Don Juan et Faust*, was shut down near the end of shooting (after its costs had soared to 800,000 francs) and was subsequently released in an oddly truncated form early in 1923.[36]

At Pathé-Consortium, the superproduction strategy was already in doubt by the end of 1922. Receipts on the three big films that followed *Les Trois Mousquetaires* did not measure up to expectations, especially in the case of *L'Empereur des pauvres* (1922). Although the Gounouilhou-Bourrageas faction retained control, Richaud and his associates were sacked and replaced by André Gounouilhou and Henri Mège (of the Banque Bauer et Marchal).[37] The new administration quickly adopted a restrictive policy on film production:

> The industry is going to its ruin if it continues on the path it has followed. We do not want to leave anything to chance, to the unexpected, to accident, delay, negligence, or waste. No film will be undertaken without a precise plan. A French film costs so much because we squander time and money.[38]

The policy change hit Diamant-Berger particularly hard. Pathé-Consortium had earlier agreed to produce a third and final Dumas adaptation, *Le Vicomte de Bragelonne*, and Diamant-Berger was busy transforming an abandoned Niepce airplane hanger in Billancourt into a studio, he says, "the like of which did not exist in France."[39] Besides baths, a restaurant, and a special foyer for the actors, "a veritable electric keyboard—a centralized command post for all the floodlights—would make it the most modern and best-equipped studio in Europe." When Pathé-Consortium abruptly canceled production on *Le Vicomte*, Diamant-Berger was left with a nearly completed studio and little to do. Unable to get financing anywhere else, late in 1923, he had to put Studio Billancourt up for sale to pay his mounting debts.[40] Within six months he would escape the disarray at Pathé-Consortium and seek out a new career in the United States. Much like Gaumont, for all intents and purposes, Pathé-Consortium was on the verge of becoming a film distribution company. The only major films it helped finance now were the serials produced by its new affiliate, the Société des Cinéromans. In that affiliation lay the company's rejuvenation.

Early in 1922, Jean Sapène, publicity editor of the major Paris daily newspaper, *Le Matin*, had taken over the Société des Cinéromans from René Navarre and drawn the company into an alliance with Pathé-Consortium and the Lutetia circuit of cinemas in Paris. Cinéromans would produce serials to appear simultaneously in Pathé-Consortium/Lutetia cinemas and in the cartel of Paris newspapers headed by *Le Matin*. Sapène immediately hired Louis Nalpas (freshly returned from the United States) as his executive producer and put Arthur Bernède (Feuillade's former scriptwriter) in charge of his scenario department. He also began to set up a factory line system of film production and distribution. As the Cinéromans serials, beginning with Henri Fescourt's *Rouletabille chez les bohemiens* (1922), steadily increased in number and popularity, Sapène's influence within Pathé-Consortium rose. By the end of 1923, with the active support of the Banque Bauer et Marchal (through Henri Mège) and Pathé-Cinéma, Sapène was in a position to oust the Gounouilhou-Bourrageas faction, bring back Charles Pathé, and take control of Pathé-Consortium. Behind this takeover, suggests Georges Sadoul, was a power struggle between the cartel of Rightist Paris newspapers (represented by Sapène) and the Rightist provincial newspapers financed by Gounouilhou and Bourrageas. One of Sapène's first measures was to expand the company's production base by buying and renovating (electrifying) the Levinsky studio at Joinville-le-pont (built by Gaumont's old set designer), turning its five stages into the most modern in France. By the end of 1924, Sapène had reorganized Pathé-Consortium into a vertically integrated corporation again, thus making it the most powerful company in the industry.[41]

12. Jean Sapène

The Cinéromans serials—such as Jean Kemm's *L'Enfant-Roi* (1922) and *Vidocq* (1923), Gaston Ravel's *Tao* (1923), Fescourt's *Mandarin* (1923), Leprince's *L'Enfant des halles* (1924), and Luitz-Morat's *Surcouf* (1925)—provided a solid production base for Pathé-Consortium. Secured by their profits, in 1924, Sapène (much like Gaumont after the war) launched a new series under the aegis of "Films de France." These films would be shown in a single *séance*, or performance, and would have preferred treatment in the Pathé-Consortium and Lutetia circuit of cinemas. For the 1924-1925 season, Louis Nalpas announced no less than ten Films de France, including Luitz-Morat's *La Cité foudroyée*, Fescourt's *Les Grands*, and Dulac's *Le Diable dans la ville*.[42]

Yet Cinéromans was only the most important of several French film production companies that, from 1922 to 1924, attempted to compensate for the production cutbacks at Pathé-Consortium, Gaumont, and Film d'Art. If "production in abundance is the sign of industrial power," wrote René Clair, then Louis Aubert was certainly next in line.[43] In an interview with André Lang in 1922, Aubert had offered this famous definition of the cinema: "Two drawers—one for receipts, the other for expenses, and this little mysterious box in which films are filed on index cards. . . ."[44] As one of those drawers turned into a cornucopia of profits, from an expanded circuit of cinemas and from the

13. Cinéromans studio at
Joinville-le-pont (late 1920s)

sensational distribution of Feyder's *L'Atlantide*, Aubert decided, in his words, to boldly play "the French film card."[45] He would do his part to revive the French film industry by investing his fortune in an expanded film production. After hiring C. F. Tavano as his executive producer, Aubert gathered René Hervil, Louis Mercanton, René Le Somptier, E. E. Violet, Donatien, Charles Maudru, as well as Vandal and Delac of Film d'Art into a loose consortium to co-produce a series of films.[46] This new "French Effort" opened with Mercanton's *Phroso* (1922), followed by a half dozen other films, including Hervil and Mercanton's *Sarati-le-Terrible* (1923) and Le Somptier's *La Bête traquée* (1923) and *La Dame de Monsoreau* (1923). By the summer of 1924, Aubert had more than a dozen films in various stages of production, and *Cinéa-Ciné-pour-tous* devoted a full issue (1 September 1924) to the company's upcoming season.

After Cinéromans and Aubert, the most important French production companies were two that developed out of the Russian emigré colony in Paris. In 1922, Joseph Ermolieff left Paris for Berlin and sold Films Ermolieff to his associates, Alexandre Kamenka and Noë Bloch.[47] Kamenka reorganized the company into Films Albatros and quickly initiated a half-dozen film projects. Under his direction, Albatros's production soon shifted to more expensive, more prestigious films—e.g., Tourjansky's *Le Chant de l'amour triomphante* (1923), Volkoff's *Kean* (1924) and *Les Ombres qui passent* (1924), Nadejdine's *Le Chiffonnier de Paris* (1924), and Epstein's *Le Lion des Mogols* (1924). Recently, the scriptwriter, Charles Spaak, described Kamenka, for the consistency of his work, as perhaps the greatest French producer of the 1920s.[48] The second company was financed by a young Russian emigré in the steel industry by the

24

name of Grinieff. It was founded in 1923 by the popular novelist, Henry Dupuy-Mazuel, and by Jean-José Frappé, who christened it the Société des Films Historiques (S.F.H.).[49] The name was apt, for their grandiose scheme, according to André-Paul Antoine, was "to render visually the whole history of France."[50] The company's first project dwarfed, in scope and budget, anything previously attempted by the French film industry. It was an immense reconstruction of the period of Louis XI (late fifteenth century) and of the famous legend of Jean Hachette. Directed by Raymond Bernard, *Le Miracle des loups* became the most popular film of 1924 and the first film ever to be premiered at the Paris Opéra.

14. Alexandre Kamenka

Another sign of the French film industry's regeneration during this period was the continued proliferation of independent production units, most of them small and geared to a particular director. Yet even here there were losses. Germaine Dulac had managed to sustain Films D.-H. for five years through a varied selection of film projects and financial arrangements with other producers and distributors (Harry, Eclipse, Film d'Art, Louis Nalpas, Aubert, André Legrand).[51] In 1921, she dissolved her company and, after a trip to the United States, tried her hand at free-lance work. When that failed (projects in Germany and Italy), Vandal and Delac arranged for Film d'Art to finance her personal production of *La Souriante Madame Beudet* (1923). Then, through the intercession of Louis Nalpas and Henri Fescourt, Dulac signed on with Ciné-romans to direct a serial and one of the first Films de France.[52] The young critic-cinéaste, Louis Delluc, worked independently for three years, from 1920 to 1922, through two separate production companies, Parisia Films and then Alhambra Films—both of which he supported with an inheritance; box office receipts; money from Elena Sagrary, who was allowed to star in *Fièvre* (1921); and financial or administrative assistance from his friends, Henri Diamant-Berger, Louis Nalpas, Jacques de Baroncelli, and Léon Poirier.[53] The budgets for his films were ridiculously low, but the receipts were even lower, so that *La Femme de nulle part* (1922) brought him close to bankruptcy.[54] He had to sell *Cinéa*, the important film journal which he had founded, and abandon all film projects for over a year. Delluc literally worked himself to exhaustion and died prematurely of pneumonia in April, 1924.

Nearly a dozen other film producers and directors, however, set up production companies in Dulac's and Delluc's place. The more successful of these included several of Delluc's mentors. Jacques de Baroncelli, for instance, left Film d'Art to work independently when he was assured production capital from a Belgian financier, Arthur Mathonet. His consistent success with literary adaptations—*La Légende de Soeur Béatrix* (1923), the Prix Goncourt *Nêne* (1924), and *Pêcheur d'Islande* (1924)—made Films de Baroncelli an unexpectedly respectable enterprise.[55] After leaving Gaumont, Léon Poirier set up Films Léon Poirier, apparently modeled on Baroncelli's company, to produce and direct another Prix Goncourt adaptation, *La Brière* (1925). Even the popular dramatist, Tristan Bernard, established his own film production company so that his son Raymond Bernard, from 1921 to 1923, could direct a series of psychological and sentimental comedy scenarios.[56]

While these filmmakers were successful as their own producers, others experienced difficulties or unusual risks in deciding to work independently. After *L'Atlantide*, Jacques Feyder deliberately turned away from superproductions

25

and approached André Legrand to produce a small, realist film adaptation of *Crainquebille* (1923) at a fraction of the cost (only 300,000 francs) of his desert epic.[57] In September, 1923, together with the Max Linder, who had returned a second time from the United States, Feyder announced the formation of Grands Films Independents, a production company financed by two Lausanne businessmen, Dimitri de Zoubaloff and François Porchet.[58] Linder's stay with the company was unusually brief, and the venture quickly collapsed when Feyder and his financiers quarreled over *Visages d'enfants* (1925), whose editing and distribution were held up for a year.[59] For Julien Duvivier, the means to film production was Celor Films, a small company he founded in 1922. On shoestring budgets from diverse sources, Duvivier turned out a variety of films over a three-year period, including the earliest compilation documentary on cinema history, *La Machine à refaire la vie* (1924).[60] Although René Clair came to filmmaking through the intercession of others, he, too, got by on paltry means.[61] Early in 1923, Baroncelli read a script by Clair, who was then his assistant, and sent it on to Henri Diamant-Berger. Still flushed with success from his two superproduction serials, Diamant-Berger arranged a miniscule budget to finance Clair's first film, *Paris qui dort* (1924). In order to continue his independent status through another three films, Clair accepted the patronage of René Fernand and then Rolf de Maré, publisher of *Théâtre et Comoedia Illustré* (for whom Clair wrote as a film critic) and owner-manager of the Théâtre de Champs-Elysées.

15. Marcel L'Herbier

Two other young filmmakers were even more lucky than Duvivier or Clair. On the basis of a surprisingly successful fictionalized documentary film—*Pasteur* (1922)—and the double recommendation of Louis Nalpas and Abel Gance, Jean Epstein won an extraordinary ten-year contract with Pathé-Consortium late in 1922.[62] The contract called for Epstein to make four films a year for Pathé, but he would have complete freedom in his choice of scenarios and in his manner of filming, within a limited budget. Although this arrangement lasted for little more than a year, it produced three important small films—*L'Auberge rouge* (1923), *Coeur fidèle* (1923), and *La Belle Nivernaise* (1924). The most reckless of all the neophytes, Jean Renoir, was also the most wealthy. In 1923, after seeing Mosjoukine's *Le Brasier ardent*, he dropped his work in ceramics and decided to pursue a career in the cinema. Drawing on an immense fortune from his father's paintings, Renoir set up his own production company and began paying for his apprenticeship as a producer and director with *Catherine {Une Vie sans joie}* (1927) and *La Fille de l'eau* (1925).[63]

Finally, there was one independent enterprise whose ambitions loomed larger than any other of the period. This was Cinégraphic, which Marcel L'Herbier founded (with the help of Jean-Pierre Weller, Latigny, and others) when he left Gaumont in 1922. L'Herbier's intention was to create "a kind of workshop [or atelier] of creativity" as an alternative artisanal or cooperative practice to what he saw as an exhausted, timid, unimaginative capitalist production system in France. One of L'Herbier's strategies was to encourage young filmmakers with their films—Jaque Catelain's *Le Marchand de plaisir* (1923) and *La Galerie des monstres* (1924) as well as Claude Autant-Lara's experimental short, *Faits-Divers* (1924). Although unsuccessful in convincing his distributor to back René Clair's script for *Le Fantôme du Moulin Rouge* in 1923, he had Cinégraphic produce Louis Delluc's last film, *L'Inondation* (1924). However,

L'Herbier's own projects were at the center of Cinégraphic's operation, and they were designed to bring together artists and artisans from various disciplines to create special "synthetic" films. Cinégraphic's offices at 9, rue Boissy d'Anglais (in a building owned by the literary patron, le Vicomte de Noailles) became "a school without precedent" where L'Herbier and Philippe Hériat presided over the study and execution of scenarios, decors, costumes, camera setups, and editing. The list of films in preparation included adaptations of Racine's *Phèdre*, Maurice Barrès's *Le Jardin sur l'Oriente*, Oscar Wilde's *The Picture of Dorian Gray*, Pierre Mac Orlan's *La Cavalière Elsa*, and Leo Tolstoy's *Resurrection*. With the decision to go ahead on *Resurrection* and then on a Mac Orlan scenario for *La Femme de glace*, Cinégraphic helped initiate the first era of international co-productions.[64]

The outcome of the French superproduction strategy of 1919-1922 was decidedly mixed. With the exception of *L'Atlantide*, as we will see, none of the big French films made a dent in the large American market. And at home, they failed to ease the near stranglehold of American films in the cinemas. Consequently, at the same time that Jean Sapène set out to strengthen the industry (and his position in it) by revitalizing the serial format, several other major companies and independent producers embarked on a grander strategy to challenge the world cinema markets. The strategy was simple: to produce films that would have international appeal, one must make the basis of their production international. Writing in *Cinémagazine*, Paul de la Borie put the economic basis of this strategy quite bluntly:

the film industry is ruled by economic conditions which do not allow one to treat it nationally, since no nation—except perhaps America—is in a position—cinematographically—to live on its own resources. And because this is so, because all the European markets (whether it please us or not) are constrained to strict interdependence, the conditions of existence for the film industry can be boiled down to this inflexible formula: it will be international or it will not be at all.[65]

So although the foreign policies of the *Bloc national* were still in force and although the Poincaré government had taken the extreme measure of occupying the Ruhr in January, 1923 (to force the Germans to make some kind of war reparations), the French film industry began to seek out alliances with the Germans and Austrians. From American capital and film techniques, the French now turned to German capital and/or studio facilities for the co-production of so-called international films. Although untried by the film industry, this strategy was not without precedent—before the war, one faction of the French government had sought a reconciliation with Germany through various financial collaborations.[66]

This shift in alliances was partly defensive, the result of Paramount's shocking—to the French—invasion of the French film industry. Apparently, the way was prepared by Léonce Perret who, in 1920, had returned from the United States to France and, with Paramount's assistance, had made several independent films under the rubric of Perret Pictures. The most successful of these, *Le Démon de la haine* (1922)—shot in Texas, New York, Paris, London, the French Alps, and along the French-Spanish border—was heralded by *Cinéa* as the "first international film." Perret went on (with or without the help of Paramount is unclear) to set up a new production company for the sole purpose

27

of directing a major superproduction adapted from Pierre Benoit's best-seller, *Koenigsmark* (1923). Showcasing spectacular sets, Bavarian landscapes and castles, and Huguette Duflos in magnificent costumes, *Koenigsmark* had a success that rivaled Feyder's *L'Atlantide*, breaking all the box office records set previously by American films in France. According to Marcel L'Herbier and Léon Moussinac, it became a new model for French superproductions.[67]

On the strength of Perret's success, Paramount opened a new branch office in Paris in 1922 and named Adolphe Osso its director, with orders to implement a policy of film production in France. Osso soon engineered a major coup by releasing one of the most popular French films of the 1922-1923 season, Henry Roussel's *Les Opprimés* (1923). Although this story of a sixteenth-century Flanders peasant girl was shot in France (and Belgium) by a major French director, employing a French crew and cast (excepting the star, Spanish singer Raquel Meller), it was produced and distributed entirely by Paramount.[68] That an epic reconstruction of French history should be made with American money piqued the French no end. While Roussel went on to form an important production company, Lutèce Films, in order to exploit his partnership with Raquel Meller in another epic historical reconstruction, *Violettes impériales* (1924), Paramount initiated a second more contemporary co-production, Robert Boudrioz's *L'Epervier* (1924). When First National announced plans, shortly thereafter, to film a co-production of *Le Collier de la reine* (with Norma Talmadge) on location at Versailles, the French film press exploded in rage.[69] No French film company had ever been accorded that privilege. Pride as much as money was at stake.

Paramount's involvement with a fourth French filmmaker brought grief of a different sort. In the summer of 1922, Adolphe Osso had asked Marcel L'Herbier to prepare for Paramount a script on *Notre-Dame-de-Paris*. When that project failed to develop properly, Osso agreed to a contract with Cinégraphic by which Paramount would handle the international distribution of L'Herbier's adaptation of *Résurrection*. When one-fourth of this ambitious film had been shot at the Epinay studio and on location in Lithuania (at a cost of 300,000 francs), L'Herbier fell ill with typhoid, and the project closed down. After his recovery, Marcel Lapierre writes, L'Herbier worked tirelessly to put together 2 million francs and was about to resume shooting on the film. At that moment, however, Universal reported that it was preparing an American version of *Résurrection* on a budget the equivalent of 20 million francs! Paramount promptly reneged on the distribution of L'Herbier's film, and the Cinégraphic project collapsed for good. Undaunted by this demonstration of American power and self-interest, L'Herbier was not to be denied. The following summer, he signed a contract with the singer-actress, Georgette Leblanc, and Otto Kahn (the prominent American patron of the arts and Paramount's principal banker) to produce a film starring Leblanc that would be destined for American as well as European audiences. Director and star clashed repeatedly over Pierre Mac Orlan's scenario—the one wanting to "present a synthesis of the modern decorative arts," the other demanding more emphasis on her character and the story. The result was a "modernist fantasy," *L'Inhumaine* (1924), whose mixed critical reception and soft returns ended Cinégraphic's status as a fully independent production company.[70]

The conjunction of these film projects with the political tide that was building to the *Cartel des gauches* victory in the 1924 elections spurred Aubert and Pathé-Consortium to seek a rapprochement with the German film industry. Aubert's own experience with Franco-American productions gave him added incentive. In 1923, he repeated Vandal and Delac's strategy of hiring American stars for French films. Aubert hired another eclipsed American actor, Sessue Hayakawa, to star in two major superproductions, Violet's *La Bataille* (1923) and Roger Lion's *J'ai tué* (1924). Although the first had considerable success in Europe, the second flopped badly. The owner of the Fordys cinema chain made the same mistake by engaging the old serial queen, Pearl White, for a film entitled *Terreur* (1924)—with disastrous consequences. In April and May, 1924, while marketing his films in Germany, Aubert developed a fresh tack in negotiations with UFA and Erich Pommer. A new German production company by the name of Vita-Film had constructed a studio in Vienna and was anxious to collaborate with the French film industry on co-productions. Aubert and Pommer arranged for the big spectacle film, *Salammbô* (1925), to be shot there, with a French director and cast. The path to this co-production was probably laid down by Jacques Feyder who, after the debacle of *Visages d'enfants*, had accepted the position of "artistic director," as well as a three-film contract, at Vita-Film. Certainly it was Feyder who persuaded Vita-Film to produce Max Linder's *Le Roi du cirque* (1925), which Violet directed and Aubert distributed. Of the three films in production in Vienna during the summer of 1924, however, *Salammbô* and Feyder's own *L'Image* (1926) did poorly at the box office. Their failure coincided with the fall of the Austrian currency, and Vita-Film was thrown into bankruptcy. Although the experience was anything but fortuitous, Aubert's alliance with UFA and Pommer remained intact, momentarily.[71]

The most spectacular example of this international strategy, however, involved Pathé-Consortium in an alliance with two new firms in France and Germany. In 1923, the important German financier, Hugo Stinnes ("the coal merchant of Mülheim"), and a wealthy Russian emigré, Vladimir Wengeroff, conceived the idea of a grand European film consortium. Together, the two speculators formed the Westi Corporation in Berlin and began setting up affiliated companies throughout Europe, the most important being Ciné-France in Paris, directed by Noë Bloch, the former associate of Kamenka and Ermolieff. Late in 1923, Pathé-Consortium joined the group and gave its authority to the strategy. The first contract was between Westi, Pathé-Consortium, and Films Abel Gance. This was for Gance's mammoth project, a six-part *Napoléon*, for which Westi created a separate administrative firm, Wengeroff Films. Gance's immediate response was to buy and complete Diamant-Berger's studio at Billancourt, where *Napoléon*'s shooting commenced in January, 1925. The next contract was between Westi and Ciné-France for a project announced in March, 1924, *Michel Strogoff* (1926), to star Ivan Mosjoukine under the direction of Léonce Perret. Another Westi-Ciné-France project starring Mosjoukine was signed and begun the next summer, *Le Prince charmant* (1925), directed by Tourjansky. When difficulties cropped up over the production of *Michel Strogoff* (Perret signed a contract with Paramount), Tourjansky also agreed to direct the second film after completing *Le Prince charmant* at the Billancourt studio of Abel Gance. Finally, late in 1924, a third Westi-Ciné-France project put Germaine Dulac under contract to direct what would become *Âme d'artiste* (1925). Pathé-Consortium agreed to distribute all of these co-productions in France; for its part, Westi contracted to distribute the Grinieff-financed *Le Miracle des loups* in Germany and Eastern Europe. The magnitude of this Franco-German consortium, much of it financed by Russian emigré money and employing some of the best French directors and technicians, dwarfed even Aubert's alliance with Erich Pommer and UFA. So much so that the axis of Pathé-Consortium, Ciné-France, and Westi seemed to offer the possibility of a genuine European challenge to the American film industry's dominance.[72]

Yet strong political and economic forces were already in motion to undermine the strategy of these alliances. The rapprochement foreign policy of the *Cartel des gauches* government certainly gave sanction to the cooperative enterprises of the French and German film industries. Its economic policies, however, had a double-edged effect. The bank capital strike and the high rate of inflation produced by these policies forced the industry to look beyond its national borders for production financing and thus indirectly fostered co-productions. But not many French producers were in a position to attract foreign capital—the major corporations, yes; the smaller firms and independent producers (with an exception or two), no. More and more money was going to fewer and fewer films. The consequence was that only fifty-five films were released in 1926, the lowest number until the transition year of 1929.[73]

Furthermore, the co-production strategy of the major corporations was thwarted by what was happening in Germany. In the summer of 1924, the Allies set up what was called the Dawes Plan to stabilize the Deutschmark (after Germany's rampant inflation threatened the international financial community) and to give the Weimar Republic economic control over all of its territory (ending French occupation of the Ruhr), both of which were designed to provide Germany with the means to pay off its reparations debt.[74] The Dawes Plan, in effect, encouraged the investment of American capital in Germany to shore up most sectors of its economy, including the film industry.[75] One by one, the German film companies found themselves indebted to the Americans, partially absorbed by them, and then systematically robbed of many of their best personnel.[76] By early 1927, according to Léon Moussinac, 75 per cent of German film production was financed by American money.[77] Although the Dawes Plan may have helped deflect American film investment from France to Germany, it also disrupted the French-German efforts to create a truly European consortium. Consequently, the period from 1925 to 1926 saw a good deal of change in the production sector of the French film industry.

The American influence in French film production grew slowly but steadily. Under Adolphe Osso's (sometimes token) stewardship, Paramount's Paris office presented the most lavish spectacle film of the 1925-1926 season, Léonce Perret's *Madame Sans-Gêne* (1925), starring Gloria Swanson as the legendary eighteenth-century rags-to-riches duchess. Its 14-million-franc budget clearly separated the fat from the lean, for a similar sum could have produced ten French films. To the consternation of the French film industry, *Madame Sans-Gêne* had a tumultuous reception and was awarded the Jury Grand Prix at the famous Paris Exposition des Arts Décoratifs. Released six months earlier, in a much shortened version, in the United States, however, it drew faint praise and less than expected grosses. Although some in the industry began to question the whole strategy of international films, Paramount itself went ahead with two smaller film projects for the following year.[78]

Metro-Goldwyn's alliance with Gaumont countered French film production in a different way. Its distribution contract of April, 1924, led to even further reductions in Gaumont's own filmmaking. When Louis Feuillade died in March, 1925, the company had no other directors or projects and La Cité Elgé was turned into a rental studio. Within six months, Gaumont had become Gaumont-Metro-Goldwyn, controlled by the American corporation as an outlet for MGM films.[79]

Aubert found itself being co-opted by the Paramount and MGM interests on another front, in Germany. Although German film production declined steadily during the first half of the decade (from 646 to 228 films per year) according to Georges Sadoul, the cost and the quality of its films just as steadily mounted. What specifically affected Aubert was the unsuccessful attempt by UFA, Germany's largest production company, to challenge the growing American hegemony with a series of monumental films for export—e.g., Lang's *Nibelungen* (1924) and *Metropolis* (1927), Murnau's *The Last Laugh* (1924), *Tartuffe* (1925), and *Faust* (1926). This strategy soon had UFA impossibly overextended—with vast studio holdings, scarcely any liquid assets, and an increasing indebtedness to American interests. In a joint agreement, signed in December, 1925, Paramount and MGM became controlling partners in a reorganization of the German firm. Each of the three partners would produce twenty films annually for distribution through a subsidiary, Parufamet. No longer its own master, UFA began using its contract with Aubert, as well as others, merely as one way to fill its production quota of films.[80]

The alliance between Pathé-Consortium, Ciné-France, and Westi suffered an even greater shock. Early in 1924, Hugo Stinnes died suddenly, and Wengeroff was left as sole director of Westi Corporation and its far-flung affiliates. It was he who had initiated all the projects in France: Gance's *Napoléon* and the three films under Noë Bloch of Ciné-France. He had even persuaded Jean Sapène to let Westi help finance Henri Fescourt's four-part adaptation of *Les Misérables* (1925-1926). Sapène needed the Westi money because *Les Misérables* was the biggest film Cinéromans had attempted, with a budget of nearly five million francs and a cast that included fifteen major and fifty minor roles. In the spring of 1925, however, the Stinnes empire was disclosed to be deeply in debt. After a quick examination, the German banks decided to liquidate all the Stinnes companies, among them the Westi Corporation, which was dissolved in August, 1925. Suddenly bereft of financing, Gance's *Napoléon* was halted in mid-shooting, a shutdown that would last six months. Cinéromans' *Les Misérables* and *Michel Strogoff* were also severely cut back near the end of production. Unable to operate on its own, Ciné-France disappeared. The dream of a European consortium was in ashes.[81]

For most of the smaller French producers, ironically, the domestic and foreign policies of the *Cartel des gauches* also spelled the end of independent film production.

Considered on the commercial level, [films] must inevitably become a kind of factory product. More and more, film directors are condemned to bend to the exigencies of companies—there is only one option: to submit or to be sent packing—and it is because they have not yet been able to replace this system that they support it.[82]

As their sources of financing dried up, the more commercial independent filmmakers, such as Julien Duvivier, Henry Roussel, and Jacques de Baroncelli, moved within the spheres of influence of Aubert/Film d'Art, the Société des Films Historiques, or Cinéromans. After the Westi collapse, Abel Gance kept his own company alive in name only. Bled white by his ill-fated Franco-American productions, Marcel L'Herbier allied Cinégraphic with Films Albatros on a project starring Mosjoukine, *Feu Mathias Pascal* (1925). Successful though the film was, Cinégraphic remained in debt, and L'Herbier was forced to accept a six-film contract with Cinéromans. After his Swiss and Austrian debacles, Jacques Feyder reluctantly signed on with Albatros. He was joined there by René Clair, whose independent productions with René Fernand and Rolf de Maré were commercially unsuccessful. Finally, Jean Renoir's fortune began to run out. With Pierre Braunberger, the former director of Paramount's publicity department in Paris, Renoir arranged to produce a film adaptation of *Nana* (1926), in conjunction with a German studio. When the film failed through a quirk in distribution, much of Renoir's one-million-franc investment was lost. Desperate to direct a more commercial project, he accepted financing from actress Marie-Louise Iribe (the wife of Pierre Renoir), who set up Les Artistes Réunis so she could star in *Marquitta* (1927).[83]

Against this tide of retreat and consolidation, only a few producers and filmmakers could pursue their own way. Of the old guard, only Léon Poirier was fortunate enough to find independent financing. From 28 October 1924 to 26 June 1925, he and Georges Specht documented the Citroën-sponsored automobile race across Africa (from Morocco to Madagascar) in *La Croisière noire* (1926). After that, however, Poirier was able to complete just one major fiction film during the last half of the decade, *Verdun, vision d'histoire* (1928). In 1925 and again in 1927, Germaine Dulac interrupted her contractual assignments at Ciné-France and Cinéromans to produce three small films on her own, none of which received more than scant circulation—*Folie des vaillants* (1925), *L'Invitation au voyage* (1927) and *La Coquille et le clergyman* (1928). Intrigued by his experience of starring in Raymond Bernard's *Le Miracle des loups* (1924) and *Joueur d'échecs* (1927), the famous Théâtre de l'Atelier director and actor, Charles Dullin, formed his own film production company, Société Charles Dullin. The company functioned much like L'Herbier's Cinégraphic, gathering together a small group of artists, including the documentary filmmaker, Jean Grémillon, to make its one and only superproduction, *Maldone* (1928).[84]

Perhaps the most important of the independent production companies were those of Jean Epstein and Pierre Braunberger. Late in 1925, Epstein left Films Albatros, where he had directed four films, after breaking his contract at Pathé-Consortium nearly two years before. Several months later, with the backing of Marguerite Viel (another Russian emigré) and the indirect support of Abel Gance, he established Films Jean Epstein and gathered around him a group of young film enthusiasts as assistants, one of whom was Luis Buñuel.[85] His company produced four major films over the next four years, none of which had much success except in the limited circuit of specialized cinemas throughout Europe. After the disappointment of *Nana*, Pierre Braunberger founded Néo-Film to both produce and distribute French films. Néo-Film was conceived even more along the lines of L'Herbier's earlier Cinégraphic. While financing major commercial projects by Jean Renoir and Alberto Cavalcanti (L'Herbier's former assistant and set designer), Braunberger also sponsored documentaries and experimental short films.[86] Much like Epstein's work, his productions also (but not exclusively) often appeared in the specialized cinemas. What Braunberger did to support several avant-garde filmmakers of this period provided a model for his later support of the young New Wave filmmakers, especially from 1954 to 1958.

The political and economic changes that occurred in France in 1926 reversed the downslide or slump that was spreading gloom throughout the French film industry. The *Union nationale* foreign policy of conciliation continued to encourage international co-productions. But, more important, conservative fiscal policies finally ended the high rate of inflation and stabilized the value of the franc. Even the rate of unemployment fell drastically. As more capital became available again in France, the level of film production rose accordingly—from fifty-five films in 1926 to seventy-four in 1927 and ninety-four in 1928. Although the forty-three producers and twenty-five distributors responsible for those films evidenced much the same fragmentation and disorganization as before, the future looked bright.[87] France seemed embarked on an era of prosperity and the easy life.

The four major production companies all went through changes in management and orientation. Albatros lost most of its Russian emigré base—Mosjoukine signed a contract with Universal to work in the United States and then Germany; Tourjansky and Volkoff both transferred to Films Abel Gance and then to Noë Bloch's Ciné-France. To continue his policy of quality films at Albatros, Kamenka engaged Jacques Feyder, René Clair, and Henri Chomette (Clair's older brother and Feyder's assistant) to direct films that were more specifically French. His dividend was a series of brilliant comedies, the best of the decade. By contrast, the Société des Films Historiques shifted to a non-French subject by putting a second epic historical reconstruction into production, Raymond Bernard's *Joueur d'échecs* (1927). Grinieff held up its shooting to divert funds to Gance's stalled *Napoléon*; and after that risky adventure, Films Historiques resumed its own orientation. Its last projects included Roussel's life of Chopin, *Valse de l'adieu* (1928), and two historical films by Jean Renoir, one of which, *Le Bled* (1929), marked the centennial celebration of French colonization in Algeria. Louis Aubert did both more and less. Although he tried valiantly to sustain the high level of production he had initiated in 1924, his 1925-1926 season of films contained some dreadful disappointments, such as *Salammbô*. In February, 1926, he ceded administration of the Aubert cinema chain to a M. Cari and, like Pathé and Gaumont before him, began to take a less active role in his company's operations.[88] Production was cut back slightly, but without disturbing the alliance with Vandal and Delac of Film d'Art. Although the company lost its major director in René Hervil, Aubert himself signed up the new film production team of Jean Benoît-Lévy (an educational filmmaker) and Marie Epstein (Jean Epstein's sister), and Film d'Art took Julien Duvivier under contract.[89]

After the collapse of Westi and Ciné-France, Jean Sapène's Cinéromans was left as the central house of production within Pathé-Consortium. The company's announcement for the 1926-1927 season was down a bit from the previous two years: four serials, of course, but only four new Films de France, plus a special co-production with Cinégraphic.[90] Was Sapène concerned about this slippage? Did he now believe himself better qualified than Louis Nalpas to run most phases of Cinéromans' operation? For whatever reasons, "around 1926-1927," according to Henri Fescourt, "Sapène personally took charge of the preparation of all the films his company was going to produce."[91] What particularly obsessed him was reading and revising all the *découpages*, especially rewriting the intertitles. This intervention even led him to the extreme of launching a publicity campaign around a series of films to make a star of his wife, Claudia Victrix (was he thinking of William Randoph Hearst and Marion Davies?). In effect, Sapène took over Nalpas's position as executive producer. Jean-Louis Bouquet concludes that, though audacious in his business enterprises, Sapène was unusually cautious and even retrograde in his artistic tastes and that he failed to encourage and promote the best of his young staff within the company.[92] Despite such innovations as a far-ranging campaign to advertise his film production schedule nearly a year in advance of its release date, the Cinéromans films began to suffer from his lack of taste and judgment.[93] As he himself admitted later, "Having entered the film industry by error, I remained there out of pride."[94]

Coupled with this leveling off or incipient stagnation of the major French film producers (which, some have argued, provided a climate of security), the stabilization of the French economy stimulated the development of several new production companies.[95] Besides Pierre Braunberger's relatively minor Néo-Film, the two most important firms were Production Natan and Franco-Film, both of which seem to have developed out of associations with Paramount. Early in 1926, Bernard Natan, the director of a film processing company and publicity agency (Rapid-Film and Rapid-Publicité), turned his speculative sights on the opportunities in film production. First, he arranged distribution rights through Paramount for a film adaptation of Pierre Benoit's novel, *La Châtelaine du Liban* (1926). Then, after meeting Henri Diamant-Berger, just back from two years in the United States, Natan agreed to produce two of his films, one of which, *Education de Prince* (1927), was lucky enough to star Edna Purviance. Based on the success of these films as well as his association with Paramount, Natan purchased one of the old Eclair studios at Epinay and constructed another completely modernized one, the Studio Réunis, on rue Francoeur in Montmartre. From René Fernand, he secured the rights to produce Marco de Gastyne's *Mon coeur au ralenti* (1928) and Maurice Gleize's *La Madone des sleepings* (1928). Then came his most ambitious project, the popular historical reconstruction that took two years to complete, Marco de Gastyne's *La Vie merveilleuse de Jeanne d'Arc* (1929). By this time, the *Cinématographie française* was calling Natan one of the most important French film producers.[96]

Early in 1927, Robert Hurel, another French producer at Paramount, formed a consortium called Franco-Film out of a number of small firms—Films Léonce Perret, Jacques Haik (Gaston Ravel), and Paris-International (actor-director Léon Mathot and Italian actress Soava Gallone). Within as many months, Hurel announced at least six films for the upcoming fall season, headlined by Perret's *Morgane la sirène* (1927). What helped the consortium get under way was Perret's reputation plus the profits from *La Femme nue* (1926), which had been financed by Natan, perhaps with Paramount's assistance. By the summer of 1928, Franco-Film was so prosperous that it took over the former Louis Nalpas studios at Victorine (which Rex Ingram had been using for several years). Even though two of its affiliates had close ties to England and Italy, Franco-Film professed its commitment to "the development of French cinematography" with "programs composed of French films."[97] The commitment was far from empty in the context of international co-productions.

Despite the collapse of the Westi consortium, the costliness of Aubert's agreement with UFA, and a number of outcries from within the industry itself—René Clair, for one[98]—the strategy of international co-productions continued in vogue. Georges Sadoul sums it up well:

16. Bernard Natan

In the last years of prosperity, the French productions evolved toward huge set pieces with sumptuous costumes and decors, in hopes of rivaling Hollywood. For these "prestige" films, the last big French producers resorted, especially after 1925, to formulas which drew them into associations with various foreign countries, Germany mainly, but also England, Sweden, sometimes Italy, and more rarely the United States. For the powerful German cartel UFA, the co-production strategy was a means of enlarging its position in the French market. Collaborations between Berlin and Paris developed considerably.[99]

In fact, international co-productions threatened to monopolize the production capital and energy of the French film industry.

Much of this investment went into one corporation that emerged from the ashes of Westi and Ciné-France. Late in 1925, Grinieff, the Russian emigré financier behind the Société des Films Historiques, along with Henry de Cazotte, founded the Société Générale des Films (S.G.F.), on whose board sat none other than Charles Pathé. The occasion of S.G.F.'s formation was Grinieff's decision to finance the remaining production schedule for Abel Gance's *Napoléon* (1927). Although only Part I of the six-part epic was completed, S.G.F.'s largesse seemed limitless. By the time *Napoléon* premiered at the Opéra in April, 1927, it had become the most expensive French film of the decade—at a cost estimated somewhere between 15 and 19 million francs. Soon after *Napoléon* resumed shooting at the Billancourt studio, S.G.F. announced a second project, *Casanova* (1927), which drew most of its personnel from Albatros and Ciné-France: Bloch (producer), Volkoff (director), Lochakoff (set designer), Bilinsky (costumes), and Mosjoukine (star). Finally, during the later stages of *Napoléon*'s shooting, S.G.F. offered the Danish filmmaker, Carl Dreyer (whose *Master of the House* [1925] had just had a big success in Paris), the chance to make a film on a famous woman who might complement Napoléon in French history. Dreyer accepted and began work on *La Passion de Jeanne d'Arc* (1928), importing his cinematographer and set designers from Germany.[100]

The fascinating thing about S.G.F. was, as Harry Alan Potamkin put it, that, among the major French corporations, it alone allowed "the director, and not the fiscal policy, to set the pace" and character of its film production.[101] Although restricted to historical reconstruction projects, Grinieff offered the filmmaker unbelievable conditions: total control over all phases of production and an almost unlimited budget. Overwhelmed by a screening of

La Passion de Jeanne d'Arc, G. W. Pabst confessed that the German film industry could never be that experimental with so much money.[102] This was
atelier filmmaking raised to a level that even Marcel L'Herbier had not dreamed
possible at Cinégraphic. It was an incredible risk, especially on the eve of the
sound film revolution. Perhaps inevitably, the result of this concentrated be-
neficence was financial disaster for the company.

International companies and cross-cultural contracts now proliferated in the
place of independent French production units. Henry Roussel's Lutèce Films,
apparently aided by S.G.F., invited Maurice Tourneur back from the United
States for a major French superproduction on the war, *L'Equipage* (1928).[103]
For his part Jacques Feyder signed a contract with DEFU-Deutsche First National to direct a French-German cast in a Berlin studio production of *Thérèse
Raquin* (1928).[104] The Société des Films Artistiques, SOFAR, which had been
based in Italy and Germany, initiated a series of modern studio spectaculars
directed in France by the Italian director, Augusto Genina.[105] By now, however, the Russian emigré talent and money were shifting substantially to Germany. Late in 1927, *Cinématographie française* announced a six-film contract
between UFA and Ciné-Alliance, a new company headed again by Noë Bloch.
The first film was a lavish spectacle film, Volkoff's *Schéhérazade* (1928), shot
in UFA's Berlin studio.[106] Besides Volkoff, this project tied up Lochakoff,
Bilinsky, and Nicolas Koline, all formerly of Albatros and Ciné-France.

Either out of necessity or speculative desire, the older French majors were
drawn into the international strategy again. In 1927, no less than three Cinéromans films were co-productions: Robert Wiene's *La Duchesse des Folies-Bergère*
(filmed in Vienna, Berlin, and Paris), Gaston Ravel's *Le Roman d'un jeune
homme pauvre* (shot in Berlin), and Marcel L'Herbier's *Le Diable au coeur* (made
in conjunction with UFA and Gaumont-British).[107] Aubert tried to recover
from *Salammbô* with another film directed by Wiene, *Der Rosenkavalier* (1927),
which was shot in Vienna under the baton of Richard Strauss himself.[108] Late
in 1927, Vandal and Delac, Aubert, and Wengeroff-Films signed an accord
to produce a series of films jointly.[109] The first of their projects was Julien
Duvivier's *Le Tourbillon de Paris* (1928). About the same time, Albatros and
Sequana-Films (a production company newly established at the Billancourt
Studio) announced "a French-German-Spanish-Swedish collaboration," which,
after several comedies, culminated in *Cagliostro* (1929), with a French-German
cast under the direction of Richard Oswald in Paris.[110] And, despite its commitment to French films, even Franco-Film hired the German director, E. A.
Dupont, to shoot *Moulin Rouge* (1928) in Paris and London as an Anglo-French
production.[111]

As older production companies such as Cinéromans and Aubert seemed to
mark time, newer companies such as Franco-Film and Natan's Studio Réunis
grew apace. In February, 1928, Gaumont severed its alliance with MGM, by
common consent, and began developing its optical sound-on-film process for
feature film production.[112] The stage was set for the transition to sound films.

At least three conclusions can be drawn at this point about French film
production during this period. First of all, the production sector of the industry underwent a kind of compression-explosion that created a multitude of
large-, medium-, and small-scale enterprises. Although Pathé-Consortium,

Gaumont, Cinéromans, and Aubert (at certain moments) could claim that they made more films than any other company, clearly the majority of French films were produced by small firms and independent producers. In one sense, this dispersion of film production was a regression from the consolidated system that had marked the French film industry before World War I. It even looked archaic compared either to the corporate capitalist structure of the American film industry (with its model of division of labor and scientific management, instituted by Thomas Ince, as well as its half-dozen vertically integrated monopolies, spurred by Zukor's Paramount Pictures and perhaps modeled on the old Pathé-Frères company) or to the state-supported (through favorable legislation) structure of the German film industry.[113] Heterogeneous and internally competitive, the French companies were hardly in a position to challenge the larger, more homogenous, more financially endowed corporations in the United States and Germany—though they doggedly persisted in doing so. In another sense, however, this decentralized system of small French production companies depended on an unusual degree of entrepreneurial independence and artisan- or atelier-based praxis.[114] That independence and praxis fostered an attitude of risk-taking, experimentation, and concern for Frenchness, not only in certain individual filmmakers, but even in such large companies as Albatros, Cinégraphic, Ciné-France, S.F.H., and S.G.F. On that basis alone, the French film industry could be said to rival its competitors in the United States, Germany, and the Soviet Union.

Second, a good portion of the production sector's investment came from outside France. Less came from the United States than one might have expected, at least until the last couple of years of the decade. But then, the British and German film industries and markets offered greater opportunities for the Americans.[115] More came from Germany, after 1924, but gradually that investment amounted to the use of German capital and studio facilities for co-productions in Germany. The extraordinary thing was the high incidence of Russian emigré money in French film production. The heavy French investment in prewar Russia had not been lost entirely after all. The Russian emigré money supported a variety of production strategies—from Albatros and S.F.H.'s commercial quality films to Ciné-France's international co-productions, from Abel Gance's epic *Napoléon* to Jean Epstein's narrative experiments. Without this lavish financing (through Grinieff, Wengeroff, Bloch, and Kamenka), the French production efforts of Sapène and Aubert might not have been sufficient to counter the American and German product. Nearly all of this foreign investment, however, went directly into individual films. For modernizing their production base in studios and equipment, the French had to rely on themselves. Technologically, they tended to lag behind the Americans and Germans, from a lack of capital, certainly, but perhaps also from a lack of industrial research, research that linked investor and entrepreneur.[116] Consequently, the work of Debrie and Eclair (on camera equipment) and of Diamant-Berger and Sapène (on studio facilities), for instance, was all the more important for the industry's survival.

Finally, the heady champagne of internationalism, which dominated the latter half of the decade, failed to strengthen and broaden the industry as had been hoped. The Americans could not have been more pleased with the results than if they had concocted the strategy themselves and unashamedly sold the

French on it. As modern studio spectaculars began to rival in number the historical reconstruction films, the French co-productions increasingly mirrored American films, reflecting a modern style of life whose characteristics of material well-being and conspicuous consumption were basically American. As early as 1926, an American analyst reported:

> The peoples of many countries now consider America as the arbiter of manners, fashions, sports, customs and standards of living. If it were not for the barrier we have established, there is no doubt that the American movies would be bringing us a flood of the immigrants. As it is, in a vast number of instances, the desire to come to this country is thwarted, and the longing to emigrate is changed into a desire to imitate.[117]

As Marcel Braunschvig conceded, "film is in the process of Americanizing the world."[118] Increasingly also, the American and German film companies were encroaching on French terrain (in 1928, United Artists and First National joined Paramount as French film producers) or siphoning off its talent (e.g., Feyder, Volkoff, Mosjoukine). More and more French resources seemed to be involved in projects whose profits went to the Germans or Americans (and sometimes both together). This encroachment and exploitation were even stronger in the distribution and exhibition sectors of the French film industry.

Distribution: The Divided Country

If the French government's attitude toward French film production was strictly laissez-faire, its attitude toward film distribution and exhibition was a bit more ambiguous. That ambiguity is apparent in the government's fitful attention to film censorship and to film imports regulation.

Before the war, according to Paul Leglise, the control of film distribution and exhibition, like that of theatrical performances, was in the hands of local authorities.[1] In 1906, the Chamber of Deputies abandoned the system of a national commission to control spectacles in France and delegated the power of censorship to local mayors and police chiefs. This system led to a crazy quilt of standards and wild fluctuations in censorship practices. The southeast provinces, including Lyon, were especially prone to ban films, and even the Minister of the Interior would step in occasionally to recommend the censorship of films "susceptible of provoking demonstrations that might disturb the public order and tranquility." The advent of the war brought further crackdowns, particularly on the crime serials.

Finally, after continued protests from film distributors and cinema owners, the Minister of the Interior established a temporary national Commission du Contrôle des Films in June, 1916.[2] The principal purpose of the commission was to review the weekly *Annales de la guerre*, which was produced by the army's section on photography and cinematography. The head of that section, J.-L. Croze, remembers two examples of the commission's censorship practice. It banned shots of General Pétain grimacing at the taste of the common soldiers' wine, and, in 1918, it eliminated all references to the approaching armistice.[3] The commission's jurisdiction also extended to the rest of the French film production and even to film imports, thus paralleling the power of local mayors and police chiefs, which remained in force. Marcel Lapierre has argued that another reason for the commission's creation was the popularity of the crime serials and their supposedly harmful effect on the young who, under lessening parental control, were flocking to the cinemas.[4] Yet the commission allowed most of the serials to pass uncut in Paris, while some provincial authorities banned the Pearl White serials and even Gaumont's *Judex* (which, ironically, was quite properly moralistic compared to the previous criminal celebrations of *Les Vampires*). What the commission did do, however, was halt the distribution of such American films as Griffith's *Birth of a Nation* and *Intolerance* (which was screened privately within the industry in 1917, perhaps when Griffith himself visited France in May and October), forbid the production of "bloody" dramas such as *Othello*, and cut from Thomas Ince's *Civilization* Christ's words to his disciples, "Let peace be with you!"[5]

In 1917, the Minister of the Interior appointed a committee to recommend a national regulation system for film distribution and exhibition that could be instituted after the war. As both Leglise and Diamant-Berger have pointed out, the primary motivation of the committee was to protect the film industry from the vicissitudes of local censorship in the provinces. After two years of wrangling, on 25 July 1919, the government established a central commission of thirty members, headed by Charles Deloncle and including Charles Pathé, Léon Gaumont, and even Abel Gance. Henceforth, all films except newsreels would have to obtain visas from the commission to permit their distribution in France. The visa system applied equally to French films and imports, and several films soon came under fire. In 1920, and again in 1921, the Interior Minister personally banned one of Aubert's early film productions, *Li-Hang le cruel*. In 1920, the exhibition run of Marcel L'Herbier's *L'Homme du large* was interrupted to excise shots of violence and eroticism from several sequences in the village café. Louis Delluc's *Fièvre* (1921) had to be recut for similar reasons. Despite the central commission's status, film bannings continued in the provinces, again especially in the southeast; and, surprisingly, several court rulings upheld their legality. Film journals (*L'Ecran, Ciné-Journal*), newspapers (*Comoedia*), as well as filmmakers such as André Antoine (who had fought censorship in the theaters two decades earlier), protested both the national and local forms of film censorship. However, the industry generally downplayed the issue, and these protests fell on deaf ears in the National Assembly. Sanctions continued against such films as L'Herbier's *Don Juan et Faust* (1923), Epstein's *Coeur fidèle* (1923), Feyder's *L'Image* (1926), and Cavalcanti's *Rien que les heures* (1926).[6]

Finally, in 1926, various segments of the film industry, particularly the distributors and exhibitors, began to agitate for more equitable controls. Their pressure eventually led to Edouard Herriot's "Decree of 18 February 1928," which strengthened the central commission and limited the power of local authorities. Individual French filmmakers, however, did not escape further reprimands—e.g., L'Herbier's *L'Argent* (1929), Dreyer's *La Passion de Jeanne d'Arc* (1928), Benoît-Lévy/Epstein's *Peau de pêche* (1929). Jacques Feyder had the most difficult time with *Les Nouveaux Messieurs* (1929), which was prohibited because it allegedly insulted the French National Assembly (at one point, the satirized hero was made up to look like the president). For the commission's second review, the film was presented by Henry Roussel, who had gained the support of influential friends in the Assembly. In order to save face, the censors asked Albatros, the film's producer, to cut just twenty meters of intertitles during the love affair scenes, and *Les Nouveaux Messieurs* was approved.[7]

39

However, the primary targets of control were the foreign imports. German films, beginning as early as 1922, with Lubitsch's *Madame Du Barry*, routinely were re-edited or banned outright—e.g., Pabst's *The Joyless Street* and *Pandora's Box*, Lang's *Spies*, and May's *Asphalt*. Even some American films came in for excisions. René Jeanne recalled that Griffith's *Intolerance*, for instance, was shorn of its St. Bartholomew's Day massacre story (because it depicted an unpleasant period in French history); and Louis Delluc saw prints of the same film that had been reduced in length from three hours to a mere one and a half hours. But the real brunt of French censorship was borne by the Soviet films. First Eisenstein's *Battleship Potemkin* and then Pudovkin's *Mother* were banned, only to circulate widely in special screenings legally organized by the Ciné-Club de France and Les Amis de Spartacus. After the rightist victory in the 1928 elections, the ban on Soviet films became total. In 1929, *Cinéa-Ciné-pour-tous* listed six Soviet films which had been forbidden distribution: Kuleshov's *Dura Lux*, Eisenstein's *Battleship Potemkin*, Wiskousky's *Black Sunday*, Pudovkin's *Mother*, Eisenstein's *October*, and Pudovkin's *End of St. Petersburg*. As it turned out, the central commission on film censorship operated indirectly as France's chief means of limiting film imports.[8]

During the 1920s, the distribution sector of the French film industry was determined, to a large extent, less by its own production than by the quantity and quality of foreign imports. Although imports, primarily from the United States, comprised 75 percent or more of the films marketed in France by 1918-1919, most of them were still distributed by French companies (with the exception of Vitagraph). As the American film industry consolidated into a half-dozen vertically integrated corporations, it began to intervene directly in the French film economy. One after another, the major American firms set up offices in Paris or strengthened their alliances with French distributors. In 1920 came Paramount and Fox-Film, not only with their feature films but with newsreels as well.[9] Jean Mitry recalls the sensation caused by the huge posters that suddenly materialized everywhere, depicting a tripod and camera straddling the globe: "It's a Paramount film!"[10] A year later, they were joined by Associated Artists (United Artists) and Erka Films (First National).[11] In 1922, it was the turn of Universal, which offered a special premiere of Metro's *The Four Horsemen of the Apocalypse* at the Théâtre de Vaudeville.[12] Meanwhile Goldwyn and Metro signed exclusive distribution contracts with Gaumont and Aubert, respectively. By 1923, *Cinématographie française* was often listing the weekly releases of Paramount, Universal, and Fox-Film ahead of those of the French distributors. Even the two largest companies, Pathé-Consortium and Gaumont, were distributing fewer French films than imports. France had become a veritable dumping ground for the American film industry. After turning a profit in the United States, films could be sold cheaply and easily on the French market for an added bonus.

At the same time, German films began to appear in the Paris cinemas, for the first time since before the war. Breaking the barrier of prejudice and hostility was Robert Wiene's *Cabinet of Doctor Caligari* (1919), which Louis Delluc arranged to have screened at the Colisée cinema in October, 1921. Others soon followed in 1922, imported chiefly by Cosmograph and screened at the Ciné-Opéra: Lang's *Destiny* (1921), Wiene's *Genuine* (1920), Pick's *Shattered* (1921) and Murnau's *Nosferatu* (1922). To oppose this invasion, the Comité de défense du film français was formed by director Gérard Bourgeois and actor Jean Toulout, with the support of Germaine Dulac, René Le Somptier, René Hervil, Armand Tallier, and others. The National Assembly even tried to ban Lubitsch's *Madame Du Barry*, claiming that it was an insult to French history. Neither measure was successful. The walls were down, and the possibilities of exchange were once more open.[13]

For their part, the French were attempting to rebuild the foreign markets they had lost in the war, especially the more lucrative ones in Germany and the United States. The meager range of their common export market can be gleaned from *Ciné-pour-tous*'s publication of the balance sheet on a moderately expensive (310,000 francs) Pathé-Consortium film, Pierre Caron's *L'Homme qui vendait son âme au diable* (1921).[14] Twenty-five prints had been sold in France, about twenty in England and its colonies, ten in South America, four in Eastern Europe, three in the Scandinavian countries, two in Belgium, and one each in Switzerland, Holland, Spain, Portugal, Greece, Turkey, Egypt, and Japan. None in the United States, Germany, or the Soviet Union. With those sales, the film barely turned a profit; had it been released just a year or two later, when the American industry had taken control of the British market, it would not have done so.

As their first goal, the French distributors blithely took on the herculean task of breaking back into the American market. Several ambitious efforts quickly ended in failure: Diamant-Berger's film with Adolphe Osso, Vandal and Delac's films with Fanny Ward, and the embezzled Franco-American Cinematographic Corporation. Yet some French films seem to have made their way into the United States just after the war—e.g., Mercanton's *Bouclette* (Eclipse), L'Herbier's *Rose-France* (Gaumont), and Dulac's *Le Bonheur des autres* (A.G.C.). Unfortunately, it is still unclear whether any were actually screened. In 1919, for instance, Abel Gance discovered that Pathé-Exchange did have a print of *J'Accuse*, but they had done little to sell it. Nothing drastic was done until 1921, when the French heard that German films were being shown with some success in New York. In October, 1921, Gance finally sold a second version of *J'Accuse* (for $192,000) to United Artists, who at least exhibited it in New York and Los Angeles. A month later, Louis Nalpas personally sold his two biggest films, *La Sultane de l'amour* and *Mathias Sandorf*, to First National. After successfully blocking United Artists from showing Douglas Fairbanks's *The Three Musketeers* (1921) in France in order to leave the market open for his own production, *Les Trois Mousquetaires* (1921-1922), Henri Diamant-Berger also went to New York and sold his film there in the spring of 1922. On his return, he reported on half a dozen French releases, including Feyder's *L'Atlantide* (retitled *Missing Husbands*), Mercanton's *Miarko* and *Phroso* (all three exported by Aubert), Poirier's *Narayana* (Gaumont), and Ermolieff's *L'Ordonnance* (Pathé-Consortium). A year later, André Capellani returned to France and reported on several more—Baroncelli's *Le Rêve*, Henry Roussel's *La Faute d'Odette Maréchal* and *Visages voilés . . . âmes closes* (retitled *The Sheik's Wife*).[15]

In those three years, however, only three films enjoyed any measure of success in the United States: *L'Atlantide*, Boudrioz's *L'Atre* (retitled *Tillers of the Soil*), and Feyder's new film *Crainquebille* (*Old Bill of Paris*).[16] Simply put, the French films never really caught on because the French export efforts were poorly financed, independent of one another and uncoordinated, and because their American distributors did not push them. As Marcel Lapierre concludes,

The Americans had no intention of establishing a current of exchange. They produced films in overabundance: therefore, they had no need of ours, even if excellent. They had no interest, either material or moral, in opening their doors to our film exports. Of course not, otherwise how can one explain the fact that they mutilated or bowdlerized some of our films which were presented to the American public?[17]

No more than a dozen French films were exhibited annually from 1920 to 1925, and few reached cinemas outside New York, Los Angeles, and a couple of other large cities. Even in New York, according to Diamant-Berger, there were only five or six small cinemas that consistently screened foreign (let alone exclusively French) films.[18]

Disillusioned by their repeated failures in the United States, the French turned their attention to Germany and, almost immediately, were rewarded. Operating independently, Diamant-Berger made *Le Petit Café* (with Max Linder) the first successful French film in Germany since before the war. In November, 1922, Vandal and Delac of Film d'Art opened talks with Erich Pommer about distributing French films on a regular basis in UFA's cinema circuit. The following year, Film d'Art and Aubert films began appearing in German cinemas—e.g., Feyder's *L'Atlantide*, Baroncelli's *Le Rêve*. By early 1924, Aubert and Film d'Art had a lucrative contract with Pommer and UFA, and twice as many French films (forty-four) were being shown in Germany as there were German films (twenty) in France. Although the French figure included films produced over several years, it still represented a good percentage of overall French film production. Within a year, according to *Tout-Cinéma*, the number of French exports (thirty) to German imports (twenty-three) was nearly reciprocal.[19]

A similar arrangement also developed about the same time with the Soviet Union, probably stimulated by the Herriot government's recognition of the U.S.S.R. in 1924.[20] Little is known yet about this export agreement—who arranged the sales, the number of film prints that were sold, where and how often they were shown. According to Russian sources, however, the flow of French exports to the Soviet Union rivaled and perhaps surpassed those going to Germany.[21] Beginning with just one film, *Judex*, in 1921, the number increased to more than fifty by 1925.[22] As might be expected, these included most of the films produced by Films Ermolieff and Films Albatros—the most interesting entry perhaps was *Le Brasier ardent* (soon after its release in 1923). Other important films included *La Dixième Symphonie* (in 1922); *L'Atlantide* and *Don Juan et Faust* (in 1923); *J'Accuse* and *Les Trois Mousquetaires* (in 1924); *L'Atre, Crainquebille, Cœur fidèle, La Cité foudroyée, La Brière*, and *Le Diable dans la ville* (all in 1925). Surprisingly, *La Roue* is not mentioned as being imported until 1926. What kind of impact might these particular films have had on the nascent Soviet cinema?

The question of foreign film imports so divided the French film industry that it took quite a while to develop any kind of organized effort to control them. Although producers obviously favored controls, most cinema owners actually opposed them; and the distributors were somewhere in between. Consequently, writes Georges Sadoul, it was not until the threatening invasion of

German films that a debate over film imports finally surfaced in the National Assembly. Pressured mainly by Pathé-Consortium and the Confédération Générale du Travail (C.G.T.), Aristide Briand had decreed, early in 1922, an ad valorem tax of 20 percent on all imported films. So benign was it, however, that the new tax had little effect, since most French distributors and exhibitors could still make more money by marketing American films than French ones. Under continued pressure, in 1922, Marcel Bokanowski, the Minister of Finance, included in his budget request to the Assembly a proposal that would have charged a surtax on cinemas whose programming consisted of more than 80 percent foreign films and that would also have raised the ad valorem tax to 50 percent. When the budget was rejected and Bokanowski removed, the original proposal was modified by Taurines in order simply to establish a quota system that would reserve 33 percent of all cinema programs for French films. The idea for this quota system had come from the Comité de defénse du film français, which persuaded some of the distributors (notably Aubert) to accept a minimum quota of 25 percent. However, another faction of the distributors (with Gaumont as its spokesman) argued that they would be hard pressed to fulfill even the lower quota figure. That faction was joined by the national organization of cinema owners (led by Léon Brézillon) in even more vehement opposition. In the confused debate of the Assembly's last days, during which the Radical party's fears of creating a new bureaucracy seem to have carried the day, the Taurines measure went down to defeat. The Comité de défense du film français, together with various labor unions and professional groups (writers, actors, cameramen, etc.), protested in vain.[23] French films would remain unprotected from the flood of American imports. More important, a schism had opened between two major factions of the French film industry: Pathé-Consortium and Aubert on one side, Gaumont on the other.

In 1923-1924, either responding to the French threat of import quotas or taking advantage of the weakness of that threat, several of the American film distributors in Paris made a further incursion into the French industry. Under Adolphe Osso, Paramount began producing and distributing its own French films—Roussel's *Les Opprimés* (1923), Boudrioz's *L'Epérvier* (1924), Perret's *Madame Sans-Gêne* (1925). Besides, it allied itself with Cinégraphic to distribute (and perhaps deliberately undersell?) L'Herbier's *Résurrection* (unfinished), Jaque Catelain's *Le Marchand de plaisir* (1923), and, in the United States, L'Herbier's *L'Inhumaine* (released in 1926, finally, as *The New Enchantment*). Vitagraph also expanded its distribution practice by releasing Volkoff's *Kean* (1924), before its network was bought out by Warner Brothers.[24] Although not directly linked to these transactions, Gaumont moved steadily into the American orbit, seeking financial security and even survival. In 1922, Léon Gaumont finally conceded defeat to the American cinema:

The American market is completely closed to us while our screens are cluttered with American films. We can do nothing about it—it's a battle between the clay pot and the iron kettle.[25]

With the company's financiers now in control, production was cut back and contracts signed with Metro, Goldwyn, and others to distribute and exhibit more American films. In 1924, when even Louis Feuillade's serials began to lose their appeal, Gaumont tied itself more closely to Metro-Goldwyn as the new American combine's exclusive distributor in France.[26] Within a year, however, the larger of the partners easily gained control, and Gaumont became Gaumont-MGM. In all but appearance, the once French giant was now MGM's branch office in Paris.

Throughout the first half of the 1920s, Pathé-Consortium was the bulwark of opposition to any threat of American hegemony in France. Besides distributing its own films, either the superproduction serials or the literary adaptations of S.C.A.G.L., it was also the major outlet for the smaller firms and independent producers. From 1921 to 1923, the following producers and filmmakers channeled their work through Pathé-Consortium: Films Ermolieff, Films Tristan Bernard, Films Abel Gance, Productions Léonce Perret, Productions H. Pouctal, Films André Legrand, Films Luitz-Morat and Pierre Regnier, Films André Hugon.[27] In 1923 and 1924, as the level of French production dropped, it took the lead in re-releasing older films, especially during the summer months. Then, as Jean Sapène rose to power with Cinéromans, the company began to consolidate its distribution. Cinéromans serials and Films de France became the single most important source of Pathé-Consortium products.

The Cinéromans serials, particularly, seem to have played an important role in the French film industry. Their regular, increasingly popular distribution through Pathé-Consortium came precisely at the moment when, fresh from their conquest of the British film industry and just before their intervention in the German industry, the American film companies made an effort to gain control in France. According to Jean-Louis Bouquet,

The large American firms really wanted to impose a *blockbooking* system, a kind of annual programming deal, thanks to which they had already gained control of the British exhibition market. The serials shattered these attempts at a monopoly. . . .[28]

His colleague, Henri Fescourt, continues the argument:

the serial episodes offered exhibitors the guarantees of a long series of weeks of huge returns from a faithful mass public hooked on the formula. Thus assured of a program base for three-quarters of the year, the cinema owners could resist the foreign film salesmen. . . .[29]

Without the Cinéromans serials, French film exhibitors might, like the British, have turned their screens over entirely to American films. Consequently, during a crucial period, Pathé-Consortium and Cinéromans shored up the French film industry.

Perhaps anticipating the coming American investment in Germany and definitely encouraged by the *Cartel des gauches'* foreign policy, Sapène began cutting down the number of American film imports that Pathé-Consortium still distributed (the company kept its options open) in favor of German imports and Franco-German productions. In this new strategy, Sapène was following the lead of the second largest French film distributor, Louis Aubert. In 1921, Aubert had the foresight to take over the distribution rights to *L'Atlantide* when Jacques Feyder's financiers became alarmed over its soaring costs. The film made a fortune for him, playing at the prestigious Madeleine Cinéma alone for one year, a record eclipsed only by *Ben-Hur* in 1927-1928. Within a year, Aubert had taken over most of the distribution contracts from A.G.C.

and formed an alliance with Vandal and Delac of Film d'Art as well as with Films de Baroncelli. Prospering from these alliances, from an expanded circuit of cinemas, and now from his own productions, Aubert opened two initiatives in 1924. One was the agreement with UFA in Germany for a reciprocal exchange of French film exports and German imports—e.g., Violet's *La Bataille* and Hervil's *Paris* for Lang's *Niebelungen* and Murnau's *The Last Laugh*.[30]

The other initiative complemented Sapène's serial strategy at Cinéromans. For the 1924-1925 season, Aubert organized what he called "Festivals of French films," a program of recent and current French releases (primarily Aubert/Film d'Art productions) to be distributed in the provinces over a two- or three-month period. According to Aubert's own publicity sheet, the typical program ran as follows:

Week 1 *Frou-Frou*
Week 2 *Les Premières Armes de Rocambole*
Week 3 *Le Secret de Polichinelle*
Week 4 *Le Voile du bonheur*
Week 5 *Le Crime d'une sainte*
Week 6 *La Sin-Ventura*
Week 7 *La Bataille*
Week 8 *La Légende de Soeur Béatrix*[31]

Although *Ciné-Information-Aubert* used several of these festivals for promotional purposes (Cinéma-Palace de Joigny [Yvonne], Grand-Théâtre d'Antibes), their overall success was apparently mixed.[32] For his next season, Aubert seems to have dropped the idea. Still, this festival concept was important because it represented one of the few French attempts at a form of blockbooking.

With Pathé-Consortium and Aubert concentrating on their own films, and the once powerful A.G.C. nearly defunct, the many smaller production companies and independent producers created a demand for new distributors. In 1924, Kamenka took over the distributor E. Girard, which became Films Armor, to release his films from Albatros. Soon Armor was being hailed as the third largest distributor of French films.[33] Another new company, Grandes Productions Cinématographiques (G.P.C.), started out as a production effort to make French films along the lines of Vandal and Delac and Aubert; but all it could come up with were small films by Gaston Roudès. In 1924, it turned to distribution and released a half-dozen films, most of them Cinégraphic productions.[34] Its development was bound up with that of an important regional producer-distributor, Phocéa, in Marseille. On the strength of its box-office bonanza with the serial, *Les Mystères de Paris* (1922), Phocéa enjoyed a momentary prominence, even to the point of opening a foreign exchange office.[35] By 1926-1927, both Phocéa and G.P.C. had become production units in a small consortium called Interfilm.[36] Along with Phocéa, which was originally formed to distribute American films during the war, several other foreign import companies began releasing French films. Another American importer, Georges Petit, for instance, distributed most of Julien Duvivier's early films; and a German importer, Mappemonde Films, agreed to handle René Clair's *Le Fantôme du Moulin Rouge* (1925).[37]

One of the chief distribution problems during this period was the relative lack of independent distributors and their weak position within the industry.

Although independent producers proliferated, their counterparts in distribution grew more slowly. With the exception of Armor, none of them had much influence in the French exhibition market. Furthermore, they tended to operate separately and were often at odds with one another. The only one, apparently, to have sought some kind of power base to coordinate the release of independent films was Jean de Merly, Henry Roussel's producer on *Les Opprimés* (1923). Somewhat like Aubert, de Merly made a small fortune from handling a single film, Roussel's *Violettes impériales* (1924).[38] The following year, he sank most of his profits into the distribution of a supposedly balanced program of half a dozen independent films by Roussel, Feyder, and Gaston Ravel. When all but one of those films showed a net loss, de Merly's drive toward a consortium of independent distribution stalled. In 1926, he was forced to reorganize his company in association with Fernand Weill.[39] All the other important independent distributors were geared to individual filmmakers or films. Léon Poirier, for instance, founded the Compagnie universelle cinématographique in order to distribute *La Brière* (1925) as well as Jean Epstein's first independent film, *Mauprat* (1926).[40] Even smaller distributors were Georges Loureau (perhaps allied with Mappemonde?) who handled Clair's *Entr'acte* (1924) and *Le Voyage imaginaire* (1926), and Maurice Rohier, who released several films by Epstein and Dmitri Kirsanoff.[41]

In 1927, the French film industry received another shock that spurred renewed efforts to impose some form of import quotas and that led to a further round of reorganization within the distribution sector. During the middle 1920s, the level of American imports declined steadily as films became bigger—from 589 in 1924 to 368 in 1927.[42] However, that decline was offset by an increase in the level of German imports. From 1924 to 1926, the number of French exports to German imports had decreased, but not drastically, to a level that was just less than reciprocal. Suddenly, in 1927, German imports tripled, without any corresponding increase in French exports. In fact, more films were imported from Germany (ninety-one) than were produced by the entire French film industry (seventy-four). This jump in German imports might have been foreseen in the spring of 1926, when the Alliance Cinématographique Européene (A.C.E.) was set up in Paris.[43] Although linked to S.G.F., as the distributor of Dreyer's *La Passion de Jeanne d'Arc* (1928), for instance, A.C.E.'s primary objective was to distribute the films of UFA and other German firms in France. Bypassing Aubert and Pathé-Consortium, A.C.E. quickly became the chief French distributor of German films.[44] The German drive (supported by American money) to infiltrate much of the French market was on the verge of success. Cinematographically, France was in danger of being colonized a second time over.

The French film export market, by contrast, remained substantially unchanged. A good number of films were now being exported, especially to Germany and the United States, but they were having little impact on either market. In Germany, although certain titles were quite profitable, the French films never comprised more than 5 percent of the total distribution market. The situation was worse in the United States. The number of cinemas exhibiting foreign films, even in New York, was still quite low. And many of the French films had a limited audience because they were distributed only through the Film Arts Guild.[45] According to George Pratt, Feyder's *Visages d'enfants* and Clair's *Paris qui dort* were shown for one evening only, 29 June 1926, at the Cameo cinema in New York.[46] Moreover, the American distributors sometimes sabotaged the more commercial French films. The classic example is Gance's *Napoléon*. In its shortened triple-screen format, *Napoléon* was exhibited in twelve different cities across France and in eight major European capitols (where, in just twenty-one days, allegedly, it nearly made back its colossal costs).[47] When MGM paid $450,000 for distribution rights to the film in the United States, Gance was hopeful of a worldwide success.[48] But the American company cut the film drastically (from seventeen to just eight reels), concentrating solely on producing a coherent narrative.[49] They reduced the triple-screen images to miniatures on a single screen and, according to Kevin Brownlow, ended the film with the Ghosts of the Convention sequence—including among the shots of Marat, Danton, and Robespierre, a similar soft-focus insert of George Washington![50] Ignorant of the film's origins, exhibitors were baffled and infuriated.[51] Metro's publicity campaign could not disguise the fact that they had turned Gance's powerful epic into a dull period film. Only recently, therefore, has *Napoléon* been shown here in anything resembling its original form.

Yet the French themselves sometimes undermined their own efforts. The marketing of Fescourt's *Les Misérables* (1925-1926) offers a case in point. Assuming that the American distributor would automatically exhibit the film in its four-part format, Pathé-Consortium shipped all twenty-two reels of it (about six or seven hours) to the United States. "It required eight months of the most difficult and expensive efforts," wrote Howard Lewis, "to rework and remodel this product of French studios into a shape suitable for American audiences."[52] Besides, by the summer of 1928, the American film industry was already entering the transition period to sound films; silent films could no longer attract audiences in the large cities where French films would have been shown.

Acutely aware of its continuing import/export imbalance, especially in light of the now favorable ratio in the general French economy, the film industry organized an intensive campaign in October, 1927, to protect its film production once and for all through a quota system that would really control film imports.[53] The campaign was led by influential men like Sapène and Aubert, representing most of the French producers and distributors, and was supported by the unions and professional groups (including many of the same people as in 1922-1923). This time they were victorious, if only for a short time, and the new government adopted the Herriot decree of February, 1928: for every seven foreign films imported into France (four American, two German, one British), one French film would be purchased and exhibited overseas. Moreover, in an effort to indirectly subsidize French film production, a system of import permits was instituted that favored French distributors at the expense of the American branch offices in Paris.

The American film industry quickly retaliated by calling a boycott on further distribution contracts in France; and, in an unprecedented move, Will H. Hays sailed to Paris to lobby personally for the industry. The boycott divided the French again, with exhibitors, especially in the provinces, loudly opposing the new decree. After a series of joint conferences between representatives of the two industries, along with a timely objection from the League of Nations, within two months, the French capitulated. The seven-to-one quota system would continue in force, but the import permit subsidy was dropped. American films could still comprise up to 60 percent of the French market, while French films exported to the United States would remain at a level of ten or twelve per year. There were even those, such as Léon Moussinac, Jean Tedesco, and Hubert Revol, who argued that, since the original Herriot decree contained enforcement clauses that were clearly unworkable and that favored the major French producers (including Paramount), it may not have been in the best interests of all segments of the industry anyway. One year later, at a most inopportune moment, the French again tried to reduce the import-export ratio (this time to 3:1), but to no avail. Confronted by another American boycott, from April to September, 1929, which coincided with a growing demand for sound films, the government retreated to the seven-to-one ratio once more.[54]

By the end of the silent film period, the distribution sector of the industry was divided into three major factions. The American faction, led by Paramount and Gaumont-MGM, controlled probably the largest share of the French market (certainly in numbers of films released). Included in that number were more French films than ever before, since First National, Fox-Film, Universal, and United Artists had all joined Paramount to produce and/or distribute French projects in 1928-1929. The German faction, headed by A.C.E. and Luna-Film, had an influence above and beyond its small size. Securely within its orbit now were two of the largest French companies, Aubert and Armor, whose programs increasingly were given over to German films. The embattled French faction still stood its ground. Pathé-Consortium continued to release more French films than most of the other firms put together. Aubert and Armor were next in line, but much of their profit now came from German releases. Jean de Merly and Fernand Weill joined together in a loose consortium to distribute Marie-Louise Iribe's *Hara-Kiri* (1928) as well as some of the bigger historical reconstruction films at the decade's end: Bernard's *Joueur d'échecs* (1927), Poirier's *Verdun, visions d'histoire* (1928), and Fescourt's *Monte-Cristo* (1929). Another new firm, Jean de Venloo, established itself by first distributing *Le Miracle des loups* abroad and then releasing several of Baroncelli's films—*Pêcheur d'Islande* (1924), *Veille d'armes* (1925), *Le Réveil* (1925)—as well as a new shortened version of Diamant-Berger's *Les Trois Mousquetaires*.[55] By 1927, de Venloo was in a position to bargain with several important independent producers: Charles Dullin—Jean Grémillon's *Maldone* (1928), the Société des Films Historiques—Roussel's *Le Valse de l'adieu* (1928), and Lutèce Films—Cavalcanti's *Le Capitaine fracasse* (1929). Finally, through Néo-Film, Pierre Braunberger began to interest himself in the distribution of French avant-garde films (both narrative and non-narrative) in France and abroad.

There is little doubt that the distribution sector, through the efforts of Pathé-Consortium and Aubert, helped save the French film industry from complete capitulation to the Americans, especially during the period from 1922 to 1925. However, that sector also proved to be the weakest component of the industry. It failed to develop a systematic or coordinated pattern of film booking, other than the serial format, to counter the glut of American films. It failed to come up with an organized consortium or network to distribute the large numbers of independent films. And it wavered, divided, in its attitude toward a government system of controls on foreign imports, eventually always siding with the exhibitors, whose profits depended on those imports. The consequence of these failures was that the Americans and Germans had a secure foothold within the French film industry at the crucial moment of the transition to sound films.

Exhibition: "We're in the Money"

The French cinema owners often seemed to operate quite separately from the other two sectors of the film industry. From the industry's beginnings, most of the cinemas constructed in France were independently, even individually, owned (the figure consistently hovered around 80 to 90 percent). During the war, as American films replaced French films in number and popularity, imports became the chief source of the exhibitors' revenues. Because that condition persisted throughout the 1920s, the exhibitors repeatedly opposed any form of government control on imported films, especially from the United States. Their position was strong enough, most importantly with the government, to defeat all proposals offered by the French film producers and distributors. Compared to the rest of the industry, furthermore, the exhibition sector was unusually secure financially. The degree of that security is suggested by the steady rise in box office receipts, in Paris alone, throughout the decade:

1923 85,428,746 francs
1926 145,994,959 francs
1929 230,187,461 francs[1]

Although the 1926 figure may be deceptive because of the high inflation, the 1929 figure represents an astounding jump in the cinema's popularity. Despite this prosperity, sometimes at the expense of the rest of the industry, the French cinema owners had their share of problems.

The most serious problem, in the minds of the exhibitors, was taxation. If the French government showed scant concern for film production and distribution (except on the matter of imports and exports), it quickly included film exhibition among the sources of added and increased taxes that the war seemed to have demanded. As audiences flocked to the cinemas during the first year of the war, the National Assembly debated various proposals to institute a national tax on spectacles. What was finally agreed to, on 30 December 1916, imposed a fixed tax rate on theaters and music halls and a progressive tax rate on the cinemas.

5 percent of monthly receipts under 25,000 francs
10 percent of monthly receipts of 25,000 to 50,000 francs
20 percent of monthly receipts of 50,000 to 100,000 francs
25 percent of monthly receipts over 100,000 francs

This was in addition to the ancient "poor tax," which was set at 9.5 percent for all three spectacles. By 1920, the government had grown so used to this new tax base that it was sanctioned in peacetime as well. Lobbied by the theaters and music halls, which wanted to reverse the wartime advantages enjoyed by the cinemas, on June 25, 1920, the National Assembly adopted a new tax law which reduced their tax rate and increased the rate on the cinemas even more.

10 percent of monthly receipts under 15,000 francs
15 percent of monthly receipts of 15,000 to 50,000 francs
20 percent of monthly receipts of 50,000 to 100,000 francs
25 percent of monthly receipts over 100,000 francs

The new law also authorized municipalities to levy a local tax on cinema admissions up to 50 percent of the national tax. After all, the Finance Minister is reported to have said, "Because of its current vogue, the cinématographe can bear taxation more easily than any of the other spectacles."[2]

The French exhibitors, especially the smaller owners, were outraged by this new increase, particularly since it came during a period when high unemployment and a general strike threatened to erode their audience. Moreover, they began to object to the rental rates demanded by the French film distributors, which they considered draconian compared to the cheap American rates. In 1921, a good number of the smaller cinema owners even threatened to close their cinemas for the summer. This "strike" turned out to be poorly organized, however, and had little effect. Simultaneously, the larger exhibition circuits organized a committee (headed by Edmond Benoît-Lévy and Edgar Costil) to work with Marcel Bokanowski in getting the National Assembly at least to lower the tax. Although Bokanowski's measure failed, a second proposal to reduce the national tax was introduced by Taurines and passed (without its original import quota restrictions) in the National Assembly on 1 July 1923.

6 percent of monthly receipts under 15,000 francs
10 percent of monthly receipts of 15,000 to 30,000 francs
15 percent of monthly receipts of 30,000 to 50,000 francs
20 percent of monthly receipts of 50,000 to 100,000 francs
25 percent of monthly receipts over 100,000 francs

Yet less than a year later, most of these small gains were lost when the *Cartel des gauches* government increased the taxes on all spectacles by 20 percent. Opposition to the tax began to fade, and the exhibitors accepted an overall tax rate of from 17 percent to 40 percent of gross receipts in Parisian cinemas and from 15 percent to 31 percent in the provinces. Throughout the 1920s, the cinemas contributed 50 percent of all spectacle tax revenues in France; by 1930, according to André Chevanne, their share had grown to over 300 million francs per year.[3]

Although the French film exhibitors were financially well-off, in spite of a heavy tax load, the scope and mode of their operations were quite restrictive for the production and distribution sectors of the industry. In 1918, according to Georges Sadoul, there were only 1,444 cinemas in France, nearly 200 of which were located in Paris.[4] By 1920, their number had almost doubled to 2,400. Even so, the French exhibition market still ranked behind England (3,000), Germany (3,730), and the United States (18,000).[5] By 1929, the number of French cinemas had grown to 4,200, but their position worldwide was the same as before.[6] As if that were not bad enough for French distributors, "less than 40 percent operated daily," reported *Film Daily Yearbook* (1929), "and only 900 had a capacity of 750 seats or more."[7] Many of the rest in the provinces, adds Sadoul, "offered only three or four screenings a week."[8] The insufficient number of cinemas, argued André Delpeuch, resulted from the French public's relative lack of appreciation for the new spectacle.[9] And André

Chevanne's statistics seemed to confirm that: despite the stereotypical notion that France is a nation of cinéphiles, only 12 percent of the French population regularly attended the cinema in 1928 (up from 7 percent in 1919), just half the percentage of regular customers in the United States.[10]

Yet the French publicity strategies did little to entice that public into the cinemas to see French films. In 1919, Henri Bousquet writes, only a dozen or so of the eighty French films produced that year received special advertising campaigns. Pathé, for instance, devoted an unusual effort to Gance's *J'Accuse* and especially to Pouctal's *Travail*, lavishing on the latter a full year of publicity before its first episode even premiered. Most others, including Feuillade's *Tih-Minh*, oddly enough, were advertised the week of their opening, and that was all. The situation improved slightly the following year, with the films of Baroncelli, Poirier, Le Somptier, Mercanton, Hervil, and Roussel singled out for special attention. In 1921, however, French publicity contracted to focus on less than a dozen films, including Feyder's *L'Atlantide*, Diamant-Berger's *Les Trois Mousquetaires*, Bernard-Deschamps' *L'Agonie des aigles*, and Leprince's *L'Empereur des pauvres*.[11] Although much more needs to be known about French film advertising during this period, it seems consistently to have performed below the level of American advertising. This may account for the rapid rise of such men as Robert Hurel, Pierre Braunberger, and Bernard Natan (all associated with the Paramount publicity office); and it may explain why the specialized film journals—e.g., *Cinéa* and *Cinéa-Ciné-pour-tous*—considered it so important to sponsor film poster contests.

French film programming practices were determined in part by a system of film rental contracts which was standardized by the early 1920s. Cinema owners could rent a new feature film according to one of three basic contracts:

Première vision confers on the lessee this privilege—that no other cinema owner can screen the film before him in a predetermined city or zone. But the *première vision* rental can be made simultaneously with many cinema owners.

Priorité (or *antériorité*) grants to the lessee the privilege of screening a film before all other competing cinemas in a predetermined city or zone, and of designating his choice of cinema locations.

Exclusivité is understood as a booking strictly reserved to one cinema for a predetermined zone or period of time, along with the exclusive right of related publicity.[12]

Although each year after 1921, more and more French films were released *en exclusivité*, only a limited number of cinemas in Paris and in the provinces (Lyon, Marseille, Bordeaux, Toulouse, Nice) could exhibit them.[13] In Paris, these were five of the most prestigious cinemas: the Marivaux, Madeleine, Aubert-Palace, Max-Linder, and Caméo.[14] An *exclusivité* or *priorité* film usually played several weeks to a month in one cinema and then shifted to *première vision* status for its general run. The majority of films, however, were released under *première vision* contracts. As early as 1919, this meant a release pattern of anywhere from several weeks to several months. A film would begin playing one week at, say, several dozen major cinemas and then, if successful enough, week by week, would work its way through the smaller urban and rural cinemas.[15] Programming schedules for the larger cinemas were prepared from several months to a year in advance but usually could be juggled to accommodate the exceptionally popular film—e.g., *L'Atlantide* (one year at the Ma-

51

deleine), *Mathias Sandorf* (six months at the Cirque-Hiver), *Ben-Hur* (over one year at the Madeleine). An exception to this practice ruined Renoir's *Nana* (1926). After a surprisingly good late summer run *en exclusivité* and *en priorité*, it was withdrawn to make way for Aubert's fall season of films. [16]

The serial and the *film à époques* or multipart film provided a unique product for cinema programming. By 1918, Louis Feuillade had standardized the French serial format at twelve episodes of about a half-hour each. This meant that a cinema could run a single serial film title for nearly three months, screening one episode a week. In 1923, Jean Sapène modified this format when he ordered the Société des Cinéromans to produce serials of eight episodes each so that they could be released at two-month intervals, from September to May. Although Sapène's format dominated the rest of the decade, public opinion apparently forced some distributors eventually to market two versions of the same serial—a "condensed" version for the larger cinemas and a complete version for the smaller urban and provincial cinemas. [18] The unusually sustained popularity of the serial in France seems to have spawned a peculiar hybrid form, the *film à époques* or multipart film. These films were made up of two to four parts or "acts" (lasting one or two hours each), none of which, taken separately, could be accepted as complete; and they were intended to be screened in single *séances* or performances over a period of consecutive weeks. Perhaps the earliest example of this format was Louis Feuillade's war film, *Vendémiaire*, whose two parts of 1,680 and 1,350 meters, respectively, were released on 17 and 24 January, 1919. [19] Several other films were shown similarly within the next year—e.g., Gance's *J'Accuse* (four parts), Gérard Bourgeois's *Christophe Colomb* (two parts), Pouctal's *Travail* (eight parts)—and the format saw rather extensive use throughout the decade, generally for expensive historical or biographical films. [20] Perhaps the most prominent films were Henri Diamant-Berger's *Les Trois Mousquetaires* and *Vingt Ans après* (twelve parts each), Gance's *La Roue* and *Napoléon* (four parts each), Henri Fescourt's *Les Misérables* (four parts), and the same director's 1929 remake of *Monte-Cristo* (two parts). Apparently, each part would play just one week in a cinema until the whole film was recycled for another screening. Here, too, was a fairly successful strategy that assured the exhibition of French films in the face of the American film onslaught.

Programming practices were probably determined as well by the location of cinemas and thus by the clientele they served. Unfortunately, there is no study yet of early French cinema locations to compare with the rigorous analyses of early American cinemas performed by Russell Merritt, Douglas Gomery, Robert Allen, and Charlotte Herzog. [21] However, André Antoine offers a place to begin. In 1921, Antoine did an informal survey of the cinemas in Paris according to the seven or eight quarters (and stereotypes) that comprised the city. [22] The Left Bank cinemas then were frequented by students, teachers, lawyers, and civil servants who preferred "films marked by the qualities of dispassionate observation and truthfulness." The cinemas of Grenelle, on the other hand, catered to the bourgeois audience that enjoyed the serials and historical films, which swelled them with pride and respect. The elegant cinemas of Passy, Auteil, and Étoile were becoming social playgrounds for the idle rich to carry on affairs and talk of affairs. The cinemas of the working-class quarters (République, Bastille, Pointe-Saint-Paul) were thronged by people who, though passionately interested in the crime serials and in sentimental melodramas, could also discern an exceptional film when they saw one. The new cinemas of the Boulevards were supplanting those around the Place de Clichy as "the center of cinema life," for they were crowded with shoppers from the nearby Printemps and Galeries Lafayette, day and night, weekdays and weekends.[23] It was here, where cinema-going was becoming linked to the consumption patterns of the big department stores, that the industry could determine how successfully a film could attract the general public. Or whether, as André Delpeuch so blithely put it, a film could satisfy "this need that we sometimes feel to escape, if only for a brief flight, the conditions of our bourgeois existence."[24]

A typical French cinema program just after the war, according to Louis Delluc, looked like a "programme-salade."[25] The recipe consisted of a half-dozen different kinds of films: a newsreel, a comic short, a serial episode, a feature-length drama or comedy, and either a travelogue, another serial episode, or a second comic short. Here are some examples from *Le Journal du Ciné-Club* (30 April 1920):

Gaumont-Palace	*La Fête espagnole* (short drama)
	La Bretagne pittoresque (cinematographic study)
	Barrabas, 9th episode (serial)
	Charlot apprenti (comic short)
	Les Environs du Caire (documentary in color)
Pathé-Palace	*Pathé-Journal* (newsreel)
	Houdini, 10th episode (serial)
	Le Secret d'Argeville (police drama)
	Fritzigli (comic short)
	Le Duel de Max (comic short)
Folies-Dramatiques	*Dernières actualités* (newsreel)
	Barrabas, 9th episode (serial)
	Bigorno cireur (comic short)
	La Révélation (Rio Jim western)
	Les Chansons filmées (film songs)

These were mixed in various combinations and presented *en bloc*, beginning at a certain hour of the afternoon or evening, with no indication of exactly when a specific film would appear or even if it would be repeated. The only thing one could be certain of was that the course would last from two to three hours, since the films' total length usually ran from 3,000 to 3,500 meters.[26] The young Dadaist and Surrealist poets loved the chance encounters this system created, but people of more regular habits complained.[27]

Filmmakers and critics complained about this system as well, because exhibitors exercised a right to alter films to suit their needs. Feature films were already measured on the bed of Procrustes, according to Antoine, since distributors often cut them to a standard length of 1,350 to 1,700 meters each, whether the story demanded it or not.[28] Then the cinema owner could tailor any film to fit his particular program—cutting out scenes that might displease his clientele or shortening it in such a way that he could add the special attraction of an extra film. Even the "enlightened" manager of the Caméo and Artistic cinemas, Lucien Doublon, defended the exhibitor's need to heed the demands of his patrons.

53

When the manager of a "permanent" cinema cuts a film, he knows what he is doing; he is eliminating useless things, repetitions in a scene, evocations, etc. But, I must add, he pays the same metrage rate to the distributor. There is not one single manager of a "permanent" who cannot lighten a program in such a way that the spectator doesn't notice it.[29]

Another irritating exhibitor practice, which was just as common in the United States, was to project films in the cinemas at faster than their "taking speed" (initially, 16 to 18 frames per second), presumably to squeeze in an extra daily program.[30] This, along with other factors, tended to slowly increase the "taking speed" of films during the decade. Yet the speed of French films, according to Barry Salt, still lagged behind most others—whereas American films, for instance, had reached a speed of 22 frames per second by 1924, the French films did not reach that speed until 1929.[31]

By the middle of the decade, programs were being organized around the exhibition of one feature-length film and a serial, with perhaps the addition of a newsreel and a short. Now they were standardized at from two to three hours in length and were presented regularly according to an announced schedule. The only change in this format was Paramount's introduction of double-bill programming (which the French also used sparingly) and the same company's 1928 decision to adopt a policy of continuous screenings.[32] To suggest the range of programs, the following examples are drawn from *Cinémagazine* (16 March 1928):

Madeleine-Cinéma	*Ben-Hur*
Omnia-Pathé	*Le Chauffeur de Mademoiselle*
Sèvres	*L'Esclave blanche*
	La Sirène des tropiques
	Poker d'as, 1st episode (serial)
Hôtel-de-ville	*Princesse Masha*
	Gribouille veilleur de nuit (comic short)
Impérial	*Paname n'est pas Paris*
	Paris il y a vingt ans (documentary)

In the provinces, the practice of changing programs twice a week was introduced; and, in Perpignan, at least, this included reruns of many films released earlier in the decade.[33] Exhibitors everywhere, however, continued to alter films as they saw fit.

Although most French cinemas were owned and operated independently, several large circuits controlled important segments of the French market. Their association with the major film producers and distributors went back to the industry's formative years before the war. Nearly fifty cinemas were operated by Pathé-Frères/Pathé-Cinéma, through six regional circuits—five in France and Algeria, plus another in Belgium and Holland. Edmond Benoît-Lévy had an administrative interest in four of them. The most important of the company's early Paris cinemas were the Pathé-Palace (600 seats) and the Omnia-Pathé, "in the purest Louis XIV style" (1,000 seats), the latter of which probably initiated the *exclusivité* screening practice in 1916 with *The Cheat*. Gaumont controlled the next largest circuit of cinemas in Paris and the provinces. The flagship of the company was the Gaumont-Palace, formerly the Hippodrome Theater, on Place Clichy. Under the management of Edgar Cos-

17. Omnia-Pathé interior

til, the huge theater (nearly 6,000 seats) was transformed with a mammoth moveable screen that was surrounded by "an immense architectural frame in a Greco-Roman style." The orchestra area was remodeled to seat eighty musicians, and two great "Aeolian" organs were installed on each side. Opening in 1911, the Gaumont-Palace became the first French cinema to provide automatic projection equipment. Louis Aubert's circuit was quite small at first, comprising just five cinemas in Paris. In contrast to the major companies, however, Aubert was the only one during the war period to construct new cinemas: the Electric-Palace (500 seats) and the Nouveautés-Aubert-Palace (800 seats), which was laid out in the shape of a drawing compass.[34] Consequently, by the end of the war, despite these few exceptions, the French cinemas were in lamentably poor condition.[35]

All that began to change in 1919. While the production and distribution sectors of the film industry hesitated or reorganized in the face of American film imports, the exhibition sector embarked on a three-year binge of cinema construction (nearly doubling the number of cinemas in France). If anyone was going to make money, it would be cinema owners. They were encouraged in this boom by the nationwide adoption, in 1919, of an eight-hour workday and the "English week" (five and a half days of work per week).[36] The undiminished growth in cinema attendance fueled the industry's desire for more and better cinemas. Pathé-Cinéma/Pathé-Consortium expanded its circuit in the outer districts of Paris and in the provinces, constructing the first *grandes*

18. Gaumont-Palace façade (left) and Madeleine Cinéma façade (right)

salles in many regions. Aubert continued to expand its circuit with new cinemas in Paris, Lyon, and Brussels. Soon nearly every Parisian quarter had a 1,500- to 2,000-seat cinema.[37] However, what most fascinated the French film press was the marvelous apparition of a half-dozen or more luxurious "super-cinemas" in Paris.

The center of the cinema district in Paris now was the department store and theater area of the Right Bank Boulevards, and most of the new super cinemas were constructed there from 1919 to 1921. The first and grandest of them all was the Salle Marivaux (1,050 seats), which opened in April, 1919, with Griffith's *Intolerance*.[38] Built by the independent Compagnie générale française de cinématographie circuit (whose founder, Benoît-Lévy, linked it briefly with Vandal and Delac's grand scheme of a vertically integrated French film company), this new cinema was a peculiarly satisfying blend of sober lines, comfortable elegance, and ostentatious decor. Much of its atmosphere was "calculated on the play of light from three ranks of 5,000 lamps."[39] But its decor was decidedly byzantine:

Side by side with Ionian columns are vaguely Egyptian ornaments, all of which are illuminated in old rose and ochre, with green and gold motifs. One has the impression

19. Salle Marivaux interior

of swimming in a gigantic ice cream mixture of strawberries and vanilla adorned with pistachios.[40]

Related in style to the classical hardtop cinemas that were flourishing in the United States, with generous touches of the atmospheric, the Salle Marivaux seems an early example of what Dennis Sharp has called the Continental search for a distinctive and modern architecture in cinema design.[41] Under Francis Aron's management, it quickly became the most prestigious of all the *exclusivité* cinemas in Paris. The Marivaux was soon joined by another luxury cinema, the Ciné Max-Linder (900 seats), which had been a showcase for the French comic's own films and for the earliest American film imports during the war. In 1919, Linder himself spent two million francs to completely renovate the cinema in order to exhibit a series of films that he planned to make in France.[42] Although the Ciné Max-Linder reopened with the smash hit, *Le Petit Café*, Linder failed to get a second film project under way. Sold to an independent circuit, the cinema bearing his name soon became one of the few *exclusivité* cinemas in Paris. Another cinema that opened with a bang was the 850-seat Madeleine-Cinéma (also financed by Benoît-Lévy), which started *L'Atlantide* on its way to a worldwide success.[43] It, too, became an *exclusivité* cinema. Finally, Louis Aubert kept expanding his Paris circuit with a half-dozen cinemas, including the rebuilt 2,000-seat Tivoli-Cinéma.

While this construction boom went on, several exhibitors and distributors experimented with special programming formats. For instance, the only cinema on the Champs Elysées at the time, the Castillan-owned Colisée, began to devote its programming regularly to German films, to re-releases, and to the work of filmmakers such as Delluc, L'Herbier, and their "circle." The Mogodor-Palace followed suit with a series of re-releases inaugurated by *The Cheat*. The 4,000-seat Trocadéro theater had film projection equipment installed for several gala presentations by Pathé-Consortium—for Bernard-Deschamps's *L'Agonie des aigles* (April, 1921) and Diamant-Berger's superproduction serial, *Les Trois Mousquetaires* (September, 1921).[44] This screening of *Les Trois Mousquetaires* became the first highly publicized premiere in French cinema history. It was organized for the benefit of the men wounded and handicapped by the war, and its presiding hosts were five government ministers and the war hero, Marshal Foch. Pathé-Consortium even consigned Jean Sapène (then advertising editor of *Le Matin*) to direct a massive publicity campaign for the film's premiere as well as for its general release in sixty cinemas two months later.[45] One year later, on 6 November 1922, Pathé-Consortium organized a similar special premiere for Diamant-Berger's *Vingt Ans après* at Rolf de Maré's Théâtre des Champs-Elysées, where the Ballet suédois and Diaghilev's Ballets russes performed.[46] At the same time, Universal held a special preview for Metro's *The Four Horsemen of the Apocalypse* at the Théâtre de Vaudeville.[47]

From 1922 to 1925, the construction of new cinemas in France fell off a bit. Although construction continued in the provinces—e.g., Aubert-Palaces in Lille and Marseille—the mushrooming of big new cinemas in Paris ceased. Instead, the major circuits began to consolidate their holdings. In 1924, Aubert bought the Mogodor theater and converted it into a cinema; Gaumont, shifting its concern to distribution and exhibition, bought out the Madeleine. Pathé-Consortium formed an alliance with a new circuit based in Paris, Lutetia-Fournier. The highest-grossing cinemas in Paris, and in France, were nearly all controlled by one of the major chains: the Salle Marivaux (now 1,400 seats), Gaumont-Palace, Caméo (formerly Pathé-Palace), Aubert-Palace, Max-Linder, Madeleine, Lutetia-Wagram, Omnia, Palais de Fêtes (Brézillon), and Tivoli-Cinéma. Finally, the industry reached a new stage of public acceptance when the management of the Paris Opéra agreed, after several years of debate, to premiere special French films. The first film to be so honored was Bernard's historical epic, *Le Miracle des loups*, in November, 1924. The premiere became a national event when the president of the Republic presided over a select audience of ministers, diplomats, and celebrities in the arts and sciences from around the world. A year later, the Opéra initiated a series of such premieres with Aubert's *Salammbô*.[48]

During the last four years of the decade, the stabilization of the French economy and the continued high risks of film production led to another round of super cinema construction, which paralleled a similar expansion in Germany and slightly preceded an even larger boom in England. Among the French circuits, Pathé-Consortium opened the era with two new Paris cinemas in

1926—the Empire, where it now screened all of its new releases for the exhibitors and critics, and the Impérial, which soon became one of the topgrossing Paris houses. Its circuit was augmented further when Lutetia constructed three Paris cinemas in 1927. Aubert kept pace by purchasing the prestigious Caméo and Artistic cinemas. In September, 1927, the Théâtre des Champs-Elysées became a combination concert stage, music hall, and cinema. A month later, finally, a new independent super cinema, the Rialto, was dubiously inaugurated with Jean Sapène's tribute to Claudia Victrix, *La Princesse Masha*.[49]

All this activity was probably also spurred by Paramount's decision to invade the French exhibition market. In 1925, Adolphe Osso approved the purchase of the Théâtre de Vaudeville and its reconstruction as a super cinema. During the next two years, the American company either built or bought outright eight major cinemas in the French provinces. And it completed the Paramount-Palace (2,000 seats), located on the same spot as the old Théâtre de Vaudeville, just in time for the Christmas period of the 1927-1928 film season. The spacious art deco interior, the unusually comfortable main floor and loge seating, and the sophisticated underground electrical generating system—all forced the French to admit that the Paramount-Palace was the best of the super cinemas in Paris. Paramount also knew how to advance its own cause. It paid for a special supplement in the *Cinématographie française* (13 August 1927), and it regularly stunned the French distributors and exhibitors by spending up to one million francs to advertise a single film. By 1928, the Paramount-Palace accounted for 20 million francs or almost 10 percent of the total cinema receipts taken in Paris.[50]

The record grosses taken in by the exhibitors and the publicity given to this cinema construction boom helped provide the French film industry with sufficient capital, when the Americans and Germans forced the issue, to make the transition to sound films.

Silence in the Face of Sound

As the decade began in a state of crisis for the French film industry, so did it end in a crisis of a slightly different sort. To the conditions that determined the industry's ambiguous position throughout the 1920s, another was added to create the crisis of 1928-1929: the failure to encourage industrial research that could produce a marketable technology for the sound film.

The technology for sound film production and exhibition was developing very quickly by the early 1920s, particularly in the United States and Germany, but few perceived or pushed its commercial value.[1] In France, Gaumont had experimented with various synchronized sound systems from 1900 to 1913, but none of them became marketable for lack of economic and technical feasibility. By the 1920s, the company was in retreat and projected its occasional short sound films only as novelties. This lack of commercial foresight and financing was all too characteristic of the French film industry. Of the basic technologies forming the cinema's base, the French bridged the gap between invention and industrial manufacture and marketing in only a single one with any kind of consistency—camera and projection equipment. In the case of electronic sound recording, they faced an added drawback—the slow development of their electrical industry. Here the United States and Germany had a distinct advantage. For the incentive to convert to sound film production came from the powerful new electrical industries.

By early 1928, ERPI (Electrical Research Products Incorporated—a subsidiary of Western Electric) and RCA (an affiliate of General Electric) had acquired control of the American rights to sound film systems, signed contracts with the major film producers, and were beginning to push into the European market.[2] Within six months, two large patent groups, Tobis (controlled by Dutch financiers) and Klangfilm (in the hands of the German electronics industry) had emerged to challenge the Americans. The French were caught completely off guard in this confrontation. Gaumont was the only company to come up with an alternate sound film system, one developed by two Danish engineers working in France. Although technically advanced, the Gaumont-Petersen-Poulsen system proved commercially unfeasible, at least in its initial format. In March, 1929, Tobis and Klangfilm pooled their assets as a German corporation, and opened a year-long war with ERPI and RCA over control of the world market. When an agreement was finally reached in July, 1930, France officially became an open territory where the three corporations continued to vie for control.

Consequently, the French film industry was ill prepared for the sound film revolution. To survive, to make the conversion to sound film systems, it would have to depend on the monopoly of American or German technology. *Cinéa-Ciné-pour-tous* reported that Western Electric was charging up to 600,000 francs to install its sound projection equipment in a single cinema.[3] And that would be costly, doubly costly, since the money would not circulate back through the economy. Furthermore, the American boycott of film exports to France (from April to September, 1929) delayed the installation of sound systems in the cinemas.[4] The industry also found itself strapped by other costs. In 1926, Pathé sold its film-stock factory at Vincennes to Eastman-Kodak. Although the sale netted Pathé-Cinéma a tidy profit, the French film industry now had to depend on either Eastman-Kodak or Agfa film stock. Given such bleak material conditions, the French came through the transition period better than one might have thought. The sound film turned out to be an unexpected godsend—for it reintroduced the national barriers of spoken language.

The subject of the new sound films came up in the French press as early as 1926. By 1927, film journals were printing reports on the various formats that were being tried out in the United States—Paramount's singing film shorts with Raquel Meller, Fox-Movietone newsreels (using the ERPI system), and Warner Brothers' projected series of "feature-length talkie productions."[5] They were also debating the relative merits of *films sonorisés* and *films parlants* or talkies. The consensus was, according to Marcel Lapierre, that the sonorized film would eliminate poor orchestral accompaniment (or monstrosities like the "mechanical brouhaha" used for sound effects in the Paris screening of *Ben-Hur*) and, therefore, was preferable to the less familiar talkie.[6] By 1928, more and more reports came in, saying that the new sound films, especially the talkies, were setting box office records in both the United States and England. While passing through Europe, René Clair recalls drolly, Jesse Lasky confirmed the rumors.[7] French producers, directors, and scriptwriters immediately took off across the Channel to London to study the "savage invention" firsthand. All complained about the quality of sound reproduction and the static nature of the films, but none could deny that the monster would be victorious. For, as one put it, "[if] silence is silver . . . the word is golden."[8]

It was not until late in 1928, two years after Warner Brothers introduced its Vitaphone sound-on-disc system and just as the entire American film industry was deciding to convert to sound, that feature-length sound films began to appear in Paris.[9] Drawing on its long experience and its new optical sound-on-film process (Petersen-Poulsen), Gaumont was able to present the first French sound film before any American films could be released in France. The film was Marcel Vandal's colonial adventure, L'Eau du Nil, projected at the Caméo on 19 October 1928. Although the sound track of L'Eau du Nil consisted only of music and songs, the French press realized a "revolution" was at hand. Cinématographie française even compared Gaumont's presentation to the first public projection of Lumière's L'Arrivée du train and Sortie des usines Lumière. A month later, at the Madeleine-Cinéma, MGM screened an American sound film, Ombres blanches (White Shadows by Van Dyke and Flaherty), which used a Movietone optical sound accompaniment of Hawaiian guitar music. At the same time, Paramount released a newly sonorized version of Les Ailes (William Wellman's Wings). In early January, 1929, at the Ciné Max-Linder, Pathé-Consortium hesitantly joined the advance by releasing Marcel L'Herbier's L'Argent, accompanied at one point by phonograph recordings of Bourse crowd noises and an airplane roar. For a few heady weeks or months, it seemed as if the French film industry was on the cutting edge of the sound film revolution. But the euphoria proved illusory.

As in the United States, the turning point came with the release of Warner Brothers' The Jazz Singer (1927), on 26 January 1929, at the Aubert-Palace. Although presented in English (with one scene of dialogue) and restricted by the Vitaphone sound-on-disc recording system, The Jazz Singer was a smash hit. It played at the Aubert-Palace for almost a full year and doubled the cinema's previous year's receipts. In March, at the Théâtre de l'Apollo, Tobis-Klangfilm premiered the first German sound film, a popular music-hall film, La Revue Nelson, using its excellent optical sound process. At the same time, Paramount and Fox-Movietone began to exhibit their sound newsreels. In June, Paramount finally had its first genuine success (using Movietone optical sound) with Richard Wallace's A Song of Paris, starring the popular French singer, Maurice Chevalier. The demand reached the point where French film producers were forced to initiate sound film projects as a regular feature of their production schedule. In the process of changeover, the level of French film production fell steeply from ninety-four films in 1928 to fifty-two in 1929. Taking advantage of the five-month American boycott of film exports, however, the industry unloaded most of the last big French silent films (to limited competition) during the spring and summer months and prepared as best it could for the new fall season.[10]

Because French studios were still equipped for silent film production only, the earliest French sound films were simply sonorized in France or made in England or Germany. The 1929 fall cinema season included a hodgepodge of French sound films.[11] In October, at the Caméo, Aubert screened its first sound feature, a period film by Gaston Ravel and Tony Lekain, Le Collier de la reine, whose lone sequence of dialogue—a comic finale between Marat and

Robespierre—was postsynchronized, using the Tobis-Klangfilm process. At the Marivaux, Natan presented his first talking film, André Hugon's lackluster re-make of *Les Trois Masques*, which was recorded (with RCA optical sound) in England. The real hit of that program, however, was not Charles Méré's creaky bourgeois melodrama, but Walt Disney's energetic cartoon, *Mickey virtuose {Opry House}*. Pierre Braunberger contributed *La Route est belle*, which Robert Florey also recorded in England. Pathé-Consortium weighed in with Marcel L'Herbier's *Nuit de princes*, which was shot in France and then sonorized by Sequana Films in Berlin. And Abel Gance was sent to London by the Société de l'Ecran d'Art to shoot the sound sequences for his expensive new project, *La Fin du monde*.

By the end of the year, French talkies were finally coming out of French studios.[12] Natan led off a series of productions with L'Herbier's melodrama, *L'Enfant de l'amour*, and Pierre Colombier's boulevard comedy, *Chique*. Tobis-Klangfilm responded with a series headed by Henri Chomette's *Le Requin* and René Clair's *Sous les toits de Paris*. In December, *Pathé-Journal* began to appear as a sound newsreel. Within a year, the changeover was nearly complete: of the ninety-four French films produced in 1930, seventy-six were talkies.[13] And most of the others were silent films re-released with awkwardly synchronized sound tracks. Although silent film production in France did continue almost to the end of 1929, the transition seemed much sharper than it actually was because most of those films—e.g., Jean Epstein's *Sa Tête* (1930)—were virtually ignored in the French press.[14]

The major corporations in the French film industry suffered a crisis of leadership just before the sound film conversion got under way.[15] Charles Pathé wanted to retire again from Pathé-Cinéma and Pathé-Consortium, where he still wielded some power. Jean Sapène was disillusioned after his personal intervention at Cinéromans, especially by the failure to make his wife a star. When Louis Nalpas finally quit to organize his own production company once more, Cinéromans seemed to lose momentum. In 1929, after a period of sporadic activity, Léon Gaumont arranged for Edgar Costil to take over the directorship of Gaumont. Louis Aubert was elected to the National Assembly in 1928 and soon began to seek a buyer for his company. After its disastrous international films, S.G.F. was acquired by Serge Sandberg in the summer of 1928. Although Abel Gance and Carl Dreyer were retained nominally as directors, the only film S.G.F. produced (perhaps at Gance's insistence) was Jean Epstein's *Finis Terrae* (1929). Alexandre Kamenka abandoned Albatros's studio in Montreuil and closely allied his company with Sequana Films at Billancourt. With American and German interests poised to begin dividing up the French market, several spectacular upheavals seemed to reorder the French film industry structure completely.

The principal impetus for this upheaval came from Bernard Natan, Robert Hurel, and Edgar Costil. The leadership crisis at Cinéromans and Pathé-Consortium presented Natan with a speculator's dream, especially since his own company apparently was secretly in debt. In February, 1929, he bought out Pathé's controlling interest in Pathé-Cinéma and had it simply absorb his debts. With the active support of the Banque Bauer et Marchal, plus that of the Banque Conti-Gancel, Natan soon had control of Pathé-Consortium as well. In August, he pulled into his new conglomerate the Lutetia chain of

cinemas. The giant consortium that emerged from this systematic takeover,
Pathé-Natan, was hailed, with some irony, "as the witness of a renaissance in
the French cinema!" That same summer, Franco-Film picked up the option it
held on Aubert, and Hurel renamed the combined companies Franco-Film-
Aubert, Half a year later, in February, 1930, with the financial backing of
the Crédit Industriel et Commercial and the Swiss electrical industry, Gaumont absorbed Franco-Film-Aubert. A second consortium was born, Gau-
mont-Franco-Film-Aubert (G.F.F.A.), and Edgar Costil had himself appointed its director. According to Henri Diamant-Berger, there was even an
attempt to merge the two giants, but Hurel's financiers considered Natan a
"primitive" (a racial slur?) unworthy of sitting at the same conference table
with them. Even separate, however, the two looked formidable. As Jean Mitry
remarked, the French film industry seemed to have reconstituted itself as the
powerful force it once was before the war.[16] However, the resemblance proved
ironic. In five years, through poor management and speculation, both would
be bankrupt.

By the end of 1929, the French film industry had been pared to a half-
dozen companies with the resources and equipment necessary to begin full-
scale sound film production.[17] Immediately after taking over Pathé-Consortium, Bernard Natan enlarged the studios at Joinville-le-pont from four to six
stages, equipped each with RCA sound, and turned them into some of the
best in Europe. Similarly, he also converted his studio at rue Francoeur to
sound. At Paramount, Jesse Lasky and Walter Langer decided to concentrate
their European operations in Paris and named Robert Kane to take over direction of their Paris office from Adolphe Osso (who was soon to set up his own
production firm). In a grand splurge, they acquired the old Réservoir studios
in Saint-Maurice and built six new sound stages (using Western Electric
equipment) that surpassed even those at Joinville. Tobis-Klangfilm set up an
affiliate in Paris (under Georges Loureau), purchased the Eclair-Menchen studios at Epinay, and converted them with its optical sound system. Jacques
Haik built a new sound studio north of Paris at Courbevoie, while Franco-
Film reequipped the Victorine studios near Nice. For its part, Gaumont converted its huge studio to sound. Finally, the independent producer Pierre
Braunberger merged Néo-Film with a new production company set up by
Roger Richébé, a regional film distributor in France. Films Braunberger-Richébé took over the former Abel Gance studios at Billancourt and converted
them with Western Electric sound equipment. The other major companies—
Albatros, S.G.F., S.F.H., Louis Nalpas—were assimilated, reorganized, or
ceased production.

The co-production "internationalism" that so marked the latter half of the
1920s in France carried over into the early practice of sound film production.[18]
Following the pattern quickly established in the United States (by MGM) as
well as in England and Germany, nearly all the French studios produced not
one but several versions of each film, in the languages of their principal markets: French, German, English, and sometimes Spanish and Italian. Occasionally, translated dialogue was simply postsynchronized, but the standard practice at first was to hire a separate cast and director for each different version
of the film. Marcel L'Herbier's *La Femme d'une nuit* (1931) was an extreme
case: in French, it was a psychological drama—in Italian, a light comedy—in

63

German, an operetta! But Paramount, under Robert Kane, was the center, the fabulous Babel, of multiple-version film production. Beginning in the spring of 1930, Paramount's Joinville studio became a veritable "League of Nations" of directors, writers, actors, and technicians (including such French filmmakers as Louis Mercanton, Julien Duvivier, Alberto Cavalcanti, and Claude Autant-Lara), sometimes operating on a twenty-four-hour factory schedule, churning out some 100 features and 50 shorts in up to fourteen languages. This strategy was hopelessly costly, compared to the practice of dubbing and subtitling, initiated by MGM again, that eventually became standard. Consequently, after a loss of three million dollars over less than two years, Paramount converted its Joinville studio into Hollywood's dubbing center for Europe. Although the practice of making several complete versions of individual films disappeared, the American and German production/distribution companies retained a strong presence within the French film industry.

A similar form of dependency, attrition, and consolidation marked the exhibition sector.[19] Throughout 1929, French cinema owners experimented with various kinds of sound film systems (Mélovox, Synchronista, Idéal-Sonore), and those that chose sound-on-disc systems often projected silent films accompanied by their own choice of phonographs, without regard for synchronization. However, most soon followed the Paramount, Madeleine, Caméo, and other big cinemas in accepting the standardization provided by Western Electric, RCA, and, to a lesser extent, Tobis-Klangfilm. Although the major cinemas in Paris and the larger provincial cities could afford to make the costly changeover to sound (and were forced to do so quickly), many of the smaller cinemas could not. By 1932, sound projection equipment had been installed in 95 percent of the Paris cinemas but in less than 50 percent of French cinemas nationwide. The number of small provincial cinemas declined as a result, and the larger circuits strengthened their hold on the exhibition market. The consortium of Pathé-Natan controlled a total of 166 cinemas (69 in Paris, 35 in the outer districts of the city, 91 in the provinces, and 2 in Brussels). G.F.F.A. controlled 46 cinemas (20 in Paris and 26 in the provinces). Together these two concerns controlled the best cinemas in the country. "By the end of 1931," according to the figures of André Chevanne, "France had nineteen different circuits, whose 630 cinemas comprised [the most important] 15 percent of the total number of cinemas."[20]

Jacques Feyder, Henri Diamant-Berger, Henri Fescourt, Henry Roussel, Augusto Genina, and others within the French film industry saw the sound film revolution as an opportunity, a source of renewal.[21] Despite the presence of Paramount and Tobis-Klangfilm as major French producer-distributors and the modernization of most French cinemas with RCA and Western Electric synchronized sound systems, the triumph of the talkies gave the French one distinct advantage. They could make films in French and about French culture more easily and more effectively than anyone else. And that was what the French public was beginning to demand. When *Fox Follies 1929* was shown in English at the Moulin-Rouge-Cinéma, in December, 1929, for instance, the near riot that ensued was a clear sign of that demand.[22] So was the high profit margin (five to six times production costs) on most of the first French sound films—e.g., Roussel's *La Nuit est à nous* (Tobis-de Venloo), Robert Florey's *La Route est belle* (Braunberger-Richébé), Pierre Colombier's *Le Roi de resquilleurs* (Pathé-Natan), Julien Duvivier's *David Golder* (G.F.F.A.), and Marcel Pagnol's *Marius*, directed by Alexander Korda (Paramount).[23] The French cinema screens could be theirs again, for the first time since 1914. And they would be regained, not by any new stratagem of the French film industry, but by default. Ironically, by promulgating the sound film revolution, the American film industry divested itself of some of the French market. Furthermore, the French were helped by the relatively slow reaction of the country's economy to the Depression that staggered the United States and Germany. To the optimists, therefore, the French film industry seemed to have reached a position analogous to that of the American film industry in 1921—consolidation into several large corporations that could monopolize the horizon of their concern. There were differences, of course—less vertical integration, smaller markets, fewer capital resources, the presence of foreign producers and distributors, an approaching Depression. But the French industry appeared to be on the verge of realizing some of the hopes it had first articulated at the end of the Great War. It seemed closer to resolving its persistent state of crisis.

Others in the industry, particularly the formerly independent filmmakers, were pessimistic. After seeing *The Jazz Singer*, Marcel L'Herbier confessed, "When the cinématographe said to us all of a sudden: 'Look here, I, too, am going to talk,' I said to myself, 'So the catastrophe is coming.' "[24] Gance, Dulac, Clair, and L'Herbier, at one time or another, all thought it was "the end of the world." And they had cause for alarm, not about the new technology itself, but, as Clair put it, about "the deplorable use our industrialists will not fail to make of it."[25] "We are attending a death or a birth," concluded Alexandre Arnoux[26]—but which would it be?

As it turned out, the sound film did not really break with the silent film; the "perfection" of the latter was not entirely lost. But many important people in the industry and a whole way of filmmaking were adversely affected. The men who had shaped the industry for fifteen years or more were displaced—Pathé, Aubert, Sapène, Nalpas, and the unheralded Russian emigrés (Kamenka, Bloch, Grinieff). For every filmmaker who was able, financially and technically, to carry on and improve his or her work, there were far more whose work was abruptly cut off, constrained, or deflected. The reason for this was simple: the higher costs of film production and increased standardization. The kind of small- or medium-budget project financed by independent producers quickly became impossible. As a consequence, the entrepreneurial independence so characteristic of the 1920s abated, while the debilitating interest in speculation increased all the more. Ironically, as if still slavishly imitating the American cinema, a uniformity of style and social vision spread throughout the industry. As Bernard Eisenschitz has written,

> The talkie, by imposing a clumsier, more expensive infrastructure, by putting in question the narrative modes of silent film, cut short their *élan*—for it represented a knockout blow to all the avant-gardists and their advanced practices. . . .[27]

Only in the middle and late 1950s would the industry return to the rather diversified, artisanal conditions of the 1920s. And the New Wave would arise out of conditions similar to those of the First Wave.[28]

FRENCH CINEMA

II The Commercial Narrative Film

No, the cinema is not an art. . . . It is chemistry, physics, optics, mechanics, industry. And, above all, it is commerce.—Jacques de Baroncelli (1923)

Neither an art nor a business, the cinema is a craft.
—Alexandre Arnoux (1945)

What is the best way to come to grips with the hundreds of commercial French narrative films, from 1915 to 1929? That question depends on another, prior question: What, to the French, exactly was a *commercial* film? The one anticipates the answer to the other. To be commercial, paradoxically, a film need not have been profitable. If profitability were the issue, then René Clair's *Paris qui dort* (1924) would be commercial whereas Aubert's extravaganza, *Salammbô* (1925) would not. Similarly, the means of production financing hardly provided a clear-cut criterion. Many of the films one could include as part of a narrative avant-garde, for instance, were actually initiated or under-written as commercial projects by the major production companies—e.g., Abel Gance's *La Roue* (1922) and *Napoléon* (1927), Marcel L'Herbier's *El Dorado* (1921) and *L'Argent* (1929), Germaine Dulac's *La Souriante Madame Beudet* (1923), Jean Epstein's *Coeur fidèle* (1923), and even Carl Dreyer's *La Passion de Jeanne d'Arc* (1928).

Several filmmakers from the period offer a way to resolve these contradictions. "In cinema jargon," quipped Jean Renoir, "a commercial film is not one which necessarily makes money, but one which is conceived and executed according to the principles of businessmen."[1] But what were those principles? In one of the earliest books on French film, *Le Cinéma* (1919), Henri Diamant-Berger argued that, first, the producer, not the filmmaker, made the crucial decisions that determined a film's production.[2] Henri Fescourt, one of Ciné-romans' most consistently successful directors, agreed: "With few exceptions, it was not the filmmaker who chose the subject. In most cases, that was the prerogative of the producer. . . ."[3] Second, the essential element of a film, for the producer, was the scenario or story. In fact, said Diamant-Berger, "it *was* the film."[4] And what kinds of stories did he tend to choose? Here is Fescourt again: "The story most crammed with events or spectacular elements—a story with a recognizable title, which had already garnered accolades in the theater or in the bookstalls."[5] Diamant-Berger was more precise. Even if "roughly [and childishly] defined," such stories were formulas or *genres* that could be duplicated for mass circulation, exactly as were the products in "a grocery or lingerie shop."[6] As a site of pleasure, therefore, the French cinema seemed to attract and hold its audience, not with the images of popular stars (which was much more common in the United States), but with the familiarity or noto-riety of a film's subject or story.[7]

These statements suggest that the best way to analyze the commercial French narrative films of the period is to consider them within the framework of a loosely defined genre system in French film production.[8] Such an approach offers more than the convenience of labeling; it imposes certain questions. What film genres dominated the French cinema? What were the material conditions of each genre's development? What were the privileged conventions of its form—its fundamental structural components of character, setting, ac-tion, style? What was the social or ideological function of its tacit contract with the audience? Which specific films were most characteristic of a genre, which were most popular and profitable, and which were especially effective either in resolving a genre's representation of cultural conflicts or in changing its conventions? Finally, which genres in particular provided the context of accepted conventions within which and against which the narrative avant-garde tended to position itself?

The distribution of film genres within the French film industry seems to have had its origins in the kinds of films produced on a regular basis prior to the Great War, when the cinema was establishing itself as a form of spectacle entertainment. According to Georges Sadoul, by 1908 Pathé-Frères had "defined, classified, organized, and developed" a catalogue of film forms that would consistently attract a mass clientele. The most important of these were "the newsreels, 'dramatic and realist scenes,' 'Biblical stories,' and . . . comic films with their 'wild and woolly' chases."[9] Several others (associated more with Georges Méliès) had already declined in popularity and nearly disappeared—the trick film and the fairy tale or fantasy.[10] During this period, two of Pathé's products underwent significant changes. The comic film, of course, came to focus on the misadventures of a single clown or comic type—André Deed, Prince Rigadin, Max Linder. The "dramatic and realist scene," on the other hand, became a label for several different kinds of films that reflected divisions within French society. There were "social" films about the working classes, "sentimental dramas" about the bourgeoisie, and crime films ("dramas of passion") involving either class as well as bands of outsiders.[11] These latter films provided the basis for the rapid emergence of the series film and the serial. About the same time, one last format was tested successfully—the Film d'Art and S.C.A.G.L. adaptations of literary classics, especially those from the theater.

During the war, in the face of competition from the American cinema, which threatened the viability of much of their production, the French abandoned the comic short almost altogether—to Sennett, Chaplin, Arbuckle, Lloyd, and Keaton—and concentrated most of their production efforts on the serial and particular kinds of feature-length films. The popularity of the serial quickly led to a standardized format of half-hour episodes projected weekly over a period of several months, a format that could handle stories of crime, sentimental melodrama, and historical adventure and intrigue. In contrast to the serial, the term *grand film* designated a film of at least an hour in length, designed to be shown complete in a single *séance* or performance. By 1920, the average French feature was anywhere from four to six reels or 1,200 to 1,800 meters long.[12] Since the format encompassed a variety of genres that shifted in priority as the decade advanced, their development demands more specific attention.

Prior to the war, the first feature films had been literary adaptations, many of them drawn from theatrical productions. However, by the war's end, the plays that now were turned into film scenarios tended to be modern or contemporary—principally boulevard melodramas—typifying a shift away from the classic dramas, which had already been pretty well rummaged through. Simultaneously, a further shift was underway to film adaptations of novels and short stories, especially nineteenth-century realist fiction. During the early years of the twenties, therefore, the bourgeois melodrama and the realist film, followed by minor genres such as the fantasy, the Arabian Nights adventure story, and the boulevard comedy, had precedence. These were superseded rather quickly, however, by larger and longer superproductions. After the phenomenal success of *Les Trois Mousquetaires* (1921-1922), *Les Opprimés* (1923), and *Koenigsmark* (1923), the French turned more and more to large-scale historical reconstructions, which soon became the "top line" of production. As the nation rebuilt the northern provinces devastated by the war, so too did the film industry reimagine and thus give representation to ideologically significant figures and events in certain periods of French history. This genre was challenged in turn, around 1926-1927, by the development of studio spectaculars in a generalized modern European decor. These films of contemporary life played out in the new chic restaurants, nightclubs, theaters, and resorts sought to position the French within an emerging worldwide consumer society. When the industry finally changed over to talking films, in 1929-1930, the preference for adaptations from fiction ebbed once again in favor of contemporary theatrical productions.

This brief overview of French film genres provides a point of departure. The classification schema I offer is obviously tentative, in the absence of much prior research; and it is perhaps less than consistent—but then my purpose does not include a theoretical consideration of genre. As Henri Diamant-Berger confessed, "most of the really successful films prove the instability of any rigid classification."[13] Still, the schema can be valuable if it helps to mark out areas of intertextual relations among disparate films and to suggest ways that the films may be read contextually within the structures and processes of French culture.

In one sense, the serial was simply a transformation or retooling of the **Serials** prewar series film. Initially, there were several kinds of series films—some concocted in imitation of story serializations in the popular magazines, others drawn from imported dime novels and their French equivalents. They included westerns (*Riffle Bill, Arizona Bill*) and burlesque (*Onésime, Bout-de-zan*), but the most lasting was the police or criminal series.[1] Its period of formation was 1908 to 1914, from Victorin Jasset's *Nick Winter, Le Roi des détectives* (Eclair, 1908)—which soon had imitators in Britain, Denmark, and the United States— to Jasset's *Zigomar* (Eclair, 1911), *Zigomar contre Nick Winter* (Eclair, 1912), and *Zigomar, peau d'anguille* (Eclair, 1913); Georges Denola's *Rocambole* (Pathé-Frères, 1913); and Louis Feuillade's *Fantômas* (Gaumount, 1913-1914).[2] The criminal heroes of these films were especially popular, which made Arquillière, as Zigomar, and René Navarre, as Fantômas, early French film stars.

It would be imprecise to call the series film simply a serial in another guise. Each film in the series format was complete in itself, and the series was released, more often than not, in an irregular pattern. For example, *Fantômas* was really five separate films involving the same major characters (Fantômas, Inspector Juve, the journalist Fandor), and they were released over a one-year period at intervals of two to four months.[3] There were exceptions to this format—the most important probably was Léonce Perret's *L'Enfant de Paris* (Gaumont, 1913)[4]—but nothing to anticipate the abrupt change that occurred late in 1915 with the conjunction of two famous films.

First came Feuillade's *Les Vampires* (starring Musidora and Edouard Mathé), which opened at the Gaumont-Palace, 13 November 1915. From then until 30 June 1916, its ten semi-independent parts were released anywhere from three weeks to two months apart.[5] Although quite popular, its success was quickly superseded by Pathé-Frères' *Les Mystères de New-York* (starring Pearl

20. An early poster for
Fantômas (1913-1914)

White), which opened three weeks later, on 4 December 1915. This French-American import caused a sensation not unlike that caused by Eugène Sue's novel, *Les Mystères de Paris* (1842), from which it slyly drew its title.[6] To distribute the film, Pathé compiled episodes from the first three Pearl White serials which its New York counterpart, Pathé-Exchange, in partnership with William Randolph Hearst, had made as part of a popular new trend in American films.[7] Following the American format, *Les Mystères de New York* was made up of linked episodes, twenty-two in number, released in a continuous weekly series until 29 April 1916. Furthermore, its story was transposed by Pierre Decourcelle and printed daily, weeks in advance, in one of Paris's largest newspapers, *Le Matin*, as well as in several provincial papers.[8] La Renaissance du livre then published Decourcelle's novelization, episode by episode, in a series of "volumes" that together could constitute a book—the first of their *Collection des Romans-Cinémas*.[9] From that moment on, the French adopted the practice with enthusiasm, and the series film became the serial, the *ciné-roman*, or the "film in episodes."

For nearly four years, the epidemic of serials developed according to the parameters established by *Fantômas, Les Vampires,* and *Les Mystères de New-York.* These included a contemporary milieu with many shifts in setting (some exotic); a series of ingenious crimes, searches, entrapments, and escapes; and a clutch of characters distinguished by their fascination with (or revulsion from) evil (sometimes defined sexually) and by their position in a social class or ethnic group. Nearly every French producer turned out several such films on crime and/or detection annually, and distributors imported even more from the United States. In 1916, for instance, Abel Gance made several thrillers (*Les Gaz mortels, Barberousse*) for Film d'Art in order to take advantage of the genre's popularity. The following year, also for Film d'Art, Henri Pouctal filmed Arthur Bernède's patriotic diatribe, *Chantecoq*, as a serial (published in *Le Petit Parisien*); and Germaine Dulac directed *Ames de fous* (starring Eve Francis) in six episodes.[10] But there were some differences among all these films, differences which were most apparent in the products of the two major companies, Gaumont and Pathé-Frères.

Most of the serials made by Pathé-Exchange and imported into France had women as their central characters. The major heroines were Pearl White—*Les Exploits d'Elaine {The Perils of Pauline}, Le Masque aux dents blanches {The Iron Claw}, Le Courrier de Washington {Pearl of the Army}, La Reine s'ennuie {The Fatal Ring}*—and her chief rival Ruth Roland—*Who Pays?, The Red Circle*.[11] Usually the heroine was the victim or threatened victim of an outlandish scheme—the assassination of her father, her own murder for inheritance money, corruption and criminal implication by her fiancé—but she was also the one who tracked down or outwitted the villains and defeated them. Pearl White especially was a resourceful, agile, intrepid adventuress, willing to take on a gang of toughs as easily as a cream tart. In her optimistic blend of naïveté and natural strength (in this she resembled another favorite actress of the French, Mary Pickford), she may have seemed to the war-pressed French populace a kind of modern-day Jeanne d'Arc (her villains often were German actors or had German names). Francis Lacassin suggests another, darker reason for the success of her serials and of the others imported by Pathé-Frères. It was less her triumphs than her persecutions that drew the crowds—persecutions so often inflicted in subterranean worlds that they reminded Lacassin of the Marquis de Sade and his notorious chateaux. Was she a kind of Justine who "fell into the arms of vice all the while believing that she was protecting herself?"[12] It is difficult to decide whether the heroine of these serials is a "new woman," a model of emulation, or simply a reconstituted image of the "classical" figure of violation.

The serials that Louis Feuillade made for Gaumont during this period shared a kind of schizoid interest in women characters, but the scandalous success they acquired came initially from their fascination with crime. The black-clad criminals of *Fantômas* and *Les Vampires* are almost magically adept at manipulating, to their own advantage, the spaces in and around Paris. In *Les Vampires*, they can commandeer automobiles, scramble about moving trains, disappear around corners and down manholes, and creep unseen over the rooftops of the city. They can anesthetize a whole party of wealthy Parisians and rob them of their jewels or pluck a woman from an apartment window and drop her into a car waiting below. In the long-take, deep-space, long shots that characterize these films, Feuillade and his cameraman, Guérin, come close to celebrating a revolutionary underworld force against society. At the time, some people were disturbed particularly by the close correlation between Fan-

21. A publicity photo of the
ballet sequence in the first
episode of *Les Vampires* (1915-
1916)

tômas or the Vampire gangs' exploits and the activities of the anarchist Bonnot
band that terrorized Paris in 1912.[13]

Yet, as Richard Roud has observed, in *Les Vampires*, "the battle is not only
political and social, but also sexual."[14] The Vampire gang goes through several
leaders during its twelve episodes—the Grand Vampire, Satanas, and Vene-
nos—but the original French screen femme fatale—Musidora as Irma Vep—
outlasts them all. In episode after episode, this sorceress appears and vanishes
in a different disguise: as a demure family maid, a young male secretary, a
laboratory assistant, a wealthy widow, and a street tough. Gradually, the
reporter hero, Guérande (Edouard Mathé), becomes infatuated with her, especially when she helps kidnap his own wife. But Musidora's end already is
figured in the opening episode when a black bat-winged dancer (Stacia Napierkowska) hovers threateningly over a white-gowned woman, only to collapse and die of poison. Sure enough, in the final moments of the film, in
another *ballet fantastique*, the kidnapped wife guns down Musidora in a rescue
attempt, and Guérande lingers longingly over her dead body.

All this is conspicuously absent from Feuillade's most popular serial, *Judex*
(1917), and its successor, *La Nouvelle Mission de Judex* (1918). Perhaps frightened by the temporary banning of several episodes from *Les Vampires*, Gaumont
and Feuillade deliberately gave *Judex* an "uplifting moral tone." Although
Musidora was revived as the villainess, Diana Monti, the real star now was
the detective hero (René Cresté), whose status was epitomized in the transfor-

22. René Creste as Judex in
Judex (1917)

mation of the Vampire gang's sinister black costumes into Judex's black cape.
"That majestic cape that he threw over his shoulder in such a noble gesture
. . . *was Judex*," wrote Bardèche and Brasillach, "the rest was of little importance. . . ."[15] Louis Delluc, despite his admiration for Feuillade's technical
skill, was considerably less charitable: "*Judex* [and] *La Nouvelle Mission de Judex*
. . . are crimes certainly more serious than those which have been condemned
as traitorous by the Military Tribunal."[16] The only relief came in Marcel Levesque's antics as Judex's confidant, Cocantin.

It is worth pausing a moment on Feuillade's crime serials. Although they
were less popular in their time than was the police serial, *Judex* (which did
not protect them, nonetheless, from criticism by the young film critics and
cinéastes around Delluc), the crime serials have had their champions—from
the Surrealists in the 1920s to more recent figures as diverse as Alain Resnais
and Annette Michelson. The Surrealists were struck by Feuillade's vision of "a
defamiliarized reality." The conjunction of fantastic acts in recognizably real
spaces induced, for them, a peculiar state of disorientation, evoking the *marvelous*. "There is nothing more realistic and, at the same time, more poetic
than the serial," wrote Breton and Aragon, "in *Les Mystères de New-York* and
Les Vampires, one discovers a real sense of our century."[17] For Resnais, conversely, "Feuillade's cinema is very close to dreams—and therefore . . . perhaps the most realistic kind of all."[18] For Michelson, according to Roud, his
films reveal the architectural structure of bourgeois Paris as everywhere dan-

23. Suzanne Grandais in
L'Essor (1920)

gerous, threatened with being undermined or subverted.[19] I myself wonder if, in their conjunction of the real and the unreal, the banal and the unexpectedly terrifying, the films also convey, through displacement, the French experience of the war—the absurd proximity of normal life to the ghastly horrors of trench warfare.[20]

From the beginning, the serial was an easy target for parody. In fact, Jacques Feyder did his filmmaking apprenticeship on one of the earliest and best of these parodies, *Le Pied qui étreint* (1916).[21] In this four-episode film, the gang's signal of recognition is a raised wriggling foot (ridiculing episode one of *Les Mystères de New-York*: "The Clutching Hand"), and the gang boss is carted about in a baby carriage. In the fourth episode, he even imitates Chaplin in a robbery scheme. Finally, the hero and his boy sidekick watch themselves pursue the gang on a cinema screen, followed by their models—Marcel Levesque, Suzanne Grandais, Musidora, and Edouard Mathé. Such parodies, however, only seemed to whet the public appetite for the genre.

From 1919 to 1922, the serial's continued popularity began to form a bulwark against the onslaught of American films that threatened to displace French films from the cinemas. In the process, the formula underwent some changes. Perhaps these changes came about because, in the postwar society, a central commission now licensed and thus exercised some control over all commercial films. Perhaps they paralleled, through imitation or example, the development of subjects in feature films. Whatever the cause, although the format had become standardized at a dozen episodes, each from 600 to 900 meters in length, the parameters of the serial shifted and were redistributed in several different modes.[22]

As a backdrop to these changes, plenty of films still held to the familiar formula of the war period. From its New York branch office, Pathé-Cinéma and then Pathé-Consortium continued to import serials starring Pearl White, Ruth Roland, Marguerite Courtot, Irene Castle, and even Harry Houdini.[23] Pathé-Consortium also distributed film adaptations of popular novels by Pierre

24. The Vampire gang leaders in *Tih-Minh* (1919)

Decourcelle and Jules Mary: Pouctal's *Gigolette* (1921), Burguet's *Baillonnée* (1922), Etiévant's *La Pocharde* (1921) and *La Fille sauvage* (1922).[24] Through his own personal company, Société des Cinéromans, René Navarre starred in a half-dozen films of espionage, such as Edouard Violet's *La Nouvelle Aurore* (1919), in which he tried vainly to recapture his old fame as Fantômas.[25] For Phocéa, the small Marseille production company, Suzanne Grandais appeared in several serials, regaining her earlier status as France's first female star.[26] She was the only French film actress who could rival Pearl White. Even Louis Delluc admired her: "Oh, how charming she is. Not all of her films may be good, but she is always good in them, that is to say, smiling and amusing."[27] In 1920, her career was cut short when, working on a film by Charles Burguet in Alsace, she was killed in an auto accident. The most promising of these films, however, was Alexandre Volkoff's *La Maison du mystère* (1922-1923), produced by Films Ermolieff. Its chief surprise, according to Jean Mitry, was the multiple disguises of Ivan Mosjoukine. His "erudite, concise, synthetic" acting "contrasted sharply with the exaggeration of most French actors" and made critics compare him favorably with Sessue Hayakawa.[28]

A real break in the genre, interestingly enough, came in the work of Louis Feuillade. His first two serials after the war, made in and around the Nice studio he had taken over for Gaumont, surprisingly returned to the criminal world. In *Tih-Minh* (1919), a French explorer (René Cresté as Jacques d'Athys), his servant (Biscot as Placide), and an English diplomat (Edouard Mathé as Sir Francis Gray) are in search of a secret document that will lead them to an immense war treasure. Their antagonists include a Doctor Gilson (actually the German agent, Marx, played by Gaston Michel), a Hindu fakir, and the resurrected Vampire gang, who have taken over a villa named Circe along with its "living dead." Jacques falls in love with an Indochinese princess, Tih-Minh (Mary Harald), a young woman (and orphan) who has taken refuge with his family; and the villains kidnap her (several times) in hopes she can direct them to the treasure.[29] Although Francis Lacassin has described the world of *Tih-*

77

25. A kidnapping on the
grounds of the estate in
Barrabas (1920)

Minh as a kind of tourist's nightmare of exotic locales,[30] the schematic narrative seems most striking for the way it replays the nationalist and imperialist conflicts of the Great War.

In *Barrabas* (1920), the criminal gang is even more international in scope, operating behind the cover of an important banking corporation. Rudolph Strelitz (Gaston Michel) is the head of this double organization whose main bank leads directly to a health clinic, a luxury hotel, and a simple guesthouse on the grounds of a lost chateau—which is really a fantastic universe ruled over by the mysterious figure of Barrabas. The intrigue develops slowly from the guillotining of an innocent man to the revelation of Barrabas as an imposter and to his condemnation. For Lacassin, the title suggests the continuing, ineradicable existence of evil, for it is "the password that allows the gang members to move back and forth from the world of appearances to the parallel nightmare world."[31] Could *Barrabas* bear comparison with Fritz Lang's *Dr. Mabuse, der Spieler* (1922)?

In 1920, either because Feuillade's last two serials declined in popularity or because the Commission du Contrôle des Films was censoring film violence, Gaumont decided that the public no longer wanted to see crime serials, no matter how fantastic, and Feuillade went along with him.[32] Where previously he had shown either a fascination for the criminals or a moralizing interest in the "dispenser of justice," now, in three straight serials—*Les Deux Gamines* (1921), *L'Orpheline* (1921), and *Parisette* (1922)—Feuillade redirected his at-

26. René Clair and Sandra
Milowanoff in *Parisette* (1922)

tention to the victims, all young women. These victims, however, were a far
cry from the robust, combative characters of Pearl White or Suzanne Grandais.
As embodied in the Russian emigré actress (and former St. Petersburg ballerina), Sandra Milowanoff, they were closer to the exquisite purity and fragile
innocence of a Lillian Gish.[33] To match this usually orphaned ingenue heroine
(doubled in *Les Deux Gamines*), the figure of the detective gave way to a
"sentimental hero" (one played by René Clair).[34] The narrative became less an
accumulation of bizarre and baffling intrigues and more a character-oriented,
dramatic structuring of separation, adventure/misfortune, and reunion. The
former exotic or urban settings were replaced by family dwellings, villages,
and convents in the provinces. Older people and children became prominent.
And in the end, the long-suffering characters realized their undying hopes in
marriage. "A simple shift in the poles of attraction," writes Lacassin, "was
sufficient to transform a powerful magnetic field into a pool of tears."[35] In
their frankly romantic and sentimental appeal, Feuillade's serials had become
lengthy bourgeois melodramas.

Although the few film critics and historians who have seen these melodramatic serials find them much less interesting than *Les Vampires, Tih-Minh,* and
Barrabas, the French public of the early 1920s, most film reviewers, and
Feuillade's own friends were delighted. The three films coincided with a wave
of sentimental popular novels that held French readers enthralled just after the
war—*Les Deux Gamines* even drew its title from two of them, D'Ennery's *Les
Deux Orphelines* and Pierre Decourcelle's *Les Deux Gosses*.[36] Often these novels
were stories of orphans, and Feuillade's new serials were among the first films—
along with Pouctal's *Travail* (1919), Bernard's *Le Petit Café* (1919), Baroncelli's *Le Secret du Lone Star* (1920), L'Herbier's *El Dorado* (1921), and Poirier's
Jocelyn (1922)—to establish as a dominant subject in the French cinema of the
1920s the situation of the abandoned child or of the lone adult faced with
abandoning or adopting a child/orphan.[37] The collective French interest in,
even obsession with, this subject may have a simple historical basis—the terrible loss of men in the war as well as the decline in marriages and births
during and after the war, both of which perpetuated a situation that was well

79

27. Léon Mathot (left) in *Le Comte de Monte-Cristo* (1917-1918)

established by 1900.[38] To the film industry, however, Feuillade's postwar serials also served as models in their desperate attempts to set off the "Frenchness," the cultural superiority or sensibility, of French commercial films from the American competition. In the words of Aladin,

Ah! how ridiculous and infantile the American serials seem when we attend the preview of a serial such as *Les Deux Gamines*. . . . Here, in a word, is no silly story, but one governed by rational imagination, by logical dramatic development, rigorous, well-designed, and magisterially executed.[39]

That concern for Frenchness was equally apparent in the films resulting from a second shift in the parameters of the serial. This change probably had its origins in Henri Pouctal's 1918 version of Alexandre Dumas's *Le Comte de Monte-Cristo* (starring Léon Mathot in his most popular role), produced by Louis Nalpas at Film d'Art and released in eight episodes.[40] Till then, the serial had been restricted to current *cinéromans* and to the subject of criminal activity in the modern, mostly urban world. Suddenly it expanded to include "a pseudo-historical subject, full of costume adventures embroidered with a facile fabulism."[41] "*Monte-Cristo* is very good," wrote the usually reserved Louis Delluc, "very well conceived in its fabulous action and its dramatic interest. I have never before seen such fine understanding of just what a popular film should be like."[42] Georges Sadoul was also complimentary: "The story is simple, clear, direct. The editing is concise and intelligent, the lighting advanced [the cameraman was Guérin] but without an excessive precision. A lovely sense of natural landscapes gives a poetical quality to many episodes. . . ."[43] In due time, especially after a rerelease late in 1920, the way opened by *Le Comte de Monte-Cristo* was seized on by two newly independent producers.

Louis Nalpas had left Film d'Art in 1918 to set up his own production company in Nice. One of his most ambitious projects was Henri Fescourt's *Mathias Sandorf* (1921), an adaptation of Jules Verne's transposition of the same Dumas novel. A story of intrigue and adventure involving a Hungarian independence hero, *Mathias Sandorf* was released early in 1921 in nine weekly episodes. It became so popular, however, that it was recut later in the year and rereleased as a single-*séance* film that ran for seven months at the Cirque d'Hiver.[44] Francis Lacassin speaks of it in terms similar to those he used to praise the Frenchness of Feuillade's serials:

An "adventure film," certainly, but one that differs from the stale and uneven resale items that the Americans dispense—because of its strong dramatic structure, the quality of its acting based on a well-established psychology, the intelligent choice of landscapes, and the splendor of its photography. . . .[45]

At the same time, an even more ambitious project was initiated by Henri Diamant-Berger. His plan was to film the most popular French adventure novel, Dumas's *Les Trois Mousquetaires*, complete in twelve unprecedented hour-long episodes. The role of D'Artagnan was offered first to Douglas Fairbanks, but Fairbanks refused to work in such a vulgar genre as the serial.[46] Stimulated by the idea, nonetheless, he counteroffered by inviting Diamant-Berger to Hollywood to direct him in a two-hour American version of the novel. Refusing to cut his scenario so drastically, and with Charles Pathé's financial blessing, Diamant-Berger went ahead with his plan (as did Fairbanks), using an entirely French cast (Aimé Simon-Girard, Edouard de Max, Armand Bernard, Henri Rollin, Vallée, Charles Dullin) and shooting much of the film on locations, particularly in the old fortified city of Pérouges in the hills above Lyon.[47] Initially projected for three consecutive gala evenings at the Trocadéro in September, 1921, *Les Trois Mousquetaires* was shown over a three-month period all over France, accompanied by its publication in *Comoedia* and many provincial newspapers.[48] Its phenomenal success—17 million francs against a cost of 2.5 million—convinced Diamant-Berger and Pathé-Consortium to make a second adaptation from Dumas, *Vingt Ans après*, which was released in ten episodes late the following year.[49] The success of these two films, in fact, also helped establish the genre of historical reconstructions.

By 1922-1923, the serial had become both an economic strategy and an umbrella concept covering various kinds of narratives of adventure and intrigue: police (Fescourt's *Rouletabille chez les bohemiens*, 1922), criminal (Feuillade's *Le Fils du flibustier*, 1922), sentimental (Feuillade's *Parisette*, 1922), costume (Burguet's *Les Mystères de Paris*, 1922, starring Huguette Duflos), and, for want of any better label, a lackluster hodgepodge (René Leprince's *L'Empereur des pauvres*, 1922).[50] There were even more parodies: L'Herbier's "humoresque," *Villa Destin* (1921), and Mosjoukine's *Le Brasier ardent* (1923). More and more critics and producers realized that the serial had reached a dead end. There were complaints about the length of time required to see one serial, about their monopolization of cinema screens to the disadvantage of other French films, about the stagnation of repeated formulas.[51] In 1922, Pathé-Consortium stopped importing American serials when Pathé-Exchange was sold to a group of Merrill Lynch investors in New York. In September, troubled by less than anticipated grosses, the company abandoned its expensive costume serials.[52] In the summer of 1923, after Pathé-Consortium had rereleased *Le Comte de Monte-Cristo* (a second time) and Gaumont had rereleased *Judex* in a reduced, single-*séance* format, Louis Feuillade admitted to physical and artistic exhaustion.[53] During this period, *Ciné-Journal*, *Mon-Ciné*, and *Cinémagazine* engaged in a lengthy public debate on the discredited serial format. *Mon-Ciné* even conducted an extensive survey among its readers and concluded that the serial indeed was desperately in need of reform.[54] What the public wanted, wrote Pierre Desclaux, was a serial of six to eight episodes on an historical subject.[55] And that is precisely what they got when Jean Sapène, the advertising editor of *Le Matin*, turned film producer.

Sapène's prescription for reviving the genre depended chiefly on organization.[56] After taking over the Société des Cinéromans from René Navarre in 1922, he built up a double-barreled distribution system of *ciné-romans* that involved Pathé-Consortium in association with the Lutetia cinema chain and the major Paris newspaper consortium of *Le Matin, Le Journal, L'Echo de Paris*, and *Le Petit Parisien*.[57] His new production team was led by Louis Nalpas (chief producer or "artistic director") and Feuillade's former scriptwriter, Arthur Bernède (scenario department head).[58] Their task was to engage reputable directors, scriptwriters, and actors for an annual production schedule of four serials, standardized in eight episodes, to be released evenly throughout the year. They were aided in their efforts by a spirited defense of the serial format by Pierre Gilles in the pages of *Le Matin*.[59] From 1923 to 1927, outside of an occasional film by Gaumont (Feuillade's last films), Aubert, Phocéa, and Albatros, the serial became the exclusive property of Sapène's Cinéromans.

The films themselves, beginning with Henri Fescourt and Gaston Leroux's *Rouletabille chez les bohemiens* (1922), adhered basically to the parameters already established—with one important difference. Some, such as Germaine Dulac's *Gossette* (1923) and René Leprince's *L'Enfant des Halles* (1924), continued the pattern of combining elements of the police and sentimental serials. These still made much of children and orphans. Others exploited the exoticism of adventures in the colonies—e.g., Le Somptier's *Les Fils du soleil* (1924). However, they were all outnumbered by costume adventures drawn from original scenarios rather than from popular literary classics. Now, more often than not, the hero was an historical figure. War heroes and adventurer-brigands from the period of 1750 to 1850 were especially popular—e.g., Gaston Ravel's *Tao* (1923), Jean Kemm's *Vidocq* (1923) and *L'Enfant-Roi* (1923), Fescourt's *Mandarin* (1924), Luitz-Morat's *Surcouf* (1925) and *Jean Chouan* (1926).[60] In their return to a rich French world and an optimistic, valiant hero, both belonging to a supposedly more glorious past, these latter films can be read as part of a collective attempt at an ideological restoration or redefinition that is even more visible in the expensive historical reconstruction films.

At least two of the Cinéromans productions survive and allow us more than a passing glance at the last important serials. *Mandarin* (1924), one of the most well-received of Cinéromans' serials, had as its hero a kind of Robin Hood of tax-collecting (Fairbanks's *Robin Hood* had been very popular in France the year before), whose exploits were based on an historical figure operating in the Dauphiné region around 1750.[61] Claude Beylie and Francis Lacassin describe his particular brand of derring-do:

Declaring himself the enemy of the landowners, attacking their collectors to whom he sold contraband tobacco in exchange for their cashboxes, benefiting from the complacent indifference of the local gendarmes, Louis Mandarin, in less than three years, disrupted the French fiscal system and escaped all the soldiers ordered to pursue him.[62]

Perhaps in anticipation of a sequel, Bernède and Fescourt allowed their hero to avoid capture and the guillotine, through the intercession of Voltaire, no

82

less (who actually did support him in several writings and letters). Instead of emphasizing complicated intrigues or the sentimentality of suffering, according to Beylie and Lacassin, *Mandarin* seems to have gone for a deft combination of action and atmosphere:

It is a fast, concise film, intercut with spectacular horseback chases and explosive confrontations. In the exterior shooting, Fescourt has used the ravines and gravel slopes of the Niçois back country to remarkable effect. . . . [It] remains a model of the *French* adventure film, full of a sweeping epic inspiration whose secret is perhaps lost.[63]

A critic writing at the time of its release, however, was much less enthusiastic: ". . . the technique of *Mandarin*—especially that which involves 'montage'— is regressive by several years. . . . If you wish to follow innovations in the serial, look again at *Gossette* and *La Maison du mystère*."[64]

Indeed, *Gossette* (1923) does differ markedly from *Mandarin*, but its avant-garde status is highly suspect. The story that Dulac was assigned to film was in the tradition of Feuillade's *L'Orpheline* or *Parisette*: the sentimental hero, who is falsely accused of murder, disappears; the ingenue heroine (already an orphan) is taken in by the hero's parents who then are killed, abandoning her again to misfortune; the hero and heroine team up to discover the "truth"; the real villain is unmasked; the old parents' spirits bless the young couple's union.[65] This tearful tale is complicated by frequent flashbacks (the lack of intertitles in the only existing print does not help), but several choices that Dulac makes in the narrative are of interest.[66] Most of the film was shot in the old Pathé studio at Vincennes and then at the Levinsky studio in Joinville-le-pont, so it eschews the natural landscapes that function so prominently in *Mandarin*. Instead, the film relies heavily on close shots (MSs to CUs) of the characters—often starkly or flatly lit against dark backgrounds (a lighting technique which had become rather standard practice in French silent films). It also occasionally uses a subjective montage, including soft-focus images (e.g., the hero's hours of half-drunken peregrinations before he is accused of murder) and a montage of objects (e.g., the narration of the initial murder by means of a glass, a cigar, hands, and shadows). However, these supposedly avant-garde devices are awkwardly integrated into the film, and Dulac herself felt deceived and unduly compromised by Cinéromans after making it.[67]

It was during this period, also, that one of the best parodies of the genre appeared in Jean Epstein's *Les Aventures de Robert Macaire* (1925), produced by Albatros. For his scenario, Epstein drew on the legendary character of the fictional Dauphiné highwayman created by Frédérick Lemaître as well as by the famous series of caricatures by Daumier.[68] The narrative reminds one of Fescourt's in *Mandarin*—five separate intrigues and adventures (beginning in 1824) involving Macaire (Jean Angelo), his sidekick Bertrand (Alex Allin), and a bevy of women and victims.[69] Epstein's concern for atmosphere, however, is much more pronounced than Fescourt's. In fact, the authentic and sometimes exquisite Corot-like landscapes (photographed by Paul Guichard), together with the realistic interiors (designed by Lazare Meerson), tend to counterpoint the adventures and reduce their significance.

But there was method in Epstein's apparent mania. According to Pierre Leprohon,

28. Alex Allin and Jean Angelo in *Les Aventures de Robert Macaire* (1925-1926)

In choosing this picaresque hero of popular literature, the filmmaker could—by juxtaposing the intelligence and cunning of his two comrades Robert and Bertrand with the stupidities of the other characters—both amuse the general public as well as amuse himself by parodying the genre that he seemed to serve.[70]

Jean Angelo plays Macaire with a blithe hauteur that belies his often well-worn and changing costumes. He saves aristocratic ladies from death, rescues good people from the gendarmes, and steals fortunes to set up young couples in marriage; but he is not above picking Bertrand's pocket. Bertrand, on the other hand, fails at nearly everything he tries, but that does not deter him. Begging for food, he is scared off by a farm family that includes a tough old woman, a mangy dog, and a boy picking his nose. After Macaire rescues Mlle. de Sermeze (Suzanne Bianchetti) from drowning, Bertrand whistles for her horse and watches it scamper away. Lovesick over a maid, who keeps reappearing with a different man, he tries to drown himself in an inches-deep fountain and, then, with a huge blunderbuss, succeeds only in blasting his hat. Finally, he is defeated in a duel with the sentimental hero (Nino Costan-

84

29. Sarah Bernhardt in *Jeanne Doré* (1915)

tini) and then is beaten up for good measure. Macaire and Bertrand, however, sometimes do make a good team, as when, in their hilarious robbery of a farmer's wife, they disguise themselves as St. Anthony and a half-blind, purse-snuffling pig. In the end, on a ridge road overlooking a picturesque valley, they swear to become honest men and stride off over a hill, picking one another's pockets.

By 1927-1928, the serial had all but disappeared, as it had even earlier in Germany and the United States. Its once prominent position in Cinéromans' production schedule had passed to the Films de France series and to the expensive spectaculars the company was co-producing with Ciné-France and others. As more and more publicity was given to these bigger films and as American and German films consolidated their hold on the French public, cinema programs increasingly were geared to the single-*séance* films and even to the American double-bill format. As a consequence, the serial declined in popularity and profitability. Here the history of the French film serial seems to close off. But the study of that history, despite the fine work of Francis Lacassin and François de la Breteque, has hardly begun.

As the *grand film* developed into a major production strategy during the war, it defined itself initially within the tradition of literary adaptations established by Film d'Art and S.C.A.G.L. Producers at Pathé-Frères, Eclipse, and Film d'Art could now more easily mobilize the reputable actors of the Comédie Française as well as their slightly less illustrious colleagues from the boulevard theaters and music halls to lend some measure of respectability either to their patriotic films or to their condensed versions of the current theater. Thus, the appeal of these films, for a short time anyway, derived from the presence of famous stage actresses and personalities. The music hall star, Mistinguett, for instance, had her greatest success in *Fleur de Paris* and *Chi-*

Bourgeois Melodramas

85

gnon d'or (both 1915).[1] Réjane made one of her rare film appearances in Pouctal's *Alsace* (1916), which reprised her prewar theatrical performance and ran
for two consecutive (and unprecedented) weeks at the Gaumont-Palace. Sarah
Bernhardt posed before Jeanne d'Arc's statue and the ruined Rheims cathedral
in Hervil and Mercanton's *Les Mères françaises* (1917); and in Mercanton's adaptation of Tristan Bernard's *Jeanne Doré* (1915), she gave an unusually restrained performance that is affecting even today, partly because of her ravaged
face and nearly immobilized body.[2] At Pathé-Frères, Gabrielle Robinne, who
had performed in the original version of *L'Assassinat du duc de Guise* (1908),
was now starring in her own series of films (most of them directed by René
Leprince) in which, according to René Jeanne, she did a lot of loving and
suffering, with dignity.[3] In 1918, she was still representative enough for Louis
Delluc to hold up her mannered style of acting for ridicule against the robust
spontaneity of Pearl White.[4]

Most of these early feature films were drawn from a particular form of
drama, the popular melodrama. There had been instances of the genre in the
prewar cinema, say, in Pathé-Frères' adaptations of several Henri Bernstein
plays.[5] But the genre did not come into its own until after 1916, once the
ground had been prepared by the Italian melodramas starring Francesca Bertini
and by De Mille's *The Cheat* with Sessue Hayakawa (whose success, in part,
depended on its French bourgeois melodrama origins).[6] The bourgeois melodrama had long been the favorite of the *boulevardiers*, whose life revolved around
the theaters, nightclubs, and cafés on the Grand Boulevards of Belle Epoque
Paris. Motivated perhaps by the war restrictions on theater performances in
Paris, the film industry eagerly expropriated the genre to itself and began to
expand its audience with a new clientele.

The bourgeois melodrama film generally took its subject from the socioeconomic context of the high and middle bourgeoisie.[7] The *boulevardiers* and
Opéra-season ticket-holders could find familiar settings here: Renaissance dining rooms, Louis XV bedrooms, and Empire offices.[8] There were the familiar
plots, full of lurid intrigue and violent action usually predicated on the "eternal love triangle." And at the center was the question of a woman's loyalty or
social function as wife and mother as well as the consequent affirmation of the
family as the locus of moral and spiritual value and, hence, of social stability.[9]
The attraction of the bourgeois melodrama, according to Jean Mitry, was that
it produced the world of "a society drawn from the theater . . . not the
reflection of the actual bourgeoisie, but the image of the privileges that they
no longer enjoyed except in the fictions that were made for them and which
they greedily devoured."[10]

Several films preserved at the Cinémathèque française provide a good index
of the early feature-length bourgeois melodrama. Camille de Morlhon's *Maryse*
(1917) tells the story of a young woman (Maryse Dauvray, Eclair's star) who
accepts a brief liaison with a doctor in order to keep up an apartment for her
mother.[11] Later she becomes the model and mistress of an up-and-coming
young painter, who just happens to be the doctor's son. The climax comes in
a recognition scene between the two men; the painter attempts suicide, unsuccessfully, and father and son are reconciled. Yet the last shot is of the
young woman alone once more. The narrative sacrifices passion for family
harmony (between father and son), but the surviving print makes it uncertain

whether the woman is an immoral temptress or the real victim. *Maryse* uses a
limited number of flatly lit sets (several apartments, the painter's studio, the
Opéra) but divides up many of its scenes, in the manner of American continuity editing, into a range of shots from LS to ECU (with most of them falling
between FS and MCU). However, the rhythm of the editing is not always
smoothly paced; and the acting, though quite restrained for a French film of
that time, relies on theatrical clichés at highly emotional moments. In comparison, Jacques Feyder's early two-reeler about a double love triangle, *Têtes
de femmes, femmes de tête* (1916), looks even more restrained and original—it is
played out almost entirely in MSs.[12]

Abel Gance's *Le Droit à la vie* (1917) tells a similar, though less ambiguous,
story. A young woman (Andrée Brabant) is in love with a stockbroker (Léon
Mathot) but is forced to marry an older financier (Paul Vermoyel) to pay the
debts of her dying mother. The financier discovers the young couple's love
and then an embezzlement by one of his assistants. When the assistant shoots
and wounds him, the enraged financier pins the blame on Mathot. Finally, in
the midst of a heated trial, he confesses Mathot's innocence and, soon after,
conveniently dies so the young couple can be reunited. Gance's film is distinguished from *Maryse* by much more sophisticated lighting and editing, both
of which probably derive (as does some of the story) from *The Cheat*.[13] In
several key sequences, the characters are isolated in close shots and sculpted
by side lighting against black backgrounds. This technique, mastered by Gance's
young cameraman, L.-H. Burel, also appears in other bourgeois melodramas
such as Aubert's *Notre Faible Coeur* (1916) and Germaine Dulac's *Venus victrix*
(1917).[14] Significantly, the moral and psychological condition of the central
characters (but only the men) is emphasized through several subjective images.
The suspense of the shooting climax is heightened by a strategy of parallel
editing (using crude wipes) between the confrontation of men in one room
and a progressively more unrestrained masked ball in another.[15] The trial is
articulated almost entirely in MCUs that depend on eyeline matches and shot/
reverse shots; in fact, the film as a whole is marked, even more than is *Maryse*,
by frequent MCUs and CUs. Finally, there is one fascinating fetishistic gesture
whose repetition almost turns it into a rhetorical figure. In linked sequences,
Mathot lovingly caresses the young woman's hair, and then the financier dreams
of caressing her in the same way as he prepares his marriage plan. After the
wedding, however, as she stands by the bedroom window, the young woman
refuses to let him touch her.

The potential of the bourgeois melodrama is probably most clearly demonstrated in Gance's *Mater Dolorosa* (1917), said to be the most popular French
film of the 1917-1918 season.[16] Although an original scenario, *Mater Dolorosa*
follows the dramas of Paul Hervieu, Henri Bernstein, Charles Méré, and,
perhaps more specifically, Henri Kistemaecker's *L'Instinct*.[17] Much like *Le Droit
à la vie*, it also owes a good deal to *The Cheat*. The narrative is predicated on
a love triangle involving Dr. Gilles Berliac (Firmin Gémier), a pediatrician,
his wife Marthe (Emmy Lynn), and her lover, his brother Claude (Armand
Tallier).[18] Overcome with guilt for her affair, Marthe tries to commit suicide
and, in a struggle with Claude, accidentally shoots him. When Gilles is informed of his brother's death (through a humpbacked blackmailer!), he believes Marthe guilty of murder and leaves her, taking their young son with

30. (left) Emmy Lynn and
Armand Tallier in *Mater
Dolorosa* (1917)

31. (right) Emmy Lynn
at the window

him. Uncertain of his fatherhood, Gilles agonizes over caring for the boy when
suddenly the latter falls ill. Finally, a letter comes that exonerates Marthe,
and Gilles recognizes her suffering. The couple is reunited; the son, restored
to health. As in the other films belonging to the genre, the emphasis throughout this narrative is on the psychological condition and moral state of the two
central characters. But here, quite clearly, the health of the individual as well
as the society literally depends on the health of the family or the condition of
a marriage.

Besides the social or ideological implications of its narrative, *Mater Dolorosa*
exhibits most of the stylistic conventions of the bourgeois melodrama. The
settings are confined to the lover's study, several rooms in the couple's comfortable parkside house, the hospital ward, the doctor's apartment (only these
last two deviate a bit from convention—the hospital ward, for instance is
unusually realistic in its detail) and a few exterior shots. The range of shots
used in the film's dozen or so segments—from LSs to CUs, from straight-on
shots to various angled shots—is not all that different from *Maryse* or *Le Droit
à la vie*. Nor is the number of shots deployed uncommon. Most of the sequences are composed of many separate shots, yet they do not add up to the
nearly "400 shots" in André Antoine's comparable crime melodrama, *Le Coupable* (1917).[19] In Gance's film, however, the cutting within and between
sequences is exceptionally clear and economical, the more so since there are
quite a number of inserts, short flashbacks, and brief subjective sequences,
along with several sequences of parallel action. By contrast, *Maryse* and *Le
Coupable*, the latter of which tries to narrate a past story within the context of
a trial, display much less economy, smoothness, and clarity.

Yet *Mater Dolorosa* transcends its genre conventions in several ways. Com-
menting on its mise-en-scène, Jean Mitry neatly sums up the judgment of
French film historians:

Mater Dolorosa . . . surprises, astonishes, by means of lighting effects, the knowing
use of light and shadow to intensify dramatic scenes, the intimate fidelity of the
decors, singling out particular details, and a thousand unusual qualities for a French
film.[20]

88

Gance and Burel used a good deal of sidelighting and low-key spot lighting on faces and parts of figures against dark backgrounds, creating even softer images than in *The Cheat* or *Le Droit à la vie*. Here the effect serves not only to model the characters in a three-dimensional space but also to heighten their emotional expressiveness. Figures are framed in silhouettes at windows and behind curtains—a technique that owes a debt not only to *The Cheat* but to earlier French films such as Léonce Perret's fascinating *L'Enfant de Paris* (1913), photographed by Georges Specht.[21] As Colette first noted, the film also evidences "a new use of the *still life*, the poignant use of props, as in the fall of a veil to the floor."[22] The slightest movements within the frame resonate metaphorically: Emmy Lynn backing off into the darkness after the shooting, a single window opening outwards (with no person visible) in a LS of the apartment building, a MS of the doctor behind a curtain as he touches his wife's veil, which echoes the earlier CU of the same veil falling beside the window through which she watches him leave the house. More obvious metaphors are evoked in a shattered mirror (in the sequence of doubted fatherhood) and in a painting of the *mater dolorosa* which provides the prior image or figure recognized by the doctor and replicated in his wife's suffering. Here, in embryo, is the possibility of a sustained pattern of rhetorical figuring.

Film adaptations of the bourgeois melodrama continued to be an important asset to the French film industry into the early 1920s. Especially popular were the plays of Bernstein, Kistemaecker, and Méré. When Gaumont, for instance, wanted Marcel L'Herbier to prove himself commercially after the total failure of *Rose-France* (1919), he told him to consider the success that Louis Mercanton and Gaby Deslys had made of his previous scenario for *Bouclette* (1918); and he assigned him to direct Bernstein's *Le Bercail* (1919). L'Herbier agreed, as he put it, "to practice his scales."[23] The result was that Gaumont made a tidy profit and L'Herbier could go on making films. Film d'Art produced several more melodramas starring Emmy Lynn, that "victim of passion and mother love": Gance's *La Dixième Symphonie* (1918) and Henry Roussel's *La Faute d'Odette Maréchal* (1920).[24] When the company determined to make films marketable in both France and the United States, it chose as its first projects Bernstein's *La Rafale* (1920) and Kistemaecker's *Le Secret du Lone Star* (1920), both directed by Jacques de Baroncelli and starring the American actress, Fanny Ward, and Gabriel Signoret of the Comédie Française. Despite risking most of its capital on expensive serials and multipart films, Pathé-Consortium also distributed popular melodramas such as Henry Krauss's adaptation of a Méré play, *Les Trois Masques* (1921).

However, much like the serial, the genre was under a great deal of pressure that was pushing it in several different directions at once. Abel Gance, for instance, was reshaping it with his technical experimentation as well as his philosophical pretentions. His original scenario for *La Dixième Symphonie* (1918) tried to transform a bourgeois melodrama plot of marital fidelity by posing the problem of artistic creation—an idea, Kevin Brownlow writes, that was inspired by a quotation from Berlioz: "I am about to start a great symphony in which my great sufferings will be portrayed."[25] The composer Enric Damor (Séverin-Mars), a widower with a grown daughter, Claire (Elisabeth Nizan), marries Eve Dinant (Emmy Lynn), who has an untold, compromised past— she is being blackmailed by a former lover, Frédéric Ryce (Jean Toulout) for accidentally killing his sister. When Ryce courts Claire and Eve opposes their announced marriage (without explanation), Damor believes his wife is secretly in love with the suitor. In despair, he writes and performs his symphony, and Eve prepares to sacrifice her own happiness if Ryce will leave Claire alone. Claire discovers what is happening, and, after a flurry of threats and counter-threats, Ryce shoots himself. Claire defends Eve to her father (without telling all), and Damor relents and forgives. Two years later, André Hugon would rework this dual problem of marital fidelity and artistic inspiration, with Séverin-Mars as a poet cursed by alcoholism, in a much more conventional melodrama, *Jacques Landauze* (1920).[26]

What is admirable in *La Dixième Symphonie* extends the techniques of *Mater Dolorosa*: the mysterious elliptical opening of the past accidental shooting, the repetition of gestures for psychological effect, the lighting and placement/ movement of characters, the rhythmic clarity of the action. But Gance's attempts to relate his artistic intentions to the classics (e.g., comparing Eve to the Winged Victory of Samothrace, citing numerous literary quotations) and to represent the act of artistic creation itself (for Damor's performance, he films an "Isadora Duncan" dancer [Ariane Hugon of the Opéra] in a series of natural settings, masked by a horizontal vignette of Greek vase designs) provoked critics to misleadingly brand the film "inaccessible to the public."[27] Today, these moments merely seem embarrassingly simplistic. Furthermore, Eve's suffering is much greater, ironically, than that of her composer husband, and Damor never discovers the full extent of her discontent.

J'Accuse (1919), Gance's first superproduction for Pathé-Cinéma, transformed the genre almost completely by thrusting the melodrama plot into the disturbing context of the war. Here, even more than in *La Dixième Symphonie*, the love triangle intrigue is but a pretext for a fiercely emotional personal statement and for further cinematic experimentation. Paradoxically pacifistic and nationalistic at the same time, *J'Accuse* was a stunning commercial success, especially considering its release several months after the Armistice. As will be demonstrated in Part IV, it was also technically and rhetorically much in advance of any other French film of 1919. The same blend of family melodrama, personal statement, and experimentation would also mark Gance's next epic, *La Roue* (1922-1923).

In contrast to Gance's "epic symphonies," Raymond Bernard, a protégé of Jacques Feyder, oriented the genre toward the "chamber music" of a more intimate drama. Drawing primarily on a series of plays and scenarios by his famous father, Bernard concentrated on the psychological possibilities of the bourgeois melodrama—in *Le Secret de Rosette Lambert* (1920), *La Maison vide* (1921), and *Triplepatte* (1922). The subject of *Le Secret de Rosette Lambert* was a conventionally "cruel and violent story," adapted from Tristan Bernard's *Coeur de Lilas*.[28] In it, a businessman sets a trap for the wife of his partner in order to ruin him. When the villain dies, his proxy keeps up the intrigue, only to be unmasked by a family friend of the victims. Unlike previous bourgeois melodramas, however, this film situated its story in quite modern decors designed by the young master architect, Robert Mallet-Stevens. Mallet-Stevens's sets simply and starkly validated Bernard's psychological interest as well as creating a suitable atmosphere for informal dancing (which was then undergoing a new wave of popularity in Paris).[29] For the first time, apparently, mod-

32. A Robert Mallet-Stevens decor for *Triplepatte* (1922)

ern interiors were constructed specifically for a film and not merely chosen from the stock of traditional studio decors.[30] Despite fine acting from Henri Debain, Sylviane Grey, and Charles Dullin (in debut), the film was compromised by its star, an unknown American actress, Lois Meredith.[31] Still, Bernard's direction, according to Louis Delluc, resulted in "one of the most splendid manifestations of *photogenic plasticity* in the cinema."[32]

La Maison vide, the first film to come out of Bernard's own independent production company, was an original scenario that he devised from a banal love story. In his unpublished memoirs, Bernard has confessed that his ambition in the film was to make the audience aware of subtle mental states of which the characters themselves were not always conscious.[33] Henri Fescourt remembers the film vividly:

An impalpable story of grays. Hesitations, subtle nuances, slight incidents. A timid entomologist, suspended over his precious collections, falls in love with his secretary. Scarcely anything happens. A bouquet on a table, displaced by an angry kick, falls to the floor. A microscope that reveals darkened images. Is it the fault of the lens? No, the eye that observes, an eye darkened by a tear. . . . No hands clutching the breast, no long sighs. Very few intertitles. It was enough to watch the images and Henri Debain.[34]

Unfortunately, Bernard's choice of a title, *La Maison vide*, failed to attract audiences to the cinema, and the film ended up appealing to only a few

91

33. (left) Eve Francis, Jean
Toulout, and Gaston Modot
in *La Fête espagnole* (1920)

34. (right) Ginette Darnys in
Le Silence (1920)

filmmakers and critics.[35] In *Triplepatte*, Bernard fared much better by retreating to one of his father's stock of well-known plays, which allowed Henri
Debain to mildly satirize a similar "hero of indolence and indecision."[36]

Bernard was not alone in creating "chamber music" films during this period, for the analogy (it is Henri Fescourt's) also fits a small group of films
produced by filmmakers involved in the narrative avant-garde. Several of Louis
Delluc's earliest films, for instance, develop a refined psychological irony from
rather conventional bourgeois melodrama plots. *Le Silence* (1920) can serve as
an example, even though it survives only in the form of a published, deceptively simple scenario.[37] Pierre (Signoret) is awaiting his lover Susie (Eve Francis) alone in his rooms. Suddenly, in a chance comparison of letters, he realizes
that she was responsible for an anonymous letter in the past that inflamed his
jealousy and incited him blindly to kill his young wife. When Susie finally
arrives late, Pierre is dead in his chair, the victim of the same revolver with
which he shot his wife. Since the action takes place almost entirely within
Pierre's consciousness, *Le Silence* has been aptly described as "a monologue in
images."[38] The "dramatic theme" (to use Delluc's own phrase) unfolds through
the alternation of Pierre's memories and his perception of certain key objects
in his possession. Elliptical and full of ironic twists, this alternation seems to
have been, in contrast to the usual bourgeois melodrama, more intellectual
than emotional in its effect.

Germaine Dulac shared Delluc's interest in the psychological states of characters, and not only in their collaborative film, *La Fête espagnole* (1920)—where
two suitors kill one another over a bored Spanish lady (Eve Francis again) who
ignores them and, drunkenly awakened to life once more in a festival dance,
gives herself to a third man.[39] The rather dense narrative structure of this
short film will be discussed later; for now it is worth mentioning that Eve
Francis's costume was one of the first designed specifically for film.[40] *La Mort
du soleil* (1922) is perhaps more characteristic because its scenario, written by
André Legrand, resembles that of *Mater Dolorosa*. While it celebrates the struggle

of Doctor Lucien Faivre (André Nox) against tuberculosis—epitomized in recurring shots of supplicating diseased children in some barren place—it also focuses on the conflict dividing Marthe Voisin (Denise Lorys), who is dedicated to helping Faivre but is equally devoted to her family, especially her young daughter.[41] Given this scenario, Dulac wanted in her words, "to describe the inner workings of the mind or soul, within the theme of the action."[42] Consequently, she uses her plot, with its several misunderstandings, to explore the subjective life of both the woman and the doctor, separately and in combination. The most unusual of these moments is a strange conjunction of the two characters as the doctor lies near death early on in the film. Images of Faivre's delirium and of Marthe's inner thoughts are intercut to produce a "communion of souls" whose significance oscillates between escape, shared passion, and awakening dedication to a scientific discipline. Unfortunately, according to Charles Ford, "this eminently cinematographic scene was cut in nearly all the cinemas {because} the spectators {and the exhibitors} would not let the action of a film be encumbered with psychological notations."[43]

By 1922, the bourgeois molodrama had been so transformed—and separated from its theatrical origins—that it no longer existed as a distinct genre. Perhaps this transformation was due to an apparent rivalry (or lack of cooperation) between the cinema and theater as much as it was to the pressure of the interests of the narrative avant-garde.[44] Perhaps, too, Charles Pathé's warning about adaptations from the theater had proved true:

. . . the author and director should consider not only the title of the play they want to adapt, or the intensity or violence of the series of well-linked actions, but also—and this is not current practice—the nature of the emotions that are expressed. The extreme plot situations of prominent playwrights, unless substantially amended, will fail to pass censorship, particularly in the Anglo-Saxon countries. . . . The audiences of these countries will not appreciate the spicy, risqué plots that Bernstein and, preeminently, Bataille have established as the norm.[45]

In any case, this change was actively supported by a new film journal, *Mon-Ciné*. Within months of its appearance in February, 1922, *Mon-Ciné* embarked on an educational campaign to encourage the development of a "cinema of quality" in France. Its purpose was twofold and implicitly ideological: to forge a link between film and fiction and to dignify the cinema by displacing the serial or *cinéroman*, in the popular taste, with the *roman-ciné* or something very much like the bourgeois melodrama.[46] To that end, each issue of *Mon-Ciné* was devoted to a serialized novel and to the novelization of a current "serious" film, which novelization soon became as important as the film itself. Largely ignoring the work of the narrative avant-garde as well as the serials, *Mon-Ciné* singled out for praise such filmmakers as Bernard, Roussel, Feyder, Fescourt, Robert Boudrioz, and Léon Poirier.[48] Their films, and especially Poirier's *Jocelyn* (1922) and *Geneviève* (1923), came closest to realizing what Maurice Roelens has identified as an "aesthetic of emotion"—"a [logical] series of naturally melodramatic situations, apt to arouse emotion and especially 'the voluptuousness of compassion' that one usually associates with melodrama."[49] Although terminologically vague—and thus capable of infusing various genres, as we shall see—this was one answer to the question of what was peculiarly French about the French cinema.

35. Three shots from the delirium sequence of Doctor Faivre (André Nox) in *La Mort du soleil* (1922)

In the course of *Mon-Ciné*'s polemic, most of the filmmakers who had come into the cinema from the theater before or during the war turned exclusively to adapting fiction or writing their own scenarios. And those theatrical melodramas that did become films were usually subsumed in one of several other genres.[50] Some, such as René Hervil's *Blanchette* (1921) or Fescourt's *Les Grands* (1924), evoke the atmosphere and ambience of natural location shooting and are best seen as realist films. Others, such as L'Herbier's "melodrama," *El Dorado* (1921), or Julien Duvivier's *Maman Colibri* (1929), became part of the cycle of exotic or colonial films. Still others, such as Dulac's *Ame d'artiste* (1925), L'Herbier's *Le Vertige* (1926), or Perret's *La Femme nue* (1926), create elaborate sets and an international milieu that make them early examples of the modern studio spectacular. Otherwise, the only truly theatrical adaptation to replace the bourgeois melodrama in the 1920s was the boulevard comedy, especially as represented by the plays of Labiche and company. But the boulevard comedy is important enought to be treated separately.

The exceptions to these changes were few and far between. Germaine Dulac's *Antoinette Sabrier* (1927), produced by Cinéromans from a play by Romain Coelus, which Réjane had made popular, is one of the sole surviving examples.[51] Its subject is a busy industrialist (Gabriel Gabrio) who cannot decide which of two women he loves, his wife (Eve Francis, who had not made a film in four years) or a younger woman "whom he believes to be the incarnation of Love" (Yvette Armel).[52] According to Charles Ford and René Jeanne, the film was too close to being a Comédie Française production.[53] Julien Bayart pinpointed one of the reasons: "the decors . . . produce an impression of artificiality, an impression of coldness accentuated even more by the way they are lit. . . ." *Antoinette Sabrier*, he concluded, "is a theatrical, a terribly theatrical . . . story. . . ."[54] The genre had come back to its origins.

Realist Films

As the Great War drew to a close, a number of French films appeared— André Antoine's *Le Coupable* (1917) and *Les Travailleurs de la mer* (1918), Louis Feuillade's *Vendémiaire* (1919), and Jacques de Baroncelli's *Ramuntcho* (1919)— all of which challenged the prominence of the class-conscious, studio-bound evasions of the bourgeois melodrama. These films mark the beginning of a broad genre of feature films that developed in the French cinema of the late 1910s and early 1920s. At the time, they were identified in the press under different labels—e.g., "simple dramas," "atmosphere films," or just *plein air* films." Despite the problematics of the term, let me call them realist films, for the designation seems to have some historical basis.

First of all, these films were not without precedents in France. Before the war, after all, as a counteraction to the Film d'Art literary adaptations, Louis Feuillade had produced a series of sixteen short films under the high-sounding title, *La Vie telle qu'elle est (Life as It Is)*. In a statement introducing the series, in April, 1911, Feuillade spoke of his films as "slices of life"—"they eschew any fantasy and represent men and things as they are, not as they should be."[1] As Francis Lacassin has shown, despite Feuillade's invocation of Zola and Maupassant, most of these sketches were violent, intimate melodramas, stripped down to a handful of characters in a few simple, stereotypical settings.[2] Another, perhaps unlikely, precedent can be seen in some of the prewar crime

films and serials. Léonce Perret's *L'Enfant de Paris* (1913) and Georges Denola's
La Jeunesse de Racombale (1913), for instance, already exhibited the same sensitivity to natural light and open air that would characterize the later films.[3]
Like several of Perret's early films, *L'Enfant de Paris* was shot on location (by
Georges Specht), in the back streets of the Paris *faubourgs* as well as in and
around a villa above Nice.[4] In these early serials, however, the conjunction of
fantastic crimes and deceptions with recognizably real spaces induces a peculiar state of disorientation or dislocation that differed radically from the effect
of the postwar realist films.

Georges Sadoul has argued that Feuillade and his colleagues at Gaumont
were influenced in these efforts by the Vitagraph films then being imported
into France and by the *verism* that characterized French literary naturalism.[5]
Even more marked by that *verism*, however, were similar films by Victorin
Jasset and Maurice Tourneur at Eclair and by some of their colleagues at
S.C.A.G.L.[6] The best of Jasset's *Les Batailles de la vie* series, *Au pays des ténèbres*
(1912)—inspired by Zola's *Germinal*—was no less melodramatic and conform-
ist in its moralism than were the Feuillade films. But it did seem to have a
surface verisimilitude as a result of being shot in the northern coal-mining
regions.[7] At S.C.A.G.L., Zecca assigned René Leprince and Camille de Morlhon to produce a comparable series, *Scènes de la vie cruelle*,[8] but the company's
major realist productions were two early feature-length films. The first was
André Capellani's adaptation of Hugo's *Les Misérables* (1912), which Antoine
later cited as one of "the first accurate realizations of the cinema."[9] The second
was Gérard Bourgeois's remake of *Les Victimes de l'alcool* (1911), based on Zola's
L'Assomoir. This film stuck more closely to Zola than did any of the others,
although it depicted alcoholism as an individual vice rather than as a social
phenomenon. Its real interest, however, according to Sadoul, lay in its mise-
en-scène.[10] Each sequence was filmed in the old-fashioned style of the tableau
(and in studio decors), yet the movements of the actors often carried them
from LS to MS within the space of a single take. Here was one of the earliest
sustained instances of a realism based on deep space.

The man probably responsible for this initial influx of *verism* into the French
cinema was none other than André Antoine. His work in translating the aesthetics of naturalism from fiction to theater—through the Théâtre Libre (1887-
1896) and then the Théâtre Antoine (1897-1906)—had provided an incentive,
particularly for the filmmakers at S.C.A.G.L.[11] This should not be surprising
since some of them—Tourneur, Capellani, Desfontaines, Denola, and Krauss—
originally had been members of his theater companies. In 1914, Antoine's
position of influence increased dramatically when, out of financial exigency,
he accepted a contract to direct films for S.C.A.G.L.[12] Apparently, he thought,
as did Charles Pathé for a time, that he might transform the French cinema
the same way he had the French theater a generation before. Although that
mission proved unsuccessful—and his age (sixty), abrasiveness, cantankerous
nature, and sense of self-importance alienated many of his colleagues—Antoine
did articulate ideas and institute practices that were fundamental to the emergence of the French realist film.

The first thing Antoine insisted on was shooting on location. As early as
1917, in response to a question on the crisis in the French cinema, he argued
that

The cinema would make real progress if it abandoned the studios to work in nature just as the Impressionists did. Instead of improvising an artificial milieu for the camera, we should transport the cameraman and his instruments into real buildings and interiors, as well as develop mobile electric generators for lighting.[13]

In part, these words were provoked by the economic and material conditions of the wartime French film industry. The studios were operating at less than full capacity, and they were clearly now inferior to the American studios, especially in lighting and set design. Furthermore, neither Pathé nor Gaumont seemed willing or able to provide the capital needed to renovate their facilities. So filming on location was a viable response to the industry's limitations. Antoine's own production of *Les Travailleurs de la mer* (1918) seems to have set a precedent. Within two years, many of the French film companies, particularly the independents, had dispersed into the countryside, using mobile or on-location studios for their productions.

More important to the specific development of the realist film was Antoine's concept of location shooting and the new acting style that it demanded. When motion pictures first appeared, Antoine was fascinated by the filmed documents and then by the newsreels.[14] What struck him was the plasticity of these images, the natural landscapes and real figures in those landscapes, rendered in relief through natural gestures and movements as well as through the direction, intensity, and texture of natural light. For his naturalistic theatrical productions, it should be remembered, Antoine had often taken photographs of their alleged locations, photographs which his set designer then used as an index of verisimilitude. Now the cinema seemed to offer the possibility of enacting and recording the story or scenario in those very locations. Just as he opposed the painted sets and reusable decors of the studios, so did he object to good theater actors becoming grimacing film stars: "these performers must be exclusively plastic. . . ."[15] Because of the difference between theater and film, Antoine also advocated the formation of a special troupe of actors who would work only in the cinema.[16] And he suggested that, wherever possible on location, "real types" among the local inhabitants enact the smaller roles— in effect, play themselves. Finally, he had the novel idea that, instead of making the actors play to the camera (which was usually immobile), the camera should be free to follow the actors. "[It] should follow them step by step, to surprise their looks, from whichever angle they present themselves."[17]

The last thing Antoine stressed was the importance of the scenario, the subject of the film. Despite his interest in the plasticity of the film image and in what he called "impressionistic tableaux," he believed that "photography was no more than a means."[18] The principal factor in a film's appeal and success was its subject. For Antoine, the best subject was either an existing realist or naturalistic work of fiction or an original scenario by a like-minded contemporary novelist. This would allow the narrative cinema to represent life "as it really was," to hold up a window or mirror for the spectator. Antoine's own choice of scenarios is significant. Those that he chose, rather than those he was assigned, were stories of peasants and working-class people, adapted from major nineteenth-century narrative poems and novels. His production of Hugo's *Les Travailleurs de la mer* (1918) and his decision, in 1919, to film Zola's *La Terre* (1921) established precedents for representing something other

than the life of the French bourgeoisie in Paris or in the southern coastal
playgrounds.

Thus, in its exploration of geographical areas and provincial cultures, the French realist film developed a mode of representation which differed somewhat from that of realist and naturalistic fiction. The critical, even fatalistic, representation of the social order so crucial to that fiction was tempered in the realist film by several influences, among them French landscape painting, reaching from the Impressionists back to Millet, his more conventional contemporaries, and even Corot. Instead of analyzing the relationships among individuals or groups in the social order, the realist film tended "to record the verities of nature *en plein air*" and to celebrate natural landscapes as a presence that encompassed and affected the characters, usually with a sense of gentle melancholy.[19] The genre seemed to subordinate social analysis to a concern for the pictorial and even the picturesque. Were these French landscapes displayed as so many scenes or documents for the disinterested aesthetic pleasure of a spectator, a touring bourgeois spectator, for whom, in John Berger's words, "the landscape [was] *his* view, the splendor of it *his* reward"?[20] Or was that pleasure perhaps more than disinterested—did such landscapes accurately represent a France that was still predominantly rural (until 1931)[21] or did they deflect attention from the harrowing reality of the war-devastated regions of northeastern France? Whichever, in contrast to the serial and the bourgeois melodrama—whose love triangle plots it sometimes shared—the realist film tended to invest less in narrative and more in description. More precisely, it emphasized the emotional and connotative relationship between landscape and character, sometimes to the point where a particular landscape or milieu became the central character of the film.

It is tempting to characterize the realist film as having two broadly different subjects. The distinction is a simple one—life in the city, usually Paris, and life in the country. Something of the deep social/ideological division in France between Paris and the provinces, between a bourgeois society dependent on a state apparatus, industry, and a proletariat (as well as the unemployed) and one dependent on the land and a peasant class of farmers and artisans, between the locus of the "modern" and the locus of the "traditional," does seem to undergird the genre. Yet the division is perhaps less significant than one that distributes the more numerous films set in the provinces according to different landscapes and regions—the seacoasts, the mountains, the rivers and canals, the agricultural plains. Along with the modern urban milieu, each of these regions and their local customs is represented by some half-dozen films in the early 1920s. Interestingly, they correlate somewhat with the regions that had been the subject of a folklorist concern of the nineteenth-century Realist art, what Linda Nochlin calls, "picturesque regional genre painting"—e.g., Provence, the Pyrenees, and especially Brittany.[22] Whatever the geographical area or culture, however, the realist films, much like their forerunners in painting, tended to turn to the past or to more traditional ways of life in presenting positive images of France and of the French social order.

One of the earliest areas to be explored was the coastal region of Brittany. After making *Les Frères corses* (1916) and *Le Coupable* (1917), Antoine refused to shoot another film in Paris. Deliberately, he chose to adapt Victor Hugo's *Les Travailleurs de la mer* (1918) so that he, his assistant Georges Denola, and cameraman Paul Castanet could work almost entirely on the western tip of Brittany.[23] Recently, his son talked about the production:

Antoine had a villa at Camaret. He loved that spot very much. It is there that he shot the essential parts of the film . . . it was an occasion to photograph the sea. For the real character of the film is the Sea.[24]

The stills that remain of Antoine's film evidence his obvious love for the "filmed document . . . this quality of ubiquity and presence, of the cinema's omnipotence."[25] Yet the film did not always achieve the naturalness that Antoine desired. Delluc criticized its scenario (for which trick shots had to be used in a climactic battle between the hero and an octopus!) and pointed to the contradiction of Comédie Française actors (Romauld Joubé, Armand Tallier, Andrée Brabant) playing Breton fisherfolk in the midst of the real thing.[26]

Ah, how I wish he had a story of his own, a scenario that was alive, new, modern. Say, a story about workers or, even better, about peasants. . . . Perhaps the characters could be acted by their real-life counterparts. I would like a peasant to be played by a peasant.[27]

That was a practice, however, which S.C.A.G.L. apparently refused to let Antoine indulge in. Still, *Les Travailleurs de la mer* was unusually popular—the readers of *Comoedia*, for instance, voted it one of the top five films of the decade—and it seems to have stimulated the production of a number of coastal realist films.[28]

Two of the most interesting of these early films were Marcel L'Herbier's *L'Homme du large* (1920) and Louis Mercanton's *L'Appel du sang* (1920). Mercanton, in collaboration with René Hervil, had directed L'Herbier's first scenario, *Le Torrent* (1918), whose theme, L'Herbier says, was "a raging river in the middle of France, in a village at the water's edge, with thickets of little dramas that are nourished by the torrent."[29] Their strategy, however, was to film it with Comédie Française actors, such as Henry Roussel and Gabriel Signoret (with Jaque Catelain in debut), against the rather tame gorge of the Loup river on the Côte d'Azur.[30] Although Léon Gaumont thought highly of the film when it previewed at the Ciné-Opéra in November, 1917, L'Herbier himself did not even recognize his story and characters in Mercanton and Hervil's images.[31] Three years later, the young cinéaste returned to the theme of *Le Torrent* with a Breton film that caused a brief scandal.

L'Homme du large (1920) was a rather free adaptation of a short philosophical story by Balzac, *Un Drame au bord de la mer*.[32] Following his habit of designating the genre of his films, L'Herbier christened it "a seascape." The narrative, told in a long flashback, caused a stir by contrasting two children of a Breton fisherman (Roger Karl)—the daughter Djenna (Marcelle Pradot) is pious and obedient; the son Michel (Jaque Catelain) is profligate and afraid of the sea.[33] Infatuated with a new singer in a local café and egged on by his friends (including young Charles Boyer), Michel refuses to attend his dying mother and, in a drunken fight, stabs the singer's lover. Then he tries to steal the money which his mother has entrusted to Djenna—he threatens both his sister and father with a knife but is entangled in a fishing net as he attempts to

 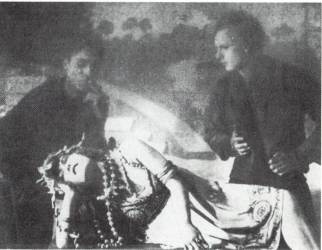

36. (left) Roger Karl and Jaque Catelain in *L'Homme du large* (1920)

37. (right) The cabaret singer

escape through a window. The father punishes him by putting him, bound and alone, into a small boat and pushing it off into the sea. Then he and Djenna separately take vows of silence—the one living in a sea cave, the other becoming a nun. Michel survives the ordeal and, one year later, returns a changed man; and in turn his father and sister are freed from their vows. Another kind of notoriety attached to the film, soon after it opened in Paris on 3 December 1920,[34] when several sequences in the rough café were censored as excessively violent and sexually provocative.

Much of *L'Homme du large* was shot by Georges Lucas and Jean Letort in the early summer along the southern coast of Brittany, from Quiberon to Penmarch.[35] Like Antoine, L'Herbier's intention was to have "the sea as a protagonist." As he himself wrote of the experience, "the awesome subject of elementary forces, when they reach a high level of pure expressiveness, has been, is, and will be the privileged subject of the cinématographe."[36] However, just as in *Les Travailleurs de la mer*, there is an obvious contradiction in the film between the overwhelming images of the seacoast and village and those of the actors, who simply are not convincing as a Breton family. More surprising is the artificial nature of the frequent wipes, irises, superimpositions, and stylized intertitles supered over shots of the sea—taken at the time as a sign of L'Herbier's concerns as a literary aesthete, carried over from *Rose-France* (1919) and *Le Carnaval de vérités* (1920).[37] Despite these real and apparent limitations, *L'Homme du large* does succeed sometimes in creating an atmosphere that is both convincing and aptly connotative—through its choice of seascapes and village landscapes (with Djenna's white figure, in LS, gliding along the dark walls and across the rocks), its low-key interior lighting (especially during the mother's death and during Michel's pathetic theft), its views of actual Breton life, and its exotic seething café (where L'Herbier first seems to have used a juxtaposition of soft and sharp focus within a single

99

38. Gabriel de Gravone,
Phyllis Terry, Le Bargy, and
Ivor Novello (background) in
L'Appel du sang (1920)

shot). Perhaps Juan Arroy sums up the film best: "It produced exceptional
visual harmonies, through the alternation of great waves of images, animated
and aerated by the sea, and the feverish rhythm emanating from a sailors'
café."[38]

After Antoine abandoned film production in 1921, the leading proponent
of a realist cinema in France, according to René Jeanne, was Louis Mercanton.[39] Mercanton had been one of the first filmmakers, after Antoine, to adopt
location shooting in earnest. By 1919, he had developed a model mobile
studio "of four motorized trucks and two trailers (carrying a generator capable
of producing 12,000 amps) along with eighty lamps of all sorts. . . ."[40] With
this newly devised equipment, he shot several films in England and France;
for one, he even ventured out across the Mediterranean. *L'Appel du sang* (1920),
adapted from a Robert Hitchens novel, tells a story similar to *L'Homme du
large*, but with a different class of characters, in a very different locale—the
dry rocky shores of Sicily. It also combines a lot more narrative complications
with a much less exciting visual style. The film was a resounding commercial
and critical success—*Ciné-pour-tous* judged it one of the three best French films
of the 1919-1920 season.[41] Even Louis Delluc, who appreciated "the open air"
of Mercanton's films, found it more than the usual "remarkable album of
photographs" and praised the acting of its international cast.[42]

The narrative (articulated in frequent intertitles) begins with Hermione Les-
ter (Phyllis Neilson Terry), an Englishwoman who lives in Rome, deciding to
marry a younger man, Maurice Delarey (Ivor Novello), unaware that her good
friend, the novelist Emile Artois (Le Bargy), is deeply in love with her.[43] The

couple go to live at Hermione's villa in Sicily, and Maurice takes a liking to her servant, Gaspare (Gabriel de Gravone). Enchanted by the culture and by the sea (his grandmother was Sicilian), he is soon drawn into an affair with an island siren, Maddelena (Desdemona Mazza). Her fisherman father, Salvatore (Fortunio Lo Turco), begins to blackmail him; and when Maurice decides to break off the affair, the old man kills him and throws his body in the sea. Hermione discovers what has happened only when she confronts Maddelena grieving at her husband's grave. Released from his promise of silence to Maurice, Gaspare tries to take revenge on Salvatore; their struggle in his island cottage is interrupted by a knock at the door, and the old man accidentally shoots his own daughter. Hermione finally realizes Emile's love for her, and the two are engaged to marry—even though the novelist priggishly reprimands her for transferring some of the flowers from Maurice's to Maddelena's grave.

Viewed today, *L'Appel du sang* looks more like a slightly exotic bourgeois melodrama than a realist film. Although it was shot by Emile Pierre entirely on location, the images rarely suggest the ambience of life in Sicily. Many shots of the characters posed against the Sicilian hillside or seacoast look as if they could just as easily have been filmed on the Côte d'Azur or even in Southern California. Only occasionally is there an inkling of what attracts Maurice to the culture—the men dancing the "Pastorale"; the torchlight fishing (perhaps one of the earliest sequences of location shooting at night); the village festival, which ends in a huge fireworks display (culminating in a superimposed image of a flaming religious icon, smokestacks, wheel frames, and tiny silhouetted human figures). Maddelena, on the other hand, is at first more Aldonza than Dulcinea, but she gradually earns our attention and even our sympathy (she really does love the bloody Englishman). For brief moments, both Maurice and Emile are given subjective images, yet none captures the emotional state of the characters as well as do either the shots silhouetting the illicit lovers in a small boat (framed by a sea cave) and, later, against the fireworks display (framed by a hotel room balcony) or the shot of the sea and rocky shore where Hermione first catches sight of Maurice's body in the distance. Overall, the film seems more interested in clarity of action than in the evocation of an atmosphere or in the representation of emotional states. Yet despite its conclusion in a proper bourgeois marriage, *L'Appel du sang* remains ambiguously drawn to the tragic passion that Sicily awakens in its unfortunate hero.

Mercanton also seems to have initiated a short-lived vogue for films shot in the region of Arles and the Camargue in southern France.[44] There, in the early summer of 1920, he filmed *Miarka, la fille à l'ourse* (1920), with the famous actress Réjane, Ivor Novello, and Charles Vanel.[45] Although the technical facilities of the on-location production work were not the best, *Miarka* seems to have been quite successful—largely because of Réjane's understated, agonizing performance which exacerbated her illness and led to her death just two weeks after the shooting ended.[46] Soon after, André Hugon directed a string of low-budget films with Jean Toulout and Claude Mérelle in the Camargue— *Le Roi de Camargue* (1921), *Diamant noir* (1922), and *Notre Dame d'amour* (1922).[47] Even Antoine agreed to shoot his last film there, an adaptation of Alphonse Daudet's novel (not the popular play), *L'Arlésienne* (1922).[48] His interest was less in the story of passion and its attendant action on horseback than in the landscapes of flat marshes and huge skies. But one decision directed audience attention elsewhere. The legendary Arles girl would actually be seen on the screen, played by Fabris, a famous nude dancer at the Casino de Paris![49] Some colleagues and critics were aghast, but *L'Arlésienne* proved to be one of Antoine's more profitable films.[50]

Another series of landscapes to be explored by the realist film was, first, the mountains of the Pyrenees and then, the French Alps. After at least one successful film set in the provinces—*Le Retour aux champs* (1918)—Jacques de Baroncelli seems to have made the first of the cycle of mountain films with his adaptation of Pierre Loti's 1897 novel, *Ramuntcho* (1919). The film was shot by Alphonse Gibory in the Basque region of the Pyrenees, in the area where the action of the novel was located. There, the engagement between Ramuntcho (René Lorsay) and Gracieuse (Yvonne Annie) is broken when he is sent off to Indochina to do his military service; subsequently, she enters a convent. When he eventually returns, in a final encounter, Gracieuse rejects her vows in order to renew their engagement.[51] Henri Fescourt was especially struck by *Ramuntcho* when he returned from the war to begin working for Films Louis Nalpas.[52] But Louis Delluc was even more enthusiastic: the film was successful precisely in the way that, unfortunately, Antoine's films were not.

Here is a *metteur-en-scène* who has perceived the harmony between things and living creatures, the *sensibility* of a landscape, the distinctive light of a sky that is at once awesome and finely nuanced.[53]

Baroncelli has taken a great leap forward. Perhaps the entire French cinema will take that leap forward with the same conviction. We approach here that animated impressionism which will be, I believe, the unique property of the French cinema—the day when the French cinema will fully merit being called French.[54]

If the terms *impressionist* or *impressionism* meant anything to Delluc and his colleagues in the French cinema in 1919, they defined the emerging realist film. And if the French cinema was going to distinguish itself from the American cinema that threatened to overwhelm it, here was one way to do so. Delluc himself attempted to follow Baroncelli's example in *Le Chemin d'Ernoa* (1921), whose narrative of criminal intrigue becomes secondary to a documentarylike description of hauntingly empty Basque landscapes.[55]

But *Ramuntcho* alone was not enough to interest the French in their mountain regions. That took the appearance of several Swedish landscape films, such as Sjöström's *Les Proscrits* (1918) and Stiller's *Trésor d'Arne* (1919) and *Dans les remous* (1919)—all shown in Paris during the 1919-1920 season—which much impressed them with the evocative power of their snowscapes.[56] As a consequence, several filmmakers began to explore the mountainous regions of the French Alps, apparently unaware of the early German mountain films—e.g., those of Arnold Frank, who would become Leni Riefenstahl's mentor. In *Jocelyn* (1922), one of the first French films to be shot in the Alps, Léon Poirier took advantage of the snowy wastes around Mont Pélat for a number of dramatic and rhetorical effects.[57] Although Henri Fescourt called *Jocelyn* merely "an illustration" of the famous Lamartine poem of the same title,[58] and its

39. Mlle. Myrga and a mountain village in *Geneviève* (1923)

story is set in the period of the French Revolution, the film is firmly rooted in the realist genre. Its narrative depends upon an unequal opposition between the revolutionary turbulence of Paris and the tranquil solitude of a mountain retreat, which allows for "a dramatic scherzo," as Poirier conceived it, with "a largo responding in echo."[59] In a mountain cavern, Jocelyn (Armand Tallier), who has fled the Terror, gives refuge to an orphaned boy, whom he later discovers is a disguised young woman (this Mary Pickford type is played by Mlle. Myrga). He falls in love, but that love is denied him by his religious superiors. Thinking she has been abandoned, the young woman throws herself into a life of pleasure in the Paris of Napoléon, as a way of forgetting Jocelyn. Years later, their separation is recapitulated in a single poignant encounter.

Under her windows, the hero espies the woman he no longer is permitted to love; she appears on her balcony, leans there a moment and drops a rose which falls in the pebbled stream at Jocelyn's feet; he reaches for it, but the flower is carried off by the current, escapes the hand that pursues it.[60]

When she finally returns to the mountains, exhausted, to die with Jocelyn at her side, in Poirier's delicate tableaux, their souls are joined as one in his simple room and then in adjacent graves on a high mountainside.

Impressed by *Jocelyn*'s commercial and critical success (the conservative Société des Auteurs des Films voted it the Best French film of 1922), Gaumont asked Poirier to put together another film based on Lamartine.[61] Drawn from a lesser-known novel, *Geneviève* (1923) was even more clearly a realist film. Uncommonly, unrelentingly pessimistic, the narrative is little more than a

103

series of episodes that chronicles the life of a pious orphan girl (Mlle. Myrga).[62] She is refused in marriage; raises her sister only to have her die in childbirth; is unjustly imprisoned for abandoning the child; wanders in the mountains as a beggar; becomes the servant of her old fiancé, who then dies in an epidemic; is restored by Jocelyn; and finally becomes head of a hospital where she rediscovers her sister's grown child. For the four months of location shooting in the region of Dauphiné, Poirier used nonactors consistently in the secondary roles.[63] He also seems to have aimed for a painterly quality in his exterior and interior tableaux, which reviewers much remarked on at the time. "Betrothed, Geneviève looks like a Sargent; as a servant, a Holbein; as a traveler entering the village, a Millet."[64] The overall effect, wrote *Cinémagazine*, was to produce a Corot-like "study of Nature's magnificence: wooded landscapes, fields, and mountains" that tempered the tragic experience of "the poor peasant girl."[65] Léon Moussinac, usually a harsh critic of Poirier's films, found in *Geneviève*,

a unity of direction, a very successful equilibrium. . . . Certain passages are remarkable: the mother's death in the beginning . . . the story of the [abandoned] child and the servant's wanderings in the snow, among the most terrible landscapes imaginable.[66]

As an "atmosphere film," *Geneviève* may bear comparison with Henri Fescourt's *Mandarin*, also shot in the Dauphiné region several months before, as well as his *Les Grands* (1924), which documented the life of several schoolboys abandoned to their own devices during a vacation period in Aix-en-Provence.[67]

The best of these mountain films, and arguably one of the best realist films of the decade, was Jacques Feyder's *Visages d'enfants* (1925). As I mentioned earlier, this film was the victim of production disagreements and distribution caprice that caused a delay of two years in its release and hence a limited commercial run of scant success.[68] "Simple, intimate, lacking any special attractions, stars, or prestigious sets," to quote Georges Sadoul,[69] it deftly, even subtly, narrated a well-acted story of sustained emotional poignancy. French critics generally thought highly of it, and Feyder proudly noted, in his slim autobiography, that, in 1926, the Japanese press called it the best European film of the year.[70]

Visages d'enfants was Feyder's first original scenario since his apprenticeship days at Gaumont during the war. He wrote it specifically to use the talents of Jean Forest, the young actor he had discovered for *Crainquebille* (1923), as well as the location of the Haut Valois region of Switzerland. Basically the scenario integrates the character study of a young boy who must learn to accept a new stepmother and stepsister with the social study of an isolated Catholic community's rituals and customs, in a landscape that alternately separates, endangers, and forces people closer together.[71] In the village of Saint-Luc, in the Haut Valois, the mayor's wife (Suzy Vernon) dies unexpectedly, leaving her husband, Amsler (Victor Vina), with two young children, Jean (Jean Forest) and Pierrette (Pierrette Houyez). Jean is especially affected by his mother's death, and, when his father marries a widow (Rachel Devirys) with a daughter his age, Arlette (Arlette Peyran), he bitterly opposes their presence in the house. One day, while the family is returning home in the sleigh, no one notices as Jean maliciously tosses Arlette's favorite doll into the snow. When the girl goes to search for it alone in the evening, a sudden spring avalanche

40. Jean Forest and Victor Vina in the village cemetery in *Visages d'enfants* (1925)

buries her in a tiny mountain chapel. Although she is rescued, Jean is beside himself with remorse. He writes a note to his father and goes off to drown himself in the nearby river. Reading the note, Arlette tells her mother, who catches him just as he is about to be swept over a waterfall. Recognizing their concern and love for him, Jean finally relents and accepts his stepmother and stepsister.

The first thing that, even now, impresses one about *Visages d'enfants* is the unusual authenticity of its natural and social milieu. It has one of the most beautiful and most efficient film openings of the decade. Several ELSs introduce the village, nestled beside a waterfall in a boulder-strewn mountain valley. There is an LS of the mayor's long house, constructed of hewn logs and ornately-carved dark wood, and then several shots of villagers walking up to it. In the large central room, the major characters are singled out (Amsler, Jean, Pierrette), and the occasion is finally identified—the funeral of the mayor's wife. Her coffin is carried down a flight of wooden stairs (a CU of shoes on the steps conveys the difficulty), and a HA shot describes its shadow passing across the bare wooden floor. Outside, the funeral procession (the men and women are in separate groups; Jean and his father precede the priest) moves slowly down the narrow, stone-cobbled streets, past rows of log buildings whose first stories begin at the height of the winter snows. The cemetery is in a grove of trees some distance away, but several LSs there situate the village clearly in the background against the mountains. So consistent is the texture of the lighting and decor here (the cameraman was L.-H. Burel), it is difficult to distinguish the studio from the location footage. Smoothly, succinctly, and in some detail, the sequence establishes a particular natural landscape, a social community drawn together in an important ritual, a family in that community, and, as we now see, one figure who is already given some psychological depth.

The only thing missing from this description is Jean's subjective experience of the funeral. As soon as he is introduced, the sequence singles him out by linking his figure with POV shots and with various optical effects. Before the coffin even appears, a shot of his morose face is followed by a MS that blurs in as it tilts up to reveal his father. Other shots also seem to be his POV: that of his little sister blowing bubbles, the CU of shoes descending the stairs. In the HA shot of the coffin's shadow, he is the one who follows its path across the floor. Even the procession through the street is described in several handheld moving shots that either take his POV or dolly ahead of him. Finally, at the cemetery, when they start to fill in the grave, he is isolated in several CUs until a brief series of rapidly cut swish pans erupt. At the end, he faints, and his father has to carry him back to the house unconscious. This judicious pattern of subjectivity quickly determines Jean as the film's central character and his acute sensitivity to his mother's death—his inability to cope with her loss—as the film's primary subject.

The overall narrative structure of the film is a model of rigor and balance. It divides into four major segments of alternating sequences, connected by transitions, all of which produce a narrative line that ascends steadily through two sets of complications to a doubled climax. The first segment of alternation separates father and son. At Amsler's request, the village curate takes Jean over the mountains (in a series of breathtaking shots) to Voissay in the next valley. In the meantime, Saint-Luc celebrates Amsler's wedding with a ritual dance. Finally, at the end of several alternating sequences, while the two rake hay one late afternoon, the curate tells the boy about the marriage. The magnificent mountain spaces, through which Jean first seemed to move harmoniously, now offer little solace. The mountains now stand as a barrier, dividing him from his family and community, and the lush hayfields of Voissay lie open to the sun in mute contrast to his misery. He is out of place, in both society and nature.

As Jean returns alone now to Saint-Luc, the sequences that had narrated his father's wedding shift focus to the stepmother and stepsister Arlette. Here the pattern of alternation juxtaposes Jean and the two intruding women (the father is deemphasized) in different parts of the house. Jean soon finds himself displaced in his own home—Arlette uses his crayons and takes over his room. While she and her mother go about their work, Jean spends his time clinging to his mother's memory through such things as a portrait and some clothing stored in the attic. Jean's hostility to Arlette grows until it climaxes in the avalanche segment. After the sleigh ride, Arlette runs out into the snow to look for her lost doll while Jean turns restlessly in bed. The avalanche now separates her from the family/community, replicating the mountain barrier that had cut off Jean earlier. As Jean and Arlette, separately, pray to figures of the Madonna, the villagers search the darkness with lanterns and discover the chapel's cross projecting from the snow. This miraculous conjunction, across distant spaces, restores Arlette, but Jean still considers himself an outcast for his "criminal" act.

41. Arlette Peyran in *Visages d'enfants* (1925)

Three short sequences with all the characters together in the large central room serve as a bridge from this first climax to the concluding one. The distance that still separates Jean from the family is articulated in several HA/LA shots, with the boy looking down from the top of the stairs to the others around the table. As he prepares to do away with himself, the final segment of alternation begins, intercutting the stepmother milking cows on the hillside, Amsler driving off in a cart to the local lumber mill, and Jean saying goodbye to Arlette and asking her to give the note to his father. Appropriately, Jean heads for the stream, to drown himself in the run-off from the snow that buried Arlette earlier. When he reaches his destination, the alternation shifts to exclude first his father and then Arlette. In a final paroxysm of rapid cutting, Jean falls from a tree limb, and his stepmother wades into the swollen current above the waterfall to snatch him up as he is carried by.

The final image of Jean and his stepmother, restoring the lost mother-son relation, is prepared for in an interesting pattern of rhetorical figuring. That figuring associates Jean with a number of objects, as if forcing him to come to grips with reality. His dead mother's possessions especially obsess him, either as a means of sustaining his closeness to her or as a sign of his separation. At first, the most important of these is the portrait of his mother, which he takes into his new room and to which he prays daily. Early on, her image had even seemed to smile down on him momentarily. Then, over Sunday dinner, during the stepmother's first week in the house, Jean notices a brooch at her neck. When he breaks down crying, his father (even more ignorant than we are) orders him out of the house. Only as he lies in the fields do we understand the threat literalized in this object—a single subjective CU of the brooch tilts up to reveal his mother's face. Several days later, Jean tries to revive the presence of his mother through one of her dresses which he finds in the attic. In a brief, eerie scene (LS, FS, MCU), he literally fetishizes the dress, draping it over a chest of drawers against the wall, caressing it, and finally laying his head in its lap. When the stepmother finds the same dress and makes plans to use it for smaller articles of clothing, Jean savagely hacks it to pieces. Again the father shows surprising insensitivity and orders him out of the house. Either this lack on the father's part is so exaggerated as to be a projection of the son's (consistent with the Oedipal relation at the center of the film) or it raises disturbing questions about his actual feelings and attitudes.

Jean's destruction of the fetish, to deny the transfer of desire, raises the possibility of his doing actual violence to one of the intruding women or even to himself. This comes to pass through another object that appears just prior to the mother's dress—Arlette's doll. Arlette takes the doll with her whenever she tends goats on the hillside. One day, when Jean brings her some lunch, he grabs the doll and attaches it to the horns of one of the goats, which begins to prance about wildly. His teasing has a disturbing edge—with the doll serving as a metaphorical substitute for Arlette, it raises the specter of violence, even rape. The conjunction of this action with the fetishization of the dress that follows produces an extraordinary mirror image—of desire for the mother versus repression of desire (through violence) for either the stepmother or daughter who would replace her. Several days later, to punish Arlette for reporting his cutting of the dress to her mother, Jean throws away the doll, as if to erase her image, her presence. The avalanche then literalizes the metaphor by burying Arlette with her doll. Suddenly pushed to the extreme, the sexual symbolic of this rhetorical figuring is resolved, or displaced, by a religious one. That displacement is articulated in the miraculous conjunction that restores Arlette. At that moment, Jean exchanges one mother for another, as the object of his praying. From the faded portrait of his dead mother, he turns to a small statue of the Madonna in his room. The disturbing sexual antagonism within the family is suppressed, even in Jean's decision to commit suicide. For there in the stream the stepmother appears as a *deus ex machina*, the Madonna come to life and made flesh. The transformation is complete. In the raging waters, Jean is baptized and born again. Nature, the community, and the family are in harmony once more. And the portrait of the dead mother smiles down on them in the end, blessing the restoration.

Feyder's achievement in *Visages d'enfants* was diminished by its commercial failure and then almost obliterated by another provincial realist film very much like it which was highly successful less than a year later. That film was Julien Duvivier's *Poil de carotte* (1926), whose scenario was adapted from a Jules Renard novel—ironically, by Jacques Feyder.[72] Because it was a small production for Phocéa, Duvivier shot the film in the Morvan mountains of central France rather than in the Hautes-Alps (which lessened the impact of the landscape considerably).[73] The narrative is complicated, focusing not only on a young misunderstood boy, Carrot-Top (André Heuzé), but on his deceitful brother (Fabian Haziza), his frightful stepmother (Charlotte Barbier-Krauss), his rather ignorant father (Henry Krauss), a cabaret singer who seduces the brother, and a family maid who befriends the outcast.[74] Greed, cruelty, ugliness, and a hypocritical piety are concentrated in this most stereotypical of stepmothers, one of the most offensive images of women in the French cinema of the decade. Furthermore, the film's resolution is oddly fractured: father and son are reunited, as are the stepmother and stepson; yet the reunions are separate, and the family does not seem to be restored. Despite all the conflicts and contradictions, this narrative is located in a rather detailed village setting, so that Duvivier is at least partially correct in calling *Poil de carotte* an "atmosphere film."[75] And, in 1932, he had the commercial acumen to make a sound film version of his scenario that was even more popular.

The last two geographical areas to be represented by the realist film genre may well have been initiated by one of Louis Feuillade's more original works, *Vendémiaire* (1919). It starred two of his chief serial actors, René Cresté and Edouard Mathé, in a contemporary story divided into a "prologue and three parts (the vineyard, the vat, and the new wine)".[76] The narrative is predicated on the displacement of refugees (with two disguised German spies among them) from the war zone to the vineyards of Bas-Languedoc. The film stresses the allegorical, almost Biblical, elements of this narrative and operates according to an alternation of sequences that obsessively juxtapose war and peace. Yet, at times, it is surprisingly realistic, even lyrical—perhaps, as Francis Lacassin suggests, because Feuillade chose to set the film in the landscape of his own childhood.[77] Particularly moving are the prologue that follows a boat of refugees down the Rhône river and a documentarylike sequence on the sense of community that develops among the peasants during the grape harvest.

108

42. A frame still from *La Terre* (1921)

These two sequences seem to lead into two fairly distinct sets of realist films—the peasant film and the river or canal film.

The many peasant films that were produced in the early 1920s tended to cultivate a feeling for landscape in the agricultural regions of western, central, and southern France (the north and east having been destroyed by the war). Most of these films narrated rather simple stories and tried to document as economically and authentically as possible the land-holding bourgeois and peasant milieu.[78]

Once again it was Baroncelli and Antoine who spearheaded the effort. Baroncelli seems to have initiated this cycle of films with *Le Retour aux champs* (1918), which Delluc praised for bringing to the screen the peasant and the "truth" of his way of life with a characteristic "impressionism."[79] The following year, Antoine decided to film an adaptation of Zola's *La Terre* (1921). This time Antoine was uncompromising. As was his practice, he and L.-H. Burel shot the film entirely on location, in the Beauce region below Chartres (presumably, in the summer and winter of 1919). The results Paul de la Borie described as meticulously painterly, almost Millet-like, in their realism.[80] There were repeated HALSs which literally positioned the peasants as part of the earth, carefully composed "deep space" LSs sensitive to natural and man-made patterns in the fields and pastures, and many CUs of animals and farmyard machines and objects that gave the film a material weight. Although Comédie Française actors once again played the principal roles, the acting was uniformly excellent, with Armand Bour particularly effective as Old Fouan. Above all, Antoine refused to dilute the unrelenting pessimism of Zola's story of greed

109

43. A publicity photo of the threshing sequence in *Nêne* (1924)

and deception among small landowners. An old farmer, Old Fouan, is slowly robbed of his land, his farmhouse, and his money by his own sons, "Buteau" (Jean Hervé) and Hyacinthe (Milo). At the same time, a young newlywed neighbor woman, Françoise (Germaine Rouer), whose sister Lise (Jeanne Briey) has married "Buteau," discovers the plot against Fouan and is brutally attacked one day in the fields. In the final sequence, these stories come together in a cross-cut series of grimly poignant images. In a bitter snowstorm, Fouan drags himself across the parched earth that was once his until he collapses, while Françoise dies alone in her simple husband's house, without denouncing or implicating anyone.

René Hervil contributed two of his best films to the genre, both shot by Amédée Morin, *L'Ami Fritz* (1920) and *Blanchette* (1921), the latter adapted from a play by Eugène Brieux.[81] *L'Ami Fritz* told the story of Fritz Kobus (Léon Mathot), a rich and propertied Alsatian, who falls in love with the daughter (Huguette Duflos) of one of his tenant farmers (de Max). Set in his bachelor ways, Fritz, after a long struggle, grudgingly relents to marriage. Disturbed by all the attention to what he considered a poorly crafted film (there was no electrical illumination and scant time to film), Hervil himself preferred *Blanchette*.[82] According to Fescourt, *Blanchette* combined impressive winter landscapes and unusually natural acting (by Maurice de Féraudy, Léon Mathot, Pauline Johnson, and Thérèse Kolb) with a reactionary subject—"the danger to a peasant family that comes from giving their daughter an education above their social level."[83] Much like his mentors, Antoine and Mercanton, however, Hervil was criticized for a rather monotonous mise-en-scène, an absence of rhythm in the editing, and a gaping discrepancy between the intrigue and "the depiction of a way of life."[84]

Several other peasant films seem to have avoided these shortcomings. One is only marginally about peasant life—Louis Delluc's *L'Inondation* (1924)—and its rhetorical and narrative complexity carry it well beyond the conventions of the genre. Others include Protazanoff's *L'Ombre du péché* (1922) and a recent rediscovery that has yet to be fully reappraised—René Le Somptier's *La Bête traquée* (1923), adapted by Michel Carré from Adrien Chabot's novel, *Marielle Thibaut*.[85] The best known, at least at the time, was Baroncelli's *Nêne* (1924), probably because it was drawn from a Prix Goncourt novel by Ernest Perrochon.[86] In it, Sandra Milowanoff played a peasant girl who cares for the house and two children of a widowed farmer named Corbier (Van Daële). Threatened by a jealous hired hand, a scheming village seamstress (France Dhélia), the drunken vengeance of her own brother Jean (Gaston Modot), and the blind egoism of her master, Nêne is finally told to leave the farm; and, heartbroken, she tries to drown herself in a stream. Corbier rescues her and comes to his senses, accepting the woman whom his children now consider their mother. Some of the best moments in *Nêne* depend on well-chosen natural locations. Having searched out the most suitable landscapes in the Vendée region of western France, Baroncelli lodged his cast and crew (including cameraman Louis Chaix) for a month of shooting in a tiny hamlet, "in the midst of actual peasants," where they took "their meals in a communal house."[87] The results were remarkable, especially in the hay-baling sequence (where Jean loses an arm in the threshing machine) and in several dramatic encounters in the region's vast wheatfields and pastures. And they were complemented by interior night scenes of minimal lighting and by poignant exchanges of looks in CU. Here, as in *Ramuntcho*, Baroncelli seems to have produced the synthesis of realism and impressionism that so marks the genre.

Perhaps the best of these peasant films was *L'Atre* (1923), an almost forgotten work by Robert Boudrioz, who had once worked before the war as a scriptwriter for Maurice Tourneur.[88] With the financial backing of Abel Gance's new production company, Boudrioz (and his cameramen, Gaston Brun and Maurice Arnou) shot the film during the spring and summer months of 1920.[89] However, the edited film was withheld from distribution for almost three years, perhaps because of the double whammy strategy of serials and superproductions which then gripped Pathé-Consortium.[90] Although *L'Atre* was only marginally successful commercially, *Cinéa-Ciné-pour-tous*'s readers included it among the ten best films of 1923.[91]

The scenario for the film was drawn from *La Chevauchée nocturne*, a "peasant tragedy" written by Alexandre Arnoux.[92] The story begins with a desperate young woman who, on Christmas Eve, abandons her baby girl at the farmhouse window of an old peasant couple (they already have two grandsons to raise) and then drowns herself in a nearby stream. Several years pass. The younger boy gives the girl one of his whittled wooden dolls, and the two boys fight over her on their way to school. Days later, all three watch puzzled and terrified as their grandmother (Renée Dounis) dies in her chair. Again time passes. The elder son, Bernard (Charles Vanel), now does most of the work on the farm while his brother Jean (Jacques de Féraudy) loafs about and carves clay sculptures—for instance, an ugly bust of the cruel, oafish servant boy.

111

44. (left) Maurice Schutz and
Renée Dounis in *L'Atre*
(1923)

45. (right) A landscape
publicity photo

Jean has fallen in love with Arlette (another Mary Pickford type played by
Renée Tandil), and Bernard watches them sullenly at a village dance. When
Bernard threatens to leave the farm, his grandfather (Maurice Shutz) suddenly
decides to make him his principal heir and marry him to Arlette; then he
orders Jean off the farm. Heartbroken, Jean goes off to the city, where his
sculptures eventually win acclaim at an exhibition. Arlette reluctantly agrees
to marry Bernard, and the couple takes over the farm when the grandfather
dies. However, Arlette's continuing love for Jean enflames Bernard's jealousy,
and the two fight bitterly one day when he discovers that she has written to
his brother. Learning that Jean is returning to the farm, Bernard spirits Arlette away to an abandoned mill. On reaching the farm, Jean threatens the
servant boy (who has sided with Bernard earlier) and, when he rides off toward
the mill, is shot in the back. He struggles into the mill just as Arlette is
about to turn a knife against herself. Bernard's fury dissolves into shame at
the sight of his brother's condition, and Jean "remarries" Arlette to his con-
trite rival with his dying breath.

Viewed today, in a 35mm nitrate print at the Cinémathèque française,
L'Atre is something of a revelation. "Simplicity," wrote René Clair, "that is
the quality, the chief quality of the best parts of *L'Atre*."[93] Indeed, its lovingly
composed images (often framed in oval or arched iris masks) have a meditative,
lyrical power that remind one of Tourneur as well as of F. W. Murnau's *Sunrise*
(1927) and *City Girl* (1929). At the beginning of the third time period of the
film, for instance, the grandfather admires his farm in a slow montage of
images that ends with shots of a bullock plowing a field (including a CU of
the plow slicing through the soil) intercut with shots of the old man picking
up a clod of earth to hold in his hands. Just before he turns the farm over to
Bernard, they move to the farmhouse window—where his vision becomes Bernard's—and the transfer is sealed in a CU of their clasped hands. This natural
relationship between the peasant and the land even marks the sequence of the
grandmother's death (handled in a few restrained shots of her sitting by the

window, the children standing in the doorway, and the grandfather called back from walking across the fields and into a wood). Her funeral procession is described in just one long-take LS—stretched out along a country road, it is silhouetted against an immense sky as well as reflected in the still waters of a marsh. Jean's relationship to the land is strangely one of ignorance—even though he reworks the earth for his sculptures. Only when he is forced to leave does he really seem to see it—in one shot, he looks out sadly (from some trees in the foreground) over an unplowed field stretching off into the distance. But the image he carries with him and which finally inspires his art is a LS of Arlette, as she crosses the stream on a wooden bridge, carrying a water jar on her shoulder. Significantly, the figure seems to derive more from classical sculpture than it does from his life on the farm.

Indeed, the most moving moments in the film are those articulating a sense of loss or tragic confrontation. The sequence that follows Jean's expulsion from the farm is particularly eerie. From the barn Jean longingly watches Arlette at her bedroom window, and his hand twists and retwists a rope at his side. When her light goes out, he puts a ladder against the house and climbs up and inside. The servant boy spots him and tells Bernard, who steals up the inside stairs and opens the bedroom door to see Jean crouched over Arlette (what was he going to do?). Stealthily they pull knives and face one another across her bed. When she moves in her sleep, they stare at her; the tension ebbs, and they go off silently to argue downstairs. At least two later sequences involve the poignant conjunction of separate characters' heightened emotional states. At the precise moment, for instance, when Jean is inspired in his work by the memory of Arlette carrying the water jar, she is looking through a storage drawer filled with the wooden figures he carved as a boy. The sight seems to rekindle her love; but when Bernard discovers her, he angrily tosses the figures into the hearth fire and, in CU, crushes one under his boot. After their fight in the kitchen (the staging is surprisingly brutal), Bernard leaves Arlette and walks out to the stream. For the first time, we begin to share his dejection as he sits (with his back to us in HALS), tearing up her letter to Jean and dropping it in the water. Simultaneously, Arlette writes another letter to Jean and starts when a cat suddenly appears in the doorway. Their separate miseries are ironically matched in back-to-back shots: a HALS of Bernard slouched beside the stream; a HALS of Arlette going through an arch in the village street, on her way to post the letter.

Despite its power, the resolution of *L'Atre* is less than satisfying. "The sculptor hesitates" / "The farmer never does" / "The earth remains most significant"—so read the final intertitles. But the opposition has not been that simple. Jean and Arlette's passion for one another has been less responsible for the tragic chain of events than has Bernard's and his grandfather's blind adherence to the land and to its possession. In fact, the earth that feeds and protects the peasant also produces the blind passion that divides and destroys. The hearth fire that brings the children together in the beginning (where the boys replace the Christmas manger doll with Arlette) also serves later to shatter the bonds that join them. Although the film attempts to celebrate the earth and its bounty, it gives more attention to the loss and sacrifice that precludes its continued sustenance. Boudrioz once said in an interview that "the ideal purpose of the cinema" for him, was "to record as simply as possible the simplest, yet most powerful things."[94] In *L'Atre*, he achieved that simplicity with a degree of artistry that renders it darkly ambiguous.

The landscapes and peoples of the French rivers and canals were the last to be explored by the provincial realist film. Less than a year after Feuillade's *Vendémiaire*, Antoine conceived the idea for a film devoted entirely to the life of the boatmen on the canals. His friend, Gustave Grillet, was persuaded to write a scenario, *L'Hirondelle et la mésange*, which simply "followed the journey of a barge," from the canals of Flanders all the way to Paris.[95] In the winter of 1920-1921, Antoine finally got permission from S.C.A.G.L. to film the scenario in Belgium, integrating his main actors, Henry Krauss and Pierre Alcover, with the crews of two canal barges.[96] In an interview with André Lang, he gave this account of the experience:

We left on our barge from Anvers and went up the Escaut to Bruges. . . . Magnificent! . . . Since everything was shot during the trip, all the footage was in sharp contrasts. . . . The story was solid . . . a very simple drama . . . it ended with a man sinking out of sight in the cargo hold one night . . . and the next morning the barge threaded its way up river, quietly, in the sunlight and silence. . . . It was very beautiful. . . ."[97]

Yet the film was never released—for one of two reasons. Antoine told his son that the new directors of Pathé-Consortium were indignant over the footage and refused to let him finish editing the film for distribution.[98] Grillet's son, however, reports that, because of the constant fog and rain that hampered shooting, Antoine was not satisfied with the lighting—it was he who refused its release.[99] Whatever the case, Antoine's son concludes, *L'Hirondelle et la mésange* was to have been "a poem in images."[100]

Several years later, a number of films more or less fulfilled Antoine's ambitions. In *Le Carillon de minuit* (1923), Baroncelli also went to Belgium to document the milieu of a canal town and its religious mission work. René Jeanne and Charles Ford especially praised Baroncelli's half-tone and gray monochrome images for the way they perfectly complemented the story's discreet feeling of resignation.[101] In *La Fille de l'eau* (1925), Jean Renoir used the banks of the Loing river near Montigny to provide a painterly context for the beginning and ending of a picaresque series of wild adventures involving Catherine Hessling. But Renoir's film was much more than a realist film, and its exuberant experimentation demands further discussion later. The most sustained evocation of barge life on the canals occurs in Jean Epstein's *La Belle Nivernaise* (1924).

This charming film was adapted from Alphonse Daudet's popular 1886 novella—a simple, even banal, staccato-styled tale of an orphan boy adopted by a river barge family. In his scenario, Epstein updated the story to the present, altered the narrative structure a bit, added some dramatic conflict at one point, and generally "poeticized" his material.[102] Here, in brief, is his version of the plot. On one of his biannual runs to Paris, Louveau (Pierre Hot) finds an abandoned child and, with police consent, takes him back to his barge, "La Belle Nivernaise," and his unsuspecting wife and daughter. Ten years later, the boy, Victor (Maurice Touzé), has become "Père Louveau's right arm" on the barge and is close to being in love with his daughter Clara

114

46. The benediction ceremony
at the end of *La Belle
Nivernaise* (1924)

(Blanche Montel). Called to Paris by the authorities, Louveau discovers that
Victor is actually the son of Maugendré (David Evremont), one of his charcoal
shippers on the Nivernaise canal (connecting the Loire and Seine rivers in
central France). Sometime later, as he and his wife make arrangements to
return the boy, Victor defends Clara from an attack by the barge mate (who
has become jealous of his position) and barely saves the barge from crashing
into a lock. Maugendré sends him off to a *lycée*—"to make something of
him"—but Victor pines away from loneliness. Recognizing his error, Maugendré reverses his decision and offers Victor and Clara a river barge of their
own, "La Nouvelle Nivernaise."

Unfortunately, *La Belle Nivernaise* had only a modest success with the French
public and disappointed many critics who were expecting to see some spectacular moments of rapid cutting which Epstein had become known for.[103] Wrong-
headed though that expectation may have been, there was reason for disappointment. For instance, the sequence that depends most on rapid cutting
turns out to be one of the least effective in the film. This is the moment when
the barge mate attacks Clara and the barge drifts dangerously close to a canal
lock. Yet the motivation for this attack is hardly plausible, and the rapid
cutting does little more than sustain suspense. Perhaps the sequence would
work halfway effectively if projected with the music intended to accompany
it; but, as is, the moment seems expanded to an exhausting length, to the
point where discrepancies between the position of the barge in different shots
are surprisingly obvious.

When *La Belle Nivernaise* does work effectively, which indeed is much of the time, it does so by refining the conventions of the realist film genre. Of all Epstein's early narrative films, it most privileges description over narrative, as if it were simply documenting a way of life or a character's emotional state in the context of a particular space and time. One sign of this is the frequency with which Epstein and his cameraman Paul Guichard employ LSs. Nearly all of the sequences on the barge include them, either positioning the characters in a deep space stretching from stern to bow or in a somewhat flattened space (shot from a 90° angle) as they walk along the barge edge. As a young boy, Victor is initially defined in LSs—as he walks back and forth in front of an *épicerie* or sits by a lamppost in a narrow street (where Louveau happens on him). The best of these moments is a marvelous long-take ELS of an empty square with a small central park of bare trees, through which the boy slowly meanders in the early morning air, as if wavering between fear and awe. The combination of wide stretches of river and grassy fields, in the area where Maugendré lives, have a very different ambience in LS. Repeatedly, the characters come and go through the high grass, moving in harmony with its undulations. When Maugendré decides to return Victor to the Louveaus, the sequence of their agreement concludes in a magisterial LS of the group on the barge silhouetted against the fields and sky. The film finally ends in the same area with a benediction ceremony for "La Nouvelle Nivernaise," which includes the implication of Victor and Clara's marriage as well (a bird cage passes from one to the other to be hung in a small arbor of vines and flowers). A HALS of the barge and surrounding countryside, as a priest comes on board, produces an image of harmony that is almost paradisiac.

As early as *Bonjour Cinéma* (1921), Epstein had echoed Delluc and others in writing, "A landscape can embody a state of mind. Especially a state of repose."[104] *La Belle Nivernaise* gave him the chance to capture the spirit of one particular landscape—the Seine river between Paris and Rouen. This section of the river, along which most of the film was shot (in the late summer months of 1923), Epstein later described as "the greatest actor, the strongest personality that I have known intimately."[105] There can be little doubt that "the heart and soul—the living axis and artistic center" of the film, in the words of Paul Ramain, is the Seine.[106] Its languid current provides the "landscape dance" on which the film's slow, limpid rhythm depends. It is a rhythm accentuated by the LSs, by the gentle landscapes and character movements, by the dissolves and graphic match cuts (e.g., a short sequence in the fog), but principally by a host of smooth tracking shots, taken from a camera mounted on the barge or on one close by moving parallel to it. Fixed and flowing at the same time, this camera movement has a descriptive rather than a narrative function, operating as an extension of the river itself. Those critics who initially praised *La Belle Nivernaise* noted the rhythmic fluidity generated by its landscape and mediated by Epstein's camera; and they compared it favorably with the early masterworks of the Swedish cinema.[107] Ten years later, a similar landscape and rhythm, much inspired by it, would animate Jean Vigo's *L'Atalante* (1933).

Despite the peaceful harmony of the film's ending, the river's presence is not without some ambiguity. In the beginning, for instance, it seems a rather neutral backdrop to the quarreling that initially marks the Louveau family.

Briefly, in the fog sequence, it even poses a physical threat. Perhaps the best evidence of this ambiguity, and of the hypnotic shifting perspective so characteristic of Epstein's films, is the first subjective sequence in the film, the family's departure from Paris after Louveau has learned of Victor's identity. The sequence opens with a fluid series of tracking shots from the barge (linked by dissolves): the river's edge, smokestacks, trees, cottages among the trees. Then comes another series (linked by dissolves again): a shot of open water, a CU of Victor's face, a MS of Victor at the tiller, a LS of Louveau (from behind) walking toward the barge bow, and a tracking shot (from the bow) of the river ahead. This measured pattern of movement seems to elide the time passing and produce a continuous moment interrelating man and nature, with Victor easily controlling the barge in the river's current—except for one thing. Between the two series of shots comes an intertitle describing Louveau's emotional state: "Troubled, Louveau had hastened his departure from Paris." The intertitle makes the shots problematic. Are they Victor's POV shots (juxtaposing a visual to a verbal subjectivity) or an omniscient description which gradually becomes anchored in Louveau? Or are they both? Victor's relation to the river turns ambiguous—he is both subject and object, ironically unaware that his movement on the river will separate him from it. As shots of the prow and water now alternate with shots of Louveau in the bow, the latter wavers between duty and love (in an intertitle): to give the boy up or keep him as his adopted son. He turns to look at Victor and Clara, who has joined him, and the backward-looking POV shots suddenly look almost like memory shots (since they echo the first images of the young couple together). When he turns once more to face the poplar-lined river ahead, he turns away from an image that is already past (it is the last he will see of Victor until the end). Although Louveau's look seems to dominate the sequence (as his choice seems to determine Victor's destiny), he, too, is determined—by the knowledge he bears and by the very motion of the barge and the river. His subordinate position within a larger design is confirmed in the final shots of the sequence: a LS of the barge bow, with Louveau as a small figure (frame right), and a FS of the barge mate (who has just written to Maugendré), squatting by the rail. As in Jean Renoir's films, the lovely, seductive rhythm of the river sometimes carries with it an ominous undercurrent.

By 1924, the realist provincial film reached a kind of apotheosis in two large-scale productions which combined the French love for the ambience of river or canal landscapes with their interest in the culture of Brittany. One was Léon Poirier's *La Brière* (1925), which was adapted from a recent Prix Goncourt novel by Alphonse de Chateaubriand and starred two of his popular actors from Gaumont, Armand Tallier and Mlle. Myrga. Although an independent production, its commercial status was confirmed by an exclusive month-long run (following L'Herbier's *L'Inhumaine*) at the prestigious Madeleine-Cinéma.[108] Yet the narrative was predicated on a bitter dispute over whether or not to drain marshland for a brick factory in La Brière, a famous salt marsh at the mouth of the Loire river in lower Brittany. Poirier shot most of the film around Saint-Joachim in the Brière region over a period of several months and chose an obscure actor named José Davert—who had appeared opposite René Navarre in *La Nouvelle Aurore* (1919)—for his central character, Aoustin,

47. (left) José Davert in *La Brière* (1925)

48. (right) A landscape publicity photo

the old watchman of the marshes, who opposes the drainage plan.[109] The result was a solemn, impeccably crafted, but somewhat uneven film which had a very successful run.

For the most part, *La Brière*'s rhythm is slow, magisterial, in correspondence with the calm, flat landscape of the salt marsh and the lives of its rustic inhabitants. With his large solid physique and expressionless weathered face, Aoustin becomes an icon of the people's determined resistance to change. His quiet, stolid figure is in perfect harmony with the serene marsh landscape he slowly poles his skiff across; and his silence intensifies the conflicts he has with his less obstinate wife and daughter, Théotiste, and her peasant fiancé, Jeanin. At the film's preview in August, 1924, one viewer was heard to remark, "Doesn't it seem that you can actually see the silence."[110] This documentary-like diegesis, as well as the film's technical facility, is disturbed, however, by several misplaced rhetorical conventions. For example, there is one sequence of accelerating montage to bring the daughter and fiancé together (by means of a stampeding horse) and another to intensify the stalking climax between Aoustin and Jeanin. At three points, the film also abruptly inserts into the narrative a strange young woman (a variation on the Arles's girl?) in order to give support to Aoustin. In the end, as Léon Moussinac argues, the basic conflict underlying the film is simplified into a nostalgic contrast between "modern mechanics" and a "rough mysticism."[111] The socioeconomic conflict is displaced almost completely into the family, where it is resolved tragically in a romantic, moralistic plot that turns the old man's rebellious vision into a form of blindness. Théotiste bears a dead child illegitimately; Aoustin loses a hand that is replaced by a wooden one; the salt marsh turns into bricks—all because a daughter won't obey her father.

118

49. (left) Charles Vanel in *Pêcheur d'Islande* (1924)

50. (right) Sandra Milowanoff

Even more prestigious than *La Brière* was Jacques de Baroncelli's *Pêcheur d'Islande* (1924), which preceded Raymond Bernard's *Le Miracle des loups* at the Salle Marivaux and then continued for another month at the new Mogodor cinema.[112] Pierre Loti's novel had been set in Paimpol on the northern coast of Brittany, and Baroncelli took his cast and crew there (again his cameraman was Louis Chaix) for several months of shooting in the spring and summer of 1924.[113] For a while, the sailing ship Marie became a veritable studio in the harbor and on the seas; and the people of Paimpol joined the production to enact the story of what they considered to be their book. The story is a simple one. Gaud Mevel (Sandra Milowanoff), a young woman from Paimpol, falls in love with a fisherman, Yann Gaos (Charles Vanel), who is wary of reciprocating her love. Only after she is orphaned in poverty does he relent and marry her, just days before he must sail on the Marie for a summer of fishing in the North Atlantic. Gaud waits for him into the late autumn; but the ship never returns.

Jean Mitry remembers *Pêcheur d'Islande* merely as "an album of photographs."[114] But Henri Fescourt recalls images—"the crucifixes on the hills, the crosses in the cemeteries, the slopes of heather, the low fishermen's houses under sad cloudscapes, a vast horizon of waves"—which embody "a particular kind of sensibility as well as the social customs of the epoch when the novel was written that have persisted up to the beginning of the twentieth century."[115] Frame stills taken from the few surviving prints (which are all I have seen of the film) confirm its "carefully composed photography of the Breton coast and its affectionately observed details of the customs of Brittany. . . ."[116] Several critics at the time wrote of its psychological acumen in depicting the characters, especially through the performance of Charles Vanel; while another was struck by the omnipresence of the sea, which, even more than in *L'Homme du large*, actually seemed to be the film's central character.[117] Baroncelli himself saw the film as "the story of a fisherman and not the collective drama of all fishermen," acted out before "the deep enveloping backdrop" of the sea.[118]

His words describing Loti's novel aptly describe his own film: "the views, the visions that follow one another like waves, are bound up, commingled, multiplied in a 'simultaneism,' that expresses a profound psychological and mental truth. . . ."[119] Much like *Visages d'enfants* and *La Brière*, this film was a quasi-documentary of a remote French society as well as a slowly accumulating, impressionistic tableau of character and landscape co-existing in harmony.

So popular was *Pêcheur d'Islande* that the readers of *Cinéa-Ciné-pour-tous* voted it the second best film of 1924.[120] This success led Baroncelli to embark on a cycle of film adaptations of sea stories—*Veille d'armes* (1925), *Nitchevo* (1926), *Feu* (1927)—that one critic personified as "the various faces of the sea."[121] But these latter are no longer realist films. *Feu* was a sea adventure about a gunboat captain during the recently ended colonial war against the Rifains in Morocco. And *Nitchevo* was a drama about men trapped in a submarine off the French naval base at Bizerte, Tunisia. As Baroncelli shifted away from the genre of the realist film, he found himself working on films set up to advance the careers of young actresses as well as relying on the facilities of Cinéromans' new studios. The representation of Brittany's seacoasts and the life of its fishermen was left to younger filmmakers such as Jean Epstein and Jean Grémillon.

On the basis of this survey of the genre so far, the French realist film offers an interesting contrast to the realist cinema that developed in Germany about the same time. Perhaps because the German film industry modernized its studios more quickly and on a grander scale than did the French, their films tended to be shot in studio sets that reproduced reality. There were exceptions, of course—Lulu Pick's *Shattered* (1921), for example, and Gerhard Lemprecht's *Children of No Importance* (1926)—but nearly all, whether shot on location or in the studio, gave representation to a distinctly urban milieu.[122] Influenced by *Kammerspiel* theater, perhaps especially through Carl Mayer, and to a much lesser extent by Expressionist art, architecture, and drama, these realist films created city spaces that were enclosed, intimate, and sometimes claustrophobic.[123] Their preoccupation with rendering *Stimmung* (mood) seems to have depended heavily on the use of artificial light.[124] By contrast, the French films tended to open out into expansive (if no less deterministic) landscape spaces and to rely on recording the nuances of natural light. The German realist films were tied more to the lower and middle classes of the city (often a limited number of characters living in an everyday ambience), which gradually led to an important subgenre of street films during the last half of the decade.[125] The French realist films, on the other hand, found their locus more often in the natural landscapes and villages of the provinces and in their bourgeois, peasant, and artisan classes.

This does not mean that there were no French realist films whose environment was the city, but they were less numerous and, with a few exceptions, not as popular as the provincial realist films. Toward the end of the war, at least three films grounded the genre in the milieu of the city, in the modern. The earliest of these was Antoine's *Le Coupable*, which was interrupted in its shooting by the battle of the Somme (during the summer of 1916) and then not released until 1917.[126] Because the surviving print of the film lacks intertitles, its complicated narrative, which alternates a court trial with a past story

120

51. A frame still from *La Coupable* (1917)

in which an abandoned woman (a flower girl) bears a child and later turns to crime, is now close to incomprehensible.[127] Yet *Le Coupable* still holds some interest for its grim images of wartime Paris (the cameraman was Paul Castenet) and for its deliberate contrast of the bourgeois and little-known proletarian milieux. René Prédal, in fact, calls it "the first authentic [film] document about Paris."[128]

Another quasi-realist film set in the newly built industrial belt around Paris was Henry Roussel's adaptation of a propagandistic war novel, *L'Ame du bronze* (1917). According to Georges Sadoul and others, most of the film was "an abominable melodrama."[129] Harry Bauer played an engineer who let a rival fall to his death in a crucible of molten bronze. After the metal is forged into a cannon, the engineer is called to serve in the war; there he is forced to use the very same cannon in a climactic battle. Despite this heavy-handed irony, the film's initial sequences created a sensation. They were shot entirely in a huge ironworks factory, by Paul Castenet again, in an almost documentary fashion. Louis Delluc was particularly struck by the evocative authenticity of this setting:

The most powerful character in *L'Ame du bronze* is not an actor; it is a factory. Astonishing images reveal to us the modern marvels of metallurgy. It is as beautiful as a page of Verhaeren. Here is a real poetry, the best that the cinema can aim for. . . .[130]

Probably the most important of these early city films was Henri Pouctal's eight-part adaptation of Zola's *Travail*, the most publicized and probably the most successful French film of the 1919-1920 season.[131] According to Jean

121

52. Léon Mathot in a factory location in *Travail* (1919-1920)

Galtier-Boissière, Pouctal smoothly resolved the problem of integrating two different film modes—"the documentary and the scripted or dramatic film."[132] The workers looked and acted like workers, whether in the factory or in the bistros and poorly paved streets surrounding it. And the chief actors (Léon Mathot and Huguette Duflos) seemed to blend in with them. Most impressive was the factory itself, where much of the film was shot by Louis Chaix:

the factory in action, with its tall smoking chimneys, with its pulsating entrails . . . the blast furnaces, the streams of incandescent iron, the blind steam pistons, all this gigantic machinery, around which scurry, sometimes illuminated by the light of a purple flame, the human pygmies, the galley slaves of industry.[133]

Jean Mitry argues that,

with its well-composed images, its detailed atmosphere, its relative authenticity, *Travail* helped orient the French cinema toward subjects inspired by everyday life, illustrating the social problems of the proletariat as opposed to the pleasures of an idle class.[134]

Viewed today, at least in the well-preserved tinted print of chapter one, *Travail*'s tableaux sequences of human figures struggling to achieve parity in an industrial landscape are still impressive.[135] Yet the film's explicit though muted class conflict and resolution (already sentimentalized in the manner of Lang's *Metropolis* [1927]) is masked by the melodramatic story of a victimized young woman, an orphan, and her eventual marriage into wealth. Reformist throughout in its ideology, Marcel Oms writes, *Travail* articulates its sense of national reconciliation, capitalist-worker accord, and social justice in the context of a moral rejuvenation. An even more simplified ideology marked René Le Somptier's *La Croisade* (1920), in which a "reborn" factory owner (a returning war veteran) was pitted against an anarchist worker who conveniently goes mad at the end.[136]

On the strength of *Travail*'s success, several producers tried to turn other works of nineteenth-century urban fiction into profitable realist films. After its American-style productions failed to find American distribution in 1920, Film d'Art assigned Baroncelli to direct an adaptation of Balzac's *Père Goriot* (starring Signoret), which was released in 1921. Although some critics praised *Père Goriot* for its detailed reconstruction of the shabby Vauqier pension, the scenario did not allow Baroncelli to exercise his sensitivity to natural landscapes.[137] The film was but the first of a series of studio-bound adaptations of Balzac that included Gaston Ravel's *Ferragus* (1923), Jacques Robert's *Cousin Pons* (1924), and Max de Rieux's *Cousine Bette* (1924).[138] Even less distinguished film adaptations were made of several Zola novels—Bernard-Deschamps's *La Nuit du 11 septembre* (1920) and Marsan and Maudru's *L'Assommoir* (1920).[139] Yet the latter, Louis Aubert confessed to André Lang, was one of his most profitable films that year.[140]

Several realist films from this period actually straddle the distinction I have been making between the provincial and urban environments by locating their stories in a major city in the provinces. Louis Delluc's *Fièvre* (1921) and Jean Epstein's *Coeur fidèle* (1923), for instance, are both set in the down-and-out waterfront sections of old Marseille. Drawn from original scenarios, both have simple, rather melodramatic narratives, predicated on love triangles; and both make much of the atmosphere of their milieu, though by different means. Delluc was confined to a Gaumont studio but had a finely detailed set designed by Robert Garnier. Epstein was able to film in several deserted areas of the Marseille harbor and created a famous sequence of rapid cutting out of a local carnival. In rhetorical complexity, however, the two films deviate quite a bit from the standard realist film.

Certainly the most impressive of these genre deviations was Abel Gance's *La Roue* (1922-1923). The scenario was inspired initially by Pierre Hamp's working-class novel, *Le Rail*, but it soon took off from its source in several different directions. At first glance, *La Roue* seems like an epic, highly melodramatic modernization of the Oedipus story. Its subject is a locomotive engineer named Sisif (Séverin-Mars) who falls in love with his adopted daughter, Norma (Ivy Close), whom he had rescued as a girl from a train wreck in Nice. To protect her from his obsession, and even from his son Elie (Gabriel de Gravone), he marries her to a wealthy railroad inspector. Still maddened by guilt, he fails in several attempts to commit suicide and then is blinded

53. (left) Gabriel de Gravone
and Ivy Close in the railyard
house in *La Roue* (1922-1923)

54. (right) Séverin-Mars

by an accidental blast of steam from his own locomotive. Demoted to running
the funicular railway on Mont Blanc, the aging man is confined with his son
to a mountain cabin. When Norma and her husband visit a nearby resort, Elie
is drawn into a fight with the husband, and both are killed. After blaming
her for his son's death, Sisif finally relents and allows Norma to live with him.
In the end, while she joins in the peasants' spring dance in the snows, Sisif
dies peacefully at his cabin window.

There are several features which distinguish *La Roue*—its moments of subjectivity, its techniques of rapid cutting or accelerating montage and their
multiple function, its patterns of rhetorical figuring, its doubled narrative
structure—all of which carry it well beyond the standard French film. But one
feature is of particular interest here. That is the hybrid form of its realism,
combining elements of both the urban and provincial realist films. In the first
part of the film, this realism stems largely from the location shooting in the
Gare Saint Roch railyards near Nice, in which Gance tries to reproduce the
proletarian ambience of the railway workers' milieu. In the final section, however, that realism depends on the location shooting in the French Alps. Here,
the mountain landscape, which initially dwarfs Sisif and accentuates his suffering, is finally transformed in the peasants' dance in the vast expanse of the
snow fields. Somewhat as in *Jocelyn*, a human community has become one with
a natural landscape.

Most of the commercial urban realist films, however, were different from
La Roue. For one, they focused exclusively on the French capital of Paris. In
some, the idea of documenting the daily life of the city became as important
as narrating the story. Léon Poirier had wanted to make just such a film as
early as 1921. "I dreamed of a great symphony about Paris, modern Paris, the
magnetic pole, the human crucible which produced both geniuses and criminals. The subject was vast."[141] Poirier's prologue had already been shot when
Gaumont decided that he could not release two films with the same title—

55. A street scene publicity
photo for *Paris* (1924)

and Louis Feuillade's *Parisette* would certainly make more money. Perhaps the
first film to actually employ the city's name alone in its title was René Hervil's
Paris (1924), which was based on an original scenario by Pierre Hamp. According to *Cinéa-Ciné-pour-tous*, Hamp's scenario constituted a sort of "synthesis of modern Paris, the city of work as well as the city of amusement."[142] It
followed several different characters—a dressmaker's assistant, a fruit-seller, a
mechanic, an industrial magnate, a music hall star, a fashionable young woman,
and an inventor—as they circulated around Paris.[143] "The cinema too often
forgets its real goal," Hamp said during its production, "which is life itself
and the reproduction of life."[144] Unfortunately, though quite profitable in
Aubert's cinemas, Hervil's film seems to have sacrificed its documentary mode
and exaggerated its plot that called for the hero (Alibert) to foil the theft of
the inventor's designs for a new locomotive and then to convalesce side by side
with his fiancée (Dolly Davis).[145]

By 1925, the urban realist film, much like its provincial counterparts, was
undergoing a transformation. The change becomes clear if one examines several

125

56. (left) Jean Forest in
Crainquebille (1923)

57. (right) Maurice de
Féraudy

films directed by Jacques Feyder and Jean Epstein—*Crainquebille* (1923), *L'Affiche* (1925), and *Gribiche* (1926).

With *Crainquebille*, Feyder was taking more than the risk of independent financing for a small film. The film trade press considered the classic Anatole France story on which it was based too interiorized, too subjective, for the cinema; and they thought that audiences would remember only too well Lucien Guitry's popular performance of the old man's role in its theatrical adaptation.[146] *Crainquebille* is "a simple human story" (says the American version of the film) about an old vegetable cart vendor (Maurice de Féraudy) who has worked the rue Saint-Antoine area of Paris for nearly forty years.[147] One day, a gendarme misunderstands the old man and arrests him, thinking he has been insulted. Powerless in court, Crainquebille is sentenced to several weeks in jail, which he quickly adapts to—as he does to most things. After his release, however, his old customers (petit-bourgeois shopkeepers) reject him, and he takes to drinking. Finally, one rainy night, when on the point of throwing himself in the Seine, the old man is befriended by "The Mouse" (Jean Forest), a young orphan who lives in an abandoned shed near the river. This is a neat reversal of the conventional orphan plot denouement—the plucky kid (lighting a cigarette butt at the end) saves the old man from suicide and restores his desire to live.

Crainquebille opened in March, 1923, and, despite the odds, soon was successful—worldwide—and even influential.[148] For instance, it helped persuade Albatros to produce a modern adaptation of *Le Chiffonnier de Paris* (1924), starring the Russian emigré actor, Nicolas Koline, in one of his best roles as Père Jean (a role that Frédérick Lemaître had made famous in 1847).[149] No doubt *Crainquebille*'s success depended to a great extent on the performances of Féraudy and Forest, who was making his acting debut. When the film was previewed for a special audience of vendors from Les Halles, Lucien Doublon exclaimed, "That's Crainquebille himself!"[150] Even the vendors acknowledged the authenticity the two actors gave to their characters. But *Crainquebille* was exceptional, too, in L.-H. Burel's location shooting around Les Halles and in the Marais (then still one of the oldest communities in Paris).[151] Particularly evocative of this milieu are the sequences of Féraudy pushing his cart through the narrow streets, an early one of the boy selling newspapers, and another of the old man drinking at a café while outside the door vendors gather in the huge market area. In the film's opening and closing, some of the shooting was done at night—for the sequence of market wagons rolling into the city and for Crainquebille's suicide attempt. This combination of naturalistic acting and location shooting gives Feyder's film adaptation of the story a significance that synthesizes the social and psychological—the naïveté and supposed inferiority of the main character balances the indifference and inhumanity of the social order that victimizes him.

Some film historians have accepted *Crainquebille* as an avant-garde film, because, in several sequences, it resorts to subjective fantasy in depicting the old man's victimization. Although these moments deviate from the film's dominant mode of representation, they do so in a way which is somewhat different from the narrative avant-garde film practice. Both moments occur during sequences when Crainquebille is in unfamiliar surroundings—in the courtroom and in jail. There is some logic and consistency, consequently, in the fact that they are set off from the representation of his everyday life. The first moment represents his perception of the trial—articulated through blurred, distorted shots (of the judge and prosecutor), multiple exposures (of a gigantic gendarme and a tiny defense witness), mise-en-scène tricks (a statue bust turns to look down on him), and camera movement (an erratic dolly shot through the courtroom crowd). The second moment represents a nightmare that assaults him after he has been convicted. Though the rhythm of its editing is ragged, this sequence is quite unique since it includes not only slow-motion shots and superimpositions of the tiny defense witness and judges (who leap down from their benches) but also negative images (of the chief judge) and a brief flurry of rapid cutting. There is some question whether this second sequence actually was part of the original film.[152] Even if it was, however, the nightmare serves little function in the film's narrative. It simply repeats, in different images, the terror Crainquebille experienced during the trial, and it has absolutely no effect on nor parallel with any later sequence in the film. The subjective moments of the trial may function with slightly more justification. Yet they serve less to reveal something about Crainquebille (his ignorance of the legal system and his terror before "superior beings") than to narrate the course of the trial by aggrandizing one side at the expense of the other (even across social lines—for instance, the defense witness is a gentleman). Consequently, both sequences seem roughly imposed on the film.

All in all, however, *Crainquebille* is probably the best of the 1920s realist films about the French capital. Upon seeing it in New York, D. W. Griffith is said to have remarked, "I have seen a film which, for me, precisely symbolizes Paris."[153]

A different kind of near tragedy and amalgam of modes marks Epstein's *L'Affiche* (1925), which was drawn from a rather sentimental scenario by his sister, Marie.[154] Albatros was pleased enough with its success to ask the pair to duplicate their efforts six months later in *Le Double Amour* (1925).[155] *L'Af-*

127

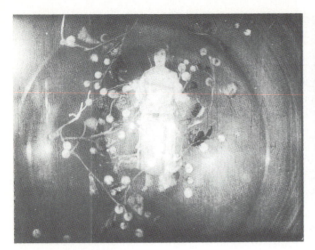

58. (left) Nathalie Lissenko in the opening of *L'Affiche* (1925)

59. (right) The riverside cabaret

fiche tells the story of Marie, a Paris flower girl (Natalie Lissenko), who is disturbed to realize that her youth is passing and so spends the night with a young man (Genica Missirio) she meets one evening at a riverfront cabaret. He turns out to be a rich playboy who disappears the next morning, leaving her pregnant. Once her child is born, she is desperate for money and enters its photo in a real estate company's contest for Paris's "most beautiful baby." She wins the 15,000 francs prize, but, soon after, the baby sickens and dies. Her grief becomes all the more poignant when an advertising campaign covers the walls of Paris with thousands of posters of her baby. Once the company director (Camille Bardou) recognizes her plight, it is revealed that the man who abandoned her is none other than his son, who now realizes his "sacred debt of love" and proposes marriage.

Compared to *Crainquebille, L'Affiche* integrates the subjective experience of its central character into its diegetic flow almost effortlessly. The opening creates a simple emblem of Marie's desire: a series of superimpositions in which she lifts her arms (in FS) through a revolving floral design and then (in CU) looks at something just off-screen and starts. Thereafter, the subjective appears at crucial moments, as in the distorted shots of a cross when she visits her child's gravesite;[156] but the most effective moments occur when she confronts the multiple images of her dead child, from which the film derives its title. In these sequences, Marie's own memory becomes visible, concrete; and her inner torment literally echoes, as in a nightmare, throughout the real world of Paris's streets.

Even more crucial, however, to the development of the realist film genre is the vivid, if facile, dichotomy that *L'Affiche* sets up between proletarian and bourgeois milieux. The one is characterized by the simple decors of Marie's workplace and apartment and, especially, by the riverfront cabaret. For there, in a leisurely montage of LSs, natural landscape and social community seem to co-exist in harmony.[157] The other is characterized by stark, spacious offices, restaurants, and townhouse interiors. For these interiors, Boris Bilinsky's black-

128

and-white decors, which are echoed in the repeated motif of checkerboard floors, seem cold and sterile, almost antagonistic. Yet it is here that the narrative is resolved, in a highly conventional fashion, exactly as in the sentimental serial or bourgeois melodrama. Could Epstein be concocting a deliberately false happy ending?

A similar dichotomy marks Feyder's *Gribiche*, which opened *en exclusivité* at the Aubert-Palace in late March, 1926, and which soon became even more popular than *Crainquebille* in France.[158] This time, the film belongs almost entirely to Jean Forest, whom one viewer described as a French synthesis of Charles Ray and Jackie Coogan.[159] The narrative, based on a short story by Frédéric Boutet, is an interesting variation on the orphan subject.[160] A young boy accepts adoption by a rich American woman (Françoise Rosay) so that his working-class mother (widowed in the war) can remarry. Puzzled and intimidated by his new environment, and then repulsed by it, the boy escapes during the Bastille Day festivities and wanders through Paris at night to his old apartment, where he is discovered and reunited with his mother and her new husband. Somewhat facilely, the film juxtaposes the working class and the wealthy, the French and the American—and clearly celebrates the one at the expense of the other. The most effective articulation of this idle fantasy comes in the story of the boy's returning the American woman's lost purse, which sets up the adoption. The woman tells the story several times to different friends, and each time (presented in flashback) it becomes more exaggerated, more melodramatic, until finally the boy is dressed in rags, and his mother is nearly dying of starvation in a garret!

Many film critics praised the film's sensitivity in conveying the boy's awareness of his own and his mother's situation.[161] Except for one awkward section of rapid montage in a fairground sequence (imitating the carnival sequence in Epstein's *Coeur fidèle*), the initial and concluding parts of *Gribiche*, shot mainly on location, still confirm that judgment. The sensitivity falters, and the ideological contrast is nearly reversed, in the long middle half of the film, which is played out in the modern decor of the wealthy American's apartment, designed by Lazare Meerson. As photographed by Maurice Forster and Maurice Desfassiaux, that decor is both sumptuous and sterile, fascinating and off-putting. The reason seems to lie in an apparent contradiction between the mise-en-scène and the narrative. Although the film celebrates Meerson's craft (its release coincided with the famous architectural designs at the Paris Exposition des Arts Décoratifs), it also condemns the fictional world his decors represent. In its heavy reliance on studio sets rather than on location shooting, *Gribiche*, even more than *L'Affiche*, clearly evidences the enervation of the urban realist film in the face of growing interest in the modern studio spectacular.

After 1925, the simple realist film nearly disappeared from the French cinema programs. Adaptations from nineteenth-century fiction continued to be made, of course, but now they assumed a different form. Some, such as Jean Renoir's adaptation of Zola's *Nana* (1926), were expensive, finely detailed historical reconstruction films as well as examples of the growing pattern of French-German co-productions. Others, such as Marcel L'Herbier's *L'Argent* (1929) and Julien Duvivier's *Au bonheur des dames* (1929), both contemporary adaptations of Zola novels, were important films in the new cycle of modern studio spectaculars. Several films, however, despite their conception as large-scale productions, attempted to maintain some degree of simplicity and some attention to either natural landscapes or bourgeois and proletarian or peasant milieux. The most prestigious of these was Cinéromans' big film for the 1925-1926 season, Henri Fescourt's adaptation of *Les Misérables*.

Initially, Cinéromans wanted to reduce Victor Hugo's novel to a single film like the rest of its Films de France series. But Fescourt, who had been assigned to direct it, fought determinedly to win acceptance of his own adaptation "in four parts, each of which would correspond to a complete film."[162] Those four parts closely followed the divisions of the novel: "L'Evasion de Jean Valjean," "Fantine et Cosette," "Marius," and "L'Epoque de la rue Saint-Denis." Fescourt was also allowed complete freedom in choosing his large cast. The only difficulty arose when he selected a rather unknown actor, Gabriel Gabrio, for the leading role. However, Gabrio proved to be "an excellent peasant at heart," wrote Fescourt, "he was Jean Valjean, Jean Valjean completely. . . . Victor Hugo would have been pleased."[163] Finally, Cinéromans budgeted the project at the considerable sum of six million francs, which allowed Fescourt to shoot much of the film on location.[164] Four months into the shooting, however, the sudden bankruptcy of the German company, Westi, led to a serious curtailment in finances. In order to finish the film, Cinéromans frantically cut corners everywhere, which is why, according to Fescourt, certain sequences in the last two parts seem sketchy. "Authentic town centers, authentic streets were to have served as a frame for the riot scenes: we recreated them in the studio. . . . That is the reason for the inequalities in the film."[165] Most audiences did not seem to mind, for its success, which was worldwide, exceeded all expectations; and it won a 1926 Gold Medal from *Cinémagazine*'s Amis du Cinéma.[166]

The narrative of *Les Misérables* covers almost a twenty-year period, from the end of Napoléon's reign to the Paris insurrection of 1832.[167] During that time, Jean Valjean, a peasant and convicted thief in Provence, becomes a small textile factory owner and the mayor (by changing his name to Madeleine) of the northern town of Montreuil-sur-Mer, and then is exposed and reduced to factory work and thievery again in Paris. Paralleling his story is that of Fantine (Sandra Milowanoff) who, abandoned with a child after the battle of Waterloo, has to turn to factory work and, eventually, to prostitution in order to pay the money-grubbing Thénardiers (Georges Saillard and Renée Carl) to raise her daughter Cosette (Andrée Rolanne). Once she dies, Cosette is protected and supported by Valjean until she grows into a young woman (Sandra Milowanoff again) who falls in love with Marius (François Rozet) and is taken into his aristocratic family. Valjean's chief antagonist during much of this time is the grim soldier-turned-lawyer, Javert (Jean Toulout), while his spiritual benefactor is Monseigneur Myriel (Paul Jorge), a priest in Digne who inspires him initially to renounce his criminal past.

In contrast to most previous realist films, *Les Misérables* is concerned primarily with the slowly building action of its narrative and with the conflicts that logically determine its course. "For Fescourt," write Beylie and Lacassin, "the cinema remained essentially the *art of narrative*; all the embellishments (the decors, the photogenic quality of the actor, the montage) should only serve, and never supersede, the narration."[168] As a consequence, the film's mise-en-scène (decors, costumes, lighting) is consistently simple, even primitive, in design. Interiors (whether they be the priest's rectory, Javert's office, or Marius's townhouse) are spare and unadorned; the lighting tends to be full and even. The editing relies heavily on a conventional continuity system of establishing shots and then closer shots of the characters' interactions. Long shots and full shots predominate, while middle shots and close-ups are reserved for moments of tension or conflict and for individual character reactions (as when Madeleine/Valjean saves Fantine from arrest by Javert). For such a lengthy film, Fescourt keeps the narrative under rather tight control, which is one reason Jean Mitry still thinks highly of it.[169] For instance, Fantine's descent in Montreuil-sur-Mer closely parallels Valjean's systematic rejection by the townspeople of Digne after he gets out of prison; and her rescue by Madeleine echoes Valjean's rescue earlier by Monseigneur Myriel. Even in the flashbacks, which economically narrate certain stages of Valjean's life, actions are paralleled: Valjean frees a mired wagon in the prison rock quarry; later as mayor he lifts a wagon that has tipped over on a man. Finally, in the climactic last reels, Fescourt and his editor, Jean-Louis Bouquet, intercut several different actions together as Valjean's story merges with the Paris insurrection: the fighting at the barricades (including the death of a boy named Gavroche and the wounding of Marius), the arrest of Javert as an Orléanist spy, and Valjean's flight through the Paris sewers with the injured Marius on his back.[170]

Despite the primacy of its narrative, *Les Misérables* does evidence some concern for atmosphere and for the evocative power of certain landscapes. The opening sequence functions much like a documentary of a quiet, peaceful southern French provincial town. But when Valjean first appears, he is framed against bare trees that are "bowed down and splitting like the weight of his own past."[171] Ironically, the town rejects him, and, after he has stolen from the priest and been forgiven, he is sent back out into the same mountain landscape to redeem himself. Sitting by a gnarled tree on a mountain top, he undergoes a long night of penance. If natural landscapes provide a simple

62. (left) A street in
Monteuil-sur-mer in *Les
Misérables* (1925-1926)

63. (right) Gabriel Gabrio
in the opening of
Les Misérables

connotative context for significant moments of Valjean's life as well as Fantine's later on, another strategy marks the last trying moments of Javert's
existence. Finally struck by remorse, after Valjean secretly has released him
from execution as a spy, Javert undergoes an agony of conscience in his office.
That agony is articulated in MCUs and CUs of his face, intercut appropriately
with subjective intertitles that increase in size: Authority, Law, Duty, Justice.
As the latter word suddenly shrinks in size, Javert looks straight at the camera,
and GOODNESS and then GOD expand to fill the screen. In the very next
sequence (deluded by his own judgment?), he throws himself from a bridge
into the Seine.

Although apparently critical of Restoration France and empathetic for the
victims of its social inequities and injustices, Fescourt's film is ultimately quite
conservative or at least contradictory. While it celebrates the people manning
the barricades against Louis Philippe's loyal troops, it also turns the battle
into a sewer of blood and offal through which Valjean must struggle with his
ward's fiancé. By saving Marius, he restores an aristocratic family, and allows
Cosette to return to the class from which her mother had fallen years before.
Only as he is dying does the couple learn of his sacrifice (the identity of
Marius's savior was unknown), and Monseigneur Myriel (in a subjective insert)
seems to bless Valjean on his deathbed. Victor Hugo may not have been
pleased with such a reactionary happy ending.

Another commercial project that subordinated atmosphere to the brutal
demands of its narrative was Jacques Feyder's *Carmen* (1926).[172] Its source was
Prosper Mérimée's novel, and Feyder went to a lot of trouble to recreate the
1830 period of Spanish Seville. Some of the best sequences of the film were

132

64. Raquel Meller in *Carmen* (1926)

shot on location by Maurice Desfassiaux: the tobacco factory of women employees, the climactic bullfight (staged according to the different bullfighting practices of the early nineteenth century), the gypsy bandits' flight through the desert, the gypsy mountain camp (especially in ELSs taken at night).[173] The interiors by Lazare Meerson were designed with an exacting sense of detail to complement the authenticity of the location shooting.[174] The best example is the café where Carmen and Don José meet, which has an ambience similar to the saloons of American westerns and to the bars of other French films such as *Fièvre* and *Coeur fidèle*.

Unfortunately, the presence of Raquel Meller as Carmen (and the unknown Louis Lerch as Don José) guaranteed her supremacy over both atmosphere and story. Feyder complained after the film's completion that Albatros was only interested "in making something with Raquel Meller in *Carmen*"—as with Gloria Swanson's *Madame Sans-Gêne* (1925), the film was primarily a vehicle for the star.[175] Furthermore, his star was not at all well disposed toward her character.

[Since] Raquel Meller intended to play only completely sympathetic characters . . . [she] deplored the immorality of the bohemian girl. She rejected her "bad ways," her amorous glances, refusing any shameless kiss on the mouth, and, through safeguards in her contract, so discouraged the director that he grew accustomed to little more than a rough idea of the lover of robbers, soldiers, and bullfighters.[176]

The result was a film oddly lacking in spirit (what Feyder needed was an actress such as Pola Negri in Lubitsch's *Carmen* [1918]), and with a rhythm

133

65. A street scene in *Thérèse
Raquin* (1928)

that slackened too often into monotony. When it opened at the Salle Mari-
vaux, in November, 1926, Feyder's film had the misfortune to follow Douglas
Fairbanks's swashbuckler, *The Black Pirate*.[177] Needless to say, *Carmen* was
Raquel Meller's first commercial flop.

The most successful of these big films to reconcile atmosphere, narrative,
and star apparently was Feyder's *Thérèse Raquin* (1928), which opened at the
Ciné Max-Linder in September, 1928.[178] The film was produced by DEFU-
First National and put together entirely in DEFU's Berlin studios. But Feyder
made it truly a French-German collaboration with a contract that allowed him
to rewrite the prepared scenario adaptation from Zola's novel and to use a half-
French, half-German cast: Gina Manès (Thérèse), Jeanne-Marie Laurent (the
mother), Wolfgang Zilzer (Camille), and Hans-Adalbert von Schlettow (Laurent).[179]

Feyder chose a structure, according to Léon Moussinac, that allowed him

in the first half, to create an atmosphere, to resurrect, while critiquing it, the milieu
where the heroine is formed, to evoke the daily life that thoroughly conveys the petit-
bourgeois spirit against which Thérèse is in continual revolt. . . .[180]

This sordid, oppressive atmosphere was chiefly the work of André Andrejew,
a Russian emigré set designer (who would later do Pabst's *Three Penny Opera*),
and the German cameramen, Frederick Fugelsang and Hans Scheib.[181] In the
stills that remain of the film, the Expressionist/*Kammerspiel* elements of the
decor and lighting are carefully blended according to an overriding concern

134

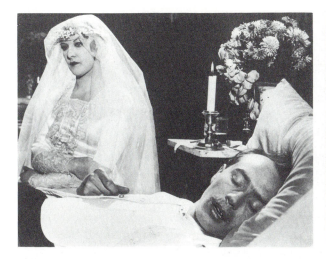

66. (left) Gina Manes and Wolfgang Zilzer in *Thérèse Raquin* (1928)

67. (right) The domino party, with Jeanne-Marie Laurent in the center

for the ambience of a certain social environment. Marcel Lapierre remembers several striking sequences and images:

the dimly lit Pont-Neuf bridge; the Raquin apartment, the domino parties on Tuesdays, solemn meetings whose ennui is analyzed by a high angle camera; the languid life of Thérèse compared to the slow hopeless turnings of a goldfish in a glass bowl. . . .[182]

And Victor Bachy describes "a strange black and white symphony" in the bridal bedroom:

Black: the dressers, the bedboard—and most sinister—the husband's nightgown. White: the wife's makeup table, the veil, the crown of orange blossoms, the bed sheets and the handkerchief with which Thérèse moistens her husband's forehead.

Several vials of medication are arranged on the bedstand; and the light plays with stunning, morbid reflections on the polished black wood and the icy satin of her dress.[183]

These images were all the more striking because *Thérèse Raquin* was one of the few French films in the 1920s to be printed exclusively on black-and-white rather than on color-tinted filmstock.[184]

In the second part of the film, wrote Moussinac, "Feyder comes to the melodramatic action, without trying to falsify and reduce the odious and cruel nature of the characters."[185] According to Charles Ford, "the spectator accepted everything that could be repulsive in the manner of this woman because Feyder had placed her so precisely in the milieu which explained her actions."[186] And Gina Manès made the character all the more credible by giving one of the best acting performances of the decade—wrote Pierre Leprohon, "This is what is called living a role."[187] For Jean Mitry, "the culminating scene [was] the one where Thérèse and Laurent, after the murder, experience the faint beginnings of anguish and remorse as they face the silent accusation of the old infirm mother."[188] The characteristic motif of Andrejew's decor now became the dirty windows covering the passageway between the flower shop

68. Le Petit Jimmy imitating
Maurice Chevalier in *Peau de
Pêche* (1929)

and the tiny apartment. In this unhealthy greenhouse, this "sort of glass jar
. . . a trio of petit bourgeoisie festered and decomposed."[189]

As a work of sustained power that depended on a synthesis of much of the
narrative avant-garde practice, *Thérèse Raquin* was one of the more uncompromising of the realist films and, for some, a masterpiece of the French silent
cinema.[190] Yet the critics as well as the public were far from unanimous (the
film was a commercial failure in France).[191] Some, such as Moussinac, re-
proached Feyder with showing "nearly too much elegance in a theme which
demanded, it seemed, less circumspection and a more willingly developed
vulgarity."[192] The social criticism, he argued, was muted and tamed in an
artful period piece, as if within its own glass jar. Others, such as Jean Dréville,
praised Feyder for transposing Zola "according to the principle of an accumulation of psychological details."[193] For them, the film was a relentless,
totally plausible, psychological study. Unfortunately, we may never be able
to decide for certain because, despite the high praise it won from both cinéphiles and cinéastes, *Thérèse Raquin* remains one of the most famous of lost
films.

Bucking this trend toward large-scale productions were a few scattered low-
budget films. There was Fescourt's adaptation of *La Glu* (1927), set in "a
milieu of rough Breton fishermen" and shot in a freakish month of sunshine
around the Pointe de Croisie (just west of La Brière).[194] There was Duvivier's
Le Mariage de Mademoiselle Beulemans (1927), which apparently achieved some
degree of atmosphere through location shooting in the streets of Brussels.[195]

Perhaps the most interesting of these small films, however, were done by the new writer-director team of Marie Epstein and Jean Benoît-Lévy.

Ames d'enfants (1928) and *Peau de pêche* (1929), both produced by Aubert, followed the format of films about children developed by Feyder and Duvivier. The more successful of the two was *Peau de pêche*, which opened at the Electric-Cinéma in March, 1929.[196] It is a rather conventional moral tale about a Poulbot orphan from the streets of Montmartre whose natural generosity is allowed to flourish in the open air of the French countryside.[197] As a reward for returning a necklace that she lost on her wedding day, Mme. Defleures (Denise Lorys) sends Peau de pêche (petit Jimmy) out to her cousin's farm in Charmont-sur-Barbuise where he grows up to fall in love with his "cousin" Lucie (Simone Mareuil). But his best friend, La Ficelle (who once saved him from drowning), seems to desire Lucie as well, and Peau de pêche (now Maurice Touzé) sacrifices his love and returns to Paris. Once she learns of his despair, Mme. Defleures counsels the young man and arranges his marriage to Lucie. *Cinéa-Ciné-pour-tous* found *Peau de pêche* quite refreshing:

Finally, here is a film that leaves behind the stifling, miserable limits of the studio, with its conventional decors and illusory techniques, a film where one can breathe the vigorous outside air . . . a film where there are no dance clubs, music halls, or worldly salons, but where, by contrast, there are admirable and restful perspectives of fields, of lovely rivers, and farm houses, so marvelously peopled that one would like to remain there the rest of one's days.[198]

More specifically, the film's charm is suggested in the sequence where petit Jimmy does a classic Maurice Chevalier imitation, in a circle of delighted village children (the film's only color tinting appears here in a slight reddening of the boy's cheeks—hence the name, "Peachskin"). And its poignant evocation of desire is evidenced in the opening wedding ceremony (emphasizing the impression the bridal veil makes on the boy) and in the sequence where the spring run-off fills the dry river bed of the village and where Lucie's image, reflected on the water's surface, comes between the two young men. Several years later, the emotional poignance, economical storytelling, and generally "poeticized" discourse that so marks *Peau de pêche* would return in Epstein and Benoît-Lévy's highly acclaimed *La Maternelle* (1933).

Otherwise, the simple realist film survived, interestingly enough, in the work of the narrative avant-garde. And there it flourished in a series of major works to be examined later—Dmitri Kirsanoff's *Menilmontant* (1926), Alberto Cavalcanti's *Rien que les heures* (1926) and *En rade* (1927), Jean Grémillon's *Tour au large* (1927) and *Gardiens de phare* (1929), and Jean Epstein's *Finis Terrae* (1929). Most of these films, however, were scarcely seen outside the network of specialized cinemas and ciné-clubs.

Based on this survey of the genre, the French realist films of the 1920s can be seen to have a significance that rivals that of the more highly budgeted genres of the historical reconstruction and the modern studio spectacular. For one thing, they provided the basis for the more publicized achievements in the genre in the 1930s. Their concern for the ambience of working-class Paris and for the relationship between environment and character fed into the important cycle of city films by Clair, Grémillon, Duvivier, Renoir, and Carné—

Prévert. Their interest in the different milieux of the provinces and in the relationship between landscape and character was resurrected in such films as Jean Epstein's *L'Or des mers* (1932) and *Chanson d'amour* (1934) and Jean Renoir's *Toni* (1934) and *Une Partie de campagne* (1936) as well as transformed in the enormously popular films of Bas- and Haut-Provence by the Marseille dramatist, Marcel Pagnol.

But the 1920s realist films were more than precursors, either to the French films of "poetic realism" or to the Italian "neo-realist" films after World War II. For the genre produced a body of work that constitutes a unique achievement on its own terms. It was the earliest consistent attempt to ground film art in reality, an attempt unfairly neglected by nearly all cinema histories, perhaps because it was superseded by the seemingly more radical concept of reality in the Soviet films later in the decade. Furthermore, the realist genre provided the context for most of the work of the French narrative avant-garde. Delluc, Epstein, Kirsanoff, Cavalcanti, and Grémillon—all have their roots in the genre. And Gance, L'Herbier, Feyder, and Renoir produce some of their most interesting or successful films from within it. That work, as will become clear in Part IV, consisted of extending the genre parameters, especially through experiments at the rhetorical and narrative levels of film discourse.

Fairy Tales, Fables, and Fantasies

In contrast to the realist film, the *féerie*—the fairy tale or fantasy—had been one of the earliest and most popular of French narrative films. Around 1900, Georges Méliès virtually created the genre with his magic shows, trick films, fantastic adventures "à la Jules Verne," and adaptations of classical and not-so-classical fables. Méliès's films were widely copied and imitated, not only in France but also in England and the United States. Their chief characteristic was the creation of an *other* world by means of uniquely cinematic techniques (superimposition, stop motion, fast motion, reverse motion, etc.) used in conjuction with deliberately unreal, often mobile sets. This was a world of the marvelous or the uncanny, in Tzvetan Todorov's terms, usually distinct from but connected to reality, a world whose laws were often determined by the camera apparatus itself.[1] Although interest in the genre soon waned, in comparison to the comic shorts, police and crime series, and literary adaptations, it never disappeared entirely in France.[2] When the war ended, the fantasy returned as a minor genre, but transformed in several different ways. Although the industry generally considered it "démodé" and unpopular in the 1920s, the fantasy is at least important for providing a point of departure for several filmmakers involved in the narrative avant-garde.

From 1918 to 1922, most of the French fantasy films were produced at Gaumont, especially in its Séries Pax, where they coincided briefly with Feuillade's exotic and fantastic serials, *Tih-Minh* (1919) and *Barrabas* (1920). Most of the Séries Pax fantasy films were predicated on the juxtaposition of two different worlds, usually a real world and an imaginary one or sometimes an imaginary world and one even more imaginary. And they tended to be marked either by a Symbolist aesthetic or by the attempt to represent an individual character's mental or hallucinatory experience.

Gaumont's major successes in the genre seem to have been the films of Léon Poirier. One of the most discussed French films of 1920, for instance, was

Poirier's *Le Penseur*, "a story of the fantastic," based on an original scenario by the *Nouvelle Revue Française* writer, Edmond Fleg.[3] *Ciné-pour-tous*, in fact, voted it one of the top three French films of the year.[4] The scenario was inspired by the cult that was then forming around Auguste Rodin's famous statue. Pierre Dartigue (André Nox) is an artist who, one day meditating beside *The Thinker*, discovers a means of seeing into people's souls. Soon this leads him to develop a method by which he can paint the inner states of his models. "But that which he apprehends and represents," writes Henri Fescourt, "shocks him deeply, forces him into isolation, and finally drives him completely mad. Having discovered the universal deceptiveness of appearances, he dies in his studio, paralyzed in the posture of *The Thinker*."[5] According to various critics, Poirier compensated for the inherently static nature of his subject with a great number of dissolves and superimpositions, with superbly composed images that involved a seductive play of light and shadow (the work of his cameraman, Specht), and with finely nuanced acting from André Nox.[6] However simplistic its irony, *Le Penseur* did seem to develop useful strategies for representing and integrating several different modes of perception.

Poirier followed *Le Penseur* with a more realistic fantasy film, *L'Ombre déchirée* (1921), in which a mother (Suzanne Desprès), "who foresees what would become of her sick daughter if she committed suicide," is tormented by conflicting desires.[7] *Jocelyn* (1922) also continued this pattern, but in a different framework, with astonishing commercial success (as discussed previously). Here the other world is an historical past of opposites—the upheavals of the Revolution and the peaceful solitude of the mountains.[8] These opposites are mediated by the repeated image of Jocelyn's deathbed (a visual motif not unlike the rocking cradle in *Intolerance*) and resolved in a secret mountain cavern, if only temporarily. The whole film is tied rather conventionally to Lamartine's poem, on which the scenario is based, and to the figure of the poet himself, who sits reading Jocelyn's memoirs beside the deathbed.[9] It is as if the artist in *Le Penseur* had been replaced by Lamartine, and the earlier frightening images of duplicity and suffering had given way to images of a spiritual odyssey toward eternal peace.

There were other more obviously symbolic fantasy films, ranging from the sublime to the ridiculous. One was a lost experimental work, *Le Lys de la vie* (1920), directed by Gabrielle Sorère and Loïe Fuller, the famous though aging dancer who was best known for her illuminated fire-dance. Léon Moussinac called their film "the first attempt to transpose a poem to the screen."[10] In this fairy-tale ballet of a princess and a marvelous lily, Fuller employed the magical lighting techniques she had developed on stage with an original conjunction of such cinematic techniques as slow motion and the alternation of tinted positive and negative images.[11] Another sort of transposition was René Le Somptier's *La Montée vers l'Acropole* (1920), one of Louis Aubert's first major film productions.[12] Le Somptier's story seemed overtly political: a socialist journalist by the name of Lesieur (Van Daële) contests and defeats a reactionary bourgeois politician, Labrousse (André Nox). And the French censors were offended enough to force Le Somptier to delete any mention of "the proletariat" or "the working class."[13] Drawing its title from Renan's famous *Prière sur l'Acropole*, the film sought to dramatize, in Marcel Oms's words, "the conflict between generations in the succession of political power."[14] The overall effect,

69. (left) Philippe Hériat and Vanni Marcoux in Autant-Lara's costumes for *Don Juan et Faust* (1923)

70. (right) Marcelle Pradot

however, came across as pseudophilosophical: "the Parthenon looked down, from the heights of eternity, at several smartly dressed French film actors at its feet [including a miscast France Dhélia]."[15] Henri Fescourt summed up its mongrel nature well: it was "ambitious, psychological, sometimes boring, seething with lighting effects, and clotted with what seemed to be an infinite number of intertitles."[16] Besides being out of step politically in 1920, *La Montée vers l'Acropole* was overly static and pretentious (the cameraman was Amédée Morin), and Le Somptier turned to direct less controversial films.

Several of Marcel L'Herbier's early films for Gaumont oscillated wildly between these extremes, at least according to his boss. Anticipating Loïe Fuller, whom he much admired, L'Herbier conceived his first film, *Rose-France* (1919), as a poetic work and subtitled it "a cantilena in black and white."[17] *Rose-France* has a narrative that is as slight as it is highly symbolic: a young man (Jaque Catelain) discovers that the pure French woman he loves (Aïssé) has been writing poems of passionate love to someone else. Finally, she reveals that her love is for France, menaced by the war. The film's discourse, however, is marked by a strange combination of effete actors and decadent decors, collages of optical effects, verse intertitles signed by Charles d'Orléans and Charles Péguy, and experimental forms of narrative simultaneity. The combination proved a commercial disaster, and L'Herbier's third film for Gaumont, *Le Carnaval des vérités* (1920), was much more conventional.[18] He called it a "realistic fantasy," since it combined a Symbolist mask drama with a melodramatic intrigue enacted in the Villa Madone on the Basque coast.[19] In order to reverse their financial losses, the Comtesse Della (Suzanne Desprès) and her

140

lover (Paul Capellani) attempt to seduce and blackmail a rich neighbor, Jean (Jaque Catelain), who is in love with a naïve young friend of theirs, Clarisse (Claude France). The plot ultimately fails; the Comtesse commits suicide; and her lover re-covers her face with its mask. The Symbolist drama was carried out by means of superimpositions and color contrasts as well as Claude Autant-Lara's decors, especially a fantasmagorical garden where the masked ball is held. Louis Delluc appreciated it all the same: "The paradoxical charm, both deft and deep, that enlivens this modern fresco, so audacious in its halftones, pleases me no end."[20]

L'Herbier's *Don Juan et Faust* (1923) was the most ambitious of these films. This was no literary adaptation but an original scenario of two juxtaposed stories and conflicting symbolic forces. Faust (Vanni Marcoux) and Don Juan (Jaque Catelain)—the opposed figures of *libido sciendi* and *libido sentiendi*—vie with one another over Dona Anna (Marcelle Pradot), the daugher of the Commandant of Castille.[21] With the help of his devilish servant, Wagner (Philippe Hériat), Faust carries off Dona Anna to his castle while Don Juan is tricked into a duel with her father whom he finally wounds mortally. Unable to locate Dona Anna, Don Juan and his sidekick Colochon (Lerner) embark on a quick series of adventures in which he returns to his old ways, seducing nuns, servant girls, and aristocratic brides. Meanwhile, Dona Anna is locked in some kind of time warp with Faust until, with the assistance of Wagner (who by now is disappointed in his master's scientific endeavors), she stabs him to death and returns to her dying father. At the end, in the midst of an orgy he has arranged for all his women, Don Juan is attacked en masse by their husbands, lovers, and assorted male relatives. But Dona Anna saves him, and together they repent and take vows of humility and chastity within the church.

This juxtaposition of contending forces determines, in part, the visual style of the film, which L'Herbier himself has described as a meeting of "Velasquez and the Gothic."[22] The interiors for Faust's castle (designed by Robert Garnier) and the costumes for Faust and Wagner (designed by Autant-Lara) were marked by a peculiar mixture of Cubism and "Caligarism"—a rare instance of the German film's influence in the French cinema.[23] Yet the other costumes and interiors as well as the location exteriors were straight out of the Spanish period of Philip II, and they were often composed (by cameraman Georges Lucas) in ensemble tableaux inspired by the classical school of Spanish painting.[24] The friction between these modern and historical styles, though admired by critics such as Canudo and Clair,[25] proved disconcerting to French film audiences, and still does today, partly because the conflict is resolved so easily by the elimination of Faust's world and then by a pat religious conversion. But there may be another, simpler reason. The version of *Don Juan et Faust* released by Gaumont was incomplete and rather obviously patched together near the end; as a consequence, L'Herbier apparently had his name removed from the credits. Furthermore, the company delayed the film's previews until October, 1922, and then downplayed its exhibition run early in 1923.[26]

Despite its flaws, let alone its commercial and critical failure, *Don Juan et Faust* is still provocative on at least one point. Once Don Juan learns that Dona Anna is with Faust, he sets out to prey on the nuns in the convent where he has gone to seek her. To seduce one, interestingly, he uses the letter and medallion (from Wagner) which has just convinced him that Dona Anna went off willingly with Faust. To intensify the perverseness of this moment, L'Herbier alternates shots of Don Juan seducing the nun in a country inn with those of Faust hypnotizing Dona Anna (apparently in an alchemist's attempt to produce gold). While Faust seems to invest Don Juan's passion with a magical power, reciprocally, Don Juan seems to invest Faust's passion with sexual malice. The alternation concludes in the convent courtyard with a dreamlike sequence of softly-focused, eyeline-matched MSs and CUs, in which Don Juan and Dona Anna seem to gaze longingly at one another—as if they have emerged from parallel dark recesses. Do lust and passion merely mask a transcendent pure desire? As if in answer, a similar transformation occurs at the film's climax when Dona Anna rescues Don Juan. The threatened orgy of female bodies around one man quickly changes into a formal ceremony in which the same man confirms his faith in the company of veiled nuns. As Don Juan finally recognizes Dona Anna, through an intercutting of CUs that echo the earlier dream sequence, the film ends in a chaste coupling that is, if in no other way, at least aesthetically satisfying.

When Gaumont reorganized its production in 1922, the genre lost its primary support within the industry. For the next several years most of the French fantasy films—excepting the short puppet animation films produced independently by the Russian emigré, Ladislas Starevich[27]—can be attributed to four men: L'Herbier, Jaque Catelain, Jean-Louis Bouquet, and Ivan Mosjoukine.

L'Herbier's Cinégraphic briefly provided a haven for the genre with two radically different films. Le Marchand de plaisir (1923), Jaque Catelain's first film for his mentor's company, was a fable that owed less to previous French fantasy films than it did to Chaplin and Griffith.[28] Its schematic story brought together Mary-Ange (Marcelle Pradot), a wealthy young woman staying at a seaside resort, and Gosta (Catelain), a simple "seller of novelties," who lives with his poor family in a shack in the sand dunes. Gosta's love, however, is no match for Mary-Ange's engagement to a young adventurer named Donald (also played by Catelain); and it is compromised by a plot perpetrated by his drunken father (Philippe Hériat), who robs Mary-Ange and incriminates his own son. The climax is brutal—Gosta has to kill his father as the latter is trying to strangle his mother. Arrested and then released (when his sanity is questioned), in the end, he and his mother are sent off on a train. Compared to such films as The Vagabond and Broken Blossoms, Le Marchand de plaisir, unfortunately, is overlong and lacks an emotional center (Catelain is no Chaplin or even a Richard Barthelmess); and in style, it combines, all too predictably, American continuity editing, simple subjective superimpositions, and unmotivated moments of rapid cutting.

L'Herbier himself was much more ambitious in L'Inhumaine (1924), an early science fiction film that juxtaposes two worlds much more successfully than did Don Juan et Faust.[29] The infamous singer, Claire Lescaut (Georgette Leblanc) lives in an ultramodern mansion (designed by Mallet-Stevens) that includes a cavernous, geometrically furnished, moat-encircled banquet hall and a winter garden of Méliès-like artificial plants. Einar Norsen (Jaque Catelain) has a spacious scientific laboratory (designed by Fernard Léger) with an experimental television system and an elaborate process for resurrecting the dead.

142

Both places seem to lie on the outskirts of Paris, overlooking the city from the vantage point of the near future. The narrative builds to Einar's apparent suicide (out of unrequited love for Claire) and his resurrection, which is then replicated inversely with Claire's apparent murder and her resurrection. The final climactic sequence of the film, in which Einar brings Claire back to life, employs a barrage of cinematic techniques (superimpositions, rapid montage, brief flashes of pure color film stock) to represent the impossible as possible. Here the display of technical virtuosity is so awesome as well as self-reflexive that it places *L'Inhumaine* well beyond the limits of the conventional fantasy film.

Jean-Louis Bouquet was an architecture student who came to the cinema as a scriptwriter, editor, and critic.[30] His first scenario was directed by Luitz-Morat for Pathé-Consortium, as *La Cité foudroyée* (1924), which, simultaneously with *L'Inhumaine*, created a different kind of ancestor for the science fiction film.[31] Its narrative involves a young engineer, Richard Gallée (Daniel Mendaille) who hopes to win the hand of his cousin, Huguette Vrécourt (Jane Marguenet).[32] Her father has been ruined financially, and Richard concocts a plan to reverse his misfortunes. He makes a pact with the neighborhood "Bad Man," who then constructs a strange factory on his property. The project turns out to be an elaborate scheme by a master criminal who threatens the destruction of Paris unless he is paid a huge ransom. In the end, Richard publishes his confession as a successful novel (the strange factory is a printing press) and marries Huguette. But what about Paris and its apparent destruction? The film depicts the apocalyptic disaster in several sequences and stages, and Robert Gys's miniatures and Daniau-Johnson's slow-motion cinematography produced quite believable effects for the period—all the major Paris monuments, including the Eiffel Tower, collapse in varying stages of ruin. The irony of the film is that, through the delay of information as well as through the cross-cutting of real and fictional action, the audience is deceived into thinking that the novel (and its images) is a confession of something that has already happened in the past—that the engineer who goes about his publishing scheme is really the master criminal! In *La Cité foudroyée*, therefore, fantasy and reality are ambiguously, bafflingly intertwined. Bouquet attempted a similar confusion of the real and the fantastic for satirical effect in his scenario, *Le Diable dans la ville* (1925), but Cinéromans persuaded Germaine Dulac to change its setting from the modern world to the fifteenth century.[33] The change resulted in a considerable loss of force, since the film's uncanny events now had a simple explanation in witchcraft.

Ivan Mosjoukine, Albatros's principal star, also dabbled in the genre, for instance, in his scenario for Protozanov's *L'Angoissante Aventure* (1920),[34] likewise for purposes of irony and satire. His eccentric film, *Le Brasier ardent* (1923), engages the fantastic at several crucial points.[35] Its opening is a stunner—an inexplicable adventure of violence and eroticism in which a woman (Natalie Lissenko) flees a man (Mosjoukine) through a half-dozen very different settings, only to encounter him each time in a different guise. An abrupt cut to a bedroom sequence reveals that this strange journey into the marvelous has been a nightmare, inspired by a detective novel. This shift from the fantastic to the comic announces the general drift of the film, and these nightmare episodes provide a loose framework for the narrative that follows. Later, the

71. (left) A poster for *La Cité foudroyée* (1924)

72. (right) Ivan Mosjoukine doubled in *Feu Mathias Pascal* (1925)

nightmare is even reenacted as comedy when the woman is chased by her husband (Nicolas Koline), who literally falls into a detective agency where he, too, meets Mosjoukine and ironically hires him to investigate his wife. From there on, the fantastic disappears, and the narrative turns to satirize other genres—e.g., the police serial and the bourgeois melodrama. For its mixture of styles and genres alone, *Le Brasier ardent* is worth considering separately.

Late in 1924, L'Herbier and Mosjoukine teamed up to make perhaps the biggest fantasy film of the decade and the first film adaptation of a work by the Italian writer, Luigi Pirandello—*Feu Mathias Pascal* (1925). In comparison to the two men's previous films, *Feu Mathias Pascal* reversed the shift from the fantastic to the comic in *Le Brasier ardent* and anchored the fantastic in the narrative much more securely than did *L'Inhumaine*. L'Herbier himself called it "a fantasmagoria with a realistic premise."[36] The narrative premise is clearly Pirandellean: a falsely reported death seems to free the central character Pascal (Mosjoukine) from a dull married life in the provinces for a second life of adventure and romance in Rome. Some of the film's fascination, as in *Le Brasier ardent* and *L'Inhumaine*, comes from its fanciful play with settings, especially the interiors designed by Cavalcanti—from the dark, cluttered rooms of the provincial home to the hallucinatory open spaces of an apartment build-

144

ing in Rome. It is here that the fantastic finally becomes dominant. In a long imaginary sequence that includes several abrupt shifts, Pascal contends not only with a rival and his brother but also with a gigantic double of himself. The disconcerting uncertainty and ironic twists that characterize this second half of the film place *Feu Mathias Pascal* as well beyond the limits of the conventional fantasy film.

After *Feu Mathias Pascal*, Mosjoukine and L'Herbier were caught up in the tide of expensive period films and modern studio spectaculars, and the fantasy genre was left momentarily to one man—René Clair. Clair was opposed to what he saw as aesthetic pretension in Poirier and L'Herbier, among others. Instead, he saw his first films as a conscious renewal of the early French comic shorts and of Méliès fantasy films. Although independent productions, they were certainly conceived as commercial projects.

Paris qui dort (1924), which was released in the wake of *La Cité foudroyée* and *L'Inhumaine*, makes an interesting contrast to them.[37] It, too, is an ancestor of the science fiction film. But where the other two films opt for spectacular effects and rhetorical or narrative complexity, Clair's film chooses the simple and direct (also partly, of course, because of budget limitations). His scientist's laboratory looks like a cardboard set for a Keystone comedy. The shot explaining how the airplane passengers and the Eiffel Tower watchman escape the scientist's invisible, immobilizing rays is the most rudimentary animation imaginable. Yet for the crucial idea of a paralyzed city, Clair's simple strategies of slow-motion footage, deserted streets, and frozen human figures are remarkably effective. Besides being a comedy of manners and situations, *Paris qui dort* opens onto another, marvelous world. The stillness of the city strangely sets off the slightest movement of the six characters who wander through it. And their movement seems to reproduce that magical moment when photographs first "came to life" in the movies.

In *Le Fantôme du Moulin Rouge* (1925), which followed *L'Inhumaine* and *La Brière* at the Madeleine-Cinéma, Clair was inspired even more directly by Méliès: "Trick shots amused me, interested me, a lot during that period."[38] The original scenario allowed him and his cameraman Louis Chaix a great deal of play with superimpositions—which eventually does get repetitious. Through a misunderstanding, Julien Boissel (Georges Vaultier) believes that his fiancée, Yvonne (Sandra Milowanoff), no longer loves him—actually, her father (Maurice Schutz) is being blackmailed by a rival (José Davert). In despair he gives himself over to a doctor (Paul Olivier) who is experimenting with a "Cartesian machine" that separates the spirit from the body. The experiment works, and Julien cavorts about Paris as a disembodied apparition, invisible to all but the doctor (and the audience). He plays tricks on people on the streets (lining up top hats beside a lamppost), at the Moulin Rouge (stealing coats), and at the Louvre (painting a mustache on the Mona Lisa—in homage to Marcel Duchamp). Finally, he refuses to come back to his body and takes up residence at the Moulin Rouge and at a cafe with a distinctly Cubist decor. Then comes the ironic twist. Suddenly made aware that Yvonne really does love him, Julien discovers that the doctor has been jailed for murder and that his own body has been confiscated for an autopsy. There ensues a frantic race to release the doctor (only he can reunite body and spirit) before the fatal operation. Success comes at the last moment. Julien's body revives in front of the aston-

73. (left) Sandra Milowanoff and Georges Vaultier in *Le Fantôme du Moulin Rouge* (1925)

74. (right) Albert Préjean and Jim Gerald in Robert Gys's fairyland set for *Le Voyage imaginaire* (1926)

ished doctors; he clears up the intrigue; he and Yvonne are reconciled. The real world proves a safer, more pleasant place after all.

As a metaphysical fantasy, *Le Fantôme du Moulin Rouge* exhibits a mood and style characteristic of the French films which contrast quite neatly with those of their German genre counterparts.[39] In *The Cabinet of Doctor Caligari* (1919), *Destiny* (1921), *Nosferatu* (1922), or *The Hand of Orlac* (1924), the phantom is a creature of menace, ultimately threatening death. Here, he is a mischievous character whose gaiety compensates for a deep-seated sadness and whose condition of freedom and power ironically turns illusory. In the German films, the settings tend to be shadow-laden with tension, claustrophobic, palpably ominous. Here, the sets (interiors by Robert Gys) are light and simple, open to Julien's playfulness as well as blandly normal in their indifference to his suffering. The overall style is lighthearted, exuberant in its technical facility, and given to rapid shifts and ironic twists. Perhaps the only thing lacking, as Léon Moussinac first observed, is "an emotional center . . . the sense of a director attentive to express that which is humanly poignant in the simplest and most banal of our actions, just as in the greatest dramas."[40] More precisely, whereas the central character of *Le Fantôme du Moulin Rouge* achieves a balance of sorts—the union of body and spirit—the narrative resolution seems to contradict the film's free-wheeling, exuberant discourse.

Clair's next film, *Le Voyage imaginaire* (1926), was written expressly for Jean Borlin, the leading dancer of the Ballet suédois, whom Rolf de Maré wanted to star in a film (he had already appeared in Clair-Picabia's *Entr'acte*, 1924).[41] Jean Mitry has argued that its subject was influenced by Harold Lloyd's *Grand-*

146

ma's Boy (1922)—a long dream miraculously invests a timid hero with the strength and courage to win his love.[42] But the imaginary voyage itself is clearly inspired by Méliès. If the film as a whole is only half successful, the fault may lie not in the scenario but in some of the acting (especially Borlin's) and in the limited budget that forced skimping on some of Robert Gys's sets as well as Amédée Morin's camerawork.[43]

Jean (Borlin), Albert (Préjean), and Auguste (Jim Gerard) are all clerks in love with their typist, Lucie (Dolly Davis). One afternoon, while everyone in the office is napping, Jean dreams of rescuing an old woman from two toughs. She tells him that his kiss has restored her powers; and she leads him down an Alice-in-Wonderland tunnel, through castrating doors of jagged teeth, over the ceiling of a room (done with an upside-down set), and into a fairyland. This fairyland, however, is no ordinary place. It's a rest home for old fairies (no one believes in them anymore), and the set is appropriately "démodé": a tawdry baroque collection of seashells, serpents, coral reefs, bijoux, and papier-mâché flowers—an outright parody of Méliès's fairy kingdom sets. With his special kiss, Jean transforms all the old hags into lovely young women (an apt metaphor for Clair's own transformation of the genre); but, unfortunately, the decors change scarcely at all. The grateful fairies bring Lucie to their world so Jean will be happy, but an evil fairy (a racist stereotype in blackface) complicates matters by bringing Albert and Auguste as well. Intrigues develop—Lucie turns into a white mouse and is chased by Puss-in-Boots (a tongue-in-cheek play on sexual appetite), and the fairies give Jean one of their store of wishing rings so that he and Lucie can return safely to the real world. All four characters somehow materialize on the towers of Notre Dame, where Jean promptly gets himself changed into Lucie's pet bulldog (an ironic twist on the sexual chase), and the other two men fight over the ring. The struggle carries over into the Musée Grévin, where Lucie recognizes Jean among the mannequins and falls over in a faint. At night, the Revolutionary mannequins put both of them on trial, threatening the guillotine (a mannequin hand gets chopped off and the bulldog begins chewing it up); but just then a *deus ex machina* intervenes—in the form of Charlie Chaplin and the Kid! Jean and Lucie are freed; Albert and Auguste are dismissed; and Jean is restored—end of dream. Now bursting with self-confidence, Jean breaks through Lucie's resistance, and he sharply heels her dog as they walk off down the street together—in a parodistic image of the petit-bourgeois couple. Placed in the service of bourgeois conventionality, the marvelous simply empties that conventionality of substance.

Neither *Le Fantôme du Moulin Rouge* nor *Le Voyage imaginaire* fared very well with the French public so Clair, much like his predecessors, turned away from the fantasy genre to more assuredly commercial projects. His first film for Albatros, *La Proie du vent* (1927), contained elements of fantasy, but they were embedded in an adventure narrative based on a popular novel, Armand Mercier's *L'Aventure amoureuse de Pierre Vignal*, which could have been done just as easily as a serial.[44] An airplane pilot (Charles Vanel) loses his way and crashlands near a mysterious castle where a madwoman (Sandra Milowanoff) and a suspected spy (Lillian Hall Davis) involve him in an intricate series of puzzling, half-developed intrigues.[45] Critics and historians praised the film's technical facility in creating a finely detailed atmosphere (this was the first collaboration between Clair and set designer Lazare Meerson) and a light, balanced rhythm overall. However, subordinating the fantasy to an almost American-style adventure was what apparently made *La Proie du vent* Clair's most profitable silent film.[46]

As the French film industry turned almost exclusively to period films and modern studio spectaculars, often in co-productions, the genre of fantasy films passed largely into the hands of the narrative avant-garde as an alternative to the realist film. They, too, would account for some of the uniquely French films produced during the latter half of the decade. For instance, Jean Renoir's *Charleston* (1926) and *La Petite Marchande d'allumettes* (1928) carry on Clair's interest in a Méliès-style fantasy. Jean Epstein's *La Chute de la maison Usher* (1928) transforms the genre according to an eccentric fantastic mode and a very personal form of pantheism. Germaine Dulac's *La Coquille et le clergyman* (1928) and Luis Buñuel's *Un Chien andalou* (1929) revolutionize it according to the Surrealist aesthetic. All three of these latter films are remarkable in creating a fantastic world whose events cannot be explained naturally. But more about them later.

Only two of these filmmakers could be said to have worked commercially as well as experimentally in the fantasy film genre. Jean Epstein did so in the first film he made for his own production company. *Mauprat* (1926), loosely adapted from a Georges Sand novel, is a curious blend of generic elements.[47] Its subject is a mysterious intrigue among the eighteenth-century provincial aristocracy in the upper valley of the Creuse River, on the northern edge of the Massif Centrale.[48] Epstein shot his exteriors there around several different chateaux, especially the ruins at Chateaubrun. Some of this footage has a freshness and charm undeniable even today: for example, the deft rapid montage of Bernard's flight into the woods after being confined in the civilizing chateau; a MS of the train of Edmée's gown gliding across tiny wildflowers by a pond; a LS, after she has been wounded (shot while on a hunting party), of Bernard proclaiming his innocence to his friend under a huge arching tree. Marie Epstein has even called the film "a forest ode."[49] The interiors are strikingly different: the Mauprat chateau is soberly conventional, but the Roche Mauprat ruins contain immense dark spaces with a rich gothic atmosphere. In the sets for these latter spaces, Epstein and his designer, Pierre Kéfer, relied heavily on a limited number of arc lights: for instance, in one shot, the motif of "two converging pencils of light concentrate attention on a strange canopy bed."[50] This obvious concern for natural landscape links *Mauprat* closely to the provincial realist film, but the film also works as a modest historical reconstruction, faithfully rendering the surface of eighteenth-century provincial life.

The narrative, however, along with the gothic atmosphere, situate *Mauprat* within the fantastic. It is predicated on a simple but rather interesting dichotomy. The Mauprat family has two branches, a good one and bad one. That the one darkly mirrors the other is clear in the decision to have Maurice Schutz play both fathers, Tristan and Hubert. Bernard (Nino Constantini) is the bad family son who is awakened by the beauty of Edmée (Sandra Milowanoff), the good family daughter. In exchange for helping her escape his treacherous family (as in a fairy tale, she loses her way and simply wanders in), she promises to give herself to no one but him (the sexual sense here is

148

75. Alex Allin and Nino Constantini in the forest in *Mauprat* (1926)

as strong as the marital). After falling in love with Edmée, Bernard is taken from his original family, civilized, humiliated (she reinterprets her promise), honored (through service in the army), accused of trying to kill her, and finally exonerated when a trial reveals that his evil father, Tristan, actually uses Bernard's gun to perpetrate the deed. Edmée recovers and eventually admits her love for Bernard, and the two are united at last.

This dichotomy of families and fathers that converges in the double-natured son creates a curious psychoanalytic fable. Is the conflict one of fathers over possession of the son? It would seem so, if one considers the flashback sequence where, beside the strange bed that holds the corpse of his mother, the orphaned boy moves back and forth between the two brothers, only to be wrapped in Tristan's huge cloak and spirited off. Or is the conflict an interior one, involving a son who does not really know his nature? Aligned with one family, he means to rape and destroy a woman; aligned with the other, he falls in love and is repeatedly denied her. Can the repression of love so easily produce the return, displaced through the father, of the son's murderous desire? The final shots seem to evade an answer with a conventional ending: the young couple, by a window, look out on a pair of swans on a pond. Yet the previous sequence demands to be read in conjunction with it. Bernard's friend, determined to do away with Tristan "with his own hands," journeys to the ruined chateau only to watch the old man cavort about the heights and finally walk out onto a rock outcropping over a lake and, with a wave, dissolve away. If a different figure of desire still exists repressed and dispersed in nature, can that pond of swans really be so idyllic? An abyss gapes in *Mauprat*, just as it does, even more disturbingly, in Murnau's *Nosferatu* (1922).

Germaine Dulac also worked both sides of the fantasy genre. Two of her films were produced independently and were consciously organized as visual ballets or musical compositions. *La Folie des vaillants* (1925) was adapted from a Maxim Gorky story about a wandering violinist and Bohemian woman with whom he falls in love. According to Charles Ford, their story was paralleled throughout by the Russian fairy tale of the eagle and the snake.[51] Still, Harry Alan Potamkin found it full of a "sentimental *poésie*."[52] *L'Invitation au voyage* (1927), on the other hand, was based on just a few lines from the famous Baudelaire poem. In a sailor's bar, a woman seems on the threshold of a dream romance until her "inviting" officer notices that she is married. Most of the film's attention is focused on the milieu of the bar and on the imaginary escape, each of which is articulated in a contrasting montage of visual motifs. Its rhetorical complexity will warrant further scrutiny later.

Dulac's third film in the genre was a commercial venture for Alex Nalpas and Louis Aubert. The fantasy in *La Princesse Mandane* (1928), adapted from a Pierre Benoit novel, sounds similar to that of the Arabian Nights world of *Salammbô* (1925).[53] But the subject and spririt of the film are closer to Clair's *Le Voyage imaginaire* (and perhaps also to Keaton's *Sherlock Jr.* [1924]). Dulac herself summarizes the story this way:

In my film, Benoit's hero became a victim of the cinema. An obsession with all the glories of the screen persuades him to abandon his peaceful life and seek through the world. He thinks, at one point, that he is transported into a wonderful country, a marvelous kingdom over which a fairy princess reigns.[54]

As in the Clair film, this fantasy kingdom is enveloped, Dulac continues, "in a fine web of comedy; a constant obsession with adorning the ways of reality in dream is interwoven with a wish to transform the gravity of any conflict with laughter."[55] Despite Clair's failure with Jean Borlin, Dulac chose to emphasize the ethereal balletic quality of this fantasy by also starring dancers in two of the film's leading roles: Ernest Van Duren and Edmonde Guy. However, *La Princesse Mandane* ends with "a moral" that has none of Clair's irony: "After his many adventures, my hero chooses to find happiness in simple things."[56] The conservative, self-congratulatory ending, Charles Ford concludes, helped to make the film a profitable one for Aubert at the end of the 1928 election year.

Throughout the next decade, the French film industry continued to refuse to exploit the fantasy genre. There were exceptions, of course. L'Herbier returned to the "realist fantasy" for one of his best early sound films, *Le Parfum de la dame en noir* (1931), but it was little more than a romantic idyll. Clair, of course, used a fantasy format for one of his best social satires, *A nous la liberté* (1931). And, if the Surrealist fantasy culminated in Luis Buñuel's *L'Age d'or* (1930), it was also conventionalized, mythified, in Jean Cocteau's *Le Sang d'un poète* (1930-1932). Only the adverse conditions of the German occupation during World War II forced the French to revive, and to see the advantages of reviving, the genre once more—and on a much larger scale.

Arabian Nights and Colonial Dreams

Throughout the 1920s, in at least one important genre, the French cinema displaced its concern with its own culture through fictional adventures in a different kind of *other* world—one outside France, especially in North Africa and in the eastern Mediterranean. At first, the genre drew on the *conte arabe* tradition of *A Thousand and One Nights*, recently made fashionable, for instance, by Diaghilev's Ballets russes, especially by his *Schéhérazade* (1910). It also drew on Biblical stories, which had fascinated many French writers of the nineteenth century. Exotic tales of romance and adventure offered an acceptable escape from the economic and ideological problems wracking postwar French society. But the French colonies of North Africa (especially the well-settled territories of Tunisia and Algeria), according to Pierre Boulanger, provided appropriate settings for similar "stories of bloody conflicts, sensual pleasure, and mystery."[1] The genre quickly reoriented itself, and a number of melodramas and romances that could just as easily have been set in France instead took advantage of the local color and exoticism of North Africa.

The earliest successful adaptation of the *conte arabe* originated with Louis Nalpas, one of the men who later sustained the French production of serials. This is less than surprising when one considers that the producer had been born and raised in Smyrna. When Nalpas established his own film production company in Nice in 1918, according to Henri Fescourt, "he thought of the 'Thousand and One Nights' stories [and decided] to make a film that would resurrect a fabulous Orient."[2] The result was *La Sultane de l'amour* (1919), directed by René Le Somptier and Charles Burguet from a scenario by the French translator of Omar Khayyám, Franz Toussaint. After a sensational spring preview, the film's fall release was extremely successful. So popular was Nalpas's first production that Pathé-Consortium included it among its re-releases in 1923.[3]

The distribution of stereotypical characters in *La Sultane de l'amour* suggests that the film may have been a hybrid outgrowth of the bourgeois melodrama, the serial, and the exotic "Arabian Nights" tales. For there was "Marcel Levesque with his comic finesse; Gaston Modot whose strong features took on a ferocious character under his [soldier's] helmet; Sylvo de Pedrelli, the lovesick Emir, imposing and handsome; France Dhélia, the fiery sultaness; [and] Vermoyal with his pathetic glances."[4] Louis Delluc called it *the* best French film" of the season—"a remarkable synthesis . . . because the film is composed of many films and its diversity [including documentary inserts as well as magical trick shots] could just as well be called complexity."[5] The film's technical limitations—it was shot without any artificial lighting at the Villa Liserb outside Nice, using painted sets (by Marco de Gastyne) and a large diorama with miniatures in order to represent vast expanses—were obviously outweighed by the gusto of the acting (especially the athletic prowess of Modot),

151

the complicated intrigue, and the unusual decision to use the stencil-color Pathé process (which was normally reserved for newsreels) in the final prints.[6]

Capitalizing on Nalpas's success, Léon Poirier produced a series of Oriental films (also set in Persia, or farther east, and shot in Nice) for Séries Pax at Gaumont: *Ames d'orient* (1919), *Narayana* (1920), and *Le Coffret de jade* (1921). All three films narrated tales of brutal, mysterious, tragic passion; and the Oriental woman was consistently typecast as the deadly seductress. *Le Coffret de jade*, according to René Jeanne, affirmed the dubious maxim: "Life is a rosebush, and woman is the thorn."[7] *Narayana* (a transcription of Balzac's *La Peau de chagrin*) Louis Delluc described as "an enticing dream—more suggestive than complete."[8] To the genre's racial and sexual misogyny, here religious idolatry was added in a sequence where a shot of the hero (Van Daële) kissing the neck of the Oriental seductress (Marcelle Souty) is followed by another of a Buddha statue over which a skull is superimposed.[9] What fascinated French audiences as much as these tales of forbidden, destructive desire, however, wrote Fescourt, was the "exotic luxury" of Poirier's "Persian 'tapestries.' . . . They oohed and aahed over the composition of the decors, the arrangements of the furniture, the wallpaper, the knickknacks, the paintings."[10] The sets for these films, designed by Robert Jules Garnier, were obviously an advance over *La Sultane de l'amour*, but the genre quickly passed on to the real thing.[11]

The popularity of Nalpas's and Poirier's films encouraged the Russian emigré colony that had settled in Paris and begun to produce films. The first major success for Films Ermolieff, in fact, was Tourjansky's *Les Contes des milles et une nuits* (1922).[12] In this three-part film, the Princess Goul-y-mar (Natalie Kovanko) is traveling to the neighboring palace of her sister when she is captured by barbarians and carried off. Accused of heresy, she is prepared for torture by Prince Soleiman (Nicolas Rimsky), who instead falls in love with her. Together they survive a number of misadventures in his land and eventually return to the princess's father's kingdom where the prince is accepted as the sultan's legitimate heir. In contrast to the earlier films, Kovanko's Oriental woman exhibits a benevolent power that transforms uncivilized barbarians. Yet, as before, what apparently appealed to French audiences was the location shooting (done in Tunisia by Bourgassov and Toporkov) as well as the rich, coordinated decors (created by Ivan Lochakoff) and costumes (designed by Tourjansky himself). *Cinémagazine*, for instance, was mesmerized by "images that evoke the lush splendor that we imagine must constitute the mysterious world of Islam."[13] Two years later, for Films Albatros, Tourjansky returned to his version of the *conte arabe* formula with *Le Chant de l'amour triomphante* (1923), again starring Natalie Kovanko (as Valéria) with Jean Angelo, Nicolas Koline, and Jean d'Yd.[14] Here Lochakoff's decors were even more stunning, especially during the sequence of Valéria's dream.

The success of these films led to Tourjansky's first big film for Ciné-France, *Le Prince charmant* (1925).[15] Although set in the present or recent past, the narrative basically offered a pretext to explore (or fabricate) the exotic and sinister world of the Orient. A European prince (Jaque Catelain) and his fiancée (Claude France) are sailing a yacht through Middle Eastern waters when they witness the shooting of a young man trying to reach a high window in the local caliph's palace. The prince soon discovers a beautiful young woman (Natalie Kovanko) hidden in the palace and falls in love with her. Through a chain of intrigues and counterintrigues, the prince and his servant (Nicolas Koline) succeed in freeing the young woman. Returning to his own country (where his father has died), the prince ascends to the throne, and defies protocol by taking his new-found love for his bride. Again love conquers all—with the aid of brute force and treachery in the Orient and civilized diplomacy in Europe. Since most of the narrative takes place in the Middle East, Lochakoff's spectacular decors for the caliph's palace, especially the huge reception hall, are the film's chief showcases.[16] *Cinéa-Ciné-pour-tous* praised them unequivocally for creating "a marvelously consistent world of complete fantasy."[17]

The crown jewel of these *conte arabe* films was to have been Aubert's *Salammbô*, which premiered at the Paris Opéra on 22 October 1925.[18] This was the most expensive of the productions that Aubert had arranged to make, during the heady early days of international production strategies, in the film studios of Vienna.[19] Pierre Marodon was assigned to direct, but soon discovered that he had to serve as scriptwriter, set decorator, costume designer, and God knows what else.[20] Despite his problems, Marodon continued to be respectful of his author; his express purpose, he said, was, "to illustrate Flaubert's novel."[21] Perhaps recalling the formula of *Quo Vadis?* Aubert encouraged him to turn his scenario into a Biblical film in the Italian operatic manner. Consequently, the tragic story of the Carthaginian princess, Salammbô (Jeanne de Balzac), her father King Hamilcar (Victor Vina), and her two rivals, Mâtho (Rolla Norman) and Narr'Havas (Raphael Liévin), apparently was narrated almost exclusively in LSs that focused on mammoth decors (both exteriors and interiors) and on great masses of people. The central narrative action—Mâtho's attempt to seize Salammbô, which ends in death for them both—seems to have gotten lost in an endless series of marches, battles, and celebrations.[22] "Though shorn of any poetry," René Jeanne and Charles Ford write, "Marodon's formula did achieve, at moments, a sort of wild grandeur that one could not find in the Italian films, even in *Cabiria.* . . ."[23] Flaubert, of course, would have been appalled by all of this (given his distaste for "illustrations," if nothing else), but Aubert probably believed that he was righting a wrong done the novel during the war by an Italian film adaptation, in which Mâtho succeeds in marrying Salammbô at the end.[24] Critics generally were not kind to the film, and some even suggested that only Florent Schmitt's specially composed score saved it from being an absolute disaster.[25] Its luster considerably tarnished, *Salammbô* marked an end rather than a beginning. Thereafter, the French abandoned ancient history and the Middle East to the Americans—e.g., *Ben-Hur* (1926) and *King of Kings* (1927).

The initial success of the *conte arabe* film stimulated several different variations in the genre. The first might be called the Spanish film, which enjoyed a brief vogue in the early 1920s.[26] Louis Nalpas again produced the first of these, Germaine Dulac's *La Fête espagnole* (1920), from a Louis Delluc scenario about a femme fatale (Eve Francis). Others included Musidora's *Pour Don Carlos* (1921) and Dal-Film's *L'Infante à la rose* (1921).[27] But the cycle peaked in Gaumont's production of *El Dorado* (1921), by Marcel L'Herbier, which provoked an outburst of praise and outrage. While critics unanimously accepted *El Dorado* as "an advance" in film art, some viewers booed what they took to be virtuoso technical effects.[28] Yet its poignant tale of fatalistic love (in which

153

Eve Francis commits suicide behind the stage curtain of a cabaret), its vivid use of tinted film stock, and its location shooting within the famous Alhambra (previously off-limits to filmmakers)—all won for it a considerable audience and big box-office grosses, at least in France. After 1922, however, especially after the commercial failure of L'Herbier's symbolic fantasy set in Spain, *Don Juan et Faust* (1923), the Spanish film—with the exception of Feyder's *Carmen* (1926)—nearly disappeared.

The other variant was much more important, for it led to a redefinition of the genre into something best called the colonial film. The key film in this transformation was Jacques Feyder's *L'Atlantide* (1921).

At least one film sparked Feyder's initial interest in North Africa—Luitz-Morat's *Les Cinqs Gentlemen maudits* (1919), which was produced independently from a scenario by journalist André Heuzé.[29] The subject was a mixture of sleuthing, adventure, and the occult. One of five French tourists visiting Tunis tears the veil from a young woman's face, and a beggar accompanying her prophesies their deaths within a month. One by one, four do disappear, but the last discovers that the beggar is actually a bandit plotting to acquire his fortune. With the villain punished, the hero can fall in love with the niece of a colonist. Although Luitz-Morat did not insist on an oriental touch, according to Pierre Boulanger, he shot most of the film on location in Tunis. Costing but 137,000 francs, *Le Cinq Gentlemen maudits* brought in more than a million, enough to impress Feyder and several others.[30]

Early in 1919, Pierre Benoit had published a novel which rapidly became the first best-seller in modern French literature. *L'Atlantide* described the lost paradise of a beautiful Circe-like queen in the Sahara Desert, where she took European explorers as her lovers and then turned them into golden statues. After the success of *Ames d'orient*, Léon Poirier got Benoit's permission to adapt his best-seller for film. But Gaumont refused Poirier's stipulation to shoot on location in the Sahara—Fontainebleau had been good enough for Feuillade, and besides, what about all that sand?[31] Feyder then snapped up the rights to the book (with only a vague notion of how he would adapt it), just weeks before Léonce Perret tried to buy it for Paramount in Hollywood.[32] After securing independent financing (which had to be resecured time and again), early in 1920, Feyder marched his crew and cast—Stacia Napierkowska (Antinéa), Jean Angelo (Capitaine Morhange), Georges Melchior (Lieutenant Saint-Vit), Mary-Louise Iribe (Tanit Zerga)—into Algeria for eight months of shooting around Touggourt, in the Aurès Mountains, and finally at Djidjelli, on the Mediterranean coast. Instead of returning to Paris for interior shooting, he had the Italian painter Manuel Orazi improvise a huge tent studio at Babel-Oued just outside Algiers.[33] The production's ordeal was well publicized in the press; and when all 4,000 meters of the completed film were previewed at the Gaumont-Palace, in June, 1921, it caused a sensation. Released in October *en exclusivité* first at the Gaumont-Palace and then at Aubert's newly opened Madeleine-Cinéma, *L'Atlantide* ran for a full year and was shown around the world.[34] Rereleased by Aubert in 1928, perhaps because of André Delpeuch's accolades to it in his survey of the French film industry, the film had a similar success.[35] Jean Mitry has called it "the first really successful postwar French film."[36]

The femme fatale figure, the idealistic passionate Frenchman (or his stand-

in), the narrative of desire that leads to death—*L'Atlantide* shares all this with films such as Poirier's earlier Persian tapestries. There is even a short sequence that echoes *Narayana*: a shot of Saint-Vit dissolves into a gong over which, as it is struck, are superimposed first the face of Morhange, then a cheetah (Antinéa), and finally a skull. What *L'Atlantide* adds is a sense of nature not found within France itself (or in its studio properties). "It began with a sense of torpid heat and rhythm that was lacking in *La Sultane de l'amour*," Delluc pointed out.[37] "Here," wrote another critic, "the Aurès mountains provided unusual rock formations and wind-eroded foothills; and, even more strikingly, the desert offered the slow undulation of its rippled dunes."[38] "The one central character in *L'Atlantide*," Delluc concluded, "was the desert sand," which "spoke with [an] undisguised eloquence. . . ."[39] In contrast to the harmony of character and landscape in the realist film, in *L'Atlantide*, the desert becomes the locus of a test. The infernal sun, the expanse, the solitude provoke an encounter with pure beauty, mystery, and death. Before this landscape, the colonized North Africans vanish like a mirage, only to reappear transformed in a perverted paradise in order to measure the power and idealism of the French. The testing produces a guilt to be expiated (maddened by Antinéa, Saint-Vit kills his friend, Morhange) through suffering (he wanders in the desert with his rescuer, Tanit Zerga) and revenge (in the final shot, he returns to the desert in search of Antinéa and her kingdom). As the first important colonial film, *L'Atlantide* establishes the landscape of North Africa as a special site for the resolution of specifically French crises of the individual, of comrades-in-arms, and, later, of the family.

Viewed today, *L'Atlantide* retains some of its fascination.[40] The early sequences of the caravan traveling across the desert and entering Timbuktu, the exploration of caves in the mountain canyons of the Hoggar, a corridor sequence during the Frenchmen's first night in Antinéa's kingdom—these still hold one's interest in their choice of location, their composition, their lighting, their ambience (much of this is due to the chief cameraman, Georges Specht). However, the film seems even longer and more slowly paced now than it did then. Its rhythm is steady, even monotonous, interrupted only by a few sequences with frequent intertitles. Feyder structures the film to narrate the story of Antinéa in a long flashback which ends in such a way (emphasizing Saint-Vit's powerlessness and suffering) that the final sequence of his immediate return to the desert loses much of its credibility and force. The sets for Antinéa's palace, in the words of Georges Sadoul, are a puzzling concoction of styles—"Carthaginian, Black African, President Fallières, and Kaiser Wilhelm II"[41]—as if someone had visited *fin-de-siècle* France and Germany and then reproduced them from a nightmare twenty years later. Although most of the acting is more than acceptable—even quite good, especially given the shooting conditions—Napierkowska's Antinéa nearly ruins the film. An internationally known dancer and actress before the war, Napierkowska had been imposed on Feyder by his financiers (he himself had wanted Musidora).[42] Unfortunately, no one realized that she had gained thirty pounds; and, instead of diminishing her appetite, as Feyder hoped, the Sahara whetted it all the more.[43] Consequently, in contrast to her pet cheetah, Antinéa lounges around much like a comfortable, extremely well-fed tabby.

Out of *L'Atlantide*'s phenomenal success, which was complemented by Valentino's romp in *The Sheik* (1921), came a whole series of French films that were shot in Tunisia, Algeria, and even Morocco.[44] In Franz Toussaint's *Inch' Allah* (1922), directed by another Italian painter, Marco de Gastyne, Napierkowska appeared as the desirable dancing daughter of a sultan, for whom a suitor kills the requisite number of seven rivals.[45] In Luitz-Morat's *Le Sang d'Allah* (1922), Gaston Modot plays a Frenchman who rescues Yasmina, the rebellious wife of a sultan, and then is saved by her suicide in the desert (Yasmina seems a reformed version of Antinéa).[46] In André Hugon's *Yasmina* (1926), a French doctor (Léon Mathot) returns the favor by saving a Tunisian (half-French) princess (Huguette Duflos) from the horror of marrying a rich old Moslem.[47] Jean Vignaud, editor of the tabloid, *Ciné-Miroir*, specialized in whipping up popular romances set in the colonies: Mercanton and Hervil's *Sarati-le-Terrible* (1923), Fescourt's *La Maison du Maltais* (1927), and Mercanton's "à la mode" *Venus* (1929).[48] Finally, Pierre Benoit tried to repeat *L'Atlantide*'s success with an adaptation of *La Châtelaine du Liban* (1926), an international co-production, directed by Marco de Gastyne and starring Arlette Marchal, for Bernard Natan and Paramount.[49]

Even the subject of the bourgeois melodrama began to infiltrate the genre. In Dmitri Kirsanoff's *Sables* (1927), a separated husband and wife (Van Daële and Gina Manès) are reconciled over the sickbed of their daughter (Nadia Sibirskaia), who has driven alone across the Tunisian desert in a sandstorm to find them.[50] Kirsanoff himself condemned his film as "terrible, childish, stupid, merely amusing . . . an imbecile wrote the story."[51] In Julien Duvivier's adaptation of Henri Bataille's old sex play, *Maman Colibri* (1929), an unhappily married woman (Maria Jacobini) falls in love with the best friend of her eldest son, a young lieutenant of the Spahi. After following him to sunny Algeria, where he abandons her for a younger woman, she returns, chastened, to snowbound Paris, to be pardoned.[52] *La Revue du cinéma* called it "a senile platitude, an absolute void of thought and feeling, a total incomprehension of cinema."[53]

In this catalogue of mayhem, villainy, suffering, and sentiment, at least two films made slightly more serious attempts to understand the largely Islamic Arab population. *Visages voilées . . . âmes closes* (1921), written and directed by Henry Roussel and partly shot in Algeria, had the honor of being shown to the French Chamber of Deputies as an official example of national film production. The daughter of a high colonial administrator (Emmy Lynn) and a mighty caliph (Marcel Vibert) fall passionately in love, but their cultures separate them. One critic wrote:

Here is one of the best psychological studies that I have seen on the very different mores of the Europeans and the Arabs. Besides the intimate scenes between the principal characters, there are the beautiful frescoes of the nomadic life of the southern Algerian tribes. They remind one of masterful paintings, of the picturesque frescoes of our best orientalists. Harka's attack on the French fort and his defeat particularly recalls Horace Vernet's famous painting, the capture of the family of Abd-El-Kader.[54]

The Arab culture is unable to escape French stereotypes, however, for, as another critic wrote, "where love, for us, logically should triumph, there the Koran triumphs over it" (an opposition that conveniently ignores one of the medieval origins of romantic passion).[55] By articulating "the irreducible antagonism that exists between the Orient and the Occident," in Pierre Boulanger's words, *Visages voilées . . . âmes closes* easily assents to French superiority.[56]

Henri Fescourt's ill-fated *L'Occident* (1928), based on Henri Kistemaecker's scenario for his own play, reverses the characters in a story of love between a young Moroccan woman (Claudia Victrix) and a French naval officer (Jaque Catelain). Here, the subject is doubled: Can an Oriental woman become an Occidental? And will the officer's passion or duty triumph in the end?[57] The first question is undermined by the fact that the Moroccan woman is already a French actress (and a bad one at that). The second is resolved against love once again, but the rulebook that thwarts it this time is hardly the Koran. Complaining of "the fundamental banality of *L'Occident*," *On Tourne* also remarked "that the characters confirm our hypocrisy."[58] In the climactic battle between the French legions and the rebellious Chleuhs—filmed "in the best western style"—the leader of the legionnaire extras even complimented the director: "Monsieur Fescourt, your manner of treating the Berbers has done a good deal for their pacification."[59] Years later, Fescourt realized that

the idea never occurred to any of the directors of this warlike spectacle that, among the crowd of retreating Moroccans, perhaps there were some who were angry at the role that we asked them to play. . . .[60]

The genre would not begin to redeem itself until Marie Epstein and Jean Benoît-Lévy's *Itto* (1934).

An interesting feature of the colonial film in the 1920s was its general lack of attention to the French foreign legion and the Moroccan war, which concluded with the surrender of the Riftains in 1926.[61] Perhaps the negative public reaction to the war, which provoked increasingly frequent demonstrations in the middle 1920s, made the film producers wary of the subject—as happened to the American film industry during the Vietnam War. In any case, an American film, *Beau Geste* (1926), became the first film devoted entirely to the legion, and the Americans devoted more films to the subject than did the French, even into the 1930s.[62] Except for *L'Occident*, the French seemed more drawn to the sea dramas associated with the Moroccan war, as in Baroncelli's *Feu* (1927) and *Nitchevo* (1926). However, it was in a film reconstructing an earlier period of the Moroccan war that the subject of individual redemption in the North African colonies was first articulated. The film was one of Cinéromans's more lavish serials, René Le Somptier's *Les Fils du soleil* (1924), which turned the Moroccan independence fighters into a particularly villainous Emir and his hordes, who team up with an unscrupulous French financier. One of its plots involved a young man falsely accused of theft who is exonerated through service in the legion.[63] Despite so-called documentary sequences of Moroccan life and its major festivities, *Les Fils du soleil* celebrated "France and its sons as friends come to collaborate in a great civilizing mission."[64] The subject of redemption comes to the fore again in René Hervil's *Le Prince Jean* (1927), adapted from a Charles Méré play, which was set in the milieu of aristocratic gamblers.[65] But it assumes its clearest expression in Jean Renoir's *Le Bled*, which had a prestigious opening at the Salle Marivaux in June, 1929.[66]

Produced by the Société des Films Historiques, *Le Bled* (1929) was commissioned for the French government's centennial celebration of the conquest or pacification of Algeria. Its purpose was to encourage tourists and immigrants by propagandizing "the productive energy of Algeria in all its manifestations as well as the beauty of its landscapes."[67] With the Algerian government's full cooperation, Renoir's crew filmed in some of the country's principal tourist and commercial centers: the port of Algiers, the Bardo Gardens, the Mitidja Plains, a model farm at Staoueli, and the desert around Sidi Ferruch.[68] In fact, *Le Bled* opens with a documentary prologue of brief sequences (each tinted differently) depicting tourist sites, industrial plants, and various agricultural lands before focusing on Algiers, where the hero and heroine arrive on a ship from France.[69] The exploration of a large coastal farm allows an imaginary re-creation of the French colonization process: beginning with the 1830 landing of troops, who dissolve into marching soldiers in more and more modern uniforms (done in-camera with tracking shots), who in turn become plows and finally tractors that cover the fields (and overrun the camera) in a choreography of machines quite similar to that in Eisenstein's *The General Line* (1929).[70] This civilizing process is not complete, for the later sections of the film document the archaic but exciting falcon-hunting practices of the nomadic Arabs.

The scenario, written by Henri Dupuy-Mazel and André Jaeger-Schmidt, narrates the healthful (and economically enriching) effect of the country on a dissolute young Frenchman. Having dissipated his inheritance and his health in Paris, Pierre Hoffer (Enrique de Rivero) comes to Algeria to borrow money

78. Arquillière and Enrique
de Rivero in *Le Bled* (1929)

from an uncle (Arquillière) who has made a fortune in farming. The money is
promised on the condition that Pierre work the farm for six months. Claudie
Duvernet (Jackie Monnier), a young woman Pierre meets on the boat, simultaneously collects an inheritance, only to fall victim to a plot by her envious,
perfidious cousins (Manuel Raabi and Diana Hart). Pierre rescues her; they
marry and plan to remain in Algeria. As in *L'Atlantide*, the desert becomes
the locus of an ideological testing: the technical skills of French industry and
commerce and the moral/physical measure of the individual Frenchman. The
indigenous Arab population conventionally makes up part of the decor, with
two exceptions. Pierre's closest friend is Zoubier (Berardi Aïssa), an Algerian
he knew in the army; and in order to finally rescue Claudie, Pierre has to
resort to nomadic falconers whose birds blind the camel on which Manuel is
fleeing.[71] Although the villains are not Algerian, but lazy, disgruntled Frenchmen, the Algerians in the film all assent to this best-of-all-possible French
worlds. Yet, in 1929, the struggle for Algerian independence was but a few
years away.

There is a tongue-in-cheek quality about *Le Bled* that disconcerted some
critics at the time—and perhaps some audiences, for its success was only
moderate—a quality that now makes the film a bit interesting. Pierre is set
off from his uncle's milieu by a comedy of costumes: while everyone else sits
down to dinner in peasant garb, he comes down in Parisian evening clothes;
for a tour of the farm, he dresses in a sporting jacket, jodhpurs, and tie.
Through the simple juxtaposition of a ladle of mush and a cocktail shaker, he

is even associated with the villainous cousins. His romantic involvement with Claudie is as comic as it is serious. On the way to his uncle's farm, Pierre is nearly hit by Claudie's car—the accident throws them together in a kind of parodic embrace. Their actual discovery of mutual love is handled just as unconventionally. It happens out in the fields one day when, suddenly drenched by rain, they take shelter in a hut with several Algerian shepherds. Jacques Rivette has spoken of this moment as if it were already glistening with drop-lets from Renoir's later film, *The River* (1951),[72] but the realistic detail (and the allusion to Dido and Aeneas) creates, for me at least, a peculiar balance of the lyrical and the farcical. In the climactic chase, done with all the verve of American action films (and lots of tracking shots), the pursuit uses up cars, horses, camels, and finally falcons; and Pierre is miraculously transformed into an athletic Douglas Fairbanks. Then he and the villain flail about absurdly over the fainted Claudie much like McTeague and Marcus over the dead horse and the money at the end of Stroheim's *Greed* (1922). The grotesquerie turns to comedy again when a shot of a horizontal bar swaying back and forth near the rear end of a horse is cut into the final sequence, where hero and heroine sit together coyly on a barn swing. One could argue that *Le Bled* is just as much satire as celebration.

Although several of these films attempted to illustrate or undermine the division between cultures in the North African colonies, generally, the colonial film was ideologically quite comforting. As Pierre Boulanger has argued, the rigid hierarchy and repressive contradictions of the French social order were replaced by a fictional society simplified into "a caste of masters (large or small) and . . . a multitude of lesser men"[73]—who were either villains or just part of the decor. Here was a world where the dropout or prodigal son (who would become the dominant hero of the genre) could find "the magic ladder of assistance that would permit him to climb back into the social hierarchy that had been hostile or inhospitable to him in the metropolis."[74] Even in battles or intrigues with the villainous natives, a Frenchman could still find some measure of glory (which the Great War had obliterated with ghastly irony in France itself). By the end of the decade, the subject of the colonial film had coalesced into the "myth of redemption."[75] That myth would find its apoth-eosis in French films of the 1930s—films such as Feyder's *Le Grand Jeu* (1934) and Duvivier's *La Bandera* (1935).

Historical Reconstructions

One might expect that the French, with their rich legacy of history and many extant chateaux, along with their achievements in the genre of historical painting, would be pioneers in the development of period spectacle films or historical reconstructions. But such was not the case. In comparison to other national cinemas, in fact, the French came rather late to the genre.

Before the war the French had made just one briefly sustained attempt to develop a genre of historical reconstruction films. That was between 1910 and 1912, when Film d'Art, Film biblique, and S.C.A.G.L. (the latter two affil-iates of Pathé-Frères) produced a small number of feature-length, tableau-style period films among their literary adaptations. Three of the most successful of these exploited crucial periods in French history: the late medieval period—

Andréani's *Siège de Calais* (1911); the French Revolution—Pouctal's *Camille Desmoulins* (1912); and the mid-nineteenth century—Capellani's *Les Misérables* (1912).[1] The most famous, however, had a non-French subject—Desfontaines and Mercanton's *Queen Elizabeth* (1912), starring Sarah Bernhardt, for which Adolph Zukor and Edwin S. Porter raised sufficient money to distribute it widely across the United States.[2] Perhaps because its share of the world market was declining, the French film industry had already begun to scale back this kind of production when the war broke out in 1914 and curtailed it altogether.

It was the Italian cinema which virtually created and then dominated the historical reconstruction film genre before the war, with the earliest feature-length films that resurrected the exploits of ancient heroes against the backdrop of mass crowd movements and mammoth, elaborately constructed sets. Especially notable were De Liguoro's *Inferno* (1909), Guazzoni's *Quo vadis?* (1912), and Pastrone's *Cabiria* (1913), with its hero, the giant Maciste.[3] Under the influence of these films (as well as several of the French), the American cinema took up the genre in such films as Griffith's *Intolerance* (1916) and De Mille's *Joan the Woman* (1917) and *The Woman God Forgot* (1917). Under the same Italian influence, as well as that of Max Reinhardt's theatrical stagings, the German cinema produced a flood of historical films from 1919 to 1923-1924.[4] Especially prominent were Lubitsch's *Köstumfilmen: Madame Du Barry* (1919), *Sumurun* (1919), and *Anna Boleyn* (1920). All of these genre examples finally began to stimulate French interest again by 1919-1920. *Cabiria* and its sequels had an extended run in Paris after the original version opened at the Vaudeville Théâtre in 1915;[5] *Intolerance* was shown in Paris in the spring of 1919; in the United States, the German films were seen and remarked on by visiting French producers and filmmakers. The French interest, however, took a course rather different from that of the German and American.

There seem to have been at least two major reasons for what eventually became a heavy French investment of energy and capital in the historical reconstruction genre. One was frankly economic. Most of the prominent figures in the film industry were quickly convinced by the end of the war that the American superproductions now determined the course of world film production, distribution, and exhibition. In order to survive, even in their own cinema circuits, the French would have to engage as much as possible in large-scale productions—they would have to go beyond the budgets of their serials, bourgeois melodramas, and realist films. Such large-scale productions might also create the breakthrough that would allow them to reenter the lucrative American exhibition market. In his typically blunt fashion, Charles Pathé summed up the challenge: "the Americans will accept nothing from Europe but costume films, historical films."[6] And according to a *Cinémagazine* story (early in 1922), the success of the German historical films in breaking into the American market provided the French with a model.[7]

The other reason was ideological. Much like the realist film, but to an even greater degree, the historical reconstruction answered a postwar collective French need. If I may simplify matters, the war had brutally divested France of its ideological trappings, and the country found itself questioning its own collective identity.[8] By resurrecting past historical moments of French glory, and tragedy, the historical reconstruction film contributed to the process of national restoration and redefinition. The effect, as one might expect, was deeply nostalgic and often escapist. As Marc Silberman has argued with regard to the German costume film, the dominant tendency of these films was toward a mass spectacle that displaced the contemporary historical process.[9] This escapism did not sit easily with some in the narrative avant-garde wing of the French film industry. But for most, the period spectacle film provided an answer to the question, first raised by Louis Delluc, of what was peculiarly French about the French cinema. The fact that most French films in the genre were about French historical subjects clearly distinquished them from the more international subjects of their German and American counterparts.

When the first French period spectacle films appeared after the war, however, this was not yet apparent. Gérard Bourgeois's *Christophe Colomb*, for instance, which began production in 1916, was done in imitation of the Italian films. Shot mostly in Spain, supposedly using 40,000 extras (is that possible?) and costing 800,000 francs, it was finally released in two parts during the summer of 1919—and found a rather indifferent reception.[10] Louis Nalpas's six-part *Tristan et Yseult* (1920), directed by Maurice Mariaud from a Franz Toussaint scenario, met a similar response.[11] But, then, Nalpas had simply dispensed with the Atlantic mists and the oaks and granite of Cornwall and done it in the Italian manner on the Côte d'Azur.[12] The only major film with a French subject was Pouctal's serial adaptation of Dumas's *Le Comte de Monte-Cristo* (1918), which Film d'Art had been ready to put into production when the war intervened. Four years later, the project was revived and completed (with Léon Mathot starring) to become the most popular French film of the 1918-1919 season. Two years later, it was re-released to similar acclaim.[13] By 1921, then, partly because of the success of *Monte-Cristo*, the French film industry began to settle on specifically French historical reconstructions.

Two films that year established some standards for the genre. They were Dominique Bernard-Deschamps's *L'Agonie des aigles* and Henri Diamant-Berger's *Les Trois Mousquetaires* (the latter, though distributed as a serial, was premiered as three separate, sequential four-hour films). Both were produced by Pathé-Consortium, at unusually high budgets of two and two-and-a-half million francs, respectively. And both were given special gala premieres at the Salle de Trocadéro (which could hold 4,000 people), with high government officials in attendance. The publicity for and national sanction of these premieres were unprecedented in the French cinema. Moreover, Denis Richaud, the new director of Pathé-Consortium, boasted that these films would serve as an important instrument of education and socialization. "How excited we are to represent our history cinematographically, to reconstruct each period's architecture, costumes and manners, and, at the same time, recall the high points of our National Unity."[14]

Accordingly, *L'Agonie des aigles* was an explicitly political film. Adapted from the novel, *Demi-Solde*, by Georges d'Esparbès (who was the chief curator at Fontainebleau), it espoused the cause of Napoléon's followers in a conspiracy to restore his son as the Emperor of France (and as ruler of most of Europe).[15] The first half of the film narrates a secret meeting between the conspirators, led by Colonel Montander (Séverin-Mars), and Napoléon's son, the "Eaglet," in Austria, where the latter is confined. This meeting prompts a long flashback

162

THE STOLL FILM C⁰.
LIMITED

THE AGONY
OF THE EAGLES.
FILM DE FRANCE

79. A publicity photo of
Napoléon's farewell at
Fontainebleau in *L'Agonie des
aigles* (1921)

chronicling the last reigning years of Napoléon (also played by Séverin-Mars), which focuses on his farewell address to loyal troops at Fontainebleau. The second half narrates the betrayal of the conspiracy by an actress who has caught Montander's eye (Gaby Morlay, in one of her first major screen roles). In the end, the conspirators go proudly to their execution by a firing squad.

There are at least two points worth making about *L'Agonie des aigles*. One involves its royalist, ultra-conservative ideology which was attacked by the Socialist and Communist press and by some film journals, with justification, for at least two of Pathé-Consortium's financiers at the time were *Bloc national* members in the Chamber of Deputies.[16] But the ideology of the film's narrative is most interesting in the context of France's victory in World War I. In the film, the authority figure responsible for Napoléon's son's confinement is the German minister, Metternich. And the French fail to liberate him (once more, a woman is the traitor), to restore him as a symbol of the national spirit (historically, the boy wanted only to die in peace).[17] All the conspirators can

163

do is die nobly, defiantly—one combs his hair at the last moment, another blows his nose nonchalantly, a third turns to the wall so that his face (once kissed by the emperor) won't be disfigured. It is as if the conflicts of the Great War had been transposed a hundred years earlier, and the victory turned into a defeat. The old heroic gestures, rendered absurd by the real war, return in this reconstruction of past suffering (Henri Fescourt remembers this finale as very moving at the time).[18] L'Agonie des aigles, therefore, seems to represent, through a kind of displacement, the French mood of defeatism after the war. And it indirectly supported the Poincaré government's intransigent policy toward Germany, epitomized in the empty slogan: "Germany will pay!"

The second point concerns the film's discourse. Much of L'Agonie des aigles seems to have been shot in Pathé-Cinéma's old studio at Vincennes. In contrast to later historical reconstruction films, the studio work here is undistinguished, probably because of inadequate facilities. The sets are skimpy and uniform; the arc lighting is simple and disposed according to rather static character positions (for instance, Gance's Mater Dolorosa [1917] is much more sophisticated). In fact, the most interesting sequences are those shot on location—the farewell at Fontainebleau (involving mass troop movements before the famous chateau), the almost realistic executions at the end. Overall, the film has a repetitious, monotonous rhythm in which images often illustrate the frequent and lengthy intertitles, which actually produce most of the narrative. Sequences rely heavily on long shots—even extreme long shots—creating a static, tableau style of representation that evidences few of the advances made in filmmaking (even in France) during the previous five years. Cutting to and between medium shots and (rarely) close-ups is done without regard for consistent matches in eyeline or even in character position. Conventional literary symbols provide the film's only use of metaphor: the fallen eagle for Napoléon's defeat, a crashing oak tree for his death. In contrast to the other French film genres, consequently, the historical reconstruction seems quite regressive, at least initially, in its deployment of narrative film discourse.

At least one shot, however, raises a question about the conventions that then marked imaginary or subjective sequences. As Napoléon's son pores over a map of the world and dreams, there is a fade to a *negative* image of a group of cavalry riding across a plain. Finally, in the battery of fades, irises, and masks that mark off many shots and sequences, one moment at the end stands out: on the execution wall, above the heads of the conspirators, there appears the superimposition of a cavalry charge led by Napoléon—a reversal of the famous shot in Gance's 1919 *J'Accuse*, where (on the screen's top half) the French army marches through the Arc de Triomphe while (on the bottom half) the dead rise up from the battlefield in anger. Here, the soldiers in the firing squad hesitate at this apparition, and then put down their muskets; ironically, the Swiss Guard is ordered up to perform the executions. The gesture will reappear, in a very different conflict, in Eisenstein's *Potemkin* (1925).

Les Trois Mousquetaires offered another form of national inspiration and evasion with the mock-heroic rapiers of d'Artagnan and his companions. For three long months during the winter of 1921-1922, as this mammoth serial of seventeenth-century adventures swept through the country, the French could divert themselves from their mounting unemployment and inflation and from their government's constant bickering with England and the United States

80. Martinelli, Aimé Simon-Girard, Henri Rollan, and Marcel Vallée (left to right) in *Les Trois Mousquetaires* (1921-1922)

about German reparations.[19] For the development of the period spectacle film, neither the serial format nor the staid, monotonous rhythm and theatrical mis-en-scène of Diamant-Berger's film (which complemented *L'Agonie des aigles* only too well) was particularly crucial. Slightly more important were its narrative of intrigue piled upon intrigue and its well-chosen cast: Aimé Simon-Girard (D'Artagnan), Armand Bernard (Planchet), Henri Rollin (Athos), Martinelli (Porthos), Marcel Vallée (Aramis), Edouard de Max (Cardinal Richelieu), Charles Dullin (Père Joseph), Claude Mérelle (Milady de Winter). However, *Les Trois Mousquetaires* differed sharply from its sister production in at least two ways—ways that would much affect the genre.

As if he were following the precepts of Antoine, Mercanton, Delluc, and others, Diamant-Berger decided to shoot most of his film on location.[20] In the once-fortified city of Pérouges, near Lyon, he and his cameraman Maurice Desfassiaux found streets and alleys that could represent old Paris. The chateaux of Périgueux, Chenonceau, Azay-le-Rideau, and Chissay served as royal quarters for the English and French. The church at Montbazon held the wedding of Milady and Athos; Chartres cathedral provided the backdrop for a major duel; and the port of Coisic functioned as both Boulogne and Dover. Finally, on a tract of land near Pathé-Cinéma's studio at Vincennes, Diamant-Berger constructed Richelieu's camp at La Rochelle and the fortifications of Saint-Gervais. The result was that *Les Trois Mousquetaires* gained, along with the picturesqueness of its landscapes, some measure of authenticity that turned it into a gigantic pageant celebrating seventeenth-century France. The effect would not be lost on later filmmakers. Furthermore, Diamant-Berger assigned

Robert Mallet-Stevens—"the uncontested master of the young school of French architecture"—to construct decors and costumes for the interior shooting at the Vincennes studio.[21] Diamant-Berger himself remembers that

Mallet-Stevens . . . was enthusiastic about the Musketeers; we stylized the decors and costumes, deciding on a clean, simple, unadorned figure, quite the opposite of the Louis XIII style, which was rather well known and "unappetizing." For the court costumes, we used furniture velour because its stiffness gave them an imposing look.[22]

All this was designed to be spectacular and also to allow for some fast-paced action. There were those, of course, who were not impressed. Ricciotto Canudo, for one, ridiculed the film as a travesty of "four swaggering petty officers caught up in drunken revelries, badly mounted horseback rides, and an unspeakable naval battle allegedly before La Rochelle but actually filmed in the pools of the Luxembourg Gardens!"[23]

In his second adaptation from Dumas, *Vingt Ans après* (1922),[24] Diamant-Berger added a new element to this combination of exterior and interior shooting, again with Desfassiaux and Mallet-Stevens. This was an enormous set construction outside the studio, of which the filmmaker is still immensely proud.

In the huge Niepce and Fetterer factory yard at Billancourt, which furnished us plywood for the decors, we "constructed" the facade of Notre-Dame de Paris, up to the height of the King's Gallery. . . .

I was going to film the Te Deum given by the queen in honor of the battle at Lens; on the occasion of this ceremony, the Paris mutineers tried to disrupt the royal cortege in order to seize the King. . . . I collected 3,000 extras [for the scene]. . . . I placed ten cameras along the course. A telephone system allowed me, while perched on a platform, from which I could control the action, to order in sequence the different groups of demonstrators to shout and throw rocks . . . made of cork.[25]

From the technical point of view, Diamant-Berger told André Lang, *Vingt Ans après* was even better than *Les Trois Mousquetaires*.[26] But both films were important. In their emphasis on numerous location sites, on expensive breathtaking set constructions and costumes, on ritualistic pageantry involving great masses of people, on intrigues or conflicts that could be resolved in the action of battle, they laid the foundations of the French historical reconstruction film genre.

Still, the French film industry hesitated to commit itself completely. Small-scale adaptations of classic nineteenth-century fiction continued in favor. Pathé-Consortium, for instance, assigned Antoine to film an adaptation of a Jules Sandeau novel, *Mlle. de la Seiglière* (1921), starring Huguette Duflos, Romauld Joubé, and Charles Lamy.[27] His son says that Antoine accepted only because he was interested in re-creating, in a chateau near Paris, "a sense of daily life in the eighteenth century in a certain [aristocratic] milieu."[28] *Ciné-magazine* found the result meticulously accurate in its details, certainly lovely to look at, but rather static and old-fashioned in style.[29] Film d'Art, likewise, assigned Baroncelli to direct low-budget films drawn from Zola and Balzac novels. Antoine roundly condemned *Le Rêve* (1921) because Film d'Art constructed a cheap cathedral facade for Baroncelli rather than let him shoot on location.[30] But *Le Rêve* was unusually popular—it played for almost a year in and around Paris—and briefly made Andrée Brabant a star.[31] Less successful was Baroncelli's *Père Goriot* (1921), starring Signoret. Still, Georges Sadoul remembers that it reconstructed quite accurately the novel's shabby Vauquier pension.[32] As I mentioned earlier, Baroncelli's film was the first of a series of low-budget adaptations of Balzac novels. Of these, one deviates radically enough from its genre conventions to be set aside for later discussion—Jean Epstein's *L'Auberge rouge* (1923).

Perhaps the reason for what seemed to be industry hesitation lay in the internal changes that forced the scaling back of film production at both Film d'Art and Pathé-Consortium in 1922. Certainly one direct consequence was that Diamant-Berger's third adaptation of Dumas never got beyond the preparation stage. But other companies quickly took up the slack, and at least two films seem to have convinced the industry to pursue the large-scale production of period spectacle films. Both were released early in 1923, in conjunction with the Paris premiere of Douglas Fairbanks's *Robin Hood* (with its magnificent sets by Wilfred Buckland), and that film's extraordinary popularity in France must have confirmed the industry's commitment.[33]

When Aubert plunged into film production in 1922, his company's biggest project was René Le Somptier's *La Dame de Monsoreau* (1923).[34] This six-part adaptation of yet another Dumas novel was calculated to exploit the interest generated by Diamant-Berger's two films. It was released close on the heels of *Vingt Ans après* and received an unusual publicity buildup that included a full issue of *Cinémagazine*.[35] Furthermore, it was distributed in a stencil-tinted version that often processed two or three colors within a single frame. The print of *La Dame de Monsoreau* that survives at the Cinémathèque française is a revelation—it is both breathtakingly gorgeous and incredibly dull.[36] Le Somptier and his cameraman Amédée Morin rely heavily on LSs of landscapes, chateau exteriors and interiors, and a parade of costumes to produce one spectacular tableau after another. And he sustains the tableaux with a simple continuity editing similar to that in *L'Agonie des aigles*. Finally, he tells his story almost completely in the intertitles, and their absence in the surviving print quickly renders the film incomprehensible—Geneviève Félix, Gina Manès, Jean d'Yd, and the other actors become so many mannequins drifting about in a brightly colored museum. Story and spectacle are kept strictly separate; the latter does not merely illustrate the former, sometimes it literally overpowers it with a nostalgic resurrection of the genre of historical painting.

Even more crucial in spurring the industry's commitment to historical reconstructions was a Paramount production, Henry Roussel's *Les Opprimés*, one of the most popular films of the 1922-1923 season.[37] Roussel's story of a spunky sixteenth-century Flanders girl apparently was not unlike opera, with flamboyant gestures, elaborate costumes, and passionate characters placed in schematic oppositions.[38] Wrote Canudo,

The austerity and implacable arrogance of the Duke of Albe; the goodness of the provost marshal whose daughter, Conception, falls in love with Philippe de Hornes, a young Flemish patriot; the diplomatic generosity of Don Luis de Zuniga, the King's ambassador and suitor to Conception, who in the end marries her to the young patriot—all are worked skillfully into an intrigue of persecution and passion embroidered onto a background of suffering and thundering revolt by an oppressed people.[39]

The film's real surprise, however, was the Spanish singer-actress, Raquel Meller,

167

81. Huguette Duflos in a
Boué Soeurs gown in
Koenigsmark (1923)

whose performance as Conception made her an immediate star, almost on the level of an Asta Nielsen. According to the French film journals, *Les Opprimés* was a magisterial reconstruction of Flanders during the reign of Philip II and demonstrated to the world that the French, too, could make successful large-scale films.[40] Still, that it should be made with American money piqued the French a bit. Besides, its appearance also happened to coincide with the belated release in France of Lubitsch's "scandalous" treatment of French history in *Madame Du Barry* (1919).[41]

Within a year, the French film industry produced no less than three major films that consolidated the conventions and confirmed the new status of the historical reconstruction genre. The appearance of these films coincided with Cinéromans' revival of the costume adventure serial that celebrated historical figures as their heroes. However, the characteristics of the historical reconstruction films set them off distinctly from the smaller-budgeted Cinéromans' productions. Those characteristics can be summarized as follows: 1) a subject calling for the reconstruction of an historical period (usually French and aristocratic); 2) elaborate, sumptuous, authentic decors and costumes; 3) a narrative that emphasizes climactic set pieces—of dazzling tableaux and/or sensational sweeping action; and 4) major stars in the leading roles.

82. Jaque Catelain and
Huguette Duflos in a
Ménessier interior in
Koenigsmark (1923)

The most successful of these films was Léonce Perret's *Koenigsmark* (1923).
An independent production (though Paramount may have been involved in its
financing behind the scenes), *Koenigsmark* was a very calculated project.[42] Perret capitalized on the success of *L'Atlantide* by adapting his scenario from
another best-selling novel by Pierre Benoit which had just been translated into
several languages. At the film's premiere at the Salle Marivaux, in December,
1923, he predicted confidently that it would have a worldwide success—and
it did.[43] The subject was a tragic French-German romance between a young
poet-tutor, Vignerte (Jaque Catelain), and Princesse Aurore (Huguette Duflos)
in a small German court on the eve of World War I (displaced slightly by
involving the Austrian, not the Prussian, aristocracy). After discovering a
mysterious crime committed by the grand duke (her father) years before, the
couple flee to France where Vignerte enlists as a pilot in the war and is killed
in combat. Perret carefully suppressed all the later war scenes in the novel, in
order to emphasize the prewar court spectacle and intrigue and to allow for a
bittersweet epilogue at the French tomb of the unknown soldier, where Princesse Aurore (with "six drops of glycerine on the edge of her eyelids") could
whisper, "Perhaps it is he!"[44]

Although certain elements align it with another film genre, the emerging

83. Raquel Meller in *Violettes
impériales* (1924)

modern studio spectacular, *Koenigsmark* is principally an historical reconstruction, intent on recreating an aristocratic period that had just been obliterated
by the war. Much of the film was shot on location in Bavaria, taking advantage
of "the romantic decor of a feudal chateau"; but Perret and his set designer,
Henri Ménessier, also used Levinsky's new Joinville studio to create several
lavish interiors.[45] Baldly put, the film was nothing less than a showcase for
grand spectacle (the discovery of the skeleton in the gothic fireplace, the burning of the chateau, the Court Ball, the hunt, the marriage banquet on Montmartre); extravagant costumes by the Boué Soeurs (demonstrating that Paris
was indeed the capital of fashion); and France's number-one star at the time,
Huguette Duflos.[46] As Léon Moussinac admitted, along with Aubert's naval
epic starring Sessue Hayakawa, *La Bataille* (1923), *Koenigsmark* provided the
industry with a model for French superproductions:

Such successes are encouraging not only for the producers of French films but also for
the investors. Certainly these are super-films worthy of the name [they can say]. . . .
They will re-invigorate [the industry] and give us mastery of the whole world.[47]

The readers of *Cinémagazine* confirmed its stature by naming *Koenigsmark* the
best film, by far, of 1923.[48]

170

Following *Koenigsmark*'s three-month run at the Salle Marivaux came Henry Roussel's second big film with Raquel Meller, *Violettes impériales* (1924).[49] Also independently produced, it, too, was a cleverly calculated operetta-style project, much like *Les Opprimés*. At the time, "Raquel Meller had made a popular song, 'Violettera,' so much her own that the mass public no longer saw her as anything but a melodious flower girl."[50] So Roussel's scenario contrived to place the singer as a simple flower-seller named Violetta in the period of the Second Empire.[51] In Seville, Violetta is rescued from a life of petty thievery by Eugénie de Montijo de Guzman (Suzanne Bianchetti), who, three years later, marries Napoléon III. Taken to Paris and given a career at the Opéra, Violetta falls in love with Count Saint-Affremond (André Roanne) but must abandon her suitor to save Eugénie from scandal in a court intrigue. Later, she learns that her brother Manuel (San-Juana) has become part of a plot to blackmail and kill the empress. Refusing to betray him and unable to divert Eugénie, Violetta employs a ruse to take her place in the royal carriage and sacrifices herself instead.

A narrative of regeneration and of almost Corneillan sacrifice, *Violettes impériales* was also a nostalgic return to a milieu of luxury and splendor long since past. The location shooting took Roussel, Jules Kruger (his chief cameraman), and his cast from the sun-drenched streets and peasant dwellings of Seville to the magnificent ceremonial receptions at Compiègne and in the Tuilleries. Critics were especially impressed with the scrupulous reconstruction of the pageantry:

. . . the scenes that the filmmaker has shot in the actual locations, inspired at one moment by a famous painting by Winterhalter, are full of such freshness that they can be counted among the most gracious tableaux that we have been privileged to admire on the screen.[52]

"But beyond these photogenic seductions," added Henri Fescourt, "the luminescence that emanated from the film . . . derived above all from the presence of Raquel Meller."[53]

The third film was an expensive production from Films Albatros, the company organized around the Russian emigré film colony in Paris. Previously, Albatros had been known for its serials, Arabian Nights fantasies, and satirical comedies. Now came Alexandre Volkoff's *Kean*, released in February, 1924.[54] Its subject was the last years of Edmund Kean, the illustrious English Shakespearean actor, and the historical period was 1830 London. The star was one of the more popular French film actors at the time, Ivan Mosjoukine. A mercurial actor, Mosjoukine made Kean one of his most successful film roles, playing him as a multifaceted character who envisioned and lived life-as-theater. Like most French film historians, René Jeanne and Charles Ford consider this film "the high point of the collaboration between Volkoff and Mosjoukine [and cameraman J.-P. Mundviller] as well as of the Albatros productions."[55] *Cinéa-Ciné-pour-tous*'s readers agreed by voting it the third best film of 1924, just ahead of *Violettes impériales*.[56]

The scenario for *Kean* was adapted from Dumas père's *fils*'s, written for the famous French actor, Frédérick Lemaître, just three years after Kean's death; unlike its source, however, it ends in tragedy or, more accurately, in bathos.[57] In the opening sequences, during a performance of *Romeo and Juliet*, Kean falls

171

84. Nicolas Koline and Ivan
Mosjoukine in the Coaly Hole
tavern in *Kean* (1924)

in love with one of his admirers, the Countess de Koeleld (Natalie Lissenko),
the wife of the Danish ambassador to England. But he is in no condition to
carry on such a love affair. Hounded by creditors, Kean and Solomon (Nicolas
Koline), his good friend and servant, have to disguise themselves as a sailor
boy and his mother (after Solomon has done a neat turn as a tiger) in order to
escape to Hyde Park (where the countess rides by on horseback and says,
tauntingly, she prefers him as Romeo). At the Coaly Hole tavern, the two
men drink themselves silly, burn up the floor with several jigs and dances,
and fall asleep until morning. Soon after, in back-to-back intrigues, Kean has
to save the reputation of a young woman, Anna Damby (Mary Odette), who
is infatuated with him, and then has to suffer an apparent rejection (of his
roses) by the countess, while he is carousing at a men's club. When his rival
for her love, the Prince de Galles (Otto Detlefren), appears with the count
and countess in the theater box one night, Kean becomes enraged and breaks
off his performance in *Hamlet* to insult them. The count protects his wife (and
keeps her from reaching the actor), and when the crowd boos and yells at him,
Kean collapses on stage. In a long coda, he retires from the theater, ill and
penniless, holes up in Solomon's run-down cottage on the outskirts of London,
and wastes away. There, of course, the countess comes to confess her love just
before he dies.

From its opening, *Kean* displays an especially effective classical continuity
style of editing—the admiring glances of more than a half-dozen women in
the theater audience are integrated clearly into the space of Kean's performance
in *Romeo and Juliet*. And the performances of Mosjoukine, Koline, Lissenko,

172

85. Ivan Mosjoukine as Kean
dying in *Kean* (1924)

and Odette are strong and affecting throughout. It is surprising, therefore, that the film's handling of the two Shakespeare plays is so mundane. So undistinguished are these moments that an intertitle has to tell us that Kean (and Mosjoukine) is a marvelous Hamlet. But the choice of the plays performed resonates aptly in the narrative. The actor first sees the countess—an exchange of privileged looks initiate his tragic desire—during the balcony scene between the star-crossed lovers. And he breaks down, mad with envy and grief, during Hamlet's tirade to Ophelia on marriage. What seems to have struck the French reviewers and audiences most about these moments, however, was the illusion of being in the old Drury Lane Theater. This, one of the major spectacles of the film, owed much to the work of Albatros's chief set designer, Ivan Lochakoff. In the old Montreuil studio, Lochakoff meticulously reconstructed the interior of the Drury Lane Theater (from designs and photographs he found in the Bibliothèque nationale).[58] "Its dimensions {were} enormous," wrote *Cinémagazine*, "twelve meters high, and twenty-five meters long. It {was} perfectly furnished: loges, boxes, gallery fans; nothing was missing."[59]

The moments accepted as classic set pieces by the ciné-clubs, however, were the final sequence of Kean's death and the night-long carousing in the Coaly Hole tavern.[60] Viewed today, Kean's dying seems to go on interminably—much like Hernani's, Jeanne and Ford confess.[61] Only Mosjoukine's restrained acting in MCU and CU, as well as the intercut exterior shot of several frail trees whipped about in the wind, save the sequence from falling completely into bathos. The Coaly Hole sequence is something else again. Kean's drunken dancing is described in ensemble shots (where several black sailors are prominent), hand-held CUs, shots of a dog and cat backing off, swish pans, all of which are edited together in a rhythmic montage that changes according to his emotional state, accelerating at several points into short bursts of rapid cutting. At the end, a pattern of subjective inserts culminates in several superimpositions of the countess on horseback riding (almost threateningly) toward him. Later, in a parallel sequence at the men's club, Kean's hallucinations reach a feverish climax. Told of the countess's rejection (the long-take CU of his reaction is marvelously poignant), he drunkenly imagines a distorted version in which his gift of roses is scorned and crushed, and then he is confronted by superimpositions of his rival and the countess (culminating in ECUs of her mouth) that seem to fill the room. If anything in *Kean* deviates from the conventions of the historical reconstruction genre, it is certainly these sequences in the Coaly Hole and the men's club.

The impressive interior decors of *Koenigsmark* and *Kean* raise an intriguing point about the development of the historical reconstruction film in France. Its elevation to prominence in French film production coincides with and probably derives from a major change in set design. According to Léon Barsacq, it was not until about 1922 that a technical evolution in film scenery freed the set decorators from *trompe-d'oeil* painting and other conventions of *fin-de-siècle* theater so that a new group of architect-designers could enter the profession. "In general," Barsacq adds, "through their exacting demands and their achievements, the Russian designers [especially] contributed to raising the status of film designers to one of close collaboration with directors."[62] Interestingly, the newcomers were not employed by the older production companies of Pathé-Consortium, Gaumont, Aubert, and Film d'Art. Instead they were made important members of recently established, often independent companies: Diamant Films had Mallet-Stevens; Films Albatros had Lochakoff, Boris Bilinsky, and later Lazare Meerson; the Société des Films Historiques also had Mallet-Stevens. One can argue, I think, that the work of these architect-designers was a key factor in the success of the historical reconstruction genre, as it would be later in that of the modern studio spectacular.

This change in set design, among other things, clearly differentiates the two major period films of the 1924-1925 season: Raymond Bernard's *Le Miracle des loups* (1924) and Germaine Dulac's *Le Diable dans la ville* (1925). Both, interestingly enough, are set in the fifteenth century.

The source for *Le Diable dans la ville* was an original scenario by Jean-Louis Bouquet, entitled *La Ville des fous*.[63]

> The story involved a case of sudden terror that seized an entire village. . . . This contagious fear was provoked by inexplicable phenomena that superstition soon attributed to the devil. The mystery was explained by the presence of a happy band of robbers who, haunting the underground caverns of the old town, duped the inhabitants in their houses at nightfall . . . for their own profit.[64]

Initially, the setting and time were to have been unspecified (yet modern), but the Cinéromans producers convinced Dulac that a fifteenth-century French village would provide a properly plausible context. Because it was a moderately budgeted Films de France production at Cinéromans, the film was shot by an undistinguished cameraman, Stuckert, entirely in the studio, using rather old-fashioned stock sets and costumes by Pathé-Consortium's chief set designer, Quenu.[65] The resulting "démodé" look fails to mesh with Dulac's emphasis on cinematic rhythm (sometimes to the point of abstraction), and both vitiate the narrative's satire and social criticism. In fact, one could argue, as Dulac herself did, that *Le Diable dans la ville* is really not a period spectacle film at all.[66]

By contrast, the Russian-emigré-financed Société de Films Historiques decided to make *Le Miracle des loups* the most expensive historical reconstruction ever mounted by the French film industry. The director, Raymond Bernard, confessed that he was stunned by the project:"I had the possibility of employing means that had never been used up to that time in France."[67] For example, in the newly renovated Levinsky studios at Joinville-le-pont, he and Mallet-Stevens reconstructed the spectacle of a medieval mystery play with "more than a thousand extras."[68] For the siege of Beauvais, actually filmed in the fortified city of Carcassonne (which André Antoine apparently convinced the producers to use rather than studio decors),[69] Bernard said,

every morning I had four thousand people ready in costumes; I had hundreds of horses in period harnesses; I shot with fourteen or fifteen cameras and usually one of my assistants [including Maurice Forster and Daniau-Johnson] was behind each camera. . . . I myself remained above the battlefield . . . in the place where I could see everything.[67]

Le Miracle des loups became a national event when the producers arranged for its premiere, along with a special orchestral accompaniment composed by Henri Rabaud, at the Paris Opéra, on 13 November 1924.[71] Presiding over the event was the president of the Republic, and in the audience were his ministers, the diplomatic corps, and celebrities in the arts and sciences from around the world. It was "a stunning success," wrote one film journal, "a veritable official consecration of the cinématographe."[72] Within two weeks, the film opened a three-and-a-half month *exclusivité* run at the Salle Marivaux.[73] One year later, the readers of *Cinéa-Ciné-pour-tous* voted it the best film of 1925 (topping Chaplin's *The Pilgrim*, Fairbanks's *Thief of Bagdad*, and De Mille's *The Ten Commandments*).[74]

The subject of *Le Miracle des loups*, adapted by André-Paul Antoine from Henry Dupuy-Mazuel's novel, took French audiences back to a period when their own national unity was being forged.[75] The time was 1461-1472, the historic years of conflict between Louis XI (played by the famous Atelier actor, Charles Dullin) and his brother, the Duke of Bourgogne, Charles le Téméraire (Vanni Marcoux)—a conflict that was mediated and resolved, according to legend, by the figure of Jeanne Hachette (Yvonne Sergyl) and "the miracle of the wolves." The film opens with an epigraph from Michelet: "History is a resurrection" (written in a stylized medieval script, as are most of the intertitles). Then a prologue establishes Charles's desire for the crown and the mutual love between Jeanne and one of Charles's noblemen, Robert Cottereau (Romauld Joubé). However, another of his retinue, de Lau (Gaston Modot), is also enamored of Jeanne and plots her abduction during the performance of the mystery play. Louis XI foils the plot and wins Jeanne's allegiance, but Charles breaks off with him, and Robert dutifully has to follow his master. This antagonism between brothers leads to an indecisive battle at Montlhery (during which Robert saves Charles from death) and an uneasy truce. Soon, however, Charles comes to believe that Louis is guilty of inciting an insurrection against him at Liège and makes him a virtual prisoner at Perrone. Jeanne and her father set out to help Louis (with a document proving his innocence); but de Lau pursues them, kills the old man, and chases Jeanne through the snowbound mountains into a pack of wolves, who miraculously ignore her and attack him and his men. Upon reaching Perrone, she and Robert stay Charles

86. The siege of Beauvais in
Le Miracle des loups (1924)

from ordering Louis's death. Several years later, Charles's army, led by Robert
and de Lau (who alone survived the wolves), attacks the city of Beauvais where
Jeanne is now living. She rallies the peasants and townspeople, but they are
driven back into the cathedral tower, which is set afire. Robert unknowingly
wounds Jeanne and then defends her against de Lau in a duel that takes them
to the tower ramparts, where de Lau falls to his death. Remembering Robert's
service to him in the past, Charles refuses to kill the reunited couple, and
Louis's army finally arrives to put him to flight. Louis, at last, is undisputed
king.

The legend of Jeanne Hachette bears a striking resemblance to that of Jeanne
d'Arc (even Louis here corresponds to Charles VII, his father), and the film's
phenomenal success probably inspired the production of two later historical
reconstructions: Carl Dreyer's *La Passion de Jeanne d'Arc* (1928) and Marco de
Gastyne's *La Merveilleuse Vie de Jeanne d'Arc* (1929). However, here the characters are probably more interesting in the context of earlier films such as
L'Agonie des aigles and *Violettes impériales*. Except for his inadvertent foiling of
de Lau's plot and his brief leadership during the battle of Montlhery, Louis is
a strangely passive, meditative king, not at all like the ruthless, prevaricating
historical figure. In one of the best film performances of the decade, Charles
Dullin plays him like an older, laid-back Hamlet or a milder, gentler Richard
II (in two sequences with Charles, he adopts a mocking half-supercilious, half-
subservient attitude, and he is fascinated by objects of power and by his own
powerlessness).[76] Much like Napoléon's son in *L'Agonie des aigles*, his function
in the film is not to restore but to be restored. Three times, Robert and
Jeanne, separately and then together, save him from defeat and death. Even
more than Louis perhaps, Jeanne at Beauvais incarnates the spirit of France—
a feminine replication of Jeanne d'Arc or of Delacroix's goddess of liberty
during the Revolution. But she, too, must be saved twice, first by a kind of
divine intervention in the miracle of the wolves and then by her lover-antag-
onist. No conflict of nations, of classes, here. Instead, a civil conflict of brother
against brother, of fiancé against fiancée, that is resolved by the code of suffering and sacrifice. If this is the French equivalent of the American *Birth of
a Nation*, the royalist conclusion is unexpectedly muted, but historically prescient. Sitting alone before a chessboard, Louis grabs the king, impulsively
sweeps all the other pieces away, and, smiling, plumps his piece down in the
center of the board. But his final gesture is to raise one hand anxiously to his
neck as his face takes on a quizzical, disturbed expression. Does he know where
the monarchy will end?

Much like *Koenigsmark* and *Violettes impériales*, Bernard's film was a showcase
for spectacle. But here, I would argue, it is integrated even more effectively
into the narrative. The first battle of Montlhery is brief but shockingly realistic—and looks ahead to Gance's *Napoléon* (1927), Orson Welles's *Chimes at
Midnight* (1966), and Kevin Brownlow's *Winstanley* (1976). In a succession of
graphic shots, the film catalogues nearly a dozen different ways that the armored horsemen and foot soldiers are wounded or killed. Its effect is registered
immediately by Louis's hasty signing of the treaty. Although slightly extended
in length, the attack of the wolves is also presented in realistic detail—with
MCUs and CUs of the wolves gripping and tearing at the men's bloody necks
and faces. Henri Fescourt, for one, criticized the sequence for failing to convey

87. Mallet-Stevens's interior
for the Beauvais Cathedral
tower in *Le Miracle des loups*
(1924)

the moment of grace; and the means are rather mechanical: horizontal frame
maskings simply shift from black to white.[77] But there is a rhetorical rightness
at the end in the juxtaposition of a CU of de Lau's bloody face (the predator
has become prey) and an ELS of Jeanne running off across a vast snow-covered
valley.

The climactic siege of Beauvais is a set piece of spectacular action, staged
on a scale clearly reminiscent of the Babylon section of *Intolerance*. The sequence is orchestrated clearly, vividly, using an unusual variety of shots (from
ELSs, looking past the defenders on the wall toward the attackers swarming
over a small hill, to MCUs of a cannon firing or a woman protecting her
child); and it shifts the narrative focus smoothly from army versus army, to
small group versus small group, to Robert versus Jeanne, then to Robert
versus de Lau (all the while intercutting Charles's soldiers pillaging the town
as well as Louis's soldiers advancing). For the interiors of Louis's court, of
Charles's rooms at Perrone, of Beauvais's cathedral tower, "Mallet-Stevens
eliminated all unnecessary details: splendid, shiny floors and high fireplaces
are the only visually rich areas."[78] The effect was to create a regal but almost
monastic space for Louis and, in the Beauvais cathedral, to conjure up a kind
of magical emblem—a LS of two armored knights poised over the wounded
Jeanne in a high-ceilinged, shimmering, debris-filled chamber.

The film employs metaphor sparingly but effectively—as in Louis's swift,
then suddenly hesitant, gestures over the chessboard at the end or in his
paradoxical behavior at the beginning—greeting Charles with open brother-

liness and then teasingly shooting a crossbow arrow into the shield of his coat of arms. The most extended sequence that relies on metaphor is that of the elaborately staged early mystery play, *The Game of Adam* (strangely reminiscent of a Méliès fantasy film). As the stage serpent seduces Eve who seduces Adam with the apple (and their clothes drop off), in a side room, Charles sends de Lau outside to bring Jeanne to him. Nimble, cavorting devils push Adam and Eve to the huge dragon mouth of hell, and Jeanne stands before Charles, who orders her to go with de Lau. As she struggles to resist, the king's crown which is nearby falls to the floor, and Louis (who has also been watching the play) suddenly enters the side room. In an economical, measured, dramatically charged montage of shots, Louis looks at de Lau, at the crown, at Charles, and then seizes the crown before his brother can reach it. As he does so, one of his retinue pulls back a curtain, and the crowd stands to face this new side stage that has displaced the mystery play. Slowly, pointedly, the king addresses his antagonist (in an intertitle): "Crowns are like women." And as Charles kneels obediently before him, Louis mischievously raises the crown to his brother's head, only to grab it back. Thoughtfully, he rubs one of the jewels and laughs: "It's cracked!" Charles stares, and the people realize that war is at hand. It is a marvelous moment, worthy of the Shakespeare it echoes—*Richard II* (Act IV, scene i)—and suggests perhaps better than any other sequence how effectively *Le Miracle des loups* works even today.

After 1924, the genre of historical reconstruction seems to have developed along two different lines. In part, these developments were linked to the *Cartel des gauches* policies which encouraged the strategy of international co-productions. But they were also determined by rival groups within the French film industry. One group had its base in the Paramount production center in Paris. It included Léonce Perret and Henry Roussel (producer-directors who had already worked for Paramount), Robert Hurel (a former Paramount producer who founded Franco-Film with Perret), and Bernard Natan (an ambitious speculator with ties to Paramount, who built his own studio and eventually took over Pathé-Consortium). Most of the period spectacle films this group produced had one thing in common—they focused on a major historical figure in the period just before or after the French Revolution.

The first of these films was Perret's second blockbuster, *Madame Sans-Gêne* (1925), which opened at the Salle Marivaux in December, 1925.[79] This Paramount production was made, during the winter of 1924-1925, largely because of Gloria Swanson. The central role of the famous Sardou play, written originally for Réjane, appealed greatly to the American actress.[80] She enlisted the aid of film critic André Daven to persuade the French film industry and government to accept the project, whose support in turn convinced Paramount to accept her wishes. Ostensibly, the subject of the film was not unlike that of *Violettes impériales*: a woman's ascent from washerwoman to marshal's wife and finally to duchess. Actually, write René Jeanne and Charles Ford, Paramount gave Perret a 14-million-franc budget to "Americanize" the play and make "something appropriately gorgeous for Gloria Swanson."[81] A good percentage of that money went to the nouveau-riche costumes designed by René Hubert and to a month of location shooting at Compiègne and Fontainebleau.[82]

179

All of France with its artistic and historical resources was mobilized to serve the star. Having at his disposal the huge Henri II gallery at the Fontainebleau palace, how could Léonce Perret resist the temptation to add a cortege of five hundred extras in court regalia and set off a fireworks display over a pool of carp, since they were there, awaiting the pleasure of the cameraman? . . . Here the rich, intricately balanced work of Victorien Sardou disappeared under a mass of ornaments. . . .[83]

Yet *Madame Sans-Gêne* received a tumultuous reception at its Paris premiere; it won the Jury Grand Prix at the 1925 Exposition des Arts Décoratifs; and Gloria Swanson still considers it one of the best films in which she appeared.[84] Although some French critics denigrated Perret's work as no more than "a charming armchair fantasy," others described it as the first great film of the French-American collaboration.[85] Their reaction was complicated by the fact that the shortened American version of the film was released six months earlier than the French and received far less glowing reviews.[86]

Another quite similar historical tableau was *Madame Récamier* (1928), which Gaston Ravel directed for Franco-Film. To mount the story of the most brilliant salon hostess of the early Napoleonic years as well as of the Restoration period, Ravel took his large cast and crew to the actual historical sites of the action: the Folie de Saint-James park, the Coppet chateau, and, of course, Fountainebleau.[87] The story begins during the Terror of 1793, when Juliette Bernard (Marie Bell) becomes the young wife of the wealthy M. Récamier (Victor Vina).[88] The marriage is a chaste one because Récamier is actually Juliette's father who has decided to atone for his past affair with her mother (Madeleine Rodriguez). Mme. de Staël (Françoise Rosay) soon becomes a good friend of Mme. Récamier and spirits her off to Germany when Napoléon and his minister Fouché (Van Daële) threaten her life. There she falls in love with a Prussian prince (François Rozet); but, when her aging husband refuses a divorce, she sacrifices her love and returns dutifully to him. This whole story is a long flashback, framed by an evening late in the life of Mme. Récamier (Nelly Corman) as she discreetly explains to her close friend, Chateaubriand (Charles de Bargy), why she cannot marry him. René Jeanne remembers Ravel's film as respectful, tasteful, but, unfortunately, not particularly satisfying.[89]

Perhaps the most interesting thing about *Madame Récamier* was its source and the timing of its production. Ravel drew his adaptation from a biography by Edouard Herriot, the prominent leader of the Radical-Socialist party, former prime minister (in 1924), and current minister of art and education. Shot late in 1927, *Madame Récamier* was premiered at the Opéra, on 12 June 1928, just after the spring national elections—which the Radical-Socialists lost.[90] It also followed the Herriot Decree (in February), which adopted a very weak quota system for the importation of films into France. This conjunction of events raises some interesting questions. Did either Herriot or Franco-Film consider the film as a political instrument before the elections? Was Franco-Film soliciting the minister's favor, for themselves or for the film industry in general? Whatever, the film was successful enough for Ravel to nearly repeat its subject in a celebrated, but mediocre, sonorized version of Dumas's *Le Collier de la reine* the following year.[91]

"The mystery of the queen's necklace" was also the subject of *Cagliostro* (1929), an Albatros-Wengeroff (French-German) production based on Dumas's

88. Gloria Swanson in a
Fontainebleau interior in
Madame Sans-Gêne (1925)

novel, *Joseph Balsamo*.[92] Jules Kruger and Jean Dréville shot the film in Paris, under the direction of the German *metteur-en-scène*, Richard Oswald.[93] In it, Cagliostro (Hans Stüwe) was an Italian doctor at the court of Louis XVI (Van Daële) and Marie-Antoinette (Suzanne Bianchetti). Implicated in the celebrated affair with the Prince de Rohar (Alfred Abel), he was not exiled in the film, as Raymond Villette complained, but transformed into "the architect of the French Revolution."[94] This was a blatant example of rewriting history in the service of film industry internationalism. Perhaps as a consequence, the film's great number of decors (some forty in all), designed by Lazare Meerson and Firenzi, were notable for their sobriety and balance. In style, they were much closer to the simple clarity of Mallet-Stevens than to the extravagances of Lochakoff and Bilinsky.[95] *Cagliostro* was rushed into release in late June, 1929, and had the dubious fortune to share a double bill at the Paramount-Palace with the new talkie hit, *A Song of Paris* (starring Maurice Chevalier).[96]

The most successful period spectacle films, however, came from a second group within the French film industry. Their common denominator was a loose network of financiers, producers, directors, and set designers whose center was the Russian emigré colony in France and Germany. One faction included the directors (Tourjansky and Volkoff) and set designers (Lochakoff and Bilinsky) initially associated with Alexandre Kamenka at Films Albatros and then with Noë Bloch at Ciné-France (financed by Stinnes and Wengeroff) and the Société Générale des Films (financed by Grinieff). The other was the Société des Films Historiques (also financed by Grinieff), whose major director was Raymond Bernard. The films that these two factions produced tended, at least initially, to look outside France for their subjects—to eighteenth-century Italy and especially to eighteenth- and nineteenth-century Russia. Although generally ignored in film histories (partly because only incomplete prints seem to have survived), they deserve some attention. And not only because their assured direction, magnificent sets and costumes, and fine acting (led by Mosjoukine and Dullin) made them quite successful in France and the international market, but because they created benchmarks of spectacular action and sumptuous tableaux in the genre that provided a context for the work of Gance, Dreyer, and others in the late 1920s. And, perhaps equally important, they allowed the Russian emigré colony to celebrate—and criticize in their own way—the country and society from which they had fled when the Bolsheviks set about transforming Russia into the Soviet Union.

The first of these films was Tourjansky's *Michel Strogoff*, an epic Ciné-France-Westi production which, after delays in financing, premiered at the Impérial Cinéma in December, 1926.[97] The scenario was drawn from the Jules Verne adventure novel about a czarist courier who carries out a dangerous mission in Siberia.[98] The Tartars, aided by several Russian rebels, are threatening czarist control of the area between Omsk and Irkutsk in south central Siberia. From Moscow, Czar Alexander II (Gaidaroff) sends Strogoff (Mosjoukine), because he was born in the region, to order the Irkutsk governor to seize the rebel commander Ogolieff (Chakatouny) and rout the Tartars. Coincidental with this mission, two journalists, Blount and Joulivet (Henri Debain and Gabriel de Gravonne), decide to journey through Siberia to Irkutsk. As their path continually intersects with Strogoff's, they provide some comic relief (which may not be all that necessary) to the narrative. On his way down the Volga river, Strogoff befriends a woman by the name of Nadia (Natalie Kovenko), only to lose her to a Tartar band which seizes their boat, wounds him, and dumps him overboard. After his escape and recovery, Strogoff disobeys orders and visits the chateau of his mother (Jeanne Brindeau) near Omsk. Inadvertently, she betrays his presence to the rebels, and both of them are seized separately and taken to the Tartar encampment at Enofer, where a major festival is in progress and where Nadia is also held captive. When both mother and son continue to deny one another's identity, the Tartars temporarily blind Strogoff with a red-hot sword, and his mother dies from the shock. After the Tartars depart, Nadia and Strogoff struggle through the snowbound mountains to Irkutsk, only to discover that Ogolieff is impersonating the courier in the palace. Confronting him alone, Strogoff suddenly regains his sight and defeats his rival in a hand-to-hand combat. He then proves his identity to the governor and helps repulse the Tartars who have begun to attack the city. Returning to Moscow, he is rewarded by the czar and marries Nadia, his "dearest prize," in a richly detailed Russian Orthodox ceremony.

89. (left) Ivan Mosjoukine in *Michel Strogoff* (1926)

90. (right) The Tartar encampment

Although the ideology this narrative serves is quite regressive—a Russia ruled by the czar and by the Russian Orthodox Church, in which a heroic individual such as Strogoff can perform herculean tasks and be rewarded in kind—Tourjansky's film is much more interesting than it may seem. Most of the production was filmed in Latvia and Norway by Bourgassov, Toporkov, and chief cameraman L.-H. Burel, who had just finished shooting Feyder's two films in Switzerland and Austria, *Visages d'enfants* (1925) and *L'Image* (1926).[99] The skirmish on the river boat, the Tartar attack on Omsk (with a magnificent HAELS of hundreds of white-robed soldiers rising en masse and charging up and over the slope of a hill), Strogoff's escape from Omsk (shot quite skillfully at night), the arduous mountain journey—all gain a naturalness and rough immediacy from the authentic location shooting. Given the conditions and the mode of the narrative, Lochakoff's sets, especially the Tartar village at Enofer, are unusually restrained, almost realistic. Perhaps the proximity to their homeland curbed the Russian emigrés' penchant for the fantastic, which usually characterized their films. Whatever the reason, even in the three-reel 9.5mm Pathéscope version that alone seems to survive, the sober cinematography and swift, economical rhythm of *Michel Strogoff* are quite impressive.

Both Tourjansky and Burel came to *Michel Strogoff* fresh from several months of work on the early stages of Abel Gance's *Napoléon*. That experience was partly responsible for the range of technical effects in the film, especially the use of unconventional camera movement. The most sustained example of techniques usually associated with the narrative avant-garde occurs in the opening

183

91. The wedding ceremony at
the end of *Michel Strogoff*
(1926)

sequence of a grand ball at the czar's palace in Moscow. The Pathéscope version
of the film opens with a HALS looking straight down on the dancers and then
a long dolly out from the orchestra box perched over the ballroom floor. The
major set piece of the sequence, however, is a subjective moment involving
the czar, after he has spoken with one of his generals about the Irkutsk crisis
in a room adjacent to the ballroom. Alone now, he pores over a map, and a
series of shots depicts the Tartar horsemen sweeping across the landscape (in
several swift tracks and dollies) and rampaging through a village. Suddenly,
to the intercutting between a MS of the worried czar and various shots of the
Tartars is added LA shots of the ballroom dancers' feet and CUs of the cymbals
in the orchestra. The rhythm accelerates into rapid cutting, and the sounds of
the dance ironically seem to impress the Tartar threat on the czar's consciousness. The moment leads immediately to his decision to send off Strogoff on
his mission. A similar moment occurs later to Strogoff at a way station when

184

a blustering Russian officer seizes the horses that have been reserved for his use. The camera dollies swiftly into a MS of their confrontation; then, after the officer strikes Strogoff, there is a LA dolly in from LS to MS on the czar as he stands in the shadows of his study. The subjective insert (in which one camera movement parallels the other) keeps Strogoff from returning the blow and perhaps revealing his identity.

Compared to *Michel Strogoff,* Volkoff's *Casanova,* which also premiered at the Impérial, in September, 1927, is much less tightly constructed and much more fantastical in style.[100] Its narrative is drawn from Casanova's *Memoirs* and is little more than an episodic series of adventures, oscillating from comedy to tragedy, from melodrama to satire. It begins in Venice with Casanova (Mosjoukine) threatened by a bailiff who has come to take possession of his house. With a bit of phony magic, he delays the threat and then arranges a rendezvous with the Baroness Stormont (Olga Day). The baron surprises them, however, and takes his case to the governing council of Venice, which orders Casanova's arrest. When a trap to capture him on the Rio San Traverse Bridge fails (the prey makes a spectacular dive into the canal), Casanova enjoys a night of love with the baroness (while the baron sleeps peacefully in the next room). Sometime later, Casanova organizes a dinner for the famous Venetian dancer, Corticelli (Rina de Liguoro). An uninvited guest, the Russian Count Orloff (Paul Guide), tries to gain her attention (as he tosses roses at her, Casanova spears them neatly, one by one, with his rapier), and Casanova challenges him to a duel. After he has won easily, Corticelli joins their hands in friendship, and the orgy, presumably, continues. Still pestered by the council, Casanova escapes to Austria in the company of a black boy servant whom the baroness has given him. One night in an inn, he rescues a young woman, Carlotta (Jenny Jugo), whose mother has sold her to a rich brute of a man. However, the rescue proves ineffectual—the man's henchmen simply follow them and take her back again. Now penniless, Casanova meets the royal dressmaker of Paris, on his way to the court of Peter III in Russia. The adventurer promptly steals his papers, money, and clothes and goes off in his place. In St. Petersburg, he meets Orloff again, who protects him from the emperor when he shows some interest in the Empress Catherine (Suzanne Bianchetti). After the coronation of Catherine (Peter is assassinated mysteriously), Casanova wavers in his affection between Catherine and Bianca (Diana Karenne), newly arrived with her father from Venice. Finally, he flees with Bianca for a brief tryst in her carriage (interrupted by soldiers) and leaves Catherine his black servant (which apparently pleases her). Returning to Venice at the time of the Carnival, Casanova finds Bianca among the revelers and spends the night with her in a covered gondola. The next morning, awakened by the screams of a young woman, he rescues Carlotta all over again. Pursued by the bailiff (who appears out of nowhere) and Carlotta's husband, Casanova hesitates between the two young women. When he chooses Carlotta, Bianca shoots and wounds him. From prison, he is forced to watch her execution. Just before he, too, is to die, Carlotta and several of his friends help him to escape and set off to sea on a sailing ship. At the last moment, he almost cannot resist taking a young gypsy woman with him.

The character of Casanova was well suited to Mosjoukine. It allowed him to exploit his penchant for multiple personalities through disguises and play-acting, and he gave perhaps the best performance of his career, equaling his portrayal of Strogoff and even Edmund Kean. All in all, he plays Casanova like a Douglas Fairbanks adventurer, with more sophistication, irony, and cool sexual presence. His disguises range from the fantastical magician who deceives the bailiff early on (parodying the magicians in several German films— e.g., *The Golem* [1920], *Waxworks* [1924]) to the clown and sailor costumes he uses to escape at the film's end. When disguised as the royal dressmaker in Russia, he even indulges in a bit of drag comedy, dressing up for Catherine in a wide floppy hat, corset, bustle, and fan. The character's sexual exploits also provide the film with several voyeuristic sequences that are rather unusual for the period. To check the bailiff's bluff of a threat, for instance, Casanova lets him gaze on Corticelli half-naked against the fine, cascading drapery of her couch. Later, at the dinner he arranges for her, she and a dozen other women perform a nude dance—described mostly in silhouette against a set of windows. The erotic nature of the dance is suggested in Corticelli's gestures and facial expressions (in MCU), intercut with Casanova's, in a shot of the men staring forward as the women's shawls descend over them, in another shot of them handing over their rapiers to the outstretched women's hands, in the silhouetted figures of the women dancing in pairs and playing with the rapiers. At the climax, Casanova carries Corticelli naked through the group of men and sets her like a draped statue on the steps above them.

With its concern for spectacle and sometimes heroic adventure, *Casanova* also exploits some of the strategies and techniques associated with the narrative avant-garde film practice. The film opens, for instance, with a brief subjective shot. A HALS of swirling women dancers and a LS of a Venice palace are superimposed over a CU of Casanova's sleeping face—as a dream site of pleasures. Near the end, a similar subjective moment appears more ominously. In a MCU of the gondola interior, Bianca leans over to kiss him awake, and her image dissolves briefly into the image of Carlotta. Other sequences are marked (the cameramen were Bourgassov and Toporkov) by deformations, unusual camera angles, and esoteric lighting effects. In one, the magician is made grotesquely mammoth in several distorted shots and then deflates like a punctured balloon (cf. the balloon travelers on the metro in Clair's *Entr'acte* [1924]). In another, Casanova and the Baroness Stormont are bathed in the most romantic of lights. The CU of their kiss (she on the left, he on the right) floods her face with a key light from the right, while his is nearly silhouetted (still dripping beads of water from the canal) with a back light from the left. When they part later, it is in a FS of a highly decorative grille, sharply etched with a single light from the right rear.

There is even an effective sequence of rapid cutting that employs several unusual CUs. The sequence occurs as Casanova paces his quarters in the Austrian inn and hears a struggle in the next room. Intercut with CUs of Casanova listening and looking one way and then another, before he leaps to the door, are a series of dimly lit shots—an ECU of a mouth opening, a CU of a woman's white shoes backing off to the right, a CU of a man's hands reaching in from the left, a HAMCU of shadows on the floor and then a woman's shoes crossing to the left, a CU of her hands clawing at a wood panel, a CU of boots pausing and then moving to the right, a CU of an arm struggling in a flash of white cloth, and an ECU of a hand coming away from the open mouth.

92. (left) Olga Day and Ivan Mosjoukine in Bilinsky's costumes in *Casanova* (1927)

93. (right) The Petersburg palace exterior

Although these shots never last less than a second or two, they are perfectly selected to describe the near rape and, simultaneously, to evoke Casanova's subjective experience. The sequence operates more effectively perhaps than does a similarly experienced attack in L'Herbier's *Feu Mathias Pascal* (1925), where Mosjoukine is in a similar position.

More than anything else, however, *Casanova* is a showcase for the spectacle of Lochakoff's decors, Bilinsky's costumes, and Venice itself. According to Barsacq, "Lochakoff and Bilinsky directed their efforts toward the spectacular aspect of scenery, toward an overall effect rather than atmosphere or the search for exact detail."[101] An important element in Lochakoff's decors was the *maquette plastique*, an intricate scale model, usually representing the upper portion of the filmed image. He employed this latest technique from the German film studios in conjunction with sets constructed according to the designs of seventeenth- and eighteenth-century Italian operas.[102] The Venice and St. Petersburg settings, consequently, took on the decorativeness of a Diaghilev ballet. Complementing these fabulous decors were Bilinsky's rich variety of costumes. Compared favorably with Bakst's work for Diaghilev, Bilinsky's costumes became the major attraction at the second Exposition du cinéma (Galerie d'Art de la Grande Maison de Blanc) organized by the Ciné-Club de France in the spring of 1927.[103] Finally, both sets and costumes were embellished by an exquisite stencil-color process that included as many as three or four sharply distinguished colors in a single frame.[104]

The most stunning effects were carefully withheld until the last two major

187

94. The bedchamber of
Catherine II in *Casanova*
(1927)

episodes of the film—the sequences in Catherine's court and the Carnival of
Venice. The principal exterior for St. Petersburg was a vast snowy expanse in
front of the palace, produced by means of a *maquette plastique* and a simply
decorated snow-covered landscape. It is here that Casanova's carriage collides
with that of the Count, and he and Bianca can use the ensuing chaos to flee
together. The best sets, however, are the interiors: the throne room where
Catherine sits under the golden emblem of the czars and an immense white
dome with statues projecting from the columns, the cavernous main hall where
the banquet and the coronation ball are held (with the guests dressed in blue-
greens, light reds, and golds). For her ascent to the throne, Catherine wears
the most fabulous of Bilinsky's costumes. In a HAELS of the throne room,
with people lining both side walls in an arching curve, she enters from the
bottom of the frame, trailing a magnificent dark cloak (was it deep blue in
the original?) emblazoned with the gold patterns of the czar's emblem. As she
moves farther into the frame, the cloak stretches longer and longer behind

188

III

95. Casanova's gondola at the
end of the Carnival sequence
in *Casanova* (1927)

her, supported by as many as two dozen servants, until it nearly fills the entire
floor space of the room.

The climactic sequences of the Carnival in Venice were apparently even
more spectacular than these. *Cinéa-Ciné-pour-tous* waxed ecstatic over the finale:

The Carnival of Venice is, in one sense, the culmination of this historical and
artistic reconstruction. It is also one of the masterpieces of set design in world film
production. Jewels glittering everywhere, brilliant red costumes, gondolas passing
rhythmically over the still canal waters, everything encompassed in the magnificent
orderly movement of the seething crowd. [105]

Even Jean Dréville was impressed with "this remarkable ensemble of images—
remarkable for its movement and the rhythm of that movement." [106] Unfortunately, the only surviving print of *Casanova* in the United States has suffered
some radical recutting (probably for its distribution here), especially in the
final reel. The Carnival is reduced to little more than a sketch, and Casanova's

escape from prison is a bit of a jumble. Perhaps the sequence that still works most effectively is the execution of Bianca (even despite a confusion in the plot). The sequence alternates MCUs of Casanova behind the bars of his cell and LSs of Bianca with the executioner and a priest silhouetted on a raised plaza in front of an immense arch. In the foreground of the LSs is the blurred silhouette of a bar pattern, which, together with Casanova's anguished face pressed to the cell bars, makes her death shockingly poignant. A similar moment would be utterly transformed a year later in Dreyer's *La Passion de Jeanne d'Arc*.

Much like *Casanova*, Raymond Bernard's second film for the Société des Films Historiques, which cost six million francs and opened to box office records at the Salle Marivaux in January, 1927, also tended more to the decorative and spectacular.[107] Its title, *Joueur d'échecs* (1927), could be seen as a clever takeoff on the final sequence of *Le Miracle des loups*, but the subject was an intrigue involving legendary independence fighters in Poland and Russia in 1776. The narrative is worth summarizing.[108] Two young Polish aristocrats in Vilno, Boleslas Vorowski (Pierre Blanchar) and Sophie Vorowska (Edith Jehanne), are pupils of the Baron de Kempelen (Charles Dullin), an inventor of life-size mechanical mannequins. Although both are leaders of the independence movement and Boleslas loves Sophie, she is attracted to Serge Oblonoff (Pierre Batcheff), a young officer in charge of the Russian forces in Poland. When Boleslas is wounded in a spontaneous insurrection in Vilno, she elects to stay by his side—even though he has a price on his head. Kempelen comes up with a stratagem to hide him in a new chess-player mannequin which he sends to the Polish court at Warsaw; but a Major Nicolaieff (Camille Bert), who recognizes Boleslas's chess moves, diverts the mannequin to St. Petersburg. There, Catherine II (Mme. Charles Dullin) challenges the mannequin, is accused of cheating, and promptly orders it shot. With Oblonoff's assistance (for he now realizes Boleslas's greater love for Sophie), Kempelen substitutes himself in his own mechanical creation and dies in Boleslas's place. Struck by the young couple's love, Catherine allows them to return to Vilno, where they are pursued by Nicolaieff. When he steals into Kempelen's house at night, suddenly the doors lock, and he is methodically dispatched by a small army of sword-bearing mannequins. The prophecy of an old gypsy thus comes true—Poland's freedom will come in the shape of a woman. Sophie and Boleslas unfurl the flag of the Polish eagle and (according to an intertitle) "go off bearing high once more the colors of Polish history."[109]

Since only certain parts of *Joueur d'échecs* could be shot on location in Poland (using the Polish army for the Vilno insurrection), the scenario demanded that Bernard's set designers, Mallet-Stevens and Jean Perrier, and his chief cameraman J.-P. Mundviller construct a number of mammoth decors at Joinville:

the gallery of the palace of Catherine II . . . the streets and squares of Vilno and Warsaw, and the grandiose court of the Winter Palace [at St. Petersburg], which alone covered an area of 8,800 square meters. . . .[110]

There were thirty-five decors in all, and the Winter Palace set was described at the time, by G.-Michel Coissac, as one of the three largest ever constructed for the cinema worldwide.[111] Perhaps the most interesting feature of Perrier's work, according to Barsacq, was that he "developed a rational concept of film

96. The Russian patrol in
Vilno at the opening of *Joueur
d'échecs* (1927)

set design as a function of the position of the camera and the lenses. . . . The
movements of the camera and actors [could be] determined in advance. . . .[112]
The result was a "complicated labyrinth of multiple sets, with passageways
behind the decors, in which one set sometimes served as a frame for the
previous one, with intersections of all sorts that formed a welter of details. . . ."[113] Consequently, *Joueur d'échecs* is full of spectacular effects: "the
uprising in the streets of Vilno, the battle of encirclement [where in one LS,
scores of cannon camouflaged on a hillside fire simultaneously], the masked
ball in the court of Catherine II, the night celebration at Vorowski's."[114] But,
as in *Le Miracle des loups*, these are integrated smoothly into the narrative.

Despite all the spectacle, Bernard's film is marked by an extremely concise
form of editing. The opening sequence, for instance, establishes the conflict
between the Russians and Poles in a tense, economical pattern of intercutting.
While Russian horsemen patrol the night streets of Vilno, members of the
Polish resistance meet in a nearby chateau. The Russians are introduced as
huge shadows gliding over the city walls, then in MCUs of the horses' hooves,
and in dolly shots describing their slow methodical progress. One horseman
nonchalantly raises a whip, and an old woman crouched by the wall spins
around and collapses from its lash. Inside the chateau, the Poles pause in their
singing, waiting for the patrol to pass. Boleslas reaches across the piano to
take Sophie's hand, but she looks at him askance. Later, in a much-admired

191

97. Charles Dullin and the
chessplayer mannequin in
Joueur d'échecs (1927)

sequence, she imagines the insurrection is victorious as she sings the national
anthem at the same piano.[115] As the camera dollies in on her, a superimposition dissolves in of horsemen charging off to the right. Again the camera
dollies in on her, and the horsemen seem to sweep out of her hands across the
piano top toward the left background. As her excitement fades, Sophie gazes
at the necklace Oblonoff had recently bestowed on her, and a subjective image
of him is cut in momentarily. She looks up and seems to see the next shot of
Boleslas falling wounded in the rocks of the battlefield. Abruptly she rips the
necklace from her neck and, in MCU, lets it fall from her hand. Cognizant
now of the insurrection's failure, her choice is made—her love will be sacrificed to her duty to her country and its freedom.

The film's celebration of Polish independence from the Russian monarchy
in a period just prior to the French Revolution tempts one to read it as a
displacement of the one onto the other. With a few exceptions—e.g., Gance's
Napoléon—the French cinema generally avoided its country's own revolution,
just as the American cinema has avoided its period of revolution. Both stand
in marked contrast to the Soviet cinema of the 1920s, which functioned as a
major collective ritual in celebrating (sometimes also by displacement) the
construction of a new society. *Joueur d'échecs* thus seems to affirm the spirit of
independence and revolution (and sacrifice) by safely packing it away to another land. The figure of the Baron de Kempelen, however, introduces a curious disruption. He is really half-mad—this teacher, this substitute father—

98. The mannequin attack at the end of *Joueur d'échecs* (1927)

a genius who lords it over his own fictional empire. But history intervenes to give his mannequins a double purpose. There is a rather fascinating metaphorical schema operating in the transformation of this man into a mechanical chess-player, after which the rest of his mannequins change briefly into men. The master takes on the role of one of his subjects and sacrifices himself so other subjects can live. He loses one game so they can win another. The creator/teacher dies so his children can be born. But when they come to life, they take revenge; they destroy a master (albeit a different one) all over again. Does this revenge of the mannequin men substitute for the victorious revolution of the children? And can this be a revolution—this bizarre, half-Christian, half-Oedipal fable of sacrifice and revenge?

Bernard's last silent film epic, *Tarakanova* (1930), returned to the world of Catherine II's court to narrate the tragic end of Elizabeth Tarakanova (Edith Jehanne), a young pretender to the throne, and her lover Prince Orloff (Olaf Fjord), Catherine's court favorite. Wishing only to punish Orloff by separating him from Tarakanova, the Empress inadvertently sends him off to die with his love.[116] Shooting on the film (the cameramen were Kruger and Lucas) was

193

99. (left) A production photo, with *maquette plastique*, for *Monte-Cristo* (1929); (right) an interior shot produced by the *maquette plastique*

completed in February, 1929, but the editing was delayed so it could be released in a sonorized version during the summer of 1930. The delay pushed the cost of the film to almost seven million francs.[117] Bernard once told Kevin Brownlow that he himself considered *Tarakanova* his best film by far, but no print has been rediscovered to confirm or deny his judgment.[118]

The success of these big films by Tourjansky, Volkoff, and Bernard prompted several other producers to try to capitalize on these genre subjects, but with less satisfying results. Henry Roussel, for instance, took a less active French-Polish subject, and in a rather different mode, in *La Valse de l'adieu* (1928). Subtitled "A page in the life of Frederic Chopin," this was a biography, wrote one critic, "more spiritual than chronological."[119] Roussel tried to make Chopin into a symbolic figure, wrote another: "In the desperate youth and sublime death of a musician {was} the story of a misunderstood genius destroyed on the calvary of a love that was both passion and Passion."[120] The result, most agreed, was a ponderous, sentimental film whose only saving grace was the acting of Pierre Blanchar and Marie Bell. Jean Sapène tried another, more obvious tack by hiring Henri Kistemaecker to compose an original scenario about an intrigue among the Russian aristocracy on the eve of the revolution. *La Princesse Masha* (1927) was adapted expressly for Sapène's wife, Claudia Victrix, whom he desperately wished to make a star; and it was given, according to Sapène's publicity, a lavish budget for set reconstructions "of the Russian revolution, palaces and Chinese gardens, sumptuous interiors, picturesque snow scenes, and innumerable crowds."[121] However, Sapène did not have a set designer at Cinéromans of Lochakoff or Bilinsky's caliber; and René Leprince's mediocre direction, together with Victrix's frightful acting, merely produced a bowdlerized imitation. Even an inaugural premiere at the new Rialto Cinéma, in October, 1927, could not save it from derision.[122]

By contrast, one of Sapène's associates, Louis Nalpas, succeeded simply by hiring the Russians to work for him. After losing production control at Cinéromans in 1927, Nalpas formed his own production company again and decided to remake *Monte-Cristo* on a mammoth scale—with Jean Angelo (Edmond Dantès), Lil Dagover (Mercédès), Bernhard Goëtzke (Abbé Faria), Pierre

194

Batcheff (Albert de Morcerf), Jean Toulout (Villefort), Henri Debain (Cadérousse), Mary Glory (Valentine), and Gaston Modot (Fernand Mondego).[123] His production team was headed by an incongruous trio: the sober, story-oriented Henri Fescourt as director, the spectacle-minded Boris Bilinsky as set designer, and Daniau-Johnson as technical director.[124] The combination apparently gelled, for most French film historians agree that *Monte-Cristo* (1929) was one of the best historical reconstructions of the decade. According to Barsacq,

In the winter palace set . . . Bilinsky re-created a vision of the palace as it might have been conceived by Italian opera designers of the eighteenth century, by Bibiena or Piranesi, with a monumental stairway, colonnades, arcades, and balconies; but it was a constructed set, at least up to a certain height: the upper part consisted of a scale model and the base was painted in *trompe-d'oeil*.[125]

Fescourt himself remembers with pleasure how he and Bilinsky used this same process to film an 1815 sailing ship entering "the old port of Marseille on a busy day in 1929 without the public's noticing the least bit of contemporaneous movement on the quay or in the harbor. . . ."[126] Wrote *Cinémagazine*,

In the set pieces such as the evening at the Opéra or the Count's celebration, [Fescourt produced] a charming evocation of the aristocratic life in 1845; the crinolines, the tasteless men's fashions, the decorum that reigned at these ceremonies gave to the images a sort of vapid grace. . . .[127]

The dominant characteristic of this *Monte-Cristo*, however, seems to have been a sense of movement that, even more than in *Casanova*, evoked the ballet. Unfortunately for Nalpas, the film was released in October, 1929, just as the first French talkies were hitting the cinemas.[128]

   The biggest of the French historical reconstruction films sponsored by the Russian emigré money, of course, was Abel Gance's *Napoléon* (1927). Beside it, Henry Roussel's much heralded *Destinée* (1926), an opportunistic but comparatively tepid, lifeless look at Napoléon during the Revolution, has paled into oblivion.[129] Gance's project, initially, was colossal in scope—six separate films on the life of Napoléon Bonaparte. Yet only the first film of the project actually was completed; and its enormous expense (15 to 19 million francs) and epic length (six hours) quickly dispelled the commercial hopes of Gance's financiers.[130] Moreover, the film turned out to be profoundly personal and highly experimental, and the filmmaker had the audacity to title it *Napoléon, vu par Abel Gance*. The version that premiered at the Opéra, on 7 April 1927, was a condensed film of close to 5,000 meters (including several tryptich sequences).[131] The following October, the complete version of 12,000 meters (but without the tryptichs) opened *en exclusivité* at the Salle Marivaux and ran for nearly three months.[132] This full-length film was not widely shown, however, and, according to Kevin Brownlow, the three-hour condensed version was generally released throughout France and the rest of Europe.[133]

   Whatever its variations and excesses, *Napoléon* fulfills all the conventions of the historical reconstruction film. With Alexandre Benois (Diaghilev's chief set designer) and the Russian-born architect Schildknecht,[134] Gance meticulously recreated the period of Napoléon's boyhood at Brienne and his young manhood in Corsica, the period of the Revolution in Paris and of his courting

195

100. Vladimir Roudenko and
Albert Dieudonné in *Napoléon
vu par Abel Gance* (1927)

and marriage to Josephine de Beauharnais, and the period of the Italian campaign. Much of the film was shot on location (Corsica, Briançon, Toulon, Nice), but most (even the sea journey from Corsica and the night battle in the rain at Toulon) was done in the huge new Billancourt studio which Diamant-Berger, with Mallet-Stevens, had built in 1923. Gance's team of assistant directors (including Volkoff, Tourjansky, and Henry Krauss) and cameramen (Jules Kruger, L.-H. Burel, J.-P. Mundviller, Roger Hubert, Emile Pierre, and Lucas) produced enough spectacle for a half-dozen films: the snowball and dormitory fights at Brienne, the escape from the army in Corsica, the Marseillaise sequence in the Club des Cordeliers, the long night battle for Toulon, the Victims' Ball, Napoléon's confrontation with the dead heroes of the Revolution. And, of course, there were the famous tryptich sequences of the Double Tempest (at sea and in the Convention in Paris), the military descent over the mountains into Italy, and the climactic victory at Montenotte. Besides this, *Napoléon* had some forty major roles for what seemed to be half the number of available French actors. They included Albert Dieudonné (Bonaparte), Vladimir Roudenko (Bonaparte *enfant*), Antonin Artaud (Marat), Edmond Van Daële (Robespierre), Alexandre Koubitsky (Danton), Pierre Batcheff (Hoche), Maxudian (Barras), Nicholas Koline (Tristan Fleuri), Armand Bernard (Jean-Jean), Philippe Hériat (Salicetti), Chakatouny (Pozzo de Borgo), Gina Manès (Josephine de Beauharnais), Annabella (Violine Fleuri), Eugénie Buffet (Letitia Bonaparte), Suzanne Bianchetti (Marie-Antoinette), Marguerite Gance (Charlotte Corday), Suzy Vernon (Madame Récamier), Damia (La "Marseillaise"), and Gance himself (Saint-Just).[135]

The complete version of *Napoléon* was a grandiose paradox. Gance once said that he made the film because Napoléon was "a paroxysm in a period which was itself a paroxysm in time."[136] Conceived in the ideological ferment of the early 1920s, his rhapsodic celebration of a single, powerful leader or mover of history (a sort of Gallicized Hegelian ideal) seemed anachronistic, chauvinistic, and even dangerous. Rewriting history, the film depicted Bonaparte as the legendary fulfillment of the French Revolution—"the soul of the Revolution." For Gance, the French hero (much like himself) must have seemed the Romantic artist in apotheosis, a towering figure who made the real world, not an imaginary one, his own province of action. For others, such as Léon Moussinac, this figure was the embodiment "of military dictatorship," frighteningly close to the image of the emperor then held by political groups of the extreme right.[137] Moreover, the film's conclusion in political and military triumph, in victory (admittedly, a result of the project's incompleteness), went against the French pattern of suffering and sacrifice that so marked even the historical reconstruction genre. Yet Gance's technical innovations alone—e.g., the range of camera movements and the multiple screen formats—influenced French filmmakers for the rest of the decade. Time and time again, as we shall see later, his imaginative handling of both the spectacular and the intimate transcended the conventions of the genre.

The difference between period spectacle films produced by the two rival groups in the French film industry are probably no more blatant than in the two films that mounted the story of Jeanne d'Arc in the late 1920s. The maid of Orléans had been the subject of several books after the declaration of her sainthood in 1920, and her life seemed a logical "property" for a French film,

101. The Convention Hall in
Napoléon vu par Abel Gance
(1927)

especially after the success of *Le Miracle des loups*, with its celebration of Jeanne
Hachette. The more conventional and decidedly more commercial of the two
was produced by Bernard Natan—Marco de Gastyne's *La Merveilleuse Vie de
Jeanne d'Arc*. This ambitious project took nearly two years to shoot (at a cost
of between eight and nine million francs), finally premiered at the Opéra late
in 1928, and was showcased at the Paramount-Palace in April, 1929.[138] Jeanne
was played by a well-known tomboy actress, Simone Genevois, supported by
expert villains such as Philippe Hériat as Gilles de Rais and Gaston Modot as
Glasdell. The scenario, by Jean-José Frappa, traced Jeanne's story from 1428,
when she first had her visions in Domrémy (visualized in a circle of white-
robed women dancing in slow motion, superimposed over a tolling tower
bell), to 1430, when she was burned at the stake in Rouen. Gastyne's interest
lay primarily in moments of grand spectacle—the coronation of Charles VII
at Notre Dame, the capture of Jeanne at Compiègne, and especially her successful siege of Orléans. The latter was filmed almost entirely on location at

197

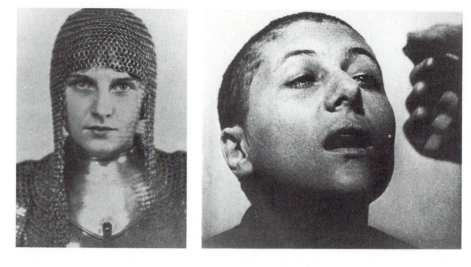

102. (left) Simone Genevois
in *La Merveilleuse Vie de Jeanne
D'Arc* (1929)

103. (right) Falconetti in *La
Passion de Jeanne D'Arc* (1928)

Carcassonne and was staged on a scale that rivaled the similar siege in *Le
Miracle des loups*. The action is brisk and clear, punctuated by LA shots of
horsemen crashing over a line of barricades and by a LAFS of Jeanne halfway
up a scaling ladder as she is struck by an arrow. But Gastyne did not ignore
other more poignant moments of Jeanne's solitude—a MCU of her praying,
after the Orléans siege, between a dead soldier's head and a wooden post from
which is suspended a heavy iron chain; a HALS of her alone, head bowed, on
a small stool in the empty space of the trial chamber. Although Simone Genevois's Jeanne is angry enough to accuse her interrogators in Rouen's public
square, she is also plainly afraid to suffer burning at the stake.

The other film, of course, was Carl Dreyer's *La Passion de Jeanne d'Arc*,
which opened in Paris at the Salle Marivaux on 25 October 1928.[139] Apparently, the Société Générale des Films engaged the young Danish filmmaker to
make a vast fresco that would complement its production of *Napoléon*. If Dreyer
is to be believed, the choice of Jeanne d'Arc as the film's subject was decided
in a match draw—ironically, because he picked the headless match.[140] As early
as May, 1927, *Cinémagazine* quoted one of the project's financial backers, the
duc d'Ayen, as saying, "We want to reproduce the most accurate and the most
poignant events in the life of Jeanne d'Arc, the heroic emblem and mirror of
the people."[141] Despite an extraordinary budget of over seven million francs,
two mammoth set constructions (one of great white interiors near the Billancourt studio, the other a reconstruction of the medieval village of Rouen),[142]
and major actors (René Jeanne Falconetti as Jeanne, Eugène Silvain as Cauchon, Maurice Schutz as Loyseleur, Antonin Artaud as Massieu), *La Passion de
Jeanne d'Arc* was also a deeply personal, experimental film, some of whose
uniqueness comes from its deliberate inversion of the genre conventions. It is
clearly an anti-historical reconstruction. Dreyer's scenario focuses neither on
the pageantry of the times nor on Jeanne's military and political successes, but
on her spiritual journey during the last day of her life (the time of her trial
and execution is condensed into what seems a single day). Based closely on

104. The jousting tournament
in *Le Tournoi* (1929)

the records of the trial at Rouen, the film is simultaneously a documentary of
Falconetti's ordeal as Jeanne and a symbolic progression of faces within an
unusually disjunctive space-time continuum. As we shall see later, *La Passion
de Jeanne d'Arc* was one of the crowning achievements of the French narrative
avant-garde.

Finally, two period films fall somewhat outside these two camps of production, but both more or less counter the conventions of the genre, although
quite differently than does Dreyer's film. The more conventional of the two is
another production of the Société des Films Historiques, Jean Renoir's *Le
Tournoi*, which opened at the Salle Marivaux in February, 1929.[143] Set in the
court of Charles IX and Catherine de Medici, the scenario by Dupuy-Mazuel
is predicated on the Protestant/Catholic conflict of the period, which is resolved here in a tournament. The exteriors were shot by Marcel Lucien and
Maurice Desfassiaux in Carcassonne (again) during "the Bimillennial celebrations," and the tournament was staged specially for the occasion.[144] Mallet-
Stevens's interiors and Georges Bargier's costumes were noted for their authenticity; and the presence of a former world fencing champion, Aldo Nadi,
in the leading role corroborated this impression. In fact, despite the intrigue
between the Protestant François de Baynes (Nadi) and Catholic Henri de Ro-
gier (Enrique de Rivero) over the favor of Isabelle Ginori (Jackie Monnier) and
the consequent jousting combat that deteriorates into swordplay and mace-
swings, *Le Tournoi* seems to have been marked by an unusual degree of realism.

199

As one of the few film critics recently to have seen the film, Raymond Durgnat was struck by the weight and feel of the weapons and banquet ware, by the detailed cumbersomeness of the knights on horseback, and by the presence of a blacksmith watching over the lovers—a shot that "locates their idyll in an everyday society."[145] André Bazin remembered the violence and cruelty of the duels—"the blood from the sword wiped on Lucrèce's hair [de Baynes's mistress]."[146] Perhaps most disturbing was the ambiguity of de Baynes's character—highly skilled in combat and thoroughly profligate, perfidious and yet finally noble in death. As in *Le Bled*, the hero seems to mock the genre from within. Although Renoir himself considered the project little more than an exercise in technique (e.g., the construction of an overhead dolly shot down the length of a long banquet table),[147] *Le Tournoi* can be seen as one more instance of a general pattern of genre subversion in his work.

That subversion is even more apparent in Renoir's earlier *Nana*, an ambitious film that got out of hand. Aubert released the film in the summer of 1926 (it premiered at the Aubert-Palace) to good reviews and large audiences and then shelved it to make way for its fall releases.[148] When the company tried to redistribute a slightly shortened version in December, interest in the film had passed.[149] That sabotaging of *Nana*'s commercial success contrasts with a different kind of sabotaging within the film itself.[150]

Before making *Nana* (with his wife, Catherine Hessling, in the starring role), Renoir had discovered Stroheim's *Foolish Wives* and had engaged in a study of French gestures in the paintings of his father and others of his generation.[151] In adapting Zola's novel, he determined to produce his own study of a society through a combination of strategies. First, Renoir eliminated most of the first half of the novel and concentrated on Nana's life in the theater and her affairs with three men: Count Muffat (Werner Krauss), Count Vandeuvres (Jean Angelo), and Georges Hugon (Raymond Guérin).[152] The narrative opens comically, with Nana's last successful theatrical performances, gradually darkens, and ends with her death from smallpox. Renoir also conceived of a unique juxtaposition of the decors and the characters. Much of the film's million-franc budget, in fact, went for the construction of elaborate sets that resurrected the final years of the Second Empire: the giant staircase, drawing room, bedchamber, and dressing room in Count Muffat's townhouse; the racetrack stands at Longchamps; the Variety Theater; the Mabille dance hall (all designed by Claude Autant-Lara at the Gaumont studio in Paris and then reconstructed in Berlin).[153] Yet Renoir deliberately consigned these decors to secondary importance in the film itself. And he underlined their "démodé" quality by having Autant-Lara design rather Impressionist costumes according to the later fashions of 1871 and after.[154] Moreover he emphasized the acting of his three main characters (in contrast to what he considered a weakness in the French cinema of the time) to the point of "constantly shooting them in American-style two-shots"—a strategy that effectively eliminated the decors.[155]

His most important strategy, however, was to have the actors employ quite divergent acting styles.[156] Werner Krauss (the star of *Caligari*) plays Count Muffat in a humorless, ponderous, pathetic German manner—almost an aristocratic variation on Emil Janning's hotel doorman in Murnau's *The Last Laugh* (1924). By contrast, Jean Angelo plays Count Vandeuvres in a suave detached manner, as if he has just stepped out of an Oscar Wilde comedy. And Ray-

105. (left) The central staircase in Count Muffet's townhouse in *Nana* (1926)

106. (right) A publicity photo of Catherine Hessling

mond Guérin plays Georges Hugon with such a self-effacing, drooping timidity that his character scarcely exists. As Nana, Catherine Hessling clearly dominates the film. No sensuous blonde seductress (as in Zola), she plays Nana as a sulky, cajoling, irrational child-woman who reverses the class- and male-dominated patterns of her time. Hessling developed a strange style of acting, derived from pantomime, for the role: syncopated rhythms and crisp, mechanical gestures, like those of an automaton or an animated doll.[157] She fascinates and upstages her men just as all of them, seconded by a couple of silent voyeuristic servants (Harbacher and Valeska Gert), upstage the period decors. In this stylized character study, a whole society is revealed in the process of self-destruction.

Some years ago Noël Burch called *Nana* "a key film in the development of a cinematic language" because its "entire visual construction depends on the existence . . . of a [*fluctuating*] off-screen space."[158] *Nana* was the first film, according to Burch, to exploit the structural use of that off-screen space systematically. Along with Alexander Sesonske, I am afraid I cannot agree. Actually, Burch is less interested in proclaiming *Nana*'s originality than in using the film to exemplify the various ways that off-screen space can be defined and be said to function. There are many earlier instances of off-screen space functioning significantly in the diegetic process of a film. Sesonske cites D. W. Griffith's films, specifically, *The Lonedale Operator* (1911); but one could go back as early as *The Lonely Villa* (1909) as well.[159] Furthermore, as Sesonske argues, off-screen space is not all that influential in *Nana*. And Burch tacitly admits this in his later writings on the French cinema of the 1920s by avoiding any mention of the film.[160] Sesonske, in fact, suggests something of much more importance which operates structurally in *Nana*—the enactment of theatrical performances at crucial moments of the narrative. Specifically, there is Nana's comically sensual performance of Venus in the opening sequence, the opening night flop of Muffat's production of *La Petite Duchesse*, her star turn at Longchamps, and, near the end, her hysterical abandon and collapse at the Bal Mabille. As the fiction that has been her life fails, writes Sesonske, Nana "turns to art, a spectacle, a performance, as a refuge from, and . . . a solution to, life's problems."[161] Within this satirical inversion of the historical reconstruction film lies the germ of an idea for Renoir—performance as an act of mediation and resolution.

There is one other subgenre of the historical reconstruction film that bears mentioning—the war film, or the reconstruction of World War I. After Abel Gance's *J'Accuse* (1919)—which will be discussed in Part IV—the Great War vanished from French films except for brief references (e.g., *La Croisade, Koenigsmark*), as if there were a tacit taboo on the subject. But in 1927, several films appeared to break the silence. Their immediate inspiration probably was the extraordinary success of King Vidor's *The Big Parade* (1925), released in France early in 1927. But also approaching was the tenth anniversary of the Armistice (11 November 1928). In advance of the anniversary, the association of war veterans put together two documentaries from the war footage stored at the Archives d'Art et l'Histoire: *Pour la paix du monde* and *Verdun*.[162] Several fictional films with the war as their setting were initiated; of these, the most important was Maurice Tourneur's adaptation of a Joseph Kessel novel, *L'Equipage* (1928), which premiered at the Impérial Cinéma in April, 1928.[163]

Even though produced by the Société Générale des Films and released by A.C.E., *L'Equipage* was called a Franco-American production because Tourneur and his leading actress, Claire de Lorez, were considered American while the rest of the cast was French (Jean Dax, Daniel Mendaille, Georges Charlia, Camille Bert, Pierre de Guingand).[164] Its story revolved around the friendship of two pilots near the end of the war, the one unaware that his mistress is married to, but separated from, the other. When he is killed in combat, the friend forgives his wife, and they resume their life together.

This tragedy of the war has none of the habitual faults of the films that evoke memories of those terrible years and contemplate the struggle of millions of combatants. Here is a truly cinematic production where the image is master and where all the effects are visual.[165]

Interestingly, Tourneur's film focused on the air war, just as did William Wellman's *Wings* (1927), which was released almost simultaneously in the United States. Both undoubtedly drew on the interest generated by Charles Lindbergh's solo flight across the Atlantic. Although the French film press considered *L'Equipage* one of the more beautiful films of the 1927-1928 season, the French public was less impressed. They remembered that Tourneur had not returned to France for the actual war, and (according to Kevin Brownlow) his return to re-enact it created such a hullabaloo that he beat a retreat to Germany.[166]

The major historical reconstruction film on the war, however, was Léon Poirier's *Verdun, visions d'histoire*, whose premiere at the Opéra, 10-18 Novem-

107. A symbolic tableau in
Verdun, Visions D'Histoire
(1928)

ber 1928, was timed to commemorate the tenth anniversary of the Armistice.[167] The following summer, it was released for an exclusive run at the Impérial Cinéma.[168] At first, Poirier had the patronage of the French government to reconstruct the strategic but costly defense of Verdun in the spring of 1916. Although that patronage was eventually withdrawn either for financial or political reasons (the 1928 elections), the government gave its complete, though unofficial, support by allowing Poirier to film on the actual battlefields and to use documentary footage from the Archives d'Art et l'Histoire. With an eerie concern for authenticity, Poirier recalled soldiers who had survived the war to re-create some of the major battles. For instance,

the survivors of the Driant Huntsmen themselves participated in the reconstruction of those terrible days from 21 to 25 February, where, after having been pounded by a twenty-four-hour bombardment, they were assaulted by a mass of soldiers ten times their number who finally gained the position after four days of battle and the death of Colonel Driant, and penetrated the Verdun defenses like a wedge as far as the fort of Douaumont.[169]

Their almost incomprehensible willingness to undergo the horror of that experience, again and again, testifies to the importance for the French of that historic moment at Verdun. Even German soldiers volunteered for the re-enactment. Wrote one, "Your film will do much to promote peace by bringing together France and Germany because we both need to better understand the spectacle of our common suffering."[170]

Poirier's scenario integrated a chronological progression of documentary footage with re-enacted sequences of battles and of various individuals engaged in or affected by the war. Instead of following a single continuous storyline in the re-enacted sequences, he chose to focus on "symbolic characters"—the French soldier (Albert Préjean), the German soldier (Hans Brausewetter), the peasant (José Davert), the son (Pierre Nay), the husband (Daniel Mendaille), the young man (Jean Dehelly), the intellectual (Antonin Artaud), the chaplain (André Nox), the German officer (Tommy Bourdelle), the old marshal (Maurice Schutz), the wife (Suzanne Bianchetti), the mother (Jeanne-Marie Laurent)—who, according to René Jeanne and Charles Ford, "would enlarge the scope of the battle, transform it into tragedy. . . ."[171] "Here," Poirier added, "there would be no story, no rousing or extravagant adventure, no sentimental or easily edifying intrigue."[172] The film's three parts—"La Force, L'Enfer, Le Destin"— would be a tribute to the collective suffering of the French people.[173]

Although critics and historians generally praise the smoothness of this integration of the dramatic and the documentary as well as the carefully restrained use of symbolic figures, the 1932 sonorized and re-edited version of the film (which is the only print I have seen) looks rather rough and uneven (Poirier himself preferred the silent version).[174] The changes from re-enactment footage to authentic documentary footage (or vice versa) are sometimes obvious; some sequences are unusually brief and others verge on incoherence; the overall rhythm of physical movement and narrative seems lax and uncertain. Still, there are stunning and poignant moments: the realistic detail and concise cutting in the initial German attack, a grisly night encounter in "no man's land," the final image of seed-sowing in the devastated earth. Much more technically conventional than *Napoléon*, say, *Verdun, visions d'histoire* was also more ideologically suited in subject to the French public of 1928—and it was no less popular. The French spirit was defined in terms of suffering, sacrifice, respect for one's enemies, and a desire to return peacefully to the past (where it still might be possible to cultivate one's garden). As *Close Up* suggested in 1929, taken as a work of propaganda or ideological statement, if not as an achievement, *Verdun* clearly bears comparison with Eisenstein's *October* (1927) and Pudovkin's *The End of St. Petersburg* (1927).[175]

For the French film industry, the genre of period spectacle films or historical reconstructions was clearly the most prestigious of the decade. Year after year, its films were among the finest commercial productions: *Les Trois Mousquetaires* (1921-1922), *Les Opprimés* (1923), *Koenigsmark* (1923), *Violettes impériales* (1924), *Kean* (1924), *Le Miracle des loups* (1924), *Michel Strogoff* (1926), *Joueur d'échecs* (1927), *Casanova* (1927), *Verdun, vision d'histoire* (1928), *Monte-Cristo* (1929). And, until *Madame Sans-Gêne* (which was more American than French), *Napoléon*, and *La Passion de Jeanne d'Arc* (which both deviated sharply from the norm), the genre was also consistently profitable, justifying, at least financially, its high percentage of capital investment. Moreover, except for the earlier films, almost all were produced and/or financed by Russian emigrés. The significance of the Russian contribution to the French cinema of the 1920s is perhaps nowhere more evident than here. These 1920s films set the basic conventions for the genre and defined its standards. In the 1930s, the genre's prestige declined slightly as many earlier films were re-made as talkies, though not as well: Diamant-Berger's *Les Trois Mousquetaires* (1932), Richébé's *L'A-*

gonie des aigles (1933), Gance's *Napoléon Bonaparte* (1934) and *J'Accuse* (1937), Tourneur's *Koenigsmark* (1935), Baroncelli's *Michel Strogoff* (1937). But there were at least two clear successes within the conventions: Bernard's reconstruction of the Great War in *Croix des bois* (1932) and Feyder's reconstruction of seventeenth-century Flanders (with a distinctly collaborationist plot) in *La Kermesse héroïque* (1935). Besides, in *Grande Illusion* (1937) and in *La Marseillaise* (1938), Jean Renoir continued to subvert the genre, to turn it to other ends.

Two decades later, a survey of the French public's preferences in film would show that the popularity of the historical reconstruction genre had continued unabated. [176]

Modern Studio Spectaculars

During the latter half of the 1920s, the French film industry discovered a new genre to invest in that soon challenged the priority of the historical reconstruction film. Perhaps more than previous genres, the modern studio spectacular had quite definite political, economic, and cultural origins. The modern studio spectacular was a product of the cultural internationalism which by then characterized urban life in most of the industrialized countries of Europe. Its development in France coincided with the shift in historical reconstructions after 1924 and also can be attributed in part to the French film industry's increasing involvement in international co-productions. In order to reach as many exhibition outlets as possible, especially the American market, the industry sought formats and subjects beyond those of the period films, that would appeal not just to French audiences but also to Americans and other Europeans. The American craze that was sweeping France by the mid-twenties offered a kind of model. While American tourists flocked to the new casinos, dance halls, and beach resorts, the French stood in line to see American jazz musicians, singers, and dance troupes. [1] At La Revue Nègre in the Théâtre des Champs-Elysées, for instance, they gaped at Josephine Baker, "The Nefertiti of Now," performing a "stomach dance" before "pink drops with cornucopias of hams and watermelons." [2] The modern studio spectacular was designed to exploit such "cross-cultural" exchanges. And it was encouraged by the success of the American "flapper" films—e.g., *Flaming Youth* (1923), *The Masked Bride* (1925), and *Dancing Mothers* (1926)—and that of the studio spectaculars produced by Paramount and UFA. [3]

The parameters of the genre were clearly fixed by 1926-1927. The milieu was the key ingredient for this genre of the Parisian nouveau riche, especially younger men and women, who sported and played at the newest nightclubs, restaurants, dance halls, resorts, or at their own art deco mansions. According to Gérard Talon, these films pictured the good life of a new generation and helped define what was modern and "à la mode" in fashions, sports, dancing, and manners generally. [4] Instead of looking to the past and to venerated traditions, or to some *other* land or culture, the studio spectacular looked to the present and the future. But this present or future was not particularly French. For the genre tended to produce either a picturesque image of contemporary France according to American stereotypes or a kind of generalized milieu that was socially and aesthetically neutral. [5] Stylish set designs and costumes (sometimes as elaborate as those in the period films) were showcased in sensational set pieces. International casts were common, but they were natural to this

108. Méssenier's Montmartre
restaurant set for *Koenigsmark*
(1923)

kind of neutral decor where actors could easily replace one another as types.
The overall effect of the genre was a fantasy of internationalism that denied
the specificity of French culture and acceded to the hegemony of the American
cinema and the new ideology of consumer capitalism or conspicuous consumption.[6] The modern studio spectacular, therefore, was probably the least French
of all the genres deployed by the French film industry.

Isolated elements of the genre can be found in the French cinema at least
as early as Perret's *Koenigsmark* (1923) and Mosjoukine's *Le Brasier ardent* (1923).
Perhaps the major set piece of *Koenigsmark* was the wedding-night celebration
in a lavish Montmartre restaurant constructed by Henri Ménessier at the new
Levinsky studio in Joinville-le-pont. Ménessier's work in the United States for
Maurice Tourneur and then Metro Pictures—he had just returned to France
with Pearl White for *Terreur* (1924)—led him to design the Montmartre set
specifically as "an amusing attraction with a little color for America!"[7] Its
central pool-enclosed dance floor and art nouveau/deco walls provided the prototype of an essential setting for the modern studio spectacular. Besides, sev-

206

eral of Huguette Duflos's costumes, designed by Boué Soeurs, were advertised as the latest in fashionable elegance.[8] A shorter but similar sequence occurs in *Le Brasier ardent*. Designed by Lochakoff on a smaller scale at Albatros's Montreuil studio, its setting is an underground Parisian café where Mosjoukine incites a group of chorus girls to a marathon contest of faster and faster dancing.[9]

The genre almost gelled in Robert Boudrioz's *L'Epérvier* (1924) and, more importantly, in Marcel L'Herbier's *L'Inhumaine* (1924). A Paramount production based on a popular melodrama by François de Croisset, *L'Epérvier* told the "tragic" yarn of a card-sharping Hungarian couple in Rome, who separate when the wife falls in love with a diplomat.[10] Unfortunately, Boudrioz's cast of Sylvio de Pedrelli and Nilda du Piessy was almost unknown (in contrast to L'Herbier's 1933 version, starring Charles Boyer), and the film had little impact. *L'Inhumaine*, which premiered at the Madeleine-Cinéma in late November, 1924, on the other hand, caused a sensation, but an unfavorable one.[11] Produced independently by Cinégraphic and financed almost entirely by American money through its star, Georgette Leblanc, L'Herbier's film was deliberately designed to showcase the most modern French painting, sculpture, architecture, costume design, and music (as well as cinema) to the American public.[12] The milieu was contemporary Paris—more specifically, art deco mansions (exteriors by Mallet-Stevens, interiors by Autant-Lara and Cavalcanti), the Théâtre des Champs-Elysées (with the Ballet suédois), and a scientific laboratory (designed by Fernand Léger). All these sets were constructed at the new Levinsky studio, with an airy lightness that contrasted sharply with the dark decors of conventional films.[13] The characters included the famous singer, Claire Lescot (Georgette Leblanc), and a cosmopolitan group of men attracted to her—Einar Norsen (Jaque Catelain), Maharajah Djorah (Philippe Hériat), Frank Mahler (Kellerman), and Tarsky (L. V. Terval)—whose offers of love and wealth she accepts with glacial, impartial indifference. The first part of the film narrates Einar's apparent death (by suicide) and "resurrection," which almost breaks Claire's composure. The second part narrates her actual death (from a viper hidden by the jealous Djorah) and her miraculous resurrection in Einar's laboratory, which causes her to admit her love for him at last.

Most of the genre elements come together in *L'Inhumaine*: the milieu, the ultramodern decors (although they are quite specifically French), the cosmopolitan characters (and cast), the narrative of a modern woman who is celebrated, defeated, and transformed. However, there was both too little and too much in the film for 1924. The "démodé" nature of the narrative—it is not much different from some of Feuillade's and Pearl White's wartime serials— blatantly contradicts the ultramodern settings.[14] And the decors themselves seem to exist independently of one another (almost in separate fictions), never quite producing contingent spaces (one could argue that they were never meant to). Besides, just as in *L'Atlantide*, the aging figure of Georgette Leblanc makes a rather unconvincing Circe-like seductress, a very problematic object of desire, even for the spectator.[15] Yet L'Herbier also used the project to deploy and experiment with all the technical devices of film discourse then available to him—that is, various forms of montage, including accelerated montage; various forms of masking; superimpositions; brief flashes of solid-color film stock; the fragmentation of objects. The result is a film that, some-

207

109. (left) Georgette Leblanc
in *L'Inhumaine* (1924)

110. (right) Bilinsky's poster
for *Le Lion des Mogols* (1924)

what like Gance's *La Roue*, was as outdated as it was avant-garde. And the combination was not commercially advantageous.

Another film which opened, at the Mogodor-Palace, about the same time as *L'Inhumaine* combined fewer elements of the genre somewhat more conventionally and with a rather cool facility. That was Albatros's *Le Lion des Mogols* (1924), directed by Jean Epstein from a Mosjoukine scenario, with sets by Lochakoff and costumes by Bilinsky.[16] The scenario juxtaposes a fantastical Arabian Nights palace and modern Jazz Age Paris, neatly mediated by the presence of a film production company. As a consequence, Mosjoukine gets to play the rebellious son of the Grand Khan, a mysterious naïve celebrity in Paris, and a movie actor in various heroic roles. More than half of the film takes place in Paris, and two major set pieces there develop the prototypical sequences from *Koenigsmark* and *Le Brasier ardent*. These are a night of drunkenness at the popular Jockey Bar (also reminiscent of the Coaly Hole sequence in *Kean*—the chief cameraman again is Mundviller) and a climactic masked ball at the fashionable Hotel Olympic. The film's attitude toward this final sequence is not exactly fashionable: the masked ball itself masks a murder in the rooms above, and it finally serves to unmask the real nature of the hero

208

and heroine (brother and sister), who return to the country of their origin and to the fantasy palace.

Henry Roussel's *La Terre promise* (1925), which opened at the Ciné Max-Linder in January 1925, was much more serious in its juxtaposition of old and new worlds.[17] It had a seriousness that was acknowledged by most film critics and even honored by official bodies such as the Comité français du cinéma. And it became the subject of the first issue of *La Petite Illustration* (4 April 1925), a deluxe variant of the popular magazine novelizations, published by the prestigious biweekly, *Illustration*.[18] For the film's subject was unique: the conflicts within a Jewish family, with one branch in London and the other in a ghetto village in Poland.

The story begins in the Polish village of Scaravaloff on the eve of the war, as Moise Sigoulim (Maxudian), a London financier, makes his annual pilgrimage to celebrate Passover with his brother, Rabbi Samuel (Bras), and his two daughters, Lia and Ester. A business deal ensues—an arrangement to drill oil on the land of the provincial governor, Count Orlinsky—and Moise invites Lia and Ester to London where they can receive a suitable education. Ten years later, Moise has become a millionaire oil baron; Lia (Raquel Meller) has taken a degree in engineering; and Ester (Tina de Yzarduy) has become a vain coquette. On a visit to London, the count's son, André Orlinsky (André Roanne), finds himself attracted to Lia over Ester, despite his antipathy, as a Christian, toward the Jews. In Scaravaloff, meanwhile, Count Orlinsky, who now manages Moise's oil holdings, has decided to lay off many of the Jewish workers; and Samuel travels to London to appeal directly to Moise on their behalf. When they all return to Scaravaloff, the family conflicts intensify: Ester vows to avenge André's rejection of her love, and Moise asks to marry Lia, who reluctantly agrees, even though she loves André. On the day of the wedding, however, the Christian workers threaten to attack the oil wells, fearing that the Jews are about to be hired in their place (a rumor started by Ester). Lia and André find themselves jointly trying to calm the workers and, then, with the help of Samuel's assistant David (Pierre Blanchar), saving the oil wells from a fiery destruction. In the end, Moise and Ester admit their errors and ask for forgiveness, while Lia and André recognize their mutual love and plan to marry.

At least two points could be made about this audacious film. Although the set decors for the London townhouse sequences, especially Moise's Friday evening reception dinners, were as lavish as any that had yet been constructed for a French film, critics were particularly astonished by the detailed evocation of the Jewish ghetto milieu.[19] And the film's attitude toward this juxtaposition of milieux was intriguingly ambiguous. Moise's London world is roundly condemned—through Ester's addiction to it as well as Samuel's disapproval of the risqué costumes, jazzband music, and dancing couples. But the Scavaraloff ghetto scarcely draws unequivocal praise—Samuel is willing to accept an incestuous marriage, and he apparently refuses to bless the marriage of Lia and André at the end. This ambiguity raises questions that are central to the film, for it seems unusually concerned with the representation of religious, ethnic, and class differences and their resolution. Moise's seeming denial of his ethnic and religious heritage pits him against his brother, while Samuel's rigid ad-

209

herence to that heritage brings him into conflict with his daughter. At the same time, the two brothers are separated by class tensions that threaten to destroy their family as well as the larger community. The distribution of these conflicts reaches a point where the contradictions seem irresolvable, except through the displacement common to melodrama—a climax of near catastrophe and individual heroic action. Created by the vengeful jealousy of one woman, this catastrophe is dispelled by the love and self-sacrifice of her sister, abetted by the man who loves her. In Lia and André, then, all conflicts and contradictions seem to be mediated and resolved, much as they will be two years later in Fritz Lang's *Metropolis*. But here the mediation remains momentary, even suspect, as Samuel's recalcitrance attests.

Despite its critical and commercial success, *La Terre promise* did not put in play all of the elements that were coming together to constitute the modern studio spectacular. That honor probably goes to Ciné-France-Westi's *Ame d'artiste* (1925), which premiered at the Salle Marivaux in July, 1925.[20] Directed by Germaine Dulac, it was adapted by the director and Alexandre Volkoff from a contemporary Danish play by Christian Molbeck. The cosmopolitan nature of the production—its financing was French, German, and Russian emigré— also extended to the cast, which included English, French, and Russian emigré actors. Dulac's way of handling this diverse group was quite opposite Renoir's in *Nana* and may well have set a precedent for the genre: she imposed a uniform style of acting which effectively neutralized any cultural differences among them. *Ame d'artiste* was set in modern London, in the milieu of the theater, probably, as Charles Ford suggests, in order to capitalize on the success of *Kean* from the previous year.[21] However, this image of London was created almost entirely in the studio with Lochakoff designing the sets and Jules Kruger doing the camerawork. There was a complete theater set (as in *Kean*), a huge hotel set for a masked ball (as in *Le Lion des Mogols*), a luxurious townhouse (as in *La Terre promise*), a simple cottage on the city's outskirts (again as in *Kean*), and a cheap hotel and bar. And there were elegant costumes for the two principal actresses and for nearly everyone at the masked ball. Yet, except for the names and exterior shots designating London, all these settings could just as easily have been French or American.

The melodramatic narrative of *Ame d'artiste* has some affinity to *L'Inhumaine* but also has the advantage of being more plausible and more emotionally authentic.[22] The film opens rather cleverly in a series of FSs and CUs: a domestic quarrel between a husband and wife (with two children in the background) climaxes with her picking up a knife to stab him. Suddenly, an ELS reveals the previous action to be a play, a play whose dramatic conflict ironically sets up expectations quite opposite to what actually happens in the film. For a while thereafter, the narrative develops rather conventionally through contrasts between the frivolous life of a famous actress, Helen Taylor (Mabel Poulton), and her lenient father (Nicolas Koline) and the rather sedate life of the Campbells—Herbert (Ivan Petrovich), an aspiring dramatist, his wife Edith (Yvette Andréyor), and her mother (who owns the cottage they live in); between the power of the rich theater-owner, Lord Stamford (Henry Houry), and the naiveté of Herbert, who falls in love with Helen. However, the masked ball sequence, in which Stamford discovers Herbert and Helen embracing, has several nice touches: Herbert is disguised as a clown, and Stamford's falling

210

111. Ivan Petrovich in the
bar sequence in *Ame d'artiste*
(1925)

cigar ash is intercut with the confetti that descends over the lovers. The sequence in which Herbert asks Edith for a divorce is unusually poignant: it
ends with a LS of Herbert going out the front gate into an empty street and
then a MCU of Edith closing the door to simply stand there waiting. The
sequence between Helen and Edith has a similar poignance, but its narrative
function is stronger: Edith brings her Herbert's supposedly lost play, and they
consider who loves him most.

The climax of the film comes in a melodramatic but quite effective alternation between Helen's performance of Herbert's play, *Ame d'artiste* (with
Edith in the audience) and Herbert's attempted suicide in a cheap hotel room
(he believes Helen has gone back to Stamford). The alternation is complicated
and intensified by subjective shots of Herbert's delirium, and his rescue by
Edith is delayed until the final shots of the film. Thus, the subject ultimately
is sacrifice: that of Edith for her husband's career as a playwright and that of
Helen, who, transformed by Edith's action, yields Herbert to her while also
advancing her career. In the end, Helen has her career, Edith has her love,
and Herbert has both love and career—through the sacrifice of the two women.
The "artist's spirit" transcends her milieu to articulate a typically French theme,
one in which Dulac must have taken little pleasure.

In one major aspect, however, *Ame d'artiste* differed from most of the modern studio spectaculars that followed—beyond the fact that it is still quite
watchable even today. Its milieu depends on the theater rather than on the

211

112. A production photo of
L'Herbier (right of camera)
and his crew in Mallet-
Stevens's restaurant set for *Le
Vertige* (1926)

1920s phenomenon of nightclub restaurants, dancing, and automobile touring. In the next two years, through several big films released by three of the
top French film production companies, the genre anchored itself securely in
these modish settings and activities.

The first of these was Cinéromans' Films de France production of *Le Vertige*
(1926), adapted by L'Herbier from a celebrated boulevard melodrama by Charles
Méré.[23] The film's popularity so unnerved L'Herbier, who had given much
more of himself to *L'Inhumaine* and *Feu Mathias Pascal*, that he avoided further
film projects for several months.[24] According to Jaque Catelain, *Le Vertige* was
a rather simplistic drama in which Countess Svirski (Emmy Lynn) escapes her
tyrannical and—just for good measure—criminal husband (Roger Karl) through
the intervention of the hero (Catelain himself).[25] In record time, L'Herbier
shot the exteriors at the fashionable resorts of Eden-Roc and Eze on the Côte
d'Azur.[26] More time was taken for the interiors—especially an ultramodern
house for Catelain and a late night restaurant—designed by Mallet-Stevens
and furnished by Jacques Manuel.[27] L'Herbier even got Robert and Sonya

212

Delaunay to donate several of their large canvases to decorate the house, and the set was so striking that Cinéromans used it as a set piece in one of their current serials, René Le Somptier's chic, sporty *Le P'tit Parigot* (1926).[28] Now that the 1925 Paris Exposition des Arts Décoratifs had legitimized the art deco style, these interiors were "à la mode." Despite L'Herbier's own reservations, several critics at the time accepted *Le Vertige* as "a prodigious synthesis" of the avant-garde and the commercial.[29] Even *Cinéa-Ciné-pour-tous*'s readers voted it fourth on the 1926-1927 list of best films shown in Paris.[30]

When L'Herbier had recovered sufficiently from the experience, Cinéromans naturally asked him to repeat *Le Vertige*'s success, this time in a joint production with Gaumont-British. The result was *Le Diable au coeur* (1928), starring Betty Balfour and Jaque Catelain in another "marvelous decor for dancing."[31] L'Herbier himself remembers it only as his first exposure to panchromatic film stock—which, in the shift from interior to exterior scenes, led to peculiar changes in his star's eyes and costumes.[32]

Despite the relative failure of Boudrioz's *L'Epérvier* (1924), Paramount also did its part in establishing the genre by backing its chief French director, Léonce Perret, in an adaptation of one of Henry Bataille's best sex plays, *La Femme nue* (1926). Updated to the twenties, the film told the story of a young painter who, once having achieved success, abandons his wife and model who, in turn, tries to commit suicide and is rescued by a friend. The subject allowed Perret to pose his stars, Louise Lagrange and Ivan Petrovich, against a series of chic Parisian tableaux, such as Montmartre cafés and Sacré-Coeur. Despite his reservations about its theatricality, Jean Dréville considered *La Femme nue* Perret's best film; and *Cinéa-Ciné-pour-tous* devoted nearly half an issue to the film when it opened at the Madeleine-Cinéma, in December, 1926.[33] Later the magazine's readers agreed with all that attention by voting it ninth on their list of 1926-1927 top films.[34] Just over a year later, Perret repeated the combination in *La Danseuse orchidée* (1928) for Franco-Film.[35] Both films were instrumental in elevating Louise Lagrange to the position of "Princess of the French cinema" in 1929.[36] Another co-production (by SOFAR) very similar in format to these two films was Augusto Genina's *L'Esclave blanche* (1927)—in the words of Dréville, "one of the better *commercial* productions from which the artistic sense has not been completely excluded."[37]

The third company to invest heavily in the genre was Aubert, with Julien Duvivier's adaptation of a popular Pierre Frondaie novel, *L'Homme à l'Hispano*, which opened at the Salle Marivaux, in January, 1927.[38] Raymond Chirat sums up the film's narrative quite aptly:

It is a common story where the old theme of the handsome knight, pure and invincible, who frees the captive princess, is adapted to the decors of luxury hotels, chateaux set in large gardens, and vast estates. A young and charming woman, badly married to an English lord, is attracted to an emotional young man, the owner of a new sportscar, and, after a good number of incidents of middling interest, finds herself passionately, happily, in love.[39]

According to Aubert's publicity, Duvivier took advantage of the new resorts in "the loveliest spots along the Côte d'Argent and in the Basque country" to shoot his exteriors, and Aubert himself bragged about spending a million francs on the interiors of the Oswill villa.[40] In fact, Aubert was so impressed

113. (left) Jaque Catelain in a Mallet-Stevens's interior in *Le Vertige* (1926)

114. (right) Louise Lagrange and Ivan Petrovich in *La Femme nue* (1926)

with the film—or worried about its costs—that he told an interviewer, "Here's the first French film which makes me want to sail to America just to show the Americans what we are capable of doing. . . ."[41] Julien Bayart was less ecstatic: it was "a good narrative film" which at least included a dandy race between a train and the famous Hispano, with some exciting, nicely edited tracking shots.[42] Along with Bernard Natan, Aubert also helped Diamant-Berger dabble in the genre in one of his first films after returning from two years of filmmaking in the United States.[43] *Education de Prince* (1927) was apparently an awkward synthesis of sentimental melodrama, American-style adventure, and studio spectacular. Only the presence of Edna Purviance in the starring role kept it from falling apart completely.[44]

By 1927, the modern studio spectacular was so popular that, when several filmmakers associated with the narrative avant-garde wanted or needed to make a film with supposedly commercial appeal, they turned to the new genre. Jean Epstein, for instance, placed his doubled story of lost love, *6½ × 11* (1927), in the milieu of the Théâtre des Champs-Elysées (singers, chorus girls, and clowns) as well as the spacious winter residences on the Côte d'Azur. Yet today, the sequences in the theater seem almost irrelevant to the film's fascinating rhetorical and narrative experimentation. Similarly, Jean Grémillon situated much of the second half of *Maldone* (1928) in the plush hotels and casinos of the Côte d'Azur. Yet his purpose was to convey the sterile conventions of this noveau riche milieu in contrast to the natural simplicity of the vagabond barge life that his central character (Charles Dullin) had previously enjoyed and to which he returns. *Maldone*, much like *6½ × 11*, was marked by unusual rhetorical and narrative strategies; and neither film did all that well commercially. Apparently the only film in this group to be successful

214

with the public was Jean Renoir's *Marquitta* (1927), which premiered at the Aubert-Palace, in July, 1927.[45]

Taking its title from a currently popular song, *Marquitta*'s scenario by Pierre Lestringuez conceived a Pygmalion story with suitably French and American twists. Among the reviews and reminiscences on this lost film, there is a curious lack of agreement about what exactly happened in it; but the main lines of the narrative seem clear enough.[46] Marquitta (Marie-Louise Iribe) is a young street singer in the working-class district of Paris. One day she is discovered by a foreign prince, Vlasco (Jean Angelo), whom she christens Coco; they become lovers, and she scandalizes the casino society of Cannes with her vulgar behavior. Her father, however, steals an enormous sapphire from Vlasco; Marquitta is accused and thrown out—with a bit of money. She goes on to become a star in the luxurious new nightclubs performing the same tunes she once sang on street corners, while Vlasco loses his money and property in a revolution and degenerates into a Russian dancer in a Nice cabaret.[47] There she finds him in a sequence with a neat comic reversal: "She invites him to dine, and the audiences cracked up when they saw the prince throw himself like a dog on a leg of chicken . . . while Marquitta, very properly, delicately, peeled a pear."[48] When Vlasco tries to commit suicide in a taxi driven by his former valet-secretary (Henri Debain), Marquitta and her 22CV Renault save him after a long chase along the cliff roads above the Mediterranean. The sapphire is recovered; the couple restored. More amicable than tongue-in-cheek or caustic in tone, *Marquitta* was probably just the kind of "high life daydream fairy tale," to quote Raymond Durgnat, that epitomized the genre.[49] Renoir himself best remembers the opening sequence, where he had a large-scale model of the Barbès metro station reflected in a huge mirror with small unsilvered areas behind which several actors were deployed (a technique that was similar to the Shufftan process).[50] The film's success, however, seems to have spurred Marie-Louise Iribe to direct her own exotic melodrama variation on the genre, the recently rediscovered *Hara-Kiri* (1928).[51]

About the same time, one of Renoir's close friends, Alberto Cavalcanti, made a very different studio spectacular, with a correspondingly opposite audience response. Produced by Pierre Braunberger, who was using the genre's popularity to shift from short film to feature film production, *Yvette* (1928) was a contemporary adaptation of a Maupassant story enacted by a half-French, half-British cast.[52] The narrative is unusually slight. Yvette (Catherine Hessling), a young woman known for her skill as a dancer, falls in love with a shallow young man of her own class, Jean de Servigny (Walter Butler). When she realizes that he does not mean to marry her and is just as interested in her mother (Ica de Lenkeffy), Yvette tries to commit suicide. She is found in time; Jean seems to pledge his love; and her mother nonchalantly returns to her lover, Jean's friend Saval (Clifford McLaglen).

In one sense, *Yvette* is a vehicle for Catherine Hessling, who gets to exhibit several different dance numbers (including one in a Black African mask for a West Indian Night party, which prefigures Marlene Dietrich in *Blonde Venus*), do a half-dozen imitations, and die in a lovely full-length white gown in a luxurious bedroom. However, she is far more subdued here than in her previous films, perhaps because just as much attention seems to be given to Eric Aës's incomparably suave set constructions: a large sunken-floor room for danc-

215

115. Catherine Hessling in
Yvette (1928)

ing and dinners, an art deco house exterior, and a spacious bar with an elevated
dance floor.[53] The opening sequence juxtaposes rather too obviously the old
and the new: an afternoon tea for the queen of England and then a modern
evening party of club sandwiches, drinks, and dancing. Thereafter, each sequence seems to document another aspect of the modish good life, from swimming at an exclusive pool to trying out every new form of dancing. The film's
attitude toward all this is anything but sympathetic and goes directly against
the genre's expectations. Yet the overall effect is not really disturbing; in fact,
it is rather distasteful and numbing. The pathos of the central character and
the sometimes acute social and psychological observations are gradually submerged and neutralized in an impeccably American mise-en-scène and montage whose unvaried rhythm finally proves wearyingly monotonous. By imitating the style of American studio spectaculars to a fault, Cavalcanti seems
to have found a consistent means of satirizing the boredom and emptiness of
this milieu; but that very consistency enervates the film itself. Audiences seem
to have responded to *Yvette*'s cool, humorless cynicism with a reciprocal cool-
ness. Today, its air of elegant sterility reminds one a little of Feyder's *Gribiche*.

Full-scale exploitation of the modern studio spectacular was underway just
before the French film industry changed to sound films. After a couple of
mediocre period spectacle films, Paramount committed its whole French film
production to the genre. In 1928, it released Maurice Gleize's adaptation of a
Dekorba novel, *La Madone des sleepings* (with Claude France and Olaf Fjord).[54]
In 1929 came contemporary adaptations of two more Henry Bataille plays—
Luitz-Morat's *La Vierge folle* (starring Emmy Lynn, Jean Angelo, and Suzy
Vernon) and André Hugon's *La Marche nuptiale* (starring Louise Lagrange and
Pierre Blanchar)—and Roger Lion's short *Une Heure au cocktail bar*, which sim-

ply used a modern bar decor, writes Gérard Talon, to intermingle "a complete set of stereotyped characters."[55] The same year, SOFAR, an Italian-German-French company, mounted two big productions by Augusto Genina: *Quartier Latin* from another Dekorba scenario (starring Carmen Boni, Ivan Petrovich, and Gina Manès) and *Prix de beauté* from a René Clair scenario (starring Louise Brooks).[56] At the same time, Cinéromans devoted a good portion of its production budget to Henry Roussel's *Paris-Girls* (with Suzy Vernon) and, especially, to L'Herbier's *L'Argent*. Aubert invested perhaps more heavily in the genre than anyone else. In 1928, the company released René Hervil's *Minuit . . . Place Pigalle* (starring Nicolas Rimsky and Renée Héribel) and H. Etiévant's *La Sirène des tropiques*, from another Dekorba scenario (Josephine Baker in debut, with Pierre Batcheff).[57] It also helped produce two major films by Julien Duvivier: *Le Tourbillon de Paris* in 1928 (with Lil Dagover) and *Au bonheur des dames* in 1929. At least two films from this extensive "catalogue" survive and offer quite different transformations of Zola novels into the modern studio spectacular.

Duvivier's *Au bonheur des dames* (1929) is much the less costly and more conventional of the two films.[58] Its narrative is predicated on the inexorable movement of progress and the unequal conflict between an old-fashioned clothing shop and a new department store (which Zola had based on the Bon Marché, then the world's largest department store),[59] conveniently located on the same street opposite one another. From the provinces, Denise (Dita Parlo) comes to Paris to work for her uncle Baudu (Armand Bour), only to find his once prosperous shop nearly abandoned. Baudu's competitor, Octave Mouret (Pierre de Guingand), hires her for his department store across the street, and they fall in love. After several secondary intrigues involving Mouret's mistress, Mme. Desforges (Germaine Rouer), Denise's cousin Jouve (Albert Bras), who runs off with a model (Ginette Maddie), and another cousin Geneviève (Nadia Sibirskaia), who dies abandoned by her fiancé—after all this, Baudu goes berserk and charges into the department store with a gun. After shooting at Mouret, the store manager, and several women customers as well, he tries to return to his shop and is promptly run over (accidentally) by one of Mouret's delivery trucks. Mouret has to sell his business, and both he and Denise end up in the now deserted old shop.

Perhaps because of the Zola source, *Au bonheur des dames* is much more critical of the modern milieu than are either of Duvivier's earlier films in the genre. But the overall tone is less antagonistic than pathetic and nostalgic—the tragic deaths, the desolation of the shop (increased by the demolition of buildings on either side), the disappearance not only of the family business but of the family itself. Despite itself, the film also cannot control its admiring attention to the department store (designed by Christian Jacque, later to become an important commercial filmmaker), the modeling and shopping that are its chief activities, and the vacation resort of L'Isle-Adam (with a bathing-suit contest) in the then fashionable Seine-et-Oise district north of Paris. Baudu's ineffectual attack and demise become an apt metaphor for the film's own compromised critical position. Distinctly German, American, and French elements combine here in a way quite characteristic of the genre. "The street scenes," writes Raymond Chirat, "nicely echo the German films of the era."[60] The attention to crowd scenes in the street and in the department store, with

116. Pierre Alcover and
Brigitte Helm in a Lazare
Meerson interior in *L'Argent*
(1929)

one serving as the context for the violent climax (as in a misguided western),
imitated American films whose crowd scenes the French took as standards of
veracity and authenticity.[61] Peculiarly French, however, were the numerous
and often elaborate tracking shots, employed usually in long takes rather than
in short clusters of shots or in isolated moments. Denise's movement into
Paris and through the streets to her uncle's boutique is marked with tracking
shots, as is Baudu's assault on the department store and his withdrawal. The
film thus exhibits quite well the synthetic nature of the modern studio spectacular.

The Cinéromans-Cinémondial production of *L'Argent* (1929), with its budget
of nearly five million francs, was one of the biggest French films of the 1928-
1929 season.[62] It was immediately embroiled in controversy when, at the start
of the production, André Antoine reported that L'Herbier's transposition of
the narrative from 1868 to 1928 would betray and disfigure Zola's novel.[63]
Antoine's argument hinged on locating the real, the authentic, in the source
text, which would have produced a period atmosphere film such as *Thérèse
Raquin*. But L'Herbier was interested in the overwhelming power of money or
capital in contemporary society and so used Zola's novel basically as a pre-

218

text.[64] In one sense, however, the question of verisimilitude or authenticity was germane, for *L'Argent* was much more an international production than was *Au bonheur des dames*. Although its narrative was situated clearly in Paris, the characters were generalized types (played by a French-German-English cast) that did not really represent French society. Nicolas Saccard (Pierre Alcover) looks like a stolid, ambitious German who has acquired an American sense of mental and physical quickness. His rival in financial speculation is a coldly calculating reclusive German, Gunderman (Alfred Abel), and his partner-betrayer is the equally cool blonde Baroness Sandorf (Brigitte Helm). The aviator hero, Jacques Hamelin (Henry Victor) and his threatened wife, Line Hamelin (Mary Glory), act like innocent foreigners (American or English) caught up mistakenly in Saccard's schemes. This form of character typing makes *L'Argent* an exemplary film in the genre of modern studio spectaculars. But it also raises the question, first expressed by Jean Lenauer, about whether the dramatic conflict between Saccard and Gunderman distracts an audience from the insidious power of money at the base of that conflict.[65]

There were other exemplary features as well. During the three days of Pentecost in 1928, L'Herbier was allowed into the Paris Bourse (the first filmmaker accorded that privilege) to shoot several spectacular set pieces for the film.[66] For one night, he also electrified the Place de l'Opéra in order to shoot crowd scenes that would later be intercut with Hamelin's record-breaking solo flight from Paris to Cayenne, French Guyana. Lazare Meerson and André Barsacq constructed several magnificent interiors, including an enormous bank interior, several banquet and party halls, and an unusual circular room decorated with a wall-size world map. Apparently, L'Herbier intended *L'Argent* to be critical of all these sumptuous fashionable images, more critical than was *Marquitta* or even *Yvette*. However, there is some question as to which is more pronounced—the critique of the milieux or the celebration of the set decors and what they represent. The film seems much more effective in creating patterns of disruption in the genre by means of several highly original formal strategies. Perhaps no other commercial narrative film seems so conspicuously marked by camera movement—of all kinds. And that insistent movement is paralleled by unconventional editing patterns that are no less striking.[67] The result is a peculiarly uncommercial, experimental work that, very much like *La Passion de Jeanne d'Arc*, presents itself as a major text of the French narrative avant-garde.

From his analysis of the French cinema in 1928, and especially the genre of the modern studio spectacular, Gérard Talon concludes that "the ambition to make French films no longer existed in France."[68] Ideologically and technically, the French film industry was bent on reproducing the studio spectacular of the United States and Germany. By presenting on the screen, "under the guise of a universal spectacle, a reality that was no longer specifically theirs," writes Talon, the French were admitting implicitly to failure—an economic failure to challenge the American cinema's hegemony and an ideological failure to reconstitute a sense of national identity.[69] The argument is harsh but generally persuasive. The attitude of many French studio spectaculars toward the modern good life they showed may have been ambiguous, but the alternative they usually offered was nostalgia for the past. There were

219

exceptions, to be sure, almost exclusively in the films of Epstein, Cavalcanti, Grémillon, and L'Herbier; but none of these (with perhaps the exception of *L'Argent*) were commercially successful. The coming of sound—and French voices, French speech—tended to reverse this pattern and gradually returned the genre to a more distinctly French base, but with its own stereotypes. During the first years of the sound film period, the genre sustained its prominence in films such as L'Herbier's *L'Enfant de l'amour* (1930) and *Le Mystère de la chambre jaune* (1930), Pierre Colombier's *Le Roi des resquilleurs* (1930), Duvivier's *Allo Berlin . . . ici Paris* (1931), and René Guissart's *Tu seras duchesse* (1931).[70] Together with the boulevard melodrama, and often in conjunction with it, the modern studio spectacular soon came to dominate French film production.

Comics and Comedies

Before the Great War, when the French film industry was not turning its national literary heritage into solemn celluloid tableaux, it was usually falling all over itself, anticipating Arthur Freed's credo, "Make 'em laugh, make 'em laugh, make 'em laugh!" As most film historians agree, it was the French who almost singlehandedly created film comedy. From 1906 to 1914, according to Francis Lacassin, more than fifty series of short comic films were produced in France, most of them by Pathé-Frères and Gaumont.[1] Their one-reel *comiques* used teams of vaudeville clowns and circus acrobats often to stage one kind of chase or another which usually ended in a triumphant, destructive furor. But soon each film had at its center a single comedian who, throughout the series, developed a singular comic type. Outside the particular skills of comedians, directors, and scenario writers, the only difference between the two rival companies' productions was Gaumont's preference for shooting location films—in order to keep the tricks and gags cheap.

The period between 1911 and 1914 was especially productive. At Pathé, André Deed (the first major French film comic) had returned from Italy to resume his *Boireau* series about a comical idiot, with an unruly shock of hair, who resorted to gags based on mechanical effects.[2] In the United States, he was dubbed Foolshead. The Variétés actor, Prince (Charles Seigneur), was appearing in the popular *Rigadin* series about "a comic simpleton."[3] Rigadin was a plump, hapless Pierrot with a lugubrious clown face and upturned nose who was hopelessly in love and at odds with everything.[4] The top-liner at Pathé, however, was the *Max* series with Max Linder. In contrast to his predecessors and rivals, who were basically clowns, Max was a trimly turned out bon vivant whose nuanced acting made him the first real star of the French cinema.[5] "A proper young man, impeccably dressed," writes Georges Sadoul, "Max lived in fine apartments, was served by domestics, frequented salons, but never worked."[6] His adventures often were prompted by the women he was infatuated with or bound to, and thus his actions were psychologically (if simply) motivated and frequently involved self-mockery. But his comedy was predicated chiefly on the contrast between his dapper figure and an unusual or unexpected situation.

When Linder's assets all came together in a scenario of cleverly structured gags, his one-reel comic shorts could be the equal of any short Chaplin film. In *Max, victime du quinquina* (1911), for instance, Max gets high on an overdose of quinine he has taken for an illness.[7] In rapid succession, he gets into a quarrel with the Paris police chief, an ambassador, and the war minister, each of whom presents a calling card and challenges him to a duel. With equal speed, a succession of policemen try to arrest him for drunkenness; but when Max blithely produces a card, they respectfully escort him in turn to the homes of the police chief, the ambassador, and finally to bed with the minister's wife. In each case, his puppetlike behavior is misperceived, and he is carried off like an overgrown baby or an expensive piece of luggage. In the end, the minister returns and tosses Max out a bedroom window and onto the street, where he lands on top of all three policemen. Simultaneously, they snap to attention, but, once recognized, he is tossed about like a bundle of laundry. Here, a vaudeville routine, assorted visual gags (Max is pinned to a lamppost when he puts on his topcoat while leaning against it), and a series of obsessively repeated situations are skillfuly woven into an economical social satire. As with Chaplin, writes Sadoul, everything for Linder depends "on the scenario, the play within the scene, the gags and the comic timing. The film technique, which remains secondary, is as simple as possible."[8]

At Gaumont, even more filmmakers were caught up in the rage of comic shorts. Léonce Perret was developing a series after a character named Léonce, which he himself played:

He was a jolly fat fellow, full of good spirits, less intelligent than Max Linder and possessed of a short temper (whose aptness kept him from being imbecilic), not very forward with women (whom he could not give time to anyway), and who, after walking about a little, concluded that he was better off than most: a sympathetic type of ordinary Frenchman—more bourgeois than Max—who had a good chance of pleasing the masses.[9]

Much like the American comic, John Bunny (Vitagraph Films), Léonce was usually married, so most of the series' comedy grew out of domestic squabbles with his wife. Louis Feuillade was writing and directing two different series for Gaumont. One was *Bout-de-Zan*, the most popular of the comic shorts centered on the antics of a precocious child. As Bout-de-Zan, René Poyen was a real *enfant terrible* who terrorized his parents, nurses, and anyone else who ventured near. W. C. Fields would have crossed the street to avoid him. The other series was called *La Vie drôle* and starred Marcel Levesque, a new comedian who had made a name for himself in the boulevard comedies of Tristan Bernard.[10]

The most interesting Gaumont comedies, however, were those done by Jean Durand. Durand created his best comic shorts in the *Onésime* series, which starred Ernest Bourbon, an outrageously costumed, acrobatic Auguste. Onésime was usually a hard-pressed buffoon who got his way through hare-brained schemes or luck. But the real fascination of these films, according to Sadoul, was the accelerating rhythms of their gags and "the imperturbably logical development of an absurd situation."[11] *Onésime horloger* (1912), for example, presents Onésime with the problem of collecting an inheritance his uncle has stipulated cannot be distributed for twenty years.[12] He merely rewires the main clock in the Paris Central Bureau, and undercranking or pixilation takes care of the rest: studies, marriage, children, a new house, a seat at the Opéra and at the Café de la Paix. By the end of the reel, Onésime has the inheritance

117. Max Linder

as well as more than his share of responsibilities and ways to spend it. As Bardèche and Brasillach first noted, *Onésime horloger* may be the germ of René Clair's *Paris qui dort* (1924).[13]

The war nearly killed off French film comedy. Several of the comics, such as Deed and Linder, volunteered for military service. Perret and then Linder accepted offers to make films in the United States, and Deed went back to Italy. Alone, Prince continued the *Rigadin* series for Pathé, but his character was becoming tiresome. While Feuillade regularly ground out *Bout-de-Zans* until his actor outgrew the role, Durand turned to literary adaptations and patriotic films. By the close of 1916, Gaumont's only regular comic short was Feuillade's retitled series, *Pour remonter le moral de l'arrière*, with Marcel Levesque.[14] The flood of imported American comic films starring Charlie Chaplin or "Charlot," Fatty Arbuckle, Mabel Normand, and Harold Lloyd quickly filled the vacuum. Outside of Levesque and the aging Prince, there were no French comics who could even begin to challenge them—and there was precious little money to do it with. Besides, the war made it difficult for the French to laugh at themselves, at least in the ways they used to. It was easier for someone else to provide the slapstick and the embarrassing situations; and the American films had a level of zest, inventiveness, and cinematic construction that created a new standard in film comedy. Perhaps the French comic short would have been superseded by Charlot and company anyway, but the war eliminated any chance that the genre could have been sustained and revitalized.

After the war, there were a few feeble attempts to resurrect the one- and two-reel comic films. At Gaumont, Durand directed a short-lived series with Marcel Levesque called *Serpentin* (1919-1920). This series found favor with the critics (even Louis Delluc); but, denied distribution beyond the small French market, it could not generate enough profits.[15] After *Serpentin* was dropped, Feuillade built a series called *Belle Humeur* (1920-1922) around another vaudeville actor, Georges Biscot. However, in the words of Lacassin, "replacing the calm immobility of Levesque with the tremblings [of Biscot] produced [occasional] guffaws rather than [sustained] laughter."[16] At Pathé, the *Rigadin* series wound down slowly until it was finally halted in the company's reorganization in 1920. Max Linder returned briefly from the United States (by way of a Swiss sanitarium, after convalescing from double pleurisy) and allowed Diamant-Berger to re-make one of his earlier one-reelers as *Le Feu sacré* (1920).[17] Nothing seemed to work. After 1922, the French comic short simply disappeared except for an occasional sortie by one of the narrative avant-garde filmmakers, none of which had more than limited distribution: Gance's *Au secours!* (1923) with Max Linder, Clair's *Entr'acte* (1924), Renoir's *Charleston* (1926), Cavalcanti's *La P'tite Lily* (1927) and *Le Petit Chaperon rouge* (1929).

The death of the comic short, however, did not mean the end of French film comedy. For two things happened during the decade after 1915 to reposition it. One was the integration of the comics into the police serial, the Arabian Nights film, and the historical reconstruction. Louis Feuillade and Marcel Levesque were instrumental in this transformation. For both *Judex* (1917) and *La Nouvelle Mission de Judex* (1918), Levesque developed a character named Cocantin who served as a comic foil and befuddled assistant to the hero. In *Tih-Minh* (1919) and *Barrabas* (1920), Feuillade gave a similar role to Biscot who, in one, was even called, ironically, Placide. It was Levesque who carried the comic role into feature films in Louis Nalpas's production of *La Sultane de l'amour* (1919). And it was Armand Bernard who made the role a viable part of the historical reconstruction film in his reluctant performance of Planchet, d'Artagnan's valet, in Diamant-Berger's *Les Trois Mousquetaires* (1921-1922).[18] Thereafter, the comic confidant, usually a male sidekick, became a prominent fixture in the French cinema of the early 1920s. Along with Levesque and Bernard, certain actors became identified with the type: Lucien Tramel, Henri Debain, Nicolas Koline, Alex Allin.[19]

The other strategy to transform the comic short was the attempt to produce a feature-length film comedy. Apparently, the idea originated with Diamant-Berger who, in 1919, had just returned from studying, at Pathé's insistence, production and distribution techniques in the United States.[20] Caught up in the dream of restoring the French cinema to international status, Diamant-Berger got Pathé's consent to film a sure-fire property with an international star. He chose Tristan Bernard's most popular boulevard comedy, *Le Petit Café* (which had played over a year at the Palais-Royal), and asked Max Linder (whom the French now considered an American) to head its cast.[21] For a director, he took a chance on Raymond Bernard, the playwright's son, who had been Feyder's assistant at Gaumont and who had directed a number of short films based on his father's scenarios.[22] Max Linder, writes Sadoul,

was perfectly cast in the role of the café waiter who, on suddenly becoming a millionaire, was still bound by contract to the bistro and so passed his evenings as a pleasure-seeker and his days as a mere garçon.[23]

Henri Debain also made an auspicious debut as a café dishwasher in the kind of secondary comic role that would become his trademark.[24] As for Raymond Bernard, he knew full well the spirit of his father's work, according to Ricciotto Canudo, and "the slight but quite funny comedy was translated intact onto the screen, with its characters and situations, its ironies and gaiety."[25] *Le Petit Café* seemed to have just the right blend of physical, social, and psychological comedy.

Everything went smoothly until the completed film was shown to a group of distributors—and no one wanted it. Diamant-Berger complains, perhaps disingenuously,

the exhibitors were unanimous! A Max Linder without fast chases, without slapstick, a comedy that lasts as long as a drama . . . how could one hope to spark the audience's laughter and sustain it for such an unusual length of time?[26]

Only four cinemas agreed to open *Le Petit Café*, in December, 1919: the Omnia-Pathé, Tivoli, Colisée, and Ciné Max-Linder, which the star was then in the process of selling.[27] Against all odds, the film was a smash and soon was playing everywhere in Paris, in the provinces, and across Europe. In Germany, it was the first French film to receive acclaim after the war. Costing just 160,000 francs, it accumulated over a million in grosses.[28]

Astonishingly, nothing came of this success. All of the principals went on to other things—Diamant-Berger began preparations for *Les Trois Mousquetaires*; Linder returned to the United States to do a parody of Fairbanks in *The Three Must-Get-Theres*; Bernard became engaged in a series of psychological

223

"chamber music" films scripted by his father—and no one else in the industry seems to have had the courage or desire to make another *Petit Café*. This is all the more puzzling since the French theater at the time was in the midst of a popular revival of boulevard comedy.[29] Why did this happen? Was there a rivalry between the theater and the cinema which restricted the chances of presenting a comedy simultaneously on stage and on film? Were the theatrical comedies so verbally oriented that it was difficult to adapt them to the visual film medium? Was the industry so overwhelmed by the American film comics and so despairing of its own comic actors?

Whatever the exact combination of reasons, the feature-length film comedy developed fitfully over the next several years. The most consistent formula was also the most retrograde: Robert Saidreau's series of vaudeville comedies, a dozen of which were released from 1920 to 1925. The least interesting were Feuillade's uninspired adaptations of boulevard comedies such as Bayard and Vanderbuch's *Le Gamin de Paris* (1923) and Labiche's *La Fille bien gardée* (1924), both of which starred a grown-up Bout-de-Zan.[30] Much more promising were two sets of films that were closed off by untimely deaths. Pathé-Consortium seemed to have given the go-ahead to a series of comedies, starring Lucien Tramel, based on the Bouif character of de la Fouchardière: *Le Crime du Bouif* (1922) and *La Résurrection du Bouif* (1922).[31] But the director of the series, Henri Pouctal, died suddenly early in 1922. Several years later, Aubert launched Max Linder's last film, *Le Roi du cirque* (1925), a French-Austrian production which was shot by E. Violet at the Vita-Film studios in Vienna.[32] The subject, a succession of amusing episodes loosely organized around the circus arena, foreshadowed and may have influenced Chaplin's more tightly structured film, *The Circus* (1927). But Linder's suicide, in late October, 1925, unfortunately closed off what promised to be a series of fine comedies and a new stage in his career.[33] The most important effort of all, as it turned out, had little to do with either the boulevard comedy, the vaudeville, or the circus. Instead, it represented an original synthesis of American film comedy and earlier French fantasy films, interpolated with parodic elements from other film genres. Two writer-directors were principally involved in this strategy: Ivan Mosjoukine and René Clair.

Ironically, it was the young Albatros company formed of Russian emigrés that initiated this renewal of French film comedy. Apparently, their model of comedy construction was the story of a naïve provincial fellow come to the sophisticated city, which suggests a parallel to the company members' own transposition from Russia to France and Paris. This juxtaposition was the basis for linking together all sorts of mocking episodes in different milieux. For instance, in Tourjansky's *Ce Cochon de Morin* (1924), adapted from a Maupassant story, Morin (Nicolas Rimsky), a lawyer from La Rochelle, has a series of drunken adventures in Paris that carry him from a jazzband dance hall to court. Perhaps overstating the case, Jean Pascal saw the film as "high comedy" in contrast to "the heavy-handed burlesque too often employed in American comedies."[34] An even better film was Volkoff's *Les Ombres qui passent* (1924), from a scenario by Mosjoukine.[35] Louis Barclay (Mosjoukine) and his young wife Alice (Andrée Brabant) live simply and sanely in Happyland, the country estate of Louis's father, Professor Barclay (Henry Krauss). In order to collect an inheritance of several million francs, the young innocents travel to Paris, where Louis is quickly seduced by the vamp Jacqueline (Natalie Lissenko) and becomes the victim of numerous misadventures. *Les Ombres qui passent* seems to have been a fantastic tale, a pastiche parodying various genres, from Griffith's sentimental country melodramas to the French bourgeois melodrama.

Mosjoukine's most interesting contribution, however, was *Le Brasier ardent* (1923), which he wrote, directed, and performed in as the leading character. Although not all that successful commercially, *Le Brasier ardent* was unquestionably one of the most bizarre films of the decade. *Cinémagazine* called the film a labyrinth whose every turn opened onto a different genre.[36] Some of the comedy comes from Lochakoff's strange set designs—e.g., the detective agency, which the husband literally falls into, or the woman's bedroom, which operates much like a Mack Sennett set. But most of it is produced by Mosjoukine's conception of the detective, who rapidly regresses from his initial heroic image through a shifting parody of disguises to a mama's boy who lives with his adoring mother and her pet bulldog. Mosjoukine was never again to be more mockingly exuberant than in this film. Within a year, stardom had tamed him into respectability.

Just as *Le Brasier ardent* was being previewed for the critics and exhibitors, René Clair was engaged in a similar attempt to revive French film comedy. His first project, based on an original scenario, *Paris qui dort* (1924), was an unexpected commercial success, despite a certain roughness in its mise-en-scène and editing.[37] Here Clair quite consciously wanted "to revert to the prewar tradition, that is to say, the tradition of the first French comic shorts . . . films [that] address directly the greatest number of spectators."[38] His narrative was predicated on the inverse of Durand's *Onésime horloger*. An angry scientist invents an invisible-ray machine which he uses to stop time and immobilize all Paris. The only people not affected are the scientist himself, his daughter, a planeload of five people from Marseille, and the caretaker atop the Eiffel Tower. Paris becomes simultaneously an immense waxworks museum and a rich, ripe world for the six characters to wander through—and plunder. Their wanderings are both comic and magical. A whole society of manners, character types, public and domestic situations lies exposed to their scrutiny and ridicule. They themselves, however, repeat those gestures and actions by taking whatever they desire and by cavorting and then fighting among themselves while suspended over the city on the Eiffel Tower. The exuberant, mocking spirit of playfulness in *Paris qui dort*, along with that in *Le Brasier ardent* and Clair's second film, *Entr'acte* (1924), carry all three films well beyond the conventions of the commercial cinema.

Although Clair's next few films do not really renounce this comic renewal, they tend more and more to experiments in fantasy. *Le Voyage imaginaire* (1926) probably most exhibits his continued interest in comedy. Much of the comedy here evokes *Le Brasier ardent* and Clair's first films. It opens, for instance, with the hero being chased by a bulldog who in turn is being chased by its master; and its long fantasy section ends with the hero transformed into a toy bulldog before the eyes of the disappointed heroine. Early on, the film also includes some effective satire of French bureaucracy—especially in the way a bouquet of flowers passes round and round a small town bank office, in order to define all of the characters and their relations with one another. However, *Le Voyage imaginaire* was no more a commercial success than was *Le Brasier ardent*.[39] The

225

Mosjoukine-Clair renewal seemed little more than a minuscule eddy in the stream of profitable period films and emerging modern studio spectaculars.

After Mosjoukine moved on to lavish spectacle films, Albatros turned to Nicolas Rimsky to sustain its film comedy projects. Rimsky was not a major comic actor; in fact, he looked and acted like a milquetoast version of Marcel Levesque. His films, done in collaboration with Pierre Colombier and Roger Lion, depended heavily on comic situations and on wholesale borrowings from other films, both French and American. One of the first of these films, Colombier's *Paris en cinq jours* (1926), revives the story of provincial characters in the city, but in a new format.[40] Here Rimsky is teamed with Dolly Davis as a New York couple (he loves *The Three Musketeers*; she is a swimmer) who win $10,000 in a contest, get engaged, and set sail for Paris. This sets the stage for five days of comic adventures. In later films, such as *Le Chasseur de Chez Maxim's* (1927)—which originally was to have starred Max Linder— *Cinéa-Ciné-pour-tous* argued that Rimsky was able to transpose completely "American methods—gags, touches of imaginative detail, comic gestures drawn from Chaplin and Lloyd—into an atmosphere of French gaiety."[41]

Jim la Houlette, roi des voleurs (1926), the only one of these films that I have seen, illustrates how well, and not so well, this actually worked.[42] Rimsky plays Jacques Morton, the lowly secretary to a popular novelist, Brettoneau, whose daughter Pauline (Gaby Morlay) he loves madly. Much like a latter-day Orlando, he writes anonymous poems to her and attaches them to lamp shades around the Brettoneau's chic ultramodern villa. Brettoneau's agent, an American-style advertising maniac, conceives a plan to reverse the slumping sales of his books—throw a party and have Jim la Houlette, a Fantômas-like character who has terrorized Europe for ten years, steal his latest manuscript. Morton is bamboozled into disguising himself as Jim (Pauline says she could love such a man), but the real thief appears and leaves him to take the rap. In the court trial (a kind of parody of *Crainquebille*), Brettoneau and his agent testify against their own duped accomplice—the publicity campaign has worked; the new novel is a best-seller. But when Pauline confesses that she loves him, Morton proudly accepts his criminal name. At the last moment, his lawyer (who turns out to be the real Jim) allows him to escape from prison. On a train bound for the lawyer's country estate, Morton disguises himself as a priest and performs a few routines imitating Chaplin in *The Pilgrim*. The lawyer invites Brettoneau to his estate, and Morton pretends to haunt him (once more disguised, as a ten-foot-tall figure perched invisibly on a servant's shoulders). Pauline shows up unexpectedly, just as her father (threatened with disclosure) has made out a blank check for 500,000 francs. Suddenly, the police arrive. The lawyer and his wife go off in one underground tunnel; Morton and Pauline go off (with the check) in another. There the film ends, as improbably as a serial, as she sums up her love: "The things I loved in Jim, I love in you—bravery and daring; but besides you are kind and honest." So it goes, indeed.

After the success of Max Linder's *Le Roi du cirque* (1925), Aubert decided to revive the Bouif character in a series of films starring Lucien Tramel. According to *Cinéa-Ciné-pour-tous*, the most important of these was the six-part serial, *Le Bouif errant* (1926): "Sly and naturally optimistic, without overzealous outbursts, without theatrical effects, Tramel provokes laughter through

226

the aptness of his gestures and expressions to the situation of the scenario."[43]
His production team was also quite supportive: an original scenario from de la Fouchardière, competent direction by René Hervil, and solid comic acting by Albert Préjean and Jim Gerald. Aubert's attempt to exploit Tramel in a double role in Duvivier's *Le Mystère de la Tour Eiffel* (1927), however, frittered away a chance to sustain momentum.[44] Clearly, one problem in most of these films was an enervating tendency to exploit sumptuous modern decors, as if comic appeal were not enough to generate public interest. That tendency was so marked in Aubert's *Les Transatlantiques* (1928), directed by Diamant-Berger and Colombier, that a satire of Yankee tourists became little more than a puff of charming pleasantries in the chic milieux of Paris and Deauville.[45] Much like the modern studio spectacular, the French film comedy seemed on the verge of losing even the remotest connection with its own national identity, its own social structures.[46]

In the last two years of the decade, the genre suddenly flowered in a quick succession of films, most of them produced by Albatros. Unlike the previous films, they were deft adaptations of classic or current boulevard comedies. These films were grounded solidly in French society, and they consistently subordinated fantasy and psychological responses to it, integrating them into the representation of a specific milieu. They also announced a new generation of comic actors: Albert Préjean, Pierre Batcheff, Michel Simon. The first two films to begin the cycle were directed by the filmmaking brothers, Henri Chomette and René Clair.

Le Chauffeur de Mademoiselle (1928), which opened at the Omnia-Palace in April, 1928, seems to have been a carefully calculated project written for Dolly Davis and Albert Préjean.[47] Chomette himself freely admitted this, but distinguished this, his first feature film, from the then current "league of nations" productions:

In the *Chauffeur de Mademoiselle*, a film that I made in full knowledge of the commercial concessions I decided were acceptable, I have tried to achieve a homogeneity by using French elements only.[48]

Among others, Jean Dréville remarked on the comedy's singularity:

Ah yes, a charming film, full of good taste and balance, and according to the French formula. For once, the formula seems to me excellent. *Le Chauffeur de Mademoiselle* is indeed a French film; the publicity is not lying.[49]

Although the film seems to have been modestly profitable, most film historians have accepted the critic's disappointment at Chomette's failure to carry over the array of techniques manifested in his few short experimental films, *Jeux des reflets et de la vitesse* (1925) and *Cinq Minutes du cinéma pur* (1926). René Jeanne and Charles Ford, for instance, conclude that, in *Le Chauffeur de Mademoiselle*, "Chomette was no more than a good craftsman."[50] Dréville, however, valued the film precisely for this restraint and notes several images which suggest that the film was more than hack work: "It is definitely interesting to study; the design produces some striking dissolves between disparate images, a sky that progressively 'eats' half a tree in the background, etc."[51] The *découpage* of one sequence published in *Cinégraphie* also reveals a rather effective use of multiple exposures or split-screen framing for comic effect: a couple's tele-

118. (left) Albert Préjean,
Olga Tschekowa, and Vital
Geymond in *Un Chapeau de
Paille d'Italie* (1928)

119. (right) Jim Gerald and
Albert Préjean

phone conversation ("Don't come yet. I haven't dared break the news of our marriage to my aunt") is gradually overheard by a half-dozen people listening in on the party line.[52] The moment has a Lubitsch-like touch that combines the technical facility of Gance's *Napoléon* and a typical gag from the prewar French comic shorts. Unfortunately, no print of the film seems to have survived so that we could resolve these critical contradictions.

René Clair's *Un Chapeau de paille d'Italie* (1928) presents no such problem. It was Alexandre Kamenka who bought the rights of this clever Labiche play from Marcel L'Herbier and then asked Clair to adapt and direct it for Albatros.[53] The film pleased the critics more than it did French audiences (an exclusive run at the Omnia-Palace, early in 1928, lasted only three weeks), but it was just successful enough—and without a single major star.[54] Clair's adaptation was brilliant in at least two crucial ways. The play's early Second Empire setting (1851) was transposed to that of the Belle Epoque bourgeoisie (1895), specifically, to the Charenton suburb of Paris bordering on the Bois de Vincennes. Keeping the Second Empire setting, reasoned Clair, would have created a period film of nostalgic beauty; to produce properly ridiculous costumes and decors for a 1928 audience, the *fin-de-siècle* period was perfect. Sepia film stock provided an appropriate period color-tone (the chief cameraman was Maurice Desfassiaux); and Lazare Meerson's interiors, with their ornamental Henri II funishings, caricatured early Pathé film sets.[55] Thus the society which enjoyed Labiche's play is itself satirized in the film. Furthermore, Clair perceived that Labiche's verbal comedy was based on a comedy of situations, a burlesque of movement. His task was to drop the verbal comedy and graft onto this "burlesque intrigue . . . , transposed cinematically and treated like a ballet, . . . a series of striking visual observations."[56] The result, although perhaps indebted to Lubitsch and Chaplin, was a truly French film comedy—without a single comic caption. At its summer preview, Edmond Epardaud dubbed it a "comedy of observation."[57]

The narrative of *Un Chapeau de paille d'Italie* intermeshes two simple plots in a delightful web of complications. On the afternoon of his marriage to Hélène Nonancourt (Marise Maia), Fadinard (Albert Préjean) crosses the Bois de Vincennes to inspect his new apartment and nuptial chamber. On the way, his horse nonchalantly munches on a lady's hat in a bush; from behind the bush quickly come Anäis de Beauperthuis (Olga Tschekowa) and her lover, Lieutenant Tavernier (Vital Geymond). In a rage, Tavernier orders Fadinard to find another Italian straw hat exactly like the half-eaten one or he will destroy his apartment. For the lady is married and must return home "intact." Throughout the day, as he anxiously goes through the series of social ceremonies, Fadinard and his servant Felix (Alex Allin) pursue the elusive duplicate hat. Tipped off by a saleswoman, he finally goes to the home of Beauperthuis (Jim Gerald) and explains his predicament, only to discover the man is Anäis's husband. When the hat eventually shows up, aptly enough, it has been there all along—the first of the bride's wedding presents. After a final ballet of circulating objects, running figures, and desperate glances, Anäis returns safely to her own bedroom and husband, while Fadinard sends Tavernier off and goes to Hélène in the nuptial chamber.

The marvelous play of visual observation which this narrative accrues makes for an unrelenting attack on the society of the Belle Epoque bourgeoisie. Clair's method is clearly an extension of the bureaucratic satire in *Le Voyage imaginaire*. The characters are all recognizable types with different objects to define them, and they behave like marionettes going through the motions of social interchange. Tavernier is all strutting uniform, with a ridiculously obsolete sense of decorum and gallantry. Nonancourt, the bride's squat father (Yvonneck), is stuffed into a new shirt front and boots that pinch. Tall, thin cousin Bobin (Pré *fils*) is at loose ends over a lost glove. Uncle Vesinet (Paul Olivier) has a blocked earhorn and cannot hear or see anything that is going on. Felix, on the other hand, sees entirely too much. At one point, every time he peeks into Fadinard's sitting room, the lovely but powerless Anäis is in a different man's arms. When the huge blustering Beauperthuis is finally introduced, his feet are soaking in a pan of hot water, which at last allows Nonancourt to pilfer some comfortable footwear.

Each social ceremony is undermined by a parody of conventions. The mayor's speech to the wedding party, for instance, is interrupted by a loose tie—everyone straightens his own, including the mayor, until finally an uncle discovers that it was his tie that initiated the ricocheting comedy.[58] Then the mayor is cut off in the middle when the increasingly nervous Fadinard interprets his lifted arms as a sign of conclusion and leads the whole family off past the astonished officials. Later, while a drunken Nonancourt delivers his homily on marriage to Hélène and the family in what he thinks to be the new apartment, Fadinard is in the next room unwittingly revealing to Beauperthuis Anäis's affair with Tavernier. Even the objects gain an importance of their own as possessions, an importance that is ridiculed in several wedding gift

120. (left) The final recovery of the hat in *Un Chapeau de paille d'Italie* (1928)

121. (right) Pierre Batcheff as the defense lawyer fantasizing in *Les Deux Timides* (1929)

exchanges. Momentarily mystified, Tavernier accepts the present of a clock, which turns out to be a replica of one in the bedroom; just as the prim couple who offered it prepare to drive off in their carriage, the clock sails through the second-floor window and smashes on the sidewalk beside them. When the exasperated Nonancourt tries to annul the marriage at the end, the relatives immediately attack Felix and grab their gifts back—inadvertently exposing the hat, the source and resolution of all the troubles.

Un Chapeau de paille d'Italie neatly sets in opposition the reality and illusion, the emptiness and hypocrisy, of the French bourgeois marriage. Although initially juxtaposed to the newlyweds, the adulterous couple soon literally replaces them. It is they who occupy the new apartment and who finally hole up in the nuptial chamber (although nothing untoward happens). While the relatives come bearing gifts to adorn the apartment, Tavernier methodically destroys some of the things that are already there. In a brief sequence (using wild camera movement, slow motion, and fast motion), Fadinard even imagines a whole set of furniture disappearing. But Tavernier and Anaïs only prepare for the pattern of doubling that succinctly closes the film. While Tavernier runs off to rescue the hat, first from the police and then from an inconveniently placed lamppost (its last resting place), Hélène hides Anaïs behind her full wedding dress and Fadinard blocks Beauperthuis's vision with a raised umbrella. In their attempt to preserve a marriage, the newlyweds provide an innocent front for deception. The implication is clear—it is only a matter of time before that deception is embodied in them. The final images

230

confirm it. While Anaïs smiles in her sleep, Beauperthuis sits bewildered in his bedroom chair, gazing at her hat (actually Hélène's). Because the hat seems intact, is she really in his possession? This illusory emblem of "the proper marriage" (fitting woman to man) is then matched by its corollary—the floral wedding wreath placed on the bedroom mantel and preserved by a glass cover. How soon will Hélène find her Tavernier?

After *Un Chapeau de paille d'Italie*, Clair had wanted to direct a realist film based on a recent criminal case; but early in 1928, Chiappe, the new *préfet de police* in Paris, began to concern himself with cinema exhibition (e.g., Les Amis de Spartacus), and Clair abandoned the idea.[59] Since Albatros had a contract with Maurice de Féraudy, he decided to use him in another adaptation of a Labiche play. *Les Deux Timides* (1929) was less successful than its predecessor, perhaps because its release coincided with the first sound films late in 1928 and early in 1929.[60] But the film itself was rather different, and critics have been divided on its merits ever since.[61] *La Revue du cinéma*, for instance, found it deftly charming in its caricature, but not really ferocious enough.[62]

The two timid characters are Frémission (Pierre Batcheff), a young provincial lawyer, and an old landowner, Thibaudier (Maurice de Féraudy), whose daughter Cecile (Vera Flory) is the object of Frémission's inept courting.[63] His rival, Garadoux (Jim Gerald), is a former wife-beater (which no one knows, since he has resettled) whom Frémission had defended in his first court case several years before. After a multiplication of misunderstandings that culminate in a near siege of the Thibaudier estate, plus another court trial, Frémission and Cecile are married.

Several things distinguish *Les Deux Timides* from Clair's earlier films. This is the first film in which Clair shot exteriors outside Paris, and several sequences—for example, the young lovers meeting in an open pasture—have a charm and freshness usually associated with the provincial realist film.[64] The interiors, again by Meerson, were designed to complement the authenticity of the location shooting and emphasized exact details—such as the old sewing machine in Garadoux's first apartment, the mixture of comfortable and uncomfortable chairs in Thibaudier's drawing room. A comedy of situations structures this film as well, but the comedy is less socially determined and more interior, that is, focused on the psychology of character types—harmonizing with the more realistic decors.[65] In the opening trial sequence, for instance, a mouse interrupts the proceedings much as did the loose tie at the wedding ceremony in *Un Chapeau*; but here the effect is to so unhinge Frémission that he becomes a blathering fool who condemns his own client, Garadoux. When the young suitor calls on Thibaudier to broach the subject of marriage, the two men are so afraid to speak that three hours later, when Cecile enters the room to turn on a light, she startles them both out of a sound sleep. Batcheff's stylized but finely nuanced performance as Frémission (his shy courting and frantic avoidance of danger are clearly modeled on Chaplin) is just right for this psychological comedy, but the other principal characters either shade off toward naturalism (Thibaudier) or broad caricature (Garadoux and his family who come to visit Thibaudier).[66] In fact, as Jean Mitry argues, the caricature and physical comedy—which are strongest in the final sequences, especially in the siege and second trial—do tend to throw the film slightly out of balance.[67]

Finally, *Les Deux Timides* contains several inventive gags that ridicule the

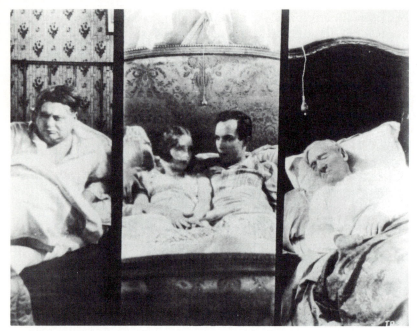

122. The final triptych
sequence in *Les Deux Timides*
(1929)

mental state of its characters, using optical effects and the split-screen concept
Henri Chomette had recently exploited in *Le Chauffeur de Mademoiselle*. The
film opens with shots of Garadoux cruelly beating his wife, which are suddenly
revealed to be the representation of the prosecutor's speech at the beginning
of the trial (this seems to cleverly incorporate Clair's original plan for a realist
crime film). In contrast, Frémission's defense envisions a gentle, generous
Garadoux and culminates in five overwhelmingly sentimental images within
one shot. After the mouse wreaks havoc in the courtroom, however, Frémission becomes flustered. And his lapses are conveyed in shots of Garadoux and
his wife that slow and freeze, then speed up and freeze again, then reverse;
finally, when the lawyer's mind fails, Harry Alan Potamkin writes, "the domestic scene explodes [in a spiral] from the screen leaving it blank."[68] In
another sequence, after they have recognized one another outside Thibaudier's
house, the two rivals go through a mock battle in separate rooms—each victorious within his half of a split screen. The final shot is a delightful parody
of Gance's triple-screen in *Napoléon*. Frémission and Cecile are in bed in the
center panel, flanked by Garadoux and Thibaudier, separately in theirs. The
two lovers embrace and look shyly off to the left and right. Thibaudier dutifully turns off his light; they embrace again and turn off their overhead light;
Garadoux looks startled and angrily throws down his lamp. Simultaneously,
the center light pops on, and a much vexed Frémission bolts upright and pulls
down a shade in front of the camera.

The last silent film comedy produced by Albatros was Jacques Feyder's *Les
Nouveaux Messieurs* (1929), adapted from a current play by Robert de Flers and
Francis de Coisset.[69] Both the play and the Charles Spaak/Feyder scenario were

232

123. Gaby Morlay and Albert
Préjean in *Les Nouveaux
Messieurs* (1929)

overtly political, which made the film rather unique in the French cinema of the 1920s. Jean Gaillac (Albert Préjean), chief electrician at the Paris Opéra and an important labor union official, is interested in Suzanne Verrier (Gaby Morlay), a prima ballerina at the Opéra and mistress of Comte de Montoire-Grandpré (Henry Roussel). Jean is elected to run for the Chamber of Deputies and, in a left landslide, defeats his opponent, Montoire-Grandpré. Suzanne becomes his mistress, and soon he has accepted all the trappings of authority and power. When the government is overturned in a crisis, Jean accepts a diplomatic post in the colonies (arranged by his rival), and Suzanne reluctantly returns to Montoire-Grandpré. The French government responded to this subject by refusing Albatros a license to distribute the film. Their objection was not to the narrative, which seemed to satirize the labor union movement (a topical subject after the left lost the elections of 1928), but to the disrespectful depiction of the Chamber of Deputies and its members.[70] After months of haggling and several brief cuts, the film was exhibited at the Paramount-Palace, in April, 1929, with its basic satirical structure intact.[71] Perhaps because of its notoriety, Feyder's film was quite successful. The readers of *Cinéa-Ciné-pour-tous* even voted it second to *The Jazz Singer* as the best film of 1929.[72]

Les Nouveaux Messieurs can be described as a sentimental romance or melodrama in a comic mode that synthesizes many previous film comedies. On the one hand, it continues the pattern of most Albatros and Aubert comedies of 1926-1927. There are several large decors (again by Meerson) straight out of the modern studio spectacular: a detailed set reconstruction of the Chamber of Deputies and a sumptuous modern townhouse for the Comte de Montoire-Grandpré. Moreover, the heroine is a star and has the role of a dancer at the

233

Opéra, where the film's long opening sequence of a rehearsal takes place. However, the light comic observations are closely modeled on Clair. The count is first defined by his lapel pin, his monocle, his coat and cane, and the overall image reflected in his chauffeured car. Jean becomes what he opposes by using the same poster design as his opponent and by blithely donning a top hat and tails. And, like Clair, Feyder and his cameramen, Georges Périnal and Maurice Desfassiaux, also employ technical devices for comic effect. The dedication of a workers' city ends in a Sennett-like fast-motion parade and speech so Jean can return to the crisis-wracked capital.[73] In the Chamber itself, the Minister of Art falls asleep and dreams his colleagues have been transformed into ballerinas in tutti. On the crucial vote of confidence for the government, a soft focus area keeps moving back and forth over the chamber, signaling the capricious shifts in voting.

The comedy, as one can see, is not quite the equal of Clair's, and the film does drag in some sequences.[74] Perhaps it is most effective in the way the overall mode shifts from romantic comedy to ironic, or even tragic, satire.[75] The ultimate subject of the satire is not the blindness and corruption of the working class or labor union movement but rather the social and political system that remains unchanged and easily co-opts them. Jean and Suzanne enjoy a brief idyll on the morning of the leftist victory—driving along the Seine (with the Billancourt factories behind them and the Eiffel Tower off to the side) and impulsively going for a swim—but the rest of the film reveals the moment to be an illusion. Perhaps the real victim of the film and its central character is Suzanne. She only accepts Montoire-Grandpré's favors because it is the "right thing" to do. Although she genuinely likes Jean, he pays little attention to her once he is launched on a career. It is she who suffers on his politicking trips: struggling with the baggage while he is greeted ceremoniously at the station, sleeping away the afternoon in a cheap hotel room, finding dirt in her luncheon coffee cup. In order to enjoy even a bit of the good life, Suzanne seems to have no other choice than to go back to Montoire-Grandpré. For her, too, "the new masters" are no different from the others. That Moussinac and his Socialist-Communist friends defended Feyder's film against the government's censorship made perfect sense.

There was one more French film comedy of a very different sort—Jean Renoir's most underrated silent film, *Tire au flanc* (1928).[76] Although an independent production, financed by Pierre Braunberger, *Tire au flanc* was definitely a commercial project, predicated on the appeal of Mouézy-Eon and Sylvanie's vaudeville comedy about army barracks life, which had played at the same Paris theater for twenty years.[77] According to Alexander Sesonske, Renoir added a new character to the play, the big-hearted, bumbling servant set off against a blithely assured, self-centered master.[78] As in *Nana*, the contrast between the two central characters was established by divergent acting styles: the smooth grace of dancer Georges Pomiès versus the awkward, grotesque fumblings of Michel Simon. And here, in a comedy, it worked perhaps even more effectively.

Jean Dubois d'Ombelles (Pomiès), a naïve, pacifist poet, is about to be conscripted into the army, along with his servant Joseph (Simon), who, allegedly, is going to protect him. A dinner party given by Jean's aunt, Mme. Blandin (Maryanne)—to pull a few strings for him—goes awry; and the guests,

Colonel Brochard (Felix Oudart) and Lieutenant Daumel (Jean Storm), leave convinced that he is an idiot. Once at Casserone, Joseph makes himself at home while Jean quickly becomes the "Sad Sack" butt of the barracks pranks led by Muflot (Zellas). Both men's fiancées visit Casserone, with predictable results. Mme. Blandin's maid, Georgette (Fridette Fatton), becomes the whole barrack's sweetheart and causes a near-riot that sends Jean and Muflot to prison. Her daughter, Solange (Jeanne Helbling), to Jean's chagrin, falls in love with Daumel. But he soon discovers Solange's sister Lily (Kitty Dorlay), who has loved him all along. Promising to reform, Jean is released from prison and performs with Joseph at the colonel's annual barracks party. When a fire breaks out, he proves himself a hero at last, by capturing the arsonist, Muflot. In the end, there is a triple wedding celebration—Mme. Blandin and Colonel Brochard toast Jean and Lily as well as Daumel and Solange in the dining room, while several enlisted men revel with Joseph and Georgette in the kitchen.

Tire au flanc was shot rapidly in the early summer of 1928, just before the opening of the Carcassonne festival that would provide the locations for *Le Tournoi* (1929).[79] Even more than in *La Fille de l'eau* (1925), this was a co-operative enterprise that established the model of community filmmaking for much of Renoir's work in the 1930s. Renoir stuck to simple, realistic sets designed by Eric Aës, and he and his cast and crew apparently improvised a great deal. Following the tendency of several French films made in the wake of Gance's *Napoléon*, some of this improvisation took the form of extensive and elaborate camera movements. Their peculiarly rough, erratic nature may be explained by a curious story Renoir once told Kevin Brownlow:

I had an electrician [Louis Née]. He used to tell me what to do. He had some very good ideas. So I gave him a handheld camera and I let him stand by the main camera [Jean Bachelet] and shoot the scene however he liked. And I used a lot of his material. He became a famous cameraman.[80]

Complementing this camera movement (which included all manner of tracks, dollies, and pans) is a pattern of foreground/background juxtapositions (of characters and parts of the decor), both of which recur prominently in Renoir's 1930s films—e.g., *Boudu sauvé des eaux* (1932).[81] The episodic narrative, the carefree acting, the "wild" camerawork, the seemingly slapdash editing—all gave *Tire au flanc* an unruly look and an unbridled, off-balance rhythm that set it apart from Clair and Feyder's smoothly crafted films.[82] At the time of its premiere at the Electric Cinéma, in December, 1928, the vaudeville comedy source did indeed guarantee the film's success; and later its playful exuberance much impressed the French New Wave filmmakers.[83]

There are several levels of comedy operating in *Tire au flanc*. Physical comedy dominates the satire on barracks life, in short mock-documentary sketches that made François Truffaut compare Renoir's film to Jean Vigo's satire on boarding school life in *Zero de conduite* (1933).[84] Arriving at Casserone, for instance, Jean walks from his chauffeured car with a briefcase and a respectfully raised hat only to be immediately pummeled by his fellow soldiers—not once, but twice. At bayonet practice, he gently pokes the enemy dummy until, prodded suddenly from behind, he hysterically attacks everything and everybody in sight. Then, on maneuvers one day, the recruits don gas masks in response to an imaginary attack. While their leader struts off confidently

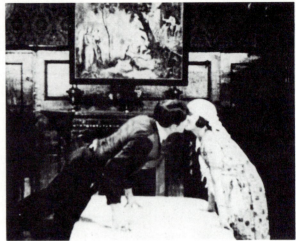

124. (left) The "gas attack" in *Tire au flanc* (1928)

125. (right) The opening shot of Michel Simon and Fridette Fatton

in one direction, they stagger off in the other, stumbling about the woods like blind men using their rifles as canes. Finally, they all roll down a long hill and, like frightening (and frightened) prehistoric monsters, scatter a class of schoolchildren on a nature study outing. All this is a bit daring because Renoir dressed his soldiers, not in the usual silly Belle Epoque uniforms, but in World War I blue.[85]

The sexual comedy involving both masters and servants, which is even more important, depends on ironies of situation and juxtaposition. Perhaps its high point comes during Jean's incarceration, in several variations on a "midsummer night's dream." Outside the barracks one night, Joseph and Colonel Brochard circle in and out of a clump of trees—in a clockwork pattern, each ignorant of the other—awaiting their lovers. When Georgette and Mme. Flechois appear, they mesh with the wrong men. While the Colonel presents a poem to the startled maid, Joseph realizes the error, although Mme. Flechois seems not to mind. Georgette simply pockets the poem, finds Joseph, and pulls him off. Another master has become a poet, ergo, an idiot. The night before, however, had seen a more bittersweet encounter. Daumel and Solange are strolling through a "forest" of drying men's shirts just outside the barracks prison. From a bush beside Jean's cell window, he plucks a rose and they kiss. Noticing the hand mysteriously appear in the moonlight, Jean is drawn to the high window, where he watches in despair, his body spread-eagled against the wall (in André Bazin's phrase) "like a great nailed bird."[86] As Sesonske points out, this supposedly Stroheim-like moment is quickly reversed four short sequences later.[87] Smuggled into the barracks, Lily tosses pebbles at Jean's prison window, which he ignores (he is reading a book on how to be audacious!). Finally, she stands on a cart to get his attention, and Jean again pulls himself up to the bars, but joyfully, to a very different apparition. When the guard comes to release him at that moment, Jean reaches for a rose; and, while Lily watches, he dances merrily out of the cell, presenting the rose to

236

126. Michel Simon as an
angel in *Tire au flanc* (1928)

his captor. Jean's character has finally undergone the change necessary for both
his survival and happiness.

For all its roughness and exuberance, *Tire au flanc* exhibits a remarkable
symmetry in its structure.[88] The end circles back to the beginning in a series
of clever reversals on master-servant relations. In the initial dinner sequence,
the characters of master and servant are neatly juxtaposed. The first shot opens
on a Daumier print depicting a fat gentleman kneeling eagerly before a young
buxom woman whose hand is daintily touching his balding head. The camera
dollies out and over the dinner table as Joseph and Georgette arrange the linen
(a toss of the cloth momentarily whitens the frame completely) and pause to
stretch over it and kiss. After the camera dollies back into the Daumier print,
the second shot repeats the movement of the first, only now Jean is standing
at the head of the table, practicing his speech for Solange, who seems less
than interested—the image will be echoed and transformed in the cell window
encounter between Lily and Jean. A third shot extends the contrast by having
Joseph and Georgette reenter the dining room and kiss, shocking Jean, who
orders them out. The formal parallels set master against servant, movement
against immobility, overt affection against repression, action against words.[89]
The arranged dinner quickly deteriorates into chaos when Joseph drops the
meat off the platter, drips sauce on the Colonel's precious uniform, and then
casually tosses a glass of Benzine (brought out to clean the uniform, but which
the Colonel mistakenly drinks instead) into the fireplace. The resulting roar
of flames drives everyone into the hall, where the guests try respectfully to
take their leave.

At the barracks party, master and servant play ironically reversed roles. Jean
now is an exuberant satyr, scampering about in a short fur piece and a crown
of laurel, piping on a flute. Joseph, however, is a large, gangling, bemused
angel, dressed in a full white dress with flimsy paper wings. He is dropped,
wriggling, from the flies just as Nana was in Renoir's earlier film. When this

ballet is disrupted by a fire set deliberately backstage, it is Jean who manfully douses it with a water hose (some satyr) and who now pummels the arsonist, his prankster nemesis, Muflot. Unlike Nana, Jean both proves and discovers himself in this performance. An epilogue of just a half-dozen shots carries the reversal one step further. Joseph leaves his wedding banquet in one room to serve at the banquet of his superiors in the next. Yet both tables are decorated with the same castle cake. And the final tracking shot comes to rest on Jean and Lily kissing below the table (he has dropped something again)—echoing Joseph and Georgette in the beginning of the film. *Tire au flanc* is more than a tuneup for such films as *Boudu sauvé des eaux* and *La Règle du jeu* (1939); it is a first-rate social satire on a favorite Renoir theme—the comic interaction of masters and servants.

By the end of the decade, the French film industry evidenced little concern for producing French films, except in the genre of film comedy. The period spectacle film generally was reconstructing historical eras elsewhere; the modern studio spectacular was producing a luxurious "no man's land" milieu; while the realist film and the fantasy film had been abandoned to the narrative avant-garde. Only the comedy presented the French as they saw themselves— through mockery. With the development of the sound film, the genre gained added prominence. Some films—such as Jean Choux's *Jean de la lune* (1932), starring Michel Simon and René Lefevre; Marc Allegret's *Mam'zelle Nitouche* (1931), with Raimu; and Renoir's *On purge Bébé* (1931), with Simon and Fernandel—merely imitated the conventions established by the Aubert and Albatros films of the middle 1920s. Others, however—such as René Clair's *Le Million* (1931), with Lefevre, and *A nous la liberté* (1931); Renoir's *Boudu sauvé des eaux* (1932), with Simon; and Jean Vigo's *Zero de conduite* (1933)—all extended the biting and caustic mockery of the late 1920s comedies. It was through these films, like it or not, that the film industry began to regain its Frenchness.

FRENCH
FRENCH
CINEMA

III The
Alternate
Cinema
Network

We are witnessing the birth of an extraordinary art. The only truly modern art perhaps, assured already of its place and one day of astonishing glory, because it is simultaneously . . . the child of technology and of human ideals.
—Louis Delluc (1918)

People are only barely beginning to realize that an unforeseen art has come into being. One that is absolutely new. We must understand what this means.
—Jean Epstein (1921)

The dominant faction of the French film industry, from 1915 to 1929, defined the cinema as a spectacle entertainment—a commercial product in the system of economic exchange. Certain kinds of films or genres, particular stars, certain methods of production and exhibition were developed to gain profits within that system of exchange. Another smaller, but quite articulate, segment of the industry conceived of cinema differently. For it, the cinema was a cultural product, an art—or something that could become an art—and the individuals and organizations who believed so considered themselves engaged in the avant-garde of its creation. Some thought of the avant-garde chiefly within the context of a narrative cinema; others thought of it as a "pure cinema"; still others thought of it in terms of documentary. Yet whatever the mode or theoretical base, their efforts depended on an alternate means of exchange. As Jean Tedesco succinctly put it:

> The actual exhibition market of the film industry . . . is almost completely closed to one category of films. We have called them avant-garde films only for the purpose of better distinguishing them from the current production and not because of any preconceived idea of a chapel or school. . . .
> We must extend the marketplace of the intellectual cinema in Paris for such films.[1]

That marketplace depended on a specific material base—an interrelated network of film critics, cinema journals, ciné-clubs, and specialized cinemas, all somewhat independent of the major companies in the industry. It was this alternate, essentially cooperative system of cultural exchange, often diametrically opposed to that of the dominant industry, which provided much of the impetus for the alternate cinema that was the French avant-garde.

The first area of struggle for an alternate cinema was located in the press—in the newspapers, literary magazines, and specialized film journals. The key figure in conceiving and promoting such a cinema was Louis Delluc.

The major journals that provided professional information and publicity about the French film industry during this period were launched either before or during the war, at the moment when the industry was being forced to adapt to the interests of the American cinema. They included *Ciné-Journal* and *Filma* (both of which published the earliest annual summaries of cinema activity in France), *Le Courrier cinématographique, Cinéopse* (whose editor, G.-M. Coissac, had founded the first popular industry organ, *Le Fascinateur*, in 1903), and, finally, the most important of all, *La Cinématographie française*.[1] Among this group was a small but influential weekly journal published by Henri Diamant-Berger, beginning in 1916, *Le Film*.[2] In its pages the concept of an alternate cinema seems to have had its beginnings.

The significance of *Le Film* lies in its nurturing of an autonomous film criticism, a criticism that assumed film could be a form of art and that began the attempt to isolate its specific features in order to analyze and evaluate individual works. Most film historians attribute this new practice initially to Louis Delluc, who had been a poet, novelist, dramatist, and drama critic for *Comoedia Illustré* before becoming editor-in-chief of *Le Film* in June, 1917.[3] But Delluc had an important precursor in another young French writer, Colette.

Introduction

The Beginnings of a Film Criticism

241

It was Colette who started the "Critique des films" column for *Le Film*, on 28 May 1917. Diamant-Berger had asked her to write for his journal, not only as a friend but because she had a keen interest in the cinema and had connections in the industry.[4] Colette was a close associate of Musidora, the famous villainess of *Les Vampires* (1915), and the two women had just collaborated on a film shot in Rome early in 1917, *La Vagabonde*. Besides, she had already written several film reviews for the Paris daily newspapers. One of these, in *Excelsior* (7 August 1916), was crucial, according to Delluc, in proclaiming the "artistic merits" of Cecil B. De Mille's *Forfaiture* [*The Cheat*] (1915), starring Sessue Hayakawa.[5] Within eight days of its opening, *Forfaiture* was elevated to *exclusivité* status at the Omnia-Pathé cinema.[6] That one film persuaded Delluc and Marcel L'Herbier, respectively, to become a film critic and a filmmaker; and it heavily influenced Abel Gance's first artistic success, *Mater Dolorosa* (1917). In Colette's own words, *The Cheat* was a veritable art school to which writers, painters and dramatists came nightly like students. It offered "the profound, if less than crystal clear, pleasure of seeing the crude 'ciné' groping toward perfection, the pleasure of divining exactly what the future of the cinema must be when its makers would want that future. . . ."[7]

Seven of Colette's columns appeared regularly in *Le Film*, from 28 May to 21 July 1917, and most were devoted to American films, especially the Triangle films of Thomas Ince. When she quit the journal—"because there was no money in it"[8]—Louis Delluc was already acting as editor-in-chief and was publishing, concurrently with her column, his own articles on particular films. From his first column (25 June 1917),[9] Delluc perpetuated Colette's interest in American films at the expense of French serials and literary adaptations, and he began to proselytize for a truly French cinema art. His witty, acerbic, trenchant pieces won a small but enthusiastic following among young writers and artists suddenly awakened to the cinema's potential. Within a year or so, the members of this "circle" had expanded and had begun to function on their own.

In the summer of 1918, Delluc ceased publishing his own critical work in *Le Film* (with a couple of exceptions) but continued functioning as editor-in-chief, a post he held until 1919 when Diamant-Berger sold the journal to Georges Quellian and went into film production. Throughout this period, *Le Film* became a forum for several other young writers to take up Delluc's challenge. In April, 1918, he published the full text of L'Herbier's "Hermès et le Silence," a philosophical rhapsody on the cinema's paradoxical ability to document life with acuity and exactitude (e.g., the war newsreels) and, at the same time, to create a "new symphony" of landscape, gesture, light and shadow.[10] In September, he introduced Louis Aragon's provocative essay, "Du Décor," which celebrated the cinema's transformation of reality through magnification/ isolation (e.g., the close-up) and through the subordination of set/landscape to character (e.g., Chaplin).[11] "It is indispensable," wrote Aragon, "that film take a place in the preoccupations of the artistic avant-gardes."[12] In December, Delluc persuaded his friend Léon Moussinac (they had spent schooldays together at the Lycée Charlemagne), to begin writing on the cinema.[13]

All this was possible in part because Delluc had been able to satisfy his own desire for an even larger reading audience.

He succeeded in convincing Léon Parsons that the time had come for a major newspaper to provide its readers with a serious cinematographic criticism alongside its dramatic criticism and, on 1 June 1918, he gave *Paris-Midi* his first article devoted to Douglas Fairbanks.[14]

Paris-Midi was not the first Paris newspaper to publicize or report on the cinema. Beginning in 1908, *Comoedia* and, later, *Le Journal* once a week had listed cinema programs in the capital and occasionally carried brief reviews and articles (as did others, such as *Excelsior*). Then, late in 1916, *Le Temps* had begun to publish a biweekly film review column by its music critic, Emile Vuillermoz.[15] In fact, before it accepted Delluc's work, *Paris-Midi* had been printing, since January, 1918, a sometimes weekly, sometimes biweekly column, "Les Spectacles," by Jan de Merry. But Delluc's column, "Cinéma et cie," was the first critical appraisal of the cinema as art to appear weekly, on a regular basis. After January, 1919, it became a daily event. For a full year or more, Delluc was the single most important voice in the cinema marketplace. And he consolidated that position by publishing two collections of his film criticism (the earliest in France): *Cinéma et cie* (1919) and *Photogénie* (1920).

127. Louis Delluc by Beçan

Delluc's early film criticism was certainly not systematic or highly theoretical, but his columns and books were more than "mere bouquets of impressions," as he ironically described them.[16] The significance of his writings becomes evident when compared to Henri Diamant-Berger's concurrent survey of the cinema as a craft in *Le Cinéma* (1919).[17] As an admirer of American films as well as a protégé of Charles Pathé, Diamant-Berger advocated a film practice in France based on the production methods and aesthetic conventions of the American cinema. No less an enthusiast of American films, Delluc, however, sketched out, through repeated insights and ideas, a framework for an alternate *French* cinema.[18] For one, he singled out certain French films and filmmakers who were developing a form of film discourse in parallel with, but differing from, the Americans: Jacques de Baroncelli's *Ramuntcho* (released February, 1919), Abel Gance's *J'Accuse* (released April, 1919), Marcel L'Herbier's *Rose-France* (released July, 1919), and Germaine Dulac's *La Fête espagnole* (released May, 1920). For another, he advocated a different concept of filmmaking. The filmmaker should be the *auteur* of the ideas and stories he films rather than, as Diamant-Berger and André Antoine would have it, the *metteur-en-scène* of a scenario developed by a recognized writer.[19] And those ideas and stories should originate in the real world of contemporary life rather than be adapted from the theater or from fiction.[20] Finally, he suggested the possibility of alternate methods of film distribution and exhibition. Attacking the then current "salad" of cinema programs (which he compared to an uncoordinated jumble of skits, excerpts, and one-act plays in a theater), Delluc asked for programs of separate individual screenings, at definite times.[21] More important, in opposition to the industry's initial reluctance to re-release films, he began to consider the idea of a repertory of significant films that could be collected for repeated screening.

Within three years of Delluc's pioneering efforts in the pages of *Paris-Midi*, the concept of a regular film review column was adopted by all of the major Paris daily newspapers. André Antoine's clarion call—"it is necessary to create a veritable, independent screen criticism, as now exists for the theater"—

seemed to announce the capitulation.[22] Following *Le Temps* (Vuillermoz) and *Comoedia* (J.-L. Croze), most of the Paris newspapers had inaugurated a weekly film column or page by the autumn of 1921: *L'Information* (Lucien Wahl, editor of *Eclair-Journal* newsreels), *Le Matin* (Jean Gallois), *Le Journal* (Jean Chastaigner), *Le Petit Parisien* (J.-L. Croze), *L'Intransigeant* (Boisyvon), and *L'Humanité* (Léon Moussinac).[23] However, the most important of these, because it brought together a circle of writers and filmmakers, probably was *Le Petit Journal*. In addition to his own column there, René Jeanne printed a series of articles by Diamant-Berger, Gance, Delluc, Ricciotto Canudo, Léon Poirier, and the art critic, Charles Léger. By 1922, the cinema was accepted as a permanent form of popular spectacle by the press, and certain critics (Vuillermoz, Wahl, Jeanne, Moussinac) were writing as if it were an autonomous art.

128. Ricciotto Canudo

Delluc's example also had an impact on the literary magazines of Paris. Before the war, Guillaume Apollinaire's avant-garde monthly, *Les Soirées de Paris*, had expanded its provocations with a regular film review column by Maurice Raynal—which culminated in the whimsical "Société des amis du Fantômas," based on the famous Louis Feuillade serial. Two small journals founded during the war—Pierre Albert-Birot's *SIC* and Pierre Reverdy's *Nord-Sud*—tried to sustain and extend Apollinaire's interest with a few notes, essays, and interviews.[24] In 1919, however, three literary magazines that would have some influence in the 1920s instituted regular essays and/or review columns on the cinema. One was *Littérature*, an irreverent new magazine edited by the young poets, André Breton, Louis Aragon, and Philippe Soupault. Their interest coincided with Delluc's, but it led to a series of playful "cinematographic poems," based especially on Chaplin and William S. Hart films. Another highly polemical, but more long-lived magazine was *Le Crapouillot*, edited by the robust eccentric, Jean Galtier-Boissière.[25] As early as 1919, Galtier-Boissière published a seminal essay on film by the painter, Marcel Gromaire; and, in March of 1920 and 1923, he devoted special issues exclusively to the cinema.[26] Between those dates, *Le Crapouillot* emerged as an important forum for film criticism, especially when Léon Moussinac became its regular film reviewer in September, 1921. Before writing for *Le Crapouillot*, as well as for *L'Humanité* (the Communist Party newspaper), however, Moussinac had joined the staff of *Le Mercure de France*. For six years, beginning in May, 1920, this prestigious literary magazine published Moussinac's trimonthly film review column along with early articles by young writers such as Jean Epstein and Alexandre Arnoux.[27] In one of his first reviews, Moussinac prophesied:

A new art is born, develops, discovers one by one its own laws, progresses toward perfection, an art which will be the expression—bold, powerful, original—of the ideal of a new age.[28]

The most flamboyant prophet of the new art was Ricciotto Canudo. In Paris before the war, this polemical Italian writer had published *Montjoie!*, a small review devoted to modern tendencies in the arts, and had actively encouraged filmmakers to join his circle of artist contributors.[29] To that end, he had written one of the first credos on the cinema—"Manifesto of the Sixth Art" (1911).[30] After being demobilized from the French army, Canudo founded a

244

second journal, *La Gazette des sept arts*, consecrated more specifically to the aesthetics of the cinema.[31] The purpose of this journal was twofold:

—the conquest of intellectual and artistic milieux, until now recalcitrant to the cinema;—the amelioration of the quality of film production.[32]

Canudo's connections in the arts world were even more extensive than Delluc's, and *La Gazette des sept arts* (which appeared irregularly until its founder's death in late 1923) included a host of important articles by writers (e.g., Alexandre Arnoux, Jean Cocteau), painters (e.g., Fernand Léger, Robert Mallet-Stevens, Marcel Gromaire), musicians (e.g., Arthur Honegger on his score for selections from Gance's *La Roue*), filmmakers (e.g., Jean Epstein on shooting his first film, *Pasteur*), and critics (e.g., Moussinac). To advance his ideas on a more regular basis, beginning in October, 1922, Canudo also initiated a film review column in the new literary weekly, *Les Nouvelles littéraires*. This "missionary of poetry in the cinema," as Jean Epstein later called Canudo, like Delluc, proselytized the idea of the filmmaker as an *auteur* or *écraniste*.[33] And, more consistently than any other writer, he articulated an expressive or Symbolist theory of the cinema, emphasizing the film image's evocation of the filmmaker's as well as of a character's feeling, imagination, or state of mind.[34]

Soon other magazines began opening their pages to the cinema—some, appropriately, to Delluc himself. One of *Le Mercure de France*'s chief rivals, *La Nouvelle Revue Française*, initiated the practice of publishing film scenarios as literary works, the most famous of which was Jules Romains's "Donogoo-Tonka" (November and December, 1919).[35] Another avant-garde journal, Le Corbusier and Ozenfant's *L'Esprit nouveau*, from 1920 to 1922, published three Delluc pieces championing the cinema (one of them devoted to Chaplin).[36] During the same period, the journal also accepted an early essay on the aesthetics of cinema by B. Tokine, a second piece on Chaplin by the art historian Elie Faure, and one of Jean Epstein's first essays on current French films.[37] *Les Choses de théâtre* (first issue) and *Le Monde nouveau* published important essays by Delluc which were to form the basis for a book tentatively titled "Les Cinéastes," but which he left unfinished at his death.[38] Finally, two monthly review journals established short-lived, but influential columns. One was *Paris-Journal* which, in 1923, began printing the reviews of Georges Charensol and the young Surrealist poet, Robert Desnos.[39] The other was the deluxe *Théâtre et Comoedia Illustré*, now published by Rolf de Maré, who also managed the Théâtre des Champs-Elysées where the famous Ballet suédois performed.[40] For over a year and a half (from December, 1922), *Théâtre et Comoedia Illustré* included a special film supplement in which René Clair wrote a comprehensive review of the month's films in Paris while twenty-year-old Jean Mitry (in between assignments as a publicity poster artist) transcribed some half-dozen interviews with major French filmmakers.[41]

Film Journals

The Paris newspapers were now providing information and increasingly sophisticated film reviews to the public, and certain literary magazines were educating their elite audiences to the value of the cinema. Could there be a publication format, a form of organization, to bridge the gap between these two—to create a popular movement which could put pressure on the French

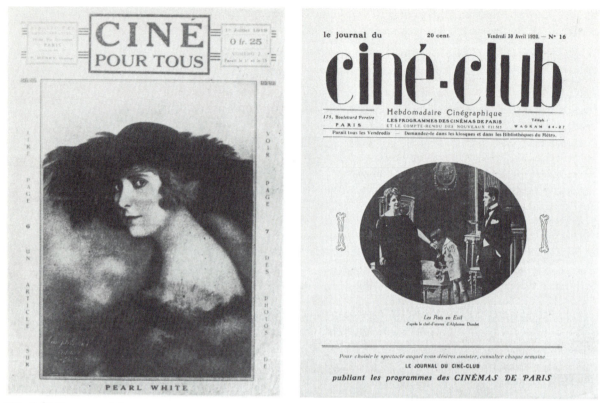

129. (left) The cover of the first issue of *Ciné-pour-tous*

130. (right) The cover of *Le Journal du Ciné-Club*

film industry and influence the direction of its operations, or which (failing that) could establish an alternative to it? To this task, Louis Delluc and several other writers now turned their efforts.

On 15 June 1919, a new film journal appeared with a masthead which proposed all Paris for its audience. Edited by Pierre Henry, *Ciné-pour-tous* ran eight tabloid-sized pages and cost but twenty centimes (old currency). Each fortnightly issue included a list of French films in production, notes on current releases, a half page of credits and reviews on a selected film (usually French), a two- or three-page essay on a film star (usually American), information on a particular area of the film industry, letters from readers, and an editorial by Henry. In *Paris-Midi*, Delluc drew attention to the journal by devoting a full column to it.

The "grand public"—which loves the cinema and which gives it life—wants someone to address it. I have always thought that would happen one day. So it begins with *Ciné-pour-tous*, a biweekly review which is not content to address the public occasionally but wants to address it exclusively. This ambition pleases me. Everything in it has *intelligence, taste, precision, force.* Sadly, the pages are limited. But it will grow, and you will find again, by waiting, all that you want to know about films, about actors, about the present and sometimes the future of the cinema.[1]

According to Jean Mitry, who began his cinema education by surreptitiously reading *Ciné-pour-tous* at school and then became one of its writers, words cannot do justice to "the role that it played, the influence that it had on the formation of young minds and the first cinéphiles."[2]

Ciné-pour-tous undoubtedly spurred Delluc's own interest in publishing a magazine for the growing number of film enthusiasts. With the help of friends such as Charles de Vesme, Georges Denola, and Léon Moussinac, he prepared a weekly film magazine whose first issue appeared on 14 January 1920.[3] Its title, *Le Journal du Ciné-Club*, was more prophetic than accurate. Actually there was no ciné-club or formal organization of cinéphiles. *Le Journal du Ciné-Club* was essentially a magazine whose purpose was "[to help build] relations between the public and the 'cinématographistes,' [to support] the work of all the young filmmakers" and "[to organize] lectures accompanied by projected film clips, dealing with the history of the cinema, its achievements, its artistic nature, [and] its social and educational ends. . . ."[4] Through its readers, wrote Charles de Vesme, "in an epoch in which the masses played such a large role and exerted on all things such a great influence, [Delluc hoped] to mobilize a cadre of the elite and the professional, together with an army constituted of the vast public who were passionate about the cinema."[5] Published twice as often as *Ciné-pour-tous*, *Le Journal du Ciné-Club* also included more pages (twelve) and more information: complete listings of cinema programs in Paris, the suburbs, and even some of the provinces; brief reviews of all the new Paris releases of the week; and articles on filmmakers as well as film stars.

Despite their intentions, neither *Ciné-pour-tous* nor *Le Journal du Ciné-Club* ever appealed to more than a small elite of the French film audience, much like the elite readers of the literary and art magazines. A truly popular film magazine did not emerge until January, 1921, when Jean Pascal and Adrien Maître launched *Cinémagazine*. This one-franc weekly journal of some fifty pages aligned itself quite closely with the commercial film industry and catered to the tastes of the mass cinema audience.[6] *Cinémagazine* served as a major publicity outlet for the French and American film producers and distributors by reviewing the week's new releases and previews, doing several articles in each issue on popular stars, publishing episodes from a filmed serial or novel, printing a great number of publicity stills and advertisements, and providing a gossipy information column. So quickly did it become popular that, within eight months of its founding, *Cinémagazine* had its own correspondent in the United States, a former assistant to Louis Feuillade, Robert Florey. But Pascal and Maître did make some effort to bridge the gap between the masses and the elite, between the dominant industry and the alternate cinema advocates. Important critics such as Moussinac, Jeanne, Wahl, and Vuillermoz were printed frequently enough in the magazine; and independent French filmmakers often reported on their production or distribution activities and problems. *Cinémagazine* also did tend to single out independent narrative films for their artistic value.

Cinémagazine's success quickly generated some rivals. Within two years, at least two more popular weekly film magazines became available in Paris: *Mon-Ciné* and *Ciné-Miroir* (published by *Le Petit Parisien*).[7] Both of these proto-fan magazines concentrated on stories about stars, filmmakers, and particular film productions, as well as novelizations of current films, at the expense of actual film reviews and cinema program listings.[8] The simultaneous release of a film

131. (left) The cover of
Cinémagazine

132. (right) The cover of
Cinéa: Rio Jim poster by
Beçan

and its novelization in a newspaper or popular film magazine had become so profitable by 1922 that several publications—e.g., the weekly *Le Film Complet* and the biweekly *Les Grands Films*—did nothing but package *récits* of current films.[9] The most expensive of these—*Cinéma-Bibliothèque* (published by Jules Tallandier)—appeared actually as a small booklet, with inserted specially printed sheets of production and frame stills.[10] All of these magazines now constitute an important, if approximate, record of lost and incomplete films; at the time, however, they served as little more than organs of the industry.

The most influential alternate film journal had its origins in Louis Delluc's last critical venture. In April, 1920, Delluc turned over the editorship of *Le Journal du Ciné-Club* to Georges Denola when he himself became involved in directing films. When the journal was forced to cease publication one year after its inception, Delluc persuaded Arkady Roumanoff (a Russian emigré collector and amateur artist) to finance a deluxe weekly review, *Cinéa*, which would be for the cinema what *Comoedia Illustré* was for the theater.[11] Directorship of the new journal was first shared by Delluc and Roumanoff and then handled by Delluc alone; but there were many collaborators: critics (Moussinac, Wahl, Vuillermoz, and especially Lionel Landry), poets (Canudo, Jean

Epstein, and Ivan Goll), filmmakers (L'Herbier, Baroncelli, Poirier, Louis Nalpas, Henry Roussel, and Alberto Cavalcanti), actors (Philippe Hériat and André Daven, and graphic artists (Serge and Beçan).[12] For nearly two years after its first issue (6 May 1921), *Cinéa* would be the most consistent, outspoken denigrator of the commercial French cinema and advocate of a national cinema art.

In *Cinéa*, Delluc and his colleagues began to sketch out a loose set of criteria for determining film art. Chief among them was the elusive term, *photogénie*, which Delluc used to point to the sometimes artless, sometimes artful, transforming power of film in relation to reality, but which became a kind of "floating signifier" that recurred frequently throughout the 1920s.[13] Delluc himself came to focus on the filmmaker's "composition" of a central idea or theme, described sometimes in terms of an analogy then current, that of musical orchestration, which he used to define "cinegraphic rhythm."[14] Although the musical analogy was quite prominent in early French film theory (e.g., Canudo, Gance, Dulac, and even Epstein),[15] another formulation probably would be more precise—"poetic composition." For the process was similar to that of rhetorical and rhythmic patterning in poetry, a kind of poeticization of the process of representation. On a more practical level, Delluc's analyses of individual films, along with those of Moussinac, Vuillermoz, and Clair, became models of an informed film criticism.[16] Delluc also became more insistent in promoting the re-release of older films and the exhibition of innovative new films, especially those from Sweden and Germany. He was now sketching the outlines of a history of cinema art that was both national and international. A library or repertory of significant films was needed, he argued, not only to preserve but to promulgate the idea of cinema art and to educate cinema audiences in order to support further innovations and the cinema's eventual achievements.

Of the contributors to *Cinéa*, the one who developed the implications of Delluc's work most thoroughly and imaginatively was the young poet and essayist, Jean Epstein, whom Jean Mitry recently admitted was "the first real theoretician of the cinema."[17] Epstein's ideas emerged full-blown in a peculiar blend of poetic and scientific language, in the last chapter of his first book, *La Poésie d'aujourd'hui: un nouvel état d'intelligence* (1921), and especially in *Bonjour Cinéma* (1921). In its original design format, *Bonjour Cinéma* was a witty parody of a film program. It included poster photographs of film stars, adulatory "fan" poems, a serial episode, and several "features"—the essays, "Le Sens 1 bis," "Grossissement," and "Ciné-Mystique."[18] More important was the book's correlation to the work done by Apollinaire, Blaise Cendrars, and even the Dadaists during the war and the postwar period. It combined a variety of different materials—three major essays, a half-dozen poems printed in free typography, photographs and posters of several American stars, and Cubist-style paintings and drawings. In a sense, Epstein was already playing with the idea of "editing" together the diverse strands of modern life into something analogous to a film. And in his essays was the germ—or quantum theory, if you will—of a cinema of discontinuity or, rather, of a continuity quite different from that developed by the American cinema.

Delluc's own film practice during these years—especially *Fièvre* (1921) and *La Femme de nulle part* (1922)—cut short his work as a film critic and editor.

133. The cover of *Bonjour Cinéma* (1921)

134. Jean Epstein

135. The cover of *Cinéa-Ciné-pour-tous*: Arlette Marchal

After the commercial failure of *La Femme de nulle part*, in October, 1922, Delluc sold his interest in *Cinéa* to Jean Tedesco (a young editor of women's magazines) and gradually yielded the editorship to him. A year later, Tedesco bought out *Ciné-pour-tous*, which was in financial trouble due to the proliferation of film magazines, and the two journals merged. In November, 1923, *Cinéa-Ciné-pour-tous* appeared in a glossy, beautifully laid out, thirty-six-to-forty-four-page format that boasted a special section of tastefully mounted photographs. Under Tedesco's editorial control, the new journal included reviews and articles by Edmond Epardaud, Pierre Porte, Dr. Paul Ramain, Pierre Henry, Juan Arroy, René Jeanne, and Léon Moussinac as well as statements by such filmmakers as L'Herbier, Epstein, Henri Chomette, Fritz Lang, and Lulu Pick. It had an immediate and lasting impact. Throughout 1924, Tedesco and others, such as Jeanne and Moussinac, agitated for Delluc's idea of a repertory cinema; and both *Cinéa-Ciné-pour-tous* and *Cinémagazine* gave extensive coverage to the special lectures and exhibitions such filmmakers as

L'Herbier, Dulac, Epstein, and Clair were beginning to give. In a short time, especially through the writings of Epstein, Porte, Ramain, and Tedesco himself, *Cinéa-Ciné-pour-tous* became the principal forum for the theories and arguments that engaged the French avant-garde.[19]

Ciné-Clubs

This broadly sustained development of independent cinema journals and an embryonic film theory/criticism were unique to France. Nothing much like this existed in the United States or Germany, let alone Great Britain, Italy, or the Scandinavian countries. Only the revolutionary society of the Soviet Union had a somewhat comparable phenomenon. But the Soviet writings came slightly later and developed quite differently. There, filmmakers such as Lev Kuleshov, Dziga Vertov, and Sergei Eisenstein were the ones to initiate discussions of film theory and practice in *Kino-fot, Kino-Gazeta*, and especially *LEF* (1923-1925).[1] Within a couple of years, in the pages of *Novy LEF* (1927) and in several books, most notably *The Poetics of Cinema* (1927), the Russian Formalist literary theorists and critics (Boris Eikhenbaum, Viktor Shklovsky, S. Tretyankov, and Yuri Tynyanov) then took up the aesthetics of the cinema, the practice of film criticism, and even scriptwriting.[2] In France, the movement had a broadly based constituency (crossing several classes and professions), but it was more exclusively cultural than political (as the critics saw it) and more oriented (at least initially) toward a conception of cinema based on the film-viewing process rather than on filmmaking. Its purpose was to encourage, first of all, an informed audience that would support advances in film art and, only secondarily, real social change. Whereas Soviet film theory and practice were stimulated by an exhibition system that included mobile agit-trains and steamers,[3] the French development was supported by the unprecedented rise of ciné-clubs and special film lectures and exhibitions in Paris. Again Delluc, along with Canudo, Moussinac, and a few others, were crucial instigators.

The idea of a ciné-club or an organization of cinéphiles dedicated to the advancement of cinema art seems to have occurred simultaneously to Delluc and Canudo. Although Delluc coined the term *ciné-club* in 1919 (from the groups called *Touring-Clubs*, according to Sadoul)[4] and published *Le Journal du Ciné-Club*, he never really organized any club or circle that would meet regularly and engage in concerted activity. Instead, he tried out several ideas which would later become standard practice in the ciné-club movement. The first was a *conférence* or special program that would provide a retrospective look at the work of a particular filmmaker. Under the rubric of *Le Journal du Ciné-Club*, on 12 June 1920, at the Pépinière-Cinéma, Delluc organized a special program devoted to the animator, Emile Cohl (most of whose short French films had been made between 1907 and 1912), and to the theater director turned filmmaker, André Antoine, whose lecture on "The cinema of yesterday, today, and tomorrow" was illustrated with film clips.[5] Soon after, Antoine broached the idea of redirecting the programming of one particular cinema in Paris for the clientele of cinéphiles—to have a kind of "Vieux-Colombier of the cinema."[6] Delluc's second idea was to present an unreleased film (the work of a cinéaste) to a limited audience. Now under the rubric of *Cinéa*, on 14 November 1921, at the Colisée cinema, Delluc organized a charity matinee screening for "Tout-Paris." The film shown was a shock—*The Cabinet of Doctor*

Caligari (1919).[7] It was the first German film to be seen in France since before the war, and the director of the small Ciné-Opéra cinema was interested enough by it to arrange an exhibition of German films the following year. Two months later (22 January 1922), again at the Colisée, Delluc hosted a matinee session for an art circle, "Idéal et Réalité." The program brought together the twin interests of the young cinéphiles into sharp juxtaposition: while he himself spoke on "Cinema, the popular art," L'Herbier screened his short experimental film, *Promethée . . . banquier*, as a kind of *entr'acte*.[8] Once having tested his ideas, however, Delluc seems to have pursued them no further—either out of a deep commitment to his film practice or, more likely, because of financial and emotional difficulties (e.g., his marriage to Eve Francis).[9] But his friends would not let those ideas drop.

The first actual ciné-club seems to have grown out of the informal gatherings of artists, writers, and professional filmmakers at the Café Napolitain in 1920. At their head was Ricciotto Canudo who, by April, 1921, had dubbed the group C.A.S.A., "Club des amis du septième art."[10] Its members included some of the most prominent of the avant-garde in the arts: filmmakers (Delluc, Dulac, Poirier, L'Herbier, Cavalcanti, Epstein), critics (Moussinac, Wahl, Landry, Jeanne, Pierre Scize), writers (Faure, Arnoux, Cendrars, Cocteau), artists (Gromaire, Mallet-Stevens, Léger), musicians (Honegger, Ravel, Roland-Manuel, Maurice Jaubert), and actors (Eve Francis, Jaque Catelain, Jean Toulout, Harry Bauer, Gaston Modot).[11] This was a ciné-club that fulfilled Delluc's expectations.

The principal activity of C.A.S.A., at first, involved little more than dinner speeches and discussions, at the Poccardi restaurant or at Canudo's spacious apartment, 12 rue du Quatre-Septembre, much in the manner of the famous Belle Epoque banquet celebrations before the war.[12] However, C.A.S.A. members were the major contributors to Canudo's *La Gazette des sept arts*; and several filmmakers associated with the group (Gance, Dulac, Nalpas, René Le Somptier) took part in a series of lectures on the cinema given early in 1921.[13] Canudo himself published an important manifesto for C.A.S.A. in the second issue of *Cinéa* (13 May 1921). Several of the principles laid down there were harbingers of the future:

> . . .
> b. To raise the intellectual standard of French cinematic productions, for aesthetic as well as commercial ends. . . .
> d. To consider as urgent the establishment of a "hierarchy" of cinemas such as exists in the theater: popular cinemas and elite cinemas. . . .
> f. To agitate, by every propagandistic means, so that equitable laws and reasonable supports be provided by the State to the "Art of the Screen," in the same measure at least as they are accorded the "Art of the Stage."
> g. To attract public attention to the origins and evolution of the Cinema in France, through the organization of a first French Cinematic Festival.[14]

Apparently, Canudo organized several private film screenings for C.A.S.A. in the hall of the "Syndicate de la Grange-sur-Belles" (about the same time Delluc was presenting *Doctor Caligari* at the Colisée).[15] But his real coup, achieved with the aid of Moussinac, was to persuade the president of the prestigious Salon d'Automne, Franz Jourdain, to hold a special exposition of film screenings in 1921 and again in 1922 and 1923.[16] At the first exposition, following an address by Jacques de Baroncelli (read by the actor, Signoret), Canudo arranged the screening of "a selection of films by Baroncelli, Feyder, Roger Lion, Henry Roussel, [and Edouard] Violet . . . as well as several fragments from *La Roue.* . . ."[17] Two years later, he selected excerpts from the best films of the year which drew attention to what he considered to be the major cinematographic styles: "1. Realism, 2. Expressionism, 3. 'Essays' in cinematic rhythm, 4. Pictorial Cinema."[18] Canudo's film programs were particularly significant because they represented the first attempt, in Jean Epstein's words, "to present to the public specifically chosen film sequences, to constitute an anthology of cinema."[19] These expositions thus marked the earliest semi-official recognition of the cinema as art. To cap this work, just before his death in November, 1923, Canudo also arranged for a similar program of screenings in Lyon (the birthplace of the Lumière brothers).[20]

In the words of Henri Fescourt,

Ricciotto Canudo's influence was decisive for the recruitment and education of curious, newly fascinated spectators everywhere. His propagandizing effort had a special, courageous character since it tried no less than to build a bridge of communication and sympathy between the traditional arts and the young, unruly, but promising savage that was the cinema. That effort bore fruit.[21]

136. Léon Moussinac

Alongside the dinners and private screenings of C.A.S.A., which continued into 1922 and 1923, there appeared a number of other clubs and special events. In imitation of Canudo's club, in December, 1921, the editors of *Cinémagazine* created an informal group called simply "Amis du cinéma."[22] Throughout the next two years, the group held monthly lunches and occasional lectures, including sessions with Bernard-Deschamps and Diamant-Berger.[23] In June, 1923, Marcel L'Herbier was invited by Robert Aron to speak to the Students' International Circle at the College de France.[24] His speech, "Le Cinématographe contre l'art," was in such demand that he repeated it during the next few months in Geneva, La Haye, and Lausanne.[25] Inspired by this mushrooming activity, young Georges Sadoul invited Jean Epstein to give a lecture at Paris-Nancy, in December that same year, a lecture which Epstein then repeated a month later at Montpelier.[26]

The most important new organization to emerge from this wave of interest was started by Léon Moussinac, either late in 1922 or early in 1923.[27] The "Club français du cinéma" was a semi-professional organization which seems to have formalized and recharged the loose circle of people Delluc had brought together around *Le Journal du Ciné-Club* and *Cinéa*. Directed by Léon Poirier, who along with L'Herbier had just been fired at Gaumont, its agenda was set up explicitly to defend filmmakers as artists (or cinéastes, to use Delluc's term) and to attack the restrictions of the commercial industry. They demanded

1) that film writers and directors enjoy the benefits of artistic copyright; 2) that they cease being at the mercy of production companies who too often ignore the subjects of their films or, at least, distort them; 3) that film writers and directors, like their actors, have contact with public opinion, by means of an independent criticism, such as exists for the theater, literature, or painting. . . .[28]

Toward these ends the club organized a number of evening screenings of both

French and other European films, in order to "unleash new initiatives, fervent convictions, creative energies—*élans* even—which, by breaking the restrictions of mercantilism and routine, will propel the art of silence to the heights of its predecessors."[29] These screenings included Delluc's *La Femme de nulle part* (1922), Epstein's *La Coeur fidèle* (1923), Lulu Pick's *Sylvester* or *New Year's Eve* (1923), the earliest Soviet feature film, *Polikouchka* (1919), and a new version of Gance's *La Roue*.[30] The drive for an alternate cinema was reaching a new stage of militancy.

That drive seemed to accelerate rather than diminish after both Canudo and Delluc died suddenly within five months of one another (November, 1923, and March, 1924). For one, the Amis du cinéma group expanded its activity. Affiliated clubs were organized in several provincial French cities.[31] In May, at the Artistic cinema, the Paris club sponsored a special preview of Jaque Catelain's second film, *La Galerie des monstres* (1924); and in November, at the Colisée cinema, it sponsored major lectures by Germaine Dulac and René Clair.[32] For another, C.A.S.A. itself underwent a transformation. Early in March, 1924, at the club's first meeting since its founder's death, René Blum proposed the revival of the weekly members-only dinners and, more important, the sponsorship of regular public film screenings and lectures.[33] With the help of Moussinac, Tedesco, and others, Blum organized a biweekly series of evening film programs at Raymond Duncan's dance studio on the rue Colisée.[34] The first program, on 11 April, was dedicated to Delluc. Blum read an homage (prepared by Dulac) introducing a rescreening of *Fièvre*, and then Jean Epstein projected his short montage film, *Photogénies*, edited specially for the occasion.[35] Two weeks later, C.A.S.A rescreened Epstein's controversial film, *Coeur fidèle*, along with what Tedesco called "Sélections Symbolistes"— selected fragments from *La Roue* and Mosjoukine's *Le Brasier ardent*.[36] For its third program, the club took the risk of presenting Dmitri Kirsanoff's first film, *L'Ironie du destin* (1924), which had received scant commercial distribution.[37]

Although this series of special C.A.S.A. screenings was something less than an unmitigated success with the public, it seems to have encouraged several different lines of activity. Tedesco's selection of film excerpts and Epstein's *Photogénies* most likely helped stimulate the avant-garde production of short non-narrative films—e.g., Léger's *Ballet mécanique* (1924), Clair's *Entr'acte* (1924), Autant-Lara's *Fait-Divers* (1924), and Chomette's *Jeux de reflets et de vitesse* (1925). More certainly, the weekly exhibition strategy convinced Tedesco to begin looking around for a permanent cinema to provide continuous programming in the fall. Meanwhile, Blum and Moussinac turned their attention to an upcoming exposition.

In the winter of 1923-1924, Moussinac had pulled off a major coup at the Musée Galliera. The Galliera's director, Henri Clouzot, had become a member of the Club français du cinéma, and Moussinac persuaded him to form a commission in order to mount a full-scale exhibition devoted to the cinema— in effect, realizing one of Canudo's dreams.[38] On that commission were Louis Lumière, Gaumont, Pathé, Gance, L'Herbier, Mallet-Stevens, Jean Benoît-Lévy, Vuillermoz, and Moussinac himself. The resultant "L'Exposition de l'art dans le cinéma français" extended from May through October and included displays of film stills and scripts from particular filmmakers, animation draw-

254

ings, examples of film titles and credits, set design models and sketches, costumes, posters, film books and periodicals. It also boasted two series of lectures, one lasting a month (May through June), the other in October. The first amounted to a veritable seminar of ten lecture-presentations on the cinema as art.

Tuesday May 27
M. G.-Michel Coissac: The history of the cinema—prophets, precursors, filmmakers.
Friday May 30
M. Léon Moussinac: The characteristics of this new art—modern, popular, international. The styles of cinema. Descriptive cinema and the cinegraphic poem. Genres. Relations between cinema and the other arts.
Tuesday June 3
M. Léon Moussinac: The visual idea, its specific character, its development in the scenario (adaptations). The importance of scriptwriting and mise-en-scène—elementary techniques. Cinegraphic rhythm and balance.
Friday June 6
M. Marcel L'Herbier: *Photogénie*. The important role of light, interior and exterior lighting methods.
Tuesday June 10
M. Jaque Catelain: The interior rhythm of images. Acting—expression, movement, makeup.
Friday June 13
M. Mallet-Stevens: Decors. Costumes. Props. The cinema—the means of popularizing the modern forms. Intertitles and posters.
Tuesday June 17
M. Jean Epstein: The expressive techniques of the cinema—the function of different shot distances and angles. Dissolves. Lap dissolves. Superimpositions. Soft focus. Deformations. Animation.
Friday June 20
M. Lionel Landry: French cinema; its characteristics, its aesthetic development. Foreign influences. The function of the critic.
Tuesday June 24
M. René Blum: Cinema and music. Composers. Orchestra conductors. Synchronizing machines.
Friday June 27
M. Luchaire: French film industry—its impact on French ideas worldwide.[39]

Substituting for Epstein, Germaine Dulac wrote one of her most persuasive essays of the decade on the possibilities of a subjective cinema.[40] If the ciné-club movement still exerted less influence on the industry and on the mass French audience than it would like, it was well on the way to establishing film as an equal in the world of the arts.

The consequences of the Galliera exhibition were twofold. For one, early in 1925, it led to the merger of C.A.S.A. and Moussinac's Club français du cinéma into one body, the "Ciné-Club de France."[41] At the core of the new group were Moussinac, Blum, Poirier, Feyder, and Henri Clouzot. According to its charter, the Ciné-Club de France sought

. . . to advocate the study, development, and defense of the cinema as Art.
. . . to coordinate all the intellectual, artistic, technical, and economic structures capable of enriching the international landscape of the cinema with films.
. . . to encourage the sincere effort of artists from all countries, whatever their

tendency or style, and to further, by any means possible, that which provides special publicity to the manifestations of its activity.[42]

With Moussinac providing much of the impetus, the new club embarked on an extensive schedule of monthly public film screenings—first at the Colisée and then at the Artistic cinemas—especially with the aim of reviving older films unjustly ignored (e.g., Stiller's *The Legend of Gosta Berling*) and previewing completed films (e.g., Feyder's *L'Image*, Léger's *Ballet mécanique*), fragments (e.g., L'Herbier's *Résurrection*), and films rejected by the commercial distributors or by the censors (e.g., Eisenstein's *Potemkin*).[43] Under Dulac's guidance (with support from Epstein and L'Herbier), in the winter of 1925-1926, the club also organized another major series of *conférences* at Jean Tedesco's new Théâtre du Vieux-Colombier.[44] Entitled "The Creation of a World through the Cinema," the announced twelve lecture-presentations, from 28 November to 20 February, complemented those at the Musée Galliera the year before:

137. Charles Léger

1. The meaning of the cinema	Léon Pierre-Quint
2. *Photogénie* of the machine world	Pierre Hamp
3. The psychological value of the image	Docteur Allendy
4. The external world as revealed by sunlight	Jean Epstein
5. Human emotion	Charles Dullin
6. Fantasy and humor	Pierre Mac Orlan
7. The comic	André Beucler
8. Cinema and time	Jean Tedesco
9. The formation of sensibility	Lionel Landry
10. The shackles of the cinema	Germaine Dulac
11. *Photogénie* of the animal world	Colette
12. The cinema in modern life	André Maurois[45]

Although there were changes in this program (e.g., L'Herbier seems to have substituted for Colette), the series was so successful that the Ciné-Club de France added several Friday evening lectures which lasted at least into March.[46]

The Ciné-Club de France's emergence out of the Galliera experience impelled a second group to form around Charles Léger—"Le Tribune libre du cinéma." Here was a younger generation of cinéphiles, including Marcel Carné, Jean Dréville, Edmond T. Greville, Bernard Brunius, Robert de Jarville, Jean Mitry, Jean Arroy, and Jean-Georges Auriol.[47] Jean Dréville tells me that the Tribune libre had its origins in a number of meetings and discussions in a hall on the Avenue Rapp, late in 1924.[48] Soon after, the group established a biweekly series of public film screenings.[49] One of Charles Léger's first and most difficult accomplishments was to organize (with Moussinac's assistance) an even larger cinema exhibition for the famous Paris Exposition des Arts Décoratifs et Industries Modernes in the summer and autumn months of 1925.[50] The highlight of the exhibition, at "La Maison des artistes," was a series of screenings of selected French films with each filmmaker present for individual discussion sessions.

So Mme. Germaine Dulac's last film project, *La Folie des vaillants*, René Clair's *Paris qui dort, Entr'acte,* and *Le Fantôme du Moulin-Rouge,* Lulu Pick's *Shattered,* Louis Delluc's *Fièvre,* Jean Epstein's *L'Affiche,* etc. . . . received an enthusiastic response from a mass cosmopolitan public.

256

The film programs changed every Thursday, and for the inauguration of each new film, at a gala *séance* on Thursday evening, the filmmaker himself spoke about his film—his intentions and ideas; after the screening, the filmmaker solicited the opinion of opponents, and debates ensued, directed and animated by Charles Léger, the delighted program organizer. There one could finally see drawn together, discussing the same subject, the artisans of the cinema, men of letters, painters, sculptors, architects. . . .[51]

After this astonishing success, Tribune libre immediately set up a second season of biweekly public film screenings at the Salle des Ingénieurs civils and then at the Salle Adyar, Square Rapp.[52] Following the format developed at the Exposition, Léger applied the combination of short lecture, projection (of excerpts or a complete film), and public discussions on a systematic basis.[53] This strategy quickly opened up the ciné-club movement to a wider audience.

Specialized Cinemas

This upsurge of ciné-club activity coincided with the institution of the first specialized cinema in Paris. The man to implement Delluc's original idea of a repertory of films, perhaps naturally enough, was Jean Tedesco. In his search for some nook or cranny to project films on a permanent basis, late in September, 1924, Tedesco discovered to his surprise (did he remember Antoine's suggestion of three years earlier?) that Jacques Copeau's famous but recently abandoned Théâtre du Vieux-Colombier was available for rent. Initially, according to André Brunelin, he and an entrepreneur by the name of Simon Gantillon concocted a scheme to use the Vieux-Colombier for alternate evenings of theater performances and avant-garde film screenings.[1] Gantillon soon pulled out of the venture, but Tedesco persisted. Although Copeau himself disdained the cinema, he was sufficiently interested (apparently Gantillon smoothed the way) to give the young madman a year's lease on the 500-seat auditorium.[2] In less than a month, Tedesco and his friends transformed the theater—installing a projection booth and screen, repainting the façade and interior, printing posters and invitations. Since Copeau, in his retreat to Bourgogne, had taken along the original pair of Florentine doves which marked the theater's entrance, Tedesco was in need of a new emblem. One day by chance he found just what he wanted—the simple circular design of the aperture shutter in a film projector.[3] On 14 November 1924, the Vieux-Colombier finally opened its doors as the beacon of cinema art.

On the posters and advertisements announcing his new cinema, Tedesco set forth a few simple principles. The Vieux-Colombier's programs would be comprised of avant-garde works and a film repertory. In that repertory would be included "quality films that the commercial industry had not allowed the majority of the public to see" as well as "films of such value that they merit a second screening under the title of Cinema Classics."[4] The first week's program established a format for those that followed: André Sauvage's *La Traversé du Crepon* (a documentary on mountain-climbing), Marcel Silver's *L'Horloge* (an experimental film without intertitles), and Chaplin's short feature, *Sunnyside* (1921).[5] The films were projected nightly and ran for one week. And they were accompanied by a secluded chamber orchestra of just three or four instruments whose musicians prepared the music specially for each program.[6]

For seven months, until the first week of June, 1925, the Vieux-Colombier

257

fulfilled its mission of a full season of film screenings. Most of the films shown were revivals—from the United States (Chaplin's shorts, Griffith's *Way Down East*, Fairbanks's *The Mark of Zorro*), Sweden (Sjöström's *The Phantom Coach* [in a new print], Stiller's *Trésor d'Arne*), Germany (Wiene's *Doctor Caligari*, Lulu Pick's *Shattered*, Lang's *Destiny*), and France (Feyder's *Crainquebille*, Epstein's *Coeur fidèle*, and Roussel's *Les Opprimés*).[7] But there were also several new films—Carl Grune's *The Street* (1923) and the Soviet feature, *Polikouchka*—and excerpts projected as set pieces of the narrative avant-garde film practice: "Sélections de rythmes" from *La Roue*, "Etude d'Expressions" from *L'Affiche*, and fragments of accelerating montage (from *La Roue, Coeur fidèle,* and *Kean*).[8] Although Tedesco sometimes organized a double bill of feature films or a selection of excerpts, his programs almost always included a short film, usually a documentary.[9] At first, "Tout-Paris" came to the little cinema out of curiosity, but the public interest waned, particularly after Tedesco tried to screen Arthur Robinson's *Warning Shadows*.[10] Perhaps a more serious problem for him was a lack of publicity. Except for his own announcements in *Cinéa-Ciné-pour-tous*, a diatribe from Moussinac in defense of the Vieux-Colombier in *L'Humanité*, and a brief reference by Emile Vuillermoz in *Le Temps*, the Paris newspapers and film magazines either ignored or took little interest in Tedesco's operation.[11] By the end of the first season, the Vieux-Colombier was in danger of closing down once again.

Yet Tedesco continued to believe in his exhibition strategy, and he convinced Copeau to extend his lease on the Vieux-Colombier for one more year. Several factors were now in his favor. The Exposition des Arts Décoratifs had excited, both among the masses and the elite, a wider interest in cinema art. Following the Exposition, with the support of the Ciné-Club de France and the literary magazine, *Les Cahiers du mois*, Tedesco hosted a series of lectures and screenings on the "Creation of a world through the cinema"—each Saturday afternoon, at 4:30, from 28 November 1925 to 20 February 1926.[12] The speakers included writers Pierre Mac Orlan and Pierre Hamp, critics Lionel Landry and Tedesco himself, filmmakers Dulac and Epstein, and the actor Charles Dullin. For Pierre Hamp's lecture, Jean Grémillon even projected a short film, *Photogénie mécanique*, comprised of excerpts from his documentaries, apparently edited in the manner of Epstein's *Photogénies* and Léger's *Ballet mécanique*.[13] This lecture series provided the Vieux-Colombier with a good deal of prestige. Futhermore, the opening film in Tedesco's second season of programs played upon the interest generated by the series and was an immediate sell-out. The film was Dmitri Kirsanoff's *Menilmontant* (originally entitled *Les Cent Pas*), which the commercial distributors had offered to him because they did not know what to do with it.[14] Its success was assured, in part, by Vuillermoz's enthusiastic one-column review in *Le Temps* and by its co-billing with Chaplin's *The Pilgrim* (which *Cinéa-Ciné-pour-tous* readers had voted the second best film of 1925).[15] Finally, Tedesco added to his schedule a Monday matinee screening for students in the Latin Quarter.[16] This, too, proved a success, and the students became passionate defenders of the *Vieux-Col*.

Inspired by Tedesco but independent of him, another cinéphile nurtured the dream of opening a specialized cinema to show films unlike the others.[17] Armand Tallier was a well-known actor who had worked with Copeau at the

138. (left) Advertisement for the Théâtre du Vieux-Colombier

139. (right) Armand Tallier in *Jocelyn* (1922)

Vieux-Colombier and who, with Myrga, his constant companion, had starred in several Gaumont films, the most important being Poirier's *Jocelyn* (1922). In the summer of 1925, the two found a small (300-seat) cinema for rent behind the Panthéon and prepared to finance a season of film programs with what they called "a light truck, . . . some money left over from an African tour, certain trinkets which would fetch a little money on the flea market, and . . . for the rest, admission tickets. . . ."[18] On 21 January 1926, the Studio des Ursulines opened its doors with this profession of faith:

We propose to enlist our audience from the elite of writers, artists, and intellectuals in the Latin Quarter and from those, ever increasing in number, whom the poverty of commercial film production has driven from the cinemas. Our programs will be composed of diverse tastes, styles, and schools: anything which represents originality, value, *effort* will find a place on our screen.[19]

Like the Théâtre du Vieux-Colombier, the Studio des Ursulines had a secluded chamber orchestra of just a few instruments.[20] But the new cinema was quite different in its programming: "twenty minutes of prewar cinema, twenty minutes of avant-garde cinema, and an unreleased film of a more accessible character and aesthetic."[21] Tallier and Myrga's first program included Léonce Perret's comic *Mimosa la dernière grisette* (1906), René Clair's reedited version of *Entr'acte* (1924), and G. W. Pabst's *The Joyless Street* (with Asta Nielsen and Greta Garbo). The latter film was an immediate sensation, especially after Tallier provoked the audience with an inserted intertitle—"The images that you should see here have been cut by order of the censors"—which forced the attending minister of education to beat a hasty retreat from the cinema.[22] Two months later, Tallier's second program revived Clair's *Le Voyage imaginaire* (1926) and then a third presented the first Japanese film in France, *Musumé*, along with Claude Autant-Lara's short, *Fait-Divers* (1924).[23] In just a few months the Studio des Ursulines was astonishingly "à la mode," and the ciné-philes were rubbing elbows with the young nouveaux riches.

Proliferation and Crisis

By 1925 or 1926, a network of film critics, cinema journals, ciné-club lectures and exhibitions, and specialized cinemas was well established in Paris. This loose cooperative system of cultural exchange and persuasion had staked out several areas of concern. It was promoting the production of formally radical, modern films by its own members (Delluc, Gance, L'Herbier, Dulac, Epstein, Feyder, Clair), both within the French film industry and on its margins. As a corollary, it was educating and expanding the audience for such films. It was also articulating key issues in the attempt to define an aesthetics of film and produce a sophisticated critical practice. And it was taking the first steps to preserve older films and establish a tradition of cinema art. The last five years of the decade were marked by a proliferation of these efforts and a number of significant crises.

In 1925, several books were published in Paris which clearly revealed the divisions that had developed between the dominant industry and the various advocates of an alternate cinema. Against G.-M. Coissac's *Histoire du cinéma-tographie*, which surveyed the technological and industrial evolution of the film industry, Léon Moussinac's *Naissance du cinéma* contended that a new narrative art had been created.[1] In a polemical but clearly reasoned analysis, Moussinac summed up the argument for a film aesthetics based on a conjunction of plastic and rhythmic elements (the mise-en-scène, framing, and editing of a cinematic discourse) and then sketched the stages of development in each of the major national cinemas (American, Swedish, German, and French). And like Delluc before him, he reiterated the belief that "the cinema will be popular or it will not be at all."[2] Against the polemical essays advocating a "pure cinema," published principally in *Cinéa-Ciné-pour-tous*, Henri Fescourt and Jean-Louis Bouquet's *L'Idée et l'écran: opinions sur le cinéma* (1925-1926) defended an up-dated and more sophisticated concept of the commercial narrative film.[3] Although admitting the value of lighting and rhythm, for instance, Fescourt and Bouquet contended that the principal basis of film art was its subject, meaning the logical development of a story.[4] Along with the publicity generated by the film exhibitions at the Musée Galliera and the Exposition des Arts Décoratifs, these books stimulated the publication of other works over the next several years.

In 1926, Les Ecrivains réunis alone published two books on the cinema. In one, a slim volume entitled *Le Cinématographe vu d'Etna*, Jean Epstein collected

several of his lectures together with a new theoretical essay. In the title essay,
Epstein developed a concept of the cinema apparatus as a machine of the
Imagination, producing its own epiphanies of revelation—"one of the most
powerful forces of the cinema is its animism."[5] In another, however, he called
for "a new avant-garde" and a mode of filmic construction that would direct
the polysemic play of associations in a chain of images. That play, as rhetorical
figuring, could be controlled through patterns of simultaneity and alternation
(or, more generally, through paradigmatic and syntagmatic relations), in what
Stuart Liebman has called a "thematic montage of associations."[6] In the second
book, *L'ABC du cinéma*, Blaise Cendrars, the idiosyncratic poet who had helped
Abel Gance shoot and edit *La Roue*, finally published the full text of his essay
on the modernity of the cinema.[7] In his elliptical, telegraphic prose style,
Cendrars argued that film's fragmentation of reality gave the viewer an intensified experience of the simultaneous flux of life and that the worldwide exhibition of a film created a kind of "global village" of simultaneous audience
participation.

The following year, a Geneva publisher collected many of Ricciotto Canudo's published and unpublished essays into *L'Usine aux images* (1927). The
most important of these, "Réflexions sur la septième art," which articulated
Canudo's expressive theory of film, seems to have been written in 1921, while
the reviews of film genres and individual films that complete the book date
from 1922-1923. As the decade drew to a close and the silent cinema to an
end, several books attempted to sum up the historical development of the era:
Moussinac's own *Panoramique du cinéma* (1929), Alexandre Arnoux's *Cinéma*
(1929), Georges Charensol's *Panorama du cinéma* (1929), and Henri Fescourt's
Le Cinéma des origines à nos jours (1932).

There was even more activity among the film journals and literary magazines. Several literary magazines, such as *La Revue nouvelle*, followed *Le Mercure
de France* in establishing film review columns; but the most important phenomenon was the increase in special issues, modeled after *Le Crapouillot*. *Les
Cahiers du mois* put out the most significant of these. In 1925, it devoted two
special book-length issues to the cinema: #12 on scenarios, #16/17 on film
aesthetics and criticism. The latter included essays—some from the Ciné-Club
de France lectures at the Vieux-Colombier—by most of the critics, filmmakers, artists, and writers associated with the ciné-club movement. There were
major statements by Epstein, L'Herbier, Clair, and Dulac, as well as summary
critical pieces by Tedesco, Vuillermoz, Charensol, Henry, and Moussinac.
Two other literary magazines came out with important special issues—*La
Revue fédéraliste* (November, 1927) and *Le Rouge et le noir* (July, 1928)—both
of which focused more on the cinema itself as an art than on its relation to
literature.[8] In 1926, René Jeanne convinced the Librairie Félix Alcan to publish and market a special collection of essays on the cinema in a serial format,
much like the issues of a magazine.[9] *L'Art cinématographique* (1926-1929) ran
to six book-length volumes and collected most of the lectures given at the
Vieux-Colombier in 1925-1926, along with additional pieces by Gance,
L'Herbier, Vuillermoz, and others. Several are notable as summary or original
statements: Dulac's "Les Esthétiques, les entraves, la cinégraphie intégrale,"
Landry's "Formation de la sensibilité," Moussinac's "Cinéma: expression sociale," and André Levinson's "Pour une poétique du film."

This phenomenon of special issues was paralleled by the emergence of several specialized, rather deluxe film journals, all of them edited by filmmakers and ciné-club leaders. Although none lasted more than a few years, they were important organs for the exchange of ideas on an alternate cinema. Germaine Dulac's *Schémas* (1927), which appeared but once, was envisioned as a theoretical journal modeled after *Les Cahiers du mois* (#16/17). That one issue contained a cross-section of critical debate (and no photographs): Hans Richter and Dulac herself advocating a "pure cinema" analogous to music, Henri Fescourt and Jean-Louis Bouquet again defending the narrative cinema, Dr. Paul Ramain celebrating the "oneiric incoherence" of film, Dr. Commandon explaining the value of scientific films, and Jules Romains rhapsodizing in a poetic epilogue. Jean Dréville edited no less than three film journals over a two-year period: *Photo-Ciné* (1927), *Cinégraphie* (1927-1928), and *On Tourne* (1928). Of these, *Cinégraphie*, which ran only five issues, had the most impact.

140. The cover of *Cinégraphie*

Printed in a folio-sized format, it was the most deluxe film journal of the decade, reproducing large-scale stills from major films along with Dréville's own exquisite landscape and portrait photographs. It was also the only film journal to publish excerpts from actual shooting scripts: Dulac's *La Folie des vaillants* (1925) and Epstein's *6½ × 11* (1927).[10] In Switzerland, Kenneth McPherson edited a monthly English-language film journal, *Close Up* (1927-1930), which provided continuing coverage of the avant-garde French cinema through Jean Lenauer. Finally, there was the monthly *La Revue du cinéma* (1928-1931), edited by Jean-Georges Auriol and addressed to the elite clientele of Gallimard and the *Nouvelle Revue Française*.[11] Besides the comprehensive film criticism by Paul Gilson, Louis Chavance, Bernard Brunius, and himself, Auriol published several of Robert Desnos's scenarios as well as Buñuel and Dali's scenario for *Un Chien andalou* (1929).[12] Although large (forty to eighty pages) and rather expensive, *La Revue du cinéma* took consistently leftist political positions, especially after Janine Bouissounouse and Robert Aron joined the editorial staff. It was the only film journal, for instance, which, following Moussinac, envisioned an alternate cinema in political as well as aesthetic terms.

Coincident with the first issue of *La Revue du cinéma*, late in 1928, the field of popular film journals expanded with the appearance of two new rivals to *Cinémagazine* and *Cinéa-Ciné-pour-tous*. The first was *Cinémonde*, edited by Gaston Thierry, a slim twenty-page folio-format weekly. *Cinémonde*'s attention was focused on the major commercial films then in release or in production, and it was filled with publicity photographs, sometimes artfully arranged according to the whims of an imaginative graphics designer. Although it defended the work of several filmmakers associated with the narrative avant-garde, their work and that of the avant-garde generally received even more attention in the other new magazine, *Pour Vous*. *Pour Vous* was edited by Alexandre Arnoux, who hoped to make it an inexpensive, independent film journal: "In this magazine, our readers will find not a single line of film industry publicity, whether blatant or disguised (as is too often the case)."[13] To that end, *Pour Vous* used a newspaper-size format of only sixteen pages (much like *Cinémiroir*). And Arnoux and his writers—e.g., Wahl, Charensol, Roger Régent, Nino Frank, Jean Lenauer, and Lucie Derain—devoted a good deal of space not only to industry matters and the latest commercial films but to the broad range of avant-garde film practice as well as to the exhibition activities of the ciné-clubs and specialized cinemas. Although it could not sustain the level of independence that Arnoux initially desired, *Pour Vous* survived, along with *Cinémagazine* and *Cinémonde*, to become the major weekly film journals of the 1930s.

For all that Delluc, Canudo, Moussinac, and others had done to create a specialized/popular press devoted to the cinema and, in the words of Harry Alan Potamkin, "a body of critics, as authentic and authoritative as the critics of the other arts,"[14] their legal status was less than clearly defined. To the industry, the press served as a kind of publicity department extension; to the critics, it served as an educational forum, an arena of exchange on aesthetic values and on the social function of the cinema. These conflicting attitudes came to a head in March, 1928, when a state court finally handed down a decision on a suit that Jean Sapène and Cinéromans had brought against Moussinac for one of his columns in *L'Humanité* (26 September 1926). The charge was that he had maligned a film they were then distributing, *Jim le Harponneur* [*The Sea Beast*, starring John Barrymore], as "the perfect example of a bad American film or, simply, a bad film."[15] Incredibly (or perhaps not—given the results of the recent national elections), the court decided against Moussinac and accepted Cinéromans's demand of 100,000 francs in damages.[16] Moussinac and *L'Humanité* appealed the verdict, but it was not until 12 December 1930 that the Court of Appeals overturned the lower court's decision and, in effect, granted the film critics freedom of expression.[17] After more than a decade of struggle, film critics could finally enjoy the same legal rights as their colleagues in literary, theater, and art criticism.

Moussinac found himself at the center of an even more important struggle in the ciné-club movement in 1928.

The success of the Ciné-Club de France and the Tribune libre had been phenomenal. Early in 1927, alongside its regular public film screenings, the Ciné-Club de France organized, for the College libre des sciences sociales, a series of lectures called "The Cinema in modern life and thought":

January 7:	M. Charensol—The state of the cinema
January 14:	M. A. Berge—Literature and cinema
January 21:	M. A. Obey—Music and cinema
January 28:	M. Moussinac—The social expression of the cinema
February 4:	M. Levinson
February 11:	M. Jean Laran—The documentary and instructional cinema
February 18:	M. René Clair—The cinématographe vesus intelligence
February 25:	M. M. L'Herbier—The cinématographe as a cosmic medium.[18]

A month later, it sponsored a second "Exposition du cinéma" for the Galerie d'Art de la Grande Maison de Blanc.[19] And during the commercial exhibition of Gance's *Napoléon* at the Madeleine-Cinéma, the club held a special screening of the triptych sequences that had been cut from the film.[20] Meanwhile, the Tribune libre opened its third season of weekly public film screenings with Kirsanoff's *Menilmontant*.[21] In April, it sponsored Robert de Jarville's series of avant-garde film screenings and lectures, held on Saturday afternoons at the Théâtre de Chateau d'Eau.[22] Later that same year, for the Salon d'Automne,

Jarville also delivered a lecture on "Images du monde" and screened several undistributed Soviet films.[23] Finally, for its fourth season, the Tribune libre began with what it called "the most characteristic specimens of each country's production": Feyder's *L'Image* (France), Lulu Pick's *Sylvester* (Germany), Sjöström's *L'Epreuve du feu* (Sweden), and Kuleshov's *Dura Lux* (Soviet Union).[24]

All of this activity soon had repercussions throughout France and the rest of Europe. In Paris itself, a host of small ciné-clubs grew up—with names like Club de l'Écran (Pierre Ramelot), Phare tournant (Raymond Villette), Régards, Le Lanterne magique, L'Effort, Les Spectateurs d'Avant-Garde.[25] Outside the capital, as early as 1925, Dr. Paul Ramain had organized the first provincial ciné-club at Montpelier.[26] Over the next few years, others were started in Agen, Lyon, Reims, Strasbourg, Bordeaux, Chalons, Lille, Tours, Grenoble, and Marseille—Jean Vigo's Amis du cinéma, Ciné-Club d'Avant-Garde.[27] In London, in 1925, there was the Film Society organized by Ivor Montagu and Hugh Miller and run by Iris Barry; in Lausanne and Geneva, in 1926, the "Ciné d'Art," partly sponsored by the Vieux-Colombier.[28] The most active ciné-club outside France, yet still associated with the French groups, was in Brussels. Organized by Albert Valentin in 1925, as "Cinégraphie Fridays" at the Cabinet Maldoror, the Brussels ciné-club soon changed its name to "Visions fortis" and held an extensive series of lecture-presentations late in 1926 at the Salle de L'Union Coloniale.[29] The list of speakers reads like a directory of the French avant-garde: Dulac, L'Herbier, Epstein, Gance, Poirier, Clair, Feyder, Chomette, Kirsanoff, Dr. Comandon, Moussinac, Vuillermoz. By 1927, the film critic Carl Vincent, who took over from Valentin, had transformed the group into the "Club du cinéma," which held weekly screenings at Sever House both Friday and Saturday evenings.[30]

By the end of the decade, the ciné-club movement had proliferated to such an extent that it climaxed in two major international events. In September, 1929, Robert Aron and Janine Bouissounouse organized a ten-day International Congress on the Independent Cinema at the Chateau de La Sarraz in Switzerland.[31] The congress gathered together filmmakers and critics from France (Aron, Bouissounouse, Auriol, Cavalcanti, and Moussinac), Germany (Hans Richter and Walter Ruttman), England (Ivor Montagu and Isaacs), Austria (Béla Balázs and Fritz Rosenfeld), Holland (H. K. Franken), Italy (Enrico Prampolini and Alberto Sartoris), Spain (Giménez Caballero), Switzerland (Robert Guye, Arnold Kohler, Georg Schmidt, Alfred Masset, and Jean Lenauer), the United States (Montgomery Evans), and the Soviet Union (Sergei Eisenstein, Edward Tissé, and Gregory Alexandrov). Two months later, in Paris, Germaine Dulac, Charles Léger, and Robert de Jarville organized a Congress of Ciné-Clubs, out of which emerged the first international Fédération des Ciné-Clubs.[32]

Despite this expansion, the ciné-club movement remained basically elitist, appealing to a restricted number of artists, intellectuals, cinéphiles, and (to use an unflattering label from the period) "boisterous snobs."[33] But there was one exception—"Les Amis de Spartacus." Two events in 1926 and 1927 finally led Moussinac and several of his Communist friends to wed their interest in an alternate cinema with their political ideology. On 13 November 1926, at the Artistic-Cinéma, Moussinac and Dulac arranged a Ciné-Club de France screening of the banned Eisenstein film, *The Battleship Potemkin* (1925).[34] It

264

was one of the most successful of all their programs and aroused a keen interest among some Parisians to see more Soviet films. Then, in 1927, a workers' cooperative took over the Bellevilloise, a popular cinema in the 20th *arrondissement*, to screen "exceptional films considered 'uncommercial' by the majority of cinema owners."[35] By the early 1930s, the Bellevilloise would become an important outlet for workers' newsreels.[36] Its early success convinced Moussinac to attempt a similar venture in the form of a ciné-club.

In July, 1927, along with Jean Lods, Francis Jourdain, Paul Vaillant-Courturier, and Georges Marrane, Moussinac organized the "Club des Amis de Spartacus" with the purpose of creating a mass cinema movement.[37] Their first step was to acquire the Cinéma du Casino de Grenelle, the largest cinema in the 15th *arrondissement*.[38] The second step was to arrange for the rights to project a series of provocative films. The third was to publicize their principles:

> To the public that loves and understands the cinema, that foresees its destiny, there remains only a single means of battling this dictatorship of money: to band together.
>
> Henceforth, it is the purpose of "Amis de Spartacus," through the organizaiton of restricted screenings, to assure the distribution of major works of the French, German, American, and Soviet cinema.
>
> The future of the cinématographe is entirely in the hands of the public.
>
> It is indispensable that every film advocate work against commercial publicity, against French protectionism, against American colonization.[39]

The cinema would be conceived, not as an end in itself, but as a means of combat and of social liberation.

Finally, on 15 March 1928, the Casino de Grenelle cinema opened with the first of six months of weekly programs. Four thousand people reportedly showed up to vie for the 2,000 available seats.[40] "We couldn't believe our eyes," said Jean Lods, "when we found ourselves with a few thousand members after several weeks; we didn't know what to do."[41] One strategy they tried was scheduling simultaneous screenings at the Bellevilloise as well as at the Casino de Grenelle. Within three months, membership in Les Amis de Spartacus had swelled to at least ten thousand.[42] Soon the club was organizing efforts in the suburbs and provinces until, within another couple of months, the membership had quadrupled.[43] Just what films was the group exhibiting that could cause this phenomenon? Older film classics, such as Delluc's *Fièvre* and Stiller's *Trésor d'Arne*, recent popular films, such as Flaherty's *Moana* and the Swedish film, *Charles XII*, and, most important of all, three banned Soviet films—Eisenstein's *Potemkin* and Pudovkin's *Mother* (1926) and *The End of St. Petersburg* (1927).[44] According to Jean Lods, as many as twenty-five to thirty thousand people saw *Potemkin* alone.[45] What was the group planning for its fall season in 1928? Series of French, American, and German films, and, in honor of the tenth anniversary of the Soviet revolution, Eisenstein's new film, *October* (1927).[46]

Les Amis de Spartacus was the one overtly political organization in the French ciné-club movement of the 1920s. And it was the only organization to come close to making that movement a mass movement, to lay the groundwork for a truly popular alternate cinema which could confront the dominant industry with any degree of force. As long as the ciné-clubs and specialized cinemas were restricted to small audiences, the industry could ignore them or even offer mild encouragement. But when a club could compete on a par with the largest commercial cinemas in Paris, that was another matter. Les Amis de Spartacus was also making a mockery of the government practice of permitting officially censored films to be projected privately in the ciné-clubs but forbidding them in the commercial cinemas.[47] That most of these films were Soviet in origin made them a highly visible target of the political attacks on French Communists that reached a peak in 1928. In September, Jean Chiappe, the dapper, devious Paris chief of police, called Jean Lods into his office and told him the Spartacus group was on a collision course with his duty to protect the public order. He even threatened to have his agents (who had infiltrated the group) disrupt any further Soviet film screenings at either the Casino de Grenelle or the Bellevilloise.[48] Given Chiappe's power, Moussinac and Lods had no legal recourse. By October, Les Amis de Spartacus was disbanded, and the energy that had gone into the organization dispersed among the other film groups and into other political activities. Although the Spartacus group never reached the point of engaging in film production, the Soviet films it exhibited had a decided impact on a number of French avant-garde filmmakers.

Another crisis of sorts occurred among the specialized cinemas as they expanded in number and scope to the point of threatening the apparent unity of the alternate cinema network. Jean Tedesco steadily continued to build up a film repertory at the Vieux-Colombier and promoted his effort in the pages of *Cinéa-Ciné-pour-tous*.[49] For the most part, his programming consisted of re-screening films, whether successful (e.g., L'Herbier's *Feu Mathias Pascal*, Lang's *Siegfried*) or unsuccessful (e.g., Murnau's *The Last Laugh*, initially booed at the Aubert-Palace),[50] which had contributed to the development of film art. His choice of films struck a fairly equal balance among the American, German, and French cinemas. In the second and third seasons, however, Tedesco began to introduce new films as well (e.g., *Menilmontant*, Cavalcanti's *En rade*).[51] Most of these were documentaries—by Sauvage, Boge, Chaumel, and Jean Grémillon—a preference that soon distinguished the Vieux-Colombier from the other specialized cinemas in Paris.[52] That preference seems to have coincided with, and possibly fed, a growing public interest in documentary films—e.g., Poirier's *La Croisière noire* at the Salle Marivaux (April, 1926), Cooper and Schoedsack's *Grass* at the Madeleine (June, 1926), and Flaherty's *Moana* at the Electric (August, 1926).[53] In November, 1926, Tedesco offered a special screening of *Moana*, which had to be rescheduled twice to meet audience demands.[54] In early 1927, he presented André Gide and Marc Allegret's film on central Africa, *Voyage au Congo*, and then Grémillon's *Tour au large*, a lyrical celebration of trawler fishing off the Brittany coast.[55] For the latter, Grémillon himself constructed an experimental sound synchronization system using Pleyela player piano rolls. The popularity of the Vieux-Colombier persuaded Tedesco, early in 1927, to lease the first floor of a building on the Right Bank of Paris, the Pavillon de Hanovre. There, at the Pavillon du cinéma, until the summer of 1928, he could screen films that had been programmed at the Vieux-Colombier one or two weeks before.[56]

Tedesco's example and the expanding activity of the Tribune libre led to the transformation of a small cinema near the Mouffetard area in the same year the Pavillon opened. This was the 300-seat Ciné-Latin, owned by José Miguel Duran, whose model for programming strategy was Charles Léger.[57] Much like the Vieux-Colombier, the Ciné-Latin specialized in repertory programs, but its emphasis was on the French cinema. In February, 1928, for instance, following the exclusive run of *Napoléon*, Duran rescreened Gance's early war epic, *J'Accuse*.[58] In March, he devoted several weeks to a retrospective of films by René Clair; in June, he persuaded Marcel L'Herbier to project, along with *L'Inhumaine*, his incomplete version of *Résurrection*.[59] The Ciné-Latin is even credited with rediscovering, and so preserving, Louis Delluc's *La Femme de nulle part* and *L'Inondation* as well as Max Linder's *L'Etroit Mousquetaire*.[60] Just as did the Tribune libre, Duran scheduled discussions, every Thursday evening, for the spectators to debate the films shown during the past week.[61] The audience of the Ciné-Latin guaranteed a lively dialogue, for it was comprised equally of students and working-class people from the neighborhood. Paul de la Borie reports on one of the summer programs:

Seated side by side, intellectuals and workers fraternize in front of the screen. I cannot say that the films they are watching produce the same impression on one and the other. They are not, evidently, in the same state of receptivity. The comic film preceding the *pièce de resistance* provokes among the common people of the audience a hilarious outburst in which the university students do not share. Instead, the students amuse themselves over the naïve delight of their neighbors. But the second part of the program begins, and soon there is a silence that is absolute. The entire audience follows the unfolding of the images and the development of ideas with unfailing attention. But, in general, the common people applaud very little. They are trying too hard to understand. And the fact is that they do understand for they don't get annoyed. . . . And they come back for more.[62]

Much like the Bellevilloise cinema across Paris, then, the Ciné-Latin served as a precedent for Moussinac's Les Amis de Spartacus.

The Studio des Ursulines flourished even more than did its two companion cinemas. By late 1927, Tallier told the *Cinématographie française*, his cinema had drawn 23,000 to 25,000 people to its programs.[63] His programming format of prewar films, avant-garde films, and unreleased films distinguished it from both the Vieux-Colombier and the Ciné-Latin. And Tallier's choice of newly released German and American films, along with French experimental shorts, catered to the snobs of his audience. Ironically, that snobism affirmed the very status quo the alternate cinema movement was trying to combat: that the French cinema merely existed on the margins of the American and German cinema. An unspoken rivalry seems to have arisen between Tallier and Tedesco, perhaps because the latter saw himself as a founder or father confronted by a usurper.[64] The rivalry is implicit in *Cinéa-Ciné-pour-tous*'s relative neglect of the Studio des Ursulines in its pages and perhaps explicit in Tedesco's abandonment of a joint exhibition of G. W. Pabst's *Secrets of a Soul* (1926), planned for May, 1927.[65] In its second and, especially, its third season, the Studio des Ursulines shifted its programming to include more and more new French films—but with no letup in the rivalry. In the fall of 1926, Tailler had countered Tedesco's screening of *Moana* by being the first in Paris to exhibit Cavalcanti's semi-documentary, *Rien que les heures* (1926).[66] Late in 1927, he countered *Le Voyage au Congo* and *Tour au large* at the Vieux-Colombier with Léon Poirier's new documentary on Africa, *Amours exotiques*. That same year, Tallier scored another coup by offering *en exclusivité* two of Jean Epstein's independently produced films, *6½ × 11* and *La Glace à trois faces*. The latter had an exceptionally successful run, for a French film, of nearly three months.[67]

What really made the Ursulines distinctive, however, was short avant-garde films. It was the single Paris cinema to consistently offer an outlet for young independent filmmakers. By exhibiting Clair's *Entr'acte*, Autant-Lara's *Fait-Divers*, and Léger's *Ballet mécanique* on its earliest programs, the Ursulines built up a loose corpus of short experimental films which were first projected publicly on its screen. Besides those mentioned, they included Chomette's *Jeux des reflets et de la vitesse* (1925) and *Cinq Minutes du cinéma pur* (1926), Duchamp's *Anemic cinéma* (1926), Cavalcanti's *La P'tite Lily* (1927), Clair's *La Tour* (1928), and Man Ray's *Emak Bakia* (1927) and *L'Etoile de mer* (1928).[68] Tallier even made room in this corpus for several short documentaries: Georges Lacombe's striking study of the ragpickers of the Clignancourt flea market, *La Zone* (1928), Marcel Carné's *Nogent, Eldorado du dimanche* (1930) and Jean Vigo's *A propos de Nice* (1930).[69] At least one of his selections, however, embroiled the Ursulines in considerable controversy. This was *La Coquille et le clergyman*, which Ciné-Club de France had screened privately as early as October, 1927.[70] Thinking that Antonin Artaud (the author of the scenario) had denounced Germaine Dulac's production of the film, the Surrealists provoked a near-riot when the film was shown in February, 1928.[71] The so-called scandal demeaned *La Coquille et le clergyman* at the time, but so marked it historically as to create continued interest in it.

During the last two years of the decade, at least four more specialized cinemas sprang up in Paris. The popularity of the Ursulines's programming convinced a M. Querel, late in 1928, to open another little cinema, the 550-seat Salle des Agriculteurs.[72] According to Jean Dréville, *Autour de l'argent*, his short documentary (and montage study) on the making of L'Herbier's *L'Argent* (1929), was the main attraction of the inaugural program—even more than Ralph Ince's *Shanghaied* (1927).[73] For its first half year, the Agriculteurs had a shaky existence. *La Revue du cinéma* alternately praised and damned its programming—they especially supported an early festival of Cavalcanti films.[74] In May, 1929, Tallier and Myrga announced that they were going to take over management of the cinema, and for the next six months or so they seem to have run the Agriculteurs successfully as a repertory cinema.[75] Even more successful than the Agriculteurs was Jean Vallée's L'Oeil de Paris, located near the Place de l'Etoile. Although less luxurious than some of the other cinemas, L'Oeil de Paris had a chic Argentinian decor and was conveniently inexpensive.[76] Its inaugural program, in May, 1929, was modeled on the Ursulines—Dulac's *Arabesques*, Robert Florey's *Life and Death of a Hollywood Extra*, excerpts from the old serial *Les Mystères de New-York*, and Jean Epstein's new film, *Finis Terrae*.[77] Within months, L'Oeil de Paris had become the meeting place for the biweekly sessions of the Club de l'Écran.[78] The only specialized cinema to fail during this period was the Studio Diamant. Ever the opportunist, Henri Diamant-Berger conceived this cinema as part of an ambitious art center for the avant-garde.[79] All he completed, however, was the 160-seat cinema and an adjacent bar. Perhaps because of his former position in the commercial industry, his rather unfocused programming included very few

French films.[80] Although Diamant-Berger says that his mismanagement of the bar caused him to close the Studio Diamant, Harry Alan Potamkin suggests another reason (besides the programming): it was so designed (with steel stalls, a leveled or stairlike ceiling, and a distant screen) as to distract and trouble one's vision.[81]

The last major specialized cinema was Jean Mauclaire's Studio 28. Mauclaire opened his 337-seat cinema in January, 1928, not on the Left Bank, but halfway up the hill of Montmartre.[82] His programming format aligned the Studio 28 closely with the Ursulines: unreleased or newly released features plus short prewar and avant-garde films. The inaugural program he put together—a documentary on the making of Gance's *Napoléon* and a new Soviet film, Abram Room's *Bed and Sofa* (1927)—was so successful that it ran for five weeks.[83] That summer, Studio 28 featured Epstein's new film, *La Chute de la maison Usher, en exclusivité*, with similar success.[84] Like the L'Oeil de Paris, it, too, became a favorite meeting place for several ciné-clubs.[85] From the beginning, Mauclaire's ambition was to equal or surpass the prestige of the Vieux-Colombier and the Ursulines. To that end, according to Potamkin, before each program he projected color slides on the cinema's silver-toned walls and then accompanied each film with "an arranged selection of music from a mechanical piano."[86] Within a short time, Studio 28 was acknowledged as the most attractive and "à la mode" small cinema in Paris.

On one occasion, however, Maucliare's programming actually endangered his own cinema. In April, 1929, at the Ursulines, the Surrealists had arranged a private screening of the unknown *Un Chien andalou*, along with Man Ray's *Les Mystères du château du Dé*.[87] Initially skeptical, they came away enthusiastic advocates of the Buñuel-Dali film. When Mauclaire agreed to premiere *Un Chien andalou* at Studio 28 the following autumn, André Breton decided to make it a gala event, with a foyer exhibition of paintings by Masson, Miró, Ernst, Man Ray, and others.[88] Rumor and the usual polemical publicity led to an ugly confrontation at the early November premiere. Members of the right-wing Jeunesse patriote and Camelots du Roi stormed into the cinema, attacked the film, and retreated, slashing some of the paintings. This scandal assured *Un Chien andalou*'s success, and for nine months at Studio 28 it played off and on to capacity crowds whose responses oscillated wildly from outrage to enthusiasm and hysterical laughter.[89] Cyril Connolly, for instance, reports that

The picture was received with shouts and boos and when a pale young man tried to make a speech, hats and sticks were flung at the screen. In one corner a woman was chanting, "Salopes, salopes, salopes!" and soon the audience began to join in.[90]

As the ciné-clubs and specialized cinemas multiplied in the second half of the decade, there was a reciprocal increase in the demand for avant-garde films. The problem was how could the production and distribution of more and more French films be financed? The production of a short silent film was not all that expensive—Carné's *Nogent, Eldorado du dimanche* (1929) reportedly cost but 5,000 francs—but that was beyond the means of most avant-garde film-makers.[91] One source of capital was a wealthy patron whose interest in the cinema made him susceptible to dabbling in the new art. Rolf de Maré, for instance, financed Clair's *Entr'acte* as an interlude for one of the 1924 Ballet suédois programs at his Théâtre de Champs-Elysées. To compete with de Maré, the following year, the Comte de Beaumont asked Henri Chomette to make several short films for his famous ballet productions, "Soirées de Paris."[92] Perhaps through his indirect involvement in L'Herbier's Cinégraphic company, the Vicomte de Noailles became enamored of the cinema and hit upon the idea of producing one film each year as a gift to his wife: Man Ray's *Les Mystères du château du Dé* (1929), Luis Buñuel's *L'Age d'or* (1930), and Jean Cocteau's *Le Sang d'un poète* (1930-1932).[93] But the whole French production of avant-garde films could hardly depend on the whim and largess of a couple of latter-day Maecenases.

In contrast to Germany, where both UFA and the state helped finance short avant-garde films,[94] capital was not forthcoming from the French commercial film industry, especially after the tight money conditions of 1925. Perhaps inevitably, the specialized cinemas began to venture into film production. As early as 1926, Jean Tedesco turned the loft above his cinema into the "Laboratoire du Vieux-Colombier" for the production of short scientific films—e.g., *Etoiles et fleurs de mer, Papillons et chrysalides.*[95] A year later, Jean Renoir's production team joined Tedesco to expand the laboratory's meager facilities for their fantasy film, based on a Hans Christian Andersen fable, *La Petite Marchande d'allumettes* (1928).[96] The atelier now had its own electrical generator, specially built reflector lamps (for panchromatic film stock), wooden tanks and an old Pathé camera (for processing the negative and making the initial positive prints).[97] After more than six months of work, *La Petite Marchande d'allumettes* was projected in the very place of its creation, in June, 1928.[98] Unfortunately, the film's exhibition and distribution was halted almost immediately by Maurice Rostand (the author of a 1914 operatic adaptation of the same fable), who charged Renoir and Tedesco with plagiarism.[99] Although the filmmakers won their case, it was in litigation for more than a year; and Tedesco was unable to develop the Vieux-Colombier laboratory into the major production facility he had envisioned.[100] Still, it was used occasionally, at least until 1930, when the Hungarian animator, Berthold Bartosch, worked there on his film version of a book of woodcuts, *Une Idée* (1934).[101] Besides these few studio films, Tedesco also seems to have helped finance Kirsanoff's short experimental sound film, *Brumes d'automne* (1928), and Epstein's short documentary, *Le Pas de la mule* (1930).[102]

The Ursulines and L'Oeil de Paris also sponsored several short films, notably the abstract experiments of Germaine Dulac—*Thémes et variations* (1928) and *Arabesques* (1929). But the most assiduous practicioner of independent film production financing was Jean Mauclaire of Studio 28. Even before he opened his cinema on Montmartre, Mauclaire had signed a contract with Abel Gance that gave him exclusive exhibition rights to several short triptych films.[103] In May, 1928, Dréville identified three of these works (which have since disappeared) as *Galop, Danses* and *Marine*—the last of which, he said, was "with *Tour au large*, the most beautiful poem that has been created about the sea."[104] During the next two years, Mauclaire provided financing to several young filmmakers for their first films: Henri d'Arche and Georges Hugnet's *La Perle* (1929), Lucie Derain's *Harmonies de Paris* (1929), Eugène Deslaw's *Marche des machines* (1928) and *Nuits électriques* (1929), and A. Sandy's *Lumières et ombres*

(1929) and *Prétexte* (1929). According to one source, he also partially underwrote Epstein's *La Chute de la maison Usher* as well as his last silent film, *Sa Tête* (1929).[105]

Just as they were forced into film production, the Vieux-Colombier and Ursulines both found themselves involved very quickly in film distribution. By 1926, Tedesco was shipping films off to Switzerland and Belgium to provide current programs for outpost cinemas and ciné-clubs. Tallier soon followed his example, and, by the summer of 1928, he was advertising that the Ursulines could supply a program of films, a projector, and a projectionist to any provincial cinema on payment of costs and a moderate fee.[106] The two primary distribution agencies for young avant-garde filmmakers, however, were set up independently of Tedesco and Tallier. One was the "Cooperative du Film," directed by Robert Aron, a newly appointed editor for *La Revue du cinéma*.[107] The other was run by Pierre Braunberger. Braunberger's production company, Néo-Film, had already financed short films by Renoir and Cavalcanti—e.g., *Charleston* (1926) and *La P'tite Lily* (1927)—as well as the latter's feature film, *En rade* (1927).[108] In May, 1929, he announced the formation of Studio-Film to distribute and sell "all the films of artistic quality (experimental films, documentary films, films called 'Avant-Garde')."[109] In just a few months, Braunberger had compiled a list of available films that summed up much of the current French and foreign avant-garde film practice:

A. Cavalcanti—*En rade, Rien que les heures, La P'tite Lily.*
Man Ray—*L'Etoile de mer, Emak Bakia, Les Mystères du château du Dé.*
E. Deslav—*La Nuit électrique, La marche des machines, Montparnasse.*
D. Kirsanoff—*Brumes d'automne.*
E. Deslav—*La Nuit électrique, La marche des Machines, Montparnasse.*
L. Buñuel—*Le Chien andalou.*
G. Lacombe—*La Zone.*
René Clair—*Le Voyage imaginaire.*
Henri d'Arche—*La Perle.*
J. Renoir—*La Fille de l'eau.*
C. Lambert—*Voici Paris, Voici Marseille.*
J. de Casembroot—*Ernest et Amélie.*
R. Landau—*Rhythmes d'une cathédrale.*
S. Silka—*Le Mâle mort de Canart.*
Duhamel—*Paris express.*
O. Blakeston—*I Do Love To Be beside the Seaside.*
P. Sichel—*Bithulite.*
C. Heymann—*Vie heureuse.*
Gide et Allegret—*Voyage au Congo.*
Allegret—*Les Troglodytes.*
V. Blum—*Wasser.*
A. Strasser—*Partie de campagne.*
Robert Florey—*Symphonie des gratte-ciels.*
Kenneth Macpherson—*Monkeys, Moon.*
Michel Gorel—*Bateaux parisiens.*
Pierre Chenal—*Un Coup de dé.*
C. Autant-Lara—*Construire un feu.*
Jean Lods et Boris Kaufmann—*Aujourd'hui.*[110]

Even Pathé-Cinéma inadvertently became part of this alternate cinema distribution circuit through its sale of 9.5mm copies of films to collectors and the smaller ciné-clubs.[111] Unfortunately, this distribution effort was quickly undermined and diverted by the sound revolution sweeping the film industry.

Preservation

The change to sound films in France, from 1929 to 1930, had a disrupting effect on two crucial areas of the alternate cinema network—production and exhibition. The proliferation of independent avant-garde film production was halted and reversed by the expense and inaccessibility of material and equipment. Only a few filmmakers were able to work briefly—and independently—in sound: Buñuel's *L'Age d'or*, screened at Studio 28 for several weeks before it was banned on 11 December 1930; Jean Cocteau's *Le Sang d'un poète*, made in 1930, but not screened until 20 January 1932, at the Vieux-Colombier; and Jean Vigo's banned *Zero de conduite* (1933), which was screened only once publicly at the Artistic cinema. Epstein tried to maintain his independence with a little-known three-reel semi-documentary on Brittany fisherman, *Mor-Vran* (1930), but he had no control over its musical soundtrack. Most filmmakers were soon forced to join the dominant industry to work on commercial feature films (L'Herbier and Grémillon at Natan-Pathé, Clair and Chomette at Tobis-Klangfilm, Cavalcanti at Paramount, Renoir at Braunberger-Richébé) or newsreels (Dulac for Gaumont) or singing interlude films (Epstein for Synchro-Ciné). Of the specialized cinemas, only two survived beyond 1930. Tedesco sonorized the Vieux-Colombier with an eccentric system, Equipment Synchronista, and kept the cinema open until 1932 with his repertory films plus a few new foreign releases.[2] Tallier also sonorized the Ursulines in 1930 and was lucky enough to premiere Sternberg's *The Blue Angel* (with Marlene Dietrich), which played for a record fourteen months.[3] When his staple of German films dried up by 1934, the Ursulines reverted to a repertory program that alternated with the usual commercial releases.

The ciné-clubs also changed their orientation. Where before they had focused on educating film viewers and supporting independent filmmakers, they now became sanctuaries for the masterpieces of the Belle Epoque of silence. For some, a period of nostalgia set in. For others, more serious, the impulse to establish a heritage of cinema art and to preserve a body of films from the economic cycle of production and destruction (negative film stock melted down for chemical extractions) or from blind neglect (negative and positive prints thrown away or stored haphazardly and carelessly) suddenly became paramount. A precedent of sorts had been set by the educator, Victor Perret, in establishing an educational cinema library, the Cinémathèque de la ville de Paris, in 1925.[4] The repertory film concept of Tedesco, Léger, Clouzot, and others had yielded a small collection of films of widely varying conditions. Cinéphiles such as Jean Mitry and Jean Mauclaire agitated among filmmakers and critics for a national cinémathèque, not for educational, technical, or military purposes, but to honor the cinema itself.[5] As evidence of his concern, Mauclaire managed to organize a retrospective of Louis Delluc's films (April, 1929) and, with Jean-Georges Auriol of *La Revue du cinéma*, sponsored a special program devoted to Georges Méliès, with eight newly reconstructed, tinted prints (16 December 1929).[6] In his book, *Panoramique de cinéma* (1929), Mous-

sinac joined in to argue at length for an international *bibliothèque* and *cinéma-*
thèque.[7]

According to Raymond Borde, however, it was not until 1933 that a Cinémathèque nationale was established and installed in the old Trocadéro palace.[8]
The impetus came not only from ciné-club lobbying (Maurice Bessy, for instance) but from the public outcry in the press over the loss of films. Moussinac recounts the story well.

A number of cinema owners, in effect, faced with the lamentable mediocrity of the
talkies available to them, still resist reequipping their cinemas and, in order to offer
"silent" programs, specifically seek out *quality films* released during the past five or six
years. Their interest leads them to compose a kind of program sharply different from
that of their competitors and thus serves to maintain an existing clientele. Certain
other cinema owners, even though equipped for sound, continue to screen silent films
from time to time, preferring to schedule an interesting nontalkie rather than an
imbecilic talkie.

Such actions cannot agree with the interests of the large companies which need to
circulate their production schedules through the greatest possible number of cinemas
in order to write off, at least, the cost of the films.

Hence, the recent offensive which translates itself into the sabotage of the good
silent films that still exist.

We have already mentioned that, for a great number of these films, the distributors
are resisting any rentals and that, if a rental is allowed, the prints provided are so
scratched, spliced, and deteriorated, that a public screening provokes the ire of spectators. In that way, the masters of the international film industry hope they can force
all the "rebellious" cinema owners—if they want to avoid closing down—to screen
"their" programs of sound films, however mediocre they may be.

They are going so far—and even the bourgeois press is scandalized, for appearance's
sake—to *destroy* certain works which truly deserve preservation for the history of the
cinema.[9]

Unfortunately, the Cinémathèque nationale proved little more than a name
since it lacked any funding. To rectify its inaction, two years later, Mitry,
Georges Franju, and Henri Langlois organized the Cinémathèque française
under the nominal direction of Paul-Auguste Harlé, a top administrator of *La
Cinématographie française*.[10] Thus did the ciné-clubs and the few cinéphiles who
collected films, along with key industry figures such as Alexandre Kamenka
and Germaine Dulac as well as second-hand film distributors, become the
primary sources for what has been preserved of the French silent cinema art.

The French movement to establish an alternate cinema in the 1920s seems
to have gone through three fairly distinct stages. The first can be marked off
by Louis Delluc's assumption of the editorship of *Le Film* in 1917 and by the
deaths of Canudo and Delluc, respectively, in 1923 and 1924. Those six or
seven years saw the founding of independent film journals, regular newspaper
film review columns, and the earliest ciné-club organizations. From the writings and conversations of Delluc, Canudo, Moussinac, Vuillermoz, and others
emerged the theory and praxis of an embryonic film criticism and the concep-
tualization of an alternate cinema. The second period can be marked off from
1924 to 1926 or 1927. For two or three years, a loose network of ciné-clubs,
specialized cinemas, and film journals seemed to present a united front in
actively promoting an alternate cinema. Popular exhibitions at the Musée Gal-

liera and the Exposition des Arts Décoratifs, lectures at the Vieux-Colombier, and regular public screenings by the Ciné-Club de France and the Tribune libre—all these activities encouraged independent filmmakers in their work, built up a permanent audience, and began to articulate a history of cinema art. The third and final period can be marked off from 1927 to 1930. In these three or four years, the proliferation of organizations and the intensification of activity had two major consequences. With the founding of Les Amis de Spartacus, the cooperative system supporting an alternate cinema verged on becoming a mass political/socioeconomic movement. The threat was grave enough to the dominant industry and the state that the Paris police reacted quickly to dissolve and disperse its force. Simultaneously, the alternate exhibition system established by the ciné-clubs and specialized cinemas expanded to include film production and distribution. This, too, was swiftly curtailed by the industry's transformation to sound films. Stymied by political and economic conditions, what was left of the alternate cinema system redirected its energies into the cinémathèque movement and into limited subversion from within the industry itself—e.g., the films of Clair, Renoir, Dulac, Vigo, and Jacques Prévert.

This history of an alternate cinema structure in France also reveals certain internal contradictions or oppositions which the movement failed to resolve. What was conceived as a mass movement, a popular cinema, consistently functioned as an elitist operation. Despite Delluc and Canudo's expressed wishes, their journals and clubs (and Delluc's films, for that matter) attracted only a small cultured audience. Léger's Tribune libre and Moussinac's Les Amis de Spartacus came closest to fulfilling those initial dreams, but their work was outweighed by the elite-oriented programs of the Ursulines, Studio 28, and even the Vieux-Colombier. The "à la mode" audiences of the Ursulines and Studio 28, especially, led to repeated charges that the French avant-garde merely provided excitement and entertainment for snobs. The elitism of the alternate cinema structure also depended in part on its overriding interest in aesthetic and even epistemological questions raised by the new medium of film. The debates that animated the pages of *Cinéa-Ciné-pour-tous, Les Cahiers du mois, Cinégraphie*, and others often revolved around the possibility of a "pure cinema" or a non-representational cinema, the definition of cinematic specificity and cinematic rhythm, the relationship between cinema and the other arts. especially music. At their best, they explored the ways that film could expand human perception and knowledge. Only Moussinac, and Clair to a lesser extent, consistently argued in writing that an alternate cinema had to be conceived politically and economically. It would depend on a strong alternative to or a transformation of the dominant industry. That did not, and perhaps could not, happen in the French society of the late 1920s.

Moussinac's bitter conclusion has some validity: "because it envisioned the problem according to the point of view of aesthetics only, because it wanted to ignore the economic laws which determined it, the avant-garde is dead."[11] Yet the avant-garde did not really die. If it failed to sustain a lasting cultural revolution on the scale it had hoped for, its counterpart in the Soviet Union was hardly more successful in its mission. One should not forget that, even with all of its contradictions, the French alternate cinema movement produced a good deal of valuable work, in theory and practice, that has not been without

274

descendants. Its heritage is visible in the British documentary movement of the 1930s, in the film theory and criticism of André Bazin and Jean Mitry (though unacknowledged and somewhat obscured), in the American avant-garde that finally developed after World War II, and in the French film activity in the 1950s that eventually became known as the New Wave. In this current period of rediscovery and reinterpretation, may that heritage once more make a useful intervention.

FRENCH
FRENCH
CINEMA

IV The Narrative Avant-Garde

One does not make films according to theories; one constructs theories after the films.
—Jean Epstein (1924)

As far as signs are concerned, man is always mobilizing many more of them than he knows.
—Jacques Lacan (1978)

The "First Avant-Garde" or the "Impressionist Cinema"—these are the labels that have long been attached to the French narrative avant-garde films of the 1920s. Yet unless one is interested in a rather limited number of filmmakers and films, neither term seems appropriate to cover the extent and diversity of the narrative avant-garde film practice. Nor is either all that useful in understanding the significance of that practice. As P. Adam Sitney has suggested, these labels represent an "insidious distinction . . . [that] has helped to perpetuate a distorted picture of this period."[1] Let me try to explain why.

The First Avant-Garde is a term that began to emerge as early as the 1930s, when Germaine Dulac wrote probably the earliest historical sketch of avant-garde French filmmaking.[2] Since then, historians and critics have used it to distinguish one group or "wave" of filmmakers and their films from several other later ones.[3] That group usually includes Abel Gance, Marcel L'Herbier, Louis Delluc, Germaine Dulac, and sometimes Jean Epstein, all of whom made feature-length narrative films within or on the margins of the commercial film industry between 1919 and 1924. As Emile Vuillermoz put it, this was the first generation to "think spontaneously in animated images."[4] They are to be distinguished from a Second Avant-Garde of Pure Cinema advocates and Dada/Surrealist films as well as from a Third Avant-Garde of documentaries. All of these supposedly are shorter non-narrative films produced outside the industry, from 1924 to 1929. When history gets this neat, you suspect something may be wrong with the terms and categories.

When Jean Epstein called for "a new avant-garde," late in 1924, neither he nor his colleagues meant that they were giving up on a narrative cinema.[5] Independent production companies within the dominant industry may have shrunk in number, but avant-garde narrative films did not vanish when the short non-narrative films first appeared, in 1923-1924. In fact, one can argue, they continued to flourish in the form of both short and feature-length works until the end of the decade. Moreover, they were made not only by members of the so-called First Avant-Garde but by others as well: e.g., Dmitri Kirsanoff, Alberto Cavalcanti, Jean Renoir, Jean Grémillon, and Carl Dreyer. As a critical term, therefore, the First Avant-Garde may be limited; but at least it is relatively neutral. That is hardly the case with its more prominent synonym, the Impressionist Cinema.

"Impressionism" and "Impressionist" are terms that some of the filmmakers themselves used to describe certain kinds of films during the 1920s. But look at the way they used them, the way their meaning shifted. As I have already indicated, these terms first came into parlance near the end of the war to describe the early French realist films set in the provinces, particularly the way they represented or evoked a landscape or milieu's atmosphere through a series of visual "impressions." Through its emphasis on the contemporary, the pictorial, and the natural harmony of characters and landscapes, wrote Louis Delluc, "the impressionism of the cinema parallels in its blossoming that astonishing period of painting [French Impressionism]."[6] For his part, Marcel L'Herbier made a somewhat different association, between the "musicality of the image [as rhythmic discourse]" and musical Impressionism.[7] By 1925-1926, however, the terms were being used to define a particular kind of film and a specific stage in the development of French film art. According to Germaine Dulac, the Impressionist era commenced about 1920 and was characterized by the "psychological film," which placed a "character in a particular situation . . . in order to penetrate into the secret domain of his inner life. . . ."[8]

Impressionism made us see nature and its objects as elements concurrent with the action. A shadow, a light, a flower had, above all, a meaning, as the reflection of a mental state or an emotional situation, then, little by little, became a necessary complement, having an intrinsic value of its own. We experimented with making things move through the science of optics, tried to transform figures according to the logic of a state of mind.[9]

From then on, even though Dulac is speaking about her own films perhaps more than those of her colleagues, Impressionism became linked indissolubly with the concept of a subjective cinema. Through Henri Langlois and Georges Sadoul, principally, the term has come into conventional historical parlance.

The way we understand, and judge, this so-called French Impressionism, however, also seems to depend on a broader context, on a specific moment or shift in the history of art, especially French art. Briefly, that moment is marked by the divergent transformations of the aesthetic imperative of nineteenth-century Realism—to be truthful to one's individual perception of the physical or social world. According to Linda Nochlin, the initial transformation provided the impetus for both Impressionism and Symbolism (in painting and literature). Here the emphasis shifted to "the demands of one's inner 'subjective' feelings or imagination" over and above the demands of external reality.[10] The latent subjectivity implied in the Realist concept of nature as viewed through a temperament or personality became overt, privileging the unique perception or transcendent imagination of the individual. Subsequently, a second transformation led to what has become a chief tenet of Modernism. There the emphasis fell on "the reality of the pictorial *means* at the expense of the reality of the external world depicted by . . . these means."[11] The nature or specificity of the material (e.g., in painting, the flat surface and the substance and technique of application) became the proper subject of art. While Impressionism and Symbolism seemed to maintain a position within the context of a system of representation and narration, Modernism seemed to adopt a more advanced position that advocated a system of pure presentation and formal construction which was both anti-illusionist and anti-narrative. Dubiously appropriated to describe the French avant-garde cinema of the 1920s, it is this apparent difference that has determined the choice of most film historians to celebrate the "Modernist" non-narrative films at the expense of the "Impressionist" narrative films.

To some extent, the theoretical and critical writings of the period support this simple opposition and abet the elevation of one term (and group of films) over the other. But if one looks at the actual avant-garde film practice, the matter is less clear-cut. For the diversity of that practice raises questions not only about these labels but about exactly what was avant-garde in the French narrative cinema. If Impressionism as a critical concept is misleading or even suspect, that comes less from its instability as a term of definition than from its failure to encompass the range of French narrative avant-garde film practice. Defining the narrative avant-garde, as I would prefer to call it, solely as an attempt to create a subjective cinema, through so-called Impressionist techniques or devices, greatly simplifies or excludes much of what is going on in the discourse and narrative processes of the major films.[12] To cite just a few instances here, there were experiments in developing a mixture of styles or modes, different systems of continuity, "plastic harmonies," patterns of rhetorical figuring, and complex narrative structures. Besides, what was taken for subjectivity in some films is not at all an individual character's state of mind or inner life, but something else—either a kind of collective consciousness, an interrelation of several characters' perceptions and feelings, a shifting experiential flow of the subjective and the omniscient, or, in Fredric Jameson's broad reframing of Impressionism, "the exercise of perception and the perceptual recombination of sense data as an end in itself."[13] Furthermore, as Ian Christie has noted, and I have described in detail, the infrastructure that was developed in conjunction with the early avant-garde narrative films provided a basis for all subsequent avant-garde film practice.[14] Consequently, many of the films usually associated with the later avant-garde groups actually depend on strategies and systems of signification that they share with the narrative avant-garde films. Films such as *Entr'acte, Rien que les heures, La Coquille et le clergyman, Un Chien andalou*, and perhaps even *Ballet mécanique* can be read quite profitably within the context of narrative avant-garde film practice.

It is my contention that the French narrative avant-garde's contribution throughout the decade to what Bernard Eisenschitz has called the search for "a new artistic practice" in the cinema has been much misunderstood and undervalued.[15] In choosing to rethink the significance of that contribution, I do so, not only because I agree with Jameson that "the all-informing process of *narrative*" can be taken as "the central function or *instance* of the human mind,"[16] but because that contribution has been undermined and eclipsed by a rather uncritical acceptance of a narrowly defined Modernism. Accordingly, the following pages are devoted to an assessment of several critical perspectives on the French narrative avant-garde filmmakers and their films, to a new working definition of narrative avant-garde film practice that challenges the narrow confines of Impressionism, and to a series of close readings of what I consider to be the major film texts of that practice. The short non-narrative French films are excluded from analysis here, except for those instances when they can be linked closely to or realigned with the narrative avant-garde films. Most of these films, I assume, already have claimed a good deal of attention in English-language histories and critical studies—because of their obvious historical value, their unique connection to the visual arts, and their long availability in the United States.[17] By contrast, the film practice of the narrative avant-garde, I contend, cries out for a critical reevaluation. As Noël Burch realized, more than ten years ago.

Obscured by the great national cinemas of the silent period (the German, the Russian, the Scandinavian, the American, even the Italian), the French movement in the twenties . . . is today, incontestably, the most misunderstood, the most scorned—by critics, historians, and cinéastes.[18]

By reexamining at some length the practice of only those filmmakers who chose to work within the various forms of narrative cinema, I hope to correct an imbalance, to recover something lost.

The Alternate Cinema Network, Genres, and Auteurs

During the 1920s, the alternate cinema network of film critics, film journals, ciné-clubs, and specialized cinemas certainly provided the most visible means of constituting the French narrative avant-garde. If a commercial filmmaker was an active member of several ciné-clubs or lectured frequently, he or she was perceived as a leader or model for the French avant-garde. If a narrative film became part of the Vieux-Colombier's repertory or was shown at one of the other specialized cinemas, and if it was judged by Léon Moussinac or some other major critic to be an advance in film art or even a masterpiece, that was a sign of its status as an avant-garde work. Although inconsistencies abounded in this personally engaged, fluctuating process of defining the narrative avant-garde, the judgments passed and selections made during the 1920s influenced the number and quality of film texts that have come down to us as well as the kinds of readings performed on them in film histories. Consequently, it is worth drawing some conclusions from this process in order to recover some sense of that historical record.

Who were the independent or commercial filmmakers most deeply involved in the ciné-club movement of the 1920s? Although men such as Abel Gance, Jacques Feyder, Robert Boudrioz, René Clair, Alberto Cavalcanti, and others took part in the movement, none played anything like a major role. That was left to a handful of filmmakers: Louis Delluc, Léon Poirier, Marcel L'Herbier, Jean Epstein, and Germaine Dulac. Delluc's involvement, together with that of Ricciotto Canudo, of course, was crucial in initiating and developing the whole concept of a ciné-club. Léon Poirier provided leadership for both the Club français du cinéma and the Ciné-Club de France in their early stages. Marcel L'Herbier and Jean Epstein lectured and projected excerpts from their work quite frequently in all sorts of *conférences* and special screenings. Germaine Dulac's commitment was perhaps the strongest and certainly the most long-lasting of all. An original member of Delluc's first informal ciné-club and a frequent lecturer herself, Dulac presided over the Ciné-Club de France for several years and was instrumental in establishing the first international Fédération des Ciné-Clubs in 1929. Because of their committed ciné-club work, all five filmmakers, at one time or another, were considered prominent figures in the narrative avant-garde.

Which French narrative films were privileged by repertory screenings or premieres at the specialized cinemas in Paris? The most extensive repertory was built up at Jean Tedesco's Théâtre de Vieux-Colombier, from 1924 to 1930. Although Tedesco's principal interest was in documentary films—e.g., Grémillon's *Tour au large* (1927), Allegret's *Voyage au Congo* (1926)—the Vieux-Colombier collected and screened a good number of French narrative films. On the poster announcing the Vieux-Colombier's first season, that repertory included the following:

Robert Boudrioz, *L'Atre*, 1923
Abel Gance, *La Roue* (short version), 1923
Louis Delluc, *Fièvre*, 1921
Jean Epstein, *Coeur fidèle*, 1923
Marcel L'Herbier, *El Dorado*, 1921
Ivan Mosjoukine, *Le Brasier ardent*, 1923
Marcel L'Herbier, *Don Juan et Faust*, 1923
Léon Poirier, *Le Penseur*, 1920

Abel Gance, *Mater Dolorosa*, 1917
Léon Poirier, *Jocelyn*, 1922
Henry Roussel, *Les Opprimés*, 1923[1]

Four years later, the number of narrative films had more than doubled to include:

Germaine Dulac, *La Souriante Madame Beudet*, 1923
Jean Epstein, *La Belle Nivernaise*, 1924
Jean Epstein, *L'Affiche*, 1925
Jacques Feyder, *Crainquebille*, 1923
Jacques Feyder, *Visages d'enfants*, 1925
Jacques Feyder, *L'Image*, 1926
Alexandre Volkoff, *Kean*, 1924
Jacques de Baroncelli, *Pêcheur d'Islande*, 1924
René Clair, *Paris qui dort*, 1924
Marcel Silver, *L'Horloge*, 1924
Marcel L'Herbier, *Feu Mathias Pascal*, 1925
Dmitri Kirsanoff, *L'Ironie du destin*, 1924
Dmitri Kirsanoff, *Menilmontant*, 1926
Alberto Cavalcanti, *Le Train sans yeux*, 1926
Alberto Cavalcanti, *En rade*, 1927
Jean Renoir, *La Petite Marchande d'allumettes*, 1928[2]

The bewildering variety of this collection is probably due to Tedesco's rather catholic tastes as well as to the availability of film prints. At the Studio des Ursulines, Armand Tallier and Myrga screened fewer French narrative films for their "à la mode" audiences, but most of them were premieres rather than revivals. These included, chronologically:

René Clair, *Le Voyage imaginaire*, 1926 (revival)
Alberto Cavalcanti, *Rien que les heures*, 1926
Jean Epstein, *6½ × 11*, 1927
Jean Epstein, *La Glace à trois faces*, 1927
Léon Poirier, *Amours exotiques*, 1927
Jean Epstein, *La Chute de la maison Usher*, 1928
Germaine Dulac, *La Coquille et le clergyman*, 1928[3]

For a while, Ursulines even provided an exclusive exhibition outlet for Jean Epstein's films; then Studio 28 and L'Oeil de Paris assumed that status—for *La Chute de la maison Usher* (1928), *Finis Terrae* (1929) and *Sa Tête* (1929).

During the last half of the decade, several filmmakers were also honored with retrospective screenings in the ciné-clubs and cinemas. Louis Delluc's films were repeatedly revived: *Fièvre* at the 1925 Exposition des Arts Décoratifs and at Les Amis de Spartacus, *La Femme de nulle part* and *L'Inondation* at the Ciné-Latin, and all three films at Studio 28. Several of Jean Epstein's films were similarly rescreened: *L'Affiche* at the 1925 Exposition, *Coeur fidèle* at the Ciné-Latin, and *La Belle Nivernaise* and *6½ × 11* at the Ciné-Club de France. René Clair's early films—*Paris qui dort*, *Entr'acte*, *Le Fantôme du Moulin Rouge*, and *Le Voyage imaginaire*—were also exhibited at the 1925 Exposition or at the Ciné-Latin. Several of Jacques Feyder's films—*Visages d'enfants* and *L'Image*— were projected for the Tribune libre and the Ciné-Club de France. Other retrospective screenings included L'Herbier's *L'Inhumaine* and Dulac's *La Folie des vaillants* at the 1925 Exposition, Poirier's *La Brière* for the Ciné-Club de France, and Kirsanoff's *Menilmontant* for the Tribune libre. All of these films were being lifted out of the cycle of commercial cinema distribution for the purpose of educating audiences to the possibilities of film art, establishing a tradition or history of that art, critiquing that tradition, and stimulating further explorations.

Going by these screenings alone, one can conclude that, by the end of the silent film period, Jean Epstein was the most prominent, and controversial, filmmaker in the French narrative avant-garde. And Louis Delluc was already being celebrated as a kind of progenitor as well as a prophet. Also interesting was the attention accorded Clair and Feyder. For various reasons (more commercial work, fewer films), Gance, L'Herbier, and Dulac had all fallen from their once prominent positions in the early 1920s. Apparently replacing them, Clair and Feyder had been elevated to the point where certain critics considered them the best, if not the most advanced, filmmakers in France. Several books published during the period reflected this shift clearly. Moussinac's *Naissance du cinéma* (1925) singled out the following French narrative films as benchmarks in the development of film art:

Delluc-Dulac's *La Fête espagnole*, 1920
Delluc's *Fièvre*, 1921
L'Herbier's *El Dorado*, 1921
Gance's *La Roue*, 1922-1923
Epstein's *Coeur fidèle*, 1923[4]

Two years later, in *La Crapouillot*, he added Clair's *Entr'acte* (1924) and Feyder's *L'Image* (1926) to that list.[5] And in his *Panoramique du cinéma* (1929), Moussinac selected four new French films for extensive, generally positive reviews:

Gance's *Napoléon*, 1927
Dreyer's *La Passion de Jeanne d'Arc*, 1928
Feyder's *Thérèse Raquin*, 1928
Clair's *Un Chapeau de paille d'Italie*, 1928[6]

In his own *Panorama du cinema* (1929), Georges Charensol basically supported Moussinac's judgment by drawing special attention to the films of Delluc, Gance, L'Herbier, Epstein, Clair, and Feyder.[7]

To some extent, the privileging of these particular filmmakers and films also depended implicitly on a 1920s version of the *politique des auteurs*. As early as 1918, in opposition to Charles Pathé, Henri Diamant-Berger, and André Antoine, Louis Delluc had made a distinction between filmmakers (*auteurs*) who wrote scenarios for the films they directed and those (*metteurs-en-scène*) who adapted other writers' work for their films.[8] Supposedly, *auteurs* were thus able (or could attempt) to exercise greater control over their films and to approximate more closely the Romantic concept of the individually unique artist, using the medium of his choosing for his own personal expression. Although the idea was never developed into a theory or isolated as a major criterion of evaluation during the period,[9] Delluc's distinction, in fact, does tend to separate members of the French narrative avant-garde from the commercial filmmakers.

Because the commercial film industry was predicated so heavily on literary adaptations, especially from fiction, filmmakers were generally discouraged from writing original scenarios.[10] Consequently, all the important commercial filmmakers were principally *metteurs-en-scène*: Jacques de Baroncelli, Henri Fescourt, Henry Roussel, Léonce Perret, Raymond Bernard, Henry Diamant-Berger, Alexandre Volkoff, Victor Tourjansky, Julien Duvivier, André Antoine, Louis Mercanton, René Hervil, René Le Somptier, and others. Those filmmakers who wrote their own scenarios were the exception. Louis Delluc, for instance, wrote the scenarios for all but one of his films, consistently working variations on a single theme: the effect of past desires and actions on the present condition of one or more characters. This obsession led him to some rather complex forms of narrative construction and rhetorical figuring. Abel Gance, though often inspired by books for his film projects, always wrote his own scenarios about the moral dilemmas or philosophical problems that passionately concerned him at the moment. From *J'Accuse* on, his films also revealed a constant interest in achieving ever more striking effects with various technical innovations. Jean Epstein also conceived several of his own films—*Coeur fidèle, Finis Terrae, Sa Tête*—and wrote an equal number in collaboration with his sister, Marie Epstein—*L'Affiche, Le Double Amour, 6½ × 11*. Moreover, all but one of his other films were based on his own adaptations. Much like Gance, Epstein was fascinated by the technical side of filmmaking, but he turned that fascination either into epistemological explorations or, like Delluc, into experiments in narrative construction and rhetorical figuring. Both Marcel L'Herbier and René Clair composed the scenarios of their early films and usually wrote their own adaptations, but their personal interests were diametrically opposed. L'Herbier also showed an interest in unusual forms of narrative construction and in experiments with various technical innovations, sometimes for their own sake. Clair, on the other hand, subordinated his technical facility to a coolly satirical social vision.

Although a *politique des auteurs* may set Delluc, Gance, Epstein, L'Herbier, and Clair somewhat apart from the commercial mainstream of French filmmaking, it leaves many others in a kind of limbo. Germaine Dulac, for instance, ran the gamut from directing production-line serials or personal scenarios by others (Irene Hillel-Erlanger, Louis Delluc, André Obey, Jean-Louis Bouquet, and Antonin Artaud) to writing adaptations and even several of her own scenarios—*Ames de fous, La Cigarette, L'Invitation au voyage*. Yet a good number of her films, despite their differing sources, consistently examine the suffering and frustration of women in various social conditions as well as exhibit an interest in technical innovations. Some filmmakers, such as Jean Renoir, Alberto Cavalcanti, and Dmitri Kirsanoff, started out writing a scenario or two and then were forced to become, more and less, *metteurs-en-scène*. Others, like Jacques Feyder and Léon Poirier, were known chiefly for their excellent adaptations, but each wrote at least one important scenario of his own—*Visages d'enfants* and *Verdun, visions de l'histoire*. Ivan Mosjoukine presents a more singular case: an actor who wrote scenarios and who also directed several himself, the most important being *Le Brasier ardent*. Finally, the distinction between *auteurs* and *metteurs-en-scène* is complicated by the fact that several commercial directors—e.g., Bernard, Roussel, Duvivier—also dabbled in writing their own scenarios.

If a *politique des auteurs* offers an important, if limited, method of privileging certain films and filmmakers, the study of *film genres* offers another just as important. In Part II, I have already suggested that the film genres popular during and after the war established a significant context for positioning the narrative avant-garde film practice. One characteristic of that practice was the consistency with which filmmakers worked within certain genres in their experimentation with the nature and limits of film discourse. Early on, the bourgeois melodrama and the realist film provided a basis for advances by Gance, L'Herbier, Dulac, and Delluc. Particularly important were explorations of psychological or subjective experience in the bourgeois melodrama and of relations between landscape or decor (including specific objects) and character or action in the realist film. Throughout the decade, the realist film continued to function as a conceptual base, particularly in the work of Epstein, Feyder, Renoir, Kirsanoff, Cavalcanti, and Grémillon. But other genres also became important: the fantasy and comedy, especially for Poirier, L'Herbier, Mosjoukine, Dulac, Clair, Feyder, and Renoir.

Besides extending and redefining the parameters of film discourse, the narrative avant-garde filmmakers also tended to undermine or subvert the conventions within particular genres. This critique took the form of either denying the conventions and expectations of a genre or undermining their signification. The genre most critiqued was the dominant one, the historical reconstruction film; and the most extreme cases of its subversion were Renoir's *Nana* (1926), Dreyer's *La Passion de Jeanne d'Arc* (1928), and perhaps even Gance's *Napoléon* (1927). Many of the other genres also suffered attacks from within: the serial—Epstein's *Les Aventures de Robert Macaire* (1925); the colonial film—Renoir's *Le Bled* (1929); the fantasy film—Dulac's *La Coquille et le clergyman* (1927) and Buñuel's *Un Chien andalou* (1929); the modern studio spectacular—Grémillon's *Maldone* (1928) and L'Herbier's *L'Argent* (1929). Significantly, this practice of subversion was most pronounced after 1924, when economic conditions and industry consolidations forced many of the narrative avant-garde filmmakers to forfeit independent film production and work for the major companies.

Stylistics and Subjectivity

Until recently, most film historians have defined the French narrative avant-garde almost exclusively in terms of style or stylistics. According to this view, an overriding concern for *cinematic essence*, specifically an interest in certain features or formal techniques unique to the cinema, seemed to determine what was advanced in film practice and to separate the avant-garde filmmakers from their more commercial colleagues. Originating in various reviews and critical writings of the 1920s, especially in Henri Fescourt and Jean-Louis Bouquet's pseudo-Socratic attack on the "new aesthetic" in *L'Idée et l'écran* (1925-1926)[1], this conception of an avant-garde has been widely accepted. For instance, in his personal history of the French cinema, Jacques Brunius uses a catalogue of such techniques to disparage the work of Germaine Dulac, Abel Gance, Jean Epstein, Marcel L'Herbier, and Carl Dreyer.[2] In his eclectic study of experimental cinema, Jean Mitry is more kind, but he limits the value of their work to a "search for a rhythmic structure significant in and of itself, that is, a pure rhythm."[3] In their large-scale histories, both Mitry and Georges Sadoul also depend on this conception and its assumptions, often implicitly, as a means of constituting the narrative avant-garde. In the United States, these assumptions inform the most comprehensive study of the French narrative avant-garde film practice—David Bordwell's doctoral dissertation, "French Impressionist Cinema" (University of Iowa, 1974).[4]

What exactly are these formal techniques? It would be tempting to try to answer this question by pointing to a series of innovations and experiments in French film technology. Both Marcel L'Herbier and Abel Gance have given credence to this view. In a recent interview, for instance, L'Herbier joked about how, in 1926, the industry expected him to "do something" with the new panchromatic film stock. They said to themselves: "L'Herbier will be our guinea pig!"[5] Gance, on the other hand, has always been quite serious about his role as an innovator.

As for me, I loved the cinema that way. . . . It was a joy, you know, we were excited about going to see the rushes, to see what we had done. We went as if to a magic show, because it had never been done before. . . . That's what the cinema should be! It should be reinvented each moment.[6]

In fact, his insatiable appetite for new discoveries makes one of the strongest arguments for Gance's inclusion in the French narrative avant-garde.

There are two problems, however, with such a link between technology and film practice. One is that a comprehensive history of French film technology remains to be written. Although both Sadoul and Mitry, in their voluminous histories, provide information on the changes made in the various components of the cinematic apparatus in France, their accounts are too sketchy, enumerative, and atomistic. Neither has the thoroughness that characterizes, for instance, Barry Salt's ongoing research into the relationship between film technology and film style, primarily in the American cinema and secondarily in the German, Soviet, French, and British cinemas.[7] The second problem is that, given what is known, the French narrative avant-garde filmmakers seem to have been working with the same basic technology that other filmmakers were using. In fact, if anything, the French industry lagged behind the American industry in technology and thus put the French filmmakers at a disadvantage. The question for them became: what could they do differently with what they had?

The best definition of a stylistics of formal techniques and of their function in French narrative avant-garde films still comes from David Bordwell. Put simply, Bordwell defines those techniques within the context of Impressionism, particularly as conceived by Dulac, Langlois, Sadoul, and Mitry. Thus, the French narrative avant-garde film practice becomes a paradigm of marked elements or privileged features serving one principal function—the expression or representation of subjectivity or subjective experience.[8] Through the transformation of recorded reality, certain privileged elements of film discourse can evoke, in Canudo's words, "the feelings that envelop things" or convey an individual character's psychological state.[9] A story, consequently, merely provides the basis for expressing—intermittently, momentarily—a subjective experience or vision. As Bordwell argues, this expressive theory and its concern for the fleeting impression, the oblique suggestion, the sentient process of consciousness reveals as implicit debt to a Symbolist aesthetic as well as to

287

Impressionist art.[10] This basically idealist conception of film can validate either a heightened degree of consciousness (defined variously) or individual perceptions and feelings as a special kind of truth.

Bordwell's analysis has two major components—one synchronic, the other diachronic. His initial aim is to establish a paradigm of stylistic features (based on a family-resemblance model) that can encompass all the French narrative avant-garde films. In that paradigm, he includes the following specific features:

1) Camerawork	Use of close-ups as synecdoches and symbols
	Use of close-ups as subjective images
	Use of camera angles to indicate optical subjectivity
	Camera movement independent of the subject
	Camera movement for purely graphic effects
	Camera movement representing a character's point of view
2) Mise-en-scène	Single light-source
	Shadows indicating off-screen actions
	Variety of lighting situations
	Variety of decor styles, usually undistorted and naturalistic
	Some interplay of foreground and background arrangement and movement of figures in space
3) Optical devices	As transitions
	As magical effects
	As emphasizing significant details
	As pictorial decoration
	As conveyors of abstract meanings
	As indications of subjectivity
4) Editing	Temporal relations between shots:
	Flashbacks or fantasy
	Spatial relations:
	Occasional synthetic building up of space from specific detail
	Glance-object editing
	Crosscutting
	Rhythmic relations between shots:
	To convey psychological and physiological states.[11]

Valuable as this paradigm is in directing attention to the texture of French narrative avant-garde films, it has some problems which keep me from employing it as a model for this study.

First of all, Bordwell tends to assume a narrative avant-garde stylistics and then posit a conventional cinema style through negation or opposition rather than perform the reverse operation. It now seems more likely, as his later work testifies, that the narrative avant-garde film practice was a loosely related series of extensions of, variations on, and deviations from an existing paradigm of conventions.[12] Secondly, the Bordwell paradigm is atomistic, far from exclusive of conventional film practice, and unclear on the question of pertinence. Thirdly, it depends heavily on the assumption that these formal techniques primarily serve the cause of subjectivity. Although subjectivity may be an important tenet, it is only one of several in the full range of French narrative avant-garde film practice. Even though the paradigm offers evidence of particular features serving other functions—the abstract, the decorative, and the symbolic—it fails to account for them except insofar as they tend toward "pure cinema." Finally, Bordwell does not attempt to analyze how these stylistic features function in the construction of film narrative, how the avant-garde practice operates structurally within the diegetic and narrative processes of specific film texts.

The second, diachronic component of Bordwell's analysis, though more tentative, is perhaps more useful. Here, he postulates a periodization scheme for the French narrative avant-garde's development of certain stylistic features. The scheme he comes up with is a definite advance on the simple, sometimes imprecise divisions offered previously—by Dulac, Langlois, Sadoul, and Mitry—and it also avoids the eccentric compartmentalization erected by Brunius. Bordwell's framework divides into three distinct periods. The first, from 1918 to 1922, was marked by what he calls pictorialism. Recurrent pictorial techniques were used to suggest a character's perceptions and psychological states.[13] The second period, beginning in 1923, was marked by the proliferation of a rapid-cutting form of rhythmic montage, whose immediate source was Gance's *La Roue* (1922-1923).[14] By 1925, the repertory of narrative avant-garde stylistics had crystallized and, according to such disparate figures as Jean Epstein and René Clair, had even begun to appear excessive, repetitious, or clichéd.[15] The third period, therefore, from 1926 to 1929, was marked by stylistic diffusion.[16] Certain filmmakers pursued new techniques—the handheld camera, long tracking shots, widescreen formats, the absence of intertitles—while others continued to work with the existing stylistics. Finally, avant-garde filmmaking began to diverge into distinct but interrelated modes—documentary, abstract, Surrealist.

This periodization scheme bears an interesting correlation to already established patterns within the French film industry, both in the development of film genres and in the ciné-club and specialized cinema movement. The first period of pictorialism, for instance, corresponds to the years when certain industry figures—e.g., Pathé, Gaumont, Nalpas—were supporting original or experimental work and when the bourgeois melodrama and the realist film were prominent as genres. It was also stimulated by the critical writings of Delluc, Canudo, Moussinac, Vuillermoz, and others. The second period was sustained, in part, by conditions that allowed independent and semi-independent film production to thrive and by the appearance of a new exhibition outlet through the first ciné-clubs and specialized cinemas. It also coincides with an increased interest in the renewal of several different film genres, the fantasy and comedy. The third period of what Bordwell calls "stylistic diffusion" corresponds to the years of industry consolidation, which, although curtailing large-scale independent production (with a few exceptions), led to narrative avant-garde work in nearly all the existing film genres. It was also sustained by the phenomenal growth of ciné-clubs and specialized cinemas, which created a viable network of small-scale independent film production, distribution, and exhibition.

Recent film studies, in France especially, provide a different way of positioning the narrative avant-garde film practice of the 1920s. To describe the avant-garde in terms of a stylistics serving one or even several principal functions tends to produce a reductive analysis, simplifying the diverse strands of theory and practice during the period. To describe it, instead, as an exploration of the processes of representation and signification in narrative film discourse seems to offer both a more precise and a more inclusive strategy. Using the methodologies developed by recent structuralist, semiotic, and ideological studies, Noël Burch, in particular, has sketched out a schema for repositioning and reevaluating the French narrative avant-garde.

In a major essay first published in *Cahiers du cinéma* (1968), Burch and Jean-André Fieschi rethink the First Avant-Garde film practice in terms of its similarity to, rather than its difference from, the theory and practice of the Second Avant-Garde.[1] Accordingly, they single out for discussion the work of Jean Epstein, Marcel L'Herbier, Germaine Dulac, and, to a lesser extent, Louis Delluc. Against Fescourt and Bouquet's defense of a representational cinema dominated by the story or narrative (of which the prime example was the American cinema),[2] Epstein, L'Herbier, and Dulac all advocated some form of an alternate cinema whose subject and mode was quite different. Specifically, Burch and Fieschi isolate and extend L'Herbier's remark on the practice he considered most common among his colleagues: "None of us—Dulac, Epstein, Delluc or myself—had the same aesthetic outlook. But we had a common interest, which was the investigation of that famous *cinematic specificity*. On this we agreed completely."[3] Quoting Epstein on L'Herbier's *L'Inhumaine* (1924), they interpret that investigation as an attempt to redefine the very subject of film as art: "a subject thus conceived as a 'bass clef,' permitting the construction of plastic harmonies."[4] Or, as Bernard Eisenschitz put it, a bit differently, "a destruction of the taboo of the image as a transparent, total, inviolable reflection of the world, and the construction of a distinctly filmic space-time."[5] For the French narrative avant-garde, in other words, the story served as a means or framework, not only to discover the "supposedly unique visual and kinetic aspects of cinema,"[6] or to explore the so-called expressive capabilities of film, but to investigate what we could call broadly the signifying processes of film as a discourse. Thus, in parallel with, rather than in opposition to, the Modernist impulse in the visual arts, literature, and even the Pure Cinema movement, the material of narrative film discourse, as a "language" or system of signification, often became the actual subject of avant-garde film practice. At its furthest advance, that practice involved some form of self-reflexivity.

As David Bordwell has argued, the Burch-Fieschi essay is "a critical rather than an historical study and lacks both concreteness and documentation"; but that is scant grounds for dismissing it.[7] The essay's major problem is that it sacrifices a precise, consistent, thorough analysis for a highly polemical statement. As Burch and Fieschi admit, the essay has "no other ambition but to pose several points so as to give to this movement more than mere historical dignity. . . ."[8] What they hypothesize is a broad functional definition of the narrative avant-garde film practice (in an historical context) and a consequent network of relations among several filmmakers, their theoretical writings, and their films. Jean Epstein is described as the theoretician who speaks to them most directly and to their interest in the signifying process of film. L'Herbier,

Epstein, and, to a lesser extent, Dulac, are singled out as the filmmakers most committed to the concept of a formal renewal of film discourse, based on the redefinition of the subject of film. The most sustained, coherent examples of that renewal are L'Herbier's *L'Argent* (1929) and Epstein's *La Glace à trois faces* (1927)—the latter, they argue, is "rhythmically, compositionally, structurally, dramatically, one of the best films of the silent period, and not only in France."[9]

Six years later, in a longer essay in *Afterimage* (1974), Burch and Jorge Dana rework this definition within a broader, but more detailed, ideological analysis of film practice. First they begin with a tentative paradigm of conventional film practice, well established by 1918-1919 (in both the American and European cinemas), according to the codes of representation (e.g., contiguity, continuity, the illusion of spatial depth) and of narrativity (e.g., the subordination of objects to characters, the verisimilitude of acting, the stylistic homogeneity of costuming, the linearity of the narrative).[10] Then they hypothesize a taxonomy of variations on or reactions to that practice:

A. Films totally accounted for and informed at all levels by the dominant codes . . .
B. Films totally accounted for by the codes, but in which this fact is masked by a stylistic (which the dominant ideology describes as 'form') . . .
C. Films which intermittently escape the ideological determination of the codes . . .
D. Films which are informed by a constant designation/deconstruction of the codes which, however ideologically determined at the strictly diegetic level, implicitly question this determination by the way they situate the codes and play upon them.[11]

According to this taxonomy, Burch and Dana single out only two French films which intermittently escape these conventions. About *La Passion de Jeanne d'Arc* (1928), they write,

by doing away entirely with the pro-filmic frame of reference and using the eye-line match almost to the exclusion of any other type, Dreyer brings to the fore the flat image as such, creating a filmic space which designates itself as a succession of shot-frames, as a fictional and "autonomous chain."[12]

In *L'Argent* (1929), they assert, L'Herbier is the first filmmaker "to divert camera movement away from the universal functions ('descriptive,' 'subjective,' 'dramatic,' 'revelatory,' etc.) . . . as alternatives to syntagms of montage. . . ."[13] By implication, the rest of the French narrative avant-garde films would seem to be no more than instances of mere formal stylistics. Yet Burch and Dana do not discuss the French cinema of the 1920s in anything but the most marginal way.

In the following pages, I want to formulate a slightly different taxonomy as a means of contextualizing the French narrative avant-garde film practice. In my view, that practice can be seen as a series of breaks with, additions to, and reconstitutions of the parameters of conventional narrative film discourse. "[It is] an effort of work on cinematographic language," as Jacques Petat puts it. "It tends to be a critique, a redistribution of the elements of that language. . . ."[14] That redistribution Barthélémy Amengual sees as an attempt "to analyze or fragment reality, reconstruct the fragments into quasi-hieroglyphs, and organize these *ideograms* into systems of signs and graphic-rhythmic structures."[15] To sketch out those parameters and their redistribution more clearly, I propose a schema that focuses on several different levels of narrative film discourse: referentiality, narration, syntactical continuity, rhetorical figuring, and narrative structure.[16] In each of these five selected areas, I will note some of the conventions of that discourse, as they were established by 1918, and the French narrative avant-garde deviations from and reconstitutions of those conventions. Although buttressed by statements from Jean Epstein and others, this schema does not depend on a comprehensive synthesis of the theoretical writings of the period. As Bordwell discovered, the bewildering and contradictory variety of those writings makes difficult any attempt to turn them into a systematic account of film either as a medium or an art.[17] This may be because, as Stuart Liebman argues, the French "understood theory as a speculative instrument" whose function was "to generate hypotheses for the sake of argument and investigation. . . ."[18] For them, theory was closely tied to praxis, and, according to Epstein, the actual film practice of the French narrative avant-garde was often in advance of their theoretical writings. Nor does this schema pretend to be all-inclusive. Its purpose is simply to provide a rough framework for encompassing the rich diversity of French narrative avant-garde film practice.[19]

Referentiality

Referentiality was determined conventionally by literary texts (either from theater or fiction), and by particular genres of texts at that—the bourgeois melodrama, the realist or naturalist novel, the historical epic, and so on. Against this practice, the narrative avant-garde adopted several major strategies. One was the attempt to substitute reality, actual contemporary life (either in documentaries or original scripts), for literature as the principal ground of referentiality. As Louis Delluc once admonished his colleagues: "So you have nothing to say? Walk about, look around you, really look. The street, the subway, the streetcars, the shops are filled with a thousand dramas, a thousand good and original stories."[20] The question, of course, is how was this reality conceived and represented? A favorite answer was the concept that Delluc himself introduced, that free-floating signifier, *photogénie*, which seemed to mysteriously animate certain images.[21] For some, such as Marcel Gromaire and Canudo, *photogénie* was an expression on film of the affective, creative imagination of the filmmaker.[22] For Epstein and others, sometimes it became a sign of the uncanny or a core of enigmatic mystery in the natural world provoked by a quasi-epistemological quest.[23] Wrote Epstein at one point,

the camera lens . . . is an eye endowed with inhuman analytical properties . . . an eye without prejudice, without morality, free of influences, and it sees in the human face and gestures traits that we, burdened with sympathies and antipathies, habits and inhibitions, no longer know how to see.[24]

Another strategy was to deemphasize the story or narrative as the principal referent and foreground the elements of film discourse as referents unto themselves. "The decomposition of an event into its photogenic elements," wrote Epstein again, "is the first law of film, its grammar, its algebra, its order."[25] At its extreme, this could become either a nonrepresentational spectacle of plastic forms in movement, a visual symphony analogous to music, or a playful critique of the process of representation itself.[26] One further strategy, much less radical than the others, was the effort to rehabilitate "démodé" genres such as the fantasy or *féerie*.

Narration and representation

Here the conventional source of the narrative was the intertitles.[27] Furthermore, an uninterrupted, clear, direct, narrative flow, in which all elements were diegeticized, resulted in a so-called objective focus on the action of the narrative. To counter these conventions, the narrative avant-garde developed a number of strategies of reorientation and disruption. One was the privileging of the image and image relations as the exclusive source of the diegesis and narrative. As Epstein and others believed, "the cinema is made to narrate with images and not with words."[28] This led to attempts to produce films with few or no intertitles. A major strategy, of course, involved privileging one or more characters' subjectivity, by means of a variety of techniques, reorienting the diegetic flow from the action to perception, feeling, and thinking.[29] But that shift soon expanded to include what Gérard Genette would call "narrative focalization" that depended on more than a single character's consciousness. In one form, Epstein's "objective and subjective" combined in such a way as to dissolve the differences and multiply the connections between one or more individuals and, say, the surrounding natural world.[30] A related strategy involved privileging description over narrative (already prominent in the realist film genre) or, in Roland Barthes's terms, the semic code (including character and landscape) over the proairetic. Other disruptions came from generally emphasizing the nondiegetic elements of the discourse and from making problematic the narrating position of the text.

Syntactical continuity

The principal convention was linearity or sequentiality, predicated on a logic of causal relations, using the "classical" spatial-temporal continuity style of editing that had developed primarily in the American cinema.[31] Against this convention, the narrative avant-garde developed a variety of syntactical systems of continuity that could be deployed either in some sort of coherence or in playful incoherence. They were certainly interested in what Léon Moussinac called "visual rhythm" or patterns of rhythmic relations within and between shots,[32] and they especially favored syntactical forms of both conjunctive and disjunctive simultaneity. The latter involved alternations not only between actions in different spaces or periods of time, between reality and either memory or fantasy, but also between multiple image chains—in paradigmatic relation. "The quick, jagged succession" of rapid montage, for instance, came close to fulfilling one of Epstein's dreams: "the perfect circle of an impossible simultaneity."[33] Marcel L'Herbier was more graphic: "everything blended in a vast rainbow of vitality—a cocktail of powerful forces. . . ."[34] Generally, the narrative avant-garde developed patterns of continuity that depended on a combination of graphic, rhythmic, and associative or connotative relations. We have found a "visual language" wrote Epstein, that "juxtaposes and combines the simplest images according to rhythmic variations, cross-cuttings, repetitions, and [other] layers to produce meaning."[35]

Rhetorical figuring

Conventional film discourse borrowed most of its rhetorical figures from verbal language and literature. Against this practice, the narrative avant-garde explored the connotative possibilities of *photogénie* in networks of motifs and metonymical/metaphorical associations.[36] "[We were] interested in telling a story," wrote Alberto Cavalcanti, "by using to the maximum, with a liberty which the public considered revolutionary, the cinematic means of expression and by going to extremes in the choice of analogies, comparisons, and metaphors."[37] "The image is a sign, complex and precise, like that of the Chinese alphabet,"[38] concluded Epstein; its meaning depended on its shifting context among other images. In the films themselves, this can perhaps best be described as the articulation of a rhetorical figuring that involved privileged elements of the mise-en-scène (especially ordinary objects and parts of the body) as well as patterns of framing, camera movement, and editing. This figuring depended on such textual operations as repetition and variation, condensation and displacement, metonomy and metaphor.[39] Through these processes, the narrative avant-garde sometimes sought to produce a system of connotative or symbolic relations paralleling and intersecting with the narrative.

Narrative structure

Finally, the narrative avant-garde experimented with various narrative structures which could synthesize these deviations from conventional film discourse or could play them off against one another. These structures seem to have taken at least five principal forms: 1) a sequential or linear structure of segments, each of which was determined by a different stylistics or set of genre conventions;[40] 2) a basically paradigmatic structure of past/present narrative relations; 3) a doubled narrative structure, in which the actions of the second half paralleled or recapitulated those of the first half; 4) a "dream" structure modeled on (but not reproducing) the vaguely perceived structures and operations of the unconscious; and 5) a structure predicated, in Burch's words, on "a dialectization of the principal modes of spatio-temporal continuity."[41]

With this schema or taxonomy providing an initial frame of reference, what follows is a series of close readings of those films I consider the major texts of the French narrative avant-garde film practice. At appropriate junctures, certain films are tied to or inscribed by specific theoretical writings, but the focus throughout is on the actual discursive and narrative operations of the film texts. Although the organization of these readings is generally chronological, I have isolated, paired, and otherwise combined films in such a way as to emphasize the most pertinent patterns and strategies of that practice. While some readings tend to analyze the texts so as to chart the development of those strategies; others focus on the particular textual significance of discontinuity, incoherence, or excess; and still others take up particular patterns of textual synthesis and coherence within an interpretative framework. It is essential, I believe, to encompass both the homogeneity and heterogeneity of this film practice, as articulated in specific texts, in order to reposition and hence recuperate the French narrative avant-garde in cinema history.

Some years ago, Henri Langlois argued that Abel Gance's short film, *La Folie du Docteur Tube*, which Film d'Art allegedly refused to release in 1915, was the first French avant-garde film.[1] Many film historians have accepted this view, and even Gance himself has defended the film for its supposed introduction of subjectivity into the French cinema. As Jean Mitry and Kevin Brownlow attest, it probably did nothing of the kind.[2] Nor was it particularly advanced. Gance's story of a mad scientist (Albert Dieudonné looking something like Prince Rigadin), who discovers a powder that changes the appearance of people and things—first his dog, his black boy assistant, and himself, then two young women next door, and finally two men who call on them—and who reluctantly agrees to change them all back to normal, is merely the premise for a lighthearted, rather mediocre comedy of camera tricks.[3] Actually, the changes are all achieved by means of distorting mirrors.[4] More than anything, *Docteur Tube* tries to re-create the magical world of Georges Méliès or Onésime and looks ahead feebly to René Clair's *Paris qui dort* (1924).

Although some might argue, with more validity, that Gance's *Mater Dolorosa* (1917) or possibly even *La Dixième Symphonie* (1918) mark its beginning, the French narrative avant-garde does not really develop in earnest until after the Great War. From the start, however, its interests and strategies are already multiple. By 1917, according to Sophie Daria, Abel Gance was pressing Louis Nalpas at Film d'Art to let him make "psychological films, where he could express emotions or a state of consciousness rather than merely lay out facts."[5] "We need to make something more interesting," Brownlow quotes Gance as telling Nalpas. "We'll make real dramas about real feelings. That's the sort of thing that will catch the public's imagination."[6] At the same time, Marcel L'Herbier was arguing that the distinctive feature of the cinema was its mechanical reproduction of reality—especially as evidenced in the newsreels—while he was also advocating the transformation of that reality—in a "new symphony composed of leitmotifs of landscapes, counterpoints of gestures, fugues of shadow. . . ."[7] Unmediated documentary versus stylized system of "musical" signs—these were the twin poles that would preoccupy L'Herbier, as well as others, for the rest of the decade. As Jean Epstein rather bluntly put it,

French films seemed destined to be no more than albums of poses and catalogues of decors, when the first major works of Gance, then L'Herbier, and then Delluc revealed a new tendency which accepted the lesson of American realism, perhaps too hastily and to an excess, in order to submit it to personal interpretations, to deformations, but also to artistic standards, to all sorts of unconscious indelible traces of high culture.[8]

The extent to which Gance's and L'Herbier's work began to redefine the parameters of narrative film discourse can be seen in the films they released immediately after the war: *J'Accuse* (1919) and *Rose-France* (1919).

The trade press advertisement for Gance's film featured a four-page-wide fold-out of a black background against which the title stood out in blood-red letters that oozed heavy white drops.[9] The film itself provided the basis for this design, beginning with the HAELS of thousands of French soldiers in an open field spelling out the title in mammoth letters—*J'Accuse*.[10] The allusion

295

141. The title shot from
J'Accuse (1919)

to Emile Zola's famous attack on the court-martial that condemned Dreyfus
some twenty years before was brilliant as well as a bit presumptuous. It announced a provocative film treatment of the war, completely different from
the propagandistic and pacifist films previously seen in such abundance. And
it did so with the assistance of the French Army. Yet *J'Accuse* could hardly be
described as radical or rabble-rousing, at least ideologically. In fact, it caught
rather well the mood of the French public just after the war and was a huge
success. First released in four parts (of approximately 1,200 meters each), the
film was re-edited into several single-*seance* versions from 1919 to 1921 (Gance
loved to correct his work).[11] Apparently, prints of these shorter versions are
the only ones preserved.[12]

Gance began writing the scenario for *J'Accuse* in the summer of 1917, under
several different influences. One was Henri Barbusse's devastating novel on
the war, *Le Feu, Journal d'une escouade* (1916), which had just won the popular
Prix Goncourt.[13] Another even stronger was the desperate rage he felt at the
deaths of so many of his friends in the trenches (nine out of ten, he would say
later).[14] And finally, there was the creative and competitive surge he experienced at seeing Griffith's *Intolerance* (privately in Paris, in 1917) and at knowing that Griffith was then at work on his own film about the war, *Hearts of
the World* (1918).[15] This combination of anger and ambition produced a confused, poignant, and absurdly grandiloquent narrative. Edith (Maryse Dauvray) is married to a paradoxically violent yet tender man, François (Séverin-

Mars), but she is loved by the poet, Jean Diaz (Romauld Joubé). Both men are mobilized for the war and serve in the same battalion, where they are reconciled and agree to let Edith choose between them. Jean returns home on leave to his dying mother, and Edith (sent to François's parents home in the Ardennes) returns from German captivity with a child—the result of rape. On his return, François attacks Jean in a jealous rage until Edith intervenes to explain. For vengeance, both men go back to the front, where François is killed and Jean is shellshocked into madness. Back home again, Jean invokes the war dead and calls forth a vision of phantom soldiers rising up and confronting the startled villagers. Then he, too, dies, re-reading his prewar poems, *Les Pacifiques*, after accusing even the sun for its complicity in the war's destruction.

Although this mixture of the epic, the melodramatic, and the didactic sometimes threatens to disintegrate, much of *J'Accuse*'s very real power comes from moments of intense feeling produced by means of several different strategies that Gance worked out with his chief cameraman, L.-H. Burel. One extends the practice of his previous two films, *Mater Dolorosa* and *La Dixième Symphonie*, and is predicated on the perceptual, emotional, and mental activity of certain characters. Early in the film, for instance, Jean reads to his mother from one of his poems, "Hymn du Soleil," and his words are replaced by a "cinematographic poem," a slow montage of pastoral drawings and shots of a sunrise over the sea, all tinted in yellows and blues. Though still quite derivative and simplistic, the sequence works more effectively than does the musical performance in *La Dixième Symphonie* because the images not only join the two characters in a shared feeling (that will be obliterated by the war) but also make the audience experience something like that feeling as well. Later, when Edith is forced to defend Jean from her husband and reveal the paternity of her child, the experience of her rape by a German soldier is suggested in just three flashback images (a restrained variation on current propaganda posters):[16] the shadow of a helmet, the shadow of a pair of hands reaching out, and finally that of a man's shape filling the room. More simply, our allegiance to Edith is marked from the very beginning. When François first appears, he throws the carcass of a deer across the kitchen table and, grabbing his hound, tries to make it lick the dripping blood. There is a cut to a POV shot of Edith, who, from her seat at the window, turns and flinches. From that moment on, as Kevin Brownlow notes, the spectator sees François as Edith sees him.[17] Gance even plays with the shock effect of the POV shot when he has François discover Edith and Jean together in the woods. After a shot of François raising his shotgun, there is a shot looking down the gun barrel, which is aimed directly at the couple. In a reverse shot, François fires—cut to a bird falling dead at Jean's feet. The forced spectator identification with the villain and the deliberate ellipsis of the gun's movement away from the couple startle us far more than the metaphorical threat of the dead bird. Much later, when François has returned home on leave from the war, he is a changed man. And the film shifts our attention and sympathy to his awkward attempts to be reconciled with his wife. His puzzlement over the child living with Jean culminates in a sequence at his own house that reminds one of *Mater Dolorosa*. In a series of POV shots, he discovers what he reads as a sign of Edith's guilt in several ordinary objects: a child's doll and then (in CU) a pair of tiny shoes.

A second strategy that recurs in *J'Accuse*, and which may have been inspired by *Intolerance*, works by means of a shocking or ironic juxtaposition of narrative actions, sometimes articulated in alternation. One of the earliest of these moments, which comes just as Jean finishes reading his poem, condenses two extreme figures of sentimental melodrama. Intercut with the peaceful scene between mother and son, which is generated by the "high art" of poetry, are several charged images of sexual brutality: a woman lies half-naked on the floor beside a bed; François gloats over a pair of panties in his hand; the woman is revealed as Edith (in MCU), her hair clutched by François's other hand and her breast bared. After this sexual threat has been shifted to the Germans—in the three-shot flashback of Edith's rape—a more complicated juxtaposition occurs as Jean and François return to the front. In the departure scene, the conflict between the two men seems resolved when François notices Jean and Edith's clasped hands (in MCU) and orders them to embrace. Instead of cutting immediately to the battlefield, where the superimposed figure of Charlemagne seems to stalk ahead of the troops that Jean exhorts to victory, a very different representation of the war is inserted. Here the village children put a German helmet on Edith's child and a wooden gun in his hand, then begin to taunt him, and finally beat him to the ground. The playful intolerance of their action, which surprisingly echoes the earlier attacks on Edith herself, subverts the subsequent heroic images of battle and gives a raw edge to the conventional melodramatic figure of suffering mother and child.

In certain key sequences, a third strategy is visible—rhythmic montage marked by extensive camera movement. Sometimes this functions much like the fast cutting in Griffith's films, especially *Intolerance*: it plunges us into the action, to make us participants, as Gance would say later. The most sustained instance of this strategy occurs in the last major battle, in which François is wounded. The daylight fighting progresses through shots of Jean laughing madly at the letters that he will never send and an alternation of cannon fire and troops massing to attack; and it crescendos in huge explosions, smoke-blurred images, fast cutting, and wild tracking shots. The night battle that follows shifts to a rough rhythmic pattern of blinding flashes from artillery shells in the dark and ends in a single shot of a body thrown back into a trench and then a slow tilt down from a cathedral window to bodies heaped in its crypt. Besides evoking something like a collective consciousness of trench warfare, Gance's strategy also functions at least once in a moment of subjective hallucination—when François maliciously tells Edith that her child has drowned. There a short montage of dolly shots of her running, intercut with brief water images, intensifies her fear and anxiety until she reaches the bank of the stream where Jean and the child are peacefully reading.

In other sequences of *J'Accuse*, however, rhythmic montage operates quite differently. The film opens, for instance, in the midst of a provincial festival where the villagers are dancing a farandole in the central square. Here, a social ambiance builds up before the major characters are introduced and the narrative begins. The movement of the dancers, the red firelight reflected on their faces, and the rhythmic intercutting of separate figures and groups suggest a society whose rituals already verge on belligerence. Not long after, news of the war prompts a short documentarylike sequence that brings the villagers together again, one by one, from their shops and houses to celebrate the

142. A publicity photo from a battle sequence in *J'Accuse* (1919)

mobilization order. That celebration shifts presciently at the end in two simple shots: a FS of a young woman leaning against a wall (her husband has just left) and a MS of an older woman slumped and staring forward silently in the crowd. This sequence is followed by a series of symbolic contrasts and displacements—children are shown playing in some rubble, skeletons dance, even Saint Severin rejoices, and a scythe dissolves in, replacing the book of poems in Jean's hands. Then, the men's departure is narrated in a simple synecdochal montage of hands—packing a bag, clasped together, raising a last cup of wine, praying before candles, an old man's grasping a child's. In contrast to the earlier derivative cinematographic poem, in this slow montage the film produces a poignant figure of metaphorical condensation.

Here, *J'Accuse* approaches a form of collage similar to that marking the Modernist painting (e.g., the Cubists, Léger, Delaunay) and poetry of Gance's contemporaries.[18] The collage text produced order, not so much by sequentiality or succession, but by simultaneity. At first, particularly in the work of the Futurist painters and poets, a succession of events, often objects in motion,

299

143. Jean reads to his mother on her deathbed in *J'Accuse* (1919)

was telescoped into a kind of overlay, into paradigm. In the more advanced poetry of Guillaume Apollinaire and Blaise Cendrars, however, simultaneity reached the point of assimilating, into a continuous present, quite divergent events and images, both objective and subjective, either through the representation of a single consciousness or through simple presentation.[19] In Gance's film, this simultaneity is still relatively simple—a rhythmic montage of only slightly heterogeneous elements or dislocated moments—e.g., the opening farandole, the montage of hands. But the cutting here is already determined less by the diegetic process or narrative progression than by the description of what Ricciotto Canudo called "the collective body acting as a single individual"[20] and by a play of similarities and differences—e.g., graphic matches, metaphorical relations—in the material features of each shot. Since Canudo and Cendrars were close friends of Gance at the time and since Cendrars acted as his assistant director on *J'Accuse*, it is hardly surprising that the film evidences what Standish Lawder has called "the post-war aesthetic of kaleidoscopic imagery."[21] Was it this film that led Jean Epstein to conclude that, within five years, "we will compose cinematographic poems: 150 meters and 100 images like beads on a thread whose movement imitates the flow of intelligence"?[22]

For all its disparate discursive strategies and its abrupt, almost incoherent, melodramatic narrative twists, *J'Accuse* gains a loose form of coherence through several patterns of rhetorical figuring. One such pattern is initiated by the montage sequence of hands (in CU), which sums up a set of simple human activities, a way of life, that is about to be abandoned. The motif of hands returns in another departure scene in the middle of the film, when François seems to bless the relationship between Jean and Edith. And it returns a last time when the two men are hospitalized side by side after the climactic battle.

144. Blaise Cendrars leads the "resurrection" of the dead soldiers in *J'Accuse* (1919)

Just before he dies, François reaches out to grasp Jean's hand, as a final gesture of friendship and reconciliation. And the sequence ends with a CU of their hands whose clasp a doctor is unable to break. Another pattern of rhetorical figuring undergoes a very different semantic shift. It begins with Jean's "Hymn du soleil," whose accompanying images mark the sentimental nature of his vision as well as the harmony between mother and son. Later, on her deathbed, she asks him to read from his poetry again, but now the sequence of images that accompany his words are of painted landscapes over which Edith is superimposed. Artificial and distanced, they close on a conventionally desolate snowscape. Here they seem to mark his sense of loss, of both women as well as of his poetic vision. In the end, Jean returns to his mother's house and rediscovers the "Hymn du soleil." As he reads it a last time before a window through which the sunlight streams, he turns to cursing the sun's silence and the deceptive source of his inspiration. The accompanying images change from a pastoral landscape to a battlefield of corpses and then to a peaceful valley over which the sun sets and then rises again. In this ironically charged simple image, everything is still latent. Nothing has changed, and Jean is martyred before an apparently indifferent natural order of things.

This ending rhetorical tableau, which shifts the blame for the war onto nature in an impotent protest, is preceded by another more dramatic and no less ironic attempt to resolve the question of accusation. For *J'Accuse* climaxes in a famous sequence that transforms Jean's personal vision into a symbolic confrontation for the entire village, and for all France. Here, the film's strategies of subjectivity and simultaneity intersect in a passionate, paradoxical protest. A protest all the more moving for Gance's knowledge that the hundreds of soldiers he had recruited for the scene would be returning to Verdun, a place from which, they knew well, few of them might come back alive.[23] Returning half-mad from the trenches after François's death, Jean gathers the villagers together in the fire's red light (an echo of the film's opening) and reads them his letter of accusation. His words give way now to an ELS of a flat, barren landscape under a superimposed darkening sky—a battleground covered with crosses and hundreds of soldiers. As if responding to Jean's cries, first one (Blaise Cendrars, with his amputated left arm), then another, and finally all the dead rise up and slowly begin to march forward. After another intertitle, the screen splits horizontally to boldly juxtapose this "Resurrection of the Dead" with a documentary shot (from a similar angle, on the same direction of movement) of the Armistice Victory Parade through the Arc de Triomphe.[24] The relentless march of the dead (depicted in tracking shots, superimpositions, various kinds of masks, and funereal purple toning) finally reaches the village, where, overwhelmed by the horror, the people beg their forgiveness and affirm their sacrifice. Their deaths apparently now justified, given significance, the dead regroup, move off into the distance, and disappear.

Thus, in its attempt to expose the horrors of war and to accuse those responsible, Gance's film does not avoid a conventional moralizing and a certain chauvinism. "It is less the war that is denounced," concludes Marcel Oms, "than the pleasure, cupidity, and immorality of the living as opposed to the nobility of the dead soldiers who have known true valor."[25] Seemingly critical of a patriotism that blindly ignores the death it causes, *J'Accuse* ends up celebrating the dead's sacrifice as a form of patriotism.

Rose-France was as great a financial catastrophe as *J'Accuse* was a success. With the French army's blessing, in 1918, L'Herbier set to work on a scenario which would raise the people's morale during the war. Unfortunately, the Armistice was signed before the film could be finished, and it was no longer exactly relevant.[26] But there were other reasons for its commercial failure. Although it exhibits an even more extravagant patriotism than *J'Accuse*, *Rose-France* breaks even more sharply with the conventions of a film discourse that privileged narrative action. As L'Herbier himself wrote, on the eve of the film's second release:

. . . the cinegraphic representation of a succession of actions and reactions, that is of dramatic gestures and of images representing the dreams or reflections that those gestures would provoke in the hero of the *drama*—this representation, I say, which will combine together and nearly simultaneously, the active and passive visage of life—exquisite sensibilities in black and white—will be one of the best modes of realization in French film poetics.[27]

145. Jaque Catelain and Mlle.
Aïssé in *Rose-France* (1919)

Most film critics accepted L'Herbier's attempt to constitute cinematographically the "mental or psychological states" of characters, but objected to the
film's preciosity and air of decadence.[28] Yet, even if the film depended excessively on "fin-de-siècle banalities," writes Noël Burch, *Rose-France* "opens out
towards us" by producing "a series of symbolic actions which converse with
the intertitles and non-diegetic inserts [in] . . . a 'music of images.' "[29]

What strikes one initially about *Rose-France* is its pyrotechnical display of
optical devices (the cameraman was Thiberville, who had worked, interestingly enough, on Méliès's early films). At various times, these function to
simulate subjective states or to divide the frame into two or three images for
symbolic conjunctions and juxtapositions.[30] Like Gance in *J'Accuse*, L'Herbier
early on deploys a poem and a montage of the visual images it evokes to join
his two central characters, a young French poetess, Francine Roy (Mlle. Aissé),
and a young American who has been demobilized because of his health, Lauris
Dudley Gold (Jaque Catelain). This sequence is marked by the transformation
of natural images through dissolves, superimpositions, and unusual masks, all
of which culminate in a literal sign of interiorization. In the next-to-last shot
of the sequence, as the lovers kiss, there is a quick dissolve into negative. The
shot fades, only to iris in on a CU of them kissing, now framed in a dark
star-shaped mask, itself superimposed with small glittering stars. This sentimental transformation places the lovers among the stars, creating a kind of
privileged microcosm for two within the universe.

Given the European naïveté about the United States, Lauris has a savage
companion, Tigre-Prince (Francis-Byron Kuhn), whom he must have picked
up during his cavalry days in the Far West (although the West Indies seem
more likely) and through whom he learns that Francine apparently loves another. Sometime later, when Lauris discovers an inscription which seems to
confirm his suspicions in Francine's book of poems, a subjective insert of the
earlier shot of the couple together grows blurred and is followed by a superimposition of her figure crossing the lawn to him (as earlier), which now meets
with his horrifying gesture of rejection. This period of seeming loss and mel-

303

ancholy culminates in a subjective triptych shot of a smoky white panel masked on each side by black. In the central panel, a blurred image of Lauris and Francine dissolves in, followed by images of Francine on the left and Lauris on the right, each turned away from the other. The central image dissolves to white, and then so do the separate side images. Clearly, this deployment of iris masks and vignettes for subjective and symbolic effects differs radically from the pictorial and narrative conventions established earlier by such film-makers as Maurice Tourneur and D. W. Griffith.[31]

More important than these moments, however, are several extended segments that narrate simultaneously two lines of action or associations, one usually real and the other subjective or imaginary. Perhaps the most complex of these is the one that begins with Lauris discovering the poetry inscription. The entire segment is predicated on an alternation between Lauris's and Francine's separate actions after she swears she loves none but him. While he paces about his house and garden, she returns to her house, visits a bookseller (to discover he has purchased her book of poems), and writes him a letter. Cut into this alternating series, however, are subjective inserts for each of the two characters as well as several generalized symbolic images. This makes the segment quite demanding to read, as it shifts quickly and often from one line of action to the other, and from the diegetic to the nondiegetic. Rather than the simultaneity of divergent actions in a continuous present, as in *J'Accuse*, *Rose-France* thus produces a simultaneity of "the active and passive visage of life" in a doubly paradigmatic narrative structure. As we shall see, this is probably the film's most original contribution to the narrative avant-garde film practice.

Another form of paradigmatic structuring depends on a pattern of rhetorical figuring that is curiously similar to the motif of hands in *J'Accuse*. Early in *Rose-France* there is an enigmatic CU of a woman's hand taking a rose from another hand that is missing three fingers and part of the palm. Inserted in the opening sequence between Lauris and Tigre-Prince, and before Francine arrives, its only reference is an intertitle: "And at the same moment in a nearby park a mutilated hand. . . ." After Lauris and Francine embrace, a rose drops from her dress, and he asks her if she is wearing it in hopes that the war will end soon. Who gave it to her?—"I don't remember." The shot of the rose and hands returns, and from then on, Lauris jealously begins to suspect a rival. The rose/hands figure recurs in a different conjunction after Lauris discovers the poetry inscription: a CU of Francine bending over the rose on her table is followed by a CU of Lauris closing his eyes with *his* hands. The next day Lauris meets two soldiers on the road, trails one along a wall, and notices his disfigured hand as the soldier follows a woman through a gate. When he finally reads Francine's letter, which explains that her inscription and poems are dedicated to "the Spirit, the Art, the Past and the Air itself— in short, the Genius of France!" (quoting the fifteenth-century poet, Charles d'Orléans), there is a MCU of him looking up, followed by an insert of the soldier passing through the gate (now blurred), and then a MCU of him tearing up the letter against a background of flower-patterned cloth. In a bold condemnation of his jealousy, the shot fades out on his own contorted hands. After their reconciliation, Francine gives Lauris "this Rose-de-France"; there is a repetition of the original giving of the rose (now in LS to reveal the soldier and Francine); and now as they kiss, the rose is superimposed between them.

146. (left) The title shot from *L'Homme du large* (1920)

147. (right) An intertitle

In the context of *Rose-France*'s slight narrative structure, this rhetorical figuring has a crucial function. The initial rose/hands figure raises the enigma that the film's narrative has to answer, and it proceeds to do so through a rather simple investigation, much as in a detective story (it is almost impossible not to compare this with the similar, more overt, yet more complicated function of the Rosebud/glass ball motif in *Citizen Kane*). And once the enigma is solved (in a simple change of camera position), the motif seems to be relocated as a sign of the couple's love. Yet something is not quite right here. French critics who reviewed the film, such as Jean Galtier-Boissière, were deeply offended by the image of the mutilated hand, reading it as a grotesque magnification of French suffering during the war.[32] Although the ostensible reason for their offense seems greatly exaggerated and prejudiced, they may be right in pointing to the grotesquerie. So powerful is the film's fascination with the hand, giving image to a disfigurement considered taboo and linking it metonymically with Lauris's love, that its metaphorical connections with the rose function rather ambiguously even today. Rather than marking a reciprocal healing through sacrifice and devotion, the rose/hands motif seems to cast a pall over the lovers, almost calling the whole romance into question.

When he first saw Marcel L'Herbier's *L'Homme du large* (1920) at a ciné-club screening in the late 1920s, Henri Langlois called it "the first example of cinematic writing."[1] That epithet might surprise those who found and still find the theatrical acting styles of Henry Krauss and especially Jaque Catelain (as the antagonistic father and son) at odds with the Brittany seascapes as well as finding the representation of a Breton community a bit fabricated and unrealistically polarized.[2] No doubt the film is more than interesting—for its camerawork and mise-en-scène (e.g., the low-key lighting, foreground/background contrasts, unusual wipes and masks), its incorporation of documentarylike footage into the fiction (much like *J'Accuse*, it begins by building up a milieu, an atmosphere), and its exploration and uneasy resolution of cultural

L'Homme du large and El Dorado

305

extremes (self-denial and profligation). Yet *J'Accuse* and *Rose-France* clearly can be seen as prior texts of "cinematic writing."

Although Langlois's judgment demands a good deal of qualification now, there is something to what he says. At least two forms of experimentation seem to be operating in the film, and both involve a double process of signification at the level of the discourse. First, unlike, say, Pouctal's and Feuillade's films, as Langlois notes, *L'Homme du large* does not merely narrate a series of events, connected and explained by intertitles.[3] It combines the images and intertitles in a unique way—instead of taking the place of the images or duplicating them, the intertitles sometimes are superimposed over them. Langlois speculates that this obvious stylization functions as a form of underlining, to fix the image in the memory.[4] It makes more sense, I think, to see it instead as an early, misguided attempt to produce a "film language" of hieroglyphs or ideograms. Second, as Noël Burch suggests, there are occasional sequences (as in the confrontation between father and son) where the montage clearly serves a double function—as a vehicle for the narrative and as a stylized rhythmic structure determined by the mise-en-scène and framing as well as the rhythm of shot transitions.[5] While the progression of shots narrates, it also presents itself as a formal construction or, in L'Herbier's terms, a "musical composition." On this basis, although the point could be contested, *L'Homme du large* seems to me still a problematical film text in the French narrative avant-garde film practice.[6]

There is no question, however, that another of L'Herbier's films from this period synthesizes the early narrative avant-garde film practice into its first masterwork—*El Dorado* (1921). L'Herbier himself considered *El Dorado* "the culmination of the five films in which [he] had experimented with a certain number of effects."[7] Henry Fescourt called its first public screening at the Gaumont-Palace, on 7 July 1921, one of the three most important film premieres in France between 1916 and 1929.[8] After that premiere, Lionel Landry wrote:

When the language of the Cinema will have stabilized and when historians look, retrospectively, for someone who is owed some merit, nothing will detract from the startling role that M. Marcel L'Herbier played in the formulation of its vocabulary.[9]

The simplest yet most memorable reaction was Louis Delluc's famous cry, "There, that's cinematic!"[10]

L'Herbier deliberately subtitled *El Dorado* "a cinematographic melodrama," making explicit the popular origins it shared with the other early narrative avant-garde films.[11] Like the Dulac-Delluc *La Fête espagnole* (1920), it was set in Spain during a holiday, specifically in Granada during Holy Week, and featured Eve Francis dancing in a cabaret. Although she is the star performer at the cabaret (a hellhole ironically dubbed El Dorado), Sybilla is obsessed with the poor health of her young son, the offspring of an earlier affair with Estiria, a wealthy impresario in the city. After her renewed pleas to him are spurned, she considers blackmailing him with her knowledge of the secret love between his daughter (Marcelle Pradot) and a Swedish painter (Jaque Catelain) for whom Sybilla has posed in the Alhambra. Shocked by their discovery of Estiria's villainy, the young couple break with him and persuade Sybilla to let them take the boy to be raised in the country by the painter's

148. Sybilla (center) among
the cabaret dancers at the
beginning of *El Dorado* (1921)

mother. Cut off from her son, probably forever (almost cruelly, at the last
minute, the painter tells her his mother will soon be leaving Spain), and
menaced by the drunken types who frequent the cabaret, particularly the piano
player (Philippe Hériat), Sybilla finally commits suicide behind the stage backdrop.

Needless to say, not all spectators shared Delluc and Fescourt's enthusiasm
for *El Dorado*, especially when it was released to the public in October, 1921.[12]
Particularly offensive were the many visual deformations (various distortions and
soft focus shots), which were done in collaboration with his chief cameraman,
Georges Lucas, and which soon made the film famous. At the first company
screening, in fact, Léon Gaumont, the producer, was much annoyed and kept
yelling at the projectionist, "Fix the focus!" However, singling out such deformations to the exclusion of all else distorts the work of the film considerably. For *El Dorado* simulates subjective experience through a wide range of
strategies, and it does much more. It was probably the first French feature
film to have an original musical score, composed by Maurius-François Gaillard, synchronized to accompany its projection. Although the complete score
now seems lost,[13] L'Herbier has said that the music was essential to the rhythm
of his montage and to the emotional states and interactions of the characters.
So important was it that he referred to *El Dorado* as a "musical drama" and
linked it to "Impressionist music." The film also employed a sophisticated
orchestration of tinted film stocks (strikingly preserved in the Cinémathèque
française print), of which L'Herbier was the narrative avant-garde's most devoted proponent. Extending his work in *Rose-France*, it also deployed editing

307

patterns involving a degree of spatial-temporal discontinuity as well as patterns of rhetorical figuring. Finally, it used a narrative structure that synthesized a mélange of discourse modes—including the documentary, the decorative, and the subjective—a structure predicated on parallels and juxtapositions even more than on narrative continuity. The best measure of the film's synthesis of narrative avant-garde film practice can be gleaned from examining the film reel by reel.

The first reel of *El Dorado* immediately intrigues the spectator with the subjective life of Sybilla's character, in L'Herbier's words, through "a dialectic that combines the real and the unreal."[14] After a series of shots (tinted yellow) that suggest the milieu of the cabaret, Sybilla is introduced as an enigma, an absence—at the center of a FS of several dancers seated on the cabaret stage, her figure alone is blurred out of focus. More of the cabaret milieu is described—some musicians, a flower girl, a woman suckling a baby, distorted shots of drinkers and of a hand fondling a woman's blouse. Sybilla now appears in MCU, again blurred slightly out of focus. As the other women prod her to dance, in FS, her figure comes into sharp focus; and she gets up to perform, but without much enthusiasm. Why is she "not there," or only partly there, in the space of the cabaret? What is she thinking? The answer comes at the end of a series of alternations between shots that sum up the ignorant world of the cabaret and shots of an isolated room where a boy lies ill in bed. The transition shots shift from a blind man to some women laughing to a blurred CU of Sybilla—it is the boy she is thinking of, her son. After accepting the excited applause of the cabaret clientele, she goes backstage, past the shadow of clapping hands on the stage backdrop (tinted rose), to what we discover is the upstairs room (black/white) where she and her son live.

The sequence that follows makes us share and come to understand Sybilla's condition through a progression of gestures and objects, subjective inserts, memory flashbacks, and a sequence of cross-cutting that involves some rhythmic montage. Once in the room, where she cradles the boy in her arms, there is an immediate cut to a shot of the curtain blowing at the window. In MS and then CU, Sybilla discovers a broken pane through which the wind is howling. This prompts a LS of the city (tinted green) and then another which blurs in distortion—a supposed POV shot turns subjective, as if an imaginary wind were leveling the world—and Sybilla stuffs part of the curtain into the gaping hole. An alternation now begins between the bedroom and the cabaret below, where the piano player is dancing clumsily, wildly on stage. As Sybilla gazes down on her son and her eyes widen in fear, several quick shots of the cabaret dancing and revelry are cut in for dramatic contrast. When she goes to the fire across the room and blows on the coals (tinted rose), the contrast turns cruelly ironic in a cut to a HALS of the activity in the cabaret as it grows more frenzied, followed by several quick shots from unusual angles of the whirling dancer, his mouth gaping wide. Into this alternation, two short flashbacks are also intercut. The first is prompted by a title (now missing) which, through a perfect example of classical continuity editing (an ELS of the city, a LS of a mansion, a LS of an interior with a man at a desk, a MS of the man reading a letter), introduces Estiria as he coolly responds to Sybilla's plea for help. The second flashback is strikingly different:

149. (left) The painter's initial view of an Alhambra interior in *El Dorado* (1921)

Fade to black.

Wipe in a MCU of Estiria (younger) speaking angrily to Sybilla (her back to the camera) in front of him.

Wipe in a MS of Estiria smoking and reading a letter at his desk.

Wipe in a FS (blurred) of Estiria at his desk; Sybilla enters the frame and embraces him.

Wipe in a MS of Estiria sealing his letter and sending it off with a servant.

Wipe to black.

Fade in.

This remarkable segment of parallel montage playing off a chronological present against a reversed chronological past briefly summarizes the relation between Sybilla and Estiria, but its discontinuity (accentuated by the wipes) emphasizes the disturbing contrast between his once enflamed passion and his now cold behavior.[15] Furthermore, since the cabaret sequence between these two flashbacks singles out the piano player (who desires Sybilla), a parallel is suggested between the two men—as if the latter were acting out a vulgar replication of the former's earlier passion. After the piano player is jeered off stage, the crowd sends him off to beg Sybilla to perform again. In her room he tries to kiss her (in contrasting CUs and HAMCUs) but is repulsed. Then, just before going on stage, she receives the impresario's letter (we assume), rejecting her and the boy, as he must have done several times before. The sequence ends as it opened, with Sybilla beginning her dance slightly out of focus. Her figure comes into sharp focus, slows, and then, after a shot of the boy calling out, her face blurs into featurelessness—suggesting a pain so great that it obliterates all expression.[16]

The next reel is marked by a dramatic shift from the active, brutal world of the cabaret to the peaceful, static world of the Alhambra, from Sybilla to the Swedish painter, from the subjective to the decorative, from color contrasts to black/white contrasts. The painter is introduced (in a dolly shot) at his mother's house, looking through a packet of photographs of the Alhambra's architecture. As the sequence alternates shots of him looking and POV shots of individual photographs, each photograph distorts slightly, assuming the elongated, broken lines of a Delaunay painting (e.g., "Saint Severin," "La Tour Eiffel"). Thus does his perception seem to transform the world around him. This playful prelude to creation is interrupted by a nondistorting photograph and then by a subjective insert of an unknown woman dressed in white (Estiria's daughter, it turns out), in which she dissolves in between fountain jets of water in a courtyard garden. The double shift seems to remind the painter of a rendezvous he has at the Alhambra, but the woman he meets there is Sybilla, his model. In a strange parallel to the previous subjective insert, the black figure of Sybilla appears on the grounds of the Alhambra against a background which metamorphosizes through several lap dissolves but which does not affect her continuous advance in the slightest (and here the dissolves seem without subjective motivation).

As the two move from place to place in the palace gardens (the transitions marked by wipes using silhouetted grillework panels), the painter is distracted twice more by superimpositions of the imaginary woman passing near the fountains and columns. Finally, he gives up his work; but as Sybilla is leaving, she notices the woman in white enter the grounds and then follows her unseen to *her* rendezvous with the painter. There follows a hypnotic sequence of figures drifting through the arches and colonnades of the Alhambra, composed in sharply etched areas of light and shadow, one figure slowly, stealthily pursuing the other two. As Noël Burch has written,

Here the diversity of camera angles and spaces, the foreground/background juxtapositions, the entrances into and exits from the frame represent an already assured affirmation of an attitude which, progressively, even at the heart of a dramatic cinema, distances L'Herbier from the "mise-en-scène," and aligns him with that which he has called the "mise-en-film.". . .[17]

These plastic or compositional harmonies, which nearly float free of the narrative, herald the hallucinatory perambulations and poses of later narrative as well as non-narrative avant-garde films. As Sybilla leaves the Alhambra (in a slow reverse dolly shot), she is haunted by juxtaposed images—a LS of her son surrounded by darkness and a FS of the lovers (do they remind her of herself and Estiria in the past?) slowly gliding out of the sunlight into shadow.

The third reel shifts abruptly, but easily, from the decorative to the documentary, from fantasy to reality, returning to the pathos of Sybilla's current position. Sometime later, Sybilla decides to confront her former lover in person; but her way to his mansion is blocked by a religious procession of the Virgin. This improvised sequence (shot during an actual ritual that year) is transformed rhetorically into a series of ironic juxtapositions.[18] On the one hand, Sybilla is a lone figure separate from and moving in the opposite direction from the religious procession; on the other hand, she is trying to save her son in the midst of a community celebrating the mother of Christ. The people's happiness and well-being (even wealth) exist apart from and are blind to her suffering, exactly in the way the revelries of the cabaret crowd are. As the statue of the Virgin on its elaborate, elevated platform stops momentarily beside Sybilla, the two mother figures (and images of adoration) mirror one another inversely (in a series of CUs)—the one seeing but unseen, the other

310

150. (left) Sybilla and the long, towering white wall in *El Dorado* (1921)

151. (right) The piano player (Philippe Hériat) attacks Sybilla

seen but unseeing. The moment passes, and Sybilla passes by. After she is thrown out of Estiria's house (for disturbing his party guests) and the glass doors to the house close, Sybilla wanders through the now empty city in a sequence that culminates in one of the most famous shots of the film. In contrast to the earlier sequence of the procession, the LSs of her wandering now alternate with a progression of subjective and perceptual inserts, condensing the despair and anger of her emotional state: a LS of her son in bed, lit by a single, small light; a LS of bells tolling in a church tower; a blurred LS of the lovers together in the Alhambra garden. The last shot is of a high white wall running diagonally from the right foreground into the distant left background, where the tiny black figure of Sybilla comes forward slowly. As she moves along the wall (and we realize there will be no further inserts), its looming whiteness metaphorically takes on all the suffering she has experienced. She pauses, nearly overwhelmed, and then continues forward until her face fills the screen. Displaced into the wall, which is itself now displaced, all that suffering rushes metonymically into the final, fading CU of her pained face.

The final reel of *El Dorado* repeats the opening with tragic effect.[19] In green-tinted shots of the cabaret's entrance, Sybilla's son goes off with the young couple on horseback, leaving her standing beside the old blind man who lightly strums a banjo. In the bedroom, absence lingers; Sybilla distractedly repeats some of her gestures from the initial sequence, and certain emotionally charged objects recur—the empty bed, the boy's clothing, the broken window pane. Cross-cut with this sequence (paralleling the earlier flashbacks of Estiria) is a series of shots (tinted green) narrating the boy's progress through the city and into the mountains. But the second shot among them is a flashback of all four characters at the cabaret's entrance. The series shifts from the omniscient to the subjective and then wavers in between. The piano player again comes up from the cabaret, but this time he attacks Sybilla in a flurry of CUs (tinted

311

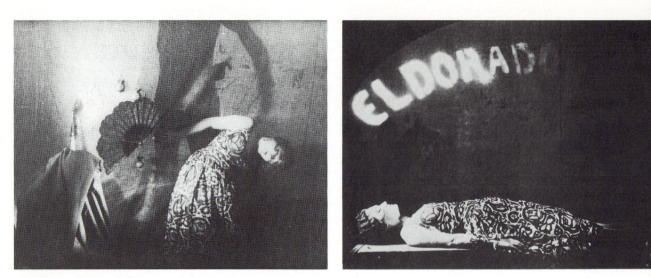

152. (left) Backstage, Sybilla staggers against the cabaret backdrop

153. (right) The final shot in *El Dorado* (1921)

blue-green) that dissolve into an elongated distortion of him lying on top of her. After she repulses him once more and briefly performs on stage (tinted yellow), Sybilla stops in the backstage area (tinted rose) behind the backdrop and writes a short note as the silhouettes of clapping hands are replaced by the huge lunging shadow of the piano player dancing.

Before this "interior screen," which reduces the cabaret revelry to a shadow-puppet play and condenses her despair and suffering much as did the great white wall earlier, Sybilla stands out sharply, realistically, as she performs her final act.[20] Drawing a dagger from her dress, she plunges it into her neck,

MS Sybilla writhes slowly, her blood flowing from the wound and smearing her dress and face.
FS Sybilla staggers backwards (almost in slow motion) into silhouette against the backdrop, her figure joined with but separate from the piano player's dancing shadow.
FS The piano player dances on stage as the backdrop buckles and bulges slightly from the unseen Sybilla's weight.
MS Sybilla flails against the backdrop.
FS of the piano player dancing.
FS of Sybilla against the backdrop.
CU of an old woman asleep (sitting off to the side, backstage).
FS of Sybilla staggering forward from the backdrop and collapsing.
MCU of a woman laughing as she suckles a baby.
FS of Sybilla on the floor.
CU of the old woman awakening with a start.

This "dance of death" stunningly sums up both the gulf between Sybilla and the world around her as well her struggle with that world. And in this image of a man and woman conjoined as silhouettes through a screen—the one performing for an audience, the other in the throes of death—the nature of the struggle becomes violently, even perversely, sexual. An ironic peace comes at last in the final shots. In a FS of the backstage area (now in black/white),

312

Sybilla is laid out on the table, her head resting on a tambourine, before a group of mourners—the piano player, the old blind man, the old woman, and several other dancers. As the shot changes to MS, they all dissolve out and the word ELDORADO dissolves in, wavering in a ghostly arc over Sybilla, whose body finally fades out, leaving only the word—emptied out, marking the site of specific absence and, now, absolute loss.

Fièvre and La Femme de nulle part

In *J'Accuse, Rose-France*, perhaps *L'Homme du large*, and certainly *El Dorado*, Gance and L'Herbier had marked out a number of ways to break with and reconstitute the conventions of narrative film discourse. Quickly, other film-makers, notably Germaine Dulac and Louis Delluc, seized on their advances. Dulac's interest at this point seems to have been restricted to strategies that could prolong or displace the narrative action by redirecting its focus to the characters' inner experience. In *La Cigarette* (1919), for instance, according to Charles Ford, she had already "enveloped the protagonist [Signoret] in a po-etic, unreal atmosphere of soft-focus images whose delicacy of touch stunned all the cinéphiles [in the audience]."[1] In *La Mort du soleil* (1922), as I have shown, Dulac expressly wanted "to describe the inner workings of the mind or soul, within the theme of the action."[2] There she explored the subjective life of her two central characters, an aging doctor (André Nox) and his female research assistant (Denise Lorys), both separately and in conjunction with one another. The work of Louis Delluc, however, was even more innovative.

As evidenced by his film criticism during this period, Delluc was pushing the concept of *photogénie* toward a sketchy theory of cinematic denotation and connotation. Film was "a median term between stylization and reality;"[3] the film image functioned simultaneously on several levels of signification—it was both iconic and symbolic, transparent and transformed. The shaping of that signification came from its sequential "composition" with other images, or-ganized according to a central idea. Like his colleagues, Gance, L'Herbier, and Dulac, Delluc was later fond of describing this composition by means of an analogy then current, that of musical orchestration. Yet his own film prac-tice, which became the chief means to explore and validate his ideas, reveals instead an interest in what might be called lyrical composition, similar to metaphorical patterning in poetry. As one might expect, his films also evi-dence a fascination with the dramatic construction of the *découpage*. For Delluc, the recurrent idea structuring his work was "that confrontation between the present and the past, between reality and memory, articulated in images."[4] Much impressed by the alternation of parallel stories in Griffith's *Intolerance*, which he reviewed a half-dozen times in May and June of 1919, Delluc, like Gance, seems to have come up with the idea of intercutting antithetical or opposing stories (or lines of action) for other than strictly narrative purposes.[5]

Noting their simple, modest appearance, film historians and even his fellow filmmakers have tended to write patronizingly of Delluc's films: they reveal a superb scenarist but "not a man of the camera lens" (Georges Franju); they represent the "sketch of a cinematic *oeuvre* which he had neither the time nor the means to complete" (René Clair); they are "much inferior to that which he would have been able to realize, had he lived" (Georges Sadoul).[6] Yet despite their faults, Delluc's few films represent a major effort in the narrative

313

avant-garde film practice, and the highly original narrative structures of his scenarios constitute one of the most important syntheses of that practice. For Jean Epstein, "they represented perhaps the most original tendency in French cinema."[7]

Although he praised both *J'Accuse* and *Rose-France* in his 1919 *Paris-Midi* reviews, Delluc was troubled by the didacticism and technical lapses in Gance's film and by the *longueurs* and hesitations of the narrative in L'Herbier's.[8] Perhaps as a consequence, his first two short films (only two reels each) were quite different. His scenario for *La Fête espagnole* (1920), actually directed by Dulac, was brief, spare, unsentimental, and even brutal.[9] Two men in love with a bored young woman (Eve Francis) kill one another in a duel, while she gets caught up in the dancing of a local festival and, rejuvenated, impulsively gives herself to a third. At least two salient points can be gathered from the published scenario and the incomplete print of *La Fête espagnole* that survives.[10] First of all, from its beginning, much as in *J'Accuse*, the film works to document the ambiance of a particular milieu, a Spanish village on holiday; so that when the main characters are introduced, in Delluc's words, they seem "less presented than incorporated into the flow of picturesque events."[11] Had they been able to shoot on location in Spain as planned rather than in Nice, he, Dulac, and cameraman Paul Parguel would have turned the scenario into even more of a documentary: the woman's story would have been merely "one component of the Spanish festival, a sudden change in character without the least bit of prominence."[12] Secondly, the film interweaves a half-dozen different lines of action, setting up a rather complex paradigmatic narrative structure, somewhat akin to that of *Rose-France*.[13] In the end, the two major lines of action come to a climax simultaneously as the film intercuts the woman's ever more exhilarated dancing with the knife fight between her two suitors. In a stunning rhetorical conjunction, one fever seems to enflame the other in an ironic juxtaposition of "resurrection" and death. As Delluc himself noted, these "final images especially, in which the scenes of passion and pleasure alternate so rapidly with those of blood and death, [are] a strikingly successful example of the 'relative synchronism' offered by the cinema."[14]

Delluc's second film, *Le Silence* (1920), has not survived; but its published scenario suggests that it deserves a quick glance.[15] Its story may owe something to Jacques de Baroncelli's *Le Roi de la mer* (1918) which Delluc praised as an "interior story that never left a shipowner's office."[16] Here Pierre (Signoret) is alone in his apartment, awaiting his lover (Eve Francis). Suddenly, a chance comparison of letters makes him realize that, several years before, she was responsible for an anonymous letter that incited him to shoot his young wife, Aimée, (Ginette Darnys) and kill her. When the lover arrives, Pierre is dead in his chair, a victim of the same revolver. Unlike *La Fête espagnole*, the salient features of this film are a metamorphosizing pattern of rhetorical figuring and an unusually disjunctive narrative structure. The "dramatic theme" unfolds through the alternation of Pierre's memories and his perceptions of certain key objects in his possession—a revolver, a bed, two photographs, and several letters. These objects are isolated and intensified, especially through CUs (the cameraman was Louis Chaix), somewhat like the details in *J'Accuse* and *Rose-France*; but their significance shifts in conjunction with the series of memory flashbacks. For instance, the revolver turns into an instrument of self-destruction when it emerges from a kind of memory store, the same drawer that produced Aimée's photograph and letters. As Jean Epstein wrote of this, his favorite Delluc film, ". . . the lens . . . discovers in the simplest and most unlikely things a new dimension of inner dynamism, of symbolic truth, of dramatic conspiracy with the action."[17]

If Delluc's choice of objects and their melodramatic significance may be dated, the intricacy of the scenario's narrative structure still seems original. The eight flashbacks or imaginary sequences, most of them concentrated in the first two-thirds of the scenario, are organized in an achronological order that withholds the key revelatory moments from the past until the end. Furthermore, several of those sequences are themselves organized in a highly discontinuous manner. The second flashback, as it appears in the scenario, can stand as representative:

28 Present—Pierre in front of a bed.
29 Past[1]—FS of Pierre sick in the same bed, now in disorder.
30 Present—Pierre asks himself why he was there.
31 Past[3]—FS of Aimée ill in the same bed.
Intertitle—"Aimée"
32 Past[3]—MCU of Aimée ill in bed.
33 Past[5]—FS of Pierre and Aimée leaving a church in wedding clothes and laughing.
34 Past[4]—FS of Pierre and Aimée embracing at the rail of a ship on their honeymoon.
35 Past[2]—FS of Aimée dead in the same bed; Pierre kneels at the bedside.
36 Past[2]—MS of Pierre mad with grief, restrained by some doctors.
37 Present—Pierre smiles at the clock pendulum.[18]

In just eight (planned) shots, the film presents flackback within flashback within flashback, summarizing Pierre's life with Aimée by layering over their happiness with several different moments of loss and grief. As may be gathered from this brief excerpt, the elliptical, achronological organization within and between sequences in *Le Silence* seems astonishing for 1920. It turns what could be the exploration of a single character's psychological condition into an intellectual puzzle, a tightly knit narrative of knowing, a narrative of bitter revelations and ironic reversals.

Because no prints have survived intact, *La Fête espagnole* and *Le Silence* remain problematical film texts within the narrative avant-garde film practice. There is no question, however, about the position of Delluc's first nearly feature-length film, *Fièvre* (1921).[19] *Fièvre* was made from an original scenario, but it drew heavily on several sources: on Antoine's theatre of naturalism and on a number of the cinéaste's favorite American films—particularly William S. Hart's westerns (the saloon became a waterfront bistro; the hero was called "the man with clear eyes"; HALs were used to encompass the full decor of the bistro) and D. W. Griffith's *Broken Blossoms* (the Oriental character, the waterfront milieu).[20] Delluc had wanted to shoot the film on location in Marseille, but lack of money confined him to Gaumont's Paris studio, where Léon Poirier was lucky to wrangle him an eight-day production schedule, in February, 1921.[21] The first four days were devoted to rehearsing and constructing the bistro set (designed by the young painter, Francis Jourdain); only the last four days were given to shooting (with Gibory and Lucas, L'Herbier's chief cam-

154. Beçan's poster for *Fièvre* (1921)

eraman). Unable to afford enough professional actors, he let one of the film's sponsors, Elena Sagrary, play a major role and called on his friends for the secondary parts—Footit (the famous clown, who died two weeks later), Léon Moussinac and his wife, Noemi Scize, and others.[22] When previewed for the critics, *Fièvre* was accompanied by a much touted piano score—"lively, rhythmic, by turns tender and passionate"—improvised by another friend, young Jean Wiener.[23] Unfortunately, when the film was finally released in November, 1921, more conventional music was used instead.

Fièvre's apparent subject can be gathered from its original title, *La Boue* (dregs or lower depths), which offended the censors. All the action takes place within a few hours one evening in a rundown waterfront bistro in old Marseille. After the local inhabitants of the bistro have been situated, a group of sailors just back from the Far East come in, among them Militis (Van Daële), whose former fiancée, Sarah (Eve Francis), is now wife and barmaid to the bistro owner, Topinelli (Gaston Modot). With him is an Oriental woman (Elena Sagrary), whom he married after she helped him recover from a long illness. The old passion between Militis and Sarah is rekindled as they dance together; but it arouses the jealousy of a petty clerk who loves her and who has been humiliated earlier. He alerts Topinelli, and a fight breaks out be-

155. (left) The opening shot of the harbor in *Fièvre* (1921)

156. (right) The opening shot of the bistro interior

tween the sailor and barowner. While Militis is overpowering Topinelli, the clerk knocks him out with a bottle, after which Topinelli finishes him off by stepping on his neck. The other sailors attack the two men and carry off Topinelli before the police arrive. Sarah, ironically, is accused of Militis's death, and the Oriental woman is left alone by the bar with a flower which had earlier captivated her. Only now does she discover it is artificial—a crucial irony that is almost lost in the titleless American print of the film.

Film critics at the time were struck by the sympathetic, even loving, attention to the milieu, the atmosphere, in *Fièvre*. Perhaps Léon Moussinac sums up this attitude best:

Fièvre, which develops in a unique decor—a sailor's bar in Marseille, whose character is revealed in a series of quick shots—proves that to make "cinema" it is not indispensable that one carry a camera to extraordinary places and that, from faces and gestures, from expressive movements in a completely integrated decor, one can produce emotional effects of real power . . . even poetry. . . .[24]

Despite its studio production, the film works from the beginning to create a realistic image of the Marseille waterfront and of the kinds of people who inhabit it, at first simply by intercutting documentary shots of the harbor with sequences of the studio-constructed bistro. Once within the bistro itself, however, a series of slice-of-life sketches introduce the characters and their attitudes succinctly—the play of looks among the men over a game of cards, Sarah's resigned exhaustion as she cleans up the bartop, the petty clerk's timid desire in following her to the wine cellar. Through this process of accumulation, the romantic intrigue seems to evolve out of the milieu itself. The development of the intrigue, however, as in the *Kammerspiel* scenarios of Carl Mayer—Lulu Pick's *Shattered* (1921) and *Sylvester* (1923)—of which Delluc was unaware, is more complex than one might at first expect.[25]

On one hand, the film pits the powerful against the powerless, the ignoble (those tied to a petit-bourgeois psychology of possession and jealousy) against

317

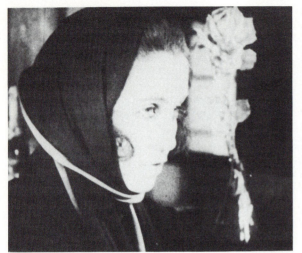

157. (left) Patience (Solange Rugiens) and the flower on the bar

158. (right) Sarah (Eve Francis) on the other side of the bar

the noble (those invested with subjectivity and the feelings of desire)—with predictable results. On the other hand, it relies on a schematic series of structural repetitions and displacements, on a configuration of looks and subjective inserts (articulating the course of desire), and on a related pattern of associations between certain characters and metonymized/metaphorized elements of the decor.[26] The latter two are especially worth examining closely together for they constitute an important effort to poeticize, to comment on, and, ultimately, to critique the narrative.

From its opening shots, *Fièvre* puts two spaces in juxtaposition, the harbor exterior and the bistro interior, in a series of alternating sequences. Within the closed, settled interior world, a diegetic process begins to develop. The character of Sarah is described as the object of Topinelli's gaze, a gaze defined (in an intertitle) as possession. Sarah's own look, which does not return his (instead she pours herself a shot of gin), is isolated, in stasis, neither desiring not desired, yet denying possession. While she remains at the bar, several other objects of the decor, besides the gin bottle and glass, come into association with her. Behind her on the wall are several posters with pictures of ships, advertising voyages to foreign lands (Brazil, Indochina). The posters confirm the position of the bistro within the space of the harbor, but they also function as corollaries of that other, exterior world. The second object is a single white flower in a vase sitting on the bar. Sarah sniffs at if briefly and then dismisses it with a gesture of scorn—what is the significance that her gestures give and then take away? The connotation of the posters and the enigma of the flower are placed in conjunction with the figure of Sarah and perhaps in opposition to the enclosed male group at the card table.

The alternating series of exterior/interior sequences begins to shift through the entrance of a young woman, Patience (Solange Rugiens), who is connected (through the editing and through her momentary placement outside) to that other world of the harbor. Positioned across the bar from Sarah, with the white

318

flower between them, Patience speaks of waiting for her sailor lover to return. Her gaze off, past Sarah, is a look of desire without an object—or, rather, a look of desire awaiting its object to materialize, to be fulfilled. Through its repeated privileged position in the CUs of Patience, the flower becomes a metonymic extension of her condition and acquires its first definite connotation, which, read backwards, places Sarah clearly in the same paradigm as her opposite. She who desires and she who denies desire (as well as possession) face one another across the flower that conjoins them.

Patience's appearance produces two further changes in the series of exterior/interior alternations. Two tracking shots of the harbor (previously described in stationary shots—like the posters) yield to a third shot of a ship moving over the water. The last shot arouses the expectation of an arrival; and, coming as it does after a CU of Patience and her intertitle on waiting, it raises questions about return, restoration, and fulfillment of her desire. The following shots—a CU of Sarah, an intertitle cynically remarking on her own past love, and a subjective insert—form an exact parallel with Patience's, but with an important difference. Though her gestures and the intertitle would seem to deny it, Sarah's past desire erupts, unexpectedly materializing in an image of herself and a sailor lover—a look, a touch, and an abundance of flowers. The exterior world of the harbor and this memory of past desire are linked in a simple equation or displacement. As the subject of desire shifts from Patience to Sarah, the shot of the ship, read backwards, raises a new possibility: is it perhaps Sarah's denial that will be answered with the return of the once desired? In the paradigmatic relations between a memory, a ship's movement in the harbor, two women's looks, and a flower, the subject of desire—and its object, somewhere in the harbor or beyond—has become active in the bistro world.[27]

From here on, the exterior and interior worlds begin to converge. After a brief sequence of docking and arrival, the sailors enter the bistro, soon followed by a group of prostitutes. In HALSs, the sailors and prostitutes take over the foreground area and begin to interact, while beyond them the bistro regulars continue their ritual—except for Patience, who has left, and Sarah, who has gone to fetch wine from the cellar. The separateness of these two worlds, which has pervaded the film from the start, is now inscribed in the distinction between foreground and background groups, setting up a tension within the room.

The development of that tension into conflict is articulated in several different ways. One simply extends the foreground/background distinctions to an extreme (perhaps as an expedient answer to the question of how to film such a large number of actors, on a single set, within such a short shooting schedule). As Georges Sadoul first noted,[28] the film employs the HALS as a means of allowing two or more simultaneous actions in different planes to unfold independently, whether in conjunction or in juxtaposition. The tension reaches its climax in the sequence where four separate actions are going on simultaneously in the depth of the frame: the sailors and prostitutes dancing, the cardplayer's drunken desire for the Oriental, Sarah and Militis's awakening love (in their movement from the foregound table to the dance floor), and the clerk's entreaties to the pipe woman and then his betrayal of the lovers to Topinelli. The gradual accumulation of spatial continuity and character rela-

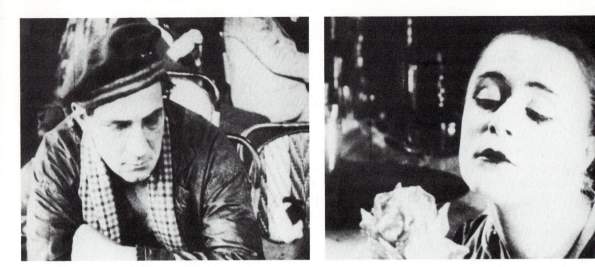

159. (left) Militis (Van Daële) sitting at a table

160. (right) The Oriental woman (Elena Sagrary) and the flower at the end of *Fièvre* (1921)

tions reaches a visual density here that parallels the dramatic tension. Each breaks when the fight erupts into two major conflicts—Militis versus Topinelli and then Sarah and the prostitutes versus the Oriental (the latter fight was reduced in the final print by the censors)—each of which is resolved in separate, but intercut, areas of the bistro.

A second articulation of this conflict appears in a further subjective eruption. After the former lovers recognize one another, Sarah moves away until the sailors and prostitutes begin to dance; then she returns to Militis, who has remained seated alone at the foreground table (though the Oriental is visible below the table to the left). To her accusation, "We loved one another, I waited for you," he seems to make no response; but then, bracketed by a MCU and punctuated by fades, comes a subjective insert that parallels Sarah's. Now it is Militis's past desire which erupts—in the same flower-laden space, he reaches out and embraces her. As he tells her of his fever in the Orient, a series of flashbacks narrate his illness (and loss of desire), his recovery attended by the Oriental, and his subsequent marriage to her, a marriage of sacrifice and repayment. The return of his past desire (for Sarah) is balanced, even outweighed, by the memory of its loss and a subsequent indebtedness (to the Oriental). This conflict is incorporated into the diegesis of the bistro as the sequence cuts steadily away from a MCU to a HALS of Militis positioned between the Oriental and Sarah. Despite his proximity to the Oriental, he decides against her, leaving the table to dance with Sarah. In the bistro milieu—with both lovers married to others—how can this reawakened desire be fulfilled?

The final articulation is primarily rhetorical and involves the Oriental in relation to Sarah and the flower on the bar. The Oriental enters the film doubly marked. On the one hand, her appearance, briefly noticed when the sailors take over the bistro's foreground table, coincides with Patience's departure. Her displacement of Patience, the film's initial subject of desire, is thus pre-

320

figured from the start. On the other hand, she is introduced as the last of the booty, a standard racial stereotype. Although identified as Militis's wife, she is an object of possession, and her placement echoes Sarah's initial introduction. She, too, is in stasis, neither desiring nor desired, and seeming to deny possession. Her relation to Sarah, as rival and double, can also be read in the figure of the French woman's reawakening desire. When Sarah positioned herself unknowingly behind Militis, she had dressed herself in a robe and parasol from among the sailor's exotic possessions. The shock of recognizing Militis makes her drop that guise and back away to position herself at the bar in a new replication of the image of Patience beside the flower. This transformation of one figure into another—emphasized by the repeated tight placement of Sarah next to the flower and close to the background voyage posters—throws her poetic status into relief and makes it seem more real.

Although introduced as the last in a series of objects, the Oriental woman, in the next sequence, is suddenly privileged with subjectivity; and her look now reorders the space of the bistro. In a new series of alternations, the bistro regulars become pitiable and insignificant objects under her gaze. But at the end of the series comes an iris-masked image of the flower on the bar, and her face brightens. The flower, which has been linked metonymically to Patience and Sarah (as subjects of desire), now itself becomes the object of desire (for the Oriental). Thus in the flower is a circle of desire, the recurrence of subject and object, doubly inscribed. A double trajectory of desire—the one metaphorically parallel to the other—has erupted into the world of the bistro and threatens to subvert or escape it. Although the sequence ends with a rhetorical question, "What is this flower?" the intertitle opening the next sequence augurs an answer: "Drunkenness." The fever of desire—is it really so different from the fever of drunkenness?

In the final sequence of *Fièvre*, that other drunkenness emerges from several points within the room as a counterthreat. Steadily, through intercutting and placement within the frame, the bistro regulars encroach upon the Oriental's movement toward the flower as well as upon the lovers' embrace and plan to escape. Here, admittedly, the film becomes awkward. In order to balance these parallel lines of action or the relationship between a diegetic and metaphoric space/time,[29] the Oriental's progress has to be delayed. As a consequence, she is reduced to crawling so slowly across the floor that the metaphorical function of her movement is almost compromised. Eventually, in an ironic juxtaposition, Militis leaves Sarah to protect the Oriental from the drunken advances of a cardplayer, and Topinelli steps in to confront him—masking his jealousy of Sarah with an accusation of Militis's brutality toward women. After the fight that ensues, Sarah is left kneeling over the dead Militis while, behind her, the dazed Oriental finally reaches the flower at the bar.

In the final shots, the parallel trajectories of the two women converge in a double negation. As Sarah gazes down on Militis, so does the Oriental gaze down at the flower in her hands. Two looks are placed in conjunction—a look of rediscovered loss and a look of discovery (of what?). The Oriental and flower now assume a foregrounded position as the police lead Sarah off—her head down, her figure framed in a background window. The more primary, narrative trajectory of desire fades away to leave the secondary, the metaphorical. The intertitle, "Nothing but an artificial flower," closes off the signification

161. (left) Beçan's poster for
La Femme de nulle part (1922)

162. (right) Eve Francis on
the road

of the flower as the Oriental lowers it in disillusionment (her position by the bar repeats, in reverse, the earlier positions of Patience and Sarah). Although the narrative seems to argue that desire is negated by the milieu, this final figure suggests something more. Not only does the flower function as a false or deceptive object, but metonymically it attaches that falseness to the desiring subject as well. As a final statement of the discourse, the figure of the Oriental and flower thus produces an ironic critique. Working and reworking the image of the flower through the looks and positions of three women, *Fièvre* has transformed the eruption of desire into loss, into absence, and placed desire itself in question. The film's strategy is complete—to diegeticize and critique the circle of desire.

After *Fièvre* gained some critical notoriety in France, if not much financial remuneration, Delluc determined to get even closer to real life by shooting his next film on location. *Le Chemin d'Ernoa* (1921) gave him the opportunity to work in a landscape he loved and considered ideal for filming, the border country of the Lower Pyrénées, where Jacques de Baroncelli had filmed *Ramuntcho* (1919). The scenario is a bit complicated.[30] The main plot involves Etchegor (Durec) and his relations with an American couple in Ernoa: he reluctantly escorts the husband (who is wanted for a bank robbery) across the border and later has to watch the wife (Eve Francis) cross over as well, after she has refused to stay behind with him. In conjunction with this intrigue, Etchegor also protects two Spanish refugees (a sister and brother) who have

322

worked for the Americans and who are unjustly implicated in the robbery. Here Delluc returned to the original plans he had conceived for *La Fête espagnole*—to deemphasize the complicated narrative and give prominence to describing and celebrating "the countryside, nature, by giving it the dominant role."[31] Although he himself considered the film a failure (perhaps because of its miniscule budget and his inexperience at location shooting), certain sequences attest to his skill (and that of his cameraman Gibory) in creating some kind of accord or resonance between character and landscape.[32] Especially notable are the opening sequence of Etchegor's walk through the village and the ending diminuendo into separate long-shot tableaux: the wife walking alone on the road, Etchegor standing alone beside his car, the refugees waiting at a tiny train station, a horse cart (into which the wife has stepped) traveling away from the camera along a river road, and Etchegor and the refugees walking slowly back through the empty village street.

Delluc's next-to-last film was much more successful in the way its narrative structure deftly and consistently conjoined landscape and character, the documentary and the subjective, the present and the past. But the aesthetic integration came at a heavy cost. Previewed in the spring and again in the summer of 1922, *La Femme de nulle part* had such a poor distribution during the fall season that its commercial failure crippled Delluc financially.[33]

Although set in the plains above Genoa in northern Italy, *La Femme de nulle part* was shot (by Gibory and Lucas again) in the region of Arles and the Camargue, where several provincial realist films had been produced the year before. The title is a homage to William S. Hart—*L'Homme de nulle part* (*The Silent Stranger*, 1915).[34] As in the American film, the main character comes out of a barren landscape, encounters a human dilemma, tries to resolve it, suffers, and returns whence she came. Delluc himself wrote of it:

A ravaged older woman, near the end of her life, makes a last pilgrimage to the house that she left, to her misfortune, thirty years before; she discovers there a young woman in the same situation that she had been in as well as the memory of her happiest moments, and she does not regret having paid so harshly for such fleeting happiness.[35]

But that is only half the story. The older woman, "L'Inconnue" (Eve Francis), arrives at the villa one morning just as the present man of the house (Roger Karl) is leaving on an overnight business trip to Genoa. His young wife (Gine Avril) meets her lover (André Daven) that evening and must decide by morning whether or not to leave her husband and small child. Reveling in her memories of past love in the gardens, the older woman persuades the younger to escape as she once did. But at the last moment, the wife hesitates over her child and stays to greet her husband's return, while the older woman goes off instead, saddened and alone.

In contrast to *Fièvre*, *La Femme de nulle part* situates its characters, not so much in a social milieu, but in a natural, unpeopled landscape (much like the Swedish films and American westerns Delluc so admired). Besides investing the diegesis with a kind of realism, the landscape articulates certain oppositions in the narrative which produce "a deep accord . . . between characters and actors." Particular images sum up this opposition quite clearly. When the older woman approaches the villa, she comes as a lone black figure on a white stone road that stretches away across flat, barren fields under a bleak sky. As in the famous white wall shot in *El Dorado*, the bleakness and loneliness of the landscape are projected onto the central character. In the harsh morning light, the open grounds and large empty house produce similar conditions and seem to threaten the young family she visits. The night sequences in the gardens, however, suggest an escape from or possible transformation of those conditions. The soft hazy light, the trees and small pavilion, the figures of the lovers (both present and past)—all conspire to produce a fragile image of an oasis or paradise. Yet the image is ever so slightly undermined by shots of the older woman walking beside a stagnant pool or past huge plane trees as the wind blows dry leaves along the ground. In the final sequences, the harsh light of day returns, and the older woman departs into the same monotonous landscape, unable—contra Chaplin—to transcend her despair. The last shot (filmed from the same distance and angle) confirms the unchanged nature of her psychological or mental condition.

La Femme du nulle part relies much more on this pattern of landscape juxtapositions than on the multiple signification of privileged objects, as in *Le Silence* and *Fièvre*. Yet Delluc does not abandon the latter practice, as evidenced in the use of objects associated with the child. After establishing shots of the road and house, an interior shot of the gate introduces the first movement in the film—a large inflated ball rolls past the camera and toward the gate, which the child quickly follows. This movement is repeated a short time later and brings the child to the gate just as the older woman arrives. At first, the ball is merely a charming detail; but it also introduces that movement toward the gate and beyond which will define the older woman's past action as well as the younger woman's present desire. In fact, at the end the child will run to the gate after her mother and bring her back to the house in a poignant echo of the way she leads the older woman up the path to the house in the beginning. Just before leaving, the older woman faces the child again (separated from the others, they are intercut several times), but now she is holding a puppet given to her by her father. As an unobtrusive replacement for the ball, the puppet is rhetorically suggestive, but ambiguous. Stationary, inanimate, yet "humanized," does it comment on the child (who has just saved her mother and preserved the family), does it foreshadow a second child to come, or does it suggest the young woman's acceptance of her condition?

As in Delluc's previous films, memory serves both as a psychological motivation for the central character and as a major force structuring the narrative. Since the older woman alone is privileged with memory (except for two shots assigned to the young wife), we experience the major portion of the film as determined by her presence, which is itself determined by her past.[36] When she first arrives at the villa and explores its rooms, brief images from her past life well up—the house as it once was, her enigmatic meeting and going off with a man. When, from the window of her second-floor bedroom, she sees the young woman reading a letter stealthily plucked from the garden steps, suddenly she remembers—a furtive man glimpsed earlier near the road and an image of herself reading a similar letter of passion at that very table. That evening she warns the young woman not to go away foolishly as she once did. But in the garden at night, her memories of past happiness there overwhelm her, climaxing in a shot of the two lovers that dissolves into one of herself and her lover in the same position and place thirty years before. Delirious with her rediscovered passion, in the morning she presses the young woman "to seize the happiness that life offers. . . . What does sadness matter, if one has experienced a moment of infinite joy? . . ." When the young woman decides to stay, the older woman's passion ebbs and her images of the past cease altogether.

In terms of its orchestration of simultaneous action in different spaces and times, *La Femme de nulle part* also seems closer to *La Fête espagnole* than it does to either *Le Silence* or *Fièvre*. The family and the two outsider characters who will act on the young wife are introduced succinctly and intercut smoothly. Before the older woman has even reached the villa, the film has suggested the gulf between husband and wife, not only through slight gestures, but by cutting from the husband alone packing in his bedroom to the older woman on the road as she notices the waiting lover. After the husband has left, the two women are presented in a series of alternating sequences that begin to establish their parallel stories. During the long night section of the film, the intercutting becomes rather complex as the film integrates at least four different lines of action, both in conjunction and opposition: the young wife's rendezvous in the garden and return to her room, the older woman's wanderings in the garden and return to her room, the memory of her own rendezvous with her lover in the past, and the husband's activities in the port of Genoa.

The Genoa sequences produce a fascinating counterpoint to the other three, the more so because they do not appear in the published scenario. At the moment the older woman goes to leave her room and the two lovers embrace in the garden, the husband rows out (on business) to a freighter in the harbor (reversing the connotation of the harbor in *Fièvre*). After the older woman has returned to the house and found the wife and child asleep, the husband is shown walking alone down a steep alley and into a crowded café where a party is going on. As the older woman debates whether to awaken the young woman, the husband angrily rejects a woman who has approached him at the bar, and he goes off alone down the alley. Immediately thereafter, the older woman is shown still dreaming of her former love and deciding to help the young woman flee. This counterpoint may at first seem morally conventional (the self-denying man versus the indulgent woman), but the mise-en-scène of the shots (natural decor, lighting, and framing) suggests something quite different. The LS of the small boat in the open water before the huge dark freighter, the LS of the narrow alley down which the husband walks between sharply etched blocks of buildings, and especially the LALS of clothes drying high up in a courtyard—all have overtones of emptiness and loneliness. Since these are being projected onto the character of the husband, his emotional state is not unlike that of the older woman at the beginning.

If these sequences draw attention to the husband in a way that is dramatically unsatisfied at the end—he returns home to find matters already decided—that is because the rhetorical function of their description is more pertinent.[37] In this, the Genoa sequences are similar to those with the Oriental and flower in *Fièvre*. By re-creating a human condition represented initially by the older woman, they undermine or call into question the reality or validity of the parallel garden sequences. Are these paradisical images (whether actual or memory) no more than delusions or fantasies? Like *Fièvre*, the film seems to raise the specter of love and fulfilled desire, only to deny its possibility.

325

But here that denial is articulated quietly, simply, emphasizing the rhetorical over the narrative, but integrating them together smoothly. After the young woman turns back to her child, there is little in the mise-en-scène, gestures, or dialogue to suggest any change in her relationship with her husband. Is she really any more happy or secure than if she had gone away? The last shots nearly repeat the beginning as the family stands reunited in front of the house while the lover and the older woman depart simultaneously but separately. The irony is almost cruel—instead of having the joy of seeing the two lovers re-create her story, she must herself repeat her past escape into a landscape of permanent exile, now more than ever fixed in her own loneliness and despair.

La Roue

Perched on a chair in the Spartan surroundings of the Centre Universitaire International in Paris, Jean Dréville grew more and more animated as he recalled the 1922 premiere of Abel Gance's *La Roue*. The entire film took three days to be projected, three consecutive Thursday mornings in December. Seven thousand people had been invited, and the nearly 6,000 seats at the Gaumont-Palace were jampacked. At the end of the third day, the audience burst into applause and rose from their seats in a wave. The applause went on and on. No one wanted to leave even though the huge cinema was none too comfortable—one could still catch the odor of horse droppings from the time when it had been a circus. Finally, a man came on stage carrying a megaphone and ordered the last reel to be projected again. The lights went down, and the rapt audience relived Sisif's death and the peasant's spring dance in the mountain snowfields. Once more the applause broke out. That had never happened before and never did again, said Dréville. "It was like a thunderclap!"[1]

Dréville's excitement, across nearly sixty years, is marvelous evidence of the response that *La Roue* provoked in its time. No film since De Mille's *The Cheat*, not even L'Herbier's *El Dorado*, had so stunned the French filmmakers, critics, and cinéphiles. Jean Cocteau supposedly even went so far as to mark off "a cinema before and after *La Roue*."[2] Such superlatives are not easy for us to understand now—for several reasons. Nor can we accept them, I think, without some qualifications. Whatever those qualifications, however, Gance's film still fascinates us, almost as much as it did that Paris audience sixty years ago. But our fascination is held now by the film's contradictions, by the conflicting demands of representation and expression that push the text toward incoherence, and by the structural designs that shape it, even roughly, into coherence.

In Emile Vuillermoz's words, "*La Roue* begins in the tragic melancholy of the coal dust and smoke and [in the end] attains the peace and purity of eternal snows."[3] Between these two sites and conditions, however, sprawls a lamentably melodramatic "shaggy dog" story. Sisif (Séverin-Mars) is a top locomotive engineer headquartered in Nice; he is widowed, with a young son, Elie (Gabriel de Gravone), and "daughter," Norma (Ivy Close), an orphaned girl he found in a train wreck. The children grow up unaware of their real relation, and Sisif falls in love with his grown "daughter." To rid himself of temptation and guilt (once he tries to commit suicide), he finally agrees to let one of the rich railway administrators, Hersan (Pierre Magnier), marry Norma, even though she dislikes him. On the way to the wedding, Sisif becomes obsessed and tries to kill himself and Norma by wrecking the train; but his fireman, Machefer (George Teroff), averts the accident. Elie (now a violin-maker) discovers the truth about Norma and accuses his father of destroying his own love for her. Shortly after, Sisif is nearly blinded in a locomotive steam-valve accident, and he tries to kill himself again by wrecking his locomotive. He survives, however, and is reduced to driving the funicular railway on Mont Blanc. Elie joins him and one day sees Norma at a nearby resort (where one of his violins is being used in a concert). His passion rekindled, Elie sends her a love letter, which Hersan discovers. He challenges Elie, and the two men fight in the mountains: Hersan is shot, and Elie falls to his death just as Norma runs up to the rocky point from which he is suspended. Alone now in his mountain cabin, Sisif goes completely blind, and Norma moves in with him, although she keeps her presence secret from him for a while. Peace finally comes to them, and one spring evening the local people invite Norma to join their annual farandole for the festival of Saint Jean. Sitting in the window, Sisif dies quietly, listening to the dancers circling in the snow.

One of our difficulties with *La Roue* is that, like Gance's *Napoléon* (at least until recently), it has come down to us in shortened, mutilated versions. At its premiere and general release (in February, 1923), the film was thirty-two reels long, or 10,500 to 11,000 meters, and ran for almost nine hours.[4] It was divided into a prologue and three parts: "Un Crépuscule écarlate," "La Rose du Rail," "La Mort du Norma Compound," and "La Tragédie de Sisif."[5] Although this complete print no longer exists, the Soviet filmmakers (Eisenstein, Pudovkin, Dovzhenko, Ekk), according to Kevin Brownlow, told Gance that they had learned their craft by studying it at the Moscow Academy.[6] Apparently, Charles Pathé also asked Gance to edit a condensed version of the film, in fourteen reels or 4,200 meters, which premiered at the Colisée cinema in February, 1924, and then was distributed elsewhere.[7] Four years later, Pathé-Consortium re-released this condensed version or perhaps even a third version, following the European triumph of *Napoléon*.[8] These shorter versions, as well as the 17.5mm copy produced by Pathé-Baby, seem to explain why there are very different prints preserved in the Cinémathèque française (Georges Sadoul says their print was acquired in 1937), the Museum of Modern Art in New York (their print is drawn from the National Film Archive print), the George Eastman House, the State Historical Society of Wisconsin, and Em Gee Film Library.[9]

Another difficulty for us is that a significant personal context, well-known at the time, has long since been forgotten. For *La Roue* was completed against great odds, in the face of personal tragedy. While preparing the film, Gance learned that his young wife, Ida Danis, after surviving the influenza epidemic in Paris that followed the war, had contracted tuberculosis. So that she could have the advantage of the Mediterranean climate, Gance changed his film's setting from Paris to Nice and then rewrote the scenario again to move his crew to the French Alps, when doctors disclosed that her only chance of recovery was in the rarefied mountain air. There was no hope, however, and she died the very day Gance finished shooting the film, 9 April 1921. During the shooting, Séverin-Mars, his chief actor and close friend, also became seriously ill, though he kept working. He, too, died shortly after the film was edited. Probably because of these personal losses, the film seems literally obsessed with death. During this period, Gance has confessed, two other close friends sustained him—Blaise Cendrars, who again worked as an assistant director, and Arthur Honegger, who arranged the film's musical score.[10] Whether it was the suffering Gance endured or the internal problems wracking Pathé-Consortium that kept the film from being released for over a year is still not clear. But for French audiences in 1922-1923, La Roue's ending was taken as an indirect tribute to Gance's young wife (through Norma's assimilation into the dance in the snow) and as a literal record of Séverin-Mars's dying.

Despite La Roue's immediate acceptance, in France, as a benchmark in the history of the cinema, nearly everyone found some fault with the sprawling epic. Léon Moussinac drew up a list of "all that . . . is insupportable or even odious: the confusion of symbols, the exaggeration of effects, the forced excess of the images, the literary intertitles which did not work in the context of the visual eruptions, the extreme bad taste. . . ."[11] Most film reviewers, such as René Clair and Vuillermoz, reduced these reproaches to 1) an overly melodramatic scenario with "long, slow passages," a "superficial psychology," and "ridiculous puppet figures"; and 2) "chapter" quotations drawn from a bewildering variety of literary texts: Sophocles, Omar Khayyám, Pascal, Chamfort, Shelley, Byron, Baudelaire, Hugo, Kipling, Zola, D'Annunzio, Claudel, Pierre Hamp, Cendrars, and Canudo.[12] Commercial considerations—the need to make a popular film—were responsible for the first, they thought; the second was merely a misguided attempt at high seriousness. Yet in an interview with Jean Mitry, in 1924, Gance defended himself and the film on both counts—they were personal choices.[13] Whatever the case, separating the melodramatic story from spectacular climaxes and extraordinary lyrical moments—as was done at the time and is usually done still in film histories and auteur studies—does little more than simplify La Roue's contradictions. The matter is a bit more complex if one looks at the textual operation of the film from a number of different perspectives.

To begin with, La Roue is predicated on not one but several competing conceptions of film then emerging in France. In part, it depends on a half-sketched realist film aesthetic developed, just after the war, by André Antoine, Louis Delluc, and others. Perhaps the closest Gance comes to producing this kind of realism is in the early segments of the film, shot by his favorite cameraman, L. H. Burel, in the Gare Saint Roch railyards near Nice.[14] Sisif's house, for instance, is squeezed into a tiny, fenced-in plot between a main rail line and several switching tracks, so that locomotives are either constantly steaming past (and rustling the window curtains) or being worked on in the background. The figures of Sisif, Norma, Elie, and others seem small and vulnerable, especially in long shots, in a barren habitat more suited to the huge mechanical creatures and their cargoes. Norma and Elie's play takes them over the coal piles, around the tenders, and into the repair pits—where once, to Elie's horror, Norma ducks down at the last minute as a locomotive passes over her. As he ponders what to do with his adopted daughter, Sisif wanders off more and more frequently alone, his sadness projected into the empty spaces of the yards and the long lines of the rails.

Pushed to an extreme, certain of these moments seem to realize in practice a very different aesthetic, the embryonic aesthetic of a pure cinema, first ar-

ticulated in France by Leopold Survage, Marcel Gromaire, and others.[15] In brief, this aesthetic privileged the film medium's graphic and rhythmic relations and the formal strategies that might structure those relations. Sometimes in *La Roue*, the machines of the railyards—the locomotives, their dials and levers, their pistons and wheels and blasts of steam, the control shack instruments, the rail switches and signals—almost seemed animated with a life of their own. Orchestrated across a montage of shots, the rhythm of these mechanical elements produced what Fernand Léger (in a famous essay based on the first part of the film) called "plastic compositions" more or less independent of the diegesis.[16] In other words, they were ruptures of nonrepresentational patterning in the film's more conventional representational discourse. "For the first time on the screen," wrote Moussinac,

we have seen an artist, with original and essentially cinematographic means, mold a new material whose photogenic qualities are clearly apparent: the mechanical world of iron and steam, of rails and smoke, of wheels and manometers, of connecting rods and regulators, of signals and switches, order and accuracy, desire and love.[17]

To cinéphiles, such as Léger, Ricciotto Canudo, Jean Tedesco, Germaine Dulac, René Clair, and others, these were the most interesting passages of the film. And they were singled out for projection in excerpt form—as "La Chanson du Rail" and "La Danse des Roues"—at the 1923 Salon d'Automne exhibition and at a special C.A.S.A. public screening in April, 1924.[18] As I noted earlier, this selection of excerpts from *La Roue*, along with Jean Epstein's *Photogénies*, helped stimulate the avant-garde production of short non-narrative films—e.g., Léger's *Ballet mécanique* (1924), Clair's *Entr'acte* (1924), Autant-Lara's *Fait-Divers* (1924), and Chomette's *Jeaux de reflets et de la vitesse* (1925).

Besides this concern for documenting real spaces and for constructing "plastic compositions," the film also drew on Pierre Hamp's *Le Rail* (the proletarian novel on which Gance based part of his scenario) to produce a realism that depended on the social ambiance of the railway workers' world.[19] Probably the

165. (left to right) Norma (Ivy Close) framed in the doorway [between Elie and Hersan] in *La Roue* (1922-1923); Hersan framed by imaginary images of wealth; Norma framed in the mirror after shutting the door on Hersan

best example of this proletarian milieu is the engineers' café, "L'Horloge des gueules noirs" (The Coal Miners' Clock). Their world is summed up in the first shot of the café interior—a long dolly shot that begins on Sisif sleeping in a corner and draws back along the length of the bar to a number of tables where the men, all of them begrimed with dirt and coal dust, are drinking and playing cards. The engineers and stokers who frequent the café make an odd mixture of types and caricatures, quite similar to those in Eisenstein's early films. There is a quiet, mousey runt, in a rumpled suit and crushed hat (with a scraggly beard, one blind eye, and tiny spectacles), who keeps a record of the men's drinking habits for the railway company. Opposite him is the enormous, chubby-cheeked bartender who crawls out of a trapdoor in the floor (knocking over a man sleeping on a chair) with a half-dozen wine bottles in his huge arms. His equal is the jolly giant of an engineer who swills mugs of beer while prancing nimbly around the café tables. There is a long-faced, balding old man who can hardly see anymore, but who reads the men's palms. Then there is the brutish, smooth-faced fellow who cheats at cards and who ridicules Sisif, now sitting dazedly in the corner, as a barroom Christ (because of the light from a window glowing behind his head). Finally, there is Machefer, Sisif's wiry little stoker, who, in between pulls on his wine bottle, keeps reading at *La Vierge du trottoir*. To make certain that this part of the film was as authentic as possible, despite this typecasting, Gance had it projected, in rough cut, to special audiences of the Fédération des cheminots and then made several revisions, according to their reactions.[20]

Even more prominent than this social realism, however, is a concern for the subjective or psychological, a commitment to the aesthetic that sought to represent and celebrate the inner life of characters. Perhaps unexpectedly, this offers one of the best measures of *La Roue*'s paradoxical nature. Frankly, sometimes Gance's handling of the subjective is nothing short of pedestrian. Elie, for instance, envisions an imaginary world for himself and Norma that looks strangely like a prewar cliché: a medieval cottage where he prospers making

330

musical instruments and a nearby garden where she walks among doves and roses. Much later, at a window in the mountain cabin, Norma appears to him as a superimposition from which he recoils in horror. Unfortunately, we accept her image, not as an object of desire or temptation, but as an image of suffering; and his gesture appalls. A very different superimposition of Norma appears earlier, after she has married Hersan. To compensate for her loss, Sisif names his locomotive after her (tacking up her nameplate in the cab), and Norma's smiling face races, unblemished, in the smoke streaming from its stack.

Yet, at other times, the subjective is articulated, as Gance himself believed, with freshness and psychological nuance.[21] The sequence where Norma and Elie play in the railyards, for instance, ends with him pulling her about on a coal shovel. The joy she can find in this oppressive life is conveyed in several dollying shots of her, crouched on the moving shovel, waving and laughing as if she were speeding along on a snowsled. Later her dilemma of choosing between Elie and Hersan is intensified by positioning her (strongly backlit) in a doorframe. She looks off to the left foreground, and there is a cut to Elie munching on bread and water as he toils over a violin. As she turns to look back through the door, there is a cut to Hersan seen from behind—and images of jewelry, cars, clothes, money, and rich foods fade in around him in a dazzling halo. She turns again and leans back, closing the door; and the quiet despair in her face is reflected in the fragment of a broken mirror (frame left). In the mountain cabin, Norma's near-starvation is even more simply conveyed in the alternation of just two shots—a close-up of her gaunt, bedraggled face and another close-up of her hands reaching hesitantly for a crust of bread. In contrast, Sisif's memory of Elie's death (related to Machefer, who has come to visit him) still evidences his trauma—its sequence of brief shots is dizzyingly interrupted by swish pans. Finally, the injury to his eyes prompts a tour-de-force sequence of out-of-focus shots, when Sisif returns to the cabin after having his eyes checked a last time in the resort village. A slow montage of close-ups and extreme close-ups of his face and eyes, intercut with blurred point-of-view shots of table objects, the pipe in his hand, a wall clock, his face in a mirror, and the distant mountains through a window, ends in a fade to white as his eyesight fails utterly. This sequence of simple objects, fading into nothingness, contrasts poignantly with the earlier sequences of railyard machines and instruments over which Sisif once exercised control.

From this series of perspectives, *La Roue* may indeed seem an incoherent text, in which the demands of various aesthetics clash uneasily. Incoherence, of course, need not be condemned per se. Overriding the conventional notion of coherence here may be a principle of play for its own sake, a form of playing that involves a mélange of aesthetic modes. That would not be unusual given the varying degrees of success L'Herbier had already had with a mixture of styles in *El Dorado* and *Don Juan et Faust*. But it is more likely, I think, that there are structural designs that set coordinates for such play, that shape it into a more or less coherent network of narrative and rhetorical relations.

Let me point the way toward sensing some coherence by focusing on the innovations for which *La Roue* has best become known—the new form of continuity editing which Gance created through a rhythmic montage of rapid cutting and accelerating montage. Actually this was less a breakthrough than

166. The first shot of the locomotive wheel in *La Roue*

the culmination of one line of technical experimentation he had begun in *J'Accuse* and which some of his colleagues were also exploring—e.g., Marcel L'Herbier in *El Dorado*.[22] Gance has said often enough that these forms of montage were based on an analogy with music. As late as 1972, he was telling Armand Panigel

. . . that the images had syncopations, accelerating movements, pauses, simultaneities, all of which produced, ultimately . . . [a form of] musical writing. . . . In *La Roue*, I constructed my montage without any aids, without an editing machine . . . and I cut absolutely as if one image was a violin, another was a flute, a third an oboe, that's to say, everything was organized in my head according to this concept of the musicality of light.[23]

However essential this analogy may have been in the actual process of editing the film as well as to the developing concept of pure cinema, it is less than helpful in getting at the *narrative* significance of Gance's innovations. For, in the sequences where it appears, the technique of rapid cutting seems to function in more ways than one and sometimes in several ways simultaneously. Rather than expressing an individual character's psychological state (as most critics have assumed), it tends to integrate or synthesize an individual's perceptions and feelings into a larger design.[24]

For Ricciotto Canudo, the film's larger design represented "the collective human body as well as the powerful mechanical forces of which man remains both creator and victim. . . ."[25] No better words could introduce the extraordinary opening sequence of *La Roue*, which synthesizes machines, a seething mass of people, and two central characters into a titleless visual paroxysm. The sequence begins *in medias res*, with a speeding locomotive. A masked forward-tracking shot of a single rail opens up to include a set of rails slashing through several cross-points, then a tracking shot beside the locomotive dissolves nearer and nearer to a close-up of the huge wheels and drive rods in motion. The smooth, consistently paced movement of this short sequence

332

167. (top left) Rescuers in the opening train wreck in *La Roue*; (top right) survivors; (bottom left) the dead woman hanging from the window; (bottom right) Sisif (Séverin-Mars) trying to move the locomotive wheel blocking the switch

suddenly breaks with the brief long shot of an unexpected train wreck. The next minute or two literally explodes with images (apparently tinted red in the original print)[26]—cars tilted in the air, people caught in the wreckage or struggling along the tracks or over an embankment, billowing smoke, lights flashing across the control shack, figures in silhouette before a flaming car, a woman hanging lifeless from a window, another collapsing beside a squalling baby, a hand grasping out of twisted metal, locomotive wheels lying about, a close-up of a rose lying against a rock, and a begrimed, staring Sisif holding a little girl (Norma). All of these shots are intercut so rapidly and jarringly that it is difficult to take them in. The simultaneous presentation of so many disparate images is almost kinesthetic, disorienting enough that one seems to be undergoing the experience oneself.[27]

Suddenly, a second catastrophe threatens. One signal has not changed, and another train is fast approaching. Sisif moves Norma to safety and then rushes over to try to lift a set of wheels blocking the main switch. The sequence

333

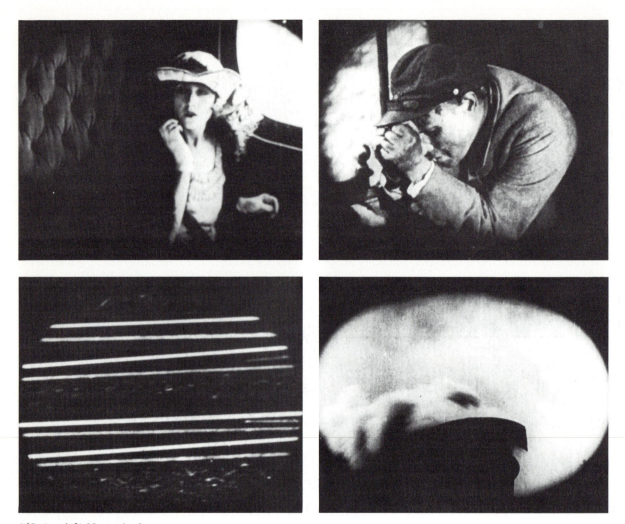

168. (top left) Norma in the
train compartment; (top
right) Sisif in the locomotive
cab; (bottom left) a tracking
shot of the rails; (bottom
right) a tracking shot of the
locomotive smokestack;

alternates shots of him straining at the wheel, the train coming on (several
shots looking ahead over its cab), the engineer hanging out his side window,
and a wrecked car with people looking up anxiously—accelerating to shots of
a half-second or less in length. Just in time (in a quick series of shots), the
switch mechanism smoothly changes the signal, and the engineer reacts by
slowing and stopping his train. The final shot is of the rock and the rose,
which irises out and in to reveal Norma ("La Rose du Rail") huddled on the
ground. Here the story of Sisif's heroism and discovery of Norma (whom he
soon adopts) is first set against and then integrated into a tragic collective
experience. The subjective merges with the objective, to use Jean Epstein's
terms, in a landscape dance or, more precisely, a symphony of machine movement.[28]

In contrast to the deliberately ragged, discordant rhythm of this opening
accident, the sequence of Sisif's attempt to wreck his own locomotive (as it

334

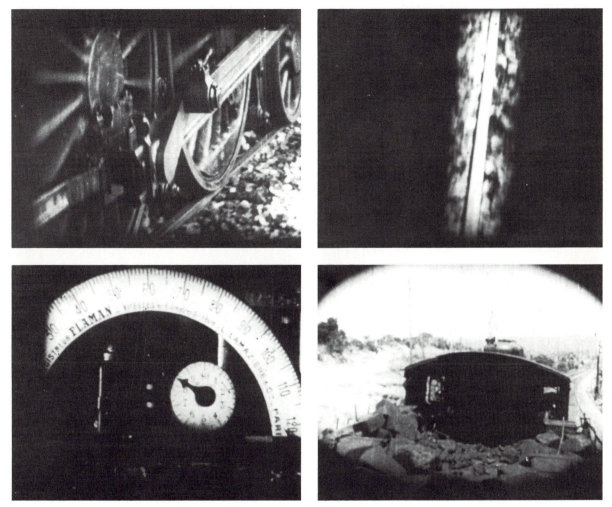

(cont.) (top left) A tracking shot of the locomotive wheels; (top right) a tracking shot of a single rail; (bottom left) the locomotive speedometer; (bottom right) a dolly shot of the landscape ahead of the locomotive cab

carries Norma to her wedding) moves smoothly, unswervingly, to a climax of suspense. It comes close to embodying the Purist concept, then held by Cendrars and Léger, of an aesthetic order animated by the "geometric spirit."[29] The sequence begins by orchestrating four basic shots (in various combinations)—the train wheels revolving, Sisif on the left side of the cab, Machefer on the right, and Norma seated in her first-class compartment. Soon after Sisif opens the throttle, and Machefer takes a swig of wine, a new shot is introduced—a close-up of the speedometer needle rising. Then another shot joins the alternation—a forward-tracking shot of a single rail, masked on each side into a vertical strip. When the needle hits 120 (kilometers per hour) and Norma begins to glance out her window, three more shots break in—a shot past the cab to the landscape into which the locomotive is racing, a tracking shot of the rails from the side as they blur by, and a shot of smoke billowing from the stack. At this point, a regular series of shots is repeated five times, and each time the shot lengths become shorter and shorter—from eighteen to nine to six to four frames each. This accelerating montage culminates in a longer shot of the wheels jumping and blurring (because of the speed) until, suddenly, Machefer discovers the open throttle and slows the train down. This sequence may work as a projection of Sisif's desire as well as a mesmerizing montage of simultaneous objects and actions. But its overall effect is to submerge both Sisif's and Norma's subjective states in the machine "dance of death" that Sisif has set in motion.

Sisif's final suicide attempt is constructed according to a similar form of accelerating montage. Only this time, he is alone in his locomotive, Norma Compound, as they hurtle through the station and onto the rail siding. Because of its limited focus, the cutting is simpler, more concentrated, more orderly in its rhythm, and perhaps less interesting. The shot lengths decrease at regular intervals by units of four frames—"I could make the images," Gance boasted, "alternate like verses."[30] At the climax, the alternation is between close-ups of Sisif's staring face and close-ups of the driving wheels ("8-4, 8-4, 8-4, 4-2, 4-2 . . ."). Man and machine become one in a headlong rush of agony. The locomotive smashes into an embankment, but Sisif survives, bathed suddenly in a strong sidelighting of sunshine. He crawls to the front of his locomotive to find it deep in a bed of flowers. Even more clearly than the others, this sequence organizes itself around Sisif's desire. But it, too, places the subjective within a larger context—a miraculous intervention that ends in a rather simplistic symbolic tableau.

The last major sequence of accelerated montage, "La Mort d'Elie," also differs from the others. This, too, is a moment of suspense, as were the two suicide attempts, but it lacks any machine images and at first seems conventionally tied to a single character's subjective state. The sequence begins with Elie clinging to a shrub on the side of a cliff, after his duel with Hersan, and Norma trying desperately to reach him. The intercutting between them focuses on Elie's face and hand (in a gray oval iris) and on Norma (in a black circular iris) running ahead of Sisif (who is left behind). The regular alternation of close-ups of Elie and Norma quickens (from two seconds to a half-second each), and then the rhythm slackens ever so slightly in a final oval-masked long shot of the cliff above the village and valley (fifteen frames) and a circular-masked close-up of Elie (twelve frames). As he opens his mouth to scream, the film seems to erupt in a rush of images. The shot alternates with a myriad of midshots and close-ups of Norma in the past—in her old scrubbing clothes, in her medieval costume, in tights, in a little girl's dress, in her wedding gown and veil, or simply with her face backlit (and the rhythm quickens from four or five frames to two or three frames per shot). At the end of this alternation, there is another brief pause as the past shots of Norma turn into an extreme close-up of her eyes. Then the climax comes in a single-frame montage—the shot of Elie alternating with shots of Norma in her medieval headdress, of her face backlit, and of just her eyes. A three-frame shot of Elie screaming (in a gray oval iris again) jars that rhythm slightly just before he falls (in long shot). As she reaches the cliff edge, Norma's face is now framed (in close-ups) in a blurred circular mask that changes from gray to white. The sheer speed and density of this accelerating montage clearly functions as a representation of Elie's last moments of consciousness, as he remembers images of Norma from various periods of her life. Yet the very rapidity of the cutting (making the two characters synonymous), the pause on her eyes, and the shifting association of the several masking devices seem to include her changing emotional state as well. Through this interchange of shots, Elie's love and pain seem to coalesce magically in Norma. Their subjective states become so intermeshed that they literally seem wedded in an expanded instant just before the moment of his death. Face to face with this image of a woman, which almost seems to break free of the diegesis in a paroxysm of fragmentation, Elie's cry seems to ring with Gance's own personal cry of suffering and loss.

No matter how extraordinary one considers these epiphanies of simultaneity, in which opposites are dissolved and/or transformed, they provide but one of several patterns shaping *La Roue* into coherence. The classical myths of Oedipus and Ixion, for instance, offer another—the figure of a hero who undergoes a long period of suffering for a forbidden desire. Sisif is just such a figure, and his forbidden desire constitutes the melodramatic crux of the film. For what drives *La Roue*'s narrative is Sisif's "incestuous" passion for Norma and his desperate attempts to repress that passion. The clearest sign of this comes in the confession he blurts out one night to Hersan. In the last of several explanatory flashbacks, Sisif looks up from his workbench to see Norma rocking back and forth on the flower-garlanded swing in the front yard. In the alternation between the two, Sisif's POV shots focus on her skirt and legs, and, in despair, he closes the window and then draws the curtain across it. The sequence ends with a close-up of him holding onto the curtain as if it were her skirt and sobbing into it. Yet, if Sisif's passion seems unnatural, his repression is even more so, for it rests on the perpetuation of a falsely constituted family (after the train wreck, instead of returning Norma to relatives, he destroyed a letter identifying her and her dead mother and then made her his own). The more he asserts the "law of the father" and tries to maintain Norma's false identity, at the expense of any other possibility (to the point of marrying her off to Hersan instead of his own son), the more he suffers. And his suffering engenders psychological conflicts that infect the other characters. As a consequence, in order to preserve the relation of father to "daughter" and, by extension, the Oedipal bonds within the family, the repression he imposes on himself perversely almost destroys them.

For all its peculiar contradictions, the relationship between Sisif and Norma does come to a resolution. On the one hand, it forms the paradigm of a narrative transformation that joins and then separates a man and a woman, in a doubled fictional structure whose second part replicates the first through inversion and displacement. By means of substitutions, this even includes the repetition of specific narrative actions—e.g., Sisif undertakes a funeral march after the destruction of Norma Compound and then another after the death of Elie; he attempts to separate Elie and Norma when she listens to the music of his violin, and later Hersan does likewise. On the other hand, even more intriguingly, especially in such a massive film, their relationship is bound up with a system of rhetorical figuring that marks a major advance over Gance's previous work—e.g., *Mater Dolorosa* and *J'Accuse*. Although remarked on at the time, this rhetorical figuring has largely been forgotten, perhaps because the existing prints are in such mutilated condition.

337

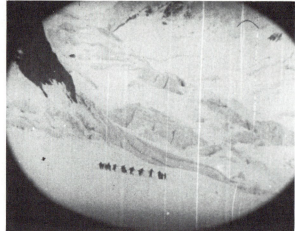

169. (left) Sisif framed in the cabin window at the end of *La Roue* (1922-1923)

170. (right) One of the groups of peasant dancers circling in the snowfields

At least two major interrelated patterns of rhetorical figuring govern the shape of *La Roue*, and both are initially articulated in the opening sequences. In a bold stroke of vision, they wed the Modernist to the sentimental or melodramatic. Here, again, the paradoxical nature of the film becomes clear. The first pattern can be summed up in one of the intertitles—"La Rose et le rail." In the opening train wreck, Norma is introduced in conjunction with a rose blossom, juxtaposed beside the rocks and rails. Two elements are set in a rather conventional opposition, and Sisif seems to offer the one protection from the other. Several other sequences continue this nexus of relations—the vision of Norma in Elie's fantasy, the moments when she sits by the flower-garlanded well. But then, suddenly, the distribution shifts when Sisif gazes at her, surrounded by flowers, swinging against the background of rails and steaming locomotives. The one-time protector turns potential violator, as threatening as the engines he is supposed to control. Later, after Elie has learned that his sister was adopted, Sisif shouts at him that there will be no more flowers beneath the rails. But when he wrecks Norma Compound, the embankment it comes to rest on is literally covered with them. The tragic irony of his action—overcome by guilt, he destroys Norma again, in the form of his engine—is neatly reversed by this exaggerated pastoral symbolism. The flowers create a kind of natural funeral bier for the engine and protect him—or force him to go on with his guilty existence—as if the "Rose" he had saved in the beginning has multiplied to repay the debt.

The last part of *La Roue* would seem to offer poor ground for this pattern of rhetorical figuring to flourish. Yet two major sequences draw it out further. The prominent shadow of the dying locomotive on the flower bank echoes in the frequent shadows of the cross Sisif carries up the mountain to Elie's grave on the anniversary of his death. The parallel suggests that the cross bears metaphorically the weight of Sisif's guilt in separating and destroying his son and adopted daughter. At the gravesite, Norma scatters flowers over the rocky

338

point and kneels on them at Sisif's feet. But he denies her, so locked is he in his own blind suffering. Only in the final sequences do the flowers reappear, to mark the end of his penance. On the day of the peasants' spring dance, he takes up some pampas grass plumes and shakes them to create a dreamlike snowfall filling the cabin. It is a magical moment of transformation, like the moment when the room fills with pillow feathers in Chaplin's *The Gold Rush* (1925). Norma goes off with his blessing, and Sisif dies seated at the window, framed by the locomotive model he holds in his hands and by the backlit pampas grass plumes. In the double displacement, "La rose et le rail" seem to bless his passage to peace.

The other pattern of rhetorical figuring is tied to the film's central metaphor—"la roue," the tragic wheel of fate. If the metaphor smacks a bit too much of Gance's literary pretensions and sometimes grows clotted with signification, it is boldly envisioned, marvelously sustained, and strikingly multiple.[31] On one level, it operates simply as a visual motif in the recurring image of the locomotive wheels. Inert, lifeless, they mark the opening cataclysm; and, until Sisif struggles with one set blocking a switch, they threaten a second catastrophe. Whereas in one brief montage they seem to convey his love of his work, in another they carry him rapidly toward the death he so desires. And it is the steam that drives them that causes his blindness. At the end of his last day at the roundhouse, after he has watched the Norma Compound being broken up for scrap, the wheel appears transposed in a shot of his resigned figure, set against the background of a 360° pan of the silent engines. On another level, it functions as the locus of symbolic reference. The Victor Hugo quotation that opens the film points the way: "Creation is a Great Wheel which does not move without crushing someone." The chariot wheel that Ixion was tied to (for desiring Hera) becomes the locomotive wheel that Sisif is bound to, first out of love and then as a form of punishment. It is this crushing punishment that the film hammers out, over and over, in repeated sequences of suffering, separation, and loss. In fact, the wheel even seems to become a figure for the film itself. As a series of structural variations on the initial tragedy, the narrative acts exactly like a wheel revolving round and round in a great circle or spiral.

"The first cinematographic symbol," Jean Epstein christened this great wheel of *La Roue.*

On predestined tracks of fortune that bode less good than ill, the wheel rolls on while one heart yet beats. The cycle of life to death has become so painful that it has to be forged lest it be broken. Hope radiates from the center, a prisoner.[32]

At the end, that hope breaks forth as the metaphor undergoes a transformation. Separation turns into union; loss, into gain. The circle of suffering is replaced by a circle of joy as the peasants dance round and round in the rocks and snow fields. The once barren mountains no longer seem threatening. Norma is drawn into a human community that is one with nature. And Sisif can die in peace—"the man of the rails" positioned in the midst of light and flowers. Against a last panning shot of the mountain clouds, in superimposed negative images, gigantic locomotive wheels seem to roll across the sky. All "Pursue their pattern as before / But reconciled among the stars."

La Roue's spectacular premiere in December, 1922, marked another break with and reconstitution of the parameters of narrative avant-garde film practice. Two years later, Jean Epstein could still call it "the formidable cinematic monument in whose shadow all French cinematic art lives and believes."[1] However, not all French filmmakers immediately leaped at the chance to ape Gance's advance. Two who did not, interestingly enough, were Germaine Dulac and Louis Delluc. One of Dulac's best films, La Souriante Madame Beudet (1923), offers a good point of departure.

Despite her own enthusiasm for La Roue, Dulac conceived and executed La Souriante Madame Beudet much more in line with her previous work, especially La Mort du soleil. It was already surprisingly short for a narrative film released in late 1923—barely 800 meters or thirty-five minutes in length.[2] As if restricting, condensing, and refining the subject of La Mort du soleil, La Souriante Madame Beudet focused exclusively on a provincial woman trapped in an unsatisfying bourgeois marriage. To articulate Madame Beudet's condition and her response to it, Dulac eschewed those techniques that had given La Roue its notoriety—any form of rapid cutting and accelerating montage—and depended instead on patterns of subjectivity and rhetorical figuring like those developed in her earlier films and in those by Delluc and L'Herbier. Introducing the film at the Musée Galliera, on 17 June 1924, she spoke of the conceptual basis of her strategy, singling out the editing or montage.

The shot is an image isolated for its expressive value, emphasized by the frame of the camera lens. . . . The shot is at once space, action, thought. Each different image juxtaposed to another is named: shot. The shot is a fragment of drama; it is a nuance which converges on the conclusion. It is the keyboard on which we play. It is the single means that we have to create, in a progression, an inkling of a character's inner life.[3]

As Dulac herself admitted, La Souriante Madame Beudet engaged her personally, passionately, and that engagement shows in the film's masterful simplicity and ironic poignancy.[4]

Unlike the other films so far singled out, La Souriante Madame Beudet was based on a stage play. However, this particular play, by André Obey and Denys Amiel, already differed from the standard bourgeois melodrama adapted for the cinema. This was a contemporary work, a psychological drama written according to "the theory of silence," according to principles that seem to have paralleled those of Dulac and her avant-garde colleagues in the cinema as well as those of the German Kammerspiel.[5] Within two years after having been first performed in 1921 by an avant-garde theatrical group, the Canard Sauvage, it had won the Paul Hervieu Prize, had been staged at the Odéon, and had become a modern classic.[6] The narrative, basically unchanged in the film, is unusually simple. Madame Beudet (Germaine Dermoz) is a cultured, outwardly happy woman who is suffering from ennui as the wife of a provincial clothing merchant (Arquillière). One evening, overwhelmed by M. Beudet's insensitivity and lack of understanding (his idea of a joke is to put an unloaded revolver to his head and pretend suicide), she surreptitiously puts several shells in the chamber. The next morning, he aims it playfully at her, unawares, fires and misses. The shock makes him suddenly realize her state—but not her intention—and promise to renew their marriage. Today, this uneventful narrative sounds like a stripped down, muted version of *Hedda Gabler* or *Madame Bovary*, with an ambiguous ending.

Dulac and Obey's adaptation altered the play in at least one significant way. That alteration did not involve an opening out into the real world through location shooting, for all but a couple of sequences were shot by Paul Parguel and Maurice Forster in Film d'Art's Neuilly studio (in this, the film resembles *Fièvre*). Rather, it took the form of an opening inward, a sustained exploration of the inner life or the subjective experience of Madame Beudet. Through the character's perceptions and imaginings, the spectator is made to identify and empathize with a sensitive, remorseful woman whom her husband utterly fails to comprehend, even at the end. Here is a bourgeois marriage criticized from within, from the perspective of its most unwilling victim.[7]

To set up this critique, the film actually provides each of the major characters a degree of subjectivity. For instance, M. and Mme. Lebas, who initiate the narrative by inviting the Beudets to a performance of Gounod's *Faust*, define themselves as stereotypical bourgeois by imagining the clothes they will wear that evening. M. Beudet's first subjective shot likewise defines him through his image of the opera: a MS of Marguerite set off against a group of singers. This conventional male fantasy (later he dreams of her ankle or foot) is juxtaposed to Madame Beudet's subjective image of the opera: a MCU of Mephistopheles (frame foreground left) singing at Marguerite (frame background right), who holds up a hand to her face in horror. The hidden misogyny of the woman-as-fetish is suddenly, succinctly, explicit. Even the maid is given a brief, ambiguous subjectivity as the figure of her fiancé dissolves in at her shoulder when she asks Madame Beudet to be let off for the evening. Is Madame's reluctant assent a sign of envy (the maid can escape the house with another) or of disquiet (will the maid's marriage be any better than her own)?

Not long into the film, however, Madame Beudet is privileged with entire sequences of subjective shots articulated through a wide range of technical effects—dissolves, distorted lenses, double exposures, slow motion, handheld camera movement—and unusual patterns of continuity editing. After refusing to accompany M. Beudet to the opera, for instance, Madame Beudet reads a magazine that has just arrived in the mail. Glancing several times at her irate husband, who is muttering and pounding his desk across the room (conveyed in separate CUs and MSs of the two, intercut through the eyeline matches), she looks at a photo of a champion tennis player who suddenly, in slow motion superimposition, breaks out of a serving stance. As if acting out her desires, this imaginary figure moves slowly behind the husband's desk and begins choking a supered double of him, then lifts him up and carries him off toward a background window. At the end of this imaginary attack and displacement (as if revenging the victimization in *Faust*), there is a HACU from behind her head as she leans back slightly sideways and laughs. The unexpected camera angle that frames her gesture is disorienting, disturbing; and the threat suddenly seems more than fanciful. In response to this laughter, M. Beudet takes an empty revolver out of his desk and jokingly threatens suicide—"a simple and often repeated pleasantry," says one of the film's few intertitles. As in *Le Silence*, one wonders how this key object will eventually be used.

The privileged degree of Madame Beudet's inner life and its difference from that of the other characters clearly establishes one dimension of the film's

341

central conflict or opposition. But that conflict is articulated from the very beginning through several patterns of rhetorical figuring as well. In her lecture at the Musée Galliera in 1924, Dulac offered a rare close analysis of the film's opening.[8] After several LSs of Chartres—"Observations of melancholy in the empty streets, in the quaint, tiny human figures. The province . . ."—a CU in split screen: "two hands playing a piano and two hands feeling the weight of a silver knife. Two characters. Contrary ideals . . . different dreams, we already know it; and without seeing a single person." There follow several shots associating Madame Beudet with the piano, a piece of sheet music (Debussy's "Piano à deux mains," on which she writes her name), a vase of flowers, and an imaginary image of (to return to Dulac's language) "the sunlight playing on the water among the reeds . . . a book . . . Intellectualism." Then comes a sequence of shots associating M. Beudet with money, a clothing shop counter, a desk, a calendar, and "a clutch of clothing samples . . . Materialism." A series of metonymical relations has become charged metaphorically. When M. Beudet enters the room where Madame is reading, Dulac writes,

the characters have already been established through images isolating their different gestures, sharply outlined and put in opposition. All of a sudden, a long shot of the room brings them together but in a deep space of foreground/background distinctions. Abruptly, all the disparity of a marriage is revealed.

The cutting, framing, mise-en-scène, and choice of objects have all conspired to produce a clearly defined network of cultural oppositions, and sexual differences, within the marriage.

Like *Le Silence* and *Fièvre*, then, Dulac's film relies heavily on the multiple signification of selected objects. The vase of flowers, for instance, plays a central role in depicting the habitual discord between M. and Mme. Beudet. The flowers are first linked to Madame's piano playing and reading, where their prominent position in the margin of the frame parallels the way she places the vase near the edge of the table (as if for an Impressionist still life). This off-center arrangement bothers M. Beudet no end, for he repeatedly moves the flowers to the table's center, as if this small gesture will produce order in his home. Conversely, while Madame is alone on the evening of the opera, she discovers that her husband has locked up the piano, denying her one of her few pleasures. The clocks associated with his work now begin to bother her, monopolizing her attention, so that they seem to be placed wherever she turns. Her entrapment, in time as well as space, is finally summed up in a single image: a MS of her mirrored figure (frame left) as she rests her head on a clock cover (frame right).

All these patterns of subjectivity and rhetorical figuring culminate in Madame Beudet's decision to retaliate and her consequent remorse. Deprived of her piano for the evening, she begins reading a poem from Baudelaire's *Fleurs du mal*—"La Mort des amants." For each line that she reads, a corresponding shot of imagined objects in the house undermines the words and yet reinforces the title.

"We have beds suffused with delicate odors"
FS of Beudet's empty bed.
"Divans deep as tombs"
MS of two stacked, unused pillows.

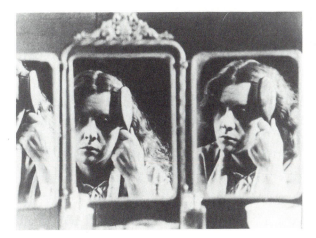

171. (left) Madame Beudet (Germaine Dermoz) reflected in her dresser mirror in *La Souriante Madame Beudet* (1923)

172. (right) Monsieur (Arquillière) and Madame Beudet at the end of *La Souriante Madame Beudet*

"And strange flowers on the shelves"
CU (masked) of the contested vase of flowers.

After sending away the maid, she finds herself suspended in a spatial-temporal limbo. Caught between mirrors and clocks, she looks out the window: (intertitles) "Always the same horizons"—the "Courthouse and Prison." Across the street, an actual prison facade mirrors her metaphorical one. To escape, she turns inward, imagining the blurred figure of a man coming through the window with his arms open (as if completing the earlier tennis-champion fantasy). Glancing at a photograph of M. Beudet and impetuously casting off her wedding ring, she suddenly finds her imaginary lover displaced by M. Beudet, who climbs through the window in slow motion, his huge ugly grin blurred and distorted in several MCUs. Denied escape now even through her imagination, she goes behind the desk and gets out the revolver; the sequence fades out as she reaches into a second drawer (where the bullets are stored). The trap is set. Her impotence has given her husband an ironic potency.

The next morning, Madame Beudet's agitated state verges on delirium. Appropriately, M. Beudet has come in late and fallen asleep on a bedroom chair. Tossing and turning on the bed, Madame awakens to several intercut shots which suggest the sounds she is hearing—a MS of shoes passing on the street, a CU of a clock ticking.[9] This sequence shifts to fantasy in a LS of the bedroom over which a superimposition of a pendulum (in CU) moves back and forth in slow motion. As she looks down at the pillow beside her, the figure of her husband dissolves in and out, only to be replaced by a subjective insert of the threatening courthouse. With economical precision, this stream-of-consciousness sequence condenses the experience of the night before and foreshadows what may come. As Madame starts in fear and moves to the edge of the bed, M. Beudet awakens, and she lies back again. Abruptly, the level of narration turns omniscient, and several exterior shots of the streets mark a transition to a slightly later time. After M. Beudet goes downstairs for breakfast, Madame sits before her dressing mirror, combing her hair. Fragmented

343

into three reflected images, she looks at herself and combs more and more slowly and finally stops. Self wars against self in the tense calm of immobile replicated faces. Will M. Beudet play his suicide joke now? Will he find the revolver loaded? Should she try to reach the revolver first and unload it? Should she confess her guilt?

As the film moves toward the climactic gunshot, both M. and Mme. Beudet's actions contribute to the suspense. While searching for a misplaced invoice, M. Beudet pauses to ridicule his wife's taste in music and pounds the piano in exasperation. Growing more and more vexed, he turns his anger against all women ("Women: Do you know what's to be done with them? . . .") and seizes a doll from one of the bookshelves. Almost without realizing it, he crushes its head with his fist. This unexpected violence raises a frightening possibility—will the gun be turned on Madame Beudet?—a possibility underscored by a cut to his wife, now dressed in the bedroom. As she decides to go downstairs, subjectivity returns in an unusual HA shot looking down the stairs, a handheld POV shot (with an anamorphic lens) that wavers back and forth and moves forward slightly. She reaches the room with the desk only to be interrupted by M. Lebas, by the maid, and finally by M. Beudet himself. As he works on his accounts, she sits nervously in her chair nearby; when he pulls out the revolver, suddenly he appears in POV shots—distorted FSs of him pointing the revolver at his head and then straight ahead. In an irised CU the revolver fires, followed by a masked shot of the flower vase falling over. Released at last, the violence remains rhetorical.

The film ends differently, and quite consciously, from Obey and Amiel's play. As M. Beudet tries to comfort his wife—mistakenly thinking that she wanted to kill herself—she simply stares off straight ahead, expressionless. Side by side, in MS, their separate figures parallel the opening split-screen image of opposing hands. To emphasize this lack of reconciliation (a bit crudely perhaps), Dulac adds a further shot of the Beudets with a puppet couple behind them in a picture frame or stagelike mirror. In a parody of the bourgeois melodrama happy ending, the puppets hug and wave gaily, and a curtain with THÉÂTRE emblazoned on it drops in front of them. The film's first intertitle reappears, "In the provinces . . . ," with an added phrase, "Joined by habit . . . ," confirming the return of the Beudets' initial relationship. In a LS of a gray, deserted street, M. and Mme. Beudet greet a priest whom they pass and then walk slowly off, side by side but separate, their backs to the camera. In this extraordinarily concise juxtaposition, genre is played off against genre, convention against reality, theater against cinema. And the final starkly realistic image closes off our identification with Madame Beudet and defines her condition—in a provincial, sexist, church-oriented, bourgeois society—as *unchanging*, without future and without escape.

Another provincial realist film that, like *La Souriante Madame Beudet*, eschewed the technical effects of *La Roue*, was Louis Delluc's last film, *L'Inondation* (1924). Contrary to his usual practice, Delluc adapted the scenario for *L'Inondation* from a contemporary novella by André Corthis, a fact which, unfortunately, led most French film critics and historians to give it scant attention.[10] Although released just weeks after the filmmaker's untimely death,

L'Inondation came close to disappearing altogether.[11] Both the film and the filmmaker deserved better.

What probably inspired Delluc to film this particular work was a Swedish film by Victor Sjöström, which he had reviewed in Cinéa two years earlier.

Karen, Daughter of Ingmar (1920) is a film whose principal character is a river.
The river is so powerful that it floods the country—and it has so much talent that it overwhelms the film.[12]

From Sjöström's example and Corthis's material, writes Marcel Tariol, Delluc produced a true "peasant drama integrated into a natural field . . . where the elements erupt with destructive force."[13]

The story involves four main characters in an unspecified village in the Vaucluse: Alban (Philippe Hériat), the principal farmer in the district; his fiancée Margot (Ginette Maddie); Broc (Van Daële), the aging secretary to the mayor; and his grown daughter, Germaine (Eve Francis), whom he has not seen since her mother left him for another man many years before. Germaine's appearance in the village revives her father's spirit and attracts the attention of Alban. She, too, is attracted, but Margot forces Alban to reject her. Stunned, Germaine falls ill just as the flooding Rhône River engulfs the countryside. Margot disappears; and when the waters recede, her body is found at the river's edge. Alban is accused by his dead fiancée's mother, but Broc finally confesses to the murder, first to Germaine and then to the police.

Because Delluc and Gibory shot the film mainly on location on the lower Rhône River, L'Inondation has an unusually authentic physical surface.[14] At least a fifth of the film's footage is given over to describing the Vaucluse countryside, the village center, a local festival dance (held inside because of the rain), the flood (shot at the last minute under actual conditions), and the search for Margot's body. The interiors are rich in details of the commonest sort—from the airy spaciousness of Alban's kitchen to the rough Spartan comfort of Broc's small cottage. To emphasize the realism, Delluc employs particular lighting effects—lighting Broc's room at night from the fireplace, framing the dance through the doorway and lighting the scene almost entirely from within (an effect which is repeated ironically when Margot's body is laid in a nearby room by her mother), lighting the search for Margot with lanterns in the trees and on the water. For the same reason, apparently, he also uses several tracking shots for the first time, and not without a certain technical awkwardness. In the beginning, there is a relatively long HALS dollying into the busy village square, followed shortly by shots slowly tracking the rows of market stalls. Similar shots occur at the beginning of the flood sequence: a HALS dollying forward through crowds of men in the square and a tracking shot that parallels the water lapping the edge of a street. The structural parallelism between these two series of documentary shots simply and clearly articulates one dimension of the film's initial narrative condition and its reversal.

The main characters come to the fore unobtrusively within this milieu, and the action evolves gradually as they become more fully defined. To facilitate this integration of character and milieu, Delluc asked each of his four actors to play against the type they had become associated with in French films.[15] In

173. Germaine (Eve Francis) resting near Alban's farmhouse in *L'Inondation* (1924)

the opening market sequence, several villagers are congratulating Alban and Margot while Broc walks alone through the streets to the mayor's office. Germaine enters the village much the same way the older woman came to the house in *La Femme de nulle part*. An insignificant figure in a dreary landscape, Germaine's isolation is at first more physical and social than psychological. This is confirmed when Alban notices her resting in a doorway and invites her into his kitchen for bread and soup. In a series of CUs and MSs, she observes the objects on the table and stove and by the hearth, all of which succinctly convey both his ample way of life and her alienation from it. Falling asleep at the table, she is rudely awakened by Margot's humiliating laughter. Broc's situation is no better—"The people of the village treat [him] with ridicule," and his house is furnished with the barest essentials. The first objects we see are a bed and mirror, a fireplace, a bowl and water jar, and a photograph of Germaine as a child. His life is suggested in the simplest of gestures—after looking at the photograph, he removes a speck of dirt from the water.

This socioeconomic contrast is uncommon in Delluc's work and perhaps may be traced to Corthis's novel. Even so, the class conflict is far from extraneous. In fact, it operates in parallel with the romantic intrigue, providing a second motive for Margot's attitude toward her rival. The conflict is developed most explicitly, however, in connection with Germaine's character. Alban attracts her, but so does his way of life as represented by his possessions. She becomes acutely conscious of her own drab clothes and, while looking at the store window full of posters and magazine covers, fantasizes herself (through superimposition) into the costume on one. After having to sew her own dress and scarf, she tries them on before the fire and Broc's old mirror. The CU of Germaine looking at her reflection in its dull fogged surface is a perfect synthesis of physical object and inner being. And it follows quickly and inevitably on its corollary—a LS of her scrubbing the floor and turning to gaze out the window. Window and mirror both frame her desire to escape her condition.

For such a simple story, *L'Inondation*'s narrative structure is as complex as anything else Delluc wrote. That complexity depends, in part, on some half-dozen flashbacks and subjective sequences positioned at crucial junctures in the film. Their operation, both internally and as a part of the overall narrative structure, is unusually varied. Of the four main characters, only Germaine and Broc, as the underclass, are privileged with subjectivity. Perhaps the most startling sequences are those associated with Germaine. Here Delluc returns to the pattern of achronology that he first employed in *Le Silence*. When Germaine returns to the cottage, in stunned disbelief after being rejected by Alban, she goes up to the mirror before which she had dressed herself earlier. Following an intertitle, "An attack of fever," a quick series of shots erupts, repeating previous shots of Margot, Alban, and herself, but in reverse chronology and moving from MS to LS. Then, just as abruptly, the sequence changes chronology and distance once more with a cut to the FS of Alban rejecting her and then to a shot of the river. Germaine's face returns, in MCU, only to be transformed by a series of dissolves (CU, ECU, CU); and finally, in FS, she collapses out of the frame onto the floor. The moment may be melodramatic, but the order and rhythm of shots effectively equates our perception with the flow, no, the rush of Germaine's consciousness.

A similar moment erupts for Germaine just before Broc follows Margot off as she passes the cottage. Here, however, the sequence of subjective images shifts unexpectedly from memory to fantasy.

MS (from the side) of Germaine in bed; she raises herself up, leans against the wall, and falls back. Fade
FS of Germaine in her new dress, embraced by Alban. Cut
MS (straight on) of Germaine in bed; she sits up and looks around. Fade
MS of Germaine and Alban; he disengages his hand and pushes her away. Fade
CU of Germaine in agony; she falls back in bed. Cut
FS of Germaine and Alban dancing at the festival. Cut
MS of Germaine and Alban dancing. Cut
FS of Germaine and Alban dancing. Cut
MCU of Germaine sitting up again in bed; she lifts her arms as if to ward off something and falls back, calmed. Suddenly she struggles up again, only to fall back.

This shift, together with Germaine's repeated movement, rising and falling, produces a hypnotic, suspended sense of disorientation. That disorientation is doubled by a curious pattern in the transitions between shots. The first shift from present to past is marked by a fade while the return to the present comes with a cut. The second shift to the past is also marked by a fade, but so now is the return to the present. The third shift is to fantasy; it comes with a cut, but so now do the transitions between shots in the fantasy. Although the fade retains its consistent transitional function throughout, the cut functions in three different ways. By midway through the sequence, we don't know, with a cut, what kind of time shift to expect. Consequently, by disrupting the then conventional codes of transition, the sequence seems to heighten the distortion of Germaine's condition.[16]

Although less striking initially, Broc's subjective sequences are even more crucial to the narrative. The first comes when Germaine introduces herself as his daughter. A brief flashback informs us of Broc's past life and how the two were separated: in the foreground of a spacious, comfortable room, Broc plays with a child while his wife greets a man in the background. The next sequence occurs as Broc sits in his cottage, just out of the firelight, after he has found Germaine ill and put her to bed.

MS of Broc seated frame center, with the fireplace in the left background.
FS of Alban walking through a crowd of men clustered by the archway to the dance hall.
MS of Margot chatting with her girlfriends.
FS of Broc and Germaine meeting Alban in front of a cafe.
LS of Alban and Margot walking away down an alley toward the square.
CU of Margot laughing.
LS tracking to the right past flooded fields and farm buildings.
LS tracking to the right past a flooded farm.
MS of Broc; he moves slightly and puts down his head.

This sequence is interesting because it is composed of shots used earlier in the film, only one of which has been associated with Broc. The order is chronological until the CU of Margot, which comes from a time much earlier when Germaine was awakened in Alban's kitchen by her laughter. Then, rather than cutting back to Broc immediately, the sequence ends with two tracking shots of the flooded river. The effect of all this seems less psychological (cf. the delirium sequences of Germaine that soon follow) than analytical. The sequence stresses Broc's conclusion (based on what he has learned from Germaine?) that Margot is responsible for her illness, but it also links Margot metonymically with the river at its destructive flood stage. That association will prove crucial.

The last subjective sequence is also Broc's, when he finally confesses his guilt to Germaine. His delayed narration of Margot's murder consists of a flashback of just a dozen shots. Mist or fog obscures the action, deemphasizing the suspense, as do shots like the LALS of the road and guardrail posts (from the side) as the characters' feet cross the top of the frame. When the murder does come, its quick, elliptical cutting echoes the Temptation sequence in Jean Epstein's *L'Auberge rouge* (1923) and looks ahead to the murder that opens Dmitri Kirsanoff's *Menilmontant* (1926).

CU of Broc's face.
". . . And . . . driven by your despair . . ."
MS of Broc (frame left) holding out his hand toward Margot's back (frame right); river and sky in soft focus in the background.
Shot of the river surface, the current flowing to the right.
MS of Broc pushing Margot.
MS of Margot (from the front) falling feet first.
Shot of the river surface.
FS of Broc standing by a guard post, looking down toward the right background.
MCU of Germaine and Broc facing forward.
CU of Germaine showing signs of suffering; she closes her eyes.

The alternation suggests how, to Broc's mind, eliminating Margot allows Germaine to recover and live again. As the sequence shifts focus to Germaine, emphasizing the effect of Broc's action on her condition, Alban is restored to her (an intertitle suggests), but at the expense of her father and, of course, Margot.

174. A publicity photo of Margot (Ginette Maddie) and Broc near the bridge in *L'Inondation* (1924)

The real achievement of *L'Inondation* comes from what Delluc would have called its lyrical composition, the intricate pattern of signification that arises from the association of all four characters and the waters of the Rhône. This association is precisely what critics seized on to attack the film when it was released. William Bernard put the argument almost contemptuously, writing in *La Tribune de Genève*:

. . . the drama has no direct connection with the cataclysm which forms the basic theme of the visual poem. For the unleashed elements have nothing to do with the murder of the coquettish Margot—it could have been accomplished just as well without them. There is always, I think, enough water in the Rhône to drown a little girl. [17]

Only Marcel Tariol has perceived the flooding river differently:

. . . its true function is more poetic than dramatic: the slow, crafty inundation, which invades everything little by little, which insidiously suppresses all trace of life, is the backdrop—a funereal accompaniment of the voices of nature to the tragedy of the heart. [18]

Its function is indeed poetic, but hardly as the literary convention of a lament by nature over human suffering. Instead, the river serves as the coordinate of a network of metonymic/metaphorical relations.

One of the principal associations is prepared for early on in at least two sequences. The first occurs when Broc looks at the photograph of Germaine (who is not yet identified) and notices some dirt in his cup of water. The subtle link between Germaine and water (and Broc's discovery of something in it that disturbs him) is marked by a CU and MCU, the only ones in the sequence. The second occurs when Broc tries to retrieve Germaine's letter (also unidentified until she arrives) which the postman drops before his cottage. In a series of shots, the wind blows it along the road and Broc follows it to the edge overlooking the river. The letter blows off and is carried away by the current (anticipating Germaine's delirium), but the sequence is shot and cut much like the later murder sequence.

FS of the road edge, with the river below and beyond, as the letter blows off.
FS of the letter falling in the air.
FS of the road edge, with the river below and beyond, as Broc comes in from the left.
MS of Broc, looking toward the right background and holding out his arms.
FS of the river surface as the letter is carried off to the right.
MS of Broc, resigned, looking toward the right background.
FS of the river surface, with the current flowing to the right.

In retrospect, the river is functioning here already as a metaphorical extension of Margot, eliminating the sign of Germaine's presence and identity.

This oblique association finally becomes explicit in the sequence that simultaneously narrates the river flooding and Germaine's illness. Just as she collapses after Alban's rejection, the film cuts to a church bell (ironically) sounding the alarm and then to a series of shots of men gathering, dam gates opening, and water engulfing the countryside. Thereafter, Broc's discovery of his daughter and his attendance on her is intercut with shots of the flood waters as they reach their peak. While sustaining the analogical properties of these alternating images, the sequence also equates their connotative significance. The flood becomes a metaphorical corollary to the fever of grief and sadness that engulfs Germaine, and her gestures of delirium become those of one drowning.

A second major association is introduced even earlier, in the sole exception to the film's pattern of subjectivity. As he stands on the village bridge spanning the river, Alban imagines a CU of Margot superimposed on the water's surface. This conventional romantic image soon shifts, however, into a very different metonymic equation which only gradually accumulates significance. Traced over a series of sequences—the letter sequence, Broc's subjective sequence by the firelight, the rendezvous with her cousin by the bridge, the sequence where her body is carried up from the river's edge—Margot's association with the river culminates in Broc's confession of her murder. Whereas earlier Broc had watched helplessly as Germaine's letter was carried off, now at flood crest and on the same spot he pushes Margot into the river. The elliptical cutting that alternates between Margot and the river, denoting her death by obliteration, also completes the metonymic equation between the two. That equation simply and succinctly inverts the initial romantic superimposition.

Margot's disappearance, doubly narrated in the film, first releases Germaine from her illness and then frees Alban of misplaced guilt. Their embrace in the final shots is quite muted, however, for visual and emotional dominance is given to Broc's separation from her. Whereas in the preceding confession the two had been repeatedly shown side by side in MS, now they are separated, first by foreground/background differences within the same shot and then by intercutting. The two LSs of Broc going off between the gendarmes, stopping to look back toward the camera, and then continuing away along the muddy road, overpower both the MS of Alban taking his place beside Germaine and the intertitle, "The two of us will save him. . . ." Germaine continues to look off to the right, deflecting our attention from her and Alban, while Broc's

350

movement directs our attention deep into the center of the frame and then reflects it backwards in his gaze. That gaze is all the more poignant because he has not once looked at Germaine since beginning his confession, and he now breaks the look in turning away. The distance, the look, the emotional paradox, all are echoed, probably unconsciously, in the final shots of separation in Claude Chabrol's *La Femme infidèle* (1968).

L'Auberge rouge and Coeur fidèle

When Jean Epstein began making films, he had two masters as mentors— Louis Delluc and Abel Gance. His first fiction film, *L'Auberge rouge* (1923), was conceived more along the lines of Delluc's film practice. The main link between Epstein's work and, say, *Le Silence* or *La Femme de nulle part*, is in the construction of the scenario, which presents a complicated narrative structure simply and economically.[1] More precisely, that narrative structure is predicated on a confrontation between the past and the present, between fiction and reality, between one world and another. It is this kind of structure, along with particular syntactical patterns and rhetorical figurings, that makes the film much more than the adaptation of a minor literary classic. Pathé-Consortium, however, simply dropped it among its summer re-releases, in August, 1923.[2]

The subject of *L'Auberge rouge* comes from the novella of the same title by Balzac. The novella already provides the structure of a double narrative—"two overlapping stories that progress in parallel to a conclusion in which the epilogue of the past story constitutes the end of the present story."[3] In Epstein's version of *L'Auberge rouge*, the double narrative runs as follows. In 1825, a Paris banker gives a dinner for his son André (Jacques Christiany) and his fiancée, Victorine, accompanied by her uncle, Jean Frédéric Taillefer (David Evremont), a former supply contractor for the French imperial army. Among the guests is an important merchant named Hermann, who tells a story about two young doctors who, one rainy October night in 1799, had to put up at an inn in Alsace. One of them, Prosper Magnan (Léon Mathot), becomes interested in the inn's maidservant (Gina Manès). The innkeeper (Pierre Hot) intervenes but soon attends to a new arrival, a Dutch aristocrat, who turns out to be a diamond broker (in Balzac, he is a French pin manufacturer, carrying gold and diamonds). Next morning the aristocrat is found murdered and his diamonds missing; the other doctor has vanished, and Magnan is arrested. He is tried, convicted, and finally executed, despite the testimony and pleas of the maidservant, who asks a traveler to take a last letter from Magnan to his mother. Hermann, it turns out, was that traveler (in Balzac, he is Magnan's temporary jailer). Over a card game after dinner, André (Balzac's primary narrator) confronts Taillefer, who had become increasingly nervous during Hermann's story. Through a series of quick maneuvers, Taillefer is unmasked as the other doctor at the inn, the one who perpetrated the crime and then left his friend to die for his guilt.

Epstein's distinctive manner of introducing his characters and the spaces of their action is already apparent in *L'Auberge rouge*. Nearly a dozen shots occur before several intertitles identify the characters and period of the 1825 story.[4] These shots describe a half-dozen or more people in a drawing room and an adjacent dining room (beyond the brilliantly lit table, all else is dark) at the

351

175. A production photo of Jean Epstein shooting the first sequence in *L'Auberge rouge* (1923). Notice the old Pathé camera and the primitive dolly which is steadied by the weight of Epstein and three of his crew

moment when a butler calls them to dinner. A young couple remains separate from the others in the drawing room, and in a soft-focus CU, the young man gently tries to kiss his fiancée. As they enter the dining room, a woman, already seated at the table, looks up, and the fiancée glides forward in a dolly-back CU. After the four major characters have been identified (the couple comes last), a tracking MS begins to slowly circle the table. As it moves from Hermann to the banker, an intertitle requests that he tell a story that will make them all shudder, and a reverse track circles back to him. The formal costumes and decor, "the splendor of the jewelry, the candles, the crystal, sharply outlined against the black backgrounds,"[5] the smooth movement of the figures and camera, the seamless editing, all produce an almost idyllic milieu of bourgeois elegance, family harmony, and discreet romance. The only disturbing element is the initial shot—an enigmatic white-masked CU of Léon Mathot, unidentified and unintegrated into the sequence that follows.[6] Who is he and how will he affect this world, especially, perhaps, the anticipated marriage of the young couple?

Hermann's story is introduced quite differently. After an intertitle—"20 October 1799, two young doctors proceed in short daily advances to their posts in Alsace"—two horsemen seem to explode from the screen.

FS dolly back before two horsemen riding in the rain.
LAMS of the horses as they pass on a diagonal.
CU of the hooves splashing through the mud (diagonally).

The last two shots are quite brief and immediately give way to a LS of the interior of the inn where several soldiers and women sit among the tables while the innkeeper paces back and forth. This juxtaposition of exterior and

176. (left) The 1825 dinner table setting in *L'Auberge rouge* (1923)

177. (above) The opening CU of Prosper Magnan (Léon Mathot)

interior is repeated with more rapidly cut shots of the horses and then closer shots of the various soldiers and women at the inn (much as in *Fièvre*). When the horsemen reach the inn, the innkeeper tells them there is nowhere to sit—the camera pans over the tables, following his hand, in MCU, as it points out all the people. No intertitles identify the horsemen (but we recognize one as Léon Mathot); instead, several shots single out one's wet coat and boots and, after some coins are offered, his boots and hands are stretched out to the fire. The foul weather, "the inn's cramped space swarming noisily with the usual types," the open antagonism between the characters, the abrupt juxtapositions between shots—all produce a milieu that contrasts sharply with that of the 1825 dinner.[7] That contrast was heightened, according to Pierre Leprohon, by "tinting contrasts" which are not present in the surviving prints.[8] Several conflicts are already set in paradigmatic relation. Will the horsemen (with their energy and desperate condition) threaten or disrupt the world of the inn or, instead, will they be threatened? Will the conflict emerging in the 1799 Alsatian inn somehow threaten or disrupt the ambiance of the 1825 Paris dinner? Finally, do these oppositions in some way parallel the opening juxtaposition of Léon Mathot (in CU) and the 1825 milieu?

About two dozen sequences alternating between these two different milieux form the narrative structure of *L'Auberge rouge*. Until the final ten minutes of the film, the narration of the past story and its tragic mystery dominates. Instead of developing Magnan's story conventionally through dramatic confrontations with the diamond broker, the authorities, and innkeeper, or the maidservant, Epstein emphasizes simple patterns of rhetorical figuring and several ambiguous sequences of privileged subjectivity.

One pattern of rhetorical figuring arises from an old woman and a deck of cards at the inn (absent in Balzac). When Magnan agrees, without much interest, to have his fortune told, she begins shuffling the cards, an action intercut with shots of an accordionist playing nearby and a young woman swaying to his music, all of which are slowed slightly to produce a mesmerizing rhythm of movement (amplified by the editing). This rhythm carries over into the fortunetelling, presented primarily in CUs of Magnan, the old woman, and her hands turning the cards. The sequential order of the turned-up cards metaphorically narrates the story to come: the ace of diamonds ("Gold"), the seven of clubs ("Crime"), and the ten of clubs ("Death"), the last of which is followed by a blurred CU of a cloaked skull. At key moments in the story, thereafter, each of these three cards recurs as if to confirm what is already determined. When the diamond broker displays his jewels, for instance, the ace of diamonds dissolves in and out over an ECU of one large diamond, linking Magnan to it, even though he does not seem to be one of the rapt onlookers. Then, when Magnan discovers blood on his hands and the broker's dead body nearby, the seven of clubs dissolves in and out over a CU of his terror-stricken face. Finally, after the judge pronounces sentence, the ten of clubs dissolves in and out over a blurred CU of Magnan's face. And as he is led outside the courtroom and past the maidservant, a last CU of his face dissolves into the blurred CU of the skull. Instead of representing Magnan's subjective experience, this pattern of rhetorical figuring somewhat conventionally suggests a fatalistic force beyond the control of any character; but it does not determine the story, nor is it beyond the characters' manipulation.

Throughout the first four segments of the past story, subjectivity is distributed among almost all of the major characters, but only in the form of POV shots. In the fifth segment, however, marked off by the intertitle, "Temptation," Magnan undergoes a remarkable nightmare experience of nearly killing the diamond broker. The segment opens with a series of rhythmically cut exterior shots (long shots and closer shots) of wind and rain sweeping the tree-shrouded inn. Cut into this rhythmic "drumming" are CUs of the diamonds and then CUs of Magnan awakening, as if he were being roused simultaneously by the sound of the rain and by the diamonds glistening in a dream image. Shots of the inn's exterior lashed by the storm continue to alternate throughout the segment as Magnan looks about the crowded guestroom, spots the Dutch gentleman, imagines the diamonds once more, and then from his pouch slowly draws a scalpel. We anticipate a violation, the slashing of one body, the opening of another, to extract the jewels. Instead, unable to act, Magnan backs away toward the door in a shot that is interrupted repeatedly by quick fades, producing a kind of hallucinatory strobe-light effect. In effect, his own body seems slashed by light in the darkness. In a LS of the inn's central room, he crosses to a window; there, in MCU, his face, through the window, seems beaten and streaked by rain. As if roused again, he returns to the guestroom, resolved to carry out his murderous intentions. This time an intertitle halts him as he is about to strike: "He hears something like a voice within and realizes the horror of his action." Again Magnan backs away—in a chain of CUs and MCUs of his face drifting and blurring within the frame,

178. (left) Prosper Magnan
backs away through the
doorway in the "Temptation"
sequence in *L'Auberge rouge*
(1923)

179. (right) The recurring
HACU of the table
centerpiece

accentuated by a slow reverse dolly—the shots alternating with images of the storm-lashed inn exterior. Finally, in a rhythmic "drumming" of long and close shots (that echo the opening shots), he leans, head in hands, against the outside wall of the inn and lets the rain wash over him. The last shots return him to the inn—a MCU of his head (shot from behind) dollies toward the door, and once inside he collapses.

No doubt this segment is organized to convey the different stages of Magnan's heightened emotional condition. A number of cinematic devices combine to articulate those stages—the chain of MSs and CUs of Magnan's face (first irised in white, then sharply defined and later blurred against the darkness), a chain of MSs and CUs that changes in accordance with the CUs of objects (imagined and real), the quick slashing faces at one point, and the hallucinatory camera dollies.[9] However, what is even more interesting is the pattern of rhetorical figuring produced by the repeated shots of the storm elements intercut with Magnan's gestures and movements. Here is the earliest instance in Epstein's films of what he had envisioned, in *Bonjour Cinéma* (1921), as "the linking together [or merging] of the objective and the subjective."[10] The significance of one shifts in relation to the other, for the images of the rainstorm carry a contradictory or paradoxical charge. Initially, the storm serves to rouse Magnan to his murderous desires—even producing, it seems, the dream image of the diamonds. Yet twice the lightning drives him back in horror from enacting his desire. Again the storm seems to goad him on, as he stares out the rain-streaked window. In the end, however, that same rain washes over him, almost as a sign of penitence. Or is it a sign of his destiny as a victim? In the beginning, after all, it was the storm that forced him to put up at the inn.

The segment that narrates Magnan's execution, which concludes the past story, involves a different form of simultaneity, a doubled conjunction of "the objective and the subjective." The sequence leading up to the execution raises the possibility of rescue or reprieve. Shots of Magnan's progress to the stake (these shots change gradually from LSs to MSs) alternate with shots of the maidservant's journey across the bare autumn fields to the prison. But the fact

355

that her progress changes inversely to Magnan's—from MSs, including one shot of her feet coming through the mud, to an ELS—dissipates the possibility. The execution is narrated in a simple metonymic series: a CU of Magnan's face, soldiers in a diagonal line, lowered rifles, a drum roll, an officer's sword falling. Instead of returning to a shot of Magnan, however, the editing pattern is disrupted by the reintroduction of the maidservant.

FS of the maidservant (in profile) at the prison gate.
CU of her face.
FS of leafless trees silhouetted against the sky. Dissolve to
FS of leafless trees silhouetted against the sky, tilt up.
MS of Magnan lying on the ground near the stake.
CU of the maidservant's face.
FS as she turns away from the prison gate.

Spatially, temporally, these shots are ambiguous. Does the maidservant see the execution, merely hear the presumed gunshots, or arrive at the gate too late? Whichever the case, the moment of Magnan's death, metonymically prepared for, is displaced metaphorically in the shots of the trees and sky (echoing the night of his temptation in the inn). Now, as the maidservant slowly returns across the same fields, the shots of her lone figure alternate with those of the silhouetted trees. But the latter are marked by up-and-down wipes, and her movements within the frame are masked off into a narrow vertical space. This series of transformations or displacements—from one facial CU to another, from one alternation to another, from metonymy to metaphor (and back?)—this double linking of "the objective and the subjective," seems to function as an uncanny moment of communion and exchange. The tragic suffering of one character shifts onto the other. As in the "Temptation" segment, this transposition occurs within and is mediated by a natural landscape. The human drama of the film's past story seems circumscribed within some larger, strangly ambiguous, natural design.

As it progresses, this past story impinges, at first imperceptibly, on the 1825 dinner guests. A visual motif (somewhat like the image of the rocking cradle in *Intolerance*) repeatedly marks the transition between the two stories— a HACU of candles and wine glasses around a glass fruit bowl on the dinner table. Here is one of Epstein's earliest and purest examples of *photogénie* in a single shot—the unusual camera angle renders the image both literal and transformed.[11] Besides denoting the passage of time (the candles burn down), the recurrence of this shot connotes a sense of permanence and stability, as if this single image of light, glass, and decorative food summed up the 1825 bourgeois world. But that permanence and stability prove illusory.

After the first segment of the past story, the present story returns in a HAFS of the dinner guests, a shot whose slight disorientation registers as a vague disturbance. André and Victorine look at one another and, in CU, his hand moves away from hers and clenches. Not until after the second segment does Hermann finally give his hero a name, Prosper Magnan, and Victorine innocently asks her uncle (who has downed some water and put his hand to his head) if he is feeling ill. In the brief sequence that follows the segment introducing the diamond broker, Taillefer turns down the diamond ring on his finger (in CU), a small movement which André seems to notice. While the past story links Magnan to the diamonds (through the ace of diamonds), the present story sets up a different, as yet ambiguous, association. Prior to the "Temptation" sequence, Hermann confesses that he cannot remember the name of the second doctor in his story; only after the murder is narrated does it spring unconsciously to his lips—Frédéric. The sudden emergence of the name (as if called up by the act itself) produces another link between Taillefer and the past. But it already has been planted in the brief sequence that bridges Magnan's temptation and the discovery of the murder. That sequence has only three shots: a MS of Taillefer with his hands over his face, a CU of Hermann talking, and a HACU of the candles and fruit bowl. Here, at the precise point where the past crime is elided, the present story implicates the real culprit. Yet we may not notice it, so wrapped up have we been in Magnan's nightmare. Throughout the narration of Magnan's trial and execution, the intercut sequences of the dinner continue to focus on Taillefer as he grows more anxious (and finally runs out of water); but none of the characters seem as suspicious of him as we in the audience may be. That is delayed until the final segment of the film.

When Hermann's story ends, so ends the dinner (only one old man, ignoring the story, seems to have eaten anything at all), and the guests retire to the drawing room. Victorine and her uncle walk arm in arm, followed by André. Suddenly, although it has been prepared for, subjectivity is invested in André.

MCU of André looking forward.
MCU of Victorine from behind. Dissolve
CU of her face.
MCU of a drink in her hand.
CU of a necklace circling the back of her neck.
CU of André's face.

An intertitle even reveals his thoughts—"Was he going to marry the niece of a criminal?" Victorine has now become suspect in his eyes, the source of her status and wealth uncertain. Yet the subjective level of narration and the CUs of faces and selected objects here form a curious parallel to the sequence of Magnan's temptation. That parallel reinforces the structural relationship that has developed between the two men and the women they love. André and Victorine's near embrace in the film's opening, for instance, is replicated in Magnan and the maidservant's embrace in the inn, just before everyone goes to sleep. The two opposing objects of Magnan's past desire are fused here paradoxically in André's image of Victorine with the jewels that seem to mark her with guilt. Victorine's position becomes even more ambiguous when she keeps André from approaching her uncle but then herself asks him if he was once in Alsace. At that point, André invites Taillefer to a game of cards, and they settle down for the denouement.

The metaphorical pattern of the cards returns, but manipulated now for a very different purpose. André points to Taillefer's diamond ring—"That ring is rather large and turns easily"—and begins to deal. As if by magic, the three cards that once came to Magnan now turn up for Taillefer. As he looks at the fatal cards, Magnan's eyes dissolve in over them, and then a shot of the old fortuneteller is cut in. Taillefer stands up, staggers, and falls (the camera,

180. Magnan's eyes dissolve
in over Taillefer's card hand
at the end of *L'Auberge rouge*
(1923)

behind him, dollies forward and tilts down on his movement), as if, across twenty-five years, repeating Magnan's collapse. Instead of "consuming" Hermann's story (it seems to replace the dinner) and forgetting it, André engages in an "interpretation" which he puts to use. In a sense, he reinvents the story to reveal what was repressed and to define himself and his situation more clearly. But the film does not allow him to determine its end, at least without a touch of ambiguity. Victorine leans on a man's shoulder until André comes over beside her; then, in a MCU, her head shifts over to his shoulder. Is this the embrace which was denied and delayed in the beginning? The ambiguity is heightened by the final shot—a HACU of the fruit bowl and candles, now burned down to nothing. Besides the story, what else has ended? What will now begin?

At this early stage of French film history, *L'Auberge rouge* is quite unusual for the way it intercuts two stories from different periods of time. The simultaneous narration of separate stories was not itself unusual—Antoine's *Le Coupable* (1917), as well as other films by Baroncelli and Delluc, had employed the strategy several years before. But in Epstein's film, the two stories interact with one another, changing the audience's response to each; and the real enigma of one is neatly resolved in the denouement of the other. Moreover, the discourse of the film does more than set in opposition two different stories and milieux. Its mixture of styles seems to free certain discursive elements to play off one another in a rich variety of combinations. That play is organized or controlled within a chain of signification, through structures of simultaneity or alternation, to produce ambiguous patterns of rhetorical figuring. Besides, *L'Auberge rouge* is interesting as an ideological construction, for the way it juxtaposes one historical period against another. As Epstein articulates it, this is less an historical juxtaposition—of the Bourbon Restoration versus the Revolutionary Directory—than a socioeconomic one—of a bourgeois society versus a society of aristocrats, soldiers, and peasants (almost a pre-Revolutionary world). The peace and prosperity of the bourgeois world rest on the wealth and power gained from a past violent crime—against an aristocrat (is this a displaced

358

reenactment of the Revolution in miniature?). Through an act of betrayal, the guilt for that crime is displaced and repressed. The film, therefore, seems to out-Balzac Balzac, by unmasking the violence and deceit on which the French bourgeois society is predicated. That it ends so ambiguously may suggest Epstein's own uncertain attitude, or that of his contemporary society, toward that unmasking and its consequences.

Epstein's second film, *Coeur fidèle* (1923), was conceived, much more than was *L'Auberge rouge*, in the wake of Abel Gance's film practice, specifically *La Roue*. Gance's film had appealed to Epstein for personal as well as formal reasons. As a young poet and friend of Blaise Cendrars, he had visited Gance several times during the years of its shooting and editing; and when Epstein produced his first film, *Pasteur* (1922), a fictionalized documentary marking the centenary of the famous doctor's birth, Gance had encouraged him with suggestions about how to handle the editing.[12] Although Epstein had reservations about Gance's work, he was enthusiastic about *La Roue*, especially its rapid cutting and its creation of "the first cinematographic symbol"—the Wheel. "If I had not seen it," he later wrote, "I undoubtedly would have conceived . . . *Coeur fidèle* differently."[13] *Coeur fidèle* also quickly became famous for its sequences of rapid cutting and accelerating montage, as witness the carnival sequence which was anthologized by the C.A.S.A. ciné-club. This notoriety, however, did not keep Epstein's film from being an unmitigated commercial failure. Its exclusive run at the Salle Marivaux was halted after just three days because of the fights that broke out between factions in the cinema—a response that pleased Epstein immensely.[14] Even at the Théâtre du Vieux-Colombier, late in 1924, the film played to fewer and fewer spectators until, on the last night, there was just one bewildered man, on whom Tedesco and Epstein took pity and refunded his ticket.[15] To his detriment as a commercial filmmaker, Epstein was no mere imitator. *Coeur fidèle* not only deployed Gance's new editing techniques in an original manner, it synthesized most of the then current narrative avant-garde film practice.

At the time of its release, *Coeur fidèle* seems to have been accepted as a realist film.[16] Its story involved marginal workers, down-and-out types, in the milieu of cheap bistros, piers, and dilapidated apartment buildings on the old Marseille waterfront. Following the practice then standard for the genre, Epstein and his chief cameraman Paul Guichard shot much of the film on location in Marseille in May, 1923. By doing so, he accomplished what Louis Delluc had wanted so badly to do in *Fièvre*. In fact, at first glance, *Coeur fidèle* seems to resemble Delluc's film quite closely. It opens in a waterfront bistro with the heroine working as a barmaid, and she is in love with a man linked with the sea. It also quickly accumulates a sense of atmosphere, of place—"this poetry of the waterfront and misery, this rather sordid realism"—out of which the narrative seems to evolve naturally.[17] Together, these two films established what became a subgenre of the so-called poetic realist film over the next fifteen years: it would include Cavalcanti's *En rade* (1927), Grémillon's *La Petite Lise* (1930), Feyder's *Le Grand Jeu* (1934), Duvivier's *Pépé le moko* (1936), and Carné's *Quai des brumes* (1938).[18]

Epstein, however, conceived of *Coeur fidèle* as a simple melodrama, and he confessed to a group of students at Montpelier, in January, 1924, that he had

359

written its scenario in a single night.[19] The story is certainly simple and extreme in its conflicts. Marie (Gina Manès) is trying to escape from her job and also from her lover, an unemployed drunk named Paul (Van Daële); her dream is to go off with another man, a dockworker named Jean (Léon Mathot). The two men quarrel in the bistro where Marie works and again at a local carnival, but Paul retains control over her. Sometime later, Marie has a baby who falls ill. Jean and a crippled neighbor woman (Marie Epstein) try to aid the child, but Paul, in a stupor, nearly causes its death. In a final struggle, the crippled woman seizes Paul's gun and shoots him dead.

Why indeed did Epstein choose to film such a banal, brutal tale? For two reasons, he said.

> First of all, to win the confidence of those, still so numerous, who believe that only the lowest melodrama can interest the public. . . .
>
> The second reason which decided me on this story is that, on the whole, I would be able to conceive a melodrama so stripped of all the conventions ordinarily attached to the genre, so sober, so simple, that it might approach the nobility and excellence of tragedy. And in fact, by means of an insistent, studied, concentrated banality, I have made a rather strange film that is a melodrama in appearance only.[20]

This sounds strangely similar to Gustave Flaubert's position just before he began work on *Madame Bovary* (1857). There, to represent contemporary life in all its banality, ugliness, and mediocrity undistorted, he shifted his aesthetic interest from what was represented to the means of representation.[21] In a famous letter to Louise Colet (16 January 1852), Flaubert wrote,

> What seems beautiful to me, what I should like to write, is a book about nothing, a book dependent on nothing external, which would be held together by the internal strength of its style . . . a book which would have almost no subject, or at least in which the subject would be almost invisible, if such a thing were possible. . . .
>
> It is for this reason that there are no noble subjects or ignoble subjects; from the standpoint of pure Art one might almost establish the axiom that there is no such thing as subject—style in itself being an absolute manner of seeing things.[22]

For Epstein, according to Pierre Leprohon, style owed

everything to those essential features of a cinema discovered through the study of its materials and means: the expressive value of the image through the systematic use of CUs, the rhythmic rapport of images through a rigorous montage, in which the mobility of camera angles intervenes as a dynamic element, which is likewise always orchestrated and significant.[23]

In other words, as Leprohon continues, in *Coeur fidèle*, "the melodrama served as the pretext for an experimental film."[24] Although Epstein may not have achieved the perfect fusion of the popular and the experimental that he so envied in *El Dorado* and *La Roue, Coeur fidèle* certainly justifies Léon Moussinac's designation—"a considerable . . . advance."[25]

The opening sequence of *Coeur fidèle* is nearly as striking as that of *La Roue*, but its mode is different—understated and intimate. The sequence introduces the waterfront bistro and Marie's position there in a series of alternating CUs that deviate rather sharply from the conventional patterns of continuity editing.

360

HACU of a table surface as a hand clears it of a plate and a cigarette and then wipes it with a rag.

ECU of Marie's face (45° angle).

MCU of a hand picking up a glass and bottle while another hand wipes the edge of the table.

CU of Marie's face (straight on).

MCU of wine being poured from a bottle into a glass, beside which a hand rests on the table.

CU of Marie's face looking down.

MS of Marie pouring wine for a man seated at the table; she corks the bottle, and he lights a cigarette; he begins talking to her.

LS of the bistro interior: Marie and the man are at a table in the right background, behind a couple at another table, while the edge of the bar is in the left foreground. The bistro owner pushes Marie toward the man at the table and then exits (foreground left); his wife enters (foreground left) and shakes her head at Marie, who comes over to the bar with a paper in her hand.

If, as Epstein wrote two years earlier, in *Bonjour Cinéma*, "the close-up, the keystone of the cinema, is the maximum expression of [the] photogeny of movement . . . is drama in high gear . . . ," what "drama" is already in motion here?[26] Isolated and magnified, this face, this hand, this table surface, this bottle and glass take on unusual importance. In fragmentary images, a world of mundane objects comes into existence (is Epstein constructing something like the early Cubist paintings?). A hand works among these objects, its action seemingly at their service—cleaning, rearranging them. And then there is Marie's face, inhabiting its own space, detached from the action but dominated by it (her face is intercut in brief shots of fifteen, twenty, and twenty-four frames each). What is she thinking? Or can she be thinking? With extraordinary economy, the film presents Marie as a divided character— her doing separate from her seeing, her body separate from her consciousness. She is both in the world and other. Yet that otherness is circumscribed in the editing chain of alternation (the quick cutting) and in the ever-widening space of the frame. Her subservience to objects is redefined as subservience to the proprietors of the bistro.

Marie's otherness, her consciousness, quickly finds expression, however, as she walks over to the bistro door. The following sequence of shots is deceptively simple:

MCU/LS past Marie's blurred head and door frame onto the harbor.

CU of Marie's face (straight on) aslant in the window. Dissolve

LS of the harbor where a ship is coming forward. Dissolve

LS of a ship at dock. Dissolve

FS of smoke. Dissolve

LS of a truck coming along the dock. Dissolve

LS of a truck going off the other way. Dissolve

MS of flotsam in the harbor water. Dissolve to

CU of Marie's face (straight on) through the window.

The alternation of the initial shots prepares us to see what Marie sees outside the bistro, perhaps something quite different from the world she seems trapped in. We expect, as in *Fièvre*, a contrasting description of that harbor

181. Marie's face (Gina Manès) dissolves in over the harbor flotsam in the opening of *Coeur fidèle* (1923)

world; yet the exterior space turns out to be no less constricting than the interior one. Moreover, the harbor shots suggest the beginning of narrative. The sequence of shots arouses an expectation of arrival (the ship approaching, the ship docked, the truck approaching)—is someone coming to Marie from the sea? But the possibility fades as the truck moves away and is replaced by the flotsam. Finally, the dissolves seem to signal a shift to subjective fantasy, and the first dissolve suggests that the harbor world also functions as a corollary to her consciousness, as an expression of desire. Instead of a fantasy of escape (connoted by the ships), however, we infer from these images that her mind is so resigned, so paralyzed by her environment, that she can imagine nothing other. The possibility of escape turns into residue, waste—the image of flotsam superimposed briefly over her expressionless face. In the final shot, as Marie seems to awaken and look directly at the camera, we are both identified with her and separate, bound up in an ambiguous conjunction of "the objective and the subjective."

The narrative that seemed on the verge of development erupts in the next sequence. After the CU of Marie's face at the window, as if by magic, comes a FS of Paul (from Marie's POV) walking directly toward the bistro door. Instead of someone who might free her, take her away, the harbor world produces the major character who will oppress her. The sequence alternates shots of Marie backing away into the bistro interior and of Paul coming through the door and advancing on her (in 180° shot/reverse shots). Once again she is circumscribed within the bistro world. Rhyming with the opening shots of the film, the sequence closes off, ironically, with CUs of Paul's arm across Marie's back and finally of his fist on the bar top. Much like *Fièvre* and *La Souriante Madame Beudet*, *Coeur fidèle* succinctly defines its heroine's position in society.

Only in the second major segment of the film is Marie offered any kind of alternative to her life with Paul in the bistro. Here, as toward the end of *L'Auberge rouge*, the focus is on a doubled conjunction of "the objective and

362

the subjective," but with some important differences. Excusing herself to get more wine, Marie leaves the bistro to meet Jean on one of the harbor quays. On the way there, she stops on a bridge to fix her hair, looking at her reflection in a scarred fragment of mirror (an echo of *La Roue*). Dissolves link the four shots of this brief sequence, underscoring its subjective nature. And the ECU of her roughened mirror image isolates and magnifies her eyes, emphasizing her desire, in rhyming contrast to the earlier CU of her "dead" face superimposed with flotsam. When she and Jean finally embrace on the harbor rocks, their shared emotional state is briefly suspended in time and space. Particular elements of the discourse come to the fore—long lap dissolves, superimpositions, slow wipes, white iris fades, reversed camera angles, and graphic textures (of the calm, open sea surface). Instead of enacting a transfer or exchange, this moment of communion is transformed into a "plastic composition" that almost floats free of the narrative. Soon after, when Jean is left alone by the sea, multiple images of Marie perform a hypnotic "stream-of-consciousness" ballet. Marie's face drifts slowly back and forth, dissolving in and out, over the surface of the water, which alternately seems to support and suppress her image. Here, too, the sea, it seems, carries a paradoxical charge.[27]

Just as in *La Roue*, the set pieces of rapid cutting in *Coeur fidèle* never function in exactly the same way. Besides the celebrated carnival segment, there are several other sequences that rely heavily on this technique. One depicts the initial confrontation between the two men when Jean follows Marie back to the bistro only to find himself facing Paul and three of his friends. The confrontation is presented entirely in CUs of faces (including Marie and the proprietor) and hands/fists. Instead of using an accelerating montage to build suspense, Epstein produces a fairly regular pattern of longer and shorter shots (3:1 or 4:1) but shifts their reference.[28] The sequence begins with several alternating shots of Paul and Jean (of nearly equal length), then shortens the shots of Jean (to four to ten frames each), and alternates them with shots of the other characters (twenty-two to twenty-five frames each). The effect is similar to the film's opening shots, subordinating Jean to a numerically superior force. Suddenly the shorter shots shift reference to Paul and his friends and alternate with longer shots of their hands and fists.[29] Only now does the rhythm of alternation break and signal the climax:

CU of a hand going into a pocket (twenty-three frames).
ECU of Marie, her hand to her mouth (twenty-one frames).
CU of a fist (twelve frames).
ECU of a fist (twelve frames).
ECU of Marie (twenty-seven frames).
FS of the group, looking past Paul to Jean, who moves slightly forward, speaks
    to Paul, and walks off into the background.

The threat of violence dissipates, for the moment, but not before its target has shifted from Jean to Marie. In a way, then, the sequence repeats Paul's initial attack on Marie; it is she, not Jean, who remains trapped in the bistro.

The carnival segment, which concludes the first half of the film, is more sustained and much more complex in its operation. So unusual was it, in fact, that it, more than any other sequence, provoked uncomprehending boos from the audience at the Salle Marivaux.[30] The germ of its conception can be traced

182. A strip of film from the carnival sequence in *Coeur fidèle* (1923)

to a passage in *Bonjour Cinéma*: "I long for a drama about a merry-go-round or, more modern yet, with airplanes. The carnival below and its surroundings would be progressively confounded. Centrifuged in this way, and adding vertigo and rotation to it, the tragedy would increase its photogenic quality tenfold."[31]

The segment begins as an alternation between Paul forcing Marie up the road to the carnival and Jean asking a drunken old woman at the bistro where they have gone. This basic alternation between the couple and Jean continues throughout the segment until Jean also reaches the carnival, when the two sequences merge into one. The carnival itself is introduced in a series of rapidly cut shots (with a general rhythm of 2:1).

CU of a mechanical organ music card looping upward (forty frames).
MCU of a merry-go-round horse head moving against a blurred background (thirty
    frames).
FS of the merry-go-round circling (forty-eight frames).
FS of the merry-go-round ceiling circling (twenty-three frames).
CU of the music card looping downward (twenty-two frames).
FS of a swing set whirling (forty-eight frames).

Once the atmosphere and general rhythm of the carnival are established, CUs of Marie and Paul are cut in, and a LS finally situates them in front of the airplane ride. Paul tries to persuade Marie to go on the ride—in the midst of LAFSs of the circling planes, HALSs of the carnival crowd, and CUs of objects and parts of the carnival decor in motion. This pattern of editing parallels that of the film's opening, and its function is similar. It clearly places the actions and desires of the characters within the multiple rhythms of a larger design. This initial sequence is complicated, however, by the fact that it is framed by blurred shots of the old woman laughing. Presented as her narration, apparently, the motion of the carnival takes on the connotations of a drunken frenzy. The couple's experience is submerged in what René Clair has described as a "beautiful visual intoxication, an emotional dance in space."[32]

As with the symbol of the wheel in *La Roue*, however, the syntactical design governing this vertiginous dance has ominous implications. The continual circling movement of the planes, the often-repeated shots, the mechanically produced "sound"—all set up a regularized, almost machinelike rhythm that is sustained through numerous variations. One such variation, foreshadowing Renoir's *La Règle du jeu* (1939), is a sequence of CUs and ECUs of tiny carved musicians on a calliope. It is followed by shots of the circling planes and then Marie and Paul seated in one, its streamers blowing in the wind. The two characters react quite differently to the carnival's pleasure machines. While Paul expresses interest and delight in almost everything, Marie is expressionless, withdrawn, even sullen. Their opposing attitudes and behavior suggest that the carnival is a metaphorical extension of the bistro world and a sharp contrast (especially the plane as it slashes through a glittering confettilike stream of people on the ground) to the seascapes that once joined Jean and Marie. Gradually, as the segment progresses, the carnival turns into a mechanical amusement prison.

While the couple is confined in the circling plane, the cutting begins to accelerate—to shots of six, seven, and eight frames each—simulating the in-

364

creasing speed of the ride. Suddenly Paul tries to kiss Marie, but all we see are quick swish pans of the ground, of the plane ride's central support pole, of the merry-go-round. The double function of the segment intensifies, goading Paul on and impinging more and more on Marie. Just before Jean reaches the carnival, the shots of Paul and Marie tilt at a 30° angle, and the cutting accelerates again—to four-frame and finally two-frame shots. In the midst of this barrage, Paul finally kisses Marie; and the segment pauses ironically on a sign of their union—a CU of a baker's hand spelling "Amour" on a pig-shaped pastry. At that moment, Jean appears near the merry-go-round. Now, not two, but three separate characters—two of them paired (one against her will)— are encompassed within the intoxicating dance of the carnival. The cutting shifts into an erratic rhythm of irregular shot lengths and threatens to disintegrate—until the plane ride slows and Paul and Marie descend (in a marvelous long-take track). Jean finally recognizes Marie from a distance, and there is a final burst of rapid cutting:

MCU of Jean yelling.
CU of Jean yelling (thirty frames).
CU of the music card looping downward (nine frames).
LAFS of the circling planes (twelve frames).
CU of the drum (fifteen frames).
CU of the face of the mechanical organ (fifteen frames).
FS of the swing set whirling (ten frames).

At the moment of their anticipated reunion, the mechanical movements and "sounds" of the carnival erupt as a substitution, a quick suppression. And with that last burst of drunken frenzy (echoing the first carnival images), the segment closes off. In effect, the centrifugal montage of the carnival has actually enforced the conjunction of one couple at the expense of the other. Nothing has changed.

The final sequence of *Coeur Fidèle* seems to recapitulate the editing patterns that concluded the carnival segment, but with Jean and Marie now reunited. Yet several unusual juxtapositions and ellipses make the "happy ending" a bit unsettling. The final image of Paul, for instance, is a horrible CU of his dead face lying in the crib beside the sick child.[33] This is followed by a night shot of a fountain brightly spotlit and then by a MS of Jean and Marie in the same plane ride at the carnival. Marie smiles for almost the first time in the film, but now Jean is curiously expressionless. The last image of the crippled neighbor woman is a FS, as she cradles Marie's child on the apartment stairs. Cut into the shots of Marie and Jean on the plane ride, its significance is puzzling (How has she escaped punishment? Has she taken the child permanently or just for the day?). The sequence ends with a barrage of technical effects—a LS of fireworks bursting over the carnival crowd, superimposed faintly with drifting flowers; a kaleidoscope image of a superimposed pair of eyes dissolving in and out; a CU of Marie and Jean with "forever" superimposed across their faces, which dissolves out, leaving the word alone (an echo of *El Dorado*). Because of the questions and associations that precede it, this conclusion is not entirely persuasive.

The parallel between the conclusion of the carnival segment and the final sequence of *Coeur Fidèle* caps a whole range of paradigmatic relations that point

183. (left) Marie is kissed by Paul (Van Daële) on the airplane ride in the carnival sequence

184. (right) The crippled woman (Marie Epstein) and Paul (Léon Mathot) on the apartment building stairs near the end of *Coeur fidèle* (1923)

to the doubled nature of the film's narrative structure. Like *La Roue*, in fact, Epstein's film divides rather neatly into two equal parts. Accorded different spaces (bistro, quay, carnival/bistro, street, apartment), each part works several variations on the melodrama conflict indigenous to the love triangle plot. Indeed, the second half of the film seems to begin all over again, at least a year later. The first part limits itself almost entirely to the three central characters, focusing on Marie's entrapment and desire to escape. It develops a number of patterns of simultaneity and rhetorical figuring, articulating the inner life of the individual within the context of an oppressively determined social world. The second part introduces several more characters—the sick child to burden Marie (almost as a metaphorical extension of her relationship with Paul) and two different women to aid/hinder the opposing male characters. If anything, it focuses more now on Paul and Jean, giving a greater degree of subjectivity, strangely enough, to Paul—is Epstein trying, unsuccessfully, to humanize his villain? The patterns of simultaneity, subjectivity, and rhetorical figuring seem diminished and less complex in this second half; and the melodramatic conflict between the characters is much more pronounced and drawn out.[34]

Perhaps the most interesting feature of the film's climax and resolution is that the villain is destroyed (with his own gun), not by the hero, but by the crippled woman. The internal division that had marked Marie's character from the beginning now seems redistributed in these two women. It is as if all of her suffering were projected onto the crippled woman, who then assumes all the guilt of revenge—of the oppressed against the oppressor, of woman against man. Through this schematic displacement, Marie is free to be positioned in the fiction of the romantic couple. The schematic division, along with the disturbing resonances, makes *Coeur Fidèle* seem to waver at the end, questioning, much like *L'Auberge rouge*, the certainty of that romance.

A very different film made in the wake of *La Roue* was Ivan Mosjoukine's *Le Brasier ardent* (1923). In the Russian emigré film colony in Paris, Mosjoukine was a versatile figure, writing scenarios and performing as an actor—and rapidly becoming a major French star. When Films Ermolieff was reorganized as Films Albatros, Mosjoukine convinced Alexandre Kamenka to let him direct a scenario of his own as one of the company's first productions. The result was *Le Brasier ardent*, his only major work as a film director, which opened at the Salle Marivaux, in August, 1923.[1] Perhaps the rough, uneven quality of the film, together with its bizarre plot and tonal shifts, antagonized cinema audiences, for it was a quick commercial failure. Yet Mosjoukine's work intrigued French critics and cinéphiles, who puzzled over exactly what kind of complicated concoction they had before them. Jean Renoir, for one, was absolutely dazzled by it.

> One day at the Colisée cinema, I saw *Le Brasier ardent*, directed and acted in by Ivan Mosjoukine and produced by the courageous Alexandre Kamenka of Albatros Films. The audience howled and whistled, shocked by a film so different from their usual fodder. I was ecstatic. Finally, I had before me a good French film.[2]

Ricciotto Canudo found the film as "stunning as the first ballets of Diaghilev."[3]

Mosjoukine's original scenario for *Le Brasier ardent* may seem slapdash and wildly inconsistent, a recipe of oddly contradictory ingredients that do not really blend. But it was written, in part, as a vehicle for his own mercurial presence as an actor. His penchant for eccentric fantasy and comedy made him a Protean master of disguise, a synthesis of character types. Here is a brief synopsis.[4] A woman, named simple "Elle" (Nathalie Lissenko), and her husband, a wealthy industrialist (Nicholas Koline), are not on the best of terms. While she enjoys the way he caters to her every whim, she wonders whether he really loves her. He, on the other hand, torments himself by imagining rivals. One morning she awakens from a nightmare in which she has been pursued by a man in various guises (Mosjoukine), who turns out to be the famous Detective Z, whose memoirs she has been reading. When she and her husband quarrel over leaving Paris permanently for a country estate, he goes to the "Trouve Tout" Agency and hires, of all people, Detective Z, to win back her affection. She promptly steals their marriage contract. Z tracks down the document and is nearly seduced in the process, but he resists her and returns to the comforts of home, his adoring mother, and a pet bulldog. In a chic restaurant one evening, she challenges him to a dancing duel, which he wins. After her confession of love, he goes home with a toothache. The contract is returned, the married couple plan to go away on a trip—all is ending as it should. Suddenly, she runs off to Z's home where his mother accepts her and Z himself jumps for joy. The husband, meanwhile, sails off alone, relishing his freedom. Not the "usual fodder," indeed.

Among French films of the 1920s, *Le Brasier ardent* certainly has the most extravagant mixture of styles or modes prior to Marcel L'Herbier's *L'Inhumaine* (1924). That is due, in part, to Mosjoukine's performance as nearly a dozen different characters. In the opening nightmare alone, he plays a heretic burning at the stake, an elegant gentleman, a bishop, and a beggar. In the rest of the film, he shifts among a series of contradictory personae—a brilliant detective, a silly buffoon, a cruel dancing master, a shy lover, and a mama's boy. The decors, designed by Lochakoff (assisted by Schildknecht and Bilinsky), also change radically to complement these and other character shifts. The nightmare city is transformed in a simple cut from a realistic space into a *Caligari*-style street. The woman's bedroom looks like a Mack Sennett set—a small makeup table descends from the ceiling to rest in front of her, breakfast trays pop out of the walls on either side of the bed, a circular dish of puppies is carried in by the maid, and her husband is stashed conveniently behind a Leonardo da Vinci portrait. The detective agency, which the husband literally falls into, is a labyrinth of revolving doors, conveyer-belt corridors, and rooms, one of which, the chamber of "Missing spouses," metamorphoses along with its disguised detectives (who materialize as twelve informed psychologists!). The restaurant interior, on the other hand, is a stark, sober prototype of the dancing decors of the modern studio spectacle films. No wonder critics like Léon Moussinac could not figure out what to call this film—"a dramatic comedy? a fantasy? a fantastic comedy?"[5] Jean Tedesco even dubbed it a "psychological dream."[6] Now, perhaps, it is much easier to read *Le Brasier ardent* as a conscious synthesis of current French, American, and German films as well as a send-up of several major French film genres—the serial, bourgeois melodrama, and fantasy.

In some ways, Mosjoukine's film operates conventionally enough. It is heavily titled, so that words produce much of the narrative. Like *Crainquebille* (1923), it has few subjective sequences, and, with only a couple of exceptions, these are uncomplicated and rather awkwardly inserted in the narrative. Also, like *Crainquebille*, but in reverse, it integrates several documentary-style sequences uncertainly into its predominant fantasy. Although the narrative is hardly predicated on a logic of causal relations, it is largely sequential; those instances of simultaneity simply propel the narrative forward, alternating two actions in different spaces. However, the film does develop several structural relations (semantic and syntactic rather than rhetorical) which give its discontinuous discourse some degree of unity.

There are at least two segments of the film which are strikingly original in conception and execution. One is a short subjective sequence, the morning after the nightmare, in which the woman remembers (in intertitle) "her tragic past and the first sight of her future husband." She is a young peasant woman being attacked by a man in a small fishing boat. Her husband-to-be is taking photographs with a camera in a boat nearby, and he rescues her when she leaps overboard. In just five shots, separated by fades, the sequence narrates their meeting and marriage—a MS of them inside a carriage as they embrace and look fondly at one another, a FS of her in the midst of a half-dozen women tailoring an outfit to suit her, a FS of her answering the questions of two teachers at opposite ends of a desk, a MCU of the couple kissing after they have exchanged wedding vows, and a FS/LS of them standing before the Place de la Concorde in Paris. What makes this sequence particularly interesting is the way it is framed. The woman is looking at photograph negatives in bed, and the sequence begins with a negative image of her and a man in the fishing boat. The still negative turns into a moving negative image of them fighting which then dissolves into a positive image. The sequence ends by reversing the process. A MCU/LS of her standing alone before the Place de la Concorde fountain turns into a negative image, and then that image freezes into a still negative. Here is a rags-to-riches story, summed up in two simple images, whose unreality calls attention to its fictional nature. The discourse is highly reflexive here, a point which is underscored by the presence of the husband's camera within the diegesis of the past story.[7]

The other segment is much more sustained and establishes several major structural patterns for the whole film. This is the opening nightmare sequence, which is as stunning, in its way, as the initial train wreck in *La Roue* and which looks forward to the murder sequence that opens Dmitri Kirsanoff's *Menilmontant* (1926). After a FS of a darkened room (a veil covers a lamp in the right center background), where a woman lies writhing in bed, an intertitle announces, "The woman tries vainly to escape the grip of a frightening nightmare." Although the intertitle directs our expectation, it scarcely prepares us for the barrage of rapid cutting and bold lighting contrasts that Mosjoukine and his cameraman, J.-P. Mundviller, fire at us. At first, the sequence alternates shots of glaring eyes (masked by darkness), then it shifts to CUs of Mosjoukine's savage face (staring slightly toward the right foreground) and Lissenko's face (looking slightly toward the left foreground) in a flickering light. Finally, there is a FS establishing the implied space: Mosjoukine naked to the waist and tied to a stake (frame left) in the middle of a blazing fire, Lissenko standing in a diaphanous white dress (frame right), and Koline—also naked to the waist—crouched (frame center, in the background), blowing on the flames. Again the faces alternate; Lissenko glances down almost in fascination, and there is a cut to a MS of the flames licking up to Mosjoukine's feet. His hands reach across the smoke (in MCU); more shots of their faces are intercut, and then (in MCU), their hands touch. Suddenly, she screams and (in MCU) puts her hands to her head, and each of Mosjoukine's hands (in MCU) grips a strand of her hair. The sequence integrates more and more shots with the previous ones and accelerates in rhythm—to shots of a half-second to a second each. There are MSs of his hands gripping her hair as she flails about wildly, MCUs of her feet near the flame, MCUs of Koline puffing excitedly, FSs of the threesome as Lissenko is drawn toward Mosjoukine and the flames. Suddenly (in MCU), her hair breaks in his hands, and she escapes (in FS) and runs off in a halo of top back lighting.

The rest of the nightmare sequence works a number of variations on this initial encounter, but without the rapid cutting. As Lissenko (now dressed in black) wanders a city street at night, she sees two prostitutes in the company of men. In one instance, the CU of a man's hazy profile is followed by a MCU of the prostitute's leg as a cane unrolls her stocking. In the other, a woman leaves a fat gentleman in a taxi, and then (in consecutive MCUs) her hand reaches toward his jewel-encrusted fingers resting on a cane—and he passes her a wad of francs. As Lissenko passes a beggar (Koline) near a flight of stairs, he seizes the dark veil from her neck. Running off through a stark, unpeopled street, she comes face to face with a blank wall; and Mosjoukine approaches her out of the darkness as a coldly staring gentleman in top hat and tails. The wall opens in a zigzag slash and she squirms through into the light, then under a heavy curtain, and finds herself in an opium den (a HACU of a hand lighting an opium pipe) among a group of scantily clad women lounging about some low tables. The curtain now bursts into flames at the bottom and

369

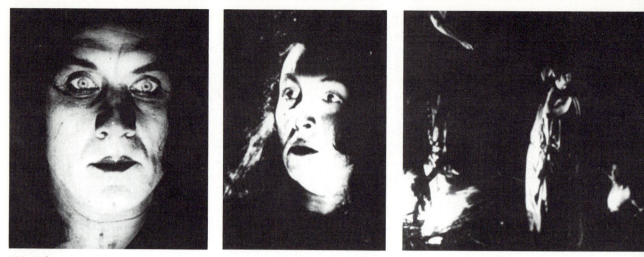

185. (left to right) Ivan Mosjoukine as the burning heretic in the opening sequence of *Le Brasier ardent* (1923); Nathalie Lissenko stares at Mosjoukine (off); Mosjoukine reaches down from the burning stake (left) to pull Lissenko's hair as Nicolas Koline (right background) blows on the flames; Lissenko's feet are drawn toward the flames; Lissenko escapes and runs off over a rocky landscape

wipes upward, revealing Mosjoukine (in FS) on a slightly raised stage. The women—young and old, European, African, and Oriental—crawl toward him, but he passes through them and stands over Lissenko. As he leans down to kiss her (in MCU), the women form a semicircle (in FS) before them. Suddenly (in FS), Lissenko comes out of a doorway and walks forward in the darkness, now cloaked in black. Just as suddenly, she is in a cathedral (in ELS) as the bishop (Mosjoukine) and his attendants turn from the altar to face the suppliants. Her face is intercut with the bishop's and she lifts her veil (in MCU) to kiss his outstretched hand. He blesses her and orders her out into the foyer, where (in LS) a beggar (Mosjoukine again) accosts her. He asks her for love, not money (in MS), and when she rejects him, he stabs himself in the heart. In horror, she faints (in LS) and falls into the arms of the first beggar (Koline). Dissolve to Lissenko alone writhing in the same position in her bed.

Although this marvelous nightmare is immediately explained as a harmless fantasy, the explanation proves illusory. The woman looks about her and concludes that she has simply transformed several objects in her room: a heavy curtain before the window with light slitting the middle and edging the bottom, a statuette of a savage squatting before an incense cup, Detective Z's memoirs that contain photographs of him in several disguises. The nightmare sequence, however, is no rude shock which is quickly over and forgotten. Z does appear in the body of the film, and he does pursue her, for one purpose, while she pursues him, for another. In fact, the nightmare sketches out in paradigm what will occur at certain moments later in the real story. It provides a rough structure of actions and relations for the narrative that follows. For instance, the husband's appearance in the detective agency replicates, in part, the sequence in the opium den. Here the husband undergoes a kind of assault—he is tossed about by masked men in black tights, his head is stuffed through windows where he sees a myriad of eyes and ears in the darkness (through multiple exposure) as well as a diagonal line of hands poised over typewriters. Mosjoukine appears, not as the master of a harem of women, but

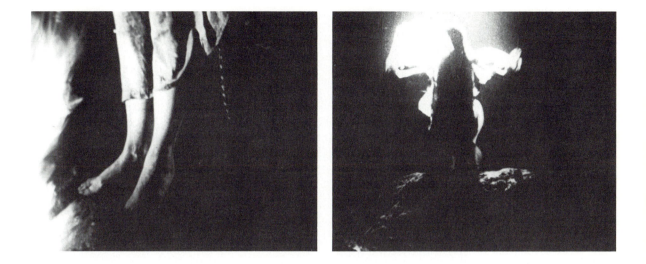

as the best of a dozen detectives. Because of the nightmare, the husband's choice of him as the pursuer is ironically portentous. The dancing duel in the restaurant, in a different way, also replicates the opium den sequence. Here the woman's dancing arouses the men's desire, reversing the relation between Mosjoukine and his den of women. Z challenges her power by organizing a competition among the restaurant women—3,000 francs for the one who can outlast the others. As he plays the piano, accelerating the rhythm, the speed of the dancers increases—in fast motion shots and rapid cutting (although the rhythm of the editing is a bit rough). When the last dancer collapses, Z has to save the woman from an attack by the crowd of men. Finally, in the sequence where Z discovers the marriage contract hidden under the woman's bed (where else?), several actions and images are repeated from the stake-burning and city street sequences. When the woman sees his legs sticking out from under the bed, she takes a cane and begins whipping him, reversing the provocative act in the nightmare. Instead of hands struggling over flames and strands of hair, here, ironically, they struggle over a briefcase containing the contract.

The main function of the nightmare—"positioned structurally in the film much like the thematic prelude to a symphony," as Canudo says[8]—is to establish a nexus of semantic relations for the narrative to play with. It is an explicitly sexual fantasy, articulating both the fascination for and fear of sexual desire, a fable of eruption and suppression. Whether she abandons herself to desire (at the stake-burning, on the street, or in an opium den) or seeks atonement in the church (is this a typical Catholic story?), it positions the woman as the threatened object of man's desire and power. The real story of the narrative seems to reverse this relation between the sexes. The woman lords it over her husband. She arouses desire in the detective, which he tries vainly to suppress. Yet her power is tenuous, illusory. It is her husband who is the source of money and social status (she was just a peasant fisherwoman). It is he who possesses the law and who is its subject (e.g., the marriage

186. Mosjoukine confronts Lissenko before the zig-zag slash door in the *Caligari*-style street in the opening sequence of *Le Brasier ardent* (1923)

contract that she steals). And it is the detective whose money bests her in the dancing duel. Thus, the film narrates her oscillation between two conditions, as a wife and a free woman, neither of which is much different from the other.

Eventually, however, her story is subordinated to the detective's. She will end up serving one man or another. Whereas the nightmare defined Z as a figure of daemonic power, in reality he is a sexual naïf. His encounters with the woman are fraught with suppression and evasion. The horror of the nightmare turns to comedy—the whipping, the guilty return of the briefcase, his boyish mannerisms, his toothache (which the bulldog shares), his love for mother. Only indirectly can he exercise power over the woman. In the restaurant, his money controls the dancers, and his detective's revolver protects (but does not threaten) her. For him, the ending is a comic resolution to an apparently long-delayed Oedipal crisis. He is asleep beside his mother on the couch when the woman arrives. Quietly, one woman simply replaces the other. Awakening, Z leaps about in a frenzy of delight, overjoyed to discover that he can have both mother and lover at the same time. The new relationship is summed up in the last bit of mockery. Before the final kiss, the woman takes her coat off and coyly buttons up his jacket to the neck. What did the Surrealists think of this outrageous parody of *l'amour fou*?

Le Brasier ardent may begin in the cauldron of savage passion, but it ends on the couch of domestic inhibition and motherly love. So much for scorching fires. A woman's nightmare has been transformed into a man's fantasy. Tragedy has been turned into comedy. If the resolution seems contrived and unconvincing, the point seems deliberate. For there is one short sequence left—

372

the husband sailing off on his cruise. On deck he notices a woman alone at the rail. As he sidles closer to her, the boat whistle sounds (as if in alarm); he looks up and sees a life preserver emblazoned with LIBERTÉ (and the sign of the C.G.T.). In a FS/LS, he walks quickly off down the deck, and the woman at the rail turns to the camera and laughs. Who indeed has the last laugh? This is not a film that resolves its conflicts smoothly or that closes off by masking its contradictions. Just the opposite—they are all left dangling openly at the end.

To hear Jean Renoir tell it, *La Fille de l'eau* (1925) was the offspring of a bizarre coupling, in the summer of 1924, between his young wife, Catherine Hessling, and the forest of Fountainebleau.[9] At times in the film, Renoir seems to have been working in the shadow of his famous father, Pierre Auguste Renoir. Catherine had been the painter's last model, and Renoir admits that his initial interest was to explore, with his cameraman Jean Bachelet, "the plastic qualities" of her face and figure. The locations chosen for the exterior shooting, on Cezanne's old estate at Marlotte (where Jean had a house) and along the river Loing near Montigny, also echoed some of his father's paintings. Yet Renoir's cinematic interests really lay elsewhere.

The scenario for *La Fille de l'eau* was an original one, written in collaboration with his friend, Pierre Lestringuez. It was a slapdash affair, much like *Le Brasier ardent*, concocted from fairy tales, American serials and comedies, French melodramas and realist films.[10] When her father, a canal bargeman, drowns accidentally, Virginia (Catherine Hessling) comes under the brutal care of her Uncle Jeff (Pierre Philippe, alias Lestringuez) who soon drinks away what little inheritance there is, including the barge. After he tries to rape her one morning, she runs off and joins a young poacher, nicknamed "The Ferret" (Maurice Touzé), who undertakes her education and brings her to live with his mother in a gypsy encampment. One day they antagonize a wealthy farmer, Justin Crepoix (Pierre Campagne), and are protected by Georges Raynal (Harold Livingston), the college-educated son of an eccentric landowner in the neighborhood (he has a passion for motor cars). The conflict flares up again, however, until one night the local farmers burn the gypsy wagons. Virginia escapes, only to fall into a quarry, where Georges finds her and takes her to a miller's cottage to convalesce. Later, Jeff turns up and demands money from her, which she is forced to steal from her benefactor. Georges overhears her arguing with Jeff, leaps over a wall to do battle, and throws him into the river. Since the family is being sent to Algeria, for business reasons, he asks Virginia to join them.

According to Renoir and Lestringuez, this nonsensical story was of little importance. "It was no more than a pretext for shots of a purely visual value."[11] At the time, Renoir considered himself quite *au courant* in his conception of film art. Later, he would change his position radically, but the change would not affect his perception of *La Fille de l'eau*. If the film was of interest at all, it was only for his fascination with certain technical effects—besides what he learned from its production about filmmaking. Although the results of this fascination do indeed place *La Fille de l'eau* in the context of the narrative avant-garde film practice, they are not the only elements of the film that do so.

187. Catherine Hessling and Harold Livingston in *La Fille de l'eau* (1925)

La Fille de l'eau was released just as Jean Epstein was announcing that certain "strategies of cinematic expression" were becoming clichéd, that is, part of conventional French film practice.[12] One of these techniques was rapid montage, which was now appearing in such commercial films as Volkoff's *Kean* (1924) and Epstein's own *Le Lion des Mogols* (1924). Renoir was obviously fascinated by it, for *La Fille de l'eau* contains two sequences of rapid montage clearly derived from Gance's *La Roue*, Mosjoukine's *Le Brasier ardent*, and Epstein's *La Belle Nivernaise* (1924).[13] Neither mark an advance in the function of the technique, but they work effectively enough. The first is used to describe Jeff's attack on Virginia in the cabin of the barge. That montage gets down to six to eight frames per shot at one point and includes CUs of Jeff and Virginia, high angle shots of her crying for help at a window, and interspersed shots of a barking dog tied on deck as well as of a clock alarm going off. If this sequence is chiefly omniscient in its narration, incorporating a number of separate actions simultaneously, the second is completely subjective. In a state of shock after her fall into the quarry, Virginia hallucinates back to the attack on the gypsy camp. Shots of a wagon burning (from different distances and angles) alternate rapidly with shots of Crepoix and the other farmers (who seem to loom out of the darkness and flames) and of her own face in a wagon window.[14] The alternation changes very little in rhythm or choice of shots, however; and the sequence simply ends with Virginia stumbling off, her hair flaring out in a daemonic halo.

Certain in-camera optical effects apparently enchanted Renoir even more than did rapid montage.[15] He was especially taken with various kinds of multiple exposure and slow motion shots. In the parody of a heroic battle at the end, for instance, Georges is nearly knocked unconscious (rendered in several

374

188. (left) Catherine Hessling
asleep at the beginning of the
dream sequence in *La Fille de
l'eau* (1925)

189. (right) Catherine
Hessling falls through the sky
at the end of the dream
sequence

out-of-focus shots and double exposures) before he tosses Jeff into the river. The major display of these techniques, however, comes in Virginia's fantasy the night after she falls into the quarry. Much like the nightmare that opens *Le Brasier ardent*, this fantasy undergoes a series of startling ruptures and transformations. Their effect is to turn it into an overtly sexual version of *Alice in Wonderland*.

At the beginning, against the trunk of a large tree, Virginia is asleep in the rain, dressed mysteriously in a diaphanous gown whose overexposed whiteness contrasts sharply with the darkness around her. In superimposition, she rises to discover Jeff suspended from a rope in the tree. Suddenly he is alive beside her, the noose becomes a snake coiled around his neck, and she backs away in slow motion. Now the fantasy begins again with her double image leaping backwards onto a tree limb (in reverse slow motion) where Jeff and Crepoix dissolve in menacingly beside her. When Crepoix slowly swings under the limb like an animal, Virginia leaps down and bounds off. A series of dissolves takes her through a landscape of rocks and bare stunted trees to a large hall with huge phallic pillars lying about on their sides. The two men reappear, along with a lumbering dragon (a magnified chameleon with absurdly tiny wings) that crawls among the pillars. Seemingly pursued by monstrous beasts threatening rape, Virginia runs toward a wall opening, and several handheld tracking shots heighten her desperate flight. Suddenly back at the tree, the fantasy resumes for a third and last time as Georges appears astride a galloping white horse with Virginia beside him. Through a series of slow-motion tracking shots (actually 360° pans within a black cylindrical set at Gaumont studios),[16] supered over silhouetted trees and clouds, the pair race off into the heavens. The threatened rape turns into an ecstatic seduction. There, Virginia slips off the horse and falls gently through the air, the veil of her white gown billowing about her. Dissolve to the figure by the tree and fade out. It was this magical, almost surrealistic sequence which, one week in 1925, Jean Tedesco screened at the Vieux-Colombier in a program of extracts from recent French films. The night Renoir and Catherine Hessling attended, the audience was so enthusiastic that the piano accompaniment was eventually drowned out by their applause. "For the first time," wrote Renoir later, "I experienced the intoxication of success."[17]

There is more to *La Fille de l'eau* than these set pieces of technique, however. Despite Renoir's disclaimer, its narrative construction is interesting and bears some similarity to that of other narrative avant-garde films. There are crucial moments of ellipsis, for instance, as in Epstein's films. The death of Virginia's father occurs in a LS of the barge (we can barely see someone fall) and a shot of a splash, some bubbles, then stillness on the water. The theft of Georges's money is described in a single shot (marked off by fades)—a CU of Virginia's hand passing francs to Jeff's, seen against a dusty road surface crisscrossed by the shadows of tree limbs. There are also segments organized in alternating sequences. The most surprising of these occurs in the beginning of the film as, first, Virginia's "family" and, then, the Raynals are introduced. When Georges and his father appear alongside the canal, we expect the alternation to bring them together. But it doesn't. That is delayed until almost midway through the film, and the alternation instead juxtaposes two classes, two ways of life. Both are treated somewhat comically: the megaphone Virginia uses to talk with her father while she cooks leaves a black circle around her mouth (Hessling's spunkiness here reminds one of Mary Pickford); M. Raynal trundles his car off in a cloud of smoke to search for botanical specimens along the canal. The alternation suddenly turns tragic and mocking when Virginia's father drowns. At the precise moment that happens, Georges is taking a photograph of the canal with a box camera. Because of the juxtaposition, his ignorance of the accident becomes metaphorical—a stigma of blind complacency attaches to him and his class. Since Renoir's own socioeconomic position was much like Georges's at the time, the sequence looks like a very conscious attempt to separate his own personal vision from that of his fictional character.

La Fille de l'eau also shares with several other narrative avant-garde films an eclectic combination of film styles or modes. Like *Le Brasier ardent*, it leaps and oscillates from one extreme to another. Documentary-style realism is juxtaposed to comic caricature; bourgeois melodrama to wild flights of fantasy. An early reviewer called special attention to these shifts:

. . . the alternating cadence of its tableaux, where the limpid freshness of the streams and canals is opposed to visions of nocturnal horror in which the water is no longer the mirror of a clear sky but the somber shroud of the drowned, where the calm existence of a little provincial village contrasts with the ravings of a mob drunk on vengeance, where the feverish sleep of a child turns into a whirling nightmare that ends in a fantastic horseback ride through a stormy sky and over the twisted tops of blackened trees. . . .[18]

These stylistic oscillations all seem determined by a particular axis of opposition: a surface texture of social harmony or natural beauty that masks conflicting forces and the threat of violence. The forces continually disrupting the placid calm of the characters and their environment are clearly socioeconomic, racial, and sexual in nature. But their distribution across the film is ambiguous, even contradictory.[19] The Ferret, for instance, provides Virginia with a natural environment for love and play, yet he and his mother desert her. The

Raynals are bumbling fools, yet Georges gains the physical strength and generosity of spirit to protect her. Strangely, the peasant farmers and craftsmen are unequivocally vilified. Jeff and Crepoix are the real villains. As the most broadly caricatured figure—almost like an Eisenstein villain, notes Raymond Durgnat[20]—Crepoix, particularly, is the locus of every kind of threat. Angered by Ferret's playful disrespect and poaching on his land, Crepoix punishes him, and their conflict escalates into a vengeful conflagration in which the Ferret sets Crepoix's haystacks ablaze and the band of farmers burns the gypsy camp. Ending this sequence is a FS of one bullheaded farmer (Pierre Renoir) silhouetted against the flames, holding out a pitchfork as if it were a weapon (aimed at Virginia?). Condensing all the forces of violence into a single shot, this is probably the most frightening image in the film.

This ideological matrix of oppositions would concern Renoir for most of his film career. How far away he still is from clearly defining these conflicts and resolving them in a satisfactory form can be gathered from *La Fille de l'eau*'s conclusion. Despite his blindness at the beginning, Georges turns into the sentimental hero—love allows him to hear and see. Jeff is exposed and defeated, but he swims away in the river, as if only temporarily repressed (Renoir will redefine the character and action radically in *Boudu sauvé des eaux*, 1932). Crepoix and the farmers, on the other hand, are simply forgotten. With all the disreputable attributes of her class sloughed off (in Jeff's disappearance), Virginia can be accepted into the Raynal family, conventionally resolving the sexual and socioeconomic conflicts. *Lumpen* wanderer and landed gentry achieve an illusory form of harmony, camaraderie, and freedom. And yet the film seems acutely conscious of its implausibility, for the whole family is quickly packed off to Algeria. Either the conflicts, once resolved, can exist only in an exotic other world or they will be exported intact in a colonial adventure.

Paris qui dort and Entr'acte

Like *Le Brasier ardent*, René Clair's first film, *Paris qui dort* (1924), is a comic fantasy which synthesizes much of the then current narrative avant-garde film practice. Clair's shooting schedule, from June to September, 1923, coincided exactly with the premiere and general release dates of Mosjoukine's film.[1] The actual shooting, mostly on location in Paris, came in bits and pieces, however, because there were frequent interruptions whenever producer Henri Diamant-Berger could not provide enough money.[2] These production conditions show clearly in the relatively simple cinematography (by Maurice Desfassiaux and Paul Guichard) and rough continuity editing of the released film, which unaccountably was withheld from exhibition until late 1924.[3] The most circulated American print, which Clair has disowned, in fact looks like it has been overextended to feature-length.[4] Yet Clair himself considered *Paris qui dort* little more than an apprentice film. Its roughness testified to his desire to revive "the prewar tradition, that is, the tradition of the French comic shorts" and of Méliès's *féeries*.[5] Although he shared the narrative avant-garde filmmakers' fascination with "the cinematograhic machine," Clair disapproved of what he believed to be their excessive aestheticism and redirected the apparatus toward different ends. In *Paris qui dort*, consequently, the narrative avant-garde film practice is placed explicitly in the service of an amusing fantasy and a wittily satirical social vision.

377

The scenario for *Paris qui dort* is an original one, cleverly exploiting the cinematic production of movement as the crux of its narrative.[6] One morning, Albert (Henri Rollan), the night watchman on the Eiffel Tower, awakens to discover nothing at all moving in the city below. In some places, the streets are completely empty; in others people and vehicles seem frozen in a state of immobility. As he is about to despair of this mystery, a carload of five people pulls up—a pilot (Albert Préjean), a "woman of means" (Madeleine Rodrigue), an industrialist (Stacquet), a detective (Pré *fils*), and his prisoner, a thief (Marcel Vallée). All have just arrived by plane from Marseille. The six characters wander about Paris together, gradually deciding that they can simply take anything they want; but, as a precaution, they continue to live on top of the Eiffel Tower. One day, a radio S.O.S. directs them to a house where a young woman (Myla Seller) is trapped. Her father is a scientist (Martinelli), who has invented a ray machine that can paralyze the whole world. And that is just what he has done. The group of survivors surprises the scientist and forces him to return the world to normal. However, all is not well. When he tries to court the scientist's daughter, Albert discovers that he has no money left. Surreptitiously, the two use the ray machine to immobilize the world again and then set off to acquire some. The scientist notices what has happened, reverses the process, and Albert and the daughter are promptly arrested. When they try to explain, the police toss them in with the other five mad characters who have preceded them to the station. Quickly abandoning their obsession with telling the truth, all seven are released. While the scientist waits on a park bench below, Albert and the daughter go to the top of the Eiffel Tower, where he finds a pearl ring (the only souvenir of their adventure) and slips it on her finger.

None of the characters in this story is more than a type. "Each assumes a pure *essence*," writes Barthélemy Amengual, "that is represented perfectly with neither ambiguity nor bravura."[7] Except for hero and heroine, each has a particular tic or trait. The pilot carefully lowers a ladder and then jumps out of his plane in a leather jacket, goggles, and tastefully disheveled hair; on the Eiffel Tower, he goes off by himself and performs gymnastics on the steel beams. The woman lounges about like a nonchalant fashion model, once even posing like Delacroix's figure of liberty against the cityscape (in one of the few lovingly photographed images of the film). The industrialist is a short-tempered, compact little man, who runs in quick, short steps; he is solely concerned to find his mistress Lisette (who turns out to be with another man). The detective is thin, long-faced, with a drooping mustache; he is, of course, the slowest of all of them to catch on to anything. The thief, on the other hand, is an exuberant, quick-witted, generous fellow, who cannot keep his hands off playing cards, money, or precious objects. It is he who turns out to be the most useful member of the group—picking locks to get into houses, demonstrating how to get what one wants in a restaurant, and topping their festivities with speeches.

The thief's changed status in this "paradise" is but one of a series of ironic reversals whose interrelation seems to provide some structure to the film. A rich, ripe Aladdin's Cave of a world lies open to plunder, and all six characters become thieves in order to survive—and prosper. Although a whole society of manners, mores, and public and private situations lies exposed to their scru-

190. (left) Albert Préjean on
the Eiffel Tower in *Paris qui
dort* (1924)

191. (right) Madeleine
Rodrique and Henri Rollan
on the Eiffel Tower

tiny and ridicule, they find themselves reproducing that society on the Eiffel
Tower. Albert and the woman stroll around the platforms in chic white sporting outfits, like advertisements of the modern good life. The others play poker
or rummage through the hockshop of goods they have carried up from below.
Soon the easy life bores them—the woman idly tosses pearls off the Tower,
and the pilot sails paper airplanes cut out of thousand-franc notes. Finally,
the men begin quarreling after they realize there is only one woman left on
earth. When these "masters of the world" reenter normal society, they find
themselves threatened on every side. A gendarme tickets the car they have
been driving; a tiny old lady attendant forces Albert and the scientist's daughter out of some park chairs, and a flower girl pursues them along a walk.
When the authorities finally hear their story, they promptly lock them up as
madmen—in a comic variation on the conclusion of *Caligari*. Only by denying
their difference from society (which has turned out to be no difference at all)
are they accepted into the world again. And the pearl that has symbolized
both their greed and boredom concludes the film as a not-so-innocent token
of love.

Like some of its predecessors, *Paris qui dort* concocts a mixture of the real
and the unreal, of reality and fantasy. Its combination of the two, however,
is quite unlike that of L'Herbier's, Epstein's, or Dulac's films. And it involves
nothing like the complexity of rhetorical figuring or syntactical relations that
characterize their work. Much of Clair's film is documentary footage of Paris—
of its famous monuments, of the inhabitants and vehicles traveling its streets.
There are even several brief, awkward attempts to record the elevator's movement up and down the Eiffel Tower, a subject Clair would return to in his
short documentary on the celebrated steel structure, *La Tour* (1928). However,
the function of these shots and sequences, whether realistic or fantastical,
depends entirely on their placement in the narrative discourse. Occasionally,
there are moments when the two modes are peculiarly fused. For instance, an

379

obviously fictional space is produced by intercutting several HAFSs of Albert (looking in three different directions on the Pont Alexandre III) with shots of the Place de la Concorde, the Madeleine, and the Champs-Elysées. The same is true of certain stylistic elements. Tracking shots, fast-motion shots, and rapid cutting—all are associated with both the real and the fantastic. When Albert remembers the past unparalyzed city (he assumes the position of Rodin's statue, in a deliberate parody of Poirier's *Le Penseur* [1920]), there is a short subjective sequence of tracking shots among the vehicles on the streets. When the men begin to quarrel on the Tower, several fast-motion shots of their fighting produce a little minimalist film of a repeated kick in the pants. In contrast to these moments, when the scientist argues near the end with one of his colleagues about his experiment's success—and they cause the machine accidentally to go haywire—a sequence of rapidly cut, fast-motion tracking shots erupts, describing a totally different world on the brink of physical catastrophe. It is as if the accelerating train sequence in *La Roue* had been expanded to include the entire world (or all of Paris, at least).

The primary visual opposition in *Paris qui dort*, however, is not between reality and fantasy or between one stylistic and another. Rather, it is simply between immobility and movement, between stasis and motion, between the still and moving image.

It was probably because I was interested in the movement produced by the cinematographic machine that I tried to demonstrate the value of that movement through the absurd, that is, to paralyze Paris in order to emphasize how different was Paris, animated and alive.[8]

For the crucial concept of a paralyzed city, Clair's simple strategies are remarkably effective—shots of deserted streets, shots that metamorphose from freeze frames to moving images (and vice versa), shots of inanimate human figures juxtaposed in the same frame with animate ones. The stillness of the city strangely sets off the slightest movement of the six characters who wander through it—shades of Pirandello.[9] This new world is like a Musée Gravin of photographs—especially Atget's vacant Paris spaces, as Annette Michelson has noted[10]—whose reference has been redirected from the past to the present and future, a space that opens into another time. In reproducing that first moment when photographs "came to life," *Paris qui dort* recovers the magic of the cinema with a simplicity that reminds one of Buster Keaton's *Sherlock Jr.* (1924). Though its scientific laboratory looks like a cardboard set even Mack Sennett would reject, its magic nearly rivals the panache of Marcel L'Herbier's *L'Inhumaine* (1924). For all of its *longueurs* and flaws of execution, Clair's film offers a truly fresh vision of an *other*, marvelous world.

Clair's second film, *Entr'acte* (1924), is a comic fantasy of a different order. As Clair himself has said, there were two versions of this film which was hastily shot (by Jimmy Berliet) and assembled in October, 1924.[11] The first played an integral part in Francis Picabia's ballet *Relâche*, which, performed by Jean Borlin's Ballet suédois, premiered at the Théâtre des Champs-Elysées on 4 December 1924.[12] The performance opened with a short film prologue that featured Picabia and the ballet's composer, Erik Satie, descending from the sky in slow motion to load a cannon. The cannon shot signaled the begin-

192. A "still life" from *Paris qui dort* (1924)

ning of the ballet on stage. At the *entr'acte*, the rest of Clair's film was pro-jected—to a rising storm of boos, whistles, howls of disgust, and scattered applause. In the end, a character breaks through the "End" title (in slow motion), and Rolf de Maré, the Théâtre des Champs-Elysées manager, kicks him back through—to signal the beginning of the ballet's second act. Just one year later, these two parts were combined into a twenty-two minute film for the opening of the Studio des Ursulines.[13] This second version of the film now exists in general circulation, and it has recently been legitimized by the synchronized recording (under Clair's supervision) of Satie's original score.[14]

Most critics accept *Entr'acte* as possessing two loosely related parts of equal length. The first half owes most to Picabia's single-page scenario or sketch, allegedly dashed off one night at Maxim's. It is virtually plotless, except perhaps for the shooting (by Picabia) of the hunter figure (Jean Borlin). De-nying logical connections and diegetic continuity, the images offer instead a continuity of graphic and rhythmic relations as well as a stream of comically provocative associations. The lights of a Paris nightscape blur into a pair of boxing gloves (in negative) that rapidly spar with one another until one seems to punch out the camera. A chess game played by Marcel Duchamp and Man Ray suddenly dissolves into the Place de la Concorde and is immediately awash in water. A paper boat begins tossing and turning against a panning shot of the Paris rooftops. A ballerina, photographed in slow motion from below through glass, is transformed into an opening and closing flower, matching the inflating/deflating balloon heads of some dolls in a shooting gallery. The hunter shoots an artificial egg suspended in a jet of water, and, in its place, a pigeon flies off. Animating this series of colliding, metamorphosing, dispar-ate visual elements is a Dadaist spirit of intentional mystification and mocking provocation.

The second half of the film, however, owes more to Clair's improvisation with narrative. A Mack Sennett-like chase involving a vast crowd of funeral mourners (perhaps for the hunter) and a camel-drawn hearse, it is organized like a whimsical study of cinematic movement and a celebration of motion

381

over stasis.[15] The funeral procession begins in slow motion with a long line of mourners following the hearse in marvelous leaps. When the hearse escapes the camel (or vice versa), it quickly draws these single-minded figures into a vortex of ever-increasing speed. The climax comes in an accelerating montage of fast-motion tracking shots of the streets filled with racing cars, of trees streaking by overhead, and finally of a vertiginous rollercoaster ride. When the coffin spills out and comes to rest in a field, a magician (Jean Borlin again) pops out and makes the few remaining mourners and himself disappear, one by one. The brilliant tour de force of rhythmic cutting in this sequence gives a wry parodic twist to the famous accelerating montage set pieces (of suicide) in Gance's *La Roue* and L'Herbier's *L'Inhumaine*.[16]

Several critics, however, have interpreted *Entr'acte* as an integral whole. For Noel Carroll, the film is "a coherent, purposively directed assault" on the social practices and beliefs, the rationality, of the French bourgeois culture.[17] It affronts high art, for example, by burlesquing ballet. "The repeated crotch shots of the ballerina suggest a well-known pornographic interest in the art," while the substitution of a rather greasy and unattractive man for an ideal image of female beauty is "akin to drawing a mustache on the Mona Lisa." The solemnity of a funeral turns into farce—a carnival air hose on the doorstep lifts the skirt of each grieving woman. Paris itself turns pejoratively meta-phoric—as a boxing match, a chess game, a turbulent sea. Finally, Clair emphasizes the velocity of the climactic game, the chase, seeming to suck the whole city into pursuit of the hearse. Ultimately, that chase becomes self-destructive, a kind of ironical death race, "that breaks up society under the pressure of its own reckless propulsion."

For Paul Sandro, more plausibly, this assault is set in the context of "an extensive parody of cinematic reality [and] cinematic discourses."[18] The first part of *Entr'acte* teases us with the possibility of diegetic continuity and caus-ality through several pairs of eyes—those of the man who scratches his head (igniting matches), those superimposed on a water surface, and those of the balloon-head dolls. But these multiple POVs prove unstable, just as the chess game gets out of control and the "drunken boat" seems to go nowhere or around in circles. We are caught up in an interplay of deceptions. The second part of the film finally produces a linear action, but diegetic space-time con-tinues to be parodied. The hearse as well as its pursuers change screen direc-tions frequently. Shots of the ballerina are cut into the chase, as disruptive excess. Furthermore, the film parodies its own production of narrative. Picabia himself performs the act of violence to initiate the chase and then has his and Satie's initials put on the vehicle that will propel it to a climax. As undertakers behind the scenes, as proprietors in absentia of the (narrative) vehicle, they embalm their characters in the diegetic space-time of the story. And, in the end, the narrative corpus, like the corpse in the story, refuses to be put away and must suffer one last repetition and reversal.

If Picabia believed that *Entr'acte* respected nothing except "the desire to burst out laughing,"[19] Clair seems to have had more in mind. For all its debunking and denunciation, *Entr'acte* is a narrative text of pleasure, in San-dro's words, "one that celebrates old forms and reinscribes them in a ludic space."[20] The magical, marvelous world of *Paris qui dort* is turned inside out here in a witty, audacious, slapdash thrill ride.

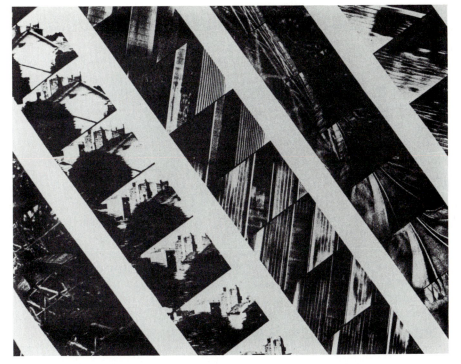

193. Strips of film from
Entr'acte, from the cover
of *Théâtre et
Comoedia Illustré*

L'Inhumaine

Marcel L'Herbier's *L'Inhumaine* (1924) is one of the more disreputable forgotten films of the 1920s. For reasons that are still unclear, L'Herbier chose not to submit his film to the usual previews for exhibitors in the summer of 1924.[1] Instead, *L'Inhumaine* opened cold at the Madeleine-Cinéma, in November, in the midst of *Le Miracle des loups, Pêcheur d'Islande* and *The Ten Commandments*.[2] The response was overwhelmingly negative: "The audience whistled and yelled . . . and at certain screenings some people even broke up their seats. . . ."[3] A financial catastrophe in France, the film only recouped a good portion of its costs after a year or more in worldwide distribution.

Most film historians and critics have ridiculed *L'Inhumaine* as a disastrously misguided attempt to celebrate film as art or to reconcile the popular and the elitist.

The adventure that it narrates in images under the name of Pierre Mac Orlan is unusually ordinary, simply standard fare. It could just as easily be signed Jules Mary, Pierre Decourcelle, Jean de la Hire.[4]

If the action of *L'Inhumaine* is situated in 1950, the characters are situated in something more like 1910, in a rapturous world where the Italian "divas" . . . and other "belles dames sans merci" live.[5]

Glossing an imitation modernism over a cock-and-bull story in which Georgette Leblanc and Jaque Catelain are rivals in guile and artifice, this film, which must be the end of the end of art for art's sake and today is nothing short of ridiculous, was then no more than the ultimate expression of vanity in the midst of falsehood envisaged through a welter of resemblances.[6]

383

As Noël Burch suggests, the film "does not merit such scornful excess."[7]

Like *La Roue*, the scenario for *L'Inhumaine* was paradoxically "démodé." Even L'Herbier admits it was not very prestigious. The original version, written in collaboration with Pierre Mac Orlan, was entitled *La Femme de glace*. But it had to be radically revised and custom-tailored for the American singer-actress, Georgette Leblanc, on whom the project's financing and distribution hopes depended. What the film might have been like had another more accomplished, less inflexible actress been available (L'Herbier later remarked that Brigitte Helm would have been perfect for the role)[8] is difficult to surmise. As it is, the film's narrative does seem a concession—condescension may be closer to the mark—to popular taste. The celebrated singer, Claire Lescaut (Georgette Leblanc), is engaged to marry a wealthy American entrepreneur, Frank Mahler (Fred Kellerman). At an evening salon in her spacious mansion outside Paris, she suddenly rejects Mahler as well as the attention of several other international guests who have come to court her: a Russian prince, Tarsky (L. V. Terval), the Maharajah Djorah (Philippe Hériat), and finally a Swedish inventor, Einar Norsen (Jaque Catelain)—"A young engineer in love with machines, sports, and the magic of modern science." Told that she will go off on a world tour unless "something" happens, Einar threatens suicide. As he leaves the salon early, she coolly drops a tiny knife in his hand. Later that night, he is apparently killed when his sports car goes over a cliff. A peasant woman (Marcelle Pradot) reports the accident to Claire, who shows little emotion at all. The next day, she is called to identify the body—after successfully countering the efforts of the other three men to disrupt her performance at the Théâtre des Champs-Elysées. When she breaks down and prays before the corpse, Einar miraculously revives (he had faked the death), and Claire reluctantly admits her love for him. They tour his laboratory, and she returns to the Théâtre. Jealous of her new fascination for the inventor, Djorah disguises himself as a chauffeur and concocts a plan to kill her with a viper hidden in a basket of flowers. The plan succeeds, and he cruelly deposits her body in front of Einar's laboratory. There, in an agony of passion, Einar undertakes several dangerous experiments and restores her to life . . . and love.

For L'Herbier, however, this serial-style science fiction adventure romance (aptly subtitled a "fairy tale") was of little consequence. What concerned him was how it was narrated—or not narrated. He used the scenario, he told Jean-André Fieschi,

. . . a little like composers use what they call the bass clef. On this bass clef, I constructed chords, plastic chords, and what was important for me was not the horizontal parade of events but vertical plastic harmonies.[9]

Very much like *Coeur fidèle*, then, the scenario of *L'Inhumaine* serves as a pretext for an experimental film. What marks it most conspicuously is a barrage of ruptures or breaks with the conventions of narrative film discourse. These ruptures advance, retard, suspend, and even deflect the narrative systematically, in a variety of ways. As a consequence, they produce a narrative structure that is organized paradigmatically rather than syntagmatically. Equally important, they call attention to the materials of film discourse and to their graphic, rhythmic, and connotative relations.

The systematic nature of *L'Inhumaine*'s break with conventional narrative film discourse justifies L'Herbier's repeated description of the film as his most deliberately synthetic work. The adjective fits aptly in more ways than one. From the production's inception in the summer of 1923, as a French showcase for the American market, L'Herbier and his colleagues at Cinégraphic planned to make it "a sort of summary, a provisional summary, of all that was artistically advanced in France two years before the famous Exposition des Arts Décoratifs."[10] This included the work of (besides Pierre Mac Orlan) the painter Fernand Léger, the architect Robert Mallet-Stevens, the composer Darius Milhaud, the furniture designer Pierre Chareau, the fashion designer Paul Poiret, the young set designers Alberto Cavalcanti and Claude Autant-Lara, and, of course, his new chief cameraman, Georges Specht.[11] Through this conjunction of artistic activity, L'Herbier also made his most ambitious (but not entirely successful) attempt to produce a narrative structure guided by one particular strategy of the narrative avant-garde film practice—the mixture of film styles or modes.[12] In this, *L'Inhumaine* represented the culmination of a whole line of films that included *El Dorado, Don Juan et Faust, La Roue, Le Brasier ardent,* and even *L'Auberge rouge.* Finally, like *El Dorado* and *Coeur fidèle,* L'Herbier's film synthesized most of the techniques then current in the narrative avant-garde film practice. In the final climactic moments of the film, in fact, those techniques were pushed to a kind of cinematic apotheosis.

A good measure of *L'Inhumaine*'s deviation from conventional narrative film discourse can be gathered from its opening. The subject is perfectly normal— the description of a place and several major characters—but the manner of presentation is highly unusual. The titles begin it with a Léger machine drawing (including a revolving disk, upper frame right) against which the elegant white letters of *L'Inhumaine* glide across from right to left. What kind of conjunctions and juxtapositions are condensed here? The first shot (perhaps echoing *La Roue*) is a rapid tracking shot of a roadside slope which tilts up slightly to reveal, far below in the background, a river and bridge and city beyond. Already the camera track, unattached to any character, calls more attention to the frame and the speed and direction of its movement than to the space it is moving through. As the slope rises and blots out the view, the shot cuts (the effect is like a wipe) to a simple De Stijl-style painting of an ultramodern house. This blatant juxtaposition of the three-dimensional and the two-dimensional, the documentary and the fictional, the real and the artificial, is bridged by the intertitle, "Dominating the city." The next shot is a HAELS of the same city which slowly pans left until the river begins glinting in the sunlight. Suddenly the movement turns into a swish pan, and an invisible cut carries the pan left to a model of the house with all of its windows lit. Again there is the juxtaposition, the gap, that is "healed" now by a cinematic device which calls attention to its compression or literal blurring of space and time. Here lives Claire Lescaut, another intertitle narrates, and a series of dissolves takes us closer to the house until the model gives way to a full-scale set as several cars drive up and their passengers disembark. Before we even see her, the central character has been defined in a position of dominance, on the side of the geometrical, the static, and the artificial. Who will be defined as her opposite? And how will the machine world of the title drawing be bound up in that opposition?

Once inside, the first shot is a soft-focus LS of several men standing before

385

an archway. A wipe removes the soft focus, and the men move off to the side—as if prompted by the device. Several soft-focus transitions fix them in MS, looking at a poster of Claire Lescaut. Again, she is defined as a two-dimensional, artificial figure, this time as the object of men's looks. As the first three rivals for her affection are introduced (Einar is absent, delayed), in a series of shots (FSs, MSs, MCUs) and intertitles, the sequence does not so much define them in a three-dimensional space, related by looks and movement, as it spreads them out in a kind of abstract mosaic. Instead of establishing a realistic space, the sequence constructs a nonreferential space (delimited by the frame) and positions and repositions the men within it. Only after Djorah is introduced does this pattern change:

MCU of Djorah starting forward.
HALS of the room, with men gathered (frame left); detaching themselves from them, Tarsky and Mahler go over to take a poster from a bearded man (frame right).
MCU of Djorah; he looks around and starts to move forward.
HALS of the room; Mahler and the bearded men exit right; Djorah enters from the left and goes to Tarsky, takes the poster, looks at it, and hands it to another man; all of them drift off toward the right.

The abrupt shifts in camera distance and angle single out Djorah as a special character but curiously provide little more sense of a referential space. Finally, just before Claire appears, a HAELS reveals an immense banquet hall—whose center is a geometrically designed black-and-white marble platform surrounded by a moat of water. The men are but small figures (frame left), and Claire is visible in a strongly lit arched area (at the focal point of the center background), as if she were already at the head of the table. With this shot, the sequence's construction of space climaxes in spectacle. The next shot continues the effect—a FS of a half-dozen butlers clustered in the center, who, after a white dove flies into the frame and out, spring apart to reveal Claire on a kind of throne. And each butler has on an identical white mask: Do they suggest the symbolic position of the men—anonymous replications of one another and subservient to her wishes? Finally, there is the inevitable slightly soft-focus CU of Claire, smiling against a dark background. As the center of the spectacle, she is both its most desirable object and its subject, its governing figure.

The sequence that finally introduces Einar Norsen defines him as both Claire's equal and her opposite. His house, which is similar to Claire's, suggests a parallel to her; but the sports car he roars off in, inscribing the machine world of the opening title, produces a crucial contrast. A brief series of camera and figure movements extends this initial ambiguity.

HALS of the sports car traveling left along a curved road on a hill above the river beyond.
HAFS of the banquet table; pan right from Claire to the guests on the right side of the table and then pan left back to her.
FS dolly ahead of the sports car traveling rapidly along a wet road.

Einar moves into the same space as described in the beginning of the film, which seems to position him on the opposite side of the paradigm from Claire. The lateral camera movement in the second shot, however, which first sets

194. Alberto Cavalcanti's set for Claire Lescaut's banquet hall in *L'Inhumaine* (1924)

her apart from him, also places her in the direction of his movement. Suddenly the tracking shots of his sports car turn subjective: a HAELS track left above the river bridge, which turns into a swish pan, and then a rapid forward dolly shot, past Einar's head (in MCU), to the road ahead—conveyed by a split image of trees whipping by on the left and right. As his head dissolves out and the trees continue to whip by, the shot seems to shift (as if following the Futurist aesthetic) into a pure experience of speed and unrelenting change. The model house reappears, with all of its windows lit; and a series of forward dolly shots, with repeated quick pans to the right, seem to carry Einar to it. The POV tracking shots single out Einar as a potential subject opposite Claire, but they also replicate the omniscient description of the film's beginning. This replication puts Einar on the verge of shifting into the position of controlling the narrative, a position he will occupy at crucial points later. By fusing the omniscient and the subjective, it also foregrounds the speed and direction of the frame's movement and propels them into a vertiginous visual rhythm, a cinematic dance. Two forms of spectacle, two film styles, have been set in opposition—the one static and artificial, the other dynamic and natural.

This systematic privileging of paradigmatic relations and the materials of film discourse gives *L'Inhumaine* a decidedly operatic quality. The sharply different decors and styles of acting confirm this impression. Mallet-Stevens's house exteriors, in De Stijl ultramodern, mask contrasting interiors. Cavalcan-

387

ti's geometric banquet hall—where jugglers, fire-eaters, musicians, and even Claire herself perform—and Autant-Lara's winter garden of fantastical plants are both linked to the Théâtre des Champs-Elysées.[13] These are the decadent kingdoms of the solitary "Princess." Léger's laboratory (perhaps influenced by Friedrich Kiesler's sets for *R.U.R.*)[14]—where men and machines work in tandem—is linked to the natural world by means of an experimental television system and the sports car's passage through the natural landscapes. These are the realms, embodying the Purist ideal of science and nature in harmony,[15] of the solitary "Prince." As neutral areas, Cavalcanti's dark underground vault (where Einar reappears) and stark monumental hall (where Claire is resurrected) become spaces that resolve their opposition. Against the smiling, cold-blooded capriciousness of Claire's mezzo-soprano vie the nimble calculations and nervous energy of Einar's tenor and the murderous, single-minded passion of Djorah's basso (this is no conventional Italian opera). Hériat's tall hulking figure and heavy face with large staring eyes, complemented by his appearance several times as a foreground silhouette (as in a shadow play), make him a perfect embodiment of the stock villain.[16] But Georgette Leblanc is too old and unskilled as an actress to project the proper luminance as Claire, and Jaque Catelain is a bit lightweight and too youthful opposite her. The acting, unfortunately, is much less effectively synthesized than are the decors. It is a weakness that, coupled with the absurdities of the plot, indeed does dissipate the film's power.

Perhaps, as Noël Burch suggests, Darius Milhaud's score for *L'Inhumaine* may have given the characters more consistency and force.[17] We may never know, for, like most other scores for 1920s French films, it seems to have disappeared. Even the special revival screening of the film (November, 1976) for the Paris "Cinquantenaire," celebrating the 1925 Exposition, lacked it. Apparently, however, just as a different score had been for *El Dorado*, the music of Milhaud was essential to the rhythm and structure of the film. This was especially so for the sequences of rapid cutting and accelerating montage which probably were *L'Inhumaine*'s most noted feature at the time and which still work surprisingly well, even silent. These sequences were much more than tour-de-force set pieces of technique. Like similar sequences in *La Roue, L'Auberge rouge,* and *Coeur fidèle,* they functioned as major structural components of the film's narrative.

The first such sequence narrates Einar's apparent death in the car accident. It is remarkable for its variety of tracking shots—dollying in front of the sports car, looking forward through the windshield, looking at the trees streak by and at the river below, focusing on the spinning tires and on the jittering steering wheel—and for its superimpositions—a double image of his profile (in CU) buffeted by the wind, tracking shots of the foliage overhead (distorted by the speed) over a straight-on CU of his determined face. This is the most subjective sequence so far in the film, and it plunges us into the experience with an exhilaration that is matched by its threat of danger. What is more remarkable, however, is that this flight is but one-half of an alternating sequence. The other narrates the last performance of the evening at Claire's mansion—one of her own songs. Intercut with the subjective shots of Einar's movement are MSs and CUs of her singing (what is the song?). The alternation turns her into a kind of modern-day siren whose extraordinary voice seems to

195. (left) Maharajah Djorah (Philippe Hériat) in Claude Autant-Lara's "winter garden" in *L'Inhumaine* (1924)

196. (right) Fernand Léger and his laboratory set

lure the traveler to his death. As the butler brings her Einar's note (written as he left), the shots of his flight begin to change. She takes the note in her hands, and now there are HALSs of the sports car speeding along the curving cliff road. Suddenly, at the shot of a strummed guitar (does a different musical rhythm take over here?), the cutting accelerates to a crescendo, alternating between LSs and FSs of the car and MCUs of Claire holding the note—twelve, twelve, twelve, ten, nine, seven, six, frames each. The rhythm slackens on several shots tracking toward and over the cliff, and then a half-second image of Claire precedes the sports car's long fall to the river. Only then does she read what he has written. As the focus of the sequence shifts near the end to Claire, it articulates the cruel nonchalance, even ignorance, of her power.

The second major sequence which involves rapid cutting is the one that most satisfied L'Herbier himself "at the plastic and poetic level."[18] Here Claire comes to the vault wherein the body lies and finds that Einar is alive. The sequence begins with HALSs down a long narrow corridor of stairs as Claire descends, spreading her cape against the high backlight. Entering the room, in LS (frame right), she discovers (in a niche frame left) the corpse covered by a white sheet and set off against a black curtain. A brief interchange of closer shots isolate the two in separate indeterminate spaces. A sudden pan right from the corpse to a MS of Claire (at a 45° angle) then introduces an alternation between CUs of a phonograph playing and Claire looking about in wonder. How nicely ironic if this song were the one she had sung when Einar's car crashed. As the corpse is reintegrated into the alternation, the cutting accelerates—twenty-three, thirteen, eleven, six, fifteen, seven, thirteen, nineteen frames each—and Claire rushes back to the stairs. Again she approaches the corpse and, when the sheet begins to move, comes closer still. Two superimposed CUs of Einar's blood-stained face against the black curtain signal a further change, this time in the intercutting between the two figures. The

389

MCU of Claire and the CU of the sheet over the corpse's face are taken from angles that deny any subject-POV shot organization. What Burch calls "the discrepancy in camera angles and the differences in frame space"[19] here seem to serve a double function. They obviously represent Claire's subjective experience, verging on an hallucinatory trance in which she is positioned as subordinate, submissive—the very antithesis of her position in the opening sequence in her mansion. At this point, suddenly (in LS), Einar glides down the stairs (frame right background) and stops at the bottom, framed starkly in the doorway. L'Herbier himself sums up the odd tone of the sequence better than I can: "After a silent, rather pathetic dialogue, they both ascend the stairs toward a kind of gibbet or guillotine. . . . That's the moment I love."[20]

These two sequences constitute the major turning points in the first half of the film. In one, the heroine (as villainess) destroys the hero; in the other, she seems to restore him. Einar briefly takes over the position of the narrator, however, and explains, in flashback, that his death was a ruse. The real change, we see now, has been in Claire—from villainess to heroine. He has revived her humanity, her capacity for feeling. This highly symmetrical, overt (and sentimental) pattern of reversal is replicated exactly in the second half of the film. Only now it is the villain who apparently destroys the heroine, and the hero must once more restore her, this time to life. Again the turning points are marked by sequences of rapid cutting.

The first of these doubled sequences narrates Claire's death from the viper. This occurs in the back seat of her touring car as Djorah drives it along the same cliff road (but in the opposite direction) where Einar had crashed his sports car. The sequence reminds one of Sisif's first attempt to destroy his train in *La Roue*. Some dozen or more shots are repeated with variations: a dolly before the car, tracks of the landscape and trees streaking by, a MS of Claire (frame left background) and Djorah (frame right foreground), CUs of each, a CU of the flowers, a CU of her hand, a track of the road under the car from near one of the wheels, a HA track of the road surface (from the briefly opened car door), a HALS of the car speeding along the cliff road (panning to the right until it tilts at an angle), and finally a dolly behind the car. The cutting accelerates to a climax, with shots of only a half-second each, just before Claire tries to open the door and then slumps back paralyzed. Less regular than in the sequence in *La Roue*, the pattern of repetition here—the same shots recur but constantly shift their order—is closer to that of the carnival sequence in *Coeur fidèle*. The characters' actions and inner life are subsumed in a larger design. Although Claire's subjectivity is emphasized, she is an object as well, enmeshed in the pulsating rhythm that Djorah has set in motion. Caught up in this whirlwind of camera movement and cutting, their juxtaposed faces—in which agony contends wildly with a malicious glee—create an extravagant operatic duet. Could Milhaud have scored it that way?

In the final climactic sequence of Claire's resurrection, *L'Inhumaine* presents a stunning synthesis of narrative avant-garde film practice. Einar lays her body on a raised platform of massive blocks, with symmetrically placed zig-zag lighting fixtures on either side. It is like some monumental altar to science or, more specifically, to electricity and electronics. Rushing into the laboratory—a labyrinthine forest of machines and bold geometrical forms—he dons a helmet and white coat, stands over the control switchboard (posted with the

197. Einar Norsen (Jaque Catelain) on the stairs leading down to the vault in *L'Inhumaine* (1924)

warning "Danger of death"), and directs several technicians (like metallurgical workers) encased in shiny black uniforms. Once, twice, "The huge laboratory pulses with activity." The first attempt to revive Claire is cautious, brief. It is marked by flashes of light, blurring LSs of Claire, MCUs of Einar and the technicians, and several CUs of the switchboard and revolving machine discs. The second attempt is longer and more dangerous. It is marked by LSs and FSs of the activity in the laboratory (now including electrical sparks and smoke), closer shots of the technicians' quick gestures (their hands flipping levers, pouring liquids [of course], immersed in flares of light), CUs of Einar's frantic looks, and rapid shifts in camera distance and angle. The cutting accelerates in two separate crescendos—the one (seven, nine, three, three frames) involving Einar, the technicians, and his switchboard; the other (seventeen, five, two, ten, two, eight, fourteen, seventeen frames), the "Danger" sign, Einar, Claire, and several flashes of light. But Claire remains still. A third and even more risky experiment is needed.

This last attempt produces, in L'Herbier's own words, "a series of explosions, an over-revving of the machines."[21] Milhaud apparently scored the sequence for percussion instruments only, and the montage was geared to that rhythm. The effect still seemed insufficient to L'Herbier, so he decided to add color, but in a novel way.

198. Einer and Claire
(Georgette Leblanc) in the
"resurrection" hall at the end
of *L'Inhumaine* (1924)

. . . what you no longer see in the prints now was not only a film stock tinted red,
but something else. At certain moments of excitement, I inserted fragments of film
stock of different colors, so that suddenly you seemed struck by flashes of pure white,
and two seconds later, flashes of red, or blue, before the image reappeared. . . .[22]

Even deprived of this rhythmic interplay of music and color, the sequence
retains much of its power. At the beginning, several separate shots of Einar
and the technicians end with the brief flash of a superimposed dial gauge.
Then in a LS of the laboratory, a pendulum dissolves in, swinging slowly
forward and away, as the background space alternately brightens and dims. In
rapidly cut shots, Einar dashes around from one machine to another, and
several quick CUs of the pendulum, discs, and revolving arm levers appear.
The shots of machine parts begin to blur, white out, and dissolve into one
another; and the cutting rhythm accelerates to one-second and half-second
shots and finally to shots of just two to eight frames apiece. Into this choreographed vertigo of machine movement, punctuated by two-frame flashes of
color, shots of Claire (in MS and CU) and Einar (in ECU) are integrated. Einar
begins to laugh, and (in a single shot) Claire's face smiles. Now the sequence
shifts entirely to shots of the pendulum, the dial gauge, the "Danger" sign
flashing, bursts of color, and a spiral which begins to blur and finally concludes the montage. Einar rushes to Claire; she moves her head and looks up
at him. In the words of the German film critic, Alfred Loos, this finale made
L'Inhumaine "the only film for which Tristan's cry makes sense: I hear the
light!"[23]

392

Noël Burch argues that this famous sequence is based on an erroneous concept of montage:

. . . to render movement, to create "visual rhythms" by means of the strictly musical assemblage of very short shots representing *inanimate* objects, depends ultimately, it seems to me, on the belief that the duration of a static shot must be pure, and thus comparable to the length of a musical note.[24]

Its flaw is that it is not an "organic articulation of organic movement." Instead, Burch continues, ". . . in *La Roue* and *L'Inhumaine*, the mechanical rigidity of the shots, even in their movement and despite wild accelerations, ends in a strained stasis that is now almost insufferable." My own analysis suggests that Burch's argument is overly simplistic and leads me to several different conclusions. If one examines this sequence according to its diegetic and nondiegetic functions, an important transformation emerges. The narrative function of the sequence is, of course, to represent Claire's resurrection, to present the impossible as possible. Because the display of technical virtuosity is so awesome, however, that function seems to get lost or more precisely, it gives way to a nondiegetic function, a "poetic" one, foregrounding the graphic and rhythmic materials of the discourse. In this cinematic dance, the locus of the marvelous shifts from the representational level to the presentational, and, by analogy, to the cinematic apparatus itself. The laboratory that resurrects becomes a metaphor for the cinema, the machine that reproduces, that re-animates life. *L'Inhumaine*, therefore, ends up producing a metaphor to celebrate the apparatus of its own production. This act of self-reflexivity, however, unlike that of Clair's *Paris qui dort*, continues to uphold the magic and mystification of the cinematic machine.

If one examines the sequence as an ideological construction, however, as the culmination of the whole film's operation, something quite different emerges. More than poor acting and absurd plotting are regressive, even grotesque, in *L'Inhumaine*. Although the characterization of Djorah (the dark-skinned colonized non-European as an exotic figure of evil) raises questions about racial and geopolitical myths, the film's principal grotesquerie lies in its characterization of Claire in relation to Einar. Its misogyny, like that in serials such as *The Perils of Pauline*, is monstrously excessive. Reversing the conventional relations of power between men and women, she becomes a modern Circe, an international "belle dame sans merci," whose profession serves to attract men in order to subjugate or destroy them. She must be punished for this, specifically for causing the hero's death. When that death turns out to be false, it doubly inscribes the hero's power over her. That power extends even to a measure of control over her profession, her singing. While Claire can enchant crowds at the Théâtre des Champs-Elysées, Einar has invented a television system that can send her voice and image around the world.[25] In a demonstration sequence (presented by means of back projection or matting), it documents her appearance at the Folies-Bergère while people (in different parts of the world) listen to her voice on radios. The last image, in fact, is of a sick woman who responds to the song, in ironic parallel to the sequence of Einar's "restoration" as well as to Claire's own position at the end of the film. This sequence gives image to Blaise Cendrars's concept of the cinema as a revolutionary technology of simultaneity, producing "a new synthesis of the human spirit . . . in all the worlds' capitals, millions of hearts stop beating at the same instant, and in the remotest villages, bursts of laughter shatter the countryside."[26] But that technology also serves to subordinate woman to man, the human to the machine, as well as the rest of humanity to Europe and the civilized world. Claire's humanization and subjugation is not complete, however, for she must be punished further by undergoing the destruction or erasure that she herself was accused (falsely) of committing. Only in the condition of lifelessness can she be re-formed, re-created anew. Like a modern god or Doctor Frankenstein, Einar literally charges her with life. Man produces woman, as if reversing childbirth, in an operation with strangely necrophilic undertones. Reinventing her image, he turns her absence into presence. To be human, *L'Inhumaine* concludes, woman must be positioned in the proper relation to man.

A brief note on Fernand Léger and Dudley Murphy's *Ballet mécanique* (1924). According to Standish Lawder, the idea for this short non-narrative film occurred shortly after a specially arranged Georges Antheil concert at the Théâtre des Champs-Elysées, on 4 October 1923, which was recorded by L'Herbier for the near riot at Claire Lescaut's performance in *L'Inhumaine*.[27] Made sometime between the winter and summer of 1924, *Ballet mécanique* had its premiere in late September or early October, in Vienna at Friedrich Kiesler's Internationale Ausstellung Neuer Theatertechnik.[28] Thereafter, it was shown in Berlin (3 May 1925), then simultaneously in London and New York (14 March 1926), and soon became a much-circulated film on the ciné-club and specialized cinema circuit.[29] Strangely, its public screening in France did not come until the late spring or summer of 1926, when it followed Clair's *Entr'acte*, Chomette's *Les Jeux des reflets et de la vitesse* and *Cinq Minutes de cinéma pur*, Autant-Lara's *Fait-Divers*, and Ruttman's *Film absolu* at the newly opened Studio des Ursulines.[30] Jean Tedesco, much to his later chagrin, actually saw the film with Léger shortly before the Vieux-Colombier opened, on 14 November 1924, but decided not to include it in his programming.[31] Perhaps the rejection so angered Léger that he refused to consider its screening in Paris for some time.

Ballet mécanique deserves mention here for several reasons. First, its study of motion and speed, both cinematic and extra-cinematic, makes it a good companion piece to Clair's *Entr'acte*. In this film, however, the analysis is more purely "plastic" (though consistently representational in its use of everyday objects) and eschews any social critique. Even more than Clair, Léger celebrates openly the kinetic activity, the pulsating dynamism, of modern urban life.[32] More importantly, though one of the earliest French non-narrative films, *Ballet mécanique* clearly derives from the then current narrative avant-garde film practice. The germ of its conception, as Lawder has demonstrated, can be seen in Léger's analysis of Gance's *La Roue*, where he focuses on the sequences of machine movement and "the intrinsic plastic value of the object."[33] Several of those sequences, in fact, were projected by C.A.S.A. (of which Léger was a member), on 25 April 1924, during the time when *Ballet mécanique* was being shot and edited.[34] Léger also had the example (executed simultaneously with or just prior to his film) of the final resurrection sequence in *L'Inhumaine*, which used machine parts and elements of the laboratory decor that he had constructed for L'Herbier. Finally, Jean Epstein's theoretical writings, especially his emphasis on the close-up and photogeny of movement, in *Bonjour Cinéma* (1921), coincided with Léger's own ideas, as Epstein himself suggested in an astute essay on the painter in *Les Feuilles libres* (1923).[35] Besides the carnival segment in *Coeur fidèle*, another of Epstein's films provided Léger with a model—the lost *Photogénies*, compiled for a special screening organized by C.A.S.A., on 11 April 1924.[36] Consequently, through *Ballet mécanique* and *Entr'acte*, the French non-narrative avant-garde films owe more to the narrative avant-garde than generally has been acknowledged.

Menilmontant and Rien que les heures

The urban milieu of the working class and unemployed had provided the basis for several early narrative avant-garde films—Delluc's *Fièvre*, Epstein's *Coeur fidèle*, and, some might add, Feyder's *Crainquebille*. In the middle of the decade, while most of the leading filmmakers (e.g., Gance, L'Herbier, Dulac, Epstein) were being compromised by the film industry's consolidation and single-minded investment in historical reconstruction films and modern studio spectaculars, two young filmmakers chose to explore that same milieu (in Paris) in their first films. The films were Dimitri Kirsanoff's *Menilmontant* (1926) and Alberto Cavalcanti's *Rien que les heures* (1926).

To be accurate, *Menilmontant* was actually Kirsanoff's second film. From 1921 to 1922, while performing in the orchestras of several cinemas (the Cluny, the Artistic, and the Danton), the young Russian emigré had managed to shoot a short feature film, *L'Ironie du destin*, with the help of Arnou (the cameraman who had filmed Boudrioz's *L'Atre*) and Nadia Sibirskaia (his wife who was the principal actress).[1] *L'Ironie du destin* (no print survives) had a simple subject "which is none other than life," wrote *Cinéa-Ciné-pour-tous*—a double story of love lost and regained.

The story is that of a child who becomes a woman after having known her first suffering, then a lone woman who falls in love, finally a broken old creature. And that is all. A young man, similarly, is the plaything of an undeserved love for a prostitute; he experiences all the despair possible, even to the point of doubting himself. He, too, becomes an old man, and, on a common park bench, he rediscovers the old woman who had once been young and beautiful and who always has loved him secretly. They retell their story without forced irony—sad destiny dictated by chance and unmarked by marvelous interventions. This story is the film.[2]

Refused distribution for nearly a year, the film finally played in just three Paris cinemas and failed to recoup even the modest amount it had cost.[3] But several things about the film caught Jean Tedesco's eye—Sibirskaia's subtle acting, the Paris location shooting (there were scarcely any interior decors), the simplicity of the narrative, and the film's complete lack of intertitles (perhaps the first such French film).[4] Tedesco was impressed enough to feature *L'Ironie du destin* in the biweekly series of Friday film programs organized by C.A.S.A. in April and May of 1924. When the Paris distributors rejected Kirsanoff's next film, initially entitled *Les Cents Pas*, Tedesco snapped it up, in January, 1926, to open his second season of film programming at the Vieux-Colombier. *Menilmontant*, as it came to be called, helped assure the success of the Vieux-Colombier and soon became a major film on the ciné-club and specialized cinema circuit.[5]

Like *L'Ironie du destin*, *Menilmontant* tells its story entirely in images. There

395

are no intertitles. But the story it narrates is complicated and ambiguous.[6] After the unexplained murder of their parents, two sisters leave their provincial village and move to Menilmontant on the eastern edge of Paris, one of the poorer working-class districts in the 20th *arrondissement*. Although they work together at first in the flower market, the older sister (Yolande Beaulieu) soon turns to prostitution and goes off on her own. The younger (Sibirskaia) falls in love with a young man (Guy Belmore) who quickly abandons her and eventually takes up with her sister. Burdened with an illegitimate baby and nearly starving, she comes close to drowning both the child and herself in the Seine. Finally, one night on the street, she rediscovers her sister, who has grown relatively rich in her profession, and the two are reunited. At the same time, the young man who had deserted her is killed in a street mugging by another woman and a male accomplice.

This brutal, melodramatic story reminds one of Delluc and Epstein's work in several ways. Kirsanoff shot most of the film himself on location in Menilmontant during the winter of 1924-1925.[7] The narrow blackened streets, the cheap hotels, the deserted parks, the beckoning water of the Seine (or is it the Canal St. Martin?)—all produce the realistic ambiance of a wretched milieu, out of which the story (or at least part of the story) seems to evolve naturally. One brief sequence will suffice to note the detail of the film's description. It opens with a LS down a drab alley where a woman stands waiting in the distance. In a closer HA shot, water flows forward over the rough cobblestones along a low curb. A young man comes up the alley alone and stops; in MS, he raises one foot to polish his shoe on the back of his other pant leg. The two sisters get off the metro (reflected in its glass doors); Sibirskaia follows her older sister up the alley and, from around the corner in LS, watches her go off with the man. However, *Menilmontant* is much more than a realistic "slice of life." As in *Coeur fidèle*, the banality of its story seems to serve Kirsanoff as a pretext for experimentation. The flow of images, as René Jeanne and Charles Ford suggest, reminds one of a Baudelaire prose poem, say "Le Spleen de Paris."[8]

Like several other narrative avant-garde films, *Menilmontant* is marked by a mixture of styles or modes, a pastiche of techniques. There are sequences of violence in rapid montage, of dreamlike multiple superimpositions and lap dissolves (all done in camera), of documentarylike impressions (e.g., a description of the neighborhood around the sisters' apartment on a quiet Sunday morning), of classical continuity editing (e.g., the poignant moment in the park when an old man silently puts down beside him on the bench a piece of bread for Sibirskaia, sniffling and teary-eyed from the cold, to pick up and eat—echoing a moment in *La Roue* when Norma first comes at night to Sisif's mountain cabin), and, unfortunately, of exaggerated sentiment (e.g., the two sisters excitedly jumping up and down on their bed, incongruously imitating Griffith's stereotype of little Southern belles). At first, this mélange, especially in such a short film (of only thirty-five minutes), may appear to break down into isolated, loosely related fragments—as if it were already an anthology of avant-garde set pieces. The narrative, after all, has a number of puzzling gaps, and its beginning and ending seem separate from the rest.[9] Yet, as Noël Burch has written, *Menilmontant* can be seen as a systematic and sophisticated attempt "to refine existing codes of *découpage* to a point where it becomes possible to dispense with the disrupting titles and yet maintain *the control of the flow of signification*. . . ."[10] Specifically, I would argue, the film achieves its coherence through a strategy of structural parallels and repetitions.

Along with the opening minutes of *La Roue* and *Le Brasier ardent*, the first sequence of *Menilmontant* is one of the most startling and disorienting in 1920s French cinema. It begins *in medias res*, without warning or preparation. A CU of a lace curtain which suddenly moves; a MS of the curtain (now clearly through a door window) as a man rips it aside and gestures frantically (a woman and another man are glimpsed briefly behind him); a CU of the door-knob twisting; another brief CU of the curtain "wiping" away to reveal a woman's face as a hand yanks her hair from behind; a MS of the door opening as the first man struggles out, yelling, followed by the woman. In little more than a minute, in a montage of some thirty shots (of faces, upper torsos, and arms), the second man pursues the two others, seizes a nearby hatchet, and, in a rage, kills them. As his arm strikes down through the frame one last time, the shot holds momentarily on a line of bare trees blurred in the background. Cut to a HAFS of a shallow mud puddle—the hatchet drops in it. So the sequence ends. This opening is unusually striking for its lack of establishing shots, its spatial ambiguity, its almost subjective shot/reverse shots whose immediacy forces our involvement with unidentified characters, and its shocking elimination of those characters. Lacking a context in space and time, the rapid montage transforms the specificity of the CUs and MCUs into a kind of generalized dance of death that both fascinates and appalls. The violence seems senseless and is never explained—the murderer disappears from the film altogether. At most, the sequence implies that this is a world of sexual distrust, deception, and jealousy, and, consequently, of brutal victimization.

In the next few sequences, the film's diegetic flow is redirected toward Sibirskaia's character, only to shift and diverge in peculiar ways. Juxtaposed sharply to the murder is a sequence in which, outfitted in simple short white dresses, the two girls (in imitation of the Gish sisters?) are playing in a park. As they run forward gaily, the sequence cuts to a MS of workers in a semicircle, all looking down (presumably at the bodies). Suddenly, the camera focuses on Sibirskaia alone, stopped in MS and staring forward. Four quick jump cuts of her face, moving in from MS to ECU, simulate the shock of her recognition of what has previously been shown us but is here elided. In this relocation of the subjective, our knowledge becomes hers. After another quick cut to MS, she turns in fright and runs off down a park path. In the village cemetery, sometime later, dissolves link shots of the two girls, of a cross and a wreath (one each for a father and mother), of a low fence chain, of the two girls' faces superimposed together in CU like a Janus head. This shared subjectivity in mourning carries over, across another ellipsis in time—a brief description of the overgrown cemetery—to the young women's departure. They walk off, hand in hand, down a bleak poplar-lined lane, their black figures diminishing in a series of lap dissolves that seem to hold them back momentarily as well as propel them on their way.

The rest of *Menilmontant* works a number of variations on this pattern of loss or separation (through sexual deception and victimization) followed by some kind of replacement. For a while, the two sisters are equally, if ambiguously, the center of attention, even though their paths begin to diverge.

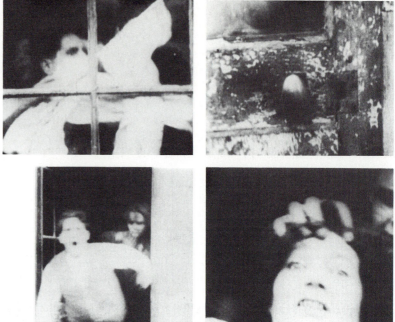

199. Selected frames from the murder sequence that opens the existing print of *Menilmontant* (1926)

Another juxtaposition introduces Paris: instead of slow lap dissolves of a country lane, there are several rapid tracking shots of fast-moving cars, then still shots of the flower girls and a CU of the two sisters among them (an intriguing parallel to the opening of Epstein's *L'Affiche*). Are these tracking shots omniscient clichés of the city or imaginary images suggesting something of the women's desires? After Sibirskaia has met, several times in a park, the young man who claims to love her, she reluctantly agrees to spend the night with him in a hotel. In a haunting ELS, they come forward together down a grimly glistening alley and then, in MCU, pause in the narrow hotel doorway almost in silhouette.

The two interrelated sequences that follow are among the most ambiguous in the film. The first begins with a HALS, as the couple enters the hotel room. A dissolve leads to a HAMCU looking over the man's shoulder to Sibirskaia. The camera angles and dissolves both conspire to force the young man on her. In CU (eye-line match cuts), however, she refuses him; the camera cuts back to MS, as she pushes him away, and to HALS again, as he pursues her and is granted a kiss before she runs to the window and stops. The sequence ends in this same HALS, with the man now in bed and Sibirskaia standing by the door. A dissolve shifts her across the room to kiss his head, and another shifts her back to the doorway through which she exits. Instead of compromising her, as before, the dissolve now bestows her blessing. In the middle of this sequence, however, another is interpolated, simultaneous with it, of Sibirskaia's sister asleep in bed. A slow montage of shots ensues: a clock, a book she has been reading, a cat prowling down some stairs, a CU of feet

398

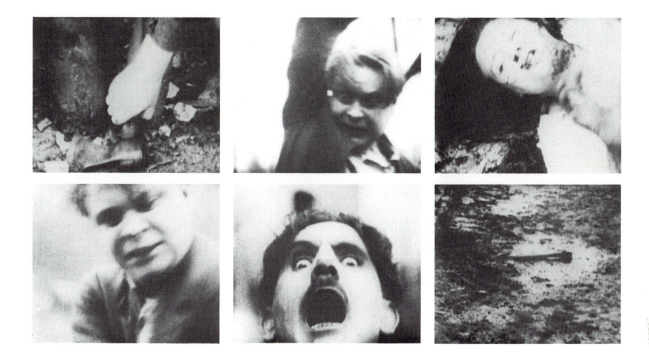

walking along an alley, car wheels passing. These seem to be simply descriptive shots until a MS of the sleeping woman blurs into a series of dissolving multiple superimpositions: tracking shots of cars and tires on the streets, pointillistic light and shadow patterns, the clock, and the naked torso of a woman lying in different positions. The montage ends in a MS of the sister as she turns over in her sleep, and the shot pans right to reveal an empty pillow (apparently Sibirskaia's). Is this onmiscient description, an autonomous chain of graphic and rhythmic patterns, or a semiconscious imagining of the sister's?[11] And, if the latter only, does it convey her own repressed desire or her apprehension over Sibirskaia? The significance is all the more puzzling because it clearly substitutes for the couple's love-making. Why should the film disrupt the diegesis or shift into the sister's consciousness precisely at this moment, expecially since she disappears soon after from the narrative? Would such a "dream" stand in opposition to a lack on Sibirskaia's part? Is the sequence somehow articulating the difference that separates them?

Until nearly the film's end, the diegetic flow now focuses on Sibirskaia. After leaving the hotel room, she pauses on the Pont Neuf. A CU of her lovely, delicate face (framed within the curving brim of a soft hat) is followed by a shot of spinning trees and then shots of her playing as a child in a wooded park. This brief eruption of memory condenses two earlier moments in the film: her innocent play at the time of her parents' death and her pensive look in the cemetery. In ELS, the child pauses at a shaded shallow pond deep in the woods and then runs off (another echo), her image doubled on the water surface as if emerging from a dazzling burst of sunlight. At the end of this

200. The alley leading to the hotel in *Menilmontant* (1926)

201. Nadia Sibirskaia on the Pont Neuf in *Menilmontant* (1926)

rearticulation of loss, Sibirskaia starts down the steps to the Seine and stops; in CU, her feet turn and ascend out of the frame. The water, repeatedly associated with death, now seems to strangely draw her. After another ellipsis, in which her baby is born, Sibirskaia walks along the Seine (in a long tracking CU of her desperate, tear-stained face). Again she pauses on a bridge (the same one?), and over a slow panning shot of the water surface is superimposed a CU of her face—echoing the shot of Gina Manès early in *Coeur fidèle*. Her baby cries and prompts her to continue walking. A montage of superimposition and tracking shots leave her standing on the same steps leading down to the Seine. There she sits, facing the river in a HAFS, and leans against the iron and stone railing. What keeps her from committing suidice? As if in answer, the young man who deserted her is shown sitting on a park bench. He gets up to leave, and Sibirskaia and her baby dissolve in, sitting next to the spot he has just left. Is this an imaginary image, suggesting her final recognition of his abandonment, or an ironic condensation of time, creating a near meeting and reconciliation that never occur? Whatever, the young man's place on the bench is quickly occupied by an old man with a cane. This stranger who replaces him discreetly offers her part of his lunch—in a series of CUs, bread passes from one to the other. Though they briefly acknowledge one another's presence, the two remain separate in their cold, lonely spaces.

The final sequences of *Menilmontant* resolve the narrative in a series of disturbing and disorienting repetitions. At night, a man and woman enter the familiar hotel. From the doorway they enter, the shot tilts up to the HOTEL sign and to a lighted window; then it tilts down to catch the young man going in the door. An elliptical montage of shots sets up a curious parallel

400

and an expectation. First comes a CU of coins in a hand, then a shot of a woman, never seen before, at the street-level window. In MCU, a pair of hands moves stealthily among the wine bottles, crusts of bread, and cigarette butts on a table. The last shot shows the woman quickly drinking from a nearly empty bottle. Like Sibirskaia, this woman seems on the verge of starving; unlike her, however, she lives from what she can steal. If she has seen the young man's money, what will she do? Again the subjective is being relocated. Meanwhile, Sibirskaia is crouched with her baby in the darkness under a bridge. Glancing off, she spots her sister in LS, pacing back and forth in a full-length fur coat. A MCU of her legs mercilessly describes her high heels moving awkwardly about in a thin layer of mud. When Sibirskaia comes up, she adds to her sister's surprise (in shot/reverse shots) by offering her the baby. Just then, the young man appears at a distant corner (has he come to pick up the sister?). From his point of view, the two women embrace and go off together. Through a redistribution of the three characters, this reconciliation "heals" the split between the women, first announced in the alley sequence when Sibirskaia watched her sister go off with the same young man. Circumscribed within his glance, the diegetic flow shifts one last time.

The sequence of the young man's death forms a close parallel to the opening of the film, with a difference.[12] Here, the triangle is inverted, and the couple attacks the single man in an action that erupts without warning and is soon over. CUs of the young man coming up an alley are intercut with CUs of the starving woman creeping forward down another. Their confrontation ironically echoes his first meeting with Sibirskaia's sister. As they begin to struggle—over money? Has she known him before? Is she another woman he has deceived?—he tries to escape through a nearby door that suddenly shuts. Quickly, a second man comes up to assist the woman. In a brief flurry of shots (of faces, upper torsos, and arms), which expand the moment and prolong the horror, she picks up a loose cobblestone and bashes in his head. The two then drag his body around a corner, and the sequence ends as abruptly as it began. Several shots here almost literally repeat those of the initial murder—the woman's arms striking down, the man's head falling back. And the image of hands picking up the cobblestone produces an ironic parallel to the hands passing bread on the park bench. This is poetic justice with a vengeance. More important, the editing, as in the initial murder, is almost subjective. We in the audience are implicated, not on the side of the victim, but on that of the

401

murderers. It is as if our desire for punishment is being enacted. After all, the young man has not only deceived Sibirskaia; he has broken our identification with her and robbed us of our pleasure. In this cycle of betrayal and violence, our gaze is caught up and compromised.

Perhaps *Menilmontant*'s ending may be read as a gloss on Epstein's *Coeur fidèle*. The starving woman replaces Sibirskaia, taking on her suffering and the guilt of vengeance, just as the crippled woman replaced Marie in the earlier film. But here, the outcome is quite different. The young man has been eliminated, but has the attitude that motivated him (whether displaced onto us or not)? Besides, Sibirskaia still has an unwanted child, and her sister is still a prostitute. The system of sexual exchange and deception remains in place. *Menilmontant* thus breaks off in such a way that the audience is disturbingly suspended. The conclusion resolves nothing and seems to return to the beginning. The final shots are enigmatic; several images of gaslights and bridges at night, a swish pan to the hands of the girls making flowers, then a swish pan to blackness. Has Sibirskaia gone back to being a flower girl? Or is the same story about to begin again, in yet another guise? Against the ending of *Coeur fidèle*, as well as *L'Affiche*—where the expected romantic convention produces the loving couple—*Menilmontant* aligns itself with Delluc's *Fièvre* and the critique of that convention.

"*Rien que les heures* was an accident," Alberto Cavalcanti told Elizabeth Sussex recently.[13] A very fortunate accident. After working as Marcel L'Herbier's chief set designer for Cinégraphic—on *Résurrection* (unfinished), *L'Inhumaine* (1924), and *Feu Mathais Pascal* (1925)—the Brazilian-born Cavalcanti wanted to try his hand at directing. His first film, *Le Train sans yeux* (from an old scenario by Louis Delluc), which he took over from Julien Duvivier, was shot in Germany and then withheld from distribution because the producers could not pay their bills.[14] To make sure that he would have a film released by the end of the year, Cavalcanti says that he got together with a few friends to concoct the script for *Rien que les heures*. They worked quickly, shooting all their footage on location in the streets of Paris and assembling it into a short film of just 600 meters in length.[15] The cost: a mere 35,000 francs. In October, 1926, *Rien que les heures* premiered at the Studio des Ursulines.[16] Within a year or two, it was making the rounds of the ciné-club and specialized cinema circuit; and, at a 1928 Film Society screening in London, it had a considerable impact on, among others, John Grierson.[17]

Rien que les heures is a peculiar hybrid of a film, combining the fictional and the factual in several fascinating ways. As early as 1922, Cavalcanti was engaged in an attempt to integrate what he simplified into the two poles of French film theory—Delluc's interest in the real (with its "pragmatic" or denotative value) and L'Herbier's interest in the ideal (with its "lyrical" or connotative value).[18] Curiously, in his own filmmaking, he chose to emphasize the realistic, the documentary, as if in reaction against his previous work with L'Herbier on what were primarily fantasy films. Above all, *Rien que les heures* has become known as one of the first films to document systematically the daily life of a modern city. "This film does not need a story," reads the opening intertitle, "it is no more than a series of impressions on time passing. . . ."[19] As in Walter Ruttmann's *Berlin* (1927), which was made some

203. (left) The newspaper woman in *Rien que les heures* (1926)

204. (right) The pimp (Philippe Hériat) waits while the prostitute dances with the sailor

months later but screened earlier in England and the United States, those impressions follow a dawn-to-dusk pattern of organization, albeit somewhat loosely. After a prologue (more on that in a minute), daybreak reveals several late revelers coming home drunk in a limousine as well as the earliest workers—a water truck spraying the streets, mice nibbling some refuse, and a man opening the gates of the metro. Later in the morning, a shopowner opens the shutters on his window, a woman selling brooms and feather dusters walks up a street, and a man washes some clothes in the river. At noon, ragged men stand in line for a bowl of soup while a proper young gentleman in an elegant restaurant polishes off a beefsteak. In the evening, the factory machines stop, a concierge sits down with her cat, and men congregate in a café to drink and play cards. Later at night, couples flock to the cinemas, amusement parks, and dance halls. Throughout, *clochards* continue to sleep in niches along the walls of the buildings. At irregular intervals in this "flow of life," CUs of a clock face are inserted, indicating the change of hours.

Despite the opening intertitle, *Rien que les heures* does produce a narrative of sorts. Out of a milieu much like that of *Menilmontant*, a diegetic process evolves, yet much more slowly and schematically than in previous realist films. In the morning, along with the water truck and mice, a prostitute (Blanche Bernis) is introduced already walking the streets. At noon, after several shots of a shanty town of unemployed men (one of whom "plays" a stringless violin), a pimp (Philippe Hériat) awakens and steps out on a tenement balcony. In the evening, another woman appears hawking newspapers on a street corner (in one brief sequence of accelerating montage, a tracking shot of her running along the street is intercut with the spinning titles of her papers). Shortly thereafter, a sailor (Clifford MacLaglen) meets a small boyishly tailored woman at an amusement park. Only now, nearly two-thirds of the way through the film, does a story develop out of the interaction between these characters. The newspaper woman has her fortune told by a gypsy woman and receives a death card. Then the pimp and prostitute briefly meet and kiss in an alley, and he sends her off. Later that night at a dance hall, the prostitute dances with the sailor (their figures multiplied in superimpositions) while the pimp waits patiently in the doorway. Afterwards, the pimp tells the prostitute to act as a lookout while he waylays the newspaper woman. At this point, the fictional discourse of *Rien que les heures* shifts into prominence, the factual slips into the background, and the few intertitles disappear altogether.[20]

This sudden conflict forms the climax of the film, articulated in several different modes of representation. The pimp's attack on the newspaper woman closely parallels the murder at the end of *Menilmontant*. As he confronts her at the corner of an alley, the discourse shifts abruptly into a rapid montage of eyeline match cuts.

CU of the woman's face moving away.
ECU of her mouth opening.
CU of the pimp's face.
CU of the woman's face.
CU of the pimp's face.
ECU of the woman's mouth biting his hand.
CU of the pimp's face in pain.
FS of the woman stepping back.

Just then, the prostitute sees the sailor coming toward her up another alley, and she leaves her post to divert his attention. The CUs of the pimp and newspaper woman return, and he begins to beat her brutally. As she loses consciousness, the CU of her face blurs and splits into two shots that alternate rapidly at half-second intervals. A swish pan of newspaper titles is superimposed across one while the surface of the other is increasingly scratched and daubed. At the moment of her death, the film image itself literally begins to deteriorate. Signified and signifier undergo a simultaneous disintegration.

After the prostitute has gone off with the sailor and the pimp has stolen some money from the dead woman, the story ends with two ironic juxtapositions. A black cat looking down from a wall is intercut with the woman's body; then two gendarmes pedal up on bicycles in LS, look briefly over a railing into a sunken alley, and ride off. After another shot of the dead woman, the prostitute and sailor (with obvious relish) prepare to go to bed together. This sequence is articulated in just four shot setups that alternate in such a way as to produce a concise model of spatial-temporal contiguity. Eyeline match cuts link a CU of the sailor and a CU of the prostitute as she, one by one, takes off her hat and coat and dress. Intercut now with the CU of the smiling sailor is a FS of a bed, then a CU of one of her boots as it is untied and slipped off. In CU, the prostitute winks and turns, and her look positions the bed just behind her and to the left. The alternation ends with a CU of the sailor beaming and glancing off to the right—cut to a shot of the bed. Though perhaps too broadly played, this sequence is doubly disturbing. Not only does it jarringly follow the newspaper woman's death, but its mode of subjectivity parallels the near subjectivity of the attack. Thus does the murder coldly infect the couple's gaze and compromise their desire. In this "best of all possible worlds," the poor prey blindly, it seems, on their own kind.

Throughout the film, a lame old woman appears as a fifth character, isolated from the others, often in single shots.[21] This pathetic creature is introduced in a HALS, just before the morning segment, moving slowly up a narrow alley that runs vertically between two buildings. Next she is seen in a closer HALS, dragging herself from left to right along the same route. Later, in LS,

205. The old woman in the construction or dumping site in *Rien que les heures* (1926)

she staggers away from the camera along a wall and down another twisting alley. By this time (just prior to the pimp's appearance), she alone among the various people in the film is beginning to arouse some expectations—where is she going and will she get there? Is there a story emerging, even if it is one fit only for a Samuel Beckett fiction? Or is she some symbolic figure of hopeless misery and isolation, suturing together the different strands of the film as does the figure of Lilian Gish rocking the cradle in *Intolerance*? As the pimp and prostitute's story begins, the old woman reaches a construction site or storage/dump area near the Seine river, where she collapses in the shade of a wooden scaffolding. Once there—"indifferent to time passing," reads an intertitle—her role in the film seems to shift. With scraggly white hair obscuring her face, she sits numb and exhausted in a MS that links the sequence at the dance hall to the sequence of the attack and murder. Then, between the shot of the gendarmes leaving and the shot of the dead body that precedes the sequence of seduction, there is a final CU of her head nodding back and forth slowly, enigmatically. In the alternations of the narrative's climax, she seems to have become an ironic figure of fate, seeing and not seeing, knowing and yet unable to do a thing. A National Film Theater screening several years back gives credence to this reading. Juxtaposed with an incongruous accompaniment of light Parisian songs, which Cavalcanti himself selected, according to Elizabeth Sussex, the old woman emerged as a bizarre, almost comical character.[22]

405

Such contrasts and shifts in perception and signification are evident from the very opening of *Rien que les heures*. It is important to realize that the prologue operates as a whimsically reflective discourse on image-making and representation. After an intertitle saying, "All cities would be alike if their monuments did not distinguish them," the discourse presents a toy replica of the Eiffel Tower (with a thermometer inlaid), a shot of the Madeleine super-imposed within a glass ball, and a map of Paris so blurred that it looks like a cloudy complex molecule. A normal shot of the Place de la Concorde appears (an audience may sigh in relief, in recognition), only to be obliterated by a hand soaping over the camera lens! With these cliché images removed, what will we see of the city? "Not the fashionable, elegant life," says another intertitle. A FS of impeccably costumed women (on the steps of the Opéra?) suddenly turns into a photograph which is torn to pieces by a pair of hands and then scattered, along with other fragments, on the sidewalk. Gone, too, now are a certain socioeconomic class, a kind of woman (a kind of cinema?), and another image of the advertising age. Instead, we will see ". . . the common life of the lowly, the downtrodden"; and the shot of a limousine dissolves into a donkey cart which is slowly driven off.

The discourse of *Rien que les heures* thus situates itself consciously in the context of representational images already present in French society. Later, appropriately, when various cinema posters are reproduced, they are all of adventure films and serials. The film's strategy will be to allow other images to emerge that have been masked or repressed by those already dominant. Instead of going directly to the representation of actual life, however, the discourse offers an interlude of various paintings of Paris streets (e.g., Chagall, Delaunay). At first, we might take these as models of representation, but they are followed by a shot of some two dozen eyes in rows of little oval irises (opening and closing like a bed of tiny clams) and then an intertitle, ". . . only a succession of images can reconstitute life for us." Although painting reproduces spaces and things, only the cinema reproduces movement and the illusion of life. An old and dubious argument, at best; but there is more. This discourse is not content merely to give image and movement to the oppressed. For the succession of images that constitutes the film keeps shifting between the contiguous or coherent and the apparently fragmentary or incoherent. Consistently, however, what at first seems incoherent turns out not to be—through various patterns of juxtaposition and unexpected conjunction. Thus does the film oscillate between the real and the surreal, between the simple representation of a wretched milieu and the production of a reality constituted of multiple maskings and juxtapositions.

One such pattern of juxtaposition involves the production and consumption of food. In the morning segment, for instance, one sequence describes the array of produce in the markets. In the middle of this description, a series of crude wipes (back and forth, from left to right) alternates between shots of vegetables and fruits in their display cases and shots of market refuse in garbage cans and boxes. Lettuce, cauliflower, onions, beans, pears, currants, bananas—each turns into refuse, which immediately turns into something fresh again. The effect is ambiguous. Does the juxtaposition critique a systematic wastefulness in the midst of want? Or is this a sardonic sign of the inevitable decay hidden in the image of all living things? A later sequence is more clear-cut. The "noon meal" intertitle is followed by the shot of a limousine parked in front of a poster advertising the Tasserre restaurant. Suddenly, the car pulls away, revealing a meter man who is sitting on the curb and munching on some sausage and bread. One image of privileged sustenance masks another less proper. This unmasking is followed by another. A young gentleman (in CU) is eating a steak (HACU of his plate). Suddenly, the steak is displaced by a soft iris image—a LS of a side of beef being butchered. Cut to the gentleman chewing contentedly, then back to the butchering going on "behind" his plate. Here the film jokingly reveals an interrelationship to which the character is oblivious. This simple ironic critique of his ignorance (and of his class?) is similar to, yet nowhere as complex as that of a similar sequence in Vertov's *Kino-Eye* (1924), where the meat in a market (through the technique of extended reverse motion) is turned back into a bull and returned to its pasture—to emphasize the physical and socioeconomic process of food production and distribution.

Another pattern involves shifts in perception on the subject of sexual desire. Near the end of the morning segment, a series of CUs seems to set up a mildly erotic scene.

CU of a woman's leg sheathed in stocking and garter.
CU of a sleek-haired man's face looking down and to the right.
CU of the woman's leg, a man's hand brushes by.
CU of the man's face, impassive yet intent.

But this voyeuristic moment proves deceptive when a MS of the woman's legs tilts up to reveal that her body is a mannequin. The man's hands are arranging a new outfit for sale. Cut to a LS of the man standing before several mannequins in the display window of a boutique. This witty unmasking presents the erotic as a construction of looks (of subject and object); the sequence simply reverses the process that functions in advertising, where the customer's look would replace that of the window dresser. A further deconstruction of sexuality occurs just after the newspaper woman has her fortune told. This sequence, in which the sailor first appears, is loosely organized around a bizarre alternation between various couples and foods. The foods include an ECU of absinthe poured over some sugar into a glass, chestnuts boiling in a street-corner tub, potatoes cooking in a pot, and a platter of baked fish. The couples shift from a silhouette of a man and woman kissing to the sailor and his girl at the amusement park, a woman and a man who must stand on tiptoe to kiss her, a Rodin sculpture of lovers, and the pimp and prostitute meeting in an alley. If the potatoes and fish are not enough to demystify the Rodin, then the pimp and prostitute clinch it. Consequently, the final seduction sequence between the sailor and prostitute caps a whole series of perceptual deceptions and demystifications.

Rien que les heures may seem to end with a rather lame epilogue. A couple of intertitles produce a conventional conclusion: "We can fix a point in space, stop a moment in time . . ." / ". . . but space and time both elude our grasp." The discourse of images, however, presents a rough challenge to an audience's perception and understanding. Clichés abound—a simple globe of the world (singling out Paris and Peking), an aerial shot of the Arc de Triomphe, several snapshots of pagodas, a French mother and child before a white curtain, a man chasing a woman before an abstract Cubist screen (the action comically repeated several times). Why should we accept these images per se any more than those at the film's beginning? For a film that has examined, whimsically as well as coldly, both a wide range of images and the image-making process, such an epilogue would be patently silly as a transparent succession of images. It is not, I would argue. As the final shots divide and fragment (through multiple exposure, mattes, and camera movement), the work of deconstruction that the film has engaged in is shifted onto the audience. How will we now perceive the representational images of our culture all around us?

En rade and *L'Invitation au voyage*

Cavalcanti's second film to be released in France, *En rade* (1927), differs markedly from *Rien que les heures*. For one, commercial considerations played a role in its production. The producer was Neó-Film, Pierre Braunberger's fledgling semi-independent company. The cast included several prominent film actors: Nathalie Lissenko, Philippe Hériat, and Catherine Hessling. The scenario, written by Cavalcanti in collaboration with Claude Heymann (one of Jean Renoir's assistants), was more exclusively narrative in mode.[1] Unlike his earlier film, *En rade* was first distributed commercially by Super-Film, in September, 1927, and then was quickly picked up by the specialized cinemas, beginning with the Vieux-Colombier, in November, 1927.[2] Apparently, there was some discrepancy between the commercial and Vieux-Colombier versions of the film—"numerous cuts, in effect, were made" in the latter—but the print preserved at the Cinémathèque française is presumably complete.[3]

The story that *En rade* tells is familiar, so familiar that one critic lumped it together with the "junk of the old naturalist scrap heap."[4] It is a simple, melancholy story of failed romance and yearning for adventure in a seaport slum. Bored with his life in the old port of Marseille, and chafing at the possessiveness of his laundress mother (Lissenko), a young man (George Charlia) dreams of going to sea as a sailor. He befriends a retarded old man who inhabits the docks (Hériat) and, through him, meets and falls in love with a local café waitress (an unusually restrained Hessling). The couple make plans to elope, but Lissenko discovers her son's hidden seaman's kit and boat ticket. Thereafter, everything goes awry. In the café, one stormy night, Charlia is strangely provoked into trying to seduce Hessling; shocked, she repulses him and sends him away. He returns to his mother, and Hessling stays on in the café. In a small rowboat, Hériat alone sets off to sea, only to drown.

Indeed, why should Cavalcanti have chosen such a banal tale? Surely not, like Epstein and Kirsanoff before him, as a pretext for experimentation. No, what impresses one about *En rade* is its sustained sense of atmosphere, the deft balance of its narrative structure, and the simplicity and poignancy of its rhetorical figuring. In this, Cavalcanti seems (as Feyder does, one could argue, in *Visages d'enfants*) to be consolidating some of the strategies of previous films, especially *Fièvre*, *Coeur fidèle*, and *L'Inondation*. "Nothing and everything," wrote Jean Dréville, "its development and technique are clear and accessible to all."[5] *En rade* is simply, plainly, poetry, on the order of a folk ballad.

Dissolving out of a blurred shot of swirling water, the title of *En rade* ("Moored" or "Aground at low tide") appears as a sign washed by rain. Just the right touch to evoke this film's atmosphere of despair, false hopes, and evasion. For the sake of authenticity, Cavalcanti had Jimmy Rogers shoot all of the exteriors on panchromatic film stock in the Old Port area of Marseille.[6] And the interiors, constructed with the assistance of Eric Aës, he designed meticulously to blend in with the location footage. As in *Fièvre*, the opening shots of *En rade* succinctly set two spaces in opposition—a ELS (blurred) of ships in the harbor and a LS of Lissenko's apartment, with drying shirts and sheets hung from the ceiling like castoff sails. Located in the one cramped, cluttered world, the laundress, in MCU, looks off frame left. In the other open world, near a dock crane that obscures an ocean liner and tug, Charlia, in MS, looks off frame right. Though separate, the two characters are inter-related, through the alternation of shots and the direction of their looks. A suggestive shot follows the boy's gaze—the doors to a nearby warehouse close shut. Soon after, the mother's position (as authority and provider) is confirmed in a few brief shots in the apartment, as Charlia sits at the table.

MCU of Lissenko giving a stern silent look.
HAMCU of Charlia looking up slowly.
MCU of Lissenko as before.
HAMCU of Charlia glancing down and chewing on a piece of bread.

Before this, however, a third space is established—the run-down café where Hessling waits on sailors and dockworkers and cleans up after them. The café is a long, bare, narrow room (holding perhaps a half-dozen rough tables), with a grubby service and storage area at the back (up two steps), where a window in one wall opens onto the kitchen. The big woman who owns the café and runs the kitchen is rarely visible except for a huge arm that pounds the window ledge. While Hessling (dressed in a dirty sweater and skirt) is washing some plates, Hériat comes into the café. There is an exchange of looks between them, and he sits down at a table near the door. Already parallels are forming—between the apartment and the café, as closed worlds opposite the harbor and sea, and between the two pairs of characters.

To sustain the ambiance of old Marseille, *En rade* is unusually restrained in its deployment of technical effects. It relies, instead, on the mise-en-scène (decors, lighting, and actors), a slow rhythm of editing, and, in Dréville's words, "the skillful choice of camera angles to delimit the frame space."[7] The latter, which also characterizes Jean Epstein's later films, is particularly evident in an extended morning segment that, almost without intertitles, develops the relationship between mother and son. While walking down to the harbor, for instance, Charlia stops before a shop window that is displaying a model ocean liner. The cutting here is a bit unusual: from HAELS to MCU and back to HALS. Also, dividing the MCU in two is a brief double exposure of Charlia and the boat, which suggests his desire to become one with it, to project himself into a fantasy voyage.[8] As he moves on, the reality of the harbor area stands in mute contrast to his fantasy. The direction of his movement counterpoints that of the freighters and ocean liners, and (in ELS and HAELS) his figure is diminished before the huge ships. Returning to the apartment, Charlia stops in the street to speak briefly with his mother who is on a second-floor balcony. Again the cutting is unusual: a LALS of Lissenko standing beside the drying wash, a CU of her looking down, a HALS of Charlia looking up, a closer shot as he opens a bag of something he has bought, then an ECU

206. (left) Nathalie Lissenko
on the apartment balcony in
En rade (1927)

207. (right) Philippe Hériat
and Georges Charlia on the
dock

of several utensils from the bag in his hand. Lissenko's position and look, in conjunction with the shot that reveals the hidden objects, subtly articulates her control over her son. Her curiosity piqued (as is ours), she soon goes into the curtained-off corner which serves as Charlia's bedroom and rummages through a sack. There she "discovers his secret"—a sailor's mess kit. Although her guilty intrusion advances the narrative (and gives us knowledge), does she realize not only her son's desire to leave, but also his need to sustain himself independently (literally, to feed himself)? And what is her need that demands such close watch over him?

After this discovery, the first major break in the narrative occurs, altering this pattern of alternating spaces and characters. One day, while Charlia is leaning on an anchor cable, watching a crane load a freighter, Hériat sits down near him on the dock. Curious, he goes over to the cable to follow his gaze. In a brief intercutting of CUs and MCUs, Charlia says, "And you, too, would like to leave." Although Hériat makes no reply, the boy's words seem to project his dream onto him. Still silent, he soon goes off, in LS, beneath the spidery legs of the crane, leaving the boy, in ELS, again posed before a tug shepherding an ocean liner out to sea. Whether imagined or actual, Charlia now has an accomplice. After another sequence in the café, where Hessling is nearly attacked by one of the dockworkers (in a series of CUs and camera dollies that remind one of the opening of *Coeur fidèle*), Charlia goes to find Hériat among the men working on the docks. Suddenly, his mother appears and separates them (does she fear that he is arranging boat passage?). The next Sunday, Charlia follows Hériat through the slum streets and alleys to the café (in one LALS, as if still dogged by his mother, they pass under some washing

410

hung out to dry). There, they sit and watch the next table where a dockworker has asked Hessling to have a glass of wine with him. In a frank exchange of MCUs and CUs, Hessling stares at Charlia, who hesitantly stares back. When she gets up to set a table for a family that comes in, the sequence ends with a MCU of him bathed in the sunlight falling through the door. Even nature seems to bless their meeting. In this turn of events, Hériat has acted as a mediator, linking the different worlds of the diegesis and leading Charlia to do the same. And, perhaps without knowing it, in exchange for the dream, he seems to have given Charlia his place near Hessling in the café. Will the love suggested here in their looks conflict with this dream or will it release her, too, from servitude and confinement?

According to the next two sequences, the answer seems assured. Sometime later, Charlia takes Hessling down to the docks, where she now replaces Hériat as his accomplice. Nervous about their attraction to one another, they stand awkwardly beside some unloaded bags of coffee beans. While Charlia picks at the burlap on one of the sacks, Hessling shyly turns up the brim of her hat and leans back against it. Finally, he touches her hair, and the label revealed on the side of the sack neatly substitutes for his words: "Constanzia." How poignant is this gentle foreshadowing of *café au lait* in the morning after love-making. Here the romantic is reimagined in the commonest things.[9] Yet there is an edge to these images. What does it mean to have the romantic articulated so clearly by commodities in the system of economic exchange? The next time the lovers meet on the waterfront, Hessling arrives early, walking in the same area Charlia has walked before, linking herself with the ships and the sea. Among the timbers beneath one of the docks, they plan their departure (a boat ticket and letter—of employment?); then she kisses him and runs off. Are they really on the verge of escaping, and where and to what?

At this crucial moment, Lissenko once more searches Charlia's corner and discovers the boat ticket and letter. Her action now sets up the second major break in the narrative, which reverses the previous process of mediation and exchange. In a sequence marked off from the rest by long tracking shots, she searches the waterfront area at night for her son. At one point, she stops close by the raised piece of canvas on which he lies sleeping (an ironic parallel to the apartment with its drying sheets and curtained-off corner). A strong wind suddenly comes up, as if provoked by her efforts, and she shivers and walks off, in LS, past the tall dock cranes. Instead of one sleeper, she finds another— Hériat asleep in an alley. The displacements are beginning. Dazed by her questions (they have told him nothing of their plans), he is beaten, madly, savagely, in the first instance of rapid montage in the film. Then, just as suddenly, Lissenko stops, stunned, and slowly walks off. The effect of this attack on Hériat is ambiguous. In a LS marked by gusts of wind, he runs up to the café—cut to a strange HAFS (through the top of the door frame) of Hessling down on her knees scrubbing the floor. Has he come to protect or threaten her? Just then, Charlia comes up, and the two men glance briefly at one another—what passes between them? Charlia goes inside to Hessling, and they sit on a table to embrace, rocking back and forth, and sing softly to-gether. Outside, Hériat watches them through the doorway—what does it mean for us to see them through his eyes? In CU, his face moves toward the

411

door and stops (paralleling Lissenko earlier?); in a reverse angle LS, he stands resigned for a moment, buffeted by the wind in front of the café, and then lopes off. As if on cue, in a flurry of CUs and ECUs, Charlia leaps at Hessling.

There is something uncanny about this apparently unmotivated act. Has Charlia realized that he is not really going to leave, that he will never go to sea? Is his attack, then, an act of frustration or desperation? Perhaps so, but the discourse of the film at this point provides no such psychological explanation. Instead, it foregrounds a series of narrative displacements in conjunction with a curiously inverted form of rhetorical figuring. In separate incidents, one of the initial pairs of characters attacks the other:

Lissenko————————Charlia
Hessling ◄———————► Hériat

The mediation that previously realigned them (substituting Charlia for Hériat and Hessling for Lissenko) is reversed by the victim of that realignment, the abandoned mother. And her agent, strangely enough, is the initial mediator, Hériat. Relayed through Hériat, Lissenko's fear and rage flare up paradoxically, self-destructively, in Charlia. As if by magic, his love turns villainous. Through this series of displacements, a mother's possessiveness effectively destroys her son and those around him. Even the wind seems to serve as her agent. Touching first one then another, moving from the harbor to the café, it finally coincides with (and provokes?) Charlia's madness. In this instance, a metonymical relation turns into metaphor, and the wind seems to generate its own literal human storm.

The final images of *En rade*, like those of *Fièvre*, shift into tableaux. Charlia and Hessling are once more juxtaposed in their separate worlds. He is posed on the dock, watching a ship (in ELS) leave the harbor westward toward the setting sun. She is sitting (in MS) on the steps near the back of the café, filling her scrub bucket from a wall faucet. Yet the images of water and light, which once seemed to unite them, now coalesce again into a form of correspondence. The sea glitters with the reflected light of the sun, while the café tap water glows strangely (even Hessling gazes at it) like a long candle flame. Although the dream still seems alive, the next sequence confirms its deceptiveness. From a cliff overlooking the sea, Charlia watches Hériat push off in the rowboat. In the final HALS of him rowing away across an empty expanse of sea, the water has turned ominous, the light deathly pale. Charlia returns to his mother's apartment and, ignoring the meal she has prepared, goes immediately to his corner. She stands at the curtain and looks in one last time as he sobs into a pillow. The sequence ends in two dolly shots, moving away from the curtain to the window across the room, a transition which leads us to see what Lissenko does not.

FS of Hériat's body washing up slowly on a beach.
ELS of the sea and beach.
LS of rowboat overturned on the beach.
LS of the sun setting.

As a consequence of enacting Charlia's dream, Hériat demonstrates its futility, its inevitable end. He drowns in the sea which supposedly would have given him new life. Yet his death metaphorically parallels Charlia's condition, con-

412

208. Catherine Hessling at
the end of *En rade* (1927)

fined now to live in a world of poverty and constriction. Unlike *Fièvre*, *En rade* has no need of an intertitle such as "Disillusion" to close off its circle of signification.

Germaine Dulac's *L'Invitation au voyage* (1927) makes a strangely apt companion work to *En rade*. It takes up the same subject of evasion or *ressentiment*, but in a very different mode and context. Whereas Cavalcanti's film was shot, in part, on location and enjoyed reasonably adequate financing, Dulac's film was shot quickly on a shoestring budget (by Paul Guichard), with minor actors in rather tacky studio decors. Perhaps that was inevitable, for it was a short film (about thirty minutes) produced independently, along with *La Coquille et le clergyman* (1928), between commercial assignments—somewhat like Renoir's *Charleston* (1926) and Cavalcanti's *La P'tite Lily* (1927).[10] Despite its production base, Dulac and her assistant, Marie-Anne Malleville, arranged for a limited distribution commercially. But the film's length apparently gave exhibitors the option of screening or not screening it as part of their programs—and they tended not to.[11] Within a year, like *En rade*, it, too, found its way into the circuit of specialized cinemas and ciné-clubs.[12]

Ostensibly, as Charles Ford has written, *L'Invitation au voyage* is a free, visual adaptation of the Baudelaire poem of the same title, especially the lines,

Mon enfant, ma soeur,
Songe à la douceur,
D'aller vivre ensemble.[13]

Yet the film's narrative as well as its discourse actually owes almost nothing

413

to Baudelaire.[14] Leaving her husband and child one evening, a married woman (Emmy Gynt) adventures into a rather stylized cabaret (the locale is not specified) frequented by marine officers and chic young women. There she catches the eye of a young officer (Raymond Dubreil); and after they dance together, he tells her of his tropical sea voyages. Just as they are about to go off together, he notices that she is married. Another woman leads him off to dance, and the married woman—her dreams dashed—returns stealthily home.

Despite their admiration for Dulac's writings and lectures as well as for some of her previous films, French critics were not very kind to *L'Invitation au voyage*. One complained that "its images convey a concept of evasion more worthy of Monsieur Paul Géraldy and the Comédie Française."[15] Another charged the film itself with an evasion of sorts, particularly in comparison to the straightforwardness of *En rade*: "we have the constant impression, at each and every moment, that it conjures away (quite easily) its principal subject."[16] There is something to these objections, no doubt, but I am not sure the film can be dismissed so easily. Could a feminist and socialist of Dulac's position suffer such a failure of imagination or mistaken concession to popular taste that she would seriously endorse this "pale bourgeois nostalgia"?

Partly out of budgetary limitations and partly out of Dulac's own interests in montage, *L'Invitation au voyage* relies heavily on a visual orchestration of looks, gestures, and objects, in relatively close shots, with few intertitles. That orchestration apparently once depended on a musical accompaniment, which the cabaret provided diegetically—a sailor singing and playing an accordion, a violinist, a small jazz combo.[17] Because of its absence now, the rhythm of the film seems a bit rough and ragged in the surviving prints. As in Dulac's previous films, *L'Invitation au voyage* gives special emphasis to the representation of subjective moments. None of these, at least initially and separately, is particularly original. A flashback early on briefly defines the woman's position in marriage—her husband goes out each evening on a business appointment; much like Madame Beudet, she sits knitting in her chair, listens to the clock, and looks out the window. The sequence of dancing, although geared to the jazz combo more than to her, follows a well-established model of intoxication—accelerating montage, superimpositions, quick pans and tracks, out-of-focus shots, and fast motion. From this comes a dream sequence in which the officer opens a porthole in an imaginary space, a miniature ship "comes to life" in the surf, and she joins him on board. Her look (like that of the Oriental in *Fièvre*) alternates briefly between the surf and what has now become "refuse" in the cabaret. Finally, as the violinist comes to play by their table, the real and the imaginary interweave to produce a double trajectory of desire—she sees the surf, the blurred sails, and clouds; he reaches out to caress her hand.

Two things mark the discourse of *L'Invitation au voyage* from this point on and disturb a conventional reading of the ending. One is a shift in the locus of the subjective, from the woman to the officer, or, more precisely, to a juxtaposition of the two. When the woman leaves the cabaret, there is an exchange of looks between her and the officer. Then he is left alone at the bar before some roses which he looks at and touches (the end of *Fièvre* returns reimagined). As he imagines the two of them on the ship of *her* fantasy, her figure dissolves away. In her absence, her fantasy has become his. A few brief shots follow, succinctly placing the woman at home before her husband's arrival (his foot enters a door, his hat is placed on a rack). The final image in this series shows her drawing a blanket up over her in bed. How much is she hiding from her husband and how much is she burying herself and her vision? The film ends with a last brief sequence back in the cabaret. The officer puts the roses aside, looks at the locket he has taken from her (an ECU of her photograph), and closes it. Finally, his gaze falls on a toy boat. Why should the officer be given this final act of seeing?

This conjunction of objects concludes an important pattern of rhetorical figuring that marks the later sections of the film. The locket is the crucial object which reveals the woman's status to the officer. Its appearance coincides with that of a tray of toy boats which a woman is selling in the cabaret. As the married woman reaches out to take one of the boats, the locket falls from her bracelet into the officer's hand. He examines it closely while she gazes at the boat. When she reaches for his other hand now, he moves it away. Thus, simultaneously, two images suffer a reduction and transformation—the fantasy sailing ship becomes an easily purchased toy, and the woman becomes a tiny enclosed photograph (an object of possession?). And the oval of the locket frame is neatly juxtaposed to the image of the porthole offered for her vision. On such simple economies the narrative turns.

The ending merely confirms what has already changed. But what does it mean for the officer's look and gestures to circumscribe these objects—the rose, the locket and photograph, the toy boat? Does the knowledge of his gaze render the married woman's dream of escape ridiculous? Does the film then satirize the "pale bourgeois nostalgia" it has been accused of embracing? Or does the officer's look reaffirm the primacy of the male vision? Is the woman-as-subject, and the desire she looses, doubly contained—in both the opening of the porthole as well as the closing of the locket? After all, what stimulates her imagining but the sailor's song, the violinist's music, and the officer's stories. Is this woman trapped, not only in a social space, but in a way of seeing, a way of imagining?

Feu Mathias Pascal and *Maldone*

In *L'Inhumaine*, Marcel L'Herbier had transformed an admittedly "démodé" scenario into an original, if uneven, experimental film. In *Feu Mathias Pascal* (1925), he took a step sideways, adapting a modern novel into a slightly more conventional, more consistent work. At the time of its premiere at the Salle Marivaux, in September, 1925, L'Herbier's film was considered avant-garde by some simply because of its source, an early Luigi Pirandello novel, *The Late Matthew Pascal* (1904).[1] Pirandello's plays were then the rage of "Tout-Paris", thanks to the productions staged by Pitoëff and Dullin.[2] What made the film a financial and critical success, however, was undoubtedly the presence of Ivan Mosjoukine in the title role. One of the most popular actors in the French cinema at the time, Mosjoukine became available when Films Albatros agreed to co-produce the project with Cinégraphic. His performance here has much in common with his Protean character in *Le Brasier ardent*, and L'Herbier takes advantage of (and even indulges sometimes) his actor's penchant for eccentric behavior.

Most film historians consider *Feu Mathias Pascal*, after *El Dorado*, L'Her-

415

bier's best realized film, and even Pirandello seems to have thought highly of it.[3] That judgment, Noël Burch argues, only means that the film is retrograde, compared to *L'Inhumaine*, since it places "[the] mise-en-scène in the service of a story."[4] Burch's argument may be overly polemical, yet, within the context of the narrative avant-garde film practice, certainly the film is much more a work of synthesis than one of experimentation. L'Herbier himself called it "a fantasmagoria with a realistic premise."[5]

The premise of *Feu Mathias Pascal* is clearly Pirandellian (although L'Herbier admits to an autobiographical basis);[6] a falsely reported death seems to free the central character for a second life. Pirandello's novel provides the basic structure for the narrative, and L'Herbier's adaptation follows its source quite closely. Only at the end does he deviate considerably from the novel, which has Pascal return to his old life (but not his wife) and to his job at the library, where he writes the memoirs that constitute the book.[7]

In the film, Mathias Pascal (Mosjoukine) is an eccentric dreamer, dabbling at writing *The History of Liberty*. Suddenly, he is forced to make his own way in the world when his mother naïvely loses the family estate to an unscrupulous lawyer. Asked by his timid friend Pomino (Michel Simon) to court a young woman, Romide (Marcelle Pradot), by proxy, Mathias ends up marrying her instead. Circumstances force them to live with her tyrannical mother in a cramped house in Miragno, and Mathias goes to work at the little-used town library. After the sudden deaths of his mother and baby daughter, he flees to Monte Carlo, where a run of luck at roulette wins him a small fortune. Reading a newspaper report of his own suicide (a body found on his former family estate has been identified as his), he leaps at this chance for freedom and embarks on a new life in Rome. Calling himself Adrien, he moves into an apartment building and soon falls in love with Adrienne Paléari (Lois Moran), the daughter of his spiritualism-obsessed landlord. She is engaged, however, to an odious archeologist, Terence Papiano (Jean Hervé), whose brother Scipion (Pierre Batcheff in debut) steals his money during a rigged seance. Unable to seek help from the police, Mathias agrees to let the brothers off if they leave Rome. Cognizant of his lack of freedom again, he himself returns to Miragno. There he discovers that Romide has already remarried his old friend Pomino. Mathias decides to leave the couple in peace (with the mother-law and a new baby) and return as Adrien to Rome and Adrienne. "To live happily," the film concludes, "it is necessary to live in concealment. . . ."

Feu Mathias Pascal is particularly successful in its balanced mixture of styles. As in *L'Inhumaine*, this depends largely on the decors, both natural and constructed—the latter by Cavalcanti and Lazare Meerson, with the assistance of Eric Aës.[8] Miragno's stagnant provinciality is defined by two particular sets. One is the house interior which Noël Burch aptly describes as "*Kammerspiel* rural."[9] It is a crowded split-level space with a tiny unprivate bedroom for the young married couple. The other is the library, housed in an abandoned church, a huge Gothic chamber full of dust, disorderly piles of books everywhere, and mice nibbling the pages. Mathias takes a puppeteer's delight in tossing leashed cats at them. The only exception to this oppressive atmosphere is an evening festival (shot documentary-style by Paul Guichard against the white medieval walls and towers of San Gimignano),[10] where, on a grotto beach, Mathias courts Romide. Against these decors are ranged the ultramodern Monte Carlo

casino (with its elegant frenzy) and the otherworldly streets and interiors of Rome. Mathias first sees Adrienne at the train station and then follows her through a city that is largely empty. Their journey is described in a series of HALs and LALs across terraces, down flights of steps, and past piazza fountains. Spotted by a gendarme, Mathias checks into an expensive hotel and immediately ducks out a window. In a series of dissolves, he makes a miraculous descent down a long flight of steps to find Adrienne again and follow her home (MCUs and dolly shots now intensify his interest). The Paléari apartment building has a hallucinatory sense of space produced by a wide, deep, strangely arched corridor which nearly replicates the main spiraling stairwell. Its large bare rooms are also reminiscent of Mathias's mother's estate, and the parallel suggests that the film's resolution will somehow repeat its beginning.

The smooth, even progress of *Feu Mathias Pascal* is disrupted at certain moments when Mathias is most aware of his potential for freedom and happiness or of his lack of both. These moments of subjective hallucination happen to be crucial turning points in the narrative—near the end of the first story in Miragno and at the climax of the second story in Rome. Together they underscore the doubled structure of the film.

The first of these turning points resonates in several ways as it draws together a series of sequences in a nexus of structured relations. It is perhaps the closest the film comes to a sustained pattern of rhetorical figuring. The first sequence involves Mathias's reaction to the simultaneous deaths of his mother and his child. He has visited his dying mother one evening and is returning to his house after having promised to let her see the child once more. His disoriented state of mind is conveyed in a series of panning and dollying shots (connected by dissolves) through the village streets. There he discovers his

417

own child deathly ill, and he wanders distractedly about the small courtyard as the doctor leaves. Instead of going in, he moves to a window and gazes in at the child's dark room as the shadows of tree limbs crisscross his face. Suddenly, a light appears inside, illuminating a woman kneeling by the crib and another coming to close the window curtain, and Mathias's face backs off into deep shadow. When Mathias does reenter the room, his near hysteria makes him imagine the child is alive (a slight movement). In LS, he carries the body, trailing a long veil from the crib, past the silhouettes of the women and out into the night. A series of alternating shots (leaves blowing in the wind, a MCU dolly in front of him) describe his fantastic night journey, bearing the corpse to his mother's house. In an eerie HAMS/LS, he moves through a group of mourning women gathered around her bed and places the body in his dead mother's arms. In so doing, he unconsciously produces a shocking image of his double loss. Simultaneously, paternal and filial love are denied him.[11] And the image of the dead mother and child concisely evokes his own feeling of entrapment and approaching "death."

The second moment of disturbance occurs shortly thereafter, in Monte Carlo. Here two sequences are juxtaposed—the night in the casino and the following morning in the train station post office. At the casino, Mathias wins a fortune while the man who gave him his lucky tip shoots himself in the casino garden. Shots of the revolving roulette wheel alternate with those of the croupier, until he announces Mathias the winner. Then the alternation shifts to a CU of hands counting out money along with shots (progressing from CU to FS) of the man in the garden shooting himself in the head. Again a death seems to prefigure Mathias's own. But his ignorance of the man's suicide, in the midst of his good fortune, contrasts disconcertingly with his earlier reaction to his mother and child. This contradiction deepens when, in the very next sequence, he decides not to send a telegram to Romide about the mistaken newspaper report of his own suicide in Miragno. After an intertitle, "To be dead was to be *free*," the shadow of the post office window grating (echoing the shadows at his own child's death) suddenly disappears from his face, and LIBERTÉ in waving block letters spreads across the screen. How are we to read Mathias, a character whose sensibility seems so paradoxical and whose freedom depends perversely on others' deaths?

The most extended moment, of course, occurs just before the narrative climax of the film, in Mathias's confrontation with Papiano and Scipion. Mathias discovers that a drunken spiritualist who lives in the apartment building has convinced Paléari to marry his daughter to Papiano against her will. Deprived of identity and doubtful of his position, Mathias has a fantasy about Adrienne that quickly turns into nightmare. The sequence, in effect, inverts the sexual fantasy that opened *Le Brasier ardent*. When Adrienne materializes in Mathias's room, he kisses her hand, only to be interrupted by a double of himself which dissolves in, laughing at him. As he struggles with the image, grown twice his size, against a black void, the figure seems to retreat and blur out. Suddenly, Mathias, with revolver drawn, is advancing on an elevated door marked "Two Witnesses." As he rips a white paper cover off the door, several superimpositions of his double reappear to threaten him, and (in LAMCU) he finds himself framed by an arch marked "MARRIAGE." The futility of his

action is underscored by a series of shots that have alternated with this elliptical fantasy—a white horse drawing a carriage, inside of which Adrienne sits
smiling at Papiano. Now Mathias faces an image of Papiano in profile: the
latter is smoking a cigar and repeatedly whipping down his raised arm. Against
a corridor background that replicates the spiraling stairwell, he seems to slam
a door in Mathias's face. Within the fantasy of Mathias's life in Rome, a
second parallel fantasy metamorphoses into a nightmare of entrapment and
impotence.

Although the following sequences bring Mathias closer to Adrienne, they
also confirm his powerlessness and lack of freedom. Through the window shutters of his room (in several angled MSs), he listens to Papiano talking with
the drunken spiritualist about himself and Adrienne (in Pirandello's novel, the
whole sequence is narrated from Mathias's limited point of view).[12] When the
young woman is brought to her fiancé and seems to be attacked, Mathias
springs through the shutters to her rescue. But Papiano is ingratiating, offering a cigar, and inviting him to Paléari's spiritualist seance. All Mathias can
do is fantasize himself leaping (in slow motion) on Papiano and strangling
him. Again his fantasy turns against him. In a series of shots that blur in and
out of focus, now Adrienne bursts into laughter, and two gendarmes suddenly
appear and take him off when he cannot produce identification papers. The
seance that immediately follows is also treated like a fantasy: the soft single-
source lighting from the table produces silhouetted figures and singles out
faces and hands against the darkness. The many HALSs and HAFSs, intercut
with MSs and CUs, heighten the sense of unreality. Both hero and antagonist
undermine the seance's alleged purpose—to find out if Adrienne will be happy.
While Mathias uses the darkness to show his affection for Adrienne—kissing
her hand, interlocking his fingers comically with hers—Papiano sends Scipion
off to steal his money. After the seance is disrupted, Mathias again realizes
his inability to act and accepts the loss of his money in exchange for Adrienne's
freedom. The magical exchange reverses the narrative operation in the Monte
Carlo sequence and leaves Mathias with nothing but a false identity and the
option of dying once more.

As a doubled narrative of loss, powerlessness, and deception, *Feu Mathias
Pascal* proves quite fascinating.[13] The hero's fantastical second life replicates
his first—with important differences. In the beginning, Mathias suffers a loss
of money and status and gains a woman's love through deception. The result
is his own subjugation, especially to a tyrannical mother-in-law. He escapes
this condition by another deception—his apparent suicide. But that death or
absence coincides with the chance acquisition of money, allowing him to establish a second life, representing himself in a status similar to that which he
had in the beginning. His freedom to define himself, however, seems intimately bound up with an escape from mortality (at the expense of others) and
with a miraculous gift of money. In place of a threatening mother-daughter
duo, he now finds a father and daughter threatened (as his mother had been)
by an arch-deceiver, Papiano (who parallels the lawyer). To save them, he
accepts another loss of money, which threatens to expose his deceptive identity. Although he has gained the daughter's love, and an "ideal family," he is
an imposter and no longer himself free. The freedom he has so desired (even

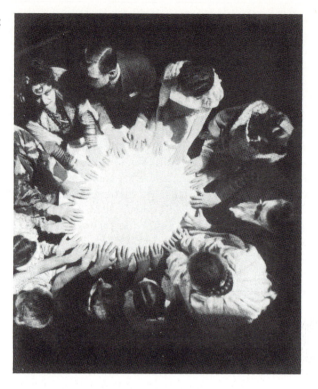

211. A publicity photo of the spiritualist sequence in *Feu Mathias Pascal*

more than the woman or family?) remains elusive and perhaps illusory. Mathias seems unable to free himself from a condition of either powerlessness/ impotence or deception.

The film's attitude toward Mathias's search and his unchanging condition is confusingly ambiguous. Is this simply an evasion—an escape from real social conditions through fantasy (Miragno versus Rome)? Is it an analysis of the problematic condition of psychological wholeness and integrity? Or is it a contradictory ideological construction which questions the role of mortality and money (capital) in a definition of the self in society and then blithely forgets it? The final sequences detail that ambiguity in a series of repressions. The question of money vanishes completely, and Mathias somehow returns to Miragno like a ghost or spirit come back to revenge himself on his enemies. Briefly, he considers resuming his legal right as Romide's husband, but, on seeing her child by Pomino, he relents. Does he withdraw out of graciousness or does he leave them to live out guiltily their own deceptive existence? Before departing from the village, however, he visits the lawyer, who is preparing a campaign speech for the mayoral election. In a mocking, metaphorical reversal of the film's opening, Mathias lashes him to a chair and takes his place before a large crowd in the piazza, giving a short impromptu speech that wins their enthusiastic approval. The sequence celebrates Mathias's new-found powers of impersonation, on which his life will now be based; and, by extension, it celebrates the actor Mosjoukine (not the cinematic apparatus, as in *L'Inhumaine*). Before the spectacle of a double impersonation, a double audience

420

applauds. Mathias now pays his respects to his own gravestone and walks away a free man. But what other graves—other deaths—are conspicuous by their absence? Framed within a "Souvenirs" booklet, a photograph of Mathias and Adrienne in wedding costume comes to life and closes off the narrative in a final spectacle of deception. The film's conclusion thus neatly represses, one by one, all its disturbing contradictions.

Another doubled narrative film, Jean Grémillon's *Maldone* (1928), makes an interesting contrast to *Feu Mathias Pascal*. The project that led to *Maldone* was conceived by the actor Charles Dullin for his newly formed film company early in 1927. Dullin would be the star, of course, the film's major commercial asset. But he took a considerable risk by engaging inexperienced, though talented, newcomers to head the team responsible for the film.[14] The original script was written by one of Dullin's friends, the poet and playwright, Alexandre Arnoux, who had done the scenario for Boudrioz's *L'Atre* (1923). The film's direction was given to Jean Grémillon, a young documentary filmmaker, some of whose short poetic works Jean Tedesco had screened at the Vieux-Colombier. His assistant was Georges Lacombe, who had been assistant director on most of René Clair's film. The cinematography, using the new panchromatic film stock, was handled by Grémillon's principal cameraman, Georges Périnal, assisted by Christian Matras. The set decors were constructed by André Barsacq, a young set designer at Dullin's l'Atelier Théâtre. And the music was compiled from pieces by Debussy, Jaubert, Satie, Milhaud, Honegger, and Grémillon himself (an accomplished violinist who had played in several cinema orchestras—e.g., the Max-Linder and the Parisiana). The production team of *Maldone* thus resembled an apprenticeship school.

Although Dullin's expensive gamble did not pay off very well financially, the film was a major critical success. There is some discrepancy about the precise basis of that success, however, for the film was projected in two different versions. First previewed at the Salle Pleyel, on 29 February 1928, it ran to 3,800 meters in length.[15] Responding to criticism that the film had "an awkward montage and unbearable dull passages," the distributor, J.-P. de Venloo, with Dullin and Grémillon's permission, had the film shortened to 2,800 meters and re-cut considerably, for a second preview in June.[16] It is this second version of *Maldone*, opening at the Omnia-Palace in October, which survives in a few copies today.[17]

Arnoux's scenario was about a character in whom "two men co-existed . . . the savage and the civilized, the free man and the submissive."[18] This double character has a striking affinity to Mathias Pascal and to Bernard Mauprat in Jean Epstein's *Mauprat* (1926). The older son of a wealthy landowner, Olivier Maldone (Dullin) has renounced his inheritance many years before to enjoy the life of a vagabond and itinerant worker along the rivers and canals of France. While towing a barge one day, he meets a young gypsy woman, Zita (Gênica Athanasiou), whose image gradually charms him and who seems to reciprocate his interest. About the same time, Olivier's brother is killed in an accident, and an old servant, Leonard (Georges Séroff), is dispatched to inform the prodigal that he must now manage the family estate. Leonard finds him one evening at a village dance, where he is playing the accordion and laying claim to Zita by winning a fight. The news stuns Olivier, and Zita slips away.

212. A publicity photo of
the opening sequence of
Maldone (1928)

Three years pass (five years in the script). Olivier has now settled into a comfortable bourgeois life with a young wife, Flora (Annabella), and her father,
Levigné (Roger Karl). Restless and dissatisfied, he embarks with his wife on
a voyage, which the family hopes will distract and cure him. On the Côte
d'Azur, however, he again meets Zita, who has become a prominent music-
hall dancer. They have dinner together, but she tells him she now has her
own life and leaves with a young man. Saddened, he and Flora return home,
where he slowly goes mad with longing for his former life. Finally, breaking
with his wife and father-in-law, Olivier dons his old vagabond's outfit and
gallops off across the fields toward the canals he loves.

In 1928, French film critics most praised in *Maldone* those moments which
epitomized the ambiance of a natural landscape or which overpowered them
with displays of technical virtuosity. The opening sequences offer probably the
best examples of Grémillon and Périnal's eye for documentary-style filming on
location. One reviewer described these images as "sometimes like etching,
sometimes like engravings, often strangely recalling the texture of two-color

gelatine photographs. . . ."[19] The subject is the Canal de Briare (connecting the Loire and Loing rivers in central France) on a hot summer afternoon, strongly reminiscent of the canal milieux that opened *La Belle Nivernaise* and *La Fille de l'eau*. The first shots are all LSs—of the still canal water, the narrow white towpath flanked by a line of poplars, a small barge being pulled slowly along by a plodding horse, a wagon pausing at a crossroads near the flat, sun-drenched fields of a farm. Into this peaceful, almost sleepy, landscape, Maldone is introduced (in MS), walking beside the tow horse, followed by a man poling the barge (in FS) and then Zita alone (in CU, superimposed, a bit conventionally, with playing cards), her image associated with the wagon as it approaches the canal. As the wagon passes over a bridge and Zita gets out, this slow, steady alternation of shots leads to a silent encounter, an exchange of looks. There is a shot past Zita to the horse moving off down the towpath, an interchange of HA and LA shots between her and Maldone as she moves off the bridge, a shot of the barge moving off down the canal, and a MCU of Zita as she looks back and then turns to follow the wagon off down the road. The narrative emerges out of this milieu in a simple, momentary conjunction. Maldone's look is curious, admiring, raising the possibility of desire, and so does hers as she glances back in the last fading shot.

The ripple of narrative expectation carries through the next sequence of shots, which dissolve together as in a dream—the barge coming forward down the canal, a woman chopping vegetables on deck, a dog sleeping, a smokestack emitting steam, a child sitting at the barge edge, the prow slicing through the canal water, tree limbs drifting by overhead, reflected light and leaves shimmering on the water surface—and ending in a CU of Maldone's face. Will the relation that promises to develop between them disturb this vision of a harmonious relationship between man and nature or can the two be integrated? And how does this vision compare with the later sequence where Leonard gets off the train (which puffs away under an immense sky) and pauses, in LS, at a crossroads gravesite to orient himself in an incredibly flat landscape?

The moment most singled out as "an astonishing demonstration of [Grémillon's] virtuosity"[20] was the Grand Ball (21 July 1928, says a poster) in the bargemen's bistro. Not only is it one of the best film dance sequences of the decade (perhaps even better than the Coaly Hole dance in *Kean*), borrowing several techniques from Gance's *Napoléon*, but it embodies perfectly an idea of Jean Epstein's, first articulated in *Bonjour Cinéma* (1921):

I would like to see a dance shot successively from the four cardinal directions. Then, with strokes of a pan shot or of a turning foot, the room as it is seen by the dancing couple. An intelligent *découpage* will reconstitute the double life of the dance linking together, if I may say so, the viewpoints of the spectator and the dancer, objective and subjective.[21]

In contrast to the usual practice, here as elsewhere in the film, André Barsacq designed the decors as a full four-walled set.[22] This allowed Grémillon much more freedom in positioning his camera and his actors. As one reviewer wrote, in terms of "the camera position and angles . . . never have we seen such diversity."[23] In fact, much of the narrative avant-garde film practice is deftly drawn into this kinaesthetic synthesis of narrative and spectacle.

213. Production photos of the Grand Ball sequence in *Maldone* (1928)

In the beginning, there are HALSs, through paper streamers hung from the ceiling and through the railing of an inner balcony, of a multitude of couples crowding the dance floor that takes up most of the bistro. Maldone is identified, in a HAMCU, drinking at one of the tables along the wall. In a dolly-back shot, several dancers drag him to a small raised platform, where he begins playing the accordion, and the camera dollies back in among the dancers, its handheld movement paralleling their quickened rhythm. The alternation of HALSs, close shots of the dancers, and LAMSs of Maldone smiling above their heads synthesizes the omniscient and the subjective (doubly inscribed) in a marvelous spectacle of simultaneity. Zita is introduced first as a silhouette at the window, then from outside looking in at the dancers (much like Chaplin outside the dance hall in *The Gold Rush*); and a backward dolly shot finally brings her into the bistro. This last shot alternates with a close shot of Maldone, and then a HAELS of the bistro merges the two into the crowd—as the narrative is subsumed in the spectacle, the subjective in the omniscient. A farandole is announced, and Maldone leads the long line of dancers up several flights of stairs, around the balcony, and down onto the dance floor again. This is a stunning moment—conveyed in slightly HALSs, in a HALS directly above the stairs that tilts and pivots to follow the dancers along the balcony, and in shots from a handheld camera moving "freely" with the dancers. It positions Maldone clearly as the subject of the spectacle (like a Pied Piper directing its rhythm) and ends with Zita its central object as she dances before him in a circle the other dancers have made for her. At that moment, in a HALS, Leonard enters the bistro, and a young man asks Zita to dance with him—two different characters threaten to disrupt the union produced by the spectacle. As Maldone begins to speed up his playing, the shots shift to MCUs and CUs and the cutting accelerates. There are circling HA and LA shots of the couple dancing, 360° pans (changing to swish pans) of their legs, their shoulders, all of which blend smoothly into one continuous movement, even when alternating with CUs of the accordion expanding and compressing and with CUs of Maldone's grinning face—as if he is relishing this maelstrom of

424

motion. In this double inscription of the subjective (Maldone's and the dancing couple's), the narrative threat is, simultaneously, intensified and suppressed—and thus suspended. The rhythm slows and pauses, allowing the man
to kiss Zita, and Maldone stops playing (in HALS) and advances on them. A
tossed glass of wine leads to a fight between the two men, erupting in a second
montage of confused handheld camera shots and swish pans. The confusion
ends with Maldone triumphantly carried back to his platform and accordion.
But not for long. Sitting now at a table, he and Zita are interrupted by
Leonard, who shows him a photograph of his dead brother. The short union
with Zita is unexpectedly broken by this intervention of the familial past.
After all the frenzy of movement, which Maldone seemed able to control, the
break is described quietly in a simple CU of separating hands. All in all, this
"Grand Ball" sequence is one Jean Epstein would have been proud of.

Although most critics were intrigued by *Maldone*'s story, they found fault
with its lack of originality and its awkward construction. They particularly
objected to the three-year break which divided the film into equal parts and
to the comparative banality of the second part—which, admittedly, is overlong and perhaps overly static.[24] Marc Allegret, for instance, wanted to know
how and why Maldone had let himself be ensnared in such a monotonous
life.[25] This objection has some validity, if one's primary interest in narrative
is the psychological development of character. But it ignores the structural
relations (semantic, syntactical, rhetorical) between the two parts of the narrative. The second part does more than set up an opposite image of Maldone,
developing the other half of his character. Like *La Roue, Coeur fidèle*, and
L'Inhumaine, it works a number of interesting variations or structural rhymes,
on the space and action of the first half of the film.

First of all, there is the contrast of decors, classes, and ways of life. As
vagabond characters, lone figures on the margins of French society, Maldone
and Zita live in harmony with the provincial milieu of canals, farms, and
village bistros and inns. While the canals and fields are constantly open to the
sun and air, the bistro interiors are comfortably rough-hewn and worn and,
in the case of the Grand Ball, bursting with movement. It is a milieu which
supports their ceaseless wandering (even allowing Zita to poach chickens from
the farms) and which encourages the eruption of emotion. Their "free" life is
thus defined very much in the tradition of a Romantic individualism. Both
characters, however, move into a different world in the second half of the film.
Maldone is now a wealthy landowner, a settled family man, living uneasily at
a respectable socioeconomic level of French society. His home is defined as a
dark closed space with the family seated around a central, well-lighted table
(echoing the 1825 dinner setting in *L'Auberge rouge*). This is a sober, orderly
space which lacks movement (except for a system of dolly shots that open and
close sequences) and suppresses any kind of emotion. The only place where he
feels happy is out in the fields or among the farmhands and threshing machines—e.g., in a brief documentary sequence of men and machines working
in an air thick with dust and chaff. This milieu also includes the elegant
modern hotels and restaurants on the Côte d'Azur; but here, too, where he
finds Zita, the decors are closed, self-contained, inhibiting his movement and
his rekindled desire. Zita seems quite different, at ease in this new world,
perfectly accommodated to it. If money alone has raised up Maldone but left

him unchanged, how and why has she changed? Was she never really part of the natural landscapes the way Maldone was? But the film is not interested in the story of her transformation, except to set up her image as a slightly disreputable opposite to Maldone.

This structural rhyming, through similarity and difference, includes several major actions in the two halves of *Maldone*. The Grand Ball sequence, for instance, recurs—with a number of reversals—in the restaurant sequence. The latter begins, and ends, as a displaced extension of the former. Maldone and Zita are seated at a table, their hands clasped together, talking and looking at the dancers. As before, a young man asks Zita to dance, but Maldone now merely sits and watches them, his face angry and then anguished. Long after she, along with the other dancers, has gone, he walks slowly across the empty restaurant (in a HALS), through layers of confetti (echoing the paper streamers before) that cover the dance floor. Although abrupt shifts in camera position and angle carry over from the Grand Ball sequence, there is neither rapid cutting nor camera movement here; and all the subjective experience is focused, confined, in Maldone.

The other rhymed sequences involve horses at full gallop. While riding across the family estate, Maldone's younger brother is killed when his horse brushes him against a tree limb. This is described in several short sequences of rapid cutting and tracking shots, which alternate with sequences in the bistro where Maldone and Zita's family seem to agree on the couple's betrothal. After the disastrous voyage, much later, Maldone rides one of the horses bearing the carriage and Flora back home, in a sequence whose cutting accelerates into CUs of the horses' heads and hooves, jiggling handheld shots of the carriage, multiple exposures of the horses, and fast tracking shots before and beside the horses and carriage. The sequence resonates with the threat of danger to both characters and, echoing the techniques of the Grand Ball, with the likelihood of the couple's separation. Later, Maldone rides out alone into the hills overlooking the valley estate, much as his brother had done before. His action not only evokes the threat of danger once again but also suggests the possibility that his madness will drive him to suicide. It even reflects backwards, raising the question of whether the younger brother also felt Maldone's desire to escape. Coupled with Zita's mother's remark to Maldone, "Your enemy is yourself," the brother's ride foreshadows his own possible tragic end.

If, in the first half of *Maldone*, the world of the bourgeois family intervenes, through the intercutting, to pluck Maldone from his relaxed life along the canals; in the second half, that intervention is reversed. The means are an extended series of subjective images, brief flashbacks, as Maldone's past life erupts into the present. The strategy is not unlike that of Delluc's *Fièvre* and *La Femme de nulle part*. These eruptions begin when Maldone encounters Zita again. Along with several shots of Flora waiting alone in a hotel room, they punctuate the restaurant sequence, retelling the past story in a few succinct images—a CU of Zita's face superimposed over a shot of water dripping from blades of grass, a HALS of the barge in the canal, and several shots from the Grand Ball dance and fight. Maldone realizes that the past is repeating itself in the restaurant milieu, but now he can do nothing. In the carriage ride home, again the past erupts. First comes an image of the restaurant encounter

and then shots of his initial vision of Zita and their betrothal agreement in the café. It is this achronological flashback, emphasizing his loss, which provokes the accelerating montage of the carriage ride. That night, as he sits with the family around the table and Flora brings him coffee (the shots are marked now by frequent pans, tilts, and dollies), more images of his past life on the barge return. When Flora comes over and gently puts her arm around his neck, it is Zita he sees—in a CU of her face and then an ECU of her mouth. He closes his eyes (in ECU) and tears himself (in FS) from her embrace. The shot pans right to follow him out the door and then pans back to Flora, terrified, and her father. Just as his brother's death propelled Maldone away from Zita and back to the family, so does the (recognized) loss of Zita propel him away from the family and back to his old life. But the reversal reverberates with a poignant dissonance. The image of the past that most provokes him to act is the one he can not return to, and his anguish is echoed in the family, especially in Flora, who is given no chance to understand him.

Maldone's decision to return to nature and a vagabond's life is marked by further anguish—a confrontation with Levigné, in which he raises a whip against him, and a later HALS of his doubled-up figure pausing on the spiral staircase to the attic. The juxtaposition of past and present, itinerant work and bourgeois wealth, reaches a climax in the sequence in the attic. As Maldone looks at himself in an old floor-length mirror, the image of his former

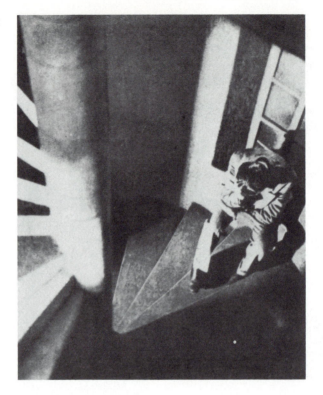

216. Maldone on the attic
stairs

self dissolves in, spitting and raising a whip to him. Maldone searches a trunk
nearby for his old clothes, and as he dresses, shots of the barge and canal are
intercut. Finally, in a reversal of images, dressed in his vagabond's outfit, he
faces his bourgeois figure in the mirror. Suddenly he pulls a gun from his
pocket and shoots, shattering the glass. The duality is resolved, at the level
of the individual, by simple elimination. As he flees the house for the second
time, the shots of his speeding horse and tense face give way to shots of
swirling water, billowing clouds, and finally, repeating the beginning, to an
image of calm water. The clouds and calm water come as a relief, smoothing
the agitation into a continuous motion that ends in a state of rest. Does it
metaphorically represent Maldone's psychological condition, articulating his
success in finding peace of mind? Or does it operate deceptively? Can Maldone
ever be the same as he was in the beginning, enjoying the same harmony with
the canal landscape? If not, the calm water surface simply erases, submerges,
all that he has lost or abandoned. And this becomes another resolution that
masks profound dissonances.

Napoléon vu par
Abel Gance

The Walker Art Center, Minneapolis, Minnesota, 14 March 1980. Looking
much like the third phase of the Sphinx's riddle to Oedipus, a small, stooped
figure, his eyes twinkling under a swept-back thatch of white hair, introduces
the Midwest premiere of Kevin Brownlow's meticulous reconstruction of *Napo-*

428

léon (1927). It is the film's maker, Abel Gance. "Why would anyone want to spend a whole evening watching an old movie?" he begins. Suddenly spotting a KCTA cameraman recording the event, Gance brandishes his cane like a rapier and charges the camera with a spryness that belies his ninety-year-old frame. Then he backs away in feigned defeat, accepting the power of a machine whose ancestor he did so much to develop. Delighted by an enthusiastic, admiring crowd, he builds his oration, phrase by lofty phrase—"I am alive because I think always and only of the future"— and ends by dancing a jig to mime his pleasure. He refuses to leave—"there are too many beautiful women in the audience." But eventually he is persuaded, and the special screening begins. Nearly six hours later, the famous triptychs (in perfect synchronization) draw to a climax that yields to a wave of applause and bravos. Rarely have I seen a film audience so charged, so "high."[1]

To see this new reconstruction of *Napoléon* is nothing less than a revelation. That has been said before, I know, of other versions of the film. In 1955, at the Studio 28 cinema in Paris, François Truffaut and his colleagues at *Cahiers du cinéma* discovered Gance's two-hour sound version of *Napoléon* (1934), which integrated new footage with postsynchonized portions of the silent version, including a brief sequence of the final triptychs.[2] Some years later, the Cinémathèque française revealed Marie Epstein's painstaking reconstruction of the silent version of *Napoléon*, which, though far from complete (absent were much of the opening snowball fight, the sequences with Violine, the triptychs), included nearly all of the major sequences.[3] Then, on the occasion of Bonaparte's Bicentennial (with financial assistance from André Malraux and Claude Lelouch), Gance came up with a four-hour version (again mixing old and new footage), *Bonaparte et la révolution* (1971).[4] For this last project, Marie Epstein discovered, to her horror, Gance blithely set about re-cutting some of an original positive print that the Cinémathèque française had returned to him.[5] Now comes Kevin Brownlow's reconstruction, some twenty years in the making, drawn from a dozen archive and private prints (especially those of the Cinémathèque française, C. K. Elliot, and MGM).[6] Inevitably, there are distortions and gaps: the image quality is sometimes inconsistent (due to sections of enlarged 17.5mm footage), the extensive tinting and toning of the original prints is gone, and nearly a half hour of the total footage is still missing.[7] But Brownlow's reconstruction is unquestionably marvelous—the most complete version yet assembled and the first to include the full final reel of triptychs.[8] To be accurate, there are two versions of Brownlow's work—a complete version (projected at 20 fps), produced by the British Film Institute and Images Film Archives in association with Thames Television, and a slightly shortened version (projected at 24 fps) sponsored by Francis Coppola's Zoetrope Studios.[9] Although the "Coppola" *Napoléon* has been widely screened in the United States, I have used the longer, more authentic version as the basis for this analysis.

Impressive as Brownlow's reconstruction is, Gance's initial plans for the project were even more colossal in scope. As early as 1924, he had sketched out no less than six separate films on the life of Napoléon Bonaparte. The first film was envisaged in three parts: "La Jeunesse de Bonaparte," "Bonaparte et la Terreur," and "La Campagne d'Italie." The other five were to be titled *D'Arcole à Marengo, Du 18 brumaire à Austerlitz, D'Austerlitz aux cent-jours,*

Waterloo, and *Saint-Hélène.*[10] Through a consortium of French-German companies and later the Société Générale des Films (both financed largely by Russian emigré money), Gance commenced shooting the first stage of his project early in 1925 and finally finished eighteen months later. Because of its enormous expense (15 to 19 million francs) and epic length (six hours), only the first film was actually completed, and even then, its third part had to be condensed.[11] On 7 April 1927, a three-hour version of the film, audaciously titled *Napoléon vu par Abel Gance* and highlighted by several triptych sequences, premiered at the Paris Opéra with an orchestral score composed by Arthur Honegger.[12] The following October, the complete six-hour version (apparently programmed in two consecutive segments, but without the triptychs) opened at the prestigious Salle Marivaux and ran for three months. This full-length version was not widely shown, but the three-hour condensed version was released selectively throughout France and the rest of Europe.[13] In a sense, then, by integrating these two different films into a single spectacle, Brownlow not only re-creates but enlarges Gance's vision. As Bernard Eisenschitz notes, Brownlow's work has produced both a literal and an ideal reconstruction of the film.[14]

In order to situate the analysis that follows, let me summarize the narrative of *Napoléon* briefly, sketching the major plot lines and the distribution of characters. As a pupil at the military college of Brienne, young Napoléon is persecuted as an outsider by the teachers and other students.[15] His only friends during his tribulations and first triumph (in a snowfort battle) are the cook, Tristan Fleuri, and a pet eagle. Some ten years later, in 1789, during the early days of the Revolution in Paris, Napoléon is little more than a marginal character, listening with interest to Rouget de Lisle's "Marseillaise" sung at the Club de Cordeliers but troubled by the lynch mobs roaming the streets. By the time of his return to his family home in Corsica, in the summer of 1793, however, he has become a supporter of the Revolution and an opponent of the Corsican patriot Paoli and his secretary, Pozzo de Borge, who have concocted a plan to annex the island to England. Their plan succeeds, and Napoléon is forced to flee by rowboat in a storm (and eventually on the good ship Le Hasard) to France. Assigned to the French army laying siege to Toulon (which is controlled by the English), Napoléon reencounters Tristan Fleuri, whose daughter Violine is "bewitched" by him. General Dugommier makes him commander of the artillery, and Napoléon leads several assaults on the larger English army and finally is victorious in a battle fought at night in a torrential rainstorm. In Paris, the Reign of Terror begins. Marat is murdered in his bath by Charlotte Corday; Danton, Robespierre, and Saint-Just are all condemned to the guillotine.[16] Accused by Salicetti, a fellow Corsican, and imprisoned, Napoléon is miraculously saved—Tristan Fleuri, imitating his friend La Bussière, literally eats the decree that condemns him. After refusing several posts with the army, Napoléon is finally called by General Barras to take command of the defense of Paris against the Royalist Rebellion. The rebellion is put down, and celebrations break out all over the city. At the Victims' Ball, Napoléon is mesmerized by Josephine de Beauharnais and wins her away from his friend, General Hoche. The whirlwind courtship ends in marriage, after Barras makes him commander of the Army of the Alps. Buoyed by a vision of the ghosts of the Revolution, Napoléon assumes command of a

bedraggled army at Albenga and quickly inspires the soldiers to victory at Montenotte. So the narrative ends as (an intertitle says) "Napoléon laughingly opens the gates of Italy."

As this summary suggests, *Napoléon* is, first of all, a grand example of the French historical reconstruction film, the most popular film genre in France during the 1920s. Although a good part of the film was shot on location (Corsica, Briançon, Toulon, Nice), most was done in the brand-new studio at Billancourt, on the outskirts of Paris. There, with Alexandre Benois (Diaghilev's chief set designer), the Russian-born architect Schildknecht, and Ivan Lochakoff, Gance meticulously (for the most part) re-created the period decor and costumes of the late eighteenth century—e.g., the school at Brienne, the Club des Cordeliers and the Convention Hall in Paris, the battleground at Toulon. Together with an unusually talented team of assistant directors (Alexandre Volkoff, Victor Tourjansky, Henry Krauss, Henri Andréani, Marius Nalpas, Anatole Litvak) and cameramen (Jules Kruger, L.-H. Burel, J.-P. Mundviller, Bourgassov, Lucas, Roger Hubert, Emile Pierre), he produced enough moments of spectacle for a half-dozen films. The acting was consistently first-rate and sometimes inspired. Albert Dieudonné played Napoléon as a lean, active, decisive strategist, sometimes given to public posturing but also blindly naïve in love. Gina Manès brought to Josephine's opportunistic character a matronly assurance and quick intelligence that made her behavior with Napoléon and his rivals fascinatingly ambiguous. The "Three Gods of the Revolution" were perfectly cast. Alexandre Koubitsky was a fiery, voluable, plump Danton; Antonin Artaud made Marat a sullen ascetic with a brilliant, mad stare; Van Daële was utterly transformed as the slouching pock-marked Robespierre, his eyes mere slits above tightly drawn lips. And Gance used his own sense of self-importance ironically by casting himself as the cold, cruel, slightly effeminate theoretician Saint-Just. Yet, all in all, like Carl Dreyer's *La Passion de Jeanne d'Arc* (1928), which the Société Générale des Films also produced as a complement to it, *Napoléon* was much more than a well-crafted, well-acted costume film.

At the time of its original release, the French film critics' reviews of *Napoléon* corresponded closely to their reactions to Gance's earlier epic, *La Roue*. The film was a monumental paradox—conventional yet unorthodox, anachronistic yet radically advanced. Again the critics objected, with reason, to the number and mode of the film's intertitles, which included countless quotations from historical sources—a misguided attempt to invoke the mantle of authority—which merely labeled and affirmed, as if on parchment, what was presented in images.[17] The intertitles were also full of rhetorical declamations, especially Saint-Just's discourse on the Revolution, which critics found reminiscent of Edmond Rostand and literary pretension.[18] Once more the critics objected to irrelevant, uneven sequences and to "dissembling tirades" of "repetitions, redundancies, and overprolonged effects."[19] And they were aghast at the way Gance rewrote history, depicting Napoléon as the legendary fulfillment of the French Revolution—a nationalistic messiah who saved France from the Revolution's destructive excesses and then provided his countrymen with a kind of Manifest Destiny to "liberate" (read "conquer") Europe.[20] Harry Alan Potamkin called Gance simply a "Hugo without Hugo's vision."[21] To a man, however, the critics heaped praise on the cinematic qualities of the film. "The unrepentant lyricism, the vertiginous technical strategies, the generous abandon, the photogenic delicacies, the acting in certain roles"—all more than made up for the film's numerous faults.[22] Specifically singled out, of course, was the innovation of the triptychs, the Polyvision triple-screen system, which produced a concluding visual symphony of extraordinary power. Perhaps Léon Moussinac summed up the critical reaction best. If Gance's subject and scenario were presumptuous, sometime ridiculous, and dangerously chauvinistic,

From the cinematic point of view, *Napoléon* was the occasion . . . to put in play original ideas that succeeded in enlarging the resources of cinematography, in sum, an incontestable advance: a date in the history of the technical development of the cinema.[23]

The contradictions in *Napoléon* are, if anything, now even more apparent. But their locus and distribution seem to have shifted. Take the most celebrated feature of the film—its technical innovations and achievements. It is clear that, from the beginning, Gance was preoccupied with questions of cinematic technique. For instance, Alexandre Volkoff, one of his assistant directors for a time, was astonished to find that

he was continually haunted by the idea of doing more and then more again, of surpassing himself and all others. Incessantly, he tried out cinematic innovations, combining new technical methods. He strove to go ever farther and higher.[24]

This effort is clearly evident even now in the remarkable film record of the production which Gance instigated, preserved under the title, *Autour de Napoléon*.[25] But how successful, exactly, was Gance with his innovations? One of the earliest segments to be filmed, the snowfort battle at Brienne, provides an ambiguous answer.

Like the opening train wreck of *La Roue*, this sequence was orchestrated, in Gance's words, "to make the otherwise passive spectator an actor. He would not only look at but participate in the action."[26] In *La Roue*, he had relied on the rapid cutting of many disparate images to simulate the aftereffects of the

432

219. A production photo of
Jules Kruger (center left) and
Abel Gance (dark glasses)
with the sled-mounted camera
for filming the opening
sequence in *Napoléon*

crash, to integrate Sisif's perceptions and feelings into a larger conceptual design. Here, he privileges the character of young Bonaparte—to the point of making the flow of images his subjective experience—but reduces the number of disparate images and multiplies the technical strategies of combination and intensification. Initially, Gance superimposes a CU of young Bonaparte over shots of his battling cohorts, to convey the passion and force of his counter-attack (after the boy is bloodied by a snowball with a rock inside). To this, Gance then adds an unconventionally mobile camera. He had Jules Kruger (with a hand-cranked camera) sit on a sled that was pushed rapidly toward one of the two snow forts. Then at Gance's insistence, Kruger also ran into the thick of the fighting with another hand-cranked camera strapped to his chest and supported by a brace around his waist.[27] The only thing he did not do was what legend has attributed to him—throw the camera about like a snowball.[28] Finally, Gance resorts to a form of rapid cutting—wildly fast tracks, dollies, and swish pans—in conjunction with a repeated static CU of young Bonaparte. At the climax, the cutting accelerates to a rush of single frames, with the boy's smiling face appearing every four frames.

Despite the novelty of handheld mobile camera shots in alliance with the by-then conventional technique of rapid montage, this sequence is less than astonishing. In part, if I may presume, the problem lies in its conception. Compared to the opening of *La Roue*, this sequence seems regressive—it limits itself to the representation of a single character's subjective state. More important, perhaps, the representation of that state, organizing the world around Bonaparte, is relatively simplistic (his enemies, Philippeaux and Peccaduc, are cruel buffoons; the counterattack is easily carried out). The single-minded diegetic flow of the images quickly becomes repetitive, wearyingly so, as the action is expanded in time. The longer the sequence goes on, the more excessive and empty it becomes. What could have been an exciting, riveting opening, in which the spectator shares young Bonaparte's intoxicating discovery of his skill and ambition as a leader, comes close to lapsing into bombastic cliché.

At least two conclusions can be drawn from such close analysis of the technical innovations in *Napoléon*. First of all, they tend to improve in quality and effectiveness as the film progresses. The combination of fast tracks, dollies, and swish pans, for instance, is much more controlled in the later sequence of Napoléon's journey to Albenga to join the Italian Campaign army. Here, even more than before, some of the camera movements deliberately call attention to themselves. The opening LS of the road down which Napoléon's coach and flanked horsemen race away suddenly turns into a following dolly shot; the movement allows for a smooth cut to a tracking shot of the countryside which then pans 60° to become a dolly shot following the advance horsemen. The spectator is caught up, quite deliberately, in the diegetic process. After Napoléon has issued a number of orders, sent off a letter to Josephine, and changed to horseback, the sequence ends with a series of rapid dollying shots ahead of his pounding white horse, each of which becomes shorter and shorter as it is punctuated by quick swish pans. Here, the camera movement (in conjunction with the rapid cutting) functions less to convey Napoléon's subjective experience of the journey than to equate, through the accelerating rhythm, his driving ambition with the "flow of history" and, at this point, with the lightning speed of the narrative. This combination of camera movements will reach a climax in the final segment of the triptychs.

Secondly, Gance's technical achievements, for me at least, often depend on a striking economy and symmetry of articulation. The school dormitory battle, for instance, produces a visual assault even more effective than the opening snowfort battle. One snowy night, Philippeaux and Peccaduc vengefully release Bonaparte's pet eagle, and he storms into the dormitory to find the culprits.

LS dolly back ahead of Napoléon as he enters the room.
MCU dolly forward past one boy shaking his head, then a second, and a third.
LS dolly forward behind Napoléon as he speaks to one boy after another.
MCU dolly forward past a boy yawning and then another shaking his head.
LS Napoléon stops at the end of the room, turns, and throws a pile of boys' clothes.
MCU Napoléon shouts.
Intertitle: "So all of you are guilty!"
FS dolly back ahead of Napoléon as he attacks one boy after another, systematically; they come out and surround him.
FS dolly forward behind Napoléon and the boys as they begin to fight—pillows and feathers fly about.
Four split-screen images of the fighting.
Nine split-screen images of the fighting.
A half-dozen superimpositions of the fighting.

What is interesting about this sequence is how succinctly it works through repetition and variation. The first series of movements, rhythmically matched, end in Bonaparte's angry gesture and accusation. The second series begins to repeat the first and then oscillates quickly into a crescendo of simultaneous multiple images. Bonaparte's fury, metaphorically, tears the boys to pieces (clothes-pillows-feathers) and transforms the room into a dense cloud of feathers and white-robed figures.[29] It is as if the snowball fight is recapitulated in miniature.

Still, whatever one thinks of these "highlights," an exclusive focus on Gance's technical innovations and achievements can be misleading. It tempts one to

434

conclude, as do Jean Mitry and most film historians, that *Napoléon* is incoherent, "a chaos traversed by lightning flashes."[30] To my mind, however, that
supposed incoherence actually provides a basis for the film's appeal. In fact,
in terms of narrative structure and syntactical continuity, it may not be incoherence at all. Let us admit, for instance, that the film deploys, throughout
its narrative, a cacophony of styles or modes of representation. There are posturing "theatrical" characters such as Paoli and Salicetti, "naturalistic" characters such as Josephine and General Hoche, comic buffoons such as the recurring Tristan Fleuri, and bold caricatures such as L'Oeil-Vert (the one-eyed
master of the guillotine lists) and Couthon (a decrepit old man who creeps
about in a wheelchair with a white rabbit in his lap). There are reproductions
of famous mass spectacle paintings of the Revolution and its aftermath, documentary moments (such as a bread line of women and children in a snow-
covered street), American-style chases on horseback, an oddly anachronistic
moment of modern dancing at the Victims' Ball (including a line of flappers
and shots of naked breasts and buttocks), and highly subjective visions articulated in a barrage of cinematic techniques. This kind of mixture we have
seen before—in such diverse films as L'Herbier's exquisite melodrama, *El Dorado*; Mosjoukine's satirical comedy, *Le Brasier ardent*; Kirsanoff's poetic "slice-
of-life," *Menilmontant*; and Cavalcanti's cruelly witty documentary, *Rien que les
heures*. If the cacophony in *Napoléon* seems deliberate, then perhaps overriding
the usual conventions of coherence is a principle of play for its own sake, a
playing that involves a mélange of styles. Or, even more likely, perhaps there
is in the film, as there was in *La Roue*, a conception of structural unity that
sets coordinates for this play, that shapes it into a coherent network of narrative relations.

Similarly, throughout its length, *Napoléon* deploys a variety of syntactical
systems. In the Victims' Ball, for instance, Gance relies basically on the "classical" style of editing that creates a spatial-temporal continuity to ensure a
clear chain of character action. At several points, this involves a subtle alternation of eye-line matches between Napoléon, Josephine, and Hoche—when
they first meet and when Napoléon takes Hoche's queen in a chess game. In
a dramatic sequence during the Royalist Rebellion (as well as in other sequences), however, Gance sets up a different form of spatial continuity, shifting back and forth between matched and "mismatched" shots that define the
relations between Barras, Napoléon, and a Captain Murat. Finally, in Napoléon's journey to Albenga, as has been noted, the spatial-temporal continuity
is sacrificed in order to emphasize a system of graphic, rhythmic, and connotative relations. Because of its inconsistent adherence to the "classical" continuity system developed by the American cinema, Noël Burch, among others,
has called *Napoléon* a "primitive" film.[31] Even if Burch means to reverse the
pejorative sense of the word (to celebrate early film practice), the label seems,
to me, inappropriate. For what Gance and his colleagues in the narrative
avant-garde seem to have developed and/or accepted was a discourse that was
deliberately plural. At his disposal for *Napoléon* were several different or alternative systems of syntactical continuity. Again, the question is, do they simply provide another means for play or are there patterns to the deployment of
these syntactical systems that coalesce into coherence?

Let me point the way toward grasping the film's integration of these modes of representation and continuity systems by focusing on that portion devoted to the relationship between Napoléon, Josephine, and her maid Violine. At the time of *Napoléon*'s release, critics tended to ignore this part of the film, presumably on the grounds that it was a sentimental digression. That attitude still persists for most of the cuts in the "Coppola" version now circulating in the United States are made here.[32] That is unfortunate, because these sequences achieve a high degree of rhetorical complexity and emotional poignance and, in the process, reveal a nexus of coherence in the midst of incoherence. Furthermore, they introduce a disturbing note of discord, another level of contradiction, into the text of *Napoléon*.

The courtship between Napoléon and Josephine is marked by a mixture of high and low comedy until one day Napoléon calls unexpectedly at her tiny chateau. While her son and daughter chat with the awkward suitor in an antechamber, Josephine tarries in the bedroom with Barras (whose mistress she has been and may still be), receiving his permission to marry. The children engage Napoléon in a game of blindman's bluff; and as he fumbles about, blindfolded, Barras escapes by tiptoeing past him and out the door. Napoléon is caught up in the game (articulated in an accelerating montage of fast panning CUs) until Josephine sneaks up behind him and allows herself to be captured. Instead of taking off the blindfold, however, he tells her that he has no need of eyes to know whom she really loves in her heart. At this she does a warily slow double take, as if suddenly fearful that he may realize her actual feelings and motives and the extent of her duplicity. This sequence is remarkable in several ways. The accelerating montage sets up an implausible continuity, the subjective vision (all are POV shots) of a character who is blindfolded. Yet the function of that implausibility is to call into question Napoléon's ability to see and hence to know. The subsequent series of shots reinforce that questioning by juxtaposing (in matched CUs) the blinded lover and his all-too-seeing-and-knowing beloved. In the context of his skill as a military strategist and his inheritance of the visionary principles of the Revolution (which he accepts immediately after the wedding), Napoléon's blindness here takes on disturbingly grand proportions. If his love for Josephine can be mocked so cruelly and easily, can his devotion to the Revolution be any less of a delusion?

The wedding ceremony introduces a further sense of questioning and disturbance. In contrast to several brief sequences where the couple stroll in the gardens around her chateau (photographed in exquisitely glowing images that soften at the edges), the wedding is a lackluster affair of waiting (Napoléon arrives late) in a tacky civil chamber (the spotlighting on the walls is even blatantly inconsistent). Intriguingly, however, this ceremony is almost displaced by the wedding (identified as such in an intertitle) that Violine stages for herself. This young woman has appeared repeatedly in the second half of the film—in the Convention as Robespierre and Saint-Just are condemned, in the bread line of women in the snow, at the Victims' Ball as a coat-check girl. She becomes infatuated with Napoléon (at one point buying a wooden statuette of him that is hawked in the streets of Paris) and finally arranges her hair like Josephine's and gets herself hired as one of her maids. On the evening of the marriage, Violine dresses herself in white before a mirror in her room, then slowly gets up onto her bed and kneels in a position of prayer. In place of a headboard is a small cabinet that she opens, revealing a tiny altar to

Napoléon that includes the statuette, some flowers, several candles, and one of his white gloves.[33] The sequence then cuts to Napoléon and Josephine in their bridal chamber. For a moment he stands alone by the bed, which is thinly veiled by a full-length curtain, and then she comes to the opposite side and touches one of the garlands encircling the curtain. He joins her, and they kiss (in CU) as veil after veil falls diagonally across their faces until the image fades to white. The sequence then returns to Violine, who has left her bed to stand by the wall. The left portion of the frame, which has been blurred out of focus, suddenly clears, revealing the statuette on a small table. Violine's hand moves the figure slightly and its enlarged shadow appears on the wall. In a final MS, she moves to the projected shadow and presses her lips to it.

This double wedding transpires in a mysterious world, half real, half fantasy. In its startling white-on-white mise-en-scène, Moussinac writes, Violine often seems "to fade away into the gray mists of a magical background."[34] Yet the sequence is also unusually perverse, pushing passion and sentimentality to excess. Something like this had occurred earlier when Napoléon was taking lessons in courtship. At the end of that sequence, he faced a globe of the world and imagined Josephine's face superimposed inside it. When he moved to kiss her, she turned away; turning the globe brought her back again. But as Napoléon covered her face with his and seemed to caress her hair, Josephine's look was reluctant, even resistant. Here, in Violine's chamber, the situation is reversed. A woman produces her own image of the man she loves (or the image her society offers her) and manipulates that image for her own ends. But the man is absent, the manipulation a delusion. What does this suggest, not only about the "mad" character of Violine, but about perception and power in sexual relations? Does Violine's passion parallel and reflect on Napoléon's relation to Josephine? And does her fetishistic projection make us even more conscious of the film's representation of Napoléon?

The motif of testing that marks these sequences of courtship and marriage provides, I would argue, a basis of coherence for the film as a whole. The scope of *Napoléon* may be too large for its disparate parts to be organized into anything like the tightly-fitted, Chinese box-like construction of a short work such as Jean Epstein's *La Glace à trois faces* (1927). Yet there does seem to be an overall design that depends on more than the chronology of historical events (which already has suffered several major shifts and lacunae). To grasp that design is to see Napoléon propelled through a double series of increasingly more crucial tests and confrontations whose paradigmatic relations are as important as their syntagmatic progress. For in the reversals and transformations of those tests, the character of Napoléon undergoes a kind of deconstruction.

The first half of *Napoléon* introduces the motif of the test or confrontation at the outset, in the snowfort battle which is then recapitulated in the dormitory pillow fight. That segment ends in an image which condenses elements of the previous action and presages what is to come. Young Napoléon is alone in an empty storeroom, sitting on an old cannon, when his pet eagle returns through an open window from the snowy night to join him. This rhetorical form of closure—the lone figure, the imperial eagle, the military hardware, the glittering particles in the air—establishes a pattern that will recur at several key moments in the film. The next segments, during the onset of the Revolution, delay any further test. The retreat to Corsica, however, sets up a confrontation between the island factions, especially between Napoléon and Paoli, who has sided with England. The confrontation begins in a local café (articulated in a slow montage of marvelous faces in CU), builds to a face-off in front of the actual Bonaparte family home (photographed with a special "brachyscope" lens to make up for space limitations), and then to a horseback chase that ends in his escape by sea. All of this culminates in two major tests—the storm at sea and the siege of Toulon—which climax the first half of the film. Both demand close scrutiny.

The first of the two begins with a stunning image that transcends cliché. In a small boat Napoléon has taken to escape the Corsican gendarmes, he attaches to the mast the huge French flag he has seized from Paoli and unfurls it as a sail. With one hand grasping the flag and the other guiding the tiller, he quickly puts out to sea—for France. This image culminates a series of simple similes in the film: young Bonaparte and the eagle, Danton and the flames of a blacksmith's forge, Pozzo and a snake (which, as in a prewar serial, incongruously coils about his shoulder). But it also marks the transition to an even grander simile. Apparently inspired by Victor Hugo's line, "To be a member of the Convention is like being a wave of the ocean," Gance concludes the Corsican period with a sequence that intercuts Napoléon's storm-tossed boat and the surging melee of the Convention—hence its title, the Double Tempest.[35] Following Moussinac, Mitry has argued that this sequence is flawed because it simply visualizes a preexisting idea—a mere literary symbol, no more.[36] However, the tumult of the Revolutionary assembly in Paris is not only paralleled to but transformed by the turbulent sea through which Napoléon navigates to his "destiny." The point of the charged equation, it seems to me, is to suggest that the Convention will soon test Napoléon as well and that he will survive it just as he survives the storm at sea. He will triumph over forces both cosmic and human, natural and political. In fact, the latter forces are diminished, and almost obliterated, by the former in this rhetorical process of mystification.[37]

The significance of the Double Tempest depends, in part, on its use of the celebrated Polyvision triple screen or triptych system. As originally conceived, this system was intended simply to record panoramas several times wider than the normal frame area. Gance had André Debrie mount three identical Parvo-Debrie cameras on top of one another, aim the top and bottom ones to record the fields adjacent to that recorded by the middle camera, and synchronize all three to run automatically.[38] Despite a slight parallax problem in joining the three images, the results were so stunning that Gance used the technique several times in *Napoléon*, not only for panoramas near the end (as initially planned) but for other effects as well. Here, in the Double Tempest, the shots of the Convention are marked by the vertiginous movements of pendulum camera shots—"the camera was placed at the end of a metal rod some ten meters long, which oscillated like a gigantic pendulum, imparting to the lens a forward and backward movement, similar to some sort of swing's rising and falling."[39] Similarly, the shots of the storm are marked by wildly tilting images of the boat as it is deluged with water, CUs of Napoléon's bloody hands, and both positive and negative images of enormous roiling waves (photographed from a glass box submerged in the surf). According to Gance, the sequence crescendoed in a rhythmic montage involving all three panels of the

220. Napoléon and his
Tricolor sail at sea

triptych, along with an increasing number of superimpositions, until it climaxed in sixteen images spaced across the triple screen.[40] Even in its present fragmentary form, one can see here the recapitulation of the earlier snowball and pillow fights literally enlarged to epic proportions.

The siege of Toulon extends the epic mode of this testing, but it also introduces the earliest discordant note of ambiguity. The first assault begins at midnight, and all the fighting thereafter is conducted at night. Furthermore, it begins in a downpour of rain that persists unrelentingly throughout the fighting. Together these conditions produce a shifting combination of "heroic" and "unheroic" images, in conjunction with which Napoléon is both larger-than-life leader and sharer of the suffering. Early on, especially, close shots of his face are intercut with the attacking soldiers and artillery firing. And in the climactic moments, several shots are divided into a miniature triptych, with Napoléon in the center panel seeming to direct the fighting at his sides. But the battle is also unusually brutal. In the first assault, a soldier is blown up in a water-filled ditch and a second soldier falls in dead after him; a third is wounded in the head, while a fourth has his foot run over by a cannon.[41] In the second assault, two soldiers struggle in a sea of mud until one drowns the other—the last image is that of an arm reaching up desperately, futilely, out of the murky water. In the aftermath of the siege, in several HALSs, Napoléon stands hunched in the rain on a mound surrounded by scores of dead soldiers in the mud. Yet the last shots condense and transform these elements from the battle, along with some from Brienne and Corsica.

221. The Parvo-Debrie cameras set up to record a triptych panorama. Albert Dieudonné is in costume (right foreground)

The master shot is a LS of a hill on which sit a house (frame right) and a low wall (frame left), near which, under a bare tree, Napoléon falls asleep on a drumhead. As smoke rises from the right foreground, the dawn light of the sun breaks in from the left background. On General Dugommier's orders, soldiers cover Napoléon with several French flags, and an eagle alights in the tree overhead. All these tests thus climax in a heavily symbolic tableau that "resolves" any sense of contradiction.

The second half of *Napoléon* is constructed somewhat like the first; there are a number of confrontations early on and then another more important series at the end. The beginning segment covers the period of the Reign of Terror, during which Napoléon again is a marginal character, especially during the time when the "Three Gods of the Revolution" disappear. But when the Royalist Rebellion breaks out, Barras calls him to the Convention to take command of Paris's defense. With a few words, Napoléon distributes arms to the citizens, and the rebellion is quickly crushed. As the segment climaxes in a moment of spectacle at the Convention—in a series of huge shot/reverse shots that will be echoed in the film's final reel—Napoléon announces to the cheering throng, "I am the Revolution!" Yet this expected triumph is torn by contradictions. On the one hand, it recapitulates and transforms the sequence

440

of the Double Tempest. The new storm that threatens the Convention has been stilled—in place of tumult, there is stasis and order; in place of several squabbling leaders, there is now a single figure of authority. On the other hand, Napoléon's position is even more ambiguous than at the siege of Toulon. As savior of the Revolution, he has turned into its dictator, its new God. In the Convention Hall, whether fully lit or silhouetted, he is an overdetermined subject—the focal point of framing and editing, the source of powerful words (e.g., "Justice" hangs over him in the air). Before taking command, however, for one long moment, his shadow falls ominously over "The Declaration of the Rights of Man." And in the Convention's aftermath, his body is disguised and then fetishized in statuettes hawked in the streets. Oscillating between Great Man of History, puppet, and menacing shadow, the figure of Napoléon has become plural, paradoxical.

If this Convention triumph displays an ever increasing sense of discord, the sequences of courtship and marriage that follow push the character of Napoléon to the brink of incoherence. There, a different form of testing, involving the dynamics of sexual politics and degrees of knowledge, raises disturbing questions about the Napoléonic hero and his position as subject in the narrative and in history. At the point of dissolution, the film suddenly backs off and recovers a form of coherence by displacing its questions and contradictions in the mystification of spectacle. The shift occurs in the long (and sometimes tedious) sequence in the now empty Convention Hall where, before going off to Albenga, Napoléon faces the dead heroes of the Revolution (in a series of superimpositions). Their interrogation turns into a warped, simplistic affirmation (read "betrayal") of the Revolution, and the dead begin to sing the "Marseillaise," echoing the film's very first moments in the Club de Cordeliers. The sequence modulates into an even montage of MCUs, commingling both leaders and common people in one continuous image that blurs all distinctions. The final shot is a masterpiece of condensation through superimposition. It begins with a LACU of Napoléon listening intently (against the darkness of the hall); a superimposition of the wind-whipped tricolor (echoing the Double Tempest) dissolves in *behind* him; then a canted LAFS of La Marseillaise (in place of Josephine?) dissolves in, replacing Napoléon—she calls off to the right and then points left into a strong wind that billows her garments; finally, the initial image of Napoléon dissolves back in but replaces the flag *behind her*. Thus does the film, in an incredible stereoptic deception, equate Napoléon with the spirit of the Revolution, placing him at the still center of its swirling, dynamic charge. Now the challenges of Brienne, Corsica, Toulon, and the Convention can reach their apotheosis in the final reel, in a stunning series of triptych effects, all of them geared to Napoléon as the uncontested narrative and rhetorical subject par excellence.[42]

The final reel opens at the Albenga encampment (a crater surrounded by rock walls and crowned by a ruined castle) with a series of sequences edited primarily according to the "classical" continuity system. Several panorama shots establish the location as Napoléon rides his white horse back and forth among the troops, his movement linking the massed units of soldiers as well as the three panels of the triptych. His first brief speech to them confirms his dominance—an intertitle in the central panel is followed by a MCU of Napoléon, flanked by hundreds of soldiers in each side panel, and then by several

441

222. (top) Napoléon overlooks the Albenga encampment (in panorama triptych)

223. (bottom) A publicity photo of the reverse shot of the Albenga encampment

224. The central panel of a triptych, in which Napoléon gazes down on his troops at Albenga

panorama shots as he leads them forward and off-screen (the horses flash by impressively in MS). The following morning that dominance is reestablished with a triptych MCU of Napoléon against dark clouds moving across the sky and a triptych LS of the troops arising (the panorama shot tilts up to include soldiers appearing on the castle walls above the rock face). Throughout his main speech to the army, the sequence generally alternates triptych MCUs of Napoléon with LSs of the soldiers responding to his words and gestures (in eyeline-matched shots). But the pattern varies to include gigantic shot/reverse shots as well as FSs of the soldiers and MCUs of Napoléon flanked by LSs of the massed army. And the speech climaxes in a series of reverse panorama shots, with a CU of Napoléon's look serving as the pivot of control and direction, linking the French army to the other side of the mountain with its "rich provinces and great towns" spread over the fertile Italian plains. In the deep space of the final shot, the soldiers charge forward (from ELS to MS) en masse.

For the descent into Italy that follows, the film shifts to a "musical" continuity that stresses graphic and rhythmic relations as much as the representational. Leaving the Albenga encampment, the army divides (in triptych) into three different lines of troops that march forward past ruined castle walls and through a valley of vast fields. As the central panel changes to dollying FSs of the marching soldiers and wagons, the left and right panels (inversions of one another) describe, in LSs, the advancing infantry, cavalry, and cannon. At Montenotte, a "classical" continuity returns in conjunction with a split screen of connotative parallels. In several panorama shots, the army descends a hill

442

225. Triptychs of the descent from Albenga: the central panel of the second triptych includes a CU of Josephine (Gina Manès) and a silhouette of Napoléon superimposed over a map of Italy

to attack and capture the town; while in gigantic reverse shots, a CU of Napoléon is flanked first by parallel tracking shots of the cavalry and then by ELSs as they race forward across the plains. The battle is quickly dispatched, and Napoléon is propelled ahead of his army and then, in a brief shot echoing the Double Tempest, is joined with the wildly applauding Convention crowds in Paris—by means of an intertitle that explodes across the triple screen: "Hearing of / this sudden entry / into Italy // the Parisians / burst the bounds / of their enthusiasm."

In its final minutes, the film shifts once again into a continuity system that is graphic, rhythmic, and highly connotative. Recapitulating the beginning as well as all the other moments of testing, this climax enacts the ultimate transformation and mystification of Napoléon's vision. It begins with Napoléon stalking the heights of Montezemolo, inscribing "in the Italian sky all his desires and all his victories." As he looks out over the mountains and valleys, three separate sequences erupt simultaneously onto the triple screen, the images metamorphosing through superimpositions, dissolves, and iris masks that shift back and forth from panel to panel in what Mitry has called

443

226. (top) The Convention crowd in Paris (one image in triplicate)

227. A triptych from the final sequence of *Napoléon* (1927)

"a fuguelike movement of dizzying rhythms."[43] Initially, they include a FS of Napoléon, LSs of the army attacking across the plains, a LS of his white horse, and a suspended CU of Josephine. Soon, in addition, appear the revolving globe, LSs of the valleys and mountains, maps of Italy and England, insignia, cannon fire, and attacking cavalry. Finally, the sequences shift into rapid montage, drawing together closer and closer shots of the victorious marching soldiers, CUs of Napoléon as a boy and man, ECUs of his eyes, blurred shots of the Revolutionary leaders, a beating drum, flashes, cloud rifts, streaming water, and waves exploding in sunlight. Suddenly, the vanguard of the army sees the shadow of a bird preceding them on the road, and there is a head-on FS of a soaring eagle extending its wings across the triple screen. The sequence shifts to CUs and ECUs of Napoléon again, and the film ends in a rush of images—blurred figures, swish pans, ECUs of Napoléon's eyes, and streams of light. Then, in a last twist, the panels of streaming light turn red, white, and blue, transforming the final triptych into a gigantic French tricolor. Although Napoléon is the apparent subject or source of this whirlwind of resonant images, this projection of the "Revolutionary spirit," he becomes, in fact, the object or figure restored by its charge. For what begins as his vision shifts deceptively into an omniscient barrage that "devours" its subject and, through that deception, subsumes the paradoxical nature of his character and all the contradictions of his seeing and knowing. Consequently, this celebratory restoration of Napoléon's power can be seen as the product of a cinematic spectacle whose operation renders its own resolution problematic.

What position can one take toward this rhapsodic celebration of a single

444

powerful leader, a sort of Gallicized Hegelian ideal of the hero in history—anachronistic, chauvinistic, and perhaps even fascistic? For Gance, his hero must have seemed the Romantic artist in apotheosis—as he saw himself—a towering figure who made the real world, not an imaginary one, his province of action.[44] For his contemporary, the critic Moussinac, this figure was the embodiment of military dictatorship, frighteningly close to the image of the Emperor then held by political groups of the extreme right.[45] On these grounds, some argue, *Napoléon* could join the ranks of such films as Griffith's *Birth of a Nation* (1915) and Riefenstahl's *Triumph of the Will* (1934) for the way it weds a pernicious ideology to an innovative and/or masterfully persuasive discourse.[46] Yet, ironically, in its structural repetition of narrative and rhetorical motifs, the film works much like Eisenstein's *Potemkin* (1925-1926)—culminating in a rush of images in which past, present, and future implode and seem to burst the bounds of the screen. And in the wake of that rush, for the spectator turned analyst, wash a welter of contradictions. Or, in other words, there remain several textual levels of incoherence suspended in a deceptive form of coherence. The overall effect of *Napoléon* may be mystification on a grand scale, but the text goes a long way toward producing the basis of its own critique.

To Gance's despair, the impact of his technological advances in *Napoléon* was severely curtailed by circumstances beyond his control. Soon after the film's release, the American film industry determined to back the sound film revolution at the expense of other innovations. Because Gance's Polyvision process required special screening facilities and because many of his other innovations were costly in time and money, neither he nor the French film industry were in a position to promote them or carry them further. Some years later, in fact, in a fit of depression, Gance destroyed all but one reel of the original triptych negatives.[47] Yet his Polyvision concept was the most important forerunner of the Cinerama format that the American film industry finally began to exploit in the 1950s. It was also a precursor of the split-screen techniques developed worldwide in the 1960s. According to Brownlow, Gance and L.-H. Burel even experimented with a color 3-D process one day while shooting some of the panorama triptychs.[48] The only thing that kept Gance from using the 3-D footage was that it attracted too much attention to itself and did not seem to support the graphic and rhythmic patterns he had established in the film.

Despite the industry's implicit rejection of Gance's work, several narrative avant-garde filmmakers did try to adapt and extend his experimentation. Only one, however, Claude Autant-Lara, worked on a variant of the Polyvision process. That process, called Hypergonar, was quite different from Polyvision, since it used an anamorphic lens (a wide-angle viewfinder invented for World War I tank drivers) which Henri Chretien adapted to an optical printer soon after he had seen *Napoléon*.[49] The fate of Autant-Lara's short film, *Construire un feu* (1928-1930), and the Hypergonar process were as ignominious as *Napoléon*'s. More than a year after the film's completion, Autant-Lara still had not found an exhibition outlet in Paris beyond several private screenings.[50] Discouraged, he signed a contract with MGM to work in Hollywood. Once there, in 1930, he writes,

I rushed to the front office and submitted to them the new process (then still called "Hypergonar" for wide screen). . . . After six months, the "Research De[partment]" of MGM gave me the answer: "This process is of no interest."[51]

Ironically, that very Hypergonar lens is rumored to have been used years later to shoot Twentieth-Century Fox's *The Robe* (1953), which gave birth to Cinemascope.[52] While Autant-Lara remained in Hollywood to direct the French versions of some MGM talkies, in December, 1930, the manager of the small Studio de Paris cinema in Montparnasse finally decided to risk screening *Construire un feu*[53] After an irregular three-month run, the National Syndicate of Exhibitors forced him to halt its projection because they considered the new optical process "unfair competition."[54] Soon after, because Autant-Lara's debts remained unpaid and a letter never reached him in the United States, the laboratory in France destroyed the film negative.[55]

As a precursor of the wide-screen processes finally developed by the American film industry in the early 1950s, the historical importance of *Construire un feu* is assured. Yet the few stills that remain of the film, as well as one published page of the *découpage*, reveal that Autant-Lara was doing some unusual things with his anamorphic lens.[56] Not only was he squeezing the image from the sides; he was also squeezing it from the top and bottom—as if experimenting with the best method of recording and projecting the image. Furthermore, although some frames were composed of a single image, others were split into two or three separate images of varying sizes, sometimes arranged vertically as well as horizontally. The existing split-screen frames include juxtapositions of full shots and close-ups and of shot/reverse shots, as well as of interior and exterior shots. Because of its complexity in screen format changes and in image connections, *Construire un feu* may have presented an even greater challenge to narrative filmmaking and film viewing than did *Napoléon*.

L'Image, 6½ x 11, and La Glace à trois faces

For two years after leaving Pathé-Consortium, Jean Epstein made a string of successful commercial films for Films Albatros—*Le Lion des Mogols* (1924), *L'Affiche* (1925), *Le Double Amour* (1925), and *Les Aventures de Robert Macaire* (1925-1926).[1] Even when his own production company was formed early in 1926, he continued in that mode with his first independent film, an adaptation of *Mauprat* (1926). Only then did he hazard a return to the level of experimentation that had marked his earliest films. That experimentation was still somewhat hesitant in $6½ \times 11$ (1927) and then much bolder in *La Glace à trois faces* (1927). Although there were probably a number of reasons for this resurgence of creativity in Epstein's work, part of the impetus must have come from a film much admired at the time—Jacques Feyder's *L'Image* (1926).[2]

L'Image was based on an original scenario by the well-known writer, Jules Romains, who saw the cinema as a new medium in which to express the tenets of his belief in unanimism. Its subject was almost Pirandellian:

. . . four men differing in circumstances, scruples, and intellect—a painter, an engineer, a diamond merchant, and an ex-seminarian—fall in love with a woman they have never seen and of whom they know only "The Image" exhibited in a photograph.[3]

446

228. (left) The photographer's multiple images of the woman in *L'Image* (1926)

229. (right) The woman (Arlette Marchal) alone in the solitude of the Bakony plains

Obsessed with what they take to be an image of the ideal woman, each, unknown to the others, abandons his profession to seek her. While the painter reproduces his own vision of her image in a large portrait, the other three go off searching through the world. Chance leads them simultaneously to an inn on the Bakony plains of Hungary. Not far away, in a manor surrounded by vast open pastures and marshes, lives a woman whom her husband, his spinster sisters, and his vivacious cousin do not understand—the woman of the photograph (Arlette Marchal). That evening, as the men converse and discover that not only are they rivals but that each of their visions of the woman is different, she happens to stop briefly outside the inn and then pass on. The next morning, the men go their separate ways—"one to his death, another into meditation, the third to wander across the world."[4] And the woman continues to live out her lonely, unsatisfied existence.

Some critics faulted Romains's scenario for *L'Image* for being too literary, too schematically constructed, which caused it to fail completely at the box office. But all were impressed by the simple purity and lyrical continuity of the film's images (again, Feyder's cameraman was L.-H. Burel).[5] The high points of the film come in the sequences where the woman is defined in relation to this expansive landscape. Her emotional state draws its meaning, in part, from the mesmerizing effect of the plains and, in Henri Fescourt's words, "its horizons at dusk, its nostalgic atmosphere, its returning cattle herds, its flights of birds, its marshes, its pale tonalities of light. . . ."[6] But this image of a lone figure in the solitude and plenitude of nature draws its power in turn from at least two other sets of contrasting images. One set includes the stylized images of the woman that the men produce, epitomized in the painter's vision of an elevated figure, the worshipped object of out-stretched male hands. The other set, however, describes the stereotypical banality of provincial bourgeois family life. In other words, the film not only interweaves several converging lines of action; it also juxtaposes three different forms of representation and degrees of perception and desire.

In the final sequence, the woman remains in her natural landscape, but the meaning of her image has now changed. Jean Mitry has described this moment with uncharacteristic rapture:

And this end of all beauty; this end that does not end—which will never end. . . . On the Bakony plateau, against a horizon of oak trees at the top of a moor, close to a sheepfold and a shepherd who sings while cutting himself some bread, a perfectly beautiful woman, somberly dressed, looks off into the distance behind her, as if she is waiting.[7]

The subject of a paradoxical charge, the woman of *L'Image* is both part of nature and apart, deflecting and dissipating its unanimism into longing. Moreover, as the figure to be looked at and fetishized (yet who is unseen by the other characters) and as the bearer of the look (yet who bears an unfulfilled desire), almost fatalistically it seems, she marks the site of some sort of lack or absence at the center of things. And this is exactly what links *L'Image* to Jean Epstein's two films—the crucial object of a woman's photograph, the narrative situation of several characters vying for the attention of another, and this shared sense of melancholy, of a lack or absence.

In *Le Cinématographe vu de l'Etna* (1926), Epstein had written,

One of the greatest powers of the cinema is its animism. On the screen, there is no still life. Objects assume attitudes. Trees gesticulate. Mountains, as well as this Etna, signify. Every property becomes a character. The decors fragment and each of the pieces takes on a singular significance. An astonishing pantheism is reborn in the world and fills it to bursting.[8]

At least one critic quoted this passage back to Epstein, in order to say that he saw "nothing, absolutely nothing" of that power or pantheism in *6½ × 11* (1927).[9] Today that conclusion seems oddly obtuse, but not exactly wrong-headed. For, while the film does have a singular power, it also has an uncannily cool air about it, a rigorously measured rhythm, almost as if it were an exquisite, finely tuned machine. Perhaps Jean Dréville sums up best the sheer amazement and intense irritation most critics experienced when it was released in September, 1927. Although certainly Epstein's most interesting work yet as a filmmaker, unmatched in technical virtuosity, *6½ × 11* seemed to him "a kind of laboratory film . . . a film which played too much on our cerebral faculties to touch our sensibility. . . ."[10] Yet, as Dréville suggested, that simply meant it was even less conventional and more advanced than other narrative avant-garde films.

The scenario for *6½ × 11* was first developed by Marie Epstein, Jean's sister.[11] The idea came from a simple visual image. Two years before, the image around which Marie had organized the scenario of *L'Affiche* was a Bébé Cadum poster that one day mysteriously seemed to speak to her—"but you know that this baby is dead!" This time it was "a photo in a developing bath . . . [and she] found a dramatic situation to surround the face that little by little appeared there. . . ."[12] Hence the title—the dimensions of the Kodak print (since Kodak refused to allow its name in the title). The scenario she

and Jean then worked into a *découpage* was little more than a *fait divers*. Jean
(Nino Costantini), the younger brother of a prominent doctor, Jerome de Ners
(Van Daële), is naïvely infatuated with Mary Winter (Suzy Pierson), a singer
at the Théâtre des Champs-Elysées. For their "Palace of Love," he buys a
magnificent modern chateau on the Côte d'Azur. When she soon ditches him
for a dance man at the Théâtre, Larry Gold (René Ferté), Jean commits suicide. Unaware of what has happened to his brother, Jerome now becomes
infatuated with the singer, after treating her for a minor illness at the Théâtre.
She, too, is ignorant, at first, of the relation between the two men. One day,
he receives word that Jean is not dead but has disappeared under an assumed
name. Jerome goes to the chateau to claim his possessions, and Mary follows
him, dreading what may happen. There he finds the negatives of some photographs Jean had taken, develops them, and discovers the bitterly ironic
truth. Here, the film's principal distributor asked Epstein to produce a happy
ending—Jean returns and is reunited with his brother. For the version screened
at the Studio des Ursulines (and preserved at the Cinémathèque française),
Epstein provided his original ending—Jerome simply leaves Mary, sick with
remorse, in a room with her dance man, Gold.[13]

Several elements of this story are clearly concessions to the then growing
taste in France for film showcases of the new good life of consumer capitalism.
The chateau and gardens on the Côte d'Azur, the open speeding sports cars,
the performances and behind-the-scenes activity at the Théâtre des Champs-
Elysées—all of these were modern and "à la mode." Today, some of these
sequences seem dated and almost irrelevant. Epstein himself found them distasteful—too reminiscent, he admitted, of Pierre Frondaie melodramas.[14] His
real interest is startlingly clear in the very first sequence of the film—just four
shots, linked by slow dissolves, of the two brothers in a cemetery.

LS of a wall with several crosses projecting above it (in the bottom third of the frame),
silhouetted against a foggy sky.
FS of two men, their backs to the camera at a 45° angle, standing before a simple
tomb.
MCU of the two (full face), framed against a grave triptych behind them.
FS of the slanting, oddly convex, marble tomb surface, with a cross sculpted on it (in
the bottom half of the frame), against a foggy sky obscuring the sun. Fade out.

The original *découpage*, published in *Cinégraphie*, described this differently (a
shot of flowers, a superimposition of a smiling face), preceded it by a sequence
of their mother dying, and followed it with an intertitle—"Two years later."[15]
As changed in the film (there is no intertitle at all), the sequence seems
suspended in time, elliptical, and strangely evocative. We may assume the
death of a parent, but the fog and the massive marble block are mysteriously
ominous—their reference redirected from the past to the future. They give us
premonitions of other losses to come—the brothers' own deaths, the loss of
something important to them? So oppressive is this opening that it casts a
pall over the first sequences in the de Ners's Paris townhouse (the first intertitle begins to focus on Jean—"Monsieur Jean has not yet returned") and over
the whole "à la mode" milieu that soon becomes dominant. Somewhat like
Cavalcanti's *Yvette* (1928), *6½ × 11* thus undermines the genre of the modern
studio spectacular from within.

230. The cemetery tomb in the opening sequence of *6½ × 11* (1927)

This opening sequence also makes one quickly aware of the film's stunning visual quality, which does indeed give things and spaces "a singular significance." Of that quality, which is unusually sustained throughout, Dréville said to Epstein, ". . . you hold the cinema in your hands."[16] *6½ × 11* is narrated almost entirely by images (there are only about two dozen intertitles, posters, and letters scattered over its length), and those images are among the first in France to be recorded on panchromatic film stock (Epstein's cameraman was Georges Périnal, the documentary cameraman for Jean Grémillon). The CUs of objects seem tangibly luminous (e.g., the jewels and crystal associated with Jean and Mary); and HALSs of the de Ners's rooms shade off into fine dark grays in the backgrounds and edges of the frame. The long lap dissolves, superimpositions, and image deformations, all done in-camera, are marvelously assured. The last shot describing Jean and Mary's journey to the Côte d'Azur chateau, for instance, begins as a rapid tracking shot from in front of the sports car; a supered LS of waves moving in toward some shore rocks dissolves in at the bottom of the frame; a supered CU of Jean and Mary (veiled) dissolves in above—they kiss; both car and couple then dissolve out, and, in the LS that remains, the waves crash on the rocks. Later, in a slightly HAELS, Larry Gold's sports car drives off down a straight country highway whose thick bordering woods are blurred a soft gray at the center and far edges, creating a kind of flattened hourglass-shaped frame of road and sky. There are prescient asymmetrical compositions—e.g., a LS of Mary's bedroom as Jean opens the long window curtains (frame right background) just before he discovers her empty bed (out of the frame in the left foreground). There are unusual camera angles and abrupt, elliptical shifts in the spatial continuity of the editing. The only thing conspicuously absent are sequences of rapid montage or sustained camera movement.

Pierre Leprohon has described the style Epstein reinvents for *6½ × 11*:

. . . as devoid of sentimental emotion as of plastic "delights," [the film] essentially hinged on the vigor of its rhythms, on the resemblances among the images, and thus,

450

to a great extent, depended on the succinctness of the montage and on the images' power of evocation.[17]

This style should not be taken simply as an autonomous formal construction, however; its significance arises as a function of the film's peculiarly schematic narrative structure. Like *Coeur fidèle*, *L'Inhumaine*, *Feu Mathias Pascal*, and others, *6½ × 11* is a doubled narrative film in which the second part replicates much of what has happened in the first. It is almost perfectly symmetrical (three reels for the first part, three reels for the second) and quite deliberate in its replication—substituting one brother for the other in the same love triangle, setting the climax of both parts in the same place, and developing a nexus of image relations which define the characters and are repeated across the two halves of the film. This last pattern of replicated structural relations is crucial. Here, in a dense pattern of rhetorical figuring that is repeated, varied, and inverted to the point of reflexivity, lies the film's chief concern.

At the center of this pattern of rhetorical figuring are several forms of light and the photographic process of image reflection and representation. As Epstein himself once said, "the sun and a Kodak figured in the film's origins."[18] Through them, nature seems to make an ambiguous and "perpetual intervention," one critic wrote, defining the relationships among the characters and determining "the progress of the film."[19] The first major instance of rhetorical figuring occurs in a series of three sequences which describe the incipient breakdown between Jean and Mary. On one of their shopping trips to town, Jean stops before an optics shop to buy a camera. In the display window, an ad (in CU) promises that "this spring will last longer with a Kodak photo"—dissolve to a shot through the window past a cardboard figure of a woman to several shelves of cameras. In FS, Jean stands for a moment before the window, where two large painted eyes are now prominent. In this conventional commercial representation of the human body, the woman's figure and the man's eyes, the couple is positioned metaphorically. And their subject-object relation is already suspect—the cardboard, the painted glass. At a restaurant later, where several couples are dancing the Charleston, Jean examines the camera he has just bought, and Mary tells him, "I hate photography. . . . That sudden flash of magnesium gives me a shock. . . ." While Jean is preoccupied (frame left), a man comes up behind Mary (frame right) and begins talking to her. Suddenly (in MS), the latter two are illuminated by a flash of light, and they turn to look off toward the left foreground. The artificial illumination, Mary's lack of anxiety, and the shots of the dancing couples that follow—all suggest that the man is a rival (much later he will be identified as Larry Gold). The camera flash, however, turns out not to be Jean's (as we might have expected), for he turns to be introduced only after Mary has talked with the man for a while. Ironically, his interest in the camera blinds him to her interest in the other.

The last of the three sequences, which immediately follows, sums up this initial pattern of rhetorical figuring succinctly. Mary leads Jean into the chateau gardens where he can photograph her posing on a bench beside a pool. As Jean tries to get her to look in a particular direction, several shots are cut in of the sun glaring through the slowly waving branches of the garden's cypress trees. Mary seems restless, disturbed—by the sunlight (in opposition to the magnesium flash before) or by the photographic process itself? Does she fear the camera will expose her "real" attitude?

MCU of Jean as he steps into the frame from the left foreground (blurred out of focus at first) and stops to adjust the camera in his hands.
ECU of the camera viewfinder, with Mary's image framed in it.
MCU of Jean looking up from the camera and off to the left foreground.
ECU of his finger clicking the lever beside the camera lens.
LS of the sun glaring through the cypress trees.
ECU of his finger clicking the lever again; the camera then moves up and off to the left.
MCU of Jean looking at the camera face.
LS of Mary going off to the right through the cypress trees.
MCU of Jean looking up and off to the left foreground; a look of displeasure crosses his face. Fade out.

Again the couple is positioned metaphorically—his eyes replaced by the camera lens, his hand controlling its operation, her figure framed as the object of vision and reflection. But Jean's gaze is different from the camera's, his control illusory. Although this is the last time he will see her (the next morning she will be gone), Jean does not realize that both eye and body, subject and object, are marked by deception, are not what they seem. Ironically, he is a blind subject in the film's system of representation.

The next major instance of this rhetorical figuring climaxes the first half of the film. As Jean prepares to leave the chateau, writing a note and packing his bags, he goes into Mary's bedroom for the last time. There he sits at her dressing table and looks at his reflection in the mirror (in MCU/MS). Slowly a CU of Mary's face dissolves in (only half lit from the side), followed by an ECU of her eyes, and finally a smaller image of her face drifting in from the left. Is the deception in the image any clearer now or is the subject-object relation shifting position? Her face provokes him to pick up a powder puff and sniff it lightly, as if to recall her through the fetish of scent. He goes to her bed and strokes the curtain beside it and then picks up his camera. As he gazes at the lens, a smile crosses his face, and he unexpectedly pulls a revolver from his coat pocket.

MS of Jean reflected in the mirror; he raises the revolver and fires. Dissolve to
CU of the hole and crack in the mirror, in which Jean's image is reflected in MCU.
CU of the revolver as it turns to point at Jean's body.
MCU of Jean's face; his mouth opens; his eyes stare wide and then close.
LS of Jean slumped on the bed.
MCU of Jean's face as he looks up. Dissolve in a supered camera face on the right. A CU of a camera lens wipes in from the left. Another camera lens dissolves in in the center. All three suddenly flare and fade out one by one.
LS of Jean slumped on the bed; he falls to the floor. Iris out.

The magnesium flash and the sunlight's glare reverberate in the revolver's flash of fire and in the supered flares of the cameras. All come together in a moment of subjective recognition as Jean destroys himself both as the subject and object of the process of reflection. For him, self-reflection leads to a tragic awareness of deception. But the first part of the film does not end there. In a playful ironic twist, the sequence cuts to a MCU of a hand reaching under a desk to pick up a photograph—of Jean. It is Jerome's hand, we discover, and he looks at the empty space on the wall from where it has fallen. The analogy renders Jean's tragedy almost ridiculous. But it also suggests an uncanny correspondence between things and sets up the figure of Jerome searching for his brother through the image of a photograph.

In the second half of the film, the rhetorical figuring returns with the reappearance of that particular photograph. The pattern resembles the reappearance of the playing cards in *L'Auberge rouge*, but is here transformed into a more complicated, more consciously cinematic mode. Mary has come to Jerome's townhouse one evening shortly after her illness. Led into a room by the butler, she is left alone, applying powder to her face, when she suddenly discovers Jean's photograph on a nearby table. As she stares, a CU of the photograph dissolves in, blurs, and nearly whites out. The powder, sunlight, revolver flash, and camera flares—all echo again in that whiteness. She moves away from the table nervously, and Jerome comes in. The sequence ends in an off-balanced FS of the two sitting in separate chairs (frame left and center), which irises out on the table with the photograph (frame right). Although Jerome has replaced Jean in the position of the infatuated lover, he is disturbingly ignorant, even more so than was Jean of his rival. When he next sees Mary in her dressing room at the Théâtre, that disturbance resonates in the prominent mirrors and in the alternating shots of women dancing on the stage below. To these visual echoes of his brother's story, he is, of course, blind.

After Jerome receives the note about Jean's disappearance, he takes a train south to the Côte d'Azur. Mary follows and finds him at the chateau, sitting before a box of Jean's possessions and looking at his camera. The rhythm of the cutting (and shifts in camera distance and angle) becomes nervous, disruptive, evoking the psychological tension of both characters—the one puzzling slowly, anxiously, over the camera ("for a woman . . . a little love . . . suddenly a death . . ."); the other fearful of the secret that it may hold. The sequence shifts almost imperceptibly from one room to another and then back, as if the situation were being played out again and again in the same space. Finally, in an ECU, Jerome's fingers open the camera case, revealing a label, "My dear M . . . 12/2/26." She moves away from him to stand by the box once more, and her shoes (in ECU) step on a piece of paper dropped on the floor. It is an ad for Kodak, of which only a few words are visible—"Don't forget vacations . . . that vanish without . . . 11." Suddenly (in FS), he is sitting on the bed, almost exactly in the position Jean was in when he shot himself, and (in CU) his raised fist falls on the camera. Jerome and Mary are slowly being drawn into a doubled replication of Jean's coming to consciousness.

The process reaches an initial climax in the next sequence (tinted red in the original),[20] as Jerome develops the film he has found in the camera. The room is dark except for a rectangular viewing screen, emitting a faint light above the developing trays. When Mary comes in, she asks, hopefully, whether undeveloped film deteriorates after six months, but Jerome says simply that it can last up to a year. The revelation of the double deception now looms in a series of marvelously lit CUs and MCUs.

MS of Jerome as he runs back to look at the filmstrip.

231. (left) A publicity photo of Nino Constantini, René Ferté, and Suzy Pierson in *6½ × 11* (1927)

232. (right) A publicity photo of Suzy Pierson at the chateau bedroom window near the end of *6½ × 11*

ECU of Mary's eyes wide in the dark; they close, and her head leans back slightly.

CU of Jerome's face, barely lit from the right side, with a pinpoint of light in the right eye.

CU of the filmstrip moving upward, against the light, revealing a woman clearly in three frames.

MCU of Jerome staring at the filmstrip, turning it over and back.

MCU of Mary and Jerome as he holds up the filmstrip in front of her and between them.

CU of the filmstrip against the light.

LAMS of Mary as she staggers to a chair.

MS of Jerome coming over to her.

LS of the room, with the photographic light and table (frame left), Jerome and Mary (frame right); he helps her up, and she goes to the door (frame center background) and opens it.

The process that Jean unconsciously had begun in the garden months before is nearly complete. The image of Mary framed in the camera's viewfinder reappears, like a return of the repressed, in the filmstrip negative Jerome holds in his hands. In the artificial light of the developing room, the camera's "truth" begins to separate the second couple and destroy the basis of their relationship. Thus, the photographic process, in a highly reflexive manner, is made to serve the narrative of the film.

But Epstein cannot leave the matter there, and he draws out the film's resolution in an extraordinary sequence, where the photographic/cinematic process of reflection/representation becomes literally equivalent to the process of self-reflection. As Jerome walks out into the dawn, Mary watches at her bedroom window, in a LS that replicates exactly Jean's position in the room just before

454

he discovered her empty bed. She rushes out as if to follow him, but Jerome reaches a garden pavilion alone and sits down to look through the developed photographs. Suddenly, Mary is revealed laboring slowly forward on a rough beach of sand and rock—on the same beach where before she used to sing to herself (the gardener had told Jerome)—in a HAELS (framed in a gray iris) that ironically echoes those of the stage at the Théâtre. At this crucial point, the sequence begins to alternate between Mary and Jerome. When she looks up (in a MCU with the same gray iris), the alternation shifts to introduce a LALS of a cypress tree with a pale sun poised at its tip. Like the cemetery sun of the opening sequence (as opposed to the sunlight of the garden), this cold dawn light seems to strike her like an agent of revenge. Immediately, the alternation shifts back to Mary and Jerome and brings them to an incredible confrontation.

MCU of Jerome from behind, looking down at an unseen photograph.
HALS of Mary coming forward on the beach.
MCU of Jerome as he begins to turn around.
CU of Mary with her hand to her head, looking as if she is about to faint.
MCU of Jerome now turned around.
CU of Mary.
MCU of Jerome beginning to come forward.
CU of Mary beginning to fall back.
HALS of Mary falling back on the beach.
MCU of Jerome coming forward, his face twisted in anguish.
LS of Mary's bedroom; Jerome enters from a door (frame right background), looks at her empty bed.

Despite the apparent distance between the beach and the pavilion, the movement of the figures and the direction of their looks creates the illusion of a contiguous abstract space and a dramatic conjunction. The alternation works amazingly like the famous telepathic exchange between Nina and Nosferatu, separated by half of Europe, in Murnau's *Nosferatu* (1922). But here, the effect of the alternation is multiple, combining the objective and the subjective in a stunning simultaneous revelation. With Mary as subject, they act out a drama of agonized pleading and rejection. With Jerome as subject, however, her image suddenly substitutes for the unseen photograph in his hands. Light matches "light," recalling the light that created the original negative. And together, the two experience the same subjective moment of anguish in a brief cinematic dance. Mary's anguished face is replicated in Jerome's. Her falling back (diminished, almost suppressed, in the vast space of the beach) is mirrored in his movement forward. The revelation of this double deception thus ends in a double tragedy. The process of self-reflection, instigated by Jean's camera, leads to isolation and the consciousness of a lack. And nature, as in the beginning, seems to sanction this suffering, this separation, and this near paralysis.

In conclusion, 6½ × 11 offers a cold indictment of the deception marking human relations, especially sexual relations. Although the woman and, by association, the good life of consumer capitalism are made the principal sources of this deception, the film also approaches a critique of the subject-object positioning at the basis of sexual representation. Yet it ends up celebrating the disturbingly ambiguous power of nature in conjunction with the new

455

"machine eye" of photography and, by extension, cinematography. Unlike *L'Inhumaine*, however, here that power is disturbing because its revelations seem more destructive than constructive, at least given the milieu and characters of the film's narrative.

At first, *La Glace à trois faces* (1927) may seem to mark a change in Epstein's work. As far as I can tell, it premiered at the Studio des Ursulines, in November, 1927, and then was distributed within the circuit of specialized cinemas and ciné-clubs in France, Belgium, Switzerland, and England.[21] This makes it, along with Dulac's *L'Invitation au voyage* (1927), one of the first narrative films produced exclusively for the alternate cinema network that had originated in France and spread across Europe. It is also an unusually short film, of only three reels or 900 meters, which is comparable to the length of one episode in a serial or to the early films of, say, Louis Delluc—e.g., *La Fête espagnole, Fièvre*. In that short length, however, *La Glace à trois faces* manages to narrate seven different stories in the most complicated film narrative structure of the decade. It does this with a minimum of intertitles—except for numbers, character names, newspapers, signs, and telegrams, there are only ten in all. And it employs a compendium of all that Epstein had developed in the way of strategies and techniques over his five years of filmmaking. Consequently, as Noël Burch and Jean-André Fieschi have argued, *La Glace à trois faces* represents a culmination of much of the narrative avant-garde film practice.

Epstein drew the scenario for *La Glace à trois faces* from a mildly erotic short story in *L'Europe galante* (1922), by Paul Morand.[22] The scenario neatly inverts the narrative situation in Feyder's *L'Image*. Here, three different women are in love, simultaneously, with the same man. Pearl (Olga Day) is "an eccentric Englishwoman" who enjoys the luxury of the modern good life. Athalia (Suzy Pierson) is a Russian sculptress whose work is admired by "the Paris snobs." And Lucie (Jeanne Helbling) is a young working-class woman whose simplicity and naïveté set her apart from the other two. All three have scheduled rendezvous with a young, unnamed financier and playboy (René Ferté, a strained, unlikable actor) who casually ignores them in order to drive his new sports car to the fashionable beaches of Deauville, "alone and free." On the way, however, a swallow darts from a telephone line into the path of the car and strikes him, slashing its beak across his forehead. In an instant, he loses control of the car, crashes, and dies. Put this way, the story seems little more than a banal *fait divers*, with a touch of poetic justice, much as in *Menilmontant*. But Epstein transforms it into a highly original, Pirandellian narrative structure (remarked on at the time),[23] both on the general level of relations between the separate stories and on the specific level of syntactical and rhetorical relations within and between sequences. Epstein himself dubbed it a "new formula for the cinematic scenario."[24] As several critics have pointed out, it clearly anticipates the later films of Alain Resnais.[25]

La Glace à trois faces divides neatly into four parts whose titles ("1," "2," "3," and "lui," [him]) refer to the three women and the unnamed hero who are the film's principal characters.[26] The opening intertitle—"Three women love a man. But does he love one of them?"—is set off from "1" and thus acts as a prologue to pose an enigma, an initial question, involving these charac-

ters. The final intertitle—"Thus did I realize suddenly that the messages received by the three women came from one man only and that man was he"—
and a shot of a three-sided mirror (hence the film's title) are also set off as an
epilogue from the fourth part, entitled "lui." Although this intertitle does
not answer the initial question posed in the prologue (in fact, it merely confirms what we already know), the shot of the mirror, as we shall see, does—
and more.

In each of the four major sections of the film, the discourse produces a
separate narrative. The fourth narrative, however, begins in conjunction with
the first, progresses simultaneously (but briefly) with those of sections "2" and
"3," and is developed and resolved in the "lui" section. Furthermore, the first
three sections also contain embedded stories, narrated by each of the women,
about their past experiences with the hero. The relationships among all these
seven stories can be summarized as follows. In "1," the hero and the Englishwoman, Pearl, separate angrily at a pavilion restaurant, and she tells a fawning
old man the story of her exasperating past life with the hero as his mistress.
That past story advances to the point where the separation took place, and the
hero sets off in his new sports car from a multilevel parking garage—after
sending Pearl a telegram. In "2," the second woman, Athalia, also tells an
old man (but not the same one) the story of her encounters with the hero, first
in the Bois de Boulogne (where he rescues, of all things, her escaped pet
monkey) and later in her apartment. Meanwhile, the hero continues his jour-

235. (left) A frame from the tracking shot in the multilevel garage in *La Glace à trois faces* (1927)

236. (right) A shot from the boating sequence

ney through a small village (where, in ironic contrast to the sculptress, a woman is trimming cabbages in a street cart), but he is abandoning Athalia as well—and sends her a telegram. In "3," the third woman, Lucie, tells an old neighbor woman the story of how she first met the hero—she had been hired to sew some buttons on one of his coats. Then alone, she remembers a boating trip they took together, ending in the fashionable L'Isle-Adam park restaurant (where her lack of proper manners began to irritate him). In "lui," the hero stops in a second village and sends off a third telegram—to Lucie. Briefly, he acts the tourist, wandering about a local festival that is in progress, and then heads off again in his sports car. As he speeds along the highway, the swallow swoops down, causing the accident that costs him his life.

One of the first things that strikes one about this narrative structure is the way it allows Epstein to play with a rich mixture of styles and modes of representation, in perhaps the most daring concoction since *Le Brasier ardent* and *L'Inhumaine*. Each of the film's separate parts constitutes a different milieu, determined by genre and class, with its own types of characters. The first, set in the financier's art deco lodgings and in a chic pavilion restaurant, reproduces, in miniature, the ultramodern milieu of the modern studio spectaculars. The jewelry and crystal associated with Pearl, in fact, remind one of Mary Winter in $6^{1/2} \times 11$. The second part, set in the grotesque artifice of the Russian sculptress's studio and the Bois de Boulogne, parodies the *démodé* ambiance and pretentious characters of the conventional bourgeois melodrama. The parody looks like a tamer version of *Le Brasier ardent* or an ironic revision of Epstein's own *Le Lion des Mogols* (both Albatros films). The third part, set in the streets of Paris's outskirts, in Lucie's working-class apartment, and in the L'Isle-Adam riverside park, updates the realist urban milieu of *Coeur fidèle*. The initial meeting between Lucie and the hero is narrated in a surprising sequence of reverse chronology (each shot separated by flashes of gray), as if in allusion to Delluc's *L'Inondation*. And the boat ride they take on the river evokes the peaceful atmosphere of the provincial realist films, especially those

458

like *La Belle Nivernaise* documenting life on the canals.[27] The fourth part, depicting the hero's fatal journey, includes a brief "pure cinema" passage of sustained camera movement (in a single long take) as the sports car descends from the multilevel parking garage, a short documentary-style sequence on the local village festival, and a tour de force of accelerating montage that ends in a car crash. *La Glace à trois faces* thus juxtaposes genre to genre, style to style, and class to class, in a multifaceted, Chinese box construction.

Another prominent feature of the film is the concise way its discourse operates in patterns of syntactical and rhetorical relations. The patterns may not be as concentrated or as sustained as those in *6½ × 11*, but they are no less complex. Their operation is particularly evident in the opening section with its two parallel stories and one embedded story. The section is not without simple metaphorical and synecdochal relations within shots. The jewel and ring that are appropriately Pearl's, the fur coat which she drops as she leaves the pavilion restaurant, the *Finance* newspaper behind which the hero disappears as he is driven away from the restaurant—all are marks of a certain social class. Pearl's name, as well as her ring and jewel, also mark her status as a possession. Two playing cards (a three of hearts in the foreground and a joker further back) strewn among the papers on the hero's desk, "as if by chance," even offer the flicker of an answer to the initial enigma of loving. However, what is more pronounced than these metaphorical connections are rhetorical relations between shots and sequences whose significance becomes multiple through the alternation of associative image chains.

One example must suffice—from the embedded story of the hero and Pearl's past life together.[28] They are in his art deco study, apparently getting ready to go out for the evening.

MS of the hero sitting behind his desk, looking toward the left foreground and folding his hands.
MS of Pearl as she stands by a chair and puts on a dress over her head.
MS of the hero looking toward the left foreground.
LS multiple exposure of telephone lines, and then a train crossing an empty landscape from the right foreground toward the left background.
MS of the hero, leaning back in his chair, his eyes mere slits.
CU of Pearl's face as she puts her mouth to a jewel.
MS of the hero as before.
LALS double exposure of telephone lines and a train crossing an embankment from the right background toward the left foreground.
MS of the hero as before.
MS of Pearl as she lifts her hands to the back of her head, turns around and moves off toward the left background.
HAMCU of the hero touching a ring on his finger.

The beginning of the sequence establishes a pattern of alternation between Pearl and the hero, the one being the apparent object of the other's gaze. The multiple exposure shot of telephone lines and speeding train functions as a subjective vision of the hero's and as an opposite pole of attraction from Pearl. Thus the alternation produces a choice between business and romance, with the added opposition between the pleasures of speed and those of sexual satisfaction (the hero watches Pearl undress and dress).[29] As befits the film's initial question, the hero's look is enigmatic—is he fascinated, dissatisfied,

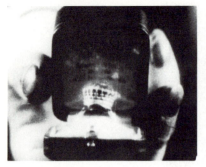

237. (left to right) René Ferté "caught" between opposite attractions: the ring he has given Pearl and the train and telephone lines that suggest his business dealings.

indifferent? And well it might be, for his choices are not unalloyed—in the repeated image of the train and telephone lines lies a buried clash of connotation. For while the train will soon be displaced by the sports car that takes the hero away from Pearl (and the other women), the telephone lines will eventually offer the swallow as the antithesis to the hero's ecstasy in his speeding "plaything." Within the imaginary of the embedded past story, the future is metonymically latent. Epstein's own words describe the sequence well—"among memories the future breaks forth."[30]

Perhaps even more important than either this mixture of modes or rhetorical figuring is the way the overall narrative structure works variations on a paradigm of character relations and functions. In the first three sections of the film, each of the women narrates her own meeting with the hero. The discourse of the fourth story, simultaneously with the other three, positions the hero as separate from the three women, and that separation is confirmed by the words of his telegram. Each woman's narration of meeting, therefore, is juxtaposed to the hero's words of separation. Instead of moving simply from presence to absence, from forming a couple to being absent or alone, the hero forms another couple of sorts. The women are displaced by the sports car (not a vehicle for business, but a chic new "plaything"). This new paradigm of relations, sustained through "1," "2," and "lui," is altered or broken by the sudden intervention of the swallow. What had occurred through one character replacing another, in *Coeur fidèle* and *Menilmontant*, here transpires through a poetic displacement. Associated with the telegrams (through the telephone lines it flies from), the swallow functions in place of a response from the women. The discourse elides them and offers the swallow as a metaphorical agent of revenge, of punishment, very much like the dawn light in $6\frac{1}{2} \times 11$. By breaking contact with not one but three women (excess through repetition), the hero is made to suffer the ultimate absence—death (excess through degree). His lack of a name is perfectly apt.

In the final shot of the film, the discourse reinvents and reflects on the schema of the hero's circulation in the narrative. This shot of the three-sided mirror functions metaphorically, in a double operation. As a metaphor of linearity, the hero's image moves forward in the mirror and dissolves away, reenacting his movement from presence to absence in each of the three stories and from life to death in the final story. As a metaphor of simultaneity,

460

238. The final shot of the three-paneled mirror in *La Glace à trois faces* (1927)

however, the mirror itself represents, in paradigm, the three stories narrated by the women. The fact that the hero, but none of the women, appears in each panel and that he appears as a reflection (his body is not visible within the space of the room) suggests an answer to the initial question raised in the film. The hero never was really present to the women; they served only as mirrors for his own self-enjoyment. Like Narcissus, he loved none but himself.

One final and crucial point. From the very beginning, *La Glace à trois faces* seems highly reflexive about the alternation and displacement that produces its narrative. For, in that production, the spectator is positioned as subject in an unusually conscious operation. The first dozen shots of the film (after the initial intertitle) demand a full description.

1. A dark, indistinct image with vague lights in the distance.
2. MS of several men who, from the foreground, go back to some shrubbery and look off toward the left background (the whole background is dark); one man laughs briefly.
3. Another dark, indistinct image; the lights are closer, fuller (an amusement park?); the camera seems to be moving to the left and slightly forward.
4. Continuation of shot 2 as another man enters from the foreground, speaks to the men curtly, and they all begin to exit.
Intertitle: "Nervous tears."
5. LS of the gate to a pavilion restaurant with two cars in the foreground left and right; a woman comes out the gate, daubing her eyes; the door of the car to the left is opened for her; she hesitates and drops the fur coat from her shoulders.
6. MS of the woman as she walks forward and exits to the right foreground; behind her a waiter picks up her coat.
Intertitle: "Pearl."
7. LS of the woman entering the frame from the left foreground and walking diagonally toward the right background, in the setting of a park; as she passes an old gentleman in top hat and tails, in the center foreground, he turns to look after her and starts to follow.
8. FS/LS as the woman comes from the park background to a bench in the left foreground; the old man follows and sits beside her.

461

9. FS of the interior of the pavilion restaurant, lattice forming a wall in the background; a man (frame center) looks to the left and then forward and begins to walk toward the left foreground—much later he will be identified as a rival.

10. LS of several men talking among the restaurant tables; from the background, the man comes forward and speaks to them.

11. LAFS between two cars at the gate to the restaurant; three men race forward and exit to the left; a fourth man, a gentleman in top hat and tails, walks forward slowly, coolly smoothing his white gloves, and follows them off.

12. MS through the side windows of a car to the other side where the gentleman steps in through the open door—he will become the hero of the film.

We read this alternation in shots 1-4 as unidentifiable observers and something they are looking at (the direction of their gaze, the camera movement). This alternation gives way to another that specifies a milieu and indirectly identifies the observers as waiters. It also identifies and emphasizes Pearl as separate from the unidentified men. By displacing the opening shots of the observers and of something seen but unknown, Pearl becomes both the anticipated subject and object of the expected narrative. But the old man who follows her initiates her gradual shift into the latter position. The men, on the other hand, seem clearly positioned as subjects of scrutiny. Their lack of identity, of difference even, of relation to Pearl—all pose an enigma. Thus the enigma of the discourse has become the enigma of the narrative. And we are there, too, in the transformation. The waiters' initial position in the frame, facing away from the camera/screen and looking excitedly at something off in the background, metaphorically, but explicitly, places the spectator as subject in the film's discourse. The dark, indecipherable images double the darkened cinema screen before us. Their looks double our looks. Their desire directs ours. Out of the darkness comes light, out of absence comes presence, out of enigma comes narrative. Consciously positioned as subjects, we become, simultaneously, seekers after enigma—ultimately the uncertain identity and desire of the hero—and observers of the swift, economical production of narrative.

Reflecting on its own initial production of narrative, *La Glace à trois faces* returns in the end to an equally reflexive resolution. The moment that metaphorically conjoined syntagmatic and paradigmatic elements within the film, its various pasts and presents, now severs film and spectator. The figure in the mirror who moves and disappears, the hero's several selves which are resolved into . . . absence. Whose reflection, whose double, is this? Is it not each one of us as (male) spectators? The reflection of a look and an absent body positions us at the breaking point, both inside and outside the film (simultaneously, the subject of enunciating and the subject of the enunciation).[31] In a crisis of recognition, the enigma of the hero's identity and desire shifts onto us. Repositioning us as subjects, now present in absence before the screen/mirror of our own divided selves, the discourse of *La Glace à trois faces* produces a reflection on the deceptive nature of *our* desire.

When it premiered at Studio 28, in June, 1928, the French film critics immediately hailed Jean Epstein's *La Chute de la maison Usher* as a masterpiece of silent film art. For Jean Dréville, it confirmed Epstein's position as "the true master of the modern cinema, the most intuitive as well as the most serious as an artist."[1] Henri Langlois remembers the film in connection with *La Passion de Jeanne d'Arc*: "They provoked the same enthusiasms, the same critiques . . . most of the critics adopted them without reservation; they were truly not only the ultimate expression of ten years of experimentation but their justification."[2] Because of this high praise as well as the Edgar Allan Poe story that provided a familiar literary subject, Epstein's film soon became a popular feature on the circuit of specialized cinemas. And its acclaim had not slackened, twenty years later, in 1950, when it was specially rescreened at Studio 28.[3] This continuing popularity may account for the film's ready availability, even here in the United States.[4]

Even so, *Usher* has sometimes been misperceived and misunderstood. At the time of its initial release, many French critics detected a German influence in the film—an Expressionist (even *Caligari*-like) style and an atmosphere of morbid fantasy.[5] And they focused on Epstein's evident fascination with slow motion as "a new, purely psychological, perspective"—"I know nothing absolutely more moving than a face, freeing itself of an expression, in slow motion."[6] Accordingly, too many historians have tended to pigeonhole *Usher* as a work of exquisite Gothic atmosphere and technical experimentation.[7] But this surely misses much of the real importance of the film. In this last film for his own production company, Epstein turns away from the contemporary world of his previous two films and reverts to period material, as in *Mauprat*; but here the mode of representation is very different. Although its narrative structure may be less complex (though no less interesting) than that of *La Glace à trois faces*, the articulation of its discourse—syntactically, rhetorically— is as unconventional as ever and unusually sophisticated. While it may represent a kind of culmination in Epstein's work, *Usher* also marks the beginning of a change in his aesthetic commitment.

Pierre Leprohon and Marie Epstein have pointed out that *Usher* is less an adaptation than an amalgam of several Edgar Allan Poe stories: the title story, of course, but also "Ligeia," "Berenice," "Silence," "The Man of the Crowd," and especially "The Oval Portrait."[8] It works much like a theme-and-variation composition "according to the motifs of Edgar A. Poe," and Epstein himself said it was "[his] general impression of Poe."[9] Synthesizing this material, Epstein made several changes in the title story: Roderick Usher is a painter; he and Madeleine are husband and wife (rather than brother and sister); and his visiting friend is both hard of hearing and terribly nearsighted. Perhaps the most important structural change eliminated the first-person narrator for a strangely fluctuating omniscient narration.

The film opens with a stranger (Charles Lamy) stopping at a country inn to ask directions to the Usher chateau; he has come to visit his old friend, Roderick Usher (Jean Debucourt), whose young wife, Madeleine (Marguerite Gance), appears to be dying. He finds Roderick painting a huge portrait of her with a feverish disregard for her health. There is a doctor in residence, baffled by Madeleine's illness. Soon she collapses and dies, but Roderick, believing she may be still alive, tries to keep the doctor and his friend from interring her body. After she is finally buried in a grotto at some distance from the chateau, Roderick sinks into an existence of torpor and monotony; yet, paradoxically, his senses sharpen to a frustrating acuteness. One night, a sudden storm erupts with terrific force. Roderick watches and listens intently at a window, and Madeleine slowly arises from the grotto and comes to him, while, simultaneously, lightning strikes the chateau and sets it afire. Just before it is consumed completely, she leads Roderick and his friend out of the inferno to safety.[10]

Despite Epstein's remark that he avoided "any plastic effects," in order to achieve a simplicity of style that matched Poe's own,[11] *Usher* strikes one as a rich film visually, especially in comparison, say, to *La Coquille et le clergyman* (1928) and *Un Chien andalou* (1929). The delicately textured natural landscapes (shot by Georges Lucas in the marshes and forests of Sologne, in February and March, 1928), are saturated with an eerie light that wavers between cold and soft, icy and moist, making the land seem, simultaneously, barren and bounteous.[12] The few interiors—Usher's two large central halls (with their marvelous deep spaces) and a long upper hallway, the inn, the grotto—are lit similarly. But in each, a deep rich blackness surrounds almost everything, often masking off the lighted spaces into narrow rectangles or multiple frames within the frame. And the objects thus singled out—the glasses on a long table, the huge stand of candles, the elaborate frame of the portrait, a full suit of armor, the mammoth fireplace (with its gargoyles hanging from the mantel)—seem to possess a peculiarly effusive glow.[13] The lack of tinting in the exhibition prints (drawn from an orthochromatic negative) must have emphasized this eerie quality of the lighting.[14] This obvious concern for the texture of the image was complemented by complex superimpositions at certain moments—as Madeleine collapses (in overlays of both positive and negative images) and as the men begin to carry her coffin across the estate (seemingly through aisles of candles and slowly drifting leaves)—and by sequences using slow motion in conjunction with camera tracks and dollies, especially during the latter two-thirds of the film. Still, this "calligraphy," as Epstein called it, was unimportant in and of itself. "The image is a sign, complex and precise," he wrote at the time of production—its shifting signification depended on its relation to other images and to the overall design of the film.[15] And in *Usher* the relation between images is indeed complex.

The opening sequence of *Usher* seems lifted out of a Dracula story, e.g., Murnau's *Nosferatu* (1922). In the inn, the stranger's request for a carriage is met by stillness, stares, repeated mutterings—"Usher?" "Usher"—and then a final "USHER" (filling the frame), which, like a thunderclap, signals the shift to the chateau. But the diegetic process, the form of spatial-temporal continuity, peculiar to the film is evident from the start. The sequence is articulated in fragments, Keith Cohen argues, that either coalesce into a continuity viewed from an unusual perspective or remain free or isolated through slight ellipses and gaps.[16] The stranger, for instance, is introduced as a small figure (in LS) struggling in the landscape of gray fields and white sky, a pair of legs and bags (stopping in MS), and a pair of gloved hands (in CU) flexing before a thick coat and scarf. He approaches the inn (described in one LS) by walking forward past a puddle of muddy water (in HAFS) and immediately knocks at a door (in a MS taken at a 60° angle from the back). Inside, again he is described in a MS of legs and bags, followed by a MS and MCU (from the back) as his head turns around halfway (so he can read a letter from Roderick, it turns out). These shots alternate with several MSs of the men in the inn looking up from their tables, in a curious reversal and denial of POV expectations (their seeing discovers almost nothing about him). The space within the inn is no less fragmented and ambiguous. There is no establishing shot, and we must guess the relationship between two separate tables and the area near the door from the eyeline-matched looks of the innkeeper, who comes up to the stranger. But where is the lantern-lit hallway and door through which, after offering him tea, a woman (the innkeeper's wife or daughter?) disappears? As Cohen says, these shots of the inn form just so many isolated spaces in which the characters seem to float or drift, under the threat of being swallowed up or obliterated.[17]

This opening also begins to establish significant patterns of alternation and repetition. John Hagan argues that they help elicit a sense of mystery and expected revelation but that the revelation (and even the subject of the mystery) is continually denied or deflected.[18] The repeated progression from longer to closer shots reveals little about the stranger, either to the men in the inn or to the spectator. When he examines the letter, for instance, he has to use a magnifying glass; and only the words "malade" and "Madeleine" waver distinctly across its surface. Though providing the hint of a motivation for his appearance, the linked words also mask the fact that Roderick is actually describing himself as "malade." In fact, the final shots of the sequence shift our attention to the enigmatic woman who, as the stranger departs, apparently watches from a window. In a shot of the inn exterior (which is encrusted with a weblike network of leafless vines), she appears first in one window (frame right) and then at another (extreme frame left) whose edge barely intrudes into the frame. Finally, a MCU of the vines and window restricts her face to a small area (frame right); and her twisted neck, wide eyes, and open mouth give her a painfully contorted look. The sequence reveals as much about the inn as about the stranger—to us, not to him (besides the magnifying glass, he also resorts to an earhorn). And what we seem to discover is a world whose principal horror is entrapment.

The first sequence in the chateau is organized even more tightly according to an alternation that foregrounds patterns of repetition and difference. An intertitle quickly establishes the Usher couple's relationship: "In this menacing ruined manor, Sir Roderick holds his wife Madeleine in a strange seclusion, dominating her with his tyrannical irritability." The next two dozen shots simply articulate the precise form of Roderick's tyranny, his malady, and its effect on Madeleine. Here a clear pattern of rhetorical figuring begins to emerge, involving isolated objects and parts of bodies, the inanimate and the animate. Epstein found confirmation for such links among the images in one of Poe's own lines—". . . there exist, undoubtedly, combinations of very simple and natural things which loose the power to move us. . . ."[19] Several schema of associated shots (mostly in CU and MCU)—Roderick's hands and a painter's palette; his look and a large, obscurely lighted painted image; his look and Madeleine—are placed in paradigm. Even before an intertitle (much later) reveals the hereditary nature of his action, Roderick's affliction is enunciated here in terms of the desire to paint. A second set of schema—Roderick's hands and Madeleine, his look and Madeleine—seems to shift the significance

239. (top, left to right) The hands of Roderick Usher; the painter's palette; the portrait of Madeleine. (bottom, left to right) The obsessive gaze of Roderick (Jean Debucourt); Roderick's clenched hands; the pained look of Madeleine (Marguerite Gance) in *Usher* (1928)

of that desire. Through repeated alternation, his nervously clenching hands (displacing his look) suggest a "blind" compulsion that seems to threaten her. When he picks up the palette at the conclusion of these shots, the act of painting is now charged metaphorically—it involves a transfer of and thus an attack on Madeleine.

This alternation between Roderick and Madeleine, as subject and object, is disturbed briefly by their opposing movements within the frame. Roderick moves left with the palette (toward the painting off-screen) while Madeleine turns to move away from him (into the right background). As he turns to look after her, she stops and turns back (her image caught, metaphorically, within the frame of a harp, which parallels the frame of his painting and also echoes the woman's entrapment at the inn). The final set of schema completes the anticipated action, with a startling effect. In a new alternation, a paint-brush displaces both Roderick's hands and his look so that the schema of hands/palette is condensed into a single shot of paintbrush touching palette while the schema of look/painted image is condensed into a shot of brush touching canvas. The two acts of touching and painting, through metonymy and metaphor, articulate a transfer from one object to another: adding to the painted image subtracts from Madeleine. As the paintbrush strokes the canvas, Madeleine reacts as if struck, as if her face were being taken away. Roderick's desire is being defined as a compulsion to transfer life to the painted image—to give life to artifice—at the expense of life itself. To enclose Madeleine living within the frame of the painting is to imprison her, to destroy her, to place her in a kind of coffin.[20]

466

With extraordinary succinctness, this initial sequence in the chateau constructs a paradigm for the narrative action in the first half of the film. Roderick transfers Madeleine (as an object of value) from reality to artifice, from a condition of freedom to one of imprisonment, from a condition of living to that of "life-in-death." This transubstantiation of Madeleine—is it actually a misogynist form of denial? Here, it seems to me, is the essential horror of Usher's world. But the horror is countered by something else. In the second half of the film, this narrative action is reversed, with an important difference. And the transition from one to the other occurs in the sequence of Madeleine's burial.

When the pallbearers (Roderick, his friend, the doctor, and a butler) reach their destination, the grotto is depicted in a single establishing shot as a double chamber framed by a glass matte of obviously painted rocks and columns (in the manner of a Méliès fantasy film). The grotto thus suggests itself as analogous to the painting that Roderick has done. Through a series of metaphorical parallels—hinging on the butler's hands hammering nails into the coffin lid in place of Roderick's paintbrush stroking the canvas—the placement of Madeleine's body in the grotto becomes at once the logical outcome of his compulsion and its reenactment. This reenactment is offset, however, by a strange enchantment. "An astonishing pantheism," to use Epstein's own words from *Le Cinématographe vu d'Etna* (1926), emerges to set the reversal in motion. Because of the grotto's distance from Usher, the funeral becomes a kind of processional through nature. The men cross a river or tarn at one point, and a long series of alternating shots (in slow motion) track them down a grassy slope and under a succession of tree branches drifting across the sky.[21] Superimposed over many of these shots are slowly falling leaves and tall flaming candles that create a kind of path or aisle through which the processional moves. Because Madeleine's burial clothes are much like a bridal costume and a long veil trails like a train behind the coffin, the journey seems to be as much wedding march as funeral—one action masks another metaphorical one.

467

242. (top left) A shot from the funeral procession

243. (bottom left) The mating toads in the grotto sequence

244. (right) Madeleine returns in Usher in the storm

It is as if nature, in its "mourning," was offering some secret cause for celebration.

Midway through the burial sequence, this metaphorical undercurrent comes to the fore in an uncanny pattern of rhetorical figuring. When Roderick is finally sent out of the grotto by his friend, an unexpected change occurs in the alternation that has organized the sequence (the butler nailing the coffin lid/Roderick reacting in pain). Instead of cutting back to a CU of the hammering, the discourse suddenly interjects a shot of a toad on wet stony ground (completely free of any POV shot). A shot of the hammering recurs, followed by another shot of the toad, only this time a second toad is on the back of the first in mating position. Given the spatial ambiguity of this association, the visual continuity produces a schema of metaphorical opposition: an entombing of the dead versus an impregnating of life.[22] Through this bizarre, almost Surrealist rhetorical figure, the discourse introduces an antidote to Roderick's compulsion. A second unexpected displacement produces a strange triplet or triadic pattern of alternation. Instead of returning to Roderick and his friend outside the grotto, the discourse interjects a negative (or high contrast) image against a black background, of an owl in a white web of branches. Again the spatial continuity is ambiguous. This repeated pattern shifts briefly into rapid montage (the shots of the toads and owl last but two seconds each) until the CU of hammering gives way to a shot of the sealed coffin lid and then to a shot of the doctor and butler ascending the grotto stairs. The repeated contiguity of the toads and owl suggests their parallel function in opposition to the nailing of the coffin. To this unusual figure of fertility, what does the image of the owl bring? Is it the sign of the "white goddess," confirming the grotto as the site of life-in-death and as the potential site of resurrection?[23] Is it the sign of some "natural" wedding or union? Whatever the precise correlations within this uncanny rhetorical figure, Madeleine's burial seems to function, simultaneously, as a withdrawal from life and as an insemination, a renewal.

The figure of metaphorical associations constructed in this sequence is crucial to the operation of the film's conclusion. The enchantment grows into a devastating conjunction of the animate and the inanimate. The storm wind rises one night against Usher, and, in fast tracks and slow motion shots, the curtains begin to billow and the leaves to blow about the interior hallway while lightning flashes in the exterior shots of the tower (and its slowly tolling bell). As Roderick drags his uncomprehending friend to the window to see, the discourse interjects that same shot of the owl in wind-whipped tree branches, followed by a LS of the exterior landscape as fire and smoke begin to appear around the chateau. Through a simple instance of contiguity (emphasized by the spatial as well as temporal discontinuity), the owl and storm are placed in conjunction; the figure of fertilizing and renewal is equated with the storm's destructive force. Shots of the logs burning and smoking in Usher's huge fireplace alternate with shots of Madeleine's coffin moving in the dark and then falling off its support. A shot of candle flames igniting a curtain is intercut with Madeleine's veil unfurling from the grotto entrance. As the chateau is engulfed in flames, Madeleine's white figure appears in the doorway (in MS), as if suspended in the air, revolving in slow motion. This magical reversal, mediated by the mating toads, the owl, and the storm, transforms her into a figure of salvation. While the storm destroys Usher (the portrait, too, is consumed by fire), Madeleine rescues Roderick from a kind of death-in-life (imprisoned within the chateau, he, too, has become the victim of his own compulsion). Whereas he had denied her life by transferring her into a painted image, into artifice, she reverses the process. Inverting the Orpheus-Eurydice myth, she restores him to life by plucking him from Usher and releasing him into the reality of the natural world.[24]

Like all narratives of the fantastic, *Usher* depends on a sustained epistemic ambiguity.[25] Seeing and knowing remain uncertain to the end. Does Madeleine really die and does Roderick then imagine her resurrection and rescue? Or does she merely sleep until natural or unnatural forces uncannily awaken her and direct her mission? This narrative uncertainty is paralleled by uncertainties in the film's discourse, not only in its spatial-temporal continuity, but even in the function of its rhythm and rhetorical figuring. At two crucial points, the discourse reaches a particularly high level of indeterminacy. Both focus on Roderick's sensibility and, in so doing, render problematic the strange animism that emerges in the film. Moreover, since the film's score is lost, that lack of diegetic music and sound prominent in both sequences makes for an added mystification.[26]

The first of these, "Roderick's Song," immediately precedes the sequence of Madeleine's collapse. Intercut with MSs of Roderick and his friend seated at a table in the central room are several LSs of the upper hallway—its curtains

469

waver and leaves blow in across the floor. As Roderick picks up a guitar (substituting for the harp that once framed Madeleine?) and begins to play, the sequence alternates LSs of the hallway with CUs of his fingers (in slow motion) plucking the strings. Does the intrusion of the wind and leaves compel him to play or does he initiate the song as a means of resistance or control? After the butler announces that Madeleine's illness will prevent her from joining them, Roderick leaves the table; and the sequence begins to alternate MCUs of his hands on the guitar strings with shots of natural landscapes—a wavering water surface, misty trees, branches blurred against the sky. Accelerating quickly from shots of two seconds to one second to a half second each, the alternation suddenly shifts into a set of four shots (beginning with the CU of his fingers) repeated four times according to a strict tempo—ten, ten, ten, and twenty-five frames each. As David Bordwell discovered, this sequence operates "musically"—besides repeating shots exactly, it varies a motif from one set to another (shot four in one set becomes shot three in the next).[27] The fifth and last set ends with a longer shot (fifty frames) of a horizon and darkening sky, and then Roderick turns (in MS) to look at his painting. In Poe's story, a similar song recounted the former glory of the Usher ancestral home; here, however, the shots (lacking music) are highly ambiguous. It is uncertain whether they are a subjective projection (excluding the friend and butler) or an omniscient montage of association. Are they imagined by Roderick, in conjunction with the music, as a means of escape from the chateau?[28] Are they images of the environment around Usher which his sensibility orders and controls through song? Are they signs of a world that also suffers, correspondingly, from his destructive, melancholy affliction? Or are they a kind of regenerative presence from which he draws strength and nourishment? Whatever the case, the experience seems to stimulate him, and Roderick turns from the guitar and these images of nature to work one last time on his fatal portrait.

The second of the sequences, paralleling the first, follows closely on Madeleine's burial. It begins with a slow montage of natural landscape shots, some of which are repeated from the earlier sequence. Then it shifts to shots of Usher's hallway where again a wind begins to move the curtains, especially around a suit of armor and a large grandfather clock (several CUs focus on its slowly swinging pendulum). Time is already protracted—as if by some uncanny natural force—when Roderick is introduced ("His nerves completely taut . . . the least noise exasperates him"), sitting in the central hall while his friend reads at a table across the room. A shot of his clasped hands is intercut with that of the guitar lying on the floor, but he seems traumatized (as immobile as the armor), unable to reach for it as he did before (or as he reached even earlier for the palette). Into this alternation of shots (including a MS of Roderick and a FS of his friend, who is engrossed in reading the story of Ethelred and the dragon) comes the CU of the oscillating pendulum, a repeated ECU of the clock gears and then a LS of the room which suddenly doubles and wavers. An uncertain animism grips the interior of these spaces and things, but is it subjective (visual correlatives for acutely perceived sounds) or natural, menacing or promising?[29] The guitar now quivers; the room glows with a strange light at its center; the clock gears stop; from the clock bell eerily fall particles of dust. The tension culminates as a tiny hammer finally strikes the bell, a guitar string snaps, and Roderick rises out of the chair and

470

245. Selected shots from the second "fantastic" montage sequence near the end of *Usher* (1928)

moves toward the portrait. But, as his friend looks up from his book, he turns away, not daring (in an intertitle) to give in to his mad desire again. Do all these images and sounds represent Roderick's insight into the mystery, the profound animism, at the heart of things?[30] Or do they evoke unknown natural forces which he can no longer control and which now verge on controlling him? And by enveloping the MS "portrait" of him (his arms beginning to lift), do the shots of the breaking strings suggest his degeneration or his liberation?[31] Perhaps the music or sound effects that originally accompanied these images would resolve the ambiguity, but what if they were projected in silence—what if the spectator was forced, while seeing, to share the friend's lack of hearing?[32] Is it significant that the gap between perceiving, knowing, and acting looms largest at the point where Roderick's compulsion seems to be broken?

In the representation of Roderick's compulsion to paint, *Usher* seems to put in question a certain aesthetic and way of seeing. Roderick is the inverse of a Pygmalion. His inherited, unexamined compulsion transfers value from the living or from reality to fiction or artifice. It seems a particularly decadent form of "art for art's sake," cut off from the real and turned in upon itself. And it denies a woman's existence, by replacing her with a painted image, in an unnatural form of union and exchange. There is something in this, the film suggests, that is blind, perverse, and ultimately self-destructive. And nature itself seems to revolt against it. Usher's destruction may deny the value of the artificial and fictional (a point emphasized by the obviously miniature set of the chateau's exterior), and a "tree" of stars (but is this any less artificial?) may "bless" the space of the disavowal. But how will Roderick see and what will he do, as an artist, in the real world of nature? And what will be his relation to Madeleine? Given the fantastic mode of the film, can the real, the natural, be anything but problematical? Although *Usher* seems to announce a break in Epstein's aesthetic commitment, the effect of that break remains unarticulated.

Another film that aligns itself with *La Chute de la maison Usher* is Jean Renoir's *La Petite Marchande d'allumettes* (1928). The history of its production is well known, although the sequence of events has often been confused. In the summer of 1927, Renoir and Tedesco began work on the film in the small studio or atelier they had built in the loft of the Vieux-Colombier.[33] Given such artisanlike conditions, their decision to use panchromatic film stock

471

246. (left) Catherine Hessling peers through the restaurant window in *La Petite Marchande d'allumettes* (1928)

247. (right) Catherine Hessling and the toy soldier officer

throughout (it was then usually reserved for exterior filming) was extremely risky. Shooting went slowly, in piecemeal fashion, but was completed successfully within six months. This pace and the corresponding attention to detail allowed Jean Bachelet (the cameraman) and Eric Aës (the set designer) to produce images of a texture similar to Epstein's in *Usher*.

Renoir and Tedesco had a rough cut of the film ready by the end of March, 1928, when the latter was invited to give a special screening for the ciné-club in Geneva.[34] But Tedesco delayed its premiere at the Vieux-Colombier until June so that the film could conclude his 1927-1928 season.[35] That initial Paris screening was abruptly cut short when the film was impounded as the result of a lawsuit brought by Maurice Rostand (charging plagiarisms of his 1914 operatic adaptation of the same title).[36] By the time the courts had decided in Tedesco and Renoir's favor, one year later, the sound film revolution was in full swing.[37] For financial reasons, presumably, both men were forced to give up any rights they may have had to the film's distribution. When *La Petite Marchande d'allumettes* was finally released commercially by SOFAR, in February, 1930, it had lost several hundred meters in length and gained a number of intertitles as well as, in Renoir's words, a "truly ridiculous" music track (a mixture of Strauss, Mendelssohn, and Wagner).[38] Unfortunately, the original silent version (which supposedly ran eighty minutes) has been lost; the shortened version (minus its score) is preserved in several film archives.[39]

As in several previous films, *La Petite Marchande d'allumettes* describes the condition of a woman's entrapment in a hostile or indifferent milieu, her dream of escape, and the failure of that dream. But it eschews the more common modes of representation of either the bourgeois melodrama or the realist film for another quite similar to *Usher*'s. For this is a highly stylized fantasy whose simple scenario is drawn from a Hans Christian Andersen fairy tale. On a cold, snowy night, around Christmas time, in an unidentified northern city, a poor girl dressed in rags and tatters (Catherine Hessling) leaves her dilapidated shanty to peddle her wares—boxes of matches—to shoppers and passers-by. Unable to sell even one, she wanders in the streets, afraid to go home, and finally settles down near a fence under the temporary shelter

472

of a plank. There she dreams of cavorting through the snow and into a toy shop window which earlier she had passed by under the watchful eyes of a policeman. The officer (Jean Storm) of a platoon of wooden soldiers befriends her; and, when Death (Manuel Raabi) suddenly appears as a Jack-in-the-box, they race off into the sky on his horse. Death pursues them, however, defeats the officer, and bears the unconscious girl away. In the morning, several people discover her lifeless snow-covered body by the fence and wonder stupidly how she would have expected matches to keep her warm.

La Petite Marchande d'allumettes divides into two distinct segments—one depicting the reality of the girl's condition; the other, her fantasy—but the distinction between them is not as sharp as one might expect.[40] Renoir has described the film overall as "an attempt at a purely exterior nonrealism.[41] This is as true of the street scenes as it is of the girl's dream. Her wanderings are described quite differently from those, say, in either *Menilmontant* or *En rade*, partly because of the studio as opposed to location shooting. The girl's look and gestures, the way her rags fit—all suggest the coldness of the night as well as her despair with an economy that reminds one of Chaplin—a "Charlot in skirts."[42] Indeed, there are explicit echoes here of the hungry bum in *A Dog's Life* (the exhausted girl going to sleep by the fence) and the lost prospector in *The Gold Rush* (the lone figure in the street, scraping the ice from a window to look in on a waitress serving food to a lady and gentleman).[43] As in Chaplin films, too, the decors are minimal, often just a few props—a simple storefront, a window frame, the tray of matches. But this film consistently keeps the characters separate, in MSs and CUs; and their glances, opening into off-screen spaces, provide the primary means of spatial continuity. Thus does the girl seem to move through a world defined principally by just two elements—darkness and snow. The tone of this first segment is delicately ambiguous. The darkness threatens in the background and off-screen. Yet the soft light and falling snow seem to transform Hessling, as if there were a magical agent already present in the world.

The dream segment of the film reenacts the street segment in several ways, producing a variation on the now familiar doubled narrative form. The toy shop window reappears as a carnival with huge balls, a merry-go-round, a host of animals (a dog, a pig, a bear, a rabbit), mechanical dolls, a ballerina, wooden soldiers, and trains. The snowfall turns into the white clouds and mist through which the officer and girl are pursued by Death. More complicated (as well as technically competent) than the flight fantasy in *La Fille de l'eau*, this chase and struggle resemble the fairy-tale adventures of a Lotte Reiniger silhouette film—e.g., *Les Aventures de Prince Ahmed* (1925).[44] Instead of black figures sharply etched against white backgrounds, however, here the figures are diaphanous superimpositions, and their actions are choreographed in a slow motion ballet. Characters also recur, but in a fabulous guise. Jean Storm, who earlier tried to buy some matches from the girl, now plays the officer who falls in love with her and offers her protection. Manuel Raabi, the policeman who had pointed out the toy window and then told her to go home, now becomes the Jack-in-the-box figure of Death.

The white magic of soft lighting and snow seems to open up the possibility of escape for Hessling, especially in a series of transformations that mark the last half of the film.[45] The shift to dream, like that in *La Fille de l'eau*, is

473

248. Catherine Hessling at
the end of *La Petite Marchande
d'allumettes* (1928)

articulated through a darkening of the background and through several superimpositions. As Hessling dances, she reaches out for snowflakes that turn into
balls which she catches in her hat and then juggles in the air. The snow turns
into a gauze curtain that swirls in slow motion and through which she passes
to jump down into the carnival of life-size toy figures. Once the officer declares
his love to Hessling, he becomes the magician of the narrative. The background changes again, and she finds herself in a simplified pastoral setting—
a single tree and a toy sheep, whose eyes move in CU when her hand caresses
its head. When she signals her hunger, the officer waves his hand, and the
sheep turns into a table filled with food and drink.[46] Suddenly Death appears
and threatens to take control of and reverse the transformations. The ballerina
collapses, the dolls' heads drop, the rabbit pops back into its sack, all the
soldiers fall—and Death stalks over them.[47] When, high on the city walls,
the officer changes the background to sky, and the couple flees on horseback,
Death merely has his own horse materialize (dissolve in) beside him. The two
male figures thus struggle, not only for possession of Hessling, but for control
of the delirious world they inhabit and of the magic that governs it.

If Death is the victor in this unequal struggle, his dominion is completed
in the final transformations—in a mysteriously simple pattern of rhetorical
figuring. In LS, carrying Hessling in his arms, Death walks out of the clouds
(left background) and lays her body down on a flat stone beside a cross (lower
right foreground). In a ritual gesture that strangely becomes an act of insemination, much as in *Usher*, he tosses a lock of her hair to the wind. The cross
turns into a rosebush, which begins slowly to grow (as trees will, coming up
through stage floors), and he walks toward and seems to dissolve into it.
Death, the creator, thus becomes part of his creation. As a CU of Hessling's
face alternates with a CU of the rosebush, its petals dissolve into snowflakes.
We are back to reality. This hypnotic transition—from death to life to death
again—articulates rhetorically the cyclical, illusory nature of the narrative.
The dream restores Hessling, lets her relive her desires, only to repeat them—
from lack to love to lack once more—and so come to the end she has evaded.
Raymond Durgnat's phrase for *La Petite Marchande d'allumettes* is perceptive—

474

"at once fairy tale and film noir."[48] The darkness and snow become one. As the rose petals of love turn into the snow flowers that kill, once again there is that disturbing echo, masked over and ignored by the passers-by, of the bitter conclusion to *Fièvre*—the end of desire. But the magic of this fantasy proves gently, almost regretfully, deceptive.

Probably the best known and most widely circulated of the later French narrative avant-garde films, at least in the United States, are two short works released within a year of one another. They are Dulac's *La Coquille et le clergyman* (1928), from a scenario by Antonin Artaud, and Luis Buñuel's *Un Chien andalou* (1929), co-authored with Salvador Dali. Besides their familiarity, there are several good reasons for examining them together. Along with Man Ray's *L'Etoile de mer* (1928) and Buñuel's first sound feature, *L'Age d'or* (1930), they are often singled out as the major Surrealist films of the period. And both were the subject of demonstrations which, intent on preventing their exhibition, actually gave them even greater notoriety. Moreover, both have been described, somewhat erroneously and simplistically, as oneiric fantasies or fictions in which a seemingly arbitrary flow of images is determined by an acute sensibility or by the mechanisms of the unconscious. What concerns me principally is their differences, as much as their similarities, particularly as to how they structure their narratives (or deconstruct them) and how they deviate from conventional narrative discourse.

Few films have been as encrusted or distorted by historical error, superficial criticism, and "scrambled" prints as the three reels of *La Coquille et le clergyman*.[1] The so-called scandal of its premiere at Armand Tallier's Studio des Ursulines is a legend still perpetuated in most film histories. Artaud is alleged to have denounced Dulac for betraying his scenario and then to have led the Surrealists in a violent demonstration against the film's exhibition. Alain Virmaux long ago concluded otherwise.

The origins of the collaboration between Dulac and Artaud on *La Coquille et le clergyman* remain unclear.[2] Although Artaud at first may have wanted to direct his own scenario, he accepted Dulac's artistic control as director of the film's production. Given the differences in their temperaments and in their concepts of cinema, the relations between the two were actually quite cordial during most of the production period, from June to September, 1927.[3] He was willing to make concessions in the scenario, and she accepted some of his added ideas for shooting. But Dulac began to perceive his increasingly persistent queries as interference and carefully excluded Artaud from the shooting and editing process (he had already been excluded from the cast). Only when he discovered this did he become angry and anxious. When first screened, for the Ciné-Club de France (on 25 October 1927), the film was announced as the "Dream of Antonin Artaud, Visual Composition by Germaine Dulac."[4] The publication of the first draft of the scenario in the *Nouvelle Revue Française* (November, 1927) coincided with this screening; and Artaud added to it a preface objecting to such "an exclusively oneiric interpretation": "This scenario is not the reproduction of a dream and should not be considered as such."[5] For the film's exhibition at the Ursulines (on 9 February 1928), Dulac, to her

La Coquille et le clergyman and *Un Chien andalou*

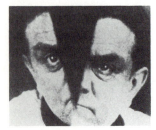

249. Attacked by the
clergyman, the face of the
general/priest (Lucien Bataille)
splits in two, in *La Coquille et
le clergyman* (1928)

credit, had the opening titles changed to "Script by Antonin Artaud, Production by Germaine Dulac." But Artaud was said to have harbored some disagreement still, apparently over the filmmaker's reliance on so-called softening technical effects (although some were already present in the scenario).[6] Convinced that their prodigal member had been maligned (after a year of estrangement, Artaud was momentarily back in the Surrealists' good graces), André Breton led his friends to clamor against *La Coquille et le clergyman* and against Dulac, in particular.[7] And their judgment of the film became history. Privately, Breton apologized to Tallier the next day; and years later, Georges Sadoul (who took part, mistakenly thinking he was attacking Artaud) confessed to the injustice they unwittingly had perpetrated.[8] Artaud himself, however, did not let these experiences color his view of the film as "the first of its genre and a precursor."[9]

Much like *L'Invitation au voyage, La Coquille et le clergyman* was an independent production whose budgetary limitations show much too obviously in its skimpy decors and sometimes awkwardly executed "special effects" (by Paul Parguel)." But a certain roughness cannot detract from the bizarre discontinuity of its narrative and from the disorienting strategies of its discourse. Artaud conceived of *La Coquille et le clergyman* (the only one of his half-dozen scenarios to be filmed) in terms that must have intrigued Dulac—it was to be "a film of pure images," developing "a series of states of mind which are derived from one another just as one thought is derived from another, without the process producing a reasonable sequence of events."[10] And he was proud of the scenario's "obvious incoherence" and "merciless cruelty."[11] From this, one might expect a film without any narrative at all, a serial composition of singular visions, a series of bafflingly connected *merveilles*, as if produced by a demonic (as opposed to the usual Surrealist euphoric) psychic automatism.[12]

Yet there *is* a narrative in *La Coquille et le clergyman*, if only a minimal one, a narrative that has undergone a sort of deconstruction. Three characters recur and interact through a number of spaces, several of which are repeated. There is the odd little man in black, the clergyman (Alex Allin), who is the primary subject and agent of the action. His antagonist is a stereotype of convention and authority—a fierce-looking, pompous, heavily-decorated general (Lucien Bataille); and the persistent object of his desire is a lovely, full-gowned lady (Gênica Athanasiou) who seems allied with the general. In the opening sequence, the general discovers the clergyman in a kind of alchemist's laboratory, pouring a clear liquid from a large seashell into flasks and then shattering them on the floor. After his shell is smashed by the general's saber (as if in punishment), the clergyman follows him and the woman to a city church where they go into the confessional. Attacked by the clergyman, the general turns into a priest and is tossed into the sea; then the clergyman seizes a talisman or trophy, a double seashell that covers the woman's breasts. Again he confronts the general and woman in a ballroom of dancing couples. After he brandishes the double seashell, they vanish; when she reappears dressed in white, he drops the shell, and his coattails grow to enormous lengths. Eventually, he chases the woman along a country road and into a room where he seems to capture and enclose her head in a large glass globe. Stalking the corridors like a jailer, the clergyman comes upon the couple once more and gives pursuit. In a ship's cabin, while the general receives the woman's kiss

476

in a corner, the clergyman fantasizes strangling her; but out of his hands emerge stalactite islands, water, mist, and a tiny sailing ship. Finally, he and the woman (in a bridal gown) enter a room occupied by servants bustling around the glass globe, in which *his* head is now enclosed. Everything vanishes except for the clergyman and the globe, which he then shatters on the floor. Placing the head on a large seashell, he puts it to his lips and drinks.

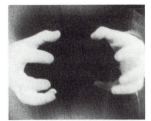

The discourse of this narrative works more consistently perhaps than any other prior to it to produce a sense of spatial and temporal disorientation. Following the scenario, the film eschews all intertitles, a stratagem that forces the images alone to provide patterns of continuity and that, correspondingly, opens up the shots and sequences to ambiguity. For instance, while the film uses a conventional punctuation system of fades to mark off the first four sections of the narrative, they suddenly disappear during the middle sections. And when the system returns near the end, the fades now operate within as well as between sequences. More important, the film rarely adheres to the continuity editing of conventional film discourse. Instead, it works to create a different kind of continuity through discontinuity. Shots shift "erratically" from normal to high angle, from in front of characters to beside or behind them, from CU to LS (without recourse to a POV system), from one fragmentary image to another—in a montage of associations and disassociations. The sequence in the church, for instance, at one point turns into a series of alternating frontal CUs of the three characters. Representational space dissolves through the lack of eye-line matches, and time is negated through the paradoxical alternation of anger and bliss on the general-priest's face. When night falls abruptly, the faces of the woman and the general revolve from left to right; as in a serial composition, the movements are then repeated in reverse. Sometimes, as here, the flow of images is marked by an excess of repetition that borders on the obsessive. The clergyman's progress in the street, for instance, is described in a half-dozen contiguous subjective dolly shots and about the same number showing him going around corners (all linked by lap dissolves). And he pursues the woman along the country road in an alternating sequence of some twenty repeated dolly shots. This obsessive repetition is quite apt, it turns out, for the desire that drives the film's narrative.

250. Three shots from the "strangling/creation" sequence in *La Coquille et le clergyman*

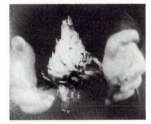

As the title suggests, this is the clergyman's story. In contrast to Dulac's previous films, however, where the representation of the subjective was given special emphasis, here the very concept of the subjective is called into question and the narrative subject put into crisis. The clergyman may be the subject of most of the looking in the film and have several explicit fantasies—e.g., when he imagines strangling the woman and a "world" emerges from his hands. But the usual differences between the omniscient and the subjective are continually being dissolved. The very first shot that dollies toward a half-open door—is this omniscient description or the general's POV (he soon peeps in on the clergyman)? When the clergyman beckons to the camera to approach the glass globe, are we to assume the POV of the woman, who seems to be caressed and then seized (invisibly) and whose head then appears superimposed in the globe? More generally, the technical effects which, by 1927, were commonly used to mark off subjective sequences—soft-focus shots, distortions, superimpositions, dissolves, rapid montage, camera movement, slow motion—here occur with an undifferentiated frequency, in a continuous, dis-

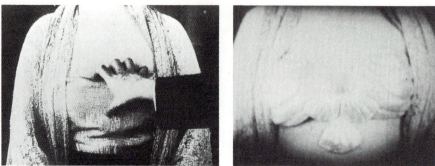

251. (left) The woman (Gênica Athanasiou) transformed in *La Coquille et le clergyman* (1928)

252. (center) The clergyman's hand of desire and violation; (right) The seashell covering the woman's breasts

orienting flow of images. Distributed throughout the discourse of the film, they disperse the subjective into its opposite and vice versa, producing a world that is both other and the same. Thus the film ends aptly in a doubled image, with the clergyman's own face both the subject and object of his seeing.

If the subjective is dispersed and the seeing subject turned back on itself in *La Coquille et le clergyman*, the sexual subject undergoes a similar deconstruction. For the clergyman is also the subject of a repeatedly thwarted desire and a deflected fulfillment. The sexual symbolic of the narrative, however, can be read in several ways. On the one hand, the clergyman, the general, and the woman seem to act out, through a series of displacements, an Oedipal situation. Repressed by the "father," the "son" attacks and destroys him, freeing the "mother" for his pleasure and possession. But the "son" is forced to reenact this conflict again and again until, in exasperation, his desire turns destructive. The expected resolution—a death, a union, an escape—never comes, and the "son" is left face to face with his own desire, and perhaps his own violently ambiguous narcissism. On the other hand, as Sandy Flitterman argues, the film seems

to reproduce the actual production process of desire—its evanescent, fleeting quality as it circulates ("ceaselessly different in [its] repeated metamorphoses") from representation to representation. By emphasizing the *fantasmatic* nature of this image of the woman—as an imaginary production, with the capacity of simulacrum, of memory, of vision—the female figure in *Seashell* touches on something . . . fundamental in the operations of the cinematic apparatus. . . . [13]

Free of the constraining conventions of narrative, desire circulates as a "lure," inviting the spectator's own participation in the production-process of meaning.

Although Artaud told Dulac that his scenario was devoid of psychoanalytical (as well as metaphysical or human) meaning, it is difficult not to read it or see the film as other than deeply personal.[14] The clergyman's shifting relations with the general and the woman closely parallel what little is known of Artaud's attitudes toward his own father and mother.[15] Furthermore, the parts of the clergyman and the woman were written specifically for Artaud himself and Gênica Athanasiou, whom he had loved (oscillating similarly between

478

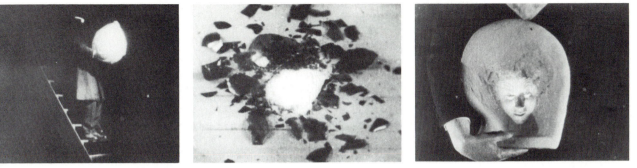

253. (left to right) The clerrgyman carries a globe/head somewhere between the ship and the ballroom; the clergyman's face lies among the fragments of the glass globe on the floor; the head of the clergyman (Alex Allin) in the seashell at the end of *La Coquille et le clergyman* (1928)

hysterical rage and desperate need) ever since their performances together in Charles Dullin's Atelier Théâtre—in a sense, this was their story as parable.[16] Dulac's choice of Alex Allin in place of Artaud for the central character, therefore, was crucial. Instead of possessing Artaud's virile, intense, even erotic presence, the clergyman is invested with Allin's awkward comic pathos. His expressions and gestures make his desire seem absurd, and the character comes close to being an adolescent. Dulac's substitution, as Wendy Dozoretz has suggested, does support a reading of the film as a feminist critique of a fetishizing male vision.[17]

Given these oscillations of eruption and repression, of disruption and resolution, what gives *La Coquille et le clergyman* a sense of coherence, as much as anything else, is the pattern of rhetorical figuring that devolves from the seashell of its title. In the opening sequence, the seashell seems the source of a fascinating clear liquid (which, paradoxically, is tossed away), a source which the general's saber shatters. Later it recurs doubled as a protective carapace which the clergyman seizes in order to expose the woman's breasts (are we to associate, metaphorically, one liquid for another?). Brandished high in the air by the clergyman, this second seashell becomes a kind of magical talisman or fetish (its waving movement seems to generate the swinging chandelier in the ballroom). When the woman appears transformed in a white dress, the dropped seashell is engulfed in flames on the floor, and the clergyman, much agitated in a LAFS (filmed through glass), clutches his crotch (is the gesture masturbatory or suppressive?), only to have his coattails expand to gigantic proportions. At the end, when the glass globe shatters (what accounts for the reversal of heads therein?), the original seashell reappears to cradle the image of his face that lies among the fragments on the floor. The face is transformed into liquid (are we to assume it is blood?); and now, in CU and ECU, it pours darkly glistening from the raised seashell into his mouth. Is this an image of purification, of self-transformation, or of narcissistic perversity? Or do the connotations of self-consumption and self-generation perhaps condense the whole film and its flow of images here into a single source or point of origin? The initial figure of seashell, liquid, and shattering glass has returned, but reversed, transformed, and no less ambiguous. While this circular pattern of rhetorical figuring neatly closes off the disruptive and disturbing narrative, its

479

significance remains enigmatic and multiple. Is this part of what Artaud meant, and Dulac would have agreed with, when he spoke of the film's "organizing current" as "a kind of intellectual music"?[18]

To the question, what is *Un Chien andalou*, there are a number of answers. The first really successful Surrealist film to be exhibited in Paris. The means by which two Spaniards, Luis Buñuel and Salvador Dali, first became visible and recognized in the world of French artists and intellectuals. The culmination of three years of work by Buñuel within and on the margins of the French film industry. The one film from the French cinema of the 1920s that has generated more criticism, in English, at least, than has any other.[19] And, despite the overlays of that criticism, a film whose "savage poetry"—to use Jean Vigo's phrase[20]—apparently still shocks, puzzles, delights, and liberates audiences as much now as it did when first screened.

The known production history of *Un Chien andalou* can be summarized briefly. After immigrating to Paris from Spain in 1925, Buñuel had worked as an assistant director in the French film industry (principally for Jean Epstein) and as a film critic for an important Spanish literary magazine, all the while trying unsuccessfully to make a film of his own—one project, perhaps influenced by Cavalcanti's *Rien que les heures*, which Buñuel admired, was "a reportage on the bric-a-brac contents of a typical magazine."[21] Finally, in January, 1929, Buñuel and Dali conceived and wrote, in their words, a "stupendous scenario" based on an irrational series of gags and "dream-residues" and labeled with the appropriately illogical title—*Un Chien andalou*.[22] Two months later, Buñuel shot the film quickly and cheaply (with money from his mother); and, by April, 1929, it was edited for a special preview arranged for the Surrealists at the Studio des Ursulines.[23] Expecting to denounce "a shameful usurpation," Breton and his comrades came away instead proclaiming it a genuine Surrealist film.[24] Their enthusiasm led to a gala premiere, with a complementary exhibition of paintings, at the Studio 28 cinema in early November.[25] When the cinema and exhibit were physically attacked by rightwing groups, Buñuel was dumbfounded.[26] Then came another surprise—Dali had arranged on his own to have the scenario published, coincidentally, in *La Revue du cinéma* (15 November 1929). Indignant, Buñuel broke with his friend, and the scenario was published a second time, in *La Révolution surréaliste* (December, 1929), with *his* authority and endorsement.[27] By then, Buñuel had embraced the Surrealists and gleefully accepted the film's notoriety and was arguing that its object was to offend, to provoke both revulsion and attraction in the spectator.[28] In a moment of excess, he even called it "a desperate and passionate appeal to murder."[29] The provocation paid off, for *Un Chien andalou* ran nine consecutive months at Studio 28, and Buñuel was soon able to secure independent financing for his next project, *L'Age d'or* (1930).[30]

Un Chien andalou exhibits a rough, even awkward, simplicity in its execution that aligns it superficially with *La Coquille et le clergyman*. But there are more substantial connections between the two films. Like Artaud before him, Buñuel argued that his film did not merely reproduce a dream. Rather, it deliberately sought a narrative incoherence, a lack of logical associations, through the mechanism of an "unconscious psychic automatism," drawing on the "free association" of uninhibited compulsions.[31] What principally links the two films,

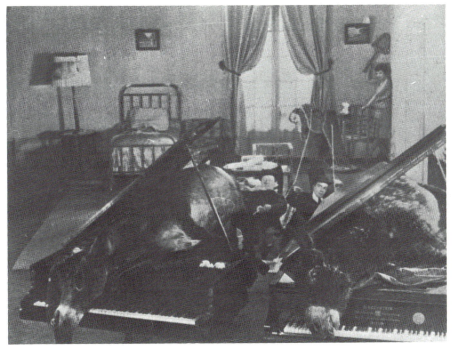

254. Pierre Batcheff's "burden" of cork mats, melons, priests, and donkey-laden pianos in *Un Chien andalou* (1929).

however, is their deconstruction of the conventions of narrative cinema. In *Un Chien andalou*, that deconstruction is unusually systematic and comic, undermining the diegetic process at all levels of the discourse.

To begin with, the film's few intertitles (there are only five) perform a witty mystification:

"Once upon a time"
"Eight years later"
"Toward three in the morning"
"Sixteen years before"
"In the spring"

Although these simple phrases offer the semblance of temporal continuity, their order oscillates wildly, illogically, to the point of absurdity. And their placement in relation to the sequencing of images fails to provide any ground for a coherent narrative. The innocuous "Once upon a time" lulls the spectator into one of the most shocking beginnings in film history—a razor slashing open a woman's eye. Then, "Eight years later," the same woman reappears as if nothing had happened. "In the spring" sets up expectations of a happy ending, but the final shot presents a puppet couple buried up to their waists in a desert of sand. On the one hand, such intertitles "constitute, in parodic form," writes Michel Marie, "a theoretical reflection on the function of intertitles in the silent cinema."[32] On the other, they also function as "break points," in William Van Wert's words, suspending the image flow to trigger another kind of incongruity in the images that follow.[33]

481

255. (left) Simone Mareuil and Pierre Batcheff look down from the apartment; (right) the androgynous figure pokes at the severed hand in the street below

These disruptions in the diegetic process are augmented by spatial discontinuities as well. The film's central setting, the apartment of the young woman (Simone Mareuil), keeps changing its contents and its position in relation to an exterior world. At first, it seems located above a quiet narrow street; later, it looks down on a busy thoroughfare. In the end, inexplicably, it opens out directly (from the ground floor) onto a beach. Once in the apartment, the young man (Pierre Batcheff) becomes the center of several metamorphoses. Writhing in pain on one side of a door in which Mareuil has caught his hand, he also lies docilely in her bed on the other side. Puzzled by her resistance to his advances at one point, he suddenly grabs two ropes and begins dragging from off-screen a bizarre collection of objects we have never seen before and won't again—a pair of cork mats, melons, priests lying flat on their backs, and a grand piano with the bloody carcasses of two donkeys draped over it. Later, in the same room, he shoots a character who, in a simple cross-cut, falls beside a nude woman (who dissolves away at his touch) on the grounds of an unidentified large estate.

Despite these incongruities, *Un Chen andalou* does narrate a story of sorts. As Phillip Drummond notes, one can read it as a "romantic tragicomedy, complete with an embattled hero and heroine, [that is] perpetually unsettled and undermined. . . ."[34] There is a central male-female relationship, between Batcheff and Mareuil, but the characters they play are unnamed, inconsistent, and, in Batcheff's case, even multiple. Mareuil's character is the more consistent of the two, but her attitude toward Batcheff undergoes several abrupt shifts. Exhibiting a loving concern for him in the beginning, when he falls off a bicycle in front of her apartment, she is suddenly alarmed by the ants that appear in the palm of his hand and that seem to fascinate him. When he attacks her, she is frightened but submits to his caresses, then flees and resists, threatening him with a tennis racket (conveniently hung on a wall), and finally slams his hand in the door. Near the end of the film, she sees him again in the room and, angrily sticking out her tongue in disgust, leaves him to obediently meet another unidentified young man on the beach. They walk off

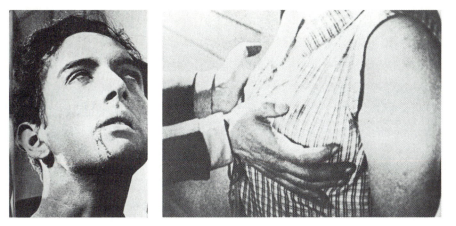

256. (left) Batcheff's face in
blissful agony; (right)
Batcheff's hands caress
Mareuil's breasts

together contentedly, arm-in-arm—to be coupled in the space of a Beckett-like spring.

The Batcheff character is much more unstable. Initially, his various selves may seem parodic forms of his earlier screen roles—the self-sacrificing heroes of *Joueur d'échecs* (1927) and *Napoléon* (1927) and the sentimental heroes of *La Sirène des tropiques* (1928) and *Les Deux Timides* (1929). He first appears cycling awkwardly through the empty streets of a city, wearing over a man's suit several frilly articles of a maid's costume. In the woman's room, his look becomes active—he is fascinated by his ant-infested hand and then excited by the figure of a woman poking at a severed hand on the busy street below. This androgynous figure bears a striking resemblance to Batcheff (is it actually Batcheff in drag?), and he/she quickly becomes a victim, run down by a speeding car. The sudden appearance and disappearance of this double provokes Batcheff to sexually assault Mareuil, and his caresses climax in facial registers of bliss and a deathlike agony. Next he is lying docilely in bed, again dressed as the cyclist, the victim of a small, hatted and suited stranger who harangues him and tosses his maid's costume out a window, piece by piece. The stranger forces him to stand in a corner like a guilty schoolboy and then himself turns into a younger Batcheff double. This meek, pleading figure beseeches him with schoolbooks; but Batcheff now turns gleefully revengeful and shoots him with a pair of revolvers—pleasure and agony return, divided in a strangely self-destructive act. In the end, Batcheff reappears in the woman's room, the subject of another metamorphosis—his mouth vanishes and is replaced by a smudge of hair (apparently from Mareuil's armpit). Ultimately, these four or five different selves exceed the conventional limits of character coherence. "The film's 'body consciousness,' " concludes Drummond, "is permitted and encouraged to explode the traditional 'containment' of psychological-dramatic continuity and logic."[35]

What makes *Un Chien andalou* unique among the French narrative avant-garde films is that this disruption of continuity even extends to the film's rhetorical figuring. Many images/objects, whether they occur only once—e.g.,

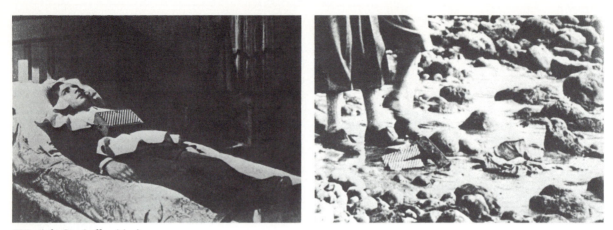

257. (left) Batcheff, with the striped box, as he lies docilely on the bed in the apartment; (right) the striped box, now broken, on the beach at the end of *Un Chien andalou*

the chain of ropes, cork mats, melons, priests, and donkey-laden pianos; the art book (opened to Vermeer's "The Lace-maker"); the death's head moth; the footprint and the sea urchin in the sand (an ironic allusion to Man Ray's *L'Etoile de mer?*)—or several times—e.g., the striped tie, the woman's armpit, the ant-infested hand—maintain an unusual degree of ambiguity or uncertainty in the flow of signification. The most shifting and deceptive of these is the diagonally striped box.[36] It first appears as part of the cyclist's costume and is singled out, in ECU, as a potent enigma. From it emerges a striped tie like that worn by the man who cuts the woman's eye in the beginning. Both box and tie become part of the costume that the woman lays out reverently on her bed. The same box (or is it a double?) next appears as a receptacle for the severed hand which the androgyne clutches to her breast. The box thus confirms a (repressive?) parallel between three characters; but it disappears with the androgyne, and fails to return later (as might be expected) to mark a similar relationship between the cyclist and the stranger/double. Finally, together with the cyclist's costume, the box reappears, now broken, on the shoreline where the woman and the unidentified young man are walking. If, connotatively, these objects may be remnants of the cyclist, the woman refuses to read them that way. Unlike the seashell in Dulac's film, the box is abandoned, somewhat like an unexplained McGuffin, in the mud of the beach.

Perhaps what does come closest to organizing or determining the disruptions in the continuity of *Un Chien andalou* is the circulation of desire. In Paul Sandro's words, "the desires of the characters are constantly frustrated . . . they are condemned to repeat variations of the same scenario."[37] This repetition is complemented, and complicated, by the phonograph music that originally accompanied the film—through the simple alternation of a pair of Argentinian tangos and the "Liebestod" theme from Wagner's *Tristan and Isolde*.[38] While the music of Isolde's death matches the deaths of the androgyne and Batcheff's younger double (both feminized versions of his self), the tangos satirize his pursuit of Mareuil and counterpoint the prologue of her eye-slashing as well as her "civilized" meeting with the man on the beach and the final image of interment in the sand. In conjunction with this alternately comple-

484

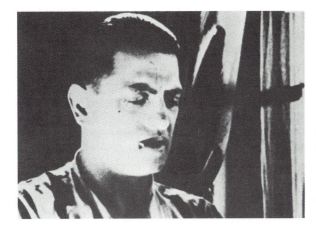 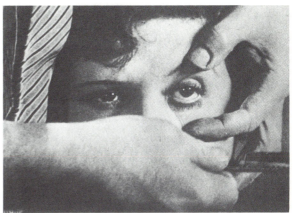

258. (left) Buñuel in the opening sequence of *Un Chien andalou*; (right) Mareuil's eye about to be sliced by Buñuel's razor

mentary and contrapuntal music, Batcheff, Mareuil, and Batcheff's doubles and rivals enact a sexual symbolic of desire, repression, and displacement. Some may still want to read this symbolic in terms of a "primitive" Freudian psychoanalysis—as a celebration of the sexual drive and its tragicomic transformations under the pressure of psychological and social constraints.[39] More recent critiques, however, conceive the process as a deconstruction of the sexual subject—an opening up of the contradictions of desire, in the circulation of looks and fetishized objects and parts of bodies.[40] Dismemberment and disintegration mark the film at all levels—in the bodies of the characters that multiply and fragment, in the body of a narrative that fails to resolve itself, in the body of meanings that refuse to cohere, in the body of the viewing subject whose desire is engaged and unfulfilled.[41]

In the end, there is the beginning. The notorious prologue to *Un Chien andalou* is both a thematic overture and an exercise in syntactical and rhetorical repositioning.[42] The alternation of objects and faces, in MCU and CU, reminds one of an Epstein film; only here the ambiguities are even more disturbing. The shots of the man smoking and the razor being stropped—are they to be read diegetically as parts of the same space or in metaphorical association (the result of "incorrect" eyeline matching)? The CU of the woman's face—is she sitting on the balcony beside the man or is she an imaginary image he conjures up? The ECU of the eye-slashing—are we to notice the punning trick of cutting (substituting another eye) or accept it as a violent assault on the woman? The trauma of this initial sequence has a paradoxical effect. Attacked and disfigured by the man (an act heightened by the fact that Buñuel himself performs it), the woman nonetheless will return unharmed and unchanged in the rest of the film. The man, however, disappears from the text (the filmmaker from his film) to be replaced by his opposite, Batcheff as the cyclist (and his striped tie will reappear in Batcheff's striped box). The spectator's position in all this is compromised. Led to identify with Buñuel's gaze (in POV shots), the spectator is confronted unexpectedly with the woman's face, at once the desired object of the look and the mirror image of his own gaze. As a narcissistic act of self-destruction, the eye-slashing sets in motion an unending cycle of repeated ruptures. In the final rupture (the "happy ending"), effigies of a man and woman are framed in a grim still life—immobile, paralyzed, castrated. This final gag makes explicit what they have been all along, the fetish objects of the spectator as voyeur.[43]

How apt is Vigo's epithet, "An Andalusian dog howls—who then is dead?"[44]

La Passion de Jeanne d'Arc

After Gance's *Napoléon* (1927), Carl Dreyer's *La Passion de Jeanne d'Arc* (1928) was, without question, the most expensive experimental French film of the decade. The young Danish director had been hired by the Société Générale des Films apparently to make a historical reconstruction film that would complement *Napoléon*. Once the subject of Jeanne d'Arc was agreed on, in October, 1926, S.G.F. budgeted Dreyer's film at seven million francs and gave him almost complete autonomy over its production.[1] "I had a free hand," he said later, "I did absolutely what I wanted."[2] Instead of a vast fresco of fifteenth-century France, which the producers expected, Dreyer set about making an intimate, psychological film—in an attempt to document the experience of the mystic.[3] To do so, wrote Léon Moussinac, Dreyer "cast aside or deviated from the normal modes of cinematic creation."[4]

With this extraordinary freedom, Dreyer assembled an international crew, a fact which made the production somewhat of an anomaly among the narrative avant-garde films. For his technical collaborators, he chose several craftsmen who, like himself, came from outside France. Rudolf Maté, who had assisted Karl Freund on several UFA films in Germany—notably Dreyer's own *Mikhel* (1924), was the chief cameraman. Hermann Warm, who had constructed the decors for several major German films—e.g., *The Cabinet of Doctor Caligari* (1919), *Spiders* (1919), *Destiny* (1921)—was the chief set designer. Warm's assistant was Jean Hugo, whose wife, the Surrealist Valentine Hugo, then designed the rough, simple, slightly stylized costumes. For his cast, Dreyer stuck with French actors, but here, too, his choices were unusual.[5] A seventy-year-old veteran of the Comédie Française, Eugène Silvain (who had never acted in the cinema), portrayed the chief trial judge, Bishop Cauchon. The Surrealist actor-playwright, Antonin Artaud, played Jeanne's young supporter, Brother Massieu. And an ordinary café owner became the English general, Warwick. The strangest casting of all was for Jeanne—Renée Jeanne Falconetti, a young Comédie Française actress, who was renowned for her roles in light boulevard comedy. Without the makeup, she was a different woman, Dreyer realized—"I found on her face exactly what I had been seeking for Joan of Arc: a rustic woman, very sincere, who was also a woman of suffering."[6] Falconetti's inspired performance (her only appearance on film) became one of the high points of this consistently well-acted film.

At S.G.F.'s request, the initial scenario for the project was written by Joseph Delteil, based on his popular, and sentimental, biography, *La Vie de Jeanne d'Arc* (1925).[7] Dreyer, however, was drawn to Pierre Champion's recent edition of the transcript of Jeanne's trial at Rouen, which he studied closely.[8] Discarding Delteil's scenario, he wrote his own script, compressing the five months and twenty-nine sessions of the actual trial into what seems to be a single day of five separate interrogations. As David Bordwell writes,

Many of the issues in the trial—Jeanne's alleged witchcraft, the magical powers of her ring, the question of her virginity—are eliminated from the film so that Dreyer focused on the principal charge leveled against her: that her persistent belief in the sanctity of her visions and the holiness of her mission constituted a refusal to submit to the authority of the Church.[9]

The narrative thus constitutes a double struggle—between Jeanne and her captors (the English army and the French clergy) as well as within Jeanne herself. In the opening section, Jeanne is brought into the Rouen court for an initial interrogation by Cauchon, Loyseleur (Maurice Schutz), d'Estivet (André Berley), and others (including Michel Simon as Jean Lemaitre), with Warwick and his soldiers in the background. Returned to her cell, she is ridiculed by her jailers and then deceptively interrogated again. Her answers confound Cauchon and Beaupère (Ravet), who has taken over the questioning, and the judges take another tack—threatening her with torture and then tempting her with communion. When she turns their accusations back on them, they lead her out into the graveyard for execution. There she wavers, out of fear and a desire to aid France, and finally signs a recantation. Sentenced to life in prison, she is forced to have her head shaved and suddenly realizes that she has denied herself and her spiritual mission. Recalled, the judges reluctantly order her to be burned at the stake, and Massieu gives her a final communion. As Jeanne goes to her death in the public square, the crowd of French peasants becomes restless and is attacked by the English soldiers. Her spiritual mission turns out to have its political effect.

Nearly a full year after shooting first began, *La Passion de Jeanne d'Arc* was previewed in late April, 1928, first in Copenhagen and then in Paris, where it was hailed by the film critics and severely attacked by the Archbishop of the city.[10] According to Moussinac, under threat of censure, the Archbishop forced S.G.F. and A.C.E. (its distributor) to re-cut the film, without Dreyer's consent.[11] As a consequence, its exclusive run at the Salle Marivaux did not begin until 25 October 1928.[12] This censorship, along with the film's lack of commercial success, led to a broken contract and finally to an unfortunate lawsuit between Dreyer and S.G.F.

The cuts and changes . . . were so serious [wrote Moussinac] that the public could only see an annoying, Catholic film in which the Rouen tribunal had become almost sympathetic and the trial was reduced to a theological discussion without any dramatic advance.[13]

Ironically, this recut version was the one released generally in France, whereas the original version, apparently, was exported. The latter, for instance, seems to have been exhibited in New York in March, 1929, but it was also specially screened (without musical accompaniment) at the Studio des Ursulines, in May, 1929.[14] Bordwell concludes that the currently available, nearly complete prints of the film (2,200 of its original 2,400 meters) probably derive from several sources.[15] One print certainly comes from a negative of the exported version, which was given to the Cinémathèque française in 1951 (and from which Lo Duca, in 1952, made a "mutilated" sound version for Gaumont).[16] And my own research confirms Bordwell's findings—there are substantial differences between this print version (collected in several American film archives) and other versions, say, the print at the National Film Archive in London.[17] Like the differences in the various archive prints of *La Roue*, these discrepancies in *La Passion de Jeanne d'Arc* demand further study.

In 1964, Dreyer told Georges Sadoul that he conceived *La Passion de Jeanne d'Arc* as a documentary. It was a literal transcription of the trial record—"All the words pronounced [in the film] were drawn from history."[18] So keen was his interest in the authenticity of these words that his original intent had been to make a talking film.[19] But no French studio was equipped with sound recording systems in 1926-1927 (what made Dreyer think they were?), and none wanted to risk the investment, so he had to resort to other means of authenticity. One of his strategies was to turn the shooting process itself into a grueling reproduction of history. The cast and crew spent five months nearly living in the court and prison sets constructed in an empty Renault assembly shop next to the Billancourt studios and in the replica of medieval Rouen erected on the southern outskirts of Paris. The process of the trial was shot strictly in sequence, and the actors spoke only the words of the transcript (there was no improvisation).[20] All makeup was forbidden so that the new panchromatic film stock could record the confrontation of naked faces. "The elimination of makeup," wrote Moussinac, "gave to the faces a strange, awesome power which openly revealed the inner play of feelings and thoughts of the characters."[21] For the bloodletting sequence that follows Jeanne's fainting in the torture chamber, Dreyer even had a doctor actually draw blood. Falconetti, especially, gave herself up to Jeanne's dilemma, undergoing unusual physical and psychological hardship. In the climactic sequence of head-shaving, her agony was shared by the entire cast and crew.

In the silence of an operating room, in the pale light of the morning of the execution, Dreyer had Falconetti's head shaved. . . . We were moved as if the infamous mark were being made there, in reality. The electricians and technicians held their breaths and their eyes filled with tears. Falconetti wept real tears. Then the director slowly approached her, gathered up some of her tears in his fingers, and carried them to his lips.[22]

An assistant director summed up the whole shooting experience best—"We were not making a film, we were living Jeanne's drama, and we often wanted to intervene to save her."[23]

But *La Passion de Jeanne d'Arc* is more than the record of a pro-filmic drama, a documentary whose realism is the product of indexical signs. Much like Eisenstein's *Potemkin* (1925-1926), which Dreyer confessed to being haunted by in the early stages of his preparation, it is a discourse on history—in the form of a poeticized narrative of oppositions.[24] Much has been written about the operation of the narrative discourse in *La Passion de Jeanne d'Arc*. David Bordwell, in an early essay, argues that the film constitutes a unique distillation of the concrete and the abstract as well as an extraordinary "implosion" of internal contradictions (as opposed to the "explosion" of "realistic" space in Eisenstein's silent films).[25] Paul Willemen sees it, within the context of commercial narrative films, as possessing a "tentative emphasis . . . on the poetic function of discursive practice."[26] More precisely, Noël Burch singles out the fact that it breaks with the conventions of "illusionist representation . . . creating a filmic space which designates itself as a succession of shot-frames,

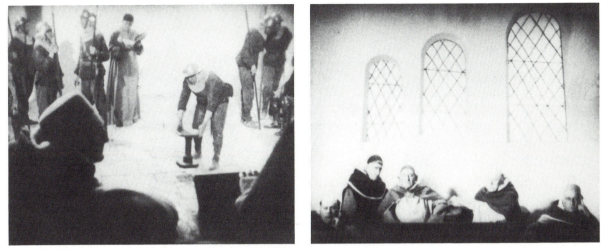

259. (left) A frame from the tracking shot that opens *La Passion de Jeanne d'Arc* (1928); (right) the judges before the white wall and irregular windows in the opening trial sequence

as a fictional and 'autonomous' chain."[27] In his recent book on Dreyer, Bordwell analyzes the film's contradictions—both spatial and representational—and its tendency to "bring space forward" through the strategies of emphasizing the face and interrogating the representation of tableaux.[28] At the risk of underestimating the film's willful gaps and dislocations, my own analysis situates *La Passion de Jeanne d'Arc* within the context of the French narrative avant-garde film practice and interprets its strategies and techniques within a reading of its narrative framework.

A complex of strategies is at work in the film, but all seem to function, more or less, for the purpose of compressing and intensifying the narrative. Their operation occurs at several levels—in the construction of a space-time continuum, in the orientation of the narrative flow, and in the systematic articulation of rhetorical figuring. The diegetic process they produce is unique, to say the least. The construction of space in *La Passion de Jeanne d'Arc* is strikingly antithetical to the conventions of the historical reconstruction film. "For the construction of the decors," Dreyer himself wrote, "I broke with tradition."[29] Instead of sumptuous tableaux, full of eye-opening period detail and teeming with movement (even as in *Napoléon*), here the images are stark and simple, to the point of abstraction. For the decors, Hermann Warm claimed, were modeled on medieval miniatures.

In a Parisian library I found the story of Jeanne d'Arc illustrated by a miniature-painter from the Middle Ages. The simple reproduction of the buildings, landscapes, and the people, the naïve lines and incorrect perspective provided ideas for the film's sets.[30]

And the starkness and simplicity of those sets were heightened by the absence of any color tinting in the release prints. In this, *La Passion de Jeanne d'Arc*, like *La Chute de la maison Usher* and *Thérèse Raquin*, stood out among the late 1920s French films for its exhibition in black-and-white.

Except for the Rouen exteriors, which are rarely seen in the film and are

260. Jeanne d'Arc (Falconetti)
in the opening trial sequence

never seen whole (much to the dismay of the producers), Dreyer reduced the
sets to the barest essentials. As Harry Alan Potamkin remarked, "There is no
extraneous detail in the film."[31] In the opening sequence, for instance, the
wall behind the judges' slightly raised platform is a flat white expanse with
three simple windows (without stained glass) whose height decreases rapidly
from right to left, but with no attempt to produce an illusion of perspective.
The opposite wall is quite similar (although the windows are unevenly scattered), and the floor is a simple design of light stone slabs. The only props
are the soldiers' spears, several large Bibles and links of chain, and a wooden
stool which one soldier places in the center of the floor for Jeanne. This space
is described initially in a single shot—a HAMS/LS tracking to the right,
parallel to the silhouettes of the judges (in the foreground) and to the soldiers
standing about in groups on the floor. The simplicity of this design—the same
neutral walls and floors—carries over into Jeanne's cell (which has a single
window and a simple cross on one wall) and even into the torture chamber
(where the torture instruments comprise no more than a revolving spiked
wheel, a hook and chain, and one table of smaller devices—although a raised
stool also momentarily looks threatening). Even the doorways and arches are
unornamented, and the doors are of dark wooden planks or bars (as in the
cell). The overall effect of this set design, in conjunction with the low camera
angles, the black-and-white film stock, and the consistently full, even lighting, is to foreground the characters, especially their faces, in what Peter Brook
has called a "delocalized space."[32] Their figures seem positioned in a dimen-
sionless, gravity-free world, a kind of void or limbo of whiteness. Consequently, the interrelationships among the characters and between them and
certain details of the decor are transformed into what Bordwell once wrote is
a "unique dialectic of specificity and generality, of [the] concrete and [the]
abstract," of the physical and the spiritual.[33]

    This is the story of Jeanne's passion, and she is at the center of the film as its primary subject. Yet, instead of privileging her with subjectivity, the discourse locates the subjective among several characters (through a variety of techniques) and only gradually restricts it to Jeanne. In the opening interrogation, for instance, there is a play of looks and POV shots which distributes the characters into opposite camps. The second shot of the sequence dollies in from a LAFS to a LAMS of Cauchon reading the charges and is followed by a LAMS of Massieu (crossing the frame from right background to left foreground), whom Jeanne then follows at a distance (both of them looking off to the left foreground). As the alternation shifts to shots of Cauchon and her, the subjective shifts from Massieu to Jeanne—and foreshadows his eventual alignment with her against Cauchon. When Warwick enters the room, he is linked to Loyseleur by an eyeline match cut; later, their conspiratorial bond (the French clergy fronts for the English army) is suggested again in a tilt-pan from one to the other.[34] As Cauchon begins the interrogation, the tension between the judges and Jeanne is articulated in a series of shock cuts and sudden movements. His question, "Who taught you [the Lord's Prayer]?" is followed by a one-second shot of his face that seems to stun her. The reverse happens after her reluctant answer, "My mother." Just before she responds to the question, "You pretend you are sent by God?" there is a two-second LAMCU of two judges leaning toward one another as a third stands up behind them (a quick dolly out pushes the shot toward vertigo). This technique seems an alternative to the abrupt changes in the scale of intertitle letters, which was then current in French films and was most developed by Soviet filmmakers.[35] When Jeanne says the English will be driven from France, except for those who die there, a soldier yells angrily in a shot that dollies in and out rapidly several times, from MCU to CU (like a rhythmic zoom). When she says that her mission is "the salvation of my soul," d'Estivet attacks her in the first outbreak of actual physical violence. In a brief moment of rapid cutting involving several unbalanced shots (LACUs of his mammoth face and ECUs of her frightened eyes), his pursing lips seem to explode in the spittle that spatters against her cheek. Finally, when one monk, de Houppeville, turns to defend her, a nod from Loyseleur leads to his expulsion (and possible execution) by the soldiers. But this brief action is observed from the point of view of an old white-haired judge—in close shots of Warwick, a messenger, Loyseleur, the soldiers' spear points filing out the door. When he tries to protest, Cauchon (in an ECU) grimly silences him. Oscillating between the omniscient and the subjective as well as between different characters' points of view and sometimes overlapping radically opposed subjective positions, this opening sequence scales down the most grandiose effects of a film such as *Napoléon* and integrates them into a series of profoundly intimate exchanges.

If the first interrogation is marked by a wide range of conflicts and by abrupt shifts in subjectivity, in which Jeanne is but one of several major participants, the rest are organized much more centrally around her. In the second interrogation, for instance, the spatial continuity and placement of the characters in Jeanne's cell is fractured and reorganized according to her spiritual condition. That reorganization is articulated in a system of looks in which the direction of her look becomes dominant. It is Loyseleur who first enters the cell, through the immense arch of a door, and whose look sets up the spatial arrangement of the characters. In the opening sequence, his inter-

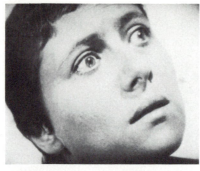

261. Selected shots from the
first interrogation sequence in
Jeanne's cell

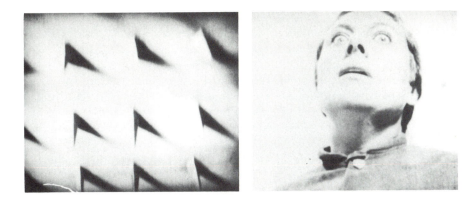

262. (left) The revolving
spiked wheel in the torture
chamber; (right) Jeanne
collapses in terror

vention between the English soldier and Jeanne had seemed to offer her support. Now he looks to the left (in CU)—cut to Jeanne gazing toward the left
foreground (as a forged letter from Charles VII is read to her); then he looks
off to the right—cut to Cauchon spying on his trickery. Eyeline match cutting
positions Loyseleur between Jeanne and Cauchon, as a deceptive mediator,
while a system of graphic matching aligns his look to the left with hers. After
the other judges enter the cell (from the right background) and position themselves looking toward the left foreground, Jeanne (in CU) turns to look toward
the right foreground. Now the eyeline match cutting of CUs sets up a clear
opposition between her on the left and Beaupère, who has taken over the
interrogation, on the right. As the questioning proceeds, she turns to look
toward the left (as if for advice), and there is a cut to Loyseleur also looking
toward the left foreground and nodding. She turns back to the right foreground, smiling and seemingly confident in her answers. The direction of her
look has now become the pivot point of the sequence and places Loyseleur
opposite the other judges as her friend and counselor, even though the direction of his look makes this problematic. It becomes even more problematic
when several FSs reveal him standing prominently behind Cauchon. Two different spaces are being constructed simultaneously—whereas one locates the
characters physically, the other distributes them psychologically or spiritually,
according to Jeanne's vision.

The climax of the interrogation comes in a series of disruptions and re-
orientations. Suddenly, when Jeanne is asked if she is already saved, Massieu
intervenes (in MS) from the left background and assumes the direction of her
look toward the right. But he backs off when Cauchon rises and angrily reprimands him. Asked finally if she is in a state of grace, Jeanne looks again
toward the left for advice, and the cut to Loyseleur now reveals him turned
slightly to the right (in CU), looking up in tight-lipped silence. His denial
and deception are shockingly clear. Yet when Jeanne turns to gaze straight
ahead and slightly upwards, an uncanny moment of peace seems to pass across
her open face. Several shots of the judges, and of Cauchon in particular, describe them looking straight at the camera and backing away stunned. Shock
follows shock as their looks mirror ours. As Cauchon and Loyseleur huddle
together (it is the latter who orders her to be tortured), Massieu speaks to

Jeanne at last, assuming the position off-frame left which Loyseleur had abandoned. In a double articulation, Jeanne's look—the sign of her soul—has triumphed over the judges' machinations and revealed the real distribution of the characters.

The other interrogation sequences are marked by different kinds of spatial continuity and discontinuity. In the torture chamber, Jeanne is fixed—as if paralyzed by fear—in a series of graphically matched CUs, whether shot from the left or right at a low angle or straight on. The interrogators, by contrast, are shown in a variety of deliberately mismatched and unbalanced shots—in LACUs, in profile, in straight-on CUs, in extreme LACUs, in ECUs of trembling lips, in tracking MSs that move swiftly from one to another, in MSs where one figure leaves the frame to the side as another enters from the bottom. Their frantic efforts burst and ebb around her like the surf pounding a lone rock outcropping. Only when she is brought before the revolving spiked wheel (linked by association to Cauchon's looming face), does Jeanne's position in space fragment, become multiple and contradictory—and she collapses.

In the fourth interrogation, just after the bloodletting, the spatial continuity is organized much like that of the first sequence in her cell, with several important differences. This sequence begins with Cauchon entering the cell (in a shot that frames him between her bedpost in the foreground and the immense arch over the doorway) to gaze at Jeanne sleeping. The scale of their faces indicates his initial dominance—a CU of him looking down toward the right foreground and a corresponding HAMCU of her looking up toward the left foreground, but from the lower right corner of the frame (as if trapped there by the heavy diagonal bedpost). Yet his position to her left implies that he, like Loyseleur, now may show some compassion for her. When Jeanne awakens, too weak to rise (her head, in CU now, remains tilted at a 30° angle), she requests of Cauchon that her body be buried in holy ground. He seems to agree, in CU, and even smiles; but then, in MS, he clumsily pulls away when her hand reaches up from the lower right corner of the frame to grasp weakly at him. Massieu and several other priests file in with a communion table, and Jeanne (in CU) turns to gaze off expectantly toward the right foreground. At the precise moment when she is about to receive the host, however, one of the judges enters and seems to take the priest's place, offering instead the recantation. What Jeanne had imagined (both left and right) to be areas of compassion and community abruptly turn threatening as Cauchon ironically tells her not to reject "the body of the Church." When she refuses once more to recant, Cauchon brusquely orders the host and communion table taken away. Her hands cover her tilted face, in CU, and she cries out, "I love God! I love him with all my heart!"

Suddenly (through intercutting), she seems surrounded by priests, shouting her down as "the devil's instrument." In a slow alternation of faces, she looks stunned at each one of them; her look shifts counterclockwise from the left and right foreground to the upper right and left, and the corners of the frame seem to function like the four points of a compass. Then, in a slightly closer shot (intercut with several fast 180° pans {to the right} across the assembled priests' blank faces), she stares off to the left foreground and softly, but defiantly, turns the charge back upon them—"It's you who have been sent to make me suffer." The alternation of faces returns with the same counterclock-

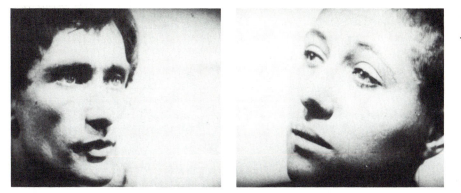

263. (left) Massieu (Antonin Artaud); (right) Jeanne d'Arc (Falconetti)

wise movement of her look, but now her eyes are glistening through her tears; and, in quick shots, the priests fall back astonished. In an abrupt FS track, Cauchon orders her execution; in another FS, the priests leave the room, diminished in scale (in the lower left corner of the frame); and the sequence ends with a CU of Jeanne sobbing almost hysterically. Cauchon may control the narrative at this point, but Jeanne's centrality to the spatial continuity of the sequence suggests that her spirit remains unbroken and that she will ultimately triumph.

Finally, in the sequence where Jeanne denies her recantation, all the framing and editing patterns, which before had operated disruptively, "repair" or "heal" the film's spatial continuity, with Jeanne securely positioned at its center. When Cauchon enters Jeanne's cell for the last time, the scale of their faces is now reversed in a simple alternation of eyeline matches—in CU, she looks off toward the right foreground while he looks off to the left, from the lower right corner of an otherwise empty frame. "So you believe you are a messenger from God?" he says almost meekly. Several of the other judges, in CU, assume Cauchon's position, their faces now subdued and even sorrowful; then all of them turn and file out to the right through the arching cell door. Jeanne calls back Massieu, however, and her look to the left repositions him in the space of psychological and spiritual support. In another simple alternation of eyeline matches, Massieu questions her sincerely, seriously, trying to understand her spiritual mission. Her eyes radiant through her tears, Jeanne finds her answer: "And the great victory?" "It will be my martyrdom." "And your deliverance?" "Death." In a sense, the whole film has been working toward this simple, almost naked, confession and communion of faces. The spatial discontinuities of the previous sequences have functioned primarily to set it off as the climax of Jeanne's spiritual journey. And the uncanny intensity both Artaud and Falconetti bring to their characters makes their confrontation a uniquely privileged moment. Pierre Audard said it well: "[Falconetti and Artaud] are immobile figures at the center of things, a look fixed on an invisible point, a hand stretched out toward the unknown."[36]

Jeanne's passion, however, is articulated further in an important series of metonymic and metaphorical associations which help bring the film to closure.[37] Several patterns of rhetorical figuring, for instance, distribute the char-

495

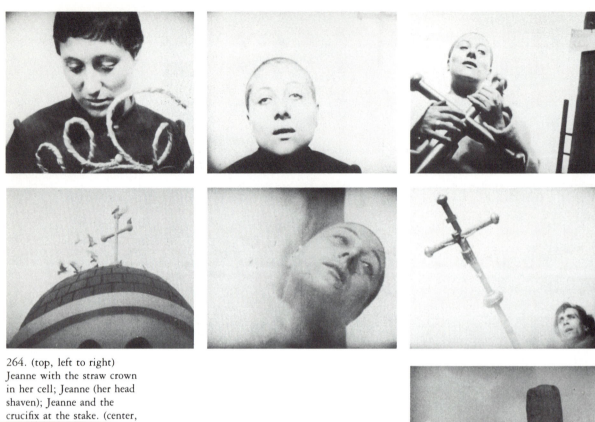

264. (top, left to right)
Jeanne with the straw crown
in her cell; Jeanne (her head
shaven); Jeanne and the
crucifix at the stake. (center,
left to right) The church
dome cross; Jeanne yearns
toward . . . the crucifix that
Massieu holds up to her.
(bottom) The final image of
the cross and stake at the end
of *La Passion de Jeanne d'Arc*

acters into opposite camps. Most of the priests, throughout, are marked by
semicircular, close-fitting caps. Those without caps are conspicuously bald,
and the shiny domes of their heads, fringed with hair, produce a similar effect.
This semicircular shape is echoed in the arching doorways of the church buildings which repeatedly frame the priests' entrances and exits. Together, these
images become a material sign of the Church itself as an institution, a sign
which designates its representatives and confers on them the illusion of power.
The pattern culminates in the final sequence, linking the domes of the church
with the wall towers from which, on Warwick's command, maces and other
weapons are dropped to the soldiers. By contrast, Jeanne, as well as Massieu,
is "unadorned." Instead, she is marked, at one point, by a simple cord-work
crown and, especially, by the sign of the cross. The cross first appears in her
cell as a faint shadow cast by the window bars, and Loyseleur treads on it as

496

265. (top, left to right) Jeanne's feet bound in chains; the Bible bound in chains; Warwick in the opening trial sequence. (center, left to right) Jeanne's bound feet as she goes to the stake; the link chain that separates the peasants and townspeople from the square and stake; warwick and his soldiers at the execution. (bottom, left to right) The judges behind bars at the execution; a mace is dropped from the tower

he comes to play Judas to her. It reappears as a rough wooden frame beside the doorway when she enters the torture chamber and then as a simple cross on the cell wall after she has denied the recantation and had her head shaved. When she reaches the stake, the executioner presents her with a smoothly carved dark crucifix; while around a cross topping the highest church dome in the square, a flock of doves settles and then (in a progression of shots) flies off higher and higher into the sky.[38] As Jeanne presses the crucifix to her bosom in prayer, there is a cross-cut to a baby suckling at the breast of a peasant woman in the crowd. The earthly sustenance of one image parallels the spiritual regeneration of the other. As the fire begins to engulf her, Massieu holds up the crucifix through the smoke so Jeanne may gaze on it one last time. Thus newly charged with meaning, the unadorned "risen" cross must be part of the film's final image—while the top of the blackened stake smoulders in the foreground, in the background (separated from the church on which it sits) a cross stands out gleaming bone white.

Another pattern of rhetorical figuring binds protagonist to antagonist as well as forges a link between the beginning and ending of the film. Our first image of Jeanne is a tracking HAMCU of her feet bound together by a single heavy chain. Four shots later, a parallel tracking HACU introduces the Bible on which she will "swear to tell the truth" it, too, is weighted down with a chain. When Warwick appears, he is wearing a similar strand of chain draped smartly around his shoulders, like a decorative remnant of chain mail. Even before the interrogation reveals his power and control, the chain images suggest concisely who and what is oppressed by whom. At the beginning of the final sequence of execution, again Jeanne is introduced in a tracking CU of her bound feet descending a few steps. Now her movement is paralleled by a shot of running peasants and townspeople, across the space of which a length of chain (hastily put up by the soldiers) hangs prominently in the foreground, creating a barrier or enclosure. Above the action, Warwick sits rigidly, like a gang warlord, fingering his long loose chain (behind him his soldiers form a phalanx of helmets). Even the once powerful priests now sit on a platform behind bars, protected from the populace, but also seemingly trapped by their own illusory decision-making. When Warwick orders weapons for his soldiers, the maces dropped from the towers (described in quick pendulumlike in-and-out camera movements) neatly condense the oppressive images of chain and spiked wheel. From this condition of enchaining or being chained, Jeanne's death by fire acts as a form of release. Or does it?

As the narrative of Jeanne's spiritual journey nears its climax, it engenders a second parallel narrative which pits Warwick's army against the French peasants and townspeople. The relationship between the one narrative and the other is a paradoxical one, for they are resolved ambiguously, unlike the narrative of Eisenstein's *Potemkin*, which apparently so influenced Dreyer at the time. The peasants make their first appearance in the film during the cemetery sequence, where they are held back by Warwick's soldiers. After Jeanne recants and is led away, one man in the crowd yells out, "Long live Jeanne!" For this political heresy, several soldiers seize him, tie his hands behind his back, and toss him into a pond. Their action, however, is described in a single FS reflected upside down on the water's surface. Hence, the shock is doubled by this body that seems to break the smooth plane of both water and frame. From this brutal, disruptive dispatch, the film cuts to snips of Jeanne's hair falling on the cell floor. Ironically, this one peasant's death is juxtaposed to her "salvation." And the irony seems to be sustained through a further juxtaposition, alternating shots of Jeanne's head being shaved (do the priests think they can rob her, like Samson, of her power so easily?) and of the peasants and townspeople entertaining themselves outside the town walls. Yet the long tracking shots that describe this spectacle reveal a grotesquerie of contorted mimes, acrobats, sword-swallowers, and clowns on display. This festive make-believe agony, this mockery of torture, throws Jeanne's submission and suffering into relief.[39] As she watches the barber sweep her hair up into a dust pan and then with it her cord-work crown, she suddenly realizes that in choosing to recant, in choosing life, she has been shorn of grace. Like the peasants, she, too, has been turned into a grotesque. By choosing death

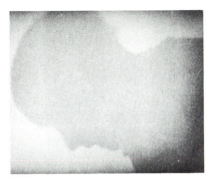

266. Jeanne's immolation and
transubstantiation

and martyrdom now, she will take their place in the square and enact a different kind of spectacle.

That spectacle literally ignites the political conflict of the second parallel
narrative. Throughout this final sequence, Jeanne's martyrdom functions as a
fixed point of reference. As she catches fire, her body is fragmented, obscured,
and finally obliterated. The spectacle of her body being broken is transformed
into a sacrificial offering, an emblem enflaming the people. The shock waves
emanating from this transformation reverse the vector of forces which climaxed
the torture chamber sequence, and rebellion breaks out. Preceded by a band
of soldiers, the peasants burst into the town in several HA upside-down shots
that tilt 120° or more to follow them through a high gate. These disruptive
shots seem to repeat, in reverse and in multiple, the earlier shot of the soldiers
tossing the bound peasant into the pond. As the cross-cutting associates the
crowd (especially the women) more and more closely with Jeanne's suffering
at the stake, again one of the peasants cries out, "You have burned a saint!"
Suddenly, Warwick orders his soldiers to attack, and the conflagration explodes into mass violence. In CUs (e.g., a stone breaking a church window,
an arm throwing a spear, the feet of a young child running up to its mother
lying dead on the cobblestones), in HA and LA shots (e.g., leaping figures
pursued by others flailing maces), in an editing rhythm that approaches rapid
montage, the soldiers brutally overpower the peasants and push them out of
the town. There, spread over a hillside, topped by a gibbeted figure in the
distance, they watch the drawbridge rise up, cutting them off as if exiled.
The rebellion fails. Having broken Jeanne's body, Warwick's army besieges
the "body" of the people. They, too, are broken and driven from the place of
her transubstantiation, now a perversion of paradise. Thus, despite Jeanne's
act of sacrifice and transcendence, the forces of oppression and death still
govern the world.

For Dreyer, *La Passion de Jeanne d'Arc* was a "hymn to the triumph of the
soul over life."[40] Jeanne's vision of God leads her to self-fulfillment; her love
consumes and transforms her. Thus does she become the first of Dreyer's possessed, inspired, daemonic figures. Yet, as the narrative of an insurgency, the
film is unusually bleak and straightforward, especially compared to its "sister"
historical reconstruction films—Bernard's *Le Miracle des loups* and *Joueur d'échecs*
or even Gastyne's *La Merveilleuse Vie de Jeanne d'Arc*. Here, the conflicts divid-

267. (left to right) The peasants rush into the town through the gate; the soldiers attack the peasants and townspeople; the peasants and townspeople are driven outside the town walls at the end of *La Passion de Jeanne d'Arc*

ing the characters remain unresolved through the ideological convention of French suffering and sacrifice. Instead, Jeanne's catching fire delineates more sharply the friction between nations, classes, and political groups. Furthermore, as the story of a woman whose body and soul are besieged by men, for the purpose of submission and even erasure, *La Passion de Jeanne d'Arc* operates as a symbolic narrative par excellence.[41] Is Jeanne's death by fire the proper end for the woman who refuses to submit? Such a representation of the position of women, in relation to men, may be read as the culmination of a long line of French narrative avant-garde films that includes Delluc's *Fièvre*, Gance's *La Roue*, Dulac's *La Souriante Madame Beudet*, Epstein's *Coeur fidèle*, L'Herbier's *L'Inhumaine*, Kirsanoff's *Menilmontant*, Dulac's *L'Invitation au voyage*, and Epstein's *La Glace à trois faces* and *La Chute de la maison Usher*.

Finis Terrae and *Gardiens de phare*

The transformation that concludes *La Chute de la maison Usher*—the destruction of the chateau and Roderick's release into the real world—parallels a change in Jean Epstein's own life and career as a filmmaker. Faced with the demise of his own production company, disgusted with the falseness of studio filmmaking, and disappointed by the slow technical development of the French film industry, Epstein left Paris, in the early summer of 1928, for Land's End, the most westward reaches of Brittany jutting into the Atlantic.[1] This break, this seeming retreat, was actually both a renewal and a means of advance. Not only did it allow him to renew his experience of spaces for which he had long nurtured a love, but it returned him to the origins of his own filmmaking, in fictionalized documentary.[2] Rather than abandon the theory and practice he had developed and refined, particularly in his previous three films, he extended it into new territory. Simply put, Epstein placed his vision and his cinematographic machine in the service of an unusual community of people and the natural world in which they lived. The result, after he returned to Paris in late autumn, was *Finis Terrae* (1929), a film unlike any he had done before. Film critics praised the new work highly, when it inaugurated the specialized cinema, L'Oeil de Paris (in May, 1929), as well as later when it opened a series of French films in London (in October, 1929).[3] But since then, Epstein's film has suffered an unjust neglect.

"I believe," wrote Epstein in announcing the film, "that we must concern

500

ourselves, more and more, with such natural actors, in all countries, in all classes of society, in all professions; that we must use natural decors, true scenarios, authentic spaces."[4] In one sense, then, *Finis Terrae* represents a culmination of the realist aesthetics articulated by Antoine, Delluc, and others ten years before. Its subject was discovered in the preparatory stages of production, and that discovery determined, to an extent, its mode of production. Specifically, the scenario developed out of several exploratory voyages that Epstein took to the islands of Bannec and Balanec, west of Ouessant, islands that were inhabited only in the summer months by small teams of kelp-gatherers. And it was written in collaboration with the islanders themselves, drawing on one particular story in their oral tradition.[5] Then Epstein and his miniscule crew (including Joseph Barth, Joseph Kottula, and Louis Née) were able to execute the shooting entirely on the islands and the sea of Iroise.[6] There were no constructed sets; and all but two or three brief sequences (the interiors of an island hut and a village house) were filmed in the open air, at the mercy of the elements. Most important of all, Epstein refused to import any professional actors for his cast. All were selected from among the inhabitants of Ouessant; they used no makeup and wore their own clothes as costumes.[7] The two central characters, in fact, were played by young men who had never even seen a film before and whose families, for a while, actually believed they had been kidnapped and sold to the gypsies or to the devil.[8] But they and their fellow islanders adapted quickly to Epstein's few directions and gave performances of a simplicity and naturalness that distinguished *Finis Terrae* from most other films of the period.

The story *Finis Terrae* enacts is a simple one, a *fait divers* of sorts, yet one that sums up a good deal about the islanders' culture. On the island of Bannec, a dispute erupts between two young men when one accidentally breaks a bottle of wine and the other accuses him of stealing his knife. Ambroise has cut his thumb on a glass fragment and soon falls ill, though he keeps the injury to himself; when he stops working, Jean-Marie and the other two men on the island, out of anger, ignore him. Eventually, Jean-Marie finds his knife on the beach, recognizes his friend's infection, and sets out with him for Ouessant in a small sailboat, despite an unusually becalmed sea. On Ouessant, meanwhile, a lighthouse-keeper notices the lack of activity on Bannec; and the villagers, particularly the young men's mothers, prompt the local doctor, Lesenin, and several sailors to venture out in a rowboat to find out what is wrong. A dense fog materializes at sea, but the two boats miraculously find one another, and Lesenin immediately lances Ambroise's wound. Through the night, the two mothers keep vigil on the rocks above the harbor cove; and at dawn, having outlasted a squall, the overcrowded rowboat struggles back to Ouessant. The men are safe; the families reconciled.

The subject—"this mystery of men devoted to a land that is nothing but rock, to a sea that is nothing but foam, to a harsh and perilous task"—and the simplicity and directness with which it is presented may remind one superficially of Robert Flaherty's early documentaries, especially *Man of Aran* (1933), which Epstein's film predates by several years.[9] But *Finis Terrae* is actually closer to several Soviet films, such as Kuleshov's *Dura Lux* (1926) and Pudovkin's *Mother* (1926), as well as Dreyer's *La Passion de Jeanne d'Arc*, all of which Epstein probably saw just before leaving Paris for the islands off Brit-

268. The kelp burning in
Finis Terrae (1929)

tany.[10] Although emphasizing the factual nature, the authenticity, of his film, Epstein also insisted that it was a psychological documentary. It focused on "the material and spiritual reality of the island life," including the characters' subjective experience of their interaction with their environment.[11] Its mode of representation employs techniques quite common to the narrative avant-garde film practice—blurred and distorted shots, extreme camera angles, rapid montage, unusual tracking shots—but with much more restraint than in Epstein's previous films. In fact, strangely enough, the most prominent, the most consistently used of these techniques is slow motion. Instead of recording certain sequences at speeds three to six times the norm, as in *Usher*, here Epstein consistently had the camera overcranked just slightly, from thirty to forty frames per second. Even this slightly slowed motion was "magical" for him—"sincere expressions and natural gestures were thus diverted, singled out, prolonged, 'held,' and stylized."[12] This concept may now sound naïve, but Epstein did not apply it naïvely. Slow motion described not only the actions of the central characters but also the dynamic flux of nature around them, especially the movement of the sea. The technique seemed to suggest, then, an unusual correspondence, an underlying harmony, between men and nature. For Epstein, the film became the work of a Magus.

The magical power that Epstein and his camera brought to the people of these islands, however, is not the only form of magic in the film. If its story is simple, the telling is hardly so. Its mystery is articulated in the strange transformations that mark the structure of the narrative as well as in the system of parallels and oppositions that mark the discourse.

The film seems to open conventionally enough, with a series of descriptive

269. Jean-Marie and
Ambroise confront one
another in the opening
sequence of *Finis Terrae*

shots of a seacoast landscape and an intertitle that identifies Bannec and then
mentions two teams of two men each gathering kelp there during the summer.
Abruptly, the focus shifts to two of them, one of whom sends the other off to
get their last bottle of wine, and (within a little more than a dozen shots, half
of them involving fast tracks or dollies, as they try to pass the bottle on the
run) the accident occurs that determines the rest of the narrative.[13] Unlike the
pattern of Epstein's earlier films, here the sudden rupture and resultant discord
are strangely subsumed in the rest of the film's first reel. Two more intertitles
appear, but they describe the kelp-gathering process and the lack of water on
the island as if the accident had never happened. Furthermore, the conflict
between the two young men almost subsides in descriptive sequences of the
teams first burning the kelp in piles (only once do they raise their fists at one
another) and then separately eating potatoes and bread for supper. The film
seems to have turned into a documentary, and the accident is forgotten or
masked over in the daily round of their lives. Yet something faintly disturbing
remains, particularly in a number of isolated CUs of simple objects. There is
the distant association between a shot of the wine soaking into the sand and
the ECU of blood on Ambroise's thumb. There is also a menacing miniature
still life—the ECU of a glass fragment framing a tiny daisy among the rocks.
Finally, there is a series of CUs intercut, much like a musical motif (free of
POV shots) within the sequence of eating—an empty wooden bowl, that once
held the potatoes, is caught in the incoming tide, overturned, and submerged.
What kind of threat does this elusive pattern of rhetorical figuring portend,
these disappearances into the ground or underwater that are both seen and
unseen? And, what should we make of this rhetorical parallel to the "submerging" of the narrative?

At the beginning of the second reel, suddenly, time becomes specific—it is
Friday, 16 August (the date is crossed off a calendar)——and the two men are
finally identified in separate brief sequences. Yet, except for a single remark
on Ambroise's loss of strength in one arm, the intertitles as well as the images
in the next several sequences continue to foreground the activity of gathering

503

and drying the kelp. Only in the evening, ironically, during the moment of relaxation, does the conflict between the two resume. Jean-Marie comes upon Ambroise (who is now experiencing some pain) soaking his hand in the water bucket and yells at him for using the drinking water so foolishly. Ambroise gets a small shallow pan for his wound, and an echo of the earlier wooden bowl emerges:

CU of Ambroise's hand in the pan water.
LS of the sea surf (slow motion).
CU of the pan nearly empty of water (its bottom is dirty and rough).

In this conjunction of the pure and the contaminated, of movement and stillness, of presence and absence, the tension between a sense of harmony and menace increases.

The next day Ambroise, now half-delirious from the infection, refuses to work; and his companion quits him to work for Jean-Marie. While the intertitles chronicle the companion's disgust with his "laziness" and the men's concern over the dangerously low level of drinking water (telling their side of the story), the images shift into another mode altogether, focusing on Ambroise. As he sits alone like a maddened animal shivering in the hut, the discourse slowly turns into a subjective experience of his hallucinations. The sequence alternates MSs and MCUs of him with shots of the sea and coastal rocks, as the latter change and multiply into shots of his diseased arm, a lighthouse (from which a ring of light seems to expand and contract repeatedly, filling and then fading from the image), clouds blotting out the sun, the incoming surf, Jean-Marie's face (upside down), bottle fragments in the rocks, a clenched fist. These are edited into a brief sequence of rapid montage—the shot lengths based musically on units of half seconds—that culminates in three quick jump-cut shots of Ambroise's hand shaking and clutching and then a series of swaying and tilting shots that match cut his movement to the apparent animation of the lighthouse. Despite its apparent subjectivity, there is something about the rigorously organized rhythm and plasticity of this sequence, its "laconic dryness," to use Philippe Haudiquet's phrase, that keeps us at a distance from Ambroise's experience.[14] Again the discourse seems intent on drawing together disparate images (now even more spatially and temporally discontinuous), but this time even the sense of harmony of the associative parallels becomes threatening. The imagined distant object of appeal—the lighthouse as a secular guardian of perception and protection—turns into a projected image that doubles and mirrors the collapsing self.[15]

Initially, these shifts and discontinuities that mark the first third of *Finis Terrae* seem puzzling. One wonders if they are calling attention to the narrative process itself in order to establish a reflexive play on narration similar to that which characterized *La Glace à trois faces*. But the shift from Bannec to Ouessant—just as the narrative conflict on the island approaches a climax (Ambroise tries to set off alone in a boat and collapses on the beach while the others silently pass him by to eat their lunch)—suggests something else. In this sudden break lies an important contiguity. The first shot of Ouessant includes a church spire in the distance (revealed in a slight boom camera movement), and the second depicts its tolling bell (in slow motion). Repeated several times in the sequence, the bell, of course, functions to bring the villagers together. But it also seems to respond, across the great expanse of sea (emphasized in an intertitle), to Ambroise's distress. It is as if his nightmare vision of the lighthouse has been transformed, in the ellipsis, into the keeper's sight (the hallucination is even echoed in a swaying dolly LS of the lighthouse) and then the sound of the bell. The conjunction resembles the storm's rising and Madeleine's awakening (which also sets off a tolling bell), in *Usher*, in order to save Roderick from a condition of which his friend is ignorant. In the ambiguously charged natural world of the island, the men's isolation, made dangerous by their silence and their blind disregard for one another, is countered miraculously by a sense of community, communication, and mutual concern on Ouessant. The horrors of solitude, as Pierre Leprohon puts it, are answered by the solidarity of the people.[16] But in its narrative juxtaposition, is not the film also suggesting that subjectivity, and the concept of the individual, literally depends, for its health and very existence, on this larger community? In *Finis Terrae*, then, the conjunction of the subjective and the omniscient that Epstein had postulated nearly ten years before in *Bonjour Cinema* seems to assume a new, more socially determined articulation.

From this point on in the film, the narrative gells into a long continuous series of alternating sequences. The resolution of the conflict between Jean-Marie and Ambroise is quickly resolved and subordinated to the focus on Jean-Marie and Lesenin as, simultaneously, they depart from their separate islands and edge out upon the sea toward one another. The climax of their encounter is one of the simplest and most effective passages in any of Epstein's films. Its articulation depends on a series of sub-sequences, each of which is marked by repetition and a different set of alternations. Shots of Jean-Marie and Ambroise become slightly blurred, and a HALS reveals white fog pools floating on the sea. Then a number of quick tracking shots (alternating to the right and left) of rocky outcroppings in the fog heighten the sense of danger, and an ELS reveals the sailboat, surrounded by fog, coming forward in the distance. The sequence shifts to Lesenin's rowboat where a montage of MSs and MCUs describes all four men rowing while they pass around a jug of water. These quick shots (lasting about two seconds each) are match-cut to the forward and backward movement of the men and their oars within the frame. While the rhythm heightens the suspense, it also describes the smoothness of their teamwork and the ease with which they spell one another. As a LS of the rowboat includes a speck on the horizon ahead, the sequence shifts again to an alternation based on camera angle and distance. A LAMS of Jean-Marie, now rowing and turning to look off to the right foreground, is intercut with a HALS of the rowboat coming forward slowly (from the right) across the foggy sea surface. The recognition comes in a marvelous series of shots that pushes this juxtaposition to the extreme and then collapses it.

MCU of Jean-Marie looking off (to the right foreground) and calling.
LS of the rowboat, now in clear view, coming forward.
LAECU of Jean-Marie's hands cupped at his open mouth.
LAMCU of a sailor and Lesenin, the latter pointing off to the left.
LAECU of Jean-Marie's hands cupped at his open mouth.
HAELS of the rowboat (frame right) moving slowly to the left; the sailboat (frame left) becomes faintly visible in the fog.
LAECU of Jean-Marie's hands cupped at his open mouth.

HAELS of the boats; the rowboat (frame right) continues to move to the left.
CU (blurred) of the doctor calling and then listening.
LAECU of Jean-Marie calling.
CU of the doctor nodding, as if in reply and recognition.
FS of Jean-Marie in the sailboat, standing and waving his arms.
FS of Lesenin in the rowboat, standing and waving his arms.

Across the expanse of space—and the juxtaposition between shots—the intimation of sound mediates, reducing difference to sameness, distance to closeness.[17] The sequence both echoes and transforms the sequence of Ambroise's desperate hallucination on Bannec. The doubled image of one sequence parallels the doubled image of the other, but now ship mirrors ship and man mirrors man in a common effort. Discord and menace have turned into a vision of mysterious harmony.

The last reel of *Finis Terrae* closes off in a diminuendo that seems to confirm this miracle. The final images edge into peaceful tableaux. There is a FS of a hallway framing the room into which Ambroise is carried and where he sleeps, with Jean-Marie dozing beside him. And then a LS of a doorway, where the women gather quietly, protectively, in silhouette, to frame the kitchen area where Lesenin pauses to eat and rest. But his rest is interrupted, in a curious narrative shift. A boy comes for the doctor—an old man is ill on the other end of the island—and they go off together. In the final shot, they are walking up and over a grassy hill, silhouetted (in LALS) against a huge white sky. This emphasis on Lesenin at the end suggests that, in this secular parable of near-death and resurrection, the doctor plays a crucial mediating role. As a figure of knowledge, power, and *caritas*, he exercises a measure of control over nature and its "illnesses" and functions as a benevolent "father" who sacrifices himself for the women (defined principally as mothers) and the young men (who become little more than children). Is there something of Louis Pasteur, the subject of Epstein's first film, in this model modern hero?[18] And does Epstein see his own work as a filmmaker within the islanders' culture as analogous to the doctor's—a mediation, in the face of sickness and death, that reveals, in Epstein's own words, "the angel in man like the butterfly in the chrysalis"?[19]

Yet this celebration of the doctor is not entirely persuasive. For the optimistic conclusion to *Finis Terrae* rests ultimately on the benevolence of the sea. The mothers' night vigil displaces the men's struggles at sea in squall conditions. Foggy shots of the turbulent surf alternate with shots of the two women huddled together under a single shawl on the harbor cove's rockface (Ambroise's mother even holds her right arm much as her son held his earlier). The juxtaposition seems to favor the mothers when shots of the slowly revolving lighthouse beacon (echoing Ambroise's hallucinations) are associated with them. But the sequence concludes with mesmerizing ominousness—magnificent slow-motion shots of huge waves crashing over the coastal rocks. The miraculous emergence of the overcrowded rowboat in the dawn thus both preserves the rhetorical emphasis of the recognition scene and seems to answer the patterns of "submerging" that were articulated in the early sequences of the film. But the "dark side" of nature's mystery—and man's—merely seems in momentary abeyance. In the others of Epstein's cycle of films set in Brit-

270. The mothers await their sons near the end of *Finis terrae*

tany—*Mor-Vran* (1930), *L'Or des mers* (1932), and *Le Tempestaire* (1947)—the darkness of that mystery becomes more evident and almost overpowering.

Just as *Finis Terrae* was premiering at the L'Oeil de Paris, a second film set in Brittany was nearing completion—Jean Grémillon's second feature film, *Gardiens de phare* (1929). Although similar to Epstein's film in subject and style, *Gardiens de phare* was very different in origin and production. The scenario was a literary adaptation, drawn from an existing play by Autier and Cloquemont, a successful work in the Grand Guignol repertory.[20] That Jacques Feyder did the adaptation (and may have intended to direct it himself, before he left to work in Hollywood) probably helped secure the film's independent financing. Despite Grémillon's background in documentary filmmaking, much of this film was shot, during the winter and spring of 1929, in Gaumont's Paris studio in simple decors designed by André Barsacq.[21] Exteriors were shot around Saint-Guénolé on the Penmarch Peninsula in Brittany, probably in the late summer of 1928 but perhaps also in the early summer of 1929 (sources are unclear about this).[22] Finally, the production enlisted a professional cast to perform the major roles. When *Gardiens de phare* was ready for release, through Films Armor, it premiered at the Ciné Max-Linder, in late September, 1929. *Tout-Cinéma* (1930) suggests that the film may have been sonorized for its exhibition, but no other reference source confirms this.[23] In any case, the only copies of the film that I have seen are silent.[24]

Much like *Finis Terrae*, *Gardiens de phare* narrates a story of illness on a remote island. Instead of the former's optimistic resolution, however, it ends in a brutal, tragic death. The film opens as Yvon (Geymond Vital) and his father (Fromet) leave the mainland for a month-long stay at the lighthouse on Saint-Guénolé. Yvon has just been wed to Marie (Gênica Athanasiou) and is reluctant to leave his young wife with her mother (Mme. Fontan). That day, a neighbor by the name of Old François takes his dog to the local veterinarian and discovers it has rabies. At the lighthouse, Yvon is bothered by a wound on his right arm and tells his father that several days before, as he and Marie

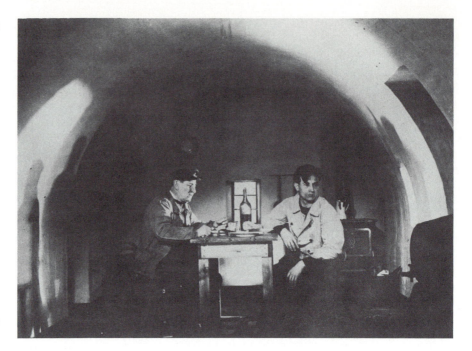

271. Yvon (Geymond Vital) and his father (Fromet) at the lighthouse table in *Gardiens de phare* (1929)

were walking among the sand dunes, François's dog attacked them and bit him. Drowsy but unable to eat or sleep, Yvon stands watch the first night and fantasizes a reunion with Marie. The next day he is irritable and seems ill, but he refuses to let his father send a distress signal. Several days later, the dog is dead, and Marie and her mother learn of the rabies threat. A storm has come up, making any rescue impossible; and that evening, as a ship flounders off the coast, Yvon attacks his father before they can ignite the lighthouse beacon. In their struggle, Yvon falls to his death.

Although slightly longer than *Finis Terrae, Gardiens de phare* seems shorter and more consistently paced. In part, that comes from the scenario's tight dramatic structure which, quite unlike Grémillon's first film, *Maldone*, moves relentlessly toward the tragic climax. But its effectiveness also depends on shifts and contrasts in the circulation of knowledge among the characters and the spectator. The dog, for instance, first emerges from beneath a tarp in Old François's cart, as Marie and her mother return home after Yvon's departure. Its snarling presence is enigmatic until we (and François) are told it is rabid. So, when Yvon tells his father of the past attack, we know his danger (as they do not) and we worry even more over their growing suspicions. But, because Marie, too, has seen the dog, we half expect and hope that somehow she will be informed of its rabidness in time. To our discomfort, however, the narrative keeps her ignorant until the last minutes of the film. Father and son gradually come to realize what we already know, and the film climaxes in a number of ironic twists. The battered ship appears, but again we alone are informed of its presence. Marie and her mother read the village mayor's order to examine all dog-attack victims (actually, a visiting pastor reads the announcement from

508

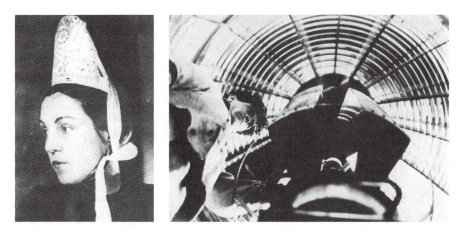

272. (left) Gênica Athanasiou
as Marie in *Gardiens de phare*

273. (right) Yvon checks the
lighthouse beacon

a local newspaper), and they hasten to the cottage window, aghast to see the lighthouse beacon unlit. Yvon's father suddenly hears the ship's distress signal, but he is attacked before he can do anything about it. And when the beacon finally comes on, it resolves the narrative with a contradictory signal. The father realizes that he has killed his son. Marie and her mother rejoice, thinking that all is well at the lighthouse. Appalled by this cruelly ironic gap, we suddenly discover that even we do not know, with certainty, what has happened to the ship. In this stunning, deftly crafted denouement, knowledge and communication break down irreparably.

The irony is all the more apparent because of Georges Périnal's marvelous cinematography in the film.[25] The interiors of the cottage are deeply shadowed and strongly side-lit (as if from the hearth fire); those of the lighthouse focus on the glass-enclosed beacon (which sometimes deforms the figures) and especially the two circular rooms below it, connected by spiral stairs and lit either by the revolving lamp (through the shadow of its blades) or by the sunlight falling in a pointillist pattern on the walls. Although shot mostly within the range of FS to CU, there is a strong sense of deep space to these interior images. Low angle shots abound, sometimes interspersed with high angle shots, and the frame often contains an object or part of a figure in focus in the foreground with an integral connection to something or someone in focus in the background. The bars of the spiral stairs are particularly prominent toward the end, in the entrapment of both Yvon and his father. This deep space is even more pronounced in the exterior sequences. The opening, in fact, establishes the concept almost immediately. After several LSs and ELSs describing the rocky coast and village, a panning LS of a wave breaking into white foam on the beach cuts to an enigmatic CU of a hand waving a white handkerchief. After another panning LS, the contrast of long and close shots is integrated within the frame of three striking shots that reveal indirectly what is happening.

MS/ELS of an arm (right foreground) waving a handkerchief toward a land mass (left background.

CU/ELS of the back of a woman's head (frame left) as she waves her arm (frame right); as the arm falls, it reveals a departing sailboat and dinghy (right background).

FS/ELS of a sail (frame left) and a man waving his arm (frame right) toward a land mass (center background); the dinghy is visible behind the stern of the sailboat.

LAMS of two women looking off to the left foreground; the younger one on the left waves.

This pattern is repeated when Yvon and his father reach the lighthouse, but now the alternation includes LA shots of the island rock and the stairs to the lighthouse as well as HA shots of the dinghy approaching a rock cove. As the two men climb the stairs, Yvon pauses to look out at the departing sailboat (in CU/ELS) and then joins his father (in a HAMS/LS and a reverse LALS). Thereafter, in the lighthouse sequences, these extreme camera angles help articulate not only Yvon's delirium but his father's fear as well as the conflict that engulfs them.

Although *Gardiens de phare* lacks the complex patterns of rhetorical figuring that characterize Epstein's and others' films, it does employ what Henri Agel has called leitmotifs in a kind of musical composition.[26] Perhaps the most important of these is the recurrence of the rabid dog. Its introduction—popping up almost like a puppet, in two dolly CUs—disrupts the smooth flow of the opening sequences, and its blackness contrasts sharply, threateningly, with the whiteness of the waving handkerchief. In Yvon's story to his father, the dog is again disruptive—a FS of the couple sitting quietly on a sand dune is suddenly interrupted by a one-second shot of the dog running forward through the dune grass and then by a half-second CU of it lunging forward. The attack is described in rapid montage until François runs up, and Yvon and Marie (in LAMCU) examine his arm. This eruption of the past into the present is then repeated as the dog invades Yvon's fantasy of Marie. Although expected, the threat is even more frightening for its inevitability. It attacks now as a shadow on the sand, as a snarling face (in multiple-exposed CU), and as a relentlessly loping figure (in a slow motion HAFS backward dolly).[27] The last times the dog appears, the threat has changed. It is the day of the storm, and in the veterinarian's office the dog is quiet now (in ECU) behind bars. In the next sequence, Yvon paces restlessly by the lighthouse stairs and, when he sits on a step, he is unable to drink the cup of water he thirsts for. A single FS reveals the dog lying dead in some straw (it is so "frostily" side-lit that the image looks like a negative). Fade to a slightly blurred CU of Yvon's head behind the bars of the stairs as he asks, "And if one of us kills the other, Father?"[28] If the diseased animal seems a simplistic figure of a horror inherent in nature, its recurrence works effectively as a motif—as a fatalistic double of the human—infecting Yvon through the cross-cutting and presaging his end.

The clear-cut spatial-temporal continuity that marks *Gardiens de phare* dissolves, at two crucial points, into a disorienting series of images that lead to mysterious subjective interrelations. Yvon's fantasy of Marie initiates this process of dissolution. It begins with blurred shots of the revolving beacon, followed by a quick montage of reverse CUs of Yvon (alternating his upward look from right to left and vice versa). The room in which he sits is transformed by a bubblelike pattern of lights drifting about the walls and floor. In an interpolated LS of a beach, Marie (dressed in her white wedding dress and traditional conical hat) picks up a large conch shell and suddenly (in a simple cut) descends the spiral stairs to circle around her husband. As she puts the shell to her mouth (in CU), the sequence turns into a kind of shadow play—hands clasping against the beach sand and then the couple kissing. At this point the dog's shadow intervenes, and the sequence shifts into a montage of alternating shots—the couple running on the beach, their hands clasping, and the multiply-exposed dog's face. At the end, shots of the dog alternate briefly with shots of incoming waves (do we read them in conjunction—as a sign of inevitability—or in opposition?). When the shot of the running dog awakens Yvon, he calls out, "Marie!"; and the sequence cuts to a LS of the kelp-drying racks outside their cottage and then to a MCU of Marie turning in her bed and looking off. The intertitle—the sound of her name—miraculously elides the distance between them; but unlike similar sequences in *Usher* and *Finis Terrae*, the poignant cross-cutting does not lead to an exchange. This is a world that denies such magical correspondences and transformations.

The second instance of dissolution follows almost immediately, but this time Yvon's father is at its center. The older man has put on his son's fur coat when he replaced him on the night watch, and now he recalls (in three brief shots) the story Yvon told him. It is as if the coat itself wrapped him in the memories. The next morning, the father climbs up to the beacon and looks out at the darkening sky and sea. He reimagines the departure from the mainland in a single image, and then his memory suddenly changes to the wedding celebration of Yvon and Marie. The sequence begins with images punctuated by fades and then shifts to a continuous montage as the wedding procession comes out of the church (with its ringing tower bells) to dance in a circle on the beach. MCUs and CUs of Yvon's father are intercut throughout in such a way that gradually his position becomes ambiguous—is he still on the lighthouse or watching on the beach? As the camera begins to pick up the movement of the dancers (a 360° pan left on Marie turns into a swish pan as the dancers change direction), shots of Yvon abruptly intervene.

CU of Yvon's father looking off right.
HALS of the frothy sea at the base of the lighthouse; in the lower left foreground, Yvon gazes down from the catwalk.
LAMS (blurred) of Yvon looking down, framed by the lighthouse behind him.
MS swish pan on the dancers moving right.
CU of the father (but slightly behind him) as he looks off to the right and smiles.
HA wild camera shot of the sea and rocks below.
CU of the father suddenly turning, startled, to look off to the right foreground.
HAMS of Yvon (from behind) leaning over the edge of a railing, the frothy sea below him.
CU of the father coming off and down (right foreground).

Initially, an omniscient interruption of the father's reverie, the HA shot of the sea suddenly turns subjective. It is as if Yvon's stare has redirected his father's look, and the latter telepathically experiences the vertigo that has seized his son. The delirium of the wedding celebration (echoing that of the country dance in *Maldone*) is shockingly transformed into a delirium of madness and death.

These patterns of cross-cutting culminate in a climax that, for rhythmic intensity and emotional power, rivals any other done during the decade. And, as in *Usher* and *Finis Terrae*, the intimation of sound is integral to its opera-

511

274. (left) The mainland church and wedding procession that Yvon's father conjures up in memory

275. (right) The cottage interior near the end of *Gardiens de phare*

tion. Three different spaces alternate initially—the lighthouse (where Yvon confronts his father in a series of tense shot/reverse shots and deep space MCU/FSs), the cottage (where the two women and the pastor are positioned in a number of diagonal and triangular compositions until the news of the rabies threat separates them into individual MCUs), and the ship (where LSs give way to closer shots of the captain and sailors drenched with spray). These alternations end in three separate shots—of the women at the window (the pastor is in CU in the background), the father on the stairs, and the captain at the ship's wheel as he gives the order, "Sound the siren!" Now the sequence shifts quickly to shots of the siren blasts intercut with shots of the startled father, and the sound seems to propel him up the stairs and, ironically, into the conflict with Yvon. Father pushes son through a door and outside onto the catwalk (in MS), and their struggle is alternately concealed and revealed by the swinging door. A sudden shot of a circular whirling image and then of waves on the rocks elides Yvon's fall, and the father remains on the catwalk (in MCU) with the door flapping behind him. Shots of the ship and its crew return, but Yvon's father dazedly reaches down to pick up his son's shirt. Again the siren blasts intervene (more insistently, in doubled and quadrupled shots), and the old man puts his hands to his ears. For a moment, the siren becomes a metaphorical extension of his own unbearable pain.[29]

In contrast to the Double Tempest sequence in *Napoléon*, this climactic struggle ends in a tragic loss. Although Yvon's father recovers himself enough to climb the ladder to the beacon, on shore the women and the pastor misread its illumination. The irony (doubled by the possibility of a displaced rejoicing on the ship) deepens the poignancy of the final images:

CU of Yvon's shirt on a chair, the shadows of the beacon blades passing over it.

512

CU of the father's face (tilted diagonally and lit strongly from the upper left); the
   shadows also pass over him as he cries.
CU of the shirt on the chair.

This alternation of light and shadow echoes the earliest images of Yvon in
that room as well as the representation of the father-and-son struggle (the
door's concealing and revealing). And it resonates with the pattern of black/
white juxtapositions that have animated the film. Reversing the handkerchief's
sign of departure and promised return at the beginning, the simple image of
the shirt marks a profound sense of absence and permanent separation. In
contrast to the amazing grace of human and natural communion in *Finis Terrae, Gardiens de phare* closes with an agonizing lack. The tragic death of a son
at the hands of a father either has terrible consequences—the possible destruction of the ship at sea—or articulates an unexpected horror at the center of
things.

Napoléon provided Marcel L'Herbier an example of sorts for his last impor-   *L'Argent*
tant film of the 1920s, *L'Argent* (1929). Choosing one of his idols, an historical
figure whom he admired and adored, Gance had made an impressive, yet
profoundly personal film. Could L'Herbier do likewise, but with something
that he hated, that he detested above all else?[1] The subject he chose would be
one only too familiar to cinéastes, one that had plagued him insidiously
throughout his career—money, or capital.[2] L'Herbier found a context for his
hatred in Zola's novel of the same title, about the 1868 crisis on the Paris
Stock Exchange. Instead of reconstructing French society during the Second
Empire, however, as some critics, particularly André Antoine, vociferously
wished he had done, L'Herbier updated the novel's narrative to the present.[3]
He would respect the spirit of Zola—"money . . . it's the dung that sustains
life"—but he wanted to depict the ideological power of capital in contemporary terms.[4] It would be omnipresent but also repressed. It would animate the
characters, marking their dialogue incessantly, but never once would it be
seen.[5] As it turned out, this representation of effects—of luxury spaces and
devious, high-risk speculation—caught rather accurately, and fortuitously, the
condition of western capitalist society on the brink of the Great Depression.
   L'Argent was previewed for the critics, in early December, 1928, as a film
of 200 minutes, divided into two parts by a short intermission.[6] Much to
L'Herbier's surprise, when it opened at the Ciné Max-Linder, on 9 January
1929, the film had been re-edited considerably and was reduced by more than
half an hour.[7] This sabotage was the result of a personal feud between L'Herbier and Jean Sapène, the head of Cinéromans, a feud which apparently started
when an exchange of insults so enraged the patron that he tried to throttle
the filmmaker in his office. Despite pressure from the Société des Auteurs as
well as the Paris film critics, Sapène refused to relent; and the truncated
version went into general release in April, 1929.[8] Although it cost nearly five
million francs, *L'Argent* seems to have done well commercially, especially in
Germany;[9] but its critical reception was mixed, to say the least. The judgment
that persisted for almost forty years, in fact, was that the film represented

L'Herbier's "cold cerebrality" to a fault (Jeanne and Ford)—it was the "ultimate expression of vanity in the midst of falsehood" (Mitry), "a romantic intrigue, in luxurious modern decors . . . where portable cameras enacted a kind of ritual dance . . ." (Sadoul).[10] However, now that the Archives du Film at Bois d'Arcy (with L'Herbier's assistance) has reconstructed the original version of the film and *L'Avant-Scène du cinéma* has published the complete *découpage* (1 June 1978), our critical sense of *L'Argent* is changing radically.[11] Noël Burch, who first championed a reevaluation of L'Herbier's work, has even called it "an absolute masterpiece, one of the great films in cinema history, and, at least, the most modern of all the silent films. . . ."[12]

Unlike *L'Inhumaine, L'Argent* offers more than a bass clef upon which the filmmaker can play with plastic harmonies and ultimately celebrate the cinematic apparatus. This is one of the few French films of the 1920s to explicitly represent the capitalist economic system that determines its actual production. Part of the film's distinctiveness, therefore, comes from the way that system and the conflicts inherent therein are represented—in other words, how the film confronts and critiques advanced capitalist society. Eschewing a straightforward political or ideological analysis (which was not L'Herbier's forte), the film instead engages in a rhetorical critique, in a subversion of narrative and discursive strategies. In the articulation of its narrative, compared to *Feu Mathias Pascal*, for instance, *L'Argent* does much more than synthesize current narrative avant-garde film practice. Here, as Burch has argued, there is a more or less systematic pattern of ruptures or breaks with the conventions of the diegetic process in narrative film discourse,[13] especially within the context of the modern studio spectacular genre. Furthermore, the film deploys a pattern of rhetorical figuring that links the sexual and the economic through fetishization and that depends, to some degree, on reflexivity. These interrelated disruptions and disturbances—putting in question both the mode of representation and what is represented—make *L'Argent* perhaps as subversive and/or experimental as *La Glace à trois faces, La Passion de Jeanne d'Arc, La Coquille et le clergyman,* or *Un Chien andalou.*

The narrative of *L'Argent* seems to focus on Nicolas Saccard (Pierre Alcover), a powerful financier consumed by the desire to accumulate more capital than his competitors. In the beginning, Saccard is humiliated by his chief rival, Alphonse Gunderman (Alfred Abel), when some mysterious maneuvering at the Bourse, promulgated by Massias (Mihalesco) and La Méchain (Yvette Guilbert), nearly undermines his Banque Universelle. To recoup his losses, Saccard, together with his secretary Mazaud (Antonin Artaud) and the journalist Huret (Jules Berry in debut), craftily concocts a scheme that involves the French aviator hero, Jacques Hamelin (Henry Victor), in a daring solo flight from Paris to Cayenne, French Guyana, where the financier has extensive oilfield holdings. Hamelin's young wife Line (Mary Glory in debut) helps secure his unwitting agreement after Saccard plays upon her fascination for him and the trappings of wealth. According to plan, when Hamelin's plane is reported (falsely) to have crashed, Saccard manipulates the sale of his own bank's stock at the Bourse. His attempt to blackmail Line into silence fails, however, and she comes close to shooting him at his celebration party. Shamed by her complicity and encouraged by Saccard's former mistress (now Gunderman's ally), the enigmatic Baroness Sandorf (Brigitte Helm), Line initiates a stock-selling spree that collapses his empire and leads to his arrest, as well as her husband's. In the ensuing trial, Gunderman discreetly intervenes to free Hamelin, and Saccard alone goes unrepentant to prison.

In its broad outlines, this narrative seems a conventional enough indictment of ambition and overreaching. Saccard is a "bad" capitalist whose appetite exceeds all bounds—he is vulgar, devious, ruthless, and immoral. Ultimately, he sacrifices everything to his desire for *l'argent*. Prominent on his desk in the beginning sequences is a black statuette of Napoléon (the ironic reverse of Gance's hero), as if to invoke the suspect grandeur of Saccard's passion and ambition. And Alcover's stocky, solid physique, together with his heavy, round, yet hatchet-featured face, seem to fulfill our expectations of the stereotypical villain. But the film undermines such an easy reading in several ways. The distribution of character traits makes Saccard's antagonist no less villainous than he. Alfred Abel turns Gunderman into a tall, thin, tight-lipped elderly gentleman whose presence exudes a sinister calm. Introduced at breakfast, he cradles a white Pomeranian (which rarely leaves his arms throughout the film) and daintily pecks at a soft-boiled egg. His cold, sterile, repressive manner contrasts markedly with Saccard's impulsive and energetic behavior. For all his deceptive rapaciousness, Saccard, of the two, is the much more appealing figure. Furthermore, despite these differences, Gunderman is no less a schemer in his speculations. He uses the Hamelins for his own ends, for instance, just as his rival does. Perhaps most important of all, as Burch notes, is the role of *deus ex machina* which the film allows Gunderman to play.[14] By acquiring the majority of stock in the Banque Universelle, he can simply dismiss the charges against Hamelin and allow the case against Saccard to proceed. In effect, the court is displaced by the "good" capitalist as a compassionate and supposedly dispassionate judge.

The relationship between these two rival capitalists, consequently, raises questions about the film's apparent happy ending. Will Jacques Hamelin's genius be able to fulfill itself under the tutelage of a "good master," as one critic wrote,[15] or has he been duped again? Does justice really triumph in Saccard's imprisonment or is it irreparably compromised by the fact that he will be released in six months and, even more, by the demonstration of Gunderman's power? If Gunderman is as representative as Saccard, if not more so, of the capitalist system of speculation and accumulation, then the fall of the lesser of the two leaves that system unchallenged and intact. With this exception. By not completely repressing the story of Gunderman's maneuverings, in favor of exposing Saccard's, the narrative unmasks the ideological basis of its repression and thus challenges that system indirectly from within.

If the conflict between Saccard and Gunderman seems primary to *L'Argent*, there is a second story that parallels and intersects with it—the story of Jacques and Line Hamelin. Their story comes into conflict with the other in two ways. First is the conflict, in L'Herbier's terms, between "the materiality of capital and the power of heroism."[16] Jacques is the modern Romantic hero par excellence—the lone adventurer who challenges the elements and the unknown with his flying machines.[17] Dangerous solo flights test his mettle, as acts of purification; and his inventions contribute to that twentieth-century ideal, technological progress. But he has little chance of exercising his heroic nature without recourse to money. Out of necessity, and love for Line, Jacques ac-

515

276. (left) A publicity photo
of Saccard (Pierre Alcover)
and Mazaud (Antonin Artaud)
in *L'Argent* (1929)

277. (right) Gunderman
(Alfred Abel) and Massias
(Mihalesco)

cepts an association with Saccard in the world of high finance and speculation
that he scorns. As if in punishment, he is nearly blinded at the end of his
flight to Guyana (he does lose an eye); and, as a consequence, he signs over
financial responsibility for his wife to Saccard. Although prison eludes him,
Gunderman's generosity hardly frees him from a compromised existence. In
the end, Jacques is not unlike Baudelaire's albatross—"Exiled to the ground
amid the jeering pack." Furthermore, because of L'Herbier's personal commitment to the film, there is every reason to believe that we are to assume an
analogy here between the aviator hero and the filmmaker as artist. Jacques's
uneasy, compromised relation to the world of finance parallels that of the
narrative avant-garde filmmaker in the French film industry. Like Daedulus
or, more precisely, Icarus, neither can escape the labyrinth of capitalist speculation that supports their efforts.

The second conflict involving the Hamelins is what L'Herbier called "life
versus capital" or, more precisely, love versus money.[18] Jacques and Line are
introduced as a rather stereotypical romantic couple—the sentimental hero and
heroine of a modern fairy tale. Both are flawed, however (the one by his love,
the other by her newly aroused desires); and both thus play naïvely into Saccard's hands. As their status and integrity are compromised, the narrative sets
up corresponding expectations—for Saccard's fall and the couple's reconciliation and restoration. The way this is articulated, however, is through an ironic
repetition. The couple now plays even more naïvely into Gunderman and
Sandorf's hands. It is these two speculators, after all, who restore the Hamelins
by using them to eliminate their rival. Furthermore, the film undermines the

516

final image of the reunited lovers. They may leave the courtroom arm in arm, but in the background of a shot that frames them between the contented foreground figures of Sandorf and La Méchain. Thus is the concept of the romantic couple, as well as the ideal of the hero, compromised and questioned, even more so than in L'Herbier's earlier *Rose-France* and *Feu Mathias Pascal*.

The interrelation of these two stories depends primarily on the relationship between Line and Saccard, and here the film develops a fascinating rhetorical nexus of economic and sexual connections. The introduction of Line and Jacques Hamelin establishes a schematic juxtaposition against which her affair with Saccard will play off. They are seated before a large map, their hands (in CU) tracing the line of a flight he must make—for money to support them. After she tells him she is afraid of the risk he is taking, the sequence closes by alternating MCUs of them kissing (their heads revolve in the frame, in the manner of the late Hitchcock) with MCUs of their clasped hands slipping off the map. This rhetorical figure of romance contrasts sharply with the voyeuristic POV shots which link Line and Saccard. They first see one another at the Restaurant Champy where Huret arranges the meeting that will lead to the Guyana flight scheme. Sitting at a separate table, Saccard notices Line in a sequence that alternates his steady, smiling gaze with shots that tilt down to her legs under the table, show her kicking Jacques lightly, and then tilt up to reveal her eyes glancing down. When she finally returns his look, only to drop her eyes and lift them again, Saccard gazes knowingly at her. This pattern of POV shots is repeated, with a difference, when Saccard comes to the Hamelin apartment to consider the Guyana flight plans. There, for a brief moment, they are alone together, sitting across from one another over a low table of maps. Line crosses the room to offer him a drink and cigarette, as he watches her intently. Returning, she stumbles slightly—cut to a MS of her legs (she smoothes a rough spot in the carpet), a shot which then tracks her legs to the table and tilts up to show Saccard accepting the drink. When he leans forward (almost leeringly) to refuse the cigarette and take out his own cigar, Line goes back across the room; and Saccard smiles at the MS of her legs as she pauses again to tap the carpet. Here, while revealing her interest in better room furnishings, Line becomes both the fetishized object of Saccard's gaze and the servant of his appetite (soon she will deliver Jacques to him); and his position is emphasized at the beginning of the scene, by the way his hands are placed on the map they have been examining.

To this figure of fetishization another is added that begins to epitomize Line's function and also raise questions about the spectator's position with respect to her. Immediately after the young couple's introduction, Line and Jacques are described against a window. Isolated in MCU, Line looks at the reflection of herself in a wall mirror, and her image seems doubly inscribed in glass. Transfixed by her own self-image, she turns to cajole Jacques into accepting Huret's offer. Later, at a stockholder's meeting (where Saccard proposes Jacques for a vice-presidency in his bank), this image returns with a vengeance. Again Line has persuaded her husband to accept the financier's scheme, and they watch the proceedings from behind a glass door. When Saccard announces the condition of Jacques's acceptance—"He will remain an aviator and embark on a long-distance flight"—her shock and pain are registered in an isolated MCU, and her hand reaches out to touch the glass (the

517

278. Line (Mary Glory)

screen?). The gesture, curiously, poignantly, suggests a character entrapped as an image. A short while later, the image returns once more, to be circumscribed within Saccard's gaze. Line has left the banquet hall at the bank to look through the windows of an upper-story office, fascinated by the crowds gathered at night on the Place de l'Opéra to hear the news of Jacques's flight. The sequence initially alternates shots of Saccard at the banquet, MSs and CUs of Line (again pressed to the glass), and panoramas of the people in the street. When Saccard discovers her, he is mesmerized by her thinly clad figure half revealed in the light that streams through the glass. A series of rapid tracking shots of the crowd seems to impel him across the room and then prompt him to caress her bare shoulder. The visual energy of the camera movement in conjunction with the crowds' excitement (generated by Jacques's heroism and Saccard's capital) seem to arouse and charge his desire.[19] When Line bursts into laughter and applause, this climax neatly masks and delays the expected seduction and speculation coup.

The patina of romance briefly surrounds these two. But it depends on Line's ignorance—the film has her sleep through the radio report of Jacques's plane crash, audaciously intercutting fragments of the news with shots of her dreaming, smiling face. When she does learn of it, Line rushes to Saccard's office and, in quick succession, discovers that Jacques is alive and that they have gained a fortune. Saccard has restored her husband, with interest. She collapses in a chair—out of joy, amazement, and horror—and lets him kneel chivalrously before her and take her hand. When Saccard puts his lips to her fingers and smiles in surprise, she ambiguously caresses his other hand. The figure of romance returns, but as the sign of a very different kind of coupling, ironically juxtaposed to the sequence of Jacques going blind in the tropics. This romance, of course, is a momentary illusion that masks their real relation. Having fed his desires, Line is rewarded—and kept as "The patron's new conquest." The next time she appears, she has a chic new outfit, and Saccard apparently has arranged her move into a larger apartment. There he gives her a bracelet (costing 125,000 francs) as well as a checkbook drawn on his account. But his attention is caught by one of Line's slips which is draped over a suitcase. In an alternation of shots, Saccard stares at the silken garment, slowly caresses it, and a superimposition dissolves in of her reclining nude figure.[20] This unusually explicit fetishizing condenses his attitude toward woman and capital—the touch of possession and mastery "slips" over an imagined body.[21] When Saccard later returns to Line's apartment, he tries again to seduce her—in a rapid montage of his hands pawing her twisting body—and ends up kneeling to kiss the hem of her dress. But she resists him now, racing off (in a fast forward dolly) through several rooms to open the front door; and their final confrontation comes at his celebration party. There Line appears for the last time as a figure reflected in glass, the object of contention between Saccard and the intervening character of the Baroness Sandorf.

Sandorf performs an interesting function in this nexus of relations.[22] For all their striking differences (the one, a childishly naïve brunette; the other, a coolly sensual blonde, sleekly costumed and coiffured), she acts as a double for the younger woman—a role that confirms Line's change of masters and her subservience to Gunderman. Sandorf's first appearance in the film comes immediately after Saccard's initial financial loss. It is his image of her—a single memory shot of her stretched out on a couch receiving the gift of a bracelet from him. This figure of the mistress will be echoed later when Line assumes her position. The two women are implicitly paralleled in a brief series of shots that follow the Banque Universelle banquet and the Place de l'Opéra celebration. The first shot is rather ambiguous—it begins on a CU of the front page of *Le Matin* falling from someone's hand, rack focuses to reveal a white line drawing of a nude couple on glass (echoing the previous glass images of Line and pointing ahead to Saccard's fetishizing of her slip), and then pans slightly to include Sandorf (in MS) as she leans back seductively on a couch. Instead of an eyeline-match shot of the person holding the paper, the next shot is a MCU of Line, her hair spread out on a pillow, dozing on a couch in her apartment. The third shot returns to Sandorf as she smiles (as if in response to a statement or look) and moves toward a phone built into the back wall, on which the shadows of aquarium fish drift about. A fade to Saccard dozing at his office desk, newspapers and telephones (plus a small statue of a hippopotamus) spread out before him, suggests that the unseen person in Sandorf's apartment is none other than Gunderman.[23] In this play of "jungle" spaces, of looks (unidentified and deflected), of fetishized women, of consciousness and unconsciousness, the positions of these four characters are succinctly defined. Controlled by an off-screen presence, Sandorf, through her glance, seems to control the sleeping Line. How will this doubled and deceptive seeing/desiring/knowing come into conflict with that of Saccard?

This pattern of doubling and difference, of economic and sexual condensation, comes to a climax in the second half of the film. The stage is set in the sequence where Saccard confronts Sandorf in the stylized jungle luxury of her apartment. It opens on a MCU of a heavily jewelled hand and arm (Sandorf's, of course) taking up a deck of cards on a casino table. While some of her friends engross themselves in a card game, setting up the context of high risk gambling, Sandorf goes to talk with Saccard in an adjacent sunken room. There, another related context—"a decor open to variations of fraudulent sexuality"—is set up by several prominent zebra-skinned couches and the shadows of fish (just off camera) that drift about the walls.[24] As he kisses her hand,

279. (left) A publicity photo of Saccard and Sandorf (Brigitte Helm) in her apartment

280. (right) One of Lazare Meerson and André Barsacq's set decors for the Banque Universelle in *L'Argent*

Saccard eyes the new bracelet Sandorf flaunts before him and soon discovers that she is now working for Gunderman (confirming his presence in the earlier sequence). His reaction is swift and brutal—he moves to strangle her. The action is choreographed almost sensuously around the two couches—in three different shifts of character position (depending on who is standing over whom), several fast tracks, and a short burst of rapid montage—with interpolated shots of the cardplayers' shadows on the ceiling. In this highly metaphorical space, this jungle clearing of combat, Saccard's revenge is thwarted by his fear of scandal—the other "players" may see and recognize him. In the very next sequence, Line becomes the object of a similar attack when Saccard tries to seduce her. There the space lacks almost any decor—it is Line who acts like a frightened mad animal—but Saccard is thwarted by his own sudden compassion for her.

By the time of the celebration party, Sandorf has visited Line, discovered her knowledge of Saccard's "grave irregularities," and won her confidence. At the party, Line appears in a sort of waiting room as a still figure in a wall mirror, pointedly associated with a small statue of a child (a cupid?) grasping a dolphin. Sandorf and Saccard alternate going to see this nearly immobile *femme de glace*, whose representation seems to sum up, metaphorically, her

520

relation to him.[25] First Sandorf, also as a reflection, approaches her, hesitantly, and withdraws. Then Saccard enters, and they struggle over the check that will pay off her debts and, reciprocally, demand a different kind of repayment. As he forceably kisses her, the shot is framed in such a way that the statue blocks Line from view, displaces her, in fact—in a perverse culmination of his fetishizing. Still she resists, and Saccard retreats into the main room where the legs of several women dancers are intercut ironically with his movements. By now Line has drawn a revolver from her purse and waits by the statue, driven to the point of accepting her own destruction if only she can destroy Saccard and the grip he has on her. It is Sandorf who sees this change in Line but who realizes that she and Gunderman can gain more from Saccard if he is kept alive and in ignorance. When he next appears before Line, Sandorf is there to control the reverberations of this mirror image, suppressing the threatened gunshot for a later, more damaging (and profitable) discharge.

Sandorf's shift of allegiance, from Saccard to Gunderman, is now repeated by Line. As a result of this maneuvering, Line goes to meet Gunderman, in a circular room whose entire wall length is covered by a world map—as if the earth itself had been turned inside out. There she divulges information about Jacques's discoveries in Guyana and his inventions—in exchange for his freedom. This image of two bargaining figures before a gigantic enclosing map of the world stands in marked contrast to the initial romantic shots of Jacques and Line. When Gunderman escorts her to an invisible door in the wall, they vanish, one after the other, into his "world."

If *L'Argent* disrupts and throws into question the conventional expectations of its narrative (along with their ideological bases), if it deploys a complex pattern of rhetorical figuring that deliberately borders on the perverse, it also seems to call attention to the process of its own "writing," to the diegetic process of its discourse. Although perhaps not always consistent or systematic, these "stylistic" breaks with convention occur in several interrelated ways. One immediately recognizable feature of the film (particularly for a work based on Zola) is the way the mise-en-scène, together with lens choices and camera placements, undermines the usual appeal to verisimilitude.[26]

Decors in the genre of the modern studio spectacular tended to be large, but those in *L'Argent* are positively immense, even monumental.[27] Part of this effect is due to the actual locations selected—the central chamber of the Bourse (rented out to L'Herbier and his 1,500 actors and over a dozen cameramen for the three-day Pentecost holiday) and the Place de l'Opéra (specially lighted for one long night of shooting).[28] But it also depends on the studio sets constructed at Studios Francoeur by Lazare Meerson and André Barsacq—the huge room in his house which Saccard makes over for the celebration party, the prison corridor with its "Piranesi-like perspectives,"[29] and especially the interior of the Banque Universalle which, one critic argued (unconscious of his aptness), might just as well be "a department store."[30] Most of these spaces have smooth, polished surfaces and are streamlined to the point of exhibiting little more than walls, ceilings, and floors. So upset was one critic by the stark simplicity of Saccard's party, for instance, that he complained about the lack of a buffet for the guests![31]

Given the deliberate immensity of these decors, what next strikes one is how they are transformed by an uncommon dynamism. Some of that dyna-

281. A high angle long shot
from the Bourse sequence

mism come from the secondary characters that continually traverse the frame.[32] Crowds throng the Bourse, the Banque Universelle, the Restaurant Champy, the Bourget airport, the Place de l'Opéra, and Saccard's party—all of them driven here and there by a passion for money and status. In order to accentuate their every movement, L'Herbier had Jules Kruger film many of these crowd sequences in HA and LA shots. This is particularly evident when Saccard's clients panic in his bank and when the stock prices twice change radically at the Bourse. L'Herbier himself described his crowds as "pygmies who, driven by their desire, teem as in an immense anthill."[33] That dynamism also depends, somewhat like that in *Maldone* and *Gardiens de phare*, on a deep-space mise-en-scène that juxtaposes characters and/or parts of the decor.[34] The Banque Universelle, for example, is usually described in HALSs, some of which include, in the foreground, a section of the balcony outside Saccard's office, an office typewriter, or the top of the tall bank-teller windows. In other HA shots, characters in the foreground are set off from those in the background or vice versa—as in the confrontation between Gunderman's spy, Solomon Massias, and the ineffectual Baron Defrance (Pierre Juvenet) in the opening sequence or in the clash between Saccard and his bank clients (after his first loss to Gunderman). Kruger accentuates this deep-space mise-en-scène even more by often resorting to wide angle lenses, including the brachyscope lens used for *Napoléon*.[35] This combination of stylized space and movement produces a world that complements perfectly the narrative conflict between the larger-than-life capitalists.

What most distinguishes *L'Argent*, however, is another kind of dynamism—what Burch has called "a mobile camera strategy absolutely without precedent,

522

quantitatively, certainly, but especially qualitatively."[36] At first, one may be struck, as in *Napoléon*, by the virtuosity of the camera movements. At the Bourse and the Banque Universelle, for instance, cameramen were strapped to low-slung carts and pushed or pulled rapidly among and alongside the crowds. At Saccard's party, camera and operator glided back and forth over the performers and guests on a platform suspended from the ceiling. Finally, at the moment of Jacques Hamelin's departure, the frenzied activity at the Bourse was recorded by an automatic camera descending on a cable from the dome toward the central bargaining ring. All these Jean Dréville has documented in detail in his exquisite short film, *Autour de L'Argent* (1928). Yet this virtuosity alone hardly suffices to mark the film off from others in the late 1920s. What is peculiar to *L'Argent* is the high visibility of these camera movements and the ambiguity of their function. That visibility depends less on their frequency and the extent of their duration—Burch has estimated that only 20 percent of the shots actually include some movement of the apparatus[37]—than on when and how they occur.

The opening sequences of the film offer a good range of its mobile camera strategies and effects. Some of the camera movements here do fall within the conventions of narrative film discourse. Several tracks and dollies, for instance, simply describe Saccard's movement from the iron gates surrounding the Bourse (which already seem to imprison him) to the entrance of the Restaurant Champy. Many others deviate from convention, however, some to the point of establishing alternatives to a strictly spatial-temporal continuity. The back-to-back sequences describing Saccard's and then Gunderman's offices, for instance, are marked by different kinds of camera movement. In the one, there are short dollies out and in, along with combination pan-tracks; in the other, a series of smooth forward dollies continually follow a servant's progress toward Gunderman. Encoded here are a restless, anxious energy juxtaposed to a placid, undisturbed command. Another kind of structural difference marks the description of the Bourse area where Massias challenges Defrance for control of one of Saccard's subsidiaries. The second shot of the sequence dollies forward up the aisle, from a LS of the hall to a FS of Defrance and several associates at a table. The second-to-last shot of the sequence repeats the movement, but at a much more rapid pace, leading to the climactic FS of Massias as he votes against Defrance's motion. This repetition and startlingly abrupt shift acts very much in the manner of a musical closure. Finally, instead of adjusting to the movement of characters, in order to reposition them in the frame, here the camera itself does the repositioning. The most unusual instance of this occurs in Gunderman's office. In the background of one LS (just before he reaches the financier), the servant moves across the room (from left to right) as the camera tracks slowly left (while also panning slightly to the right), in order to produce a strangely drifting yet anchored space that accentuates his movement. A half-dozen shots later, Massias stands (in FS) in the circular map room as the camera performs a 180° track around him to reveal a servant opening the invisible door in the wall, through which he disappears. The world literally seems to revolve around him—at Gunderman's command, we discover by the end. In *L'Argent*, largely because of these unusual camera movements, space oscillates uncannily between the fixed and the fluid.

These mobile camera strategies, together with some unconventional editing

282. A production photo of
Mihalesco and Jules Kruger in
Gunderman's circular map
room

patterns, produce a particularly effective choreography of space and movement
in two very different sequences. The first occurs just after Saccard has decided
to go ahead with the Hamelin flight scheme. It begins with a forward dolly
(matching the backward dolly on Saccard, as he leaves his office at the end of
the previous sequence) from a LS of Gunderman's office to a HAFS of a rapa-
cious-looking Sandorf seated across from him at his desk. The matching dollies
quickly set us up for a confrontation. That confrontation is played out, however, in a spacious corridor adjacent to the office, aptly covered by a marble
floor of black-and-white squares. The initial LS of this space positions Saccard
(in FS, frame center left, with his back to the camera) on the edge of a couple
of steps leading off and down in the foreground. A servant comes from across
the floor to greet him while another crosses from right to left to join a fourth
man seated in the left background. The right-angled direction of these movements act as a figural prelude to the "dance" that ensues.

FS/LS of the same space. As Gunderman and Sandorf come through a door in the
    right background, the camera dollies in to a closer shot of Saccard and the man
    who has greeted him. Simultaneously, Gunderman stops in the center background;
    Sandorf comes forward on the right; on the left Saccard starts to walk toward
    Gunderman; the man exits toward the lower right foreground. As Sandorf and
    Saccard pass one another, he turns to glance at her.
FS of Sandorf and Saccard passing one another; she takes a few steps to the left and
    stops, turning her back to the camera, and gazes back to the right, while Saccard
    continues walking and exits frame right. Sandorf stands looking for a moment, and
    then the two previously seated men cross the frame from right to left in the back-
    ground.
FS/LS of Sandorf (frame right) watching Saccard join Gunderman (in the center back-
    ground). She sidles across the frame from right to left and stops, continuing to
    watch the two men who move toward the door in the right background.
MS of Sandorf (frame right) gazing off right. As a bearded man enters from the lower
    area in the left background, the camera dollies out to a FS of him meeting a second
    man on the steps (frame left). Sandorf then turns and flounces off from right to
    left, exiting behind the two men, in the left background.

524

The camera movements that begin and end this series of shots seem to mark off a shift in attention from Saccard to Sandorf. Yet each movement, though focused on the still figure in the foreground, is prompted by a movement in the background—either Gunderman's or that of one of his assistants (the bearded man). Sandorf's surprise and her pause to wonder about Saccard's intentions is also strangely accentuated by the 90° shift in camera position that describes a 180° rotation of her body and glance (from front to back, from left to right). And in each of the last three shots, she moves laterally across the frame from right to left, her pauses disrupted by the movement of the camera as well as by that of pairs of men. Thus does a simple crossing of paths and an exchange of looks become a serial melody of movement and a game of counters or chess pieces, all within the context of Gunderman's "stage."

The second sequence comes at the moment of Jacques Hamelin's departure, near the conclusion of the first half of the film. Here, *L'Argent*'s deviation from conventional film discourse is complemented and briefly extended by sound. The sequence is predicated on the counterpoint of cross-cutting, a pattern of editing that is quite prominent in the film. What is peculiar about this instance, however, is that the relations between shots work primarily according to a metaphorical plan.[38] In effect, the sequence operates much like the sequence of Einar's supposed death in *L'Inhumaine* or the Double Tempest in *Napoléon*. It begins by alternating shots of the hectic trading at the Bourse, Jacques's plane taking off, and Line again standing at a window (in the upper story office at Bourget). This alternation is "the central pivot" of the film, according to L'Herbier—"the airplane which races into the sky after a miracle and the spectators below who bet on that miracle."[39] And Line, pressed against the glass (as if mirroring us) is caught between them. At the precise moment of takeoff, the sequence intercuts shots of the plane's ascent with aerial shots plunging dizzily toward the Bourse bargaining ring. In these juxtaposed movements, the mass tumult of speculation seems to threaten Jacques's flight— to drag it down—through a literal "montage of attractions."[40] In the original screening, moreover, this attraction was emphasized by sound recordings of "the crowd noises at the Bourse and the motorized roar of the plane."[41] Instead of being kept distinct, by synchronizing them according to the alternation of shots, these sounds were overlaid one on top of the other, blurring their differences, in one continuous simultaneous flux. Although nowhere near exemplifying the contrapuntal use of sound advocated by Eisenstein, Pudovkin, and Alexandrov (in 1928),[42] this brief segment of image-sound montage in *L'Argent* is one of the earliest practices of something other than a simple "naturalistic" synchronization.

As an instance of *L'Argent*'s originality, Noël Burch has argued that the singularity of its camera movements lies principally in "their *arbitrariness*."[43] By operating as a systematic "intervention" (because visible and artificial), they function "to justify the *arbitrary*, to critique the 'naturalness' " of narrative film discourse as standardized, particularly in American films.[44] There is no doubt of the latter. But to conceive of the arbitrary as the opposite of the conventional seems a bit simplistic—a point which Burch himself may now admit. Besides, it would seem to give primacy, implicitly, to the hegemony of the American cinema. Consequently, although the camera movements and

525

editing patterns in *L'Argent* may seem arbitrary in the context of a conventional film discourse, it seems to me that one should stress instead their integral function as part of an alternate system—or systems—of film "writing" as developed by the French narrative avant-garde. Even those instances that seem most arbitrary (and even incompetent) in the film—the joining of stable shots, each of which concludes with a slight jarring camera movement—are repeated with a consistency that leads one to accept them as an alternate system of continuity. Cumulatively, all of these patterns foreground the film's discursive process of signification in a way that reflects on the narrative and its articulation. As Burch avers, echoing Roland Barthes, the pleasure of this text was, and still remains, impure.[45]

"Is that the end of the story?" asked Christopher Robin. "That's the end of that one. **Afterword**
There are others."
—A.A. Milne, *Winnie the Pooh* (1926)

This space is usually reserved for a summary statement or closing speech. Here, the writer, and especially the historian, takes stock of his findings and rehearses once more the main lines of his narrative, his analyses and arguments. His last persuasive act often depends on the strategy of recapitulating, simplifying, and thus overdetermining his work's coherence. Instead, I would like to offer a kind of blueprint for further work. Let me explore, if only briefly, several areas of activity, sets of questions, and possible narratives, all involving the French cinema (1915-1929), that demand to be taken up as the subjects of further research and analysis. And in the process, let me lay out the assumptions of an autocritique.

One thing this book has done is to point up the need for further research on the technological base and industrial organization of the French cinema during this period. There is a surprising lack of basic information on the development and impact of film technology in France. Was the old Pathé camera, for instance, so widely used throughout the 1910s as to merit the claim that every cameraman (almost anywhere in the world) began his career with one? Were the Eclair and Debrie cameras really competitive with, say, the Bell and Howell cameras in the 1920s? And if so, what features gave them an advantage? How, specifically, did the various color and sound film processes developed by Pathé and Gaumont work; how extensively were they used; how were they encouraged or inhibited by both aesthetic and socioeconomic forces; and how did they compare with the color and sound film processes developed, say, in Germany and the United States? More generally, what changes took place in the design and use of film studios (especially in set decoration, lighting, and shooting methods) and in the techniques of editing? Finally, in light of Barry Salt's work,[1] what effect did the French technical developments have on the forms and styles of films produced and marketed by the industry?

Similarly, much more detailed information could be gathered about the organizational structures and the operational systems within the French film industry of this period. What kinds of production units and schedules, for instance, were standard in France, and how did that standard and the major deviations from it change, say, from 1915 to 1920 to 1925 to 1929? Furthermore, how did the French system compare with the American system, as delineated recently by Janet Staiger?[2] What was the full range of film distribution patterns in France, and were those patterns different for French and, say, American films.[3] How exactly were films publicized, how much proportionately was spent on film publicity, and were there differences between the publicity for French and American films? What specific changes occurred in the exhibition of films, both in Paris and the provinces, and what particular socioeconomic groups constituted the cinema audience and how did that audience's composition change over time? Was the French system of film exhibition very different from the early American system, as established by Douglas Gomery and Robert Allen?[4] Finally, what networks of socioeconomic relations connected the various film companies as well as linked them with certain banks, newspapers and magazines, department stores, theaters, and other institutions? Answers to some of these questions might arise through the study of one particular company—such as Pathé-Consortium, Film d'Art, Films Aubert, Films Albatros—or even a single individual—such as Louis Aubert, Louis Nalpas, Jean Sapène, or Alexandre Kamenka.[5]

Recent studies in England and the United States have demonstrated that a system of representation or spatial-temporal continuity was well established in the American cinema by the late 1910s.[6] Although I have assumed so, it is less than certain that this system was accepted and imitated by the French film industry. It would be useful to know, through an extensive viewing of existing film prints, if and when this system became accepted as the norm in France and just what kinds of French films were marked by it. It would also be useful to know if there was a coherent prewar or wartime system of representation that the French drew upon as an alternative to the American system. This would help determine whether, by the early 1920s, there was a single dominant system of representation or several alternatives. Whatever the number of systems over time, it would be useful as well to trace the changing function of such features as intertitles and musical accompaniment, and to know whether the French normally accepted such things as spatial-temporal discontinuities and patterns of rhetorical figuring. All this is important not only to provide a context for the French narrative avant-garde film practice but to contextualize the French narrative cinema generally as a national cinema.

My own work has shown that several film genres came into prominence in the French cinema of the 1910s and 1920s. But it also points to areas of uncertainty in the development of those genres especially during the period of the war. The serial, for instance, demands a much more thorough investigation, both as a narrative form and as a marketing strategy. The bourgeois melodrama, if defined differently (perhaps more closely aligned with the theater?), might be seen as a conceptual center around which several groups of films (some of which I have ignored or assigned to other genres) could be clustered as variations. The realist film could be more narrowly defined and then compared to the so-called realist films of later periods as well as to those of other national cinemas. The modern studio spectacular could be subsumed, as Kristin Thompson suggests, in the context of the international co-productions that characterized European and even American film production in the late 1920s. Finally, attention needs to be given to several film genres and modes that I have not even considered here—e.g., newsreels, documentary films, scientific films, educational films, animated films.[7] Moreover, most of these film genres as well as many of the narrative avant-garde film texts could benefit from a more fully developed ideological analysis than I have provided, whether based on a Marxist model as used by Noël Burch or on a somewhat eclectic "cultural studies" model as used by Rick Altman and Thomas Schatz.[8]

The French film genres also offer a context for defining the narrative avant-garde somewhat differently that I have done. Briefly, I have argued that the discourse and narrative conventions of such genres as the bourgeois melodrama and realist film were crucial to the development of a "deviant" narrative avant-garde film practice. However, it might be argued that the strategy of subversion in general—whether latently inherent in a genre such as the comedy or deliberately practiced against the conventions of certain genres—could define what is crucial to narrative avant-garde film practice. Actually I have incorporated this strategy in my analyses of several film texts—e.g., *Le Brasier ardent, Paris qui dort, Entr'acte, Rien que les heures, Napoléon, 6½ × 11, Maldone, La Passion de Jeanne d'Arc, L'Argent.* But it might also be used to defend Clair's *Un Chapeau de paille d'Italie* and *Les Deux Timides* as avant-garde works. And it could provide grounds for defending much of Renoir's early work as avant-garde—*La Fille de l'eau, Nana, Tire au flanc, Le Tournoi,* and *Le Bled.*

Another context for defining the French narrative avant-garde might be provided by recent studies in psychoanalysis. Here, one would need to set up a methodology that could account for more than the explicitly Dada-Surrealist films of Clair, Man Ray, Dulac-Artaud, and Buñuel-Dali. Crucial to such a methodology would be the construction of the subject, as both narrative agent and bearer of the look, and the related construction of spectator position. Could one then distinguish a body of French film texts in which this construction of the subject was undermined, subverted, or otherwise made problematic? As a corollary, could Jean Epstein's appeal to the unconscious in his theoretical writings (recently examined by Paul Willemen)[9] have a parallel in the representation and interrogation of unconscious process in his film texts? And could similar processes of representation and interrogation mark other film texts—e.g., those of L'Herbier, Dulac, Kirsanoff? In a similar vein, could certain French narrative avant-garde film texts, especially those of Epstein, provide a fertile ground for testing and extending Christian Metz's recent systematic analysis of rhetorical figuring in film or, more specifically, the operations of metonymy/metaphor?[10]

However one defines the French narrative avant-garde, what is badly needed at this moment is a critical history (along with English translations) of French film theory and criticism during this period. Stuart Liebman's recent hypothesis of a French Ur-theory, from 1910 to 1921, provides an excellent beginning.[11] But much more work needs to be done. On the one hand, there is the subject of intellectual currents that intersected both the writings on film and those on the other arts, in France and elsewhere. On the other, there is the relationship between the theoretical writings of the 1920s and the actual film practice. Of the latter, it would be good to confirm or counter Epstein's dictum that practice preceded theory and thus was usually in advance of most theoretical positions.

Once some of this work has been accomplished and these questions have been addressed more thoroughly, we will be in an even more secure position to take up important comparative studies. Then it will be time, for instance, to examine more accurately and insightfully the relationship between the French cinema of the 1920s and the 1930s. Did the sound film "revolution" produce a rupture that divided these decades into separate periods or did it merely mask their real similarities? No doubt the technology of film changed, but how different was the industry of the 1930s (in structure and operation) from that of the 1920s? Would our sense of the French film genres be any different if the analyses I have initiated were fully extended for another decade? With the addition of sound, did the continuity systems used by the French change that much, and in what ways? And exactly what strategies and features of the narrative avant-garde film practice continued to operate in the 1930s film texts, and how were they amended by the political developments of the decade? Likewise, it will be time to compare at some length the film theory and practice of the French and the Soviet cinemas of the 1920s. And to analyze the impact of French films in Germany and the Soviet Union, and vice versa. Finally, it will be time to extend Bernard Eisenschitz's brief comparison of this First Wave of the French cinema and the period of the French New Wave (circa 1955-1965).[12] Are the suggestive correlations between the two periods—e.g., the impact of American films, the extensive film theory and criticism activities, the independent film production methods (most specifically, in Pierre Braunberger's work as a producer), the "deviant" film practice—as significant as they seem? If so, the two periods of film writing and filmmaking could be played off one another to clarify the chief attributes and accomplishments of each. And, more important, their parallels could provide an organizational strategy for giving a different sense of coherence to the overall history of the French cinema.

Introduction

1. John Berger, *The Look of Things* (New York: Viking, 1974), 146.

2. Shoshana Felman, "Psychoanalysis and Education: Teaching Terminable and Interminable," *Yale French Studies* 63 (1982), 44.

3. A similar retrospective, organized by Georges Franju, was mounted by the Cinémathèque française in the summer of 1980.

4. Jean Mitry, "De quelques problèmes d'histoire et d'esthétique du cinéma," 115.

5. "Table ronde sur l'histoire du cinéma [Claude Beylie, Patrick Brion, Raymond Chirat, Francis Courtade, Jean-Claude Romer]," 11.

6. Walter Benjamin, "The Author as Producer [1934]," *Understanding Brecht*, trans. Anna Bostock (London: NLB, 1973), 98.

7. "Rediscovering the French Cinema: Part II," which Stephen Harvey organized for the Museum of Modern Art, includes some fifty French feature films as well as a dozen shorts, from the period of 1910 to 1929. All but about a half dozen of the feature film titles have been singled out for major attention in Parts II and IV of this history.

8. Roger Icart and Raymond Chirat are preparing a catalogue of French feature-length narrative films from the 1920s, to be published by the Cinémathèque de Toulouse, which should go a long way toward determining the number of films actually produced, how many survive, and perhaps in what condition. For comparison, see Raymond Chirat, *Catalogue des films français de long métrage: films sonores de fiction, 1929-1939* (Brussels: Cinémathèque royale de Belgique, 1975).

9. Raymond Borde, "La Gazette des Cahiers," *Cahiers de la cinémathèque* 30-31 (Summer-Autumn, 1980), xii.

10. The number of lost films may have risen once more because of the disastrous fire at a Cinémathèque française storage facility in August, 1980.

11. This conclusion is based on the research done by Glenn Myrent in various Paris archives and personal collections, from 1975 to 1976. Currently, Myrent is writing a biography of Henri Langlois, in association with Langlois's brother.

12. Henri Diamant-Berger, *Le Cinéma*, 102; Ernest Coustet, *Le Cinéma*, 161.

13. Mitry, "De quelques problèmes d'histoire et d'esthétique du cinéma," 120.

14. Coustet, *Le Cinéma*, 162-163.

Acknowledgments

1. These interviews formed the basis of a twelve-part "Histoire du cinéma" series that Armand Panigel produced for Antenne II in Paris. For some reason, the first two parts on the films of the silent period were not included in the original broadcast on French television in 1973-1974, but they were shown in a repeat of the series in 1981. Both are available through F.A.C.S.E.A., the French-American Cultural Services and Educational Aid in New York.

Note on Terms

1. Henri Diamant-Berger, *Le Cinéma*, 221.

2. Ibid., 12.

3. Barry Salt, *Film Style and Technology: History and Analysis* (forthcoming). Kevin Brownlow generally agrees with Salt's conclusion, but he also finds a consistent pattern of films being projected at speeds slightly faster than their "taking" speeds as well as numerous exceptions to a gradual increase in projection speed—"Silent Films: What *Was* the Right Speed?" *Sight and Sound* 49 (Summer, 1980), 164-167.

Part I, The French Film Industry: Introduction

1. Gérard Talon, "Cinéma français: la crise de 1928," 105.

2. This framework is based on the following historical studies: Jacques Chastenet, *Histoire de la Troisième République: les années d'illusions, 1918-1931*; D. W. Brogan, *The Development of Modern France, 1870-1939*, Vol. 2; Donald Harvey, *France since the Revolution*; David S. Landes, *The Unbound Prometheus: Technological Change and Industrial Development in Western Europe from 1750 to the Present*; Theodore Zeldin, *France, 1848-1945*, Vols. 1 and 2; Gordon Wright, *France in Modern Times*; José Baldizzone, "Des Historiens évoquent les Années Folles," 34-40.

3. Despite the fact that the Hays Office tried to argue that the film industry was the fifth largest United States industry, Douglas Gomery's research indicates that even at its peak it was never higher than thirty-fifth. Letter from Douglas Gomery, 14 May 1979.

4. Jacques Petat, "L'Avant-garde française des années vingt," 22.

5. Baldizzone, "Des Historiens évoquent les Années Folles," 35.

6. Léon Moussinac, "Panoramique du cinéma [1929]," in *L'Age ingrat du cinéma*, 238; Georges Sadoul, *Histoire générale du cinéma*, 4, 51. For convenience in these notes, the first number following the title of Sadoul's multi-volume history will refer to the volume number.

7. *Mon-Ciné* 34 (12 October 1922), 22, quoted in Maurice Roelens, "*Mon-Ciné* (1922-1924) et le mélodrame," 202.

8. Henri Diamant-Berger, *Le Cinéma*, 275.

9. Pierre Henry, "Les Films de France," *Ciné-pour-tous* 12 (22 October 1919), 2.

10. René Jeanne, "La Crise du cinéma," *Cinémagazine* 2 (21 October 1921), 14.

11 Jean Sapène, "La Politique du cinéma français," *Cinéa-Ciné-pour-tous* 34 (1 April 1925), 7.

12. Hubert Revol, "La corporation du cinéma," *Cinégraphie* 4 (15 December 1927), 64.

The War: Collapse and Reconstruction

1. G.-Michel Coissac, *Histoire du cinématographe, des origines jusqu'à nos jours*, 350-351, 359, 465-475, 482; André Delpeuch, *Le Cinéma*, 212-220; Georges Sadoul, *Histoire générale du cinéma*, 2, 241-255; Georges Sadoul, *Histoire générale du cinéma*, 3, 50-51; Pierre Leprohon, *Histoire du cinéma*, 1, 229-231; Georges Sadoul, *Le Cinéma français*, 218; Paul Leglise, *Histoire de la politique du cinéma français: le cinéma et la IIIᵉ République*, 36-37; Henri Diamant-Berger, *Il était une fois le cinéma*, 44.

2. Coissac, *Histoire du cinématographe*, 452-455; Delpeuch, *Le Cinéma*, 207-211; Sadoul, *Histoire générale du cinéma*, 2, 359-360; Leprohon, *Histoire du cinéma*, 1, 231-232; Sadoul, *Le Cinéma français*, 182; Francis Lacassin, "Alice Guy, la première réalisatrice de films du monde," in *Pour une contre histoire du cinéma*, 13-16; Jean Mitry, "De quelques problèmes d'histoire et d'esthétique du cinéma," 126.

3. Wright, *France in Modern Times*, 279-280.

4. Coissac, *Histoire du cinématographe*, 502-504; Sadoul, *Histoire générale du cinéma*, 2, 361, 363.

5. Coissac, *Histoire du cinématographe*, 498-501; René Jeanne and Charles Ford, *Histoire encyclopédique du cinéma*, 1, 114-123; René Jeanne, *Cinéma 1900*, 84-85. For convenience in these notes, the first number following the title of Jeanne and Ford's multi-volume history will refer to the volume number.

6. Jeanne and Ford, *Histoire encyclopédique du cinéma*, 113-114; Sadoul, *Histoire générale du cinéma*, 2, 350; Sadoul, *Histoire générale du cinéma*, 3, 253-254; Diamant-Berger, *Il était une fois le cinéma*, 16-17; Jeanne, *Cinéma 1900*, 104-105. René Jeanne and Charles Ford, *Paris vu par le cinéma*, 11-13.

7. Coissac, *Histoire du cinématographe*, 505-506.

8. Ibid., 492-495.

9. Sadoul, *Le Cinéma français*, 218; Tino Balio, "Struggles for Control: 1908-1930," in *The American Film Industry*, ed. Tino Balio, 103; Jeanne Thomas Allen, "The Decay of the Motion Picture Patents Company," in *The American Film Industry*, ed. Balio, 120-123. Jon Gartenberg's research on Vitagraph demonstrates that the American company distributed much of its own film product in Paris, from 1907 to 1914. Letter from Jon Gartenberg, 23 May 1983.

10. Charles Pathé, "De Pathé Frères à Pathé Cinéma," 73-77.

11. Sadoul, *Histoire générale du cinéma*, 2, 567-571.

12. Petat, "L'Avant-garde française," 22.

13. "Le Film français," *Le Film* (24 June 1914)—reprinted in *Intelligence du cinématographe*, ed. Marcel L'Herbier (Paris: Corréa, 1946), 433. Cf. V. Guillaume Danvers, Cacophonie!" *La Cinématographie française* 21 (29 March 1919), 9; Pierre Henry, "Le Film français," *Cahiers du mois* 16/17 (1925), 202; Sadoul, *Histoire générale du cinéma*, 3, 10.

14. Marcel Lapierre, *Les Cent Visages du cinéma*, 123; Henri Fescourt, *La Foi et les montagnes*, 137.

15. Georges Sadoul, *Histoire générale du cinéma*, 4, 38-39; Jeanne and Ford, *Histoire encyclopédique du cinéma*, 164.

16. Lapierre, *Les Cent Visages du cinéma*, 123-124; René Prédal, *La Société française (1914-1945) à travers le cinéma*, 49-51.

17. Philippe Soupault, *The American Influence in France*, 13-14.

18. Louis Delluc, "Cinéma et cie: ciné-romans," *Paris-Midi* (8 June 1918), 3; René Jeanne and Charles Ford, *Le Cinéma et la presse, 1895-1960*, 141-143.

19. Sadoul, *Histoire générale du cinéma*, 3, 327-357; Fescourt, *La Foi et les montagnes*, 146; Bernard Eisenschitz, "Histoires de l'histoire (deux périodes du cinéma français: le muet—le génération de 58)," 24; Claude Beylie and Francis Lacassin, "À la recherche d'un cinéma perdu: entretien avec Jean-Louis Bouquet, Henri Fescourt, Joë Hamman, Gaston Modot," 14-15, 22-25.

20. Louis Delluc, *Cinéma et cie*, 44-46; Fescourt, *La Foi et les montagnes*, 144-146.

21. Jean-Louis Bouquet, "Le Cinéma en France après la guerre," in *Le Cinéma des origines à nos jours*, ed. Henri Fescourt, 250.

22. Sadoul, *Histoire générale du cinéma*, 4, 51.

23. Jean Mitry, *Histoire du cinéma*, 2, 139. For convenience in these notes, the first number following the title of Mitry's multi-volume history will refer to the volume number.

24. *Annuaire général de la cinématographie* (1917), 44, 48, 50, 53, 55, 58-60, 73, 75, 78, 81, 83-85, 125, 135. Henri Diamant-Berger, "Nouvelles d'Amérique," *Le Film* 148 (15 January 1919), 7. For an account of Tourneur's work in the United States, see Richard Koszarski, "Maurice Tourneur: The First of the Visual Stylists," *Film Comment* 9 (March-April, 1973), 24-31, and Kevin Brownlow, "Ben Carré," *Sight and Sound* 49 (Winter, 1979-1980), 46-50.

25. Advertisements, *Cinématographie française* 9 (4 January 1919); Lapierre, *Les Cent Visages du cinéma*, 143.

26. *Cinématographie française* 26 (3 May 1919), 4.

27. *Cinématographie française* 24 (19 April 1919), 14.

28. Sadoul, *Histoire générale du cinéma*, 4, 45. During the first three months of 1919, the French position improved slightly, and French films made up 29 percent of the Paris releases.— V. Guillaume Danvers, "L'Entente industrielle, artistique, et commerciale," *La Cinématographie française* 32 (14 June 1919), 9.

29. Charles Pathé, *Souvenirs et conseils d'un parvenu* (1926), as quoted in Mitry, *Histoire du cinéma*, 2, 139. See also Charles Pathé, "Etude sur l'évolution de l'industrie cinématographique française [1918]," *Intelligence du cinématographe*, ed. Marcel L'Herbier (Paris: Corréa, 1946), 213-228; Fescourt, *La Foi et les montagnes*, 177-184; Marc Silberman, "Film and Ideology: The Structure of the German Film Industry and Films of the 1920s" (Paper delivered to the Fourth Annual Purdue Film Conference, West Lafayette, Indiana, 22 March 1979), 10.

30. Mitry, *Histoire du cinéma*, 2, 140.

31. Sadoul, *Histoire générale du cinéma*, 4, 35.

32. Pathé, "De Pathé Frères à Pathé Cinéma," 84; Mitry, *Histoire du cinéma*, 2, 140.

33. Louis Delluc, "Cinéma et cie: Questions," *Paris-Midi* (27 July 1918), 3.

34. Wright, *France in Modern Times*, 369.

35. Mitry, *Histoire du cinéma*, 2, 140; Sadoul, *Histoire générale du cinéma*, 4, 52; Pathé, "De Pathé Frères à Pathé Cinéma," 94; Charles Moraze, *The French and the Republic*, 74.

36. Pathé, "Etude sur l'évolution de l'industrie cinématographique française [1918]," 215-217. See also "Echos et information," *Le Journal du Ciné-Club* 57 (11 February 1921), 3; Fescourt, *La Foi et les montagnes*, 179-183; Sadoul, *Histoire générale du cinéma*, 4, 46.

37. "Du studio à l'écran," *Ciné-pour-tous* 43 (25 June 1920), 2; "Echos," *Cinémagazine* 1 (21-28 January 1921), 24; Pathé, "De Pathé Frères à Pathé Cinéma," 99.

38. Georges Sadoul, *Histoire générale du cinéma*, 6, 312-313. Henri Diamant-Berger offers a more personal explanation for this shocking retreat: Pathé was convinced that he had cancer of the throat, a condition which "miraculously" disappeared once he stopped wearing high collars that buttoned over the larynx! Diamant-Berger, *Il était une fois le cinéma*, 48.

39. Léon Poirier, *Vingt-quatre images à la seconde*, 40.

40. Ibid., 41; Pathé, "De Pathé Frères à Pathé Cinéma," 94.

41. Poirier, *Vingt-quatre images à la seconde*, 42.

42. "Production du film français," *Tout-Cinéma* (1922), 349-351; V.-Guillaume Danvers,

"Le Cinématographe en France de 1915 à 1920," 28. Sadoul, *Histoire générale du cinéma*, 5, 31, 413.

43. Coissac, *Histoire du cinématographe*, 504. A.-P. Richard, "Les Tendances modernes de la cinématographie," 28-29; Barry Salt, *Film Style and Technology: History and Analysis*.

44. Danvers, "Le Cinématographe en France de 1915 à 1920," 28.

45. Jeanne and Ford, *Paris vu par le cinéma*, 186; Jaque Catelain, *Marcel L'Herbier*, 29.

46. "Nos Studios," *Ciné-pour-tous* 26 (18 February 1920), 3; Howard T. Lewis, *The Motion Picture Industry*, 395.

Production: From Independent Artisan to International Consortium

1. Maurice Levy-Leboyer, "Innovation and Business Strategies in Nineteenth- and Twentieth-Century France," in *Enterprise and Entrepreneurs in Nineteenth- and Twentieth-Century France*, ed. Edward C. Carter II et al., 116-117.

2. Diamant-Berger, *Il était une fois le cinéma*, 60.

3. Ibid., 60-61.

4. Ibid., 61.

5. *Ciné-pour-tous* 33 (17 April 1920), 8; *Ciné-pour-tous* 37 (15 May 1920), 8; Fescourt, *La Foi et les montagnes*, 328.

6. "Le Monde du cinéma," *Ciné-pour-tous* 33 (17 April 1920), 2; Coissac, *Histoire du cinématographe*, 502; Fescourt, *La Foi et les montagnes*, 328.

7. "Les Faits," *Ciné-pour-tous* 32 (10 April 1920), 3; "Un formidable trust franco-américaine," *Le Journal du Ciné-Club* 34 (3 September 1920), 4-5; Steven Neale, "Art Cinema as Institution," 21, 25.

8. Sadoul, *Histoire générale du cinéma*, 5, 10-11.

9. *Ciné-pour-tous* 51 (22 October 1920), 8; *Ciné-pour-tous* 53 (19 November 1920), 6; Diamant-Berger, *Il était une fois le cinéma*, 74-78.

10. See Henri Diamant-Berger's laudatory description of such a producer in *Le Cinéma*, 72-78.

11. Bouquet, "Le Cinéma en France après la guerre," 254. Jean Girard, *Le Lexique français du cinéma, des origines à 1930*, 191.

12. These figures are based on the average length of 1,800 meters for a feature film—Ernest Coustet, *Le Cinéma*, 100. Chastenet, *Histoire de la Troisième République*, 215; Sadoul, *Histoire générale du cinéma*, 5, 8-9.

13. Louis Delluc, "Cinéma," *Paris-Midi* (31 January 1919) 2. "Au pays des milles et une nuits," *L'Illustration* (15 March 1919), 305-309; *Ciné-pour-tous* 10 (8 November 1919), 4, 8; "Le Monde du cinéma," *Ciné-pour-tous* 19 (10 January 1920), 2; "Le Monde du cinéma," *Ciné-pour-tous* 22 (31 January 1920), 2; *Ciné-pour-tous* 35 (1 May 1920), 4-5, 6; "Echos et informations," *Le Journal du Ciné-Club* 32 (20 August 1920), 5-6; *Ciné-pour-tous* 56 (31 December 1920), 4; Louis Nalpas folder, Bibliothèque de l'Arsenal; Louis Nalpas, "Lettre," *Cinématographie française* 463 (10 September 1927), 21; Fescourt, *La Foi et les montagnes*, 201; Sadoul, *Histoire générale du cinéma*, 4, 486.

14. Diamant-Berger, *Il était une fois le cinéma*, 53-67.

15. Jean Arroy, "Abel Gance: sa vie et son oeuvre," 6.

16. Sophie Daria, *Abel Gance, hier et demain*, 59; Kevin Brownlow, *The Parade's Gone By*, 613-614.

17. "Echos," *Cinémagazine* 3 (3 August 1923), 170.

18. Georges Dureau, "L'Atlantide," *Ciné-Journal* 15 (11 June 1921), 3; René Clair, "Films passés," *Théâtre et Comoedia Illustré* 13 (January, 1923), [n.p.]; Charles Ford, *Jacques Feyder*, 16-17; Fescourt, *La Foi et les montagnes*, 270-271; Sadoul, *Histoire générale du cinéma*, 5, 170.

19. Pierre Henry, "Les Idées—Petits Films," *Ciné-pour-tous* 32 (10 April 1920), 2.

20. "Du Studio à l'écran," *Ciné-pour-tous* 39 (29 May 1920), 2; Jupiter folder, Bibliothèque de l'Arsenal.

21. "Du Studio à l'écran," *Ciné-pour-tous* 43 (25 June 1920), 2; "Du Studio à l'écran," *Ciné-pour-tous* 49 (24 September 1920), 2. "Informations," *Cinémagazine* 1 (20-26 May 1921), 27; "Le Film français production," *Tout-Cinéma* (1922), 322-323. Fescourt, *La Foi et les montagnes*, 354.

22. Jay Leyda, *Kino: A History of the Russian and Soviet Film* (New York: Macmillan, 1960),

116; Jean Mitry, "Ivan Mosjoukine," 425; Richard Taylor, *The Politics of the Soviet Cinema, 1917-1929* (Cambridge: Cambridge University Press, 1979), 11, 16, 23.

23. "Du Studio à l'écran," *Ciné-pour-tous* 37 (15 May 1920), 2; "Du Studio à l'écran," *Ciné-pour-tous* 42 (19 June 1920), 2; "Louis Delluc présente Parisia-Film," *Ciné-pour-tous* 42 (19 June 1920), 4-5; *Les Nouveautés Aubert* 1 (September, 1920), 1; *Les Nouveautés Aubert* 4 (November, 1920), 1; *Les Nouveautés Aubert* 19 (August, 1921), 1.

24. Transcript of an interview by Armand Panigel with Marcel L'Herbier (1973). Marcel L'Herbier, *La Tête qui tourne*, 32-33.

25. "Du Studio à l'écran," *Ciné-pour-tous* 42 (19 June 1920), 2; André Lang, *Déplacements et Villégiatures littéraires et suivi de la promenade de royaume des images ou entretiens cinématographiques*, 158; Poirier, *Vingt-quatre images à la seconde*, 45 Catelain, *Marcel L'Herbier*, 41.

26. Poirier, *Vingt-quatre images à la seconde*, 45.

27. "Les Faits," *Ciné-pour-tous* 32 (10 April 1920), 3; "Du Studio à l'écran," *Ciné-pour-tous* 43 (25 June 1920), 2; "Du Studio à l'écran," *Ciné-pour-tous* 46 (30 July 1920), 2; "Echos et informations," *Le Journal du Ciné-Club* 37 (24 September 1920), 5; "La grande polémique au sujet de rapport de M. Charles Pathé," *Le Journal du Ciné-Club* 40 (15 October 1920), 2-3; Coissac, *Histoire du cinématographe*, 476-478; Pathé, "De Pathé Frères à Pathé Cinéma," 99-101; Philippe Esnault, "Entretiens avec André-Paul Antoine," 8; Mitry, *Histoire du cinéma*, 2, 361. Sadoul, *Histoire générale du cinéma*, 5, 12-13; Gerald McKee, *Film Collecting*, 73; François de la Breteque, "Le Film en tranches, les mutations du film à épisodes," 91, 97.

28. Diamant-Berger, *Il était une fois le cinéma*, 83. Sadoul gives the figure as three million francs.

29. Robert Florey, *Filmland* (Paris: Cinémagazine, 1923), 257; Diamant-Berger, *Il était une fois le cinéma*, 114. The first electrified studio in France seems to have been the Studio de Saint-Maurice, rue des Reservoirs, Joinville, constructed in 1920—Fescourt, *La Foi et les montagnes*, 150.

30. Diamant-Berger, *Il était une fois le cinéma*, 69-90, 113.

31. Sadoul, *Histoire générale du cinéma*, 5, 17.

32. Coissac, *Histoire du cinématographe*, 478; Sadoul, *Histoire générale du cinéma*, 5, 15-18.

33. "Le Marché européen en 1929," *Tout-Cinéma* (1930), 211. Prédal, *La Société française (1914-1945) à travers le cinéma*, 114. Sadoul, *Histoire générale du cinéma*, 5, 27.

34. *Annuaire général de la cinématographe* (1928), 566-567.

35. Jeanne, *Cinéma 1900*, 162; Sadoul, *Histoire générale du cinéma*, 5, 26-27.

36. Catelain, *Marcel L'Herbier*, 64-65; Fescourt, *La Foi et les montagnes*, 263. Claude Beylie and Michel Marie, "Entretien avec Marcel L'Herbier," 34/viii.

37. Sadoul, *Histoire générale du cinéma*, 5, 23.

38. Ibid., 24.

39. Diamant-Berger, *Il était une fois le cinéma*, 113-114.

40. Ibid., 119-120.

41. "Ce que l'on dit . . . ," *Cinémagazine* 2 (2 June 1922), 316; *Pathé-Journal* (1 September 1924), 5-8; *Pathé-Journal* (15 November 1924), 9; *Pathé-Journal* (15 December 1924), 1; Coissac, *Histoire du cinématographe*, 479; Fescourt, *La Foi et les montagnes*, 76, 356, 358; Claude Beylie and Francis Lacassin, "Henri Fescourt," *L'Avant-Scène du cinéma* 71 (June, 1967), 291; Sadoul, *Histoire générale du cinéma*, 5, 32-34; Diamant-Berger, *Il était une fois le cinéma*, 121; Breteque, "Le Film en tranches, les mutations du film à épisodes," 98-99; Jean-Louis Bouquet, "Panorama de l'activité française, 1916-1928," 62-63.

42. "Echos," *Cinémagazine* 4 (25 January 1924), 153; *Pathé-Journal* (15 October 1924), 5; *Pathé-Journal* (15 December 1924), 5; Fescourt, *La Foi et les montagnes*, 360; Bouquet, "Panorama de l'activité française, 1916-1928," 63-64.

43. René Clair, "Les Films du mois," *Théâtre et Comoedia Illustré* 22 (November, 1923), [n.p.].

44. Lang, *Déplacements et Villégiatures littéraires*, 159.

45. *Ciné-Information-Aubert* 26 (1 September 1925), 1.

46. Coissac, *Histoire du cinématographe*, 502; Fescourt, *La Foi et les montagnes*, 356.

47. Mitry, "Ivan Mosjoukine," 426; "Les projets de Films Albatros," *Mon-Ciné* (24 January 1924), 20.

48. Transcript of an interview by Armand Panigel with Charles Spaak (1973).

49. Fescourt, *La Foi et les montagnes*, 314; Sadoul, *Histoire générale du cinéma*, 5, 158.

50. André-Paul Antoine, *Antoine, père et fils* (Paris: René Julliard, 1962), 211.

51. André Bencey, "Germaine Albert-Dulac," 233-234.

52. Fescourt, *La Foi et les montagnes*, 296-297; Charles Ford, "Germaine Dulac," 20.

53. "Le Monde du cinéma," *Ciné-pour-tous* 23 (7 February 1920), 2; "Louis Delluc présente Parisia-Film," 4-5; "Du Studio à l'écran," *Ciné-pour-tous* 47 (13 August 1920), 2; Poirier, *Vingt-quatre images à la seconde*, 45; Sadoul, *Histoire générale du cinéma*, 5, 65; Transcript of an interview by Armand Panigel with Eve Francis (1973).

54. Transcript of an interview by Armand Panigel with Eve Francis (1973). Sadoul, *Histoire générale du cinéma*, 5, 76-77.

55. Jean de Mirbal, "Jacques de Baroncelli," 117; Jean Mitry, "Jacques de Baroncelli," [n.p.]. Albert Bonneau, "L'Effort français en 1924," *Annuaire général de la cinématographie* (1925), 82. Fescourt, *La Foi et les montagnes*, 328.

56. *Almanach du cinéma* (1923), 18; Lang, *Déplacements et villégiatures littéraires*, 176; Fescourt, *Les Cent Visages du cinéma*, 192.

57. Fescourt, *La Foi et les montagnes*, 273.

58. "Echos," *Cinémagazine* 3 (7 September 1923), 346; Jean Mitry, *Histoire du cinéma*, 3, 371.

59. Sadoul, *Histoire générale du cinéma*, 5, 184.

60. "*La Machine à refaire la vie*," *Mon-Ciné* (24 April 1924), 14. Raymond Chirat, "Julien Duvivier," 5-6, 122.

61. "Actualités," *Théâtre et Comoedia Illustré* 19 (July, 1923), [n.p.]. Fescourt, *La Foi et les montagnes*, 282. Catherine de la Roche, *René Clair*, 10; Jean Mitry, *René Clair*, 182; Transcript of an interview by Armand Panigel with René Clair (1973).

62. Lang, *Déplacements et villégiatures littéraires*, 177; Delpeuch, *Le Cinéma*, 251. Pierre Leprohon, *Jean Epstein*, 33.

63. Bernard Chardère, ed., "Jean Renoir," 9; André Bazin, *Jean Renoir*, 202-204; Jean Renoir, *Ma Vie et mes films*, 77-78.

64. Catelain, *Marcel L'Herbier*, 71-73, 80-81. Transcript of an interview by Armand Panigel with Marcel L'Herbier (1973); Beylie and Marie, "Entretien avec Marcel L'Herbier," 34/viii.

65. Paul de la Borie, "Le Film européen," *Cinémagazine* 5 (9 January 1925), 63. Cf. Lapierre, *Les Cent Visages du cinéma*, 192.

66. Wright, *France in Modern Times*, 314.

67. Advertisement, *Cinéa* 48 (7 April 1922), 17; Lucien Wahl, "*Le Demon de la haine*," 7; Léonce Perret, "Comment j'ai tourné *Koenigsmark*," 329-332; Moussinac, "La Naissance du cinéma [1925]," 132-134; G.-Michel Coissac, "L'Evolution du cinématographe et la réalisation de quelques grands films," 22. Transcript of an interview by Armand Panigel with Marcel L'Herbier (1973).

68. Gaston Tournier, "Les projets de nos metteurs en scène," *Cinémagazine* 2 (8 September 1922), 289.

69. René Clair, "L'Affaire du Collier de la Reine," *Théâtre et Comoedia Illustré*, 24 (December, 1923), [n.p.]; Jeanne and Ford, *Le Cinéma et la presse*, 137-138.

70. "Ce que l'on dit . . . ," *Cinémagazine* 2 (4 August 1922), ,142; "Actualités," *Théâtre et Comoedia Illustré* 14 (February, 1923), [n.p.]; "Actualités," *Théâtre et Comoedia Illustré* 22 (October, 1923), [n.p.]; Lapierre, *Les Cent Visages du cinéma*, 188; Catelain, *Marcel L'Herbier*, 72-73, 76-77; Fescourt, *La Foi et les montagnes*, 264; Sadoul, *Histoire générale du cinéma*, 5, 98; Beylie and Marie, "Entretien avec Marcel L'Herbier," 34/viii.

71. Paul de la Borie, "Une Sentence de boycottage," *Cinématographie française* 246 (21 July 1923), 1-3; "L'Activité cinégraphique," *Cinéa-Ciné-pour-tous* 9 (15 January 1924), 28; "L'Activité cinégraphique," *Cinéa-Ciné-pour-tous* 14 (1 June 1924), 26; "L'Activité cinégraphique," *Cinéa-Ciné-pour-tous* 15 (15 June 1924), 23. Paul de la Borie, "Le Film européen," 63. Jean Mitry, "Max Linder," in *Anthologie du cinéma*, 2 (Paris: L'Avant-Scène du cinéma, 1967), 311. Victor Bachy, "Jacques Feyder," in *Anthologie du cinéma*, 2, 416-417; Sadoul, *Histoire générale du cinéma*, 5, 34, 36, 433.

72. "L'Activité cinégraphique," *Cinéa-Ciné-pour-tous* 8 (1 March 1924), 28; Albert Bonneau, "M. Tourjansky tourne *Le Prince charmant*," *Cinémagazine* 4 (3 October 1924), 12-14; "Echos," *Cinémagazine* 4 (21 November 1924), 345; "Echos," *Cinémagazine* 5 (9 January 1925), 90; "Echos," *Cinémagazine* 5 (23 January 1925), 190; Mitry, "Ivan Mosjoukine," 429; Brownlow,

The Parade's Gone By, 613; Sadoul, *Histoire générale du cinéma*, 5, 157, 432-433; R. T., "Le nouveau film de Mme Germaine Dulac," *Cinéa-Ciné-pour-tous* 28 (1 January 1925), 4-5.

73. "Le Marché européen en 1929," *Tout-Cinéma* (1930), 211.

74. Chastenet, *Histoire de la Troisième République*, 124-125. Brogan, *The Development of Modern France*, 581-582. Sadoul, *Histoire générale du cinéma*, 5, 422-426.

75. Landes, *The Unbound Prometheus*, 363.

76. Sadoul, *Histoire générale du cinéma*, 5, 438-440.

77. Léon Moussinac, "La Foire du cinéma est ouverte," *Le Crapouillot* (May, 1928), 55.

78. "Léonce Perret reçoit un grand prix aux Arts Décoratifs pour *Madame Sans-Gêne*," 28; Jeanne and Ford, *Histoire encyclopédique du cinéma*, 1, 224-225; Fescourt, *La Foi et les montagnes*, 100; Sadoul, *Histoire générale du cinéma*, 5, 41; Gloria Swanson, *Swanson on Swanson*, 214-216, 222, 269, 278-279.

79. "L'Activité cinégraphique," *Cinéa-Ciné-pour-tous* 13 (15 May 1924), 28; Sadoul, *Histoire générale du cinéma*, 5, 32, 39-40.

80. Sadoul, *Histoire générale du cinéma*, 5, 435-440; Silberman, "Film and Ideology: The Structure of the German Film Industry and Films of the 1920s," 21a-22; Letter from Kristin Thompson, 22 February 1980.

81. *Pathé-Journal* (15 October 1924), 5; Coissac, "L'Evolution de cinématographe et la réalisation de quelques grands films," 25; Lapierre, *Les Cent Visages du cinéma*, 162. Fescourt, *La Foi et les montagnes*, 344; Sadoul, *Histoire générale du cinéma*, 5, 433.

82. Henri Poullaille, "L'Age ingrat du cinéma," 59.

83. "Echos," *Cinémagazine* 4 (10 October 1924), 69; "L'Activité cinégraphique," *Cinéa-Ciné-pour-tous* 37 (15 May 1925), 23; "L'Activité cinégraphique," *Cinéa-Ciné-pour-tous* 46 (1 October 1925), 30; "Echos et communiqués," *Cinéa-Ciné-pour-tous* 51 (15 December 1925), 34; "L'Activité cinégraphique," *Cinéa-Ciné-pour-tous* 54 (1 February 1926), 25; "Films présentés en France," *Tout-Cinéma* (1928), 933-940. Catelain, *Marcel L'Herbier*, 91; Chirat, "Julien Duvivier," 122. Barthélémy Amengual, *René Clair*, 175. Pierre Leprohon, *Jean Renoir*, 33; Renoir, *Ma Vie et mes films*, 72-75, 77-78.

84. "L'Activité cinégraphique," *Cinéa-Ciné-pour-tous* 88 (1 July 1927), 26; "L'Activité cinégraphique," *Cinéa-Ciné-pour-tous* 89 (15 July 1927), 25. Pierre Billard, "Jean Grémillon," *Anthologie du cinéma*, 2, 526-528.

85. "Echos et communiqués," *Cinéa-Ciné-pour-tous* 60 (1 May 1926), 26; Interview with Marie Epstein, 14 August and 13 November 1976.

86. "L'Activité cinégraphique," *Cinéa-Ciné-pour-tous* 80 (1 March 1927), 26; Jean Dréville, "Films," *Cinégraphie* 2 (15 October 1927), 37; Elizabeth Sussex, "Cavalcanti in England," 207.

87. Marcel Colin, "En 1927," *Cinématographie française* 480 (14 January 1928), 11; "Le Marché européen en 1929," *Tout-Cinéma* (1930), 211; André Chevanne, *L'Industrie du cinéma: le cinéma sonore*, 49; Lapierre, *Les Cent Visages du cinéma*, 191.

88. *Ciné-Information-Aubert* 37 (1 March 1926), 1.

89. *Ciné-Information-Aubert* 41 (1 May 1926), 1; Advertisement for Aubert, *Cinémagazine* 6 (21 May 1926), 368; "M. Louis Aubert nous parle de sa nouvelle production," *Cinéa-Ciné-pour-tous* 92 (1 September 1927), 31.

90. "Pathé-Consortium-Cinéma: la saison prochaine," *Pathé-Journal* (9 April 1926), 12.

91. Fescourt, *La Foi et les montagnes*, 361-362.

92. Bouquet, "Panorama de l'activité française, 1916-1928," 64-65.

93. Harlé, "L'Effort français," *Cinématographie française* 482 (28 January 1928), 9.

94. Fescourt, *La Foi et les montagnes*, 362.

95. Bouquet, "Le Cinéma en France après la guerre," 264; Fescourt, *La Foi et les montagnes*, 363; Sadoul, *Histoire générale du cinéma*, 6, 315.

96. *Film Daily Yearbook, 1922-1923* (New York: Film Daily, 1923), 413-414; "L'Activité cinégraphique," *Cinéa-Ciné-pour-tous* 54 (1 February 1926), 25, 28; Advertisement, *Cinéa-Ciné-pour-tous* 60 (1 May 1926), 4; "L'Activité cinégraphique," *Cinéa-Ciné-pour-tous* 66 (31 July 1926), 24; "L'Inauguration du Studio Natan," *Cinéa-Ciné-pour-tous* 78 (1 February 1927), 26; "Les Studios Réunis," *Cinématographie française* 467 (15 October 1927), 18; "Les Notabilités du cinéma," *Cinématographie française* 479 (7 January 1928), 13; Diamant-Berger, *Il était une fois le cinéma*, 148-150.

97. "Echos et communiqués," *Cinéa-Ciné-pour-tous* 55 (15 February 1926), 22; Advertisement, *Cinémagazine* 27 (17 June 1927); "Les Projets de la Franco-Film," *Cinématographie française*

453 (9 July 1927), 18; Robert Trevise, "Les Présentations," *Cinéa-Ciné-pour-tous* 89 (15 July 1927), 33; "L'Activité cinégraphique," *Cinéa-Ciné-pour-tous* 94 (1 October 1927), 23; Mitry, *Histoire du cinéma*, 2, 365.

98. René Clair, "Millions," *Le Rouge et le noir*, special issue (July, 1928), 46-47. Cf. Pierre Desclaux, "Les grands films de 1927-1928," *Almanach de Mon-Ciné* (1929), 11-12.

99. Sadoul, *Histoire générale du cinéma*, 6, 315.

100. "L'Activité cinégraphique," *Cinéa-Ciné-pour-tous* 52 (1 January 1926), 22; "L'Activité cinégraphique," *Cinéa-Ciné-pour-tous* 72 (1 November 1926), 25. Juan Arroy, "La Technique de *Napoléon*," 9. "Apres *Napoléon*, Jeanne d'Arc," *Cinématographie française* 455 (20 July 1927), 1; David Bordwell, *Filmguide to La Passion de Jeanne d'Arc*, 14; Sadoul, *Histoire générale du cinéma*, 6, 319, 382.

101. Lewis Jacobs, ed. *The Compound Cinema: The Film Writings of Harry Alan Potamkin*, 287.

102. H. D., "An Appreciation," *Close Up* 4 (March, 1929), 57.

103. "Actualités," *Cinémagazine* 8 (16 March 1928), 469; Desclaux, "Les grands films de 1927-1928," 13.

104. "L'Activité cinégraphique," *Cinéa-Ciné-pour-tous* 96 (1 November 1927), 27; Ford, *Jacques Feyder*, 28-31.

105. "Courrier des studios," *Cinématographie française* 472 (9 November 1927), 49; SOFAR folder, Bibliothèque de l'Arsenal.

106. "Les Films Ciné-Alliance U.F.A.," *Cinématographie française* 468 (22 October, 1927), 24.

107. *Pathé-Journal* (27 August 1926), 8-9; "L'Activité cinégraphique," *Cinéa-Ciné-pour-tous* 73 (15 November 1926), 17; Catelain, *Marcel L'Herbier*, 99-100.

108. Robert Trevise, "Les Présentations," *Cinéa-Ciné-pour-tous* 89 (15 July 1927), 33. Catelain, *Marcel L'Herbier*, 92-93.

109. "Accords Franco-Allemands," *Cinématographie française* 478 (31 December 1927), 8.

110. "La Production d'Albatros," *Cinématographie française* 462 (7 September 1927), 4; Gilbert Flamand, "On tourne *Cagliostro*," *Cinéa-Ciné-pour-tous* 124 (1 January 1929), 21; Advertisement, *Tout-Cinéma* (1929), 619.

111. "Les nouveaux films," *Cinéa-Ciné-pour-tous* 111 (25 June 1928), 6; Desclaux, "Les grands films de 1927-1928," 14.

112. *Cinématographique française* 484 (11 February 1928); Pierre Henry, "Le film sonore—les dates," *Cinéa-Ciné-pour-tous* 130 (1 April 1929), 8.

113. Brogan, *The Development of Modern France*, 520. Balio, "Struggles for Control: 1908-1930," 114. Sadoul, *Histoire générale du cinéma*, 5, 413-416. Janet Staiger, "Dividing Labor and Production Control: Thomas Ince and the Rise of the Studio System," 16-25.

114. Jacobs, ed., *The Compound Cinema*, 287; Henri Mercillon, "Industries du cinéma et analyse économique," *Economie et cinéma* 1 (January-February, 1955), 9; Levy-Leboyer, "Innovation and Business Strategies in Nineteenth- and Twentieth-Century France," 128-129; Letter from Jean Dréville, 5 July 1978.

115. Lewis, *The Motion Picture Industry*, 397.

116. Landes, *The Unbound Prometheus*, 482.

117. James True, *Printer's Ink* (4 February 1926), quoted in Charles Eckert, "The Carole Lombard in Macy's Window," 4-5.

118. Marcel Braunschvig, *La Vie Américaine* (Paris: Armand Colin, 1931), 356.

Distribution: The Divided Country

1. Leglise, *Histoire de la politique du cinéma français*, 27-28, 30-32.

2. Jeanne and Ford, *Le Cinéma et la presse*, 201-202; Leglise, *Histoire de la politique du cinéma français*, 33; Sadoul, *Histoire générale du cinéma*, 5, 45.

3. Jeanne and Ford, *Le Cinéma et la presse*, 202-203.

4. Lapierre, *Les Cent Visages du cinéma*, 139.

5. Louis Delluc, "Cinéma," *Paris-Midi* (12 May 1919), 2; Delluc, "Cinéma," *Paris-Midi* (18 May 1919), 2. Diamant-Berger, *Le Cinéma*, 247-248; Lapierre, *Les Cent Visages du cinéma*, 240. Kevin Brownlow, *The War, the West, and the Wilderness* (New York: Knopf, 1979), 144-149.

6. André Antoine, "Tripatouillages," 5-6; "Censure des Films," *Tout-Cinéma* (1922), 613.

Coissac, *Histoire du cinématographe*, 436; Catelain, *Marcel L'Herbier*, 45; Leglise, *Histoire de la politique du cinéma français*, 10, 61-67; Sadoul, *Histoire générale du cinéma*, 5, 45-48; Sussex, "Cavalcanti in England," 207.

7. "L'Activité cinégraphique," *Cinéa-Ciné-pour-tous* 125 (15 January 1929), 22; Marcel Carné, "Censures . . . ," *Cinémagazine* 9 (20 September 1929), 415-418; Leglise, *Histoire de la politique du cinéma français*, 67-70; Prédal, *La Société française (1914-1945) à travers le cinéma*, 205; Mitry, *Histoire du cinéma*, 3, 376-377; Paul Monaco, *Cinema and Society: France and Germany during the Twenties*, 51; Letter from Jean Dréville, 5 July 1978.

8. Delluc, "Cinéma," *Paris-Midi* (12 May 1919), 2; Delluc, "Cinéma," *Paris-Midi* (18 May 1919), 2. "Films russes interdits," *Cinéa-Ciné-pour-tous* 132 (1 May 1929), 6; Fescourt, *La Foi et les montagnes*, 224. Brogan, *The Development of Modern France*, 645; Leglise, *Histoire de la politique du cinéma français*, 67; Prédal, *La Société française (1914-1945) à travers le cinéma*, 103-104; Sadoul, *Histoire générale du cinéma*, 5, 401-403; Monaco, *Cinema and Society*, 51-52; Diamant-Berger, *Il était une fois le cinéma*, 153-154; Jeanne, *Cinema 1900*, 243.

9. Advertisements, *Le Film* 170 (April, 1920); Advertisements, *Almanach du cinéma* (1922), 6-7.

10. Mitry, *Histoire du cinéma*, 2, 361.

11. Advertisements, *Cinémagazine* 1 (28 October 1921).

12. Advertisements, *Cinémagazine* 2 (3 March 1922); *Film Daily Yearbook, 1922-1923*, 413-414.

13. "*Le Cabinet du Docteur Caligari*," *Cinéa* 27 (11 November 1921), 8; Lionel Landry, "*Le Rail*," *Cinéa* 59-60 (23 June 1922), 5; Louis Delluc, "Les Cinéastes," 43. Jean Pascal, "L'Invasion du film allemand," *Cinémagazine* 2 (22 September 1922), 351; Jean Galtier-Boissière, "Une séance d'art muet," *Le Crapouillot* (1 January 1923), 20-21; Sadoul, *Histoire générale du cinéma*, 5, 29-30.

14. Sadoul, *Histoire générale du cinéma*, 5, 9-10.

15. Louis Delluc, "Cinéma," *Paris-Midi* (5 April 1919), 2. "Abel Gance nous revient de New York," *Cinémagazine* 2 (4 October 1921), 28. "On nous écrit de New York," *Cinémagazine* 2 (4 November 1921), 33. Robert Florey, "Echos de Los Angeles," *Cinémagazine* 2 (13 January 1922), 52. Henri Diamant-Berger, "La leçon d'Amérique," *Cinémagazine* 2 (12 May 1922), 192. Albert Bonneau, "Un Entretien avec Albert Capellani," *Cinémagazine* 3 (20 April 1923), 113. *Film Daily Yearbook, 1922-1923*, 55, 57, 63, 84, 86. Poulaille, "L'Age ingrat du cinéma," 63. Catelain, *Marcel L'Herbier*, 29. Daria, *Abel Gance*, 86. Brownlow, *The Parade's Gone By*, 623-624. Transcript of an interview by Armand Panigel with Abel Gance (1973). Sadoul, *Histoire générale du cinéma*, 5, 43. Pierre Boulanger, *Le Cinéma colonial*, 61.

16. "Ce que l'on dit . . . ," *Cinémagazine* 3 (27 April 1923), 167; A. T., "Cinémagazine à New York," *Cinémagazine* 3 (28 September 1923), 454; *Film Daily Yearbook* (New York: Film Daily, 1924), 55; Fescourt, *La Foi et les montagnes*, 274.

17. Lapierre, *Les Cent Visages du cinéma*, 150.

18. Sadoul, *Histoire générale du cinéma*, 5, 28. Diamant-Berger, *Il était une fois le cinéma*, 107.

19. "Le Marché européen en 1929," *Tout-Cinéma* (1930), 210-211. Sadoul, *Histoire générale du cinéma*, 5, 36, 433. Diamant-Berger, *Il était une fois le cinéma*, 67.

20. Wright, *France in Modern Times*, 360.

21. "Frantsuzskie nemye fil 'my v sovetskom prokate [French silent films in Soviet distribution]," *Kino: vremia* 4 (1965), 348-379. Vance and Betty Kepley drew my attention to this source in their "Foreign films on Soviet Screens, 1922-1931," *Quarterly Review of Film Studies* 4 (1979), 431.

22. The number of films imported into the U.S.S.R. from Germany and the United States was even higher: respectively, 41 and 7 (1922), 137 and 101 (1923), 94 and 231 (1924), and 53 and 241 (1925). Kepley, "Foreign Films on Soviet Screens," 431.

23. Brogan, *The Development of Modern France*, 588. Leglise, *Histoire de la politique du cinéma français*, 55-56. Sadoul, *Histoire générale du cinéma*, 5, 28-31.

24. Advertisement, *Cinémagazine* 4 (8 February 1924). Albert Bonneau, "L'Effort français en 1924," 82. "Nos echos," *Mon-Ciné* (24 January 1924), 20.

25. Poirier, *Vingt-quatre images à la seconde*, 57.

26. Sadoul, *Histoire générale du cinéma*, 5, 39-41.

27. "Pathé-Consortium-Cinéma: les grandes productions françaises," *Tout-Cinéma* (1922), 68-

69, 322-323. V.-Guillaume Danvers, "La Cinématographie en France en 1922," *Almanach du cinéma* (1923), 55-58, 60-67. Delpeuch, *Le Cinéma*, 105.

28. Bouquet, "Le Cinéma en France après la guerre," 263. Also see Delpeuch, *Le Cinéma*, 96-97.

29. Fescourt, *La Foi et les montagnes*, 359.

30. *Les Nouveautés Aubert* 21 (October 1921), 1; *Les Nouveautés Aubert* 23 (November, 1921), 3; *Les Nouveautés Aubert* 27 (April, 1921), 1; *Ciné-Information-Aubert* 8 (1 December 1924), 1; *Ciné-Information-Aubert* 18 (1 May 1925), 1. Coissac, *Histoire du cinématographe*, 496-497. Coissac, "L'Evolution du cinématographe et la réalisation de quelques grands films," 14. Sadoul, *Histoire générale du cinéma*, 5, 36-37. Boulanger, *Le Cinéma colonial*, 38.

31. *Ciné-Information-Aubert* 12 (1 February 1925), 1.

32. *Ciné-Information-Aubert* 8 (1 December 1924), 1.

33. Albatros brochures, Bibliothèque de l'Arsenal. Bonneau, "L'Effort français en 1924," 73-74.

34. Advertisement, *Almanach du cinéma* (1923), 24-25. Bonneau, "L'Effort français en 1924," 76. Roger Weil-Lorac, *Cinquante ans de cinéma actif* (Paris: Dujarric, 1977), 11.

35. Coissac, *Histoire du cinématographe*, 508-513. Delpeuch, *Le Cinéma*, 98, 222. Fescourt, *La Foi et les montagnes*, 99.

36. Advertisement, *Annuaire général de la cinématographie* (1928), 516.

37. Bonneau, "L'Effort français en 1924," 79.

38. "Présentations spéciales de l'année 1924," *Annuaire général de la cinématographie* (1925), 118.

39. "Edition-Location," *Tout-Cinéma* (1926), 355. Advertisements, *Tout-Cinéma* (1928), 492-583.

40. Advertisement, *Tout-Cinéma* (1928), 550.

41. Advertisements, *Tout-Cinéma* (1926), 364, and *Tout-Cinéma* (1928), 573.

42. "Le marché européen en 1929," *Tout-Cinéma* (1930), 210-211. Chevanne, *L'Industrie du cinéma*, 105.

43. Advertisement, *Cinémagazine* 6 (21 May 1926), 375-376. *Film Daily* reported that many of these German films were accepted as reparation payments—*Film Daily Yearbook* (New York; Film Daily, 1929), 1021.

44. "Le Marché européen en 1929," *Tout-Cinéma* (1930), 210-211.

45. *Film Daily Yearbook* (1928), 511-512; *Film Daily Yearbook* (1929), 31.

46. George Pratt, ed., *Spellbound in Darkness: A History of the Silent Cinema* (Greenwich, Conn.: New York Graphic Society, 1973), 382.

47. Daria, *Abel Gance*, 116-117. René Jeanne and Charles Ford, *Abel Gance*, 52.

48. Brownlow, *The Parade's Gone By*, 631.

49. Ibid., 647.

50. Letter from Kevin Brownlow, 25 August 1979.

51. Daria, *Abel Gance*, 118. Brownlow, *The Parade's Gone By*, 650.

52. Lewis, *The Motion Picture Industry*, 408.

53. André Delpeuch, "Le Décret est publié," *La Cinématographie française* (25 February 1928)—reprinted in *Intelligence du cinématographe*, ed. L'Herbier, 456-460. Moussinac, "La Foire du cinéma est ouverte," 54. *Film Daily Yearbook* (1928), 957. Bouquet, "Le Cinéma en France après la guerre," 266, 271. Lewis, *The Motion Picture Industry*, 404, 408. Harvey, *France Since the Revolution*, 220-230.

54. Jean Tedesco, "Le Décret de M. Herriot," *Cinéa-Ciné-pour-tous* 104 (1 March 1928), 9-10; Moussinac, "La Foire du cinéma est ouverte," 55; Hubert Revol, "Le Cinéma, spectacle forain," *On Tourne* (July, 1928), 1; J. Vidal, " 'Lock-out,' on dit les Américains, pour faire échec au contingentement," *Pour Vous* 22 (18 April 1929), 2; Alexandre Arnoux, "Contingentement: Dernier Bulletin," *Pour Vous* 43 (12 September 1929), 2; *Film Daily Yearbook* (1930), 571, 1015; *Film Daily Yearbook* (1929), 1021; Lewis, *The Motion Picture Industry*, 404, 407, 410; Robert Sklar, *Movie-Made America: A Cultural History of American Movies* (New York: Random House, 1975), 222; Janet Staiger and Douglas Gomery, "The History of World Cinema: Models for Economic Analysis," 39. Garth Jowett, *Film: The Democratic Art* (Boston: Little, Brown, 1976), 204-205.

55. "Echos et informations," *Cinémagazine* 7 (24 June 1927), 624; Pierre Heuzé, "Un Animateur du film français: P. J. de Venloo," *Cinémonde* 15 (31 January 1929), 286.

1. "Echos et communiqués," *Cinéa-Ciné-pour-tous* 109 (15 May 1928), 27; Chevanne, *L'Industrie du cinéma*, 77. In 1920, the rate of exchange was about 15 francs to a dollar; in 1925, it was more than 25 francs to a dollar—Chastenet, *Les Années d'illusions*, 215.

2. "Echos-Information," *Le Journal du Ciné-Club* 16 (30 April 1920), 2. Coissac, *Histoire du cinématographe*, 437-438. Leglise, *Histoire de la politique du cinéma français*, 51-58.

3. Coissac, *Histoire du cinématographe*, 438-439. Bouquet, "Le Cinéma en France après la guerre," 257. Lewis, *The Motion Picture Industry*, 412. Chevanne, *L'Industrie du cinéma*, 81. Leglise, *Histoire de la politique du cinéma français*, 55-56. Sadoul, *Histoire générale du cinéma*, 5, 8. Bouquet, "Panorama de l'activité français, 1916-1928," 60.

4. Sadoul, *Histoire générale du cinéma*, 4, 491.

5. "Echos et informations," *Le Journal du Ciné-Club*, 57 (11 February 1921), 9. Taylor, *The Politics of the Soviet Cinema*, 80. There were only 1,500 to 1,800 cinemas in the U.S.S.R.

6. Chevanne, *L'Industrie du cinéma*, 72.

7. Lewis, *The Motion Picture Industry*, 412.

8. Sadoul, *Histoire générale du cinéma*, 6, 315.

9. Delpeuch, *Le Cinéma*, 99.

10. Chevanne, *L'Industrie du cinéma*, 82. Cf. Lewis, *The Motion Picture Industry*, 412.

11. Henri Bousquet, "Economie et publicité cinématographique dans l'immédiat après-guerre," 67-75.

12. G.-Michel Coissac, *Les Coulisses du cinéma*, 198. These contracts are quite similar to the "Règlement des usages de location des films cinématographiques," published by the Chambre Syndicale de Cinématographie Française in *Cinématographie française* 17 (1 March 1919), 16-18.

13. Chevanne, *L'Industrie du cinéma*, 72.

14. "Cinémas," *Tout-Cinéma* (1926), 107-120.

15. Diamant-Berger, *Le Cinéma*, 221-222. "La Représentation—la vie du film," *Ciné-pour-tous* 53 (19 November 1920), 2. Diamant-Berger, *Il était une fois le cinéma*, 67.

16. *Ciné-Information-Aubert* 49 (1 September 1926), 1.

17. *Pathé-Journal* (15 October 1924), 5.

18. Breteque, "Le Film en tranches," 91, 99.

19. Francis Lacassin, *Louis Feuillade*, 186.

20. Jean Girard, *Le Lexique français du cinéma, des origines à 1930*, 113.

21. Russell Merritt, "Nickelodeon Theaters, 1905-1914: Building an Audience for the Movies," in *The American Film Industry*, ed. Balio, 59-79. Robert C. Allen, "Motion Picture Exhibition in Manhattan: Beyond the Nickelodeon," *Cinema Journal* 18 (Spring, 1979), 2-15. Douglas Gomery, "Toward a History of Film Exhibition: The Case of the Picture Palace," Publix Theaters and the Chain Store Strategy," *Cinema Journal* 18 (Spring, 1979), 26-40. Douglas Gomery, "The Growth of Movie Monopolies: The Case of Balaban and Katz," *Wide Angle 3* (1979), 54-63. Charlotte Herzog, "The Movie Palace and the Theatrical Sources of its Architectural Style," *Cinema Journal* 20 (Spring, 1981), 15-37. Douglas Gomery, "The Economics of U.S. Film Exhibition Policy and Practice," *Ciné-tracts* 12 (Winter, 1981), 36-40. Douglas Gomery, "Movie Audiences, Urban Geography, and the History of the American Film," *Velvet Light Trap* 19 (1982), 23-29.

22. André Antoine, "Le Public," *Cinémagazine* 1 (18-24 February 1921), 5-7.

23. Michael B. Miller, *The Bon Marché*, 47, 236.

24. Delpeuch, *Le Cinéma*, 271.

25. Louis Delluc, "Cinéma," *Paris-Midi* (3 March 1919), 2. Compare Diamant-Berger, *Le Cinéma*, 232, and "Entretien avec Jean Mitry," *Cinématographe* 47 (May, 1979), 21.

26. Diamant-Berger, *Le Cinéma*, 221. André Antoine, "Tripatouillages," 5.

27. André Breton, "Comme dans un bois . . . ," 27.

28. Antoine, "Tripatouillages," 5-6. Compare Pathé, "Etude sur l'évolution de l'industrie cinématographique française [1918]," *Intelligence du cinématographe*, 214.

29. Lapierre, *Les Cent Visages du cinéma*, 190. Compare Moussinac's outrage at the poor condition of several re-releases of Swedish films—"Au Cinéma: Reprise," *Le Crapouillot* (1 May 1923), 30.

30. Diamant-Berger, "La Leçon d'Amérique," 192. Pierre Gilles, "Pour la cinématographie française," *Pathé-Journal* (4 December 1925), 8.

31. Barry Salt, *Film Style and Technology: History and Analysis*.

32. Lewis, *The Motion Picture Industry*, 412.

33. René Noell, "Histoire du spectacle cinématographique à Perpignan, de 1896 à 1944," 60.

34. Advertisements, *Annuaire général de la cinématographie française et étrangère* (1917), 112, 131. Coissac, *Histoire du cinématographe*, 350-351, 359, 363-364, 369, 495.

35. Diamant-Berger, *Le Cinéma*, 225-232.

36. Brogan, *The Development of Modern France*, 608.

37. "Le Monde du cinéma," *Ciné-pour-tous* 27 (6 March 1920), 2. Coissac, *Histoire du cinématographe*, 361, 497.

38. Coissac, "L'Evolution du cinématographe et la réalisation de quelques grands films," 16.

39. Coissac, *Histoire du cinématographe*, 367.

40. "L'Inauguration de la Salle Marivaux," *Cinématographie française* 24 (19 April 1919), 35.

41. Dennis Sharp, *The Picture Palace* (New York: Praeger, 1969), 70-84, 86-102.

42. Mitry, "Max Linder," 303. Diamant-Berger, *Il était une fois le cinéma*, 66-67. Florey, *Filmland*, 246.

43. Coissac, *Histoire du cinématographe*, 356, 361, 367.

44. V.-Guillaume Danvers, "*L'Agonie des aigles*," *Cinémagazine* 1 (22-28 April 1921), 13-18. Advertisement, *Cinémagazine* 1 (7 October 1921).

45. Diamant-Berger, *Il était une fois le cinéma*, 89-90.

46. Jean Pascal, "La Première de *Vingt Ans après*," *Cinémagazine* 3 (17 November 1922), 236. Cinéor, "Blancs et noirs," *Cinéa* 75 (17 November 1922), 12.

47. Advertisement, *Cinémagazine* 2 (3 March 1922).

48. André Antoine, "Le Cinéma et l'Opéra," *Cinémagazine* 1 (8-14 April 1921), 3-4. André Tinchant, "*Le Miracle des loups*," 315. Paul de la Borie, "Le Niveau monte," *Cinémagazine* 4 (21 November 1924), 337. *Ciné-Information-Aubert* 7 (15 November 1924), 1. Reginald Ford, "Statistiques des cinémas de Paris," *Cinématographie française* 355 (22 August 1925), 10. *Ciné-Information-Aubert* 29 (25 October 1925), 1. Coissac, *Histoire du cinématographe*, 464. "Cinémas à Paris," *Tout-Cinéma* (1929), 177-179.

49. *Pathé-Journal* (12 February 1926), 10-11. "Une nouvelle salle sur les boulevards: l'inauguration de l'Impérial," *Pathé-Journal* (11 June 1926), 11. *Cinématographie française* 465 (1 October 1927), 10. *Cinématographie française* 472 (16 November 1927), 1. Arnold Whittick, *European Architecture in the Twentieth-Century* (Aylesbury: Leonard Hill, 1974), 414-416.

50. *Cinématographie française* 458 (13 August 1927), 11-26. P. M., "Le Paramount," *Ciné-monde* 9 (20 December 1928), 178. Pierre Kéfer, "Revue des programmes," *Revue du cinéma* 2 (February, 1929), 72. "L'Activité cinégraphique," *Cinéa-Ciné-pour-tous* 137 (15 July 1929), 24. Coissac, *Les Coulisses du cinéma*, 204-207.

Silence in the Face of Sound

1. James Limbacher, *Four Aspects of the Film* (New York: Brussel and Brussel, 1968), 202-203. Douglas Gomery, "Tri-Ergon, Tobis-Klangfilm, and the Coming of Sound," *Cinema Journal* 16 (Fall, 1976), 52-53. Douglas Gomery, "The Coming of the Talkies: Invention, Innovation, and Diffusion," in *The American Film Industry*, ed. Balio, 193-211. Roger Icart, "L'Avènement du film parlant," 25-218.

2. Jean Tedesco, "La France et le film sonore," 7. R. L., "L'Europe contre l'Amérique—la lutte pour le film parlant," *Revue du cinéma* 9 (1 April 1930), 75. Icart, "L'Avènement du film parlant," 31-32. Michel Marie, "Les Années 30," *Défense du cinéma français* (1975), 35. Gomery, "The Coming of the Talkies," 195, 201-207. Gomery, "Tri-Ergon, Tobis-Klangfilm, and the Coming of Sound," 54-57. Silberman, "Film and Ideology: The Structure of the German Film Industry and Films of the 1920s," 24. Gomery, "Economic Struggle and Hollywood Imperialism: Europe Converts to Sound," 85-86.

3. Tedesco, "La France et le film sonore," 7. Actually the cost could run from 220,000 to 480,000 francs (RCA Photophone charged an equivalent rate; Tobis-Klangfilm's price was only half as much)—Icart, "L'Avènement du film parlant," 60.

4. *Film Daily Yearbook* (1930), 1016.

5. Lapierre, *Les Cent Visages du cinéma*, 206. Gomery, "Tri-Ergon, Tobis-Klangfilm, and the Coming of Sound," 53.

6. Lapierre, *Les Cent Visages du cinéma*, 206. Cf. Fescourt, *La Foi et les montagnes*, 369.

7. René Clair, *Cinema Yesterday and Today*, 126.

8. Fescourt, *La Foi et les montagnes*, 369.

9. Léon Abrie, "Les débuts du film parlant," *Cinémonde* 8 (15 December 1928), 143. Henry, "Le Film sonore—les dates," 8. Lapierre, *Les Cent Visages du cinéma*, 207. Catelain, *Marcel L'Herbier*, 205. Icart, "L'Avènement du film parlant," 50-51. Patrick Ogle, "The Development of Sound Systems: The Commercial Era," 200. François Cuel, "Don Juans et fous chantants," *Cinématographe* 47 (May, 1979), 5.

10. "Les nouveaux films," *Cinéa-Ciné-pour-tous* 136 (1 July 1929), 5. Henry, "Le Film sonore—les dates," 8. "Le Marché européen en 1929," *Tout-Cinéma* (1930), 211. Chevanne, *L'Industrie du cinéma*, 49. Lapierre, *Les Cent Visages du cinéma*, 207. Leglise, *Histoire de la politique du cinéma français*, 71. J. Leclerc, *Le Cinéma, témoin de son temps*, 27.

11. "L'Activité cinégraphique," *Cinéa-Ciné-pour-tous* 141 (1 October 1929), 28. "Les nouveaux films," *Cinéa-Ciné-pour-tous* 143 (1 November 1929), 4. "Revue des programmes," *Revue du cinéma* 5 (15 November 1929), 75. Pierre Scize, "Eloge de 'Mickey,' " *Cinéa-Ciné-pour-tous* 149 (1 February 1930), 23-24. "Liste des films sonores et parlants," *Tout-Cinéma* (1930), 29. Raymond Chirat, *Catalogue des films français de long métrage: films sonores de fiction, 1929-1939* [n.p.]. Beylie and Marie, "Entretien avec Marcel L'Herbier," 36/x.

12. Lapierre, *Les Cent Visages du cinéma*, 209. Leglise, *Histoire de la politique du cinéma français*, 72. Leclerc, *Le Cinéma, témoin de son temps*, 27. Chirat, *Catalogue des films français de long métrage*, [n.p.]. Beylie and Marie, "Entretien avec Marcel L'Herbier," 37/xi.

13. Chevanne, *L'Industrie du cinéma*, 48.

14. By the spring of 1930, *Cinéa-Ciné-pour-tous*'s references to silent films had shrunk to a single column—"films muets," *Cinéa-Ciné-pour-tous* 3 (May, 1930), 40.

15. "L'Activité cinégraphique," *Cinéa-Ciné-pour-tous* 112 (1 July 1928), 31. Advertisement, *Tout-Cinéma* (1929), 619. "Echos et communiqués," *Cinéa-Ciné-pour-tous* 141 (1 October 1929), 28-29. Beylie and Lacassin, "Henri Fescourt," 301. Leglise, *Histoire de la politique du cinéma français*, 82. Diamant-Berger, *Il était une fois le cinéma*, 172. Icart, "L'Avènement du film parlant," 51.

16. "L'Activité cinégraphique," *Cinéa-Ciné-pour-tous* 127 (15 February 1929), 24. "L'Activité cinégraphique," *Cinéa-Ciné-pour-tous* 135 (15 June 1929), 25. "L'Activité cinégraphique," *Cinéa-Ciné-pour-tous* 137 (15 July 1929), 22. "L'Activité cinégraphique," *Cinéa-Ciné-pour-tous* 139 (1 September 1929), 27. Advertisements, *Almanach du Mon-Ciné* (1930). Lapierre, *Les Cent Visages du cinéma*, 191. Sadoul, *Le Cinéma français*, 53. Mitry, *Histoire du cinéma*, 2, 365. Prédal, *La Société française (1914-1945) à travers le cinéma*, 49. Sadoul, *Histoire générale du cinéma*, 6, 373. Diamant-Berger, *Il était une fois le cinéma*, 175.

17. "L'Activité cinégraphique," *Cinéa-Ciné-pour-tous* 129 (15 March 1929), 27. "L'Activité cinégraphique," *Cinéa-Ciné-pour-tous* 136 (1 July 1929), 24. "L'Activité cinégraphique," *Cinéa-Ciné-pour-tous* 137 (15 July 1929), 22. "L'Activité cinégraphique," *Cinéa-Ciné-pour-tous* 139 (1 September 1929), 26. "L'Activité cinégraphique," *Cinéa-Ciné-pour-tous* 140 (15 September 1929), 28. Catelain, *Marcel L'Herbier*, 109. Fescourt, *La Foi et les montagnes*, 76. Mitry, *Histoire du cinéma*, 2, 365-366. Diamant-Berger, *Il était une fois le cinéma*, 176. Dudley Andrew, "Sound in France: The Origins of a Native School," 99-100. Denise Tual, *Le Temps devoré*, 57.

18. Lapierre, *Les Cent Visages du cinéma*, 213. Catelain, *Marcel L'Herbier*, 111. Fescourt, *La Foi et les montagnes*, 378. Mitry, *Histoire du cinéma*, 2, 366. Icart, "L'Avènement du film parlant," 68-76. Diamant-Berger, *Il était une fois le cinéma*, 177. Gomery, "Economic Struggle and Hollywood Imperialism," 83-84. Andrew, "Sound in France: The Origins of a Native School," 100-101.

19. "La Sonorisation des salles," *Cinéa-Ciné-pour-tous* 139 (1 September 1929), 22. "Etat numérique des salles équipées et en cours d'équipement en France et pays de langue française," *Tout-Cinéma* (1930), 649. *Film Daily Yearbook* (1930), 1016. Chevanne, *L'Industrie du cinéma*, 69-74. Lapierre, *Les Cent Visages du cinéma*, 208. Icart, "L'Avènement du film parlant," 58-62. Compare Hayes and Southard on American domination in David Strauss, "The Rise of Anti-Americanism in France: French Intellectuals and the American Film Industry, 1927-1932," *Journal of Popular Culture* 10 (Spring, 1977), 755, 758.

20. Chevanne, *L'Industrie du cinéma*, 75.

21. Jacques Feyder, "Je crois au film parlant," 3. Leglise, *Histoire de la politique du cinéma*

français, 81. Diamant-Berger, *Il était une fois le cinéma*, 175. Icart, "L'Avènement du film parlant," 83-86.

22. Lapierre, *Les Cent Visages du cinéma*, 209.

23. J. Bouissounouse, "*La Route est belle*," *Revue du cinéma* 8 (1 March 1930), 51. Chevanne, *L'Industrie du cinéma*, 49. Lapierre, *Les Cent Visages du cinéma*, 208. Fescourt, *La Foi et les montagnes*, 384. Diamant-Berger, *Il était une fois le cinéma*, 174.

24. Transcript of an interview by Armand Panigel with Marcel L'Herbier (1973).

25. Clair, *Cinema Yesterday and Today*, 128.

26. Lapierre, *Les Cent Visages du cinéma*, 207.

27. Eisenschitz, "Histoires de l'histoire," 29.

28. See Steven Lipkin, "The French Film Industry of the 1950s" (University Film Association, 1980).

Part II, The Commercial Narrative Film: Introduction

1. Jean Renoir, "Souvenirs," *Le Point* 18 (December, 1938), reprinted in André Bazin, *Jean Renoir*, 153.

2. Henri Diamant-Berger, *Le Cinéma*, 71-76.

3. Henri Fescourt, *La Foi et les montagnes*, 364.

4. Diamant-Berger, *Le Cinéma*, 37. Also see Henri Fescourt and Jean-Louis Bouquet, *L'Idée et l'écran: opinions sur cinéma* 1, 24-25. For convenience in these notes, the first number following the title of Fescourt and Bouquet's three-volume work will refer to the volume number.

5. Fescourt, *La Foi et les montagnes*, 364.

6. Diamant-Berger, *Le Cinéma*, 55.

7. Diamant-Berger, *Le Cinéma*, 179. André Chevanne, *L'Industrie du cinéma; le cinéma sonore*, 51.

8. Here is a selected bibliography of recent theoretical studies on film genre: Douglas Pye, "Genre and Movies," *Movie* 20 (Spring, 1975), 29-43; Tom Ryall, "Teaching Through Genre," *Screen Education* 17 (Autumn, 1975), 27-33; Bill Nichols, ed., *Movies and Methods* (Berkeley: University of California Press, 1976), 107-175; Charles (Rick) Altman, "Towards a Theory of Genre Film," *Purdue Film Studies Annual* 2 (1977), 31-44; Marc Vernet, "Genre," trans. Bill Horrigan and Janet Jenkins, *Film Reader* 3 (1978), 13-17; Stephen Neale, *Genre*, London: BFI, 1980; Thomas Schatz, *Hollywood Genres* (New York: Random House, 1981), 3-41. For related studies on literary genre, see Paul Hernadi, *Beyond Genre* (Ithaca: Cornell University Press, 1972); Tzvetan Todorov, *The Fantastic: A Structural Approach to a Literary Genre*, trans. Richard Howard (Ithaca: Cornell University Press, 1975); Tzvetan Todorov, "The Origins of Genres," *New Literary History* 8 (Autumn, 1976), 159-170; Fredric Jameson, *The Political Unconscious: Narrative as a Socially Symbolic Act* (Ithaca: Cornell University Press, 1981); Janet Altman, *Epistolary: Approaches to a Form* (Columbus: Ohio State University Press, 1982).

9. Georges Sadoul, *Histoire générale du cinéma*, 2, 328.

10. Diamant-Berger, *Le Cinéma*, 59-60.

11. Sadoul, *Histoire générale du cinéma*, 2, 341-348.

12. Pierre Henry, "Les Idées—petits films," *Ciné-pour-tous* 32 (10 April 1920), 2. Diamant-Berger, *Le Cinéma*, 36, 186. Ernest Coustet, *Le Cinéma*, 100. Pathé, "Etude sur l'évolution de l'industrie cinématographique française [1918]," *Intelligence du cinématographe*, 214.

13. Diamant-Berger, *Le Cinéma*, 55.

Serials

1. Francis Lacassin, "Le Serial," in *Pour une contre histoire du cinéma*, 116-117.

2. Albert Bonneau, "Le Film à épisodes," 125. Georges Sadoul, *Histoire générale du cinéma*, 3, 325-326. Jacques Deslandes, "Jasset," *L'Avant-Scène du cinéma* 163 (November, 1975), 292-295.

3. "Fantômas" (May, 1913), "Juve contre Fantômas" (September, 1913), "La Mort qui tue" (November, 1913), "Fantômas contre Fantômas" (February, 1914), and "Le Faux magistrat" (April, 1914)—Francis Lacassin, *Louis Feuillade*, 176-178.

4. "Concerts et Spectacles," *Le Journal* (3 October 1913), 7.

5. Lacassin, *Louis Feuillade*, 67-68. The second episode of *Fantômas* is available from several

sources in the United States. The other episodes as well as *Les Vampires* are preserved at the Cinémathèque française and Anthology Film Archives.

6. Francis Lacassin, "Pearl White," in *Pour une contre histoire du cinéma*, 130.

7. According to Lacassin, *Les Mystères du New-York* was comprised of *The Exploits of Elaine* (13 episodes), *The New Exploits of Elaine* (9 episodes), and *The Romance of Elaine* (3 episodes). Lacassin, "Pearl White," 119, 137. Sadoul says, however, that the last ten episodes came from *Ravengar (The Shielding Shadow)*—yet that serial does not even star Pearl White. Sadoul, *Histoire générale du cinéma*, 3, 337-338.

8. Maurice Bardèche and Robert Brasillach, *The History of Motion Pictures*, 113.

9. Christian Bosséno, "Le Cinéma et la presse (II)," 94-95.

10. René Jeanne and Charles Ford, *Histoire encyclopédique du cinéma*, 1, 165. Charles Ford, "Germaine Dulac," 7-9.

11. *Les Exploits d'Elaine* was comprised, confusingly, of nine or ten episodes from *The Perils of Pauline*. Sadoul, *Histoire générale du cinéma*, 3, 338. Lacassin, "Le Serial," 120.

12. Lacassin, "Pearl White," 133.

13. Sadoul, *Histoire générale du cinéma*, 3, 202.

14. Richard Roud, "Louis Feuillade: Maker of Melodrama," 10. Lacassin, *Louis Feuillade*, 71-75.

15. Bardèche and Brasillach, *The History of Motion Pictures*, 131.

16. Louis Delluc, "Cinéma," *Paris-Midi* (6 July 1919), 2. Both *Judex* and *La Nouvelle Mission de Judex* are preserved at the Cinémathèque française.

17. Louis Aragon and André Breton, *Le Trésor des Jésuites* (1929), quoted in François de la Breteque, "Le Film en tranches: les mutations du film à épisodes, 1918-1928," 89.

18. Richard Roud, "Memories of Resnais," *Sight and Sound* 38 (Summer, 1969), 125.

19. Roud, "Louis Feuillade," 10.

20. Compare Paul Fussell, *The Great War and Modern Memory* (New York: Oxford University Press, 1975), 64-69.

21. Charles Ford, "Jacques Feyder," *L'Avant-Scène du cinéma* 63 (October, 1966), 181. This brief description is based on the print of *Le Pied qui étreint* preserved at the Cinémathèque française.

22. Pierre Henry, "Les Idées: le film en épisodes," *Ciné-pour-tous* 29 (20 March 1920), 2.

23. Anthony Slide, *Early American Cinema* (New York: A. S. Barnes, 1970), 164-165, 171.

24. V.-Guillaume Danvers, "La Cinématographie en France en 1922," *Almanach du cinéma* (1923), 55-66.

25. Bonneau, "Le Film à épisodes," 127. Lacassin, "Le Serial," 121, 124.

26. Henri Fescourt, *La Foi et les montagnes*, 99.

27. Jeanne and Ford, *Histoire encyclopédique du cinéma*, 1, 456.

28. "D'un film à l'autre," *Théâtre et Comoedia Illustré* 16 (April, 1923), [n.p.]. Jean Mitry, "Ivan Mosjoukine," 426.

29. Breteque, "Le Film en tranches," 93-95.

30. Lacassin, *Louis Feuillade*, 84-85, 185.

31. Ibid., 85-86, 186. Both *Tih-Minh* and *Barrabas* are preserved at the Cinémathèque française; *Tih-Minh* can also be found at Anthology Film Archives.

32. Lacassin, *Louis Feuillade*, 94.

33. Marcel Lapierre, *Les Cent Visages du cinéma*, 180. *Broken Blossoms* was screened in Paris at the same time as *Les Deux Gamines*.

34. Bonneau, "Le Film à épisodes," 127-128.

35. Lacassin, *Louis Feuillade*, 87.

36. Louis Jalabert, "La Littérature commerciale: le ciné-roman," *Etudes* 171 (5 June 1922), 513-531; 172 (20 June, 1922), 675-689. Henri Diamant-Berger, *Il était une fois le cinéma*, 68.

37. Paul Monaco, *Cinema and Society: France and Germany during the Twenties*, 84-93. Unfortunately, Monaco vitiates his analysis by finding the "orphan story" almost everywhere in the French cinema of the 1920s.

38. Theodore Zeldin, *France 1848-1945: Ambition and Love*, 315.

39. Francis Lacassin, "Louis Feuillade," 262. Compare Bonneau, "Le Film à épisodes," 127-128.

40. Jan de Merry, "Les Spectacles," *Paris-Midi* (12 January 1918), 3. "Léon Mathot," *Cinéa-Ciné-pour-tous* 5 (15 January 1924), 5-7. A print of *Le Comte de Monte-Cristo* is preserved at the

Cinémathèque française. Unfortunately, I saw the film too late to incorporate my observations into this study.

41. Jean Mitry, *Histoire du cinéma*, 2, 249.

42. Louis Delluc, "Notes pour moi," *Le Film* 99 (4 February 1918), 15.

43. Sadoul, *Histoire générale du cinéma*, 4, 100.

44. Fescourt, *La Foi et les montagnes*, 198.

45. Claude Beylie and Francis Lacassin, "Henri Fescourt," 290.

46. Diamant-Berger, *Il était une fois le cinéma*, 86-88.

47. Ibid., 84.

48. Jeanne and Ford, *Histoire encyclopédique du cinéma*, 1, 166. Diamant-Berger, *Il était une fois le cinéma*, 89.

49. Diamant-Berger, *Il était une fois le cinéma*, 103, 113.

50. Georges Sadoul, *Histoire générale du cinéma*, 5, 20-23.

51. Pierre Henry, "Les Idées: le film en épisodes," 2. Ricciotto Canudo, "Le Ciné-Roman en *n* épisodes," *Le Film* 183 (November, 1921), [n. p.]. Albert Montez, "A propos de Ciné-Romans," *Cinémagazine* 2 (1 September 1922), 268. Léon Moussinac, "Les Films à épisodes," *Le Crapouillot* (1 March 1923), 27-29. Bonneau, "Le Film à épisodes," 125-128. Breteque's periodization schema generally coincides with my own analysis of the development of the French serial—Breteque, "Le Film en tranches," 90-91.

52. Sadoul, *Histoire générale du cinéma*, 5, 23.

53. "Echos," *Cinémagazine* 3 (7 September 1923), 346. Lacassin, *Louis Feuillade*, 96-97.

54. Maurice Roelens, *"Mon-Ciné* (1922-1924) et le mélodrame," 204. Breteque, "Le Film en tranches," 95-98.

55. Breteque, "Le Film en tranches," 97.

56. *Pathé-Journal* (15 December 1924), 1.

57. René Jeanne and Charles Ford, *Le Cinéma et la presse, 1895-1960*, 168.

58. Beylie and Lacassin, "Henri Fescourt," 291.

59. "Actualités," *Théâtre et Comoedia Illustré* 18 (June, 1923), [n.p.].

60. *Pathé-Journal* (15 December 1924), 5. *Pathé-Journal* (1 February 1925), 10. *Pathé-Journal* (1 October 1925), 12.

61. "Les nouveaux films," *Cinéa-Ciné-pour-tous* 7 (15 February 1924), 4.

62. Beylie and Lacassin, "Henri Fescourt," 295.

63. Ibid.

64. Henri Cels, "Vous pourrez voir bientôt," *Théâtre et Comoedia Illustré* 28 (15 February 1924), [n.p.].

65. Jean de Mirbel, *"Gossette," Cinémagazine* 3 (7 December 1923), 384-386. Charles Ford, "Germaine Dulac," 21.

66. This brief analysis is based on the print of *Gossette* preserved at the Cinémathèque française.

67. Ford, "Germaine Dulac," 22.

68. *"Robert Macaire," La Petite Illustration* 2.

69. Films Albatros brochure—Bibliothèque de l'Arsenal. This brief analysis is based on the print of *Robert Macaire* preserved at the Cinémathèque française.

70. Pierre Leprohon, *Jean Epstein*, 76.

Bourgeois Melodramas

1. Maurice Bardèche and Robert Brasillach, *The History of Motion Pictures*, 129.

2. René Jeanne and Charles Ford, *Histoire encyclopédique du cinéma*, 1, 164. Marcel Lapierre, *Les Cent Visages du cinéma*, 125. René Jeanne, *Cinéma 1900*, 223, 226-227. *Jeanne Doré* is preserved at the Cinémathèque française. Raymond Bernard plays the role of the young boy, as he did on the stage.

3. Jeanne, *Cinéma 1900*, 216. Jean Mitry, *Histoire du cinéma*, 2, 245.

4. Louis Delluc, "Cinéma et cie," *Paris-Midi* (20 May 1918), 3.

5. Bardèche and Brasillach, *The History of Motion Pictures*, 52.

6. *Annuaire général de la cinématographie française et étrangère* (1917), 137. Henri Fescourt, *La Foi et les montagnes*, 142. Alain and Odette Virmaux, ed., *Colette at the Movies*, 29-30. Roger Icart, "Le Mélodrame dans le cinéma muet français," 194.

7. Catherine Bodard Silver, "Salon, Foyer, Bureau: Women and the Professions in France," in *Clio's Consciousness Raised*, ed. Mary Hartman and Lois W. Banner (New York: Harper & Row, 1974), 72-85. The definition of bourgeois melodrama that I offer here is, of course, tentative and perhaps simplified. A somewhat different concept might be derived from a closer examination of the development of melodrama in the French theater. A good place to begin would be Peter Brooks, *The Melodramatic Imagination* (New Haven: Yale University Press, 1976).

8. Léon Barsacq, *Caligari's Cabinet and Other Grand Illusions: A History of Film Design*, 38. See also Theodore Zeldin, *France 1848-1945: Taste and Corruption*, 80-81.

9. Silver, "Salon, Foyer, Bureau," 78. Brooks, *The Melodramatic Imagination*, 4-5. Theodore Zeldin, *France 1848-1945: Ambition and Love*, 11-22.

10. Mitry, *Histoire du cinéma*, 2, 246.

11. *Annuaire général de la cinématographie française et étrangère* (1917), 121

12. Jacques Feyder's *Têtes de femme, femmes de tête* is preserved at the Cinémathèque française.

13. *La Droit à la vie* was released in January, 1917—"A travers les cinémas," *Le Gaulois* (5 January 1917), 4. It was made just after *The Cheat* was shown in the late summer and early autumn of 1916—Virmaux, *Colette at the Movies*, 17-20.

14. Bardèche and Brasillach, *The History of Motion Pictures*, 129. Georges Sadoul, *Histoire générale du cinéma*, 4, 398.

15. Gance had already used a series of crude wipes in *Barberousse* (1916)—Kevin Brownlow, *The Parade's Gone By*, 607.

16. Icart, "Le Mélodrame dans le cinéma muet français," 195. There is some confusion about the release date of *Mater Dolorosa*. Two sources list it as being screened in the spring of 1917—"A travers les cinémas," *Le Gaulois* (10 March 1917), 4, and Virmaux, *Colette at the Movies*, 24. But it was also shown in the spring of 1918—Jan de Berry, "Les Spectacles," *Paris-Midi* (12 April 1918), 3. The first filmography compiled on Gance dates its production, uncertainly, as October, 1917—Philippe Esnault, "Filmographie d'Abel Gance," 19. See also Charles Ford, *Abel Gance*, 22.

17. Fescourt, *La Foi et les montagnes*, 169.

18. This analysis is based on the print of *Mater Dolorosa* preserved at the Cinémathèque française.

19. Philippe Esnault, "Entretiens avec André-Paul Antoine," 12.

20. Mitry, *Histoire du cinéma*, 2, 255.

21. Juan Arroy, "Georges Specht," *Cinémagazine* 4 (18 January 1924), 93. Georges Sadoul, *Histoire générale du cinéma*, 2, 201.

22. Virmaux, *Colette at the Movies*, 25.

23. Jean-André Fieschi, "Entretien avec Marcel L'Herbier," 29.

24. "Cette semaine," *Ciné-pour-tous* 22 (31 January 1920), 8. Jeanne and Ford, *Histoire encyclopédique du cinéma*, 1, 458.

25. Brownlow, *The Parade's Gone By*, 610. This brief analysis is based on the print of *La Dixième Symphonie* preserved at the Cinémathèque française.

26. A print of Hugon's *Jacques Landauze* recently became available for study purposes at the National Film Archive in London.

27. Jean Eyre, "Nos metteurs-en-scène: Abel Gance," *Mon-Ciné* (14 February 1924), 10.

28. Henri Diamant-Berger, *Il était une fois le cinéma*, 76. Jacques Salles, "Raymond Bernard," 205.

29. J. G.-B., "Au Cinéma: Le Secret de Rosette Lambert," *Le Crapouillot* (1 November, 1920), 16-17. Léon Moussinac, "Intérieurs modernes au cinéma," 5-8. René Jeanne, "La Dance au cinéma," *Cinémagazine* 1 (17 June 1921), 22.

30. Mitry, *Histoire du cinéma*, 2, 263. For a brief description of the revolutionary change in interior decoration that occurred in Paris around 1910, and which finally became visible in French films after the war, see Hilly, "Décoration d'intérieur et cinéma," *La Revue fédéraliste* 103 (November, 1927), 36-43.

31. Diamant-Berger, *Il était une fois le cinéma*, 76.

32. Louis Delluc, "Quelques films français," *Cinéa* 18 (9 September 1921), 5. Sadoul, *Histoire générale du cinéma*, 4, 488.

33. Salles, "Raymond Bernard," 182.

34. Fescourt, *La Foi et les montagnes*, 313-314.

35. Salles, "Raymond Bernard," 182.

36. Edmond Epardaud, *"Triplepatte,"* 2-3.

37. Louis Delluc, *"Le Silence,"* in *Drames du cinéma*, 19-32. "Les Films de la quinzaine," *Ciné-pour-tous* 49 (24 September 1920), 6. Jean Mitry, "Louis Delluc," *L'Avant-Scène du cinéma*, 38.

38. Marcel Tariol, *Louis Delluc*, 60.

39. "Les Films de la quinzaine," *Ciné-pour-tous* 35 (1 May, 1920) 6. Louis Delluc, *"La Fête espagnole,"* in *Drames du cinéma*, 1-18.

40. Léon Moussinac, "Le Décor et le costume au cinéma," 133.

41. "Les Présentations," *Cinémagazine* 2 (23 December 1921), 26. Auguste Nardy, *"La Mort du soleil,"* *Bonsoir* (17 December 1921)—Germaine Dulac folder, Bibliothèque de l'Arsenal. I am indebted to Wendy Dozoretz for most of this information on *La Mort du soleil*.

42. Germaine Dulac, *"La Mort du soleil* et la naissance du film," 14.

43. Charles Ford, "Germaine Dulac," 14.

44. For instance, Gaby Morlay, the most prominent actress of the boulevard melodramas, appeared in only a couple of films before her rapid rise to star status in the 1930s French cinéma—Raymond Borde, "Gaby Morlay," *Cahiers de la cinémathèque* 23-24 (Christmas, 1977), 111.

45. Charles Pathé, "Etude sur l'évolution de l'industrie cinématographique française [1918]," *Intelligence du cinématographe*, ed. Marcel L'Herbier (Paris: Corréa, 1946), 214. Translated by Stuart Liebman. See also Charles Pathé, "De Pathé Frères à Pathé Cinéma," 87-97.

46. Maurice Roelens, *"Mon-Ciné* (1922-1924) et le mélodrame," 212-214. This strategy could be compared to the prewar projects of Film d'Art and S.C.A.G.L.

47. Ibid., 201-202.

48. Ibid., 207-212.

49. Ibid., 211.

50. Roger Icart supports this idea, implicitly, in "Le Mélodrame dans le cinéma muet français," 198.

51. Ford, "Germaine Dulac," 30. Another late bourgeois melodrama is Baroncelli's 1925 adaptation of a Hervieu play, *Le Réveil* (starring Charles Vanel, Maxudian, and Isobel Elsom), a print of which I have seen at the National Film Archive in London but too late to include in this study.

52. "Aux Cinéromans," *Cinéa-Ciné-pour-tous* 84 (1 May 1927), 27.

53. Jeanne and Ford, *Histoire encyclopédique du cinéma*, 1, 261.

54. Julien Bayart, "Ce que dit l'écran," *Photo-Ciné* 4 (15 April 1927), 66.

Realist Films

1. Georges Sadoul, *Histoire générale du cinéma*, 3, 192.

2. Francis Lacassin, *Louis Feuillade*, 43.

3. Philippe Esnault, "Entretiens avec André-Paul Antoine," 10. At least one early film reviewer had noticed the Paris cinema spectators' preference for films with natural landscapes as opposed to those with theatrical scenes—Henri Duvernois, "La Routine cinématographique," *Le Journal* (14 November 1913), 7.

4. "Concerts et Spectacles," *Le Journal* (3 October 1913), 7. Henri Fescourt, *La Foi et les montagnes*, 102. A print of *L'Enfant de Paris* is preserved at the Cinémathèque française.

5. Sadoul, *Histoire générale du cinéma*, 3, 191-192.

6. V. Jasset, "Etude sur la mise-en-scène," *Ciné-Journal* (21 October—25 November 1911)—reprinted in *Anthologie du cinéma*, ed. Marcel Lapierre, 83-98.

7. Sadoul, *Histoire générale du cinéma*, 3, 202-203.

8. Ibid., 204-205.

9. André Lang, *Déplacements et Villégiatures littéraires et suivi de la promenade au royaume des images ou entretiens cinématographiques*, 202.

10. Sadoul, *Histoire générale du cinéma*, 3, 209-211.

11. Ibid., 28-29.

12. Lang, *Déplacements et Villégiatures littéraires*, 120. Philippe Esnault, "Biofilmographie d'André Antoine," 30.

13. Philippe Esnault, "Propos d'Antoine [*Le Film* (December, 1919)]," 38.

14. Esnault, "Entretiens avec André-Paul Antoine," 7, 14-15.

15. Esnault, "Propos d'Antoine [*Le Film* (December, 1919)]," 38. René Prédal, *La Société française (1914-1945) à travers le cinéma*, 92. Antoine admitted his admiration for the acting in Thomas Ince's westerns—Lang, *Déplacements et Villégiatures littéraires*, 203.

16. Esnault, "Propos d'Antoine [*Lectures pour tous* (December, 1919)]," 48.

17. Esnault, "Propos d'Antoine [*Le Film* (December, 1919)]," 39.

18. Esnault, "Propos d'Antoine [*Lectures pour tous* (December, 1919)]," 48.

19. Pierre Leprohon, *Cinquante Ans du cinéma français*, 44. Linda Nochlin, *Realism* (New York: Penguin, 1971), 51-56, 137-139. See also T. J. Clark, *The Absolute Bourgeois: Artists and Politics in France, 1848-1851*, 2nd ed. (London: Thames and Hudson, 1982), 31-98.

20. John Berger, *About Looking* (New York: Pantheon, 1980), 76.

21. José Baldizzone, "Des historiens évoquent les Années Folles," 39.

22. Nochlin, *Realism*, 88, 112.

23. Esnault, "Entretiens avec André-Paul Antoine," 16.

24. Ibid., 22.

25. Ibid., 14-15.

26. Louis Delluc, "*Les Travailleurs de la mer*," 12.

27. Georges Sadoul, *Histoire générale du cinéma*, 4,115.

28. "Le monde du cinéma," *Ciné-pour-tous* 21 (24 January 1920), 2.

29. Claude Beylie and Michel Marie, "Entretien avec Marcel L'Herbier," 30/iv.

30. Marcel L'Herbier, *La Tête qui tourne*, 24-25.

31. Ibid., 26-27, 32.

32. Ibid., 47.

33. This brief analysis is based on the prints of *L'Homme du large* preserved at the Cinémathèque française and the George Eastman House. A fully titled print is preserved at the Royal Film Archive of Belgium.

34. "Les Films de la quinzaine," *Ciné-pour-tous* 54 (3 December 1920), 4-5.

35. Jaque Catelain, *Marcel L'Herbier*, 43, 44. L'Herbier, *La Tête qui tourne*, 48.

36. L'Herbier, *La Tête qui tourne*, 50.

37. Jean Galtier-Boissière, "Le Cinéma: *L'Homme du large*," 21.

38. Juan Arroy, "Marcel L'Herbier," 11.

39. René Jeanne, "Réalisme et cinéma," 11-15.

40. "Le monde du cinéma," *Ciné-pour-tous* 7 (1 October 1919), 2. "Le Studio ambulent de Mercanton," *Le Journal du Ciné-Club* 23 (18 June 1920), 3. "Tournera-t-on les intérieurs hors des studios?" *Le Journal du Ciné-Club* 45 (19 November, 1920), 8. Rachel Low, *The History of the British Film, 1918-1929* (London: George Allen and Unwin, 1971), 222.

41. "Les meilleurs films de l'année," *Ciné-pour-tous* 51 (22 October 1920), 4-5.

42. Louis Delluc, "*L'Appel du sang*," *Ciné-pour-tous* 31 (3 April 1920), 7.

43. This analysis is based on the print of *L'Appel du sang* preserved at the National Film Archive in London.

44. René Jeanne, "Le Maroc à l'écran," *Cinémagazine* 2 (1 September 1922), 259.

45. "Les Films de la semaine," *Ciné-pour-tous* 51 (22 October, 1920), 4.

46. Jeanne and Ford, *Histoire encyclopédique du cinéma*, 1, 423-424. Fescourt, *La Foi et les montagnes*, 335. René Jeanne, *Cinéma 1900*, 229.

47. René Jeanne, "Les prochains films," *Le Film*, 183 (November, 1921), [n.p.]. Jeanne and Ford, *Histoire encyclopédique du cinéma*, 1, 220.

48. "Les Films de la semaine," *Cinémagazine* 2 (24 November 1922), 276.

49. Esnault, "Entretien avec André-Paul Antoine," 24.

50. Fescourt, *La Foi et les montagnes*, 329-330. Esnault, "Entretiens avec André-Paul Antoine," 24.

51. Raymond Chirat, *Catalogue des films français de long métrage: films sonores de fiction, 1929-1939*, [n.p.].

52. Fescourt, *La Foi et les montagnes*, 327.

53. Louis Delluc, "Cinéma," *Paris-Midi* (2 February 1919), 2.

54. Louis Delluc, "Cinéma," *Paris-Midi* (1 February 1919), 2.

55. A print of *Chemin d'Ernoa* has been recently restored (without titles) by the Cinémathèque française.

56. "Les meilleurs films de l'année," *Ciné-pour-tous* 51 (22 October 1920), 4-5.

57. "Au Répertoire du Vieux-Colombier: l'histoire du deux grands films," 21-23. Recently

I saw a tinted print of *Jocelyn* at the Cinémathèque française, but too late to be incorporated into this study.

58. Fescourt, *La Foi et les montagnes*, 322.

59. René Jeanne, "Lamartine au cinéma," 228. *"Jocelyn," Cinémagazine* 2 (27 October 1922), 129. Léon Poirier, *Vingt-quatre images à la seconde*, 49.

60. Pierre Porte, "Le Cinéma n'est pas un art populaire," 27.

61. "Ce que l'on dit . . . ," *Cinémagazine* 3 (30 March 1923), 556. Jeanne and Ford *Histoire encyclopédique du cinéma*, 1, 376. Maurice Roelens, "Litérature, peuple, cinéma: *Geneviève* (1923)," 179-180.

62. Germain Lacan, *"Geneviève,"* 295-297.

63. Georges Sadoul, *Histoire générale du cinéma*, 5, 200.

64. *Film français* 12 (15 November, 1923), quoted in Roelens, "Literature, peuple, cinéma: *Geneviève* (1923)," 181.

65. Lacan, *"Geneviève,"* 295.

66. Léon Moussinac, "Le Cinéma: *Geneviève*," 29.

67. Fescourt, *La Foi et les montagnes*, 344. Claude Beylie and Francis Lacassin, "Henri Fescourt," 296. Henri Fescourt, "A propos de mon film, *Les Grands*," 18-20. A print of *Les Grands* is preserved at the Cinémathèque de Toulouse.

68. A.B., *"Visages d'enfants," Cinémagazine* 3 (14 September 1923), 385-388. Edmond Epardaud, *"Visages d'enfants,"* 13-14. "Les nouveaux films," *Cinéa-Ciné-pour-tous* 33 (15 March 1925), 5. See p. 26.

69. Sadoul, *Histoire générale du cinéma*, 5, 183.

70. Jacques Feyder and Françoise Rosay, *Le Cinéma, notre metier*, 24.

71. This analysis is based on the print of *Visages d'enfants* preserved at the Cinémathèque française.

72. *"Poile de carotte,"* 21. "Les nouveaux films," *Cinéa-Ciné-pour-tous* 57 (15 March 1926), 6.

73. Raymond Chirat, "Julien Duvivier," 77, 166.

74. This brief analysis is based on the print of *Poile de carotte* preserved at the Cinémathèque française.

75. Harry Alan Potamkin was much taken by this film and "its visual honesty of domestic detail"—Lewis Jacobs, ed., *The Compound Cinema: The Film Writings of Harry Alan Potamkin*, 280-281.

76. Lacassin, *Louis Feuillade*, 186. This brief analysis is based on the print of *Vendémiaire* preserved at the Cinémathèque française.

77. Ibid., 62-63.

78. This study of peasant films is perhaps oversimplified. See, for instance, a comprehensive treatment of the French peasantry in Theodore Zeldin, *France, 1848-1945: Ambition and Love*, 131-197.

79. Louis Delluc, "Cinéma," *Paris-Midi* (12 October 1919), 2.

80. "Le Film français," *Ciné-pour-tous* 5 (15 August 1919), 2-3. "Ce que l'on dit," *Cinémagazine* 1 (11-17 March 1921), 27. Paul de la Borie, *"La Terre,"* 29. Esnault, "Biofilmographie d'André Antoine," 30. For information about the print of *La Terre* (with Russian intertitles) presented at the Museum of Modern Art (in January, 1983), I thank Stuart Liebman and Sandy Flitterman. The film's narrative and rhetorical complexity would seem to demand further analysis.

81. "Cette semaine," *Ciné-pour-tous* 23 (7 February 1920), 4-5. Chirat, *Catalogue des films français de long metrage*, [n.p.]. Jean Mitry, *Histoire du cinéma*, 2, 434.

82. J. A. de Munto, "René Hervil," *Cinémagazine* 4 (2 November 1923), 170. Jacques Faure, "René Hervil," *Mon-Ciné* (15 May 1924), 8.

83. Fescourt, *La Foi et les montagnes*, 333.

84. *"Blanchette," Le Crapouillot* (1 June 1923), 20.

85. Ricciotto Canudo, "Le Cinéma," *Les Nouvelles littéraires* (13 January 1923), 4. *"La Bête traquée," Cinémagazine* 3 (2 March 1923), 421-422. Jacques Fieschi, "Entretien avec Jean Mitry," *Cinématographe* 60 (September, 1980), 23. A print of *La Bête traquée* is now preserved at the Cinémathèque française.

86. Jeanne and Ford, *Histoire encyclopédique du cinéma*, 1, 384. This brief analysis is based on a print of *Nêne* preserved at the Cinémathèque française. Unfortunately, I saw the film too late to do it justice here.

87. "Actualités," *Théâtre et Comoedia Illustré* 20 (August, 1923), [n.p.]. André Daven, *"Nêne,"* [n.p.].

88. Jean Mitry, "Robert Boudrioz," *Théâtre et Comoedia Illustré* 31 (1 April 1924), [n.p.].

89. "Le monde du cinéma—en France," *Ciné-pour-tous* 14 (16 December 1919), 2. "Les faits," *Ciné-pour-tous* 32 (10 April 1920), 4. Serge, "Robert Boudrioz," *Cinéa-Ciné-pour-tous* 6 (1 February 1924), 7.

90. "Les Présentations," *Almanach du cinéma* (1923), 116. Advertisement, *Cinéa* 82 (29 December 1922), 15. René Clair, "Films passés," *Théâtre et Comoedia Illustré* 1 (January, 1923), [n.p.].

91. "Notre référendum du plus beau film," *Cinéa-Ciné-pour-tous* 11 (15 April 1924), 5-6.

92. Serge, "Robert Boudrioz," 7.

93. Clair, "Films passés," [n.p.]. René Clair, *Cinema Yesterday and Today*, 48.

94. Mitry, "Robert Boudrioz," [n.p.].

95. Esnault, "Entretiens avec André-Paul Antoine," 25.

96. Ibid. Esnault, "Biofilmographie d'André Antoine," 31-32.

97. Lang, *Déplacements et Villégiatures littéraires*, 121.

98. Esnault, "Entretiens avec André-Paul Antoine," 25.

99. Esnault, "Biofilmographie d'André Antoine," 31.

100. Esnault, "Entretiens avec André-Paul Antoine," 25. Henri Colpi is said to be editing Antoine's footage of *L'Hirondelle et la mésange* for the Cinémathèque française.

101. Jeanne and Ford, *Histoire encyclopédique du cinéma*, 1, 384-385.

102. This analysis of *La Belle Nivernaise* is based on the 35mm print preserved at the Cinémathèque française.

103. "Les nouveaux films," *Cinéa-Ciné-pour-tous* 5 (15 January 1924), 4. Fescourt, *La Foi et les montagnes*, 307.

104. Jean Epstein, "Grossissement," in *Bonjour Cinéma*, 97, trans. Stuart Liebman, "Magnification," 10.

105. Jean Epstein, *Ecrits sur le cinéma*, 1, 60. For convenience in these notes, the first number following the title of Epstein's two-volume work will refer to the volume number.

106. Paul Ramain, "Sensibilité intelligente d'abord, objectif ensuite," 7.

107. Jean de Mirbel, *"La Belle Nivernaise,"* *Cinémagazine* 3 (21 December 1923), 465-466. Ramain, "Sensibilité intelligente d'abord, objectif ensuite," 7. Henri Langlois, "Jean Epstein (1897-1953)," 14.

108. "Les nouveaux films," *Cinéa-Ciné-pour-tous* 29 (15 January 1925), 6-7. "Films de la semaine," *Cinémagazine* 5 (30 January 1925), 230. This brief analysis is based on the print of *La Brière* preserved at the Royal Film Archive of Belgium. Recently, a print has been restored by the Cinémathèque française.

109. "Actualités," *Théâtre et Comoedia Illustré* 33 (1 May 1924), [n.p.]. René Jeanne, "En Brière avec Léon Poirier," 15-18.

110. "Films de la semaine," *Cinémagazine* 5 (30 January 1925), 230.

111. Léon Moussinac, "Les Films," *Le Crapouillot* (16 February 1925), 16.

112. "Les nouveaux films," *Cinéa-Ciné-pour-tous* 24 (1 November 1924), 5. "Ce que l'on dit . . .," *Cinémagazine* 4 (21 November 1924), 337.

113. Edmond Epardaud, "Comment Jacques de Baroncelli réalise *Pêcheur d'Islande*," 15. Oscar Cornaz, "A Paimpol avec Jacques de Baroncelli pour le départ de la 'Marie,' " 28-29.

114. Jean Mitry, *Histoire du cinéma*, 3, 389.

115. Fescourt, *La Foi et les montagnes*, 328-329.

116. Gerald McKee, *Film Collecting*, 82-83. Recently, a print of *Pêcheur d'Islande* was restored by the Archives du Film, Bois d'Arcy.

117. Jean Tedesco, *"Pêcheur d'Islande,"* 9. P. L., "Charles Vanel," *Cinémonde* 20 (7 March 1929), 365.

118. Jack Conrad, "Jacques de Baroncelli et la mer," 565.

119. Ibid., 564.

120. "Le meilleur film de 1924," *Cinéa-Ciné-pour-tous* 32 (1 March 1925), 5.

121. Conrad, "Jacques de Baroncelli et la mer," 565.

122. *Fantastique et réalisme dans le cinéma allemand, 1912-1933* (Brussels: Musée du cinéma, 1969), 58-119. Lotte Eisner, "Kammerspielfilme et tragédie psychologiques," in *Vingt Ans de cinéma allemand* (Paris: Centre national d'art et de la culture Georges Pompidou, 1978), 56-71.

Barry Salt and Kristin Thompson both have curbed my initial tendency to simplify this distinction.

123. Siegfried Kracauer, *From Caligari to Hitler: A Psychological History of the German Film* (Princeton: Princeton University Press, 1947), 97-106, 119-128. Lotte Eisner, *The Haunted Screen* (Berkeley: University of California Press, 1973), 199. Gerald Noxon, "The European Influence on the Coming of Sound to the American Film, 1925-1940: A Survey," in *Sound and Cinema* ed. Evan William Cameron (Pleasantville, N.Y.: Redgrave, 1980), 175.

124. Eisner, *The Haunted Screen*, 179.

125. Kracauer, *From Caligari to Hitler*, 157-170. Barry Salt, "From Caligari to Who?" 123. Bruce Murray, "*Mutter Krausens Fahrt in Glück*: An Analysis of the Film as a Critical Response to the 'Street Films' of the Commercial Film Industry," *enclitic* 5:2/6:1 (Fall, 1981–Spring, 1982), 44-54.

126. Esnault, "Entretiens avec André-Paul Antoine," 21. Esnault, "Biofilmographie d'André Antoine," 30.

127. This brief description is based on the print of *Le Coupable* preserved at the Cinémathèque française.

128. Prédal, *La Société française (1914-1945) à travers le cinéma*, 92.

129. Sadoul, *Histoire générale du cinéma*, 4, 487. Fescourt, *La Foi et les montagnes*, 336.

130. Louis Delluc, "*L'Ame du bronze*," *Le Film* 98 (28 January 1918), 16.

131. Louis Delluc, "*Travail*," *Le Journal du Ciné-Club* 1 (14 January 1920), 7. Henri Bousquet, "Economie et publicité cinématographique dans l'immédiat après-guerre," 69. Marcel Oms, "Histoire et géographie d'une France imaginaire," 78.

132. Jean Galtier-Boissière, "*Travail*," *Ciné-pour-tous* 31 (3 April 1920), 6.

133. Ibid.

134. Mitry, *Histoire du cinéma* 2, 250.

135. This brief analysis is based on the incomplete print of *Travail* preserved at the Cinémathèque française. Currently, the Cinémathèque française is restoring a complete version of the film.

136. Oms, "Histoire et géographie d'une France imaginaire," 78. Marcel Oms, "Une Cinéaste des Années Vingt: René Le Somptier," 208-209.

137. Sadoul, *Histoire générale du cinéma*, 5, 198.

138. André Delpeuch contrasts *Cousin Pons* with *L'Atlantide* to condemn the former for its poorly handled *action*—Delpeuch, *Le Cinéma* 117-121. See also René Jeanne and Charles Ford, *Paris vu par le cinéma*, 45-46.

139. René Jeanne, "Emile Zola au cinéma," *Cinémagazine* 2 (27 January 1922), 107-110. Jean Mitry, "Ivan Mosjoukine," 439.

140. Lang, *Déplacements et Villégiatures littéraires*, 159.

141. Poirier, *Vingt-quatre images à la seconde*, 48.

142. Edmond Epardaud, "*Paris*," *Cinéa-Ciné-pour-tous* 18 (1 August 1924), 10.

143. Jeanne and Ford, *Paris vu par le cinéma*, 162.

144. "L'Activité cinégraphique," *Cinéa-Ciné-pour-tous* 18 (1 August 1924), 21.

145. "Les films de la semaine," *Cinémagazine* 4 (26 December 1924), 583.

146. Fescourt, *La Foi et les montagnes*, 273. Charles Ford, *Jacques Feyder*, 20-21.

147. This brief analysis is based on the prints of *Crainquebille* preserved at the Museum of Modern Art and at the Cinémathèque française.

148. "Les films de la semaine," *Cinémagazine* 3 (23 March 1923), 502. "Ce que l'on dit," *Cinémagazine* 4 (13 April 1923), 81. A.T., "Cinémagazine à New York," *Cinémagazine* 4 (28 September 1923), 332.

149. Albert Bonneau, "Nicolas Koline," *Cinémagazine* 4 (19 September 1923), 449-452.

150. Lucien Doublon, "*Crainquebille*," *Cinémagazine* 3 (8 December 1922), 332.

151. Prédal, *La Société française (1914-1945) à travers le cinéma*, 75.

152. There are great discrepancies between the French and the American prints of *Crainquebille*. This second nightmare sequence only appears in the Museum of Modern Art version. And the first fantasy sequence in the courtroom is edited in a different order in the Cinémathèque française print than in the MOMA print.

153. Sadoul, *Histoire générale du cinéma*, 5, 182.

154. "Les nouveaux films," *Cinéa-Ciné-pour-tous* 34 (1 April, 1925), 5. Interview with Marie Epstein, 4 June 1977. This analysis is based on the print of *L'Affiche* preserved at the Royal

Film Archive of Belgium. I am indebted to Barry Salt for some of this information on *L'Affiche*.

155. "Les nouveaux films," *Cinéa-Ciné-pour-tous* 49 (15 November 1925), 4.

156. Paul Ramain, "Présentation à Montpellier du film de Jean Epstein: *L'Affiche*," 224. Epstein gets remarkable results here from a previously conventional cameraman, Maurice Desfassiaux.

157. Ibid., 224. Léon Moussinac, "Le Cinéma," *Le Crapouillot* (16 March 1925), 30.

158. "Les nouveaux films," *Cinéa-Ciné-pour-tous* 58 (1 April 1926), 6. Charles Ford, *Jacques Feyder*, 26.

159. Gille Anthelme, "*Gribiche*," *Cinéa-Ciné-pour-tous* 68 (1 September 1926), 33.

160. This brief analysis is based on the print of *Gribiche* preserved at the Cinémathèque française.

161. "*Gribiche*," *Cinéa-Ciné-pour-tous* 49 (15 November 1925), 7-8. Fescourt, *La Foi et les montagnes*, 274.

162. Fescourt, *La Foi et les montagnes*, 344.

163. Ibid., 345.

164. "L'Activité cinégraphique," *Cinéa-Ciné-pour-tous* 54 (1 February 1926), 26.

165. Fescourt, *La Foi et les montagnes*, 344.

166. "Echos et communiqués," *Cinéa-Ciné-pour-tous* 58 (1 April 1926), 25. Beylie and Lacassin, "Henri Fescourt," 322.

167. This analysis is based on a 35mm print of *Les Misérables* preserved at the Cinémathèque française.

168. Beylie and Lacassin, "Henri Fescourt," 298. Compare Henri Fescourt and Jean-Louis Bouquet, *L'Idée et l'écran: opinions sur le cinéma*, 1, 24-29.

169. Jacques Fieschi, "Entretien avec Jean Mitry," 23.

170. Beylie and Lacassin, "Henri Fescourt," 300.

171. Ibid., 299.

172. This brief analysis is based on the print of *Carmen* preserved at the Cinémathèque française.

173. Jean Tedesco, "Raquel Meller dans *Carmen*," 13-14.

174. Léon Barsacq, *Caligari's Cabinet and Other Grand Illusions*, 76.

175. Ford, *Jacques Feyder*, 27.

176. Fescourt, *La Foi et les montagnes*, 276.

177. "Les nouveaux films," *Cinéa-Ciné-pour-tous* 72 (1 November 1926), 6.

178. "Les nouveaux films," *Cinéa-Ciné-pour-tous* 118 (1 October 1928), 6.

179. Ford, *Jacques Feyder*, 30, 184.

180. Moussinac, "Panoramique du cinéma [1929]," 291.

181. Victor Bachy, "Jacques Feyder," 458. Barsacq, *Caligari's Cabinet and Other Grand Illusions*, 78.

182. Lapierre, *Les Cent Visages du cinéma*, 163.

183. Bachy, "Jacques Feyder," 446.

184. Both Jean Dréville and Marie Epstein confirmed this fact—Letter from Jean Dréville, 26 September 1978. Interview with Marie Epstein, 10 August 1979.

185. Moussinac, "Panoramique du cinéma [1929]," 291.

186. Ford, *Jacques Feyder*, 32.

187. Pierre Leprohon, "Une belle artiste: Gina Manès," *Cinémonde* 25 (11 April 1929), 447.

188. Mitry, *Histoire du cinéma*, 3, 375.

189. Barsacq, *Caligari's Cabinet and Other Grand Illusions*, 79. Sadoul, *Histoire générale du cinéma*, 5, 174.

190. Georges Chaperot, "L'Oeuvre classique de Jacques Feyder," 20. Pierre Leprohon, *Cinquante ans du cinéma français*, 57.

191. J. Duren, "Quand Dreyer tournait *Jeanne d'Arc* . . . ," 11.

192. Moussinac, "Panoramique du cinéma [1929]," 291.

193. Jean Dréville, "La Critique du film," 2.

194. Beylie and Lacassin, "Henri Fescourt," 301, 322. In the summer of 1982, Kevin Brownlow told me he had recently seen a condensed version (9.5mm) of *La Glu* and was much taken by it.

195. Chirat, "Julien Duvivier," 98.

196. "Les nouveaux films," *Cinéa-Ciné-pour-tous* 129 (15 March 1929), 5.

197. Lapierre, *Les Cent Visages du cinéma*, 162. Poulbot was a nineteenth-century painter who was famous for his paintings of children on the Paris streets. This brief analysis is based on a 35mm print of *Peau de pêche* preserved at the Cinémathèque française.

198. Robert Trevise, "*Peau de pêche*," *Cinéa-Ciné-pour-tous* 126 (1 February 1929), 26.

Fairy Tales, Fables, and Fantasies

1. Tzvetan Todorov, *The Fantastic: A Structural Approach to a Literary Genre*, 25, 41-44.

2. Georges Sadoul, *Histoire générale du cinéma*, 2, 328.

3. "Les films de la semaine," *Ciné-pour-tous* 36 (8 May 1920), 6. Georges Sadoul, *Histoire générale du cinéma*, 4, 486.

4. "Les meilleurs films de l'année," *Ciné-pour-tous* 51 (5 November 1920), 4-5.

5. Henri Fescourt, *La Foi et les montagnes*, 321.

6. Jean Galtier-Boissière, "La Critique des films," 16-17. René Jeanne and Charles Ford, *Histoire encyclopédique du cinéma*, 1, 375.

7. Jeanne and Ford, *Histoire encyclopédique du cinéma*, 1, 373.

8. Léon Poirier, *Vingt-quatre images à la seconde*, 49.

9. Jeanne and Ford, *Histoire encyclopédique du cinéma*, 1, 376.

10. Léon Moussinac, "La Poésie à l'écran," *Cinémagazine* 1 (13-19 May 1921), 16.

11. Jeanne and Ford, *Histoire encyclopédique du cinéma*, 1, 244. Some film reviewers apparently thought the negative images had been included by error—Ralph Stephenson and J. R. Debrix, *The Cinema as Art*, rev. ed. (Middlesex: Penguin, 1969), 148.

12. *Les Nouveautés Aubert* 5 (November, 1920), 1. "Les films de la quinzaine," *Ciné-pour-tous* 55 (17 December 1920), 15. "Les films de la semaine," *Le Journal du Ciné-Club* 50 (24 December 1920), 7.

13. Henri Bousquet, "Economie et publicité cinégraphique dans l'immédiat après-guerre," 73.

14. Marcel Oms, "Un Cinéaste des Années Vingt: René Le Somptier," 209.

15. Jeanne and Ford, *Histoire encyclopédique du cinéma*, 1, 221. Compare Louis Delluc, "Quelques films français," *Cinéa* 18 (9 September 1921), 5. H. J., "Nos metteurs-en-scène: René Le Somptier," *Mon-Ciné* (21 February 1924), 9.

16. Fescourt, *La Foi et les montagnes*, 338.

17. Marcel L'Herbier, "*Rose-France*," *Comoedia Illustré* (5 December, 1919), quoted in Noël Burch, *Marcel L'Herbier*, 61.

18. Jean Galtier-Boissière, "La Critique des films," 16-17. "Cette semaine," *Ciné-pour-tous* 40 (5 June, 1920), 4. This brief analysis is based on the prints of *Le Carnaval des vérités* preserved at the Cinémathèque française and at the George Eastman House.

19. Jeanne and Ford, *Histoire encyclopédique du cinéma*, 1, 305. Jaque Catelain, *Marcel L'Herbier*, 41. Sadoul, *Histoire générale du cinéma*, 4, 483.

20. Louis Delluc, "Cinéma," *Paris-Midi* (10 June 1920), 2.

21. Louis Delluc, "*Don Juan et Faust*," 13. Catelain, *Marcel L'Herbier*, 59. This brief analysis is based on the print of *Don Juan et Faust* preserved at the Cinémathèque française.

22. Jean-André Fieschi, "Autour du cinématographe," 33-34.

23. Ibid., 34.

24. Burch, *Marcel L'Herbier*, 80.

25. René Clair, "Les films du mois," [n.p.]. Ricciotto Canudo, *L'Usine aux images*, 134-135.

26. Louis Delluc, "Un Cheveu dans les pellicules," *Cinéa* 49 (14 April 1922), 12. "*Don Juan et Faust*," *Cinémagazine* 2 (28 April 1922), 130. Léon Moussinac, "Cinématographe," *Mercure de France* (1 June 1922), 497. Delluc, "*Don Juan et Faust*," 13. "La Production de Marcel L'Herbier," 13-18. "Les Présentations," *Almanach du cinéma* (1923), 115. Clair, "Les films du mois," [n.p.].

27. Georges Sadoul, *Le Cinéma français*, 230. See also Donald Crafton, *Before Mickey: The Animated Film, 1898-1928* (Cambridge: MIT Press, 1982), 237-242.

28. Lucien Doublon, "Les Présentations," *Cinémagazine* 3 (9 March 1923), 427-428. André Tinchant, "Les films de la semaine," *Cinémagazine* 3 (11 May 1923), 250-251. Léon Moussinac, "Cinématographe," *Mercure de France* (15 July 1923), 520-521. This brief analysis is based on the print of *Le Marchand de plaisir* preserved at the Cinémathèque française.

29. "Les nouveaux films," *Cinéa-Ciné-pour-tous* 26 (1 December 1924), 4.

30. Claude Beylie and Francis Lacassin, "A la recherche d'un cinéma perdu: Entretien avec Jean-Louis Bouquet, Henri Fescourt, Joë Hamman, Gaston Modot," 26.

31. Jean Eyre, "Les films de demain: *La Cité foudroyée*," *Mon-Ciné* (15 March 1924), 14-15. "Les nouveaux films," *Cinéa-Ciné-pour-tous* 26 (1 December 1924), 4. Jean Mitry, *Histoire du cinéma*, 2, 388.

32. Fescourt, *La Foi et les montagnes*, 239-241. Jean-Louis Bouquet, *"La Cité foudroyée,"* *Cahiers de la cinémathèque* 33-34 (Autumn, 1981), 153-154.

33. Charles Ford, "Germaine Dulac," 23.

34. A print of *L'Angoissante Aventure* is preserved at the National Film Archive in London. I viewed this print too late to incorporate it into this study.

35. "Actualités," *Théâtre et Comoedia Illustré* 20 (August, 1923), [n.p.]. Jean de Mirbel, *"Le Brasier ardent,"* 380-382.

36. Burch, *Marcel L'Herbier*, 91.

37. "Les nouveaux films," *Cinéa-Ciné-pour-tous* 27 (15 December 1924), 5.

38. Edmond Epardaud, *"Le Fantôme du Moulin Rouge,"* *Cinéa-Ciné-pour-tous* 34 (1 April 1925), 21. Transcript of an interview by Armand Panigel with René Clair (1973). This analysis is based on the print of *Le Fantôme du Moulin Rouge* preserved at the National Film Archive in London.

39. Edmond Epardaud, *"Le Fantôme du Moulin Rouge,"* *Cinéa-Ciné-pour-tous* 32 (1 March 1925), 20.

40. Léon Moussinac, "Le Cinéma," 26.

41. Edmond Epardaud, *"Le Voyage imaginaire,"* 14. Transcript of an interview by Armand Panigel with René Clair (1973). This analysis is based on the print of *Le Voyage imaginaire* preserved at the National Film Archive in London.

42. Jean Mitry, *René Clair*, 26.

43. Bernard Brunius, "René Clair," 12. Mitry, *René Clair*, 27.

44. Edmond Epardaud, *"La Proie du vent,"* 12. "Les nouveaux films," *Cinéa-Ciné-pour-tous* 86 (1 June 1927), 6. Maurice Bardèche and Robert Brasillach, *The History of Motion Pictures*, 246.

45. Catherine de la Roche, *René Clair*, 12.

46. Mitry, *René Clair*, 27.

47. Edmond Epardaud, *"Mauprat de Jean Epstein,"* 13-14. "Les nouveaux films," *Cinéa-Ciné-pour-tous* 87 (15 June 1927), 4. This analysis is based on the print of *Mauprat* preserved at the Cinémathèque française.

48. Pierre Kéfer, "En marge de *Mauprat*," 21-22. Pierre Leprohon, *Jean Epstein*, 43.

49. Leprohon, *Jean Epstein*, 77.

50. Léon Barsacq, *Caligari's Cabinet and Other Grand Illusions*, 41.

51. Ford, "Germaine Dulac," 28.

52. Lewis Jacobs, ed., *The Compound Cinema: The Film Writings of Harry Alan Potamkin*, 286.

53. Edmond Epardaud, "Les Productions Alex Nalpas," *Cinéa-Ciné-pour-tous* 118 (1 October 1928), 22.

54. Ford, "Germaine Dulac," 36.

55. Ibid.

56. Ibid., 37.

Arabian Nights and Colonial Dreams

1. Pierre Boulanger, *Le Cinéma colonial*, 45.

2. Henri Fescourt, *La Foi et les montagnes*, 189.

3. Jean-Pierre Jeancolais, *Carte blanche à la Cinémathèque de Toulouse* (Creteil: Maison des Arts et de la Culture de Creteil, 1975), 13.

4. Fescourt, *La Foi et les montagnes*, 191.

5. Louis Delluc, "Cinéma," *Paris-Midi* (21 March 1919), 2. Louis Delluc, "Cinéma," *Paris-Midi* (14 October 1919), 2.

6. "La Réalisation: *La Sultane de l'amour*," *Ciné-pour-tous* 10 (8 October 1919), 5. Georges Sadoul, *Histoire générale du cinéma*, 4, 486. For information on the print of *La Sultane de l'amour* presented at the Museum of Modern Art (in January, 1983), I thank Stuart Liebman.

7. René Jeanne, *"Le Coffret de jade,"* 19.

8. Louis Delluc, "Quelques films français," *Cinéa* 18 (9 September 1921), 5.

9. "Films de la quinzaine," *Ciné-pour-tous* 51 (22 October 1920), 4. This brief description is based on an incomplete print of *Narayana* preserved at the Cinémathèque française.

10. Fescourt, *La Foi et les montagnes*, 320.

11. Jean Mitry, *Histoire du cinéma*, 3, 511.

12. "Les Présentations," *Cinémagazine* 2 (2 December 1921), 22. Boulanger, *Le Cinéma colonial*, 189.

13. Boulanger, *Le Cinéma colonial*, 189.

14. Films Albatros folder—Bibliothèque de l'Arsenal. "Les Grands Films," *Cinémagazine* 3 (27 April 1923), 161. René Jeanne and Charles Ford, *Histoire encyclopédique du cinéma*, 1, 403.

15. Edmond Epardaud, *"Le Prince charmant,"* *Cinéa-Ciné-pour-tous* 28 (1 January 1925), 13-15.

16. Lucie Derain, "Un grand décorateur: Ivan Lochakoff," *Cinéa-Ciné-pour-tous* 28 (1 January 1925), 16-17.

17. Epardaud, *"Le Prince charmant,"* 13.

18. Edmond Epardaud, *"Salammbô* à l'Opéra," *Cinéa-Ciné-pour-tous* 47 (15 October 1925), 14.

19. *Ciné-Informations-Aubert* 13 (15 February 1925), 1. *Ciné-Informations-Aubert* 29 (25 October 1925), 1. Films Aubert folder—Bibliothèque de l'Arsenal.

20. *La Petite Illustration* 3 (19 September 1925), 2.

21. Ibid.

22. Ibid., 3-12.

23. Jeanne and Ford, *Histoire encyclopédique du cinéma*, 1, 222.

24. Ibid., 221.

25. Edmond Epardaud, *"Salammbô* à L'Opéra," *Cinéa-Ciné-pour-tous* 48 (1 November 1925), 21-23. Jeanne and Ford, *Histoire encyclopédique du cinéma*, 1, 221.

26. René Jeanne, "Le Maroc à l'écran," *Cinémagazine* 2 (1 September 1922), 259.

27. V.-Guillaume Danvers, "La Cinématograhie en France," *Almanach du cinéma* (1923), 62, 63.

28. Georges Sadoul, *Histoire générale du cinéma*, 5, 93.

29. "Les films de la quinzaine," *Ciné-pour-tous* 1 (15 June 1919 [reissue 27 August 1920]), 6. *Les Cinq Gentlemen maudits* was popular enough to be rereleased one year later—"Les films de la semaine," *Le Journal du Ciné-Club* 34 (3 September 1920), 10.

30. Boulanger, *Le Cinéma colonial*, 29-30.

31. Léon Poirier, *Vingt-quatre images à la seconde*, 46-48.

32. Sadoul, *Histoire générale du cinéma*, 5, 170.

33. Fescourt, *La Foi et les montagnes*, 271. Boulanger, *Le Cinéma colonial*, 35.

34. *Les Nouveautés Aubert* 21 (October, 1921), 1. V. Guillaume Danvers, "A Propos de *L'Atlantide*," 5-7. *Les Nouveautés Aubert* 27 (April, 1922), 1.

35. Boulanger, *Le Cinéma colonial*, 40. André Delpeuch, *Le Cinéma*, 119-121, 270-272.

36. Jean Mitry, *Histoire du cinéma*, 2, 435.

37. Louis Delluc, "Quelques films français," *Cinéa* 18 (9 September 1921), 8.

38. Boulanger, *Le Cinéma colonial*, 40.

39. Louis Delluc, "Notes," *Cinéa* 6 (10 June 1921), 9. Delluc, "Quelques films français," 8.

40. This analysis is based on the print of *L'Atlantide* preserved at the Cinémathèque française.

41. Sadoul, *Histoire générale du cinéma*, 5, 174.

42. Ibid.

43. Boulanger, *Le Cinéma colonial*, 36.

44. Jaque Christiany, *"Le Cheik,"* *Cinéa* 81 (15 December 1922), 14.

45. Boulanger, *Le Cinéma colonial*, 45.

46. Ibid., 43-44.

47. *"Yasmina,"* *Cinéa-Ciné-pour-tous* 72 (1 November 1926), 21.

48. "La mode à l'écran," *Cinéa-Ciné-pour-tous* 128 (1 March 1929), 18. Boulanger, *Le Cinéma colonial*, 69-70, 76.

49. Advertisement, *Cinéa-Ciné-pour-tous* 60 (1 May 1926), 4. "Les nouveaux films," *Cinéa-Ciné-pour-tous* 72 (1 November 1926), 6.

50. Marcel Lapierre, *Les Cent Visages du cinéma*, 181. Boulanger, *Le Cinéma colonial*, 74-75.

51. Walter S. Michel, "In Memoriam of Dmitri Kirsanov," 39.

52. Raymond Chirat, "Julien Duvivier," 99. Boulanger, *Le Cinéma colonial*, 77.

53. J.-P. Dreyfus, *"Maman Colibri," La Revue du cinéma* 9 (1 April 1930), 65.

54. Boulanger, *Le Cinéma colonial*, 61.

55. Ibid.

56. Ibid.

57. Claude Beylie and Francis Lacassin, "Henri Fescourt," 301. Boulanger, *Le Cinéma colonial*, 67.

58. A. Colombat, *"L'Occident,"* 4.

59. Beylie and Lacassin, "Henri Fescourt," 304.

60. Fescourt, *La Foi et les montagnes*, 348.

61. D. W. Brogan, *The Development of Modern France, 1870-1939*, 631. Georges Sadoul, *Histoire générale du cinéma*, 6, 309.

62. Boulanger, *Le Cinéma colonial*, 84. Apparently, after an outcry from the French press, *Beau Geste* was banned in France—David Strauss, "The Rise of Anti-Intellectualism in France: French Intellectuals and the American Film Industry, 1927-1932," 756.

63. Boulanger, *Le Cinéma colonial*, 82-83.

64. Marcel Oms, "Un Cinéaste des Années Vingt: René Le Somptier," 211-212.

65. Boulanger, *Le Cinéma colonial*, 144.

66. Robert Trevise, "Les Présentations de la quinzaine," *Cinéa-Ciné-pour-tous*, 134 (1 June 1929), 26. André Bazin, *Jean Renoir*, 221.

67. Bernard Chardère, ed. "Jean Renoir," 99.

68. Ibid., 99-100.

69. This analysis is based on the print of *Le Bled* preserved at the Cinémathèque française.

70. *Premier Plan* compared this sequence to the chariot race in *Ben-Hur*—Chardère, "Jean Renoir," 97.

71. It is the camel, not the villain, that is blinded here—compare Raymond Durgnat, *Jean Renoir*, 59.

72. Bazin, *Jean Renoir*, 223.

73. Boulanger, *Le Cinéma colonial*, 7.

74. Ibid.

75. Ibid., 8.

Historical Reconstructions

1. Georges Sadoul, *Histoire générale du cinéma*, 3, 37-38, 41-50. Jean-Pierre Jeancolais, *Carte blanche à la Cinémathèque de Tolouse*, 13.

2. Terry Ramsaye, *A Million and One Nights: A History of the Motion Pictures through 1925* (New York: Simon and Schuster, 1926), 595-597. Sadoul, *Histoire générale du cinéma*, 3, 40. A complete print of *Queen Elizabeth* is preserved at the Museum of Modern Art as well as elsewhere.

3. Pierre Leprohon, *The Italian Cinema*, trans. Roger Greaves and Oliver Stallybrass (New York: Praeger, 1972), 16-32.

4. Lotte Eisner, *The Haunted Screen*, 75, 86. Lotte Eisner, "Lubitsch et les films à costumes, l'influence de Max Reinhardt," in *Vingt Ans de cinéma allemand, 1913-1933*, 26-56.

5. Maurice Bardèche and Robert Brasillach, *The History of Motion Pictures*, 49.

6. André Lang, *Déplacements et Villégiatures littéraires*, 168.

7. D. Audollent, "Le Film allemand aux Etats-unis," *Cinémagazine* 2 (17 February 1922), 210-211.

8. Jacques Petat, "L'Avant-garde français des années vingt," 22.

9. Marc Silberman, "Film and Ideology: The Structure of the German Film Industry and Films of the 1920s," 15.

10. "Les films," *Ciné-pour-tous* 2 (1 July 1919), 2. G.-Michel Coissac, "L'Evolution de cinématographe et la réalisation de quelques grands films," 15.

11. "Les films de la quinzaine," *Ciné-pour-tous* 56 (31 December 1920), 4. Henri Fescourt, *La Foi et les montagnes*, 193.

12. Lionel Landry, "La Reconstitution historique," *Cinémagazine* 3 (14 September 1923), 368.

13. "Les films de la quinzaine," *Ciné-pour-tous* 55 (17 December 1920), 15. P. H., "Une grande vedette du film français: Léon Mathot," *Cinéa-Ciné-pour-tous* 5 (15 January 1924), 5-7.

14. Marcel Oms, "Histoire et géographie d'une France imaginaire," 82.

15. "Du Studio à l'écran," *Ciné-pour-tous* 43 (25 June 1920), 2. This analysis is based on the print of *L'Agonie des aigles* preserved at the National Film Archive.

16. Georges Sadoul, *Histoire générale du cinéma*, 5, 15, 19-20.

17. Janet Flanner, *Paris Was Yesterday (1925-1939)*, ed. Irving Drutman (New York: Popular Library, 1972), 18.

18. Fescourt, *La Foi et les montagnes*, 339. Marcel Oms suggests that several sequences in *L'Agonie des aigles* actually echo the Great War: Napoléon's farewell at Fontainebleau, for instance, recalls the ceremony of demobilization and the reconciliation of Clemenceau and Poincaré—Oms, "Histoire et géographie d'une France imaginaire," 81.

19. Advertisement, *Cinémagazine* 1 (7 October 1921), 4. Lucien Doublon, "Ce que l'on verra prochainement," *Cinémagazine* 1 (7 October 1921), 26.

20. Henri Diamant-Berger, *Il était une fois le cinéma*, 84-85.

21. Ibid., 83.

22. Ibid., 83-84.

23. Ricciotto Canudo, *L'Usine aux images*, 31.

24. Advertisement, *Cinémagazine* 3 (8 December 1922), 326. Henri Diamant-Berger, "Avant *Vingt Ans après*," *Cinémagazine* 2 (22 December 1922), 447-448. A print of *Vingt Ans après* is preserved at the Cinémathèque française.

25. Diamant-Berger, *Il était une fois le cinéma*, 98-99.

26. Lang, *Déplacements et Villégiatures littéraires*, 156.

27. "Mlle. de la Seiglière," *Cinémagazine* 1 (4-10 March 1921), 20-21. Pierre Desclaux, "Charles Lamy," *Mon-Ciné* (7 February 1924), 8-10.

28. Philippe Esnault, "Entretiens avec André-Paul Antoine," 24.

29. Lucien Doublon, "Ce que les directeurs ont vu et ce que le public verra," *Cinémagazine* 1 (11-17 February 1921), 26-27. V.-Guillaume Danvers, "La Cinématographie en France," *Almanach du cinéma* (1923), 55-56.

30. Lang, *Déplacements et Villégiatures littéraires*, 196.

31. Danvers, "La Cinématographie en France," 56.

32. Ibid., 62. Fescourt, *La Foi et les montagnes*, 328. Sadoul, *Histoire générale du cinéma*, 5, 198.

33. Albert Bonneau, "Robin des bois," *Cinémagazine* 3 (2 March 1923), 355-362. The readers of *Cinéa-Ciné-pour-tous* voted it second on their list of the year's best films (just after Gance's *La Roue*)—"Notre référendum du plus beau film," *Cinéa-Ciné-pour-tous* 11 (15 April 1924), 5-6. By this time, however, Ricciotto Canudo was already criticizing the apparent hegemony of the genre, especially since he included in it the serial adventure film format—Canudo, "Le Cinéma," *Les Nouvelles littéraires* (3 March 1923), 4.

34. *L'Effort Français Aubert* (1923)—Bibliothèque de l'Arsenal. Cinémathèque française filmography of René Le Somptier.

35. V.-Guillaume Danvers, "La Dame de Monsoreau," *Cinémagazine* 3 (26 January 1923), 135-140. "Le Scénario {La Dame de Monsoreau}," *Cinémagazine* 3 (26 January 1923), 141-145. René Le Somptier, "Comment j'ai réalisé *La Dame de Monsoreau*," *Cinémagazine* 3 (26 January 1923), 150. André Tinchant, "La Dame de Monsoreau," *Cinémagazine* 3 (20 April 1923), 104-106.

36. The Cinémathèque française print of *La Dame de Monsoreau* is a condensed two-hour version, which, according to Marcel Oms, was released in 1925—Oms, "Histoire et géographie d'une France imaginaire," 209.

37. Léon Moussinac, "Reprises et présentation," *Le Crapouillot* (16 January 1923), 14. Advertisement, *Cinémagazine* 3 (26 January 1923), 155-157.

38. Gerald McKee, *Film Collecting*, 83.

39. Canudo, *L'Usine aux images*, 126.

40. Albert Bonneau, "Violettes impériales: le réalisateur, la mise-en-scène, l'interprétation," 296.

41. Jean Galtier-Boissière, "Une Séance d'art muet," *Le Crapouillot* (1 January 1923), 20-21.

42. "Les nouveaux films," *Cinéa-Ciné-pour-tous* 3 (15 December 1923), 4. Robert Trevise, "Les présentations de la quinzaine," 33.

43. Léonce Perret, "Comment j'ai tourné *Koenigsmark*," 329-332.

44. Albert Bonneau, "Léonce Perret," 221. Léon Moussinac, "Naissance du cinéma [1925]," 134-135.

45. Léon Barsacq, *Caligari's Cabinet and Other Grand Illusions*, 227.

46. Trevise, "Les présentations de la quinzaine," 33. "L'Elégance et *Koenigsmark*," 18-19. René Jeanne and Charles Ford, *Histoire encyclopédique du cinéma*, 1, 248.

47. Moussinac, "Naissance du cinéma [1925]," 132.

48. "Résultat du concours du 'Meilleur film de l'Année' [1923]," *Cinémagazine* 5 (11 April 1924), 80.

49. "Les nouveaux films," *Cinéa-Ciné-pour-tous* 12 (1 May 1924), 5.

50. Fescourt, *La Foi et les montagnes*, 337.

51. "*Violettes impériales*: le scénario," 299.

52. Bonneau, "*Violettes impériales*," 297. In the summer of 1982, Kevin Brownlow told me that the film, at least in its condensed 9.5 mm version, was remarkably fluid, especially in its camera movement.

53. Fescourt, *La Foi et les montagnes*, 337.

54. "Les nouveaux films," *Cinéa-Ciné-pour-tous* 7 (15 February 1924), 4.

55. Jeanne and Ford, *Histoire encyclopédique du cinéma*, 1, 405.

56. "Le meilleur film de 1924," *Cinéa-Ciné-pour-tous* 32 (1 March 1925), 5.

57. Jean Tedesco, "*Kean* ou *Désordre et génie*," 13. This analysis is based on the prints of *Kean* collected at the Cinémathèque française, the George Eastman House, and Em Gee Films.

58. V. Mery, "Pendant que l'on tourne: *Kean*," *Cinémagazine* 3 (1 June 1923), 367.

59. Juan Arroy, "Ivan Mosjoukine tourne *Kean*," *Cinémagazine* 3 (30 November 1923), 335.

60. Tedesco, "*Kean*," 16.

61. Jeanne and Ford, *Histoire encyclopédique du cinéma*, 1, 406.

62. Barsacq, *Caligari's Cabinet and Other Grand Illusions*, 38, 40. Lucien Aguettand, who began as an assistant to Mallet-Stevens and Cavalcanti, also singles out the set design work of the Russian emigrés in Philippe Carcassonne and François Cuel, "Entretien avec Lucien Aguettand," *Cinématographe* 76 (March, 1982), 18-22.

63. "Les nouveaux films," *Cinéa-Ciné-pour-tous* 30 (1 February 1925), 5.

64. Fescourt, *La Foi et les montagnes*, 298.

65. Quenu, "L'Art de la décoration au cinéma," *Cinémagazine* 5 (26 December 1924), 565.

66. J.-A. de Munto, "Germaine Dulac nous parle du *Diable dans la ville*," *Cinémagazine* 4 (9 May 1924), 247.

67. Transcript of an interview by Armand Panigel with Raymond Bernard (1973).

68. Gilbert Flammand, "*Le Miracle des loups*," 346.

69. André-Paul Antoine, *Antoine, père et fils: souvenirs du Paris littéraire et théâtral, 1900-1939* (Paris: René Juillard, 1962), 216. René Jeanne, "*Le Miracle des loups*: la bataille de Beauvais reconstituée à Carcassonne," 21-25.

70. Transcript of an interview by Armand Panigel with Raymond Bernard (1973).

71. Paul Ramain, "L'Influence du cinéma sur la musique," 124. Coissac, "L'Evolution du cinématographe et la réalisation de quelques grands films," 25.

72. Advertisement, *Cinéa-Ciné-pour-tous* 25 (15 November 1924), 4.

73. "Les nouveaux films," *Cinéa-Ciné-pour-tous* 26 (1 December 1924), 4. "Les nouveaux films," *Cinéa-Ciné-pour-tous* 33 (15 March 1925), 5.

74. "Quel est le meilleur film de 1925?" *Cinéa-Ciné-pour-tous* 56 (1 March 1926), 16.

75. This analysis is based on the print of *Le Miracle des loups* preserved at the Cinémathèque française.

76. Dullin accepted this role of Louis XI reluctantly, as a means of sustaining his Atelier Théâtre—Antoine, *Antoine, père et fils*, 213-215.

77. Fescourt, *La Foi et les montagnes*, 315.

78. Barsacq, *Caligari's Cabinet and Other Grand Illusions*, 44.

79. "Les nouveaux films," *Cinéa-Ciné-pour-tous* 50 (1 December 1925), 5.

80. Gloria Swanson, *Swanson on Swanson*, 214-216.

81. Jeanne and Ford, *Histoire encyclopédique du cinéma*, 1, 224.

82. Swanson, *Swanson on Swanson*, 222-227.

83. Jeanne and Ford, *Histoire encyclopédique du cinéma*, 1, 224.

84. "Léonce Perret reçoit un grand prix aux Arts Décoratifs pour *Madame Sans-Gêne*," 28. Swanson, *Swanson on Swanson*, 278-279. Letter from Kevin Brownlow, 25 August 1979.

85. "L'Opinion de la presse sur *Madame Sans-Gêne*," 27.

86. J. T., "Une grande première au Rivoli à New York," *Cinéa-Ciné-pour-tous* 38 (1 June 1925), 22-23. Swanson, *Swanson on Swanson*, 269.

87. *"Madame Récamier," La Petite Illustration*, 12 (9 June, 1928), 2.

88. Ibid., 3-12.

89. Jeanne and Ford, *Histoire encyclopédique du cinéma*, 1, 234-235.

90. "Les nouveaux films," *Cinéa-Ciné-pour-tous* 112 (1 July 1928), 5. Daniel Abric, *"Madame Récamier," Cinémonde* 9 (20 December 1928), 170-171.

91. "Les nouveaux films," *Cinéa-Ciné-pour-tous* 143 (1 November 1929), 4. Paul Dornac, "Revue des programmes," *La Revue du cinéma* 6 (1 January 1930), 73-74.

92. Gilbert Flammand, "On tourne *Cagliostro*," *Cinéa-Ciné-pour-tous* 124 (1 January 1929), 21.

93. Films Albatros folder—Bibliothèque de l'Arsenal.

94. Raymond Villette, "Les films historiques en 1929," *Almanach de Mon-Ciné* (1930), 44.

95. Flammand, "On tourne *Cagliostro*," 21. R. T., *"Cagliostro," Cinéa-Ciné-pour-tous* 125 (15 January 1929), 24.

96. "Les nouveaux films," *Cinéa-Ciné-pour-tous* 137 (1 July 1929), 5.

97. "Les nouveaux films," *Cinéa-Ciné-pour-tous* 75 (15 December 1926), 7. This analysis is based on a three-reel 9.5mm Pathescope version of *Michel Strogoff* in the collection of Kevin Brownlow.

98. *"Michel Strogoff," La Petite Illustration*, 2-4.

99. McKee, *Film Collecting*, 176.

100. "Les nouveaux films," *Cinéa-Ciné-pour-tous* 93 (15 September 1927), 6. This analysis is based on the print of *Casanova* at the State Historical Society of Wisconsin.

101. Barsacq, *Caligari's Cabinet and Other Grand Illusions*, 40.

102. Ibid., 39.

103. "L'Activité cinégraphique," *Cinéa-Ciné-pour-tous* 83 (15 April, 1927), 23.

104. Kevin Brownlow generously allowed me to examine a short tinted and toned sequence from *Casanova* in his film collection.

105. *"Casanova," Cinéa-Ciné-pour-tous* 88 (1 July 1927), 23.

106. Jean Dréville, "Films," *Cinégraphie* 1 (15 September 1927), 11-12.

107. "Les nouveaux films," *Cinéa-Ciné-pour-tous* 77 (15 January 1927), 6. Advertisement, *Cinéa-Ciné-pour-tous* 79 (15 February 1927), [inside cover]. *"Joueur d'échecs," La Petite Illustration*, 2.

108. This analysis is based on two (French and English) two-reel 9.5mm Pathescope versions of *Joueur d'échecs* in the collection of Kevin Brownlow.

109. *"Le Joueur d'échecs*: le scénario," *Cinémagazine* 7 (14 January 1927), 62-65.

110. E. R., "En marge du *Joueur d'échecs*," *Cinémagazine* 7 (14 January 1927), 73. *"Joueur d'échecs," La Petite Illustration*, 2.

111. Coissac, "L'Evolution du cinématographe et la réalisation de quelques grands films," 27.

112. Barsacq, *Caligari's Cabinet and Other Grand Illusions*, 45.

113. J. W., "Raymond Bernard," *Cinémagazine* 7 (14 January 1927), 67.

114. Jean de Mirbel, "La Première du *Joueur d'échecs*," *Cinémagazine* 7 (14 January 1927), 70.

115. *"Joueur d'échecs," La Petite Illustration*, 2.

116. Edmond Epardaud, "Raymond Bernard," 33-34. Chirat, *Catalogue des films français de long métrage: films sonores de fiction, 1929-1939* [n.p.].

117. "L'Activité cinégraphique," *Cinéa-Ciné-pour-tous* 127 (15 February 1929), 24. "L'Activité cinégraphique," *Cinéa-Ciné-pour-tous* 139 (1 September 1929), 27.

118. Interview with Kevin Brownlow, 15 August 1979.

119. Pierre Rambaud, *"La Valse de l'adieu," Cinéa-Ciné-pour-tous* 121 (15 November 1928), 27. René Olivet, "On verra cette semaine à Paris," *Cinémonde* 6 (15 November 1928), 106. I viewed a print of *La Valse de l'adieu* at the National Film Archive too late to incorporate any further remarks into this study.

120. Pierre Desclaux, "Les grands films de 1927-1928," *Almanach de Mon-Ciné* (1929), 15.

121. *"La Princesse Masha," Cinéa-Ciné-pour-tous* 90 (1 August 1927), 28.

122. "Le Rialto ouvira le 5 octobre," *Cinématheque française* 465 (1 October 1927), 10.

123. *"Monte-Cristo," Cinéa-Ciné-pour-tous* 135 (15 June 1929), 27.

124. "Les nouveaux films," *Cinéa-Ciné-pour-tous* 143 (1 November 1929), 4.

125. Barsacq, *Caligari's Cabinet and Other Grand Illusions*, 39.

126. Fescourt, *La Foi et les montagnes*, 348.

127. *"Monte-Cristo," Cinémagazine* (7 June 1929), quoted in Claude Beylie and Francis Lacassin, "Henri Fescourt," 304.

128. "Les nouveaux films," *Cinéa-Ciné-pour-tous* 143 (1 November 1929), 4.

129. "Les nouveaux films," *Cinéa-Ciné-pour-tous* 58 (1 April 1926), 6. René Jeanne, *Paris vu par le cinéma*, 192. McKee, *Film Collecting*, 51.

130. There are discrepancies about *Napoléon*'s costs. See René Jeanne, "La Technique de *Napoléon*," *Cinéa-Ciné-pour-tous* 86 (1 June 1927), 9. Léon Moussinac, "Panoramique du cinéma [1929]," 268. Sophie Daria, *Abel Gance: hier et demain* 116. René Jeanne and Charles Ford, *Abel Gance*, 52.

131. Advertisement, *Cinéa-Ciné-pour-tous* 80 (1 March 1927). Jean Mitry, "Napoléon à l'écran," 56. Moussinac, "Panoramique du cinéma [1929]," 273-274.

132. "Les nouveaux films," *Cinéa-Ciné-pour-tous* 96 (1 November 1927), 5. "A Paris, cette semaine," *Cinématographie française* 480 (14 January 1928), 42. Georges Sadoul, *Histoire générale du cinéma*, 6, 319.

133. Jeanne and Ford, *Abel Gance*, 52. Interview with Kevin Brownlow, 15 August 1979.

134. Barsacq, *Caligari's Cabinet and Other Grand Illusions*, 40-41.

135. Abel Gance, *Napoléon vu par Abel Gance* [program insert].

136. Mitry, "Napoléon à l'écran," 55.

137. Moussinac, "Panoramique du cinéma [1929]," 267, 272.

138. Coissac, "L'Evolution du cinématographe et la réalisation de quelques grands films," 31-32. René Olivet, "On verra cette semaine à Paris," *Cinémonde* 26 (18 April 1929), 458. "Les nouveaux films," *Cinéa-Ciné-pour-tous* 132 (1 May 1929), 5. This brief analysis is based on a two-reel 9.5mm Pathescope version of *La Merveilleuse Vie de Jeanne d'Arc* in the collection of Kevin Brownlow.

139. "La *Jeanne d'Arc* de Dreyer à la Salle Marivaux," *Cinéa-Ciné-pour-tous* 119 (15 October 1928), 16.

140. Michel Delahaye, "Interview with Carl Dreyer," 155.

141. "Dossier Film #3—*La Passion de Jeanne d'Arc*," 46.

142. David Bordwell, *Filmguide to La Passion de Jeanne d'Arc* 20. Sadoul, *Histoire générale du cinéma*, 6, 384.

143. "Les nouveaux films," *Cinéa-Ciné-pour-tous* 127 (15 February 1929), 6. René Olivet, "On verra cette semaine à Paris," *Cinémonde* 16 (7 February 1929), 292. There was another film released about the same time as *Le Tournoi* that also may have countered the genre conventions: Cavalcanti's adaptation of Gautier's "swashbuckling" novel, *Le Capitaine fracasse*—see Gilbert Flamand, *"Le Capitaine fracasse," Cinémonde* 18 (21 February 1929), 331.

144. Bernard Chardère, ed., "Jean Renoir," 93.

145. Raymond Durgnat, *Jean Renoir* 54.

146. André Bazin, *Jean Renoir* 220.

147. Chardère, "Jean Renoir," 92.

148. "Les nouveaux films," *Cinéa-Ciné-pour-tous* 64 (1 July 1926), 8. *Ciné-Information-Aubert* 49 (1 September 1926), 1.

149. Advertisement, *Cinéa-Ciné-pour-tous* 74 (1 December 1926), 35.

150. This analysis is based on the print of *Nana* preserved at the Cinémathèque française.

151. Jean Renoir, "Souvenirs," *Le Point* 18 (December, 1938), reprinted in Bazin, *Jean Renoir*, 10.

152. Alexander Sesonske, *Jean Renoir: The French Films, 1924-1939*, 21. Sesonske's analysis of *Nana* is the best yet in English.

153. Edmond Epardaud, *"Nana,"* 15. Bazin, *Jean Renoir*, 207. Jean Renoir, *Ma Vie et mes films*, 72, 75.

154. Albert Bonneau, *"Nana," Cinémagazine* (29 January 1926), reprinted in Chardère, "Jean Renoir," 64.

155. Marcel Zahar and Daniel Burret, "Une Visite à Jean Renoir," *Cinéa-Ciné-pour-tous* 58 (1 April 1926), 14. Bazin, *Jean Renoir*, 208.

156. Bonneau, *"Nana,"* 63. Pierre Leprohon, *Jean Renoir*, 37. Claude Beylie, "A la recherche d'un style," 13.

157. Leprohon, *Jean Renoir*, 35, 37.

158. Noël Burch, *Theory of Film Practice*, trans. Helen R. Lane (New York: Praeger, 1973), 18.

159. Sesonske, *Jean Renoir: The French Films, 1924-1939*, 34. Charles [Rick] Altman, "The Lonely Villa and Griffith's Paradigmatic Style," *Quarterly Review of Film Studies* 6 (Spring, 1981), 123-134. Janet Bergstrom, "Alternation, Segmentation, Hypnosis: Interview with Raymond Bellour," *camera obscura* 3-4 (1979), 77-79.

160. Noël Burch and Jean-André Fieschi, "La Première Vague," 20-24. Noël Burch and Jorge Dana, "Propositions," 40-66.

161. Sesonske, *Jean Renoir: The French Films, 1924-1939*, 35.

162. Lapierre, *Les Cent Visages du cinéma*, 185.

163. "Les nouveaux films," *Cinéa-Ciné-pour-tous* 107 (15 April, 1928), 8.

164. Jeanne and Ford, *Histoire encyclopédique du cinéma*, 1, 426.

165. Pierre Desclaux, "Les grands films de 1927-1928," 11-12.

166. Letter from Kevin Brownlow, 25 August 1979.

167. Advertisement, *Cinémonde* 3 (9 November 1928), 56. Léon Poirier, *Vingt-quatre images à la seconde*, 223.

168. "Les nouveaux films," *Cinéa-Ciné-pour-tous* 136 (1 July 1929), 5. *"Verdun, visions d'histoire,"* La Petite Illustration, 2.

169. Poirier, *Vingt-quatre images à la seconde*, 221.

170. *"Verdun, visions d'histoire,"* La Petite Illustration, 2.

171. Edmond Epardaud, *"Verdun, visions d'histoire,"* 21-22. Jeanne and Ford, *Histoire encyclopédique du cinéma*, 1, 381.

172. Poirier, *Vingt-quatre images à la seconde*, 221. Maurice Schutz reports that Poirier accentuated the stark simplicity of the film by imitating Dreyer's decision in *La Passion de Jeanne d'Arc* not to use makeup on his actors—Schutz, "La Maquillage," in *L'Art cinématographique*, 6 (Paris: Librairie Félix Alcan, 1929), 65-66.

173. Gaston Thierry, "Les représentations de gala de *Verdun, visions d'histoire*," *Cinémonde* 4 (16 November 1928), 66.

174. Poirier, *Vingt-quatre images à la seconde*, 221. This brief analysis is based on a print of the sound version of *Verdun, visions d'histoire* preserved at the Cinémathèque française.

175. Hay Chowe, "Propaganda," *Close Up* 4 (January, 1929), 27-32.

176. Theodore Zeldin, *France, 1848-1945: Taste and Corruption*, 44.

Modern Studio Spectaculars

1. Henri Diamant-Berger, *Il était une fois le cinéma*, 143.

2. Janet Flanner, *Paris Was Yesterday, 1925-1939*, 3.

3. See the "Jazzmania" photograph of Mae Murray in *Théâtre et Comoedia Illustré* 17 (May, 1923), [n.p.], and the photograph of her in costume for *The Masked Bride* in *Cinéa-Ciné-pour-tous* 63 (15 June 1926), 20. Gérard Talon, "Cinéma français: la crise de 1928," 109.

4. For the special attention accorded to fashion and dancing by the French, see Theodore Zeldin, *France, 1848-1945: Taste and Corruption*, 83-95, 308-318. See also Anne Hollander, "Women and Fashion," in *Women, the Arts, and the 1920s in Paris and New York*, ed. Kenneth Wheeler and Virginia Lee Lussier (New Brunswick: Transaction Books, 1982), 109-125.

5. Talon, "Cinéma français: La crise de 1928," 107-108, 112-113. Marc Silberman, "Film and Ideology: The Structure of the German Film Industry and Films of the 1920s," 28-28a.

6. Charles Eckert, "The Carole Lombard in Macy's Window," 4-8. For a fascinating corollary study of changes in the American household of the 1920s, see Ruth Schwartz Cowan, "The Industrial Revolution in the Home: Household Technology and Social Change in the 20th Century," *Technology and Culture* 17 (January, 1976), 1-23.

7. Léon Moussinac, "Naissance du cinéma [1925]," 134. Léon Barsacq, *Caligari's Cabinet and Other Grand Illusions: A History of Film Design* 227.

8. "L'Elégance et *Koenigsmark*," 18-19.

9. The rage for jazz dance halls had quickly spread to the provinces after the war, despite attempts to tax them out of business. See René Noell, "Histoire du spectacle cinématographique à Perpignan, de 1896 à 1944," 53.

10. Albert Bonneau, "L'Effort français en 1924," *Annuaire général de la cinématographie* (1925), 79.

11. "Les nouveaux films," *Cinéa-Ciné-pour-tous* 26 (1 December 1924), 4.

12. Jean-André Fieschi, "Autour du cinématographe," 34.

13. "Que sera *L'Inhumaine*," 12-13. Barry Salt, *Film Style and Technology: History and Analysis*.

14. Noël Burch, *Marcel L'Herbier*, 25.

15. Barry Salt suggests that Georgette Leblanc's acting style may be in imitation of Asta Nielson—letter from Barry Salt, 10 December 1979.

16. "Les nouveaux films," *Cinéa-Ciné-pour-tous* 26 (1 December 1924), 4. This brief analysis is based on the print of *Le Lion des Mogols* preserved at the Cinémathèque française.

17. "Les nouveaux films," *Cinéa-Ciné-pour-tous* 29 (15 January 1925), 6.

18. *"La Terre promise,"* *La Petite Illustration*, 2-12. Gerald McKee, *Film Collecting* 84. Christian Bosséno, "Le cinéma et la presse (II)," 96-97.

19. Edmond Epardaud, *"La Terre promise,"* 13-14.

20. "Les nouveaux films," *Cinéa-Ciné-pour-tous* 40 (1 July 1925), 4.

21. Charles Ford, "Germaine Dulac," 26.

22. This analysis is based on the prints of *Ame d'artiste* preseved at the Cinémathèque française and the National Film Archive.

23. "Les nouveaux films," *Cinéa-Ciné-pour-tous* 66 (31 July 1926), 6.

24. Jaque Catelain, *Marcel L'Herbier*, 98.

25. Ibid., 93.

26. Ibid., 94.

27. Juan Arroy, "Marcel L'Herbier," 9-12.

28. "Films d'aujourd'hui," *Cinéa-Ciné-pour-tous* 72 (1 November 1926), 20. Fieschi, "Autour du cinématographe," 37. Marcel Oms, "Une Cinéaste des Années Vingt: René Le Somptier," 212.

29. "Ce que la presse étrangère pense du *Vertige*," *Cinéa-Ciné-pour-tous* 72 (1 November 1926), 12.

30. "Les meilleurs films 1926-1927," *Cinéa-Ciné-pour-tous* 102 (1 February 1928), 6.

31. Jean Dréville, "Films," *Cinégraphie* 3 (15 November 1927), 54. "Les nouveaux films," *Cinéa-Ciné-pour-tous* 106 (1 April 1928), 6.

32. Fieschi, "Autour du cinématographe," 37-38.

33. "Les nouveaux films," *Cinéa-Ciné-pour-tous* 75 (15 December 1926), 7. Edmond Epardaud, *"La Femme nue,"* 13-17.

34. Jean Dréville, "Ce que dit l'écran," *Photo-Ciné* 1 (15 January 1927), 14. "Les meilleurs films 1926-1927," 6.

35. Jean Dréville, "La Critique de film," *On Tourne* 3 (15 May 1928), 2. "Les nouveaux films," *Cinéa-Ciné-pour-tous* 110 (1 July 1928), 6.

36. René Jeanne and Charles Ford, *Histoire encyclopédique du cinéma*, 1, 460-461.

37. Jean Dréville, "Films," *Cinégraphie* 2 (15 October 1927), 36.

38. "Les nouveaux films," *Cinéa-Ciné-pour-tous* 77 (15 January 1927), 6.

39. Raymond Chirat, "Julien Duvivier," 79.

40. *Ciné-Information-Aubert* 51 (1 October 1926), 1.

41. *Ciné-Information-Aubert* 56 (15 December 1926), 1.

42. Julien Bayart, "Ce que dit l'écran," *Photo-Ciné* 2 (15 February 1927), 29.

43. Diamant-Berger, *Il était une fois le cinéma*, 149-150.

44. Albert Bonneau, "Les présentations," *Cinémagazine* 7 (17 June 1927), 585. Jean Dréville, "Films," *Cinégraphie* 1 (15 September 1927), 14.

45. "Les nouveaux films," *Cinéa-Ciné-pour-tous* 90 (1 August 1927), 6.

46. Bernard Chardère, ed., "Jean Renoir," 77-80. André Bazin, *Jean Renoir*, 210-211.

47. *"Marquitta,"* *Cinéa-Ciné-pour-tous* 90 (1 August 1927), 31.

48. Chardère, "Jean Renoir," 78.

49. Raymond Durgnat, *Jean Renoir*, 46.

50. Chardère, "Jean Renoir," 77. Bazin, *Jean Renoir*, 211.

51. *Hara-Kiri* received some attention in the Museum of Modern Art program, "Rediscovering the French Film, Part II," that opened in January, 1983.

52. This brief analysis is based on the print of *Yvette* preserved at the National Film Archive.

53. *"Yvette," Cinéa-Ciné-pour-tous* 99 (15 December 1927), 19.

54. "Les nouveaux films," *Cinéa-Ciné-pour-tous* 125 (15 January 1929), 7. Jeanne and Ford, *Histoire encyclopédique du cinéma*, 1, 428.

55. Edmond Epardaud, *"La Vierge folle," Cinéa-Ciné-pour-tous* 124 (1 January 1929), 23-24. "Louise Lagrange et Pierre Blanchar dans *La Marche nuptiale*," *Cinéa-Ciné-pour-tous* 125 (15 January 1929), 18-19. "L'Activité cinégraphique," *Cinéa-Ciné-pour-tous* 130 (1 April 1929), 24. Talon, "Cinéma français: la crise de 1928," 112-113.

56. A. D., *"Quartier Latin," Cinéa-Ciné-pour-tous* 125 (15 January, 1929), 23. Pierre Heuzé, *"Quartier Latin," Cinémonde* 22 (21 March 1929), 352-353. "Les nouveaux films," *Cinéa-Ciné-pour-tous* 131 (15 April 1929), 4. *"Quartier Latin," Cinéa-Ciné-pour-tous* 131 (15 April 1929), 12-13.

57. *Annuaire général de la cinématographie* (1928), 528, 559. "Les nouveaux films," *Cinéa-Ciné-pour-tous* 126 (1 February 1929), 5. Jeanne and Ford, *Histoire encyclopédique du cinéma*, 1, 214.

58. "L'Activité cinégraphique," *Cinéa-Ciné-pour-tous* 141 (1 October 1929), 26. This brief analysis is based on the print of *Au bonheurs des dames* preserved at the Cinémathèque française.

59. Michael Miller, *The Bon Marché*, 5.

60. Chirat, "Julien Duvivier," 81.

61. Burch, *Marcel L'Herbier*, 130-133.

62. Edmond Epardaud, *"L'Argent,"* 13-14. This analysis is based on the prints of *L'Argent* at the Museum of Modern Art and at the National Film Archive—both drawn from the reconstructed version at the Archives du Film, Bois d'Arcy.

63. "La Polémique de *L'Argent*," *Cinéa-Ciné-pour-tous* 107 (15 April 1928), 26-28. Marcel L'Herbier, "Le Droit de métamorphose," 10-11.

64. Fieschi, "Autour du cinématographe," 38.

65. Jean Lenauer, "The Cinema in Paris," 81.

66. Fieschi, "Autour du cinématographe," 38.

67. Noël Burch and Jorge Dana, "Propositions," 47.

68. Talon, "Cinéma français: la crise de 1928," 111.

69. Ibid., 113.

70. Marcel Lapierre, *Les Cent Visages du cinéma*, 212-213. Raymond Borde, "La France des Années 30," 23-45.

Comics and Comedies

1. Francis Lacassin, "Les Fous Rires de la Belle Epoque," in *Pour une contre histoire du cinéma*, 77-78. Claude Beylie and Francis Lacassin, "A la recherche d'un cinéma perdu: entretien avec Jean-Louis Bouquet, Henri Fescourt, Joë Hamman, Gaston Modot," 26.

2. Georges Sadoul, *Histoire générale du cinéma*, 2, 350, 352. Walter Kerr, *The Silent Clowns* (New York: Knopf, 1975), 53. Georges Sadoul, *Le Cinema français*, 177.

3. Georges Sadoul, *Histoire générale du cinéma*, 3, 122. Sadoul, *Le Cinéma français*, 227.

4. Maurice Bardèche and Robert Brasillach, *The History of Motion Pictures*, 77-78. René Jeanne and Charles Ford, *Histoire encyclopédique du cinéma* 1, 78-79.

5. Kerr, *The Silent Clowns*, 53.

6. Sadoul, *Histoire générale du cinéma*, 3, 115.

7. Jean Mitry, "Max Linder," *Anthologie du cinéma*, 334-335. This brief description is based on prints of *Max, victime de quinquina* preserved at the Cinémathèque française, Museum of Modern Art, and Em Gee Film Library.

8. Sadoul, *Histoire générale du cinéma*, 3, 117.

9. Jeanne and Ford, *Histoire encyclopédique du cinéma*, 1, 102.

10.Lacassin, "Les Fous Rires de la Belle Epoque," 79.

11. Sadoul, *Histoire générale du cinéma*, 3, 130.

12. This brief description is based on prints of *Onésime horloger* at the Cinémathèque française and at the Museum of Modern Art.

13. Bardèche and Brasillach, *The History of Motion Pictures*, 75.

14. Francis Lacassin, *Louis Feuillade*, 55-57.

15. Sadoul, *Le Cinéma français*, 200.

16. Lacassin, *Louis Feuillade*, 56.

17. Mitry, "Max Linder," 347.

18. Jeanne and Ford, *Histoire encyclopédique du cinéma*, 1, 480. Henri Diamant-Berger, *Il était une fois le cinéma*, 85-86.

19. Jeanne and Ford, *Histoire encyclopédique du cinéma*, 1, 210, 481.

20. Diamant-Berger, *Il était une fois le cinéma*, 47-61.

21. Ibid., 64.

22. Henri Fescourt, *La Foi et les montagnes*, 313. Transcript of an interview by Armand Panigel with Raymond Bernard (1973).

23. Georges Sadoul, *Histoire générale du cinéma*, 4, 488.

24. Fescourt, *La Foi et les montagnes*, 313.

25. Ricciotto Canudo, *L'Usine aux images*, 99.

26. Diamant-Berger, *Il était une fois le cinéma*, 66.

27. "Le Petit Café," *Ciné-pour-tous* 16 (20 December 1919), 8. Mitry, "Max Linder," 308. Diamant-Berger, *Il était une fois le cinéma*, 66-67.

28. Diamant-Berger, *Il était une fois le cinéma* 67-69.

29. Dorothy Knowles, *French Drama of the Inter-War Years, 1918-1939* (London: George G. Harrap, 1967), 274-287.

30. Lacassin, *Louis Feuillade*, 97-98.

31. "Pathé-Consortium," *Almanach du cinéma* (1922), 8-11.

32. "Les nouveaux films," *Cinéa-Ciné-pour-tous* 31 (15 February 1925), 4.

33. Fescourt, *La Foi et les montagnes*, 119-120. Mitry, "Max Linder," 311.

34. Jean Pascal, "Le Renouveau du film comique: *Ce Cochon de Morin*," *Cinémagazine* 4 (7 March 1924), 411-412.

35. Lucien Farnay, "*Les Ombres qui passent*," 389-390. Films Albatros folder—Bibliothèque de l'Arsenal.

36. Albert Bonneau, "Les Présentations," *Cinémagazine* 3 (8 June 1923), 412.

37. "Les films de la semaine," *Cinémagazine* 5 (13 February 1925), 328. Bernard Brunius, "René Clair," 11. Transcript of an interview by Armand Panigel with René Clair (1973).

38. Transcript of an interview by Armand Panigel with René Clair (1973).

39. Transcript of an interview by Armand Panigel with René Clair (1973).

40. "Les nouveaux films," *Cinéa-Ciné-pour-tous* 52 (1 January 1926), 6. Films Albatros folder—Bibliothèque de l'Arsenal.

41. Edmond Epardaud, "*Le Chasseur de Chez Maxim's*," *Cinéa-Ciné-pour-tous* 88 (1 July 1927), 21.

42. "Les nouveaux films," *Cinéa-Ciné-pour-tous* 73 (15 November 1926), 8. This brief analysis is based on the print of *Jim la Houlette* preserved at the National Film Archive.

43. "*Le Bouif errant*," *Cinéa-Ciné-pour-tous* 73 (15 November 1926), 35-36.

44. Raymond Chirat, "Julien Duvivier," 38-39.

45. "*Les Transatlantiques*," *Cinéa-Ciné-pour-tous* 101 (15 January 1928), 21.

46. Gérard Talon, "Cinéma français: la crise de 1928," 111.

47. "Les nouveaux films," *Cinéa-Ciné-pour-tous* 106 (1 April 1928), 6.

48. François Mazeline, "Opinions des cinéastes: Henri Chomette," *Cinéa-Ciné-pour-tous* 103 (15 February 1928), 13.

49. Jean Dréville, "Films," *Cinégraphie* 5 (15 January 1928), 94.

50. Jeanne and Ford, *Histoire encyclopédique du cinéma*, 1, 266.

51. Dréville, "Films," 94.

52. Henri Chomette, "*Le Chauffeur de Mademoiselle*," *Cinégraphie* 4 (15 December 1927), 65-67.

53. Transcript of an interview by Armand Panigel with René Clair (1973).

54. "A Paris, cette semaine," *Cinématographie française* 480 (14 January 1928), 42. "A Paris, cette semaine," *Cinématographie française* 483 (4 February 1928), 48. Jean Mitry, "Films," *Cinégraphie* 4 (15 December 1927), 69. Jean Lenauer, "René Clair," 37. Léon Moussinac, "Panoramique du cinéma [1929]," 293-295.

55. Léon Barsacq, *Caligari's Cabinet and Other Grand Illusions: A History of Film Design*, 75-76. Lewis Jacobs, ed., *The Compound Cinema: The Film Writings of Harry Alan Potamkin*, 30.

56. Jean Mitry, *René Clair*, 32.

57. Edmond Epardaud, "René Clair fonde un genre nouveau avec *Un Chapeau de paille d'Italie*," 15. This analysis is based on the print of *Un Chapeau de paille d'Italie* preserved at the Museum of Modern Art in New York.

58. Moussinac, "Panoramique du cinéma [1929]," 294.

59. Transcript of an interview by Armand Panigel with René Clair (1973).

60. René Olivet, "On verra cette semaine à Paris," *Cinémonde* 25 (11 April 1929), 440. Catherine de la Roche, *René Clair*, 15.

61. Mitry, René Clair, 59.

62. André Delons, *"Les Deux Timides,"* 65.

63. This brief analysis is based on the print of *Les Deux Timides* preserved at the National Film Archive. There is also a print at the Museum of Modern Art.

64. Jeanne and Ford, *Histoire encyclopédique du cinéma*, 1, 368-369.

65. Mitry, *René Clair*, 59.

66. Jean Lenauer, "The Cinema in Paris," *Close Up* 4 (January, 1929), 68. Fescourt, *La Foi et les montagnes*, 290.

67. Mitry, *René Clair*, 59.

68. Jacobs, ed., *The Compound Cinema*, 295.

69. This analysis is based on the print of *Les Nouveaux Messieurs* preserved at the National Film Archive in London.

70. Charles Ford, *Jacques Feyder*, 43-44.

71. René Olivet, "On verra cette semaine," *Cinémonde* 24 (4 April 1929), 426. "Les nouveaux films," *Cinéa-Ciné-pour-tous* 131 (15 April 1929), 4.

72. "Notre concours des meilleurs films de 1929," *Cinéa-Ciné* 1 (March, 1930), 41.

73. Victor Bachy, "Jacques Feyder," 448. Georges Sadoul, *Histoire générale du cinéma*, 5, 197.

74. Lenauer, "The Cinema in Paris," 67.

75. Jean Mitry, *Histoire du cinéma*, 3, 376.

76. Alexander Sesonske is the only film critic or historian to grant *Tire au flanc* its importance—Alexander Sesonske, *Jean Renoir: The French Films, 1924-1939*, 51-65. This analysis is based on prints of *Tire au flanc* at the Cinémathèque française and at the State Historical Society of Wisconsin.

77. Bernard Chardère, ed., "Jean Renoir," 88-89.

78. Sesonske, *Jean Renoir*, 53.

79. Chardère, "Jean Renoir," 89.

80. Letter from Kevin Brownlow, 25 August 1979.

81. Richard Abel, "Collapsing Columns: Mise-en-scène in *Boudu*," *Jump Cut* 5 (January-February, 1975), 18-20.

82. Raymond Durgnat, *Jean Renoir*, 56-57.

83. René Olivet, "On verra cette semaine," *Cinémode* 8 (13 December 1928), 150. André Bazin, *Jean Renoir*, 216. François Truffaut, *The Films of My Life*, trans. Leonard Mayhew (New York: Simon and Schuster, 1978), 36-47.

84. Bazin, *Jean Renoir*, 217.

85. Chardère, "Jean Renoir," 90.

86. Bazin, *Jean Renoir*, 218.

87. Sesonske, *Jean Renoir*, 60.

88. Ibid., 54-55, 62-65.

89. Ibid., 55.

Part III, The Alternative Cinema Network: Introduction

1. Jean Tedesco, "Le Répertoire et l'avant-garde du cinéma," 5.

The Beginnings of a Film Criticism

1. G.-Michel Coissac, *Histoire du cinématographe*, 448. René Jeanne and Charles Ford, *Le Cinéma et la presse, 1895-1960*, 75-76.

2. Henri Diamant-Berger, *Il était une fois le cinéma*, 30.

3. Jean Mitry, "Louis Delluc," 8-9.

4. Colette, *Colette at the Movies*, 20.

5. Louis Delluc, "Critique des films," *Le Film* (3 June 1918), as quoted in Colette, *Colette at the Movies*, 43.

6. André Antoine, "La Cinégraphie française," 6.

7. Colette, "Cinéma," *Excelsior* (7 August 1916), as reprinted in *Colette at the Movies*, 19.

8. Alain and Odette Virmaux, "Introduction," *Colette at the Movies*, 4.

9. Louis Delluc, "*Illusion* et Illusions," *Le Film* 68 (25 June 1917), 5-6.

10. Marcel L'Herbier, "Hermès et le Silence," 199-212.

11. Louis Aragon, "Du Décor," *Le Film* 131 (16 September 1918), 8-10. Delluc also published Aragon's first poem, "Charlot sentimental," in *Le Film* 105 (18 March 1918), 11.

12. Jean Girard, *Le Lexique français du cinéma, des origines à 1930*, 49.

13. Jeanne and Ford, *Le Cinéma et la presse*, 79.

14. Ibid., 53. Actually Delluc's column first appeared on 20 May 1918.

15. Emile Vuillermoz, "Devant l'écran," *Le Temps* (29 November 1916), 3.

16. Louis Delluc, "Les Cinéastes (uncompleted)," as quoted in Tariol, *Louis Delluc*, 42.

17. Diamant-Berger's conception of the cinema coincides closely with that of Charles Pathé in "Etude sur l'évolution de l'industrie cinématographique française [1918]," *Intelligence du cinématographe*, 213-228.

18. Louis Delluc, *Cinéma et cie* (Paris: Grasset, 1919), 282-283.

19. Louis Delluc, "Cinéma et cie," *Paris-Midi* (17 August 1918), 3. Diamant-Berger, *Le Cinéma*, 37. André Antoine, "L'Avenir du cinéma," *Lectures pour tous* (December, 1919), reprinted in Philippe Esnault, "Propos d'Antoine," 46.

20. Louis Delluc, "Cinéma et cie: Merveilles sans merveilles," *Paris-Midi* (3 August 1918), 3. See also Tariol, *Louis Delluc*, 48, and Mitry, "Louis Delluc," 25.

21. Louis Delluc, "Cinéma," *Paris-Midi* (3 March 1919), 2.

22. Antoine, "La Cinégraphie française," 5.

23. Jeanne and Ford, *Le Cinéma et la presse*, 54-62. J. Leclerc, *Le Cinéma, temoin de son temps*, 29.

24. Richard Abel, "The Contribution of the French Literary Avant-Garde to Film Theory and Criticism, 1907-1924," 25-31.

25. For a trenchant and highly amusing portrait of Jean Galtier-Boissière, see Denise Tual, *Le Temps dévoré*, 11-16.

26. Marcel Gromaire, "Idées d'un peintre sur le cinéma," *Le Crapouillot* (1919), reprinted in L'Herbier, *Intelligence du cinématographe*, 239-249.

27. Jeanne and Ford, *Le Cinéma et la presse*, 66-68.

28. Léon Moussinac as quoted in Vincent Paul, *Introduction au Ciné-Club* (Paris: Ouvrières, 1964), 22. Armand Tallier reprinted just these lines on the opening program notes for the Studio des Ursulines, in January, 1926.

29. Henri Fescourt, *La Foi et les montagnes*, 220.

30. Ricciotto Canudo, *L'Usine aux images*, 5-8—translated by Ben Gibson, Don Ranvaud, Segio Sokota, and Deborah Young as "The Birth of the Sixth Art (1911)," 3-7.

31. Fescourt, *La Foi et les montagnes*, 221. Georges Sadoul, "Bibliographie des ouvrages de l'auteur sur le cinéma," in Léon Moussinac, *L'Age ingrat du cinéma*, 379.

32. Paul, *Introduction au Ciné-Club*, 25.

33. Jean Epstein, "L'Elément photogénique [1924]," *Ecrits sur le cinéma*, 1, 145.

34. Canudo, *L'Usine aux images*, 33-40.

35. Jules Romains, "Donogoo-Tonka ou les miracles de la science," *La Nouvelle Revue Française* 74 (November, 1919), 821-829, and 75 (December, 1919), 1016-1063.

36. Louis Delluc, "Charlot," *L'Esprit nouveau* 3 (December, 1920), 349-351.

37. B. Tokine, "L'Esthétique du cinéma," *L'Esprit nouveau* 1 (October 1920), 85-89. Elie Faure, "Charlot," *L'Esprit nouveau* 5 (March, 1921), 657-666. Jean Epstein, "Cinéma," *L'Esprit nouveau* 14 (1922), 1669-1670.

38. Louis Delluc, "Les Cinéastes de Paris," 13-18. Louis Delluc, "Les Cinéastes," 34-44. Henri Fescourt has a charming story about Delluc's choice of this word to define the filmmaker as an artist in *La Foi et les montagnes*, 164-165.

39. Jeanne and Ford, *Le Cinéma et la presse*, 65. Robert Desnos, *Cinéma* (Paris: Gallimard, 1966), 95-111.

40. Jeanne and Ford, *Le Cinéma et la presse*, 64-65.

41. Jacques Fieschi, "Entretien avec Jean Mitry," 18.

NOTES

Film Journals

1. Louis Delluc, "Cinéma," *Paris-Midi* (21 July 1919), 2.

2. Jean Mitry, *Histoire du cinéma*, 2, 428, n. 1. Jacques Fieschi, "Entretien avec Jean Mitry," 18.

3. Georges Sadoul, "Préface," in Moussinac, *L'Age ingrat du cinéma*, 13. Mitry, "Louis Delluc," 19.

4. C. de Vesme, "Ce que doivent être le Ciné-Club et son journal," 2. Cf. Louis Delluc, "Cinéma," *Paris-Midi* (17 January 1920), 2.

5. Vesme, "Ce que doivent être le Ciné-Club et son journal," 4.

6. *Cinémagazine* was the only one of these magazines with membership in the industry's syndicate of cinema journals: Lynx, "Echos," *Cinémagazine* 4 (2 May 1924), 222. The nineteenth-century practice of anonymous or uncredited advertising and promotion in the French press is quite evident in *Cinémagazine* as well as other film journals—Theodore Zeldin, *France, 1848-1945: Taste and Corruption*, 163-177.

7. Jeanne and Ford, *Le Cinéma et la presse*, 80.

8. Coissac, *Histoire du cinématographe*, 449.

9. Jeanne and Ford, *Le Cinéma et la presse*, 170. In the 1970s, the practice was revived with the paperback novelizations of most American films.

10. Christian Bosséno, "Le Cinéma et la presse (II)," 95-96.

11. Mitry, "Louis Delluc," 20.

12. André G. Brunelin, "Au Temps du Vieux-Colombier de Jean Tedesco [1]," 90. Mitry, "Louis Delluc," 22.

13. See especially Louis Delluc, "D'Oreste à Rio Jim," 14.

14. Louis Delluc, *"Le Cabinet du Docteur Caligari," Cinéa* 44 (10 March 1922), 5.

15. See David Bordwell, "The Musical Analogy," 141-156.

16. Compare, for instance, Léon Moussinac, "*La Roue* d'Abel Gance," 13; Emile Vuillermoz, "*La Roue*," 329-331 and 363-366; René Clair, "Les Films du mois: *La Roue*," [n.p.]; Louis Delluc, "Abel Gance," 12. Also compare Léon Moussinac, "La Critique des films: *L'Auberge rouge*, d'après Balzac, par Jean Epstein," 16-17, and René Clair, "Les Films du mois: *Coeur fidèle*," [n.p.].

17. "Entretien avec Jean Mitry," *Le Cinématographe* 47 (May, 1979), 19.

18. "Le Sens 1 bis" is translated by Tom Milne as "The Senses 1 (b)" in *Afterimage* 10 (Autumn, 1981), 9-16. "Grossissement" is translated by Stuart Liebman as "Magnification" in *October* 3 (Spring, 1977), 9-15.

19. Pierre Porte, "L'Idée de photogénie," 14-15. Jean Tedesco, "Le Cinéma devant les arts," 6-7. Jean Epstein, "De quelques conditions de photogénie," 6-8. Pierre Porte, "La Forme et le fond," 6-7 and 27. Jean Epstein, "Pour une nouvelle avant-garde," 8-10. Paul Ramain, "Sur la musique visuelle engendrée par certains films," 12-13.

Ciné-Clubs

1. Georges Sadoul, "Bio-filmographie," in Sadoul, *Dziga Vertov* (Paris: Champs libre, 1971), 155-156. Richard Sherwood, "Documents from *LEF*," *Screen* 12 (Winter, 1971-1972), 25-58. Ronald Levaco, "Introduction" and "Bibliography of Works" in *Kuleshov on Film*, ed. Ronald Levaco (Berkeley: University of California Press, 1974), 6-10, 211-212. Richard Taylor, *The Politics of the Soviet Cinema*, 1917-1929 (London: Cambridge University Press, 1979), 124-151.

2. Ben Brewster, "Documents from *Novy LEF*," *Screen* 12 (Winter, 1971-1972), 59-91. "Russian Formalism," *Twentieth-Century Studies* 7/8 (December, 1972). Christopher Williams, ed., *Realism and Cinema* (London: British Film Institute, 1981), 115-152. Kristin Thompson, *Eisenstein's "Ivan the Terrible": A Neoformalist Analysis* (Princeton: Princeton University Press, 1981), 8-9. Boris Eikhenbaum, ed., *The Poetics of Cinema*, trans. Richard Taylor, Richard Sherwood, L. M. O'Toole, Joe Andrew, Ann Shukman (Oxford: RPT Publications, 1982).

3. Taylor, *The Politics of the Soviet Cinema*, 52-63.

4. Sadoul, "Préface," 13. Henri Diamant-Berger saw the Touring Clubs quite differently, as a means of propagandizing the world about France through films—see Diamant-Berger, *Le Cinéma*, 211-213.

5. Advertisement, *Le Journal du Ciné-Club* 20 (21 May 1920), 2. A. Antoine, "Le Cinéma d'hier, d'aujourd'hui, et de demain," *Le Journal du Ciné-Club* 24 (25 June 1920), 3-4. Emile Cohl, "Les Dessins animés et à trucs," *Le Journal du Ciné-Club* 25 (2 July 1920), 4-5.

6. André Antoine, "Le Public," 7.

7. *"Le Cabinet du Docteur Caligari,"* *Cinéa* 27 (11 November 1921), 8. Jean Galtier-Boissière, "L'Art cinégraphique," *Le Crapouillot* (16 November 1921), 2. Announcement, *Ciné-Journal* 15 (19 November 1921), 29. Brunelin, "Au Temps du Vieux-Colombier [1]," 91-93. Paul, *Introduction au Ciné-Club*, 24.

8. "Intéressante manifestation cinégraphique," *La Crapouillot* (16 November 1921), 19.

9. No one has been able to really explain Delluc's apparent diffidence—see Pierre Scize, "Le Film muet (1918-1930)," 37; Fescourt, *La Foi et les montagnes*, 226; and Brunelin, "Aux Temps du Vieux-Colombier [1]," 92.

10. "C.A.S.A.," *Comoedia* (6 April 1921), 3. "Au C.A.S.A.," *Ciné-Journal* 15 (28 May 1921), 9-10. Fescourt, *La Foi et les montagnes*, 220-221. Brunelin, "Aux Temps du Vieux-Colombier [1]," 93.

11. Jeander, "Les Ciné-Clubs," in Denis Marion, *Le Cinéma par ceux qui le font* (Paris: Librairie Arthème Fayarde, 1949), 380. Paul, *Introduction au Ciné-Club*, 25-26.

12. Lo Duca, "Notes sur Canudo," *La Revue du cinéma* 13 (May, 1948), 3. Roger Shattuck, *The Banquet Years*, rev. ed. (New York: Vintage, 1968), 1, and 24-27. Georges Sadoul, *Histoire générale du cinéma*, 5, 54-56.

13. "Cinémas," *Comoedia* (17 April 1921), 3. Jean Donzere, ' 'Littérateur cinématique," *Comoedia* (22 April 1921), 4.

14. Ricciotto Canudo, "L'Art pour le septième art," 16.

15. "Le Ciné-Club de France," *Les Cahiers du mois* 16/17 (1925), 254. Jeander, "Les Ciné-Clubs," 380.

16. A. Nazdy, "Le Cinéma au Salon d'Automne" [18-11-21]—Jacques de Baroncelli collection, Bibliothèque de l'Arsenal. Ricciotto Canudo, "Le Cinéma au Salon d'Automne," *Le Petit Journal* (4 November 1921), 4. Canudo, "Le Cinéma," *Les Nouvelles littéraires* (18 November 1922), 4. Léon Moussinac, "Cinématographe," *Mercure de France* (1 December 1922), 521. Canudo, *L'Usine aux images*, 45-47. Léon Moussinac, "Panoramique du cinéma [1929]," in *L'Age ingrat du cinéma*, 321.

17. P. Landry, "Le Ciné au Salon d'Automne," *Le Petit Journal* (18 November 1921), 4. Nazdy, "Le Cinéma au Salon d'Automne."

18. Advertisement for "Salon Annuel du film au Salon d'Automne," *Cinéa-Ciné-pour-tous* 1 (15 November 1923), 3.

19. Jean Epstein, "L'Elément photogénique," 6.

20. Paul, *Introduction au Ciné-Club*, 25.

21. Fescourt, *La Foi et les montagnes*, 226.

22. Announcement, *Cinémagazine* 2 (6 January 1922), 10.

23. "Conférence des Amis du cinéma," *Cinémagazine* 2 (8 December 1922), 346.

24. "Actualités," *Théâtre et Comoedia Illustré* 17 (May, 1923), [n.p.].

25. Noël Burch, "Bibliographie," in Noël Burch, *Marcel L'Herbier*, 176.

26. "L'Activité cinégraphique," *Cinéa-Ciné-pour-tous* 5 (15 January 1924), 28. Georges Sadoul, "Souvenirs d'un temoin," *Etudes cinématographiques* 38-39 (Spring, 1965), 9. André Thiron, *Revolutionaries Without Revolution*, trans. Joachim Neugroschel (New York: Macmillan, 1975), 67.

27. Jeander, "Les Ciné-Clubs," 380. Paul, *Introduction au Ciné-Club*, 26. Its members included Germaine Dulac, Jacques Feyder, Louis Delluc, Robert Boudrioz, Lucien Wahl, and René Jeanne.

28. Paul, *Introduction au Ciné-Club*, 26-27.

29. Ibid., 27.

30. Lynx, "Echos," *Cinémagazine* 4 (1 February 1924), 193. Léon Moussinac, "Cinématographe," *Mercure de France* (1 April 1924), 230. Moussinac, "Panoramique du cinéma [1929]," 322 n. 1.

31. "L'Activité cinégraphique," *Cinéa-Ciné-pour-tous* 5 (15 January 1924), 29.

32. Lynx, "Echos," *Cinémagazine* 4 (17 October 1924), 113. "Conférence de Monsieur René Clair," 420-422.

33. "L'Activité cinégraphique," *Cinéa-Ciné-pour-tous* 9 (15 March 1924), 27.

34. Brunelin, "Aux Temps du Vieux-Colombier [1]," 95-96.

35. "Au Club des Amis de Septième Art," *Cinéa-Ciné-pour-tous* 12 (1 May 1924), 28.

36. Advertisement, *Cinéa-Ciné-pour-tous* 11 (15 April 1924), 5. Canudo, *L'Usine aux images*, 128.

37. Advertisement, *Cinéa-Ciné-pour-tous* 12 (1 May 1924), 5. Pierre Henry, "Films d'amateurs," *Cinéa-Ciné-pour-tous* 32 (1 March 1925), 12.

38. "L'Activité cinégraphique," *Cinéa-Ciné-pour-tous* 5 (15 January 1924), 29. Léon Moussinac, "Cinématographe," *Mercure de France* (1 April 1924), 230-231. Sadoul, "Préface," 13.

39. Musée Galliera, *Exposition de l'art dans le cinéma français*, 66-67.

40. Germaine Dulac, "Les Procédés expressifs du cinématographe," 15-18, 66-68, and 89-92.

41. "Au Ciné-Club de France," *Cinéa-Ciné-pour-tous* 40 (1 July 1925), 22. Jeander, "Les Ciné-Clubs," 381. Paul *Introduction au Ciné-Club*, 27.

42. E.-L. Fouquet and Clement Guilhamou, ed., *Le Tout Cinéma* (Paris: Filma, 1926), 95.

43. Moussinac, "Panoramique du cinéma [1929]," 322, n. 1.

44. Advertisement, *Cinéa-Ciné-pour-tous* 46 (1 October 1925), 5. Advertisement, *Le Cahiers du mois* 16/17 (1925), viii-ix.

45. Advertisement, *Cinéa-Ciné-pour-tous* 51 (15 December 1925), 5.

46. Advertisement, *Cinéa-Ciné-pour-tous* 54 (1 February 1926), 5. Advertisement, *Cinéa-Ciné-pour-tous* 55 (15 February 1926), 6.

47. Jeander, "Les Ciné-Clubs," 381. Paul, *Introduction au Ciné-Club*, 28.

48. Interview with Jean Dréville in Paris, 27 June 1978.

49. "Tribune libre du cinéma," *Cinégraphie* 5 (January, 1928), 93.

50. P. A. Harlé, "Critique," *Cinématographie française* 364 (24 October 1925), 5. "Le Cinéma d'Avant-Garde à l'Exposition des Arts Décoratifs," *Cahiers du mois* 16/17 (1925), 255. Julien Bayart, "Ce que l'écran," *Photo-Ciné* 1 (15 January 1927), 15. Sadoul, "Préface," 14.

51. "Nôtre Avant-Garde aux Arts Décoratifs," *Cinéa-Ciné-pour-tous* 46 (1 October 1925), 11.

52. Jeander, "Les Ciné-Clubs," 381. Jean Mitry, "Deux manifestations peu connues," 116.

53. Paul, *Introduction au Ciné-Club*, 29.

Specialized Cinemas

1. André Brunelin, "Au Temps du Vieux-Colombier [2]," 88.

2. "Les Cinémas à Paris," *Tout Cinéma 1929* (Paris: Filma, 1930), 179. Brunelin, "Au Temps du Vieux-Colombier [2]," 92.

3. Brunelin, "Au Temps du Vieux-Colombier [2]," 95.

4. Advertisement, *Cinéa-Ciné-pour-tous* 24 (1 November 1924), 6. Jean Tedesco, "Le Répertoire et l'avant-garde du film," 5.

5. Lynx, "Echos," *Cinémagazine* 4 (14 November 1924), 297. Jean Tedesco, "Répertoire des films représentés par le Théâtre du Vieux-Colombier," 11. Brunelin, "Au Temps du Vieux-Colombier [2]," 98-99.

6. Lewis Jacobs, ed., *The Compound Cinema: The Film Writings of Harry Alan Potamkin*, 99, 549.

7. Advertisements in *Cinéa-Ciné-pour-tous*, from January to June, 1925.

8. Advertisements, *Cinéa-Ciné-pour-tous* 26 (1 December 1924), 5; 27 (15 December 1924), 3; 31 (15 February 1925), 5.

9. Brunelin, "Au Temps du Vieux-Colombier [2]," 104-105.

10. "Le Montreur d'Ombres au Théâtre du Vieux-Colombier," *Cinéa-Ciné-pour-tous* 26 (1 December 1924), 23. Brunelin, "Au Temps du Vieux-Colombier [2]," 99-102.

11. André Brunelin, "Au Temps du Vieux-Colombier [3]," 88-89.

12. Advertisement, *Cinéa-Ciné-pour-tous* 51 (15 December 1925), 5.

13. Pierre Billard, "Jean Grémillon," in *Anthologie du cinéma* (Paris: L'Avant-Scène du cinéma, 1967), 559.

14. Advertisement, *Cinéa-Ciné-pour-tous* 53 (15 January 1926), 3. Pierre Henry, "Nadia Sibirskaya," *Cinéa-Ciné-pour-tous* 54 (1 February 1926), 19-20. Brunelin, "Au Temps du Vieux-Colombier [3]," 89.

15. "Quel est le meilleur film de 1925?" *Cinéa-Ciné-pour-tous* 56 (1 March 1926), 16.

16. Brunelin, "Au Temps du Vieux-Colombier [3]," 89-90.

17. Roger Régent, "Petite histoire des 'Ursulines' dans la grande histoire du cinéma," 14.

18. "Les cinémas à Paris," *Tout-Cinéma 1929*, 178. Régent, "Petite histoire des 'Ursulines,' " 14.

19. Germaine Dulac, "Le Cinéma d'avant-garde," 362.

20. Jacobs, ed., *The Compound Cinema*, 99.

21. Armand Tallier, "La Création du Studio des Ursulines," in Pierre Lherminier, ed., *Armand Tallier et le Studio des Ursulines* (Paris: A.F.C.A.E., 1963), 3.

22. Tallier, "La Création du Studio des Ursulines," 3. Tual, *Le Temps dévoré*, 41-42.

23. "Programme des cinémas," *Cinémagazine* 6 (21 May 1926), 414. Tallier, "La Création du Studio des Ursulines," 4.

Proliferation and Crisis

1. G.-Michel Coissac, *Histoire du cinématographe, des origines jusqu'à nos jours*, 155-513. Léon Moussinac, *Naissance du cinéma*, 31-81.

2. Moussinac, "Naissance du cinéma [1925]," 33.

3. Besides several earlier essays (see Film Journals, note 19), see Pierre Porte, "Faisons le point," *Cinéa-Ciné-pour-tous* 49 (15 November 1925), 9, and "Le Cinéma pur," 12-13; Henri Fescourt and Jean-Louis Bouquet, *L'Idée et l'écran: opinions sur le cinéma*, 1-3.

4. Fescourt and Bouquet, *L'Idée et l'écran*, 1, 26.

5. Jean Epstein, *Le Cinématographe vu de l'Etna*, 13.

6. Jean Epstein, "Pour une nouvelle avant-garde," translated by Stuart Liebman as "For a New Avant-Garde," 29. Stuart Liebman, "The Sublime and the Fantastic: Jean Epstein's Film Theory" (Paper given at the Conference of the Society for Cinema Studies, Temple University, 8 March 1978).

7. According to Christopher Green, most of Cendrars's essay was written in 1917 and 1921. Earlier excerpts and versions were published in *Les Hommes du jour* (8 February 1919), *La Rose rouge* (12 June 1919), *Promenoir* (May, 1921), *Cosmopolis* (September, 1921). See Christopher Green, "Léger and L'Esprit Nouveau, 1912-1928," 81.

8. Unlike the other journals, *La Revue fédéraliste* was published in Lyon, not in Paris.

9. "Echos et communiqués," *Cinéa-Ciné-pour-tous* 55 (15 February 1926), 21. "Echos et communiqués," *Cinéa-Ciné-pour-tous* 57 (15 March 1926), 23.

10. Germaine Dulac, "*La Folie des vaillants* (fragments)," *Cinégraphie*, 1 (15 September 1927), 9-10. Jean Epstein, "*Six et demi × onze (un kodak),*" *Cinégraphie*, 2 (15 October 1927), 33-35.

11. Jeanne and Ford, *Le Cinéma et la presse*, 85. *La Nouvelle Revue Française* also should be mentioned for its publication of Antonin Artaud's *La Coquille et le clergyman* (November, 1927).

12. Robert Desnos, "Scénarios," *La Revue du cinéma* 3 (May, 1929), 70-81. Louis Buñuel and Salvador Dali, "Scénario du *Un Chien andalou*," *La Revue du cinéma* 5 (15 November 1929), 3-16.

13. Alexandre Arnoux, "[Editorial]," *Pour Vous*, 1 (22 November, 1928), 3.

14. Harry Alan Potamkin, "The Plight of the European Movie," *National Board of Review Magazine* 2 (December, 1927), 6.

15. "Ciné-justice," *Spartacus* 3 (15 June 1928), 5. Jeanne and Ford, *Le Cinéma et la presse*, 102-103. Robert Grelier, "Brève rencontre avec Jean Lods sur 'Les Amis de Spartacus,' " 75.

16. Gérard Strauss, *Cinémagazine* (30 March 1928), as reprinted in Jeanne and Ford, *Le Cinéma et la presse*, 103.

17. Jeanne and Ford, *Le Cinéma et la presse*, 104.

18. "Echos et communiqués," *Cinéa-Ciné-pour-tous* 76 (1 January 1927), 25.

19. "L'Activité cinégraphique," *Cinéa-Ciné-pour-tous* 58 (1 April 1926), 16. "L'Activité cinégraphique," *Cinéa-Ciné-pour-tous* 83 (15 April 1927), 23.

20. Jean Dréville, "Films," *Cinégraphie* 5 (15 January 1928), 94.

21. "Echos et communiqués," *Cinéa-Ciné-pour-tous* 77 (15 January 1927), 26. Julien Bayart, "Ce que dit l'écran," *Photo-Ciné* 2 (15 February 1927), 31.

22. "Echos et communiqués," *Cinéa-Ciné-pour-tous* 83 (15 April 1927), 24.

23. "Les echos," *Cinégraphie* 3 (15 November 1927), 42.

24. Jean Dréville, "Films," *Cinégraphie* 5 (15 January 1928), 93.

25. "Hollywood Notes," *Close Up* 3 (December, 1928), 77. "Avant-Garde et Clubs," *Cinéa-Ciné-pour-tous* 144 (15 November 1929), 27. Jeander, "Les Ciné-Clubs," 384.

26. Jean Tedesco, "Le Cinéma de 1926 au Vieux-Colombier," *Cinéa-Ciné-pour-tous* 52 (1 January 1926), 7.

27. "Avant-Garde et Clubs," *Cinéa-Ciné-pour-tous* 144 (15 November 1929), 27. Jeander, "Les Ciné-Clubs," 384-385. Paul, *Introduction au Ciné-Club*, 31.

28. Jean Tedesco, "Le Cinéma de 1926 au Vieux-Colombier," 7. Paul Ramain, "Le Vieux-Colombier à Genève: Ciné d'Art," *Cinéa-Ciné-pour-tous* 81 (15 March 1927), 41-42. Rachel

Low, *The History of the British Film, 1918-1929*, 34. *The Film Society Programmes, 1925-1939* (New York: Arno, 1972).

29. Albert Valentin, "Ce que le public en pense," *Cinéa-Ciné-pour-tous* 39 (15 June 1925), 25-26. "L'Activité cinégraphique," *Cinéa-Ciné-pour-tous* 74 (1 December 1926), 24.

30. "Echos et communiqués," *Cinéa-Ciné-pour-tous* 81 (15 March 1927), 31. "Ce qu'on fait," *Cinéa-Ciné-pour-tous* 84 (1 May 1927), 15. Jacobs, ed., *The Compound Cinema*, 333.

31. Freddy Buache, "Le Congrès de La Sarraz," *Travelling* 55 (Summer, 1979), 5-32.

32. "Le film muet," *Cinéa-Ciné-pour-tous* 145 (1 December 1929), 27-28. "Fédération des Ciné-Clubs de langue française," *Tout-Cinéma 1929*, 201-202.

33. Jean Dréville, "Films," *Cinégraphie* 5 (15 January 1928), 93.

34. Ida Bantiger, "Quelques notes sur *Potemkine*," *Cinéa-Ciné-pour-tous* 71 (15 October 1926), 31-32. Léon Moussinac, *"Le Cuirasse Potemkine,"* L'Humanité (1926), as reprinted in "Qu'en pense la critique," *Cinéa-Ciné-pour-tous* 74 (1 December 1926), 5-6. Sadoul, "Souvenirs d'un témoin," 15-16.

35. Jeander, "Les Ciné-Clubs," 383.

36. Bert Hogenkamp, "Worker's Newsreels in the 1920s and 1930s," *Our History* 68 (1977), 22.

37. Grelier, "Brève rencontre avec Jean Lods," 76.

38. Marcel Colin, "Spartacus," *Cinématographie française* 455 (23 July 1927), 12.

39. Spartacus, "Le décret des '32,' " *Spartacus* 1 (15 April 1928), 1.

40. Jeander, "Les Ciné-Clubs," 383.

41. "Les cinémas à Paris," *Tout-Cinéma 1929*, 184. Grelier, "Brève rencontre avec Jean Lods," 77.

42. Grelier, "Brève rencontre avec Jean Lods," 77.

43. Jeander, "Les Ciné-Clubs," 383. Paul, *Introduction au Ciné-Club*, 31.

44. Moussinac, "Panoramique du cinéma [1929]," 322-333.

45. Grelier, "Brève rencontre avec Jean Lods," 77.

46. *Spartacus* 3 (15 June 1928), 1, 3.

47. Jeander, "Les Ciné-Clubs," 384.

48. Grelier, "Brève rencontre avec Jean Lods," 77-78.

49. Jean Tedesco, "Bilan 1926-1927," *Cinéa-Ciné-pour-tous* 88 (1 July 1927), 9-12.

50. Dulac, "Le Cinéma d'Avant-Garde," 362.

51. "Les nouveaux films," *Cinéa-Ciné-pour-tous* 97 (15 November 1927), 6. Francisco Amunategul, "Les Ecrans: *En rade*," [n.p.].

52. P. H., "Le Cinéma Latin," *Cinéa-Ciné-pour-tous* 89 (15 July 1927), 15. Lapierre, *Les Cent Visages du cinéma*, 201-202. Pierre Kast, "Jean Grémillon," 36.

53. "Les nouveaux films," *Cinéa-Ciné-pour-tous* 59 (15 April 1926), 6; 62 (1 June 1926), 5; 66 (31 July 1926), 6.

54. Advertisement, *Cinéa-Ciné-pour-tous* 73 (15 November 1926), 7. In 1927, Flaherty wrote Tedesco, reporting that *Moana*'s success at the Vieux-Colombier and then throughout Paris had helped make the film a success in the United States—Brunelin, "Au Temps du Vieux-Colombier [3]," 95-96.

55. "Une Innovation au Théâtre du Vieux-Colombier," *Cinéa-Ciné-pour-tous* 82 (1 April 1927), 13. Jean Tedesco, *"Le Voyage au Congo,"* *Cinéa-Ciné-pour-tous* 88 (1 July 1927), 12-13. Brunelin, "Au Temps du Vieux-Colombier [3]," 91. Kast, "Jean Grémillon," 36.

56. "Ce qu'on dit," *Photo-Ciné* 1 (15 January 1927), 4. "Ce qu'on fait," *Cinéa-Ciné-pour-tous* 84 (1 May 1927), 14. "L'Activité cinégraphique," *Cinéa-Ciné-pour-tous* 113 (15 July 1928), 25. Lapierre, *Les Cent Visages du cinéma*, 201.

57. P. H., "Le Cinéma Latin," 15. Georges Charensol, "Les nouvelles salles spécialisées," *Pour Vous* 29 (6 June 1929), 14. "Les Cinémas à Paris," *Tout Cinéma 1929*, 178. Lapierre, *Les Cent Visages du cinéma*, 202. Jeander, "Les Ciné-Clubs," 382.

58. *Cinématographie française* 484 (11 February 1928), 44.

59. Pierre Audard, "Ce que le public en pense," *Cinéa-Ciné-pour-tous* 104 (1 March 1928), 33-34. Jean Dréville, "La Critique du film," *On Tourne* 4 (1 June 1928), 3. Claire Bernard, "Une dernière opinion sur les deux *Résurrections*," *Cinéa-Ciné-pour-tous* 111 (15 June 1928), 31-32.

60. P. H., "Le Cinéma Latin," 15.

61. Jeander, "Les Ciné-Clubs," 382.

62. Paul de la Borie, "Une Expérience à tenter," *Cinémagazine* 24 (17 June 1927), 571.

63. "Le Studio des Ursulines," *Cinématographie française* 478 (31 December 1927), 16.

64. One is reminded of the rivalry between Jonas Mekas of Anthology Film Archives and John Hanhardt of the Whitney Museum in New York in the early 1970s.

65. Announcement, *Cinéa-Ciné-pour-tous* 82 (1 April 1927), [n.p.]. "Echos et communiqués," *Cinéa-Ciné-pour-tous* 83 (15 April 1927), 24.

66. "Les nouveaux films," *Cinéa-Ciné-pour-tous* 72 (1 November 1926), 6.

67. "A Paris, cette semaine," *Cinématographie française* 478 (31 December 1927), 16. "A Paris, cette semaine," *Cinématographie française* 483 (4 February 1928), 16. Jean Dréville, *"La Glace à trois faces,"* 87-90.

68. Tallier, "La Création du Studio des Ursulines," 4-5.

69. L. D., "Avec le poète de *La Zone*: Georges Lacombe," *Pour Vous* 12 (7 February 1929), 4. Daniel Abric, *"La Zone,"* *Cinémonde* 17 (14 February 1929), 314. L., "L'Écran vous offrira bientôt: *Nogent, Eldorado du dimanche," Pour Vous* 61 (16 January 1930), 6. P. E. Salles Gomes, *Jean Vigo* (London: Secker and Warburg, 1972), 77.

70. "Un rêve à l'écran," *Cinégraphie*, 2 (15 October 1927), 32. Lucie Derain, *"La Coquille et le clergyman,"* 50.

71. Sadoul, "Souvenirs d'un témoin," 18-19. Alain Virmaux, "Artaud and Film," 155-156.

72. Jean Lenauer, "Cinema in Paris," *Close Up* 3 (December, 1928), 17. "Les Cinémas à Paris," *Tout-Cinéma 1929*, 180. Dulac, "Le Cinéma d'Avant-Garde," 363. Lapierre, *Les Cent Visages du cinéma*, 202. Paul, *Introduction au Ciné-Club*, 29. Diamant-Berger, *Il était une fois le cinéma*, 155.

73. Letter from Jean Dréville, 5 July 1977.

74. Pierre Kéfer, "Revue des programmes," *La Revue du cinéma* 1 (December, 1928), 72. "Un Festival Cavalcanti," *Cinémode* 16 (7 February 1929), 301.

75. "Revue des programmes," *La Revue du cinéma* 5 (15 November 1929), 75. "Films à voir," *Pour Vous* 58 (26 December 1929), 15. "Revue des programmes," *La Revue du cinéma* 7 (1 February 1930), 69.

76. R. H., "The Eye of Paris," *Close Up* 4 (May, 1929), 86-87.

77. "L'Activité cinégraphique," *Cinéa-Ciné-pour-tous* 132 (1 May 1929), 25.

78. "L'Activité cinégraphique," *Cinéa-Ciné-pour-tous* 144 (15 November 1929), 27.

79. Diamant-Berger, *Il était une fois le cinéma*, 155.

80. Lapierre, *Les Cent Visages du cinéma*, 202. Paul, *Introduction au Ciné-Club*, 29. Diamant-Berger, *Il était une fois le cinéma*, 155. Studio Diamant opened with Diamant-Berger's own documentary on Deauville, in December, 1928—V. B., "Une nouvelle salle," *Pour Vous* 6 (27 December 1928), 6.

81. "L'Activité cinégraphique," *Cinéa-Ciné-pour-tous* 142 (15 October 1929), 29. Jacobs, ed., *The Compound Cinema*, 11.

82. "Avant-Garde," *Cinéa-Ciné-pour-tous* 100 (1 January 1928), 28. "Les Cinémas à Paris," *Tout-Cinéma 1929*, 185.

83. Announcement, *Cinématographique française* 477 (21 December 1927), 3. Announcement, *Cinéa-Ciné-pour-tous* 103 (15 February 1928). Robert Herring, "A Letter from London," *Close Up* 2 (May, 1928), 57.

84. "Les nouveaux films," *Cinéa-Ciné-pour-tous* 112 (1 July 1928), 5.

85. "L'Activité cinégraphique," *Cinéa-Ciné-pour-tous* 144 (15 November 1929), 27.

86. Jacobs, ed., *The Compound Cinema*, 8, 11, 96.

87. Luis Buñuel, "L'Aventure cinématographique," in *Armand Tallier et le Studio des Ursulines*, 29. José Francisco Aranda, *Luis Buñuel: A Critical Biography*, 59, 288. Sadoul, "Souvenirs d'un témoin," 19. Tual, *Le Temps dévoré*, 65.

88. Tual, *Le Temps dévoré*, 65.

89. J. Bouissounousse, "Dans la salle," 74. Tual, *Le Temps dévoré*, 66.

90. Cyril Connolly, *The Unquiet Grave* (New York: Persea, 1981 [London: Horizon, 1944]), 117-118. Connolly mistakenly dates his screening 1929 rather than 1930.

91. Georges Sadoul, *Histoire générale du cinéma*, 6, 372.

92. Sadoul, *Histoire générale du cinéma*, 6, 345.

93. Sadoul, "Souvenirs d'un témoin," 22-23. Sadoul, *Histoire générale du cinéma*, 6, 372.

94. Sadoul, *Histoire générale du cinéma*, 6, 372.

95. "Ce qu'on fait," *Cinéa-Ciné-pour-tous* 84 (1 May 1927), 15. "Répertoire des film représentés par le Théâtre du Vieux-Colombier depuis 1924," *Cinéa-Ciné-pour-tous* 88 (1 July 1927), 11-12.

96. Brunelin, "Au Temps du Vieux-Colombier [3]," 91-92. André Bazin, "Filmography," in *Jean Renoir*, 213.

97. Bernard Chardère, ed., "Jean Renoir," 82.

98. "Les nouveaux films," *Cinéa-Ciné-pour-tous* 110 (1 June 1928), 6.

99. "L'Affaire de *La Petite Marchande d'allumettes*," *Cinéa-Ciné-pour-tous* 113 (15 July 1928), 6-7.

100. "L'Activité cinégraphique," *Cinéa-Ciné-pour-tous* 135 (15 June 1929), 25. Chardère, "Jean Renoir," 83. Bazin, *Jean Renoir*, 213-214.

101. David Curtis, *Experimental Cinema* (New York: Dell, 1971), 45-46. Freddy Buache, "Une présentation des films independents et d'avant-garde au Symposium de la FIAF à Lausanne (1-4 June 1979)," *Travelling* 55 (1979), 72.

102. "Les nouveaux films," *Cinéa-Ciné-pour-tous* 123 (15 December 1928), 6. Pierre Leprohon, *Jean Epstein*, 53.

103. "Une nouvelle salle," *Cinématographie française* 476 (17 December 1927), 45.

104. Jean Dréville, "La Critique du film," *On Tourne* 3 (15 May 1928), 2. Herring, "A Letter from London," 49. Were these composed of sequences from *Napoléon*, from the Corsican horseback chase, the Victims' Ball, and the Double Tempest? Cf. Jean Mitry, *Histoire du cinéma*, 3, 361-362.

105. Jeander, "Les Ciné-Clubs," 383.

106. Announcement, *Cinématographie française* 478 (31 December 1927), 16. Jean Lenauer, "How to Start a Film Club," *Close Up* 2 (June, 1928), 32.

107. Dulac, "Le Cinéma d'Avant-Garde," 363. Paul, *Introduction au Ciné-Club*, 32.

108. "L'Activité cinégraphique," *Cinéa-Ciné-pour-tous* 80 (1 March 1927), 26. Bazin, *Jean Renoir*, 209, 212.

109. Jean Lenauer, "Paris Notes," *Close Up* 4 (May, 1929), 88. "L'Activité cinégraphique," *Cinéa-Ciné-pour-tous* 137 (1 July 1929), 23.

110. "L'Activité cinégraphique," *Cinéa-Ciné-pour-tous* 140 (15 September 1929), 30.

111. Interview with Armand Panigel in Paris, 17 June 1977. Gerald McKee, *Film Collecting*, 73-108.

Preservation

1. René Gilson, *Jean Cocteau*, trans. Ciba Vaughan (New York: Crown, 1969), 177. René Prédal, *La Société française (1914-1945) à travers le cinéma*, 201-204. Aranda, *Luis Buñuel*, 70-72. Gomes, *Jean Vigo*, 135-139.

2. "Sonor equipment en 1930," *Tout-Cinéma 1929*, 649.

3. Régent, "Petite Histoire," 23.

4. Gaston Philip, "Aurons-nous enfin une cinémathèque?" *Cinématographie française* 353 (8 August 1925), 11. Leclerc, *Le Cinéma, témoin de son temps*, 33. Raymond Borde, "La Cinémathèque française: recherche de la vérité," *Les Cahiers de la cinémathèque* 22 (1977), 4.

5. Borde, "La Cinémathèque française," 4-5.

6. Oscar Cornez, "L'Oeuvre cinégraphique écrite de Louis Delluc," 6-8. Paul Gilson, "George Méliès, Inventeur," *La Revue du cinéma* 4 (15 October 1929), 4-20. "L'Activité cinégraphique," *Cinéa-Ciné-pour-tous* 146 (15 December 1929), 25. Borde, "La Cinémathèque française," 5.

7. Moussinac, "Panoramique du cinéma [1929]," 307-319.

8. Borde, "La Cinémathèque française," 5-8.

9. Léon Moussinac, "Etat du cinéma international [1933]," as reprinted in Moussinac, *L'Age ingrat du cinéma*, 345-346.

10. Borde, "La Cinémathèque française," 9-10 For a slightly different version of the founding of the Cinémathèque française, see Richard Roud, *A Passion for Films: Henri Langlois and the Cinémathèque française* (New York: Viking, 1983), 13-28.

11. Moussinac, "Etat du cinéma international," 336.

Part IV, The Narrative Avant-Garde: Introduction

1. P. Adams Sitney, "Image and Title in Avant-Garde Cinema," 101.

2. Germaine Dulac, "Le Cinéma d'avant-garde," 357-364, translated by Robert Lamberton as "The Avant-Garde Cinema," 43-48.

3. René Jeanne and Charles Ford, *Histoire encyclopédique du cinéma*, 1, 241-396. D-C D. "L'Avant-garde française (1917-1932)," *L'Age du cinéma*, 8-15. Jacques Brunius, *En Marge du cinéma français*, 66-145. Pierre Leprohon, *Cinquante Ans du cinéma français*, 39-52, 59-80. Georges Sadoul, *Le Cinéma français*, 24-43. Jean Mitry, *Histoire du cinéma*, 3, 342-352. Ian Christie, "French Avant-Garde Film in the Twenties: From 'Specificity' to Surrealism," 37-45. Barthélemy Amenguel, "Muet, années vingt: trois visages de l'avant-garde," 23-41.

4. Emile Vuillermoz, *"La Roue,"* 330.

5. Jean Epstein, "Pour une avant-garde nouvelle [1924]," *Le Cinématographe vu de l'Etna*, 55-63.

6. Louis Delluc, "Notes pour moi," *Le Film* 135-136 (21 October 1918), 19-20. Cf. Henri Fescourt and Jean-Louis Bouquet, *L'Idée et l'écran: opinions sur le cinéma*, 1, 12-14.

7. Jean-André Fieschi, "Autour de la cinématographe," 33.

8. Germaine Dulac, "Les Esthétiques, les entraves, la cinégraphie intégrale," 41.

9. Ibid., 42.

10. Linda Nochlin, *Realism* (London: Penguin, 1971), 236.

11. Ibid., 238.

12. Even the attempt to create a subjective cinema, it can be argued, was not the exclusive property of the French avant-garde; the Germans, too, developed a subjective cinema, sometimes using similar devices and techniques. Consequently, the convenient dichotomy in film history between French Impressionism and German Expressionism (a label which is also undergoing reexamination) is less than accurate and hence not very useful—see Barry Salt, "From Caligari to Who?" 119-123.

13. Fredric Jameson, *The Political Unconscious: Narrative as a Socially Symbolic Act* (Ithaca: Cornell University Press, 1981), 230.

14. Christie, "The French Avant-Garde Film in the Twenties," 37.

15. Bernard Eisenschitz, "Histoire de l'histoire (deux périodes du cinéma français: le muet—le génération de 58)," 28.

16. Jameson, *The Political Unconscious*, 13.

17. Hans Richter, "A History of the Avantgarde," 6-41. Sheldon Renan, *An Introduction to the American Underground Film*, 53-71. David Curtis, *Experimental Cinema*, 14-34. J. H. Matthews, *Surrealism and Film*, 11-91. Standish Lawder, *The Cubist Cinema*, 35-78, 117-242. P. Adams Sitney, *Visionary Film: The American Avant-Garde*, 11-15, 18-19, 57-59, 228-229, 276-277, 399-401. Paul Hammond, ed., *The Shadow and Its Shadow: Surrealist Writings on Cinema*, 1-21. Allen Thiher, *The Cinematic Muse: Critical Studies in the History of French Cinema*, 16-69. Sitney, "Image and Title in Avant-Garde Cinema," 97-112. Steven Kovacs, *From Enchantment to Rage: The Story of Surrealist Cinema*. Linda Williams, *Figures of Desire: A Theory and Analysis of Surrealist Film*. Besides these books and parts of books, there are a great number of essays in various periodicals.

18. Noël Burch and Jean-André Fieschi, "La Première vague," 20.

The Alternate Cinema Network, Auteurs, and Genres

1. Advertisement, *Cinéa-Ciné-pour-tous* 24 (1 November 1924), 6.

2. "Ce qu'on fait: le répertoire actuel," *Cinéa-Ciné-pour-tous* 84 (1 May 1927), 15. "Répertoire des films représentés par le Théâtre du Vieux-Colombier depuis 1924," *Cinéa-Ciné-pour-tous* 88 (1 July 1927), 11-12.

3. "Films présentés en première exclusivité par le Studio des Ursulines depuis sa création," *Armand Tallier et le Studio des Ursulines* [inside back cover].

4. Léon Moussinac, "Naissance du cinéma [1925]," in *L'Age ingrat du cinéma*, 41.

5. Léon Moussinac, "Etapes," 16-17.

6. Léon Moussinac, "Panoramique du cinéma [1929]," in *L'Age ingrat du cinéma*, 267-277, 284-295.

7. Georges Charensol, *Panorama du cinéma*, 171-185.

8. Louis Delluc, "Cinéma et cie: D'où viennent ou où vont nos metteurs-en-scène," *Paris-Midi* (17 August 1918), 3. See also Louis Delluc, "Prologue," vii-viii.

9. Alexandre Arnoux pays homage to the idea, however, in *Du muet au parlant: souvenirs d'un témoin*, 168-170.

10. In contrast to the American film industry, where the division of labor between director and writer was well established, in the French film industry, the director usually was also the writer who prepared his own scenario adaptations—André Delpeuch, *Le Cinéma*, 67-71.

Stylistics and Subjectivity

1. Henri Fescourt and Jean-Louis Bouquet, *L'Idée et l'écran: opinions sur le cinéma*, 1, 18-19.
2. Jacques Brunius, *En Marge du cinéma français*, 71-89.
3. Jean Mitry, *Le Cinéma expérimental: histoire et perspectives*, 63-74.
4. David Bordwell, "French Impressionist Cinema: Film Culture, Film Theory, and Film Style." Arno Press is planning to reprint this dissertation in the near future.
5. Claude Beylie and Michel Marie, "Entretien avec Marcel L'Herbier," 36/x.
6. Transcript of an interview by Armand Panigel with Abel Gance (1973), 4-5.
7. Barry Salt, "The Early Development of Film Form," 91-106. Barry Salt, "Film Style and Technology in the Thirties," *Film Quarterly* 30 (Fall, 1976), 19-32. Barry Salt, "Film Style and Technology in the Forties," *Film Quarterly* 31 (Fall, 1977), 46-57. Barry Salt, "Film Form, 1900-1906," *Sight and Sound* 47 (Summer, 1978), 148-153. This work, extended and revised, will be published soon in book form.
8. Bordwell, "French Impressionist Cinema," 144-146.
9. Ricciotto Canudo, "Réflexions sur le septième art," in *L'Usine aux images*, 39.
10. Bordwell, "French Impressionist Cinema," 95-98.
11. Ibid., 135-216, 271-292. Jean-Louis Bouquet suggests that what characterized the "French style" was a reliance on découpage and editing, but he admits that the French narrative avant-garde filmmakers were marked by more differences than similarities—Jean-Louis Bouquet, "Esquisse d'un panorama de l'activité française, 1916-1928," *Cahiers de la cinémathèque*, 33-34 (Autumn, 1981), 62.
12. David Bordwell and Kristin Thompson, *Film Art: An Introduction* (Reading: Addison and Wesley, 1979). David Bordwell, *The Films of Carl Theodor Dreyer* (Berkeley: University of California, 1981).
13. Bordwell, "French Impressionist Cinema," 220. Bordwell uses this term in such a way as to distinguish it from the pictorialism of Maurice Tourneur's films made during the same period—see Lewis Jacobs, *The Rise of the American Film: A Critical History* (New York: Teachers College Press, 1938), 206-209—and from that of the French realist films produced right after the war.
14. Bordwell, "French Impressionist Cinema," 232-233.
15. René Clair, "Films," *Théâtre et Comoedia Illustré* 34 (15 May 1924), [n.p.]. René Clair, "Conférence," *Cinémagazine* 49 (5 December 1924), 420-422. Jean Epstein, "Pour une avant-garde nouvelle [1924]," in *Le Cinématographe vu de l'Etna*, 55. Bordwell, "French Impressionist Cinema," 236-237.
16. Bordwell, "French Impressionist Cinema," 239.

The Fields of Discourse and Narrative

1. Noël Burch and Jean-André Fieschi, "La Première Vague," 20.
2. Henri Fescourt and Jean-Louis Bouquet, *L'Idée et l'écran: opinions sur le cinéma*, 1, 24-32.
3. Jean-André Fieschi, "Autour du cinématographe," 29.
4. Burch and Fieschi, "La Première Vague," 20.
5. Bernard Eisenschitz, "Histoire de l'histoire (deux périodes du cinéma français: le muet—le génération de 58)," 28.
6. Ian Christie, "French Avant-Garde Film in the Twenties: From 'Specificity' to Surrealism," 38.
7. David Bordwell, "French Impressionist Cinema: Film Culture, Film Theory, and Film Style," 6.
8. Burch and Fieschi, "La Première Vague," 20.
9. Ibid., 23.
10. Noël Burch and Jorge Dana, "Propositions," 43-44. For a more complete sketch of the conventions of film representation, see Noël Burch's "Film's Institutional Mode of Representation and the Soviet Response," 77-96, and Steven Neale's similar summary of "textual charac-

teristics" in "Art Cinema as Institution," 13-14. David Bordwell, Janet Staiger, and Kristin Thompson have been doing research recently which seems generally to confirm this paradigm of conventions—*Classical Hollywood Cinema: Film Art and Modes of Production.* (London: Routledge & Kegan Paul, 1984). A prelude to that research can be found in Bordwell, "Textual Analysis, Etc.," *enclitic* 5:2/6:1 (Fall, 1981–Spring, 1982), 125-136. Their work is complemented by that of Tom Gunning—"Weaving a Narrative: Style and Economic Background in Griffith's Biograph Films," *Quarterly Review of Film Studies* 6 (Winter, 1981), 11-25—and Charles Musser—"Establishing the Foundations for Hollywood's Mode of Representation" (Society for Cinema Studies Conference, Los Angeles, 1982), 1-29. See also Ben Brewster, "A Scene at the Movies," *Screen* 23 (July-August, 1982), 4-15, and Noël Burch, "Narrative/Diegesis—Thresholds, Limits," *Screen* 23 (July-August, 1982), 16-33.

11. Burch and Dana, "Propositions," 46-48.

12. Ibid., 44.

13. Ibid., 47.

14. Jacques Petat, "L'Avant-garde française des années vingt," 21.

15. Amengual also compares this practice to the "telegraphic" style that marked a good deal of French literature during the 1910s and 1920s—Barthélémy Amengual, "Rapports entre le cinéma, la littérature et les arts en France dans les années vingt," 163.

16. Besides those already cited, the works that have been especially helpful in constructing this schema include Raymond Bellour, "*The Birds*: Analysis of a Sequence," *Study Unit 14: Hitchcock* (London: BFI, 1972), 2-31; Roland Barthes, *S/Z*, trans. Richard Miller (New York: Hill & Wang, 1974); Raymond Bellour, "Hitchcock, the Enunciator," *camera obscura* 2 (1977), 66-91. Tzvetan Todorov, *The Poetics of Prose*, trans. Richard Howard (Ithaca: Cornell University Press, 1977); Gerard Genette, *Narrative Discourse*, trans. Jane Lewin (Ithaca: Cornell University Press, 1980); Noël Burch, *To the Distant Observer: Form and Meaning in the Japanese Cinema* (Berkeley: University of California Press, 1979); David Bordwell, *The Films of Carl Theodore Dreyer* (Berkeley: University of California Press, 1981); Kristin Thompson, *Eisenstein's "Ivan the Terrible": A Neoformalist Analysis* (Princeton University Press, 1981); Christian Metz, *The Imaginary Signifier*, trans. Celia Britton, Annwyl Williams, Ben Brewster, and Alfred Guzzetti (Bloomington: Indiana University Press, 1982).

17. Bordwell, "French Impressionist Cinema," 112-113.

18. Stuart Liebman, "French Film Theory, 1910-1921," 1-27. On several major points, this essay supersedes my own essay, "The Contribution of the French Avant-Garde Poets to Film Theory and Criticism, 1907-1924," 18-40.

19. For clarification, I offer the following brief definitions of key terms:

Discourse: the text of the film, as a system of material signs, a process of enunciation—as opposed to the diegesis and narrative that it produces.

Diegesis: the process and sum total of referencing, which is experienced by the spectator as representation, as a contiguous spatial-temporal world or environment.

Narrative: the succession of events, real or fictitious, which, through several relations of linkage, produces a chronological story.

Rhetorical figuring: the process of generating meaning through figures—a privileged nexus of signs or nodal points of metonymic and metaphorical relations—by means of patterns of repetition and variation, condensation and displacement.

20. Louis Delluc, "Notes pour moi," *Le Film* 89 (26 November 1917), 18.

21. Bordwell, "French Impressionist Cinema," 106-108.

22. Marcel Gromaire, "Idées d'un peintre sur le cinéma," 239-249. Ricciotto Canudo, *L'Usine aux images*, 31-40.

23. See, for instance, Jean Francis Laglenne, "Le Peintre au cinéma," *Cinéa* 9 (1 July 1921), 14; Canudo, *L'Usine aux images*, 41-42; and Alexandre Arnoux quoted in René Clair, *Cinema Yesterday and Today*, 99.

24. Jean Epstein, *Le Cinématographe vu de l'Etna*, 18.

25. Jean Epstein, "Réalisation de détail," 12.

26. Gromaire, "Idées d'un peintre sur le cinéma," 242. Germaine Dulac, "L'Essence du cinéma: l'idée visuelle," 64, translated by Robert Lamberton as "The Essence of the Cinema: The Visual Idea," 36-42.

27. According to Jean-Louis Bouquet, the French films of the late 1910s and early 1920s were marked by frequent and often lengthy intertitles—Claude Beylie and Francis Lacassin, "A la recherche d'un cinéma perdu: entretien avec Jean-Louis Bouquet, Henri Fescourt, Joë Ham-

man, Gaston Modot," 18-19. Jean-Louis Bouquet, "Esquisse d'un panorama de l'activité française, 1916-1928," 62.

28. Jean Epstein, "Pour une avant-garde nouvelle," *Le Cinématographe vu de l'Etna*, 57, translated by Stuart Liebman as "For a New Avant-Garde," 26-30.

29. Stuart Liebman argues persuasively that what he calls the French Ur-Theory of film was predicated on a Symbolist distinction between the emotional and intellectual capacities of the human mind, in which the former functioned independently of the latter to transform reality into art. However accurate this distinction may be in explaining the French theoretical writings on film, it does not hold up as an assumption for the narrative avant-garde film practice—nor does Liebman claim that it does.

30. Jean Epstein, "Grossissement," 98, translated by Stuart Liebman as "Magnification," 10. Cf. John Berger, "The Moment of Cubism," in *The Look of Things* (New York: Viking, 1974), 138.

31. Henri Diamant-Berger provides one of the earliest defenses of this continuity system in France, in *Le Cinéma*, 153-157.

32. Léon Moussinac, "La Naissance du cinéma [1925]," in *L'Age ingrat du cinéma*, 75-81.

33. Jean Epstein, "Le cinéma et les lettres modernes," 173-175.

34. Alberto Cavalcanti, "Doctrine," 12.

35. Jean Epstein, "Londres parlent," reprinted in Epstein, *Ecrits sur le cinéma*, 204. Cf. Pascal Bonitzer, "Here: The Notion of the Shot and the Subject of Cinema," trans. Bill Krohn, *Film Reader* 4 (1979), 108-117.

36. Cf. Sylvie Trosa, "Archéologie du cinéma," 37.

37. Emir Rodriguez Monegal, "Alberto Cavalcanti (1955)," 241.

38. Jean Epstein, "Les Images de ciel [1928]," 190.

39. Paul de Man, "Semiology and Rhetoric," in *Allegories of Reading* (New Haven: Yale University Press, 1979), 3-19. Constance Penley, "Introduction to 'Metaphor Metonomy' or the Imaginary Referent," *camera obscura* 7 (1981), 7-29. Metz, *The Imaginary Signifier*, 149-297.

40. Henri Fescourt and Jean-Louis Bouquet, *L'Idée et l'écran: opinions sur le cinéma*, 2, 26-27.

41. Burch and Dana, "Propositions," 44.

J'Accuse and *Rose-France*

1. D-C D., "L'Avant-garde française (1917-1932)," *L'Age du cinéma* 6 (December, 1951), 12.

2. Kevin Brownlow, *The Parade's Gone By*, 603. Jean Mitry, *Histoire du cinéma*, 2, 255.

3. This brief description is based on the print of *La Folie du Docteur Tube* preserved at the Cinémathèque française.

4. Barry Salt wonders if the source of the deformations was an anamorphic lens—cf. David Curtis, *Experimental Cinema*, 20, 94. I myself intend to agree with Brownlow that the distortions are produced by mirrors.

5. Sophie Daria, *Abel Gance, hier et demain*, 55.

6. Brownlow, *The Parade's Gone By*, 608-609.

7. Marcel L'Herbier, "Hermès et le Silence [1918]," reprinted in Marcel L'Herbier, *Intelligence du cinématographe*, 211.

8. Jean Epstein, "Memoires inachevées," in *Ecrits sur le cinéma*, 1, 30.

9. Advertisement, *Cinématographie française* 23 (12 April 1919), 17-20.

10. Compare the similar, but patently patriotic title formation in CPI's *America's Answer* (1918)—Kevin Brownlow, *The War, The West, and the Wilderness* (New York: Knopf, 1979), 116.

11. "*J'Accuse*," *Cinématographie française* 20 (22 March 1919), 11, 15-18. "*J'Accuse*," *Cinématographie française* 21 (29 March 1919), 17-20. "*J'Accuse*," *Cinématographie française* 22 (5 April 1919), 15-18. "*J'Accuse*," *Cinématographie française* 23 (12 April 1919), 17-20. "Ce que l'on dit," *Cinémagazine* 1 (23 September 1921), 27. Georges Sadoul, *Histoire générale du cinéma*, 5, 140.

12. This analysis is based on tinted and black-and-white 35mm prints of *J'Accuse* preserved at the Cinémathèque française. Excerpts from *J'Accuse* also are included in Kevin Brownlow's documentary on Gance, *Charm of Dynamite* (1969).

13. Georges Sadoul, *Histoire générale du cinéma*, 4, 388.

14. Brownlow, *The Parade's Gone By*, 612.

15. Brownlow, *The War, the West, and the Wilderness*, 144-145.

16. Ibid., 6-7.

17. Brownlow, *The Parade's Gone By*, 617.

18. Roger Shattuck, *The Banquet Years*, rev. ed. (New York: Vintage, 1968), 331-352. John Berger, "The Moment of Cubism," in *The Look of Things*, 133-162.

19. Shattuck, *The Banquet Years*, 346-347.

20. Ricciotto Canudo, "Préface: Paris, décembre 1922," in *La Roue, après le film d'Abel Gance*, 4.

21. Standish Lawder, *The Cubist Cinema*, 84.

22. Jean Epstein, "Le Cinéma et les lettres modernes," 177.

23. Transcript of an interview by Armand Panigel with Abel Gance (1973).

24. In a revival of *J'Accuse*, late in the 1920s, probably at the Ciné-Latin, Harry Alan Potamkin reports that the orchestra ceased playing for this particular sequence—Lewis Jacobs, ed., *The Compound Cinema: The Film Writings of Harry Alan Potamkin*, 109. Similar split-screen shots can be found in Bernard-Deschamps's *L'Agonie des aigles* (1921) as well as William Wellman's *Wings* (1927)—Brownlow, *The War, the West, and the Wilderness*, 211.

25. Marcel Oms, "Histoire et géographie d'une France imaginaire," 79.

26. Claude Beylie and Michel Marie, "Entretien avec Marcel L'Herbier," 31/v.

27. Marcel L'Herbier, *"Rose-France,"* *Comoedia Illustré* (5 December 1919), reprinted in Noël Burch, *Marcel L'Herbier*, 61.

28. Jean Galtier-Boisière, "Réflexions sur le cinéma," 2-4.

29. Burch, *Marcel L'Herbier*, 19.

30. Marcel L'Herbier, *La Tête qui tourne*, 32. This analysis is based on the print of *Rose-France* preserved at the Royal Film Archive of Belgium.

31. Barry Salt, *Film Style and Technology: History and Analysis*.

32. Jean Galtier-Boissière, "Les Films: *Rose-France*," 13.

L'Homme du large and *El Dorado*

1. D-C D., "L'Avant-garde française (1917-1932)," 14.

2. See pp. 98-99 for a plot synopsis of *L'Homme du large*.

3. D-C D., "L'Avant-garde française (1917-1932)," 14.

4. Ibid. See also, Juan Arroy, "Sous-titres," *Cinémagazine* 4 (22 August 1924), 311.

5. Noël Burch, *Marcel L'Herbier*, 21.

6. A recent viewing of the Cinémathèque française print of *L'Homme du large* suggests that its practice may be more important than admitted here.

7. Jean-André Fieschi, "Autour du cinématographe," 30.

8. Henri Fescourt, *La Foi et les montagnes*, 259.

9. Lionel Landry, "*El Dorado*," 7. *El Dorado*'s fame and influence were restricted largely to France because apparently it was not distributed abroad.

10. Louis Delluc, "Quelques films français," *Cinéa* 18 (9 September 1921), 5. Jaque Catelain, *Marcel L'Herbier*, 54.

11. Fieschi, "Autour du cinématographe," 33. This analysis is based on black-and-white prints of *El Dorado* at the Royal Film Archive of Belgium and the Museum of Modern Art and on a tinted 35mm print preserved at the Cinémathèque française.

12. Edmond Epardaud, "De Marcel L'Herbier et de son oeuvre," 4, 9. Maurice Keroul, "Les Grands Films," *Le Film* 183 (November, 1921), [n.p.]. Sommerville Story, "A Foreign Critic's Candid Views," *Le Film* 183 (November, 1921), [n.p.].

13. L'Herbier's own novelization of the film included one page from the score, the "Danse Gitane," composed for piano—Marcel L'Herbier, *El Dorado, Mélodrame cinématographique* (Paris: La Lampe merveilleuse, 1921), 34.

14. Claude Beylie and Michel Marie, "Entretien avec Marcel L'Herbier," 33/vii.

15. The Museum of Modern Art print indicates that two intertitles are missing from this sequence. Their absence makes this reading tentative.

16. Compare Jean Epstein's analysis of this sequence as the representation, not of this or that fandango, but of "*the* dancer," and "*the* fandango"—*Esprit du cinéma*, 90.

17. Burch, *Marcel L'Herbier*, 22.

18. Fieschi, "Autour du cinématographe," 33.

19. I skip the fourth reel, the most conventional of the film, in which Sybilla locks the couple in the Alhambra chapel tower, then releases them and explains her situation so that the painter goes to confront Estiria (and pummels him, to the servants' delight) while his daughter accepts responsibility for Sybilla's son.

20. A year before he died, L'Herbier was still adamant about the importance of this sequence (which played what he called "the real" against "the unreal")—Jacques Fieschi, Bernard Minoret, and Claude Arnulf, "Entretien avec Marcel L'Herbier," 40.

Fièvre and *La Femme de nulle part*

1. René Jeanne and Charles Ford, *Histoire encyclopédique du cinéma*, 1, 190. Charles Ford, "Germaine Dulac," 13. Jeanne and Ford see evidence of Dulac's interest in psychological states as early as *Ames de fous* (1917).

2. Germaine Dulac, *"La Mort du soleil* et la naissance du film," 14.

3. Louis Delluc, *Cinéma et cie*, 34.

4. Louis Delluc, "Prologue," *Drames du cinéma*, xiii-xiv.

5. Louis Delluc, "Cinéma," *Paris-Midi* (12 May 1919), 2. Delluc, "Cinéma," *Paris-Midi* (16 May 1919), 2. Delluc, "Cinéma," *Paris-Midi* (18 May 1919), 2. Delluc, "Cinéma," *Paris-Midi* (25 May 1919), 2. Delluc, "Cinéma," *Paris-Midi* (26 May 1919), 2. Delluc, "Cinéma," *Paris-Midi* (14 June 1919), 2. Delluc, "Prologue," x.

6. Noël Burch and Jean-Andre Fieschi, "La Première Vague," 24. René Clair, *Cinema Yesterday and Today*, 67. Georges Sadoul, *Histoire générale du cinéma*, 5, 80.

7. Jean Epstein, "Mémoires inachevées," in *Ecrits sur le cinéma*, 44.

8. Louis Delluc, "Cinéma," *Paris-Midi* (23 February 1919), 2. Delluc, "Cinéma," *Paris-Midi* (28 April 1919), 2. Delluc, "Cinéma," *Paris-Midi* (9 May 1919), 2. Delluc, "Cinéma," *Paris-Midi* (15 May 1919), 2. Delluc, "Cinéma," *Paris-Midi* (16 June 1919), 2. Delluc, "Cinéma," *Paris-Midi* (9 July 1919), 2.

9. Louis Delluc, *Drames du cinéma*, 1-18.

10. Originally—when it opened at most major cinemas across Paris, in May, 1920—*La Fête espagnole* was 710 meters long; but the only surviving print is a much condensed single, ten-minute reel at the Cinémathèque française. Films Louis Nalpas folder—Bibliothèque de l'Arsenal.

11. Henri Fescourt, *La Foi et les montagnes*, 158.

12. Jean Mitry, "Louis Delluc," 35.

13. Marcel Tariol, *Louis Delluc*, 56.

14. *"La Fête espagnole,"* *Le Journal du Ciné-Club* 16 (30 April 1920), 11.

15. "Les films de la quinzaine," *Ciné-pour-tous* 49 (24 September 1920), 6. Louis Delluc, *Drames du cinéma*, 19-32. Mitry, "Louis Delluc," 38.

16. Louis Delluc, *Cinéma et cie*, 30-31.

17. Jean Epstein, "Mémoires inédites," quoted in Tariol, *Louis Delluc*, 61.

18. Delluc, *Drames du cinéma*, 22-23. The numbers indicating periods of the past are added.

19. The publicity brochure on *Fièvre* labeled the film an "Etude dramatique" of about 1000 meters in length—Société Française des Films Artistiques ("Jupiter") file—Bibliothèque de l'Arsenal.

20. "L'Homme aux yeux clairs" was the French title of Hart's *Blue Blazes Rawden* (1918), which had opened in Paris in early October, 1919. The Hart western that *Fièvre* most resembled, however, was *The Narrow Trail* (1917), which Delluc saw sometime earlier in 1919—*Cinéma et cie*, 308. *Broken Blossoms* opened in Paris, in December, 1920, just two months before production began on *Fièvre*—P. H., *"Lys brisé,"* *Ciné-pour-tous* 55 (17 December 1920), 10-11.

21. Louis Delluc, "Huit jours de fièvre," 9-12. Léon Poirier, *Vingt-quatre images à la seconde*, 45.

22. *"Fièvre,"* *Cinéa* 10 (8 July 1921), 19-21. Eve Francis, *Temps héroique* (Paris: Denoël, 1949), 403.

23. Lionel Landry, "La Musique et le geste," 10-11. Philippe Carcassonne and Renaud Bezomes, "Entretien avec Jean Wiener," *Cinématographe* 62 (November, 1980), 28.

24. Léon Moussinac, "La Naissance du cinéma [1925]," in *L'Age ingrat du cinéma*, 107.

25. Initially, this analysis was written in collaboration with Dugald Williamson. It is based on the prints of *Fièvre* at the Cinémathèque française and the Museum of Modern Art.

26. This analysis focuses on the representation and circulation of desire within the code of the look, as a textual operation. A similar analysis is combined with a study of the organization of "spectatorial desire" in D. N. Rodowick, "Vision, Desire, and the Film Text [*The Pirate*]," *camera obscura* 6 (1980), 55-89.

27. The first tracking shot of a ship in the harbor, following the CU of Patience and her intertitle on waiting, is absent in the Museum of Modern Art print.

28. Georges Sadoul, *French Cinema*, 23-24.

29. Interestingly, Noël Burch analyzes the final sequence of Eisenstein's *Strike* (1925) in terms of a similar alternation—"Film's Institutional Mode of Representation and the Soviet Response," 90.

30. This brief analysis is based on the recently restored (titleless) print of *Le Chemin d'Ernoa* at the Cinémathèque française.

31. Mitry, "Louis Delluc," 43.

32. Tariol, *Louis Delluc*, 65. Mitry, "Louis Delluc," 44.

33. Léon Moussinac, "Le Cinéma," *Le Crapouillot* (16 April 1922), 17. "Ce que l'on dit," *Cinémagazine* 2 (21 July 1922), 93. "Cosmograph donnera au public, le 8 septembre, *La Femme de nulle part*," *Cinéa* 67-68 (25 August 1922), 16-17. "Les Prochains Films: *La Femme de nulle part* par Louis Delluc," *Cinémagazine* 2 (4 August 1922), 142-143.

34. Hart's *The Silent Stranger* was first screened in Paris in February, 1917. This analysis is based on the print of *La Femme de nulle part* preserved at the Royal Film Archive of Belgium. A print has recently been acquired by the Museum of Modern Art.

35. Delluc, "Prologue," xiv.

36. Two sequences in the scenario violated this focus on the central character: the wife's dream of going off with her lover and her lover's images of how they would travel. Both were eliminated from the completed film. Delluc, *Drames du cinéma*, 71-97.

37. Cf. Lionel Landry, "*La Femme de nulle part*," 69-70 (8 September 1922), 6-7.

La Roue

1. Interview with Jean Dréville, 16 June 1977. Dréville was a film enthusiast and photographer who frequented the film screenings of Charles Léger's Tribune Libre ciné-club. He went on to edit several film journals (*Photo-Ciné, Cinégraphie, On Tourne*), shoot a short documentary on the making of Marcel L'Herbier's *L'Argent* (1929), and then become a consummate craftsman as a cinematographer and director from the 1930s to the 1960s.

2. Kevin Brownlow, *The Parade's Gone By*, 625.

3. Emile Vuillermoz, "*La Roue*," 363.

4. Léon Moussinac, "Le Cinéma: *La Roue*, d'Abel Gance," 13. Juan Arroy, "Abel Gance, sa vie, son oeuvre," 7. Brownlow, *The Parade's Gone By*, 625. Georges Sadoul, *Histoire générale du cinéma*, 5, 149-150. Roger Icart's research indicates that the Paris print ran thirty-one reels while the print distributed to the provinces ran thirty-six reels—Roger Icart, "A la découverte de *La Roue*," 189-190.

5. Abel Gance, *La Roue*.

6. Brownlow, *The Parade's Gone By*, 625. This long accepted linkage between *La Roue* and the Soviet filmmakers is less than certain. Gance told Armand Panigel, for instance, that the print in the U.S.S.R. was a shortened version of only fourteen reels—transcript of an interview by Armand Panigel with Abel Gance (1973). Even more surprisingly, the film may not have reached the U.S.S.R. until 1926—"Frantsuzskie nemye film'my v sovetskom prokate [French silent films in Soviet distribution]," *Kino i vremia* 4 (1965), 370.

7. Arroy, "Abel Gance, sa vie, son oeuvre," 7. René Jeanne, "Une seconde version de *La Roue*," 342. Icart, "A la découverte de *La Roue*," 190.

8. This version of *La Roue* showed up at the Ciné-Latin cinema in November, 1928—Maurice Champel, "Abel Gance projette . . . ," *Pour Vous* 2 (29 November 1928), 14. Steven Philip Kramer and James Michael Welsh, *Abel Gance*, 16, 187. Icart, "A la découverte de *La Roue*," 190.

9. Until recently the Cinémathèque de Toulouse was restoring a twenty-one-reel version of *La Roue* quite different from those already preserved in various film archives—Icart, "A la découverte de *La Roue*," 190. Letter from Raymond Borde, 6 June 1983. Images Film Archives

may also release a long version of *La Roue* (approximately 220 minutes), copied from a recently discovered tinted and toned print in an Eastern European film archive—interview with Bob Harris, 14 March 1980.

10. Jean Mitry, *Histoire du cinéma*, 2, 438. Transcript of an interview by Armand Panigel with Abel Gance (1973).

11. Léon Moussinac, "La Naissance du cinéma [1925]," in *L'Age ingrat du cinéma*, 112.

12. Vuillermoz, "*La Roue*," 330-331. René Clair, "Les films du mois: *La Roue*," [n.p.].

13. Jean Mitry, "Abel Gance," [n.p.].

14. The use of rather old-fashioned overhead diffuse lighting is probably due to this location shooting—letter from Barry Salt, 10 December 1979.

15. Léopold Survage, "Le Rythme coloré," *Les Soirées de Paris* 26-27 (July-August, 1914), 426-429. Marcel Gromaire, "Idées d'un peintre sur le cinéma," *Le Crapouillot* (1919), reprinted in Marcel L'Herbier, *Intelligence du cinématographe*, 239-249. Jean-Francis Laglenne, "Le Peintre au cinéma," *Cinéa* 4 (27 May 1921), 17. Laglenne, "Le Peintre au cinéma," *Cinéa* 9 (1 July 1921), 14. Laglenne, "Le Peintre au cinéma," *Cinéa* 42 (24 February 1922), 12.

16. Fernand Léger, "A Critical Essay on the Plastic Quality of Abel Gance's *The Wheel* [*Comoedia* (December, 1922)]," *Functions of Painting*, trans. Alexandra Anderson, ed. Edward F. Fry (New York: Viking, 1973), 20.

17. Moussinac, "Le Cinéma: *La Roue*," 13.

18. Advertisement, *Cinéa-Ciné-pour-tous* 11 (15 April 1924), 5. Ricciotto Canudo, *L'Usine aux images*, 128. Honegger's "Pacific 231" score was composed specially for the C.A.S.A. public screening of excerpts from *La Roue*.

19. Ricciotto Canudo, "Préface," in *La Roue, après le film d'Abel Gance*, 4.

20. Sadoul, *Histoire générale du cinéma*, 5, 148. Icart suggests that Gance actually toned down some of the film's criticism of the railway administration's policies and practices—Icart, "A la découverte de *La Roue*," 189.

21. Mitry, "Abel Gance," [n.p.].

22. Roger Icart has discovered that, in comparing the original découpage with the film's final montage, Gance consistently broke up these sequences into more and more brief fragments whose rhythm could prolong and accentuate the visual dynamism of the images—Icart, "A la découverte de *La Roue*," 191.

23. Transcript of an interview by Armand Panigel with Abel Gance (1973).

24. Compare David Bordwell's articulate but, unexpectedly, conventional analysis of such "bravura passages" in "The Musical Analogy," 144-145.

25. Canudo, "Préface," 4.

26. Gance, *La Roue* (1930), 6-7.

27. Standish Lawder, *The Cubist Cinema* 91, 93.

28. Jean Epstein, "Grossissement," 98, trans. Stuart Liebman as "Magnification," 10.

29. John Golding, "Léger and the Heroism of Modern Life," in *Léger and Purist Paris* (London: The Tate Gallery, 1970), 18.

30. André Lang, *Déplacements et Villégiatures littéraires*, 144.

31. Did Blaise Cendrars and "the eternal noise of the wheel" in his long poem, *Prose de Transsibérien et de la petite Jeanne de France* (1913), inspire Gance in his choice of this metaphor? In addition, see the following lines in "Construction," the last poem (dated February, 1919) in Cendrars's *Dix-Neuf Poèmes élastiques* (1919):

And now / The painting becomes that enormous, restless thing / The wheel / Life / The machine / The human soul.

32. Jean Epstein, "Abel Gance," in *Ecrits sur le cinéma*, 1, 175.

La Souriante Madame Beudet and L'Inondation

1. Jean Epstein, "For a New Avant-Garde [1924]," trans. Stuart Liebman, in *The Avant-Garde Film: A Reader of Theory and Criticism*, 27.

2. René Clair, "Les films du mois: *La Souriante Madame Beudet*," [n.p.]. Freddy Buache, "Films indépendents et d'avant-garde," 49. This analysis is based on the print of *La Souriante Madame Beudet* at the Museum of Modern Art.

3. Germaine Dulac, "Le Procédés expressifs du cinématographe," 67.

4. Albine Leger, *"La Souriante Madame Beudet,"* 240. "Conférence de Madame Germaine Dulac," *Cinémagazine* 4 (19 December 1924), 518.

5. Buache, "Films indépendents et d'avant-garde," 50.

6. Dorothy Knowles, *French Drama of the Inter-War Years, 1918-1939* (London: Georges G. Harrap, 1967), 120.

7. Charles Ford, "Germaine Dulac," 14-20. William Van Wert, "Germaine Dulac: First Feminine Filmmaker," 55-56. Sandy Flitterman, "Heart of the Avant-Garde: Some Biographical Notes on Germaine Dulac," 58-61, 103. Georges Sadoul, *Histoire générale du cinéma*, 5, 112-117. Linda Dubler, "Deux ou Trois Choses que Je Sais d'Elles: A Look at Dulac and Her Film, *The Smiling Madame Beudet*" (Paper delivered to the Society for Cinema Studies Conference, Temple University, 7 March 1978).

8. Dulac, "Les Procédés expressifs du cinématographe," 67-68.

9. Sandy Flitterman argues that the exterior shots in the film function as an autonomous signification system independent of the narrative representation—"Montage/Discourse: Germaine Dulac's *The Smiling Madame Beudet*," 54-59. For a later, different analysis of the film, see Sandy Flitterman, "Women, Representation, and Cinematic Discourse: The Example of French Cinema" (Ph.D. diss., University of California at Berkeley, 1982).

10. Léon Moussinac, "La Naissance du cinéma [1925]," in *L'Age ingrat du cinéma*, 109. Jean Mitry, "Louis Delluc," *L'Avant-Scène du cinéma*, 48, 50. Sadoul, *Histoire générale du cinéma*, 5, 77-79.

11. Jean de Mirbel, "Les films de la semaine: *L'Inondation*," 223-224.

12. Marcel Tariol, *Louis Delluc*, 69.

13. Ibid., 70. This analysis is based on the print of *L'Inondation* preserved at the Cinémathèque française.

14. Louis Delluc, *"L'Inondation,"* 9-11. J. W., *"L'Inondation,"* *Cinémagazine* 4 (25 January 1924), 135.

15. Delluc, *"L'Inondation,"* 10-11.

16. Barry Salt suggests that this inconsistency could have come from a mistake in shooting or printing, but I still consider deliberate ambiguity more likely.

17. Mitry, "Louis Delluc," 50.

18. Tariol, *Louis Delluc*, 70.

L'Auberge rouge and *Coeur fidèle*

1. Jean Epstein, "Deux grands maitres à filmer," *La Technique cinématographique* (20 February 1947), reprinted in *Ecrits sur le cinéma*, 1, 415. Jean Epstein, "Mémoires inachevées," in *Ecrits sur le cinéma*, 1, 44.

2. Léon Moussinac, "La Critique des films: *L'Auberge rouge*," 16, 18. J. de M., "*L'Auberge rouge*," *Cinémagazine*, 3 (3 August 1923), 155-156.

3. Pierre Leprohon, *Jean Epstein*, 69.

4. This analysis is based on prints of *L'Auberge rouge* preserved at the Cinémathèque française.

5. Leprohon, *Jean Epstein*, 69.

6. This could be a conventional opening, introducing the stars of the film—except that Mathot is not identified by an intertitle or by a superimposed title and none of the other important actors are introduced.

7. Leprohon, *Jean Epstein*, 69.

8. Ibid., 72-73.

9. Epstein's practice here seems extraordinarily complex compared to, say, Kuleshov's famous "experiments"—Ronald Levaco, "Introduction," *Kuleshov on Film*, trans. and ed. Ronald Levaco (Berkeley: University of California Press, 1974), 7-11.

10. Jean Epstein, "Grossissement," trans. Stuart Liebman as "Magnification," 10.

11. Henri Langlois, "Jean Epstein (1897-1953)," 12-13. Jean Mitry, *Histoire du cinéma*, 2, 441.

12. Jean Epstein, "Mémoires inachevées," 33, 47, 55.

13. Jean Epstein, "Bilan de fin de muet," *Cinéa-Ciné* (January-February, 1931), reprinted in *Ecrits sur le cinéma*, 1, 235.

14. "Les nouveaux films," *Cinéa-Ciné-pour-tous* 2 (1 December 1923), 28. Pierre Leprohon, *Jean Epstein*, 35. Interview with Marie Epstein, 13 November 1976.

15. André G. Brunelin, "Au Temps de Vieux-Colombier de Jean Tedesco [2]," *Cinéma 60*, 51 (November-December, 1960), 102.

16. Léon Moussinac, "Le Cinéma: *Coeur fidèle*," 19. Jean Epstein, "Présentation de *Coeur fidèle* [January, 1924]," *Ecrits sur le cinéma*, 1, 124.

17. Leprohon, *Jean Epstein*, 71.

18. Marcel Tariol, *Louis Delluc*, 63-64.

19. Epstein, "Présentation de *Coeur fidèle*," 123.

20. Ibid., 124.

21. See, for instance, Charles Rosen and Henri Zerner, "What Is, and Is Not, Realism," *New York Review of Books* 29 (18 February 1982), 21-26. I am indebted for this connection to several discussions with Stuart Liebman.

22. *The Letters of Gustave Flaubert, 1830-1857*, trans. Francis Steegmuller (Cambridge: Harvard University Press, 1980), 154.

23. Leprohon, *Jean Epstein*, 71.

24. Ibid., 34.

25. Moussinac, "Le Cinéma: *Coeur fidèle*," 18. This analysis is based on the 35mm prints of *Coeur fidèle* preserved at the Cinémathèque française and the Museum of Modern Art.

26. Epstein, trans. Liebman, "Magnification," 10, 13.

27. Compare Epstein's explanation of his use of the sea here—Pierre Porte, "Une Loi du cinéma," *Cinéa-Ciné-pour-tous* 9 (15 March 1924), 12.

28. Langlois, "Jean Epstein (1897-1953)," 14.

29. The effect is not unlike the clenched fists that explode into a host of raised arms in Eisenstein's *Potemkin* (1925-1926). The motif of hand images, especially in the second half of *Coeur fidèle*, could bear further study.

30. Porte, "Une Loi du cinéma," 12.

31. Epstein, trans. Liebman, "Magnification," 10.

32. René Clair, "Les films du mois: *Coeur fidèle*," [n.p.].

33. Without any intertitles to guide me (they have been clipped from the surviving prints), initially I concluded that the child, too, had died; but Marie Epstein informed me that this was not so—interview with Marie Epstein, 10 August 1979.

34. Marie Epstein agrees that the second half of *Coeur fidèle* is less interesting or less sustained than the first half—interview with Marie Epstein, 10 August 1979.

Le Brasier ardent and *La Fille de l'eau*

1. "Actualités," *Théâtre et Comoedia Illustré* 20 (August, 1923), [n.p.]. Jean de Mirbel, "*Le Brasier ardent*," 380-382.

2. Jean Renoir, "Souvenirs," *Le Point* 18 (December, 1938), reprinted in André Bazin, *Jean Renoir*, 151.

3. Ricciotto Canudo, *L'Usine aux images*, 160.

4. This analysis is based on prints of *Le Brasier ardent* at the Cinémathèque française and at the State Historical Society of Wisconsin.

5. Léon Moussinac, "Le Cinéma: *Le Brasier ardent*," 19.

6. Jean Tedesco, "Cinéma-Expression," *Cahiers du mois* 16/17 (1925), 26.

7. This reflexivity foregrounds the means of photographic/cinematic production in a way that other silent films would explore quite differently—e.g., Renoir's *La Fille de l'eau* (1925), Epstein's *Le Lion des Mogols* (1924) and *6½ × 11* (1927), Keaton's *Sherlock Jr.* (1924) and *The Cameraman* (1927), Eisenstein's *Strike* (1925), and Vertov's *Man with a Movie Camera* (1929).

8. Canudo, *L'Usine aux images*, 160.

9. Jean Renoir, *Ma Vie et mes films*, 48.

10. This analysis is based on prints of *La Fille de l'eau* preserved at the Cinémathèque française and at the National Film Archive.

11. Renoir, *Ma Vie et mes films*, 49.

12. Henri Gaillard, "*La Fille de l'eau*," 581-582. "Les nouveaux films," *Cinéa-Ciné-pour-tous* 34 (1 April 1925), 5.

13. Renoir, *Ma Vie et mes films*, 51.

14. Compare Alexander Sesonske, *Jean Renoir: The French Films, 1924-1939*, 15.

15. Renoir, *Ma Vie et mes films*, 49-50.

16. Ibid., 50.

17. Ibid., 71.

18. Gaillard, *"La Fille de l'eau,"* 481-482.

19. Compare Sesonske, *Jean Renoir*, 12-13, 14.

20. Raymond Durgnat, *Jean Renoir*, 34.

Paris qui dort and *Entr'acte*

1. "Actualités," *Théâtre et Comoedia Illustré* 18 (June, 1923), [n.p.]. "Actualités," *Théâtre et Comoedia Illustré* 20 (August, 1923), [n.p.].

2. Catherine de la Roche, *René Clair*, 7. Transcript of an interview by Armand Panigel with René Clair (1973).

3. André Daven, *"Paris qui dort,"* [n.p.]. Jane Eyre, "Les films de demain: *Paris qui dort,"* 14-15. "Conférence de Monsieur René Clair," *Cinémagazine* 4 (5 December 1924), 420-422. "Les nouveaux films," *Cinéa-Ciné-pour-tous* 30 (1 February 1925), 5.

4. The American release print (presumably) of sixty minutes in length is available from the Museum of Modern Art. Another print of thirty-six minutes, restored and re-edited by Clair himself, is available from Films Incorporated. Celia McGerr, *René Clair*, 37, 222.

5. Transcript of an interview by Armand Panigel with René Clair (1973).

6. This analysis is based on the print of *Paris qui dort* at the Museum of Modern Art, versions of which are widely circulated in the United States.

7. Barthélemy Amengual, *René Clair*, 64.

8. Transcript of an interview by Armand Panigel with René Clair (1973).

9. Bernard Brunius, "René Clair," 11.

10. Annette Michelson, "Dr. Crase and Mr. Clair," 42-44.

11. "Un film 'instantanéiste'—*Entr'acte*," *Théâtre et Comoedia Illustré* 39 (1 November 1924), [n.p.]. René Clair, "Picabia, Satie, et la première d'*Entr'acte*," 108-112.

12. Roche, *René Clair*, 8.

13. Roger Régent, "Petite histoire des 'Ursulines' dans la grande histoire du cinéma," *Armand Tallier et le studio des Ursulines*, 15.

14. René Clair, *A nous la liberté and Entr'acte*, 116.

15. R. C. Dale, "René Clair's *Entr'acte* or Motion Victorious," 38-43.

16. Standish Lawder confuses the chronology of *L'Inhumaine* and *Entr'acte* in *The Cubist Cinema*, 103.

17. Noel Carroll, "*Entr'acte*, Paris, and Dada," 5-11.

18. Paul Sandro, "Parodic Narration in *Entr'acte*," 44-55.

19. Clair, "Picabia, Satie, et la première d'*Entr'acte*," 112.

20. Sandro, "Parodic Narration in *Entr'acte*," 53.

L'Inhumaine

1. Robert Trevise, "Les Présentations de la quinzaine," *Cinéa-Ciné-pour-tous* 36 (1 May 1925), 28.

2. "Les nouveaux films," *Cinéa-Ciné-pour-tous* 24 (1 December 1924), 4.

3. Jaque Catelain, *Marcel L'Herbier*, 82. Claude Beylie and Michel Marie, "Entretien avec Marcel L'Herbier," 35/ix.

4. Robert Trevise, "Les Présentations," *Cinéa-Ciné-pour-tous* 18 (1 August 1924), 29.

5. Georges Sadoul, *Histoire générale du cinéma*, 5, 102.

6. Jean Mitry, *Histoire du cinéma*, 2, 434.

7. Noël Burch, *Marcel L'Herbier*, 23. This analysis is based on the print of *L'Inhumaine* preserved at the Cinémathèque française. The Museum of Modern Art recently acquired a print drawn from the one preserved at the Archives du Film, Bois d'Arcy.

8. Transcript of an interview by Armand Panigel with Marcel L'Herbier (1973).

9. Jean-André Fieschi, "Autour du cinématographe," 34.

10. Catelain, *Marcel L'Herbier*, 76. Fieschi, "Autour du cinématographe," 34.

11. "Que sera *L'Inhumaine*?" *Cinéa-Ciné-pour-tous* 5 (15 January 1924), 12-13.

12. Burch, *Marcel L'Herbier*, 23.

13. Standish Lawder finds several instances (among them, this winter garden) of *Caligari*'s

influence in *L'Inhumaine*—Lawder, *The Cubist Cinema*, 103, 253. I tend to discount that influence: a similar garden had already been used in L'Herbier's *Le Carnaval des vérités* (1920); Einar Norsen's "death mask" is actually Cubist in design (as Lawder admits); and L'Herbier's previous film, *Don Juan et Faust* (1923), had included a *Caligari*-like style in decors and costumes that was not all that successful, even in the filmmaker's eyes.

14. Lawder, *The Cubist Cinema*, 108-110.

15. John Golding, "Léger and the Heroism of Modern Life," in *Léger and Purist Paris*, 18.

16. There is some resemblance between Hériat's character here and the figure of Cesare in *Caligari*.

17. Burch, *Marcel L'Herbier*, 24.

18. Fieschi, "Autour du cinématographe," 34.

19. Burch, *Marcel L'Herbier*, 24.

20. Fieschi, "Autour du cinématographe," 37.

21. Beylie and Marie, "Entretien avec Marcel L'Herbier," 34/viii.

22. Fieschi, "Autour du cinématographe," 34. Whether consciously derived or not, L'Herbier's strategy here recalls Léopold Survage's theoretical attempt to create an abstract film by restricting his means to form, color, and rhythm—Survage, "Le Rythme coloré," *Les Soirées de Paris*, 426-429.

23. Adolf Loos, *"L'Inhumaine,"* *Neue Frie Press* (29 July 1924), reprinted in Marcel L'Herbier, *La Tête qui tourne*, 105.

24. Burch, *Marcel L'Herbier*, 25.

25. Although this may have been one of the earliest representations of a television broadcasting system within a narrative film, the concept of television was already becoming well known in the public mind—compare Lawder, *The Cubist Cinema*, 113.

26. Blaise Cendrars, *L'ABC du cinéma*, 11.

27. Lawder, *The Cubist Cinema*, 114-115, 117. L'Herbier had nearly finished shooting *L'Inhumaine* in February, 1924—Edouard Roches, "Les films de demain," 6-7, 10.

28. Fernand Léger, "Film by Fernand Léger and Dudley Murphy, Musical Synchronism by George Antheil," *Little Review* 10 (Autumn-Winter, 1924-1925), 42-44. Fernand Léger, *"Ballet mécanique* [1924]," in *Functions of Painting*, trans. Alexandra Anderson (New York: Viking, 1973), 48-51. Lawder, *The Cubist Cinema*, 119-131, 183.

29. Lawder, *The Cubist Cinema*, 185.

30. Roger Régent, "Petite histoire des 'Ursulines' dans la grande histoire du cinéma," 15-16.

31. Lawder, *The Cubist Cinema*, 186.

32. Ibid., 165-167.

33. Fernand Léger, "A Critical Essay on the Plastic Quality of Abel Gance's Film, The Wheel," in *Functions of Painting*, 20-23. Lawder, *The Cubist Cinema*, 89-95.

34. Advertisement, *Cinéa-Ciné-pour-tous* 11 (15 April 1924), 5.

35. Jean Epstein, "Grossissement," in *Bonjour Cinéma*, 93-108. Jean Epstein, "Fernand Léger," *Les Feuilles libres* (March-April, 1923), reprinted in *Ecrits sur le cinéma*, 1, 115-118.

36. "Au Club des Amis de Septième Art," *Cinéa-Ciné-pour-tous* 12 (1 May 1924), 28.

Menilmontant and *Rien que les heures*

1. Pierre Henry, "Films d'amateurs," 10-11.

2. "Film sans sous-titre, film d'avant-garde: *L'Ironie du destin*," 20.

3. Henry, "Films d'amateurs," 11-12.

4. "Film sans sous-titre, film d'avant-garde," 20. See Kirsanoff's own essay, "Pour et contre le film sans texte," 8. Another possibly important titleless French film was Marcel Silver's *L'Horloge* (1925), now apparently lost. See Marcel Silver, "Du film sans sous-titre," *Cinéa-Ciné-pour-tous* 25 (15 November 1924), 14, 19, and Jean Tedesco, "A propos de *L'Horloge*," *Cinéa-Ciné-pour-tous* 25 (15 November 1924), 16-17. Henri Diamant-Berger claims that he made a titleless film, *Le Mauvais Garçon*, in 1922; but Pathé-Consortium added intertitles to it when the company distributed it with *Les Trois Mousquetaires*—Henri Diamant-Berger, *Il était une fois le cinéma* 93-94.

5. Jean Tedesco, "Pour un cinéaste inconnu," *Cinéa-Ciné-pour-tous* 54 (1 February 1926), 9-11. André G. Brunelin, "Au Temps du Vieux-Colombier de Jean Tedesco [2]," *Cinéma* 61, 52

(January, 1961), 89. Ivor Montagu, "Old Man's Mumble: Reflections on a Semi-centenary," *Sight and Sound* 44 (Autumn, 1975), 231. *The Film Society Programs, 1925-1939* (New York: Arno Press, 1972), 30.

6. Georges Sadoul, *Histoire générale du cinéma*, 6, 362, Freddy Buache, "Films indépendents et d'avant-garde," 67-68. This analysis is based on the print of *Menilmontant* at the Museum of Modern Art.

7. Walter S. Michel, "In Memoriam of Dmitri Kirsanov, a Neglected Master," 38.

8. René Jeanne and Charles Ford, *Histoire encyclopédique du cinema*, 1, 267.

9. One of the earliest descriptions of *Menilmontant* indicates that the original print may have had added sequences at the beginning and ending—"*Menilmontant* à Genève," 22-23. This may account for the differences between the lengths of the prints preserved at the Museum of Modern Art and the Cinémathèque suisse (the latter of which I have not seen)—Buache, "Films indépendents et d'avant-garde," 67. The print shown at the Film Society in London, 30 May 1926, which was the same length as the Museum of Modern Art print, reportedly had been reduced slightly—*The Film Society Programs*, 30.

10. Noël Burch, *To the Distant Observer: Form and Meaning in the Japanese Cinema* (Berkeley: University of California Press, 1979), 79.

11. Michel Goreloff, "Suggérer . . . ," 24. André Maurois, "La poésie du cinéma," *L'Art cinématographique*, 3, 28-30.

12. The print at the Cinémathèque suisse ends with Sibirskaia sitting beside the bed of her sleeping child in her sister's apartment—Buache, "Films indépendents et d'avant-garde," 68.

13. Elizabeth Sussex, "Cavalcanti in England," 207.

14. "L'Activité cinégraphique," *Cinéa-Ciné-pour-tous* 48 (1 November 1925), 24. "L'Activité cinégraphique," *Cinéa-Ciné-pour-tous* 55 (15 February 1926), 20. "Les Présentations," *Cinéa-Ciné-pour-tous* 105 (15 March 1928), 31.

15. "Les nouveaux films," *Cinéa-Ciné-pour-tous* 72 (1 November 1926), 6.

16. Sadoul, *Histoire générale du cinéma*, 6, 360.

17. Sir Stephen Tallents, "The Documentary Film (1946)," in *Nonfiction Film Theory and Criticism*, ed. Richard Meran Barsam (New York: Dutton, 1976), 59. Emir Rodriguez Monegal, "Alberto Cavalcanti (1955)," 242. *The Film Society Programs*, 110.

18. Alberto Cavalcanti, "Doctrine," 9-12.

19. This analysis is based on the prints of *Rien que les heures* at the Museum of Modern Art and the Cinémathèque française.

20. A similar shift from the factual to the fictional marks the structure of Georges Lacombe's *La Zone* (1928).

21. Harry Alan Potamkin saw "three motifs in [this] film, alternating progressively—a news vendor moving through the streets, a drunken hag drawing herself to the waterfront, the city about them"—*The Compound Cinema*, 71.

22. Sussex, "Cavalcanti in England," 208.

En rade and *L'Invitation au voyage*

1. Jean Dréville, "Films: *En rade*," 11. Some historians list Philippe Hériat as the scriptwriter—e.g., René Jeanne and Charles Ford, *Histoire encyclopédique du cinéma*, 1, 280.

2. "Les Présentations," *Cinéa-Ciné-pour-tous* 86 (1 June 1927), 33. Dréville, "Films," 11. Advertisement for the Théâtre du Vieux-Colombier, *Cinéa-Ciné-pour-tous* 96 (1 November 1927), 4. "Les nouveaux films," *Cinéa-Ciné-pour-tous* 97 (15 November 1927), 6. *En Rade* seems to have been imported into the United States as *Sea Fever*—*Film Daily Yearbook* (New York: Film Daily, 1930), 19.

3. Francisco Amunategui, "Les Ecrans: *En rade*," [n.p.]. This analysis is based on a 35mm print of *En rade* preserved at the Cinémathèque française.

4. Louis Chavance, "L'Impressionisme cinématographique," 21.

5. Dréville, "Films," 11.

6. V. Mayer, "Le Cinéma d'amateur: la pellicule panchromatique," *Cinéa-Ciné-pour-tous* 92 (1 September 1927), 26.

7. Dréville, "Films," 11.

8. There is a similar, even more crucial, image conjunction in Marie Epstein and Jean Benoît-Lévy's *La Maternelle* (1933).

9. Several years ago at the Centre Georges Pompidou (17 June 1977), this sequence opened a special program of excerpts from Cavalcanti's films, and absolutely delighted the audience.

10. "L'Activité cinégraphique," *Cinéa-Ciné-pour-tous* 89 (15 July 1927), 25. Charles Ford, "Germaine Dulac," 34, 48.

11. Amunategui, "Les Ecrans," [n.p.].

12. Apparently, *L'Invitation au voyage, La Folie des vaillants (Demented Hero)*, and *La Coquille et le clergyman* were the only Dulac films to be exhibited in the United States during the 1920s—"1928 Feature Imports," *Film Daily Yearbook* (New York: Film Daily, 1929), 31.

13. Ford, "Germaine Dulac," 34.

14. This analysis is based on a 16mm print of *L'Invitation au voyage* at the Cinémathèque française.

15. A. Colombat, *"L'Invitation au voyage,"* 10.

16. Amunategui, "Les Ecrans," [n.p.].

17. Dulac's earlier *La Folie des vaillants* (1925) as well as her later short abstract films also depended on specific musical accompaniments.

Feu Mathias Pascal and *Maldone*

1. "Au Ciné-Club de France," *Cinéa-Ciné-pour-tous* 48 (1 November 1925), 20. Advertisement for the Théâtre du Vieux-Colombier, *Cinéa-Ciné-pour-tous* 57 (15 March 1926), 4. Jaque Catelain, *Marcel L'Herbier*, 91. Claude Beylie and Michel Marie, "Entretien avec Marcel L'Herbier," 35/ix.

2. Michel Simon, in fact, made his acting debut here fresh from an acclaimed performance in *Six Characters in Search of an Author*—Georges Sadoul, *Histoire générale du cinéma*, 5, 104.

3. Jean Mitry, *Histoire du cinéma*, 3, 377-378. Sadoul, *Histoire générale du cinéma*, 5, 104. Jean-André Fieschi, "Autour du cinématographe," 37.

4. Noël Burch, *Marcel L'Herbier*, 26.

5. Fieschi, "Autour du cinématographe," 37.

6. Ibid.

7. Douglas Radcliff-Umstead, *The Mirror of Our Anguish: A Study of Luigi Pirandello's Narrative Writings* (Cranbury, N.J.: Associated University Presses, 1978), 164-165. This analysis is based on prints of *Feu Mathias Pascal* at the National Film Archive, the Museum of Modern Art, and the Cinémathèque française.

8. Catelain, *Marcel L'Herbier*, 86. Léon Barsacq, *Caligari's Cabinet and Other Grand Illusions: A History of Film Design*, 44.

9. Burch, *Marcel L'Herbier*, 26.

10. Catelain, *Marcel L'Herbier*, 89.

11. François Berge, *"Feu Mathias Pascal,"* 248.

12. Radcliff-Umstead, *The Mirror of Our Anguish*, 169-170.

13. The structural symmetry of this double narrative was emphasized by its exhibition in two parts, a strategy which L'Herbier himself thought diminished the film's impact. Catelain, *Marcel L'Herbier*, 91. Marcel L'Herbier, *La Tête qui tourne*, 121-122. For a different reading of *Feu Mathias Pascal* which takes it as "a key film for an understanding of the modes of mimesis [including subjective modes of representation] that the Impressionist directors developed," see Allen Thiher, *The Cinematic Muse: Critical Studies in the History of French Cinema*, 18-20.

14. "Maldone," *Cinéa-Ciné-pour-tous* 97 (15 November 1927), 8. "Maldone," *Cinémagazine* 8 (16 March 1928), 445-458. Barsacq, *Caligari's Cabinet and Other Grand Illusions*, 74-75. Henri Agel, *Jean Grémillon*, 180.

15. Advertisement, *Cinéa-Ciné-pour-tous* 103 (15 February 1928), 6. Pierre Kast, "Jean Grémillon," 36. Georges Sadoul, *Dictionary of Film*, trans. Peter Morris (Berkeley: University of California Press, 1972), 206.

16. R. T., *"Maldone," Cinéa-Ciné-pour-tous* 110 (1 June 1928), 31. "Revue de revues," *Spartacus* 3 (15 June 1928), 6.

17. "Les nouveaux films," *Cinéa-Ciné-pour-tous* 118 (1 October 1928), 6. This analysis is based on prints of *Maldone* preserved at the Cinémathèque française and owned privately by Armand Panigel.

18. Edmond Epardaud, *"Maldone,"* 13.

19. Jean Bertin, "La Réalisation," *Cinémagazine* 8 (16 March 1928), 447.

20. Kast, "Jean Grémillon," 32.

21. Jean Epstein, "Grossissement," trans. Stuart Liebman, "Magnification," 10.

22. G. D., "Les Décors," *Cinémagazine* 8 (16 March 1928), 452.

23. Bertin, "La Réalisation," 447. Compare Julien Bayart, "En regardant tournant *Maldone*," *Cinégraphie* 4 (15 December 1927), 61.

24. R. T. *"Maldone,"* 31.

25. Kast, "Jean Grémillon," 31.

Napoléon

1. Abel Gance introduced the second of three evening screenings of *Napoléon*, at the Walker Art Center, 13-15 March 1980. The screenings were arranged by Richard Peterson, Curator of the Walker Art Center's Film Program.

2. François Truffaut, *The Films of My Life*, 29-32. Jean Mitry, *Histoire du cinéma*, 3, 362. Kevin Brownlow, "Abel Gance's *Napoléon* Returns from Exile," 31.

3. Kevin Brownlow, *The Parade's Gone By*, 634. Brownlow, "Abel Gance's *Napoléon* Returns from Exile," 31.

4. Lenny Borger, "British Slighted on *Napoléon* . . . ," 1, 38.

5. Interview with Marie Epstein, 14 August 1976.

6. For the story of this reconstruction, see Brownlow, "Abel Gance's *Napoléon* Returns from Exile," 28-32, 68, 70-73.

7. Interview with Bob Harris of Images Film Archives, 14 March 1980. Several tinted frames from the film are reproduced in Kevin Brownlow's "How a Lost Masterpiece of the Cinema was Recreated," 34-35.

8. An early version of this reconstruction was screened by Pacific Film Archive in Berkeley, in 1973, and by the American Film Institute in Washington, D.C., in 1978—See Brownlow, "Abel Gance's *Napoléon* Returns from Exile," 68.

9. The initial screening of the complete version took place at the Telluride Film Festival in early September, 1979, with Gance himself in attendance. Since then, this version of *Napoléon* has been shown at the Walker Art Center in Minneapolis (March, 1980), at the London Film Festival (November, 1980), at the Edinburgh Film Festival (August, 1981), again at the Leicester Square Cinema in London (September, 1981), and at the Barbican Centre in London (August, 1982). The Zoetrope version (accompanied by an orchestral score by Carmine Coppola) opened at the Radio City Music Hall in New York (23-25 January 1981) and has played for limited engagements in selected cities throughout the United States as well as in Rome. An even more complete version (with additional footage that Brownlow discovered recently at the Cinémathèque française) was shown in Le Havre, in November, 1982, then in Paris, in the summer of 1983. That version is now deposited at the Cinémathèque française.

10. René Jeanne and Charles Ford, *Abel Gance*, 43.

11. There are discrepancies about *Napoléon*'s costs—see Juan Arroy, "La Technique de *Napoléon*," *Cinéa-Ciné-pour-tous* 86 (1 June 1927), 9; Léon Moussinac, "Panoramique du cinéma [1929]," in *L'Age ingrat du cinéma*, 268; Sophie Daria, *Abel Gance: hier et demain*, 116; Jeanne and Ford, *Abel Gance*, 52.

12. Carl Davis's specially commissioned score for the British version of Brownlow's reconstruction has drawn more praise than Carmine Coppola's, in part because Davis incorporated excerpts of "classical" music as well as some of the extant music composed by Honegger into his score.

13. Jeanne and Ford, *Abel Gance*, 52. Interview with Kevin Brownlow, 15 August 1979. In 1928, in the United States, MGM distributed an eighty-minute version of Gance's film which amounted to little more than a narrative sketch.

14. Bernard Eisenschitz, "From *Napoléon* to *New Babylon*," 49-55.

15. The classroom sequence probably inspired the first classroom sequence in François Truffaut's *Les Quatre Cents Coups* (1959). The cast list for *Napoléon* can be found on p. 196.

16. In the Brownlow reconstruction, the sequence of Marat's murder is moved from its original position just prior to the Battle of Toulon in order to open the second half of the film with a sudden shocking action—the first shot is a CU of a knife being concealed in the bodice of a dress. This transposition does raise the question of whether there are other differences between Gance's 1927 version of the film and Brownlow's reconstruction.

17. Jean Mitry, "Napoléon à l'écran," 57.

18. Jean Tedesco, "*Napoléon vu par Abel Gance*," 9.

19. Emile Vuillermoz, "Qu'en pense la critique?" *Cinéa-Ciné-pour-tous* 87 (15 June 1927), 6.

20. Emile Vuillermoz, "Abel Gance et *Napoléon*," 337-338.

21. Lewis Jacobs, ed., *The Compound Cinema: The Film Writings of Harry Alan Potamkin*, 126.

22. Tedesco, "*Napoléon vu par Abel Gance*," 10.

23. Moussinac, "Panoramique du cinéma [1929]," 277.

24. G.-Michel Coissac, *Les Coulisses du cinéma*, 113.

25. Copies of this documentary film are preserved at the Cinémathèque française and the UCLA Film Archive as well as in several private film collections here in the United States. Brownlow, "Abel Gance's *Napoléon* Returns from Exile," 31-32. See also Juan Arroy, *En Tournant Napoléon avec Abel Gance*.

26. Arroy, "La Technique de *Napoléon*," 9.

27. Coissac, *Les Coulisses du cinéma*, 113. Transcript of an interview by Armand Panigel with Abel Gance (1973).

28. Ronald Blumer, "The Camera as Snowball: France 1918-1927," *Cinema Journal* 10 (Spring, 1971), 37. Transcript of an interview by Armand Panigel with Abel Gance (1973).

29. This sequence probably inspired the pillow fight sequence in Jean Vigo's *Zero de conduite* (1933).

30. Mitry, *Histoire du cinéma*, 3, 355.

31. Noël Burch's remark was made in the session on Early French Film Theory, at the Ohio University Film Conference (May, 1980). Similarly, Barry Salt tends to conclude that the French films of the 1920s were "stylistically retarded"; they could not handle American "classical" continuity editing with "competence"—Barry Salt, *Film Style and Technology: History and Analysis*. Ernest Callenbach's suggestions were quite valuable here in the last stages of my revision of this analysis of *Napoléon*.

32. Most of the cuts involve the character of Violine (Annabella), whose role, in effect, is eliminated from the "Coppola" version.

33. This sequence may have inspired Antoine's "altar" to Balzac in Truffaut's *Les Quatre Cents Coups* (1959).

34. Moussinac, "Panoramique du cinéma [1929]," 276.

35. Brownlow, *The Parade's Gone By*, 648.

36. Moussinac, "Panoramique du cinéma [1929]," 269-270. Mitry, *Histoire du cinéma*, 3, 356-357. Actually, Mitry was much more positive about this triptych sequence in 1927—Mitry, "Napoléon à l'écran," 55.

37. In an essay that appeared after this analysis was written, Peter Pappas comes to a similar conclusion, by a different route—"The Superimposition of Vision: *Napoléon* and the Meaning of Fascist Art," 10.

38. "Le Procédé du triple écran," 17.

39. Arroy, "La Technique de *Napoléon*," 10. Transcript of an interview by Armand Panigel with Abel Gance (1973).

40. Brownlow, *The Parade's Gone By*, 648-649. Transcript of an interview by Armand Panigel with Abel Gance (1973).

41. There were precedents for this sequence in the battle scenes of Gance's own *J'Accuse* (1919) and Raymond Bernard's *Le Miracle des loups* (1924).

42. This analysis of the final reel of triptychs is based on a viewing table session with the film, arranged by Elaine Burrows, at the National Film Archive.

43. Mitry, *Histoire du cinéma*, 3, 361.

44. Vuillermoz, "Abel Gance et *Napoléon*," 336. See James M. Walsh and Steven Kramer, "Gance's Beethoven," *Sight and Sound* 45 (Spring, 1976), 109-111, for a study of Gance's later film on another Romantic artist, *Beethoven* (1937).

45. Moussinac, "Panoramique du cinéma [1929]," 267, 272.

46. For instance, see the insightful but ultimately heavy-handed polemic by Pappas, "The Superimposition of Vision: *Napoléon* and the Meaning of Fascist Art," 4-13.

47. Mitry, *Histoire du cinéma*, 362.

48. Brownlow, *The Parade's Gone By*, 647-648. Letter from Kevin Brownlow, 25 August 1979.

49. Brownlow, *The Parade's Gone By*, 649.

50. "Opinions des cinéastes," *Cinéa-Ciné-pour-tous* 109 (15 May 1928), 12-13. Brownlow, *The Parade's Gone By*, 649. Transcript of an interview by Armand Panigel with Claude Autant-Lara (1973).

51. Letter from Claude Autant-Lara, 20 July 1979. Barry Salt notes that various wide screen processes (56mm, 65mm, and 70mm) were being developed in Hollywood in 1929, which may partly explain their lack of interest in the Hypergonar process—Letter from Barry Salt, 10 December 1979. Furthermore, the "Realife" wide-screen format of MGM's *Billy the Kid* (1930), which used a similar anamorphic lens process, was not all that successful—Jacobs, ed., *The Compound Cinema*, 110-112.

52. Letter from Kevin Brownlow, 25 August 1979.

53. R. Lehman, "Un Film large: *Construire un feu*," 5. Marcel Oms, "Claude Autant-Lara dans l'Avant-Garde Française," 14. Jean Leclerc, "Jonas, pour de vrai," 19. Letter from Claude Autant-Lara, 20 July 1979.

54. Claude Autant-Lara, "La triste histoire de *Construire un feu*," 17.

55. Letter from Claude Autant-Lara, (20 July 1979).

56. Claude Autant-Lara, "Le premier essai de film large: *Construire un feu* (1928-1929)," 35-43. "*Construire un feu*: essai de reconstitution du film perdu à partir de ce qu'il en reste," 20-23. Georges Sadoul, *Histoire générale du cinéma*, 6, 318.

L'Image, 6½ × 11, and *La Glace à trois faces*

1. Interview with Marie Epstein, 14 August 1976.

2. This brief analysis is based on an incomplete, much deteriorated print of *L'Image* preserved at the Cinémathèque française. According to Jean Mitry, *L'Image* was the first film to be screened by the fledgling Cinémathèque française, in 1936—Jacques Fieschi, "Entretien avec Jean Mitry," 19.

3. René Jeanne and Charles Ford, *Histoire encyclopédique du cinéma*, 1, 349.

4. Jean Mitry, "*L'Image*," 253.

5. Léon Moussinac, "Le Cinéma: *L'Image*," 15. Georges Chaperot, "L'Oeuvre classique de Jacques Feyder," 20. Pierre Leprohon, *Cinquante Ans du cinéma français* 57. Georges Sadoul, *Histoire générale du cinéma*, 5, 184, 186.

6. Henri Fescourt, *La Foi et les montagnes*, 275.

7. Mitry, "*L'Image*," 253.

8. Jean Epstein, *Le Cinématographe vu de l'Etna*, 13.

9. Francisco Amunategui, "Les Ecrans: *Six et demi, onze*," 100.

10. Jean Dréville, "Films: *Six et demi × onze*," *Cinégraphie* 1 (15 September 1927), 14.

11. Interview with Marie Epstein, 4 June 1977. This analysis is based on a 35mm print of *6½ × 11* preserved at the Cinémathèque française. Apparently, *6½ × 11* was the only one of Epstein's silent films to be imported into the United States during the 1920s—"1928 Feature Imports," *Film Daily Yearbook* (New York: Film Daily, 1929), 31.

12. *L'Affiche* shares this inspiration and deployment of the popular Bébé Cadum posters with *Ballet mécanique* and *Entr'acte*, all three conceived and executed in 1924.

13. M. Gait, "Notes sur *Six et demi × onze*," 24. Pierre Leprohon, *Jean Epstein*, 43. Interview with Marie Epstein, 10 August 1979.

14. Henri Langlois, "Jean Epstein (1897-1953)," 20.

15. Jean Epstein, "*Six et demi × onze (un kodak)*," 33.

16. Jean Dréville, "Films: *Six et demi—onze*," *Cinégraphie* 3 (15 November 1927), 51.

17. Leprohon, *Jean Epstein*, 86-87.

18. Jean Epstein, *Ecrits sur le cinéma*, 1, 61.

19. Gait, "Notes sur *Six et demi × onze*," 24.

20. Dréville, "Films," 51.

21. Advertisement, *Cinématographie française* 466 (8 October 1927), 21. "Les Présentations," *Cinéa-Ciné-pour-tous* 99 (15 December 1927), 41. Jean Epstein, "L'Art d'événement," *Comoedia* (18 November 1927), reprinted in *Ecrits sur le cinéma*, 181-182. Trans. by Tom Milne as "Art of Incidence," *Afterimage* 10 (Autumn, 1981), 30, 32.

22. Epstein, "Art d'événement," 181.

23. Advertisement, *Cinématographie française* 466 (8 October 1927), 21. Jean Dréville, "*La Glace à trois faces*," 87-90.

24. Epstein, "Art d'événement," reprinted in *Cahiers du cinéma* 202 (June-July, 1968), 55.

25. Leprohon, *Jean Epstein*, 79. Noël Burch and Jean-André Fieschi, "La Première Vague," 23.

26. This analysis is based on prints of *La Glace à trois faces* at the Cinémathèque française and at the State Historical Society of Wisconsin. A print is also collected at Anthology Film Archives.

27. This sequence looks forward to the boating sequences in Jean Renoir's *Une Partie de campagne* (1936).

28. This sequence is foreshadowed in Epstein's earlier essay, "Pour une avant-garde nouvelle [1924]," *Le Cinématographe vu de l'Etna*, 62, trans. Stuart Liebman, "For a New Avant-Garde," 29.

29 The Italian Futurists and French "simultaneists" had already linked or opposed these two pleasures at least fifteen years before.

30. Epstein, "Art d'événement," 181.

31. Stephen Heath, "Film Performance," *Ciné-tracts* 1 (Summer, 1977), 12.

La Chute de la maison Usher and **La Petite Marchande d'allumettes**

1. "Les Présentations," *Cinéa-Ciné-pour-tous* 111 (15 June 1928), 26. "Sélect Présentations," *Spartacus* 3 (15 June 1928), 3. Jean Dréville, "La Critique du film," 3.

2. Henri Langlois, "Jean Epstein (1897-1953)," 24.

3. Langlois, "Jean Epstein," 23. Pierre Leprohon, *Jean Epstein*, 46.

4. In 1979, Marie Epstein re-released the film (slightly stretch-printed) with an added sound track of music using medieval instruments, arranged and performed by Roland de Candé. This analysis is based primarily on the silent prints of *La Chute de la maison Usher* preserved at the Cinémathèque française and the Museum of Modern Art. At several points, there are brief discrepancies in both prints.

5. Leprohon, *Jean Epstein*, 83.

6. Jean Epstein, "Au ralenti," *Paris-Midi* (11 May 1928), reprinted in Epstein, *Ecrits sur le cinéma*, 1, 191.

7. Langlois, "Jean Epstein," 22-24. Arthur Knight, *The Liveliest Art* (New York: Macmillan, 1957), 97. Jean Mitry, *Histoire du cinéma*, 3, 380. At least one film historian has even labeled it a "surrealist film"—Gerald Mast, *A Short History of the Movies*, 3rd ed. (New York: Bobbs-Merrill, 1981), 195.

8. Leprohon, *Jean Epstein*, 45. John Hagan, "Cinema and the Romantic Tradition," 46.

9. Jean Epstein, "De l'adaptation et du film parlant," *Pour Vous* (17 October 1929), reprinted in *Ecrits sur le cinéma*, 201.

10. André Breton's description of Antonin Artaud—he "carried with him the landscape of a Gothic novel, torn by flashes of lightning"—makes a fascinating conjunction with the end of Epstein's film. And Artaud had tried but failed to get himself cast in the film—as Roderick. What an opportunity Epstein missed there! See Antonin Artaud, *Selected Writings*, 167-168.

11. Jean Epstein, "Quelques notes sur Edgar A. Poe et les images douées de vie," *Photo-Ciné* (April, 1928), reprinted in *Ecrits sur le cinéma*, 188. Epstein, "Au ralenti," 191.

12. Leprohon, *Jean Epstein*, 177. Philippe Haudiquet, "Jean Epstein," 482. José Francisco Aranda, *Luis Buñuel: A Critical Biography*, 39.

13. Langlois, "Jean Epstein," 23-24. Haudiquet, "Jean Epstein," 474.

14. Langlois, "Jean Epstein," 23. Interview with Marie Epstein, 10 August 1979.

15. Jean Epstein, "Les Images de ciel," *Cinéa-Ciné-pour-tous* 107 (15 April 1928), 11-12.

16. Keith Cohen, *Film and Fiction*, 93.

17. Ibid., 95.

18. Hagan, "Cinema and the Romantic Tradition," 47-48.

19. Epstein, "Quelques notes sur Edgar A. Poe," 188.

20. In several shots, just before and after Madeleine's death, the image in the portrait even moves slightly, as if alive. Compare the very different effect of the single moving image in Chris Marker's *La Jetée* (1962).

21. The famous sequence of the coffin journey in Carl Dreyer's *Vampyr* (1931) may owe something to this sequence.

22. Bruno Bettelheim, *The Uses of Enchantment* (New York: Random House, 1975), 289-

291. Without any evidence at all, to Epstein's detriment, this image has been attributed to Luis Buñuel, his assistant on the film's production—see Aranda, *Luis Buñuel*, 41.

23. Robert Graves, *The White Goddess*, 2nd ed. (New York: Viking, 1958), 92, 343. Also, cf. the nexus of human-animal relations put in play in the nightmare sequence of *La Fille de l'eau*.

24. This narrative reversal also counters the story of Ethelred and the dragon which Roderick's friend is reading and which takes up a good number of the intertitles toward the end.

25. Tzvetan Todorov, *The Fantastic: A Structural Approach to a Literary Genre*, 25.

26. The musical accompaniment to the new print released by Marie Epstein tends to sustain this uncertainty and mystification.

27. David Bordwell, "The French Impressionist Cinema: Film Culture, Film Theory, and Film Style." My numbers are approximate, and they differ slightly from Bordwell's.

28. Stuart Liebman, "The Sublime and the Fantastic: Epstein's Film Theory" (Paper delivered at the Conference of the Society for Cinema Studies, Temple University, 7 March 1978), 18.

29. Liebman, "The Sublime and the Fantastic," 18.

30. Epstein, "Quelques notes sur Edgar A. Poe," 188. Leprohon, *Jean Epstein*, 84.

31. Liebman, "The Sublime and the Fantastic," 20.

32. Hagan argues that the friend's difficulty in hearing and seeing "calls attention to the act of perception and thus emphasizes the fact that the film is about the way in which the cinema allows us to experience things"—Hagan, "Cinema and the Romantic Tradition," 50.

33. Bernard Chardère, ed., "Jean Renoir," 82, 85.

34. "Avant-Garde," *Cinéa-Ciné-pour-tous* 106 (1 April 1928), 22.

35. Advertisement for the Théâtre du Vieux-Colombier, *Cinéa-Ciné-pour-tous* 110 (1 June 1928), 5.

36. "L'Affaire de *La Petite Marchande d'allumettes*," *Cinéa-Ciné-pour-tous* 113 (15 July 1928), 6-7. Chardère, "Jean Renoir," 83.

37. "L'Activité cinégraphique," *Cinéa-Ciné-pour-tous* 135 (15 June 1929), 25. "Jean Renoir et Jean Tedesco gagnent le procès de *La Petite Marchande d'allumettes*," *Cinéa-Ciné-pour-tous* 136 (1 July 1929), 7-10.

38. Chardère, "Jean Renoir," 83, 85. André Bazin, *Jean Renoir*, 213-214.

39. Claude Beylie, "A la recherche d'un style," 14. For a description of the original version, see Claude Beylie, "Essai de reconstitution d'un film perdu," *Ecran* 79 (15 April 1979). Renoir has said that the original print had no intertitles, but the Museum of Modern Art's version has nine brief intertitles.

40. Chardère, "Jean Renoir," 84. Alexander Sesonske argues for a three-part structure to the film—Sesonske, *Jean Renoir: The French Films, 1924-1939*, 44.

41. Chardère, "Jean Renoir," 84.

42. The publicity of the period exploited this connection between Hessling and Chaplin—Beylie, "A la recherche d'un style," 9.

43. Freddy Buache, "Films indépendents et d'avant-garde," *Travelling* 55 (Summer, 1979), 69.

44. Jean Tedesco publicized Reiniger's *Les Aventures de Prince Ahmed* several times in his film journal—Ed. E., "Les Aventures de Prince Ahmed," *Cinéa-Ciné-pour-tous* 64 (1 July 1926), 31. Ed. E., "Les Aventures de Prince Ahmed," *Cinéa-Ciné-pour-tous* 65 (15 July 1926), 30-31.

45. For a more optimistic reading of the film, see Dr. Paul Ramain, "Le Rêve dans *La Petite Marchande d'Allumettes*," 14-16.

46. Compare the Christmas Eve celebration in the mountain cabin in *La Grande Illusion* (1937).

47. As Armand-Jean Cauliez and Raymond Durgnat have noted, the sequence prefigures similar moments in *La Règle de jeu* (1939)—Raymond Durgnat, *Jean Renoir* 51.

48. Durgnat, *Jean Renoir*, 52. Sesonske reads this as a spiritual, even religious, ending—Sesonske, *Jean Renoir*, 48-49.

La Coquille et le clergyman and *Un Chien andalou*

1. Henri Langlois apparently rediscovered the complete version of *La Coquille et le clergyman* in 1962. That version is the basis for the print at the Museum of Modern Art, on which this analysis depends. Unfortunately, prints with the second and third reels reversed have circulated

for years and continue to circulate in the United States so that an even more incoherent text haunts the original one. Exceptions to the usual criticism of the film include Wendy Dozoretz, "Dulac versus Artaud," 46-53, and Sandy Flitterman, "Theorizing the 'Feminine': Woman as the Figure of Desire in *The Seashell and the Clergyman*," 1-18.

2. Could Louis Nalpas, Artaud's uncle, have arranged their meeting? Dulac was under contract to Cinéromans, where Nalpas was head of production; and Artaud had already acted in two of the company's productions, *Surcouf* (1925) and *Le Juif errant* (1926).

3. Alain Virmaux, "Artaud and Film," 156-157.

4. "Un rêve à l'écran," *Cinégraphie* 2 (15 October 1927), 32. Lucie Derain, "*La Coquille et le clergyman*, rêve filmé," 50.

5. Georges Sadoul, "Souvenirs d'un témoin," 18. Antonin Artaud, "*The Shell and the Clergyman*," 173-174.

6. Antonin Artaud, "Scénario II," in *Les Surréalistes et le cinéma*, ed. Alain and Odette Virmaux, 167-171. Virmaux, "[footnote #1]," *Les Surréalistes et le cinéma*, 172. Sandy Flitterman identifies the source of this misinformation as Yvonne Allendy—Flitterman, "Theorizing the 'Feminine,' " 3.

7. Roger Régent, "Petite histoire des 'Ursulines' dans la grande histoire du cinéma," 17-18. Sadoul, "Souvenirs d'un témoin," 18-19. Ronald Hayman, *Artaud and After* (New York: Oxford University Press, 1977), 63-64. Jean Mitry, "Deux manifestations peu connues," 115-116.

8. Régent, "Petite histoire des 'Ursulines,' " 17-18. Sadoul, "Souvenirs d'un témoin," 18-19.

9. Antonin Artaud, "Lettre à Jean Paulhan (22 January, 1932)," *Oeuvres complètes*, 3 (Paris: Gallimard, 1961), 270.

10. The scenario bears some similarity to the earlier "cinematographic poems" of Philippe Soupault, Benjamin Péret, Robert Desnos, and others—Richard Abel, "American Films and the French Literary Avant-Garde," *Contemporary Literature* 17 (Winter, 1976), 84-109.

11. Antonin Artaud, "Cinema and Abstraction," 173. Artaud, "*The Shell and the Clergyman*," 174.

12. Susan Sontag, "Artaud," in Artaud, *Selected Writings*, ed. Susan Sontag, xxvi-xxvii.

13. Flitterman, "Theorizing the 'Feminine,' " 7.

14. Virmaux, "Artaud and Film," 157.

15. Hayman, *Artaud and After*, 37-38.

16. Compare Artaud's two prose texts, *Héloïse et Abélard* (1925) and *Le Clair Abélard* (1927). Hayman, *Artaud and After*, 43-51, 62-63. Susan Sontag and Don Eric Levine, "Notes," in Artaud, *Selected Writings*, 610.

17. Dozoretz, "Dulac and Artaud," 51-52.

18. Artaud, "Lettre à Jean Paulhan," 271.

19. Frank Stauffacher, "Notes on the Making of *Un Chien andalou*," 29-30. Raymond Durgnat, *Luis Buñuel*, 22-37. David Curtis, *Experimental Cinema*, 30-31. J. H. Matthews, *Surrealism and Film*, 84-90. Ken Kelman, "The Other Side of Realism," 112-113. Randall Conrad, "The Minister of the Interior Is on the Telephone," 2-14. Linda Williams, "The Prologue to *Un Chien andalou*: A Surrealist Film Metaphor," 24-33. Phillip Drummond, "Textual Space in *Un Chien andalou*," 55-119. Paul Sandro, "The Space of Desire in *An Andalusian Dog*," 57-63. Virginia Higginbottom, *Luis Buñuel*, 35-39. Linda Williams, *Figures of Desire: A Theory and Analysis of Surrealist Film*, 53-105.

20. Jean Vigo, "*Un Chien andalou*," *Vers un cinéma social* (1930), trans. Marianne Alexandre, and reprinted in *L'Age d'or and Un Chien andalou*, 81.

21. Ado Kyrou, *Luis Buñuel*, 16. José Francisco Aranda, *Luis Buñuel: A Critical Biography*, 41, 48-51.

22. Kyrou, *Luis Buñuel*, 18. Aranda, *Luis Buñuel*, 58-59. Matthews, *Surrealism and Film*, 90.

23. Luis Buñuel, "L'Aventure cinématographique," in *Armand Tallier et le Studio des Ursulines*, 29. Sadoul, "Souvenirs d'un témoin," 19. Aranda, *Luis Buñuel*, 59, 288. Denise Tual, *Le Temps dévoré*, 65.

24. Sadoul, "Souvenirs d'un témoin," 19.

25. J. Bouissounouse, "Dans la salle," 74. Tual, *Le Temps dévoré*, 65.

26. Buñuel, "L'Aventure cinématographique," 29. Aranda, *Luis Buñuel*, 58-59.

27. Sadoul, "Souvenirs d'un témoin," 19-20.

594

28. Aranda, *Luis Buñuel*, 64.

29. Luis Buñuel, *"Un Chien andalou," La Révolution surréaliste* (December, 1929), reprinted in *L'Age d'or and Un Chien andalou*, 10.

30. Aranda, *Luis Buñuel*, 58, 68. Tual, *Le Temps dévoré*, 66.

31. Aranda, *Luis Buñuel*, 56, 59.

32. Michel Marie, "Muet," in *Lectures du Film* (Paris: Albatros, 1976), 171.

33. William Van Wert, "Intertitles," *Sight and Sound* 40 (Spring, 1980), 104-105.

34. Drummond, "Textual Space in *Un Chien andalou*," 61.

35. Ibid., 67.

36. Ibid., 71-72. Compare Jean Mitry's attack on the film's "filmed symbols"—Jean Mitry, *Histoire du cinéma*, 3, 349—and Paul Sandro's analysis of the film's graphic patterns (diagonal stripes and severed body parts)—Sandro, "The Space of Desire in *An Andalusian Dog*," 61-62.

37. Sandro, "The Space of Desire in *An Andalusian Dog*," 61.

38. Drummond, "Textual Space in *Un Chien andalou*," 72-73.

39. Kelman, "The Other Side of Realism," 114-117.

40. Drummond, "Textual Space in *Un Chien andalou*," 55-119. Sandro, "The Space of Desire in *An Andalusian Dog*," 57-63.

41. How much all of this can be situated within the context of Buñuel's animosity toward "the Andalusian Modernist poets who were insensible to a revolutionary poetry of social content" remains to be explored—Aranda, *Luis Buñuel*, 46n.

42. Williams, "The Prologue to *Un Chien andalou*," 24-33. Drummond, "Textual Space in *Un Chien andalou*," 91-105. Linda Williams's book, *Figures of Desire: A Theory and Analysis of Surrealist Film* (1981), appeared too late for me to incorporate her recent work on *Un Chien andalou* into this study.

43. Sandro, "The Space of Desire in *An Andalusian Dog*," 62-63.

44. Vigo, *"Un Chien andalou,"* 75.

La Passion de Jeanne d'Arc

1. David Bordwell, *Filmguide to La Passion de Jeanne d'Arc*, 20. Apparently, the film's cost increased to nine million francs—David Bordwell, *The Films of Carl Theodor Dryer*, 212.

2. Michel Delahaye, "Interview with Carl Dreyer," 145.

3. Carl Dreyer, "Ecrits: La Mystique réalisée (1930)," 35.

4. Léon Moussinac, "Panoramique du cinéma [1929]," 285.

5. Bordwell, *Filmguide to La Passion de Jeanne d'Arc*, 15.

6. Delahaye, "Interview with Carl Dreyer," 143.

7. "Dossier-film #3—*La Passion de Jeanne d'Arc*," 46.

8. Dreyer, "Ecrits: La Mystique réalisée," 35.

9. Bordwell, *Filmguide to La Passion de Jeanne d'Arc*, 23.

10. Moussinac, "Panoramique du cinéma [1929]," 285. "Dossier-film #3—*La Passion de Jeanne d'Arc*," 45.

11. Moussinac, "Panoramique du cinéma [1929]," 285.

12. "La *Jeanne d'Arc* de Dreyer à la Salle Marivaux," *Cinéa-Ciné-pour-tous* 119 (15 October 1928), 16.

13. Moussinac, "Panoramique du cinéma [1929]," 284.

14. Mordaunt Hall, "Poignant French Film," 7. Alexandre Arnoux, "Enfin nous avons vu la version intégrale de *Jeanne d'Arc* de Carl Dreyer," 2.

15. Bordwell, *The Films of Carl Theodor Dryer*, 216-217.

16. Bordwell, *Filmguide to La Passion de Jeanne d'Arc*, 20. "Dossier-film #3—*La Passion de Jeanne d'Arc*," 45. Lo Duca, "Les films vieillissent-ils?" 25-27.

17. In the first reel, for example, several short sequences are excised from the print in the National Film Archive and at least a half-dozen shots are flopped (left/right). I have relied primarily on the print of *La Passion de Jeanne d'Arc* preserved at the Museum of Modern Art.

18. Georges Sadoul, *Histoire générale du cinéma*, 6, 383.

19. "Dossier-film #3—*La Passion de Jeanne d'Arc*," 46.

20. Ibid.

21. Moussinac, "Panoramique du cinéma [1929]," 286-287. This strategy may have been influenced by Soviet films such as Eisenstein's *Potemkin* (1925-1926).

22. "Dossier-film #3—*La Passion de Jeanne d'Arc*," 47.

23. Ibid.

24. Sadoul, *Histoire générale du cinéma*, 6, 388. One might compare my analysis here with Marie-Claire Ropars's much more systematic reading of Eisenstein's *October* (1927)—Ropars, "L'Ouverture d'*Octobre*, ou les conditions théoriques de la Révolution," *Octobre: écriture et idéologie* (Paris: Albatros, 1976), 27-66, trans. Larry Crawford and Kinball Lockhart, "The Overture of *October*," *enclitic* 2 (Fall, 1978), 50-72, and 3 (Spring, 1979), 35-47.

25. David Bordwell, "Imploded Space: Film Style in *The Passion of Jeanne d'Arc*," 99-105.

26. Mark Nash, *Dreyer*, 54.

27. Noël Burch and Jorge Dana, "Propositions," 44.

28. Bordwell, *The Films of Carl Theodor Dreyer*, 66-92.

29. Dreyer, "Ecrits: La Mystique réalisée," 35.

30. Herman Warm, "Dreyer brugte sanfaerdigbeden som stilmiddel," *Kosmorama* 90 (June, 1969), 147, quoted in translation in Bordwell, *The Films of Carl Theodor Dreyer*, 212.

31. Lewis Jacobs, ed., *The Compound Cinema: The Film Writings of Harry Alan Potamkin*, 452.

32. Grigori Kozintsev, *King Lear: The Space of Tragedy*, trans. Mary Mackintosh (Berkeley: University of California Press, 1977), 26. The discourse of Peter Brook's own *King Lear* (1971) owes a great deal to Dreyer's film.

33. Bordwell, *Filmguide to La Passion de Jeanne d'Arc*, 23.

34. This particular shot is missing from the print at the National Film Archive.

35. See diverse French films such as *Les Misérables* (1925), *Jim la Houlette* (1926), *Napoléon* (1927), and *La Chute de la maison Usher* (1928). Michel Marie, "La Lettre et le cinématographe," *La Revue du cinéma*, 316 (April, 1977), 67-74. William Van Wert, "Intertitles," *Sight and Sound* 49 (Spring, 1980), 98-105.

36. Pierre Audard, "*La Passion de Jeanne d'Arc*," 67.

37. Compare Ken Kelman, "Dreyer," 146-147.

38. Werner Klinger, "Analytical Treatise on the Dreyer Film, *The Passion of Joan of Arc*, with Appendix of a Constructive Critique," 9-10.

39. The cross-cutting in this sequence is actually highly ambiguous. Are we to read the association between Jeanne and the players as one of similarity or difference? And is the physical grotesquerie of the players an analogue of their spiritual or sociopolitical condition?

40. Dreyer, "Ecrits: La Mystique réalisée," 35.

41. Paul Willamen, "Note on *La Passion de Jeanne d'Arc*" in Nash, *Dreyer*, 54-55. For an analysis of the film as "an heterogenous text," whose "uncoded material tells us what kind of stuff it is that the text represses . . . the impossible position of the feminine in the symbolic order of the patriarchy," see Deborah Linderman, "Uncoded Images in the Heterogenous Text," 34-41.

Finis Terrae and *Gardiens de phare*

1. Jean Epstein, "Les Approches de la vérité," *Photo-Ciné* (15 November–15 December 1928), reprinted in Epstein, *Ecrits sur le cinéma*, 1, 192. Pierre Leprohon, *Jean Epstein*, 46-47.

2. Leprohon, *Jean Epstein*, 15. Interview with Marie Epstein, 14 August 1976.

3. Pierre Leprohon, "Films d'aujourd'hui: *Finis Terrae*," 8. Leprohon, *Jean Epstein*, 50-51. Lewis Jacobs, ed., *The Compound Cinema: The Film Writings of Harry Alan Potamkin*, 290. This analysis is based on the print of *Finis Terrae* preserved at the Cinémathèque française.

4. Jean Epstein, "Nos Lions," *L'Ami du peuple* (11 January 1929), reprinted in *Ecrits sur le cinéma*, 1, 196.

5. Epstein, "Nos Lions," 194-195.

6. Leprohon, *Jean Epstein*, 179.

7. Epstein, "Les Approches de la vérité," 193.

8. Epstein, "Nos Lions," 194-195.

9. Epstein, "Les Approches de la vérité," 193. Henri Langlois, "Jean Epstein (1897-1953)," 25. Flaherty was interested in re-creating past "exotic" cultures; Epstein was interested in a contemporary, isolated culture.

10. *Mother* was shown in the ciné-clubs in 1927 and 1928; *La Passion de Jeanne d'Arc* previewed in late April, 1928; and *Dura Lux* was shown in November, 1927—Jean Dréville, "Films," *Cinégraphie* 3 (15 November 1927), 53.

11. Epstein, "Les Approches de la vérité," 193.

12. Ibid. Potamkin reported that some people complained about the film's slow rhythm—Jacobs, ed., *The Compound Cinema*, 286.

13. Leprohon compares this accident to the swallow hitting the man in the speeding sports car in *La Glace à trois faces*—Leprohon, "Films d'aujourd'hui," 8.

14. Philippe Haudiquet, "Jean Epstein," 482.

15. The image is similar to the central metaphor—of a circular stairway enclosed by mirrors—in Epstein's first essay in *Le Cinématographe vu de l'Etna*, 15-18.

16. Leprohon, *Jean Epstein*, 50-51. Interestingly, the mothers of the two young men are not on good terms, and their difference is resolved in a sequence which joins together separate shots of them, around an intertitle, "Bannec," which progressively increases in size until it fills the frame.

17. Jean-Marie's calling in this sequence contrasts with the "sounds" that separate Jean and Marie at the end of the carnival sequence in *Coeur fidèle* as well as with the unanswered calling voice of the hero near the end of Murnau's *Sunrise* (1927). *Sunrise* also premiered in Paris shortly before Epstein left for Bannec and Balanec—"Les nouveaux films," *Cinéa-Ciné-pour-tous* 104 (1 March 1928), 6.

18. Pasteur and Lesenin join several other doctor heroes in French literature from the 1920s to the 1950s.

19. Jean Epstein, "Le Cinématographe dans l'Archipel [1928-1929]," *Ecrits sur le cinéma*, 1, 199.

20. "Les nouveaux films," *Cinéa-Ciné-pour-tous* 142 (15 October 1929), 3. Henri Agel, *Jean Grémillon*, 31, 180.

21. An auto accident interrupted the production late in 1928—J. V., "Jean Grémillon nous entretient de ses travaux," *Pour Vous* 22 (18 April 1929), 4.

22. Pierre Kast, "Jean Grémillon," 36. The Cinémathèque française print gives the production date as 1928.

23. Alexandre Arnoux, "Un film français de qualité: *Gardiens de phare*," 8-9. "Films présentés en France du 1er janvier 1929 au 1er janvier 1930," *Tout-Cinéma* (1930), 1-32.

24. This analysis is based on prints of *Gardiens de phare* at the Cinémathèque française and in the private collection of Armand Panigel.

25. Compare Marcel Carné's tribute to Périnal—"a photography of atmosphere, gray without being flat, deliberately imprecise without being obscure, it added even more to the anguish of the characters, to the oppression"—reprinted in Mireille Latil Le Dantec, "Jean Grémillon: le réalisme et le tragique," 45.

26. Agel, *Jean Grémillon*, 32.

27. A similar slow motion image of a running dog occurs in Luis Buñuel's *Los Olvidados* (1950) just as the main character, Jaibo, dies.

28. There are only some twenty intertitles scattered throughout the film, all of them brief phrases of narration or dialogue.

29. The siren's relation to the father thus parallels the dog's to the son.

L'Argent

1. Jean-André Fieschi, "Autour du cinématographe," 38.

2. Claude Beylie and Michel Marie, "Entretien avec Marcel L'Herbier," 36/x.

3. "La Polémique de *L'Argent*," 26-28. Marcel L'Herbier, *La Tête qui tourne*, 149-150, 164-167. At the very moment L'Herbier was writing his scenario for *L'Argent*, Sergei Eisenstein was sketching out a project for a film based on Karl Marx' *Capital*—Sergei Eisenstein, "Notes for a Film of *Capital*," trans. Maciej Sliwowski, Jay Leyda, and Annette Michelson, *October* 2 (Summer, 1976), 3-26.

4. Beylie and Marie, "Entretien avec Marcel L'Herbier," 36/x. L'Herbier, *La Tête qui tourne*, 150.

5. Pierre Jouvet, "*L'Argent* de Marcel L'Herbier," 8.

6. L'Herbier, *La Tête qui tourne*, 161.

7. Ibid., 161-162.

8. "Les nouveaux films," *Cinéa-Ciné-pour-tous* 130 (1 April 1929), 6. L'Herbier, *La Tête qui tourne*, 159-160, 162.

9. Beylie and Marie, "Entretien avec Marcel L'Herbier," 36/x.

10. Noël Burch, *Marcel L'Herbier*, 136. Georges Sadoul, *Histoire générale du cinéma*, 6, 330. Claude Beylie, "Marcel L'Herbier ou l'intelligence du cinématographe," 28/ii.

11. Claude Beylie, "Sur cinq films de Marcel L'Herbier," 72. Nicole Schmitt, "Avertissement," *L'Avant-Scène du cinéma* 209 (1 June 1978), 7. The most recent screenings have been at the National Film Theater in London (7 August 1979) and at the Museum of Modern Art (January, 1980). This analysis is based on the restored prints of *L'Argent* at the Museum of Modern Art and at the National Film Archive. Unfortunately, both of these prints have been stretch-printed so that they run slightly slower and longer than when the film was originally screened.

12. Noël Burch, "Revoir *L'Argent*," 45.

13. Burch, *Marcel L'Herbier*, 138-162.

14. Ibid., 132.

15. Ibid., 131.

16. Fieschi, "Autour du cinématographe," 38.

17. The Hamelin figure, like the main characters of Tourneur's *L'Equipage* (1927) and Wellman's *Wings* (1927), plays on the then current fascination with aviator heroes such as Charles Lindbergh.

18. Beylie and Marie, "Entretien avec Marcel L'Herbier," 36/x.

19. This sequence bears some strange similarities to the sequence in *Un Chien andalou* where the man and woman watch an androgynous figure on the street below their window. Did Buñuel and Dali see *L'Argent* before they began shooting their film?

20. Again, there seem to be parallels between this sequence and others in *Un Chien andalou* as well as in *La Coquille et le clergyman*.

21. Jouvet, "*L'Argent* de Marcel L'Herbier," 8.

22. The role of Baroness Sandorf was expanded considerably when Brigitte Helm became available for the film.

23. Was this connection between Gunderman and *Le Matin*, Sapène's newspaper, one of the things that angered Sapène about L'Herbier's film?

24. L'Herbier, *La Tête qui tourne*, 156. This predatory couple and their jungle environment find a curious parallel twenty years later in Orson Welles's *Lady from Shanghai* (1948).

25. Line is the inverse of the *femme de glace* character of *L'Inhumaine*, and her mirror image functions somewhat like that of the man in *La Glace à trois faces*.

26. Burch, *Marcel L'Herbier*, 130.

27. Ibid., 140.

28. Fieschi, "Autour du cinématographe," 38.

29. L'Herbier, *La Tête qui tourne*, 156.

30. Burch, *Marcel L'Herbier*, 132.

31. Ibid., 133.

32. Fieschi, "Autour du cinématographe," 41. A similar dynamism marks Fritz Lang's *Metropolis* (1927).

33. Fieschi, "Autour du cinématographe," 41.

34. Michel Marie, "Modernité de *L'Argent*," 5.

35. Fieschi, "Autour du cinématographe," 38, 41. Burch, *Marcel L'Herbier*, 141.

36. Burch, *Marcel L'Herbier*, 141-142. Marie, "Modernité de *L'Argent*," 6.

37. Burch, *Marcel L'Herbier*, 146.

38. Fieschi, "Autour du cinématographe," 38.

39. L'Herbier, *La Tête qui tourne*, 157.

40. Burch, *Marcel L'Herbier*, 153.

41. L'Herbier, *La Tête qui tourne*, 162-163.

42. S. M. Eisenstein, V. I. Pudovkin, and G. V. Alexandrov, "A Statement [1928]," in *Film Form*, trans. and ed. Jay Leyda (New York: Harcourt, Brace, and Jovanovich, 1949), 257-259.

43. Burch, *Marcel L'Herbier*, 147.

44. Ibid., 150.

45. Ibid., 162.

Afterword

1. See p. 576, n. 7.

2. Janet Staiger, "Dividing Labor for Production Control: Thomas Ince and the Rise of the Studio System," 16-25. Janet Staiger, "The Mass-Produced Photoplay: Economic and Signifying Practices in the First Years of Hollywood," *Wide Angle* 4 (1980), 12-27. Janet Staiger, "Crafting Hollywood Films: The Impact of a Concept of Film Practice on a Mode of Production" (Paper delivered at the Society for Cinema Studies Conference, Los Angeles, 1982), 1-14.

3. Recently, Marie Epstein told me that she remembers seeing both color and black-and-white prints of the same film in the early 1920s. The color prints were exhibited in the few "showcase" cinemas, particularly in Paris; the less expensive black-and-white prints were shown elsewhere, especially in the provinces. Her remarks indicate one particular line of pursuit for further research on production and distribution practices in France during this period.

4. See p. 541, n. 21.

5. See, for instance, John Ellis, "Made in Ealing," *Screen* 16 (Spring, 1975), 78-127; Tino Balio, ed., *The American Film Industry*; Robert C. Allen, "William Fox presents *Sunrise*," *Quarterly Review of Film Studies* 2 (1977), 327-338; Vance Kepley, "Griffith's *Broken Blossoms* and the Problem of Historical Specificity," 37–48; Jackson Schmidt, "On the Road to MGM: A History of Metro Pictures Corporation, 1915-1920," *Velvet Light Trap* 19 (1982), 46-52.

6. See p. 576, n. 10.

7. See, for instance, Donald Crafton, *Before Mickey: The Animated Film, 1898-1928* (Cambridge: MIT Press, 1982), 217-258. Had I had space and time, at the end of Part IV, I would have included a comparative analysis of two short documentaries, Georges Lacombe's *La Zone* (1928) and Jean Vigo's *A Propos de Nice* (1930).

8. Charles [Rick] Altman, "Towards a Theory of Genre Film," *Film Studies Annual* 2 (1977), 31-44. Thomas Schatz, *Hollywood Genres* (New York: Random House, 1981), 3-41. Rick Altman, ed., *Genre: The Musical* (London: Routledge & Kegan Paul, 1981).

9. Paul Willamen, "On Reading Epstein on *Photogénie*," 40-47.

10. Christian Metz, *The Imaginary Signifier/Psychoanalysis and the Cinema*, trans. Celia Britton, Annwyl Williams, Ben Brewster, and Alfred Guzzetti (Bloomington: Indiana University Press, 1982), 149-297.

11. Stuart Liebman, "French Film Theory, 1910-1921," 1-27.

12. Bernard Eisenschitz, "Histoire de l'histoire (deux périodes du cinéma français: le muet—le génération de 58)," 19-33.

Baldizzone, José. "Des Historiens évoquent les Années Folles." *Cahiers de la cinémathèque* 33-34 (Autumn, 1981), 34-40.

Brogan, D. W. *The Development of Modern France, 1870-1939*, Vol. 2. New York: Harper & Row, 1966.

Carter, Edward C., Robert Forster, and Joseph Moody, ed. *Enterprise and Entrepeneurs in Nineteenth- and Twentieth-Century France*. Baltimore: The Johns Hopkins University Press, 1976.

Caute, David. *Communism and the French Intellectuals, 1914-1960*. New York: Macmillan, 1964.

Chastenet, Jacques. *Histoire de la Troisième République: les années d'illusions, 1918-1931*. Paris: Hachette, 1960.

Cobban, Alfred. *A History of Modern France. Vol. 3 (1871-1962)*. London: Penguin, 1965.

Earle, Edward Mead, ed. *Modern France: Problems of the Third and Fourth Republics*. Princeton: Princeton University Press, 1951.

Fox, Robert and George Weisz. *The Organisatin of Science and Technology in France, 1808-1914*. Cambridge: Cambridge University Press, 1980.

Harvey, Donald. *France since the Revolution*. New York: The Free Press, 1968.

LaCapra, Dominick and Steven L. Kaplan, ed. *Modern European Intellectual History: Reappraisals and New Perspectives*. Ithaca: Cornell University Press, 1982.

Landes, David. *The Unbound Prometheus: Technological Change and Industrial Development in Western Europe from 1750 to the Present*. Cambridge: Cambridge University Press, 1969.

Miller, Michael B. *The Bon Marché: Bourgeois Culture and the Department Store, 1869-1920*. Princeton: Princeton University Press, 1981.

Moraze, Charles. *The French and the Republic*. Translated by Jean-Jacques Demoest. Ithaca: Cornell University Press, 1958.

Thomson, David, ed. *France: Empire and Republic, 1850-1940*. New York: Walker, 1968.

Weber, Eugen. *Action Française: Royalism and Reaction in Twentieth-Century France*. Stanford: Stanford University Press, 1962.

Wright, Gordon. *France in Modern Times*. 3rd ed. New York: W. W. Norton, 1981.

————. *Raymond Poincaré and the French Presidency*. New York: Octagon Books, 1967.

Zeldin, Theodore. *France, 1848-1945: Ambition and Love*. Oxford: Oxford University Press, 1979.

————. *France, 1848-1945: Anxiety and Hypocrisy*. Oxford: Oxford University Press, 1981.

————. *France, 1848-1945: Intellect and Pride*. Oxford: Oxford University Press, 1980.

————. *France, 1848-1945: Politics and Anger*. Oxford: Oxford University Press, 1979.

————. *France, 1848-1945: Taste and Corruption*. Oxford: Oxford University Press, 1980.

History of the French Silent Cinema, 1915-1929

Andrew, Dudley. "Sound in France: The Origins of a Native School." *Yale French Studies* 60 (1980), 94-114.

Arnoux, Alexandre. *Du muet au parlant: souvenirs d'un témoin*. Paris: La Nouvelle édition, 1945.

Auriol, J. G. "Rudiments d'histoire du cinéma." *Pour Vous* 357 (19 September 1935), 2.

Bardèche, Maurice and Robert Brasillach. *The History of Motion Pictures*. Translated by Iris Barry. New York: W. W. Norton, 1938.

Barsacq, Léon. *Caligari's Cabinet and Other Grand Illusions: A History of Film Design*. Revised and edited by Elliott Stein. Boston: New York Graphic Society, 1976.

Beylie, Claude. "De Louis Lumière à Alain Resnais." *Cinématographe* 76 (March, 1982), 59-67.

———— and Francis Lacassin. "A la recherche d'un cinéma perdu: entretien avec Jean-Louis Bouquet, Henri Fescourt, Joë Hamman, Gaston Modot." *Cahiers de la cinémathèque* 33-34 (Autumn, 1981), 11-27.

Bilinsky, Boris. "Le Costume." In *L'Art cinématographique*, Vol. 6 (Paris: Félix Alcan, 1929), 25-56.

Blumer, Ronald. "The Camera as Snowball: France, 1918-1927." *Cinema Journal* 10 (Spring, 1971), 31-39.

Bonneau, Albert. "Le Film à épisodes." *Cinémagazine* 3 (17 July 1923), 125-128.

Borde, Raymond. "La France des années 30." *L'Avant-Scène du cinéma* 173 (1 October 1976), 23-45.

Bordwell, David. "French Impressionist Cinema: Film Culture, Film Theory, and Film Style." Ph.D. dissertation, University of Iowa, 1974.

Bosséno, Christian. "Le Cinéma et la presse (I)." *La Revue du cinéma: image et son* 341 (July, 1979), 105-114.

————. "Le Cinéma et la presse (II)." *La Revue du cinéma: image et son* 342 (September, 1979), 93-104.

Boulanger, Pierre. *Le Cinéma colonial.* Paris: Seghers, 1975.

Bouquet, Jean-Louis. "Le Cinéma en France après la guerre." In *Le Cinéma des origines à nos jours*, edited by Henri Fescourt (Paris: Editions du cygne, 1932), 249-280.

————. "Panorama de l'activité française, 1916-1928." *Cahiers de la cinémathèque* 33-34 (Autumn, 1981), 57-66.

Bousquet, Henri. "Economie et publicité cinématographique dans l'immédiat après-guerre." *Cahiers de la cinémathèque* 33-34 (Autumn, 1981), 67-75.

Breteque, François de la. "Le Film en tranches: les mutations du film à épisodes, 1918-1926." *Cahiers de la cinémathèque* 33-34 (Autumn, 1981), 89-102.

Brownlow, Kevin. *The Parade's Gone By.* Berkeley: University of California Press, 1976.

Brunius, Jacques. *En Marge du cinéma français.* Paris: Arcanne, 1954.

Canudo, Ricciotto. *L'Usine aux images.* Geneva: Office central d'édition, 1927.

Charensol, Georges. *Panorama du cinéma.* Paris: Editions Dra, 1930.

————. "Quarante Ans de cinéma: nouveaux visages." *Pour Vous* 328 (28 February 1935), 2.

Chevanne, André. *L'Industrie du cinéma, le cinéma sonore.* Bordeaux: Delmas, 1933.

Clair, René. *Cinema Yesterday and Today.* Translated by Stanley Appelbaum. New York: Dover, 1972.

Coissac, G.-Michel. *Les Coulisses du cinéma.* Paris: Pittoresques, 1929.

————. "L'Evolution du cinématographe et la réalisation de quelques grands films." In *Tout-Cinéma* (Paris: Filma, 1929), 13-32.

————. *Histoire du cinématographe, des origines jusqu'à nos jours.* Paris: Editions du Cinéopse, 1925.

Courtade, Francis. *Les Malédictions du cinéma français: une histoire du cinéma français parlant (1928-1978).* Paris: Alain Moreau, 1978.

Coustet, Ernest. *Le Cinéma.* Paris: Hachette, 1921.

Danvers, V.-Guillaume. "Le Cinématographe en France, de 1915 à 1920." In *Almanach du cinéma* (Paris: Cinémagazine, 1922), 19-30.

Delluc, Louis. *Cinéma et cie.* Paris: Grasset, 1919.

————. "Quelques films français." *Cinéa* 18 (9 September 1921), 5-6, 8.

Delpeuch, André. *Le Cinéma.* Paris: Octave Doin, 1927.

Derain, Lucie. "Décors et décorateurs dans le cinéma français." *La Revue du cinéma* 27 (1 October 1931), 26-31.

Deslandes, Jacques and Jacques Richard. *Histoire comparée du cinéma.* Vol. 2 (1896-1906). Paris: Casterman, 1968.

Diamant-Berger, Henri. *Le Cinéma.* Paris: La Renaissance du livre, 1919.

————. *Il était une fois le cinéma.* Paris: Jean-Claude Simoën, 1977.

Esnault, Philippe. "Entretiens avec André-Paul Antoine." *La Revue du cinéma: image et son* 271 (April, 1973), 7-28.

Fescourt, Henri. *La Foi et les montagnes.* Paris: Paul Montel, 1959.

———— and Jean-Louis Bouquet. *L'Idée et l'écran: opinions sur le cinéma.* 3 vols. Paris: Haberschill et Sergent, 1925-1926.

Fieschi, Jacques. "Entretien avec Jean Mitry." *Cinématographe* 60 (September, 1980), 18-23.

Ford, Charles. *Histoire populaire du cinéma.* Paris: Mame, 1955.

Franju, Georges. "De Marey à Renoir: Trésors de la Cinémathèque Française, 1882-1939." *L'Avant-Scène du cinéma* 279/280 (1-15 January 1982), 7-87.

Gevaudan, Frantz. "Entretien avec Jean Mitry." *Cinéma* 281 (May, 1981), 38-48.

Girard, Jean. *Le Lexique français du cinéma, des origines à 1930.* Paris: Centre national de la recherche scientifique, 1958.

Gomery, Douglas. "Economic Struggle and Hollywood Imperialism: Europe Converts to Sound." *Yale French Studies* 60 (1980), 80-93.

Icart, Roger. "L'Avènement du film parlant." *Les Cahiers de la cinémathèque* 13-14-15 (1974), 25-218.

————. "Le Mélodrame dans le cinéma muet français." *Les Cahiers de la cinémathèque* 28 (1979), 191-200.

Jeanne, René. *Cinéma 1900*. Paris: Flammarion, 1965.

————. "L'Evolution artistique du cinématograph." In *Le Cinéma des origines à nos jours*, edited by Henri Fescourt (Paris: Editions du cygne, 1932), 169-248.

————. "Réalisme et cinéma." *Cinémagazine* 2 (6 January 1922), 11-15, and 2 (13 January 1922), 45-48.

———— and Charles Ford. *Le Cinéma et la presse, 1895-1960*. Paris: Armand Colin, 1961.

————. *Histoire encyclopédique du cinéma*, Vol. 1, *Le Cinéma français, 1895-1929*. Paris: Robert Laffont, 1947.

————. *Paris vu par le cinéma*. Paris: Hachette, 1969.

Kovacs, Katherine. "Georges Méliès and the *Féerie*." *Cinema Journal* 16 (Fall, 1976), 1-13.

Lacassin, Francis. *Pour une contre histoire du cinéma*. Paris: Union générale d'éditions, 1971.

Lang, André. *Déplacements et Villégiatures littéraires et suivi de la promenade au royaume des images ou entretiens cinématographiques*. Paris: La Renaissance du livre, 1924.

Langlois, Henri. "Classiques de l'écran muet." *Cinématographie française* (24 August 1935), 16, 18.

Lapierre, Marcel. *Les Cent Visages du cinéma*. Paris: Grasset, 1948.

————, ed. *Anthologie du cinéma*. Paris: La Nouvelle édition, 1946.

Leclerc, J. *Le Cinéma, témoin de son temps*. Paris: Les nouvelles éditions Debresse, 1970.

Ledoux, Jacques and Raymond Chirat. *Catalogue des films français de long métrage: films sonores de fiction, 1929-1939*. Brussels: Royal Film Archive of Belgium, 1975.

Leglise, Paul. *Histoire de la politique du cinéma français: le cinéma et la IIIᵉ République*. Paris: Librairie générale de droit et de jurisprudence, 1970.

————. "Les Institutions cinématographiques des années vingt." *Cahiers de la cinémathèque* 33-34 (Autumn, 1981), 46-56.

Leprohon, Pierre. *Cinquante Ans du cinéma français*. Paris: Editions du Cerf, 1954.

————. *Histoire du cinéma: Vie et mort du cinématographe (1895-1930)*. Paris: Editions du Cerf, 1961.

Lewis, Howard T. *The Motion Picture Industry*. New York: Van Nostrand, 1933.

L'Herbier, Marcel. *La Tête qui tourne*. Paris: Pierre Belfond, 1979.

Lherminier, Pierre. *L'Art du cinéma*. Paris: Seghers, 1960.

Mallet-Stevens, Robert. "Le Décor." In *L'Art cinématographique*, Vol. 6 (Paris: Félix Alcan, 1929), 1-23.

Martinat, Jean Michel. "Le Cinéma des Années Folles vu de Carcassonne." *Cahiers de la cinémathèque* 33-34 (Autumn, 1981), 113-131.

Mitry, Jean. *Histoire du cinéma*. Vol. 2 (1915-1923). Paris: Editions universitaires, 1969.

————. *Histoire du cinéma*. Vol. 3 (1923-1930). Paris: Editions universitaires, 1973.

————. "Les Operateurs du muet." *Cinématographe* 69 (July 1981), 44-46.

Monaco, Paul. *Cinema and Society: France and Germany during the Twenties*. New York: Elsevier, 1976.

Moussinac, Léon. "Cinéma: expression sociale." In *L'Art cinématographique*, Vol. 6 (Paris: Librairie Félix Alcan, 1927), 23-49.

————. "Le Décor et le costume au cinéma." *Art et Décoration* (November, 1926), 133-139.

————. *Naissance du cinéma*. Paris: Povolovsky, 1925.

————. *Panoramique du cinéma*. Paris: Le Sans Pareil, 1929.

Noell, René. "Histoire du spectacle cinématographique à Perpignan, de 1896 à 1944." *Cahiers de la cinémathèque*, special number (1973), 38-63.

Oms, Marcel. "Un Cinéaste des Années Vingt: René Le Somptier." *Cahiers de la cinémathèque* 33-34 (Autumn, 1981), 207-213.

————. "Histoire et géographie d'une France imaginaire." *Cahiers de la cinémathèque* 33-34 (Autumn, 1981), 77-88.

Pathé, Charles. "De Pathé Frères à Pathé Cinéma." In *Premier Plan* 55 (Lyon: SERDOC, 1970).

————. "Etude sur l'évolution de l'industrie cinématographique française [conférence faite en 1918]." In *Intelligence du cinématographe*, edited by L'Herbier, (Paris: Corréa, 1946), 213-228.

Petat, Jacques. "L'Avant-garde français des années vingt." *Cinéma* 77, 217 (January, 1977), 18-31.

Poirier, Léon. *Vingt-quatre images à la seconde*. Paris: Mame, 1953.

603

BIBLIOGRAPHY

Poulaille, Henri. "L'Age ingrat du cinéma." *Le Rouge et le noir*, special issue (July, 1928), 55-72.

Prédal, René. *La Société française (1914-1945) à travers le cinéma*. Paris: Armand Colin, 1972.

Renoir, Jean. *Ma Vie et mes films*. Paris: Flammarion, 1974.

Richard, A. P. "La Technique." *L'Art cinématographique*, Vol. 6 (Paris: Librairie Félix Alcan, 1929), 67-137.

———. "Les Tendances modernes de la cinématographie." *La Revue fédéraliste* 103 (November, 1927), 28-35.

Roelens, Maurice. "Intellectuels (de gauche) et cinéma en 1928." *Cahiers de la cinémathèque* 33-34 (Autumn, 1981), 193-198.

———. "*Mon-Ciné* (1922-1924) et le mélodrame." *Cahiers de la cinémathèque* 28 (1979), 201-214.

Sadoul, Georges. *Le Cinéma français*. Paris: Flammarion, 1962.

———. *The French Cinema*. London: Falcon Press, 1952.

———. *Histoire générale du cinéma. Vol. 2, Les Pionniers du cinéma, 1897-1909*. Paris: Denoël, 1947.

———. *Histoire générale du cinéma. Vol. 3, Le Cinéma devient un art, 1909-1920 (L'Avant-guerre)*. Paris: Denoël, 1951.

———. *Histoire générale du cinéma. Vol. 4, Le Cinéma devient un art, 1909-1920 (La Première Guerre mondiale)*. Paris: Denoël, 1974.

———. *Histoire générale du cinéma. Vol. 5, L'Art muet (1919-1929)*. Paris: Denoël, 1975.

———. *Histoire générale du cinéma. Vol. 6, L'Art muet (1919-1929)*. Paris: Denoël, 1975.

Scize, Pierre. "Le Film muet (1918-1930)." In *Le Cinéma par ceux qui le font*, edited by Denis Marion (Paris: Librairie Arthème Fayard, 1949), 29-50.

Talon, Gérard. "Cinéma français: la crise de 1928." In *Synchronismes: 1928* (Paris: Editions du signe, 1975), 104-117.

Tedesco, Jean. "La France et le film sonore." *Cinéa-Ciné-pour-tous* 135 (15 June 1929), 7-8.

Thiher, Allen. *The Cinematic Muse: Critical Studies in the History of French Cinema*. Columbia: University of Missouri Press, 1979.

Tual, Denise. *Le Temps dévoré*. Paris: Arthème Fayard, 1980.

"Visages du cinéma des années vingt." *L'Avant-Scène du cinéma* 248 (15 May 1980), i/23-xvi/54.

French Film Journals, 1915-1929

Film Industry Journals:
Ciné-Journal, 1915-
Filma, 1916-
Le Courrier cinématographique, 1917-
La Cinématographie française, 1918-
Cinéopse, 1919-
Cinémagazine, 1921-
Ciné-Miroir, 1922-
Mon-Ciné, 1922-
La Critique cinématographique, 1927-

Production/Distribution Company Journals:
Pathé-Journal, 1917-1926
Ciné-France, 1927-1929

Les Nouveautés Aubert, 1918-1922
L'Effort Aubert, 1923
Ciné-Information Aubert, 1924-1927
Aubert-Ciné, 1928

Gaumont, Bulletin du comptoir ciné-location, 1920-1922
Gaumont films français, 1923-1924

Les Programmes Gaumont, 1924-1925
Gaumont-Metro-Goldwyn, Bulletin cinématographique, 1925-1927

Bulletin Paramount, 1922-1926
Paramount Journal, 1926-1929

Annuals or Yearbooks:
Annuaire général de la cinématographie française et étrangère. Paris: Ciné-Journal, 1917
Tout-Cinéma. Paris: Filma, 1922-
Almanach du cinéma. Paris: Cinémagazine, 1922-1924
Annuaire général de la cinématographie. Paris: Cinémagazine, 1925-
Almanach du Mon-Ciné. Paris: Mon-Ciné, 1929-1930

Film Journals—Serializations or Novelizations:
Romans-Cinémas, 1914-1918
Cinéma-Bibliothèque, 1921-
Le Film complet, 1922-
Mon Film, 1922-
La Petite Illustration, 1925-1930

Specialized Film Journals:
Le Film, 1916-1921
Ciné-pour-tous, 1919-1923
Le Journal du Ciné-Club, 1920-1921
Cinéa, 1921-1923
Théâtre et Comoedia Illustré, film supplement, 1922-1925
Cinéa-Ciné-pour-tous, 1923-
L'Art cinématographique, 1926-1929
Schémas, 1927
Photo-Ciné, 1927
Cinégraphie, 1927-1928
Close Up, 1927-1930
On Tourne, 1928
Spartacus, 1928
Cinémonde, 1928-

Pour Vous, 1928-
La Revue du cinéma, 1928-

Literary Journals (with an interest in film):
Le Crapouillot, 1919-
Mercure de France, 1919-1926
La Nouvelle Revue Française, 1919-
L'Esprit nouveau, 1920-1925
La Gazette des sept arts, 1922-1923
Les Nouvelles littéraires, 1922-
La Revue nouvelle, 1927-

Literary Journals (special film issues):
Les Cahiers du mois 16/17 (1925)
La Revue fédéraliste 103 (November, 1927)
Le Rouge et le noir, special number (July, 1928)

Problems in Early Film History

Allen, Jeanne. "The Film Viewer as Consumer." *Quarterly Review of Film Studies* 5 (Fall, 1980), 481-499.

Allen, Robert C. "The Archeology of Film History." *Wide Angle* 5:2 (1982), 4-12.

———. "Film History: The Narrow Discourse." *Film Studies Annual: Part Two* (1977), 9-17.

——— and Douglas Gomery. *Film History: Theory and Practice*. Reading: Addison and Wesley, 1984.

Bachy, Victor. "Critique historique et cinéma." *Cahiers de la cinémathèque* 20 (Summer, 1976) 82-93.

Balio, Tino, ed. *The American Film Industry*. Madison: University of Wisconsin Press, 1976.

Baxter, John. "On the History and Ideology of Film Lighting." *Screen* 16 (Autumn, 1975), 83-106.

Borde, Raymond. "La Cinémathèque française: recherche de la vérité." *Cahiers de la cinémathèque* 22 (1978), 3-53.

Bordwell, David. "Lowering the Stakes: Prospects for a Historical Poetics of the Cinema." *Iris* 1:1 (1983), 5-18.

———. "Textual Analysis, Etc." *enclitic* 5:2/6:1 (Fall, 1981–Spring, 1982), 125-136.

———, Janet Staiger, and Kristin Thompson. *Classical Hollywood Cinema: Film Art and Modes of Production*. London: Routledge & Kegan Paul, 1984.

Bowser, Eileen. "The Brighton Project: An Introduction." *Quarterly Review of Film Studies* 4 (Fall, 1979), 509-538.

Buscombe, Edward. "A New Approach to Film History." *Film Studies Annual: Part Two* (1977), 1-9.

———. "Sound and Color." *Jump Cut* 17 (April, 1978), 23-25.

Brewster, Ben. "A Scene at the Movies." *Screen* 23 (July-August, 1982), 4-15.

Burch, Noël. "Film's Institutional Mode of Representation and the Soviet Response." *October* 11 (Winter, 1979), 77-96.

———. "Narrative/Diegesis—Thresholds, Limits." *Screen* 23 (July-August, 1982), 16-33.

———. "Porter or Ambivalence." *Screen* 19 (Winter, 1978/1979), 91-106.

———. *To the Distant Observer: Form and Meaning in the Japanese Cinema*. Berkeley: University of California Press, 1979.

Carroll, Noel. "Film History and Film Theory: An Outline for an Institutional Theory of Film." *Film Reader* 4 (1979), 81-96.

Eckert, Charles. "The Carole Lombard in Macy's Window." *Quarterly Review of Film Studies* 3 (Winter, 1978), 1-21.

Elsaesser, Thomas. "Social Mobility and the Fantastic: German Silent Cinema." *Wide Angle* 4:2 (1982), 14-25.

Fielding, Raymond. "The Technological Antecedents of the Coming of Sound: An Introduction." *Sound and the Cinema: The Coming of Sound to American Film*, edited by Evan William Cameron (Pleasantville: Redgrave Press, 1980), 2-23.

BIBLIOGRAPHY

Gartenberg, Jon. "Camera Movement in Edison and Biograph Films, 1900-1906." *Cinema Journal* 19 (Spring, 1980), 1-16.

Gomery, Douglas. "The Movies Become Big Business: Publix Theatres and the Chain Store Strategy." *Cinema Journal* 18 (Spring, 1979), 26-40.

————. "The Picture Palace: Economic Sense or Hollywood Nonsense?" *Quarterly Review of Film Studies* 3 (Winter, 1978), 23-26.

————. "Problems in Film History: How Fox Innovated Sound." *Quarterly Review of Film Studies* 1 (August, 1976), 315-330.

————. "Toward an Economic History of the Cinema: The Coming of Sound." In *The Cinematic Apparatus*, edited by Teresa de Lauretis and Stephen Heath (New York: St. Martin's Press, 1980), 38-46.

Greenberg, Daniel. "The Reverence Shelf Shuffle." *Film Quarterly* 26 (Winter, 1982-1983), 5-16.

Heath, Stephen. "The Cinematic Apparatus: Technology as Historical and Cultural Form." In *The Cinematic Apparatus*, edited by Teresa de Lauretis and Stephen Heath (New York: St. Martin's Press, 1980), 1-13.

Holman, Roger, ed. *Cinema 1900-1906: An Analytical Study*. Brussels: Fédération Internationale des Archives du Film, 1982.

Icart, Roger. "L'Avènement du film parlant." *Cahiers de la cinémathèque* 13-14-15 (1974), 25-218.

Kepley, Vance. "Griffith's *Broken Blossoms* and the Problem of Historical Specificity." *Quarterly Review of Film Studies* 3 (Winter, 1978), 37-48.

McCreary, Eugene. "Film Criticism and the Historian." *Film and History* 11 (February, 1981), 1-8.

McKee, Gerald. *Film Collecting*. London: Tantivy Press, 1978.

Mitry, Jean. "De quelques problèmes d'histoire et d'esthétique du cinéma." *Cahiers de la cinémathèque* 10-11 (Summer-Autumn, 1973), 112-141.

Mottram, Ronald. "Fact and Affirmation: Some Thoughts on the Methodology of Film History and the Relation of Theory to Historiography." *Quarterly Review of Film Studies* 5 (Summer, 1980), 335-347.

Murray, Bruce. "*Mutter Krausens Fahrt in Glück*: An Analysis of the Film as a Critical Response to the 'Street Films' of the Commercial Film Industry." *enclitic* 5:2/6:1 (Fall, 1981–Spring, 1982), 44-54.

Nowell-Smith, Geoffrey. "On the Writing of the History of the Cinema: Some Problems." *Edinburgh Magazine* 2 (1977), 8-12.

Ogle, Patrick. "The Development of Sound Systems: The Commercial Era." *Film Reader* 2 (1977), 198-212.

Perry, Ted. "Formal Strategies as an Index to the Evolution of Film History." *Cinema Journal* 14 (Winter, 1974-1975), 25-36.

Salt, Barry. "The Early Development of Film Form." *Film Form* 1 (Autumn, 1975), 91-106.

————. *Film Style and Technology: History and Analysis*. Forthcoming.

————. "From Caligari to Who?" *Sight and Sound* 48 (Spring, 1979), 119-123.

Shepard, David. "Authenticating Films." *The Quarterly Journal of the Library of Congress* 37 (Summer-Fall, 1980), 342-354.

Sorlin, Pierre. *The Film in History: Restaging the Past*. Oxford: Blackwell, 1980.

Spellerberg, James. "Technology and Ideology in the Cinema." *Quarterly Review of Film Studies* 2 (August, 1977), 288-301.

Staiger, Janet. "Dividing Labor for Production Control: Thomas Ince and the Rise of the Studio System." *Cinema Journal* 18 (Spring, 1979), 16-25.

————. and Douglas Gomery. "The History of World Cinema: Models for Economic Analysis." *Film Reader* 4 (1979), 35-44.

"Table ronde sur l'histoire du cinéma." *Cinématographe* 60 (September, 1980), 3-14.

Thompson, Kristin. "Cinematic Specificity in Film Criticism and History." *Iris* 1:1 (1983), 39-49.

"Transcript of Discussion: International Federation of Film Archives, May 25, 1974, Montreal." *Cinema Journal* 14 (Winter, 1974-1975), 47-63.

Wollen, Peter. "Cinema and Technology: A Historical Overview." In *The Cinematic Apparatus*, edited by Teresa de Lauretis and Stephen Heath (New York: St. Martin's Press, 1980), 14-22.

Theory and Criticism of the French Avant-Garde Film, Primary Sources

Antoine, André. "L'Avenir du cinéma." *Lectures pour tous* (December, 1919). Reprinted in Philippe Esnault, "Propos d'Antoine," *La Revue du cinéma: image et son* 271 (April, 1973), 45-48.

————. "Propos sur le cinématographe." *Le Film* 166 (December, 1919), [n.p.].

Aragon, Louis. "Du Décor." *Le Film* 131 (16 September 1918), 8-10, translated in Paul Hammond, *The Shadow and Its Shadow* (London: British Film Institute, 1978), 28-31.

Artaud, Antonin. "Le Cinéma et l'abstraction." *Le Monde illustré* (29 October 1927). Translated by Helen Weaver, "Cinema and Abstraction," in *Antonin Artaud: Selected Writings*, edited by Susan Sontag (New York: Farrar, Straus, and Giroux, 1976), 149-150, 610.

————. "Cinéma et réalité." *La Nouvelle Revue Française* 170. (1 November 1927). Translated by Helen Weaver, "Cinema and Reality," in *Antonin Artaud: Selected Writings*, 150-152, 610.

Bandi, Miklos. "La Symphonie Diagonale de Vicking Eggeling [sic]." *Schémas* (1927), 9-19.

Canudo, Ricciotto. "L'Art pour le septième art." *Cinéa* 2 (13 May 1921), 16.

————. "The Birth of the Sixth Art (1911)." Translated by Ben Gibson, Don Ranvaud, Sergio Sokota, and Deborah Young, *Framework* 13 (1980), 3-7.

————. "Manifeste des sept arts." *Gazette des dept arts* 2 (25 January 1923), 2.

————. *L'Usine aux images.* Geneva: Office central d'éditions, 1927.

Carné, Marcel. "Le Caméra, personnage du drame." *Cinémagazine* 9 (12 July 1929). Reprinted in Robert Chazal, *Marcel Carné* (Paris: Seghers, 1965), 87-89.

Cavalcanti, Alberto. "Doctrine." *Cinéa* 73-74 (6 October 1922), 9-12.

Cendrars, Blaise. *L'ABC du cinéma.* Paris: Les Ecrivains réunis, 1926.

Chaperot, Georges. "Henri Chomette et le cinéma pur." *Pour Vous* 13 (14 February 1929), 14.

————. "Henri Chomette: le poème d'images et le film parlé." *La Revue du cinéma* 13 (1 August 1930), 26-36.

Charensol, Georges. "Le Film abstrait." *Les Cahiers du mois* 16/17 (1925), 81-84.

Chavance, Louis. "Symphonie visuelle et cinéma pur." *Cinéa-Ciné-pour-tous* 89 (15 July 1927), 13.

Chomette, Henri. "Cinéma pur, art naissant." *Cinéa-Ciné-pour-tous* 71 (15 October 1926), 13-14.

————. "Seconde étape." *Les Cahiers du mois* 16/17 (1925), 86-88.

Ciels, Henri. "Cinéma d'avant-garde." *Cinémagazine* 5 (20 February 1925), 363-364.

Clair, René. *Cinema Yesterday and Today.* Translated by Stanley Appelbaum. New York: Dover, 1972.

————. "Les films du mois: *La Roue.*" *Théâtre et Comoedia Illustré* 15 (March, 1923), [n.p.].

————. "Rythme." *Les Cahiers du mois* 16/17 (1925), 13-16.

Colette. *Colette at the Movies.* Edited by Alain and Odette Virmaux. Translated by Sarah W. R. Smith. New York: Frederick Unger, 1980.

Delluc, Louis. "Abel Gance." *Le Crapouillot* (16 March 1923), 12.

————. "Les Cinéastes de Paris." *Choses de théâtre* 1 (October, 1921), 13-18.

————. "Cinégraphie." *Le Crapouillot* (March, 1923), [n.p.].

————. *Cinéma et cie.* Paris: Grasset, 1919.

————. "D'Oreste à Rio Jim." *Cinéa* 31 (9 December 1921), 14-15.

————. *Photogénie* Paris: de Brunoff, 1920.

————. "Prologue." *Drames du cinéma* (Paris: Editions du monde nouveau, 1923), i-xix.

Deslaw, Eugène. "After My Premieres." *Close Up* 4 (March, 1929), 88-90.

————. "Cinéma abstrait." *Cercle et carré* 3 (30 June 1930), 10.

Desnos, Robert. *Cinéma.* Edited by André Tchernia. Paris: Gallimard, 1966.

Dulac, Germaine. "Le Cinéma d'avant-garde." In *Le Cinéma des origines à nos jours*, edited by Henri Fescourt (Paris: Editions du cygne, 1932), 357-364. Translated by Robert Lamberton, "The Avant-Garde Cinema," in *The Avant-Garde Film: A Reader in Theory and Criticism*, edited by P. Adams Sitney (New York: New York University Press, 1978), 43-48.

————. "Conférence de Madame Germaine Dulac." *Cinémagazine* 4 (19 December 1924), 516-518.

————. "Du Sentiment à la ligne." *Schémas* (1927), 26-31.

————. "L'Essence du cinéma: l'idée visuelle." *Les Cahiers du mois* 16/17 (1925), 57-66. Translated by Robert Lamberton, "The Essence of Cinema: The Visual Ideal," in *The Avant-Garde Film: A Reader of Theory and Criticism*, 36-42.

————. "Les Esthétiques, les entraves, la cinégraphie intégrale." In *L'Art cinématographique*, Vol. 2 (Paris: Librairie Félix Alcan, 1927), 29-50. Translated by Stuart Liebman, "The Aesthetic. The Obstacles. Integral *Cinégraphie*," *Framework* 19 (1982), 4-9.

————. "Films visuels et anti-visuels." *Le Rouge et le noir* (July, 1928), 31-41. Translated by Robert Lamberton, "Visual and Anti-Visual Films," in *The Avant-Garde Film: A Reader in Theory and Criticism*, 31-35.

————. "*La Mort du soleil* et la naissance du film." *Cinéa* 41 (17 February 1922), 14.

————. "La Musique du silence." *Cinégraphie* 5 (January, 1928), 77-78.

————. "Les Procédés expressifs du cinématographe." *Cinémagazine* 4 (4 July 1924), 15-18; (11 July 1924), 66-68; (18 July 1924), 89-92.

Epstein, Jean. "Les Approches de la vérité." *Photo-Ciné* (15 November-15 December 1928). Reprinted in Epstein, *Ecrits sur le cinéma* (Paris: Seghers, 1974), 1, 191-193.

————. "L'Art d'événement." *Comoedia* (18 November 1927). Reprinted in Epstein, *Ecrits sur le cinéma*, 1, 183-184.

————. *Bonjour Cinéma*. Paris: Editions de la Sirène, 1921.

————. "*Bonjour Cinéma* and other writings." Translated by Tom Milne, *Afterimage* 10 (Autumn, 1981), 8-38.

————. "Le Cinéma et les lettres modernes." In *La Poésie d'aujourd'hui: un nouvel état d'intelligence* (Paris: Editions de la Sirène, 1921), 169-180.

————. *Le Cinématographe vu de l'Etna*. Paris: Les Ecrivains réunis, 1926.

————. "De quelques conditions de photogénie." *Cinéa-Ciné-pour-tous* 19 (15 August 1924), 6-8.

————. "L'Elément photogénique." *Cinéa-Ciné-pour-tours* 12 (1 May 1924), 6-7.

————. "Grossissement." *Promenoir* (January-February, 1921). Translated by Stuart Liebman, "Magnification," *October* 3 (Spring, 1977), 9-15.

————. "Les Images de ciel." *Cinéa-Ciné-pour-tous* 107 (15 April 1928). Reprinted in Epstein, *Ecrits sur le cinéma*, 1, 189-190.

————. "L'Objectif lui-même." *Cinéa-Ciné-pour-tous* 53 (15 January 1926). Reprinted in Epstein, *Ecrits sur le cinéma*, 1, 127-130.

————. "Pour une nouvelle avant-garde." *Cinéa-Ciné-pour-tous* 29 (15 January 1925). Translated by Stuart Liebman, "For a New Avant-Garde," *The Avant-Garde Film: A Reader of Theory and Criticism*, 26-30.

————. "Réalisation de détail." *Cinéa*, 45 (17 March 1922), 12.

Faure, Elie. "De la cinéplastique." *L'Arbre d'Eden* (Paris: G. Crés et cie, 1922), 277-304. Translated by Walter Pach, *The Art of Cineplastics* (Boston: Four Seasons, 1923).

Fescourt, Henri and Jean-Louis Bouquet. *L'Idée et l'écran: opinions sur le cinéma*. 3 vols. Paris: Haberschill et Sergent, 1925-1926.

G., V. "Le Film sans text." *Cinéa* 11 (15 July 1921), 12.

Galtier-Boissière, Jean. "Réflexions sur le cinéma." *Le Crapouillot* (March, 1920), 2-4.

Gance, Abel. "Nos moyens d'expressions." *Cinéa-Ciné-pour-tous* 133 (15 May 1929), 7-9.

————. "Le Temps de l'image est venu." In *L'Art cinématographique*, Vol. 2 (Paris: Librairie Félix Alcan, 1927), 83-102.

Goll, Ivan. "exemple de surréalisme: le cinéma." *Surréalisme* 1 (October, 1924), 3-4.

Gromaire, Marcel. "Idées d'un peintre sur le cinéma." *Le Crapouillot* (1919). Reprinted in Marcel L'Herbier, *Intelligence du cinématographe* (Paris: Corréa, 1946), 239-249.

Henry, Pierre. "Evolution du cinéma: L'Art." *Cinéa-Ciné* 25 (May, 1932), 11-18.

Hugues, Henri. "Tuons l'anecdote. . . ." *Cinéa-Ciné-pour-tous* 128 (1 March 1929), 22-23.

Jacobs, Lewis, ed. *The Compound Cinema: The Film Writings of Harry Alan Potamkin*. New York: Teachers College Press, 1977.

Kirsanoff, Dmitri. "Les mystères de la photogénie." *Cinéa-Ciné-pour-tous*, 39 (15 June 1925), 9.

———. "Pour et contre le film sans texte." *Cinéa-Ciné-pour-tous* 17 (15 July 1924), 8.

Laglenn, Jean-Francis. "Le Peintre au cinéma." *Cinéa* 9 (1 July 1921), 14.

———. "Le Peintre au cinéma." *Cinéa* 42 (24 February 1922), 12.

Landry, Lionel. "A propos du livre de M. Jean Epstein." *Cinéa*, 33 (23 December 1921), 9-10.

———. "Au sujet des sous-titres: une offre intéressante." *Cinéa* 63-64 (22 July 1922), 12.

———. "Caligarisme ou la revanche du théâtre." *Cinéa* 51 (28 April, 1922), 12.

———. "*El Dorado.*" *Cinéa* 12-13 (22 July 1921), 7-8.

———. "Formation de la sensibilité." In *L'Art cinématographique*, Vol. 2 (Paris: Librairie Félix Alcan, 1927), 51-81.

———. "La Musique et le geste." *Cinéa* 27 (11 November 1921), 10-11.

———. "Le Snobisme prouvera que le cinéma est un art." *Le Journal du Ciné-Club* 1 (14 January 1920), 13.

Levinson, André. "Pour une poètique du film." In *L'Art cinématographique*, Vol. 4 (Paris: Librairie Félix Alcan, 1927), 51-88.

L'Herbier, Marcel. "Le Cinématographe et l'espace." In *L'Art cinématographique*, Vol. 4 (Paris: Librairie Félix Alcan, 1927), 1-22.

———. "Cinématographie de France." *Choses de théâtre* 2 (November, 1921), 84-89.

———. "Le Droit de metamorphose." *Cinéa-Ciné-pour-tous* 109 (15 May 1928), 10-11.

———. "Esprit du cinématographe." *Les Cahiers du mois* 16/17 (1925), 29-35.

———. "Hermès et le Silence." *Le Film* 110-111 (29 April 1918), 7-12.

Manaras, Acos. "Du Cinéma subjectif." *Cinéa-Ciné-pour-tous* 125 (15 January 1929), 9-11; 126 (1 February 1929), 10-12.

Maurois, André. "La Poésie du cinéma." In *L'Art cinématographique*, Vol. 3 (Paris: Librairie Félix Alcan, 1927), 1-37.

Moussinac, Léon. "Cinéma: expression sociale." In *L'Art cinématographique*, Vol. 4 (Paris: Librairie Félix Alcan, 1927), 23-49.

———. "Du rythme cinégraphique." *Le Crapouillot* (March, 1923), [n.p.].

———. "Etapes." *Le Crapouillot* (March, 1927), 16-17.

———. *Naissance du cinéma.* Paris: Povolovsky, 1925.

———. *Panoramique du cinéma.* Paris: Le Sans Pareil, 1929.

———. "*La Roue.*" *Le Crapouillot* (16 January 1923), 13.

Musée Galliera. *Exposition de l'art dans le cinéma français.* Paris: Prieur, Dubois et cie, 1924.

Obey, André. "Musique et cinéma." *Le Crapouillot* (March, 1927), 9-12.

Poirier, Léon. "Les Ennemis du septième art." *Le Petit Journal* (23 December 1921), 4.

Porte, Pierre. "A la recherche d'un fil d'Ariane: faisons le point." *Cinéa-Ciné-pour-tous* 49 (15 November 1925), 9.

———. "Le Cinéma, art objectif ou subjectif?" *Cinéa-Ciné-pour-tous*, 69 (15 September 1926), 25-26.

———. "Le Cinéma pur." *Cinéa-Ciné-pour-tous* 52 (1 January 1926), 12-13.

———. "Eclectisme." *Cinéa-Ciné-pour-tous* 58 (1 April 1926), 10.

———. "La Forme et le fond." *Cinéa-Ciné-pour-tous* 22 (1 October 1924), 6-7; 24 (1 November 1924), 27.

———. "L'Idée de photogénie." *Cinéa-Ciné-pour-tous* 17 (15 July 1924), 14-15.

———. "Inventaire du cinéma (Bilan de cinq ans)." *Cinéa-Ciné-pour-tous* 55 (15 February 1926), 11-12.

———. "Musique plastique." *Cinéa-Ciné-pour-tous* 68 (1 September 1926), 22-23.

———. "Une Sensation nouvelle." *Cinéa-Ciné-pour-tous* 64 (1 July 1926), 27-28.

Quesnoy, Pierre-F. "Littérature et cinéma." *Le Rouge et le noir* (July, 1928), 85-104.

Ramain, Paul. "Les chants et danses de la mort." *Cinéa-Ciné-pour-tous* 46 (1 October 1925), 23-24.

———. "De la construction thématique des films." *Cinéa-Ciné-pour-tous* 44 (1 September 1925), 9-11.

———. "Du rythme cinématographique." *Cinémagazine* 9 (22 November 1929), 310-311.

———. "Pour une esthétique intellectuelle du film." *Cinéa-Ciné-pour-tous* 58 (1 April 1926), 13-14.

———. "Sensibilité intelligente d'abord, objectif ensuite." *Cinéa-Ciné-pour-tous* 55 (15 February 1926), 7-8.

609

Rumain, Paul. "Sur la musique visuelle engendrée par certains films." *Cinéa-Ciné-pour-tous* 37 (15 May 1925), 12-13.

———. "Sur le soi-disant 'film pur.' " *Cinéa-Ciné-pour-tous*, 128 (1 March 1929), 7-8.

Richter, Hans. "Mouvement." *Schémas* (1927), 21-23.

Soupault, Philippe. *The American Influence in France*. Seattle: University of Washington Press, 1930.

———. "The U.S.A. Cinema." *Broom* 5 (September, 1922), 65-69.

Spartacus. "Le Décret des '32.' " *Spartacus* 1 (15 April 1928), 1.

Tedesco, Jean. "Une académie cinématographique?" *Cinéa-Ciné-pour-tous* 58 (1 April 1926), 9.

———. "Le Cinéma devant les arts." *Cinéa-Ciné-pour-tous* 18 (1 August 1924), 16-17.

———. "Cinéma dramatique, cinéma poétique." *Cinéa-Ciné-pour-tous* 121 (15 November 1928), 7-8.

———. "Notre Avant-garde aux Arts Décoratifs." *Cinéa-Ciné-pour-tous* 46 (1 October 1925), 11-12.

———. "Pur Cinéma." *Cinéa-Ciné-pour-tous* 80 (1 March 1927), 9-11.

———. "Le Répertoire et l'avant-garde du cinéma." *Cinéa-Ciné-pour-tous* 31 (15 February 1925), 5.

———. "Répertoire des films représentés par le Théâtre du Vieux-Colombier depuis 1924." *Cinéa-Ciné-pour-tous* 88 (1 July 1927), 11-12.

Tokine, B. "L'Esthétique du cinéma." *L'Esprit nouveau* 1 (October, 1920), 85-89.

Verney, Robert. "Composer une image." *Cinémagazine* 9 (3 October 1929), 12-16.

Vesme, G. de. "Ce que doivent être le Ciné-Club et son journal." *Le Journal du Ciné-Club* 1 [1920], 2-4.

Vuillermoz, Emile. "Devant l'écran." *Le Temps* (29 November 1916), 3.

———. "Devant l'écran: Esthétique." *Le Temps* (27 March 1920), 3.

———. "Devant l'écran: Hermès et le Silence." *Le Temps* (23 February 1918), 3.

———. "*La Roue*." *Cinémagazine* 3 (23 February 1923), 329-331; (2 March 1923), 363-366.

Theory and Criticism of the French Avant-Garde Film, Secondary Sources

Abel, Richard. "The Contribution of the French Literary Avant-Garde to Film Theory and Criticism, 1907-1924." *Cinema Journal* 14 (Spring, 1975), 18-40.

———. "Louis Delluc: The Critic as Cinéaste." *Quarterly Review of Film Studies* 1 (May, 1976), 205-244.

Amenguel, Barthélémy. "Muet, années vingt: trois visages de l'avant-garde." *Travelling* 56-57 (Spring, 1980), 23-41.

———. "Rapports entre le cinéma, la littérature et les arts en France dans les années vingt." *Cahiers de la cinémathèque* 33-34 (Autumn, 1981), 161-168.

Arthozoul, Alain. "Le Cinéma français des années vingt et la littérature." *Cahiers de la cinémathèque* 33-34 (Autumn, 1981), 169-173.

Blumer, Ronald. "The Camera as Snowball: France, 1918-1927." *Cinema Journal* 10 (Spring, 1971), 31-39.

Bonnet, Marguerite. "L'Aube du surréalisme et le cinéma." *Etudes cinématographiques* 38-39 (Spring, 1965), 83-101.

Bordwell, David. "French Impressionist Cinema: Film Culture, Film Theory, and Film Style." Ph.D. dissertation, University of Iowa, 1974.

———. "The Musical Analogy." *Yale French Studies* 60 (1980), 141-156.

Bouquet, Jean-Louis. "Panorama de l'activité française, 1916-1928." *Cahiers de la cinémathèque* 33-34 (Autumn, 1981), 57-66.

Breton, André. "Comme dans un bois." *L'Age du cinéma* 4-5 (August-November, 1951), 26-30.

Brunelin, André. "Au Temps du Vieux-Colombier de Jean Tedesco." *Cinéma 60*, 50 (October, 1960), 85-96; *Cinéma 60*, 51 (November-December, 1960), 87-105; *Cinéma 61*, 52 (January, 1961), 87-96.

Brunius, Jacques. *En Marge du cinéma français*. Paris: Arcanes, 1954.

Buache, Freddy. "Le Congrès de La Sarraz 1929." *Travelling* 55 (Summer, 1979), 5-32.

———. "Notes sur quelques films indépendants ou d'avant-garde." *Travelling* 56-57 (Spring, 1980), 142-154.

Burch, Noël. *Marcel L'Herbier*. Paris: Seghers, 1973.

———. "Narrative/Diegesis—Thresholds, Limits." *Screen* 23 (July-August, 1982), 16-33.

——— and Jorge Dana. "Propositions." *Afterimage* 5 (Spring, 1974), 40-66.

——— and Jean-André Fieschi. "La Première Vague." *Cahiers du cinéma* 202 (June-July, 1968), 20, 23-24.

Christie, Ian. "French Avant-Garde Film in the Twenties: From 'Specificity' to Surrealism." In *Film as Film* (London: Arts Council of Great Britain, 1979), 37-45.

Clair, René. *Cinema Yesterday and Today*. Translated by Stanley Appelbaum. New York: Dover, 1972.

Curtis, David. *Experimental Cinema*. New York: Dell, 1971.

D., D-C. "L'Avant-garde française (1917-1932)." *L'Age du cinéma* 6 (December, 1951), 8-15.

Decaudin, Michel. "Les Poètes découvrent le cinéma (1914-1918)." *Etudes cinématographiques* 38-39 (Spring, 1965), 75-82.

Eisenschitz, Bernard. "Histoire de l'histoire (deux périodes du cinéma français: le muet—le génération de 58)." In *Défense du cinéma français* (Paris: La Maison de la culture de la Seine-Saint-Denis, 1975), 19-33.

Epstein, Jean. "Avant-Garde, Arrière-Garde." In *Esprit du cinéma* (Pairs: Jeheber, 1955), 79-102.

Green, Christopher. "Léger and L'Esprit Nouveau." In *Léger and Purist Paris* (London: The Tate Gallery, 1970), 25-82.

Grelier, Robert. "Brève rencontre avec Jean Lods sur 'Les Amis de Spartacus.' " *L'Ecran* 25 (May, 1974), 75-78.

Hammond, Paul, ed. *The Shadow and Its Shadow: Surrealist Writings on Cinema*. London: British Film Institute, 1978.

Jeanne, René and Charles Ford. *Histoire encyclopédique du cinéma*, Vol. 1, *Le Cinéma français, 1895-1929*. (Paris: Robert Laffont, 1947), 241-396.

Kovacs, Steven. *From Enchantment to Rage: The Story of Surrealist Cinema*. New York: Fairleigh Dickinson University Press, 1981.

Kyrou, Ado. *Le Surréalisme au cinéma*. Paris: Arcanes, 1953.

Labarthe, André. "The Emergence of Epstein." *Cahiers du cinéma* 202 (July-August, 1968). Translated by Ian Christie, *Afterimage* 10 (Autumn, 1981), 6-7.

Langlois, Henri. "L'Avant-garde française." *Cahiers du cinéma* 202 (July-August, 1968), 8-17.

Lawder, Standish. *The Cubist Cinema*. New York: New York University Press, 1975.

L'Herbier, Marcel. "Introduction." In *Intelligence du cinématographe*, edited by L'Herbier, (Paris: Corréa, 1946), 11-34.

Liebman, Stuart. "The Film Theory of Jean Epstein." Ph.D. dissertation, New York University, 1980.

———. "French Film Theory, 1910-1921." *Quarterly Review of Film Studies* 8 (Winter, 1983), 1-27.

Matthews, J. H. *Surrealism and Film*. Ann Arbor: University of Michigan Press, 1971.

McCreary, Eugene. "Louis Delluc: Film Theorist, Critic, and Prophet." *Cinema Journal* 16 (Fall, 1976), 14-35.

Michelson, Annette. "Reading Eisenstein Reading *Capital*," *October* 2 (Summer, 1976), 27-38.

Milne, Tom. "The Real Avant-Garde." *Sight and Sound* 32 (Summer, 1963), 148-152.

Mitry, Jean. "Cinéma d'avant-garde—Jean Epstein." *Travelling*, 56-57 (Spring, 1980), 105-109.

———. *Le Cinéma expérimental histoire et perspectives*. Paris: Seghers, 1974.

———. "Deux manifestations peu connues." *Cahiers de la cinémathèque* 30-31 (Summer-Autumn, 1980), 115-116.

———. *Histoire du cinéma*. Vol. 2 *(1915-1923)*. Paris: Editions universitaires, 1969.

———. *Histoire du cinéma*. Vol. 3 *(1923-1930)*. Paris: Editions universitaires, 1973.

Neale, Steven. "Art Cinema as Institution." *Screen* 22 (1981), 11-39.

Penley, Constance. "The Avant-Garde and Its Imaginary." *camera obscura* 2 (1977), 3-33.

Petat, Jacques. "L'Avant-garde française des années vingt." *Cinéma 77*, 217 (January, 1977), 18-31.

Régent, Roger. "Petite histoire des 'Ursulines' dans la grande histoire du cinéma." In *Armand*

Tallier et le Studio des Ursulines, edited by Pierre Lherminier (Paris: A.F.C.A.E., 1963), 13-24.

Renan, Sheldon. *An Introduction to the American Underground Film*. New York: Dutton, 1967.

Richter, Hans. "A History of the Avantgarde." In *Art in Cinema*, edited by Frank Staffacher (San Francisco: Museum of Modern Art, 1947), 6-41.

Sadoul, Georges. *Le Cinéma français*. Paris: Flammarion, 1962.

————. *Histoire générale du cinéma*. Vol. 4, *Le Cinéma devient un art, 1909-1920 (La Première Guerre mondiale)*. Paris: Denoël, 1974.

————. *Histoire générale du cinéma*. Vol. 5, *L'Art muet, 1919-1929*. Paris: Denoël, 1975.

————. *Histoire générale du cinéma*. Vol. 6, *L'Art muet, 1919-1929*. Paris: Denoël, 1975.

————. "Souvenirs d'un témoin." *Etudes cinématographiques* 38-39 (Spring, 1965), 9-28.

Salt, Barry. *Film Style and Technology: History and Analysis*. Forthcoming.

Shattuck, Roger. *The Banquet Years*. Rev. ed. New York: Viking, 1968.

Sitney, P. Adams. "Image and Title in Avant-Garde Cinema." *October* 11 (Winter, 1979), 97-112.

————. *Visionary Film: The American Avant-Garde*. New York: New York University Press, 1976.

Stoneman, Rod. "Perspective Correction: Early Film to the Avant-Garde." *Afterimage* 8/9 (Spring, 1981), 50-63.

Thiher, Allen. *The Cinematic Muse: Critical Studies in the History of French Cinema*. Columbia: University of Missouri Press, 1979.

Trosa, Sylvie. "Archéologie du cinéma." *Cinématographe* 42 (December, 1978), 35-37.

Virmaux, Alain and Odette. "Notes et compléments pour une anthologie." *Cahiers de la cinémathèque* 30-31 (Summer-Autumn, 1980), 77-84.

————. ed. *Les Surréalistes et le cinéma*. Paris: Seghers, 1976.

Willamen, Paul. "On Reading Epstein on *Photogénie*." *Afterimage* 10 (Autumn, 1981), 40-47.

Williams, Linda. *Figures of Desire: A Theory and Analysis of Surrealist Film*. Urbana: University of Illinois Press, 1981.

Selected Filmmakers

1. André Antoine

Antoine, André, "Cinéma d'hier, d'aujourd'hui, de demain." *Le Journal du Ciné-Club* 24 (25 June 1920), 3-4.

————. "Le Public." *Cinémagazine* 1 (18-24 February 1921), 5-7.

————. "Tripatouillages." *Cinémagazine* 1 (25-31 March 1921), 5-6.

Borie, Paul de la. *"La Terre."* *Cinématographie française* 148 (3 September 1921), 29.

Delluc, Louis. "Antoine travaille." *Le Film* 75 (20 August 1917), 5-7.

————. "Notes pour moi." *Le Film* 102 (25 February 1918), 12.

Epardaud, Edmond. *"L'Arlésienne."* *Cinéa* 80 (1 December 1922), 9.

Esnault, Philippe. "Biofilmographie d'André Antoine." *La Revue du cinéma: image et son* 271 (April, 1973), 29-32.

————. "Entretiens avec André-Paul Antoine." *La Revue du cinéma: image et son* 271 (April, 1973), 6-28.

————. *"L'Hirondelle et la mésange* d'André Antoine." *La Revue du cinéma: image et son* 271 (April, 1973), 55-64.

————. "Propos d'Antoine." *La Revue du cinéma: image et son* 271 (April, 1973), 33-49.

Jeanne, René and Charles Ford. *Histoire encyclopédique du cinéma* (Paris: Robert Laffont, 1947), 1, 181-182.

Landry, Lionel. *"La Terre."* *Cinéa* 24 (21 October 1921), 5-6.

Lang, André. *Déplacements et Villégiatures littéraires et suivi de la promenade au royaume des images ou entretiens cinématographiques* (Paris: Renaissance du livre, 1924), 115-123, 183-211.

Lapierre, Marcel. *Les Cent Visages du cinéma*. Paris: Grasset, 1948.

Mitry, Jean. *Histoire du cinéma* (Paris: Editions universitaires, 1969), 2, 250-252.

Prédal, René. *La Société française (1914-1945) à travers le cinéma* (Paris: Armand Colin, 1972), 92-94.

Sadoul Georges. *Histoire générale du cinéma* (Paris: Denoël, 1974), 4, 106-118.

Vuillermoz, Emile. "Devant l'écran." *Le Temps* (7 February 1917), 3.

612

2. Claude Autant-Lara

Autant-Lara, Claude. "Le premier essai de film large: *Construire un Feu* (1928-1929)." *La Revue du cinéma* 16 (1 November 1930), 35-43.

————. "La triste histoire de *Construire un feu.*" *Cahiers de la cinémathèque* 9 (Spring, 1973), 17.

Carné, Marcel. "Les films du mois: *Construire un feu.*" *Cinémagazine* 1 (January, 1931), 65-66.

"*Construire un feu*: essai de reconstitution du film perdu à partir de ce qu'il en reste." *Cahiers de la cinémathèque* 9 (Spring, 1973), 20-23.

Gilson, Paul. "*Construire un feu.*" *Cinéa-Ciné* 11 (January, 1931), 36-37.

Leclerc, Jean. "Jonas, pour de vrai." *Cahiers de la cinémathèque* 9 (Spring, 1973), 18-19.

Lehman, R. "Un Film large: *Construire un feu.*" *Pour Vous* 108 (11 December 1930), 5.

Oms, Marcel. "Claude Autant-Lara dans l'Avant-Garde Française." *Cahiers de la cinémathèque* 9 (Spring, 1973), 12-15.

"Opinions des cinéastes." *Cinéa-Ciné-pour-tous* 109 (15 May 1928), 12-13.

3. Jacques de Baroncelli

Baroncelli, Jacques de. "Le Cinéma n'est pas un art." *Théâtre et Comoedia Illustré* 13 (January, 1923), [n.p.].

————. "Conférence faite par M. Jacques de Baroncelli aux 'Amis du Cinéma' de Nîmes." *Cinémagazine* 5 (1 March 1925), 495-498.

————. "Pantomime, Musique, Cinéma." *Ciné-Journal* 329 (4 December 1915), 41-43.

Boulanger, Pierre. *Le Cinéma colonial* (Paris: Seghers, 1975), 71-72.

Conrad, Jack. "Jacques de Baroncelli et la mer." *Cinémagazine* 7 (17 June 1927), 563-566.

Cornaz, Oscar. "A Paimpol avec Jacques de Baroncelli pour le départ de la Marie." *Cinéa-Ciné-pour-tous* 14 (1 June 1924), 28-29.

Daven, André. "*Nêne.*" *Théâtre et Comoedia Illustré* 22 (October, 1923), [n.p.].

Delluc, Louis. "Cinéma." *Paris-Midi* (1 February 1919), 2; (2 February 1919), 2.

————. "Notes pour moi." *Le Film* 116 (3 June 1918), 14, 16.

Epardaud, Edmond. "Comment Jacques de Baroncelli réalise *Pêcheur d'Islande.*" *Cinéa-Ciné-pour-tous* 12 (1 May 1924), 15.

————. "*Nitchevo.*" *Cinéa-Ciné-pour-tous* 63 (15 June 1926), 11-12.

————. "*Nitchevo,* L'Agonie du sous-marin." *Cinéa-Ciné-pour-tous* 78 (1 February 1927), 21-23.

Fescourt, Henri. *La Foi et les montagnes* (Paris: Paul Montel, 1959), 326-331.

Jeanne, René and Charles Ford. *Histoire encyclopédique du cinéma* (Paris: Robert Laffont, 1974), 1, 188, 383-387.

Lang, André. *Déplacements et Villégiatures littéraires et suivi de la promenade au royaume des images ou entretiens cinématographiques* (Paris: Renaissance du livre, 1924), 148-153.

Lapierre, Marcel. *Les Cent Visages du cinéma* (Paris: Grasset, 1948), 130-131, 155-156.

Leprohon, Pierre. *Cinquante Ans de cinéma français* (Paris: Editions du cerf, 1954), 53.

McKee, Gerald. *Film Collecting* (London: Tantivy Press, 1978), 82-83.

Mirbel, Jean de. "Jacques de Baroncelli." *Cinémagazine* 3 (20 April 1923), 117.

Mitry, Jean. *Histoire du cinéma.* (Paris: Editions universitaires, 1969), 2, 263.

————. "Jacques de Baroncelli." *Théâtre et Comoedia Illustré* 22 (October, 1923), [n.p.].

Sadoul, Georges. *Histoire générale du cinéma* (Paris: Denoël, 1974), 4, 484-485.

————. *Histoire générale du cinéma* (Paris: Denoël, 1975), 5, 198-199.

Tedesco, Jean. "*Pêcheur d'Islande.*" *Cinéa-Ciné-pour-tous* 24 (1 November 1924), 7-11.

Vuillermoz, Emile. "Devant l'écran." *Le Temps* (6 June 1917), 3.

4. Raymond Bernard

Antoine, André-Paul. *Antoine, père et fils: souvenirs du Paris littéraire et théâtral, 1900-1939* (Paris: René Juillard, 1962), 213-216.

Barsacq, Léon. *Caligari's Cabinet and Other Grand Illusions: A History of Film Design.* Revised and edited by Elliot Stern (Boston: New York Graphic Society, 1976), 44-46.

Canudo, Ricciotto. *L'Usine aux images* (Geneva: Office central d'édition, 1927), 99.

Cinémagazine (special number devoted to *Joueur d'échecs*) 7 (14 January 1927), 60-75.

Coissac, G.-Michel. "L'Evolution du cinématographe et la réalisation de quelques grands films." *Tout-Cinéma* (Paris: Filma, 1929), 13-32.

Delluc, Louis. "Quelques films français." *Cinéa* 18 (9 September 1921), 5.

Diamant-Berger, Henri. *Il était une fois le cinéma* (Paris: Jean Claude Simoën, 1977), 64-66, 74-78, 83.

Epardaud, Edmond. *"Le Joueur d'échecs."* *Cinéa-Ciné-pour-tous* 77 (15 January 1927), 14-16.

————. "Raymond Bernard." *Cinéa-Ciné* 4 (June, 1930), 33-34.

————. *"Triplepatte."* *Cinéa* 73-74 (6 October 1922), 2-3.

Fescourt, Henri. *La Foi et les montagnes* (Paris: Paul Montel, 1959), 313-318.

Flamand, Gilbert. "Le Miracle des loups." *Cinémagazine* 4 (29 February 1924), 346-348.

Galtier-Boissière, Jean. "Au Cinéma: *Le Secret de Rosette Lambert.*" *Le Crapouillot* (1 November 1920), 16-17.

Jeanne, René. *"Le Miracle des loups*: la bataille de Beauvais réconstituée à Carcassonne." *Cinéa-Ciné-pour-tous* 12 (1 May 1924), 21-24.

———— and Charles Ford. *Histoire encyclopédique du cinéma* (Paris: Robert Laffont, 1947), 1, 389-391.

"Joueur d'échecs." *La Petite Illustration* 8 (5 February 1927), 1-12.

Landry, Lionel. *"La Maison vide."* *Cinéa* 25 (28 October 1921), 7.

Lang, André. *Déplacements et Villégiatures littéraires et suivi de la promenade au royaume des images ou entretiens cinématographiques* (Paris: Renaissance du livre, 1924), 175-177.

Lapierre, Marcel. *Les Cent Visages du cinéma* (Paris: Grasset, 1948), 157-159.

Mitry, Jean. *Histoire du cinéma.* (Paris: Editions universitaires, 1969), 2, 262-263.

————. *Histoire du cinéma.* (Paris: Editions universitaires, 1973), 3, 512.

Moussinac, Léon. "Intérieurs modernes au cinéma." *Cinémagazine* 1 (25 February 1921), 5-8.

"Le Petit Café." *Ciné-pour-tous* 16 (20 December 1919), 8.

Ramain, Paul. "L'Influence du cinéma sur la musique." *Cahiers du mois* 16/17 (1925), 120-126.

Sadoul, Georges. *Histoire générale du cinéma* (Paris: Denoël, 1974), 4, 488.

————. *Histoire générale du cinéma*, (Paris: Denoël, 1975), 5, 201.

Salles, Jacques. "Raymond Bernard." *L'Avant-Scène du cinéma* 256 (15 November 1980), 177-208.

Tinchant, André. *"Le Miracle des loups."* *Cinémagazine* 4 (21 November 1924), 315-316.

5. Luis Buñuel

Aranda, José Francisco. *Luis Buñuel: A Critical Biography.* Translated by David Robinson. New York: Da Capo Press, 1975.

Aron, Robert. "Films de révolte." *La Revue du cinéma* 5 (15 November 1929), 41-45.

Bouissounouse, J. "Dans la salle." *La Revue du cinéma* 5 (15 November 1929), 74.

Brunius, J. Bernard. "La Revue des films: *Un Chien andalou.*" *La Revue du cinéma* 4 (15 October 1929), 67-78.

Buache, Freddy. *The Cinema of Luis Buñuel.* Translated by Peter Graham. New York: Barnes, 1973.

Buñuel, Luis. *"Un Chien andalou."* *La Révolution surréaliste* (December, 1929). Reprinted in *L'Age d'or and Un Chien andalou*, translated by Marianne Alexandre (London: Lorrimer, 1968), 85-116.

Conrad, Randall. "The Minister of the Interior Is on the Telephone: The Early Films of Luis Buñuel." *Cinéaste* 7 (1976), 2-14.

Curtis, David. *Experimental Cinema* (New York: Dell, 1971), 30-31.

Drummond, Phillip. "Textual Space in *Un Chien andalou.*" *Screen* 18 (1977), 55-119.

Durgnat, Raymond. *Luis Buñuel.* Berkeley: University of California Press, 1968.

Higginbotham, Virginia. *Luis Buñuel.* Boston: Twayne, 1980.

Kelman, Ken. "The Other Side of Realism." In *The Essential Cinema*, edited by P. Adams Sitney (New York: New York University Press, 1975), 112-133.

Kovacs, Steven. *From Enchantment to Rage: The Story of Surrealist Cinema.* New York: Fairleigh Dickinson University Press, 1981.

Kyrou, Ado. *Luis Buñuel.* Translated by Adrienne Foulke. New York: Simon and Schuster, 1963.

Lapierre, Marcel. *Les Cent Visages du cinéma* (Paris: Grasset, 1948), 203-204.

Lenauer, Jean. "Deux nouveaux films: *Le Mystère du château du dé* et *Un Chien andalou.*" *Pour Vous* 30 (13 June 1929), 4.

Matthews, J. H. *Surrealism and Film* (Ann Arbor: University of Michigan Press, 1971), 84-90.

Mitry, Jean. *Histoire du cinéma* (Paris: Editions universitaires, 1973), 3, 348-352.

Sadoul, Georges. "Souvenirs d'un témoin." *Etudes cinématographiques* 38-39 (Spring, 1965), 9-28.

Sandro, Paul. "The Space of Desire in *An Andalusian Dog*." *1978 Film Studies Annual* (1979), 57-63.

Sitney, P. Adams. "The Idea of Morphology." *Film Culture* 53-54-55 (1972), 1-24.

Staffacher, Frank. "Notes on the Making of *Un Chien andalou*." *Art in Cinema* (San Francisco: Museum of Modern Art, 1947), 29-30.

Thiher, Allen. *The Cinematic Muse: Critical Studies in the History of French Cinema* (Columbia: University of Missouri Press, 1980), 24-37.

Tual, Denise. *Le Temps dévoré*. Paris: Fayard, 1980.

Van Wert, William. "Intertitles." *Sight and Sound* 49 (Spring, 1980), 98-105.

Vigo, Jean. *"Un Chien Andalou."* [*Vers un cinéma social* (1930)]. Translated by Marianne Alexandre in *L'Age d'or and Un Chien andalou* (London: Lorrimer, 1968), 75-76, 81.

Virmaux, Alain. "Une promesse mal tenue, le film surréaliste (1924-1932)." *Etudes cinématographiques* 38-39 (Spring, 1965), 103-133.

———— and Odette Virmaux. *Les Surréalistes et le cinéma*. Paris: Seghers, 1976.

Williams, Linda. *Figures of Desire: A Theory and Analysis of Surrealist Film*. Urbana: University of Illinois Press, 1981.

————. "The Prologue to *Un Chien andalou*: A Surrealist Film Metaphor." *Screen* 17 (1976/1977), 24-33.

6. Alberto Cavalcanti

Amunategui, Francisco. "Les Ecrans: *En rade*." *La Revue nouvelle* 4 (December, 1927), [n.p.].

Aron, Robert. "Alberto Cavalcanti." *Close Up* 1 (October, 1927), 56-60.

Barnouw, Erik. *Documentary: A History of the Non-Fiction Film* (New York: Oxford University Press, 1974), 74.

Barsam, Richard Meran. *Nonfiction Film: A Critical History* (New York: Dutton, 1975), 29-30.

Cavalcanti, Alberto. "Doctrine." *Cinéa* 73-74 (6 October 1922), 9-12.

————. "Interviews et enquêtes." *Cinégraphie* 2 (15 October 1927), 17.

Chapman, Jay. "Two Aspects of the City: Cavalcanti and Ruttman." In *The Documentary Tradition*, edited by Lewis Jacobs. 2nd ed. (New York: Norton, 1979), 37-42.

Chavance, Louis. "L'Impressionnisme cinématographique." *Cinégraphie* 2 (15 October 1927), 21.

Dréville, Jean. "Films: *En rade*." *Cinégraphie* 1 (15 September 1927), 11.

Jeanne, René and Charles Ford. *Histoire encyclopédique du cinéma* (Paris: Robert Laffont, 1947), 1, 279-282.

Lapierre, Marcel. *Les Cent Visages du cinéma* (Paris: Grasset, 1948), 170.

Leprohon, Pierre. *Cinquante Ans de cinéma français* (Paris: Editions du cerf, 1954), 91-92.

Mitry, Jean. *Histoire du cinéma* (Paris: Editions universitaires, 1973), 3, 386-387.

Monegal, Emir Rodriguez. "Alberto Cavalcanti (1955)." In *Non-Fiction Film Theory and Criticism*, edited by Richard M. Barsam (New York: Dutton, 1976), 239-249.

Rambaud, Pierre. "Romans d'écran." *Cinéa-Ciné-pour-tous* 85 (15 May 1927), 22.

Sadoul, Georges. *Histoire générale du cinéma* (Paris: Denoël, 1975), 6, 359-361.

Sussex, Elizabeth. "Cavalcanti in England." *Sight and Sound* 44 (Autumn, 1975), 205-211.

"Yvette." *Cinéa-Ciné-pour-tous* 99 (15 December 1927), 19.

7. René Clair

Alby, Marianne. "Un Entretien avec René Clair." *Cinéa-Ciné-pour-tous* 42 (1 August 1925), 21-22.

Amenguel, Barthélémy. *René Clair*. Paris: Seghers, 1969.

Arnoux, Alexandre. *"Les Deux Timides* de Labiche par René Clair—*La Tour*." *Pour Vous* 3 (6 December 1928), 8-9.

Brunius, Bernard. "René Clair." *Cinéa-Ciné-pour-tous* 79 (15 February 1927), 11-12.

Brunius, Jacques. *En marge du cinéma français* (Paris: Arcanes, 1954), 95-100.

Carroll, Noel. "*Entr'acte*, Paris, and Dada." *Millennium* 1 (1977), 5-11.

Charensol, Charles and Roger Régent. *Un Maître du cinéma: René Clair*. Paris: La Table ronde, 1952.

Clair, René. *A nous la liberté and Entr'acte*. Translated by Richard Jacques and Nicola Hayden. New York: Simon and Schuster, 1970.

615

Clair, René. *Cinema Yesterday and Today.* Translated by Stanley Appelbaum. New York: Dover, 1972.

———. "Une Enquête à Londres: l'avenir du film parlant." *Pour Vous* 28 (30 May 1929), 3; 29 (6 June 1929), 2; 30 (13 June 1929), 7.

———. "*An Italian Straw Hat.*" In *Masterworks of French Cinema* (New York: Harper & Row, 1974), 20-70.

———. "Picabia, Satie, et la première d'*Entr'acte.*" *Figaro littéraire* (June, 1967). Translated by Richard Jacques and Nicola Hayden, *A nous la liberté and Entr'acte,* 108-112.

"Conférence de Monsieur René Clair." *Cinémagazine* 4 (5 December 1924), 420-422.

Dale, R. C. "René Clair's *Entr'acte* or Motion Victorious." *Wide Angle* 2:2 (1978), 38-43.

Daven, André. "*Paris qui dort.*" *Théâtre et Comoedia Illustré* 22 (October, 1923), [n.p.].

Delons, André. "*Les Deux Timides.*" *La Revue du cinéma* 2 (February, 1929), 65.

Desnos, Robert. "Une nouvelle formule: *Le Fantôme du Moulin Rouge*" and "René Clair et le nouveau cinéma." In *Cinema* (Paris: Gallimard, 1966), 129-132.

Epardaud, Edmond. "*La Proie du vent.*" *Cinéa-Ciné-pour-tous* 76 (1 January 1927), 12.

———. "René Clair fonde un genre nouveau avec *Un Chapeau de paille d'Italie.*" *Cinéa-Ciné-pour-tous* 90 (1 August 1927), 15.

———. "*Le Voyage imaginaire.*" *Cinéa-Ciné-pour-tous* 48 (1 November 1925), 14.

Eyre, Jean. "Les films de demain: *Paris qui dort.*" *Mon-Ciné* (7 February 1924), [n.p.].

Fescourt, Henri. *La Foi et les montagnes* (Paris: Paul Montel, 1959), 277-292.

"Un Film instantanéiste—*Entr'acte.*" *Théâtre et Comoedia Illustré* 39 (1 November 1924), [n.p.].

Gallez, Douglas W. "Satie's *Entr'acte*: A Model of Film Music." *Cinema Journal* 16 (Fall, 1976), 36-50.

Jacobs, Lewis, ed. *The Compound Cinema: The Film Writings of Harry Alan Potamkin* (New York: Teachers College Press, 1977), 401-409.

Jeanne, René and Charles Ford. *Histoire encyclopédique du cinéma* (Paris: Robert Laffont, 1947), 1, 359-369.

Jourdan, Robert. "Le Style Clair-Meerson." *La Revue du cinéma* 27 (1 October 1931), 32-33.

Kovacs, Steven. *From Rage to Enchantment: The Story of Surrealist Cinema.* New York: Fairleigh Dickinson University Press, 1981.

Lapierre, Marcel. *Les Cent Visages du cinéma* (Paris: Grasset, 1948), 166-169.

Lenauer, Jean. "The Cinema in Paris: *Les Deux Timides.*" *Close Up* 4 (January, 1929), 68-69.

———. "René Clair." *Close Up* 3 (November, 1928), 34-38.

Leprohon, Pierre. *Cinquante Ans du cinéma français* (Paris: Editions du cerf, 1954), 84-90.

Listel, Jean, "*Le Fantôme du Moulin Rouge.*" *Cinémagazine* 4 (12 December 1924), 465-468.

McGerr, Celia. *René Clair.* Boston: Twayne, 1980.

Michelson, Annette. "Dr. Crase and Mr. Clair." *October* 11 (Winter, 1979), 30-53.

Mitry, Jean. "Films: *Un Chapeau de paille d'Italie.*" *Cinégraphie* 4 (15 December 1927), 69.

———. *Histoire du cinéma* (Paris: Editions universitaires, 1973), 3, 362-370.

———. *René Clair.* Paris: Editions universitaires, 1960.

Moussinac, Léon. "Le Cinéma: *Le Fantôme du Moulin Rouge.*" *Le Crapouillot* (1 April 1925), 26.

———. "Panoramique du cinéma [1929]." In *L'Age ingrat du cinéma* (Paris: Editeurs français réunis, 1967), 293-298.

Richard, Jean. "La personnalité de René Clair." *Cinéa-Ciné* 23 (March, 1932), 15-17.

Roche, Catherine de la. *René Clair.* London: British Film Institute, 1958.

Sadoul, Georges. *Histoire générale du cinéma* (Paris: Denoël, 1975), 6, 338-344, 349-351.

Sandro, Paul. "Parodic Narration in *Entr'acte.*" *Film Criticism* 4 (Fall, 1979), 44-55.

Taylor, John Russell. "René Clair." In *Cinema: A Critical Dictionary,* Vol. 1, edited by Richard Roud (New York: Viking, 1980), 213-220.

Thiher, Allen. *The Cinematic Muse: Critical Studies in the History of French Cinema* (Columbia: University of Missouri Press, 1979), 64-69.

8. Louis Delluc

Abel Richard. "Louis Delluc: The Critic as Cinéaste." *Quarterly Review of Film Studies* 1 (May, 1976), 205-244.

———. "Reconsidering Louis Delluc." *Quarterly Review of Film Studies* 2 (August, 1977), 388-393.

Arroy, Jean. "Louis Delluc (1890-1924)." *Cinéa-Ciné-pour-tous* 81 (15 March 1927), 13-15.

Bizet, René. "Les bons films: *La Fête espagnole.*" *Le Crapouillot* (1 June 1920), 16.

Clair, René. *Cinema Yesterday and Today*. Translated by Stanley Appelbaum (New York: Dover, 1972), 66-67.

Cornaz, Oscar. "L'Oeuvre cinégraphique écrite de Louis Delluc." *Cinéa-Ciné-pour-tous* 131 (15 April 1929), 6-8.

"Cosmograph donnera au public, le 8 septembre, *La Femme de nulle part*." *Cinéa* 67-68 (25 August 1922), 16-17.

Delluc, Louis. *Charlot*. Paris: de Brunhoff, 1921.

———. "Cinéma." *Paris-Midi* (12 May 1919), 2; (16 May 1919), 2 (18 May 1919), 2; (25 May 1919), 2; (26 May 1919), 2; (14 June 1919), 2.

———. *Cinéma et cie*. Paris: Grasset, 1919.

———. "Les Cinéastes." *Le Monde nouveau* 5 (15 August-1 September 1922), 34-44.

———. "Les Cinéastes de Paris." *Choses de théâtre* 1 (October, 1921), 13-18.

———. "Cinégraphie." *Le Crapouillot* (March, 1923), [n.p.].

———. "D'Oreste à Rio Jim." *Cinéa* 31 (9 December 1921), 14-15.

———. *Drames du cinéma*. Paris: Editions du Monde nouveau, 1923.

———. "Huit jours de fièvre." *Cinéa* 20 (23 September 1921), 9-12.

———. "L'Inondation." *Cinéa-Ciné-pour-tous* 7 (15 January 1924), 9-11.

———. *La Jungle du cinéma*. Paris: Editions de la Sirène, 1921.

———. *Photogénie*. Paris: de Brunhoff, 1920.

Epstein, Jean. "Memoires inachevées." *Ecrits sur le cinéma* (Paris: Seghers, 1974), 1, 42-44.

Fescourt, Henri. *La Foi et les montagnes* (Paris: Paul Montel, 1959), 252-265.

"Fièvre." *Cinéa* 10 (8 July 1921), 19-21.

Francis, Eve. *Temps héroïque*. Paris: Denoël, 1949.

Galtier-Boissière, Jean. "Au Cinéma: *Le Silence*." *Le Crapouillot* (16 October 1920), 15-16.

Jeanne, René and Charles Ford. *Histoire encyclopédique du cinéma* (Paris: Robert Laffont, 1947), 1, 190-191, 245-252.

Landry, Lionel. *"La Femme de nulle part."* *Cinéa* 69-70 (8 September 1922), 6-7.

———. *"Fièvre."* *Cinéa* 30 (2 December 1921), 8-9.

———. "Louis Delluc." *Cinémagazine* 4 (4 April 1924), 41-42.

———. "La Musique et le geste." *Cinéa* 27 (11 November 1921), 10-11.

Lang, André. *Déplacements et Villégiatures littéraires et suivi de la promenade au royaume des images ou entretiens cinématographiques* (Paris: Renaisance du livre, 1924), 132-136.

Lapierre, Marcel. *Les Cent Visages du cinéma* (Paris: Grasset, 1948), 146-147.

Leprohon, Pierre. *Cinquante Ans de cinéma français* (Paris: Editions du cerf, 1954), 59-62.

McCreary, Eugene. "Louis Delluc, Film Theorist, Critic, and Prophet." *Cinema Journal* 16 (Fall, 1976), 14-35.

Mirbel, Jean de. "Les films de la semaine: *L'Inondation*." *Cinémagazine* 4 (2 May 1924), 223-224.

Mitry, Jean. *Histoire du cinéma* (Paris: Editions universitaires, 1969), 2, 427-432.

———. "Louis Delluc." *Théâtre et Comoedia Illustré* 30 (15 March 1924), [n.p.].

———. "Louis Delluc." *L'Avant-Scène du cinéma* 61 (January, 1971), 1-56.

Moussinac, Léon. "Au Cinéma: *La Boue*." *Le Crapouillot* (1 May 1921), 19-20.

———. "En présentation privée: *La Femme de nulle part*." *Le Crapouillot* (16 April 1922), 17.

———. "Louis Delluc." *Le Crapouillot* (16 April 1924), 16-17.

———. "Naissance du cinéma [1925]." In *L'Age ingrat du cinéma* (Paris: Editeurs français réunis, 1967), 103-109.

Ramain, Paul. "Un Précurseur: Louis Delluc." *Cinéa-Ciné-pour-tous* 127 (15 February 1929), 9-11.

Rops, Daniel. "Note sur Louis Delluc, homme du cinéma." *Cahiers du mois* 16/17 (1925), 231-239.

Sadoul, Georges. *Histoire générale du cinéma* (Paris: Denoël, 1974), 4, 393-400.

———. *Histoire générale du cinéma* (Paris: Denoël, 1975), 5, 51-80.

Tariol, Marcel. *Louis Delluc*. Paris: Seghers, 1965.

Tedesco, Jean. "Louis Delluc n'est plus." *Cinéa-Ciné-pour-tous* 10 (1 April 1924), 6-7.

9. *Carl Dreyer*

Arnoux, Alexandre. "Enfin nous avons vu la version intégrale de *Jeanne d'Arc* de Carl Dreyer." *Pour Vous* 26 (16 May 1929), 2.

Audard, Pierre. *"La Passion de Jeanne d'Arc."* *La Revue du cinéma* 2 (February, 1929), 66-67.

Bordwell, David. *Filmguide to La Passion de Jeanne d'Arc.* Bloomington: Indiana University Press, 1973.

———. *The Films of Carl Theodor Dreyer* (Berkeley: University of California Press, 1981), 66-92, 212-217.

———. "Imploded Space: Film Style in *The Passion of Joan of Arc.*" *Film Studies Annual* (1976), 99-105.

Burch, Noël. "Carl Theodor Dreyer: The Major Phase." In *Cinema: A Critical Dictionary*, Vol. 1, edited by Richard Roud (New York: Viking, 1980), 296-310.

Carl Th. Dreyer: Danish Film Director, 1889-1968. Copenhagen: Danish Ministry of Foreign Affairs, 1968.

Delahaye, Michel. "Interview with Carl Dreyer." Translated by Rose Kaplan, *Cahiers du cinéma in English* 4 (1966). Reprinted in Andrew Sarris, *Interviews with Film Directors* (New York: Bobbs-Merrill, 1967), 140-163.

Doolittle, Hilda. "Joan of Arc." *Close Up* 3 (July, 1928), 15-23.

"Dossier-film #3—*La Passion de Jeanne d'Arc.*" *L'Avant-Scène du cinéma* 100 (February, 1970), 44-58.

Dreyer, Carl. "Ecrits." *Cahiers du cinéma* 124 (October, 1961), 23-35.

Duca, Lo. "Les Films vieillissent-ils?" *Cinématographe* 36 (March, 1978), 25-27.

Duren, J. "Quand Dreyer tournait *Jeanne d'Arc.* . . ." *Pour Vous* 4 (15 December 1928), 11.

Fescourt, Henri. *La Foi et les montagnes* (Paris: Paul Montel, 1959), 292-294.

Hall, Mordaunt. "Poignant French Film." *New York Times* (31 March 1929), Sec. 8, 7.

"La *Jeanne d'Arc* de Dreyer à la Salle Marivaux." *Cinéa-Ciné-pour-tous* 119 (15 October 1928), 16.

Kelman, Ken. "Dreyer." In *Film Culture Reader*, edited by P. Adams Sitney (New York: Praeger, 1970), 141-159.

Klinger, Werner. "Analytical Treatise on the Dreyer Film, *The Passion of Joan of Arc*, with Appendix of a Constructive Critique." *Experimental Cinema* 1 (February, 1930), 9-10.

Linderman, Deborah. "Uncoded Images in the Heterogeneous Text." *Wide Angle* 3:3 (1979), 34-41.

Mitry, Jean. *Histoire du cinéma* (Paris: Editions universitaires, 1973), 3, 389-395.

Moussinac, Léon. "Panoramique du cinéma [1929]." In *L'Age ingrat du cinéma* (Paris: Editeurs français réunis, 1967), 284-288.

Nash, Mark. *Dreyer* (London: British Film Institute, 1977), 52-55.

Parrain, Philippe. "Dreyer: Cadres et mouvements." *Etudes cinématographiques* 53-56 (1967).

Pipolo, Tony. "The Poetry of the Problematic." *Quarterly Review of Film Studies* 7 (Spring, 1982), 157-167.

Potamkin Harry Alan. "Dreyer, in Theory and Practice." In *The Compound Cinema*, edited by Lewis Jacobs (New York: Teachers College Press, 1977), 132-136.

Ramain, Paul. "De *Ben-Hur* à *La Passion de Jeanne d'Arc.*" *Cinéa-Ciné-pour-tous* 121 (15 November 1928), 11-12.

———. "Les sens des décors et le mode harmonique dans *La Passion de Jeanne d'Arc*, de Carl Dreyer." *Cinéa-Ciné-pour-tous* 113 (15 July 1928), 23-24.

Sacha. *"La Passion de Jeanne d'Arc."* *Cinéa-Ciné-pour-tous* 125 (15 January 1929), 12.

Sadoul, Georges. *Histoire générale du cinéma* (Paris: Denoël, 1975), 6, 375-389.

Sémolué. Jean. "Carl Th. Dreyer." In *Anthologie du cinéma*, Vol. 6 (Paris: L'Avant-Scène du cinéma, 1971), 105-160.

10. Germaine Dulac

Amunategui, Francisco. "Les Ecrans: *L'Invitation au voyage.*" *La Revue nouvelle* 4 (December, 1927), [n.p.].

Artaud, Antonin. *"The Shell and the Clergyman."* Translated by Victor Corti. *Tulane Drama Review* 11 (Fall, 1966), 173-178.

Audard, Pierre. "Cinéma et réalité." *Cinéa-Ciné-pour-tous* 107 (15 April 1928), 31-32.

Bencey, André. "Germaine Albert-Dulac." *Cinémagazine* 2 (24 February 1922), 231-235.

Bizet, René. "Les bons films: *La Fête espagnole.*" *Le Crapouillot* (1 April 1920), 16.

Buache, Freddy. "Films indépendants et d'avant-garde." *Travelling* 55 (Summer, 1979), 49-50.

Clair, René. "Les films du mois: *La Souriante Madame Beudet.*" *Théâtre et Comoedia Illustré* 24 (December, 1923), [n.p.].

Colombat, A. *"L'Invitation au voyage."* *On Tourne* (November-December, 1928), 10.

Cornwell, Regina. "Maya Deren and Germaine Dulac." *Film Library Quarterly* 5 (Winter, 1971-1972), 29-38.

Derain, Lucie. "*La Coquille et le clergyman*, rêve filmé." *Cinématographie française* 471 (12 November 1927), 50.

Dozoretz, Wendy. "Dulac versus Artaud." *Wide Angle* 3:1 (1979), 46-53.

Dulac, Germaine. "Cinéma: L'Action de l'avant-garde cinématographique." *L'Etat moderne* 12 (December, 1931), 1057-1060.

———. "Le Cinéma, art des nuances spirituelles." *Cinéa-Ciné-pour-tous* 28 (1 January 1925), 18.

———. "Le Cinéma d'Avant-Garde." In *Le Cinéma des origines à nos jours*, edited by Henri Fescourt (Paris: Editions du cygne, 1932), 357-364. Translated by Robert Lamberton, "The Avant-Garde Cinema," in *The Avant-Garde Film: A Reader of Theory and Criticism*, edited by P. Adams Sitney (New York: New York University Press, 1978), 43-48.

———. "Conférence de Madame Germaine Dulac." *Cinémagazine* 4 (19 December 1924), 516-518.

———. "Du Sentiment à la ligne." *Schémas* (1927), 26-31.

———. "L'Essence du cinéma: l'idée visuelle." *Les Cahiers du mois* 16/17 (1925), 57-66. Translated by Robert Lamberton, "The Essence of the Cinema: The Visual Idea," *The Avant-Garde Film: A Reader of Theory and Criticism*, 36-42.

———. "Les Esthétiques, les entraves, la cinégraphie intégrale." In *L'Art cinématographie*, Vol. 2 (Paris: Librarie Félix Alcan, 1927), 29-50. Translated by Stuart Liebman, "The Aesthetics. The Obstacles. Integral *Cinégraphie*," *Framework* 19 (1982), 4-9.

———. "Films visuels et anti-visuels." *Le Rouge et le noir* (July, 1928), 31-41. Translated by Robert Lamberton, "From 'Visual and Anti-Visual Films,' " in *The Avant-Garde Film: A Reader of Theory and Criticism*, 31-35.

———. "La Folie des vaillants (fragments)." *Cinégraphie* 1 (15 September 1927), 9-10.

———. "La Mort du soleil et la naissance du film." *Cinéa* 41 (17 February 1922), 14.

———. "La musique du silence." *Cinégraphie* 5 (January, 1928), 77-78.

———. "Opinions." *Cinégraphie* 2 (15 October 1927), 40.

———. "Les Procédés expressifs du cinématographe." *Cinémagazine* 4 (4 July 1924), 15-18; (11 July 1924), 66-68; (18 July 1924), 89-92.

Fescourt, Henri. *La Foi et les montagnes* (Paris: Paul Montel, 1959), 295-303.

Flitterman, Sandy. "Heart of the Avant-Garde: Some Biographical Notes on Germaine Dulac." *Women & Film* 1 (1974), 58-61, 103.

———. "Montage/Discourse: Germaine Dulac's *The Smiling Madame Beudet*." *Wide Angle* 4:3 (1980), 54-59.

———. "Theorizing the 'Feminine': Woman as the Figure of Desire in *The Seashell and the Clergyman*." Paper delivered at the Society for Cinema Studies Conference, Los Angeles, 30 June 1982, 1-18.

———. "Women, Representation, and Cinematic Discourse: The Example of French Cinema." Ph.D. dissertation, University of California at Berkeley, 1982.

Ford, Charles. "Germaine Dulac." *Anthologie du cinéma* 31 (January, 1968), 1-48.

Galtier-Boissière, Jean. "La Critique des films." *Le Crapouillot* (1 April 1920), 17.

"Germaine Dulac." *Cinéa-Ciné-pour-tous* 41 (15 July 1925), 10-11.

Jarville, Robert de. "Les Arts contre le cinéma: Conférence par Mme Germaine Dulac." *Cinémagazine* 5 (17 April 1925), 112-114.

Jeanne, René and Charles Ford. *Histoire encyclopédique du cinéma* (Paris: Robert Laffont, 1947), 1, 188-190, 257-263.

Landry, Lionel. "*La Mort du soleil*." *Cinéa* 36 (13 January 1922), 15.

Lapierre, Marcel. *Les Cent Visages du cinéma* (Paris: Grasset, 1948), 129-130, 154-155.

Leger, Albine. "*La Souriante Madame Beudet*." *Cinémagazine* 3 (9 February 1923), 240.

Leprohon, Pierre. *Cinquante Ans de cinéma français* (Paris: Editions du cerf, 1954), 69-71.

Mitry, Jean. "Deux manifestations peu connues." *Cahiers de la cinémathèque* 30-31 (Summer-Autumn, 1980), 115-116.

———. *Histoire du cinéma* (Paris: Editions universitaires, 1969), 2, 259-260, 442-444.

———. *Histoire du cinéma* (Paris: Editions universitaires, 1973), 3, 345-347, 542-544.

Moussinac, Léon. "Le Cinéma: *La Souriante Madame Beudet*." *Le Crapouillot* (16 July 1923), 15-16.

Sadoul, Georges. *Histoire générale du cinéma* (Paris: Denoël, 1974), 4, 393-400.

———. *Histoire générale du cinéma* (Paris: Denoël, 1975), 5, 107-122.

———. *Histoire générale du cinéma* (Paris: Denoël, 1975), 6, 346-349, 523-524.

———. "Souvenirs d'un témoin." *Etudes cinématographiques* 38-39 (Spring, 1965), 9-28.

Sontag, Susan. "Artaud." In *Selected Writings* (New York: Farrar, Straus, and Giroux, 1976), xxvi-xxvii.

Van Wert, William. "Germaine Dulac: First Feminist Filmmaker." *Women & Film* 1 (1974), 55-57, 103.

Virmaux, Alain. "Artaud and Film." *Tulane Drama Review* 11 (Fall, 1966), 154-165.

———. "Une promesse mal tenue: le film surréaliste (1924-1932)." *Etudes cinématographiques* 38-39 (Spring, 1965), 103-133.

——— and Odette Virmaux. *Les Surréalistes et le cinéma*. Paris: Seghers, 1976.

11. Julien Duvivier

Boulanger, Pierre. *Le Cinéma colonial* (Paris: Seghers, 1975), 77.

Chirat, Raymond. "Julien Duvivier." *Premier Plan* 50 (December, 1968), 3-136.

Dreyfus, J.-P. *"Maman Colibri."* *La Revue du cinéma* 9 (1 April 1930), 65.

Jacobs, Lewis, ed. *The Compound Cinema: The Film Writings of Harry Alan Potamkin* (New York: Teachers College Press, 1977), 280-281.

"Poile de carotte." *Ciné-Ciné-pour-tous* 54 (1 February 1926), 21.

Wahl, Lucien. *"Au bonheur des dames."* *Pour Vous* 72 (3 April 1930), 11.

12. Jean Epstein

Abel, Richard. *"La Chute de la maison Usher*: Reversal and Liberation." *Wide Angle* 3:1 (1979), 38-44.

Allendy, Dr. "La Valeur psychologique de l'image." *L'Art cinématographique*, 1 (1926). Reprinted in *Intelligence du cinématographe*, ed. Marcel L'Herbier (Paris: Corréa, 1946), 304-318.

Amunategui, Francisco. "Les Ecrans: *Six et Demi, Onze*." *La Revue nouvelle* 31-32 (June-July, 1927), 100.

Bachmann, Gideon and Jean Benoît-Lévy, ed. *Cinemages #2. The First Comprehensive Presentation of the Work of Jean Epstein in the United States*. New York: Group for Film Study, 1955.

Bardèche, Maurice and Robert Brasillach. *The History of the Motion Pictures*. Translated by Iris Barry (New York: Norton, 1938), 161-162, 227-228.

Blakeston, Oswell. *"La Chute de la maison Usher."* *Close Up* 5 (August, 1929), 150-152.

Brunius, Jacques. *En Marge du cinéma français* (Paris: Arcanes, 1954), 75-78.

Burch, Noël and Jean-André Fieschi. "La Première Vague." *Cahiers du cinéma* 202 (June-July, 1968), 20, 23-24.

Chevalley, Freddy. "Ciné-Club de Genève." *Close Up* 6 (May, 1930), 407-411.

Clair, René. "Les films du mois: *Coeur fidèle*." *Théâtre et Comoedia Illustré* 27 (1 February 1924), [n.p.]

"Coeur fidèle et l'opinion de la presse." *Cinéa-Ciné-pour-tous* 27 (15 December 1924), 27-28.

Cohen, Keith. *Film and Fiction* (New Haven: Yale University Press, 1979), 93-98.

Derain, Lucie. "Jean Epstein: Virtuose et poète." *Cinémonde* 260 (12 October 1933), 837.

Dréville, Jean. "La Critique du film." *On Tourne* (July, 1928), 3.

———. "Films: *Six et demi × onze*." *Cinégraphie* 1 (15 September 1927), 14.

———. "Films: *Six et demi—onze*." *Cinégraphie* 3 (15 November 1927), 51.

———. *"La Glace à trois faces."* *Cinégraphie* 5 (15 January 1928), 87-90.

Epardaud, Edmond. *"Les Aventures de Robert Macaire."* *Cinéa-Ciné-pour-tous* 51 (15 December 1925), 14-15.

———. *"Mauprat* de Jean Epstein." *Cinéa-Ciné-pour-tous* 72 (1 November 1926), 13-14.

Epstein, Jean. "L'Art événement." *Comoedia* (18 November 1927). Reprinted in *Cahiers du cinéma* 202 (June-July, 1968), 55. Translated by Tom Milne as "Art of Incidence." *Afterimage* 10 (Autumn, 1981), 30, 32.

———. *Bonjour Cinéma*. Paris: Editions de la Sirène, 1921.

———. "*Bonjour Cinéma* and Other Writings." Translated by Tom Milne, *Afterimage* 10 (Autumn, 1981), 8-38.

———. *Le Cinématographe vu de l'Etna*. Paris: Les Ecrivains réunis, 1926.

———. *Ecrits sur le cinéma*. 2 vols. Paris: Seghers, 1974.

————. *Esprit de cinéma*. Paris: Jeheber, 1955.

————. "The Essence of Cinema" and "The Avant-Garde Cinema." Translated by Stuart Liebman, in *The Avant-Garde Film: A Reader of Theory and Criticism*, edited by P. Adams Sitney (New York: New York University Press), 24-30.

————. *La Lyrosophie*. Paris: Editions de la Sirène, 1922.

————. "Magnification and other writings." Translated by Stuart Liebman, *October* 3 (Spring, 1977), 9-25.

————. *La Poésie d'aujourd'hui: un nouvel état d'intelligence*. Paris: Editions de la Sirène, 1921.

————. "Six et demi × onze (un kodak)." *Cinégraphie* 2 (15 October 1927), 33-35.

Fescourt, Henri. *La Foi et les montagnes* (Paris: Paul Montel, 1959), 303-312.

Fieschi, Jean-André. "Jean Epstein." In *Cinema: A Critical Dictionary*, Vol. 1, edited by Richard Roud (New York: Viking, 1980), 328-334.

"Les films du mois: *Sa Tête*." *Cinémagazine* 2 (February, 1930), 79.

Gait, M. "Notes sur *Six et demi × onze*." *Cinéa-Ciné-pour-tous* 115 (15 August 1928), 24.

Hagan, John. "Cinema and the Romantic Tradition." *Millennium* 1 (Winter, 1975-1976), 38-51.

Haudiquet, Philippe. "Jean Epstein." *Anthologie du cinéma* 19 (November, 1966), 465-520.

Hot, Pierre. *"La Chute de la maison Usher."* *Cinéa-Ciné-pour-tous* 106 (1 April 1928), 21-22.

Jeanne, René and Charles Ford. *Histoire encyclopédique du cinéma* (Paris: Robert Laffont, 1947), 1, 271-279.

Kéfer, Pierre. "En marge de *Mauprat*." *Cinéa-Ciné-pour-tous* 72 (1 October 1926), 21-22.

Landry, Lionel. "A propos du livre de M. Jean Epstein." *Cinéa* 33 (23 December 1921), 9-10.

Lang, André. *Déplacements et Villégiatures littéraires et suivi de la promenade au royaume des images ou entretiens cinématographiques* (Paris: Renaissance du livre, 1924), 177-179.

Langlois, Henri. "Jean Epstein (1897-1953)." *Cahiers du cinéma* 24 (June, 1953), 8-31.

Lapierre, Marcel. *Les Cent Visages du cinéma* (Paris: Grasset, 1948), 159-161.

Leprohon, Pierre. *Cinquante Ans de cinéma français* (Paris: Editions du cerf, 1954), 74-80.

————. "Films d'aujourd'hui: *Finis terrae*." *Cinéa-Ciné-pour-tous* 134 (1 June 1929), 8.

————. *Jean Epstein*. Paris: Seghers, 1964.

Liebman, Stuart. "The Film Theory of Jean Epstein." Ph.D. dissertation, New York University, 1980.

Mitry, Jean. "Cinéma d'avant-garde—Jean Epstein." *Travelling* 56-57 (Spring, 1980), 105-109.

————. *Histoire du cinéma* (Paris: Editions universitaires, 1969), 2, 439-442.

————. *Histoire du cinéma* (Paris: Editions universitaires, 1973), 3, 378-382.

Moussinac, Léon. "Le Cinéma: *L'Affiche*." *Le Crapouillot* (16 March 1925), 30.

————. "Le Cinéma: *Coeur fidèle*." *Le Crapouillot* (1 December 1923), 18-19.

————. "La Critique des films: *L'Auberge rouge*." *Le Crapouillot* (1 August 1923), 16, 18.

————. "Naissance du cinéma [1925]." In *L'Age ingrat du cinéma* (Paris: Editeurs français réunis, 1967), 118-121.

Ploquin, Raoul. "Jean Epstein." *Cinéa-Ciné-pour-tous* 52 (1 January 1926), 14.

Ramain, Paul. "Pour *La Belle Nivernaise*." *Cinéa-Ciné-pour-tous* 111 (15 June 1928), 15-16.

————. "Présentation à Montpelier du film de Jean Epstein: *L'Affiche*." *Cinémagazine* 5 (8 May 1925), 224.

————. "Sensibilité intelligente d'abord, objectif ensuite." *Cinéa-Ciné-pour-tous* 55 (15 February 1926), 7.

"Robert Macaire." *La Petite Illustration* 4 (28 November 1925), 1-12.

Sadoul, Georges. *Histoire générale du cinéma* (Paris: Denoël, 1975), 5, 122-138.

————. *Histoire générale du cinéma* (Paris: Denoël, 1975), 6, 363-368.

"Sélect Présentations." *Spartacus* 3 (15 June 1928), 3.

Tedesco, Jean. *"La Belle Nivernaise."* *Cinéa-Ciné-pour-tous* 9 (15 March 1924), 22-23.

Thiher, Allen. *The Cinematic Muse: Critical Studies in the History of French Cinema* (Columbia: University of Missouri Press, 1979), 20-23.

Trevise, Robert. *"La Chute de la maison Usher."* *Cinéma* (15 March 1928), [n.p.].

Vincent-Bréchignac, J. "Les goémonniers, la mer, Ouessant, *Finis terrae*, par Jean Epstein." *Pour Vous* 22 (18 April 1929), 11.

Wahl, Lucien. "L'Acteur doit-il être l'instrument du réalisateur?" *Pour Vous* 30 (13 June 1929), 11.

621

Wahl, Lucien. "Allan Edgar Poe [sic] à l'écran: *La Chute de la maison Usher*, film d'Epstein." *Pour Vous* 24 (2 May 1929), 9.

Willamen, Paul. "On Reading Epstein on *Photogénie*." *Afterimage* 10 (Autumn, 1981), 40-47.

Z. "L'Ecran vous offre cette semaine: *Sa Tête*." *Pour Vous* 60 (9 January 1930), 5.

13. Henri Fescourt

Barsacq, Léon. *Caligari's Cabinet and Other Grand Illusions: A History of Film Design.* Revised and edited by Elliot Stern (Boston: New York Graphic Society, 1976), 39.

Beylie, Claude and Francis Lacassin. "A la recherche d'un cinéma perdu: entretien avec Jean-Louis Bouquet, Henri Fescourt, Joë Hamman, Gaston Modot." *Cahiers de la cinémathèque* 33-34 (Autumn, 1981), 11-27.

———. "Henri Fescourt." *Anthologie du cinéma* 26 (June, 1967), 277-328.

Boulanger, Pierre. *Le Cinéma colonial* (Paris: Seghers, 1975), 66-70.

Colombat, A. *"L'Occident." On Tourne* (October, 1928), 4.

Delbron, Jean. "L'Interprétation des *Misérables*." *Cinémagazine* 5 (13 November 1925).

Epardaud, Edmond. *"Les Misérables." Cinéa-Ciné-pour-tous* 50 (1 December 1925), 13-14.

Fescourt, Henri. "A propos de mon film, *Les Grands*." *Cahiers de la cinémathèque*, special number (Spring, 1976), 18-20.

———"Esprit moderne." *Schémas* (1927), 33-39.

———. *La Foi et les montagnes*. Paris: Paul Montel, 1959.

———, ed. *Le Cinéma des origines à nos jours*. Paris: Editions du cygne, 1932.

——— and Jean-Louis Bouquet. *L'Idée et l'écran: opinions sur le cinéma.* 3 vols. Paris: Haberschill et Sergent, 1925-1926.

"Henri Fescourt nous parle des *Misérables*." *Cinémagazine* 5 (10 April 1925).

Jeanne, René and Charles Ford. *Histoire encyclopédique du cinéma* (Paris: Robert Laffont, 1947), 1, 393-395.

Lapierre, Marcel. *Les Cent Visages du cinéma* (Paris: Grasset, 1948), 162.

Mitry, Jean. *Histoire du cinéma* (Paris: Editions universitaires, 1973), 3, 388.

"Monte-Cristo." Cinéa-Ciné-pour-tous 135 (15 June 1929), 27.

Sadoul, Georges. *Histoire générale du cinéma* (Paris: Denoël, 1975), 5, 201, 204.

14. Louis Feuillade

Breteque, François de la. "Le Film en tranches: les mutations du film à épisodes, 1918-1926." *Cahiers de la cinémathèque* 33-34 (Autumn, 1981), 87-102.

Delluc, Louis. "Cinéma." *Paris-Midi* (6 July 1919), 2.

Desnos, Robert. *"Fantômas, Les Vampires, Les Mystères de New York* (1927)." In *Cinéma* (Paris: Gallimard, 1966), 153-155.

Fescourt, Henri. *La Foi et les montagnes* (Paris: Paul Montel, 1959), 81-96.

Feuillade, Louis. "Manifeste de la série 'Le film esthétique.' " *Ciné-Journal* 92 (28 May 1910), and "Manifeste de 'La Vie telle qu'elle est.' " *Ciné-Journal* 139 (22 April 1911). Reprinted in Marcel Lapierre, ed., *L'Anthologie du cinéma* (Paris: La nouvelle édition, 1946), 73-77.

———. *"Vindicta*, scénario original." *Cahiers de la cinémathèque* 33-34 (Autumn, 1981), 132-152.

Florey, Robert. "Louis Feuillade." *Cinémagazine* 1 (2 September 1921), 9.

Jeanne, René and Charles Ford. *Histoire encyclopédique du cinéma* (Paris: Robert Laffont, 1947), 1, 211-213.

Kyrou, Ado. *Le Surréalisme au cinéma* (Paris: Arcanes, 1953), 55-62.

Lacassin, Francis. *Louis Feuillade*. Paris: Seghers, 1964.

———. "Louis Feuillade." *Anthologie du cinéma* 15 (1967), 217-288.

———. *Pour une contre histoire du cinéma* (Paris: Union générale d'éditions, 1972), 23-43, 55-71, 103-126, 189-194.

Lang, André. *Déplacements et Villégiatures littéraires et suivi de la promenade au royaume des images ou entretiens cinéematographiques* (Paris: Renaissance du livre, 1924), 161-165.

Lapierre, Marcel. *Les Cent Visages du cinéma* (Paris: Grasset, 1948), 137-139, 165.

Marie, Jean-Charles. "Hommage à Louis Feuillade." *La Revue du cinéma* 25 (1 August 1931), 3-11.

Mitry, Jean. *Histoire du cinéma.* (Paris: Editions universitaires, 1969), 2, 246-249.

Roud, Richard. "Louis Feuillade and the Serial." In *Cinema: A Critical Dictionary*, Vol. 1, edited by Richard Roud (New York: Viking, 1980), 348-359.

—————. "Louis Feuillade: Maker of Melodrama." *Film Comment* 12 (November-December, 1976), 8-11.

Sadoul, Georges. *Histoire générale du cinéma.* (Paris: Denoël, 1974), 4, 97-98.

"Special Feuillade, *Fantômas.*" *L'Avant-Scène du cinéma* 271/272 (1-15 January 1982), 3-92.

15. Jacques Feyder

Arnoux, Alexandre. "Crainquebille n'a pas vieilli." *Pour Vous* 7 (3 January 1929), 11.

Auriol, Jean-Georges. "La Critique des films: *Les Nouveaux Messieurs.*" *La Revue du cinéma* 1 (December, 1928), 28-29.

Bachy, Victor. "Jacques Feyder." *Anthologie du cinéma* 18 (October, 1966), 409-464.

Bonneau, Albert. "*Visages d'enfants.*" *Cinémagazine* 3 (14 September 1923), 385-388.

Boulanger, Pierre. *Le Cinéma colonial* (Paris: Seghers, 1975), 31-41.

Chamine. "Le Festival Feyder." *Pour Vous* 160 (10 December 1931), 5, 14.

Chaperot, Georges. "L'Oeuvre classique de Jacques Feyder." *Cinémagazine* 9 (September, 1931), 17-20.

—————. "Souvenirs sur Jacques Feyder." *La Revue du cinéma* 12 (1 July 1930), 29-40.

Danvers, V.-Guillaume. "A propos de *L'Atlantide.*" *Cinémagazine* 1 (14 October 1921), 5-7.

Delluc, Louis. "Quelques films français." *Cinéa* 18 (9 September 1921), 8.

Dréville, Jean. "La Critique du film: *Thérèse Raquin.*" *On Tourne* 3 (1 May 1928), 2.

Epardaud, Edmond. "*Visages d'enfants.*" *Cinéa-Ciné-pour-tous* 30 (1 February 1925), 13-14.

Fescourt, Henri. *La Foi et les montagnes* (Paris: Paul Montel, 1959), 267-277.

Feyder, Jacques. "Je crois au film parlant." *Pour Vous* 31 (20 June 1929), 3.

—————. "Transposition visuelle." *Les Cahiers du mois* 16/17 (1925), 67-71.

————— and Françoise Rosay. *Le Cinéma, notre métier.* Vésenaz-Geneva: Pierre Cailler, 1956.

Ford, Charles. *Jacques Feyder.* Paris: Seghers, 1973.

"*Gribiche,*" *Cinéa-Ciné-pour-tous* 49 (15 November 1925), 7-8.

Jeanne, René and Charles Ford. *Histoire encyclopédique du cinéma* (Paris: Robert Laffont, 1947), 1, 345-358.

Landry, Lionel. "*L'Atlantide.*" *Cinéa* 21 (30 September 1921), 4-5.

Lapierre, Marcel. *Les Cent Visages du cinéma* (Paris: Grasset, 1948), 162-164.

Lenauer, Jean. "The Cinema in Paris: *Les Nouveaux Messieurs.*" *Close Up* 4 (January, 1929), 67.

Manevy, René. "Nos metteurs-en-scène: Jacques Feyder." *Ciné-Miroir* 23 (1 April 1923), 103.

Mitry, Jean. *Histoire du cinéma.* (Paris: Editions universitaires, 1973), 3, 370-377.

—————. "L'Image." *Cahiers du mois* 16/17 (1925), 252-254.

Moussinac, Léon. "Le Cinéma: *L'Image.*" *Le Crapouillot* (1 July 1925), 15.

—————. "Panoramique du cinéma [1929]." In *L'Age ingrat du cinéma* (Paris: Editeurs français réunis, 1967), 269-292.

Ploquin, Raoul. "Jacques Feyder." *Cinéa-Ciné-pour-tous* 61 (15 May 1926), 15-16.

—————. "Jacques Feyder." *Cinéa-Ciné-pour-tous* 73 (15 November 1926), 20.

Roud, Richard. "Jacques Feyder." In *Cinema: A Critical Dictionary*, Vol. 1, edited by Richard Roud (New York: Viking, 1980), 359-360.

Sadoul, Georges. *Histoire générale du cinéma* (Paris: Denoël, 1975), 5, 165-198.

Tedesco, Jean. "Raquel Meller dans *Carmen.*" *Cinéa-Ciné-pour-tous* 73 (15 November 1926), 9-16.

16. Abel Gance

Abel, Richard. "Abel Gance's Other Neglected Masterwork: *La Roue.*" *Cinema Journal* 22 (Winter, 1983), 26-41.

—————. "Charge and Countercharge: Incoherence and Coherence in Abel Gance's *Napoléon.*" *Film Quarterly* 35 (Spring, 1982), 2-14.

Arroy, Juan. "Abel Gance, sa vie, son oeuvre." *Cinéa-Ciné-pour-tous* 3 (15 December 1923), 5-7.

—————. "L'Appareil portatif et la nouvelle technique cinématographique." *Cinémagazine* 7 (17 June 1927), 577-581.

—————. *En Tournant Napoléon avec Abel Gance.* Paris: Renaissance du livre, 1927.

—————. "La Technique de *Napoléon.*" *Cinéa-Ciné-pour-tous* 86 (1 June 1927), 9-12.

Bordwell, David. "The Musical Analogy." *Yale French Studies* 60 (1980), 141-156.

Borger, Lenny. "British Slighted on *Napoléon.* . . ." *Variety* 76 (4 November 1981), 1, 38.

BIBLIOGRAPHY

Brownlow, Kevin. "Abel Gance's *Napoléon* Returns from Exile." *American Film* 6 (January-February, 1981), 28-32, 68, 70-73.
————. "How a Lost Masterpiece of the Cinema was Recreated." *Observer Magazine* (9 March 1980), 32-40.
————. *The Parade's Gone By* (Berkeley: University of California Press, 1976), 595-651.
Canudo, Ricciotto. "Préface." In *La Roue, après le film d'Abel Gance* (Paris: J. Ferenczi et fils, 1923), 3-4.
————. *L'Usine aux images* (Geneva: Office central d'éditions, 1927), 127-128.
Clair, René. "Les films du mois: *La Roue*." *Théâtre et Comoedia Illustré* 15 (March, 1923), [n.p.].
Coissac, G.-Michel. *Les Coulisses du cinéma* (Paris: Pittoresques, 1929), 112-114.
Colette. "*Mater Dolorosa*." *Le Film* (4 June 1917). Translated by Sarah W. R. Smith, *Colette at the Movies*, edited by Alain and Odette Virmaux (New York: Frederick Ungar, 1980), 23-25.
Daria, Sophie. *Abel Gance, hier et demain*. Paris: La Palatine, 1959.
Delluc, Louis. "Abel Gance." *Le Crapouillot* (16 March 1923), 12.
————. "Abel Gance, après *La Zone de la mort*." *Le Film* 84 (22 October 1917), 7.
————. "Notes pour moi." *Le Film* 99 (4 February 1918), 13-14.
Doublon, Lucien. "*La Roue*." *Cinémagazine* 2 (29 December 1922), 444-445.
Drew, William M. "Abel Gance: Prometheus Bound." *Take One* 6 (July 1978), 30-32, 45.
Eisenschitz, Bernard. "Abel Gance." In *Cinema: A Critical Dictionary*, Vol. 1, edited by Richard Roud (New York: Viking, 1980), 404-415.
————. "From *Napoléon* to *New Babylon*." *Afterimage* 10 (Autumn, 1981), 49-55.
Epstein, Jean. "Abel Gance." *Photo-Ciné* 1 (September, 1927). Reprinted in Epstein, *Écrits sur le cinéma* (Paris: Seghers, 1974), 1, 173-177.
Esnault, Philippe. "Filmographie d'Abel Gance." *Cahiers du cinéma* 43 (January, 1955), 18-23.
Fescourt, Henri. *La Foi et les montagnes* (Paris: Paul Montel, 1959), 165-173, 243-252.
Gance, Abel. *La Fin du monde*. Paris: Tallandier, 1931.
————. *J'Accuse*. Paris: La Lampe merveilleuse, 1922.
————. *Napoléon vu par Abel Gance*. Paris: Librairie Plon, 1927.
————. "Nos moyens d'expression." *Cinéa-Ciné-pour-tous* 133 (15 May 1929), 7-9.
————. *Prisme*. Paris: Gallimard, 1930.
————. "Qu'est-ce que le cinématographe? Un sixième art." *Ciné-Journal* (9 March 1912). Reprinted in Marcel L'Herbier, *Intelligence du cinématographe* (Paris: Corréa, 1946), 91-92.
————. *La Roue*. Paris: Tallandier, 1930.
————. "Le Temps de l'image est venu." In *L'Art cinématographique*, Vol. 2 (Paris: Librairie Félix Alcan, 1927), 83-102.
Icart, Roger. *Abel Gance*. Toulouse: Institut pédagogique national, 1960.
————. "A la découverte de *La Roue*." *Cahiers de la cinémathèque* 33-34 (Autumn, 1981), 185-192.
"*J'Accuse*." *Cinématographie française* 20 (22 March 1919), 11, 15-18; 21 (29 March 1919), 17-20; 22 (5 April 1919), 15-18; 23 (12 April 1919), 17-20.
Jeanne, René. *Napoléon vu par Abel Gance*. Paris: Tallandier, 1927.
————. "Une seconde version de *La Roue*." *Cinémagazine* 4 (29 February 1924), 342-344.
———— and Charles Ford. *Abel Gance*. Paris: Seghers, 1963.
————. *Histoire encyclopédique du cinéma* (Paris: Robert Laffont, 1967), 1, 165-167, 182-188, 321-343.
Kael, Pauline. "Abel Gance." *New Yorker* (16 February 1981), 114-123.
Kramer, Steven Philip and James Michael Welsh. *Abel Gance*. Boston: Twayne, 1978.
Lang, André. *Déplacements et Villégiatures littéraires et suivi de la promenade au royaume des images ou entretiens cinématographiques* (Paris: Renaissance du livre, 1924), 137-146.
Lapierre, Marcel. *Les Cent Visages du cinéma* (Paris: Grasset, 1948), 127-128, 150-152.
Lawder, Standish. *The Cubist Cinema* (New York: New York University Press, 1975), 79-97.
Leprohon, Pierre. *Cinquante Ans de cinéma français* (Paris: Editions du cerf, 1954), 61-69.
Mitry, Jean. "Abel Gance." *Théâtre et Comoedia Illustré* 33 (1 May 1924), [n.p.]
————. "Abel Gance nous parle de *La Roue* . . . Abel Gance nous parle du Cinéma." *Cinéa-Ciné-pour-tous* 3 (15 December 1923), 8.
————. *Histoire du cinéma* (Paris: Editions universitaires, 1969), 2, 254-259, 435-438.
————. *Histoire du cinéma* (Paris: Editions universitaires, 1973), 3, 352-362.

624

————. "Napoléon à l'écran." *Photo-Ciné* 4 (April, 1927), 55-57.

Moussinac, Léon. "Naissance du cinéma [1925]." In *L'Age ingrat du cinéma* (Paris: Editeurs français réunis, 1967), 109-114.

————. "Panoramique du cinéma [1929]." In *L'Age ingrat du cinéma* (Paris: Editeurs français réunis, 1967), 267-277.

————. "La Roue." *Le Crapouillot* (16 January 1923), 13.

"Napoléon." *Cinéa-Ciné-pour-tous* 81 (15 March 1927), 26.

Pappas, Peter. "The Superimposition of Vision: *Napoléon* and the Meaning of Fascist Art." *Cinéaste* 11 (1981), 4-13.

"Le Procédé du triple écran." *Cinégraphie* 1 (15 September 1927), 17.

Sadoul, Georges. *Histoire générale du cinéma* (Paris: Denoël, 1974), 4, 375-393.

————. *Histoire générale du cinéma* (Paris: Denoël, 1975), 5, 140-161.

————. *Histoire générale du cinéma* (Paris: Denoël, 1975), 6, 317-327.

Tedesco, Jean. "Napoléon vu par Abel Gance." *Cinéa-Ciné-pour-tous* 83 (15 April 1927), 9-10.

Tinchant, André. "Abel Gance." *Cinémagazine* 3 (14 September 1923), 363-367.

Truffaut, François. *The Films of My Life*. Translated by Leonard Mayhew (New York: Simon and Schuster, 1978), 29-32.

Vuillermoz, Emile. "Abel Gance et Napoléon." *Cinémagazine* 7 (25 November 1927), 335-340.

————. "Devant l'écran." *Le Temps* (10 March 1917), 3.

————. "La Dixième Symphonie." *Le Temps* (6 November 1918), 3.

————. "Napoléon." *Cinéa-Ciné-pour-tous* 87 (15 June 1927), 5-6.

————. "La Roue." *Cinémagazine* 3 (23 February 1923), 329-331; (2 March 1923), 363-366.

17. Jean Grémillon

Agel, Henri. *Jean Grémillon*. Paris: Seghers, 1969.

Arnoux, Alexandre. "Un Film français de qualité: *Gardiens de phare.*" *Pour Vous* 46 (3 October 1929), 8-9.

Eisenschitz, Bernard. "Jean Grémillon." In *Cinema: A Critical Dictionary*, Vol. 1, edited by Richard Roud (New York: Viking, 1980), 447-449.

Epardaud, Edmond. "Maldone." *Cinéa-Ciné-pour-tous* 105 (15 March 1928), 13-15.

Jeanne, René and Charles Ford. *Histoire encyclopédique du cinéma* (Paris: Robert Laffont, 1947), 1, 284-285.

Kast, Pierre. "Jean Grémillon." *Premier Plan* 5 (January, 1960), 1-40.

Lapierre, Marcel. *Les Cent Visages du cinéma* (Paris: Grasset, 1948), 171.

Le Dantec, Mireille Latil. "Jean Grémillon: le réalisme et le tragique." *Cinématographe* 40 (October, 1978), 43-50.

"Maldone." *Cinémagazine* 8 (16 March 1928), 445-463.

Mazeline, François. "Jean Grémillon." *Cinéa-Ciné-pour-tous* 105 (15 March 1928), 9-10.

Mitry, Jean. *Histoire du cinéma* (Paris: Editions universitaires, 1973), 3, 384.

Sadoul, Georges. *Histoire générale du cinéma* (Paris: Denoël, 1975), 6, 368-370.

Trevise, Robert. "Maldone." *Cinéa-Ciné-pour-tous* 110 (1 June 1928), 31.

————. "Les Présentations: *Gardiens de phare.*" *Cinéa-Ciné-pour-tous* 142 (15 October 1929), 10.

18. Dmitri Kirsanoff

Boulanger, Pierre. *Le Cinéma colonial* (Paris: Seghers, 1975), 74-75.

Buache, Freddy. "Films indépendants et d'avant-garde." *Travelling* 55 (Summer, 1979), 67-68.

Cornaz, Louise. "Brumes d'automne." *Cinéa-Ciné-pour-tous* 124 (1 January 1929), 12.

Demeure, Jacques. "Eloge de Dmitri Kirsanoff." *Positif* 22 (March, 1957), 27-28.

"Film sans sous-titre, film d'avant-garde: *L'Ironie du destin.*" *Cinéa-Ciné-pour-tous* 7 (15 February 1924), 20-21.

The Film Society Programs, 1925-1939 (New York: Arno Press, 1972), 30.

Goreloff, Michel. "Suggérer. . . ." *Cinéa-Ciné-pour-tous* 91 (15 August 1927), 24.

Henry, Pierre. "Films d'amateurs." *Cinéa-Ciné-pour-tous* 32 (1 March 1925), 9-12.

————. "Nadia Sibirskaya." *Cinéa-Ciné-pour-tous* 54 (1 February 1926), 19-20.

Jeanne, René and Charles Ford. *Histoire encyclopédique du cinéma* (Paris: Robert Laffont, 1947), 1, 266-268.

Kirsanoff, Dmitri. "Les Mystères de la photogénie." *Cinéa-Ciné-pour-tous* 39 (15 June 1925), 9.

————. "Pour et contre le film sans texte." *Cinéa-Ciné-pour-tous* 17 (15 July 1924), 8.

Kirsanoff, Dmitri. "Les Problèmes de la photogénie." *Cinéa-Ciné-pour-tous* 62 (1 June 1926), 9-10.

Lapierre, Marcel. *Les Cent Visages du cinéma* (Paris: Grasset, 1948), 180-181.

"Menilmontant à Genève." *Cinéa-Ciné-pour-tous* 101 (1 January 1928), 22-23.

Michel, Walter S. "In Memoriam of Dimitri Kirsanov, a Neglected Master." In *Film Culture Reader*, edited by P. Adams Sitney (New York: Praeger, 1970), 37-41.

Prévost, Jean. "Le Cinéma: *Menilmontant.*" *Le Crapouillot* (1 January 1927), 34-35.

Sadoul, Georges. *Histoire générale du cinéma* (Paris: Denoël, 1975), 6, 361-363.

Sitney, P. Adams. "Dmitri Kirsanoff." In *Cinema: A Critical Dictionary*, Vol. 2, edited by Richard Roud (New York: Viking, 1980), 551-553.

19. Marcel L'Herbier

Amiyuet, Fred.-Ph. "Marcel L'Herbier, cinéaste français." *Photo-Ciné*, 2 (15 February 1927), 22-25.

Arroy, Juan, "Marcel L'Herbier." *Cinéa-Ciné-pour-tous* 72 (1 November 1926), 9-12.

Berge, François. *"Feu Mathias Pascal."* *Cahiers du mois* 16/17 (1925), 247-248.

Beylie, Claude. "Marcel L'Herbier ou l'intelligence du cinématographe." *L'Avant-Scène du cinéma* 209 (1 June 1978), 27/i-29/iii.

―――. "Sur cinq films de Marcel L'Herbier." *Ecran* 43 (15 January 1976), 71-72.

―――, and Michel Marie. "Entretien avec Marcel L'Herbier." *L'Avant-Scène du cinéma* 209 (1 June 1978), 30/iv-42/xvi.

Blin, Roger. "La Critique des films: *L'Argent.*" *La Revue du cinéma* 2 (February, 1929), 68-69.

Brossard, Jean-Pierre. *Marcel L'Herbier et son temps.* Locarno: Editions Cinédiff, 1980.

Burch, Noël. *Marcel L'Herbier.* Paris: Seghers, 1973.

―――. "Marcel L'Herbier." In *Cinema: A Critical Dictionary*, Vol. 2, edited by Richard Roud (New York: Viking, 1980), 621-628.

―――. "Revoir *L'Argent.*" *Cahiers du cinéma* 202 (June-July, 1968), 45-48.

Canudo, Ricciotto. "Le Cinéma: *Don Juan et Faust.*" *Les Nouvelles littéraires* (21 October 1922), 4.

Catelain, Jaque. *Marcel L'Herbier.* Paris: Jacques Vautrain, 1950.

"Ce que la presse étrangère pense du *Vertige.*" *Cinéa-Ciné-pour-tous* 72 (1 November 1926), 12.

Clair, René. "Les films du mois: *Don Juan et Faust.*" *Théâtre et Comoedia Illustré* 14 (February, 1923), [n.p.].

Delluc, Louis. "De *Rose-France* à *El Dorado.*" *Cinéa* 1 (6 May 1921), 13-14.

―――. *"Don Juan et Faust."* *Cinéa* 57-58 (9 June 1922), 13.

"Don Juan et Faust." *Cinéa* 57-58 (9 June 1922), 14-20.

Dréville, Jean. *"Le Diable au coeur."* *Cinégraphie* 3 (15 November 1927), 54.

Epardaud, Edmond. *"L'Argent,"* *Cinéa-Ciné-pour-tous* 125 (15 January 1929), 13-14.

―――. "La Collaboration Marcel L'Herbier—Luigi Pirandello dans *Feu Mathias Pascal.*" *Cinéa-Ciné-pour-tous* 43 (15 August 1925), 9-11.

―――. "De Marcel L'Herbier et son oeuvre." *Ciné-Journal* 15 (1 October 1921), 4, 9.

Epstein, Jean. "Mémoires inachevées." In *Ecrits sur le cinéma* (Paris: Seghers, 1974), 1, 43-45.

―――. "Naissance d'un langage." In *Esprit de cinéma* (Paris: Jeheber, 1955), 85-93.

Fescourt, Henri. *La Foi et les montagnes* (Paris: Paul Montel, 1959), 252-267.

Fieschi, Jean-André. "Autour du cinématographe." *Cahiers du cinéma* 202 (June-July, 1968), 26-42.

―――, Bernard Minoret, and Claude Arnulf. "Entretien avec Marcel L'Herbier." *Cinématographe* 40 (October, 1978), 40-42.

Galtier-Boissière, Jean. "Le Cinéma: *L'Homme du large.*" *Le Crapouillot* (16 November 1920), 21.

―――. "La Critique des films: *Carnaval des vérités.*" *Le Crapouillot* (1 April 1920), 16-17.

―――. "Les Films: *Rose-France.*" *Le Crapouillot* (1 April 1919), 13.

―――. "Réflexions sur le cinéma." *Le Crapouillot* (1-15 January, 1 February 1920), 2-4.

Jeanne, René and Charles Ford. *Histoire encyclopédique du cinéma* (Paris: Robert Laffont, 1947), 1, 192-193, 303-320.

Jouvet, Pierre. *"L'Argent* de Marcel L'Herbier." *Cinématographe* 27 (May, 1977), 7-9.

Landry, Lionel. *"El Dorado."* *Cinéa* 12-13 (22 July 1921), 7-8.

Lang, André. *Déplacements et Villégiatures littéraires et suivi de la promenade au royaume des images ou entretiens cinématographiques* (Paris: Renaissance du livre, 1924), 126-132.

Lapierre, Marcel. *Les Cent Visages du cinéma* (Paris: Grasset, 1948), 128-129, 152-154, 188.

Lawder, Standish. *The Cubist Cinema* (New York: New York University Press, 1975), 99-115.

Lenauer, Jean. "The Cinema in Paris: *L'Argent.*" *Close Up* 4 (March, 1929), 80-82.

Leprohon, Pierre. *Cinquante Ans de cinéma français* (Paris: Editions du cerf, 1954), 71-74.

L'Herbier, Marcel. "*L'Argent.*" *L'Avant-Scène du cinéma* 209 (1 June 1978), 3-4, 9-26, 43-60.

————. "Cinéclastes." *Cinéa* 73-74 (6 October 1922), 6-8.

————. "Cinématographie de France." *Choses de théâtre* 2 (November, 1921), 84-89.

————. "Le Cinématographe et l'espace." In *L'Art cinématographique*, Vol. 4 (Paris: Librairie Félix Alcan, 1927), 1-22.

————. "Le Droit de métamorphose." *Cinéa-Ciné-pour-tous* 109 (15 May 1928), 10-11.

————. "Esprit du cinématographe." *Cahiers du mois* 16/17 (1925), 29-35.

————. "Hermès et le Silence." *Le Film* 110-111 (29 April 1918), 7-12.

————. "Introduction." In *Intelligence du cinématographe*, edited by L'Herbier, (Paris: Corréa, 1946), 11-34.

————. "Résurrection." *Cinéa-Ciné-pour-tous* 90 (1 August 1927), 9-11.

————. "Sisyphes." *Le Rouge et le noir* (July, 1928), 42-45.

————. *La Tête qui tourne.* Paris: Pierre Belfond, 1979,

Marie, Michel. "Modernité de *L'Argent.*" *L'Avant-Scène du cinéma* 209 (1 June 1978), 5-6.

Mitry, Jean. *Histoire du cinéma* (Paris: Editions universitaires, 1969), 2, 260-262, 432-434.

————. *Histoire du cinéma* (Paris: Editions universitaires, 1973), 3, 377-378.

————. "Marcel L'Herbier." *Théâtre et Comoedia Illustré* 32 (15 April 1924), [n.p.].

Moussinac, Léon. "Cinématographe." *Mercure de France* (1 June 1922), 497-498.

————. "Naissance du cinéma [1925]." In *L'Age ingrat du cinéma* (Paris: Editeurs français réunis, 1967), 114-117.

————. "Les Présentations: *El Dorado.*" *Le Crapouillot* (16 July 1921), 13-14.

"La Polémique de *L'Argent.*" *Cinéa-Ciné-pour-tous* 107 (15 April 1928), 26-28.

Porte, Pierre. "Trois cinéphiles et *L'Inhumaine.*" *Cinéa-Ciné-pour-tous* 27 (15 December 1924), 19-20.

"La Production de Marcel L'Herbier." *Cinéa* 73-74 (6 October 1922), 13-18.

"Que sera *L'Inhumaine.*" *Cinéa-Ciné-pour-tous* 5 (15 January 1924), 12-13.

Rambaud, Pierre. "Actualités d'art: *Autour de L'Argent.*" *Cinéa-Ciné-pour-tous* 134 (1 June 1929), 10.

Roches, Edouard. "Les films de demain." *Mon-Ciné* (14 February 1924), 6-7, 10.

Sadoul, Georges. *Histoire générale du cinéma* (Paris: Denoël, 1974), 4, 477-484.

————. *Histoire générale du cinéma* (Paris: Denoël, 1975), 5, 80-107.

————. *Histoire générale du cinéma* (Paris: Denoël, 1975), 6, 328-332.

Tedesco, Jean. "*L'Argent* devant le public." *Cinéa-Ciné-pour-tous* 126 (1 February 1929), 9.

Thiher, Allen. *The Cinematic Muse: Critical Studies in the History of French Cinema* (Columbia: University of Missouri Press, 1979), 18-20.

Trevise, Robert. "Les Présentations: *L'Inhumaine.*" *Cinéa-Ciné-pour-tous* 18 (1 August 1924), 29.

Vuillermoz, Emile. "Devant l'écran: Hermès et le Silence." *Le Temps* (23 February 1918), 3.

————. "Le Film de la semaine: *Don Juan et Faust.*" *Comoedia* (13 October 1922), 3.

20. *The Russian Emigrés: Ivan Mosjoukine, Alexandre Volkoff, Victor Tourjansky*

Arroy, Juan. "Alexandre Volkoff." *Cinéa-Ciné-pour-tous* 60 (1 May, 1926), 21-23.

Bardèche, Maurice and Robert Brasillach. *The History of the Motion Pictures.* Translated by Iris Barry (New York: Norton, 1938), 168-171.

Bernard, Raphael. "Mme. Kovanko and M. Tourjansky." *Cinémagazine* 1 (9 December 1921), 5-8.

Bonneau, Albert. "Les présentations: *Les Ombres qui passent.*" *Cinémagazine* 4 (6 June 1924), 423-424.

Canudo, Ricciotto. *L'Usine aux images* (Geneva: Office central d'éditions, 1927), 159-160.

"Casanova." *Cinéa-Ciné-pour-tous* 88 (1 July 1927), 22-23.

Dréville, Jean. "Films: *Casanova.*" *Cinégraphie* 1 (15 September 1927), 11-12.

Epardaud, Edmond. "Une Heure avec Tourjansky." *Cinéa-Ciné-pour-tous* 28 (1 January 1925), 11-12.

Escoube, Lucien, "Alexandre Volkoff." *Cinémagazine* 11 (November, 1932), 49-51, 66.

Farnay, Lucien. "*Les Ombres qui passent.*" *Cinémagazine* 4 (5 September 1924), 389-390.

"Ivan." *Cinéa-Ciné-pour-tous* 26 (1 December 1924), 15-16.

Jeanne, René and Charles Ford. *Histoire encyclopédique du cinéma* (Paris: Robert Laffont, 1947), 1, 399-417.

Lapierre, Marcel. *Les Cent Visages du cinéma* (Paris: Grasset, 1948), 179-180.

Leprohon, Pierre. *Cinquante Ans de cinéma français* (Paris: Editions du cerf, 1954), 80-83.

"Mme. Nathalie Lissenko." *Cinémagazine* 4 (1 February 1924), 169-172.

"Michel Strogoff." La Petite Illustration 7 (7 August 1926), 1-11.

Mirbel, Jean de. *"Le Brasier ardent."* Cinémagazine 3 (14 September 1923), 380-382.

Mitry, Jean. "Ivan Mosjoukine." *Anthologie du cinéma* 48 (October, 1969), 393-440.

Moussinac, Léon. "Le Cinéma: *Le Brasier ardent*." *Le Crapouillot* (16 June 1923), 19.

Sadoul, Georges. *Histoire générale du cinéma* (Paris: Denoël, 1975), 5, 205-208.

Tinchant, André. "Les films de la semaine: *Les Ombres qui passent*." *Cinémagazine* 4 (24 October 1924), 152-153.

Tedesco, Jean. *"Kean."* Cinéa-Ciné-pour-tous 7 (15 February 1924), 13-17.

21. Léonce Perret

Bonneau, Albert. "Léonce Perret." *Cinémagazine* 3 (17 August 1923), 221-224.

Burch, Noël. "Léonce Perret." In *Cinema: A Critical Dictionary*, Vol. 2, edited by Richard Roud (New York: Viking, 1980), 778-780.

Daven, André. *"Koenigsmark."* Théâtre et Comoedia Illustré 22 (October, 1923), [n.p.].

Dréville, Jean. "La Critique du film: *La Danseuse orchidée*." *On Tourne* 3 (15 May 1928), 2.

"L'Elégance et *Koenigsmark*." *Cinéa-Ciné-pour-tous* 5 (15 January 1924), 18-19.

Epardaud, Edmond. *"La Femme nue."* Cinéa-Ciné-pour-tous 75 (15 December 1926), 13-17.

———. "Léonce Perret." *Cinéa-Ciné-pour-tous* 69 (15 September 1926), 22-23.

Jeanne, René and Charles Ford. *Histoire encyclopédique du cinéma* (Paris: Robert Laffont, 1947), 1, 223-225.

"Léonce Perret reçoit un grand prix aux Arts Décoratifs pour *Madame Sans-Gêne*." *Cinéa-Ciné-pour-tous* 48 (1 November 1925), 28.

Moussinac, Léon. "Naissance du cinéma [1925]." In *L'Age ingrat du cinéma* (Paris: Editeurs français réunis, 1967), 134-135.

"L'Opinion de la presse sur *Madame Sans-Gêne*." *Cinéa-Ciné-pour-tous*, 52 (1 January, 1926), 27.

Perret, Léonce. "Comment j'ai tourné *Koenigsmark*." *Cinémagazine* 3 (7 September 1923), 329-332.

Swanson, Gloria. *Swanson on Swanson* (New York: Random House, 1980), 214-126, 222-227, 278-279.

Trevise, Robert. "Les Présentations de la quinzaine: *Koenigsmark*." *Cinéa-Ciné-pour-tous* 2 (1 December 1923), 33.

Vuillermoz, Emile. "Devant l'écran: *Koenigsmark*." *Le Temps* (29 November 1923), 3.

Wahl, Lucien. *"Le Démon de la haine."* Cinéa 53 (12 May 1922), 7.

22. Léon Poirier

"Au Répertoire du Vieux-Colombier: l'histoire du deux grands films." *Cinéa-Ciné-pour-tous* 30 (1 February 1925), 21-23.

Chowe, Hay. "Propaganda." *Close Up* 4 (January, 1929), 27-32.

Epardaud, Edmond. *"Verdun, visions d'histoire."* Cinéa-Ciné-pour-tous 121 (15 November 1928), 21-22.

Fescourt, Henri. *La Foi et les montagnes* (Paris: Paul Montel, 1959), 319-326.

"Films de la semaine: *La Brière*." *Cinémagazine* 5 (30 January 1925), 230.

Galtier-Boissière, Jean. "La Critique des films: *Le Penseur*." *Le Crapouillot* (1 April 1920), 16-17.

Jeanne, René. *"Le Coffret de jade."* Cinémagazine 1 (4 November 1921), 18-20.

———. "En Brière avec Léon Poirier." *Cinéa-Ciné-pour-tous* 18 (1 August 1924), 15-18.

———. "Lamartine au cinéma." *Cinémagazine* 2 (19 May 1922), 227-230.

——— and Charles Ford. *Histoire encyclopédique du cinéma* (Paris: Robert Laffont, 1947), 1, 371-382.

"Jocelyn." Cinémagazine 2 (27 October 1922), 128-129.

"Jocelyn." Cinéa 57-58 (9 June 1922), 1-11.

Lacan, Germain. *"Geneviève."* Cinémagazine 3 (23 November 1923), 295-297.

Lapierre, Marcel. *Les Cent Visages du cinéma* (Paris: Grasset, 1948), 156-157, 185.

Mitry, Jean. *Histoire du cinéma* (Paris: Editions universitaires, 1969), 2, 262, 363.

Moussinac, Léon. "Le Cinéma: *Geneviève.*" *Le Crapouillot* (16 December 1923), 29.

———. "Les Films: *La Brière.*" *Le Crapouillot* (16 February, 1925) 16.

Poirier, Léon. "Les Ennemis du septième art." *Le Petit Journal* (23 December 1921), 4.

———. "L'Irréal." *Cinéa* 20 (23 September 1921), 5.

———. "Lamartine, précurseur du cinéma." *Cinémagazine* 3 (1 July 1923), 52-54.

———. *Vingt-quatre images à la seconde.* Paris: Mame, 1953.

Porte, Pierre. "Le Cinéma n'est pas un art populaire." *Cinéa-Ciné-pour-tous* 12 (1 May 1924), 27.

Roelens, Maurice. "Littérature, peuple, cinéma: *Geneviève* (1923)." *Cahiers de la cinémathèque* 33-34 (Autumn, 1981), 179-184.

Sadoul, Georges. *Histoire générale du cinéma* (Paris: Denoël, 1974), 4, 485-486.

———. *Histoire générale du cinéma* (Paris: Denoël, 1975), 5, 199-200.

"Verdun, visions d'histoire." *La Petite Illustration* 14 (24 November 1928), 1-7.

23. *Jean Renoir*

Analyse des films de Jean Renoir. Paris: IDHEC, 1966.

Bazin, André. *Jean Renoir.* Translated by W. W. Halsey II and William H. Simon. New York: Simon and Schuster, 1971.

Beylie, Claude. "A la recherche d'un style." *Cinématographe* 46 (April, 1979), 9-15.

———. "Essai de reconstitution d'un film perdu," *Ecran* 79, (15 April 1979).

———. *Jean Renoir.* Paris: Film Editions, 1975.

———. "L'Oeuvre filmée de Jean Renoir." *L'Avant-Scène du cinéma* 251-252 (1-15 July 1980), 137-165.

Boulanger, Pierre. *Le Cinéma colonial* (Paris: Seghers, 1975), 78-79.

Braudy, Leo. *Jean Renoir: The World of His Films.* New York: Doubleday, 1972.

Brunius, Jacques. *En marge du cinéma français* (Paris: Arcanes, 1954), 163-180.

Chardère, Bernard, ed. "Jean Renoir." *Premier Plan* 22-23-24. Lyon: SERDOC, 1962.

Durgnat, Raymond. *Jean Renoir.* Berkeley: University of California Press, 1974.

Epardaud, Edmond. *"Nana."* *Cinéa-Ciné-pour-tous* 60 (1 May 1926), 13-16.

———. *"Nana* avec Catherine Hessling." *Cinéa-Ciné-pour-tous* 54 (1 February 1926), 12-13.

———. *"Le Tournoi."* *Cinéa-Ciné-pour-tous* 127 (15 February 1929), 21-22.

Farnay, Lucien. "Le Scénario de *Nana.*" *Cinémagazine* 6 (21 May 1926), 383-388.

Faulkner, Christopher. *Jean Renoir: A Guide to References and Resources.* Boston: G. K. Hall, 1979.

Frank, Nino. "Notre Renoir." *Cinématographe* 46 (April, 1979), 16-19.

Gaillard, Henri. *"La Fille de l'eau."* *Cinémagazine* 4 (26 December 1924), 581-582.

Gautier, Claude. *Jean Renoir: la double méprise.* Paris: Editeurs français réunis, 1980.

Lapierre, Marcel. *Les Cent Visages du cinéma* (Paris: Grasset, 1948), 169-170.

Leprohon, Pierre. *Jean Renoir.* Translated by Brigid Elson. New York: Crown, 1971.

Mazeline, François. "Jean Renoir." *Cinéa-Ciné-pour-tous* 107 (15 April 1928), 13.

Mitry, Jean. *Histoire du cinéma* (Paris: Editions universitaires, 1973), 3, 385-386.

Ramain, Paul. "Le Rêve dans *La Petite Marchande d'allumettes.*" *Cinéa-Ciné-pour-tous* 110 (1 June 1928), 14-16.

Renoir, Jean. *Ecrits, 1926-1971.* Paris: Pierre Belfond, 1974.

———. *Ma Vie et mes films.* Paris: Flammarion, 1974.

———. *"La Petite Marchande d'allumettes."* *L'Avant-Scène du cinéma* 251-252 (1-15 July 1980), 105-120.

Roud, Richard. "Jean Renoir to 1939." In *Cinema: A Critical Dictionary* Vol. 2, edited by Richard Roud (New York: Viking, 1980), 835-845.

Sadoul, Georges. *Histoire générale du cinéma* (Paris: Denoël, 1975), 6, 352-359.

Sesonske, Alexander. *Jean Renoir: The French Films, 1924-1939.* Cambridge: Harvard University Press, 1980.

Tedesco, Jean. "L'Affaire de *La Petite Marchande d'allumettes.*" *Cinéa-Ciné-pour-tous* 113 (15 July 1928), 6-7.

———. "Jean Renoir et Jean Tedesco gagnent le procès de *La Petite Marchande d'allumettes.*" *Cinéa-Ciné-pour-tous* 136 (1 July 1929), 7-10.

———. *"Nana* à Berlin." *Cinéa-Ciné-pour-tous* 131 (15 April 1929), 11.

Wahl, Lucien. *"La Petite Marchande d'allumettes."* *Pour Vous* 66 (20 February 1930), 5.

24. Henry Roussel

Bonneau, Albert. *"Violettes impériales*: le réalisateur, la mise-en-scène, l'interprétation." *Cinémagazine* 4 (22 February 1924), 295-298.

Boulanger, Pierre. *Le Cinéma colonial* (Paris: Seghers, 1975), 61.

Canudo, Ricciotto. *L'Usine aux images* (Geneva: Office central d'éditions, 1927), 126.

Delluc, Louis. "Notes pour moi: *L'Ame du bronze.*" *Le Film* 98 (28 January 1918), 16.

Doublon, Lucien. *"Les Opprimés."* *Cinémagazine* 3 (26 January 1923), 155-157.

Epardaud, Edmond. *"La Terre promise."* *Cinéa-Ciné-pour-tous* 29 (15 January 1925), 13-14.

Fescourt, Henri. *La Foi et les montagnes* (Paris: Paul Montel, 1959), 335-338.

"L'Ile enchantée." *Cinéa-Ciné-pour-tous* 83 (15 April 1927), 21-22.

Jeanne, René. *"Violettes impériales*: Impressions d'Espagne." *Cinémagazine* 4 (22 February 1924), 291-294.

——— and Charles Ford. *Histoire encyclopédique du cinéma* (Paris: Robert Laffont, 1947), 1, 225-228.

Lapierre, Marcel. *Les Cent Visages du cinéma* (Paris: Grasset, 1948), 131-132.

McKee, Gerald. *Film Collecting* (London: Tantivy Press, 1978), 83-84.

Mitry, Jean. "Henri Roussel." *Théâtre et Comoedia Illustré* 35 (1 June 1924), [n.p.].

"Les Projets de nos metteurs-en-scène: Henry Roussel." *Cinémagazine* 2 (8 September 1922), 289.

Roussel, Henry. "Le Cinéma, c'est la guerre." *Cinéa-Ciné-pour-tous* 8 (1 March 1924), 16.

Sadoul, Georges. *Histoire générale du cinéma* (Paris: Denoël, 1974), 4, 486-488.

Tedesco, Jean. "Raquel." *Cinéa-Ciné-pour-tous* 8 (1 March 1924), 17-18.

"La Terre promise." *La Petite Illustration* 1 (4 April 1925), 1-12.

"Violettes impériales." *Cinéa-Ciné-pour-tous* 8 (1 March 1924), 12-15.

"Violettes impériales: le scénario." *Cinémagazine* 4 (22 February 1924), 299-300.

These filmographies are based primarily on my own research in French film journals and annuals, from 1915 to 1930. They include all major and most minor filmmakers with at least two narrative films each to their credit. Excluded, however, are several older filmmakers whose work in France dates chiefly from before the war (e.g., Albert Capellani, André Heuzé, Max Linder, Maurice Tourneur), several non-narrative avant-garde filmmakers (e.g., Lucie Derain, Eugène Deslaw, Marcel Duchamp, Georges Hugnet, Fernand Léger, Man Ray), several documentary filmmakers (e.g., Jean Benoît-Lévy, Paul Castelnau, Jean Lods, Jean Painlevé, André Sauvage), several animation filmmakers (e.g., O'Galop, Ladislas Starevitch), and the younger filmmakers who had made only one film by the end of the decade (e.g., Marc Allegret, Luis Buñuel, Marcel Carné, Jean Dréville, Georges Lacombe, Georges Rouquier, Jean Vigo). When necessary, I have relied on the filmographies in studies of individual filmmakers, on Georges Sadoul's *Le Cinéma français* (1962), on René Jeanne and Charles Ford's *Dictionnaire du cinéma universel* (1970), or on Pierre Roura's "Dictionnaire des réalisateurs français des Années Vingt," *Cahiers de la cinémathèque* (1981). Since the latter sources are not always consistent and complete, some of the following references, especially those of lesser known filmmakers, may be incomplete as well as questionable. All the films of an individual filmmaker are arranged chronologically, according to the year of each film's release in France.

Andréani, Henri (1872-1930)
L'Océan, 1917 (serial)
Mimi Trottin, 1922
Ziska la danseuse espionne, 1922
L'Autre aile, 1924
Flamenca la gitane, 1928
La Pente, 1928

Antoine, André (1858-1943)
Les Frères corses, 1917
Le Coupable, 1917
Les Travailleurs de la mer, 1918
Mademoiselle de la Seiglière, 1921
La Terre, 1921 (filmed in 1919)
Quatre-Vingt Treize, 1921 (filmed with Albert Capellani, in 1914)
L'Arlésienne, 1922
L'Hirondelle et la mésange, 1983 (filmed in 1920-1921)

Autant-Lara, Claude (1903-)
Fait-Divers, 1926 (short filmed in 1924)
Construire un feu, 1930 (filmed in 1928-1929)

Baroncelli, Jacques de (1881-1951)
La Maison de l'espion, 1915 (short)
Trois Filles en portefeuille, 1916 (short)
La Faute de Pierre Daisy, 1916 (short)
Le Jugement de Salomon, 1916 (short)
La Nouvelle Antigone, 1916
Le Suicide de Sir Petson, 1916 (short)
L'Hallali, 1916 (short)
Le Drame du château de Saint-Privat, 1916 (short)
Une Mascotte, 1917 (short)
L'Inconnue, 1917 (short)
Le Roi de la mer, 1917
Pile ou face, 1917 (short)
Trois K. K., 1917 (short)
Le Cas du procureur Lesnin, 1917 (short)
Une Vengeance, 1917 (short)
Le Scandale, 1918

Le Siège des trois, 1918
Le Retour aux champs, 1918
Ramuntcho, 1919
La Rafale, 1920
Le Secret du 'Lone Star,' 1920
La Rose, 1920 (short)
Flipotte, 1920
Champi tortu, 1921
Le Rêve, 1921
Le Père Goriot, 1921
Roger la Honte, 1922
Le Carillon de minuit, 1922
La Femme inconnue, 1923
La Légende de Soeur Béatrix, 1923
Nêne, 1924
La Flambée des rêves, 1924
Pêcheur d'Islande, 1924
Veille d'armes, 1925
Le Réveil, 1925
Nitchevo, 1926
Feu, 1927
Duel, 1928
Le Passager, 1928
La Femme et le pantin, 1929
La Femme du voisin, 1929
La Tentation, 1929

Bernard, Raymond (1891-1974)
Le Ravin sans fond, 1917
Le Gentilhomme commerçant, 1918
Le Traitement du Hoquet, 1918
Le Petit Café, 1919
Le Secret de Rosette Lambert, 1920
La Maison vide, 1921
Triplepatte, 1922
L'Homme inusable, 1923
Le Costaud des épinettes, 1923
Grandeur et décadence, 1923
Le Miracle des loups, 1924
Le Joueur d'échecs, 1927
Tarakanova, 1930

Bernard-Deschamps, Dominique (1892-1966)
48, Avenue de l'Opera, 1917
Hier et aujourd'hui, 1918
L'Agonie des aigles, 1921-1922
La Nuit du 11 septembre, 1922

Boudrioz, Robert (1887-1949)
L'Apre lutte, 1917
La Distance, 1918
Un Soir, 1919
Zon, 1920
Tempêtes, 1922
L'Atre, 1923 (filmed in 1920)
L'Epérvier, 1924
Les Louves, 1925
La Chaussée des géants, 1926
Trois Jeunes Filles, 1928
Vivre, 1928

Bourgeois, Gérard (1874-1944)
Protéa II, 1915
Protéa III, 1916
Protéa IV, 1917
Le Capitaine noir, 1917 (short)
Christophe Colomb, 1919
Le Fils de la nuit, 1919 (serial)
Les Mystères du ciel, 1920
Un Drame sous Napoléon, 1921
Faust, 1922
La Dette de sang, 1923
Terreur, 1924
Face à mort, 1925 (serial)

Burguet, Charles (1872-1957)
Pour epouser Gaby, 1917
Son Héros, 1917
Les Deux Amours, 1917
L'Ame de pierre, 1918
Au paradis des enfants, 1918
La Sultane de l'amour, 1919
Suzanne et les brigands, 1920 (serial)
Gosse de riche, 1920 (serial)
L'Essor, 1920-1921 (serial)
Le Chevalier de Gaby, 1920
Un Ours, 1921
Baillonnée, 1922 (serial)
Les Mystères de Paris, 1922 (serial)
La Mendiante de Saint-Sulpice, 1923 (serial)
Faubourg Montmartre, 1924
La Joueuse d'orgue, 1925 (serial)
Barocco, 1925
Martyre, 1926
Le Meneur de joies, 1929

Catelain, Jaque (1898-)
Le Marchand de plaisir, 1923
La Galérie des monstres, 1924

Cavalcanti, Alberto (1897-1982)
Rien que les heures, 1926

La P'tite Lily, 1927 (short)
En rade, 1927
Yvette, 1928
Le Train sans yeux, 1928 (filmed in 1926)
Le Capitaine fracasse, 1929
La Jalousie du Barbouillé, 1929
Le Petit Chaperon rouge, 1929 (short)

Champavert, Georges
Mea Culpa, 1919
L'Oeil de Saint-Yvès, 1919
Le Remous, 1920
L'Eté de la Saint Martin, 1920
La Hurle, 1921
Le Porion, 1921
L'Evasion, 1922
La Neuvaine de Colette, 1925

Chomette, Henri (1896-1941)
Les Jeux des reflets et de la vitesse, 1925 (short)
Cinq Minutes de cinéma pur, 1925 (short)
Le Chauffeur de Mademoiselle, 1928

Clair, René (1898-1981)
Paris qui dort, 1924 (filmed in 1923)
Entr'acte, 1924 (short)
Le Fantôme du Moulin Rouge, 1925
Le Voyage imaginaire, 1926
La Proie du vent, 1927
La Tour, 1928 (short documentary)
Un Chapeau de paille d'Italie, 1928
Les Deux Timides, 1929

Colombier, Pierre (1896-1958)
Soirée de reveillon, 1922
Le Taxi 313 x 7, 1922
Le Noël du Père Lathuile, 1922
Monsieur Lebidois propriétaire, 1922
Petit Hôtel à louer, 1923
Par dessus le mur, 1923
Le Mariage de Rosine, 1925
Paris en cinq jours, 1926
L'Ame du moteur: le carburateur, 1926
Jim la Houlette, roi des voleurs, 1926
Transatlantiques, 1928
Petite Fille, 1928
Dolly, 1929

Delluc, Louis (1890-1924)
Fumée noire, 1920 (short)
Le Silence, 1920 (short)
Fièvre, 1921
Le Chemin d'Ernoa, 1921
Le Tonnerre, 1921
La Femme de nulle part, 1922
La Pelote basque, 1923 (documentary filmed in 1920)
L'Inondation, 1924

Desfontaines, Henri (1878-1931)
La Forêt qui écoute, 1916

La Reine Margot, 1916
Chouchou, 1917
Les Bleus de l'amour, 1918
La Suprême Epopée, 1919
Sa gosse, 1919
La Marseillaise, 1920
Autour du mystère, 1920
Chichinette et clé, 1921
La Fille des chiffonniers, 1922
L'Insigne mystérieux, 1922
Madame Flirt, 1923
L'Oeillet blanc, 1923
Château historique, 1923
L'Espionne, 1923
Vers abecher la mystérieuse, 1924
L'Espionne aux yeux noirs, 1926
Belphégor, 1926 (serial)
Le Capitaine Rascasse, 1927 (serial)
Poker d'as, 1927 (serial)

Diamant-Berger, Henri (1895-1972)
Paris pendant la guerre, 1916 (documentary)
Le Feu sacré, 1920 (short)
Les Trois Mousquetaires, 1921-1922 (serial)
Vingt Ans après, 1922-1923 (serial)
Le Mauvais Garçon, 1923
Gonzague, 1923
L'Affaire de la rue de Loureine, 1923
Le Roi de la vitesse, 1923
La Marche du destin, 1924
L'Emprise, 1924
Rue de la Paix, 1927
Education de Prince, 1927

Dieudonné, Albert (1889-1976)
Son Crime, 1921
Gloire rouge, 1923
Catherine, 1927 (filmed in 1924)

Donatien
Une Histoire de brigands, 1920
L'Auberge, 1921
Les Hommes nouveaux, 1922
La Sin-Ventura, 1922
L'Ile de la mort, 1923
La Chevauchée blanche, 1923
Nantas, 1924
Princesse Lulu, 1924
Pierre et Jean, 1924
Mon Curé chez les pauvres, 1925
Mon Curé chez les riches, 1925
Un Château de la mort lente, 1925
Simone, 1926
Florine la fleur du Valois, 1926
Le Martyre de Ste. Maxence, 1927
Miss Edith, Duchesse, 1928
L'Arpète, 1929

Dulac, Germaine (1882-1942)
Les Soeurs ennemies, 1917

Géo, le mystérieux, 1917
Venus victrix or Dans l'ouragan de la vie, 1917
Ames de fous, 1918 (serial)
Le Bonheur des autres, 1919
La Cigarette, 1919
La Fête espagnole, 1920 (short)
Malencontre, 1920
La Belle Dame sans merci, 1921
La Mort du soleil, 1922
La Souriante Madame Beudet, 1923 (short)
Gossette, 1923-1924 (serial)
Le Diable dans la ville, 1925
Ame d'artiste, 1925
La Folie des vaillants, 1925
Antoinette Sabrier, 1927
L'Invitation au voyage, 1927
Le Cinéma au service de l'histoire, 1927
La Coquille et le clergyman, 1928
Germination d'un haricot, 1928 (short)
La Princesse Mandane, 1928
Disque 927, 1928 (short)
Thèmes et variations, 1928 (short)
Etude cinégraphique sur un arabesque, 1929
   (short)

Durand, Jean (1882-1946)
Berthe Dagmar et les fauves series, 1917-1918
Serpentin comic series, 1919-1920
Impéria, 1920 (serial)
Marie comic series, 1921-1922
La Chaussée des géants, 1926
Palaces, 1927
L'Ile d'amour, 1928
La Femme rêvée, 1929

Duvivier, Julien (1896-1967)
Haceldama, 1919
Les Roquevillard, 1922
L'Ouragan sur la montagne, 1922
Le Reflet de Claude Mercoeur, 1923
Coeurs farouches, 1923
La Machine à refaire la vie, 1924
   (documentary)
L'Abbé Constantin, 1925
Poil de carotte, 1926
L'Agonie de Jerusalem, 1926
L'Homme à l'Hispano, 1927
Le Mariage de Mademoiselle Beulemans, 1927
Le Mystère de la Tour Eiffel, 1927
Le Tourbillon de Paris, 1928
La Divine Croisière, 1928
La Vie miraculeuse de Thérèse Martin, 1929
Maman Colibri, 1929
Au bonheur des dames, 1929

Epstein, Jean (1897-1953)
Pasteur, 1922
Les Vendanges, 1922 (short documentary)
L'Auberge rouge, 1923

La Montagne infidèle, 1923 (short documentary)
Coeur fidèle, 1923
La Belle Nivernaise, 1924
Photogénies, 1924 (short)
Le Lion des Mogols, 1924
L'Affiche, 1925
Le Double Amour, 1925
Les Aventures de Robert Macaire, 1925-1926 (serial)
Au pays de George Sand, 1926 (short documentary)
Mauprat, 1926
6½ × 11, 1927
La Glace à trois faces, 1927
La Chute de la maison Usher, 1928
Finis Terrae, 1929
Sa Tête, 1930
Le Pas de la mule, 1930 (short documentary)

Epstein, Marie (1899-   ) and Jean Benoît-Lévy (1888-1959)
Ames d'enfants, 1928
Peau de pêche, 1929
Maternité, 1929

Etiévant, Henri
Etre aimé pour soi-même, 1920
La Poupée, 1920
Nine, 1920
La Pocharde, 1921 (serial)
Crépuscule d'épouvante, 1921
La Fille sauvage, 1922 (serial)
La Neige sur le pas, 1924
Coeur de Titi, 1924
La Nuit de la revanche, 1924
Le Réveil de Maddalone, 1924
La Fin de Monte Carlo, 1927
La Sirène des tropiques, 1928
La Symphonie pathétique, 1929
Fécondité, 1929

Fescourt, Henri (1880-1966)
La Menace, 1915 (short)
Mathias Sandorf, 1921 (serial)
La Nuit du 13, 1921
Rouletabille chez le bohemiens, 1922 (serial)
Mandarin, 1924 (serial)
Les Grands, 1924
Un Fils d'Amérique, 1925
Les Misérables, 1925-1926
La Glu, 1927
La Maison du maltais, 1928
L'Occident, 1928
Monte-Cristo, 1929

Feuillade, Louis (1874-1925)
Bout-de-Zan comic series, 1915-1916
La Vie drôle comic series, 1915-1918
Les Vampires, 1915-1916 (serial)
L'Aventure des millions, 1916
Un Mariage de raison, 1916
Notre pauvre coeur, 1916
Le Malheur qui passe, 1916
Judex, 1917 (serial)
L'Autre, 1917
Le Bandeau sur les yeux, 1917
Déserteuse, 1917
La Fugue de Lily, 1917
Herr Doktor, 1917
La Nouvelle Mission de Judex, 1918 (serial)
Le Passé de Monique, 1918
Les Petites Marionnettes, 1918
Tih-Minh, 1919 (serial)
Vendémiaire, 1919
L'Engrenage, 1919
L'Enigme, 1919
L'Homme sans visage, 1919
Le Nocturne, 1919
Barrabas, 1920 (serial)
Belle Humeur comic series, 1921-1922
Les Deux Gamines, 1921 (serial)
L'Orpheline, 1921 (serial)
Parisette, 1922 (serial)
Le Fils du Flibustier, 1922 (serial)
Le Gamin de Paris, 1923
La Gosseline, 1923
Vindicta, 1923 (serial)
L'Orphelin de Paris, 1924 (serial)
La Fille bien gardée, 1924
Lucette, 1924
Pierrot Pierrette, 1924
Stigmate, 1925 (serial)

Feyder, Jacques (1888-1948)
M. Pinson, policier, 1916 (short)
Têtes de femmes, femmes de tête, 1916 (short)
Le Pied qui étreint, 1916 (serial)
Le Bluff, 1916 (short)
Un Conseil d'ami, 1916 (short)
L'Homme de compagnie, 1916 (short)
Tiens, vous êtes à Poitiers?, 1917 (short)
Le Frère de lait, 1917 (short)
Le Billard casse, 1917 (short)
Abregeons les formalités, 1917 (short)
La Trouvaille de Buchu, 1917 (short)
Le Pardessus de demi-saison, 1917 (short)
Les Vieilles Femmes de l'hospice, 1917 (short)
L'Instinct est maître, 1917
Le Ravin sans fond, 1917
La Faute d'orthographie, 1919 (short)
L'Atlantide, 1921
Crainquebille, 1923
Visages d'enfants, 1925 (filmed in 1923)
L'Image, 1926 (filmed in 1924)
Gribiche, 1926
Carmen, 1926
Au pays de Roi Lepreux, 1927 (documentary)
Thérèse Raquin, 1928

Les Nouveaux Messieurs, 1929

Gance, Abel (1889-1982)
Un Drame au château d'acre, 1915 (short)
La Folie du Docteur Tube, 1915 (short)
L'Enigme de dix heures, 1915 (short)
La Fleur des ruines, 1915 (short)
L'Héroisme de Paddy, 1915 (short)
Fioritures, 1916 (short)
Le Fou de la falaise, 1916 (short)
Ce que les flots racontent, 1916 (short)
Le Periscope, 1916 (short)
Barberousse, 1916 (serial)
Les Gaz mortels, 1916 (serial)
Le Droit à la vie, 1917
Mater Dolorosa, 1917
La Zone de la mort, 1917
La Dixième Symphonie, 1918
J'Accuse, 1919
En tournant la roue, 1922 (short documentary)
La Roue, 1922-1923 (filmed in 1920-1921)
Au secours!, 1923 (short)
Napoléon vu par Abel Gance, 1927 (filmed in 1925-1926)
En tournant Napoléon, 1927 (short documentary)
Galop, Marine, Danse, 1928 (shorts)

Gastyne, Marco de (1889-1982)
Inch'Allah, 1922
L'Aventure, 1923
A l'horizon du sud, 1924
La Blessure, 1925
La Châtelaine du Liban, 1926
Mon coeur au ralenti, 1928
La Merveilleuse Vie de Jeanne d'Arc, 1929

Gleize, Maurice (1898-)
La Nuit rouge, 1924
La Main qui a tué, 1924
La Justicière, 1925
La Faute de Monique, 1928
La Madone des sleepings, 1928
Tu m'appartiens, 1929

Grémillon, Jean (1901-1959)
Photogénie mécanique, 1924 (short)
L'Electrification de la ligne Paris-Vierzon, 1925 (short documentary)
La Vie des travailleurs italiens en France, 1926 (short documentary)
Gratuites, 1927 (short)
Tour au large, 1927 (documentary)
Maldone, 1928
Gardiens de phare, 1929

Hervil, René and Mercanton, Louis
La Petite Rosse, 1915 (short)
La Dame du 13, 1915 (short)
Honneur passe richesse, 1915 (short)

Chacun sa destinée, 1915 (short)
Le Tournant, 1916 (short)
Suzanne, professeur de flirt, 1916 (short)
Suzanne, 1916
Oh! Ce baiser, 1917
La P'tite du sixième, 1917
Mères françaises, 1917
Midinette, 1917
Le Tablier blanc, 1917
Un Roman d'amour et d'aventures, 1918
Le Torrent, 1918
Bouclette, 1918
Sarati-le-Terrible, 1923
Aux jardins de Murcie, 1923

Hervil, René (1883-1940)
Simplette, 1919
Son Aventure, 1919
L'Ami Fritz, 1920
Blanchette, 1921
Le Crime de Lord Arthur Saville, 1922
Le Secret de Polichinelle, 1923
Paris, 1924
La Flamme, 1925
Knock, 1926
Le Bouif errant, 1926 (serial)
La Petite Chocolatière, 1927
Le Prince Jean, 1928
Minuit . . . Place Pigalle, 1928
La Meilleure Maitresse, 1929

Hugon, André (1886-1961)
L'Empreinte, 1916
Chignon d'or, 1916
Beauté fatale, 1916
Sous la menace, 1916
Fleur de Paris, 1916
Mariage d'amour, 1917
Angoisse, 1917
Le Vertige, 1917
Requins, 1917
Mystère d'une vie, 1917
Johannès, fils de Johannès, 1918
La Fugitive, 1918
Chacals, 1918
Un Crime a été commis, 1919
Jacques Landauze, 1919
Les Chères Images, 1920
La Preuve, 1921
Fille de rien, 1921
Le Roi de Camargue, 1921
Diamant noir, 1921
Notre dame d'amour, 1922
Le Petit Chose, 1923
La Rue du pavé d'amour, 1923
Gitanella, 1924
L'Arriviste, 1924
L'Homme des Baléares, 1925
La Princesse aux clowns, 1925

Yasmina, 1926
La Vestale du Gange, 1927
A l'ombre des tombeaux, 1927
La Grande Passion, 1928
La Marche nuptiale, 1929
Les Trois Masques, 1929

Kemm, Jean (?-1939)
Les Deux Marquises, 1916
Honneur d'artiste, 1917
Le Dédale, 1917
Le Délai, 1918
L'Obstacle, 1918
André Cornélis, 1918
L'Enigme, 1919
Le Destin est maître, 1920
Miss Rovel, 1920
Micheline, 1921
Hantise, 1922
La Ferme du Choquart, 1922
L'Absolution, 1922
Vidocq, 1923 (serial)
Ce Pauvre Chéri, 1923
L'Enfant-Roi, 1924 (serial)
Le Bossu, 1925 (serial)
André Cornélis, 1927

Kirsanoff, Dmitri (1899-1957)
L'Ironie du destin, 1924
Menilmontant, 1926
Destin, 1927
Sables, 1928
Brumes d'automne, 1928 (short)

Krauss, Henry
Papa Hulin, 1916
Le Chemineau, 1917
Marion de Lorme, 1918
Les Trois Masques, 1921
Fromont Jeune et Risler Aîné, 1921
La Calvaire de Dona Pisa, 1925

Lacroix, Georges (1880-1920)
L'Heure tragique, 1916
Dans la rafale, 1916
Beauté qui meurt, 1917
Les Ecrits restent, 1917
Haine, 1918
Le Marchand de bonheur, 1918
Le Noël d'Yveline, 1919 (short)
Son Destin, 1919
La Vengeance de Mallet, 1920
Passionnément, 1921

Leprince, René (?-1929)
Zyte, 1916
La Vie d'une reine, 1917
Le Noël d'un vagabond, 1918
Le Calvaire d'une reine, 1919
Les Larmes du pardon, 1919
La Lutte pour la vie, 1920

Face à l'océan, 1920
Force de la vie, 1920
Jean d'Agrève, 1922
Etre ou ne pas être, 1922
L'Empereur des pauvres, 1922-1923 (serial)
Vent debout, 1923
Mon Oncle Benjamin, 1923
La Folie du doute, 1923
Un Bon Petit Diable, 1923
Pax Domine, 1923
L'Enfant des Halles, 1924 (serial)
Le Vert-Galant, 1924 (serial)
Mylord l'Arsouille, 1925 (serial)
Fanfan la tulipe, 1925 (serial)
Le Jardin sur l'Oronte, 1925
Titi Ier roi des gosses, 1926 (serial)
Princesse Masha, 1927
La Tentation, 1928
La Revanche du maudit, 1929

L'Herbier, Marcel (1890-1979)
Rose-France, 1919
Le Bercail, 1919
Le Carnaval des vérités, 1920
L'Homme du large, 1920
Villa Destin, 1921
El Dorado, 1921
Prométhé . . . banquier, 1922 (short)
Don Juan et Faust, 1923
L'Inhumaine, 1924
Feu Mathias Pascal, 1925
Le Vertige, 1926
Le Diable au coeur, 1928
Résurrection 1928 (filmed in 1923, incomplete)
L'Argent, 1929
Nuits de Prince, 1929

Lion, Roger (?-1934)
Chansons filmées, 1917-1918
La Flamme cachée, 1918
Dagobert, 1919 (serial)
L'Eternel féminine, 1921
La Sirène de pierre, 1922
Les Yeux de l'âme, 1922
Le Fantôme d'amour, 1923
Fidélité, 1924
J'ai tué, 1924
La Fontaine des amours, 1924
La Clé de voute, 1925
Fiançailles, 1926
Le Chasseur de Chez Maxim's, 1927
La Nuit est à nous, 1927
Le Venenosa, 1928
Une Heure au cocktail bar, 1929

Luitz-Morat (? -1928)
Sa Majesté le chauffeur de taxi, 1919 (short)
Rien à louer, 1919 (short)
Les Cinq Gentlemen maudits, 1919

Monsieur Lebureau, 1920
Petit Ange, 1920
La Terre du diable, 1921
Le Sang d'Allah, 1922
Au seuil du harem, 1922
Petit Ange et son pantin, 1923
La Cité foudroyée, 1924
Surcouf, 1925 (serial)
La Course au flambeau, 1925
Jean Chouan, 1926 (serial)
Le Juif errant, 1926
La Ronde infernale, 1927
La Vierge folle, 1929

Machin, Alfred (1877-1929) and Henry
Wuhlschleger
Une Nuit agitée, 1920
Moi aussi, j'accuse, 1920
Bête comme des hommes, 1923
L'Enigme du Mont Agel, 1924
Les Héritiers de l'Oncle James, 1924
Le Cabinet de l'homme noir, 1924
Le Coeur des gueux, 1925
Le Manoir de la peur, 1927

Mariaud, Maurice
Le Crépuscule de coeur, 1916
La Marche triomphale, 1916
Larmes de crocodile; 1916
La Calomnie, 1917
La Danseuse voilée, 1917
L'Epave, 1917
Les Dames de Croix-mort, 1917
Le Nocturne à la poupée, 1917
Les Mouttes, 1919
L'Idole brisée, 1920
Tristan et Yseult, 1920
L'Etau, 1920
L'Homme et la poupée, 1921
L'Aventurier, 1924
La Goutte de sang, 1924
Mon oncle, 1925
Le Secret de cargo, 1929

Marodon, Pierre
Le Diamant vert, 1917
Mascamor, 1918 (serial)
Qui a tué, 1919
Les Femmes des autres, 1920
Le Tocsin, 1920
La Fée des neiges, 1920
Les Morts qui parlent, 1920
La Femme aux deux visages, 1920
Les Trois Gants de la dame en noir, 1920
Le Château des fantômes, 1921 (serial)
Le Diamant vert, 1923 (serial)
Buridan, le héros de la tour de Nesle, 1923-24
Salammbô, 1925
Les Voleurs de gloire, 1926
Les Dieux ont soif, 1926

Maudru, Charles and Charles de Marsan
Poilus de la 9ᵉ, 1916
Renoncement, 1917
La Mascotte des poilus, 1918
Le Droit de tuer, 1920
La Bourasque, 1920
Le Lys rouge, 1920
L'Assomoir, 1921
Un Aventurier, 1921
Le Méchant Homme, 1921
Le Talion, 1921
L'Inconnu, 1921
Près des crimes, 1921
La Fiancée du disparu, 1921
Le Roi de Paris, 1922 (serial)
Serge Panine, 1922
Le Crime d'une sainte, 1923 (serial)
Rocambole, 1923
L'Homme du Train 117, 1923
Les Premières Armes de Rocambole, 1924
Les Amours de Rocambole, 1924

Mercanton, Louis (1879-1932)
Jeanne Doré, 1916
Le Lotus d'or, 1916
L'Appel du sang, 1920
Miarka, la fille à l'ourse, 1920
Phroso, 1922
L'Homme merveilleux, 1922
La Voyante, 1923
Les Deux Gosses, 1924
Monte Carlo, 1926
Croquette, 1927
Venus, 1929

Georges Monca (1888-1940)
Blessure d'amour, 1916
L'Anniversaire, 1916
Bonhomme de neige, 1917
La Proie, 1917
Le Chanson du feu, 1917
La Bonne Hôtesse, 1918
La Route de devoir, 1918
Lorsqu'une femme veut, 1919
Madame et son filleul, 1919
Les Femmes collantes, 1920
Prince embêté, 1920
Si jamais je te pince, 1920
Chouquette et son as, 1920
Romain Kalbris, 1921
Le Meurtier de Theodore, 1921
Chante-Louve, 1921
Le Sang des Finoel, 1922
L'Engrenage, 1923
Altemer le cynique, 1924
L'Ironie du sort, 1924
La Double Existence de Lord Samsey, 1924
Sans famille, 1925
Autour d'un berceau, 1925

Le Chemineau, 1926
Miss Helyett, 1927
Les Fourchambault, 1929

Morlhon, Camille de (? -1945)
Sous l'uniforme, 1915 (short)
Coeur de gavroche, 1915 (short)
Effluves funestes, 1916 (short)
Fille d'artiste, 1916
Le Secret de Geneviève, 1916 (short)
Maryse, 1917
Miséricorde, 1917
L'Orage, 1917
Simone, 1918
Expiation, 1918
L'Ibis bleu, 1919
Eliane, 1919
La Fille du peuple, 1920
Fabienne, 1920
Une Fleur dans les ronces, 1921

Mosjoukine, Ivan (1890-1939)
L'Enfant du carnaval, 1921
Le Brasier ardent, 1923

Nadejdine, Serge
Le Chiffonnier de Paris, 1924
L'Heureux Mort, 1924
Naples au basier de feu, 1925
La Cible, 1925
Le Nègre blanc, 1925

Perret, Léonce (1880-1935)
La Voix de la paix, 1915 (short)
Mort au champ d'honneur, 1915 (short)
Françaises, veillez!, 1915 (short)
Le Héros de l'Yser, 1915 (short)
Les Poilus de la revanche, 1915 (short)
Une Page de gloire, 1915 (short)
L' Angélus de la victoire, 1915 (short)
Léonce aime les belges, 1915 (short)
L'X noir: l'énigme de la rivière, 1915 (short)
Aimer, pleurer, mourir, 1915 (short)
Le Roi de la montagne, 1915 (short)
Le Mystère de l'ombre, 1916 (short)
Dernier amour, 1916 (short)
L'Imprévu, 1916 (short)
Le Devoir, 1916 (short)
La Fiancée du diable, 1916 (short)
L'Empire du diamant, 1921
Le Démon de la haine, 1922
L'Ecuyère, 1922
Koenigsmark, 1923
Madame Sans-Gêne, 1925
La Femme nue, 1926
Morgane la sirène, 1927
Printemps d'amour, 1927
Orchidée danseuse, 1928
La Possession, 1929
Quand nous étions deux, 1929

Poirier, Léon (1884-1968)
Ames d'orient, 1919
Le Penseur, 1920
Narayana, 1920
L'Ombre dechirée, 1921
Le Coffret de jade, 1921
Jocelyn, 1922
Geneviève, 1923
L'Affaire du courrier de Lyon, 1923
La Brière, 1925
Eve africaine, 1925 (short documentary)
Zazavindrano, 1925 (short documentary)
Croisière noire, 1926 (documentary)
Amours exotiques, 1927 (documentary)
Verdun, visions d'histoire, 1928

Pouctal, Henri (1856-1922)
L'Infirmière, 1915 (short)
Le Brebis perdue, 1915 (short)
Le Mannequin, 1915 (short)
La Fille du boche, 1915 (short)
Dette de haine, 1915 (short)
Alsace, 1916
L'Affaire du Grand Théâtre, 1916 (short)
L'Alibi, 1916
L'Instinct, 1916
La Flambée, 1916
Chantecoq ou coeur de française, 1916-1917
  (serial)
Volonté, 1917
Le Roman d'un spahi, 1917
Le Comte de Monte-Cristo, 1917-1918 (serial)
Le Dieu du hasard, 1919
Travail, 1919-1920
Gigolette, 1920
Le Crime du Bouif, 1921
La Résurrection du Bouif, 1922

Protozanoff, Jacob, (1881-1946)
L'Angoissante Aventure, 1920
Le Sens de la mort, 1921
Justice d'abord, 1921
Pour une nuit, 1921
L'Ombre du péché, 1922

Ravel, Gaston (1878-1958)
Document secret, 1916
L'Homme qui revient de loin, 1917
Du rire aux larmes, 1917
Le Bon M. Lafontaine, 1918 (short)
Une Femme inconnue, 1918
La Maison d'argile, 1918
L'Envolée, 1921
La Géole, 1921
A l'ombre de Vatican, 1922
Tao, 1923 (serial)
Ferragus, 1923
On ne badine pas avec l'amour, 1924
Le Gardien du feu, 1924
L'Avocat, 1925

638

Chouchou poids plume, 1925
Amours, délices et orgues, 1925
La Fauteuil 47, 1926
Mademoiselle Josette ma femme, 1926
Le Bonheur du jour, 1927
Le Roman d'un jeune homme pauvre, 1927
Jocaste, 1927
Madame Récamier, 1928
Figaro, 1929
Le Collier de la reine, 1930

Renoir, Jean (1894-1978)
La Fille de l'eau, 1925
Nana, 1926
Charleston, 1926 (short)
Marquitta, 1927
La Petite Marchande d'allumettes, 1928
Tire au flanc, 1928
Le Tournoi, 1929
Le Bled, 1929

Robert, Jacques (1890-1928)
La Vivante Epingle, 1921
La Bouquetière des innocents, 1922
Cousin Pons, 1924
Le Comte Kostia, 1925
La Chèvre aux pieds d'or, 1926
En plongée, 1927

Roudès, Gaston
Marthe, 1919
La Dette, 1920
Les Deux Baisers, 1920
Au delà des lois humaines, 1920
La Voix de la mer, 1921
Maître Evora, 1921
Prisca, 1921
La Guitare et le jazz band, 1922
Le Lac d'argent, 1922
Le Petit Moineau de Paris, 1923
Le Crime des hommes, 1923
L'Eveil, 1924
L'Ombre du bonheur, 1924
Féliana l'espionne, 1924
Les Rantzau, 1924
Pulcinella, 1925
Les Elus de la mer, 1925
La Douleur, 1925
La Maternelle, 1925
Oiseaux de passage, 1925
Les Petits, 1925
Prince Zilah, 1926
Le Dédale, 1927
Cousine de France, 1927
L'Ame de Pierre, 1928
La Maison du soleil, 1929

Roussel, Henry (1875-1946)
Un Homme passa, 1917
L'Ame du bronze, 1918

La Faute d'Odette Maréchal, 1920
Visages voilés . . . âmes closes, 1921
La Vérité, 1922
Les Opprimés, 1923
Violettes impériales, 1924
La Terre promise, 1925
Destinée, 1926
L'Ile enchantée, 1927
Le Valse de l'adieu, 1928
Paris Girls, 1929

Saidreau, Robert (? -1925)
Chalumeau vaudeville series, 1920
Méfiez-vous de votre bonne, 1920
La Première Idylle de Boucot, 1920
La Paix chez soi, 1921
L'Etrange Aventure du Docteur Works, 1921
La Nuit de Saint Jean, 1922
Le Bonheur conjugal, 1922
Coeur léger, 1923
Ma Tante d'Honfleur, 1923
L'Idée de Françoise, 1923
Une Etrangère, 1924
Monsieur le directeur, 1924
Un Fil à la patte, 1924
Jack, 1925
A la gare, 1925
La Corde au cou, 1926

Le Somptier, René (1884-1950)
Le Pont des Enfers, 1915 (short)
Les Epaves de l'amour, 1916 (short)
L'Aubade à Sylvie, 1916 (short)
La Sultane de l'amour, 1919
La Croisade, 1920
La Montée vers l'Acropole, 1920
La Bête traquée, 1923
La Porteuse de pain, 1923
La Dame de Monsoreau, 1923 (serial)
Les Fils du soleil, 1924 (serial)
La Forêt qui tue, 1925
Les Terres d'or, 1925
Le P'tit Parigot, 1926 (serial)

Tourjansky, Viatcheslaw [Victor] (1891-?)
L'Ordonnance, 1921
Les Milles et Une Nuits, 1922
Les Nuits de carnaval, 1922
Une Aventure, 1922
La Riposte, 1922
Le 15ᵉ Prélude de Chopin, 1922
Calvaire d'amour, 1923
Le Chant de l'amour triomphant, 1923
Ce Cochon de Morin, 1924
La Dame masquée, 1924
Le Prince charmant, 1925
Michel Strogoff, 1926

Vandal, Marcel (1882-1965)
Graziella, 1926

Fleur d'amour, 1927
Le Sous Marin de cristal, 1928
L'Eau du Nil, 1928

Violet, Edouard (?-1955)
Lucien comic series, 1918
Fantaisie de millardaire, 1919
La Nouvelle Aurore, 1919 (serial)
Li-Hang le cruel, 1920
Le Main, 1920 (short)
Papillon, 1920
Les Mains flétries, 1920
L'Accusateur, 1920

L'Epingle rouge, 1921
L'Auberge, 1921
La Ruse, 1922
Les Hommes nouveaux, 1922
Le Voile du bonheur, 1923
La Bataille, 1923
Le Roi du cirque, 1925

Volkoff, Alexandre (1885-1942)
La Maison du mystère, 1922-1923 (serial)
Kean, 1924
Les Ombres qui passent, 1924
Casanova, 1927

Index of French names (individuals, organizations, places), titles (films, books, magazines, newspapers), and terms. This index includes selected references to substantive material in the endnotes.

647

Index of non-French names, titles, and terms. This index includes substantive references to selected material in the notes.

LIBRARY OF CONGRESS CATALOGING IN PUBLICATION DATA

Abel, Richard, 1941-
French cinema.

Filmography: p.
Bibliography: p.
Includes index.
1. Moving-pictures—France—History. 2. Moving-picture industry—France—History. 3. Moving-picture plays—History and criticism. 4. Experimental films—France—History. 5. Moving-pictures—Societies, etc.—France—History. I. Title.

PN1993.5.F7A64 1984   384′.8′0944   83-43057
ISBN 0-691-05408-8

Richard Abel is Professor of English at Drake University in Des Moines, Iowa.